DICTIONARY OF BASILIAN BIOGRAPHY

Lives of Members of
the Congregation of Priests of Saint Basil
from Its Origins in 1822 to 2002

DICTIONARY OF BASILIAN BIOGRAPHY

Lives of Members of
the Congregation of Priests of Saint Basil
from Its Origins in 1822 to 2002

SECOND EDITION
Revised and augmented by P. Wallace Platt

Published for the Congregation of Saint Basil
by
UNIVERSITY OF TORONTO PRESS
Toronto Buffalo London

© University of Toronto Press Incorporated 2005
Toronto Buffalo London
Printed in Canada

ISBN 0-8020-3949-9

∞

Printed on acid-free paper

Library and Archives Canada Cataloguing in Publication

Platt, Philip Wallace, 1925–
  Dictionary of Basilian biography : lives of members of the
Congregation of Priests of Saint Basil from its origins in 1822 to 2002. –
2nd ed. / revised and augmented by P. Wallace Platt

  First ed., by Robert J. Scollard, published 1969.
  ISBN 0-8020-3949-9

  1. Basilian Fathers – Biography – Dictionaries.   I. Scollard, Robert J.,
1908–1993   II. Basilian Fathers   III. Title.

BX2970.Z7P5 2005   271'.79   C2005-903121-2

University of Toronto Press acknowledges the financial assistance to its
publishing program of the Canada Council for the Arts and the Ontario
Arts Council.

University of Toronto Press acknowledges the financial support for its
publishing activities of the Government of Canada through the Book
Publishing Industry Development Program (BPIDP).

To the memory of

ROBERT J. SCOLLARD

and

FÉLIX POUZOL,

we dedicate this volume, so much the fruit of their labours.

Let us now sing the praises of those great men in their generations.
Some have left behind a name, so that others declare their praise.
They were godly people, whose righteous deeds have not been forgotten.
Their bodies are buried in peace, but their names live on, generation after
  generation.
The assembly declares their wisdom, and the congregation proclaims
  their praise.

Sirach 44

Contents

Preface ix

Introduction xv

Significant Dates of Basilian Foundations xxi

Abbreviations xxiii

Glossary xxv

Dictionary of Basilian Biography 3

Appendix: Basilians by Chronological Order of Death 699

Preface

This revised and enlarged edition of the *Dictionary of Basilian Biography* presents biographical notices of all the members of the Congregation of Saint Basil who died as ordained priests, professed scholastics, or novices in the Congregation from its origins in 1822 to the end of 2002. It also includes those priests (but not scholastics) who died after withdrawing from the Congregation. There are 629 entries – more than double the number in the first edition published thirty-five years ago by Father Robert J. Scollard in his book of the same name (Toronto, 1969). As well, it incorporates the research of Father Félix Pouzol, who, dissatisfied with the minimal attention given to the French members in the first edition, combed the archives in France in order to provide much additional information on them.

The presentation of each biography follows the pattern set by Father Scollard: (1) statistics of birth, family, death, and burial; (2) notice of schooling, entry into the Basilians, higher education, and ordination; (3) professional assignments and achievements; (4) comments, anecdotes, descriptive quotations (when relevant), and appreciation. The first three parts are informational, while the fourth part attempts to encapsulate the unique character of the person, the contribution he made, and its effect on the wider community. The goal has been to present them as the human beings they were. The accent has been on their positive characteristics; but whatever could be seen as of purely panegyric nature has been avoided. Some entries are of course more complete or detailed than others. This is a factor not only of their longevity or of their particular charisms but also of the duties entrusted to them by a religious superior.

The articles about members who died prior to 1969 are based on Father Scollard's 1969 entries, but a large number of them have been rewritten or expanded. Although Father Scollard's book is not listed in the sources given at the end of those entries, the debt owed to him is acknowledged with gratitude here and in the dedication of this book. In some cases the reader could find still additional information by consulting the list of sources. The sources are presented in alphabetical order, with the exceptions of GABF and ABA, which are placed first.

The entries appear in alphabetical order. This rule has been followed strictly by distinguishing the prefixes 'Mac' and 'Mc.' In cases where the person was commonly known by a name other than his first given Christian name, this is indicated by small capitals in the title of the entry or by a nickname cited in the text within quotation marks. For the hyphenation of French names we have almost always followed the usage indicated by Father Félix Pouzol in his 'Notices biographiques,' on which we have drawn so heavily for the French biographies. An asterisk placed before a name indicates that there is an entry elsewhere in this book devoted to that person.

In presenting the bibliographies of publications we have listed titles of books, pamphlets, and articles separately in chronological, not alphabetical, order. When a large number of articles appeared in the same journal, these have been grouped together under a single mention of its title. In cases where an authoritative and accessible bibliography exists elsewhere, we have listed only book titles, and then have referred the reader to that other source for the list of articles.

This revised edition itself has a history of more than ten years. In 1991 Father Kevin Kirley, archivist of the General Archives of the Basilian Fathers, suggested the new edition to Father Larry Finke, secretary general. He in turn recruited Father Brian Hogan to form a planning committee, which met several times but which eventually dissolved because of other demands on the time of its members. In 1997, Father Ronald Fabbro, superior general (now bishop of London, Ontario), commissioned me to compile the new *DBB* with the help of a new Editorial Committee. The devoted and painstaking work of its members, all of whom are priests of the Congregation, has greatly enhanced the completeness and interest of the book. Kevin Kirley composed most of the entries on the French confreres and has been the exacting and unfailing resource for checking many of the book's details in the archives. He has also compiled the Appendix listing the Basilians in the chronological order of death. William Young composed the biographies of the French confreres who held the office of superior general, as well as several other of the longer entries for French members. Peter Swan, with more than sixty years of Basilian life behind him, compiled most of the entries for Canadian and American Basilians who withdrew from the Congregation before they died, and has contributed other vital information to several articles. James Farge, an experienced and acknowledged writer and editor, has edited all the entries for harmony of style. He has compiled the bibliographies of the books and articles published by Basilians, and has entered into the computer all the changes at each stage of redaction. James Hanrahan's eight years as superior general and his wide knowledge of the Congregation were a steady stimulus from the start. William Irwin and Charles Principe helped to formulate policy decisions at the beginning. Brian Hogan resigned from the Committee when he left the Congregation.

In January 2001 a draft of the present work, albeit incomplete and lacking full editing, was put at the disposition of the whole Congregation, with a request for corrections and suggestions. In response, individual confreres, especially those related to the deceased by family, long acquaintance, or shared apostolate, contributed considerable aid. In a number of cases a draft was sent to one or other confrere for correction or completion. This, too, proved fruitful and encouraging. Answers to queries have been generously provided by the archivists of the dioceses of Austin, Detroit, Galveston-Houston, Hamilton, London, Peterborough, Toronto, and Sault Ste Marie; by the archivists of Assumption University, Windsor, the Sisters of Mercy, Rochester, and the Congregation of St Joseph, Toronto; and by the librarian of Sacred Heart Seminary, Detroit. The editor and his committee are grateful to them all.

For the sake of brevity the naming of Canadian provinces and American states has been omitted in the case of cities that are mentioned frequently in the entries – Toronto (Ontario), Windsor (Ontario), Detroit (Michigan), Rochester (New York), and Houston (Texas) – and for other well-known cities like Montreal (Quebec) and New York City. In the same interest of brevity the designation of the Ardèche as the French *département* in which the oft-mentioned town of Annonay is located has likewise been omitted. It should also be noted that until 1937 the district of the city of Windsor in which all four Basilian institutions are located was known as Sandwich, Ontario. 'Etobicoke' has been retained as the locale of Michael Power High School for purposes of recognition, even though the designation is no longer official for that section of the city now incorporated into the Greater Toronto Area.

We have made mention of the ecclesiastical dioceses in which Basilians were born; but, again for brevity's sake, separate mention of the diocese is not made when its name is the same as that of the city of birth (e.g., Toronto, Rochester). As well, because of their frequent appearance, the dioceses of birth are omitted for those born in Houston (diocese of Galveston-Houston [until 1959 simply 'Galveston']) and in Windsor (diocese of London).[1] Because Annonay and all other places in the French *département* of Ardèche appear so frequently here, their diocesan designation of Viviers should be presumed by the reader for all Basilians born in the Ardèche.[2]

A chronological list of significant dates of Basilian foundations has been provided. As its title suggests, the list is not inclusive of them all. Rather, it highlights the movement of Basilian ministry into new geographical areas and new expressions of the Congregation's ministry of evangelization in education.

In addition to a list of abbreviations used in this book, a glossary of canonical and ecclesiastical terms has likewise been provided to help the lay reader grasp the meaning of terms that Basilians themselves might take for granted. As well, many readers will not be familiar with certain terms used in the French system of education. The French word *collège* is generally equivalent to a secondary school, but it has a seven-year program. A *petit séminaire* is a *collège* for students intending to enter a major seminary to prepare for the priesthood. The *classe de sixième* is equivalent to grade IX, *cinquième* to grade X, *quatrième* to grade XI, and *troisième* to grade XII. *Seconde, première* (or *rhétorique*), and *classe terminale* (or *philosophie*) comprise the final or 'upper' three years. The *baccalauréat* is the diploma conferred at the successful completion of the seven years; the *licence* is roughly equivalent to the Master of Arts in North America. A *surveillant* is a prefect who presides over study hall, meals, recreation, and the dormitory.

---

1 Windsor was in the archdiocese of Quebec until 1826, then of Kingston until 1841, of Toronto until 1856, and since 1856 of London. From 1859 to 1869 it was known as the diocese of Sandwich.

2 The exception is the period 1801–22, when the *département* of Ardèche was part of the diocese of Mende – the diocese of Viviers having been suppressed by the Concordat of 1801. Pope Pius VII restored the see in 1817, and named André Molin its bishop; but the French legislature did not ratify this until 1822, and Molin was installed only on 16 May 1823. See Remigius Ritzler and Pirminus Séfrin, *Hierarchia catholica medii et recentioris aevi* 7 (Passau, 1958) 398n1; see also *Petite histoire de l'église diocésaine de Viviers*, Travail d'équipe coordonné par l'abbé Jean Charay (Aubenas, 1977) 189–210.

The French term *collège* was carried over to Basilian schools founded in North America. Thus St Michael's College, Toronto, Assumption College, Windsor, and similar foundations in Ohio, Texas, and New Brunswick that bore the name 'College' comprised both secondary and college-level education. This persisted at St Michael's College and Assumption College until the mid-twentieth century, when their high school sections separated and took the name 'College School' and 'High School' respectively.

In such a work as this, where attention to detail and thoroughness in research are so much a part of the process, there will invariably be omissions and mistakes. For these the editor takes full responsibility and asks the indulgence and pardon of the reader and of the Congregation. It has been an inestimable experience of grace and edification to review and recount the lives of so many admirable men. May our reading about their work and dedication translate into emulation and renewed courage in service to Church and society.

P. Wallace Platt
2 January 2003, Feast of Saint Basil

Introduction

The Congregation of Saint Basil (Basilian Fathers) took its origins[1] from a small group of diocesan priests in the Vivarais (Ardèche) region of southern France. Defying the anticlerical legislation passed during the French Revolution, they accepted the task of conducting a clandestine seminary in an almost inaccessible little village called Saint-Symphorien-de-Mahun. In 1802, when the danger was considered past, they moved the school to the town of Annonay,[2] some fifty kilometres south of Lyon near the Rhône River. Having leased for this purpose a former Franciscan convent, they called the school the 'Collège des Cordeliers.' At the same time they expanded their apostolate to include not only the training of priests but the Christian education of young laymen as well.

In 1822, in order to assure the viability of the school, ten of the diocesan priests who had carried on its work – Fathers Lapierre, Duret, Vallon, Polly, Tourvieille, Tracol, Martinesche, Fayolle, Payan, and Pagès – received permission from the bishop of Mende to form a pious association of priests under solemn promises, not vows. Although of Roman rite, they chose as their patron the fourth-century Greek bishop and theologian St Basil of Caesarea – partly because some of them were teaching in a minor seminary in the parish of Saint-Basile, but also because St Basil had inspired the early Church to embrace whatever in secular culture was in harmony with the Christian faith.

The new Association narrowly escaped extinction only a year later.

---

[1] The authoritative history of the origins of the Congregation is Charles Roume, *Origines et formation de la Communauté des Prêtres de Saint-Basile. Contribution à l'histoire religieuse du Vivarais* (Aubenas, 1965); trans. Kevin J. Kirley and William J. Young, *A History of the Congregation of St. Basil to 1864* (Toronto, 1975).

[2] See Adrien Chomel, *Le Collège d'Annonay, 1800–1860, Mémoires et souvenirs* (Annonay, 1902).

When the diocese of Viviers was canonically restored, the vicar general of its new bishop had formulated plans of his own for the diocesan schools. Before action was taken, however, the new bishop died, and his successor was favourable to the Basilians. The Holy See gave approval to the Constitutions of the Association in 1837, and in 1863 Pope Pius IX raised the status of the group to that of a religious congregation of simple vows.[3]

By this time the Congregation had been entrusted with the direction of minor seminaries and secondary schools in several dioceses, and its work soon expanded into French Algeria.[4] This expansion took place during the very decades when the centuries-old practice of religious priests, brothers, and sisters teaching in schools was being hotly opposed in France. The anticlerical government of the Third Republic of France, coming to power in the 1870s, passed a number of laws which affected Catholic education. Some Basilian schools had to close in 1878 and 1879. The Jesuits were dissolved in 1880 for the second time. All religious orders were required to have their statutes approved by the civil authorities. In July 1881 the Basilians were expelled from still another school, and in 1882 the community withdrew from its *collège* at Châteauroux (Indre). As a result a large number of Basilian teachers were left unemployed, although many found ministry in rural parishes. A second wave of suppression ensued in the early years of the twentieth century. In 1903 the Basilians were expelled from their principal foundation, the college in Annonay, which had been moved to a new site in 1867 and renamed 'Collège du Sacré-Coeur.' Most of the remaining Basilians in France applied for legal certificates of 'secular' status in order to be able to continue teaching – for the most part in minor seminaries. Some were incardinated as secular priests into a diocese. Still others remained Basilians while serving bishops in a wide variety of places, but their sense of community was greatly diminished.

The novitiate at Feyzin (Isère, now Rhône) had been forcibly closed by the secular authorities in 1880, leaving the Basilians with no novitiate to train new members. In 1883 a new novitiate was opened in Plymouth, England, to train candidates from both France and North

---

3 See T. James Hanrahan, *The Basilian Fathers (1822–1972), A Documentary Study of One Hundred and Fifty Years of the History of the Congregation of Priests of St Basil* (Toronto, 1973).

4 See Kevin J. Kirley, *The Community of Priests of St Basil in France, 1865–1922* (Toronto, 2000).

America. As vocations from Canada increased, however, the need for a novitiate in Canada became urgent, and St Basil's Novitiate was opened in Toronto in 1892. In the 1920s the French Congregation opened a novitiate in Bordighera, Italy, a site closer to Annonay than was Plymouth, and in 1928 it also built the Maison Saint-Joseph in Annonay as a new centre for Basilians in France.

A half-century prior to their expulsion from the Annonay school, the Basilians had accepted the invitation of a former student, Bishop François Armand de Charbonnel of Toronto,[5] to help minister to his largely Irish immigrant flock. Father Patrick Molony, an Irish-born professor of English at the school in Annonay, went first in 1850 and was followed by four others in 1852. They founded the mother house of the Basilians in North America near St Michael's Cathedral, from which St Michael's College took its name. In 1856 a permanent site for the college was chosen north of the city in a meadow known as 'Clover Hill,' located providentially near the University of Toronto. Thus the future role of St Michael's College as a federated arts college in the university was adumbrated.

The Congregation in North America expanded slowly at first. After a short-lived foundation in the United States (Louisville, Ohio, 1867–73) failed, the Basilians assumed direction of Assumption College at Sandwich (now Windsor), Ontario, in 1880, and in 1888 of Ste Anne's Parish, Detroit, which had been founded in 1701. Seeing the promise of expansion in North America, the French superior general established a Basilian provincial council in Toronto in 1883. Theological training for the new recruits was provided in Toronto and Windsor. Over the next several decades the Congregation continued to recruit new members, and the Basilians were able to found or to assume direction for secondary schools, parishes, and arts colleges in the Canadian provinces of Ontario, New Brunswick, Saskatchewan, Alberta, and British Columbia, and in the American states of Texas,

---

5 In 1860 Bishop de Charbonnel resigned his see, returned to France, and joined the Capuchin Order. During the next thirty years he came frequently to Annonay to ordain Basilians to the priesthood, the diaconate, and the subdiaconate. In 1881 he was raised to the rank of titular archbishop in response to a request from the bishops of Ontario that his contributions to the growth of Catholicism in their province be duly acknowledged. He died in 1891 and was buried in the Capuchin convent in Craix (Drôme). See Jean LeBlanc, *Dictionnaire biographique des évêques catholiques du Canada* (Montreal, 2002) 365.

Michigan, New York, Indiana, New Mexico, and California. A missionary apostolate to Mexican immigrants in Texas, begun in 1936, spread to Mexico itself in 1961 and then to Colombia in South America and to Saint Lucia in the Caribbean. The Congregation made particularly important commitments of personnel in founding or assuming the direction of colleges and universities[6] in Toronto, Windsor, Saskatoon, Edmonton, Houston, and Rochester. The Institute of Mediaeval Studies, founded at St Michael's College in 1929, was granted pontifical status in 1939.

The differences in numbers, in prospects, and in outlook between the provinces in France and North America resulted in two decades of dissension over a number of issues. The situation was further exacerbated when the new *Code of Canon Law* (1917) called for the profession of a stricter vow of poverty than the one taken by Basilians up to that time. In 1922, though few in number, the French Basilians asked and received permission from Rome to be reconstituted as a separate and distinct congregation from the Basilians in North America, who for their part had decided to meet the new provisions of canon law – although some existing members exercised the option of remaining in the community under the old vow. This separation lasted only thirty-three years, for the two Congregations were canonically reunited in 1955. By the early 1960s the Congregation of Saint Basil had grown to some seven hundred active members.

But the late 1960s and the 1970s proved to be a time of rapid sociological and ecclesial transition that brought complex challenges to both Church and society. A sudden shift in attitudes to authority, dogma, and social mores had wide repercussions in religious orders and in the Church in general. The Second Vatican Council (1962–5) worked to effect an *aggiornamento* of the Church to bring it more closely into dialogue with contemporary culture, adapting itself wherever possible but reaffirming and strengthening whatever was essential. Like all existing religious orders and congregations, the Basilian Fathers experienced the result of the turmoil of change by a serious loss of personnel, both priests and scholastics preparing for the priesthood, and by a dearth of new vocations. By the year 2000 the number of members had fallen to just over three hundred. Several Basilian schools, parishes,

---

6 Laurence K. Shook, *Catholic Post-Secondary Education in English-Speaking Canada: A History* (Toronto, 1971).

and other ministries had to be returned to the direction of bishops or confided to competent lay persons, many of whom the Basilians had trained.

The 629 Basilians in this volume came from the following nations: France 212, Canada 284, the United States 109, Ireland 14, the United Kingdom 7, Malta 1, Czechoslovakia (now Czech Republic) 1, and Mexico 1. They present the *personae* in the two-centuries-old Basilian drama. As the reader will discover, some have played a leading role but most a supporting one. The saga they lived continues to unfold.

Significant Dates of Basilian Foundations

1800　Father Joseph Lapierre is appointed to the rural parish of Saint-Symphorien-de-Mahun by Archbishop Charles-François d'Aviau; seminary classes are taught secretly in the rectory.

1802　School is moved to Annonay (Ardèche), occupying a former Franciscan college and becoming known as the Collège des Cordeliers.

1808　Sainte-Barbe minor seminary opened at Annonay for boys whose parents could not pay tuition.

1822　Association of Priests of Saint Basil founded at Annonay; Father Joseph Lapierre elected superior general at first general chapter, 21 November.

1850　Father Patrick Molony, Irish-born Basilian working at Annonay, arrives in Toronto with Bishop Armand de Charbonnel to minister to Irish immigrants.

1852　Father Jean Mathieu Soulerin and three other Basilians from France join Father Molony to develop St Michael's College.

1856　St Michael's College and St Basil's Church open at a new location on Clover Hill, north of Toronto.

1857　Assumption College, Sandwich (since 1937 Windsor), opened, becoming a permanent Basilian commitment in 1870.

1863　Our Lady of the Assumption Parish, Owen Sound, Ontario, comes under Basilian direction as mission centre for the Bruce Peninsula.

1867　St Louis College, Louisville, Ohio, opened: the first Basilian foundation in the United States.

1868　St Charles College, Blidah, Algeria, founded by French Basilians.

1883　College of Mary Immaculate, Beaconfield House, Plymouth, England, founded; site of the common novitiate for France and Canada.

1888	Ste Anne's Parish, Detroit (founded 1701), comes under Basilian direction.
1892	St Basil's Novitiate opened in Toronto.
1899	St Basil's College, Waco, Texas, founded; first Basilian foundation in Texas.
1900	St Thomas College, Houston, Texas, opened.
1928	Maison Saint-Joseph, Annonay, established by the French Basilians as site for regrouping the dispersed French community.
1928	Catholic Central High School, Detroit, Michigan, opened.
1929	Institute of Mediaeval Studies (from 1939 'Pontifical' Institute) founded in Toronto.
1936	Hispanic ministry to immigrant Mexican Catholics begun in southern Texas.
1936	St Thomas More College opened in Saskatoon, Saskatchewan.
1937	Aquinas Institute, Rochester, New York, comes under Basilian direction.
1947	University of St Thomas founded in Houston, Texas.
1951	St John Fisher College founded in Rochester, New York.
1959	Andrean High School founded in Gary (now Merrillville), Indiana.
1961	San Juan Crisóstomo Parish in Mexico City comes under Basilian direction.
1963	St Joseph's College, Edmonton, Alberta, comes under Basilian direction.
1968	St Pius X High School, Albuquerque, New Mexico, comes under Basilian direction.
1978	Bishop O'Dowd High School, Oakland, California, comes under Basilian direction.
1987	Nuestra Señora de la Asunción Parish and College, Cali, Colombia, come under Basilian direction.
1991	St Benedict's Parish, St Lucia, West Indies, comes under Basilian direction.
1999	Holy Redeemer High School, in Detroit's inner city, comes under Basilian direction.

Abbreviations

ABA	Archives basiliennes, Annonay (Ardèche).
Annals	Basilian Annals. Toronto. 1 (1943–50)–10 (2002).
Basilian	The Basilian. Toronto, 1934–8.
Basilian Teacher	Basilian Teacher. Toronto, 1957–67.
Benedicamus	Benedicamus. Toronto 1952–8.
CCHA	Canadian Catholic Historical Association.
CCR	Canadian Catholic Review. Saskatoon, 1983–99.
Centennial, St Mary's	Basilian Centennial, 1863–1963, St Mary's of the Assumption Parish. Owen Sound, 1963.
Chomel, Collège d'Annonay	Adrien Chomel, Le Collège d'Annonay, 1800–1860. Mémoires et souvenirs. Annonay, 1902.
CSB	Congregation of Saint Basil.
DBB	Robert J. Scollard. Dictionary of Basilian Biography. 1st ed. Toronto, 1969.
Forum	Basilian Forum. Toronto, 1964–7.
French Studies U. of T.	C.D. Rouillard and Colleagues. French Studies at the University of Toronto, 1853–1953. Toronto, 1994.
GABF	General Archives, Basilian Fathers (Toronto).
Giraud, Mémoires	Manuscript diaries of Father Julien *Giraud, conserved in the ABA.
Heartwood	Margaret Sanche. Heartwood. A History of St Thomas More College and Newman Centre at the University of Saskatchewan. Muenster, Saskatchewan, 1986.
Hoskin, St Basil's	Mary Hoskin. History of St Basil's Parish. Toronto, 1912.
Jubilee, Assumption	Golden Jubilee, 1870–1920, Assumption College. Windsor, 1920.

Jubilee, St Mary's	Golden Jubilee, 1871–1921, St Mary's of the Assumption Parish. Owen Sound, 1921.
Kirley, Community in France	Kevin J. Kirley. The Community of Priests of St Basil in France, 1865–1922. Toronto, 2000.
Kirley, Congregation in France	Kevin J. Kirley. The Congregation of Priests of St Basil of Viviers, France 1922–1955. Toronto, 1981.
Lajeunesse, Assumption Parish	E.J. Lajeunesse. Outline History of Assumption Parish, 1797–1967. Windsor, 1967.
Madden, St Basil's	John F. Madden. A Short History of St Basil's Parish, 1856–1956. Toronto, 1956.
McMahon Pure Zeal	George McMahon, Sr. Pure Zeal. A History of Assumption College, 1870–1946. Toronto, 2002.
M.S.D.	Doctor in Studiis Mediae Aetatis.
M.S.L.	Licentiatus in Studiis Mediae Aetatis.
Newsletter	Basilian Newsletter. Toronto, 1960– .
Pouzol, 'Notices'	Félix Pouzol, 'Notices biographiques.' Unpublished manuscript, Basilian Archives, Annonay.
Power, Assumption College	Michael Power. Assumption College. A Documentary History. 6 vols. Windsor, 1984–2003.
Purple and White	Purple and White, Assumption College. Windsor, 1925–8.
Roume, Origines	Charles Roume. Origines et formation de la Communauté des Prêtres de Saint-Basile. Contribution à l'histoire religieuse du Vivarais. Aubenas, 1965.
Shook, Catholic Education	Laurence K. Shook. Catholic Post-Secondary Education in English-Speaking Canada. A History. Toronto, 1971.
Spetz, Waterloo	Theobald Spetz. The Catholic Church in Waterloo County. Toronto, 1916.
S.T.B.	Bachelor of Sacred Theology.
S.T.D.	Doctor of Sacred Theology.
S.T.L.	Licence in Sacred Theology.
Yearbook SMC	Yearbook, St Michael's College. Toronto, 1909/10–. Appears under several names.
Yearbook STC	Yearbook, St Thomas College. Chatham, New Brunswick.

Glossary

Basilian:	The popular designation for a member of the Congregation of Saint Basil.
Basilian Fathers:	The popular designation for the Congregation of Saint Basil.
chapter. *See* general chapter.	
community:	A group of religious living together under a local superior and common rule; sometimes used informally to designate the whole Congregation.
confrere:	A fellow member of the Congregation or community.
Congregation of Saint Basil:	The official name of the religious community popularly known as Basilian Fathers.
councillor (first *or* second):	An assistant to the superior of a religious community; a member of the local council.
general chapter (*or* chapter):	A convocation of *ex officio* and elected members from the Congregation, for the purpose of electing the superior general and his council, and for reviewing, evaluating, and planning the work of the Congregation. It meets every four (formerly six) years or extraordinarily in the event of a crisis.
house of studies:	A local community of scholastics preparing for degrees in arts or in theology. *See also* 'scholasticate' and 'seminary.'
incardination:	The incorporation of a priest into a diocese, as when a religious wishes to leave his congregation to serve with the diocesan clergy under a bishop.

local council:	A group composed of the local superior and the two local councillors delegated by the general council to administer a local house.
master of novices:	The person charged with the formation of novices.
master of scholastics:	The person charged with the formation of scholastics.
novice:	A candidate living the required year and a day of spiritual formation as a trial period prior to first profession of vows.
novitiate:	The initial formation, lasting a year and a day, of young men prior to their first profession of vows; also the house where this takes place.
ordination:	Sacramental reception of Holy Orders, whether as a subdeacon (not practised since 1972), deacon, or priest.
pastor:	The leader of a parish, responsible for its spiritual and temporal well-being; he is appointed by the superior general but works under the bishop of the diocese where the parish is located.
philosophy:	The period and course of study of a member, lasting from two to four years, usually in conjunction with studies for the B.A. degree.
profession (first *or* final):	The taking of the three vows of poverty, chastity and obedience in a religious community. First profession is for a trial period of one to three years; final profession is in perpetuity.
province:	A division of a Congregation, usually territorial, no longer used in the Basilian Congregation, but used until 1922.
provincial:	The confrere appointed as superior of a province.
rector:	The head of a local community numbering less than six members.
regional representative:	A confrere elected to represent members

from one of four regions: Eastern or Western Canada, or Eastern or Western United States (used only from 1967 to 1997).

religious (noun): A member of a religious community of men or women who has taken vows.

retreat: A period of prayer and reflection, in a group or privately, of obligation annually for religious.

rule: A canonically approved set of statutes and disciplinary customs forming the way of life of a religious community.

scholastic: An unordained member in vows, usually studying philosophy or theology, or engaged in one or more years of practice teaching or other apostolic work.

scholasticate: The house or community in which the scholastics live, normally during their study of philosophy or theology. In 1937 St Basil's Scholasticate was renamed St Basil's Seminary. *See also* 'house of studies.'

seminary: The house or community in which the scholastics live, normally during their study of philosophy or theology. Prior to 1937 St Basil's Seminary was known as St Basil's Scholasticate.

superior: The head of a local community numbering six or more members.

superior general: The head of a religious congregation, elected by the general chapter, for a period of four years (formerly six years).

theology: The course of study by a scholastic consisting of Scripture, the systematic (dogmatic) and moral (ethical) principles of Christianity, and the history and legal norms of the Church. It lasts four years, at least three of which are required prior to ordination.

vicar general: A confrere elected by a general chapter

to be the first assistant to the superior general.

vocation: A 'call' to a way of life; in the present context a call to the Basilian way of life.

vows: Solemn promises to God to observe poverty, chastity, and obedience; first vows are professed for a trial period of one year (later for three years) at the end of the novitiate year; final vows are taken in perpetuity.

Western course: A year of courses offered at St Michael's College for high school graduates from the United States who lacked grade XIII. Course credit was granted by Assumption College, Windsor, through its degree affiliation with the University of Western Ontario.

DICTIONARY OF BASILIAN BIOGRAPHY

A

ABEND, Joseph John, priest, was born on 21 June 1920 at Wilkes-Barre, Pennsylvania (diocese of Scranton), the only son of Joseph Charles Abend and Mary Elizabeth Marly. He died in Toronto on 1 September 1994 and is buried in the Basilian plot of Holy Cross Cemetery, Thornhill, Ontario.

Joe Abend attended elementary school and St Leo's High School at Ashley, Pennsylvania, graduating in 1938. After two years of university studies at St Michael's College, Toronto, he entered St Basil's Novitiate, Toronto, in 1940. Following first profession on 15 August 1941, he completed his undergraduate studies at St Michael's College (B.A., University of Toronto, 1943). As a scholastic he taught at the high school section of St Michael's College, 1943–4, and at Catholic Central High School, Detroit, 1944–5, where he also earned teacher certification in the state of Michigan (University of Detroit, 1945). While studying theology, he lived one year at St Michael's and three years at St Basil's Seminary, Toronto. He was ordained to the priesthood on 29 June 1948 in St Basil's Church, Toronto, by Cardinal James Charles McGuigan.

Father Abend's first twenty years were spent in the high school apostolate: Catholic Central High School, Detroit, 1949–52; Aquinas Institute, Rochester, 1952–62 and 1969–71, where he was also master of scholastics; and Andrean High School, Gary (now Merrillville), Indiana, 1962–6, where he was first councillor for the local community. He earned an M.A. in education from the University of Detroit in 1950.

In 1966 Father Abend was put in charge of scholastics at the Basilian House of Studies at St John Fisher College, Rochester, but returned to Aquinas to teach, 1969–71, before taking up parish ministry as assistant at St Basil's, Angleton, Texas, 1971–4. In 1974–5 he worked first at St Catherine's Parish, Ithaca, New York, and then at Assumption Parish, Windsor. Four other parish appointments ensued: Ste Anne's, Detroit, 1975–7, Holy Rosary, Toronto, 1977–8, St Basil's, Angleton, 1978–9, though most of this year was spent in Ashley, Pennsylvania, tending to his ailing father's affairs and assisting at the local parish; and St Anne's, Houston, 1979–82. He served the Basilian community in Phoenix, Arizona, as councillor in 1984–5, and was assistant novice master at St Basil's Novitiate, Sugar Land, Texas, 1985–6. He entered the Basilian Fathers Residence (Infirmary), Toronto, in the fall of 1986.

Joe Abend was an affable man of great common sense, a gift which served him well as head of guidance at Andrean and in Basilian formation work. He was proud of his Pennsylvania coal miner background and of his German ancestry: hard work, neatness and order, and respect for authority were other characteristic traits. He loved language and, as a teacher of English, sought to communicate this love of words and good writing to his students. Though always pleasant, he sometimes manifested a certain nervousness and angst, perhaps a sign of interior suffering.

BIBLIOGRAPHY: 'Our Unknown Citizens,' *Basilian Teacher* 7 (February 1963) 181–3; 'Patience Is Necessary for Dialogue,' *Forum* 1 (October 1964) 6; 'This Problem Is a Real One,' *Forum* 1 (December 1965) 164–5.
SOURCES: GABF; *Annals* 1 (1948) 221, 8 (1995) 106–8; *Newsletter* (10 October 1994).

ABOULIN, Jean JOSEPH Marie, priest, was born at Saint-Alban-en-Montagne in the canton of Saint-Etienne de Lugdarès (Ardèche) on 19 March 1841, the son of Joseph Aboulin and Victoire Boyer. He died in Windsor on 30 August 1931, and is buried there in the Basilian plot of Assumption Cemetery.
After education in local schools, Joseph Aboulin did classical studies, first at the Petit Séminaire de Vernoux (Ardèche) and then the rhetoric year at the Collège des Cordeliers, Annonay. He lived at Sainte-Barbe, the Basilian minor seminary, 1860–1, then entered the novitiate at Feyzin (Isère, now Rhône) on 28 September 1861 and professed final vows on Pentecost Sunday, 15 May 1864. As a scholastic he taught at the Collège de Privas, 1862–4, and at the Collège des Cordeliers, 1864–7, while studying theology. He and five other Basilians were ordained priests on 21 September 1867 by Bishop Armand de Charbonnel, retired bishop of Toronto. They were the first ordination class at the Collège du Sacré-Coeur, the new site and name of the former Collège des Cordeliers.

With Father Pierre *Chalandard he was assigned to ministry in Canada, sailing from Brest on 15 February 1868, and was welcomed at New York by Father Michael *Mulcahy. After visiting in Toronto, he taught at St Louis College, Louisville, Ohio, 1868–70. He was the first Basilian pastor of Assumption parish, Windsor, 1870–93, was master of novices at Holy Rosary in Toronto, 1893–4 and 1895–1907, pastor of St Charles parish, Newport, Michigan, 1894–5, and assistant pastor of Ste Anne's parish, Detroit, 1907–28.

'The abbé,' as the confreres called him, was short of stature and spare of frame. A congenital defect of humped shoulders caused him to walk with an awkward gait but did not prevent him from working. Father E.J. *Lajeunesse wrote of him: 'A familiar sight on the local roadways was this shepherdly man of God, with short and plodding step, wending his way on foot even to the remotest parts of the parish. It was not uncommon for him to walk six or seven miles to visit the parishioners in Petite Côte or in the fourth or fifth concessions up Huron Line way.'

Father Aboulin loved to preach the Word of God in French, and was a popular confessor. At Ste Anne's Parish, he would pick up the evening paper and, while still standing, run through the death notices and marriages. His favourite reading was *L'Ami du Clergé*, a pastoral journal for priests published in France. An opinion expressed in it almost had the force of gospel for him. He had a singular devotion to the Blessed Virgin, writing in his will of 'my most beloved Mother, who protected me from my mother's womb, and to whom I owe the greatest graces, ... especially the grace of my vocation at Le Puy, then other graces at Fourvière and at Lourdes.' A memorial volume for Monsignor Francis Van Antwerp records that, at Father Aboulin's urging, Monsignor Van Antwerp suggested to Cardinal Gibbons that a national shrine of the Immaculate Conception be erected in Washington, D.C., and that from this conversation came the first practical steps towards the realization of this now famous shrine.

As master of novices, Aboulin was a living example of the ascetic life and the soul of punctuality. The confidence the community had in him is shown by his long tenure in the office of secretary general of the Congregation, 1910–22.

In 1922, when the Basilians split into two congregations, Father Aboulin – torn between his love of France and his love for the people he was serving in the New World – chose to remain in America, and accepted the new, stricter vow of poverty. He retired to Assumption College, where in his early years he had become interested in its history and had read a paper about the college before St Basil's Academy, Assumption College, on 12 November 1879. A fuller account was published by a local newspaper in 1899. He died at the age of ninety.

SOURCES: GABF; Charles Collins, 'Basilians I Have Known,' transcribed in Robert J. Scollard, 'Historical Notes C.S.B.' 10 1–21 (GABF); Kirley, *Community in France* 33, 37, 186, 211n507, 214n515, 218, 220n528; Kirley, *Congregation in*

France 14, 29, 31–4, 45, 53, 96; Lajeunesse, *Assumption Parish*; 'Notes on the Parish of the Assumption,' *Essays of the Historical Society* 2 (1915) 76–90; *Monsignor Van Antwerp Memorial Volume* (Detroit, 1930) 68; Pouzol, 'Notices'; *Purple and White* (15 October 1927); *Semaine religieuse de Viviers* (25 September 1931) 468; *Windsor Star*, 21 November 1959; *Yearbook SMC* 24 (1933).

ACOSTA, Rudolph, priest, member of the Congregation 1958–71, was born on 20 January 1927 in River Rouge, Michigan (archdiocese of Detroit), the son of Joseph Acosta and Remedios Niño. He died on 2 December 1983 in Los Angeles, California, and is buried in St Hedwig Cemetery, Dearborn, Michigan.

'Rudy' Acosta attended Western High School, Detroit, 1940–4. After working for eleven years as apprentice, journeyman, and foreman bookbinder (with one year, 1946–7, in the United States Army), he enrolled in evening classes at Assumption University, Windsor, in 1956. A year later he entered St Basil's Novitiate, Rochester, and was professed on 12 September 1958. He studied both philosophy and theology at St Michael's College and St Basil's Seminary, Toronto, and was ordained to the priesthood on 16 December 1962 by Archbishop Philip Pocock in St Basil's Church, Toronto.

For nine years Father Acosta worked in the Basilian Fathers mission apostolate in Texas and in Mexico, first as assistant at Our Lady of Guadalupe Church, Rosenberg, Texas, 1963–5, and then at St Basil's Church, Angleton, Texas, 1965–6. During 1966–8 he was stationed at the Mission headquarters, St Joseph's Center, Sugar Land, Texas, but worked at the Centro Cultural in Mexico, D.F. For two additional years, 1968–70, he was assistant at San Juan Crisóstomo Parish, Mexico, D.F., and in 1970–1 was administrator of the Our Lady of Perpetual Help mission in Wharton, Texas. He withdrew from the Congregation in 1971. After a brief civil marriage, he moved to California, where he lived alone. He died from a sudden heart attack, and was buried one week later from Ste Anne's Church, Detroit, by Father Enrico Bravo CSB.

SOURCES: GABF; *Annals* 3 (1963) 214.

ACTORIE, Joseph Marie Julien, priest, third superior general, 1859–64, was born at Saint-Jean-en-Royans (Drôme, diocese of Valence), on 13 April 1803, the son of Michel Actorie and Julie Julien. He died at the Basilian novitiate at Feyzin (Isère, now Rhône), on 28 October 1864 and was buried there on the novitiate grounds.

Julien Actorie received his early education in a school conducted by the curé of his native village. He came in 1816 to the Collège d'Annonay, where he was placed in the *classe de troisième* as a classmate of Armand de Charbonnel, future bishop of Toronto. After finishing the classical course, and while studying philosophy and theology, he was invited to join the staff as a junior member. When the community of Priests of St Basil was less than two weeks old, he entered the novitiate on 1 December 1822 with three others, none of whom persevered. He took final vows on 30 August 1826 when he was a deacon, and was ordained to the priesthood on 23 December 1826, not yet twenty-four years of age.

Julien Actorie was stationed at the Collège de Feyzin for twenty years, 1827–47, the whole period of that college's existence, as professor of rhetoric, 1827–31, and as the college's superior and director, 1831–47. A gifted teacher of classics, mathematics, and philosophy, he was also a splendid orator. He preached the Lenten series of sermons at the cathedral at Viviers in 1849.

The Feyzin school was closed in 1847 because the marshy terrain in the region proved unhealthy and because Hippolyte Guibert, bishop of Viviers since 1841, wanted the Basilians to take charge of his minor seminaries. Father Actorie became a close friend and confidant of Bishop Guibert, and this relationship continued even after Guibert's appointment as bishop of Tours (February 1857).

In August 1847 Father Actorie was elected to the Basilian general council, replacing the recently deceased Father Augustin *Payan. He served as master of novices at Annonay, 1847–8, as superior of the minor seminary in the Bas-Vivarais, located first at Bourg-Saint-Andéol, 1848–52, and then at Aubenas, 1852–9. On 30 August 1859 he was elected superior general with fifteen of seventeen votes. Less than a month later, accompanied by Father André *Charmant, superior of Sainte-Barbe, he went to Tours to consult Bishop Guibert about the formation of minor seminarians and novices and about the nature of the new Basilian Association and its Constitutions. Guibert, having joined the Oblates of Mary Immaculate seven years after their foundation in 1816, was in a position to share with Actorie the early experience of the Oblates.

Actorie moved quickly to make necessary renovations at the Annonay college. He then set about giving the Basilian community a canonical structure. This included establishing separate houses for the novitiate and the scholasticate and drawing up proper Constitutions.

Shortly after the death on 25 October 1859 of Father Auguste de *Montgolfier, master of novices at Privas, the general council voted to renovate the former college at Feyzin as a novitiate, which opened in 1860. At the end of January 1861, after consulting local superiors and councillors, Father Actorie purchased a house on the Montée du Château, Annonay, quite close to Sainte-Barbe, as a scholasticate. It opened in 1862. During Father Actorie's tenure, Denis *O'Connor, Francis *Walsh, and Michael *Mulcahy came from Canada to study at Annonay.

On 21 January 1863 Father Actorie circulated to the community a revised version of the Constitutions; and on 7 February, in a meeting with local superiors, the Constitutions were amended and approved. They consisted of two parts, of approximately equal length: the first, in fifteen short chapters, on organizational matters, and the second, in eight chapters, on the spiritual life of the Congregation. The first article declared that the apostolate of the Congregation included all ecclesiastical ministries compatible with the common life.

On 1 August 1863 Father Actorie went to Rome to present the Constitutions, translated into Latin by Father Louis *Monot, to Pope Pius IX. At the same time he presented the favourable recommendations of Bishop Guibert and several other bishops. Though Rome requested some revisions, the Constitutions were accepted the following September, and the Basilians became a pontifical community under the title of 'The Congregation of the Priests of Saint Basil.'

In 1864 Father Actorie sent to Bishop Louis Delcusy of Viviers a report on the Congregation that would help the bishop reply to a request by the Congregation of Bishops and Regulars in Rome for a report on the Basilian Congregation. He included with it the Basilians' pledge of fidelity to the Holy Father, which they had been taught by Archbishop Charles-François d'Aviau. He also expressed gratitude for the official recognition by Rome. Having put in place all the canonical requirements to enable the Congregation to conform to the Church's norms, Father Actorie had achieved his major goals. His accomplishments made him a major figure in the formation of the early Basilian Congregation.

In May 1864 Julien Actorie fell seriously ill but recovered after a few weeks. On 11 October he and his brother Achille set out to visit Bishop Guibert in Tours. After spending the first night of their journey at the Feyzin novitiate, Achille found in the morning that his brother had fallen to the floor and was unable to get up. Julien Actorie never recovered from this seizure, and died on 28 October 1864 of a cerebral haemorrhage. Bishop Guibert stated at this time: 'You know how close I was to this dear Superior; he was for me a true friend. Quite apart from the services he had rendered to my diocese when I was at Viviers, there grew up between him and me the bonds of real friendship because of a kinship of ideas. Moreover he had such great and beautiful qualities. I have never encountered such pure, sincere and solid virtue. He was the type of the true priest of Jesus Christ' (Roume, *Origines*, 398).

BIBLIOGRAPHY:
Books: *De l'origine et de la réparation du mal* (Lyon, 1846; repr. Paris, 1852). Two books in manuscript: 'Considérations sur la Providence,' and the other untitled.
Article: Circular letter (excerpts) of 26 January 1863, in *Basilian Vademecum*, ed. M.V. Kelly (Toronto, 1930) 94–105.
SOURCES: GABF; Chomel, *Collège d'Annonay* 56–9, 442–7; *Dictionnaire de biographie française* (Paris 1933) 1 365–6; Kirley, *Community in France* 29, 59, 239, and passim; Kirley, *Congregation in France* 226; Pouzol, 'Notices'; Roume, *Origines* 240–9, 273, 296–9, 305–13, 346, 372–84, 387–99, 405.

ADAM, Leo Joseph, priest, was born in Windsor on 19 January 1914, the only son of Joseph Adam and Rose Martin. He died in Toronto on 9 February 1987 and is buried in the Basilian plot of Holy Cross Cemetery, Thornhill, Ontario.

Leo attended Immaculate Conception parish school and Assumption College School, Windsor, and took grade XIII at Sudbury High School. After working for a time in the Sudbury mines and in the family grocery store to help support his family, he entered St Basil's Novitiate, Toronto, in August 1938, and was professed on 15 August 1939.

During his university studies (B.A., University of Western Ontario, History and English, 1943), Leo taught French, in which he was fluent, at Assumption College School. At Catholic Central, Detroit, 1943–4, he taught ancient history. He took courses in education at the University of Detroit, 1944, and at Wayne State University, 1945, leading to teacher certification for Michigan. During his theological studies at St Basil's Seminary, Toronto, 1944–8, he taught religion at St Michael's College School. After ordination on 29 June 1947 by Cardinal James Charles McGuigan in St Basil's Church, Toronto, Father Adam's priestly ministry was spent almost entirely in the Basilian mission parishes in Texas: Our Lady of Guadalupe, Rosenberg, assistant pastor, 1948–50 and 1964–7, rector and pastor 1950–4 and 1967–72; Our Lady of Mount Carmel, Wharton, rector and pastor, 1958–64, assistant pastor, 1978–82; St Basil's, Angleton, assistant pastor, 1972–7. There were two short appointments to Ste Anne's, Detroit, as assistant pastor, 1954–7 and 1977–8. His warm and playful nature resonated with the Hispanic people he served.

In 1982 a diabetic condition made it necessary for him to be assigned to the Basilian Fathers Residence (Infirmary), Toronto, where his health gradually declined. His love of travel, however, overcame his disability. From time to time he would disappear and turn up, unannounced and disarmingly cheerful, in the old haunts of his ministry, having travelled immense distances by bus. He would willingly return to the infirmary routine until the urge to travel came on him once more – an exasperating conduct that was redeemed by his ingenuousness.

SOURCES: GABF; *Annals* 1 (1943) 36, 6 (1988) 696–7; *Newsletter* (17 February 1987).

AGIUS, Grace Joseph, priest, was born on 3 September 1915 at Zebbug, Malta, the son of Joseph Agius and Mary Anne Spiteri. He died in Windsor on 18 September 1998 and is buried there in the Basilian plot of Heavenly Rest Cemetery.

The Agius family moved to Toronto from Malta in 1920. Grace enrolled in the high school section of St Michael's College, Toronto, in 1929, and in 1934 he entered St Basil's Novitiate, Toronto, making first profession on 12 September 1935. His first appointment was to Assumption College, Windsor, where, along with undergraduate studies (B.A., University of Western Ontario, 1938), he was assistant prefect of boarders. After an additional year of teaching at Assumption, he began theological studies at St Basil's Seminary in Toronto. During 1940–1 he lived at St Michael's College, and concurrently with his theological studies attended the Ontario College of Education. He was ordained a priest on 19 December 1942 in St Basil's Church, Toronto, by Archbishop James Charles McGuigan.

After teaching at St Michael's College School from 1942 to 1946, he was appointed to St Basil's Novitiate, Richmond Hill, Ontario, and assumed the management of Annesi Jersey Farm, then owned by St Michael's College. In 1951 he was appointed to Catholic Central High School, Detroit. Three years later, he was moved to Assumption College School, Windsor, where he remained until the end of his life.

Grace Agius was a self-effacing, affable, and devout jack-of-all-trades who could manage a farm or a boarders' residence, repair a watch or a building, raise funds with the Dads' Club, obtain his third-class engineering papers, teach geometry, algebra, typing, bookkeeping, religion, shop, and Latin, and serve as guidance counsellor. He loved his work, and deeply cared for the community and the school. He was at ease with working people, and they with him.

He regularly prepared and delivered homilies at Most Holy Trinity Parish, Detroit, until a few months before his death, and often said the printers' Mass in Detroit at two o'clock on Sunday morning. He also served as chaplain to the Maltese communities in Detroit and Windsor, celebrating Mass every first Friday for the Windsor group. In his last few years age and ill health brought the added pain of having to curtail work, which had been the joy and mainstay of his life.

SOURCES: GABF; *Annals* 1 (1943) 28, 6 (1986) 398, 7 (1993) 3–4, 9 (1999) 92–4; *Newsletter* (31 October 1998).

ALBOUSSIERE, Louis, priest, was born on 27 November 1873 at Tournon (Ardèche), the son of Jean Alboussière and Marie-Louise Marion. He died in Lyon in 1926. The place of burial is unknown.

Louis made his novitiate in 1895 at the Petit Séminaire de Vernoux (Ardèche) under the direction of Father Jean-Marie *Godard. He took first vows on 18 September 1896 and made final profession on 22 September 1899. He was ordained to the priesthood on 21 September 1901 at the Collège du Sacré-Coeur, Annonay, by Hilarion-Joseph Montéty, titular bishop of Beirut.

While being tutored in theology Louis worked in Basilian schools: professor at the Petit Séminaire d'Aubenas, 1896–7, recreation master at the Petit Séminaire de Vernoux, 1897–8, professor in the senior grades at the Collège Saint-Charles, Blidah, Algeria, 1898–9. After ordination he stayed another year in Blidah as home room teacher for *seconde* and then enrolled at the Faculté catholique de Lyon for graduate studies. He was slated to return to the college in Blidah, but the school was closed on 18 July 1903 as a result of the anticlerical laws in France.

The records of the Community make scant mention of him in the ensuing years. In 1903–4 he was private tutor in the home of a Monsieur Dorado in Paris. The following year he served as curate in the parish of Arcens (Ardèche), and in 1905–6 he was curate at Saint-Victor (Ardèche). He also worked in various parishes in the Drôme – Châteauneuf-de-Bordette and Montmiral being two of them. In 1910 and

1913 he was at Vercoiran, and in 1922 at Valence. He returned for the year 1924–5 to the Petit Séminaire d'Aubenas, where he was in charge of the students in first year of high school. With failing health, he underwent treatment in 1925 at the psychiatric hospital in Lyon, where he died a year later.

SOURCE: Kirley, *Community in France* 185, 210; Kirley, *Congregation in France* 72; Pouzol, 'Notices.'

ALLARD, Richard Joseph, priest, was born on 18 March 1935 in Syracuse, New York, the son of Charles Allard and Winifred Waite. He died in Houston on 31 March 1994 and is buried there in the Basilian plot of Garden of Gethsemane, Forest Park Lawndale Cemetery.

'Dick' Allard completed high school at Cathedral Academy, Syracuse. He learned of the Basilians through Father John H. *O'Loane's Sunday ministry at the Allards' parish in Syracuse. Richard entered St Basil's Novitiate, Rochester, and was professed on 15 August 1954. He attended Assumption College, Windsor (B.A. University of Western Ontario, majors in French and Philosophy, 1958). He was awarded the gold medal for French, the Marseille Bursary, the University Proficiency Scholarship, and the Pearson Bursary. He taught French and Latin for two years, 1958–60, at Aquinas Institute and for one year at Catholic Central High School, Detroit, while earning an M.A. in education (University of Rochester, 1961). After one year of theology at St Basil's Seminary, Toronto, he spent 1962 to 1964 at Maison Saint-Basile, the newly founded Basilian residence near Paris, taking classes at the Séminaire Saint-Sulpice, Issy-les-Moulineaux. During the summers he studied French at the Université de Strasbourg. He was ordained to the priesthood on 13 December 1964 in St Basil's Church, Toronto, by Archbishop George Bernard *Flahiff.

Father Allard's ministries were varied: teacher at Aquinas Institute, 1965–74; moderator of scholastics at Aquinas, 1966–8; secretary general of the Basilian Fathers and rector of the Curial House, Toronto, 1974–8; student counsellor at the University of St Thomas, Houston, 1978–80; master of novices, Detroit, 1980–1; director of associates and vocations, living at Aquinas, 1981–6; rector of the mission centre, Sugar Land, Texas, 1986–9; registrar, University of St Michael's College, Toronto, 1989–92; and registrar, University of St Thomas, 1992–4. He held permanent teaching certification (French) from the State of New York, and took graduate courses at Middlebury College, Vermont, and at Case

Western Reserve University, Cleveland, Ohio. In 1969 he obtained the New York State Permanent School Administration Certificate (Secondary School Principal).

Richard Allard's appointment to the vital areas of vocations and formation indicates the confidence the community placed in him. As mission procurator he was responsible for the renovation of the St Joseph's Mission Center in Sugar Land, Texas, and for furthering its tradition of hospitality. He shared his talents and expertise with religious communities of women, who frequently invited him to chair a chapter or to give a retreat to them.

BIBLIOGRAPHY: 'This Might Fall into the Hands of Bandwagon Basilians with Their Yo-Yo Mentality,' *Forum* 1 (May 1965) 113–14; 'Let Us Be Constantly Growing: Reflections on Father Murray Bogdasavitch's Article "Consultation and Community,"' *Forum* 3 (May 1967) 71–2.
SOURCES: GABF; *Annals* 3 (1965) 375, 8 (1995) 97–9; *Newsletter* (2 May 1994).

ALLEN, Elliott Bernard, priest, was born on 18 June 1921 in Hartford, Connecticut, the elder of two sons of Edward Allen and Elizabeth Stevenson. He died in Toronto on 21 January 1981 and is buried in the Basilian plot of Holy Cross Cemetery, Thornhill, Ontario.

Elliott, popularly known as 'Al' or as 'El Allen,' was educated at St Augustine's Elementary School, Bridgeport, Connecticut, and Cathedral Grade School, Springfield, Connecticut, and then at Basic Junior High School, Bridgeport, and Bulkeley High School, Hartford, graduating from the latter in 1939. He enrolled in Wesleyan University, Middleton, Connecticut, as a Jacob L. Fox Foundation scholar, but transferred in 1941 to St Michael's College in the University of Toronto. In 1942 he entered St Basil's Novitiate, Rochester, was professed on 12 September 1943, and then taught one year at Aquinas Institute, Rochester.

In 1944 he resumed undergraduate studies in the University of Toronto (B.A. Honours Philosophy, 1946). He studied theology at St Basil's Seminary, Toronto, 1946–50, and was ordained to the priesthood on 29 June 1949 in St Basil's Church, Toronto, by Cardinal James Charles McGuigan. Father Allen pursued graduate studies in philosophy and theology at the University of Toronto and at the Pontifical Institute of Mediaeval Studies, 1950–4 (M.A., University of Toronto, Philosophy, 1951; M.S.L., Pontifical Institute, 1951; Ph.D., University of Toronto, Philosophy, 1958, with a two-volume thesis, 'The Notion of

Being in Hervaeus Natalis'). From 1951 to 1953 he also taught theology at St Basil's Seminary. In 1955 he joined the Department of Philosophy at the University of British Columbia, Vancouver. There, in the Basilian community at St Mark's College, he served as second councillor, 1959–60, and as first councillor, 1960–2. A coronary thrombosis in the spring of 1961 ended his work in Vancouver, and he accepted a modified teaching schedule in 1962 at Assumption University, Windsor.

In 1963 Father Allen returned to Toronto to teach theology at St Basil's Seminary, and became prefect of studies there in 1964. Two years later he was appointed chairman of the Professional Division of the Faculty of Theology in the University of St Michael's College, and moved into the Basilian community at St Michael's in 1968. In that same year he was instrumental in creating the Institute of Christian Thought, a consortium of the theological programs at St Michael's, St Augustine's Seminary, and Regis College. He was one of the moving spirits on the Committee for Cooperation in Theological Education which led to the formation in 1969 of the Toronto School of Theology (TST). As dean of St Michael's faculty of theology from 1969 he played a leading role in the growth of TST into one of the leading ecumenical centres of theological studies in North America. He was a member of the co-ordinating committee on Theological Education in Canada, serving one year as chairman, 1978–9. During these years he was the local superior of the Basilian community at St Michael's, 1973 to 1976, and wrote about his perception of the role of St Michael's in the challenges of theological education in the immediate post–Vatican II period.

A recurrence of serious health problems began in 1977 with heart fibrillations, followed two years later by several heart attacks over a period of several months. Then, while recuperating in hospital from a stroke suffered in 1980, he suffered cardiac arrest while being prepared for gall bladder surgery, all of which left him greatly weakened. Nevertheless, in early January 1981, he asked to be moved from the Infirmary to St Basil's College (located in the same building) in order to do some teaching. On the morning of 21 January he suffered a heart attack and died a few hours later in St Michael's Hospital.

Elliott Allen was an energetic, not to say passionate teacher, a dedicated scholar, and an effective, clear-thinking administrator. He held his opinions strongly without losing respect for those who held different views. His common sense, honesty, and sense of humour attracted and encouraged many. Always loyal to the Church and her mission, he loved the Basilian community where he found friendship and support and where he communicated the same. The homilist at his funeral said that he was a man who, by his example, taught how to live and how to die.

BIBLIOGRAPHY: 'Obedience,' *Forum* 3 (May 1967) 71–2; 'International Congress on the Theology of Renewal,' *Basilian Teacher* 11 (October 1967) 341–3; 'The Roman Catholic Seminary: Changing Perspectives in Theological Education,' *Canadian Journal of Theology* 14 no. 3 (July 1968) 159–68; 'Resurrection,' *Aspects of Basilian Spirituality* (Toronto, 1972) 1–2.
SOURCES: GABF; *Annals* 1 (1949) 263, 6 (1982) 83–5; *Newsletter* (3 February 1981).

ALLIGNOL, Ferdinand, priest, member of the Congregation 1851–8, was born on 10 September 1829 at Saint-Pons, canton of Villeneuve-de-Berg (Ardèche). He died at Mercuer, canton of Aubenas (Ardèche) on 11 April 1900.
Ferdinand received secondary schooling probably at the Basilian Collège de Privas (Ardèche) and came to the Collège des Cordeliers, section Sainte-Barbe, Annonay, for philosophy, 1849–50. He graduated as *bachelier* in April 1851, and became a novice in the Congregation on 28 September 1851. While doing theological studies he combined teaching and prefect duties in the Collège des Cordeliers. He made final profession of vows on 1 May 1854 and was ordained a priest on 25 May that year by Bishop Joseph-Hippolyte Guibert of Viviers in the chapel of the Collège des Cordeliers.
Father Allignol taught *troisième* in the Collège de Privas (Ardèche), 1854–5, and was then appointed to the Petit Séminaire de Vernoux, where he taught *seconde*, 1855–6, and *rhétorique*, or *première*, 1857–8. He returned to the Collège des Cordeliers to teach *seconde*, 1857–8. In October 1858 he withdrew from the Congregation to engage in parochial ministry in the diocese of Viviers. He died as parish priest of Mercuer.

SOURCE: Pouzol, 'Notices,' Supplément 3.

ALLNOCH, Carl Mitchell, priest, was born in Victoria, Texas (archdiocese of San Antonio, since 1982 diocese of Victoria), on 15 December 1908, the son of Fred Allnoch and Rebecca Mitchell. He died near Port Lavaca, Texas, on 12 January 1969 and is buried in the Basilian plot of Garden of Gethsemane, Forest Park Lawndale Cemetery, Houston. A nephew, Fred Allnoch, was ordained in 1961 and later laicized.

Raised in a prosperous family of dry goods merchants, Carl was baptized and grew up in Houston, where he attended St Thomas College (later St Thomas High School). He entered St Basil's Novitiate, Toronto, making first profession on 11 August 1928. After his undergraduate studies at Assumption College, Windsor (B.A., University of Western Ontario, 1932), he studied theology at St Basil's Scholasticate, Toronto, 1932–6, and was ordained to the priesthood on 21 December 1935 by Bishop Christopher Byrne in Houston. The chalice presented to him by his family had once belonged to Jean-Marie Odin, the first bishop of Galveston (1847).

In 1936 he began his active ministry in Houston, where he was to spend the rest of his life. From 1936 to 1948 he taught English, Latin, and mathematics at St Thomas College. He obtained an M.A. in education from the University of Houston in 1943. From 1948 to 1950 he was assistant pastor at St Anne's Parish, Houston, after which he returned to teaching at St Thomas High School, where he was superior of the local Basilian community from 1959 to 1967.

A Texan to the marrow of his bones, 'Bucky' Allnoch was a tamer and rider of horses. As a scholastic he brought a team of horses to the Basilian retreat on Strawberry Island in Lake Simcoe, Ontario, to fill in the mosquito-breeding swamp on its east side. In Houston, he kept horses on the grounds of the school and once rode a horse into the school building, much to the admiration of the students and the consternation of the janitors. Named for his maternal grandfather, J.D. Mitchell, a famous Texas naturalist, Carl became a master of all the skills needed for survival and enjoyment in the outdoors. He was a sailor, navigator, explorer, hunter, fisherman, and an outstanding football coach. He learned welding in 1937 by helping to construct the school football stadium on the site to which the new school plant would move in 1941. During the Second World War he taught this vital skill at St Thomas High School.

Carl Allnoch's Texas pose and swagger were a front for a shy and kind man, beloved and admired among his students. He died suddenly on a Sunday morning shortly after saying Mass and about to go fishing near the Allnoch family cottage. Father Alfred *Caird, who was with him, administered the last rites.

SOURCES: GABF; *Annals* 4 (1970) 131–2; *Newsletter* (13 January 1969); http://www.sths.org/athletics/hof/inductees/allnochc.htm

ALLOR, Edward William, priest, was born at Mission de L'Anse Creuse, Harrison Township, Michigan (archdiocese of Detroit), on 20 April 1890, the second youngest son of Isidore Allor and Mary Forton. He died in Toronto on 12 February 1974 and is buried in the Basilian plot of Holy Cross Cemetery, Thornhill, Ontario.

After primary education at Roseville, Michigan, Edward went to work at the Ford Motor Company, Detroit. At the age of twenty-four, with the encouragement of Father Francis Van Antwerp of Our Lady of the Rosary Church, Detroit, he quit his job as foreman to begin studies for the priesthood by enrolling at Assumption College, Windsor. After completing four years of high school and one year of university in three years, he entered St Basil's Novitiate, Toronto, in September 1917, making first profession on 7 October 1918. He completed his undergraduate studies at Assumption College, Windsor (B.A., University of Western Ontario, 1919), and then took his first year of theology at St Basil's Scholasticate, Toronto, 1919–20, concurrently attending the Ontario College of Education for teacher certification (1920). His theology course was interrupted in 1921–2 to teach at St Thomas College, Houston. He was ordained to the priesthood on 22 December 1923 at St Augustine's Seminary, Toronto, by Bishop Alexander MacDonald.

Father Allor's priestly life was devoted exclusively to parish ministry: Assumption Parish, Windsor, as assistant, 1924–6, and then as pastor, 1926–37, returning there three times as assistant, 1943–4, 1954–5, and 1965–70; Ste Anne's, Detroit, as pastor, 1937–42 and as assistant, 1959–60; St John the Baptist, Amherstburg, Ontario, assistant 1944–6, 1955–9, 1960–5, 1970–January 1972; and Holy Rosary, Toronto, 1946–54.

Father Allor prepared his sermons weeks in advance and delivered them with ardent conviction. They were always practical and strictly in accord with the teaching of the Church. A special talent in dealing with people, especially in home visitations, left an affectionate memory of his pastoral devotedness. His attention to children, whether in the parish schools or his own nieces and nephews, was received by them with joy. He was also an able administrator, a practical builder, and a perfectionist. As pastor he was demanding of his assistants, though he was the first to meet the high standards he set. Bishop John Thomas Kidd of London, Ontario, described Father Allor as 'the model parish priest.'

Defective eyesight plagued him from the time he was ordained, resulting in special dispensations with regard to the reading of his breviary and the celebration of Mass. In his later years he suffered a great deal from arterial complications and headaches. He entered St Basil's Infirmary, Toronto, in January 1973. Although he found some relief in the care given him there, he spent a year of continuous suffering, from which only death one year later brought deliverance.

SOURCES: GABF; *Annals* 4 (1969) 117, 5 (1974) 8, (1975) 113–15; *Newsletter* (14 February 1974).

AMLIN, Thomas Delbert, priest, was born in Windsor on 19 August 1935, one of five sons of Malcolm Amlin and May Anderson. He died in Toronto on 2 December 1979 and is buried in the Basilian plot of Heavenly Rest Cemetery, Windsor.

Tom was educated in Windsor, first at Immaculate Conception and De La Salle parochial schools and then at Patterson Collegiate and W.D. Lowe Vocational School, where he graduated in 1955. He worked at Ford of Canada until 1962, when he entered St Basil's Novitiate, Pontiac, Michigan. After profession on 15 August 1963, he taught for one year at Catholic Central High School, Detroit, while studying accounting at the University of Detroit (B.B.A., 1964). He taught at Michael Power High School, Etobicoke, Ontario, 1964–5, and then at Catholic Central, 1965–6, before beginning theological studies at St Basil's Seminary, Toronto. In 1969 he was appointed to Aquinas Institute, Rochester, to teach part-time and to continue theological studies at St Bernard's Seminary. He was ordained to the priesthood on 13 December 1969 in St Scholastica's Church, Detroit, by Bishop Walter Schoenherr.

In 1970 Father Amlin was appointed to St Mary's College, Sault Ste Marie, Ontario. In October of the following year he underwent surgery for a malignant brain tumour, and resumed his teaching after a short recuperation. In June 1973, he was appointed to St Basil's College, Toronto, as bursar, while teaching part-time at St Michael's College School, Toronto. In 1975 he returned to St Mary's College to supervise the library and to teach.

The last year of his life was one of intense suffering. In the space of seven months he twice underwent brain surgery. He had a great desire to return to his work after the second intervention, and did so, but only for a short time. He was taken to St Basil's Infirmary in Toronto in the latter part of October 1979, and died there five weeks later.

Throughout his relatively short life as a Basilian priest, Father Amlin was thoroughgoing, steady and reliable in his work. He was an uncomplaining and deeply spiritual person. He accepted his various appointments and his illness with admirable equanimity. He enjoyed solitude, but was also a ready and affable community man. His habitual consideration of others was especially seen in his concern for those who cared for him in his suffering.

SOURCES: GABF; *Annals* 4 (1970) 126, 5 (1980) 524–5; *Newsletter* (6 December 1979).

ANGLIN, Gerald Falconbridge, priest, was born in Toronto on 22 March 1902, one of fourteen children of Arthur W. Anglin and Madeleine Falconbridge. He died in Toronto on 17 October 1996 and is buried in the Basilian plot of Holy Cross Cemetery, Thornhill, Ontario.

Gerald Anglin came from a distinguished family. His grandfather Timothy Anglin was speaker of the House of Commons, 1874–8. His aunt Margaret Anglin, an actress in the United States, was famous for her roles in Greek tragedies. Frank Anglin, an uncle, was chief justice of Canada, 1924–33; and his maternal grandfather, Sir Glenholme Falconbridge, was chief justice of Ontario in the early years of the twentieth century.

'Gerry,' as he was always called, attended primary and secondary schools in Toronto, took his B.A. at Loyola College, Montreal, in 1923, enrolled at Osgoode Hall, Toronto, and was called to the bar in 1926. He never practised law, however, for in that same year he entered St Basil's Novitiate, Toronto, and was professed on 2 October 1927. He studied theology at St Basil's Scholasticate, Toronto, 1927–31, and was ordained to the priesthood on 21 December 1930 by Bishop Alexander MacDonald. While studying theology he also attended the Ontario College of Education in Toronto, earning teacher certification for Ontario.

For the first twelve years of his priesthood he received educational assignments: St Michael's College School, Toronto, 1930–6, as principal; St Thomas More College, Saskatoon, 1936–40 and 1941–2, as cofounder with Father E.L. Rush; and St Basil's Seminary, Toronto, 1940–1. In 1942 he began parish ministry, which would occupy the rest of his active Basilian life: St Basil's Parish, Toronto, 1942–61, as assistant, and Holy Rosary Parish, Toronto, 1961–90, also as assistant. He retired to the Basilian Fathers Residence (Infirmary), afterwards named 'Anglin House' in his memory, in 1990, where he became not only the oldest living Basilian at that time but also one of the most beloved.

Father Anglin was gentle, perfectly mannered, considerate, devoted and soft-spoken, as well as witty. Noting that his family had lived on Grosvenor Street, just three blocks from the infirmary, he liked to remark, 'I didn't get very far in ninety years.' He had a way with children, and well into his eighties he was still preparing the classes for first confession and holy communion.

A man of many interests, Father Anglin was a tennis player in his youth and a lover of nature. He enjoyed particularly televised documentaries depicting the flora and fauna of the world. At the age of sixty he developed an interest in geology, and organized Basilian rock hunts to various parts of Ontario – 'Gerry's rock festivals,' as some called them. He willed his collection of minerals to the Royal Ontario Museum. He was ninety-four when he died.

BIBLIOGRAPHY: 'Ceremonies at Benediction,' *Basilian* 2 (May 1936) 100.
SOURCES: GABF; *Annals* 5 (1978) 266, 5 (1981) 538, 8 (1997) 114–15; *Newsletter* (1 November 1996); *Toronto Star*, 'Obituaries,' 19 October 1996.

ARMSTRONG, Charles Joseph, priest, was born on 10 October 1906 at Stratford, Ontario (diocese of London), one of four children of Charles Joseph Armstrong and Anne Sullivan. He died in Windsor on 29 May 2001 and is buried there in the Basilian plot of Heavenly Rest Cemetery.

'Army,' as he was familiarly known, attended St Joseph's parochial school in Stratford, did high school at Assumption College, Windsor, 1920–1 and 1923–5, Stratford Collegiate Institute, 1921–3, and Assumption College, Windsor, 1925–9 (B.A., University of Western Ontario). The presence there of Father Daniel *Dillon inspired him to become a Basilian. He entered St Basil's Novitiate, Toronto, and made first profession on 1 October 1930. He took his theology courses at St Basil's Scholasticate, Toronto, 1930–4, being ordained to the priesthood on 21 December 1933 in Assumption Church, Windsor, by Bishop Alexander MacDonald.

After one year of teaching at St Michael's College 'East End' School, Toronto, 1934–5, Father Armstrong was appointed to Assumption College School, where he was to remain for the next sixty-six years. Describing his first years there, he recounted: 'We were always poor. ...

We nearly had to close the school that year [1935] because we ran out of food. ... We worked twelve hours a day, did parish work in Detroit and Windsor on the weekends to bring in additional funds and visited Catholic homes to recruit students. It was always a struggle.' He became famous and much beloved as a coach, teacher, and ardent sportsman; many saw him as the heart of Assumption. He had a talent for attracting others by his genuine interest in them, his joyful simplicity, and his enthusiasm. Stories about him are legion, many of them based on his ingenuousness, almost a naïveté, which was partly natural and partly assumed. One student described him as 'humble, charismatic, smart as a whip, and a con artist too.' Students whose name he could not remember were invariably called 'Sparky.'

Father Armstrong became a legend in his lifetime. He died while celebrating Mass with his confreres. When news of his death reached the students, the mission collection, which had been one of his enthusiasms, doubled its normal five-thousand-dollar total. His wake and funeral were attended by hundreds of friends, students, and alumni. A plaque, placed on the seat in the gymnasium where he regularly watched all games, reads, 'Reserved for Father Armstrong – forever.'

SOURCES: GABF; *Annals* 5 (1981) 539–40, 6 (1984) 204–5, 9 (2000) 5, 10 (2002) 89; *Newsletter* (22 June 2001); McMahon, *Pure Zeal* 24, 86.

ARMSTRONG, David Linus, priest, was born on 9 August 1941 in the Irish Block, Woodford, Ontario, near Owen Sound (diocese of Hamilton), the son of John Francis Armstrong and Catherine Traynor. He died in Toronto on 10 April 1992 and is buried in the Basilian plot of Holy Cross Cemetery, Thornhill, Ontario.

After completing grade XIII at Owen Sound Collegiate and Vocational School, 'Dave' entered St Basil's Novitiate, Richmond Hill, Ontario, and was professed on 15 August 1961. He was appointed to the Basilian House of Studies, Windsor, where, along with his studies in science, he developed his musical talents of voice and violin at the Ursuline School of Music and, in the summer of 1964, at the Royal Conservatory of Music in Toronto. He won the Dr R.J. Coyle Memorial Prize in Zoology and two university in-course scholarships (B.Sc., Honours Biology, University of Western Ontario, 1965). He did a year of graduate studies in science at the University of Alberta, living at St Joseph's College; but in 1966 he withdrew from the Basilian Congregation and returned to Owen Sound to teach high school science. In

1967 he returned to the community, beginning a second novitiate at Erindale, Ontario. By indult from the Holy See he made his profession four months early on 10 April 1968, and taught for the balance of the year at Michael Power High School, Etobicoke, Ontario, and then for three years at St Joseph's High School, Ottawa, 1968–71, before doing theological studies at St Basil's College, Toronto, 1971–5, where he also directed the choir. He did his diaconate year at the Newman Centre, Toronto, and was ordained to the priesthood in the Thomas Aquinas Chapel of the Centre on 30 May 1975 by Bishop Francis Allen.

Father Armstrong taught at Michael Power High School, 1975–6, before undertaking three years of graduate studies in science at the University of Guelph, Ontario. His research during this time helped open the way to the production of an improved soy protein. In 1979 he returned to teaching, once again at Michael Power, and from 1980 to 1982 served as local superior there. His talents and zeal found their full scope in his work as chaplain at the University of Calgary, 1982–91. His rapport with the students, his vibrant sense of liturgy, and his contagious spirit of joy made his ministry effective and memorable. In 1991, at the onset of a serious blood disorder, he moved to Holy Rosary Parish, Toronto, for rest and renewal; but increasing debility necessitated transfer to the Basilian Fathers Residence (Infirmary), Toronto, where he died less than a year later.

SOURCES: GABF; *Annals* 5 (1976) 133–4, 7 (1993) 124–6; *Newsletter* (30 April 1992).

ARNOUX, Jean François Régis, priest, was born at Saint-Arcons-de-Barges, canton of Pradelles (Haute-Loire, diocese of Le Puy), on 12 February 1824. He died at Prades (Ardèche) on 21 August 1891, and was buried in the cemetery there.

Jean François interrupted his theological studies at the Grand Séminaire, Le Puy, in January 1848 and went to the Collège des Cordeliers, Annonay. He entered the novitiate on 30 September 1848, either at Vernoux (Ardèche) or in Annonay. Archbishop (later Cardinal) Ferdinand-François-Auguste Donnet of Bordeaux, a graduate of the Collège des Cordeliers, conferred the subdiaconate on him in the college chapel in Annonay on 29 September 1850. He made the customary profession and promise of stability on 28 September 1851. Bishop Joseph-Hippolyte Guibert of Viviers ordained him deacon in the chapel in Annonay on 23 February 1851 and priest on 20 December 1851 at Viviers.

For the next eight years, 1851–9, Father Arnoux conducted classes in grammar at the Petit Séminaire de Vernoux. When the Basilian community took vows in 1852, he chose at first to remain in his former state of profession with a promise of stability; but on 22 September 1865 he made a new profession, accepting the terms of the 1852 vows. After 1859 his health began to deteriorate. He taught *cinquième* at the Collège des Cordeliers, but had to be replaced in February 1861 for reasons of health. After a year of teaching *quatrième* at the Basilian school at Privas, 1862–3, he went to teach at the Petit Séminaire d'Aubenas, but again fell ill. Father Antoine *Bord came up from the Calvary Shrine at Prades to take his classes, while Father Arnoux took up residence at Prades. By 1865 his health was good enough to allow him to assume the duties of bursar at the Petit Séminaire d'Aubenas, a post he filled for the next nine years. In April 1874 he spent a short time at the novitiate at Feyzin (Isère, now Rhône), and then went to teach at the school for day scholars at Privas, 1874–6. Father Arnoux's last assignment was that of chaplain at the Calvary Shrine at Prades.

SOURCES: Pouzol, 'Notices'; Roume, *Origines* 347.

AUDIBERT, Auguste, priest, was born at Saint-Pierre-le-Déchausselat, canton of Les Vans (Ardèche) on 17 December 1840, son of Jean Audibert and Rosalie Martel. His date of death and place of burial are unknown.

Auguste made his novitiate at Feyzin (Isère, now Rhône), and worked in Basilian schools as he studied for the priesthood. In 1871–2 he was recreation and study-hall master at the Collège du Bourg-Saint-Andéol (Ardèche). From 1872 to 1884 he fulfilled the same functions at the Ecole cléricale run by the Basilians at Périgueux (Dordogne), some one hundred kilometres northeast of Bordeaux. Here he received the subdiaconate on 21 December 1872. Bishop Armand de Charbonnel ordained him deacon on 20 September 1873 in the chapel of the Collège du Sacré-Coeur, Annonay. Auguste then returned to Périgueux and was ordained to the priesthood there on 30 May 1874. He remained in charge of discipline at the school at Périgueux for the next ten years, when he came back to Annonay to assume the duties of prefect of discipline at Sainte-Barbe, the Basilian minor seminary for students who could not afford tuition. After one year he moved to the Petit Séminaire de Vernoux (Ardèche), where for the next three years he was again in charge of discipline. From 1883 to 1903, at the Collège

Saint-Charles, Blidah, Algeria, he taught successively the *classes de huitième* and *septième*. After the anti-religious laws of the Third French Republic forced the closing of the school in 1903, Father Audibert served as chaplain in Italian convents, first at San Remo in 1909 and then at Porto Maurizio in 1910 and 1913. The records of the provincial Father Noël *Durand, 1845–1922, show that financial help was sent to him regularly until 1915, after which date no mention is made of him.

SOURCE: Kirley, *Community in France* 38, 185, 208; Pouzol, 'Notices.'

AUREILLE, Edouard, priest, cousin of Father Emile *Aureille, was born at Meysse (Ardèche) on 21 September 1862. He died on 5 April 1934 near Port Saïd, Egypt, where he is buried.

Edouard Aureille, quite young when his father died, was educated at home by his mother. He had a sister in the Congregation of the Presentation of Mary. When he gave early signs of a vocation to the priesthood, the village curé taught him Latin. In 1876, at the age of fourteen, he organized a reception at Meysse for Bishop Joseph-Michel-Frédéric Bonnet of Viviers. He studied at the Collège du Sacré-Coeur, Annonay, Sainte-Barbe section, 1877–8, and at the Petit Séminaire de Vernoux, 1878–80. In 1880 he began his novitiate at Sainte-Barbe, where he also did duty as assistant prefect. He completed the *baccalauréat ès sciences* in 1882 and did theological studies, 1881–6, while teaching mathematics at the college in Annonay and serving one year as prefect at the College of Mary Immaculate, Beaconfield House, Plymouth, England. He was ordained priest by Bishop Bonnet on 15 September 1886 in the chapel of the Collège du Sacré-Coeur.

After his ordination he returned to Beaconfield House, where he remained until the college was closed in 1903. During these years he taught Latin, design, and mathematics. He was also an accomplished musician and amateur photographer. He stayed in England until 1919, becoming chaplain to the Sisters of Quimperlé who had been expelled from France, as well as chaplain to the Catholic troops of the Plymouth garrison. He was also instrumental in bringing the Sisters of the Presentation of Mary to Exeter and Plymouth. His long stay at Beaconfield and his knowledge and love of England induced his French confreres to refer to him as *'l'Anglais.'*

On his return to France he became pastor at Arcin in Médoc (Gironde). In 1923 he was at the Petit Séminaire de Saint-Charles, Annonay, and also taught at the Collège du Sacré-Coeur. In 1928–9 he supervised the renovations at the Maison Saint-Joseph, where Father Victorin *Marijon and others took up residence in the summer of 1929. Father Aureille continued his work at the petit séminaire, which had been confided to the diocesan clergy, and also served as treasurer general for the community in France, 1931–4. He loved to travel. In the spring of 1934 he undertook a trip to the Holy Land. On his way back, his weak eyesight caused him to miss his step and fall to his death from a moving train near Port Saïd, Egypt, where his funeral service and burial took place.

A man of many parts who taught many disciplines, Father Aureille also directed college choirs and served as organist. Because of his assistance in their work in England, the Presentation Sisters in Exeter, England, had Mass offered four times a year for the repose of his soul.

SOURCES: GABF; Kirley, *Community in France* 208; Kirley, *Congregation in France* 72, 85, 123, 126–7, 130, 137, 140, 143, 149, 154, 155–6, 174, 204; Pouzol, 'Notices'; *Semaine religieuse de Viviers* (18 May 1934) 239–42.

AUREILLE, Emile, priest, acting superior general, cousin of Father Edouard *Aureille, was born at Meysse (Ardèche), on 12 December 1870, the son of François and Rosalie Aureille. He died in Annonay on 2 November 1937, and is buried there in the cemetery on the grounds of the Collège du Sacré-Coeur.

Emile Aureille made his novitiate at Beaconfield House, Plymouth, England, 1889–90. He worked at the Collège Saint-Charles, Blidah, Algeria, 1890–1903, as prefect of study and professor of philosophy. He was ordained to the priesthood at the Grand Séminaire de Viviers on 11 October 1896 by Bishop Joseph-Michel-Frédéric Bonnet. After the dispersion of religious congregations in France in 1903 he went for a short time to Saint-André-de-Cruzières in the southern Ardèche and then to the Université de Grenoble, where he obtained a *licence ès lettres* (1904). After one year as assistant director at the Ecole libre Saint-Joseph in Avignon, he then spent the rest of his life, except for the time he was mobilized as a sergeant in the First World War, at the Collège du Sacré-Coeur, where he taught English and philosophy and was Director of Studies. Priests, friends, and former students had formed an association which had purchased the school building from the municipality in October 1904. The diocese took charge of the college, but there were always Basilians on the staff.

After the separation of the French Basilians from those in North

America in 1922, Father Aureille was elected second assistant to the superior general in France; and, when Father Julien *Giraud resigned that office in 1923, Father Victorin *Marijon succeeded. The 1928 chapter elected Marijon as superior general, Giraud as first assistant, and Aureille as second assistant. With the death of Father Marijon on 31 October 1931 (Father Giraud having also died in January 1931), Father Aureille served as acting superior general in France until the general chapter of 1932 elected Father Octave *Descellière as superior general and Father Aureille as first assistant.

SOURCES: GABF; Kirley, *Community in France* 185, 189, 196, 207, 240n569, 255n600, 260; Kirley, *Congregation in France* 42, 76n34, 81–2, 88, 116, 119, 139, 149, 154–5, 174–6, 205, 222; Pouzol, 'Notices'; *Semaine religieuse de Viviers* (12 March 1937) 549–50.

B

BALANDREAU, Jean, priest, was born at Roiffieux, canton of Annonay, on 26 November 1840, son of Claude Balandreau and Victoire Grenouillat. He died at Saint-Alban-d'Ay, near Annonay, on 14 November 1910.

Jean attended the school for day-pupils of the Collège des Cordeliers, Annonay, 1855–8, and then continued his studies at Sainte-Barbe, 1858–61, the Basilian minor seminary for students who could not afford the college fees. He made his novitiate at Feyzin (Isère, now Rhône), and worked in Basilian schools as he studied theology. His final profession took place on 22 September 1865. Bishop Armand de Charbonnel conferred the subdiaconate on him on 28 September 1865 and the diaconate on 22 September 1866, both in the chapel of the Collège des Cordeliers. By the time of his ordination to the priesthood on 21 September 1867, the college had been moved to the Collège du Sacré-Coeur on the Mont Saint-Denis, Annonay. Balandreau was the first Basilian to be ordained a priest in the chapel of the new school, again by Bishop Armand de Charbonnel.

In 1864–7 Father Balandreau worked as recreation and study-hall master in the Collège de Privas (Ardèche), and then assumed the same duties in the Ecole cléricale at Périgueux (Dordogne), 1867–8. On 29 September 1868 he set sail from Marseilles with a small group of fellow

Basilians to found the Collège Saint-Charles at Blidah, Algeria. Father Joseph *Martin was there already to meet them. Ten years later Father Balandreau returned to teach *cinquième* at the Collège du Bourg-Saint-Andéol (Ardèche), 1878–80, then moved to the Ecole cléricale at Périgueux (Dordogne), where he was in charge of the *cinquième*, 1880–8. In 1888 he returned to Algeria for one year to teach in another school taken over by the Basilians, the Collège Saint-Augustin in Bône, but he seems not to have taught there after 1889. Ill health brought him back to Annonay, where he worked as supply teacher in the Collège du Sacré-Coeur, 1894–6, after which he retired to Sainte-Barbe. Here his pastoral duties consisted of saying Mass for the Christian Brothers who taught in the Ecole Saint-Denis.

With the dispersal of the Basilians in 1903, Father Balandreau had nowhere to go. A nephew at Saint-Alban-d'Ay, near Annonay, offered him a room in his home, where he lived until his death. Father Balandreau donated the stained-glass window in the baptistry depicting St John the Baptist to the church there when it was consecrated on 3 October 1882.

SOURCE: Kirley, *Community in France* 34, 184, 202, 206; Pouzol, 'Notices.'

BANNON, J. MURRAY, priest, member of the Congregation 1943–73, was born in Logan, Ontario (diocese of London), on 11 February 1925, the son of Lorne Bannon and Mary Regan. He died on 9 May 1993.

Murray entered the novitiate from Assumption College School and was professed on 15 August 1943. At St Michael's College, Toronto, he took Upper School (grade XIII) before entering the Honours course in chemistry, transferring later to the general course (B.A., University of Toronto, 1948). He obtained a Type B teaching certification from the Ontario College of Education in 1949. After three years of theology at St Basil's Seminary, he was ordained to the priesthood by Cardinal James Charles McGuigan on 29 June 1952 in St Basil's Church, Toronto. He obtained a Master of Divinity degree from the University of St Michael's College in 1971. Father Bannon was afflicted with ill health most of his life.

In March 1973, after a year of uncertainty, during which he prayed for light and guidance, Murray Bannon left the priesthood and the Catholic Church. Father T.J. Hanrahan, superior general at that time, wrote the following passages in a letter addressed 'To Whom It May

Concern' (dated 23 September 1974): 'Father Bannon ... had reached a point where he could no longer believe that the Roman administration of the Catholic Church can claim to represent the true Church of Christ because he saw it as not following the Gospel and as giving no indication that it ever intends to do so. If one special area can be singled out, the question of infallibility seemed to cause Father Bannon the most difficulty. I pay tribute to Father Bannon's faultless moral life, to his zeal in the exercise of the ministry, and above all to his honesty. I cannot, of course, agree that the only way to meet his difficulty was withdrawal from the Roman Catholic Church, but I am certain that the only motive for Father Bannon's decision to leave the Church is the obligation he feels to be true to his convictions.' He subsequently joined the United Church of Canada and served as a minister until his death. He was survived by his wife, June.

BIBLIOGRAPHY: 'Limited Consultation Only,' *Forum* 3 (May 1967) 72–3.
SOURCE: GABF; *Annals* 2 (1952) 60.

BAQUÉ (or **BAQUET**), (Christian name unknown), priest, member of the Congregation 1861–c.1878.
He appears in the Basilian records in September 1861 as a novice coming from the Collège de Feyzin (Isère, now Rhône) to the Collège des Cordeliers, Annonay, where he taught *septième*. He was among those receiving minor orders on 30 November 1861 in the chapel of the Collège des Cordeliers at the hands of Bishop Armand de Charbonnel. After teaching in the Petit Séminaire de Vernoux and in the Collège de Privas (both in the Ardèche), he was ordained a deacon on 30 May 1863 at Viviers, along with Denis *O'Connor, and received the order of priesthood in the course of the next year. He taught junior classes at the Ecole cléricale de Périgueux (Dordogne), 1866–76. No other mention of him occurs in Basilian records.

SOURCE: Pouzol, 'Notices,' Supplément 2.

BARD, Jean Louis, priest, member of the Congregation 1847–52, was born on 23 April 1818 at Chalencon, canton of Vernoux (Ardèche, diocese of Mende, since 1822 of Viviers).
Jean Louis did his secondary studies at the Petit Séminaire de Vernoux, directed at that time by diocesan priests, and entered the Grand Séminaire de Viviers, where he received tonsure. In 1844 he made the

annual retreat in Annonay with the Basilians, 16–23 October, and for the next two years taught the classes of *septième* and *sixième* in the Basilian Collège de Privas (Ardèche). In 1846 he began his study of theology at Annonay, and from 1846 to 1850 worked as *surveillant* in the Collège des Cordeliers, Annonay. On 14 June 1847 he was received as a Basilian novice and was ordained a priest at Viviers on 25 May 1850. On 30 September 1850 he formally bound himself by promise to the Society of Priests of Saint Basil according to the rule at that time. He taught the preparatory class at the Petit Séminaire de Vernoux in 1850–1, and worked as *surveillant* in 1851–2 at the Collège de Privas. When the Society of Priests of Saint Basil decided in 1852 to profess vows, Father Bard withdrew from the Congregation but continued to teach for ten years with the Basilians in the Petit Séminaire d'Aubenas. The date of his death and the place of his burial are not known.

SOURCE: Pouzol, 'Notices.'

BARNES, Joseph George, priest, was born in Detroit on 16 April 1931, one in the family of two sons and two daughters of Joseph L. Barnes and Mary Cronin. He died in Detroit on 30 September 1974 and is buried there in the Basilian plot of Holy Sepulcher Cemetery.

'Joe' attended St Mary's (Redford) Parochial School and Catholic Central High School, Detroit. He entered St Basil's Novitiate, Rochester, making first profession on 15 August 1950, and began undergraduate studies at St Michael's College, Toronto, living with the community there, with the exception of one year, 1951–2, at St Basil's Seminary, until his graduation (B.A., University of Toronto, 1954). He was then appointed to teach at St Thomas High School, Houston. After returning to St Basil's Seminary in 1956 for theological studies, he was ordained to the priesthood on 28 June 1959 in St Basil's Church, Toronto, by Bishop Francis Allen.

After completing theology courses in 1960 Father Barnes was appointed to Catholic Central High School, where he spent the rest of his life enthusiastically and successfully teaching Latin and English. He was active in the Dads' Club, directed the Athletic Department, coached sports teams, supervised the cafeteria, fixed lockers and audio-visual equipment, filled in when and where needed, and served as superior of the local Basilian community from 1967 to 1970. He took up photography as a hobby about that time and became so proficient that he was called upon for all the school publications.

Joe Barnes had an engaging manner. He loved to be with people – confreres, family, friends, students, fellow priests of the archdiocese of Detroit. He was one of the founding members and the first treasurer of the Conference of Religious Priests in the archdiocese. His sudden death of a heart attack during the night of 28–9 September 1974 was a great shock and an equally great loss to the community, to his family, and perhaps most seriously to the students, who lost an excellent teacher, a friend at all times, and a man of God whose example they could follow.

SOURCES: GABF; *Annals* 2 (1959) 417, 5 (1974) 122–3; *Newsletter* (7 October 1974).

BARRY, John Patrick, priest, was born in Toledo, Ohio, on 17 March 1919, the son of Patrick J. Barry and Catherine Leahy. He died in Tucson, Arizona, on 2 June 1986 and is buried in Tubac Cemetery, Tubac, Arizona.

After primary education in Toledo and secondary education at Assumption College School, Windsor, 1934–8, John entered St Basil's Novitiate, Toronto, and was professed on 15 August 1939. He attended Assumption College (B.A., University of Western Ontario, 1943), and then taught for one year at Catholic Central High School, Detroit, while also earning teaching certification from the University of Detroit. The following year he taught at St Thomas High School, Houston, then began theological studies at St Basil's Seminary, Toronto, 1945–9. He was ordained to the priesthood in St Basil's Church, Toronto, on 29 June 1948 by Cardinal James Charles McGuigan.

Father Barry's early years of priesthood were spent teaching English and history in three places: Catholic Central High School, 1949–50, January 1952–6; St Thomas High School, Houston, 1956–62; and Andrean High School, Gary (now Merrillville), Indiana, 1962–7. Besides teaching he gave a good deal of time in all these schools to coaching track-and-field and cross-country running. In 1953 he earned an M.Ed. from the University of Detroit.

Parish experience in his early years consisted of a year and a half at St Anne's Parish, Houston, 1950–January 1952, and a stint of less than a year at Blessed Sacrament Parish, Windsor, 1967–March 1968. By 1968 the emphysema with which he had been afflicted for some years obliged him to seek a more salubrious climate. In 1970 he began work in the Santa Fe diocese as assistant at Holy Ghost Parish, Albuquerque,

New Mexico, where he also did hospital chaplaincy. Ten years later he became assistant pastor at St Francis of Assisi Parish, Yuma, Arizona, but ill health forced him to undergo treatment in Phoenix, 1981–3. He became Administrator of Missions at Tubac, Arizona, coordinating service to a number of parishes, mostly of native peoples. At the same time he worked as assistant pastor at Sacred Heart Parish, Nogales, Arizona, from 1983 until his death three years later.

John Barry was a gentle person with a great concern for the welfare of those he served. His love for liturgy led to his nomination to the Southwest Liturgical Conference Board. Archbishop Robert Sanchez of Santa Fe recommended Father Barry to Bishop Francis Green of Tucson, citing him as an excellent priest and minister to the hospitals in the area and for his good services on the liturgical commission of the archdiocese. Though he lived away from the community for his last eighteen years, his attachment to the Basilians remained strong. It is reported that Father Barry's grave in Tubac is carefully tended by the people whom he served in that area.

BIBLIOGRAPHY: 'Track Impressions,' *Basilian Teacher* 3 (April 1959) 192–5.
SOURCES: GABF; *Annals* 1 (1948) 218–19, 6 (1987) 574–5; *Newsletter* (12 June 1986).

BART, Peter John, priest, member of the Congregation 1917–35, was born in Stratford, Ontario (diocese of London), on 4 August 1897, the son of Peter Bart and Caroline La Porte. He died in Toronto on 16 November 1950, and is buried in the Basilian plot of Assumption Cemetery, Windsor.

After early education in Stratford, Peter Bart went in 1914 to Assumption College, Windsor. He entered St Basil's Novitiate in Toronto and was professed on 10 August 1918. He graduated from the University of Toronto with a B.A. in 1922 and an M.A. in philosophy in 1923. During these years he excelled on the college football team. He did theological studies at St Basil's Seminary, Toronto, and was ordained priest on 20 December 1924 in the chapel of St Augustine's Seminary by Bishop John McNally.

With teacher certification from the Ontario College of Education, Toronto, 1924–5, Father Bart's appointments were: teaching at Assumption College, 1925–6, assistant pastor at Assumption Parish, Windsor, and a second stint of teaching at Assumption College. In 1930 he attended the only summer session ever held at the Institute of

Mediaeval Studies, Toronto, and joined the staff of St Michael's College, Toronto, in 1932. He was a philosopher, and read papers at a number of professional conferences.

In 1935, following an automobile accident involving the death of a man, Peter Bart obtained leave of absence from the Congregation. After living several months with the Cistercians at the Priory of Notre Dame des Prairies, Saint Norbert, Manitoba, he was incardinated as a priest of the diocese of Sault Ste Marie, Ontario, on 6 July 1937. During the Second World War he served as a chaplain in the Canadian Army. Later he was the pastor of several small parishes, the last being St Mark's at Markstay, Ontario. At his own request he was buried with the Basilian community.

BIBLIOGRAPHY: 'Reflections on Perception,' *New Scholasticism* 3 (January 1929) 19–23; 'The Christianity of Paul Elmer More,' *Catholic World* 85 (August 1932) 542–7.
SOURCES: GABF; *Annals* 2 (1951) 42.

BATTY, Thomas DAKE, priest, was born on 15 February 1902 at Norwich, Ontario (diocese of London), the son of Clifford Batty and Ella Dake. He died in Toronto on 10 April 1986 and is buried in the Basilian plot of Holy Cross Cemetery, Thornhill, Ontario.

After early education at local schools and one year of high school at St Mary's College, North East, Pennsylvania, Dake's schooling was interrupted for several years; but in 1924, at the age of twenty-two, he enrolled at Assumption College School, Windsor, where he remained for four years, following this with two years at St Michael's College School, Toronto, 1928–30. He began his arts course at Assumption College, then entered St Basil's Novitiate in 1932 and was professed on 5 October 1933. He was appointed to Assumption College where, while taking an Honours B.A. in philosophy from the University of Western Ontario, 1935, he also taught geometry at Assumption College School. He studied theology at St Basil's Scholasticate ('Seminary' from 1937), Toronto, while concurrently teaching at St Michael's College School. He was ordained to the priesthood on 17 December 1938 in St Basil's Church, Toronto, by Archbishop James Charles McGuigan.

After completing his theology courses in 1939, Father Batty began thirty years of parish ministry, serving first as assistant pastor in the following places: Ste Anne's Parish, Detroit, 1939–42; St Anne's Parish, Houston, 1942–6; Assumption Parish, Windsor, 1946–8, 1955–7; St

Mary's of the Assumption Parish, Owen Sound, Ontario, 1948–55; Blessed Sacrament Parish, Windsor, 1957–8; and St Basil's Parish, Angleton, Texas, 1961–5. He was then appointed pastor and local superior at St Mary's of the Assumption Parish, Owen Sound, 1958–61. In February 1964 he suffered a slight stroke and moved to St Theresa's parish, Sugar Land, Texas, but in 1969 went to the Basilian Fathers Infirmary in Toronto where he lived until his death seventeen years later. There he became a familiar figure on the campus of St Michael's as he walked about in black cape and beret, earphones clamped to his head, engrossed in listening to music, lectures, and books recorded on tape.

Dake Batty was a determined man, as the history of his education testifies. He was a musician, having played in various orchestras and bands in his youth. He strove to keep abreast of developments in theology and liturgy, and was pleased that the Basilian community was implementing the teachings of the Second Vatican Council. During his long years of infirmity he devoted many hours a day to attending Masses and to prayer.

SOURCES: GABF; *Annals* 6 (1984) 210, (1987) 572–3; *Newsletter* (16 April 1986).

BAUER, David William, priest, was born on 2 November 1924, at Waterloo, Ontario (diocese of London), one of eleven children of Edgar Bauer and Alberta (Bertha) Hayes. He died in Goderich, Ontario, on 9 November 1988, and is buried in the Bauer family plot in Mount Hope Cemetery, Kitchener, Ontario.

After elementary school and then three years of high school at St Jerome's College in his home town, 'Dave' enrolled at St Michael's College, Toronto, to complete his high school course. After one year, 1945, in the Canadian Army, he did one year of university and then entered St Basil's Novitiate, Richmond Hill, Ontario, making first profession of vows on 12 September 1947. He completed his undergraduate studies at St Michael's College (B.A., University of Toronto, 1949), majoring in philosophy, with great interest in the work of Jacques Maritain and Christopher Dawson. He studied theology at St Basil's Seminary, Toronto, and also took courses at the Ontario College of Education (teacher certification, 1951). He was ordained to the priesthood on 29 June 1953 in St Basil's Church, Toronto, by Cardinal James Charles McGuigan.

In 1954 he was appointed to St Michael's College School, where he taught religion and history and coached hockey teams at various levels for the next seven years. He led the St Michael's 'Majors,' for whom he himself had played with stellar distinction, to the Junior A Memorial Cup Canadian Championship in 1961.

In that same year Father Bauer was appointed to St Mark's College in the University of British Columbia, Vancouver, to teach medical ethics to the nurses at St Paul's Hospital and to be Newman Chaplain and dean of residence. He did some coaching at the university and became the first name in amateur hockey when he formed a Canadian national team for Olympic competition. During the 1960s, at the height of the Cold War, he took the team on playing tours to Communist Czechoslovakia. He was determined to establish a counter-culture within sports by his opposition to commercial exploitation, violence, and overemphasis on winning. The sportsmanship he sought to inculcate in his players he embodied in himself. He was for several years a consulting coach for hockey teams in Japan. In 1964 he was awarded a special Olympic Medal for sportsmanlike conduct while coaching his team. He was awarded the Order of Canada in June 1967, and was inducted into the Hockey Hall of Fame, Toronto, in 1989.

Father Bauer's vision of hockey and of sport in general was far deeper than any success he achieved. His love of learning, his deep and constantly nourished spirituality, brought him to see sports and hockey in particular as an agent of human development and expression. Art, intelligence, respect, and a sublime concept of what it means to be human and Christian inspired his coaching. He put high ideals before his players and scored both in goals and in goodness.

During one of the hockey tours in the 1960s Father Bauer visited Jacques Maritain, the French philosopher he so much admired, at his retreat with the Little Brothers of the Poor near Toulouse, France, to talk about the last years and the death of their mutual colleague and friend Father Henry *Carr, with whom Father Bauer had lived in Vancouver.

Father Bauer was appointed to Notre Dame College in Wilcox, Saskatchewan, in 1982 to head the Quest Program there as a continuation of the post-secondary tradition of the college. With a group composed of fellow Basilians, friends, and former hockey players, together with his niece, Barbara Bauer-Maison, Father Bauer worked to maintain and develop the catholicity and the academic and athletic integrity of the small college in which he saw the potential for embodying the 'integral humanism' he learned from Maritain and which he always espoused. In 1987, the year he retired from Notre Dame College, he accepted the honour of having the stadium in Calgary named 'The Father David Bauer Olympic Arena.'

Upon leaving Notre Dame College he returned to St Mark's, Vancouver, where he began making plans to move to Toronto to implement a program for teaching teachers the richness of the Catholic educational vision. In July 1987, however, he was found to have pancreatic cancer and underwent surgery in Vancouver. After a lengthy convalescence there he moved to the home of his brother Ray at Bayfield, Ontario. His last months were a time of suffering but of closeness to his family and to the many young people who came to visit in appreciation of the values he had taught and the ideals he held out to them. Despite his suffering he never lost his sense of humour or his kindly manner. Father David Bauer will be remembered as a great figure in Canadian hockey but also as a great human being, Christian educator, and priest.

BIBLIOGRAPHY: 'The Old and the New,' *Basilian Teacher* 7 (March 1963) 220–1.
SOURCES: GABF; *Annals* 2 (1953) 107, 6 (1989) 801–3; *Newsletter* (16 December 1988); Joseph *Penny CSB, Rocco Volpe CSB, and Barbara Bauer-Maison.

BEATON, Peter James, priest, was born at East Point, Prince Edward Island (diocese of Charlottetown), on 21 June 1925, the son of Angus Henry Beaton and Jessie May O'Hanely. He died in Toronto on 5 August 2002 and is buried in the Basilian plot of Holy Cross Cemetery, Thornhill, Ontario.

Peter attended St Dunstan's University, Charlottetown, Prince Edward Island, before entering St Basil's Novitiate at Richmond Hill, Ontario, in 1952. After first profession on 12 September 1953 he was appointed to St Basil's Seminary, Toronto, for theology. He taught for two years at Aquinas Institute, Rochester, 1954–6, before completing theological studies at the seminary. He was ordained to the priesthood on 29 June 1958 in St Basil's Church, Toronto, by Cardinal James Charles McGuigan.

Father Beaton's life as a priest included both the teaching and the parish apostolates. His school assignments were at St Mary's College, Sault Ste-Marie, 1959–60; Andrean High School, Gary (now Merrillville), Indiana, 1960–9; St Thomas High School, Houston, 1969–70; Aquinas Institute, Rochester, 1973–5; Assumption High School, Windsor, 1985–6; St Michael's College School, Toronto, 1992–8. His parish assignments included: St Basil's Parish, Ottawa, 1970–2; Saint-Jean-de-Brébeuf, Lasalle, Quebec, 1975–8; St Basil's Church, Toronto, 1980–1; St Mary's of the Assumption Parish, Owen Sound, Ontario, 1981–5, 1986–92. There is no official record of his activity in the years 1978–80, which he spent at St Francis of Assisi Parish, Park Extension, Montreal.

What characterized Father Beaton's later years was his concern for the poor and zeal for causes of social justice. He was associated with Amnesty International, the Task Force of the Churches on Corporate Responsibility, Save the Children, and other like organizations, and was indefatigable in his efforts to awaken his correspondents to the urgency of these causes. Although by nature retiring and deferential, he was readily moved by the suffering of others and sought its relief.

His final years were not the happiest for himself or for those around him. He lived with the Orsini House community, Toronto, 1998–2001, and in Anglin House (infirmary) from 2001 until his death. His increasing physical incapacity caused him much frustration and strained his patience and natural kindliness.

BIBLIOGRAPHY:
Pamphlet: Ed. (with Marjorie Dalgaard) *Devotion to Our Lady*. Toronto, 1977.
Articles: 'Defending the Prisoner,' *Stirrings* (January–February 1993) 2; 'Migrants and Itinerant People,' *Occasional Paper* 21 (December 1994); 'Nicaragua – Poor but Hopeful,' *Stirrings* (January–February 1997) 1, 7; 'The Road to Racial Reconciliation – Truth Telling in South Africa,' *Stirrings* (May–June 1997) 1, 6.
SOURCES: GABF; *Annals* 2 (1958) 354; *Newsletter* (August 2002).

BELLISLE, Henry Stanislaus, priest, was born in Georgetown, Ontario (archdiocese of Toronto), on 12 November 1891, the son of Joseph Bellisle and Margaret Heavin. He died in Windsor on 28 December 1938, and is buried there in the Basilian plot, Assumption Cemetery.

Henry Bellisle grew up in Toronto, where he attended St Helen and St Francis Separate Schools. From 1904 until 1911 he studied at St Michael's College, Toronto, where he was a brilliant student and outstanding athlete. When he graduated in 1911 the class prophecy predicted that he would one day be head of the college. He was admitted to St Basil's Novitiate, Toronto, and made first profession of vows on 15 August 1912. After studies in theology at St Basil's Scholasticate, Toronto, he was ordained priest on 26 September 1915. Studies at the

Catholic University of America in Washington, D.C. followed, and in 1916 he obtained an M.A. degree from that university.

Appointed in 1916 to Assumption College, Windsor, Father Bellisle taught until 1919, when he returned to St Michael's College. With the exception of one year's sabbatical leave, 1927, which he spent at the University of Louvain, he would remain at St Michael's until 1934. At one time or another he taught practically every subject in the high school department, served as principal (the first appointed principal at St Michael's), 1921-7, as registrar of the arts faculty, and as superior, 1931-4. In 1934 a coronary thrombosis forced him to resign, and he moved to St Basil's Scholasticate, Toronto. In 1935 he was transferred to Assumption College, where he taught until his death from a heart attack in 1938.

As both an educator and administrator, Father Bellisle set high standards for himself and for those who worked with him. At St Michael's College School he ended the traditional practice of apprentice teaching by undergraduates. During the Great Depression years he opened branches of the high school section of St Michael's College in the east end of Toronto on Lee Avenue just above Queen Street, and in the west end on Dundas Street above Bloor Street West. At the same time he lowered the tuition fees to make it possible for more students to attend. In 1931, he was faced with a potentially disastrous economic loss when the Ontario Department of Education voted to move first-year university students into a grade XIII of high school. This would eliminate the large contingent of American students who came to St Michael's. At the suggestion of Father Basil *Sullivan, and with the co-operation of Assumption College, Windsor, Bellisle introduced the 'Western course' at St Michael's which allowed American students to get first-year college credit as extramural students through Assumption's agreement with the University of Western Ontario. As a teacher, Father Bellisle continued to participate in sports, and for some years he coached football and hockey teams at St Michael's College and gave his full support to an expanded athletic program. Father Robert *Fischette, who did his Master's thesis on Father Bellisle, wrote, 'Father Bellisle held that organized, competitive sport plays an important role in education, not merely for the physical, but especially for its moral value – training the student to hold his temper and keep steady under fire, training him in his resourcefulness and leadership and cooperation with others in a common cause.' For many years the St Michael's building at 1 Elmsley Place bore the name 'Bellisle House.'

Father Bellisle was called 'Happy,' a nickname that aptly described his joyful character. Father James *Embser observed that 'his presence in the community room was always a joy to his confreres. ... His laugh was infectious, and remarkable was his attention to the aged confreres. He seemed to enjoy their company and certainly added much joy to their lives.'

After noting in a memorial tribute that Father Bellisle was gifted intellectually to an extraordinary degree, Father Edmund *McCorkell added, 'He likewise had the patience of a research student, and this is the reason of his success with St Augustine, St Thomas and Newman.' On many students he had a lifelong influence, an achievement which Father McCorkell attributed to his personal piety and to the fact that 'he seemed to retain to an unusual extent the spirit of a boy throughout his whole life.'

BIBLIOGRAPHY:
Pamphlets: In the *Pamphlet* series (Toronto, 1931–4): 8: *Philosophy and Life;* 9: *Religion and the Office of Teaching;* 30: *Some Principles of Catholic Pedagogy;* 31: *The Institute of Mediaeval Studies* (repr. *Loretto Rainbow* 40, 2 [October 1933], 77–85).
Articles: 'Illumination Theory of St Augustine,' *Proceedings of the American Catholic Philosophical Association* 6 (1930) 106–17. In *Basilian*: 'Reminiscences of Father Robert McBrady,' 1 (April 1935) 23–4, 34; 'The Christian Concept of Peace,' 1 (December 1935) 131–2, and 2 (January 1936) 7–8. In *Bulletin of the Windsor Council of the Knights of Columbus*: 'Social Problems,' 14 (May and June 1938); 'The Pope's Encyclicals Explained,' 14 (March 1938); 'Who Is John Dewey?' 15 (November 1938); 'An Attack on the New Programme of Studies,' Special Education Issue, n.d.; 'What Can We Do about It?' 4 (March 1938) 44–5. He also published a series of 'Questions and Answers' in *Catholic Record* (London, Ontario), from 1936 to 1938.
SOURCES: GABF; J.W. Embser, 'Henry S. Bellisle,' *Basilian Teacher* 4 (January 1960) 116–19; R.M. Fischette, 'The Philosophy of Education of Father Henry S. Bellisle,' unpublished M.A. thesis (University of Detroit, 1943); E.J. McCorkell, 'In Memoriam H.S. Bellisle,' *Yearbook SMC* 1939; Shook, *Catholic Education* 168–73.

BENINGER, Donald Bernard, priest, was born on 6 February 1914, at Kingsbridge, Ontario (diocese of London), one of the three children of Michael Joseph Beninger and Katherine McPhee. His sister became Sister Marie Brébeuf in the Congregation of St Joseph, London, Ontario. He died at Owen Sound, Ontario, on 28 August 1971, and is buried in the parish cemetery there.

'Don' went to school at Dublin, Ontario, where he was taught by the Ursuline Sisters until the end of high school. At the age of fifteen he was stricken with poliomyelitis, which left him badly crippled. Two years later he experienced a cure at Martyrs Shrine, Midland, Ontario, where he left his crutches. An automobile accident some time later brought on a new lameness, which lasted all his life. This disability, however, did not prevent his university studies at St Michael's College, Toronto (B.A., University of Toronto, 1938). He entered St Basil's Novitiate, Toronto, was professed on 15 August 1939, and went directly into theological studies at St Basil's Seminary, Toronto. He was ordained to the priesthood on 19 December 1942 in St Basil's Church, Toronto, by Archbishop James Charles McGuigan.

Father Beninger had but four appointments in his life as a priest. He began his ministry in 1943 at St John the Baptist Parish, Amherstburg, Ontario. The following year he was appointed to Aquinas Institute, Rochester, where he spent eleven years, 1944–55, the last seven as assistant novice master at St Basil's Novitiate, Rochester, all the while teaching business courses, at first full-time and then part-time, at the school. In 1955 he went to Blessed Sacrament Parish, Windsor. Two years later he was moved to St Mary's of the Assumption Parish, Owen Sound, where he remained for the rest of his life.

In spite of his physical disabilities, Father Beninger did a full day's work wherever he was. For the last twenty years of his life he suffered from arthritis which grew steadily worse, yet he would go out to the various missions from Owen Sound and find ways of coping with his situation. He was for some years chaplain at the Wiarton General Hospital and at the Lion's Head General Hospital, Owen Sound. In this work, as in all his ministry, he made many friends who appreciated his devotedness and his courage in overcoming his debilities. He was a courteous, soft-spoken, hospitable man, much beloved of the children. When they would come to the parish house after school asking for 'Father,' all six priests in the house knew that they meant Father Beninger.

SOURCES: GABF; *Annals* 1 (1943) 28, 4 (1972) 252–3; *Newsletter* (1 September 1971).

BENWITZ, Donald Earl, priest, was born in Rochester on 9 November 1940, one of the three children of Gerald Frederick Benwitz and Helen

Marie La Duke. He died in Santa Fe, New Mexico, on 18 November 1983 and is buried in Holy Sepulchre Cemetery, Rochester.

Donald attended St Helen's Parochial School, 1946–54, and Aquinas Institute, Rochester, graduating in 1958. He entered St Basil's Novitiate, Rochester, which was moved to Pontiac, Michigan, in the course of the year, and was professed on 15 August 1959. His first appointment was to Aquinas Institute community to do studies at St John Fisher College, Rochester (B.A., 1963). As a scholastic he taught for three years, the first two, 1963–5, at Andrean High School, Merrillville, Indiana, and the third, 1965–6, at Aquinas Institute before beginning theological studies at St Basil's Seminary, Toronto (S.T.B., University of St Michael's College, Toronto, 1969). He was ordained to the priesthood in Sacred Heart Cathedral, Rochester, on 13 December 1969 by Bishop Joseph Hogan.

After completing theological studies in 1970, Father Benwitz was appointed once again to Aquinas Institute, where he taught until 1974. During the summers he studied Spanish (M.A., University of Notre Dame, 1974). His next appointment was to Andrean High School as principal, a position he occupied until 1983. In September of that year he began a spiritual renewal program in Santa Fe, which was cut short by a fatal heart attack two months later.

Father Benwitz, or 'Benny,' as he was popularly called, was a warm, sensitive, and humble man who cared a great deal for his community and his confreres. He was known to have special concern for students who were experiencing problems or difficulties. As an administrator he was personable and supportive of his staff, who appreciated his leadership. He was not a complex man; his lifestyle was simple and his needs few. He enjoyed hobbies of gardening, cooking for the confreres, or making repairs around the house. His ready sense of humour and habitual cheerfulness endeared him to all.

SOURCES: GABF; *Annals* 4 (1970) 137, 6 (1984) 300–1; *Newsletter* (5 December 1983).

BERGERON, Cyril Orville, priest, was born at Cloquet, Minnesota (diocese of Duluth), on 23 December 1914, the son of Joseph Bergeron and Celina Paya. He died in Detroit on 23 June 1963, and is buried in the Basilian plot of Assumption Cemetery, Windsor.

From an early age 'Cy' Bergeron's home was in Detroit, where he attended Catholic Central High School for Boys before entering St

Basil's Novitiate, Toronto. After first profession on 15 August 1934, he was appointed to live at St Basil's Scholasticate, Toronto, for undergraduate studies at St Michael's College (B.A., University of Toronto, 1939). His theological studies at St Basil's Seminary were interrupted by appointments to teach at St Thomas High School, Houston, 1940–1, and at Catholic Central, Detroit, 1941–2. In 1942 he obtained secondary school teacher certification from Wayne State University, Detroit. He was ordained priest on 15 August 1943 by Archbishop James Charles McGuigan in St Basil's Church, Toronto.

Teaching assignments took Father Bergeron to Aquinas Institute, Rochester, 1944–8, St Thomas High School, 1948–51, and Catholic Central High School from 1951 until his death, with the exception of two years, 1957–9, when he was on sick leave at Blessed Sacrament Parish, Windsor. He died in 1963 after a series of heart attacks.

History and English were Father Bergeron's favourite teaching subjects. From his entrance into the novitiate he was an energetic Basilian, active in athletics as a participant and as a coach, enthusiastic about his teaching and zealous in the discharge of all his priestly work.

BIBLIOGRAPHY: 'Crashaw's Christmas Poetry,' *Basilian* 4 (January 1938) 4–5, 7, 17; 'A Method of Teaching History,' *Basilian Teacher* 2 (February 1958) 4–7.
SOURCES: GABF; *Annals* 1 (1944) 53–4; 3 (1963) 218–19; *Newsletter* (24 June 1963).

BEUGLET, Luke Léon, priest, nephew of Father Luke *Renaud, was born at Belle River, Ontario (diocese of London), on 3 October 1878, the son of Henry Beuglet and Marie Renaud. He died in Detroit on 25 July 1955, and is buried in the Basilian plot of Assumption Cemetery, Windsor.

Luke attended Tilbury Public School and then worked for some years before going to Assumption College, Windsor, in 1902 to begin his studies for the priesthood. He entered St Basil's Novitiate, Toronto, in 1907 and, after profession on 15 August 1908, studied at St Michael's College and the Toronto Business College. He did his theology courses at St Basil's Scholasticate, Toronto, and was ordained priest on 18 September 1914, in St Basil's Church, Toronto, by Archbishop Neil McNeil.

His first appointment as a priest was to St Thomas High School, Houston, where he taught and served as local treasurer. In 1922 Father Beuglet began thirty-three years of parish ministry: Ste Anne's Parish, Detroit, 1922–5, 1944–55 as assistant; 1932–4, 1935–7 as pastor; St John the Baptist Parish, Amherstburg, Ontario, 1925–32 as pastor; Assumption Parish, Windsor, 1934–5 as assistant, 1937–44 as pastor. He returned to Ste Anne's Parish in 1944 where he was a silent, hardworking assistant until his death in 1955 after a long period of bad health.

Father Beuglet was a simple, sincere, and God-fearing priest. He had a deep personal devotion to the Blessed Virgin and to her mother, St Anne. As pastor of Assumption Parish he introduced the Legion of Mary into the diocese of London. He was not concerned with the purely social side of parish life and was a source of spiritual counsel that sprang from a heart fixed on divine things. In the midst of restless activity, he moved placidly and unhurried.

During his years as pastor of Assumption Parish, the centenary of the church building was celebrated in 1943. Of this celebration Father E.J. *Lajeunesse wrote in his *History of Assumption Parish*: 'In 1942 the chapel was painted and the interior decorations of the church were cleaned, renovated, and illuminated with touches of gold leaf. It is not clear, however, just what was celebrated. It may be that Father Beuglet had been misled by an old historical plaque on the church grounds stating that Assumption church was built in 1843. "Abuilding" instead of "built" would have been more accurate, as the church was not completed until three years later. In any case, week-long celebrations were held in the month of June. ... Very fittingly, the jubilee functions concluded on the feast of the Assumption with the unveiling and blessing of a souvenir stone placed on the grounds.'

SOURCES: GABF; *Annals* 1 (1943) 18–21, 2 (1955) 228–9; Lajeunesse, *Assumption Parish*.

BIONDI, Michael Bernard, priest, was born in Rochester on 2 April 1924, the only child of Frank J. Biondi and Elizabeth Parina. He died in Utica, New York, on 26 August 1980, and is buried in the priests' plot of Holy Sepulchre Cemetery, Rochester.

'Mike' Biondi attended Holy Family elementary school prior to enrolling in Aquinas Institute, Rochester, in 1938. Upon graduation in 1942 he entered St Basil's Novitiate, Rochester, and was professed on 12 September 1943. He began undergraduate studies at Assumption College, Windsor, and the following year transferred to St Michael's College, Toronto (B.A., University of Toronto, 1947). He taught for one year at Aquinas Institute, and in August 1948 was appointed to St Thomas High School, Houston, where he began theological studies while teaching. He returned to St Michael's the next year to continue theology, moving to St Basil's Seminary, Toronto, in 1950. He was ordained to the priesthood on 29 June 1951 in St Basil's Church, Toronto, by Cardinal James Charles McGuigan.

In August 1952, having completed theological studies, Father Biondi joined the faculty of Aquinas Institute, where he remained for the next twenty-four years. In whatever position he held throughout these years - teacher, dean of students, coach, moderator of many clubs - his deep concern for others and his infectious bonhomie were appreciated by all. He loved the Italian language, which he taught with enthusiasm. In 1958 he was awarded a grant for a year's study in Florence, Italy, and in 1960, having completed all requirements in the previous three summers, he received an M.A. in Italian from Middlebury College. In 1972 he was granted a sabbatical for further studies in linguistics at Georgetown, which awarded him an M.S. in 1974.

When he resumed his teaching at Aquinas Institute, Father Biondi began to experience a decline in his health: it was the first onslaught of the cancer which was to cause him much suffering during the next four years. In 1976, not feeling capable of continuing school activities, he asked for a change of apostolate and was appointed assistant pastor at Christ the King Parish, Rochester. He brought to parish ministry the same kindness and devotion that had marked his academic ministry. The young were particularly attracted to him. In the course of his illness he experienced two remissions of the cancer that was weakening him. In 1978, seemingly much improved, he was transferred to Holy Family Parish, Missouri City, Texas, as assistant pastor. The cancer recurred, but went into remission once more. At this time he gave himself intently to the study of sacred scripture. In 1980 he was appointed pastor of Holy Family Parish, but before he could assume his duties a tumour developed behind his eye which necessitated his resignation. Despite intensive treatment and a period of recuperation, the tumour suddenly reactivated and proved fatal while he was visiting relatives in Utica.

When consulted in 1980 about being appointed as pastor, Father Biondi accepted the appointment with these words: 'Ever since I was given the privilege to suffer for the Lord I have tried, to the best of my ability, never to use this difficulty of mine as an excuse to get out of my work. I do not say this boastfully. It is only a way of praising God, as St Paul would say, "Through the grace of God, I am what I am." *He* has made it easy for me.'

BIBLIOGRAPHY: 'Scripture and Our Students [forum],' *Basilian Teacher* 5 (December 1960) 81.
SOURCES: GABF; *Annals* 2 (1951) 35, 5 (1981) 614–16; *Newsletter* (9 September 1980).

BLACK, Frederick Arthur, priest, was born on 25 April 1924 in Toronto, the eldest of three sons and one daughter of Frederick Gerald Black and Alma Sampson, and the brother of Father James Bernard *Black. He died in Toronto on 9 March 2000 and is buried in the Basilian plot of Holy Cross Cemetery, Thornhill, Ontario.

'Freddy' was baptized in St Basil's Church, Toronto, on 12 May 1924 by Father Michael Vincent *Kelly. He attended the high school section of St Michael's College from 1936 to 1940, when he entered St Basil's Novitiate, Toronto, at the age of sixteen. He made first profession on 15 August 1941 and was then assigned to St Basil's Seminary, Toronto, where he completed grade XIII and three years of arts in the English Language and Literature Honours course at the University of Toronto. He did his final year of undergraduate studies while living at St Michael's College (B.A., University of Toronto, 1946). After graduation he returned to St Basil's Seminary for theology and was ordained to the priesthood on 29 June 1949 in St Basil's Church, Toronto, by Cardinal James Charles McGuigan.

In 1950, Father Black moved to St Michael's College, where he began graduate studies in English at the University of Toronto. He continued these studies at Oxford University during the years 1951 to 1954, where he studied under the renowned scholar and author J.R.R. Tolkien. He returned to St Michael's College in 1954 to teach and serve as librarian. In 1960 he was assigned to St John Fisher College, Rochester, where he filled the same offices of professor and librarian. In 1967 he was named superior of the Curial House in Toronto with the special assignment of writing a new rule for the Basilian Fathers, which would be, according to the directives of the general chapter of 1967, less a collection of laws and more a spiritual guide in the tradition of the rules of St Basil and St Benedict. *The Basilian Way of Life*, the fruit of Father Black's efforts in collaboration with Father James Hanrahan, is a work of solid spirituality written in a prose style completely appropriate to the subject.

In 1973 Father Black returned to St Michael's College and remained there until shortly before his death twenty-six years later. He served as the college archivist for twenty-five years and is especially remembered for the elegantly mounted displays of historical documents and photographs in connection with various college events. It was his work with the aged and infirm, however, which particularly marked his later years and evoked the admiration of so many. In 1972, he was named the first director of St Basil's Infirmary, a post which he held for twelve years, and where his gentle manner and devotedness were appreciated by both residents and staff. He also worked for twenty-five years as chaplain to the Queen Street Mental Health Centre. It was there that he was able to discern and suggest to medical personnel the proper treatment for one of the patients, which allowed the person to leave the hospital and live a more normal life under the proper medication. He remained attentive to this person, even while he himself struggled with bone cancer, as long as he was able. In 1988 he was named by the archbishop of Toronto as ecclesiastical assistant in Toronto to the Company of St Ursula of Canada, a women's secular institute, and was twice reappointed, though his third term was cut short by his death. He also served for several years as chaplain to the Sisters at Loretto College, Brunswick Avenue, Toronto.

Freddy Black loved books and loved to read. It was said of him that as a librarian he never put a book on the shelf before he had read it – a double-edged exaggeration which bespeaks his book lore and a certain procrastination in his character not always appreciated by others. What he read he savoured, and he was perceptive in conversations about literature. Father Laurence K. *Shook, himself a noted English scholar, remembered Fred Black as the student who got the most out of his courses, even though he did not attain first-class honours. Father Black's funeral was attended by many of those he had helped in his quiet and unassuming way.

BIBLIOGRAPHY:
Book: (With T.J. Hanrahan) *Basilian Way of Life*. Toronto, 1973; several later reprints. (With R.J. Scollard) *Register of the Letters of Bishop Charbonnel in the General Archives of the Basilian Fathers, Toronto*. Toronto, 1970.
Articles: 'Midnight Mass in Paris,' *Benedicamus* 5 (February 1952) 6–7; 'A Note on Chesterton and Anti-Semitism,' *Chesterton Review* 4 (1978) 1–6; 'Eric Gill and Sexual Morality,' *Chesterton Review* 10 (February 1984) 43–54; 'The Church and the Powers of Darkness,' *CCR* 3 (1985) 105–9; 'Chesterton and Madness,' *Chesterton Review* 15 (August 1989) 327–39; 'What Are We to Think about Eric Gill? Fiona MacCarthy's New Biography,' *Chesterton Review* 15/16 (November 1989 and February 1990) 607–25.
SOURCES: GABF; *Annals* 7 (1992) 5–6, 9 (2001) 89–90; *Newsletter* (22 March 2000).

BLACK, James BERNARD, priest, was born on 31 May 1926 in Toronto, the second child of three sons and one daughter of Frederick Gerald Black and Alma Sampson, and the brother of Father Frederick Arthur *Black. He died in Toronto on 14 October 1995 and is buried in the Basilian plot of Holy Cross Cemetery, Thornhill, Ontario.

'Bernie' attended St Monica's Separate School and St Michael's College Prep School, entering high school at St Michael's in 1939. After graduation in 1945 he continued at St Michael's College as an undergraduate for one year before entering St Basil's Novitiate, Toronto. After profession on 15 August 1947, he was appointed to St Michael's College, where he completed his undergraduate studies (B.A., University of Toronto, 1949) and took one year of theology. He taught for one year, 1950–1, at St Michael's College School and did one year of studies in library science (B.L.S., University of Toronto, 1952). He returned to St Michael's College School for another year of teaching before resuming theological studies at St Basil's Seminary in 1953. He was ordained to the priesthood on 29 June 1955 in St Basil's Church, Toronto, by Bishop Francis Allen. He was awarded an S.T.B. degree from the University of St Michael's College in 1955 and an M.A. in Library Science from the University of Toronto in 1956, having continued his studies in this field and in university administration through his years of theology.

In 1956 Father Black was appointed to St Thomas More College, Saskatoon, where he worked as librarian and taught in the department of English. In 1959 he enrolled at the University of Michigan at Ann Arbor for two years of study in library science. In 1961 he returned to St Michael's College, where he remained for the next twenty-eight years as librarian. He oversaw the building of the John M. Kelly Library, making it a valuable resource both for St Michael's and for the wider university community. For a time he served as chairman of the City of Toronto Library Board.

Bernard Black was an unconventional man in his profession, yet effective and personal. Deeply compassionate by nature and considerate of others, he was at the same time vulnerable and sensitive to criticism. He read widely and could converse interestingly and knowledgeably on many subjects. He supported compassionate causes such as that of battered women. He was available to persons in need. Sister Antoinette Sheehan CSJ said of him at his wake service: 'Every manner of educator called on Bernie. He provided sound theology for confirmation students, state-of-the-art practice for future librarians, spiritual encouragement for separated, divorced and widowed persons in the New Beginnings program, a message of hope for recovering alcoholics at Southdown.' Health problems, particularly of a cardiac nature, were part of his life. He was appointed to the Basilian Fathers Residence (Infirmary) in 1989. There he found the care he needed during the last six years of his life, years of steady decline with a good deal of suffering, both physical and mental.

Two trees were planted by a Jewish well-wisher in the Father Sean O'Sullivan Forest, Israel, in memory of Bernard Black, and the Toronto Public Library dedicated a book in his memory.

BIBLIOGRAPHY:
Pamphlets: *A Survey of Resources of Canadian Academic and Research Libraries.* Toronto, 1968. *Moments: St Michael's College – 125 Years; University of Toronto – 150 Years: An Exhibition of Historical Photographs.* Toronto, 1978. *Familiar Landmarks. Four Walks through the Historic Campus of the University of St Michael's College.* Toronto, 1984.
Articles: 'It's a Science,' *Benedicamus* 6 (April 1953) 9–12; 'Assumption–Essex Union,' *Basilian Teacher* 1 (April 1956) 18–19; 'The Literary Survival of Thomas More,' *Culture* 21 (1960) 186–202; 'Secular Studies and the Priesthood,' *Basilian Teacher* 5 (May 1961) 309–13; 'Father Carr and His Writings,' *Basilian Teacher* 8 (March 1964) 323–30; 'Reflections on a Retreat,' 10 (January 1966) 31–6; 'We Need Fear Only a Failure of Nerve,' *Forum* 2 (May 1966) 65–6.
SOURCES: GABF; *Annals* 2 (1955) 196, 8 (1996) 109–10; *Newsletter* (29 October 1995).

BOBICHON, Emile, priest, was born at Saint-Jean-de-Muzols, in the Rhône valley, canton of Tournon (Ardèche) on 9 March 1876, the son of Jules Bobichon and Rose Eynard. A brother, Paul, was a priest of the diocese of Viviers. Emile died at Tournon on 27 August 1959 and is buried there in the priests' vault of the cemetery.

Emile did his early studies at the Petit Séminaire de Vernoux (Ardèche) and entered the Basilian novitiate in 1896. He made first profession on 17 September 1897 and final profession on 21 September 1900. While studying theology, 1898–1902, he worked as master of discipline for the senior students at the Petit Séminaire d'Aubenas (Ardèche). He received major orders in the chapel of the Collège du Sacré-Coeur, Annonay: subdiaconate on 21 September 1900, diaconate on 21 September 1901, and priesthood on 20 September 1902, all at the hands of Hilarion-Joseph Montéty, titular bishop of Beirut. After ordination he remained three more years at the Petit Séminaire d'Aubenas as master of discipline in the senior section.

The dispersal of the Basilian community in France following on the anti-religious laws of the Third French Republic (1903) did not affect the Basilians teaching in diocesan institutions until two years later. After 1905 Father Bobichon is listed as *enseignant* (teacher), first in the Collège Saint-Stanislas, Nîmes (Gard), then in the Collège de l'Immaculée Conception at Sommières (Gard). During the First World War he served his country as an infirmarian in the ambulance corps. From 1921 to 1924 he taught *cinquième* at the Petit Séminaire Saint-Michel, located in one wing of the school that had belonged to the Marist Brothers at Aubenas before their dispersal in 1903. The community records next show him at the Collège du Sacré-Coeur, Annonay, 1932–43, where he taught the *classes de cinquième* and *quatrième* successively. In 1943, at the age of sixty-seven, he retired to the family home at Tournon, and died there at the age of eighty-three.

Father Emile Bobichon was a talented musician who played the organ in every institution in which he was stationed. Many secular priests in the diocese of Viviers received their training in plain chant and liturgical music under his direction. When the two branches of the Basilian community reunited in 1955, Father Bobichon chose not to make a new profession of vows nor to live in community.

SOURCES: GABF; *Annals* 2 (1959) 426; Kirley, *Community in France* 184, 204; Kirley, *Congregation in France* 76n35, 184, 205, 220, 256, 262; Pouzol, 'Notices.'

BODINEAU, Auguste Clément, subdeacon, was born at Saint-Clément-des-Levées, canton of Saumur (Maine-et-Loire, diocese of Angers), on 8 August 1844. He died in Annonay on 23 February 1875, and was buried there in the cemetery on the grounds of the Collège du Sacré-Coeur.

Auguste made his novitiate at Feyzin (Isère, now Rhône), probably in 1869, and final profession on 19 September 1873. From 1870 to 1874 he studied theology and worked as recreation master at the Petit Séminaire d'Aubenas (Ardèche). Bishop Armand de Charbonnel ordained him subdeacon in the chapel of the Collège du Sacré-Coeur, Annonay, on 20 September 1873. In March 1874, Auguste fell ill with tuberculosis and took up residence at Sainte-Barbe, the Basilian minor seminary at Annonay, for complete rest. He died there less than a year later. The annals of the college read simply: 'Today Mr Bodineau rendered his beautiful soul to God. The last days of his illness were very painful for our poor dear confrere.'

SOURCES: GABF; Pouzol, 'Notices.'

BOEHM, Francis Christian, priest, was born on 15 October 1926 in Rochester, the son of Christian Charles Boehm and Gertrude Rothenbuecher. He died in Phoenix, Arizona, on 30 September 1995 and is buried in the Basilian plot of Holy Sepulchre Cemetery, Rochester. 'Frank,' or 'Frankie,' attended Immaculate Conception and St Monica's elementary schools in Rochester, and enrolled at Aquinas Institute, Rochester, in 1940. In 1944 he entered St Basil's Novitiate, Rochester, where he made first profession on 15 August 1945. Appointed to St Michael's College, Toronto, he received a B.A. from the University of Toronto in 1949. He taught mathematics and physics at Aquinas Institute, 1949–50, and at St Michael's College School, Toronto, 1950–2, and took his first year of theology while teaching at St Michael's. In 1952 he resumed theological studies at St Basil's Seminary, Toronto, and was ordained to the priesthood on 29 June 1954 in St Basil's Church, Toronto, by Cardinal James Charles McGuigan.

In 1955, Father Boehm was appointed once again to Aquinas Institute, where he remained for twenty-one years as teacher and treasurer. During these years he also earned an M.Ed. at the University of Rochester. During the summers he attended the State University of New York in Buffalo, receiving an M.S. in mathematics in 1966.

In 1975 he participated in an assembly of the Marriage Encounter Movement which impressed him so much that he asked for the opportunity to become more involved in that ministry. In 1976 he was appointed to the Basilian Fathers of Phoenix and the following year to St Anne's Parish, Houston. In 1978 he went to St Basil's College, Toronto, for one year as bursar, and then served as Treasurer General for one year, while living at the Basilian Fathers curial house, Toronto; but eye difficulties made it necessary for him to abandon this work. He returned to St Anne's for the year 1980–1, and then undertook a special apostolate at St Bede's Parish in California. In 1983 he was once more appointed to the Basilian Fathers of Phoenix, where he devoted himself to the Marriage Encounter Movement, and where he served as rector from 1986 to 1989. He was then appointed to a special apostolate in Phoenix which, however, never materialized, for he died suddenly a few weeks later, alone in his home, and was only discovered some days later.

Frank Boehm was small of stature and feisty of disposition. As a teacher he was orderly and effective; but his greatest contribution was made in the Marriage Encounter Movement in which he became a nationally recognized figure.

BIBLIOGRAPHY: 'Mathematics in Basilian Schools [forum],' *Basilian Teacher* 4 (December 1959) 64.
SOURCES: GABF; *Annals* 2 (1955) 161, 8 (1996) 108–9; *Newsletter* (29 October 1995).

BOLAND, John FRANCIS, priest, was born in Toronto on 30 June 1916, the son of John Joseph Boland and Alice Caroline Fitzgerald. He died at Amersfoort, Netherlands, on Easter Sunday, 6 April 1969, and is buried in Assumption Parish Cemetery, Windsor.

'Frank' attended St Helen's and St Vincent's parochial schools and then the high school section of St Michael's College, Toronto. In 1933 he entered St Basil's Novitiate, Toronto, making first profession on 19 September 1934. During his undergraduate years he lived at St Basil's Seminary, Toronto, and St Michael's College (B.A., University of Toronto, 1938). He taught at St Thomas High School, Houston, 1938–9, and then returned to Toronto for theological studies at St Basil's Seminary, concurrently earning a specialist's certificate in history from the Ontario College of Education, 1941. He was ordained to the priesthood in St Basil's Church, Toronto, on 15 August 1942, by Archbishop James Charles McGuigan.

In 1943 Father Boland was appointed to St Michael's College School, where he taught history from 1943 to 1949. He was then transferred to St Mary's Boys' High School, Calgary, for one year, after which he returned to St Michael's for another four years, 1950–4. He obtained an M.A. in history from the University of Detroit in 1948 and a Ph.D. from the University of Ottawa in 1955, presenting a thesis, 'An Analysis of the Problems and Difficulties of the Basilian Fathers in Toronto, 1850–1960.' In 1955 he joined the faculty of Assumption University, Windsor, and shortly thereafter he became a member of the faculty of the University of Windsor. He founded the Canadian-American Seminar at the university in 1959, holding the directorship of the seminar and chief editorship of the *Canadian-American Seminar Reports* until 1967. He left an unpublished manuscript study of the seal-hunting controversy between the United States and Canada in the Pibilov Islands, early in the twentieth century.

Father Boland's love of history, his appreciation of student participation, and his talent for vitalizing his material made his classes memorable. He was a gentle and friendly man whose company was enjoyed by colleagues, confreres, and friends. Although he suffered a severe heart attack in 1959 he continued to give himself unstintingly to his teaching and to the academic community. On his way to Rome to fulfil a lifelong wish to spend Holy Week in that city, he stopped to visit friends in the Netherlands, where he suffered a second heart attack and died eight days later.

BIBLIOGRAPHY:
Book: Ed. *Seminar on Canadian-American Relations*. Windsor, 1962.
Articles: 'Legio Mariae,' *Benedicamus* 4 (April 1938) 77; 'Father Soulerin, Founder and Administrator,' *CCHA Report* 23 (1956) 13-28; 'The Attitude of the American Hierarchy toward the Doctrine of the Papal Infallibility at the Vatican Council,' *CCHA Report* 27 (1960) 35-49; 'Canadian-American Relations,' *Basilian Teacher* 8 (January 1964) 179-83. In the *New Catholic Encyclopedia* (New York, 1967): 'Callière, Louis Hector,' 2 1079; 'Cartier, Jacques,' 3 168-9; 'Champlain, Samuel de,' 3 442-3; 'Iberville, Pierre le Moyne d',' 7 312; 'La Salle, Robert Cavelier de,' 8 392-3; 'Talon, Jean-Baptiste,' 13 927.
SOURCES: GABF; *Annals* 1 (1943) 27, 4 (1970) 162-3; *Newsletter* (April 1969).

BONDY, Louis Joseph, priest, was born on 24 July 1894 at Sandwich (now Windsor), Ontario, one of the nine children of Albéné Bondy and Elmire Pageau. Three of the daughters became religious: Evangeline (Sister Mary St Louis CSJ), Mary Louise (Sister Pauline of Mary CSN), and Claire (Sister Emeliana CSN). A nephew, Paul Murphy, was ordained as a Basilian in 1968 but later withdrew from the Congregation. Father Bondy died in Toronto on 27 August 1985 and is buried in the Basilian plot in Holy Cross Cemetery, Thornhill, Ontario.

Louis Bondy attended local elementary schools in Sandwich and then Assumption College School, Windsor, 1905-11. He began his classical and philosophical studies at St Thomas College, Houston, where he also taught and took courses in theology, 1911-14. He entered St Basil's Novitiate, Toronto, in 1914, making first profession on 17 August 1915. He was then appointed to Assumption College to continue his arts and theological studies, but was transferred in 1916-17 to St Michael's College, Toronto (B.A., University of Toronto, 1917). He returned the following year to Assumption to complete his theological training, and was ordained to the priesthood in St Peter's Cathedral, London, Ontario, on 21 December 1918 by Bishop Michael Fallon.

After ordination Father Bondy spent the next six years teaching French at Assumption College, serving on the local council during the years 1923–5. During the summers he attended classes at the University of Chicago (M.A., French Literature, 1924, with the thesis 'Brunetière as a Classical Critic'). In 1925 he began doctoral studies at Johns Hopkins University, Baltimore, spending the year 1925–6 at the University of Paris (Ph.D., Johns Hopkins, 1927, thesis topic: 'Le classicisme de Ferdinand Brunetière'). He taught and served as registrar at Assumption College, 1927–8.

In 1928 Father Bondy was appointed superior of St Basil's Scholasticate, a position he held until 1934. Although strict and demanding of the seminarians in his charge, he was also just and deeply interested in their spiritual and academic progress. He was appointed to St Michael's College in 1934 to teach in the French Department, where he served as head until 1962. He was named professor emeritus in 1965.

Louis Bondy was superior of the local Basilian community and president of St Michael's College from 1946 to 1952. At the close of this term he was appointed to St Basil's Seminary. He was elected to the Basilian Fathers general council for the term 1954 to 1960. He returned to St Michael's for three years, 1960–3, and then settled for the rest of his life in St Basil's Seminary (after 1970 'St Basil's College').

Father Bondy was awarded honorary Doctor of Letters degrees by the Université de Montréal in 1942 and by the University of Ottawa in 1952. In that same year the Université de Laval conferred on him its *Doctorat ès lettres*, and the government of France appointed him *Chevalier de la Légion d'Honneur*. In 1979 he received an honorary Doctorate of Letters from the University of St Michael's College.

Apart from his unstinting devotion to teaching and administration at St Michael's and in the Basilian Congregation, Father Bondy is remembered above all as a man of strict principles and rigid self-discipline and as a master of the spiritual life. His influence on the spirituality of the Basilian Fathers was considerable and has yet to be chronicled. He opened to many his deep knowledge and love of the French spiritual writers, from the sixteenth to the twentieth centuries, and the riches of the great Spanish mystics, Teresa of Avila and John of the Cross. His study of Thomas Aquinas continued all through his life.

A close friend and disciple of Jacques Maritain, he promoted the great philosopher's works and acted as his interpreter when Maritain lectured in Toronto.

Father Bondy was frequently called upon to give retreats and spiritual direction to men and women religious of many communities. His doctrine was deep and compelling; his manner was stern while reassuring. He always referred to Jesus Christ as 'the Master,' and managed, even with that rather formal designation, to instil a personal relation with the Lord in his listeners which was authentic and joyful. He was more a talker than a listener in his spiritual direction, yet quite open to what one wished to speak of, were it a problem, an experience, or a question. He was paternal but never patronizing. He was easy to talk to, respectful of a contrary opinion, though he expressed his own clearly and unhesitatingly. In the sports of his early days and the bridge games of his later days he was competitive and he loved to win. Nor was he lacking in wit and a ready sense of humour.

BIBLIOGRAPHY:
Book: *Le classicisme de Ferdinand Brunetière.* Paris, 1930.
Articles: 'St John of the Cross,' *Basilian* 1 (June 1935) 63–5; 'Claudel and the Catholic Revival,' *Thomist* (January 1943) 171–87; 'The Legacy of Baudelaire,' *University of Toronto Quarterly* 14 (July 1945) 414–30; 'Tending to Perfection in Charity,' *Canadian Religious Conference* 37 (1956) 1–10; 'The Lord Be with You,' Radio address, Trans-Canada Catholic Broadcast, 'Man Alive' series, 9 November 1952; 'A Second Language Is Necessary, a Third Better,' *Basilian Teacher* 2 (January 1958) 3–6; 'Trois poètes français,' *Canadian Modern Languages Review* (1961) 7–12; 'The True Meaning of Religious Obedience,' *Religious Obedience and the Exercise of Authority. Donum Dei* 6 (Ottawa, 1961) 141–56; 'The Life of an Artist: Raïssa Maritain,' *Basilian Teacher* 6 (January 1962) 153–7; 'Obedience Is the Roofbeam,' *Forum* (October 1964) 6–8; 'A Basilian Debt to the Oblates,' *Basilian Teacher* 11 (December 1967) 428–33; 'Foreword,' in R.J. Scollard and J.R. O'Donnell. *Two Hundred Years of Basilian Ordinations to the Priesthood, 1782–1982.* Toronto, 1982.
SOURCES: GABF; *Annals* 3 (1965) 370, 4 (1969) 15, 5 (1979), 337, 5 (1980) 506, 6 (1986) 482–3; *French Studies U. of T.* 56, 119–20, 124–5, 127, 132, 134, 170, 177; *Newsletter* (12 September 1985); Kirley, *Congregation in France* 45n40, 231n24, 268.

BONFILS, Joseph Frédéric, priest, was born at Buis-les-Baronnies (Drôme, diocese of Valence), on 10 January 1847. He died at Sainte-

Euphémie, canton of Buis-les-Baronnies, on 13 March 1918. He was a great-uncle of Jean Bonfils, bishop of Viviers (1990–8).

Joseph received his primary and secondary education in his home diocese and entered the Basilian novitiate at Feyzin (Isère, now Rhône) in 1873 at the age of twenty-seven. He was professed on 18 September 1874 and made his final profession a year later, on 8 December 1875, at the Petit Séminaire de Vernoux (Ardèche), diocese of Viviers. Bishop Joseph-Michel-Frédéric Bonnet of Viviers ordained him subdeacon on 18 December 1875 and deacon on 23 September 1876. Two years later, on 21 September 1878, Bishop Armand de Charbonnel ordained him to the priesthood in the chapel of the Collège du Sacré-Coeur, Annonay.

After his first profession Joseph worked as recreation and study-hall master at the Collège du Sacré-Coeur, Annonay, 1874–5. Then he taught *sixième* at the Petit Séminaire de Vernoux, 1875–84. In the course of his last year there he was appointed to the Collège Saint-Charles in Blidah, Algeria, where he conducted classes in grammar from 1885 until the school was closed on 13 July 1903 as a result of the anticlerical laws enacted in France. Jean Bonfils returned to the diocese of Valence, a 'secular' priest in the eyes of the state with no connections to a religious congregation. The Basilian records list him as working first at Saint-Auban-sur-l'Ouvèze, canton of Buis-les-Baronnies, then in 1910 and 1913 at Sainte-Euphémie, where he died.

SOURCES: Kirley, *Community in France* 185, 210; Pouzol, 'Notices.'

BONNAUD, Louis, priest, was born at Chazeaux, canton of Largentière (Ardèche) on 7 November 1835. He died at Mélas, canton of Viviers (Ardèche) on 10 October 1904.

Louis received a thorough training in elementary school at Chazeaux, where his father was the schoolmaster. The local pastor taught him Latin. For his secondary education he went to the Petit Séminaire d'Aubenas (Ardèche), and then to the Grand Séminaire de Viviers (Ardèche) for further studies in philosophy and theology. In 1861 he entered the Basilian novitiate at Feyzin (Isère, now Rhône), and made first profession of vows on 8 December 1862. Bishop Louis Delcusy of Viviers conferred the subdiaconate on him on 20 December 1862, the diaconate on 19 December 1863, and finally the priesthood on 23 December 1865, in the cathedral at Viviers.

While studying theology Louis Bonnaud taught *sixième* at the Collège des Cordeliers, Annonay, 1862–3, and worked as recreation and study-hall master at the Basilian minor seminary, Sainte-Barbe, Annonay, 1864–7. His next appointment was to the Ecole cléricale at Périgueux (Dordogne), where he had charge of *seconde*, 1867–8. When Father André *Charmant, superior of Sainte-Barbe, suddenly needed help in operating the minor seminary, Father Bonnaud returned to become assistant director and bursar, a position he held for the next six years, 1868–74. Thanks to the skill and efficiency with which he ran the temporal affairs at Sainte-Barbe, he was assigned in 1874 to the same position at the Ecole cléricale at Périgueux, where he remained for the next twenty-nine years. With the closing of the school in 1903 in the wake of the anti-religious laws of the Third Republic, the Basilians were forced out of the Ecole cléricale, and Father Bonnaud went to live with relatives in Mélas, canton of Viviers (Ardèche), where he died. Fathers Noël *Durand, superior general, and Jean-Claude *Savoye attended his funeral.

Almost all of Father Louis Bonnaud's priestly life was devoted to the direction of Basilian houses of formation. He worked at the Ecole cléricale at Périgueux for thirty of the thirty-seven years that the Basilians ran that school. As a sign of esteem, not only for Father Bonnaud's administrative ability but also for the training he gave the seminarians in liturgy and religious ceremonies, Bishop Nicolas-Joseph Dabert made him an honorary canon of the cathedral of Périgueux.

SOURCES: Kirley, *Community in France* 185, 188n469, 206; Pouzol, 'Notices.'

BONNET, Pierre, priest, was born on 4 July 1830 at Vion, canton of Tournon (Ardèche). He died at Vion on 8 December 1870 and was buried there.

As a minor seminarian Pierre Bonnet studied at Sainte-Barbe, Annonay, 1845–53, and then went to the Grand Séminaire at Viviers, where he received tonsure and minor orders. In 1856 he came to Annonay as a postulant and began his novitiate with the Basilians on 29 June 1856. The master of novices, Father Germain *Deglesne, had died ten days earlier and was replaced temporarily by the superior of Sainte-Barbe, Father André *Charmant. The novices had their accommodation at that time in a house belonging to the Peloux family, near Sainte-Barbe. Other novices that year were Victor *Perbost, Adrien *Fayolle, Antoine *Bord, Hilaire *Durand, Léopold *Martin, and two others (Adrien Monnard and Claude Reynaud) who later withdrew from the Congregation. In August 1856 Father Auguste de *Montgolfier became novice master.

Pierre Bonnet made his first profession of vows on 29 September 1857 and final profession on 18 July 1858. As novice and scholastic he continued his study of theology and taught school, first in the college at Privas (Ardèche), 1856-8, and then at the Collège des Cordeliers, Annonay, 1858-9. He was ordained deacon on 18 June 1859 and priest on 25 September 1859 in the cathedral of Viviers by Bishop Louis Delcusy.

His priestly life, eleven years in all, was devoted entirely to the work of formation. He taught for seven years, 1859-66, at the Petit Séminaire de Vernoux (Ardèche), where he celebrated one of the Masses each Sunday in a nearby parish, and four years, 1866-70, at the Ecole cléricale in Périgueux (Dordogne), at first in charge of the *quatrième* but later was *professeur de seconde*. He fell ill in the course of the year 1869-70 but kept on teaching and finished the year exhausted. Doctors in Annonay and Lyon were unable to help him regain his health. He retired to his family home in Vion, where he died shortly afterwards.

SOURCES: Kirley, *Community in France* 31; Pouzol, 'Notices.'

BORD, Antoine, priest, was born on 15 December 1826 at Le Plagnal, canton of Saint-Etienne-de-Lugdarès (Ardèche). He died on 22 October 1902.

Antoine Bord entered the Basilian novitiate on 1 November 1856 at almost thirty years of age. He made his final profession of vows on 15 May 1859 and was ordained to the priesthood on 25 May 1859 in Lyon by Cardinal Louis-Jacques-Maurice de Bonald. (Bishop Louis Delcusy of Viviers had sustained injuries in an accident.) Like most young Basilians of his day, Antoine worked in various schools run by Basilians while studying theology. He worked as recreation and study-hall master at the Collège de Privas (Ardèche), 1857-8; at the Petit Séminaire de Vernoux (Ardèche), 1859-60; at the Petit Séminaire d'Aubenas (Ardèche), 1860-2; and at the Collège des Cordeliers, Annonay, 1862-3, where he was named *professeur de sixième*.

In early September 1863 Father Bord began his long association with the Calvary Shrine at Prades, a centre of pilgrimage in honour of the Holy Cross, which Bishop Delcusy had confided to the Basilians on 31 December 1858. At first he was assistant to Father Jean-Jacques *Giraud in ministering to pilgrims at the shrine. Then in September 1864 he was appointed curate at the nearby parish church of Prades. From August 1875 until his death in 1902 Father Bord was pastor of the parish and also in charge of the Calvary Shrine. The latter included a magnificent chapel made possible by a donation from Professor Raynaud, a nephew of Father Pierre *Tourvieille and a lay teacher at the Collège des Cordeliers in Annonay. Bishop Delcusy consecrated the Calvary Chapel at Prades on 13 September 1865.

Father Bord and his assistant Father Michel *Malbos worked together for twenty-seven years tending the parish and the shrine. Each year for the feast of the Exaltation of the Holy Cross (14 September) such huge crowds came to the shrine that Father Bord had to recruit several of his brother priests in the area to help with the Masses, confessions, and stations of the cross.

As the anti-religious policies of the Third Republic in France gained momentum at the turn of the century, zealous republicans at Prades denounced Fathers Bord and Malbos as members of a religious order, with the result that, on 7 December 1900, the Ministry of Public Instruction in Paris discontinued payment of the priests' salaries which had been agreed upon in the Concordat with Napoleon (1802). The ministry further decreed in 1903 that the Calvary Shrine be closed. Father Bord, however, had died on 22 October 1902 before seeing his life's work demolished. As a final mark of disdain, the municipal council of Prades refused him burial in the priests' plot in the local cemetery. The Basilian records describe Father Bord as 'a pious, modest priest,' adding that he died 'with that calm serenity which marked his entire life.'

SOURCES: Chomel, *Collège d'Annonay* 221–2; Kirley, *Community in France* 70n178, 124n305, 163n416; Pouzol, 'Notices.'

BOSC, Henri, priest, was born on 3 January 1837 at Saint-Julien-la-Brousse (Ardèche), canton of Le Cheylard, the son of Jacques Bosc and Magdelaine Moulin. He died at Saint-Jean-Chambre on 13 April 1901.

Henri made his novitiate at Feyzin (Isère, now Rhône) and was professed on 8 November 1861 at the Petit Séminaire d'Aubenas (Ardèche). While doing theological studies, 1861–6, he worked in various schools run by the Basilians. For two years, 1861–3, he was recreation and study-hall master at the Petit Séminaire d'Aubenas. The following year he taught at the college at Privas (Ardèche), and then went to the day-pupils section (*externat*) of the Collège des Cordeliers in Annonay for the year 1864–5 as prefect of discipline. He taught *sixième* in the Collège des Cordeliers, 1865-6, as a deacon, and was ordained a priest on 22 September 1866 in the college chapel at the hands of Bishop Armand de Charbonnel.

After ordination he was in the first group of Basilians in 1866 who assumed direction of the Ecole cléricale at Périgueux (Dordogne), and was appointed *professeur de sixième*. At the end of that school year he was moved to the Petit Séminaire de Vernoux (Ardèche), where from 1867 to 1875 he taught successively the *classes de sixième, cinquième,* and *quatrième*. From 1875 to 1878 he helped out in the school for day pupils at Privas, and then went to the Collège du Sacré-Coeur, Annonay, 1878-9, to teach the commercial course. During the year 1879-80 he taught *sixième* at the Basilian school at Châteauroux (Indre), diocese of Bourges. The following year he taught *quatrième* at the Collège du Bourg-Saint-Andéol (Ardèche). When the Basilians were forced out of that school by the anticlerical town council, Father Bosc returned to the Petit Séminaire de Vernoux, where he taught *cinquième* and *quatrième* for two years, 1881-3. The next school year was spent partly at Vernoux and partly in Annonay. Early in 1885 he went to the Basilian school at Blidah, Algeria, where he was *professeur de quatrième* and *troisième* for two years, 1885-7.

In 1887, at the age of fifty, he requested assignment to the parish ministry and was appointed pastor of Saint-Jean-Chambre, near Vernoux. There he protested vigorously against the practice of the local Children's Aid Society (*Assistance publique*) of placing Catholic children in Protestant families. During the Holy Week ceremonies of 1901 Father Bosc caught a chill and died of pulmonary congestion.

SOURCES: Kirley, *Community in France* 31; Pouzol, 'Notices.'

BOUCHER, Maurice, priest, was born on 23 December 1855 at Rocles, canton of Largentière (Ardèche). He died at Cadouin (Dordogne) on 6 December 1942.

Maurice completed his secondary school studies at Sainte-Barbe, the Basilian minor seminary in Annonay, associated with the Collège du Sacré-Coeur. He entered the novitiate at Feyzin (Isère, now Rhône), in 1878 and made final profession on 17 September 1880. For three years he worked in the Collège Saint-Pierre, the Basilian school at Châteauroux (Indre), diocese of Bourges, first as recreation and study-hall master, 1879-81, and then as *professeur de sixième* and *cinquième,* 1881-2. Bishop Joseph-Michel-Frédéric Bonnet of Viviers conferred the subdiaconate on him in the college chapel in Annonay on 18 September 1880, and Archbishop Armand de Charbonnel ordained him deacon in the same chapel on 24 September 1881. He was ordained to the priesthood on 3 June 1882 in Bourges (Cher).

After the Basilians closed their school at Châteauroux in 1882, Father Boucher remained for three years in the diocese of Bourges engaged in pastoral ministry. In 1885 Bishop Dabert of Périgueux confided the parish of Cadouin to the Basilians, who were already operating the Ecole cléricale at Périgueux, and Father Boucher was appointed pastor, a post he held for fifty-six years, 1886–1942. The parish of Cadouin included a shrine in which was venerated a holy shroud. It attracted pilgrims the year round, and as many as fifteen thousand came on the annual feast day, 15 September, in 1903.

Father Boucher had a Basilian curate to help him tend to the needs of the faithful in the parish and at the shrine. In 1898 he was appointed honorary canon of the cathedral of Périgueux. In 1934 the Church officially declared the Holy Shroud at Cadouin to be unauthentic and forbade any further pilgrimages in its honour. It was a blow to Father Boucher, who had laboured for so many years ministering to the pilgrims. He celebrated his diamond jubilee of ordination in June 1942 and died in Cadouin on 6 December of that year, dean of the priests of Périgueux. The bishop of Périgueux presided at his funeral on 8 December 1942, describing him in the funeral oration as 'a good and faithful priest, a son of that Catholic province, Le Vivarais, who had given himself entirely to God in the religious life of the Basilian Community.'

SOURCES: Kirley, *Community in France* 207; Pouzol, 'Notices.'

BOUCHET, Xavier, priest, was born on 25 December 1841 at Le Pouzin, canton of Chomérac (Ardèche). He died at Le Pouzin on 19 July 1919 and is buried there.

Xavier entered the Basilian novitiate at Feyzin (Isère, now Rhône), probably in 1864, and made final profession of vows on 18 September 1868. While pursuing theological studies he worked in Basilian institutions, first as recreation and study-hall master at the Petit Séminaire d'Aubenas, 1865–7, and the following year in the Collège de Privas (Ardèche) in the same capacities. Bishop Armand de Charbonnel ordained him subdeacon on 17 September 1868 in the chapel of the Collège du Sacré-Coeur, Annonay. He went to Périgueux (Dordogne) as *professeur de sixième* at the Ecole cléricale. The following year he was placed in charge of discipline at the college in Annonay. He was ordained deacon in the college chapel on 18 September 1869 by Bishop de Charbonnel and to the priesthood on 17 December 1870 in the cathedral at Viviers by Bishop Louis Delcusy.

Father Xavier Bouchet remained at the Collège du Sacré-Coeur for the next seven years, as prefect of discipline, 1870–2, *professeur de sixième*, 1872–3, *de quatrième*, 1873–6, and *de seconde*, 1876–7. He went to Bourg-Saint-Andéol (Ardèche) for three years as *professeur de seconde*. In 1880 he was assigned to the Collège de Saint-Pierre at Châteauroux (Indre), diocese of Bourges, where he was *professeur de troisième* and fulfilled the duties of bursar.

After the Basilian withdrawal from that school in 1882, he remained in the diocese of Bourges doing pastoral ministry until 1900. He is mentioned in the Basilian records as present at the annual retreat in Annonay in 1887 and as chaplain at Touvent (Charente-Maritime) in 1889. The archbishop of Bourges made him an honorary canon of the cathedral. About 1900 he returned to his home town, Le Pouzin, in the Rhône valley, to take care of a sick brother. During the First World War, when the pastor and the curate of Le Pouzin were conscripted for military service, Father Bouchet took care of the parish with zeal and dedication, though well into his seventies at the time. At his death there in 1919, his funeral was attended by a remarkably large number of the faithful.

SOURCES: Kirley, *Community in France* 184, 206; Pouzol, 'Notices.'

BOURRET, Marcel, priest, member of the Congregation c.1935–54, was born in 1908 in Boutières, near Le Cheylard (Ardèche). He died on 13 July 1989, and was buried in the cemetery at Le Cheylard.

Marcel joined the Congregation of Saint Basil and was ordained a priest in 1936. He taught with his Basilian confreres at the Collège du Sacré-Coeur, Annonay. Prior to the reunion of the two branches of the Community (1955) he sought and received incardination in the diocese of Viviers. He served as assistant pastor for one year in Châtillon-en-Diois, diocese of Valence, and then in 1954 was appointed pastor of Saint-Nazaire-le-Désert and of Boutières, diocese of Viviers. Here he lived and worked until his death.

SOURCES: ABA; Kirley, *Congregation in France* 185, 194, 196, 210, 220, 257, 271.

BOWIE, James Joseph, priest, was born in Toronto on 23 June 1923, seventh of nine children of Metropolitan Toronto Police Officer John Bowie and Catherine Ann Black. His sister Margaret became a member of the Congregation of the Grey Sisters of the Immaculate Conception. He died in Toronto on 21 August 1987 and is buried in the Basilian plot of Holy Cross Cemetery, Thornhill, Ontario.

'Jim' attended St Vincent de Paul parochial school and the high school section of St Michael's College. He entered St Basil's Novitiate, Toronto, in 1942 (first profession, 15 August 1943), and was appointed to Assumption College, Windsor, in 1943 for university studies (B.A., Honours Philosophy, 1947). He spent one year at St Thomas High School, Houston, both teaching in the school and studying theology. In 1948 he was appointed to Holy Rosary Scholasticate on Tweedsmuir Avenue, Toronto, to continue his theology and to attend the Ontario College of Education. He was ordained to the priesthood on 29 June 1951 by Cardinal James Charles McGuigan in St Basil's Church, Toronto.

Father Bowie's teaching years were spent as follows: Assumption High School, Windsor, 1952–9, St Michael's College School, Toronto, 1959–62, St Joseph's High School, Ottawa, 1962–70, Assumption High School, 1971–5, and St Charles College, Sudbury, Ontario, 1975–81, 1984–March 1987. He attended the University of Detroit for six summers, 1953–8, to perfect his knowledge of chemistry. In the early 1970s he moved into the area of guidance counselling, having done preparatory studies at Indiana University in the summer of 1969 and a full year of studies at the University of Ottawa (1970–1; M.Ed., 1971).

In 1981 his superiors asked him to take the position of assistant novice master in Detroit. He did so for three years, but in 1984 returned to St Charles in Sudbury to resume teaching and counselling. It was then that cancer was diagnosed; and, in spite of surgery, the disease advanced. On his own decision in the early weeks of 1987 he stopped treatments. When spring arrived he moved to the Basilian Fathers Residence, Toronto, where, as one close to him noted, he greeted death as a friend.

Father Bowie came from a close-knit Scottish Catholic family that meant a great deal to him and of which he was a constant support and a focus of unity. At the frequent gatherings of the Bowie-Black clan at Glenelg Church in Markdale, Ontario, he presided at the Mass. In the Basilian community he was gentle, witty, and extremely kind. His native quietness, far from being a social disadvantage, drew his confreres to him as one in whom they found a companion and a leader. The devotedness and generosity which he brought to a variety of appointments witnessed to his deep and enduring commitment to religious life, the priesthood, and teaching.

SOURCES: GABF; *Annals* 2 (1951) 35, 6 (1988) 702–3; *Newsletter* (27 August 1987); Hugh Foley CSB.

BRENNAN, Laurence, priest, cousin of Father Patrick *Ryan, was born in Lisdowney Parish, Kilkenny County (diocese of Kildare and Leighlin), Ireland, on 18 February 1847, the son of John Brennan and Mary Ryan. He died in Toronto on 30 June 1904, and is buried there in the Basilian plot of St Michael's Cemetery.

Laurence Brennan came to Canada at the age of seventeen on the invitation of his uncle, Father Jeremiah Ryan, 1808–80, of Oakville, Ontario. With him came his cousin, Patrick *Ryan. The uncle sent his two nephews to St Michael's College, Toronto, where they studied from 1864 until 1868, when both entered St Basil's Novitiate, Toronto, on 25 July. Together they made final vows on 2 December 1871, and were ordained priests on 1 May 1872.

The greater part of Laurence Brennan's priestly life was spent as pastor of St Basil's Parish in Toronto. First, however, he served as assistant at St Mary's of the Assumption Parish, Owen Sound, Ontario, 1872–4. Then he was sent to France in the hope that a change of climate would help his health, which was never robust. In 1875 he was back in Toronto teaching history at St Michael's College and serving as director of studies. Soon afterwards he became associated with St Basil's Parish and in 1880 was appointed its first full-time pastor. In 1889 he was transferred to St Mary's of the Assumption Parish in Owen Sound. Ill health shortened his stay there and he spent the winter of 1890 at Aiken in South Carolina looking into the possibility of a community foundation there. The year 1891 brought him back to St Basil's Parish, where he was pastor until his death in 1904. An obituary written for the *Catholic Register* of 7 July 1904, and reprinted in *Benedicamus* in 1950, said of him, 'To great piety and exceeding charity and generosity, Father Brennan added the intellectual gifts of an alert man of business. The results of his successful financing were seen when he wiped out the debt upon his church and erected the novitiate on St Clair Avenue. The versatile character of his mind is evidenced by the fact that amidst the work and cares of a large parish he found time to collect and compile material for a large and well-assorted hymn book. Anxious to introduce congregational singing among his people, a task he accomplished with a fair amount of success, he published *St Basil's Hymnal*, a work now generally used in Canada and the United States.'

Laurence Brennan involved the laity in every project he undertook. It was a committee of laymen who were responsible for the publication of the *St Basil's Hymnal*, which was reprinted about forty times and sold over a million copies. Lay persons were chosen to teach the catechism classes held every Sunday for the children of the parish. With the men and women of the parish behind him he made a series of major improvements in St Basil's Church: an addition to the nave, the present entrance and the Casavant organ in 1887, the steeple in 1889, and a church bell in 1895. Attention to present needs and thought for the future were ever on Father Brennan's mind. In 1903 he established a Students' Union, which later developed into the Newman Centre at the University of Toronto.

Concern for the Catholics living in the outlying parts of St Basil's Parish caused him to purchase in 1881 fifty acres of farm land on St Clair Avenue West on which in 1892 he built St Basil's Novitiate, whose chapel was the first place of worship for the new parish of Our Lady of the Holy Rosary. The farm itself provided produce for St Michael's College and later sale of parts of it for real estate development furnished valuable financial assistance. In addition to his parochial duties Father Brennan served on the provincial council from 1883 until his death in 1904. He was for some years honorary president of the Catholic Truth Society of Canada. On the first anniversary of his death the people of St Basil's dedicated a stained glass window to his memory. In 1939 St Michael's College named a new building containing a student dining hall, lounge, and a Basilian residence 'Brennan Hall' in his memory.

BIBLIOGRAPHY:
Ed. *St Basil's Hymn Book: Containing Daily Prayers, Prayers at Mass, Litanies, Vespers for All the Sundays and Festivals of the Year, a Selection of over Two Hundred Hymns, Office and Rules for Sodalities of the Blessed Virgin Mary, Preparation for and Prayers after Confession and Holy Communion.* ... Toronto, 1887, 1898, c. forty reprints. Ed. *St Basil's Hymnal: Containing Music for Vespers of all the Sundays and Festivals of the year. Three Masses and over Two Hundred Hymns, together with Litanies, Daily Prayers, Prayers at Mass, Preparation and Prayers for Confession and*

Communion, and the office and Rules for Sodalities of the Blessed Virgin Mary. Toronto, 1889; reprints.

SOURCES: GABF; *Benedicamus* 3 (January 1950) 24; *Catholic Register* 7 July 1904; *Centennial, St Mary's*; Hoskin, *St Basil's*; *Jubilee, St Mary's*; Madden, *St Basil's*; *Yearbook SMC* 9 (1918).

BRET, Jean-Marie, priest, the son of Jean Bret and Marie-Marguerite Perdriole, was born on 8 September 1872 at Préaux (Ardèche), canton of Satillieu. He died at Préaux on 5 March 1908 and is buried there.

Jean-Marie received basic Latin classes from the pastor at Monestier (Ardèche) and then went to Sainte-Barbe, Annonay, for his secondary school studies, 1888–92. He made first profession on 20 September 1895 and final profession on 21 September 1900. He received major orders at the hands of Bishop Hilarion-Joseph Montéty in the chapel of the Collège du Sacré-Coeur, Annonay: subdiaconate, 22 September 1900; diaconate, 21 September 1901; priesthood, 20 September 1902.

During theological studies he worked as recreation and study-hall master at the Collège de Saint-Charles, Blidah, Algeria, 1894–7, and taught grammar classes at the same school, 1898–1903. The year 1897–8 was spent in Annonay as a year of formation. When the school in Blidah was closed, 13 July 1903, owing to the suppression of religious in France, Father Bret returned to his family home at Préaux and stayed there until June 1904, when he secured employment as recreation and study-hall master in the Collège Saint-Joseph at Avignon (Provence), and then at the Collège Saint-Ignace in Marseille (Bouches-du-Rhône) from September 1904 to 20 February 1905. As he had not received a certificate of secularization from the diocese of Viviers, declaring him to be a secular priest in the eyes of the state, he was not authorized to hold any position in a school, which meant he had to leave the premises whenever the inspector arrived. When alerted to the awkward situation by the parish priest of Préaux, Bishop Joseph-Michel-Frédéric Bonnet of Viviers appointed him to the parish of Sanilhac (Ardèche), canton of Largentière, in March 1905. The necessary certificate of secularization could then have been granted; but because of Father Bret's failing health, this was not done. He died at Préaux at thirty-five years of age.

SOURCES: Kirley, *Community in France* 185, 209; Kirley, *Congregation in France* 67; Pouzol, 'Notices.'

BROSSE, Jean André, priest, member of the Congregation 1873–c.1900, was born 14 March 1846 at Châteauneuf-de-Galaure (Drôme, diocese of Valence).

Jean André made final profession of vows on 19 September 1873 and was ordained a priest in the chapel of the Collège du Sacré-Coeur, Annonay, on 19 September 1874 by Bishop Armand de Charbonnel. After two years at the Collège du Bourg-Saint-Andéol, 1872–4, he worked as prefect of discipline at the Petit Séminaire d'Aubenas, 1874–9. At the Collège du Sacré-Coeur, 1879–93, he taught successively the classes of *sixième*, *cinquième*, and 'Histoire et géographie.' After this date his name is absent from the list of appointments. Letters from the superior general written in February, March, and April 1900 ordering him to return to the Congregation received no reply.

SOURCES: Pouzol, 'Notices,' Supplément 2.

BROT, Lucien Jules, priest, was born at Ruoms (Ardèche) on 11 October 1914, the only child of Jules Brot, a farmer, and Lucie Chamontin. He died in Annonay on 15 February 1996 and is buried there in the Basilian cemetery at the Collège du Sacré-Coeur.

Lucien was but three months old when his father was killed in action at Bar-le-Duc (Meuse) during the First World War. His mother raised him alone, creating a very strong bond between the two. His parish priest gave him training in Latin, and he continued his secondary studies at the Petit Séminaire d'Aubenas (Ardèche), 1926–32. He entered the Basilian novitiate at Bordighera, Italy, making first profession on 22 September 1933. He studied philosophy at the Maison Saint-Joseph, Annonay, from 1933 to 1935, and earned his *baccalauréat*. After his military service in Lyon, 1935–7, he returned to the Maison Saint-Joseph and took two years of theology, 1937–9. Mobilized in 1939, he was taken prisoner at the end of May 1940 in the region of Boulogne-sur-Mer at the time of the evacuation from Dunkerque, and transported to a prison camp at Stettin, Prussia (now Szczecin, Poland). He worked first on farms there and then in a factory in Berlin. Freed in 1943, he returned first to Ruoms and then to the Maison Saint-Joseph. No one ever heard him utter an unkind or complaining word about his captors. He was ordained to the priesthood on 3 June 1944 at Viviers (Ardèche) by Bishop Alfred Couderc.

After ordination he was entrusted with the juniorate at the Maison Saint-Joseph while completing his theology course. In 1947 he began a life of teaching in the Collège du Sacré-Coeur, Annonay, which extended to 1980. At one time or another he taught mathematics, science, history, geography, classics, and religion in the junior classes. There was no professor more diligent, more given to his students – demanding, but never unkind or unjust; a master of discipline, an educator in the fullest sense of the word, cooperating in every detail with the rules and policies of the school.

Father Brot was a timid man but never one to shirk his duty, whatever it cost him. He loved to walk, and would go at least twice a week on long hikes, some ten or fifteen kilometres, in the countryside. He went regularly once a week to Ruoms in the southern part of the Ardèche to visit his mother, taking the bus until he later acquired a motorcycle and then a small automobile. He retired from teaching in 1980, moving from the college to Maison Saint-Joseph, where he cared for the gardens and the interior of the house, putting himself at the service of his confreres. He was scrupulously regular for Mass and other spiritual exercises of the community. In the early 1990s his health began to fail. An awareness of the slow deterioration of his mind caused him great anguish. On 30 September 1995, six months before his death, he woke up blind, but insisted on going to the chapel for Mass, which he concelebrated, reciting the prayers from memory. It was his last Mass. He was moved later to a facility at the Hôpital d'Annonay, where he died peacefully.

SOURCES: *Annals* 6 (1984) 209, 8 (1995) 4–5, (1997) 102–4; *Newsletter* (22 February 1996); Kirley, *Congregation in France* 194, 196, 198, 207, 209, 212, 213, 214, 218–19, 220, 256, 262, 266; Pouzol, 'Notices.'

BROWN, Francis Austin, priest, was born on 15 August 1907, at Kinkora, Ontario (diocese of London), the son of Robert Brown and Ellen McCarty. He died in Detroit on 26 March 1977 and is buried there in the Basilian plot at Holy Sepulcher Cemetery.

Austin attended high school at Assumption College, Windsor, graduating in 1920, and then worked for two years on the family farm before returning to Assumption College, where he took his first two years of university studies. He entered St Basil's Novitiate, Toronto, in September 1927, and made first profession on 2 October 1928. He was then appointed to Assumption College (B.A., University of Western Ontario, 1930). After graduation he was appointed to St Basil's Seminary, Toronto, for theological studies, attending concurrently the Ontario College of Education during the year 1931–2. He was ordained to the priesthood on 17 December 1933 in Assumption Church, Windsor, by Bishop Alexander MacDonald.

Father Brown – always known to his Basilian confreres as 'Beano' – had four appointments in his teaching career: St Michael's College School, Toronto, 1933–7; Catholic Central, Detroit, 1937–41, during which time he earned teaching certification in Michigan, 1939; Assumption High School, Windsor, 1941–53, serving as principal there for seven years, 1946–53, and earning an M.A. in philosophy from the University of Western Ontario, 1942; and finally, Catholic Central High School, 1953–71, where he served as treasurer, business manager, part-time teacher, and cafeteria supervisor. He would work far into the night. He asked at one point for permission to hire some office help, but the request was denied. When he retired in 1971 three persons were hired to replace him. He remained active in all the affairs of both house and school and did part-time chaplaincy work at Providence Hospital. He also served in his retirement as bursar of the Basilian house.

But retirement weighed heavily on this man who had been so very active, tireless, and successful. After two years it became necessary for him to seek the help of other priests and religious at Guest House, a rehabilitation and renewal institution near Detroit. This worked a striking and admirable transformation in Father Brown, who became an example and inspiration to his confreres for his practice of prayer, especially the rosary, and his peaceful, charitable manner. He always possessed a consciously cultivated talent for remembering people's names and their relationship to the Basilian community.

SOURCES: GABF; *Annals* 5 (1978) 320–1; *Newsletter* (31 March 1977); Edward Donoher CSB.

BROWN, William James, priest, was born on 15 August 1915 in Toronto, the son of William Brown and Mary Carleton. He died in Toronto on 19 March 1991 and is buried in the Basilian plot of Holy Cross Cemetery, Thornhill, Ontario.

'Bill' Brown received his elementary education in St Anthony and St James parochial schools in Toronto. In 1928 he entered the high school section of St Michael's College, Toronto, transferring three years later to Runnymede Collegiate Institute where he graduated in 1933. In the fall of that year he began a general arts course with math and physics options at St Michael's College (B.A., University of Toronto, 1937). That year he entered St Basil's Novitiate, Toronto. After profession on 12 September 1938, he was appointed to Aquinas Institute, Rochester, where he taught mathematics for one year. In 1939 he began four years of theological studies at St Basil's Seminary, Toronto, enrolling concurrently in undergraduate courses in chemistry at St Michael's and philosophy at the Pontifical Institute of Mediaeval Studies. During the year 1941–2 he lived at St Michael's College and attended the Ontario College of Education (Ontario High School assistant's certification, 1942). He returned to the seminary for his final year of theology and was ordained on his twenty-eighth birthday, 15 August 1943, in St Basil's Church, Toronto, by Archbishop James Charles McGuigan.

In 1944 Father Brown was appointed to St Michael's College to teach. He completed an M.A. in philosophy at the University of Toronto and served as assistant treasurer of the college for the last two years of his stay there, 1948–50. He was then appointed to the new St Michael's College School on Bathurst Street, where, in addition to his classroom duties, he served as treasurer of the school for his first four years. In 1955 he was appointed to St Charles College, Sudbury, Ontario, where he taught mathematics and served as first councillor for the local community. In 1961 he was moved to St Mary's College, Sault Ste Marie, Ontario, as principal and superior. He continued teaching mathematics and, as the 'new math' was being introduced, attended special classes in it sponsored by the Ontario Separate Schools Teachers Federation. When his term as principal came to an end in 1966 he asked to be relieved of administrative duties and to be assigned to classroom teaching only. He was appointed to Michael Power High School, Etobicoke, Ontario, to teach mathematics, and was granted a half-year sabbatical in 1968 to study in Ottawa towards the Ontario Type A teaching certification, which he received in 1971. After retirement from the classroom at Michael Power in 1981, he was appointed to St Michael's College, where he was elected first councillor of the Basilian community and served as Director of Student Awards until 1989. He returned to Michael Power, where he suffered a fatal heart attack in March 1991.

'Dollar Bill' was a nickname he received for his meticulous attention to financial details, and the community drew confidently on his financial acumen and experience. He demanded excellence of himself, his confreres, and his students. Teaching mostly at the grade XIII level, he frequently remained in the classroom after school to tutor and encourage his students. Bill was affable in his manner with others and much disposed to humour. He was extremely well read in British history and culture, especially the monarchy. For many years he took his annual vacation in England, staying at a convent of nuns where he said Mass daily for the sisters and in return received free accommodation.

BIBLIOGRAPHY: 'Mathematics in Basilian Schools [forum],' *Basilian Teacher* 4 (December 1959) 65.
SOURCES: GABF; *Annals* 1 (1944) 54, 6 (1989) 720, 7 (1992) 128–30; *Newsletter* (3 April 1991).

BROWN, William MacBeath, priest, was born on 14 June 1940 in Vancouver, British Columbia, the son of William MacBeath Brown and Margaret Emma Bell. He died in Montreal, Quebec, on 12 October 1984, and is buried in the Basilian plot of Holy Cross Cemetery, Thornhill, Ontario.

'Mac' Brown attended Kerrisdale Grade School and Lord Byng Junior and Senior High School, Vancouver. In 1958 he enrolled at the University of British Columbia (B.A., 1962), and entered St Basil's Novitiate, Erindale, Ontario, making first profession on 15 September 1963. During the academic year 1963–4 he studied philosophy while living at St Basil's Seminary, Toronto. In 1964 he taught at St Joseph's High School, Ottawa, while concurrently taking courses at the Ontario College of Education (high school teacher certification, 1965). In 1966 he studied theology at St Basil's Seminary, Toronto, but was then appointed to the Maison Saint-Basile, Issy-les-Moulineaux, France, where he continued theological studies. After completing his second year of theology at the Séminaire Saint-Sulpice, he transferred to the Institut catholique de Paris, where he studied for the next three years, receiving a *licence en théologie* in 1970. He received the diaconate on 18 June 1969 in the cathedral at Versailles (Yvelines), and was ordained to the priesthood on 18 July 1970 in Holy Rosary Cathedral, Vancouver, by Archbishop James Carney.

In 1970, while continuing his doctoral studies in Paris, Father Brown took up residence at the parish of Saint-Séverin in the heart of the Latin Quarter, where he functioned as an assistant and youth minister. He earned diplomas in Greek and Hebrew in 1971. From 1971 to 1973 he was an *élève titulaire* in the Ecole pratique des hautes études in the Université de Paris, and from 1973 to 1975 he was both lecturer and director of weekly conference-seminars, 'The Origins of Institutions in the

Early Church,' in the Religious Studies section of that institution. He continued to give periodic lectures there from 1975 to 1978.

In 1976 he joined the Secretariat for Non-Believers in Paris and took up residence at the parish of Saint-Nicolas-du-Chardonnet. He remained with the secretariat for four years, during which time he also served as chaplain and tour guide on pilgrimages to Israel, Jordan, Syria, Egypt, Turkey, and Greece for the Service international des pèlerinages, Paris. In 1980 he returned to Canada to work at the Canadian Centre for Ecumenism in Montreal as associate director, and from 1982 to 1984 he acted as co-ordinator for the Montreal Chapter of the World Conference of Religious for Peace, in addition to serving as liaison for the Centre to numerous peace and justice groups and activities. His premature death from a blood condition cut short a vibrant and promising work in the Church.

Mac Brown had a gift for friendship and hospitality. Passionately attached to the cause of ecumenism, he dreamed of a united Christendom by the year 2000. He spoke frequently and worked tirelessly for the cause of peace. He wrote in the journal *Ecumenism*, 'Every moment we turn our attention to the depths of our being, to our good energies in communion with those of the whole cosmos, every time we stop, *everything*, for three minutes or thirty minutes each day, every time we overcome feelings of violence, aggression within us, we will become a little more peace-full, and thereby more efficient and fruitful peace-makers.'

BIBLIOGRAPHY: '"To Be or Not to Be": Co-existence or No Existence,' *Ecumenism* (Montreal, June 1982); 'The Practicalities of Ecumenism: An Interview,' *Canadian Catholic Review* 2 (1984) 139–42.
SOURCES: GABF; *Annals* 4 (1971) 173, 6 (1985) 379–81; *Newsletter* (24 October 1984).

BRUNEL, Louis, priest, son of Jacques Brunel and Marie-Rose Gourdon, was born on 28 March 1841 in the hamlet of Urbillac, Lamastre (Ardèche). He died at Vernoux on 31 July 1913 and is buried in the cemetery of the commune of Silhac (Ardèche).

Louis was educated by the Christian Brothers, rue de Cance, in Annonay, and then went to the Petit Séminaire de Vernoux (Ardèche). During 1860–1 he taught French in the commercial class at the Collège des Cordeliers in Annonay. He made his novitiate in 1861–2 at Feyzin (Isère, now Rhône), and professed final vows on 18 September 1863.

He received major orders at the hands of Bishop Armand de Charbonnel: subdiaconate, 19 September 1863, at the novitiate, Feyzin; diaconate in 1864 and priesthood on 23 September 1865, both in the chapel of the Collège des Cordeliers.

Father Brunel spent most of his Basilian life in the teaching apostolate. During the year 1862–3 he was *professeur de cinquième* in the Collège des Cordeliers; the following year he was *professeur de troisième* at the Petit Séminaire d'Aubenas (Ardèche), and the year after that, 1864–5, he was assigned the same class at the Collège des Cordeliers. In 1865 he went to the Collège de Privas (Ardèche) as *professeur de seconde*, returning to the Petit Séminaire de Vernoux one year later, where he spent the rest of his life, with the exception of one year, 1867–8, at the Petit Séminaire d'Aubenas as *professeur de première*, and one year, 1888–9, at the Ecole cléricale at Périgueux (Dordogne) teaching the same class. When the Basilians were forced to relinquish the direction of the Petit Séminaire de Vernoux in 1903, owing to the suppression of religious in France, Louis Brunel accepted an appointment to parish ministry at Saint-Félix de Châteauroux (Indre), where he had helped out on many occasions. But in 1904 he returned to Vernoux, where the confiscation of the petit séminaire had deeply disturbed him. He died in the hostel at Vernoux and, according to his wishes, was buried in the cemetery of the commune of Silhac (Ardèche). The *Semaine religieuse de Viviers* described him as 'a pious, modest priest who, although attached to his students, loved solitude perhaps to excess.'

SOURCES: Kirley, *Community in France* 184, 203; Pouzol, 'Notices.'

BUCKLEY, Patrick L., priest, was born in Kilnamartyra, County Cork (diocese of Cloyne), Ireland, on 13 April 1844. He died at Port Huron, Michigan, on 28 March 1913, and was buried in the Basilian plot, Mount Hope Cemetery, Toronto.

Patrick Buckley emigrated at an early age to Newburyport, Massachusetts, where he matured into a broad-shouldered, sturdily built young man. He was apprenticed to a blacksmith and was practising his trade at Providence, Rhode Island, when he decided in 1874 to come to St Michael's College, Toronto, to study for the priesthood. Six years later he entered St Basil's Novitiate, Toronto. He took final vows on 20 February 1886, and was ordained priest on 22 September 1888.

At St Michael's College Father Buckley supervised study hall and recreation of the students, 1888–90. He was then appointed to St

Mary's of the Assumption Parish in Owen Sound, Ontario, where he was put in charge of St Michael's Church in the Irish Block and served on the Board of the Owen Sound General and Marine Hospital. In 1906 he was loaned to the diocese of London as pastor of St Joseph's Parish, Corunna, until his death in 1913 which occurred while visiting a clerical friend in Port Huron.

SOURCES: GABF; *Centennial, St Mary's; Jubilee, St Mary's.*

BUFFERNE, Vincent Augustin, priest, son of Antoine Bufferne and Françoise Basset, was born on 7 July 1849 at Marols, district of Montbrison (Loire, archdiocese of Lyon). He died at Marols on 19 November 1913 and was buried there.

After grade school and high school in his native diocese, Vincent entered the seminary in Lyon to begin the study of theology, and received tonsure on 20 December 1873. He entered the Basilian novitiate at Feyzin (Isère, now Rhône) in 1874 and made his first profession on 17 September 1875. One year later on 22 September 1876 he made final profession and was ordained subdeacon the following day by Bishop Joseph-Michel-Frédéric Bonnet of Viviers in the chapel of the Collège du Sacré-Coeur, Annonay. Bishop Armand de Charbonnel ordained him deacon on 22 September 1877 and priest on 20 September 1879 in the same chapel.

He worked as recreation and study-hall master for eight years, first at the Collège du Sacré-Coeur, 1875–6, and then at the minor seminary of Sainte-Barbe, Annonay, 1876–83. He was among the founding fathers of the Basilian school of Mary Immaculate at Beaconfield House, Plymouth, England, in 1884. He worked there as teacher and prefect of discipline for sixteen years, 1884–1900, and then returned to the college in Annonay, where he had charge of one *classe de sixième* and taught English, 1900–3. With the dispersal of the Community in 1903 he returned to his native village of Marcols, where he died.

SOURCES: Kirley, *Community in France* 183, 210; Pouzol, 'Notices.'

BURBOTT, Eugene Michael John, priest, was born in Rochester, on 16 August 1921, the son of Clarence Burbott and Catharine Luddy. He died in Rochester on 14 July 1962 and is buried there in the Basilian plot of Holy Sepulchre Cemetery.

'Gene' attended Holy Redeemer Parochial School and Aquinas Institute in his native city before entering St Basil's Novitiate, Toronto, in 1939. After profession on 15 August 1940, he enrolled at St Michael's College, Toronto (B.A., University of Toronto, 1944). Two years of teaching followed: 1944–5 at St Thomas High School, Houston, and 1945–6 at Catholic Central High School, Detroit. During these years he qualified for secondary school teaching certification for the State of Michigan. In 1947 he received an M.A. in education from the University of Detroit, presenting jointly with Father Harold O'Leary a thesis entitled 'The History of the Educational Work of the Basilian Fathers in Detroit, 1928–1946.' He did theological studies at St Basil's Seminary in Toronto and was ordained to the priesthood on 29 June 1949 in St Basil's Church, Toronto, by Cardinal James Charles McGuigan.

The only appointment of Father Burbott's short priestly life was to St Thomas High School, Houston, where he taught physics to fourth-year students and served as a guidance counsellor. A promise that he had made as a child never to waste a minute lay behind the numerous activities of his life and his habitually nervous and hurried manner in which he gave himself unstintingly to his duties and his students. He served as local director of vocations, and actively recruited promising students. When Texan novices were travelling to Rochester, he would ask his mother to meet them and also to visit them during the novitiate, in order to mitigate the possible homesickness of the young candidates. He died from a cerebral haemorrhage while visiting his parents during the summer vacation.

SOURCES: GABF; *Annals* 1 (1949) 261, 3 (1962) 160–1.

BURKE, James VINCENT, priest, was born in the Township of Adjala, Ontario (archdiocese of Toronto), on 30 October 1889, the son of James Burke and Margaret Mullen. He died in Detroit on 8 April 1949 and is buried in the Basilian plot of Assumption Parish, Windsor.

Left an orphan in his pre-school years, Vincent was raised by an aunt who sent him to school at Alliston, Ontario, and in 1915 to St Michael's College in Toronto. Two years later he entered St Basil's Novitiate in Toronto and was professed on 14 November 1918. In 1924 he received a B.A. from the University of Toronto in Honours English and History. The following year, 1924–5, he attended the Ontario College of Education, Toronto. After his course in theology at St Basil's Seminary, Toronto, he was ordained priest on 19 December 1925.

Vincent's first appointment as priest was to Assumption College, Windsor, where he stayed for five years. In 1931 he was named superior of a new foundation in the Newman Apostolate at the University of Illinois, Urbana, but the discovery of tubercular spots on his lungs sent him instead to a sanatorium in the Adirondack Mountains at Gabriels, New York State. Father Burke was at St Michael's College, 1932–3 and 1934–5, and at Assumption College, 1933–4, before he again took up full-time work in 1935 at St Basil's Seminary, Toronto, where he was superior and master of scholastics, 1938–43. Transferred to St Thomas High School, Houston, he served as superior and principal for three years. In 1946 he was appointed to St Anne's Parish, Houston. The love of God was a favourite theme which Vincent Burke urged upon students, parishioners, and seminarians at St Basil's Seminary, and he sought to exemplify it in his own life. In 1948 he went to Ste Anne's Parish, Detroit, where he died suddenly in 1949.

BIBLIOGRAPHY: 'Family Rosary Crusade,' *Benedicamus* 2 (March 1949) 28–9.
SOURCES: GABF; *Annals* 1 (1943–50) 237–8; *Aquin* (Yearbook, St Thomas High School, 1945); *Purple and White* (15 December 1925).

BURKE, John Aloysius, priest, was born on 9 January 1921 in Oswego, New York (diocese of Syracuse), the son of Thomas Patrick Burke and Brigid Veronica Doghan. He died in Houston, on 4 August 1995 and is buried there in the Basilian plot of Garden of Gethsemane, Forest Park Lawndale Cemetery.

John attended St Paul's Academy and Oswego High School in his home town. In 1938 he went to St Michael's College, Toronto, for undergraduate studies, entering St Basil's Novitiate, Toronto, in 1940. He was professed the following year on 15 August, and returned to St Michael's to complete his university studies (B.A. University of Toronto, 1943, Classics). He taught, first, at St Thomas High School, Houston, 1943–4, and then at Catholic Central High School, Detroit, 1944–5. He returned to Toronto for theological studies, living first at St Michael's College, 1945–6, and then at St Basil's Seminary, 1946–9. He was ordained to the priesthood on 29 June 1948 in St Basil's Church by Cardinal James Charles McGuigan.

In 1949 John Burke began forty-five years of ministry, the first half in secondary education (teaching Latin and religion and counselling students) and the second half in parish work. His eleven appointments with their various functions and offices were as follows: Catholic Central High School, 1949–53, teaching and obtaining an M.A. in education and Michigan teaching certification (University of Detroit, 1950); Aquinas Institute, Rochester, 1953–5, teaching; Catholic Central High School, 1955–9, teaching, second councillor, 1957–8, first councillor, 1958–9, obtaining a diploma from Catholic University Preaching Institute, Washington, D.C. (1956); Andrean High School, Gary (now Merrillville), Indiana, 1959–67, teaching, first councillor, 1959–61, superior and principal, 1961–7; Aquinas Institute, 1967–73, teaching; St Anne's Parish, Houston, 1973–9, assistant pastor; St John the Baptist Parish, Amherstburg, 1979–83, pastor and superior; Basilian Fathers Residence (Infirmary), Toronto, 1983–4, superior; Assumption Parish, Windsor, 1984–6, pastor and rector; Our Lady of Perpetual Help Parish, Glendale, Arizona, 1986–9, pastor; St Anne's Parish, Houston, 1989–95, assistant pastor.

'Burkie,' as he was called by his confreres, was a large man, rather stout, even-tempered and jovial. The variety of his appointments testifies to the confidence his superiors and his confreres had in his talents and readiness to serve as administrator, teacher, or local superior. Within the community he would be the centre of joviality in any gathering, enjoying the give and take but never allowing himself a word that might hurt another. His room was filled with religious and domestic bric-à-brac: statues and relics, pictures of saints, friends, and family, and all kinds of souvenirs of people or places. He was noted for his ardent devotion to the Mother of God and Ste Thérèse of Lisieux, frequently the subjects of his homilies and retreat conferences.

SOURCES: GABF; *Annals* 1 (1948) 221, 7 (1992) 6, 8 (1996) 100–2; *Newsletter* (4 September 1995).

BURKE, Richard Thomas, priest, was born in West Flamboro near Dundas, Ontario (diocese of Hamilton), on 15 February 1859, the son of Martin and Bridget Burke. He died in Toronto on 22 November 1941 and is buried there in the Basilian plot of Mount Hope Cemetery.

Richard grew up in Sheffield, Ontario. At Galt Grammar School, which had become one of the best secondary schools in Ontario under the direction of William Tassie, Richard won first prize in English literature. He obtained teaching certification, then joined the class of *Belles Lettres* at St Michael's College, Toronto, in 1878, where he won first prize in math each year as well as the second prize in general proficiency for the year 1878-9. Three years later he went to Assumption College, Windsor, to complete his philosophy course and to teach. In September 1882 he entered the Grand Séminaire, Montreal, as a student for the diocese of Hamilton. When ill health obliged him to withdraw at Christmas time, his bishop arranged for him to return to Assumption College to complete his theology course, 1883-6. He was ordained to the priesthood for the diocese of Hamilton, Ontario, on 28 August 1886 in St Augustine's Church, Dundas, Ontario, by Bishop James Joseph Carbury.

Father Burke served as assistant at St John the Evangelist Parish, Arthur, Ontario, 1886-9; Sacred Heart Parish, Paris, Ontario, 1889; St Ambrose Parish, Galt, 1889-90; and St Joseph's Parish, Macton, Ontario, 1890-2. In 1892 he was appointed pastor of St Andrew's Parish, Oakville, Ontario. Early in 1900 he resigned his parish, obtained a release from the diocese of Hamilton, and entered St Basil's Novitiate, Toronto. A biographical sketch in the *Basilian*, on the occasion of the golden jubilee of his priestly ordination, said of his religious vocation: 'From his first days as a priest it was his desire and firm intention to enter religious life with the Basilians. The delay of fourteen years was in deference to his bishop's need of his services.'

After his profession on 16 May 1901, Father Burke was appointed to the staff of St Michael's College, where he taught until 1907, with the exception of one year, 1904-5, spent at St Basil's College in Waco, Texas. He returned to the life of a parish priest in 1907 as pastor of St Mary's of the Assumption Parish in Owen Sound, Ontario, where he remained until 1916, when he was loaned to the diocese of Hamilton to serve as administrator of St Basil's Parish in Brantford. For two years, 1917-19, he had charge of the parish at St Columban, Ontario, thereby releasing a younger priest for service as a chaplain in the Canadian Army. From 1919 until 1930 he was stationed at Ste Anne's Parish, Detroit, where he served as religious superior for one year, 1929-30.

'Dodger' Burke, as he called in the community, was a full six feet in height, with an erect carriage that made him look every inch the dignified Irish pastor. He had an antique violin of which he was quite proud. He wrote some unpublished reminiscences during his retirement years.

Father Burke knew his limitations. The *Basilian Centennial* commemorative volume published at Owen Sound quoted a letter that he wrote on 23 August 1907, just after receiving his appointment as pastor of St Mary's of the Assumption Parish: 'I do not love "promotions," especially when they involve responsibilities of a trying nature. I prefer to serve rather than to be served. ... I shall have three assistants in Owen Sound, and all I desire is that we shall work harmoniously for the salvation of souls.' In 1930 he retired to St Michael's College, where he died of pneumonia at the age of eighty-two.

BIBLIOGRAPHY: Fra Tempo (pseud.) 'Piano Moving, Old Style,' *Basilian* 4 (February 1938) 29.
SOURCES: GABF; *Centennial, St Mary's*; 'Father Richard Burke,' *Basilian* 3 (April 1937) 75; 'Father R.T. Burke's Jubilee Year,' *Basilian* 2 (April 1936) 76; *Jubilee, St Mary's*; Spetz, *Waterloo*.

BURNS, Daniel Vincent, priest, was born on 8 July 1906 at Sunny Corner, Red Bank, near Chatham, New Brunswick (diocese of Chatham), the son of John Burns and Elizabeth Murphy. He died in Toronto on 12 March 1993 and is buried in the Basilian plot of Holy Cross Cemetery, Thornhill, Ontario.

'Dan' was recommended to the Basilians by his parish priest, who referred to him as a 'rare find' while he was still a high school student at St Thomas College in Chatham. Accordingly he went to Assumption College, Windsor, with the status of 'junior' to continue his high school studies. In 1927, at the age of twenty, he entered St Basil's Novitiate, Toronto, and was professed on 11 August 1928. Following profession he was appointed to St Basil's Scholasticate, Toronto, where he completed grade XIII, 1928–9. He moved to St Michael's College in 1929 to begin undergraduate studies at the University of Toronto. In 1931 he returned to the scholasticate to begin theology, which he did concurrently with his still incomplete university studies (B.A., 1933). He was ordained to the priesthood on 16 December 1934 in Assumption Church, Windsor, by Bishop John Thomas Kidd. During his fourth year of theology, 1934–5, Father Burns taught mathematics at the high school of St Michael's College.

In 1935 he began his fifty-eight-year apostolate with an appointment to Assumption College as a math teacher. After obtaining teacher certification at the University of Alberta, Edmonton, in 1937, Father Burns had the following appointments: teaching high school at St Michael's College, 1937–8, and at St Mary's Boys' High School, Calgary, 1938–50, where he was treasurer, 1941–50; teaching at Assumption College, 1950–3 and at Catholic Central High School, Detroit, 1953–6, obtaining an M.A. in education from the University of Detroit, 1956; and teaching at St John Fisher College, Rochester, also serving as treasurer, 1963–5.

From 1966 to 1971 Father Burns worked in parish ministry: St Mary's of the Assumption Parish, Owen Sound, Ontario, 1966–7, St Pius X Parish, Calgary, 1967–9, and Our Lady of Assumption Parish, Lethbridge, Alberta, 1969–71, as assistant in all three places. In 1971 he took up residence with the Basilian Fathers of Calgary, where for the next eighteen years he did chaplaincy service and served as house treasurer, 1972–86. Deteriorating health obliged him to enter the Basilian Fathers Residence (Infirmary) in Toronto in 1989, where he remained until his death four years later.

Father Dan Burns served in the Royal Canadian Reserve Naval Corps as chaplain during the Second World War and on into the 1960s, when he served on naval vessels on the east and west coasts. While stationed aboard the *HMCS Fort Erie*, one ship in a flotilla of American and Canadian warships escorting the Queen of England and the President of the United States for the official opening of the St Lawrence Seaway in 1959, he wrote to Father Robert *Fischette: 'It may sound very glamorous ... [but] I had more interesting and satisfying work during the two weeks in Halifax, especially with convert instructions. This is the work I really like.' He was awarded the Coronation Medal at the Canadian Naval Base in Windsor.

Dan Burns was a man of exceptionally gentle manners and unfailing kindness, a peaceful and joyful influence wherever he went.

SOURCES: GABF; *Annals* 5 (1979) 341, 6 (1985) 308, 8 (1994) 124–6; *Newsletter* (17 March 1993).

BURNS, Edmund Eugene, priest, cousin of Father Francis Leo *Burns, was born in Detroit on 12 July 1908, the son of Matthew Burns and Delia Walsh. He died at Strawberry Island, Lake Simcoe, Ontario, on 23 July 1961 and is buried in the Basilian plot of Holy Sepulchre Cemetery, Rochester.

Edmund, usually referred to as 'Tris' or 'Speaker' Burns, attended Holy Redeemer Grade School, Detroit, and Assumption College, Windsor. In 1926 he entered St Basil's Novitiate in Toronto, and was professed on 11 August 1927. He earned a B.A. from the University of Toronto, 1932, and teacher certification from the Ontario College of Education, Toronto, 1934. After theological studies at St Basil's Seminary, Toronto, he was ordained to the priesthood on 21 December 1935 in St Basil's Church, Toronto by Archbishop James Charles McGuigan.

Father Burns was appointed to St Michael's College School, Toronto, in 1936, and to St Thomas High School, Houston, in 1937. He earned an M.A. in education from the University of Houston in 1942. In 1947 he moved to Assumption College School; and in 1951 he was appointed to Aquinas Institute in Rochester, serving there as assistant superior. He collapsed and died on the way to evening prayer in the chapel at the Basilian summer retreat on Strawberry Island.

In both high school and college Father Burns had been an outstanding athlete. As a teacher of English, Latin, and algebra, he read extensively and took frequent summer courses to extend his academic and professional competencies. Gifted with a fine tenor voice, he loved to sing and to direct music in the schools where he taught. Love of people was a characteristic that became manifest early in his life.

BIBLIOGRAPHY: 'Charity and Love of Self,' *Basilian* 1 (June 1935) 70.
SOURCES: GABF; *Annals* 3 (1961) 89–90; *Basilian Teacher* 6 (October 1961) 36.

BURNS, Edmund Toussaint, priest, was born at Amherstburg, Ontario (diocese of London), on 31 October 1884, the son of John Burns and Mary Bastien. He died in Windsor on 12 May 1928 and is buried there in the Basilian plot of Assumption Cemetery.

After attending a local separate school, Edmund enrolled in 1900 at Assumption College, Windsor, where he was a class leader, and where he was called 'Sheriff' by his classmates, as his father was sheriff of Wayne County. He entered St Basil's Novitiate, Toronto, on 15 August 1907. After first profession he attended the University of Toronto for two years. He studied theology at St Basil's Scholasticate, Toronto, and was ordained priest on 13 August 1914 in St Basil's Church, Toronto, the first Basilian to be ordained by Archbishop Neil McNeil.

After teaching for seven years at Assumption College, Father Burns was appointed pastor of Assumption Parish in 1921. In 1926 he returned to Assumption College, where he taught for the remaining two years of his life.

As a teacher of English and French he loved to play on words in both languages. Father James *Embser wrote of him: 'Former students speak of him today as a perfect gentleman; they emphasize the word gentle; his life illustrated every facet of this virtue. Although without academic degrees, he was a studious man with a scholarly mind.' Father Ernest *Lajeunesse wrote, 'As a pastor of souls Father Burns set a shining example. His kindness, scholarliness and understanding won the love of all and incurred the dislike of no one. His sermons, in

English or in French, were simple, clear and persuasive homilies.' As an administrator he dealt wisely with questions of construction, of finance, and of everyday parish life. He renovated and redecorated the church. Two hobbies served as a diversion from his official duties, woodworking and the repairing of old clocks. A parishioner summed up his character: 'Le Père Burns, il est si bon.'

SOURCES: GABF; Charles Collins, 'Basilians I Have Known,' transcribed in Robert J. Scollard, 'Historical Notes C.S.B.' 10 95–8 (GABF); J.W. Embser, 'Edmund T. Burns CSB,' *Basilian Teacher* 2 (April 1958) 17–19; Lajeunesse, *Assumption Parish*; *Purple and White* (10 June 1928).

BURNS, Francis Leo, priest, cousin of Father Edmund Eugene *Burns, was born on 23 August 1905 in Detroit, the son of James Denis Burns and Catherine Elizabeth Welch. He died in Saskatoon, Saskatchewan, on 3 September 1979, and is buried in the Basilian plot of Heavenly Rest Cemetery, Windsor.

Frank attended Barbour Hall elementary school in Kalamazoo, Michigan, and enrolled in Assumption College School, Windsor, in 1919, graduating there in June 1924. On 1 August he entered St Basil's Novitiate, Toronto, and made first profession on 11 August 1925. As a scholastic he went first to Assumption College, Windsor (B.A., University of Western Ontario, 1928), and was then one of the founding Basilians of Catholic Central High School, Detroit, in August 1928, where he taught one year while also studying theology. He completed theological studies at St Basil's Scholasticate, Toronto, while also earning teacher certification at the Ontario College of Education. In 1929 he designed the parabolic-shaped shrine made of lake stone at the Basilian summer retreat on Strawberry Island, Lake Simcoe, Ontario. 'Beauty in solidity' was his motto for the project. He was ordained to the priesthood on 19 December 1931, in St Basil's Church, Toronto, by Bishop Alexander MacDonald.

His variety of appointments continued: Assumption Parish, Windsor, assistant pastor, 1932; Catholic Central High School, Detroit, teaching, 1932–6, earning his teaching certificate for the State of Michigan (1934); Assumption College teaching economics, beginning in 1936, with summers at the University of Michigan, Ann Arbor (M.A., Economics, 1939). He spent the year 1942–3 at this same university, earning a Ph.D. in 1947. In August 1948 he was appointed to St Thomas More College, Saskatoon, where he taught for ten years. He also served as college treasurer, 1952–8, and as local councillor, 1956–7. From 1958 to 1961 he was superior of Assumption College. He was appointed to St John Fisher College, 1961–3, and then to St Thomas More College once again, where he taught until 1970.

Shortly after retiring in that year Father Burns suffered a serious heart attack. On his doctor's advice he spent the winter months of 1971–2 at St Anne's Parish, Houston, where he underwent bypass surgery. Thereafter he spent the winter months of each year as assistant at St Anne's in Houston and the remaining months at St Thomas More. On 3 September 1979, while lunching with the confreres, he suffered another heart attack and died as he received the last sacraments.

The product of a prominent Michigan family, Frank Burns was a quiet, gentlemanly person who evinced a sense of dignity in himself and recognized it in others, whether student or peer. Although conservative by nature and a lover of tradition, he recognized the new spiritual life to be found in the post–Vatican II liturgical changes. Devout and deeply prayerful, a good conversationalist and source of knowledge, he enriched community life.

BIBLIOGRAPHY: 'Art in Our Schools,' *Basilian* 2 (March 1936) 52–3.
SOURCES: GABF; *Annals* 5 (1976) 140, (1980) 518–19; *Newsletter* (19 September 1979); E.J. Lajeunesse, *Strawberry Island in Lake Simcoe* (Toronto, 1962, 1974, 1983, 1984) 56.

BUTLER, Albert Francis, priest, was born in Toronto on 2 March 1921, the eldest of two boys and three girls born to Albert Butler and Dorothy O'Connor. He died in Toronto on 2 September 2001 and is buried in the Basilian plot of Holy Cross Cemetery, Thornhill, Ontario.

'Al' Butler attended St Michael's parochial school and the high school section of St Michael's College, Toronto. He entered St Basil's Novitiate, Toronto, in 1940 and made first profession on 15 August 1941. He was appointed to St Michael's College for undergraduate studies (B.A., University of Toronto, 1944). He taught for two years, 1944–6, at St Thomas High School, Houston, and then part-time at St Michael's College School while studying theology at St Basil's Seminary. He was ordained to the priesthood on 29 June 1949 in St Basil's Church, Toronto, by Cardinal James Charles McGuigan.

Father Butler began his teaching career at Aquinas Institute, Rochester, where he remained until 1961. He went to St Michael's College School, Toronto, as both teacher and director of studies. A heart attack in 1976 forced him to reduce his work load. In 1983 he went into the parish apostolate, first at St Basil's Parish, Angleton, Texas, 1983–7, then at Our Lady of the Assumption Parish, Lethbridge, Alberta, 1987–8, and finally at St Anne's Parish, Houston, 1988–90. In 1990 he entered the Basilian Fathers Residence (Infirmary), Toronto, remaining there two years before returning to St Michael's College School in 1992 for a period of seven years. In 1999 he once again entered the Basilian infirmary, now called 'Anglin House,' where he lived for the last two years of his life.

Father Butler was a teacher of science. He spent seven summers taking graduate courses in sciences at the University of Notre Dame. He had talents for the practical, and was called upon to help design the science labs in the new Basilian schools in Gary (now Merrillville), Indiana, and Ottawa, during the 1950s and 1960s. At Aquinas Institute he oversaw the electrical installations for the Memorial stadium. At St Michael's he guided the Quarterback Club, a group which raised funds for the sports programs. His multivalent talents, characteristic kindness, and ready sense of humour made him much appreciated within the Basilian community and among the students and friends of the institutions where he served.

SOURCES: GABF; *Annals* 1 (1949) 261, 7 (1992) 7, 9 (2000) 8, 10 (2002) 90; *Newsletter* (17 September 2001).

C

CAHILL, Frederick Wallace, priest, was born in St John's, Newfoundland, on 6 July 1920, one of four children of Frederick J. Cahill and Mary O'Leary. He died in Calgary, Alberta, on 4 January 1983 and is buried there in the Basilian plot of St Mary's Cemetery.

Fred attended the parish school of the cathedral of St John the Baptist and St Bonaventure's College, St John's, graduating in 1940. The following year he began four years of active military service as a pilot in the Royal Canadian Air Force, rising to the rank of Flight Lieutenant, and receiving several decorations for dangerous missions over enemy territory.

Towards the end of his active duty he made application to St Basil's Novitiate, Toronto, Ontario, which he entered in September 1945, making first profession on 4 October 1946. Appointed to St Michael's College, Toronto, he earned a B.A. from the University of Toronto (1949). He studied theology at St Basil's Seminary, Toronto, 1949–52, and was ordained to the priesthood on 4 July 1951 in St John the Baptist Cathedral, St John's, by Archbishop John Skinner CJM.

After attending the Ontario College of Education, Toronto, 1952–3, Father Cahill taught at Assumption College School, Windsor, Ontario, 1953–7. He was then appointed to St Francis High School, Lethbridge, Alberta, where he taught until 1962. During the summers he studied at the University of Lethbridge (M.Ed., 1959). In 1962 he was appointed to teach at St Mary's Boys' High School, Calgary. On leave from the Calgary Board of Education for the year 1967–8, he did studies in guidance. In 1969 he was granted an M.A. in theology from Fordham University.

Father Cahill served on the Basilian local council in Calgary from 1968 to 1972. In 1969 he began teaching at Bishop Grandin High School, Calgary, and continued to do so until his death. Concurrently with his teaching he was from 1971 until his death a member of the pastoral team at St Gerard's Church, Calgary, where he directed the 'Search' program for youth in the Calgary diocese and where he was waked.

In the summer of 1975 Father Cahill began living in a house in North Calgary with a group of young men seeking to live a more Christian life in community, some of whom were also discerning a vocation to the priesthood. In 1979 he began his work as chaplain to the Knights of Columbus, holding the rank of Fourth Degree Knight. In December 1983 the Knights inaugurated a new council named in his memory 'The Father Fred Cahill Council 8471, City of Calgary.' He was also for many years the chaplain of the Columbus Boys' Camp at Watertown Park, Alberta.

Fred Cahill was quiet and shy, impatient with inefficiency, and angered by injustice; but with his students and others with whom he dealt he was patience itself. Impeccable in his appearance, with a disarming smile and a ready greeting, he had a talent for attracting and influencing youth. He spoke of his wartime experiences only when prompted, and then with modesty, playing down the heroic moments which marked his military career.

SOURCES: GABF; *Annals* 1 (1951) 38, 6 (1984) 286–7; *Newsletter* (19 January 1983).

CAIRD, Alfred Page, priest, was born in Detroit on 28 August 1915, one of two sons of Alfred Caird and Ella Constance. He died in Rochester on 26 February 1980, and is buried there in the Basilian plot of Holy Sepulchre Cemetery.

Alfred attended Blessed Sacrament Elementary School and Holy Name Institute, Detroit, graduating with honours in 1933 and gaining the Robert J. Brown Scholarship. It was during these years that Holy Name Institute came under the direction of the Basilian Fathers and became known as Catholic Central High School. After university studies at Assumption College, Windsor (B.A., University of Western Ontario, 1937), Alfred entered St Basil's Novitiate in Toronto and was professed on 12 September 1938. He studied theology at St Basil's Seminary, Toronto, 1937–41, while taking an M.A. in philosophy at the University of Toronto, 1940 (thesis: 'St Bonaventure and the Existence of God'). He was ordained to the priesthood on 17 August 1941 by Archbishop James Charles McGuigan in St Basil's Church, Toronto.

Alfred Caird was appointed to Assumption College, Windsor, in August 1942, as assistant professor of philosophy, a position he filled for three years. In 1945 he resumed graduate studies in philosophy and palaeography at the Pontifical Institute of Mediaeval Studies and the University of Toronto. During the year 1947–8 he also taught at St Michael's College. He completed his doctoral studies in 1948, submitting as his thesis the topic 'The Doctrine of Quiddities and Modes in Francis of Meyronnes.'

In 1948 'Alf' joined the fledgling University of St Thomas, Houston, where he was to spend the greater part of his priestly life. He taught philosophy and theology and was chairman of the department of theology during most of his years at St Thomas. He was involved in many of the activities on campus, among these the Chapel Guild, and for many years he was the university chaplain. From 1959 to 1961 he served on the local council of the Basilian Fathers and in 1961 he was named local superior. In this office he showed admirable leadership in bringing the local community through the trying times of liturgical and theological change of the post–Vatican II era. After his term as superior he became rector of the Basilian House of Studies, 1967, while retaining his various responsibilities in the university. In June 1969, he returned to the Basilian residence on campus, teaching full time until 1976, when he was diagnosed as having cancer and underwent radical surgery. There followed a sabbatical year, 1977–8, of which the first half was spent on studies in Toronto, and the second half in Europe and the Holy Land. It was while visiting in Rome that he was contacted and asked to accept the office of master of novices. He took up his new duties at St Basil's Novitiate, Rochester, in August 1978. In January 1980, he experienced an attack of angina pectoris. On the morning of 26 February 1980 he was found dead in his room.

Alf Caird was an avid disciple of Thomas Aquinas. His teacher Etienne Gilson remarked that his appointment to Houston was a great loss to the Pontifical Institute. His gift for expressing profound concepts in a succinct, clear, and positive manner made his lectures memorable. A kind and patient man, he always had time for those who sought his advice and compassion. He was a good confessor whose serenity and disarming humour put one at ease. He maintained his simplicity and affability through his bouts of ill health and the inconvenience these periods brought with them, sustained as he was by a strong faith. He had a number of hobbies such as tropical fish, stamp collecting, woodworking, hunting, and fishing; but his priesthood was the centre of his life and the source of his joy.

BIBLIOGRAPHY: (With Armand Maurer CSB) 'The Role of Infinity in the Thought of Franciscus of Meyronnes,' *Mediaeval Studies* 33 (1971) 201–27; 'The Academic Course and Extra-Curricular Activities,' *Basilian Teacher* 1 (January 1957) 9–11; 'The Theology of Catholic Education,' *Basilian Teacher* 6 (November 1961) 43–8.
SOURCES: GABF; *Annals* 5 (1981) 601–2; *Newsletter* (7 March 1980).

CARR, Henry, priest, tenth superior general, was born at Oshawa, Ontario (archdiocese of Toronto), on 8 January 1880, one of nine children of William Carr and Margaret Quigley. He died in Vancouver on 28 November 1963 and is buried in the Basilian plot of Holy Cross Cemetery, Thornhill, Ontario.

Henry Carr attended primary and secondary schools in Oshawa, and then came to Toronto in 1897 to work for a printer. A former teacher arranged for him to resume his education at St Michael's College in return for teaching a class in German. In 1900 he entered St Basil's Novitiate in Toronto, and was professed on 8 September 1901. He returned to his studies in Honours Classics at the University of Toronto and graduated in 1903. He was stationed at Assumption College, Windsor, from September 1903 until December 1904, when he returned to St Michael's College. He was ordained priest on 3 September 1905 in St Basil's Church, Toronto, by Archbishop Denis *O'Connor.

As a priest Father 'Hank' Carr first taught at St Michael's College, 1905–25 and 1928–9, and served as its superior and president, 1915–25. He was rector of St Basil's Scholasticate, Toronto, 1925–8, superior of the Curial Residence, 1929–30, and then superior general, 1930–42.

In his positions as superior and superior general, Father Carr made three critically important contributions to Catholic education in Canada. First, he broadened the curriculum in the high school department of St Michael's College to qualify graduates for admission to university. Second, when the University of Toronto Act was being revised in 1906, he arranged for St Michael's College to become a federated arts college in the university, thus setting a model which was copied by other Catholic institutions in English-speaking Canada. The University of Toronto recognized his contribution with an honorary LL.D. on 8 June 1922. At St Michael's, a large stone building, designed by the eminent architect Ernest Cormier, was built and dedicated as 'Carr Hall' in 1954.

Carr's third contribution arose from his burning desire to promote excellence in Catholic thought and education. He brought outstanding scholars such as Sir Bertram Windle, Maurice DeWulf, Etienne Gilson, and Gerald B. Phelan to St Michael's College. In collaboration with Gilson, he founded the Institute of Mediaeval Studies in 1929 to be an international centre for scholarly research and publication. He was its first *Praeses*, 1929–36, and was instrumental in obtaining its papal charter in 1939.

Father Carr's thoughts on economics and social justice, inspired by his desire to implement papal encyclicals such as *Rerum novarum* and *Quadragesimo anno*, found expression in the 'Pamphlet' series of the Institute of Mediaeval Studies (1931), which were gathered together in his *Letters to Mildred* (see below). He became spiritual director to the Baroness Catherine de Hueck, who was working to establish in Toronto an apostolate similar to that of Dorothy Day in New York City. This led him to support social justice initiatives by Basilians such as Fathers Eugene *Cullinane, Wilfrid *Dore, Edwin *Garvey, and Michael *Oliver.

After his two terms as superior general he became superior and principal of St Thomas More College, Saskatoon, Saskatchewan, until 1949. He returned to Toronto to teach at St Basil's Seminary. In 1951, President Norman Mackenzie of the University of British Columbia invited him to teach classics and, later, philosophy and religious studies at that university. Mackenzie's openness to an affiliated Catholic college was a major development after his predecessors had repeatedly denied attempts by Father Carr and Archbishop William Duke to introduce Catholic higher education in Vancouver. Carr lived at first in the cathedral rectory, but with the arrival of Michael *Oliver a house was acquired in 1952. When St Mark's College was opened in 1958, Carr was its first principal. He taught until 1960, his eightieth year, and after his retirement he continued to live at St Mark's until his death from pneumonia in 1963.

One of Carr's students, Sister Mary Ruth Poelzer, wrote in her Master's thesis, 'In the strict sense of the word, Father Carr was not an originator of totally new thought or action in the educational field. However, he had the genius to recognize when a situation was ripe to bring an idea to fruition, and he also had the genius to adjust such ideas to existing circumstances without compromising basic principles.'

Over the years a rare gift for making friends drew to Father Carr people from all walks of life. In a sermon preached at Father Carr's funeral and published in the *Basilian Teacher*, Laurence K. *Shook attributed the effectiveness of Father Carr's work to this openness to friendship: 'He used to say that university federation was only as strong as the friendship and good-will of the participating parties. Insist on rights, he said, and you will get what you deserve – nothing. But act as a friend and be a friend among friends, and the most cumbersome legal machinery will roll smoothly on.' On the occasion of Carr's death, the Senate of the University of Toronto passed the resolution: 'He was appointed Superior of St Michael's in 1915 and retained that office for the succeeding ten years. He continued to expand the department of philosophy of which he was a member and to a great extent gave it its character; it was Christian in its background, international in its involvements, scholarly and research-conscious in its methods and orientations.'

The claims of friendship made Father Carr a faithful correspondent. In the *Basilian Teacher* Francis Leddy wrote, 'Father Carr's short one-page letters carried more information and helpful comment than most of us can compress into three or four such pages, and these brief communications, promptly received after every inquiry, were justly famous among his many friends who had occasion to turn to him for advice when he was at a distance.'

Every institution at which Father Carr taught conferred an honorary degree upon him: the University of Toronto, 1922; the University of

Saskatchewan, 1952, where he was presented as 'the leader of Roman Catholic education in Canada'; Assumption University of Windsor, 1955; and the University of British Columbia, 1956.

Father Carr was a religious superior for forty-three years of his life. As superior general he oversaw the revision of the Constitutions that received the approbation of Rome in 1938. He actively supported all efforts to improve the spiritual life of the Congregation. He was a strong man who respected other persons who were strong. He asked that individual abilities be developed, but as part of a common goal. This principle brought him success as coach of the two sports he loved, football and hockey.

A more complete and detailed view of Father Carr can be found in the biography published by his confrere and friend Edmund J. *McCorkell (see below). In June 2003 St Thomas More College, Saskatoon, hosted a symposium 'celebrating the life, work, and person of Father Henry Carr CSB.'

BIBLIOGRAPHY:

Books: (mimeographed, limited circulation): *Philosophy Ninety-One* (lectures in philosophy at St Thomas More College), ed. Eugene Cullinane. Saskatoon, c.1948. *The Heart of the Matter*, ed. M.J. Oliver (twenty papers of a projected thirty). Vancouver, n.d.

Pamphlets: *Letters to Mildred: Chats on Christian Economics*. Toronto, 1933 (collection of eleven numbers of the *Pamphlet* series), no. 5: I *The Blind Leading the Blind*; no. 6: II *Capital Sins as Capital Things*; no. 17: III *'Tis Folly to Be Ignorant*; no. 18: IV *Ownership, A Good Thing Gone Wrong*; no. 19: V *The Gold Standard*; no. 20: VI *Tariffs and Foreign Exchange*; no. 21: VII *Interest*; no. 22: VIII *Society and Order*; no. 23: IX *Labour and a Flat Tire*; no. 24: X *High Living and Low Thinking*; no. 25: XI *Economics and Religion are Married*.

Articles: 'The Function of the Phantasm in St Thomas Aquinas,' in *Philosophical Essays Presented to John Watson* (Kingston, Ontario, 1922; repr. Freeport, N.Y., 1971); 'Sir Bertram Windle, the Man and His Work,' *Catholic World* 129 (May 1929) 165–71; 'St Augustine as Philosopher,' *Proceedings of the American Catholic Philosophical Association* 6 (1930) 88–96; 'Canada: Roman Catholic Point of View,' *Educational Yearbook* (1932) 65–81; 'The Very Reverend J.R. Teefy,' *Report of the Canadian Catholic Historical Association* 7 (1939/40) 85–95; 'What It Means to Be a Catholic,' *Integrity* 2 (October 1947) 32–8; 'Christian Life,' *Integrity* 2 (November 1947) 31–40; 'History of the Devotion to the Blessed Virgin in British Columbia,' *Report of the Canadian Catholic Historical Association* 21 (1954) 39–52; 'The Church and the University,' *Chelsea Annual* 1 (1956) 13–16. In the *Basil-*

ian: 'Message from Father Carr,' 1 (March 1935) 3; three 'Letters to Richard,' 2 (May 1935) 99, (October 1936) 115–16, (November 1936) 133–4; 'An Answer to Father Lynch,' 2 (April 1936) 64; 'What Does Thomistic Philosophy Mean for Today?' 3 (April 1937) 63–4; 'Higher Learning in America,' 3 (October 1937) 87. In *Basilian Teacher*: 'The Most Important Step, St Mark's College,' 1 (May 1956) 1–2; 'The Roman Catholic Church,' 3 (February 1959) 121–33; 'Teaching the Catholic Religion in a Secular University,' 5 (October 1960) 3–12. In *Benedicamus*: 'On Reading Scripture,' 2 (March 1949) 25, 30–31, (May 1949) 24–35, 39; 'The Little Way – A Revolution,' 3 (March 1950) 34–5, 37, 39; Letter to the Editor re: 'The Birth of a Seminary,' 5 (April 1952) 8. In *Catholic Directory for British Columbia*: 'Vocation, Lines Selected from a Letter to Father Lococo,' 3 (1963) 39, 41; 'How Are We Going to Bring Christ to Unbelievers?' 4 (1964) 66–7; 'The Best Introduction to St Thomas,' 4 (1964) 68–9. In *St Joseph Lilies*: 'Dr Charles McKenna, a Tribute,' 11 (March 1923) 67–8; 'Father Francis Forster,' 19 (June 1930) 40–50. In *Yearbook* (St Michael's College): 'Higher Education – Our Needs and Opportunities,' 9 (1918) 28–39; 'Father Francis Forster, Sermon preached in St Basil's Church,' 22 (1931) 15–16, 133, 137, 148–9; 'Father Nicholas Roche, Sermon preached in St Mary of the Assumption Church,' 24 (1933) 11, 130, 132.

SOURCES: GABF; *Annals* 1 (1950) 310, 2 (1955) 225, 3 (1964) 295–7; *Newsletter* (29 November 1963). T.J. Hanrahan, 'Father Carr in Vancouver: The Beginnings of Catholic Education at UBC,' *CCR* 3 (1985) 414–20; *Heartwood* 52, 58–66, 70–8, 88–94, and passim; Brian F. Hogan, 'Salted with Fire. Studies in Catholic Social Thought and Action in Ontario, 1931–1961,' Ph.D. diss. (University of Toronto, 1986), passim; Kirley, *Congregation in France* 4, 10–12, 16, 25–7, 28, 57, 58, 88, 159, 229, 249, 252; E.J. McCorkell, *Henry Carr – Revolutionary* (Toronto, 1969); Sister Ruth (Irene Anne) Poelzer, 'Henry Carr, C.S.B. 1880–1963, Canadian Educator,' unpublished M.Ed. thesis (University of Saskatchewan 1968); R.J. Scollard, *New Catholic Encyclopedia* (New York, 1967) 3 146; Shook, *Catholic Education* 160–5. The 'Father Henry Carr Symposium' issue of *Basilian Teacher* 8 (March 1964) 287–334, carried the following: Introduction 287–90; L.K. Shook, 'Father Carr: Educator, Superior, Friend,' 291–300; E.J. McCorkell, 'Federation: The Legacy of Father Carr,' 301–7; J.F. Leddy, 'Father Carr in Saskatoon,' 308–14; M.J. Oliver, 'The Vancouver Story,' 315–22; J.B. Black, 'Father Carr and His Writings,' 323–30; photographs 331–4.

CARTAL, Julien, priest, member of the Congregation 1823–35, was born on 28 January 1800 at Yssingeaux (Haute-Loire, diocese of Le Puy).

The newly formed Association of Priests of Saint Basil admitted Julien Cartal as a novice on 1 December 1823 in Annonay. He pursued studies in theology while teaching in the Collège des Cordeliers, Annonay, *classe de cinquième*, 1822–4, *quatrième*, 1824–5. He taught at Maison-Seule (Ardèche), 1825–6, and was ordained a deacon on 30 August 1826, at which time he made his profession by promise, not by vows, as was the custom in those early years. Archbishop Joseph Fesch of Lyon ordained him a priest on 23 December 1826.

Father Cartal probably remained on the teaching staff at Maison-Seule until 1828 and then went to the Collège de Privas with the founder of that college, Father André *Fayolle. The records show that he taught *première* there in 1834–5; but, attracted by parochial ministry, he withdrew from the Association of Priests of Saint Basil and joined the diocese of Le Puy on 12 November 1835. The last mention of him in Basilian records notes that he was chaplain to the Sisters of Saint Joseph at Yssingeaux in 1836.

SOURCE: Pouzol, 'Notices.'

CARTER, Cyril Francis, was born at Owen Sound, Ontario (diocese of Hamilton), on 30 June 1913, the son of Michael James Carter and Elizabeth O'Neil. He died in Rochester on 18 March 1971 and is buried there in the Basilian plot of Holy Sepulchre Cemetery.

'Cy' attended St Mary's School, Owen Sound, Owen Sound Collegiate, and St Michael's College, Toronto, receiving his B.A. from the University of Toronto in 1935. He entered St Basil's Novitiate, Toronto, in August of that year and was professed on 15 August 1936. Theological studies followed immediately at St Basil's Seminary, Toronto, though he interrupted these studies in 1938–9 to earn teaching certification at the Ontario College of Education (1939). He was ordained to the priesthood on 15 August 1940 in St Basil's Church, Toronto, by Archbishop James Charles McGuigan.

Father Carter had but one appointment after leaving the seminary. In 1941 he went to Aquinas Institute, Rochester, where he remained until the end of his life. He held the post of Director of Athletics for over twenty-five years, combining this with a full schedule of mathematics classes and with various administrative posts in the school. In 1969, two years before his death, the complications of a long-enduring diabetic condition diminished his activity, though not his love for the school or his work.

Father Carter and athletics at Aquinas were synonymous. On 11 June 1967 the brochure of a testimonial dinner in his honour carried congratulations from every quarter of the Rochester region. Its preface reads in part: 'From the time of his arrival on the Aquinas campus, Father Carter has touched and enriched the lives of almost every student and has made many lasting friendships. Under his inspiration Aquinas became nationally known in the field of sports. As Athletic Director he has maintained the highest standards. As a champion of the youth apostolate, Father Carter has given generously of his time advising teenagers spiritually, emotionally, and always with one motive above all others – to bring these young people closer to God.'

Father Carter was gentle and affable by nature, while bearing for many years the affliction of diabetes, and never asking special consideration. The long months of illness preceding his death were borne with remarkable patience and resignation.

BIBLIOGRAPHY: 'Principles for an Athletic Program,' *Basilian Teacher* 2 (November 1957) 22–4; 'Mathematics in Basilian Schools [forum],' *Basilian Teacher* 4 (December 1959) 62; 'Basilians Become Frustrated Because Results Are Far from Apparent,' *Forum* 3 (April 1967) 59.
SOURCES: GABF; *Annals* 4 (1972) 253–4; *Newsletter* (18 March 1971).

CASHUBEC, James Francis Joseph, priest, member of the Congregation 1944–58, was born on 20 November 1924 at Forester's Falls (Ross Township), Ontario (diocese of Pembroke), the son of Francis Xavier Cashubec and Agnes Belanger. He died at Pembroke, Ontario, on 22 June 2000, four days before the death of his mother and one week prior to the fiftieth anniversary of his ordination to the priesthood. He was buried in St Columba's Cemetery, Pembroke.

Jim Cashubec attended elementary school at Hyndford and Haggerty Township public schools and at the Separate school at Rouyn-Noranda, Quebec. After graduating from St Andrew's High School, Killaloe, Ontario, he went to St Michael's College, Toronto, under the Sir Bertram Windle Scholarship in 1941. In 1943 he entered St Basil's Novitiate, Toronto, and was professed on 15 August 1944. After completing the Honours course in Latin and French at St Michael's (B.A., University of Toronto, 1946), he studied theology at the Grand Séminaire, Quebec City, 1947–8, and at the Pontifical Institute of Mediaeval Studies and St Basil's Seminary, 1948–51. He was ordained to the priesthood on 29 June 1950 in St Basil's Church by Cardinal James Charles McGuigan.

In 1951 Father Cashubec was sent with Father Matt *Mulcahy to found St Charles College, Sudbury, Ontario, and was named second councillor there in 1954. In 1955 he asked to be released from the Basilians, and was incardinated in the diocese of Sault Ste Marie, Ontario, in 1958. During the next thirty years he ministered in seven different parishes but also served as a missionary, a teacher, and an administrator. From 1962 to 1965 he was a missionary in Guatemala, then taught for three years, 1967–70, at the seminary in Tehuacán, Puebla, Mexico, and later, 1973–6, divided his time teaching in the seminaries of Tehuacán and in San Andrés Tuxtla, Veracruz, Mexico. He earned an M.Th. from St Paul University, Ottawa, 1970–1, and three degrees in canon law: J.C.B. and M.C.L. (University of Ottawa, 1981–2), and J.C.L. (St Paul University, 1982), with additional studies in canon law in 1986. He was the *officialis* at North Bay and in 1982 was on loan to the marriage tribunal in Toronto. He was also vice-chancellor and judicial vicar of Sault Ste Marie. In 1988 he resigned his administrative posts and retired in 1989 to Deep River, Ontario. He died in Pembroke Regional Hospital.

BIBLIOGRAPHY: 'A Sprouting Seed,' *Benedicamus* 5 (April 1952) 2–3.
SOURCES: GABF; *Annals* 1 (1950) 288; Archives, diocese of Sault Ste Marie.

CASTILLO, José Isidro, priest, was born at Tehuacán (Puebla), Mexico, on 4 April 1947. He died in Mexico City on 28 January 1996, and is buried in the Basilian plot of the municipal cemetery of the town of San Lorenzo Teotipilco (Puebla). He was the first Basilian to die and be buried in Mexico.

With no formal education in early life, 'Chilo' Castillo went to work in the fields to help support his family. Gentle by nature, of rather striking Aztec appearance and fine manners, he later apprenticed and qualified as an electrician. When the Basilians came to San Lorenzo Teotipilco, a village near the city of Tehuacán, Isidro helped install them in their new home. He had already been working as a catechist, in his desire to revive the faith among the people where he had been raised. He co-operated with the Basilians and with the 'Violeta' sisters in the family-based catechetical program *Catequesis familiar* and in other parish activities. In 1979, at the age of thirty-two, he was admitted as a Basilian associate in the Casa San Felipe, Mexico City. The next three years of his life were spent acquiring primary and secondary education in the open school program sponsored by the Mexican government.

Isidro entered the Basilian novitiate at San Lorenzo in 1982 and took first vows on 16 July 1983. He returned to live at the Casa San Felipe and attended the Instituto Porvenir to prepare for higher studies, graduating in 1986 with the highest average in his class. He entered the Universidad Iberoamericana to study humanities and theology, taking a diploma in theological sciences in 1990 and winning a government scholarship for further studies. He was ordained to the priesthood at San Lorenzo on 2 June 1990 by Bishops Ricardo Ramírez CSB and Norberto Rivera Carrera, then bishop of Tehuacán, later Cardinal Archbishop of Mexico City and Primate of Mexico.

Padre Isidro returned to Mexico City, to San Juan Crisóstomo parish, for what was to be a short but fruitful ministry. He revised and revitalized the catechetical program. He wrote a series of commentaries on the readings for each Sunday for the benefit of his parishioners. Named pastor in 1994, he worked to form pastoral assistants among the laity, inaugurated and directed a school for lay ministers, and implemented the new catechetical program for adults, *Camino de conversión* (*The Path of Conversion*). With material help from the parishioners, and using his considerable artistic talents, he constructed a strikingly beautiful chapel of the Blessed Sacrament which was inaugurated in October 1995.

On 2 January 1996 Padre Isidro witnessed Basilian novices take first vows in San Lorenzo. On 7 January he went into hospital in Mexico City with advanced tuberculosis and died three weeks later. The parish funeral Mass in Mexico City on the day he died was attended by an enormous assembly of shocked and saddened faithful. A second funeral Mass the next day in San Lorenzo was attended by several thousand people, with the body carried two kilometres between two 'walls' of people praying, singing, and weeping. The colourful faith of the people there demonstrated movingly the success of the efforts of Padre 'Chilo' to foster popular religion in the best sense.

SOURCES: GABF; *Annals* 7 (1991) 12–15, 8 (1997) 95–100; *Newsletter* (2 March 1996).

CAUVIN, Ernest, priest, was born on 5 March 1857 at Bédarieux (Hérault, diocese of Montpellier), to a family that originally came from Vallon (Ardèche). He died at Bandol (Var) on 2 January 1925 and is buried in the cemetery there.

A brilliant student in the Sainte-Barbe section of the Collège du Sacré-Coeur, Annonay, 1871–6, Ernest entered the Basilian novitiate at

Feyzin (Isère, now Rhône) in 1876 and took his final vows on 5 June 1881. He received the subdiaconate on 11 June 1881 in the cathedral at Viviers from the hands of Bishop Joseph-Michel-Frédéric Bonnet. Archbishop Armand de Charbonnel ordained him deacon on 23 September 1882 and priest on 22 September 1883 in the chapel of the Collège du Sacré-Coeur.

During theological studies Ernest worked in various Basilian schools: he taught *sixième* at the Ecole cléricale at Périgueux (Dordogne), 1877–8; he was assistant prefect of discipline at the college in Annonay, 1878–9; and teacher at the Collège Saint-Pierre, Châteauroux (Indre), 1879–80. The following three years he spent in Annonay: 1880–1 in the scholasticate and 1881–3 as *professeur de seconde* at the College du Sacré-Coeur.

After ordination Father Cauvin did graduate studies in humanities at the Institut catholique de Paris, receiving his *licence ès lettres* in 1884. For the next fourteen years, 1884–98, he taught the senior classes at the college in Annonay, holding the position of director of studies from 1893 to 1898. His next appointment brought him back to Périgueux, where he served as superior from 1898 to 1903. When the suppression of religious in France forced the closing of that school in 1903, Father Cauvin went into parish ministry in the diocese of Périgueux, first as pastor of Tocane-Saint-Agre, 1904, then as pastor of Le Bugue, 1906, and finally as pastor of La Cité Périgueux, 1908–24. The bishop named him honorary canon of the cathedral. Because he was an ex-religious, *un congréganiste*, the departmental prefect refused him the customary stipend to parish priests authorized by the Concordat.

Father Cauvin served briefly on the general council of the Basilians after the death of Father Jean-Marie *Tarabout in May 1910. Thus he took part in the general chapter held in Geneva, 5–10 July 1910, which officially created the provinces of France and America and established a curia at Ste Anne's Parish, Detroit. In his spiritual testament he wrote: 'I owe everything to the Basilian Community. I have loved it with a passion and have remained faithful to it. I am bound to it by ties that nothing has been able to break.'

After falling ill in 1924, Father Cauvin accepted the invitation of a former student to rest and recuperate at Bandol on the Côte d'Azur, where he died and is buried.

SOURCES: GABF; *Semaine religieuse de Viviers* (16 June 1925); Kirley, *Congregation in France* 12, 14, 72, 87.

CELETTE, Marcel Claudius, priest, member of the Congregation 1946–70, was born 17 December 1927 at Saint-Bonnet-le-Froid (Haute-Loire, diocese of Le Puy), the son of Régis Celette and Marie Bouillot. He died on 6 October 1998 and is buried in the cemetery of Saint-Bonnet-le-Froid.

After studies in the Basilian juniorate in Annonay, Marcel entered the Novitiate at Maison Saint-Joseph, Annonay, on 31 August 1945, and made his first profession of vows on 1 September 1946. After ordination to the priesthood on 21 March 1953 at Le Puy (Haute-Loire), he was first appointed to the Collège du Sacré-Coeur, Annonay, for one year, 1953–4, as *professeur de cinquième classique*, and then to Maison Saint-Joseph the next year as recreation master and English teacher for the Basilian juniors. He returned to Sacré-Coeur in 1955 and for the next eleven years was *professeur de cinquième moderne*, while maintaining charge of the juniorate. During summer vacations he worked with the local Boy Scouts of France.

Father Celette received an indult of exclaustration on 27 November 1964, and undertook various parochial ministries in the archdiocese of Lyon, first at Saint-Paul-en-Jarez and than at Loges near Condrieu in the Rhône Valley. On 18 September 1970 he was incardinated into the archdiocese of Lyon. He served as military chaplain for a time and also did parish work at Pélussin (Loire) and at Saint-Pierre, Longes (Rhône). From 1989 to 1993 he was pastor at Devesset and at Saint-Jeure d'Andaure (Ardèche), where he had a reputation for careful preparation and ardent delivery of his sermons and homilies. Details of his final years have been unobtainable.

SOURCES: GABF; *Newsletter* (25 January 2000); Kirley, *Congregation in France* 198, 256, 257n68, 262.

CHABERT, Benjamin, priest, member of the Congregation 1830–7, younger brother of Father Félix *Chabert, was born on 27 April 1807 in Les Vans (Ardèche, diocese of Mende, since 1822 of Viviers), the son of Joseph Chabert and Jeanne Sophie Dupuy. He died at Malbosc, canton of Les Vans, on 22 August 1885.

Benjamin Chabert was ordained a priest on 5 June 1829, and made his profession by promise in the Association of Priests of Saint Basil on 3 September 1830. He taught rhetoric in the Collège de Privas (Ardèche), and in 1835 preached the students' retreat at the Collège des Cordeliers, Annonay. Feeling drawn to parochial ministry, he left the Association in late August 1837. He was to serve as assistant pastor in the parishes of Les Vans and Vallon, as pastor in Malbosc, 1843–85, where he died. The archpriest of Les Vans presided at his funeral, and Father Basile *Hours, a native of Malbosc, preached the homily.

Father Chabert remained close to the Basilian community all his life, preaching students' retreats in Annonay and in other Basilian schools. It was in his rectory at Malbosc that his Basilian brother Félix died suddenly on 5 August 1873.

SOURCE: Pouzol, 'Notices,' Supplément 1.

CHABERT, Félix, priest, elder brother of Father Benjamin *Chabert, was born on 20 November 1803, at Les Vans (Ardèche, diocese of Mende, since 1822 of Viviers), the son of Joseph Chabert and Jeanne Sophie Dupuy. He died at Malbosc on 5 August 1873 and was buried there.

Félix went to Annonay in October 1835 as a postulant and worked as recreation and study-hall master at Sainte-Barbe minor seminary, 1835–6. He spent the next two years at the Collège des Cordeliers as assistant bursar. On Easter Monday, 16 April 1838, he entered the Carthusian monastery and received tonsure, but did not persevere in that vocation. He went to Rome, where he studied theology for some years. A speech impediment may explain why his ordination to the priesthood took place late in life on 1 November 1860 in Rome. On 30 September 1861 he returned to Annonay, requested admission to the Basilian community, and, after a year of probation, made first profession on 8 December 1862.

For twelve years, 1861–73, he taught theology to young Basilians. In addition to his speech impediment, he developed a weight problem. Early in August 1873 in the midst of a heat wave, he decided to spend some days of vacation with his priest brother Benjamin, who was pastor at Malbosc, canton of Vans (Ardèche). Two brothers of Father François-Régis *Hours went with horse and carriage to meet him at the train station, but the horse stubbornly refused to pull the extra weight. The hour's walk in the heat proved too much for Father Félix's heart. He collapsed on the way and died in his brother's rectory, after receiving the last rites.

SOURCES: GABF; *Ordo*, diocese of Viviers, 1864; Roume, *Origines*; Pouzol, 'Notices.'

CHALANDARD, Pierre Joseph, priest, was born in Annonay on 26 January 1841, the son of Jean-Joseph Chalandard and Jeanne Marie-Marguerite Magnard. He died in Windsor on 29 October 1915, and is buried there in the Basilian plot of Assumption Cemetery.

Pierre Chalandard was educated at the Collège des Cordeliers, section Sainte-Barbe, 1853–61. He entered the Basilian community and made his novitiate at Feyzin (Isère, now Rhône). During his study of theology he worked as prefect at the Collège de Privas (Ardèche), at the Petit Séminaire de Saint-Charles at Vernoux (Ardèche), and at the Petit Séminaire d'Aubenas (Ardèche), where he was also *professeur de sixième*. During the year 1866–7 he was *professeur de sixième* at the Collège des Cordeliers. Along with six other Basilians, he was ordained priest in the chapel of the Collège du Sacré-Coeur on 21 September 1867 by Bishop Armand de Charbonnel.

After ordination he and Father Jean Aboulin went to Feyzin to prepare for ministry in Canada. They left the port of Brest (Finistère) on 1 February 1868 and after eleven days at sea arrived in New York to be greeted by Father Michael *Mulcahy. Father Chalandard was appointed to St Michael's College, Toronto, where he had charge of the college band. In 1870–2 he was assistant at St Mary's of the Assumption Parish, Owen Sound, Ontario, then returned to St Michael's, where he was professor of Latin until 1889 and then bursar until 1891. In 1891 he went to Assumption Parish, Windsor, as assistant until his death in 1915.

The name of Father Chalandard was always associated with music. At St Michael's College, as well as directing the band for many years, he led the choir at St Basil's Church. Later he directed the choir of Assumption Parish. Mary Hoskin wrote in her *History of St Basil's Parish:* 'Sunday after Sunday for twenty years or more his fine voice led the chant in the sanctuary and the singing in the choir. With untiring zeal he would go from sanctuary to choir loft and back several times during the services.'

SOURCES: GABF; *Centennial, St Mary's*; Hoskin, *St Basil's*; Pouzol, 'Notices'; Kirley, *Congregation in France* 45; Spetz, *Waterloo*; Yearbook SMC 7 (1916).

CHALAYE, Isidore, novice, was born on 1 October 1829 at Saint-Agrève (Ardèche). He died in Annonay on 25 October 1849 and is buried there in the cemetery on the grounds of the Collège du Sacré-Coeur.

Isidore went to Annonay to study at Sainte-Barbe, the minor seminary section of the Collège des Cordeliers. In his senior years of college he worked as recreation and study-hall master for the day pupils. He began his novitiate in Annonay on 30 September 1848 with François-Régis *Arnoux and Charles *Vincent, one of the pioneers in the foundation of St Michael's College, Toronto. A year later, as he was preparing for the *baccalauréat* examination he fell ill and died, probably of tuberculosis. The community greatly mourned the loss of this brilliant student, the first Basilian to die while in formation. He was buried in the Saint-Jacques cemetery, 13 rue de Fontanes, Annonay; but his remains, along with those of other deceased confreres, were later translated in 1869 to the private cemetery on the grounds of the Collège du Sacré-Coeur.

SOURCE: ABA; Pouzol, 'Notices.'

CHAMBON, Jean-Louis, priest, elder brother of Father Léopold *Chambon, was born on 3 May 1841, at Uzer (Ardèche), canton of Largentière. He died at Uzer on 26 November 1900 and is buried in the cemetery there.

Jean-Louis made his novitiate at Feyzin (Isère, now Rhône) and professed final vows on 21 September 1866. While studying theology he worked as recreation and study-hall master and taught in the Petit Séminaire de Vernoux (Ardèche), 1864–7. During the year 1867–8 he taught the commercial class at the Collège du Sacré-Coeur. He received major orders from Bishop Armand de Charbonnel: subdiaconate on 22 September 1866, diaconate on 19 September 1868, and priesthood on 18 September 1869, all in the chapel of the Collège du Sacré-Coeur, Annonay.

In 1868 Jean-Louis Chambon joined the group of founding fathers of the Collège Saint-Charles at Blidah, Algeria. He was a deacon at the time. He served for thirty-two years at Saint-Charles, first as teacher, then as bursar. The community records describe him in this latter role as 'indefatigable ... a man of dedication, intelligence and character' (Giraud, *Mémoires*). The school at Blidah operated for the first twenty years in rented facilities, but in 1888 teachers and students moved into the splendid new and spacious building designed by the architect Maître Joly of Annonay and built under the careful supervision of Father Chambon, bursar, and Father Joseph *Martin, director. Father Chambon fell ill in the autumn of 1900 and retired to his family home in Uzer, where he died.

SOURCE: Pouzol, 'Notices.'

CHAMBON, Léopold, priest, younger brother of Father Jean-Louis *Chambon, was born on 2 January 1857 in Uzer (Ardèche), canton of Largentière. He died on 1 March 1919.

Léopold studied at Sainte-Barbe minor seminary and at the Collège du Sacré-Coeur, Annonay, making his novitiate at Sainte-Barbe during the year 1879–80. He made final profession on 5 January 1883, and was ordained to the subdiaconate the same year. Archbishop Armand de Charbonnel ordained him deacon on 19 September 1885, and Bishop Joseph-Michel-Frédéric Bonnet of Viviers ordained him to the priesthood in the college chapel in Annonay on 18 September 1886.

While studying theology he worked as recreation and study-hall master at the Collège Saint-Charles, Blidah, Algeria, 1880–4. The following year he was *professeur de septième* at the college in Annonay and shared the work of disciplinarian. In 1885 he was *professeur de septième* in the Ecole cléricale at Périgueux (Dordogne). After ordination he remained there for six years, 1886–92, successively as *professeur de sixième, cinquième,* and *quatrième*. He went back to Blidah, Algeria for three years, 1892–5, as *professeur de troisième* and *professeur de seconde* at the Collège Saint-Augustin, Bône. When the Basilians withdrew from the school in 1895 he went to the Petit Séminaire d'Aubenas (Ardèche), as *professeur de cinquième* and *quatrième* for eight years, 1895–1903. When the suppression of religious in France forced the Basilians out of the minor seminary at Aubenas in 1903, Father Chambon secured a teaching position in the Collège Urbain IV at Troyes (Aube), and later at the Collège Saint-Stanislas, Nîmes (Gard).

Father Léopold Chambon had a special talent for directing student plays in the schools in which he taught. 'His own good nature and jovial character gave him the appearance of a comic character dear to the heart of everyone' (*Semaine religieuse de Viviers*, 19 March 1919). In addition to his teaching and theatrical work he was of great assistance to the parishioners of Nîmes, whose pastors had been conscripted for military service during the war years 1914–18.

SOURCE: Pouzol, 'Notices.'

CHANTELOUBE, Alexis, priest, was born on 14 October 1837 in Annonay, the son of Joseph Alexis Chanteloube and Caroline Franc. He died at Châteauroux (Indre) on 23 May 1878 and is buried there. Alexis studied at the Collège des Cordeliers, Annonay, taking grades *sixième* to *troisième* as a day student, 1854–8, and the last two senior grades at Sainte-Barbe minor seminary, Annonay, 1858–60. He entered the Basilian novitiate in the first class at Feyzin (Isère, now Rhône) on 29 September 1860 and was professed on 29 September 1861. He received the subdiaconate at Viviers on 19 December 1863. Bishop Armand de Charbonnel ordained him to the diaconate on 24 September 1864 and to the priesthood on 23 September 1865, both ceremonies taking place in the chapel of the Collège des Cordeliers, Annonay.

Father Chanteloube was appointed to the Petit Séminaire d'Aubenas (Ardèche), where he taught for eleven years, 1864–75. The last three years of his life were spent teaching at the Collège Saint-Pierre, Châteauroux (Indre), diocese of Bourges. The Basilian records describe him as a confrere of 'simplicity, purity of intention, and unlimited dedication.' The records also describe him as a remarkably good teacher.

SOURCES: GABF; Pouzol, 'Notices.'

CHANTEPERDRIX, Jean-Antoine, priest, elder brother of Father Léopold *Chanteperdrix, was born on 28 January 1844 at Chassagne (Ardèche), parish of Coux, canton of Privas, the second-oldest of sixteen children of Auguste Chanteperdrix and Apollonie Tourasse. He died at Privas (Ardèche) on 22 May 1923, and is buried there in the Basilian plot in the cemetery.

At the age of seventeen, when Jean Antoine expressed his desire to become a priest, the pastor of Creysailles began teaching him Latin. He studied at the Basilian college at Privas and entered the novitiate at Feyzin (Isère, now Rhône) in 1868. He made his final profession of vows on 22 September 1871 and the following day received the subdiaconate in the chapel of the Collège du Sacré-Coeur, Annonay, at the hands of Bishop Armand de Charbonnel. He went to Viviers for the diaconate on 21 December 1872, and was ordained to the priesthood on 20 September 1873, once again by Bishop de Charbonnel in the chapel of the college in Annonay. During his years of theological studies he was *professeur de septième* and *sixième* at the Petit Séminaire de Vernoux (Ardèche), 1869–72, and *professeur de cinquième* at the Basilian college at Bourg-Saint-Andéol, 1872–3.

After ordination Father Jean-Antoine served in a number of Basilian schools: at Privas, day-pupils section, 1873–5; at the Collège Saint-Pierre, Châteauroux (Indre), 1875–7; at the Petit Séminaire d'Aubenas (Ardèche), 1877–9; at the Collège du Sacré-Coeur, Annonay, 1878–80; and at the college at Bourg-Saint-Andéol (Ardèche), 1880–1. In 1881 he was appointed to the Petit Séminaire de Vernoux, where he remained for twenty-two years, as *professeur de septième*, 1881–3, *professeur de sixième*, 1883–4, and *professeur de cinquième*, 1884–1903.

When the Basilians were evicted from the minor seminary at Vernoux in 1903, during the suppression of religious orders in France, he went to his home at Chassagne. For seventeen years, 1906–23, he served as assistant chaplain in the psychiatric hospital of Sainte-Marie at Privas, where he died. He is remembered in the community records as 'a faithful priest, humble, self-effacing.'

SOURCES: GABF; Pouzol, 'Notices.'

CHANTEPERDRIX, Léopold, priest, younger brother of Father Jean Antoine *Chanteperdrix, was born on 15 April 1861 at Chassagne (Ardèche), parish of Coux, canton of Privas, one of sixteen children of Auguste Chanteperdrix and Apollonie Tourasse. He died in Annonay on 31 March 1941 and is buried in the cemetery on the grounds of the Collège du Sacré-Coeur.

Léopold entered the Basilian novitiate in 1880, probably at Feyzin (Isère, now Rhône), the year the Basilians were forced to close that house in a first wave of anti-religious persecution in France. He finished his novitiate in Annonay two years later and was professed on 22 September 1882. He received the subdiaconate the same day in the chapel of the Collège du Sacré-Coeur, Annonay. He was ordained to the diaconate on 20 September 1884 and to the priesthood on 19 September 1885, at the hands of Archbishop Armand de Charbonnel in the chapel of the college in Annonay.

Apart from three years, 1881–4, when he taught at the Ecole cléricale at Périgueux (Dordogne) as *professeur de septième* for one year and *professeur de cinquième* for two years, Léopold Chanteperdrix spent his entire Basilian life as recreation and study-hall master and prefect of discipline, an apostolate of vigilance which lasted fifty-three years. He began this work at the Basilian school at Bourg-Saint-Andéol (Ardèche), 1880–1. He put in four years at the Collège du Sacré-Coeur, 1884–8. From there he went to the Collège Saint-Augustin in Bône, Algeria, for the seven years in which the Basilians were in charge of that school, 1888–95. For the next five years he was prefect of discipline at the Petit Séminaire d'Aubenas (Ardèche), 1895–1900. After one year at the Collège Saint-Charles, Blidah, Algeria, 1900–1, he returned to the minor seminary at Aubenas for two years. With the expulsion of the Basilians from that seminary in 1903 he returned to his family home at

Coux for two years and then joined the staff of the Collège du Sacré-Coeur, Annonay, when the school reopened in 1905 under diocesan direction. Here he reigned supreme as prefect of discipline until his retirement in 1936.

The students both loved and feared him. With his long white beard he was for them *'le vieux'* ('the old man') a form of address which caused him to pursue a miscreant across the playground in feigned fury, brandishing his cane, blowing his famous horn whistle, advancing clumsily in his large wooden shoes. He also had a stentorian voice which he used to advantage on occasion.

Father Chanteperdrix served on the general council of the Basilians in France from 1932 to 1938. After retirement he continued to live at the Collège du Sacré-Coeur until his death.

SOURCES: GABF; Kirley, *Congregation in France* 76n34, 81–2, 154, 174–5, 184, 206–6; Pouzol, 'Notices.'

CHAREYRE, Régis, priest, member of the Congregation 1863–c.1871, was born on 6 December 1839 at Rochessauve, canton of Chomérac (Ardèche).

After studies at the Petit Séminaire de Vernoux (Ardèche), Régis was admitted as a novice at Feyzin (Isère, now Rhône), probably in 1862–3. He made final profession of vows on 23 September 1864. While studying theology he taught *sixième* at the Petit Séminaire d'Aubenas (Ardèche), at the Collège de Privas (Ardèche), and at the Petit Séminaire de Vernoux, 1864–7. He was ordained to the priesthood on 19 September 1868 in the chapel of the Collège du Sacré-Coeur by Bishop Armand de Charbonnel. He taught *seconde* at the Petit Séminaire de Vernoux, 1868–71, and then withdrew from the Community. No other records of him have been found.

SOURCE: Pouzol, 'Notices,' Supplément 2.

CHARMANT, André, priest, was born in Annonay on 9 November 1802, the son of Dominique Charmant and Benoîte Angeniol. He died in Annonay on 24 March 1878 and is buried there in the cemetery on the grounds of the Collège du Sacré-Coeur.

André Charmant received his early education at the Collège des Cordeliers, Annonay, but interrupted his studies to work for a few years. Attendance at a mission moved him to resume his studies in 1822 with a view to entering the priesthood. In 1824 along with Julien *Tracol he entered the Jesuit novitiate at Avignon (Vaucluse), where he remained for three months. Poor health exempted him from military service. He entered the Basilian community and was ordained to the priesthood on 5 June 1830. He taught at Maison-Seule, the Collège des Cordeliers, and the Collège de Privas, where he served as treasurer. In 1841 he was loaned to the bishop of Bordeaux, where he taught for a year at the Grande-Sauve. He was master of novices in Annonay from 1842 to 1844. From 1844 until his death he was superior at Sainte-Barbe, the Basilian minor seminary. He was a member of the general council from 1850 to 1878 and vicar general from 1864 until his death. On the death of Father Julien *Actorie in 1864 he became acting superior general. In 1852 he strongly supported the taking of vows instead of simple promises. In 1856 he completed the term of Father Germain *Deglesne when the latter died as master of novices.

Father Adrien *Chomel wrote of Father Charmant: 'His judgment was always correct, and he was gifted with rare good sense. He was always calm and collected, and as a superior he united a prudent firmness with a sweetness of temper that became proverbial. He had a great spirit of faith, and was zealous in the service of God, especially in encouraging vocations to the holy priesthood. Though not an orator, he preached many successful retreats for college boys and religious communities.'

SOURCES: GABF; Chomel, *Collège d'Annonay* 478–81; Kirley, *Community in France* 28, 31, 64, 150n383; *Ordo*, diocese of Viviers, 1864; Pouzol, 'Notices'; Roume, *Origines* 265, 274, 346, 397.

CHARRON, Victorin, priest, was born on 7 March 1866 at Joannas (Ardèche), canton of Largentière, the son of Pierre Charron and Marie Salavert. He died at Bordighera, Italy, on 22 March 1931 and is buried at Joannas.

Victorin studied at Sainte-Barbe minor seminary in Annonay, completing rhetoric in 1885. He entered the novitiate at Beaconfield House, Plymouth, England, 1885–6, and made final profession on 21 September 1888. He received major orders in the chapel of the Collège du Sacré-Coeur: subdiaconate on 22 September 1888, conferred by Bishop Joseph-Michel-Frédéric Bonnet of Viviers; diaconate on 20 September 1890 at the hands of Bishop Pierre Dufal CSC; and priesthood on 19 September 1891 from Bishop Bonnet.

While studying theology, Victorin Charron taught classes and worked as recreation master at Sainte-Barbe, 1886–7, at the Collège du Sacré-Coeur, 1887–8, 1890–1, and at the Collège Saint-Charles, Blidah, Algeria, 1888–90. After ordination he continued his work as study-hall and recreation master at the Collège Saint-Augustin, Bône, Algeria, 1891–4, at the Collège Saint-Charles, Blidah, 1894–5, and at the Collège du Sacré-Coeur, 1895–6. He was then appointed to the Ecole cléricale at Périgueux (Dordogne) as *professeur de septième* for two years, 1896–8, returning to the college in Blidah as *professeur de sixième* and *cinquième*, 1898 to 1903.

With the expulsion of the Basilians from Blidah in 1903, as part of the suppression of religious orders in France, Father Charron took a position as curate in the parish of Coux, near Privas (Ardèche), and then went to the Petit Séminaire d'Aubenas (Ardèche) as recreation master, 1904–5 and 1906–7. In 1910 he was at the Institution Sainte-Marie, Seyne-sur-Mer (Var), and from 1913 to 1919 he taught at the Petit Séminaire d'Aubenas as *professeur de sixième*, 1913–14, and *cinquième*, 1914–19. In 1922 he was on the staff of the Institution Robin, Vienne (Isère). He received an appointment as assistant to the novice master at the Basilian novitiate, Villa Saint-Louis, at Bordighera, Italy, arriving there on 18 October 1929 to replace Father Gabriel *Deluche. One of the novices described him as 'a heavy-set man, placid, rather solemn, and distant in his relations to the novices, unlike the man he replaced.' While in Bordighera he also served as chaplain to various communities of French religious expelled from France.

SOURCES: GABF; *Semaine religieuse de Viviers* (10 April 1931); Kirley, *Congregation in France* 206; Pouzol, 'Notices'; Kirley, *Community in France* 185, 197, 204, 240n569.

CHAUSSINAND, Joseph, priest, member of the Association of Priests of Saint Basil 1822–c.1833, was born in 1797 at Saint-Martial, canton of Saint-Martin-de-Valamas (Ardèche, diocese of Viviers [from 1801 to 1822 of Mende]).

Prior to 1822 Joseph worked as *surveillant* at the Collège Sainte-Barbe, Annonay. On 19 December that year he was admitted as a novice into the newly formed Association of Priests of Saint Basil. He worked in the Collège des Cordeliers, Annonay, 1822–4. Basilian records show that he made his profession by promise, according to the custom at the time, not by vows, on 30 August 1826. Archbishop Joseph Fesch of

Lyon ordained him a priest in Lyon on 23 December 1826. By 1833 Father Chaussinand had withdrawn from the Association.

SOURCE: Pouzol, 'Notices,' Supplément 1.

CHAUVIN, Robert Thomas, priest, was born on 3 January 1926 in Windsor, the son of Albert Chauvin and Louise Menard. He died in Toronto on 6 August 1989 and is buried in the Basilian plot of Holy Cross Cemetery, Thornhill, Ontario.

'Bob' Chauvin attended Sacred Heart and St Francis schools and Assumption High School, Windsor, graduating in 1944. In November of that year he enlisted in the Royal Canadian Navy, where he studied first-aid and hospital work and served on several Canadian ships in eastern Canadian waters until his discharge in December 1945. In the fall of 1946 he enrolled in Assumption College, Windsor (B.A., University of Western Ontario, June 1949), and in his final year was president of the senior class. After one year spent as manager of the college cafeteria, he entered St Basil's Novitiate, Toronto, and was professed on 15 August 1951.

His first assignment was to St Thomas High School, Houston, to teach and to begin theological studies. He spent 1952–3 at Catholic Central High School, Detroit, as full-time teacher and assistant to the bursar. He was then assigned to St Basil's Seminary, Toronto to continue theological studies (S.T.B., 1955). Bishop Francis Allen ordained him to the priesthood on 29 June 1955 in St Basil's Church, Toronto.

In 1956 Father Chauvin was appointed to Aquinas Institute to teach business and theology and to do counselling. He also became head swimming coach and trainer for the football and basketball teams. Having injured his knee playing high school football, and no longer able to participate in that sport, he knew first-hand the importance of qualified athletic trainers. He thus became a certified master athletic trainer with expertise and authority in treating injuries. He expected and achieved excellence in his athletes and his students.

In 1969 Bob was appointed to Assumption College School as academic vice-principal. There he combined his administrative duties with counselling, teaching business, coaching the swim team, and training the football, basketball, and hockey teams. Six years later he was appointed to the Basilian community at Lethbridge, Alberta, to teach at Catholic Central High School, where he worked the next twelve years. During this time he suffered a severe heart attack which slowed him down but did not prevent his active participation in the life of the school. In 1987 he was transferred to Bishop O'Dowd High School, Oakland, California. Despite his doctor's prescribing rest in view of his weakened heart, Father Chauvin found his way to the training room, where he saw to the needs of the football players. He suffered a massive stroke and heart attack on 3 March 1989, which left him totally paralysed, except for the movement of his eyes and eyelids and the ability to smile. He was flown from California to St Michael's Hospital, Toronto, where he died five months later.

Bob Chauvin was a warm, steady, and peaceful man. His talents and unstinting devotion extended beyond the institutions and communities in which he worked and to which he so richly contributed. He was an active member of the Big Brother movement both in Windsor and in Lethbridge, and often brought little brothers to the Basilian house as well as to school games or civic and other sports events. He derived great happiness from receiving letters and calls from those children and young men he had helped grow into manhood.

BIBLIOGRAPHY: 'Vocation or Vacation,' *Basilian Teacher* 1 (April 1956) 12–14.
SOURCES: GABF; *Annals* 2 (1955) 196–7, 7 (1990) 118–19; *Newsletter* (11 September 1989).

CHAVANON, Jean Claude, priest, was born in Annonay on 12 February 1816, the son of Jean-François Chavanon and Marguerite Artru. He died in Annonay on 8 February 1902 and was buried there in the cemetery on the grounds of the Collège du Sacré-Coeur.

Jean Claude had been an altar boy at the parish of Notre Dame, Annonay. He was a brilliant student at the Collège des Cordeliers, Annonay, Sainte-Barbe section, 1829–36. For the next two years he was a study-hall master and teacher at the Collège de Privas (Ardèche). In 1838 he entered the Basilian novitiate in Annonay under Father Germain *Deglesne. He was ordained priest at Viviers by Bishop Alban-Pierre François Bonnel on 13 June 1840. For the next four years he taught at the Collège des Cordeliers, and then at the Petit Séminaire de Vernoux for seven years, for two of which he was superior. From 1851 to 1860 he was again at the Collège des Cordeliers, where he taught philosophy and rhetoric; and for one year he assisted Father Germain *Deglesne in the formation of novices. He took vows with the majority of the confreres on 21 November 1852, and was elected a member of the general council from 1855 to 1862. In 1860 he was appointed master of novices at Feyzin (Isère, now Rhône) but suffered a breakdown after a little more than a year and was replaced by Father Etienne *Prévost. After convalescence in 1862 he returned to the college in Annonay, where he taught philosophy and French literature. From 1872 to 1881 he was officially *Chef d'institution* there.

On 11 November 1869 Bishop John Farrell of Hamilton, Ontario, celebrated a pontifical Mass at the Collège du Sacré-Coeur on the occasion of the transferral of the remains of Basilian confreres from the cemetery of Saint-Jacques, rue de Fontanes, Annonay, to the cemetery on the grounds of the college. To mark the occasion Father Chavanon recalled the personalities of the confreres he had known. These reminiscences were completed in three manuscript volumes in 1892 under the title *Souvenirs sur les premiers membres de la communauté* (ABA), and were used extensively by Father Adrien *Chomel in his book, *Le Collège d'Annonay*. Chomel wrote of him: '[Father Chavanon] knew all the old professors of the college except Fathers Actorie and Vallon and had been close to them during many years of community life. His faithful memoir was an easy book to open and was pleasant to read. He delighted in telling stories of his college days, and giving graphic descriptions of his confreres.'

SOURCES: GABF; Chomel, *Collège d'Annonay* 306–12, 438; Chanoine Fromenton, *Le Petit Séminaire de Vernoux* (Aubenas, 1922); Kirley, *Community in France* 28, 70n178, 124n305, 163n416; *Ordo*, diocese of Viviers, 1864; Pouzol, 'Notices'; Roume, *Origines* 284, 346, 356–7, 384.

CHERRIER, Léon Edouard, priest, was born at Dundas, Ontario (archdiocese of Kingston, now diocese of Hamilton), on 29 October 1834, the son of Timothy and Julienne Cherrier. He died at Dundas on 23 December 1924, and is buried in the family plot of Holy Sepulchre Cemetery, Hamilton, Ontario.

Léon Cherrier attended local schools, then for a time worked in the family's general store. At twenty-one he enrolled in St Michael's College, Toronto, 1855–8, and entered St Basil's Novitiate in Toronto, making profession on 8 December 1859. He did theological studies partly in Toronto and partly in France in Annonay. He was ordained priest on 25 March 1863 in St Basil's Church, Toronto, by Bishop John Lynch.

Father Cherrier's long priestly life was spent at St Michael's College, with the exception of the years 1870–6 and 1889–91, when he was an assistant at St Mary's of the Assumption Parish, Owen Sound, Ontario;

of 1899–1901, when he served as pastor of Sacred Heart Parish, Lambton, Ontario; and of 1905–6, spent at St Peter's Cathedral in London, Ontario. He retired to the House of Providence at Dundas in 1906 and was active as chaplain until 1921. Since he lived prior to the time Basilians professed the new, stricter vow of poverty adopted in 1922, he always paid to retain a room at St Michael's College, and would show up unexpectedly to occupy it.

At St Mary's, Owen Sound, Father Cherrier undertook to visit scattered families in the more distant parts of the parish. He was fond of walking, and measured distance by the number of rosaries he could say on the way. He was known to have walked several times from Toronto to Hamilton, where he sometimes stayed with his friend the bishop, and then to return. Unconcerned with ordinary social conventions, he did not care what people thought about him. He had two ambitions in life: one to live to be one hundred years old, the other to escape Purgatory.

SOURCES: GABF; *Centennial, St Mary's*; *Jubilee, St Mary's*; Spetz, *Waterloo*.

CHERRY, John Thaddeus, priest, was born on 12 December 1919 in Houston, the son of John Arthur Cherry and Jessie Euphresia Moore. Two older sisters became Dominican nuns at Sacred Heart Convent, Houston, as Sister Victoria and Sister Thomas. He died in Merrillville, Indiana, on 21 February 1973 and is buried in the Basilian plot of Garden of Gethsemane, Forest Park Lawndale Cemetery, Houston.

John attended his parish school for primary education and in 1933 enrolled in St Thomas High School, Houston, graduating from there in 1937. He entered St Basil's Novitiate, Toronto, and was professed on 15 August 1938. Following his novitiate he was appointed to Assumption College, Windsor (B.A., University of Western Ontario, 1942). He taught for two years, first at St Thomas High School, and then at Catholic Central, Detroit, before returning to St Basil's Seminary, Toronto, for theological studies, 1944–8. He was ordained to the priesthood in St Anne's Church, Houston, on 22 June 1947 by Bishop Christopher Byrne.

In his twenty-five years after leaving the seminary, Father Cherry had three appointments: St Thomas High School, Houston, 1948–56, Aquinas Institute, Rochester, 1956–70, and Andrean High School, Merrillville, Indiana, 1970–3. At St Thomas he taught general science and chemistry, but there as elsewhere he gravitated to administration. In

1949, while still maintaining some teaching, he was appointed treasurer, an office he held for the next seven years. While in Texas he obtained his teacher's and principal's certificates, and in 1954 earned an M.Ed. from the University of Houston. He was all his life an avid and perceptive reader, particularly in the fields of theology, education, and the spirituality and psychology of adolescence.

At Aquinas Institute, after one year of teaching general science, he took over the full-time office of director of discipline, 1957–62, then treasurer, 1962–6, and finally vice-principal and director of student records, 1966–7. In 1970 he was appointed to Andrean High School as vice-principal and was named principal the next year.

At his first faculty meeting there he stated that his priority was to unite all the elements connected with the school – students, faculty, administration, and parents – in a Christian community, and managed in two years to progress a long way towards this goal. An excellent organizer, he planned and incorporated the Andrean Foundation, involving pastors, laity, business foundations, and other friends of Andrean in a program of annual funding for the school.

Father Cherry combined an outward aspect of unruffled calm with strong interior drives that led him to demand a great deal of himself and to set high standards for those with whom he worked. He had a look, especially on first acquaintance, that was severe – 'strait-laced and poker faced,' according to the wags – an appearance to make wrongdoers tremble. But when people got to know him better, they found him to be a man of ready humour, magnanimity, and generosity. His strong sense of justice and dignity led him to respect his students, even problem cases, and to become a kind arbiter for anyone in trouble. A special issue of the Andrean student paper, the *Acropolis*, published after canvassing the students and staff, found unanimous praise for his dedication and zeal for the school and his availability and his friendliness towards them.

BIBLIOGRAPHY: 'Director of Discipline,' *Basilian Teacher* 5 (March 1961) 211–14.
SOURCES: GABF; *Annals* 1 (1947) 150; 5 (1974) 53–4; *Newsletter* (27 February 1973).

CHOMEL, Adrien, priest, was born in Annonay on 28 April 1848, the son of François Chomel and Eugénie Dessemond. He died in Annonay on 24 December 1906 and was buried in the cemetery on the grounds of the Collège du Sacré-Coeur.

After studies in Annonay, Adrien entered the novitiate at Feyzin (Isère, now Rhône) and made first profession on 17 September 1869. He was ordained priest on 19 September 1874 at the Collège du Sacré-Coeur by Bishop Armand de Charbonnel. Almost all his life he taught mathematics, first at the Collège de Privas, 1870–2, and then at the Collège du Sacré-Coeur, 1872–1903. He was elected to the general council in 1898 and remained in this position until his death. He was known for generosity to the poor and to the seminarians at Sainte-Barbe.

In 1903 Father Chomel lost his teaching position because of the new anticlerical laws which suppressed teaching by religious. He retired to his family, where he spent a good deal of time writing. He contributed humorous common-sense articles to several local newspapers. He wrote a memoir on education which won a prize from the Association lyonnaise d'éducation. His book *Le Collège d'Annonay 1800–1880: Mémoires et souvenirs* is an invaluable resource for the history of the Congregation in France. Father Chomel died on Christmas Eve in his house at Montalivet, Annonay, after a long illness.

BIBLIOGRAPHY:
Book: *Le Collège d'Annonay, 1800–1880. Mémoires et souvenirs.* Annonay, 1902.
Unpublished: 'Father Julien Tracol, 1796–1885. The Interior Life of One of the Founders of the Congregation of Priests of St Basil,' Eng. trans. of the French original by John C. Plomer.
SOURCES: GABF; Kirley, *Community in France* ii, 142, 163n416, 172, 182n464, 184, 203, 244; Pouzol, 'Notices.'

CHRISTIAN, Michael Patrick, priest, was born in Stalybridge (diocese of Shrewsbury), England, on 12 November 1859, the son of Patrick Christian and Elizabeth Gorman. He died in Toronto, on 4 December 1934 and is buried there in the Basilian plot of Mount Hope Cemetery.

Michael Christian grew up in Binghamton, New York, and from there came in 1880 to St Michael's College, Toronto. After completing his course in philosophy, he entered St Basil's Novitiate at Beaconfield House, Plymouth, England, on 20 October 1886. Following profession he returned to North America and was ordained priest on 30 August 1890.

Father Christian's priestly life was spent at Ste Anne's Parish, Detroit, 1890–2, 1893–1907, 1925–8; at St Basil's Novitiate, Toronto, 1892–3, 1909–16, 1917–25, 1928–34, as master of novices, 1910–16, acting master at other times during the illnesses of other masters; and as pastor of St John the Baptist Parish, Amherstburg, Ontario, 1907–9, 1916–17. As novice master Father Christian's exemplary conduct, his silent bearing, and sometimes his words put the fear of the Lord into the novices. Beneath a show of strictness, the novices soon found that 'Mickey,' as he was affectionately called, had a kind and generous heart. Quiet and unobtrusive service to parishioners won him loyal friends in Holy Rosary Parish, Toronto, where the noviciate was located, and at Ste Anne's Parish, Detroit.

Slightly built, somewhat under medium height, Father Christian was for many years afflicted with stomach ulcers. His obituary in the *St Michael's College Yearbook* stated: 'He was a man of great patience and fortitude. In spite of severe bodily afflictions he maintained a heroic, saintly stoicism that was the admiration of all.'

SOURCES: GABF; J.W. Embser, 'Michael P. Christian,' *Basilian Teacher* 3 (December 1958) 76–9; Obituary, *Basilian* 1 (March 1935) 17; *Yearbook SMC* (1935).

CLAPPE, François-Xavier, priest, son of Jean Clappe and Marie Françoise Guyon, was born on 3 December 1811 in Annonay and died there on 23 September 1881. He was probably buried in the family plot in Annonay.

Xavier was a student at the Collège des Cordeliers, Sainte-Barbe section, 1826–32. The following two years he studied at the Grand Séminaire de Viviers. In 1834 he continued his theology courses in Annonay; but in February 1835 he was sent to the college at Feyzin (Isère, now Rhône) as *professeur de quatrième*. The following year he taught at the Collège des Cordeliers. He was ordained to the priesthood on 23 September 1837 at Le Puy (Haute-Loire) by Bishop Louis-Jacques-Maurice de Bonald, future cardinal archbishop of Lyon and controversial ultramontanist. He spent the rest of his life in Annonay as professor of rhetoric for eighteen years and director of studies for five years. For about twenty years he was director of the Sodality of the Blessed Virgin Mary and was the spiritual father of most of the students at the college, especially after the death of Father Augustin *Payan. He strongly encouraged religious vocations and was an excellent preacher. 'His deep voice lent itself admirably in recalling great truths,' wrote Father Adrien *Chomel of him (303). From 1854 to 1881 he was chaplain to the Ursulines de Sainte-Marie and to their boarding school in Annonay. In 1859 he had been considered as a replacement for Father Jean Mathieu *Soulerin at St Michael's College, Toronto.

SOURCES: GABF; Chomel, *Collège d'Annonay* 199, 303–6, 438; Pouzol, 'Notices'; Roume, *Origines* 347.

CLAUZEL, Edouard, priest, was born on 31 December 1860 at Privas (Ardèche). He died on 15 September 1911 at Thueyts (Ardèche) and is buried in that village.

Edouard studied at the Basilian school at Privas and then at the Sainte-Barbe minor seminary in Annonay, for the upper grades of his secondary studies. He sought admission to the Basilian novitiate at Feyzin (Isère, now Rhône) just at the time the sub-prefect of Vienne dispatched a detachment of military police to force the Basilians out and close the institution. His luck was no better at the Collège du Bourg-Saint-Andéol (Ardèche), where he taught the commercial class during the year 1880–1: at the end of that school year the town council closed the college, leaving the Basilian staff with no choice but to go elsewhere. These closures were part of a first wave of the suppression of religious which swept over France in the Third Republic. From Bourg-Saint-Andéol, Edouard Clauzel went to Annonay, where he taught preparatory classes in the juniorate of the Collège du Sacré-Coeur, 1881–4, and where he continued to receive a religious formation through private instruction and guidance. From 1884 to 1886 he worked as recreation and study-hall master at the Collège Saint-Charles, Blidah, Algeria. He made his profession of vows on 17 September 1886 and received the subdiaconate the next day in the chapel of the Collège du Sacré-Coeur at the hands of Bishop Joseph-Michel-Frédéric Bonnet of Viviers. By this time the Basilian community had opened a novitiate at Beaconfield House, Plymouth, England. Edouard went there for the year 1886–7, after which he returned to the college at Blidah for one year, 1888–9, to be in charge of the *classe de cinquième* and to serve as recreation master for the junior students. Bishop Bonnet ordained him deacon on 22 September 1888 and priest on 21 September 1889. Both ceremonies took place in the chapel of the college in Annonay.

Father Clauzel stayed on for one year at Sacré-Coeur as recreation master. The following year, 1890–1, he performed the same duties at the college at Blidah, but returned to Annonay for the year 1891–2 as prefect of discipline. In 1892–3 he worked as recreation master at the clerical school at Périgueux (Dordogne), and was then assigned to the Petit Séminaire at Vernoux (Ardèche), where he remained for two years, 1897–9, as professor for *septième* and prefect of discipline.

With the dispersal of the Basilian community in the final phase of the anticlerical laws in 1903, Father Clauzel, like many of his confreres, took on private tutoring among Catholic families, but the Basilian archives have no record of the places and dates. He taught in the archdiocese of Lyon and also at the Ecole Saint-Maurice, Vienne (Rhône). The week after his death in the presbytery at Thueyts (Ardèche), where the pastor had given him accommodation, the *Semaine religieuse de Viviers* of 22 September 1911 described him as a man who 'in spite of his small stature and feeble constitution exercised considerable authority. His sense of obedience and an innate need to change residence frequently meant that he made the rounds of practically every institution run by the Basilians.'

SOURCES: GABF; Kirley, *Community in France* 185, 210, 240n569; Pouzol, 'Notices.'

CLEMENS, Henry NORBERT, priest, was born on 5 June 1914 in Youngstown, Ohio, one of three children of Henry Clemens and Catherine Walsh. He died on 27 August 2002 in Houston, and is buried there in the Basilian plot of Garden of Gethsemane, Forest Park Lawndale Cemetery.

'Norb' attended St Patrick's elementary school in Youngstown. His parents died when he was thirteen, and he went as a boarder to Assumption College School, Windsor. He entered the novitiate in Toronto, and made first profession of vows on 15 August 1933. He was appointed to do his arts course at Assumption College (B.A., University of Western Ontario, 1938). During his first year of theology at St Basil's Seminary, Toronto, 1938–9, he also taught at the high school of St Michael's College. Father Clemens's next year, 1939–40, was an even more crowded one: while teaching at Catholic Central High School, Detroit, he continued his theological courses at Assumption College, Windsor, and obtained teaching certification for Michigan, 1939, and an M.Ed. from Wayne State University, 1940. He completed theological studies at St Basil's Seminary, 1940–2, being ordained on 17 August 1941 by Archbishop James Charles McGuigan in St Basil's Church, Toronto.

Father Clemens's name is invariably linked to Catholic Central High School, where he taught English and religion a total of forty-five years in five different periods, 1939–40, 1942–7, 1948–53, 1956–65, 1968–92. He taught also at St Thomas High School, Houston, 1947–8, and at Assumption College School, 1953–6, and worked for three years, 1965–8, preaching for the Mexican Missions and helping plan and direct work on the Centro Cultural in Mexico City. In 1992 he retired to Dillon House, Houston, doing part-time ministry at St Anne's Parish.

Father Clemens was active in moderating school clubs, in directing drama and musical productions, and in working with parents' organizations. In the homily delivered at the funeral Mass at St Anne's, Houston, Father Charles Christopher estimated that Father Clemens taught over ten thousand 'Men of Catholic Central,' and recalled that his teaching of Shakespeare and modern British poets was done with a verve that students were not likely ever to forget. A memorial service held for him in Detroit attracted hundreds of them, even though he had been absent from Detroit over ten years. A booklet with personal tributes and memories of him was prepared for that event.

SOURCES: GABF; *Annals* 6 (1984) 207–8, 7 (1992) 5; *Newsletter* (6 September 2002).

COHAS, Joseph Pierre Bonnet, priest, was born on 27 March 1844 at Salles, canton of Noirétable, Montbrison region (Loire, archdiocese of Lyon). He died at Vernaison (Rhône) on 2 May 1929 and is buried in the cemetery there.

After primary and secondary schooling in his home diocese and some training in theology, Joseph Cohas went to the Basilian college at Privas (Ardèche) for the year 1870–1, to help as recreation and study-hall master. He had already received tonsure. The following year he taught at the Collège du Bourg-Saint-Andéol (Ardèche). He made final profession of vows on 7 June 1874. Not all the records of his appointments have survived. It is certain that he taught for thirteen years at the Collège Saint-Charles, Blidah, Algeria, 1872–85, successively grades *sixième* through *troisième*. He may have been one of the three novices who accompanied Father Henri *Ladreyt to Blidah in September 1872, and thus completed his novitiate there. While there is no record of his subdiaconate, he was definitely ordained deacon on 18 September 1875 by Bishop Armand de Charbonnel in the chapel of the Collège du Sacré-Coeur, Annonay, and priest on 23 September 1876 by Bishop Joseph-Michel-Frédéric Bonnet of Viviers, also in the college chapel in Annonay.

Records about him during the next several years are lost, but the following appointments are known: Mary Immaculate College at Beaconfield House, Plymouth, England, bursar (January 1885–9); Ecole cléricale, Périgueux (Dordogne), teaching *sixième*, 1889 to 1903, the year the school was closed during the suppression of religious orders in France. After remaining for a time at Pézuls, diocese of Périgueux, Father Cohas returned to live at Saint-Romain d'Urfé, region of Roanne (Loire), in his native diocese. From 1924 until his death he lived in retirement at the Maison de Retraite at Vernaison, canton of Saint-Denis-Laval (Rhône).

SOURCES: GABF; Kirley, *Community in France* 38, 185, 207; Kirley, *Congregation in France* 158; Pouzol, 'Notices.'

COLL, Edward BLAKE, priest, was born in St John, New Brunswick (diocese of St John), on 12 June 1907, the son of Owen Coll and Florence Delaney. He died in Toronto on 28 August 1961 and is buried in the Basilian plot of Holy Cross Cemetery, Thornhill, Ontario.

Blake attended grade school in his native city, St Thomas College in Chatham, New Brunswick, 1922–3, and Assumption College School, Windsor, 1923–6, and then entered St Basil's Novitiate, Toronto. After professing first vows on 11 August 1927, he spent nine years at St Basil's Seminary, Toronto, obtaining a B.A. from the University of Toronto, 1932, attending the Ontario College of Education, 1933–4, and studying theology. He was ordained priest on 21 December 1935 in St Basil's Church, Toronto, by Archbishop James Charles McGuigan.

Father Coll's priestly life was spent in teaching French and Latin: at St Michael's College School Toronto, 1935–8, Assumption College School, Windsor, 1938–40, and St Mary's Boys' High School in Calgary, Alberta, 1940–61. While at St Mary's, Father Coll attended summer courses in education at the University of Alberta in Edmonton and was granted a B.Ed. degree in 1944 and an M.Ed. in 1955. He was principal of the school and local superior of the Basilian community, 1955–61. In Calgary he was frequently consulted on educational matters. Six weeks before his death in 1961 he was elected a member of the general council.

Although quiet in his personal life and slow to intimacy with others, he was staunch when the bond of friendship was established.

BIBLIOGRAPHY: 'The Pains of Purgatory,' *Basilian* 1 (April 1935) 33–7; 'Report on

Vocation Activities at St Mary's Boys' High School, Calgary,' *Proceedings of the First Basilian Meetings to Discuss Vocations* 1 (1955) 7.
SOURCES: GABF; *Annals* 3 (1961) 88–9; *Newsletter* (29 August 1961); *Basilian Teacher* 6 (October 1961) 36.

COLLINS, Charles, priest, was born on a farm near Maidstone, Ontario (diocese of London), on 3 December 1874, the son of Jeremiah Collins and Ann Cavanaugh. He died at Pontiac, Michigan, on 2 June 1947 and is buried in the Basilian plot of Assumption Cemetery, Windsor.

Charles Collins received his early education at Maidstone, after which he went to Assumption College, Windsor, in 1888. He entered St Basil's Novitiate, Toronto, in 1893, was professed on 20 November 1894, and was ordained priest on 15 August 1899 in St Basil's Church, Toronto, by Archbishop Denis *O'Connor. He was among the first Basilians who went to Texas, where he taught at St Basil's College, Waco, 1899–1901 and 1910–11, and at St Thomas College, Houston, 1908–10. He worked in three Basilian parishes: St Mary's of the Assumption Parish, Owen Sound, Ontario, in charge of the missions of Hepworth and the Irish Block, 1920–2, 1926–32, and 1934–5; Ste Anne's Parish, Detroit, 1924–6; and St John the Baptist Parish, Amherstburg, Ontario, 1932–3. The greatest part of his life was spent at Assumption College, 1901–8, 1914–20, 1922–4, 1935–47.

Father Collins wrote poetry for his own amusement, and liked to write about his student days (see Bibliography below). Describing himself as 'a simple country boy,' he used picturesque, bucolic figures of speech in his conversation, and his audience was always ready to laugh. He was a good speaker who used literary societies at Assumption College to encourage public speaking among the students. He always had time to recall and chat about old times. He died while visiting relatives.

BIBLIOGRAPHY:
Articles: 'Just Forty Years Ago,' *Basilides, Assumption College* (Windsor, 1930). In *Basilian*: 'Down on the Farm' (poem), 1 (April 1935) 37; 'The Shepherd of Owen Sound, Nicholas E. Roche,' 1 (April 1935) 31–2; 'Alfred J. Côté,' 2 (January 1936) 4–5; 'Patres Nostri, Neil McNulty,' 2 (April 1936) 68–70; 'Patres Nostri, Daniel Cushing,' 4 (March 1938) 48; 'Patres Nostri, Michael Mungovan,' 4 (April 1938) 73, 80; 'Patres Nostri, Denis O'Connor,' 4 (June 1938) 107, 120. He regularly contributed articles of reminiscence to the *Alumni Chatter* (newslet-

ter) of Assumption College. His memoirs of student life at Assumption 1888, written in 1926, have been published by Michael Power, *Assumption College. 2: The O'Connor Years 1870–1890* (Toronto, 1986) 76–98.

Unpublished: 'Basilians I Have Known' (eighteen biographies) (GABF); 'Reminiscences of St Basil's College, Waco'; 'My Annals of Owen Sound and Missions, September 26, 1920, to April 13, 1921'; 'Echoes of Assumption College, some traditions of the early days that have lapsed'; 'Athletics at Assumption College'; 'Order of the Day and Week at Assumption College in 1888.'

SOURCES: GABF; *Annals* 1 (1944) 41, 1 (1947) 158–9; *Basilides, Assumption College* (Windsor, 1930); *Centennial, St Mary's*; *Jubilee, St Mary's*; R.J. Scollard and J.F. Mallon, *A Bibliography of the Writings of Charles Collins* (Toronto, 1974).

COLLINS, James Joseph, priest, was born on 3 June 1919 in Detroit, the only son of James Collins and Margaret McQuillan. He died in Toronto on 1 October 1992 and is buried in the Basilian plot of Holy Cross Cemetery, Thornhill, Ontario.

'Jim' Collins attended Catholic Central High School, Detroit, 1933–7. He entered St Basil's Novitiate, Toronto, taking first vows on 15 August 1938. He was then appointed to St Michael's College for undergraduate studies (B.A., University of Toronto, 1942). There followed two years of teaching at Catholic Central. During this time he also attended the University of Detroit, where he obtained teaching certification for the State of Michigan. In 1944 he returned to Toronto for theology, living first at St Michael's College, 1944–5, and then at St Basil's Seminary, 1945–8. He was ordained to the priesthood on 29 June 1947 in St Basil's Church, Toronto, by Cardinal James Charles McGuigan.

Father Collins had a forty-year career of teaching, school administration, formation work, and chaplaincy service. From 1948 to 1961 he taught Latin, Spanish, and general science at Catholic Central and worked there as director of studies, 1950–61, as moderator of scholastics for thirteen years, and first councillor of the local community, 1960–1. He earned an M.A. in education from the University of Detroit in 1957. During all these years he also gave retreats and days of recollection for students in public schools.

In 1961 he was appointed master of novices at Pontiac, Michigan. When, in 1965, the Pontiac and Erindale novitiates were combined into one house at Pontiac, he became assistant master of novices there and oversaw changes to the chapel according to the liturgical norms of Vatican II. In 1966 he returned to Catholic Central, where he taught for one year before being appointed superior at Andrean High School, Merrillville, Indiana, where he also taught and did counselling. After one year of pastoral work in Yuma, Arizona, 1970-1, he returned to live at Catholic Central, where he served as chaplain at Burtha Fisher Retirement Home for the next seventeen years. In 1975 he became the first chairman of the Basilian Fathers Committee on Retirement, and was appointed to the Basilian Fathers Residence (Infirmary) in 1988.

The range and importance of Jim Collins's appointments are indicative of his competence and of the confidence the community placed in him.

BIBLIOGRAPHY: 'Summer School: Should We Have Our Own?' *Basilian Teacher* 2 (November 1957) 3-5; 'Retreat Renewal,' *Forum* 1 (November 1964) 13-17.
SOURCES: GABF; *Annals* 1 (1947) 151; 6 (1989) 720, 7 (1993) 140-2; *Newsletter* (11 October 1992).

COLLINS, John Bernard, priest, was born on a farm in Ops Township, near Lindsay, Ontario (diocese of Toronto, since 1882 of Peterborough), on 14 May 1853, the son of Timothy Collins and Mary O'Reilly. A younger brother, Timothy Francis Collins (1856-1909), became a priest of the diocese of Peterborough. Father John Collins died in Toronto on 24 February 1920 and is buried there in the Basilian plot of Mount Hope Cemetery.

John Collins attended a rural school for a few years only, then went to work on the family farm until he was twenty-three years old. In 1876 he resumed his education at St Michael's College, Toronto, and six years later went to Assumption College, Windsor, to study for the priesthood. On 20 October 1886 he entered St Basil's Novitiate at Beaconfield House, Plymouth, England, and then returned to Assumption College, where he completed his theological course, took final vows on 23 May 1888, and was ordained priest three days later.

After ordination Father Collins taught at Assumption College until 1892, when he was appointed master of novices at the newly opened St Basil's Novitiate, Toronto. The next year he returned to Assumption College, to teach until 1901, when he was made treasurer. Three parish appointments followed: pastor of St Mary's of the Assumption Parish, Owen Sound, 1904-7, assistant at Ste Anne's Parish, Detroit, 1907-14, and assistant at St Basil's Parish, Toronto, 1914-20, where he died from diabetes.

Father Collins was a witty teacher of religion. The *Centennial Volume, 1859-1959* of his native parish said of him, 'He was a tall, bony, red-headed Irishman, and the friend of everyone.' 'Tabellarius '01' wrote in the *Golden Jubilee, 1870–1920, Assumption College,* 'The handsome form of Father John Collins looms up, surrounded by a crowd of happy boys to listen to his latest story. He it was who helped more than any other to fill Sandwich College with students.'

SOURCES: GABF; *Centennial, St Mary's*; *Centennial Volume, 1859–1959, St Mary's of the Purification Parish* (Lindsay, 1959); *Jubilee, Assumption*; *Jubilee, St Mary's*; Spetz, *Waterloo*.

COLLINS, John Francis, priest, was born in Glasgow, Scotland, 25 September 1908, the son of Felix Collins and Ann Millmure. He died in Houston on 19 October 1969, and is buried there in the Basilian plot of Garden of Gethsemane, Forest Park Lawndale Cemetery.

The Collins family left Scotland and moved to Cuyahoga Falls, Ohio (diocese of Cleveland), when John was seven. After his early education there, he went in 1928 to Assumption College, Windsor. After one year of arts, 'Scotty,' as he came to be called, entered St Basil's Novitiate, Toronto, was professed on 29 September 1930, and returned to Assumption College (B.A., University of Western Ontario, 1932). He studied theology at St Basil's Scholasticate, Toronto, 1932–6, except for one year, 1933–4, at Catholic Central High School, Detroit, where he taught while continuing theology. He was ordained to the priesthood on 21 December 1935, and was appointed the following year to St Thomas High School, Houston. After two years there, he began an intensive study of Spanish at Hebbronville, Texas, to prepare for the hispanic ministry which would occupy the rest of his life, with the exception of a three-year stint of teaching at Aquinas Institute, Rochester, 1943–6.

In the fall of 1938 Father Collins joined Father Joseph *Dillon in the recently founded Basilian Mexican mission apostolate which was based, first, at St Anne's Church, Houston, then moved to Our Lady of Guadalupe Church, Rosenberg, Texas, in March 1939, where Father Collins served as assistant pastor until December 1943. After his time at Aquinas Institute, he returned to Rosenberg in 1946 as assistant and then as pastor of both Our Lady of Guadalupe Church and St Theresa's Church, Sugar Land, Texas, which he built. He was appointed mission director in 1951. His talents for organization, his habit of hard work, and his zeal for the good of the hispanic peoples advanced the mission work immensely. He preached tirelessly for the missions in many places in Canada and the United States, and founded the *Mission Memo*, which increased in circulation from thirty to ten thousand by the time of his death.

As mission director, Father Collins extended the Basilian mission field into the parish of San Juan Crisóstomo, Mexico City, and he was especially proud of the establishment there of the 'Centro Cultural,' a residence which provided young men with educational opportunities. Always solicitous for the Basilians doing missionary work, he organized monthly gatherings for them at which they celebrated Mass and shared a convivial meal. On Mission Sunday morning, 1969, Father Collins celebrated Mass with difficulty and in pain, and died that same evening.

BIBLIOGRAPHY:
Pamphlet: *Story of Our Lady of Guadalupe*. Sugar Land, Texas, 1965.
Articles: 'The Truth about Lying,' *Basilian* 2 (March 1936) 51–6; 'A Week-end on the Mexican Missions,' *Basilian* 4 (April 1938) 63–4; 'A Missionary Speaks,' *Benedicamus* 2 (June 1949) 46–7; 'Our Lady's Special Care,' *Benedicamus* 5 (April 1952) 9–10; 'Father Dillon – Missionary,' *Benedicamus* 6 (April 1953) 2–4. 'Joseph Dillon, CSB. *Laudemus viros gloriosos*,' *Basilian Teacher* 2 (March 1958) 24–6.
SOURCES: GABF; *Annals* 4 (1970) 166–7; *Newsletter* (20 October 1969).

COLOMB, Alphonse Marcelin, priest, was born on 21 April 1872 at Laurac (Ardèche), canton of Largentière, son of Jean-François Colomb and Marie Sophie Chastagner. He died at Laurac on 7 December 1943.

Alphonse made his novitiate in Annonay, 1894–5, under the direction of Father Léopold *Fayolle, and worked part time as recreation master. His first profession took place on 20 September 1895 in Annonay and final profession on 25 May 1899 in Blidah, Algeria. Bishop Léon Livinhac, superior general of the White Fathers, who had baptized some of the Ugandan martyrs, ordained him subdeacon on 27 May 1899 at Maison-Carrée near Algiers. Bishop Hilarion-Joseph Montéty, titular bishop of Beirut, conferred the diaconate on 22 September 1900 and priesthood on 21 September 1901, both ceremonies in the chapel of the Collège du Sacré-Coeur, Annonay.

While studying theology, Alphonse worked as a recreation master in the junior division of the Collège du Sacré-Coeur, 1895–8, and in the summer of 1898 he and Father Gabriel *Fuma were sent to study in

Regensburg, Germany. In the fall of 1898 he was appointed to the Collège Saint-Charles, Blidah, Algeria, first as *professeur de sixième* and then as instructor in German, 1899–1903. When the school was closed in 1903, owing to the suppression of religious in France, Father Colomb was appointed curate at Lablachère (Ardèche) by Bishop Joseph-Michel-Frédéric Bonnet of Viviers, who declared him legally to be a secular priest so that he could qualify for a teaching position. In October 1903, he went to the Petit Séminaire d'Aubenas (Ardèche), where he worked first as recreation and study-hall master and then as *professeur de sixième*. From 1905 to 1932 he taught at the Collège du Sacré-Coeur (at that time under diocesan administration) as *professeur de sixième*, 1905–7, teacher of German to all classes, 1907–16, *professeur de quatrième*, classics section, 1916–18, and *professeur de cinquième*, classics, 1918–32, while continuing to teach German.

In 1932 he returned to his native village of Laurac and to the family home, serving as chaplain in the Christian Brothers' school, Ecole Serdieu. He also coached pupils in Latin, including the young Georges *Reynouard of Rosières.

SOURCES: Kirley, *Community in France* 185, 196, 255n600; Kirley, *Congregation in France* 42, 68, 70, 76n34, 82, 206; Pouzol, 'Notices.'

CONWAY, John Thomas, priest, member of the Congregation 1938–60, brother of Sister Dympna (now Patricia) CSJ and Sister St Patrick (now Kathleen) CSJ, was born in Detroit on 6 August 1917, the son of Patrick Conway and Mary Kehoe. He died in south Florida on 9 November 1989 and was buried in the family plot in Toronto.

John entered St Basil's Novitiate, Toronto, in 1937 and took his first vows in 1938. He attended Assumption College, Windsor, 1938–41 (B.A., University of Western Ontario, 1941). He taught at St Thomas High School, Houston, 1941–2, and at Catholic Central High School, Detroit, 1942–3. He obtained an M.A. from the University of Houston in 1942 and teaching certificate for Michigan at Wayne State University, Detroit, in 1943. He studied theology at St Basil's Seminary, 1943–7, and was ordained to the priesthood by Cardinal James Charles McGuigan on 15 August 1946.

Father Conway taught at St Michael's College School, 1947–52, and was principal of the 'old school' on Bay Street in 1950–1. He was first councillor at St Basil's Seminary, Toronto, 1952–4, and taught moral theology there. He returned to high school teaching, first at St

Michael's College School, 1954–5, then at Aquinas Institute, Rochester, 1955–6, and finally at Assumption High School, Windsor, 1956–60, where he was moderator of scholastics, 1958–60.

In 1960 Father Conway withdrew from the Basilian Fathers, and lived and taught in south Florida.

SOURCE: GABF; *Annals* 1 (1946) 120.

CONWAY, William Joseph, priest, was born in Toronto on 30 October 1924, the youngest of three sons born to William Joseph Conway and Gertrude Bernadette Laughlin. He died in Toronto on 7 September 1961 and is buried in the Basilian plot of Holy Cross Cemetery, Thornhill, Ontario.

'Bill' attended St Vincent de Paul School and the high school section of St Michael's College, Toronto. In 1942 he entered St Basil's Novitiate, Toronto, and was professed on 15 August 1943. His undergraduate studies at St Michael's College were interrupted by a year of teaching, 1946–7, at St Thomas High School, Houston. He graduated with a B.A. from the University of Toronto in 1948, made his theological course at St Basil's Seminary, Toronto, and was ordained priest on 29 June 1951 in St Basil's Church, Toronto, by Cardinal James Charles McGuigan.

St Michael's College School was the scene of Father Conway's labours, with the exception of the year 1956–7 when he taught at St Charles College, Sudbury, Ontario. A congenial disposition, joined to inspiring teaching and coaching, enabled him to exert tremendous influence over students. 'Big Bill,' as he was affectionately called, as much for his friendly manner as for his tall stature, was reaching his peak as a teacher of English at the time of his death from inflammation of the pancreas, just ten years after ordination.

He had obtained high school teaching certification by attending summer school at the Ontario College of Education, Toronto, in 1952 and 1953, and in 1961 had qualified for a specialist certificate in English, a subject in which his students consistently obtained outstanding results. He coached the St Michael's Junior B hockey team to the Ontario championship in 1961.

BIBLIOGRAPHY: 'Scripture and Our Students [forum],' *Basilian Teacher* 5 (December 1960) 82.
SOURCES: GABF; *Annals* 2 (1951) 35, 3 (1961) 92; *Newsletter* (8 September 1961); *Basilian Teacher* 6 (October 1961) 36.

COOPER, Donald Theodore, priest, was born on 26 July 1923 in Houston, the only child of Denver D. Cooper and Gladys Koenig. He died in Toronto on 23 September 1995 and is buried in the Basilian plot of Garden of Gethsemane, Forest Park Lawndale Cemetery, Houston.

'Don,' or 'Coop,' as his confreres knew him, attended public schools before entering St Thomas High School, Houston. Upon graduation in 1940 he enrolled in the University of Houston, but the following year he entered St Basil's Novitiate, Toronto, making first profession on 15 August 1942. He was then appointed to Assumption College (B.A., University of Western Ontario, 1946). He returned to St Thomas High School in 1946 to teach and take his first year of theology. In 1948 he was appointed to St Basil's Seminary, Toronto, to complete theological studies, and was ordained to the priesthood on 29 June 1950 in St Anne's Church, Houston, by Bishop Louis Reicher of Austin, Texas.

In 1951, Father Cooper returned to St Thomas High School, where he remained for the next twenty-five years. He served as treasurer, 1959–67, second councillor of the Basilian community, 1967–8, and principal of the school, 1968–76. In 1976, changing ministry from classroom to parish, he was named assistant at St Theresa's Parish, Sugar Land, Texas, 1976–83. He was elected regional representative for the Western United States Region in 1979, a position he held for ten years. During this time he did some teaching at St Thomas High School, 1983–7, where he took up residence again; but in 1987–9 he was assistant novice master at St Basil's Novitiate, Sugar Land. In 1989 he returned to St Thomas once more, where he supervised the development office until 1995.

A Texan to the marrow of his bones, Don Cooper was gifted with fine southern manners and, although rather shy, brought a good deal of joy to any company. He was simple in his lifestyle, limiting travel to what official duties required. In 1994 he was stricken with cancer, which developed rapidly and led to his being transferred to the Basilian Fathers Residence (Infirmary) in Toronto, in September 1995, where he lived for but ten days. In accordance with his wishes his body was returned to Houston for burial.

BIBLIOGRAPHY: 'Scripture and Our Students [forum],' *Basilian Teacher* 5 (December 1960) 82.
SOURCES: GABF; *Annals* 1 (1950) 289, 7 (1993) 10, 8 (1996) 105–6; *Newsletter* (25 October 1995).

CORRIGAN, John Vincent, priest, was born at Uptergrove, Ontario (archdiocese of Toronto), on 4 December 1907, the son of Hugh Vincent Corrigan and Mary Agnes Long. He died in Toronto on 5 October 1962 and was buried in the Basilian plot of Holy Cross Cemetery, Thornhill, Ontario.

John Corrigan attended high school at Uxbridge, Ontario. In 1925 he went to Assumption College School, Windsor, to complete grade XIII. At the end of the school year he entered St Basil's Novitiate, Toronto, and was professed on 11 August 1927. After studies at Assumption College (B.A., University of Western Ontario, 1930), he went to St Basil's Scholasticate, Toronto, for theology and studies at the Ontario College of Education. He was ordained to the priesthood on 17 December 1933 in St Basil's Church, Toronto, by Bishop Alexander MacDonald.

Father Corrigan taught at St Mary's Boys' High School, Calgary, from 1934 to 1949, and was superior and principal there from 1943 to 1949. The years 1949–52 were spent in graduate studies at St Michael's College, Toronto (M.A., Philosophy, University of Toronto, 1952). After teaching at St Thomas More College, Saskatoon, 1952–5, he was forced by ill health to take up residence at St Basil's Seminary, Toronto, 1955–8, and then at St Michael's College School, Toronto from 1958 until his death.

Father 'Dan' Corrigan, as he was always called, was a big man of even temper and cheerful disposition. He was witty and humorous in his comments on life and people, but not unkind. Throughout his life he was plagued by injuries and ill health. An accident suffered as a student at Assumption College cost him the sight of one eye, while another injury necessitated major brain surgery in 1942. In 1948 he had a spinal fusion, and a further back injury in 1953 was coupled with a heart condition that left him a semi-invalid, although he continued working as he could for nine years more. From 1956 until 1960 he was director of vocations for the Congregation.

BIBLIOGRAPHY:

Book: *Vocation to the Religious Life*. Toronto, 1960.
Pamphlet: *Your Vocation*. Toronto, 1960.
Articles: 'Westward Whoa,' *Basilian* 1 (March 1935) 15; 'Vocation Recruiting,' *Occasional Papers of St Basil's Seminary* 2 (November 1956) 1–22; 'Discussion on the Theology of Religious Vocations,' *Proceedings of the Basilian Meetings to Discuss Vocations* 3 (1957) 52–66. In *Basilian Teacher*: 'Teaching the Mind of Christ,' 1 (January 1956) 2–8; 'Practical Pedagogical Pointers,' 1 (October 1956) 3–8;

'Justice in the Classroom,' 4 (November 1959) 27–31; 'Johnny Doesn't Know How to Study,' 5 (November 1959) 59–63.
SOURCES: GABF; *Annals* 3 (1962) 161–2; *Newsletter* (9 October 1962); *Basilides, Assumption College* (Windsor, 1930).

CORVISY, Lucien, priest, member of the Congregation from 1886 to 1900, was born on 23 May 1861 in Paris (Seine). He died, probably in Périgueux (Dordogne), on 21 January 1931.
Lucien enrolled at an early age in the Ecole cléricale at Périgueux to pursue secondary studies under the Basilian Fathers. He entered the Grand Séminaire de Périgueux, but after receiving the subdiaconate he entered the Basilian novitiate at Beaconfield House, Plymouth, England, on 30 January 1885, and made first profession on 1 February 1886. He was appointed to teach *sixième* at the Collège du Sacré-Coeur, Annonay, February–July 1886, and then went for one year to the French seminary in Rome for theological studies. He was ordained a priest on 9 April 1887 in the basilica of St John Lateran.

After returning to Annonay he taught French literature and grammar to the students specializing in science at the Collège du Sacré-Coeur, 1887–8, and then went to teach *quatrième* and *troisième* at the Ecole cléricale in Périgueux, 1888–92. In 1893, with the permission of the local superior and the superior general, he accepted the post of pastor at the parish of Lunas, arrondissement of Bergerac, diocese of Périgueux. In 1900 the superior general wrote him three times (February, March, and April), summoning him back to the community in Annonay; but he preferred to remain in the diocese of Périgueux to work as a parish priest. He became the pastor at Boulazac on 1 July 1902, and retired from active ministry in January 1914. He served as military chaplain in 1915, and was chaplain to the hospital in Périgueux in 1917.

SOURCE: Pouzol, 'Notices,' Supplément 3.

COSTELLO, John Joseph, priest, was born in Toronto on 12 May 1870, the son of Michael Costello and Mary Downey. He died at Waco, Texas, on 12 February 1906 and was buried in Holy Cross Cemetery, Waco. On 14 October 1960 his body was reinterred in the Basilian plot of Garden of Gethsemane, Forest Park Lawndale Cemetery, Houston.
John Costello was educated in Toronto at St Patrick's Separate School, De La Salle High School, and St Michael's College. Gifted with an

exceptionally rich baritone voice, he went to New York City in 1897 for vocal training and later moved to Washington, D.C. At a celebration for the Grand Army of the Republic, at which President William McKinley and his cabinet were present, John was chosen to sing 'We Are Tenting Tonight on the Old Camp Ground.' The song finished, there was a short moment of silence, then applause that lasted for five minutes. President McKinley rose, called for the singer, took the small flag pin from his lapel and pinned it on the breast of John Costello.

A promising career as a concert and opera singer was cut short by a lung haemorrhage. He returned to Toronto where his health improved to such an extent that Father Laurence *Brennan encouraged him to enter St Basil's Novitiate. After first profession on 11 July 1901, he was appointed to St Michael's College; but, when his health failed, he was sent to a warmer climate at St Basil's College, Waco. He returned to Toronto in 1903 and was ordained to the priesthood on 24 August 1904. His first Mass was the only high Mass he was able to sing. After ordination he went back to St Basil's College, Waco. He had to be taken out of teaching and was sent to Provident Heights Sanitarium, south of Waco, where he died two years later.

SOURCES: GABF; *Annals* 3 (1960) 18; Charles Collins, 'Basilians I Have Known,' transcribed in Robert J. Scollard, 'Historical Notes C.S.B.' 10 76–82 (GABF); Raphael O'Loughlin, *Basilian Leaders from Texas* (Houston, 1991) 88; R.J. Scollard, *Historical Notes* (Toronto, n.d.), 10 76–8.

COSTELLO, Paul, priest, member of the Congregation 1911–20, was born at Ennismore, Ontario (diocese of Peterborough), on 4 July 1888, the son of Michael Costello and Ellen McCarthy. He was a cousin of Father Simon *Perdue. Father Costello died at Peterborough. Ontario, on 8 January 1942 and was buried there in St Peter's Cemetery.

Paul received his early education in Ennismore. In 1904 he went to St Michael's College, Toronto, where he followed the classical course, took two years of philosophy, and was a good football player. He entered St Basil's Novitiate, Toronto, on 15 September 1911, made his theological course at St Basil's Scholasticate, Toronto, and was ordained to the priesthood on 26 September 1915.

Father Costello earned an M.A. at the Catholic University of America, Washington, D.C., 1915–16. He taught at St Thomas College, Chatham, New Brunswick, from September 1916 until November 1917, when he enlisted as a chaplain in the Canadian Army. He served overseas with distinction. After his discharge in July 1919, finding that he had lost all inclination for teaching, he obtained an indult of exclaustration (28 May 1920). Having joined his native diocese of Peterborough, he served as first assistant to Bishop Michael O'Brien at St Peter's Cathedral, 17 July 1919–8 July 1926, and was then rector of the cathedral from 8 July 1926 until 29 November 1935, when he was named pastor of Our Lady of Mount Carmel Parish, Hastings, Ontario, where he remained until his death. He kept in close contact with the community, declaring that he owed everything to the Basilians.

SOURCE: GABF.

COTE, Alfred Jacques, priest, was born in River Canard, Ontario (diocese of Toronto, since 1856 of London), on 27 July 1855, the son of Isidore Côté and Françoise Meloche. He died in Windsor on 9 April 1933 and is buried there in the Basilian plot of Assumption Cemetery.

Alfred Côté enrolled in second Latin at Assumption College, Windsor, in January 1872. As a student he always attained highest marks. In 1877 he entered the Grand Séminaire in Montreal, where he was advised that his vocation was to a religious community rather than to the diocesan priesthood. He entered St Basil's Novitiate, which was then located at Assumption College, Windsor. He took final vows on 17 January 1881 and was ordained to the priesthood on 16 June 1881.

After ordination Father Côté stayed on at Assumption College to teach Latin and to direct the college glee club and liturgical music in the college chapel. In 1897 he began a series of parish appointments: assistant at Ste Anne's Parish, Detroit, 1897–9, 1901–7, assistant at St John the Baptist Parish in Amherstburg, Ontario, 1899–1901, 1921–7; pastor, then assistant, of Assumption Parish, Windsor, 1907–21. He lived at Assumption College from 1927 until his death in 1933.

Father Côté served on the Basilian provincial council, 1912–22. His intimates in the community called him 'Charlie.' Students at Assumption College knew him best for his abilities in music and in athletics, particularly baseball and handball. A shrewd and prudent pastor, he was perfectly bilingual. In the early 1920s, after being diagnosed with diabetes, he was treated in Toronto with insulin as one of the patients on whom it was clinically tested before its discovery was publicly announced.

Writing about Father Côté in the *Basilian,* Father Charles *Collins described him as 'rather tall, athletic in build, and full of grace in his movements. His countenance ever bore a benign look and one could not picture him in a fit of temper. His genial smile and ever ready humour, his patience with our crudities were but surface indications of that evenness of disposition and calmness that hung about him all his life.' Father Côté grew old gracefully, a slow decline without much change in his buoyant disposition.

SOURCES: GABF; *Basilides, Assumption College* (Windsor, 1930); C. Collins, 'Basilians I Have Known, Alfred J. Côté,' *Basilian* 2 (January 1936) 4–5; Kirley, *Congregation in France* 12, 14, 34, 40, 57; Lajeunesse, *Assumption Parish.*

COTTER, George Barry, scholastic, was born in Toronto in 1851, the son of George Cotter, M.D., and Charlotte Trotter. He died at Guelph, Ontario, on 22 September 1875, and was buried in the Basilian plot of St Michael's Cemetery, Toronto.

Barry Cotter's father, the attending physician at St Michael's College, Toronto, died when his son was still young. His mother placed the boy in St Michael's College early in 1862, where he was nicknamed 'Mouse' on account of a facial expression. His mother entered the Sisters of St Joseph in Toronto in May of that year and was given the name Sister Mary Jane Frances. Barry was present when his sister entered the same convent in 1871 and received the name Sister Mary of the Sacred Heart. Barry Cotter's name does not appear in the records of St Basil's Novitiate before it was moved in 1873 from St Michael's College to Assumption College in Windsor, but his name does appear among the scholastics at St Michael's College in 1874–5. At the time of his death in 1875 he was on sick-leave, living with his uncle, Mr C.E. Romain, in Guelph. Sister Mary of the Sacred Heart died on 12 November 1889.

SOURCE: GABF.

COUGHLIN, Charles Edward, priest, member of the Congregation 1912–23, was born on 25 October 1891 in Hamilton, Ontario, the only surviving child of Thomas Coughlin and Amelia Mahoney. He died at Bloomfield Hills, Michigan, on 26 October 1979, and is buried in the priests plot of Holy Sepulchre Cemetery, Detroit.

Charles Coughlin attended St Mary's School, Hamilton, and enrolled in St Michael's College, Toronto, in 1907. Among his first teachers were

Fathers Henry *Carr, Vincent *Murphy, and Albert *Hurley. In his honours philosophy course he studied under Fathers Adolphe *Vaschalde, Robert *McBrady, and Daniel *Cushing. After graduation (B.A., University of Toronto, 1911) he took a three-month tour in Europe, then entered St Basil's Novitiate, Toronto, in September and made his profession of vows in September 1912. His studies in theology at St Basil's Scholasticate, Toronto, were interrupted by six months (January–June 1914) of sick leave at St Basil's College, Waco, Texas, where (according to an interview with Shelden Marcus) he taught philosophy and helped St Basil's defeat Baylor University in a baseball game. He was ordained to the priesthood on 29 June 1916 in St Basil's Church, Toronto, by Archbishop Neil McNeil. In his class were Fathers E.J. *McCorkell and T.P. *O'Rourke.

Father Coughlin taught philosophy and English literature for six or seven years at Assumption College, Windsor; but when the Basilians adopted a stricter vow of poverty in 1922 he exercised the option to withdraw, using the occasion to launch an acrimonious attack on the Community that was countered by an equally testy reply from Alphonse McIntyre, a lay member of the Assumption faculty (Shook 283–4).

Having already been in the habit of doing Sunday ministry to some acclaim in Detroit, Father Coughlin applied for incardination there and was accepted by Archbishop Michael Gallagher on 26 November 1923. After short appointments to St Augustine's Parish, Kalamazoo, St Leo's Parish, Detroit, and North Branch, Michigan, he was given the task in 1926 of building a new church to be named after the recently canonized St Theresa of Lisieux ('the Little Flower') in Royal Oak, a suburb of Detroit. When it opened, the Ku Klux Klan burned a cross on its lawn. To combat the Klan and to extol religious freedom and democracy, Father Coughlin began in October 1926 a trial series of sermons broadcast on the new medium of radio. Within a year he was receiving as many as three thousand letters a week, many containing money, to the extent that he paid off the church debt quickly and began construction of a large new shrine to replace the church that was already too small. In 1929 radio stations in Chicago and Cincinnati aired his sermons, and in 1930–1 the CBS network broadcast them to twenty-three states. The sermons became less religious and more political, directed against 'greed-blinded capitalists' on whom he blamed the Great Depression. He subsequently attacked President Herbert Hoover, prohibition, Communism, Wall Street bankers, and the gold standard. CBS cancelled his contract in 1931–2, but independent stations took up the slack. Franklin Delano Roosevelt, running against Hoover, sought and received support from Father Coughlin.

Coughlin's Radio League of the Little Flower organized a political arm, the National Union for Social Justice, whose 'Preamble and Principles' included some basic points of Catholic social teachings but also a heavy political agenda. Forty secretaries handled a volume of letters greater than that received by the White House. The alliance with F.D.R. did not last, and Coughlin supported a third-party candidate in the 1936 election. When the latter amassed only nine-hundred thousand votes, Coughlin stopped broadcasting for two months. His comeback in 1937 was marked by increasingly radical tirades that his critics termed crypto-fascist and anti-Semitic. Father Coughlin denied both charges. Seeing Communism as a greater menace than Hitler's Germany, he used his weekly newspaper *Social Justice* to advance an isolationist policy. In 1941, when the United States joined the War, the Post Office would no longer grant economical rates to the paper, and a grand jury was formed to look into charges of sedition. Coughlin's grass-roots support was seriously weakened by wartime patriotism and full employment. Cardinal Edward Mooney ordered an end to the radio talks in 1941. Father Charles Coughlin retired in relative obscurity at the Shrine of the Little Flower and later to Bloomfield Hills, a suburb of Detroit.

BIBLIOGRAPHY:
Books: *By the Sweat of Thy Brow. A Series of Sermons Broadcast ... from the Shrine of the Little Flower, October 1930–February 1931.* Detroit, February 1931. *Father Coughlin's Radio Sermons Complete.* Baltimore, 1931. *'What Is Truth?' A Reply to Dr. Clarence True Wilson.* Royal Oak, 1931. *Father Coughlin's Radio Discourses, 1931–1932.* Detroit, 1932. *Driving Out the Moneychangers.* Detroit, 1933. *New Deal in Money.* Detroit, 1933. *Eight Discourses on the Gold Standard and Other Kindred Subjects.* Detroit, 1933. *Eight Lectures on Labor, Capital and Justice.* Royal Oak, 1934. *A Series of Lectures on Social Justice.* Royal Oak, 1935. *A Series of Lectures ... May 5th to June 9th, 1935.* Royal Oak, c.1935. *Money! Questions and Answers.* Royal Oak, c.1936. *Series of Lectures on Social Justice.* Detroit, 1936; repr. New York, 1971. *Sixteen Radio Lectures, 1938 Series. ...* Royal Oak, 1938. *Not Anti-Semitism but Anti-Communism.* Royal Oak, 1938. *Persecution, Jewish and Christian.* Royal Oak, 1938. *A Chapter on Intolerance.* Royal Oak, 1938. *Is Christ the Messias?* Royal Oak, 1938. *Why Leave Our Own? 13 Addresses on Christianity and Americanism ... January 8–April 2, 1939.* Detroit, c.1939. *Am I an Anti-Semite?*

9 Addresses on Various 'isms,' Answering the Question. ... Detroit, c.1939. *Emmanuel, God with Us.* Royal Oak, 1941. *I Take My Stand.* Royal Oak, c.1940. *Bishops versus Pope.* Bloomfield Hills, Mich., [1969]. *Lectures on Social Justice.* New York, 1971. *Father Coughlin on Money and Gold; Three Pamphlets.* New York, 1974.
Articles: In *Social Justice National Weekly*: 'Communism, Capitalism and the Future,' 1 (10 March 1936) 8–10; 'Social Justice Applied to Labor,' 1 (27 March 1936) 8–10; 'A Week of Disasters,' 1 (3 April 1936) 8–10; 'A Message to the National Union,' 1 (17 April 1936) 8–10; 'Sham Taxation and Gag Legislation,' 1 (10 April 1936); 'The Real Issue,' 2 (21 September 1936) 2; 'Production at a Profit for the Farmer,' 2 (28 September 1936) 2; 'We the People,' 2 (5 October 1936) 8–9; 'The Story behind the President's Speech,' 2 (12 October 1936) 8–9, 14; 'Reply to a Right Reverend Monsignor,' 2 (19 October 1936) 2, 15; 'The Issue: Peace or War,' 2 (2 November 1936) 8–9; 'The Myth of Social Security,' 2 (9 November 1936) 8; 'As for the Future ...?' (16 November 1936) 8–9; 'Dictatorship and Labor,' 2 (17 October 1937) 14–15.
Audios: The Library of Congress, Washington, D.C., has a large collection of sound recordings of Father Coughlin's radio talks. See also: http://chnm.gmu.edu/courses/hist409/coughlin/coughlin.html.
SOURCES: GABF; Shook, *Catholic Education* 283–4; *Yearbook SMC* (1911). Mark Osbaldeston, 'In the Same Hour: Catholicism, Ecumenism, and Politics in the Broadcasts of Father Charles Edward Coughlin, 1930–36,' M.A. dissertation (Queen's University, 1991), includes a review of eight books and a dozen articles written about Father Coughlin, most of them negative towards him. For a balanced treatment see Shelden Marcus, *Father Coughlin: The Tumultuous Life of the Priest of the Little Flower* (Boston, 1973). For a laudatory view see Louis B. Ward, *Father Charles E. Coughlin: An Authorized Biography* (Detroit, 1933); see also Ruth Mugglebee, *Father Coughlin of the Shrine of the Little Flower* (Boston, 1933); but her later, enlarged edition (New York, 1937) takes a less positive stance in its closing pages.

COUGHLIN, Hubert Patrick, priest, was born at Mount Carmel, Ontario (diocese of London), on 16 June 1902, the son of Bartholomew Coughlin and Johanna Curtin. A sister, joining the Sisters of St Joseph of London, took the name Sister Juliana. He died on 6 May 1983 and is buried in the Basilian plot of Holy Cross Cemetery, Thornhill, Ontario.
The Coughlin family having moved to London some time before 1914, Hubert attended London Collegiate, 1916–20, and then studied at Assumption College, Windsor, for two years. He entered St Basil's Novitiate, Toronto, in 1922 and was professed on 13 August 1923. He

was then appointed to Assumption (B.A., University of Western Ontario, 1924). He began his theology that year at St Michael's College in Toronto, moving to St Basil's Scholasticate, Toronto, for the years 1925-7. During the year 1925-6 he also attended the Ontario College of Education, earning assistant's certification for high school teaching. In 1927 he was awarded an M.A. in philosophy from the University of Toronto. He was ordained to the priesthood in St Michael's Cathedral, Toronto, on 11 June 1927 by Bishop John McNally. After ordination he went to Rome to study theology at the Angelicum (S.T.L., 1928; S.T.D., 1929; thesis topic: 'The Obligation of Conscience in Civil Laws'). The remainder of his life was spent in Toronto.

'Hub' Coughlin was a dynamic teacher of theology and a shrewd administrator, and used both talents simultaneously throughout his life, seemingly without difficulty. He taught theology at St Basil's Scholasticate ('Seminary' from 1937), Toronto, from 1929 to 1947, and lived there with the exception of two years at St Michael's College, 1940-2. From 1938 to 1961 he also taught at the Pontifical Institute of Mediaeval Studies, Toronto, while also teaching religious knowledge to undergraduates at St Michael's College. His sharp mind, combined with fluency of expression and skill in dialogue, made his classes animated and satisfying to his students.

The Congregation entrusted Father Coughlin with administrative duties which he discharged efficiently and easily despite his full schedule of teaching. At St Basil's Scholasticate he served as second councillor, 1929-34, treasurer, 1931-4, and superior and master of scholastics, 1934-8. In 1936 he was elected to the general council of the Basilian Fathers, and remained a councillor for the next thirty-one years – one of the longest tenures in the annals of the Basilian Fathers. He served as vicar general for three superiors general (E.J. *McCorkell, 1942-54, George B. *Flahiff, 1954-61, and Joseph C. *Wey, 1961-7). In this post he had a major role in the yearly assignments given to Basilians. He was named secretary general of the Congregation from 1936 to 1948, and was superior of the curial house for three separate periods: 1943-4, 1949-55 and 1957-64. In those many tasks and responsibilities Father Coughlin always gave an impression of quiet control. A master organizer with keen perception of persons and problems, he was an *éminence grise* in the best sense, appreciated both by his colleagues on the council and by the community at large. He listened and he acted.

At the 1967 general chapter, when his long term on the council came to an end, Father Coughlin was extended a vote of thanks, expressed by a standing ovation from the capitulants which lasted a full five minutes. After the chapter he moved to the University of St Michael's College as assistant to the registrar and awards officer, functions which he maintained for ten years. Then from 1977 to 1980 he was in charge of allocating space for classes and other functions, while also working with the alumni. During these years he also served the archdiocese of Toronto as advocate in the marriage tribunal, 1968–72, and as judge and defender of the bond, 1972–8. He was first councillor for the local community at St Michael's for the year 1971–2. Affable and ever gracious, Father Coughlin drew the energy for his remarkable service from his love of the Basilian community. He was never happier than when playing bridge or watching sports or overseeing a community project. He enjoyed being teased, though he commanded the respect of all.

BIBLIOGRAPHY:
Pamphlet: *Sacrifice of the Mass.* Pamphlet series, 3. Toronto, 1933.
Article: 'The Study of Theology,' *Basilian* 2 (May 1936) 84–5.
SOURCES: GABF; *Annals* 5 (1974) 13, (1978) 259, 6 (1983) 292–4; *Newsletter* (16 May 1983).

COULET, Gustave, priest, was born on 22 May 1850 at Langogne (Lozère, diocese of Mende). He died on 5 December 1930.
Gustave Coulet studied at the Petit Séminaire de Méximieux (Ain), and also at the Petit Séminaire de Vernoux (Ardèche). At the end of the Franco-Prussian War in 1871 he was conscripted to fight in the army of Versailles against the Commune of Paris. He made his novitiate at Feyzin (Isère, now Rhône). While studying theology he taught at Basilian schools: Collège du Sacré-Coeur, Annonay, commercial, 1872–3; Collège du Bourg-Saint-Andéol (Ardèche), 1873–4; Collège du Sacré-Coeur, *professeur de cinquième*, 1874–7. He made his final profession on 17 September 1875 and received the subdiaconate the next day at the hands of Bishop Armand de Charbonnel. Bishop Joseph-Michel-Frédéric Bonnet of Viviers ordained him deacon on 23 September 1876; and, on 22 September 1877, Bishop de Charbonnel ordained him priest. All these ordinations took place in the college chapel.

Of his fifty-three years of priesthood, Father Coulet spent fourteen teaching, 1877–91, and thirty-nine in parish ministry, 1891–1930. His teaching years were apportioned as follows: 1877–9 at the Collège

Saint-Pierre, Châteauroux (Indre); 1879–88 at the Collège Saint-Charles, Blidah, Algeria; 1888–90 at the Collège Saint-Augustin, Bône, Algeria. In both institutions in Algeria he taught the senior classes. In his final year in North Africa he was *professeur de troisième* at the Collège Saint-Charles.

In 1891 he was appointed curate-chaplain to the Calvary Shrine at Prades (Ardèche) and ministered to pilgrims there until 17 June 1903 when, at 8:00 a.m., the chief of police and twenty-five *gendarmes*, executing the anticlerical policies of the Third Republic, expelled the Basilians and worshippers and padlocked the doors of the chapel. Father Coulet accepted an appointment from Bishop Joseph-Michel-Frédéric Bonnet as curate at Gravières (Ardèche), canton of Les Vans, where he was to remain in active ministry until his death on 5 December 1930.

The diocesan weekly *Semaine religieuse de Viviers* described Father Coulet as 'small of stature, surprisingly young-looking, with a winning smile and mild manner that endeared him to the faithful. People were edified by his piety and life of regularity.'

SOURCES: GABF; Kirley, *Community in France* 184, 186, 203; Kirley, *Congregation in France* 159; Pouzol, 'Notices'; *Semaine religieuse de Viviers* (26 December 1930) 636.

COUPAT, Henri, priest, was born on 24 December 1805 in Annonay, the son of Jean-François Régis Coupat and Marie-Madeleine Clozel. He died at Feyzin (Isère, now Rhône) on 5 August 1868 and was buried beside Father Julien *Actorie on the grounds of the novitiate at Feyzin.

Henri Coupat attended the Christian Brothers' school in Annonay and served as an altar boy in the old Notre-Dame church, which stood on what is now the Place de la Liberté. He studied at Sainte-Barbe, the minor seminary section of the Collège des Cordeliers, and went to the Grand Séminaire de Viviers for two years, 1826–8. In 1828 he sought admission to the Association of Priests of St Basil and was professed on 3 September 1830. His ordination to the priesthood took place on 17 December 1831. During theological studies he was *professeur de sixième*, 1828–30, and *professeur de quatrième*, 1830–1, at the Collège des Cordeliers.

After ordination Father Coupat taught for twenty-six years, first in the Collège des Cordeliers, as *professeur de troisième*, 1834–7, and *professeur de seconde*, 1837–57. He was one of those Basilians who readily accepted the vows of 1852. In 1857 he was appointed director of studies in the Collège des Cordeliers and remained in that office for two years. At the chapter in which his friend, Father Julien *Actorie, became superior general on 30 August 1859, Father Coupat was elected to the general council, with re-election in 1862 and 1865. For three years, 1859-62, he served as superior of the Petit Séminaire de Vernoux (Ardèche), and then went to the Collège de Privas to be assistant to the superior, Father André *Fayolle, who had fallen seriously ill. By March 1867, Father Coupat himself had fallen ill and, after fruitless consultation with doctors, retired in June of that year to the scholasticate in Annonay, where it was hoped his health would improve. In January 1868, he moved to the novitiate at Feyzin. Each day after celebrating Mass he would go to pray at the grave of his close friend, Father Julien *Actorie.

Known as 'le bon père Coupat,' he was beloved of all, a kind, generous, and deeply spiritual man. He willingly preached retreats and served as chaplain to various communities of women religious. A highlight in his life was a trip to Rome and audience with Pope Pius IX in August 1863, accompanying the superior general, Father Julien *Actorie, to seek approbation of the new version of the Basilian Constitutions.

SOURCES: Chomel, *Collège d'Annonay* 221, 296-7; Kirley, *Community in France* 28, 150n384; Pouzol, 'Notices'; Roume, *Origines* 346.

COYLE, William Ambrose, priest, was born on 13 July 1914 in Winnipeg, Manitoba (archdiocese of St Boniface, since 1915 of Winnipeg), the eldest of the five sons of Daniel Coyle and Jeannette Farrell. He died in Calgary, Alberta, on 10 June 1976 and is buried there in the Basilian plot of St Mary's Cemetery.

A member of the cathedral parish in Winnipeg, where he was baptised and confirmed, 'Bill' graduated from St Paul's College School, Winnipeg, in 1933 and went on to the University of Manitoba (B.A., 1936). The Congregation of the Holy Cross, to which he had applied, referred him to the Basilians, much to the pleasure of Archbishop Alfred Sinnott, who expressed his satisfaction to Father *Carr, then superior general. Bill entered St Basil's Novitiate, Toronto, in 1936 and was professed on 15 August 1937. He studied theology at St Basil's Seminary, Toronto, for two years, after which he attended the Ontario College of Education for one year. He was ordained to the priesthood on

17 August 1941 in St Mary's Cathedral, Winnipeg, by Archbishop Sinnott.

In 1942 Father Coyle was appointed to St Mary's Boys' High School, Calgary, where he spent the rest of his life teaching, directing the library, and promoting the arts of music and drama among the students. He served the Basilian community in Calgary as superior from 1961 to 1967. Continuing to improve his education credentials all his life, he earned teaching certification from the Province of Alberta in 1969 and a Diploma in Library Science from the University of London in 1968.

With an infectious laugh, the expression of a rich and ready sense of humour, Father Coyle seemed always in good spirits. A born entertainer, his talents found full scope in the musicals he loved to stage. He kept in touch with the graduates of the school by a group he founded, 'The Columbian Players,' who were particularly noted for their presentations of Gilbert and Sullivan operettas.

His only complaint during the long months he spent in hospital during the last two years of his life was his enforced absence from the students and from the Basilian community; but he was never heard to complain of the painful illnesses which kept him there. His thirty-four years in Calgary made him known and well loved by many thousands of Calgarians.

BIBLIOGRAPHY: 'A Few Salient Points,' *Forum* (October 1964) 8–10.
SOURCES: GABF; *Annals* 5 (1977) 248–9; *Newsletter* (15 June 1976).

CRESPIN, Jean, priest, was born on 3 February 1848 at Marvejols (Lozère, diocese of Mende). He died in Montreal, Canada, on 9 May 1919 and is buried there in the Cimetière de l'Est.

After primary and secondary school in his home diocese Jean Crespin entered the Basilian Congregation and took his first vows on 18 September 1874. During theological studies he taught commercial classes, first at the college at Bourg-Saint-Andéol (Ardèche), 1873–6, and then at the Collège du Sacré-Coeur in Annonay, 1878–80. He received the diaconate on 23 September 1876 and priesthood on 18 September 1880 at the hands of Bishop Joseph-Michel-Frédéric Bonnet of Viviers, in the chapel of the Collège du Sacré-Coeur, Annonay.

One year after ordination Father Crespin went to Canada, where he was to spend the rest of his life. He arrived at his first appointment, St John the Baptist Parish, Amherstburg, Ontario, on 5 September 1881. A few years later the first signs of a progressive mental illness appeared, and in 1888 he was transferred to St Michael's College, Toronto, where he worked as librarian until 1894 when institutional care became necessary. On 20 October 1894 he was admitted to La Retraite Saint-Benoît in Montreal, Quebec, where he lived until his death twenty-five years later.

Father Crespin was short, thickset, and tremendously strong. He was a meticulous worker, and at St Michael's College recorded the 3401 volumes then owned by the college in a carefully handwritten catalogue of over two hundred pages. One of his eccentricities was to fill scrapbooks with doctors' prescriptions, home remedies, and newspaper items on health.

SOURCES: GABF; Kirley, *Community in France* 186, 211n507, 214n516, 236n564; Pouzol, 'Notices.'

CROSS, James Francis, priest, was born in Detroit on 28 February 1915, the eldest of the four children of Charles C. Cross and Olivène Doucet. He died in Rochester on 27 February 1976 and is buried there in the Basilian plot of Holy Sepulchre Cemetery.

After attending Birmingham High School, Detroit, for two years, 'Jimmy' transferred to Holy Name Institute, which became Catholic Central High School in 1936, graduating in 1934. He entered St Basil's Novitiate, Toronto, and made his first profession on 12 September 1935. During the next four years he studied at St Michael's College, Toronto (B.A., University of Toronto, 1939). He taught for two years as a scholastic, first at Aquinas Institute, Rochester, 1939–40, and then at Catholic Central High School, 1940–1. He earned the Michigan teaching certification during his year in Detroit.

In August 1941 he entered St Basil's Seminary, Toronto, for four years of theological studies. During this time he also taught science at St Michael's College School. He was ordained to the priesthood in St Basil's Church, Toronto, on 20 August 1944 by Archbishop James Charles McGuigan.

In 1945 Father Cross was appointed to Aquinas Institute, where he taught science for the rest of his life. He pursued further studies in science for three summers at Cornell University and at the University of Rochester, earning an M.Ed. from the latter institution in 1958. He also became certified as a teacher with the State of New York.

What distinguished Father Cross was his singleness of purpose in life: an overwhelming desire to serve God with his whole being. This became the basis of all he did or spoke, whether in the classroom, with students outside of class, at Massaweepie Boy Scout Camp, at the various parishes where he assisted on weekends, or at home in the community, where he was especially attentive to older confreres. In his room were to be found all kinds of flora and fauna – all to be used to enliven his classes. His students affectionately referred to him as 'Jungle Jim.'

An indefatigable defender of the faith, he sought constantly for the truth; and, when he thought he had found it, nothing could sway him from it. He found it frequently in the writings of St Thomas Aquinas, whose poem 'O banquet most admirable' (*Opusculum* 57) he chose for the meditation at common prayer on the morning of 27 February 1976, the day before his sixty-first birthday. After teaching all that day, he collapsed and died at the foot of the statue of St Thomas which stands at the entrance to Aquinas Institute.

SOURCES: GABF; *Annals* 1 (1944) 99, 5 (1977) 245–6; *Newsletter* (8 March 1976).

CROWLEY, Clifford Joseph, priest, was born on 26 April 1916 (baptismal record; other sources indicate 1915), at Bonfield, Ontario (diocese of Pembroke), the son of John Edmund Pigeau and Marie Louise Giroux. He died in Toronto on 17 January 1992 and is buried in the Basilian plot of Holy Cross Cemetery, Thornhill, Ontario.

'Cliff' Crowley, baptized Cléophas Joseph Pigeau, was given the name 'Clifford Joseph Crowley' in 1923 when he was adopted by Cornelius and Ellen Crowley, the parents of Father Cornelius *Crowley. Cliff's natural mother had died in 1918. His natural father moved to Toronto to raise his family, but economic difficulties obliged him to return to northern Ontario, leaving his eight-year-old son to be raised by the Crowley family. Cliff attended St Anthony's and St Monica's separate schools and Northern Vocational School in Toronto. He graduated from the latter after a four-year course in mechanical drafting and junior matriculation. He entered St Michael's College in 1934 for senior matriculation, which he completed in 1936. That year he entered St Basil's Novitiate, Toronto, and was professed on 15 August 1937. He began university studies at St Michael's College and completed them at Assumption College, Windsor (B.A., Philosophy, English, and French, University of Western Ontario, 1942). As a scholastic he taught at St Thomas High School, Houston, 1942–3, then attended the Ontario

College of Education, Toronto, earning high school assistant certification in 1944. While studying theology at St Basil's Seminary, Toronto, he taught at St Michael's College School and obtained teaching certification in Industrial Arts and Crafts from the Ontario Department of Education in 1946. He was ordained to the priesthood on 29 June 1947 in St Basil's Church, Toronto, by Cardinal James Charles McGuigan.

After teaching at St Michael's College, 1948–9, Father Crowley received a series of appointments to pastoral ministry: assistant pastor, Assumption Parish, Windsor, 1949–58, and Holy Rosary Parish, Toronto, 1958–61; pastor, St Mary's of the Assumption Parish, Owen Sound, Ontario, 1961–7; pastor, Assumption Parish, Windsor, 1967–73 (also rector from 1970 on); pastor, St Basil's Parish, Toronto, 1973–5; assistant pastor, St Pius X Parish, Calgary, 1976–7. He took a year of study at the Divine Word Centre, London, Ontario, 1975–6. From 1977 to 1982 he lived with the Basilian Fathers of Lethbridge, Alberta, serving as hospital chaplain, assistant and pastor of the parish at Coalhurst, and rector from 1979 on. He was superior of St Joseph's College, Edmonton, from 1982 to 1985. He lived semi-retired at St Basil's Parish, Ottawa, from 1985 to 1988, during which time he spent a year with the Basilian community in Annonay. He lived at the Basilian Fathers Residence (Infirmary) from 1988 until his death.

Cliff Crowley was small of stature, gentle of manner, and admirably precise in his ministry, religious observance, dress, and speech. He was a skilled carpenter, builder, and 'handyman.' A professor at St Joseph's College liked Father Crowley's homilies because 'he preached the love of God.' His year of studies at the age of sixty and his months in France to improve his French at the age of seventy indicate his zeal and conscientiousness. He was affable and obliging, and readily saw the humorous side of life.

SOURCES: GABF; *Annals* 1 (1947) 151, 6 (1988) 591, 7 (1993) 117–19; *Newsletter* (12 February 1992).

CROWLEY, Cornelius Patrick Joseph, priest, member of the Congregation 1934–73, brother of Father Clifford *Crowley, son of Cornelius Crowley and Ellen Herlihy, was born in Toronto on 14 September 1914. He died in Windsor on 6 April 1995.

'Con' Crowley received both high school and three years of his university education at St Michael's College, Toronto, before entering St Basil's Novitiate, Toronto, in 1933. After making first profession on 15

August 1934 he returned to St Michael's College to complete his undergraduate work, 1934–6 (B.A., University of Toronto, 1936), winning the Governor General's Gold Medal at graduation. He studied theology at St Basil's Scholasticate, Toronto, 1936–8 (St Basil's Seminary from 1937). After teaching during the year 1938–9 at Catholic Central High School, Detroit, he completed his theology course at St Basil's Seminary, 1939–41, and was ordained to the priesthood by Archbishop James Charles McGuigan on 15 August 1940.

Father Crowley taught at the high school of St Michael's College, 1941–2, at Catholic Central High School, Detroit, 1942–3, and at the high school of Assumption College, Windsor, 1943–6. He did graduate work in English literature at the University of Michigan, 1946–51 (Ph.D., 1952). From 1951 to retirement he was engaged in teaching and administration at Assumption University, and from 1963 at the University of Windsor. He was both Dean of Graduate Studies and Head of the English Department from 1960 to 1967. He also directed the Assumption Players for over five years in such productions as *The Madwoman of Chaillot* and *The Little Foxes*. His production of *The Glass Menagerie* was one of four college plays invited to the National Catholic Theatre Conference, Kansas City, Missouri, 1957. In 1962 he gave a series of radio talks on the Canadian Broadcasting Corporation's 'Trans-Canada Catholic Hour.'

In 1973 Cornelius Crowley was dispensed from the obligations arising from the priesthood and religious profession. He married and was survived by his wife, Nancy.

BIBLIOGRAPHY:
Books: Ed. (with Neal M. Veil CSB) *Modern Catholic Poetry for Boys and Girls. An Anthology*. Toronto and Vancouver, 1938; repr. 1939. *A First Book of Modern Catholic Prose and Poetry*. Toronto 1947. *A Second Book of Modern Catholic Prose and Poetry*. Toronto, 1947. *The Human Image: Twenty-six Scripts of Radio Talks As Given on CBC*. Windsor, 1960. *The Legend of the Wanderings of the Spear of Longinus. A Medieval Irish Folk Tale*. St Louis, 1972.
Pamphlet: *The Human Image in Modern British Fiction*. Four talks for the Trans-Canada Catholic Hour, Radio League of St Michael, Toronto. Toronto, 1962 (mimeographed).
Articles: 'Why Argue?,' *Basilian* 3 (January 1937) 11; 'Thoughts by the Lake,' *Basilian* 3 (October 1937) 83; 'Summer Interlude,' *Basilian* 3 (October 1937) 96; 'A Singing Convert: Alfred Noyes,' *Basilian* 3 (November 1937) 116–18, 120; 'Idolatry – 1937 Model,' *Basilian* 3 (December 1937) 127; 'Padraic Colum,' *Basil-*

ian 4 (February 1938) 32–4; 'Songs from the Antipodes: The Poetry of Eileen Duggen,' *Basilian* 4 (June 1938) 113–15; 'The Structural Pattern of Charles Williams' *Descent into Hell*,' *Papers of the Michigan Academy of Science, Arts & Letters* 39 (1954) 421–8; 'Intuition and Tyrone Guthrie,' *Catholic Theatre* (November 1955); 'One Creative Writer Equals Five Philosophers,' *Basilian Teacher* 2 (December 1957) 6–7; 'Education and the Arts,' *Education Past the Crossroads* (Windsor, 1957) 10–16; 'Letter on the Basilian Educational Ideal,' *Two Letters* (Chapter documents) (Toronto, 1960) 1–13; 'Creativity and the Unity of the Sciences,' *Basilian Teacher* 4 (May 1960) 229–34; 'The Theological Universe of Graham Greene,' *Basilian Teacher* 7 (January 1963) 121–9; 'Canadian Literature – English,' *New Catholic Encyclopedia* (New York, 1967) 3 20–1; 'Let There Be More Light: The Role of the Artist in Contemporary Society,' *Culture* 26 (Spring 1965) 264–9; 'Science and Human Values' [part of a 'report of a seminar held... under the auspices of the Canada Council, 12–16 July 1965': 'Science, Technology and Society'], *Engineering Journal* (Montreal) 48 (November 1965) 25–30; 'Failure of Nerve: H.G. Wells,' *University of Windsor Review* 2 no. 2 (Spring 1967) 1–8.

SOURCE: GABF.

CROWLEY, John Joseph, priest, member of the Congregation 1937–70, was born on 14 March 1916 in Kinkora, Ontario (diocese of London), the son of John Crowley and Emerita Kelly. He died at Wawa, Ontario, on 15 September 1987, and was buried in Woodland Cemetery, Wawa, Ontario.

'Jack' Crowley attended Assumption High School, Windsor, 1932–6, entered St Basil's Novitiate, Toronto, in 1936, and was professed on 15 August 1937. He attended St Michael's College, Toronto, 1937–40, and completed his arts course while living at St Basil's Seminary, 1940–1 (B.A., University of Toronto, 1941). He taught at Catholic Central High School, Detroit, 1941–2. He lived at St Michael's College, Toronto, while attending the Ontario College of Education (teaching certification, 1943), and studied theology at St Basil's Seminary, Toronto, 1943–7. He was ordained to the priesthood by Cardinal James Charles McGuigan on 15 August 1947, in St Basil's Church, Toronto.

Father Crowley taught at Aquinas Institute, Rochester, 1947–8, and at St Michael's College School, Toronto, 1948–61 (first councillor 1957–61). He was superior and principal of St Charles College, Sudbury, Ontario, 1961–7, and principal of St Michael's College School, 1967–70.

Father Crowley requested a year's leave of absence from the Basilian

Fathers in 1970 and was subsequently granted laicization. He continued to exercise his administrative skills as principal of Michipicoten High School, Wawa, 1971–81. At death he was survived by his wife, Jeanne, and four children, Paul, Mary, Cathy, and John.

SOURCES: GABF; *Annals* 1 (1946) 119; *Newsletter* (1 October 1987); *Globe and Mail*, 19 September 1987.

CROWLEY, Joseph FLOYD, priest, was born at Loggieville, New Brunswick (diocese of Saint John), on 6 March 1902, the son of John Crowley and Annie Ahearn. He died in Houston on 23 September 1956 and is buried there in the Basilian plot of Garden of Gethsemane, Forest Park Lawndale Cemetery.

Floyd attended grade school in his home town and then worked for some months before resuming his education at St Thomas College, Chatham, New Brunswick, 1919–23. He entered St Basil's Novitiate, Toronto, and was professed on 11 August 1924. Classical and philosophical studies followed at St Michael's College, Toronto. He studied theology at St Basil's Scholasticate in Toronto and was ordained priest on 21 December 1932 in St Basil's Church, Toronto, by Bishop Alexander MacDonald.

All of Father Crowley's priestly life was spent in parish work, with the exception of January–June 1942, when he was treasurer of Assumption College, Windsor. He served as assistant at Assumption Parish, Windsor, 1933–4, St Basil's Parish, Toronto, 1934–5, 1936–7, Holy Rosary Parish, Toronto, 1935–6, Ste Anne's Parish, Detroit, 1942–8, and St Anne's Parish, Houston, 1937–42, 1948–56. During the last two years of his life myclo fibrosis, a disease of the blood, undermined his health and left him a semi-invalid.

Father Matthew *Killoran wrote of him: 'At St Thomas, Floyd took a very prominent part in all plays and skits which the college put on. He was a natural. If he forgot his lines he could easily substitute others that, at times, were better than the originals. ... His best work was in the confessional. He heard confessions at St Anne's, Houston, at all the Masses on Sunday. [Students at the school referred to him as 'Three Hail Marys Crowley.'] He was noted for his short, concise, five-minute sermons, which he always said would "pass with a push." The baptismal records, the instruction of converts as well as the sick-call books in Ste Anne's, Detroit, tell who did the bulk of the parish work when he was an assistant in that parish. Floyd at one time was an excellent first-baseman and a respectable hockey player, which sport he gave up entirely when he went to the seminary. He was also a great story teller. ... [and] never out of sorts' (Letter to R.J. Scollard, 25 February 1968).

SOURCES: GABF; *Annals* 2 (1956) 247–8; *Yearbook SMC* 1935.

CRU, Gustave, priest, was born on 4 January 1855 at Meysse (Ardèche), canton of Rochemaure. He died in the hospital at Montélimar (Drôme) on 23 April 1921.

Gustave Cru studied at Sainte-Barbe, the minor seminary section of the Collège du Sacré-Coeur, Annonay. After his year of rhetoric he made his novitiate at Feyzin (Isère, now Rhône), 1872–3, and took his first vows on 19 September 1873. During theological studies, 1874–9, Gustave exercised various functions at the Annonay college, such as assistant prefect, infirmarian, and *professeur de cinquième*, 1878–9. Final profession took place on 22 September 1876, and the following day he received the subdiaconate from Bishop Joseph-Michel-Frédéric Bonnet of Viviers. Bishop Armand de Charbonnel ordained him deacon on 22 September 1877 and priest on 20 September 1879, both orders conferred in the chapel of the Collège du Sacré-Coeur, Annonay.

After ordination his appointments were as follows: teaching *cinquième*, Ecole cléricale de Périgueux (Dordogne), 1879–80, *septième* then *sixième*, Châteauroux (Indre), 1880–2, prefect and teacher of commercial and *sixième*, Collège Saint-Charles, Blidah, Algeria, 1882–9, prefect of the junior division at the Collège du Sacré-Coeur, Annonay, 1889–90, *septième*, 1890–2, and *sixième*, 1892–3, Petit Séminaire de Vernoux (Ardèche), and *sixième*, Collège Saint-Augustin, Bône, Algeria, 1893–4. He taught at Mary Immaculate College, Beaconfield House, Plymouth, England, 1894–6.

The registers of the Community are not clear as to Father Cru's whereabouts from 1896 to 1903; he may have been a supply teacher at the college in Annonay. When this college was closed in 1903 in the course of the suppression of religious in France, Father Cru retired to Meysse to live with his mother. The local brigadier, in a letter to the prefect of the Ardèche at Privas (26 January 1909), wrote: 'In his situation he has little means of livelihood; he lives on his meagre resources and occasional alms. The Sisters at the convent in Meysse supply this former priest [religious] with one meal a day.' He died in the hospital at Montélimar following an operation.

SOURCES: GABF; Kirley, *Community in France* 184, 201, 206; Kirley, *Congregation in France* 68; Pouzol, 'Notices'; *Semaine religieuse de Viviers* (1 May 1921) 44–5.

CULLINANE, Eugene Augustine, priest, member of the Congregation 1933–56, was born on 7 August 1907, at Kalamazoo, Michigan (archdiocese of Detroit, since 1971 diocese of Kalamazoo), the son of Michael Cullinane and Margaret Liesten. He died at Madonna House, Combermere, Ontario, on 31 March 1997, and is buried there. Eugene Cullinane attended Lincoln School, Kalamazoo, 1913–16, St Aloysius Academy, Fayetteville, Ohio, 1916–21, Assumption High School, Windsor, 1921–4, and Assumption College, 1924–31 (B.A., University of Western Ontario, 1928). He earned an M.A. from the same university in 1931, submitting as his thesis 'The Analogy of Being in Scholasticism.' He entered St Basil's Novitiate, Toronto, in 1932, and was professed in 1933. While studying theology at St Basil's Scholasticate, Toronto, 1933–6, he was also enrolled in the Institute of Mediaeval Studies, Toronto. He was one of a group of Basilian seminarians who became enthusiastic about the Friendship House apostolate of the Baroness Catherine de Hueck, and distributed on her behalf issues of the *Catholic Worker* and *Social Forum*. He was ordained on 17 September 1936 by Archbishop James Charles McGuigan in St Basil's Church, Toronto.

From 1936 to 1939, Father Cullinane did doctoral studies at the Catholic University of America. During two of those years, 1937–9, he was hired to teach classes in sociology there. His intended thesis was 'The Function of the Catholic Priesthood as a Basic Element in the Social Order.' Bernard Daly, a former student of his, wrote in 1999 that instead of writing the thesis Father Cullinane was destined to act it out in everything he wrote and spoke.

Appointed in 1939 to teach economics at St Thomas More College, Saskatoon, he found to his dismay that the prescribed text advocated the *laissez-faire* capitalism of Adam Smith. From 1941 to 1945 he served in the Royal Canadian Air Force in Saskatoon and Ottawa. During the next three years, 1945–8, at St Thomas More College his devotion to social justice led him to commend to the Knights of Columbus the CCF (Co-operative Commonwealth Federation, the forerunner of today's New Democratic Party). At an earlier time the Catholic hierarchy had suspected the CCF of Communist leanings, but in 1943 an official statement of the Canadian episcopal conference cleared the way for Catholics to support it. Father Cullinane judged that Catholics in Saskatchewan were not aware of this new position. Bishop Philip Pocock, however, said that Father Cullinane's speeches, writings, and letters broke a 1946 agreement not to engage in political activity. Intimating that Cullinane was giving St Thomas More a reputation as a 'hot-house of Socialism' and that he was embarrassing the Church, he told the Basilians to remove him from the diocese. Father Hubert *Coughlin, vicar general, objected to the bishop's decision and resolved to arrange Cullinane's appointment to the first position of superior that became vacant. After one year, 1948–9, at St Michael's College, Toronto, he was appointed superior of Aquinas Institute, Rochester, 1949–52, one of the largest Basilian communities. When that term expired, Cullinane was appointed to teach at Assumption University, Windsor, 1952–5.

In 1949 Father Cullinane had once again met the Baroness Catherine de Hueck, who invited him in 1951 and 1953 to teach a summer class in Catholic Social Action at Madonna House, Combermere, Ontario. He was attracted to the spirituality and apostolate fostered there. In 1955 he asked for a leave of absence from the Congregation, and was later incardinated in the vicariate of Whitehorse, Yukon, where he worked in parishes, chaplaincies, and various social causes, often spending summers at Madonna House. After 1977 he was in permanent residence there.

Gregory Baum dedicated his *Catholics and Canadian Socialism* (Toronto, 1980) to Eugene Cullinane. Commenting on this Bernard Daly wrote, 'He was not first and foremost a socialist political activist [but] always primarily the priest-teacher, who saw in the CCF program at that time an exemplification of social truths that he had thought he had to teach, regardless of the cost to himself.' Noteworthy among such achievements in the North was his work with ARDA (Agricultural Rural Development Act) in the Madawaska Valley, Alaska, developing local co-operatives, a rural development association, and an adult training centre.

BIBLIOGRAPHY:
Books: Ed. *Basilides*, published by the students of Assumption on the occasion of the College's diamond jubilee, 1870–1930. Windsor c.1930. Ed. *Basilian*. Toronto, 1935–6. Ed. *Philosophy Ninety-One* (Lectures of Father Henry Carr at St Thomas More College). Privately printed. Saskatoon, c.1948.
Pamphlet: *The Catholic Church and Socialism*. Regina CCF Saskatchewan Section. Regina, Sask., 1948; repr. as *The Simple Truth*. Windsor [Guardian], 1956.
Articles: 'Things as Teachers,' *Basilian* 1 (May 1935) 50; 'Living the Truth,' *Basilian* 2 (February 1936) 33; 'Why Not Be Pioneers [conclusion to editorial series of 1935–6],' *Basilian* 2 (May 1936) 97–100; 'The Spirit of Mediaeval Sociol-

ogy,' *Basilian* 3 (April 1937) 76–8; 'Preface to C.I.O.,' *Basilian* 3 (November 1937) 107–9, 120, and 3 (December 1937) 127; 'Fatima and the Basilians,' *Benedicamus* 2 (March 1949) 26–7, 31; 'Father McGahey,' *Benedicamus* 6 (April 1953) 2–4; 'The Madawaska Development,' *Community Planning Review* 16 no. 1 (1966; repr. Ottawa: Dept. of Forestry of Canada, 1966).
SOURCE: GABF; Bernard Daly, 'A Priest's Tale: The Evolution of the Thinking of Eugene Cullinane CSB, 1936–1948,' *CCHA Historical Studies* 65 (1999) 9–27; *Heartwood* 73, 78, 83–5, 118; Brian F. Hogan, 'Salted with Fire: Studies in Catholic Social Thought and Action in Ontario, 1931–1961,' Ph.D. dissertation (University of Toronto, 1986); Combermere, Madonna House Archives.

CULLITON, Joseph Thomas, priest, was born on 9 July 1935 in Stratford, Ontario (diocese of London), the son of Thomas Culliton and Veronica Carbert. He died in Windsor on 24 November 1990, and is buried there in the Basilian plot of Heavenly Rest Cemetery.
'Joe' attended elementary schools and the first two years of secondary school in Stratford, but graduated in 1952 from Catholic Central High School, London, Ontario. He enrolled in London Teacher's College, where he obtained a First Class Certificate in 1953. That summer he attended McMaster University, Hamilton, where he earned an Elementary Physical Education and Health Certificate. For the next two years, 1953–5, he taught Latin, science, and health and physical education at St Patrick's Separate School, Sarnia, Ontario. In the summers he studied in the extension program of the University of Western Ontario, where he began a major in English and Psychology. In 1955 he enrolled as a boarding student in St Michael's College (B.A., University of Toronto, 1957). That year he also received an interim high school assistant certification, Type B, from the Ontario College of Education. He entered St Basil's Novitiate, Toronto, and took first vows on 12 September 1958.

As a scholastic he taught English at Michael Power High School, Etobicoke, for half a year and took two courses in philosophy at the University of Toronto. He was then transferred to Assumption College School, Windsor, where he taught while continuing studies in philosophy at Assumption University. He received a B.Ed. degree from the University of Toronto in 1960. In 1961 he began theological studies at St Basil's Seminary, Toronto, accompanying these with graduate courses in theology. He was ordained to the priesthood on 13 December 1964 in St Basil's Church, Toronto, by Archbishop George Bernard *Flahiff. From the University of St Michael's College he received an

S.T.B. in 1964 and an M.A. in theology in 1965 (thesis: 'Modern Exegesis of the Pauline Doctrine of the Body of Christ').

Father Culliton was appointed in 1965 to Assumption University and to O'Connor House, which were to be the focal points for his ministry for the rest of his life. For two years he was lecturer in the Department of Religious Studies at the newly founded University of Windsor, and he served at this time as chairman of the London Diocesan Liturgical Commission for the examination of the liturgy in religious houses and institutes of higher learning. From 1967 to 1971 he did doctoral studies at Fordham University (Ph.D., 1972), with a thesis on 'The Cosmic Visions of John Dewey and Teilhard de Chardin: A Comparative Study.'

During his last year at Fordham, Father Culliton made arrangements with the Basilian Fathers general council and with the local community at O'Connor House to establish, as an experiment, a house for ex-convicts on probation who were interested in returning to school. He was assisted in this by a Windsor probation officer; and, when he returned to the Faculty of Religious Studies at the University of Windsor in the fall of 1971, he lived with the ex-convicts. This apostolate had to be discontinued when he was appointed superior of O'Connor House in 1972. In this position, he helped revivify the religious life of the house. The Canadian Religious Conference asked him to assist in a study of contemporary religious life in Canada, concentrating on the area of obedience. He took a sabbatical year, 1977–8, for research. In 1980 he was named head of the Department of Religious Studies, University of Windsor, and, in 1981, full professor. He took the academic year 1983–4 for further study and research in Chicago. Returning to Windsor he resumed teaching, while at the same time studying for the Senior University Administrator's Certificate at the University of Western Ontario, which he obtained in 1985. In that year he was appointed dean of arts of the University of Windsor. Active on several university committees, he was named to the Board of Governors of both Assumption University and the University of Windsor. In 1988 he was invited to accept the presidency of St Joseph's College in the University of Alberta, Edmonton. Before he could take office, however, his lungs were found to be seriously damaged. He therefore continued at the University of Windsor as dean of arts until his steadily declining health necessitated his resignation in the fall of 1990.

A dedicated scholar, an effective teacher, and an able administrator, Father Joseph Culliton accomplished much for the Church and the academic institutions in Windsor during his relatively short career of twenty-five years.

BIBLIOGRAPHY:
Books: *A Processive World View for Pragmatic Christians.* New York, 1975. *Obedience: Gateway to Freedom.* Plainfield, N.J., 1979. Ed. *Non-Violence: Central to Christian Spirituality: Perspectives from Scripture to the Present.* New York and Toronto, c.1982. *Personal Presence: Its Effects on Honesty and Truthfulness* (Lanham, Md., 1985).
Chapters in books: 'Human Sexuality and Christian Development,' *Working Papers on the Theology of Marriage,* ed. James T. McHugh. Washington, D.C., 49–61; 'George Fox,' *Non-Violence: Central to Christian Spirituality,* ed. J. Culliton. New York and Toronto, c.1982, 111–34; 'Religious Obedience: Its "Grace and Sin" History,' *Religious Life Renewed. Formation Reviewed, Donum Dei* 28. Ottawa, 1983, 121–47 (trans. 'L'obéissance religieuse: Son histoire de "grâces et de péchés,"' *Vie religieuse renouvelée ... Formation à réinventer! Donum Dei* 28. Ottawa, 1983, 115–41.
Articles: 'The Discussion in Review (Christmas Conference 1961),' *Basilian Teacher* 6 (February 1962) 208–12; 'An Integral Guidance Program,' *Basilian Teacher* 8 (November 1963) 75–80; 'The Total Gift: A Consideration of Pre-marital Sex in Terms of Divine Revelation,' *America* 115 (December 1966) 770–3; 'Lucien Cerfaux's Contribution concerning "The Body of Christ,"' *Catholic Biblical Quarterly* 29 (January 1967) 41–59; 'The Human Body and Sexual Love,' *Homiletic and Pastoral Review* 57 (January 1967) 287–92; 'Where Does Responsibility for the Handicapped Person Lie?' *Horizons,* Ontario Society for Crippled Children (Spring 1974); repr. *National Apostolate with Mentally Retarded Persons Quarterly* 12 (Summer 1981) 10–13; 'Dewey and Teilhard,' *Teilhard Review* 11 (June 1976) 42–8; 'Rahner on the Origin of the Soul: Some Implications regarding Abortion,' *Thought* 53 (June 1978) 203–14; 'Commitment through the Personalization of Time,' *Spirituality Today* 34 (Winter 1982) 335–49; 'The Mass: Its Personal Meaning in Daily Life,' *Furrow* 34 (July 1983) 417–29; repr. AMECEA Pastoral Institute, Eldoret, Kenya, No. 286 (April 1984) 417–29; 'The Sexual Revolution: Liberation or Enslavement?,' *New Catholic World* 227 (September/October 1984) 221–7; 'Images of "Person" and Their Effects on Marriage,' *Studies in Formative Spirituality* 6 (May 1985) 183–99; 'In His Image: Pierre Teilhard de Chardin: Person of Extraordinary Faith,' *Canadian Catholic Review* 3 (1985) 339–41.
SOURCES: GABF; *Annals* 3 (1965) 376, 7 (1991) 149–51; *Newsletter* (21 December 1990).

CUMMER, William ERNEST, priest, was born in Hamilton, Ontario, on 4 December 1879, the son of William Cummer and Charlotte Louise Lockman. He died in Toronto on 14 May 1942 and is buried there in the Basilian plot of Mount Hope Cemetery.

Ernest Cummer graduated from Hamilton Collegiate Institute in 1899 and enrolled in the Royal College of Dental Surgeons, Toronto. In 1902 he obtained a Licence in Dental Surgery from this College and a Doctor of Dental Surgery degree from the University of Toronto.

Dr Cummer began the practice of dentistry in Toronto and at the same time continued his professional education with summer courses in Toronto, New York, and Chicago. He joined the staff of the Royal College of Dental Surgeons in 1904. In 1907 he married Muriel Gertrude Perry, who bore him a son and a daughter. His life was saddened by the early death of his son. During the First World War he served in the Dental Corps of the Canadian Army with the rank of major.

The development of new techniques in partial dentures brought Dr Cummer international recognition as an authority on prosthetic dentistry. He wrote frequently for professional journals and was much in demand as speaker at dental meetings. He was made an honorary member of several dental societies and in 1927 was elected a Fellow of the American College of Dentists. In 1931 he resigned as professor in the School of Dentistry at the University of Toronto to become founder and first dean of the College of Dentistry at the University of Detroit. A meeting of the Council of the Faculty of Dentistry at the University of Toronto held on 29 May 1942, in recording the death of Dr Cummer, paid tribute to his professional work and added that 'In all his relations with members of the dental profession, Dr Cummer displayed an exquisite politeness that was never found wanting and never failed to make lasting friendships. He gave unstintingly of his energies when helping others.'

'Ernie' Cummer, as he was called by his friends, was born and reared a Methodist. An accomplished organist, he attended church as a young man chiefly because of the music. A notice in *Our Tertiary* commented: 'his religious wanderings brought him into contact and participation with many of the sects. For two years, 1898–1900, he was chorister in Wesley Methodist Church, Hamilton; then for three years he became a regular attendant of Jarvis Street Baptist Church, Toronto. From 1903 to 1906 he was a chorister in St James Cathedral (Anglican, "low church"), and from 1910 to 1913 he was a member of St Thomas Anglican ("high church") choir.' Then, after singing for a year in the mixed choir at St Basil's Catholic Church, Toronto, as a non-Catholic, he received conditional baptism into the Catholic Church on 28 February 1917 at the Newman Centre of the University of Toronto.

About 1920 Dr Cummer began the practice of daily communion, and became an active member of the Third Order of St Francis. During an ordination ceremony in 1921 he experienced a longing to become a priest. After the death of his wife in 1932, he provided for his daughter Marjorie, arranged his affairs at the University of Detroit, and entered St Basil's Novitiate in Toronto. As a novice he embraced humility, claiming the lowest place in a group one-third his age. He was professed on 30 November 1934. Studies in Latin and philosophy, privately made, qualified him for admission to theology at St Basil's Scholasticate ('Seminary' from 1937), Toronto. He was ordained priest on 11 June 1938. His daughter drew a picture of St Apollonia, the patron of dentists, for his ordination memorial card.

Father Cummer's short priestly life was spent at St Michael's College, Toronto, where the state of his health limited his apostolic work to receiving the numerous visitors who came to consult him, and to the writing of letters. In May 1942 he suffered a stroke and died a few days later.

BIBLIOGRAPHY:
Pamphlet: *Life Is Failure without Religion*. Toronto, 1918, repr. 1924, 1938. He also wrote a series of pamphlets, folders on dental technology which were printed by the University of Toronto Press (1915–19) for private circulation among students of the College of Dentistry.
Chapter in book: 'Partial Dentures,' 312–90 in *American Textbook of Prosthetic Dentistry*, 5th ed., ed. C.R. Turner. Philadelphia, 1928.
Articles: A list of Ernest Cummer's fifty-eight articles on dental prosthesis is found in R.J. Scollard, *Dictionary of Basilian Biography* (Toronto, 1969) 37–8.
Other publications: Assoc. ed. *Our Tertiary*, *Apollonian* (to which he contributed a series of articles entitled 'Technical Culture for Dentists'), and *Oral Health*. He was also the author of a number of definitions in the *Standard Dental Dictionary* (Otoffy, 1923).
SOURCES: GABF; *Apollonian* 16 (January 1939); *Our Tertiary* 5 (July 1938) 2; *Who's Who in Canada* 1938–9.

CUSHING (CUSHIN), Daniel, priest, younger brother of Father John *Cushing, was born in Nichol, near Guelph, Ontario (diocese of Toronto, since 1856 of Hamilton), on 27 September 1850, the son of Maurice Cushin and Mary Duggan. He died in Toronto on 18 December 1928 and is buried there in the Basilian plot of Mount Hope Cemetery. Daniel Cushing (born 'Cushin') came in 1864 to St Michael's College, Toronto, where he won first prize in Elementary Latin and distinguished himself in succeeding years. He spent three years in France, 1868–71, at the Collège du Sacré-Coeur, Annonay, where he became fluent in French. On his return to Canada he taught at Assumption College, Windsor, and at the same time studied philosophy. Two years later he entered St Basil's Novitiate, Toronto. After profession he studied theology at Assumption College, took final vows on 1 February 1877, and was ordained priest on 26 May 1877 in Assumption College chapel by Bishop John Walsh of London, Ontario.

Father Cushing taught mathematics and science at Assumption College until 1886, when he was appointed superior of St Michael's College. Three years later he was named superior of Assumption College, 1890–1901, where his principal contribution was to pay off the construction debts incurred by his predecessor, Denis *O'Connor. He was then brought back to Toronto and placed in charge of scholastics at St Michael's College. When a scholasticate was opened at the novitiate in 1902 he served as superior there. Two years later he moved back to St Michael's College – again as superior. He resigned this office in 1906 but continued to live at the college until 1914, when he became teacher and spiritual director at St Basil's Novitiate. In 1927 he retired to St Basil's Scholasticate, Toronto, where he died in the following year.

In a biographical sketch published in the *Basilian*, Father Charles *Collins described Father Cushing as 'a man of learning. ... His solutions of philosophical problems were simple and direct, as old students tell me. His illustrations of knotty problems were drawn from his observations of daily life. ... he was a master of the classics and spoke French as readily as English. ... As a mathematician he was excellent.'

As superior of St Michael's College, Father Cushing welcomed Father Henry *Carr's proposals for changes in the academic courses and for full federation with the University of Toronto. On 8 June 1906 the University of Toronto conferred the honorary degree of Doctor of Laws upon him.

Besides his administrative duties in local houses, Father Cushing was called upon for administration on a higher level. He was a member of the provincial council during the years 1886–98, 1901–8, 1909–10, and 1915–22. Elected provincial in 1910, he resigned the following year when his advocacy of greater autonomy for the Canadian province failed to find favour with the superior general and his council. He served on the general council of the Basilian Fathers of Toronto from 1923 to 1928.

Father Cushing was generally referred to as 'Cush,' a nickname expressive of his friendly relations with all. Much sought after as a spiritual director, he was a patient listener, waiting for the person to raise the problem that was troubling him. Then he would stroke his beard and preface his reply with, 'I fancy ...' In *The Golden Jubilee Volume of Assumption College*, Father D. Egan gave the following picture of him: 'tall, grave, ascetic looking. ... Unassuming and unemotional as he appeared, even the inexperienced eye of youth seemed to discern the outward evidence of authority and power, as well as those of sincerity and worth.'

SOURCES: GABF; C. Collins, 'Father Cushing,' *Basilian* 4 (March 1938) 48; D. Egan, 'Father Cushing's Regime,' *Jubilee, Assumption*; Kirley, *Congregation in France* 4, 7, 12, 14, 39–40, 57; McMahon, *Pure Zeal* 14–15; *Yearbook SMC* 18 (1927), 20 (1929). For documentation relating to his presidency of Assumption College see Power, *Assumption College* 3 4, 14–16, 45–6, 48–8, 64, 199; see also x–xiii.

CUSHING (CUSHIN), John B., priest, older brother of Father Daniel *Cushing, was born in Nichol, near Guelph, Ontario (archdiocese of Toronto, since 1856 diocese of Hamilton), on 15 August 1834, the son of Maurice Cushin and Mary Duggan. He died in Toronto on 27 September 1868, and was buried in the Basilian plot of St Michael's Cemetery.

John Cushing (born 'Cushin') obtained his early education in a rural school, then studied classics under the Jesuit Fathers at Guelph for three years before coming in 1856 to St Michael's College, Toronto, for philosophy. He was received as a novice on 8 December 1858. As a scholastic he studied mathematics at the University of Toronto. He was ordained priest on 25 March 1863.

Father Cushing's brief priestly life took him first to St Mary's of the Assumption Parish in Owen Sound, Ontario, as pastor in the summer of 1863. As the son of pioneer settlers he was well suited to the work of this parish and its missions. The commemorative volume published on the occasion of the golden jubilee of the parish church described him as 'being quite tall, somewhat robust, of a conservative disposition, yet very pleasant in manner.' Called back to Toronto in January 1864, Father Cushing taught at St Michael's College, assisted in the work of St Basil's Parish, and regularly attended the mission parish of St John the Evangelist at Weston, a suburb of Toronto. Born and raised with the name 'Cushin,' he began during these years to use the form 'Cushing.' He died from consumption in 1868.

SOURCES: GABF; *Centennial, St Mary's*; *Jubilee, St Mary's*; Spetz, Waterloo.

D

DALEY, Joseph JAMES Edward, priest, was born on 25 July 1930, at North Stratford, New Hampshire (diocese of Manchester), the only child of Chester Daley and Marguerite Mason. He died in Missouri City, Texas, on 14 June 1993, and is buried in the Basilian plot of Garden of Gethsemane, Forest Park Lawndale Cemetery, Houston.

The Daley family moved to Detroit when 'Jim' was very young, and it was there his mother died when he was five. After attending St Mary's Academy, Windsor, St Theresa's elementary school, Detroit, and Hall of the Divine Child, Monroe, Michigan, he received his secondary education at Catholic Central High School, Detroit. Graduating in 1948, he entered St Basil's Novitiate, Rochester, and was professed on 15 August 1949. He studied at Assumption College, Windsor (B.A., Honours Philosophy, University of Western Ontario, 1953), and then taught at Aquinas Institute, Rochester, before beginning theological studies at St Basil's Seminary, Toronto, in 1954. He was ordained to the priesthood on 29 June 1957 in St Basil's Church, Toronto, by Cardinal James Charles McGuigan. In that same year he earned an M.A. in philosophy from the University of Toronto.

Apart from a year of doctoral studies at the University of Toronto, 1963–4, Father Daley taught for the next twenty years at a number of Basilian institutions: the University of St Michael's College, Toronto, philosophy and religious knowledge, 1958–9; Assumption University, Windsor, philosophy, 1959–63; St Thomas More College, Saskatoon, philosophy (summers of 1963 and 1964); St Joseph's College, Edmonton, philosophy and director of student affairs, 1964–75; University of St Thomas, Houston, philosophy and second councillor in the local Basilian community, 1975–7.

At the general chapter of 1977, Father Daley was elected First Councillor and Vicar General of the Basilian Fathers. After completing two terms in this office, he took courses in theological renewal from July to December in California, and then moved to the Basilian community in Calgary, Alberta, to participate in the feasibility study for the establishment of St Mary's College. In 1986 he was named superior and vice-principal of Catholic Central High School, and in 1989 he was appointed assistant at Holy Family Parish, Missouri City, a suburb of Houston.

As vicar general of the Congregation, Jim Daley put great personal effort into uniting the community. He was assigned the responsibility of seeking care for those suffering from emotional problems or addictions, having known himself the struggles involved. His death at the age of sixty-three, the result of a heart attack alone in his room, was only discovered the next morning by his absence from prayer.

BIBLIOGRAPHY: 'Autumn, a Poem,' *Basilian Teacher* 2 (November 1957), cover; 'T.V.: Tool of Education,' *Basilian Teacher* 5 (January 1961) 125–8; 'Give More Weight to the Freedom of the Sons of God,' *Forum* 1 (November 1965) 151–2.
SOURCES: GABF; *Annals* 2 (1957) 314–16, 8 (1994) 131–2; *Newsletter* (19 July 1993).

DAMATO, John Joseph, priest, nephew of Father Anthony *Lococo, was born on 25 July 1931 at Niagara Falls, Ontario (archdiocese of Toronto, since 1958 diocese of St Catharines), the only child of Nicholas J. Damato and Lena E. Lococo. He died in Toronto on 6 March 1985 and is buried in the Basilian plot of Holy Cross Cemetery, Thornhill, Ontario.

John attended St Patrick's Grade School, 1937–45, and Niagara Falls Collegiate and Vocational Institute, 1945–51. He began his university studies at St Michael's College, Toronto, in 1951 and after one year entered St Basil's Novitiate, Toronto. After profession on 15 August 1953, he completed his university course at St Michael's College (B.A., University of Toronto, 1956). During the summers of 1956 and 1957 he attended the Ontario College of Education (Type A teaching certification, 1956). As a scholastic he taught for one year at St Michael's College School, 1956–7, and then did theological studies at St Basil's Seminary, Toronto, 1957–62; S.T.B., St Michael's, 1961, with an interval of one year of teaching at Aquinas Institute, Rochester, 1958–9.

On 3 and 4 June 1961, John received the sub-diaconate and diaconate at the hands of Archbishop George B. *Flahiff, who had been ordained a bishop only three days previously. John was ordained to the priesthood on 29 June 1961 in St Basil's Church, Toronto, by Archbishop Philip Francis Pocock.

After receiving an M.A. in philosophy from the University of Toronto in 1962 (thesis: 'The Problem of the Eternity of the World in the Doctrine of Saint Thomas Aquinas,') John was appointed in 1963 to Michael Power High School, Etobicoke, where he was to spend the rest of his life, teaching Latin and Italian and counselling students. He was extremely conscientious in his own work and demanding in that of his students. He loved to stay at home and do his work, and thus came to be the person who usually answered the phone and the door at Michael Power. His manner was quiet and ever courteous. His opinions were clearly defined and strongly held. He enjoyed saying Mass in Latin, even after the liturgical changes inaugurated by Vatican II, because, as he said, it showed the universality of the Church. He was a priest of strong devotion and solid piety. He was well known in his home town of Niagara Falls where he visited and frequently did ministry.

In early March 1985 a severe cold obliged him to take to his bed. He suffered a heart attack in his sleep sometime in the early hours of 6 March and was found dead some hours later.

SOURCES: GABF; *Annals* 3 (1961) 82, 6 (1986) 473–4; *Newsletter* (12 March 1985).

DeBILLY, Roger Foley, priest, was born on 13 October 1917 at Lévis, Quebec (archdiocese of Québec), the son of Alexandre DeBilly and Alvina Mary Jane Foley. He died in Toronto on 30 September 1995, and is buried in the Basilian plot of Holy Cross Cemetery, Thornhill, Ontario.

Roger DeBilly (the 'De' in the family name had been restored to his grandfather by an act of the Quebec legislature in 1893 after it had been abandoned for several generations) attended Jesuits' College and later St Charles Garnier College in Quebec City, majoring in classical and modern languages, and received a B.A. from the Université Laval, 1940. In 1939 he moved into the boarders' residence at St Michael's College, Toronto, followed courses in theology at St Basil's Seminary for one year, and then entered St Basil's Novitiate, Toronto. After making first profession on 15 August 1941, he resumed theological studies, spending one year at St Michael's College and moving to St Basil's Seminary in 1942. He was ordained to the priesthood in St Basil's Church, Toronto, on 17 December 1944 by Bishop John Ryan of Hamilton, Ontario.

With the exception of six years of teaching at Aquinas Institute, Rochester, 1950–6, and two years of theological studies in Ottawa, 1971–2, and Louvain, 1989–90, Father DeBilly's forty-five years of active ministry were carried out in numerous parishes and chaplaincies: Blessed Sacrament Parish, Windsor, 1945–50, 1959–60, St Basil's Parish, Toronto, 1956–9, Assumption Parish, Windsor, 1960–1, 1973–5, Our Lady of the Assumption Parish, Lethbridge, Alberta, 1961–4, 1968–71, pastor and rector; Ste Anne's Parish, Detroit, 1964–8, pastor and rector; St John the Baptist Parish, Amherstburg, Ontario, 1972–3, 1979–81; St David's Parish, Montreal, 1975–7; St Basil's Parish, Ottawa, 1977–8; St Mary's of the Assumption Parish, Owen Sound, Ontario, 1978–9; St Mark's College, Vancouver, 1981–8, from where he served as chaplain first at St Vincent's Hospital and then at the Abbotsford prison; and Kingston Penitentiary, Kingston, Ontario, 1988–9, prison chaplain.

Roger DeBilly was small of stature and always impeccably turned out. His manner, while self-assured, was never offensive. His French-Canadian accent, which he carried to his grave, lent a certain charm to his conversation and to his preaching. His frequent changes of appointment were indicative of a certain characteristic restlessness, though his ministry was wholehearted. A desire to study was part of this restlessness. During his years at Aquinas, 1950–6, he spent summers studying business law at Manhattan College, New York City, and sociology at Fordham University. His second study year, taken at the age of seventy-three at Louvain, is revelatory of his pastoral preoccupation. He wrote to his superior: 'This total change undoubtedly gives a good shake to the whole system – culturally, physically, environmentally buffeted at all turns. Nevertheless, the effect is very salutary. Such innovative transformation brings the saying that *"La joie de vivre"* pivots much on *"La joie de croire."* Such exposure to such changes, adaptations, and confrontations, new thoughts, new cultures, generates tremendous pulsation to accept, reciprocate the many love moments. We must be conscious of the actions of Jesus' way and presence demanding from us a greater reading of the signs of the times.' Roger saw his time at Louvain as a preparation for a continued and reinvigorated ministry, and told his superiors, in the same letter, that he was open to ministry to the sick, given his experience in 'gerontology, chaplaincy to the unwanted and to cancer patients in hospitals.' But further formal ministry was not possible, for upon his taking up residence with the Basilian Fathers of Etobicoke in 1990 his health deteriorated. He entered the Basilian Fathers Residence (Infirmary) in 1992 and remained there for the last three years of his life.

SOURCES: GABF; *Annals* 1 (1945) 101, 7 (1992) 7, 8 (1994) 5, (1996) 106–8; *Newsletter* (29 October 1995).

DECOR, Joseph Louis Hippolyte, priest, member of the Congregation 1875–c.1881, was born on 17 February 1849 at Thor (Vaucluse, diocese of Avignon).
Joseph made final profession of vows on 17 September 1875. While studying theology he taught junior classes in the Petit Séminaire d'Aubenas (Ardèche) and in the Basilian school at Bourg-Saint-Andéol (Ardèche). He was ordained a priest on 20 September 1879 by Bishop Armand de Charbonnel, after which he taught *huitième* at the Collège Saint-Pierre at Châteauroux (Indre), 1879–80, and commercial class at the Collège du Bourg-Saint-Andéol, 1880–1. In a wave of political-religious upheaval in France the municipality forced the Basilians to leave the school in 1881. Father Décor, duly registered as a secular priest in the eyes of the State, sought employment as a teacher elsewhere. The records show that in 1889 he was an 'authorized' teacher at the Petit Séminaire d'Avignon, but no further mention occurs.

SOURCE: Pouzol, 'Notices,' Supplément 2.

DEGLESNE, Antoine Louis GERMAIN, priest, was born in Annonay on 14 September 1798, the son of Pierre Antoine Deglesne and Marianne Alléon. He died in Annonay on 19 June 1856 and was buried in the cemetery of Saint-Jacques, Annonay. His body was reinterred with several confreres in the cemetery on the grounds of the Collège du Sacré-Coeur, Annonay, on 11 November 1869. The monument which had marked his first grave was transferred to the college cemetery.
Germain Deglesne was a brilliant student, especially in mathematics, at the Collège des Cordeliers until 1814. He completed an apprenticeship of two years in Rouen, where his father was a master tailor. In 1816 he returned to Annonay, where he was a business administrator for several years. In November 1821 he decided to devote his life to the

education of youth and he returned to the Collège des Cordeliers, where he studied theology under Fathers Joseph *Actorie and Jean-Baptiste *Polly. He joined the Basilian community on 19 May 1823. He also taught classes during this time in French, mathematics, philosophy, and bookkeeping. During the year 1827-8 he was on loan to the diocese of Grenoble. Deep humility and a delicate conscience caused him to delay ordination, which took place on 14 March 1829.

Father Deglesne continued teaching philosophy and for several years did Sunday ministry at the chapel of Vidalon. From 1831 he was bursar at the Collège des Cordeliers. On 27 October 1838 he was elected to the general council, and he continued to be re-elected until his death in 1856. In this role he endeavoured to be a mediator between the confreres and the superior general, Father Pierre *Tourvieille, who was not always easily approached.

Father Deglesne's major work was as master of novices, 1834-47 and 1849-56, a total of twenty-three years. In 1847 he was chaplain and spiritual director of the Collège du Sacré-Coeur and to the sisters who served there. In the summer of 1851 he spent several weeks with the Oblate community at Notre-Dame de l'Osier in order to become more experienced in spiritual formation. In 1856 he succeeded in having the novitiate housed in a separate place at Sainte-Barbe but died about two months later.

In his role as master of novices Germain Deglesne was strongly influenced by Father Julien *Tracol, the companion of his youth and closest friend in the Congregation, who had spent some time at the Jesuit novitiate at Avignon. Father Deglesne was remarkably gifted in preaching and in the direction of souls. He was especially inspired by the theology of St Alphonsus Liguori. Many businessmen of Annonay chose him as their confessor. For these apostolic works he prepared by reading widely in both classical and contemporary writers on the ascetical and mystical life. In 1850 Father Deglesne published a textbook on bookkeeping that went into a second edition.

SOURCES: GABF; Chomel, *Collège d'Annonay* 256-67, 438; Kirley, *Community in France* 7n27, 9n31, 14n52, 59; Pouzol, 'Notices'; Charles Roume, *Origines* 260, 265, 268, 271, 275, 298, 302, 346, 366-8.

DELANEY, Charles William Patrick, priest, was born on 6 June 1942 at South Ozone Park, New York (diocese of Brooklyn), the eldest of four children of firefighter Charles William Patrick Delaney, Sr and Ann Elizabeth Fitzpatrick. He died in Oakland, California, on 7 November 1986 and is buried in the Basilian plot at Holy Sepulchre Cemetery, Hayward, California, the first Basilian interred there.

Born prematurely, the infant 'Charlie' was baptized by a nurse on duty at Kew Gardens General Hospital, Forest Hills, New York. He attended the parochial school in his home parish of St Clement in South Ozone, and graduated from Bishop Loughlin Memorial High School, Brooklyn, New York, in 1959. Through contact with Father Joseph Courtney CSB, a distant cousin, he entered St Basil's Novitiate, Toronto, in August of that same year, and was professed on 15 August 1960. During his university studies at the University of Windsor (B.A., 1964), he worked for two years as study-hall prefect for resident students at Assumption College School. He taught English at Aquinas Institute, Rochester, 1964–6, before returning to Assumption College School as teacher and prefect of residence, 1966–7. In both schools he gave himself to student activities, particularly the marching bands and the debating society. He began theological studies in 1967 at St Basil's Seminary, Toronto, taking his final year at Assumption, once more as a prefect in the residence. He was ordained to the priesthood on 12 December 1970 in his parents' home parish of St Boniface, Elmont, New York.

After ordination Father Delaney continued on at Assumption, where, besides teaching, he worked with the resident students. He served as local superior of the Basilian community, 1975–8, and was dean of residence, 1978–80, when he was appointed to Bishop O'Dowd High School, Oakland, California, where he remained until his death six years later.

Father Delaney served as chaplain to the fire departments both in Windsor and in Oakland. Devices on his desk and in his room alerted him to large fires, where, dressed in his firefighter's gear, he would encourage or comfort as the occasion required. He was known to enter a building in flames if he learned a fireman had been injured. After his funeral Mass, a member of the Oakland Fire Department gave a brief eulogy; and firefighters joined the students in forming a guard of honour as his body was moved from the school chapel to the gymnasium.

Father Delaney demanded excellence, but used encouragement to challenge the potential and generosity of young people. He kept in close touch with their parents, and would not hesitate to counsel and correct them about educational principles. During the last year of his life, though suffering the pain of terminal cancer, he continued his normal service to the community and the school.

SOURCES: GABF; *Annals* 4 (1971) 173–4, 6 (1987) 581–3; *Newsletter* (18 November 1986).

DELHOMME, Auguste, priest, was born on 18 March 1855 at Saint-Félicien (Ardèche). He died at Boufarik, Algeria, on 16 August 1916 and was buried there.

As a brilliant student in the Saint-Barbe minor seminary section of the Collège du Sacré-Coeur, Annonay, 1869–74, Auguste did the equivalent of grades X, XI, and XII all in the year 1871–2. Before entering the novitiate he lived at the Basilian scholasticate, Montée du Château, Annonay, and prepared for his *baccalauréat* in arts and science in the company of a future confrere, Emile *Suchet.

Auguste made his novitiate at Feyzin (Isère, now Rhône), 1875–6. Twice he was called upon in the course of this year to replace an ailing confrere, once at the Collège Saint-Pierre at Châteauroux (Indre), and once at the Ecole cléricale de Périgueux (Dordogne). He made his first profession on 22 September 1876, and then did theological studies and taught mathematics at Périgueux, 1876–9, while managing also to pursue higher studies at the Université de Toulouse. His profession of final vows on 30 June 1878 in Périgueux was followed by reception of major orders, all in the chapel of the Collège du Sacré-Coeur, Annonay: subdiaconate on 21 September 1878, diaconate on 20 September 1879 (from Bishop Armand de Charbonnel), and priesthood on 18 September 1880 at the hands of Bishop Joseph-Michel-Frédéric Bonnet of Viviers.

Father Delhomme was professor of rhetoric at the Ecole cléricale, Périgueux, 1880–2, and then taught science at the Collège du Sacré-Coeur, Annonay, 1882–3. During the years 1883 to 1885 he earned the *licence ès lettres* at the Institut catholique de Paris. Returning to Annonay, he taught rhetoric at the college for three years before being appointed to the Collège Saint-Charles, Blidah, Algeria, where he remained for nearly twenty years as professor of rhetoric, director of studies, 1892–9, and local superior, 1899–1903. He contributed greatly to the development of arts and sciences in Blidah.

When the suppression of religious orders forced the Basilians to surrender the college on 13 July 1903, Father Delhomme stayed on in Algeria working first as director of a diocesan institute of education, then as pastor in the parish of Bois-Sacré, and later as pastor of Boufarik. A Basilian to the end of his life, he was an elected delegate to the 1910 general chapter. On 16 August 1916 he suffered a massive, fatal stroke at Boufarik.

SOURCES: GABF; Kirley, *Community in France* 70n179, 110, 185, 209, 248n581; Pouzol, 'Notices'; *Semaine religieuse de Viviers* (1916–17) 262–3.

DELUCHE, Gabriel, priest, was born on 9 December 1879 at Piégut-Pluviers (Dordogne, diocese of Périgueux). He died on 30 May 1955 at Vésinet (Seine-et-Oise, now Yvelines) and was buried in the local cemetery.

Gabriel Deluche met the Basilians as a student at the Ecole cléricale de Périgueux. He made his novitiate in Annonay, with first profession on 22 September 1898 and final profession on 19 September 1902. The following day Bishop Hilarion-Joseph Montéty ordained him subdeacon in the chapel of the Collège du Sacré-Coeur, Annonay. He received diaconate at Viviers on 20 December 1902 and priesthood, also at Viviers, on 6 June 1903. Of his three fellow ordinands, only Félix *Séveyrac remained a Basilian, while Auguste Vayssade and Casimir Ceyte both later sought incardination in a diocese. Because of the suppression and dispersal of religious orders in France in 1903, theirs was the last Basilian ordination in France until the ordination of Father Charles *Roume in 1929.

During theological studies Gabriel worked in Basilian schools: as recreation and study hall master at the Collège du Sacré-Coeur, Annonay, 1898–1900, and at the Ecole cléricale, Périgueux, 1900–1, and prefect of discipline at the Petit Séminaire d'Aubenas (Ardèche), 1901–3. He said his first Mass in the chapel of the latter institution, assisted by Father Denis *Mouraret, on Sunday 7 June 1903.

After the dispersal of the Basilian community in 1903, Father Deluche stayed on at the Petit Séminaire d'Aubenas for one year, after which he returned to Périgueux in his native diocese. From 1904 to 1926 – with the exception of the war years 1914–18, when he worked as an accountant in a military headquarters – he was curate at Le Bugue, then pastor at Saint-Martial-Viveyrol and again at Saint-Pierre-de-Cole. With the opening of the Basilian novitiate at Villa Saint-Louis, Bordighera, Italy, in 1926, he returned to life in community, joining

Father Léon *Guigon, novice master, and Father Denis *Mouraret. He remained there for two years as chaplain to several French communities of sisters who had taken refuge in Italy. Relatively young, affable, and very active, Father Deluche was a favourite with the Basilian novices – more so than with Father Guigon's housekeeper, who brought about his departure from the novitiate. He became chaplain in a girls' school at Chatou and then curate at Vésinet (both in Seine-et-Oise, now Yvelines), near Paris. It was there he died on 30 May 1955 and was buried in the local cemetery.

Years later, a parishioner at Vésinet to whom Father Deluche had regularly brought Holy Communion summed up his ministry in these words to Father Félix Pouzol, a former novice at Bordighera: *'Ah! Le Père Deluche, c'était le bon chien du Bon Pasteur'* ('... he was the faithful dog of the Good Shepherd').

SOURCES: GABF; Kirley, *Community in France* 184, 255n600; Kirley, *Congregation in France* 144–6, 206–7, 220; Pouzol, 'Notices.'

DEMEURE, Louis Marie Joseph, priest, was born on 23 February 1833 in Annonay, the son of Pierre Demeure and Thérèse Grenier. He died in Annonay on 20 January 1896 and is buried there in the cemetery on the grounds of the Collège du Sacré-Coeur.

The school register shows that Louis Demeure enrolled in the *classe de huitième* of the day pupils section of the Collège des Cordeliers, Annonay, 1847–8, and that he completed his final year of philosophy there, 1854–5. He entered the Basilian novitiate on 27 September 1855, but did not make first profession until two years later, on 27 September 1857, having been called upon to supervise in the study hall and recreation, first at the Collège des Cordeliers, then at the Collège de Privas. He made his final profession on 18 July 1858 at Privas. During his study of theology in Annonay he taught commercial classes in the Collège des Cordeliers. He received the diaconate on 18 June 1859 and was ordained to the priesthood by Bishop Louis Delcusy of Viviers on 25 September 1859.

After his ordination Father Demeure served in the Petit Séminaire de Vernoux (Ardèche), 1859–65, and then received an appointment to Annonay, where he was to remain for the next thirty years. He taught in the moderns section, first at the Collège des Cordeliers, 1865–7, and then, when the Basilian school moved to the top of Mont Saint-Denis in 1867, at the relatively new Collège du Sacré-Coeur, 1867–78. He also had charge of a student confraternity called 'La Congrégation de la Très Sainte Vierge,' and served as spiritual director to many of the seminarians at Sainte-Barbe.

In 1877 he was appointed to the general council of the Basilian Congregation and was re-elected for the term 1880 to 1896. During much of this period he was also superior at Sainte-Barbe, 1878–96, succeeding such illustrious forebears in this office as Fathers Vincent *Duret, 1808–41, Auguste de *Montgolfier, 1841–4, and André *Charmant, 1844–8. In 1891 he was named Honorary Canon of the Cathedral of Viviers.

Father Demeure had a profound influence on many future priests in the diocese of Viviers while they studied at the minor seminary of Sainte-Barbe. The diocesan weekly *Semaine religieuse de Viviers* said of him: 'He died peacefully in the presence of his confreres in no apparent agony, fully conscious to the end. His death has brought tears to the eyes of many: the poor to whom he never refused help, Christian laity for whom he was a spiritual guide, students who held him in tender esteem, his own confreres who have lost a true friend.' His funeral took place in the chapel of the Collège du Sacré-Coeur, the only Basilian chapel large enough to accommodate the crowd of mourners.

SOURCES: GABF; Chomel, *Collège d'Annonay*; Chanoine Fromenton, *Le Petit Séminaire de Vernoux* (Aubenas, 1922); Kirley, *Community in France* 69 70n178, 137n347, 150n383; Pouzol, 'Notices'; *Semaine religieuse de Viviers* (24 January 1896) 681–3.

DENOMY, Alexander Joseph, priest, was born in Chatham, Ontario (diocese of London), on 21 June 1904, the son of Alexander Denomy and Mary Brisson. He died at North Scituate, Massachusetts, on 19 July 1957, and is buried in the Basilian plot of Holy Cross Cemetery, Thornhill, Ontario.

Growing up in Windsor, Alexander Denomy made his high school and college courses at Assumption College and obtained his B.A. from the University of Western Ontario in 1923, graduating at the age of nineteen. He entered St Basil's Novitiate in Toronto and was professed on 11 August 1924. After a year of teaching, 1924–5, at Assumption College and a year of study at the Ontario College of Education, Toronto, 1925–6, he did theological studies at St Basil's Scholasticate, Toronto, and was ordained priest on 30 June 1928 in St Basil's Church, Toronto, by Archbishop Neil McNeil. In that same year he obtained an M.A. in romance languages from the University of Toronto.

After teaching at St Michael's College, Toronto, 1928–31, Father Denony began doctoral studies in mediaeval literature at Harvard University. The chairman of the Department of French, J.D.M. Ford, wrote to Father Henry *Carr on 5 May 1933: 'In my forty years of service here I have never had any student superior to him in all aspects of the work that he is doing.' In 1934 he was awarded a Ph.D. for his thesis, 'An Old French Life of Saint Agnes and Other Vernacular Versions of the Middle Ages,' with high distinction; and he was awarded a Sheldon Travelling Fellowship, which provided for a postdoctoral year in Europe. In 1935 he was appointed Professor of the History of Comparative Literature in the Institute of Mediaeval Studies, a post he held until his death in 1957. From 1943 to 1956 he was also the editor of the Institute's journal, *Mediaeval Studies*. His scholarship drew international recognition. Twice, in 1938 and 1947, he was awarded a Guggenheim Fellowship to consult manuscripts in European libraries. He was appointed to the Advisory Board of *Speculum*, the journal of the Medieval Academy of America, in 1947. In 1948 he was elected to membership in the Royal Society of Canada, and he became in 1952 a Corresponding Fellow of the Medieval Academy of America. Father Denony suffered from a heart ailment for many years and was fatally stricken when convalescing in Massachusetts.

An obituary in the *Basilian Annals* noted that 'Father Denomy achieved a remarkable balance in his life as a devout priest and an educated scholar. He brought the same zeal and precision into the performance of his priestly duties, the editing of a mediaeval manuscript, and the writing of a scholarly article. And this was not surprising, since he did them equally for the love of God.'

BIBLIOGRAPHY:
Books: *The Old French Lives of St Agnes and Other Vernacular Versions of the Middle Ages*. Harvard Studies in Romance Languages, 13. Cambridge, Mass., 1938. *The Heresy of Courtly Love*. New York, 1947; repr. Gloucester, Mass, 1965. Ed. (with U.T. Holmes) *Mediaeval Studies in Honor of Jeremiah Denis Matthias Ford* (Cambridge, Mass., 1948). Ed. (with A.D. Menut) Nicole Oresme, *Le livre du ciel et du monde*. New York, c.1943; repr. Madison, Wis., 1968.
Articles: His eighteen journal articles are listed in *Mediaeval Studies* 19 (1957) i–ii, and in R.J. Scollard, *Dictionary of Basilian Biography* (Toronto, 1969) 42–3.
SOURCES: GABF; *Annals* 2 (1957) 295–6; *Basilian Teacher* 2 (November 1957) 19; *French Studies U. of T.* 124; Kirley, *Congregation in France* 235; *Mediaeval Studies*

19 (1957) i–ii; *New Catholic Encyclopedia* (New York, 1967) 4, 774; Gerald B. Phelan, obituary notice, *Minutes of the Proceedings of the Royal Society of Canada*, 3rd series, 52 (1958) 81–3.

DESBOS, Jean-Baptiste, priest, member of the Association of Priests of Saint Basil 1826–c.1829, younger brother of Jean-Pierre *Desbos, was born in 1793 at Saint-Félicien (Ardèche, diocese of Viviers [from 1801 to 1822 of Mende]).

Jean-Baptiste entered the novitiate of the newly formed Association of Priests of Saint Basil on 1 December 1822. He made his profession by promise, according to the custom of the time, not by vows, on 30 August 1826, when he was already a deacon. Archbishop Joseph Fesch of Lyon ordained him a priest in Lyon on 23 December 1826.

Father Desbos taught *sixième* in the Collège des Cordeliers, Annonay, in 1822–3, and *quatrième* in 1825–6 and 1828–9. He also taught in the Basilian college at Feyzin (Isère, now Rhône). Sometime after 1829 he withdrew from the Association to become assistant to his brother Father Jean-Pierre *Desbos, pastor at Arlebosc, canton of Saint-Félicien. When the latter died in 1831, Jean-Baptiste replaced him as pastor. Basilian records show that he attended the annual retreat with the Basilians in 1847 in Annonay.

SOURCE: Pouzol, 'Notices,' Supplément 1.

DESBOS, Jean-Pierre, priest, member of the Association of Priests of Saint Basil 1826–c.1828, elder brother of Jean-Baptiste *Desbos, was born 13 March 1782 at Saint-Félicien (Ardèche, diocese of Viviers [from 1801 to 1822 of Mende]). He died at Arlebosc, canton of Saint-Félicien, in 1831.

When the Association of Priests of Saint Basil was formed in 1822, Jean-Pierre Desbos was already an ordained priest, pastor of the parish of Saint-Basile, canton of Lamastre, and part-time assistant at the Petit Séminaire Maison-Seule. In October 1822, when Bishop Claude Jean-Joseph de la Brunière asked the Basilians to take charge of Maison-Seule, Father Desbos requested admission as a novice on 5 June 1823 and made his profession by promise, not by vows, on 30 August 1826. Two years later, when the Basilians left Maison-Seule to open the Collège de Privas (Ardèche), Father Desbos withdrew from the Association and became pastor of Arlebosc. His brother Jean-Baptiste joined him there in 1829 and succeeded him as pastor after his death in 1831.

SOURCE: Pouzol, 'Notices,' Supplément 1.

DESCELLIÈRE, Louis, priest, uncle of Father Octave *Descellière, was born on 13 May 1841 in Monistrol (Haute-Loire, diocese of Le Puy). He died at Aurec (Haute-Loire) on 22 November 1922 and is buried in the local cemetery.

Louis Descellière received primary and secondary education and part of his theological training in his home diocese. He entered the Basilian novitiate at Feyzin (Isère, now Rhône), probably in 1864 at the age of twenty-three, and made final profession on 19 December 1866 at Privas. He received the diaconate on 19 September 1868 and was ordained to the priesthood by Bishop Armand de Charbonnel on 18 September 1869 in the chapel of the Collège du Sacré-Coeur, Annonay.

During his theological studies Louis taught the commercial class at the Collège des Cordeliers, Annonay, 1865–6, and at the Collège de Privas, 1866–8. He was *professeur de cinquième* at the Petit Séminaire de Vernoux (Ardèche), 1868–70, and *professeur de quatrième*, 1870–1. For the following two years he was *professeur de troisième* at the Collège du Bourg-Saint-Andéol (Ardèche), and was then appointed to the Ecole cléricale de Périgueux (Dordogne), diocese of Périgueux, where he taught for twenty-eight years: *professeur de quatrième*, 1873–4 and 1880–2, *professeur de troisième*, 1874–6, *professeur de sixième*, 1876–80, *professeur de mathématiques*, 1872–1900, and *professeur de septième*, 1900–1.

In 1901 Father Descellière assumed full-time pastoral ministry in the diocese of Périgueux. Basilian records show him still at Périgueux in 1910 and also in 1913. Eventually he retired to Aurec (Haute-Loire), where he died. The *Semaine religieuse de Viviers* described him as a 'charming, good-natured man.'

SOURCES: GABF; Kirley, *Community in France* 30, 185, 207; Pouzol, 'Notices'; *Semaine religieuse de Viviers* (15 December 1922) 439.

DESCELLIÈRE, Marie Joseph OCTAVE, priest, superior general of the Basilian Fathers of Viviers, 1932–50, nephew of Father Louis *Descellière, was born in Bourges (Cher) on 25 July 1874. He died in Annonay on 9 August 1950 and is buried there in the cemetery on the grounds of the Collège du Sacré-Coeur.

Octave Descellière received his early education at the Ecole cléricale de Périgueux (Dordogne) from 1886 to 1892, at a time when it was under Basilian direction. In 1892 he entered the Basilian novitiate at Sainte-Barbe, where he also worked as prefect. He worked at the Collège Saint-Charles at Blidah, Algeria, 1894–8 and 1900–3, and at the Collège du Sacré-Coeur, 1898–9. He was ordained to the priesthood on 23 September 1899 at the Collège du Sacré-Coeur by Bishop Hilarion-Joseph Montéty, and then studied for a year at the Faculté catholique de Lyon.

After the expulsion of religious from their schools in 1903, Father Descellière spent a year as a private tutor and then became assistant at the parish of Laurac (Ardèche). He served a short while at the Petit Séminaire d'Aubenas, which was under diocesan direction; but after its confiscation on 11 December 1906 he became an assistant at Vals-les-Bains (Ardèche). He returned to the Petit Séminaire d'Aubenas when it was located in the building vacated by the Marist Brothers. He spent several years at the *Maîtrise* (choir school) in Viviers, where he was superior. Drafted during the war of 1914–18, he served in the army medical corps, then went to work in the Petit Séminaire de Saint-Charles, Annonay, where in 1928 he replaced Father Victorin *Marijon as superior. In 1930 he was named superior of the Collège du Sacré-Coeur, a post he held until he resigned in 1949.

During most of that tenure he also held the office of superior general of the Basilian Fathers of Viviers, having been elected in January 1932 after the death of Father *Marijon. In 1944, the French Basilian council received permission from Rome to elect him to a third six-year term, after which he was replaced by Father Charles *Roume.

As superior general Father Descellière had taken active measures to reassemble and strengthen the Basilian Community. By moving the novitiate in August 1929 from Bordighera, Italy, to Maison Saint-Joseph in Annonay and then opening a juniorate there in October to complement the scholasticate already functioning in that locale, he created a centre for the French Basilian community adjacent to the Collège du Sacré-Coeur. He lived through difficult times with the expulsion of religious orders from education in 1903, his mobilization in the Great War of 1914–18, and the occupation of the Collège du Sacré-Coeur, 1940 and 1942–3, by German troops, who then set fire to the Petit Séminaire de Saint-Charles after members of the French Resistance had occupied it.

Father Laurence *Shook attended the celebrations in Annonay of Father Descellière's golden jubilee of priesthood on 12 May 1949; and it was then that talks about reunion with the North American Basilians began. One of Father Descellière's last acts was to celebrate Mass on 4 June 1950, on the occasion of the one-hundred-and-fiftieth anniversary of the founding of the college at Saint-Symphorien-de-Mahun in 1800.

The *Semaine religieuse de Viviers* said in an obituary notice: 'He brought to the headship of the College a ripe scholarship, total dedication of self, authority and skill in handling complex situations. An austere and reserved exterior, somewhat aloof, hid a warm and tender heart.'

SOURCES: GABF; *Annals* 1 (1950) 244–6; Kirley, *Community in France* 185, 197, 210, 256n600; Kirley, *Congregation in France* ii, 42, 78, 81–2, 86–7, 137, 154–6, 159, 161, 174–6, 178–9, 179–85, 185–92, 192–4, 196–8, 200, 202–3, 207, 213, 220, 221, 227–8, 230, 264–5, 271; Pouzol, 'Notices'; *Semaine religieuse de Viviers* (September 1950) 22–9.

DESCHANEL, Jules, priest, was born on 25 May 1844 at Saint-Pierre-le-Déchausselat (Ardèche), canton of Les Vans. He was a cousin of Monseigneur Deschanel, vicar general of the diocese of Viviers. He died on 26 November 1933 at Saint-Rémy-de-Provence (Bouches-du-Rhône) and was buried in the priests' plot of the local cemetery.

Educated by the Brothers of the Christian Schools, Jules entered that community and taught in its Collège Saint-Charles, Marseilles. Attracted to the Basilian community, he worked as study-hall and recreation master for five years, 1875–80, at the Petit Séminaire de Vernoux and then at the Basilian school at Châteauroux (Indre), where he taught commercial for two years, 1880–2. During this time he was a postulant for one year, then a novice in the second year. Normally he would have made his novitiate at Feyzin (Isère, now Rhône), but it had been closed by the French military police as part of the 1880 nationwide suppression of religious orders. In 1882 he returned to the Petit Séminaire de Vernoux as prefect of discipline, 1882–4. He made his final profession on 19 September 1884 and received the subdiaconate the following day along with his confrere Marcel *Mourgue. During the next year, 1884–5, he and Marcel commuted between Vernoux and Annonay to help supervise study hall and recreation in both Basilian schools.

Archbishop Armand de Charbonnel conferred the diaconate on both candidates on 19 September 1885, in the chapel of the Collège du

Sacré-Coeur, Annonay. Then the two went to the Basilian novitiate at Beaconfield House, Plymouth, England, to spend a year in preparation for the priesthood. On 18 September 1886 Bishop Joseph-Michel-Frédéric Bonnet of Viviers ordained Jules to the priesthood, along with his confreres Marcel *Mourgue, Edouard *Aureille, and Léopold *Fayolle, in the chapel of the college in Annonay.

For the next sixteen years, 1886–1902, Father Jules Deschanel worked at the Collège Saint-Charles, Blidah, Algeria. He taught commercial classes, 1886–1900, and served as bursar of the college, 1900–2. He returned to the Collège du Sacré-Coeur for one year, 1902–3, where he taught *sixième*. With the closing of the school and the expulsion of the Basilians in 1903, he accepted a teaching position in the Institution Sainte-Marie at Riom (Puy-de-Dôme) where Father Auguste *Pouzol was also on staff. In 1909 he is listed as curate at Aramon (Gard) and seems to have remained there at least until 1922. By 1926 he had retired to the Maison Saint-Paul at Saint-Rémy-de-Provence where, almost blind and increasingly deaf, he died.

SOURCES: GABF; Pouzol, 'Notices'; *Semaine religieuse de Viviers* (8 December 1933) 500.

DIEMER, Rudolph Stephen, priest, was born on 25 September 1906, at Woodslee, Ontario (diocese of London), the youngest of ten children of Seigman Diemer and Theresa Merck. He died in Toronto on 6 April 1992 and is buried in the Basilian plot of Holy Cross Cemetery, Thornhill, Ontario.

'Rudy,' as he was familiarly known, attended St John's Separate School, Woodslee, and entered Assumption High School, Windsor, in 1921, graduating in 1925. After one year of university studies at Assumption College, Windsor, he entered St Basil's Novitiate, Toronto, and made first profession on 11 August 1927. He continued studies, living at St Basil's Scholasticate, 1927–8 and 1931–2, and at St Michael's College, 1928–30. He obtained a B.A. with a major in French from the University of Toronto in 1931. During his theological studies he obtained teacher qualification from the Ontario College of Education in 1932. He did a second year of teaching at Catholic Central High School, Detroit, 1932–3, before returning to Toronto to complete his theology course. He was ordained to the priesthood in Assumption Church, Windsor, on 21 December 1933 by Bishop Alexander MacDonald.

Father Diemer's teaching assignments were as follows: the high school section of St Michael's College, Lee Avenue branch, Toronto, as principal, 1934–5; Assumption College School, 1935–6; St Michael's College, while serving as part-time assistant at St Basil's Parish, 1939; St Michael's College School, 1939–43. His later appointments were to parochial or formation ministry: St Basil's Parish, as assistant, 1943–7, as pastor, 1947–55, and as assistant and first councillor, 1968–83; Holy Rosary Parish, Toronto, as rector and pastor, 1955–61; Ste Anne's Parish, Detroit, as superior and pastor, 1961–4; Erindale Novitiate, as local councillor and confessor, 1964–5 and 1967–8; Pontiac Novitiate, as local councillor and confessor, 1965–7; St Basil's Seminary, as councillor and novitiate confessor, June–September 1968.

In 1983 Father Diemer retired to the University of St Michael's College, Toronto. He moved to the Basilian Fathers Residence (Infirmary) in 1992, just shortly before his death.

To all his assignments Rudy Diemer brought a wealth of common sense, devotion, and spiritual insight. In community he was pleasant and jovial, noted for his sharp wit. He was a sympathetic listener who could hear beyond the words, which made him a sought-after confessor. In his preaching he could combine oratorical flourish with a simplicity reflective of his personal humility. His commentary on renewal during the difficult post-Vatican II years was typical: 'You know, this renewal is like trying to wear new shoes ... corns and bunions hurt, but after a while you get used to the shoes and like them better than the old ones.'

BIBLIOGRAPHY: 'Christian Education,' *Basilian* 2 (January 1936) 14–15; 'Our Lady's Apostolate,' *Benedicamus* 1 (May 1948) 2–3; 'Let Us Not Sell Our Teenagers Short,' *Forum* 1 (November 1965) 151–2; 'We Should Come Forth from Our Ivory Tower,' *Forum* 3 (April 1967) 60.
SOURCES: GABF; *Annals* 5 (1978) 266, 6 (1984) 203–4, 7 (1993) 122–3; *Newsletter* (23 April 1992).

DILLON, Daniel Leo, priest, older brother of Father Joseph *Dillon, was born on a farm near Burlington, Texas (diocese of Galveston, since 1947 of Austin) on 19 November 1889, one of twelve children of John Dillon and Ellen Gleason. Two sisters, Agnes and Mary, became Sister Mary Florentia and Sister Honorata in the Congregation of Divine Providence (San Antonio). A Michigan cousin, Leo Jones, became a Maryknoll missionary in China. Daniel Dillon died in Toronto on 7 December 1948 and is buried there in the Basilian plot of Mount Hope Cemetery.

Daniel attended St Basil's College, Waco, Texas, where he formed a lifelong friendship with Thomas Patrick *O'Rourke. He won the prize for excellence each of the three years he was there, 1906–9, and showed himself to be a natural leader in sports. A year at St Michael's College, Toronto, preceded his entrance into St Basil's Novitiate, Toronto. After profession on 17 September 1911, he resumed his studies at St Michael's, and was elected class president in 1913. After taking his B.A. from the University of Toronto, 1914, he obtained teacher certification from the Ontario College of Education, Toronto, 1916–17. He did theological studies at St Basil's Scholasticate in Toronto and was ordained a priest on 30 June 1917 in St Basil's Church, Toronto, by Archbishop Neil McNeil. Thomas O'Rourke preached at his first Mass in his home parish church.

Father Dan Dillon was appointed to teach Latin and mathematics at St Thomas College (High School) in Houston. Two years later he was named its superior and principal. At the same time he taught theology to two Basilian scholastics Edward *Allor and John *O'Loane. He brought the school's curriculum into conformity with state requirements for accreditation.

In October 1922 he was appointed as superior of Assumption College, Windsor, where he strengthened the bonds of affiliation, begun by his predecessor Father Joseph *Muckle, with the University of Western Ontario. Just a year later Assumption was seriously affected by the resignation of four Basilian professors – Charles E. *Coughlin, John C. *Plomer, William G. *Rogers, and John J. *Sheridan – who chose to be incardinated in the archdiocese of Detroit rather than profess the new, stricter vow of poverty adopted by the Congregation in 1922. He also had to cope with the constant efforts of Bishop Michael Francis Fallon to move Assumption College to London. Despite this continued pressure and other administrative difficulties, he succeeded in renovating several buildings and in constructing a new classroom building later named for him.

After a three-year interval as the first Basilian principal of Catholic Central High School in Detroit, 1928–31, Daniel Dillon was called back to Assumption College to cope with the financial crisis of the Depression years. The strain of this task brought on a severe heart attack, and in 1932 he went to St Basil's Scholasticate to convalesce. For the next five years he taught a reduced schedule of theology there and served in the Curial House as treasurer, 1934–6, and as superior, 1936–7. In 1937 his genius for business led to his appointment as treasurer of the new Basilian foundation at Aquinas Institute in Rochester. From 1938 to 1940 he served as treasurer at Catholic Central High School in Detroit. He returned to Toronto, where he lived at the Curial House and taught in St Basil's Seminary. During the ensuing years ill health restricted his activity but not his spirit.

The general chapter of 1928 elected Father Dillon to the general council and succeeding chapters of 1930, 1936, 1942, and 1948 re-elected him. He was a level-headed and clear-minded councillor who gave unobtrusive service to the Congregation. In a sermon preached at his funeral, Father Edmund *McCorkell said, 'Denied the opportunity to pursue graduate studies after ordination because he was needed in the school at Houston, denied the opportunity to devote himself to the South because he was needed in the North, denied the opportunity to continue active leadership because his health was broken, he accepted the humbler roles of a teacher in the seminary and a councillor, and he was highly successful in both roles.'

As an administrator, Father Dillon never seemed to be in a hurry. He was always willing to spend time in conversation with visitors. He managed, nevertheless, to get through a massive and exacting schedule of work. His work brought him few contacts among the laity, but among the clergy he had the gift for forming lasting friendships.

Father Dillon's lectures in moral theology at St Basil's Seminary showed remarkable common sense. Some were privately distributed in near-print form.

BIBLIOGRAPHY: *The Simple Vow of Poverty*. Toronto, 1949.
SOURCES: GABF; *Annals* 1 (1948) 233–6; *Basilides, Assumption College* (Windsor, 1930); J.W. Embser, 'Daniel L. Dillon, a Biography,' *Basilian Teacher* 1 (April 1957) 9–11; E.J. McCorkell, 'Sermon Preached at the Funeral of Father Daniel Dillon,' *Benedicamus* 2 (January 1949) 9–11, 15; McMahon, *Pure Zeal* 24–85; Raphael O'Loughlin, *Basilian Leaders from Texas* (Houston, 1991) 46–63; *Yearbook SMC* 5 (1914), 9 (1918). For extensive documentation relating to Father Dillon's presidency of Assumption College, see Power, *Assumption College* 5 34–105.

DILLON, Joseph Patrick, priest, younger brother of Father Daniel *Dillon, was born on a farm in Burlington, Texas (diocese of Galveston, since 1947 of Austin), on 16 April 1897, the seventh of twelve children of John Dillon and Ellen Gleason. Two sisters, Agnes and Mary, became Sister Mary Florentia and Sister Honorata in the Congregation of Divine Providence (San Antonio). A Michigan cousin, Leo Jones, became a Maryknoll missionary in China. Joseph Dillon died in Houston on 27 October 1953 and is buried there in the Basilian plot of Garden of Gethsemane, Forest Park Lawndale Cemetery.

Joseph Dillon made three years of his high school course at St Basil's College, Waco, Texas, 1912–15, then spent two years at St Michael's College, Toronto, before entering St Basil's Novitiate, Toronto. After profession on 10 August 1918, he returned to St Michael's College (B.A., University of Toronto, 1920). He attended the Ontario College of Education in Toronto, 1922–3, did theological studies at St Basil's Scholasticate, Toronto, and was ordained priest on 22 December 1923 at St Augustine's Seminary, Toronto, by Bishop Alexander MacDonald.

'Joe' Dillon's first appointment as a priest was to St Thomas College (High School), Houston, where he taught and served as treasurer in 1924–5. During the year 1925–6 he studied Spanish at the Universidad Nacional in Mexico City, paying his expenses by teaching at the Marist Brothers' Colegio Francés there. Hostility to clergy increased dramatically during the year, and he was said to be the last of the foreign priests to leave Mexico City. He taught at St Thomas College, 1931–2, but colitis and an ulcerated stomach curtailed his teaching and brought his appointment in 1932 to parochial work at St Anne's Parish, Houston. The year 1935–6 saw him back at St Thomas College.

In August 1936 Joseph Dillon eagerly accepted the invitation of Father Henry *Carr, superior general, to do missionary work with Mexican immigrants in Texas. For three years he commuted from St Anne's Parish in Houston to serve large sections of southwest Harris County, until Our Lady of Guadalupe Mission Center was opened in March 1939 at Rosenberg. From there Father Dillon exercised ministry in nine towns and numerous ranches and farms. He served as rector and pastor until 1946, when continuing poor health required his move north to work with Latin Americans in Ste Anne's Parish, Detroit. After another year of recuperation at St Thomas High School, 1947–8, he returned to Our Lady of Guadalupe Mission Center in 1948. In 1951 he moved to Our Lady of Mount Carmel Mission Center, Wharton, where he lived until his death from cancer two years later.

Writing of Father Dillon's missionary work, Father John *Collins said, 'Padre José was stern, but he had a deep understanding, a great love, and a sympathetic appreciation of the Mexican people. He had lived through poverty, he had worked on a cotton farm. He could see and feel all the problems of the Mexican sharecropper.' The people at Wharton showed their appreciation of his work by erecting an outdoor shrine to his memory.

BIBLIOGRAPHY: 'Notes from the Mexican Missions,' *Basilian* 3 (January 1937) 17, 20; 'Mexican Mission Needs,' *Basilian* 4 (June 1938) 106.
SOURCES: GABF; *Annals* 2 (1954) 151–2, (1955) 213; J.F. Collins, 'Father Dillon, Missionary,' *Benedicamus* 7 (February 1954) 4–7, 10; idem, 'Joseph P. Dillon, a Biography,' *Basilian Teacher* 2 (March 1958) 24–6; *Houston Chronicle* (29 July 1926); *New York Herald-Tribune* (20 July 1926) 2; Raphael O'Loughlin, *Basilian Leaders from Texas* (Houston, 1991) 64–77; *Yearbook SMC* 15 (1924).

DOLAN, Leonard Joseph, priest, was born at Nelson, New Brunswick (diocese of Chatham, in 1938 diocese of Bathurst, now diocese of St John), on 19 March 1899, the son of Thomas Dolan and Mary Gorman. He died in Rochester on 28 January 1948 and is buried in Holy Sepulchre Cemetery there.

'Tim' Dolan, as he was always called, received his high school education at St Thomas College, Chatham, New Brunswick, 1914–19. He entered St Basil's Novitiate, Toronto and was professed on 30 August 1920. After one year at St Michael's College in Toronto, he transferred to Assumption College, Windsor (B.A., University of Western Ontario, 1924). He did theological studies at St Basil's Scholasticate, Toronto, attended the Ontario College of Education, 1925–6, and obtained an M.A. in philosophy from the University of Toronto in 1927. He was ordained a priest on 21 December 1927 in St Basil's Church, Toronto, by Bishop Alexander MacDonald.

His first appointment after ordination took Father Dolan to St Thomas College in Houston, where he taught English. In 1936 he was assigned to St Michael's College and then, in 1937, he went to Aquinas Institute, Rochester. In 1938 he returned to St Michael's College, where he showed an increasing interest in preaching retreats and was much sought after as a confessor. Six years later he was appointed confessor at St Basil's Novitiate, Rochester. Late in 1947 cancer was diagnosed; he died within a month. He was the first confrere buried in the Basilian plot of Holy Sepulchre Cemetery, Rochester.

Father Dolan possessed an altogether uncommon personality. In conversation he was dogmatic and picturesque in his choice of language. Father John *O'Loane wrote of him, 'To his other gifts he added a droll sense of humour that could be called pleasing-sardonic.' As long as his health was good, he was full of energy and 'bounce.' He liked to preach and to train students to speak in public.

BIBLIOGRAPHY: 'Our Students and the Eucharist,' *Basilian* 1 (October 1938) 89–91; 'On Teaching the Writing of Letters,' *Basilian Teacher* 3 (October 1958) 25–6. SOURCES: GABF; *Annals* 1 (1948) 198–200; J.H. O'Loane, 'Leonard J. Dolan,' *Basilian Teacher* 1 (May 1957) 6–8; *Yearbook SMC* 19 (1928); *Yearbook, University of Western Ontario* (London, 1924).

DONLON, James Alexander, priest, was born on 15 August 1904 at Sandwich (now Windsor), Ontario, to George Donlon and Caroline Dufour. He died on 19 December 1987 in Windsor and is buried there in the Basilian plot of Heavenly Rest Cemetery.

'Jakie,' as he was familiarly called all through his life, was educated at St Francis School, Sandwich, and Assumption High School, Windsor. The family was poor, the father having died when Jakie was eighteen months old. As a youth he paid his own way by a variety of jobs, including that of proof-reader and college sports reporter for the *Windsor Star*. The experience of poverty did not prevent his becoming a remarkably cheerful, outgoing person; but it did generate in him a devotion to the poor and marginalized. In 1926, after completing four years of high school, he enrolled at Assumption College (B.A., University of Western Ontario, 1929), and entered St Basil's Novitiate, Toronto, making his first profession of vows on 12 September 1930.

As a scholastic he was appointed to St Basil's Scholasticate, Toronto, where in addition to taking his first year of theology he attended the Ontario College of Education (teaching certification, 1931). He was ordained to the priesthood on 21 December 1933 in Assumption Church, Windsor, by Bishop Alexander MacDonald. In 1934 Father Donlon was appointed to his alma mater, Assumption High School, where he taught French and served as director of athletics. In 1940 he began a forty-seven-year ministry in Basilian parishes: Ste Anne's, Detroit, 1940–4, as assistant pastor; Assumption Church, Windsor, 1944–62, as pastor; St Basil's, Toronto, 1962–70, as pastor; Assumption Church, Windsor, 1970–87, as pastor.

He was a feisty athlete, in spite of his small stature. His love of sports, combined with his devotion to the poor, prompted him in his first years at Ste Anne's to build a skating rink in the parish and, from time to time, to take groups of youth to Assumption College for a swim. To reach out further to outcasts he served for twenty years as chaplain at the Provincial Jail in Windsor. In an interview with the *Windsor Star* in 1981 he said, 'We often forget that these people behind bars are real people, with souls and fine minds. They are lonely and often fearful. ... We can rehabilitate these people if we show an interest.' Because he brought cigarettes and candy to the prisoners, he acquired the sobriquet 'candy man.' He also worked with the Goodfellows in Windsor, and could be seen on cold days before Christmas selling the Goodfellows' Christmas edition of the *Windsor Star*. He established the St Vincent de Paul Society at Assumption Parish in 1954. In Toronto he paid special attention to the Chinese new Canadians. His charity, moreover, began at home: in community he looked out for the needs of others, and a sick confrere could always count on a visit from Jakie – and a joke.

A huge crowd attended Father Donlon's funeral at Assumption Church, where he had been baptized, confirmed, ordained, and had served as pastor for a total of thirty-five years. A letter he had intended to send with his Christmas cards was read at his funeral, including these words: 'I have recovered 95% [from the heart attack] and I am back on the soul-searching trail with much gratitude to Almighty God for his goodness to me.'

BIBLIOGRAPHY: (With R.J. *Scollard) *Sources for the History of St Basil's Parish, Toronto*. Toronto, 1970.
SOURCES: GABF; *Annals* 5 (1981) 540, 6 (1984) 204, 6 (1988) 711–13; *Newsletter* (29 December 1987).

DONNELLY, Vincent Ignatius, priest, first native of the United States ordained for the Congregation, was born in New York City on 26 November 1871, the son of Edward Donnelly and Mary McKenna. He died there on 1 October 1940 and was buried in the Basilian plot of Assumption Cemetery, Windsor.

After early education in New York City, Vincent Donnelly went in 1888 to St Michael's College, Toronto. Four years later, on 23 August 1892, he became a member of the first class of novices at the newly opened St Basil's Novitiate, Toronto, on Kendal (now Tweedsmuir) Avenue. After profession in 1893 he continued his studies at St Michael's and at St Basil's Scholasticate. He took final vows on 18 September 1896, then taught for one year at Assumption College in Windsor, and was ordained to the priesthood on 24 June 1898.

Father Donnelly received successive appointments to St Michael's College, 1898–9, to the founding staff of St Basil's College, Waco, Texas, 1899–1900, to the founding staff of St Thomas College, Houston, 1900–1, and to the first Basilian staff at St Mary's Seminary, LaPorte, Texas, 1901–2. He returned to the college in Waco, 1902–3, 1910–13, and served again in LaPorte, 1903–10. In 1913 he moved again to St Thomas College, where he was superior and principal, 1914–16.

In 1916 Father Donnelly began a series of parish appointments at St John the Baptist Parish, Amherstburg, Ontario, as assistant, 1916–21, 1927–30, and Ste Anne's Parish, Detroit, 1921–7. After spending the year 1930–1 at St Michael's College, he returned to Ste Anne's, Detroit, 1931–5, before retiring to Assumption College. He died while visiting relatives in New York.

Known as 'Vinnie' to his friends, he was a born storyteller with a poet's gift for the use of words. He was an eloquent preacher who, as a young priest, was known as 'the silver-tongued orator of the South.' When he entered parish work in 1916 the purpose behind the change was to allow him more freedom to accept preaching engagements.

Father Donnelly was one of three Basilian priests who chose to remain in the Congregation without taking the new, stricter vow of poverty adopted in 1922. He loved to tell stories about his early days in Toronto and his years in Texas. None of his reminiscences ever contained an unkind word.

BIBLIOGRAPHY: 'History of St John the Baptist Parish, Amherstburg (1878–1928),' *Windsor Border Cities Star* (7 July 1928); 'Christmas' (poem), *Basilian* 1 (December 1935) 135–6; 'Madonna' (poem), *Basilian* 2 (January 1936) 19.
SOURCES: GABF.

DONOHER, Paul Bernard, priest, member of the Congregation 1945–74, brother of Father Edward Donoher CSB, was born in Toledo, Ohio, on 25 May 1927, the son of Thomas Donoher and Elizabeth Schlagheck. He died on 5 April 2000, in Stuart, Florida. His remains were cremated.

Paul attended Toledo Central Catholic High School and Assumption High School, Windsor. He made his first profession at the Rochester Novitiate on 12 September 1945. In 1949 he graduated from Assumption College with a B.A. from the University of Western Ontario. He taught at Catholic Central High School, Detroit, in 1949–50. He resided in St Michael's College School, Toronto, while taking theology at St Basil's Seminary, 1950–1. After teaching at Aquinas Institute, Rochester, in 1951–2, he studied theology at St Basil's Seminary, 1952–5. He was ordained to the priesthood by Cardinal James Charles McGuigan on 29 June 1954 in St Basil's Church, Toronto.

Father Donoher was assistant principal at Assumption High School in 1955–8 and was second councillor at Catholic Central High School, 1958–60. He taught at Andrean High School, Gary (now Merrillville), Indiana, 1960–1, at Aquinas Institute, 1961–2, and at Catholic Central High School, 1962–72. Paul was a brilliant history teacher and a master choral conductor. Under his direction, the Catholic Central Glee Club became the only high school group to be admitted to the Intercollegiate Musical Association, an organization composed of male choruses from prestigious universities.

In 1972 Paul Donoher was given leave of absence and joined the staff of Detroit Country Day School, where he taught until his retirement in 1990. In 1974 he was dispensed from all obligations of priesthood and religious life. Paul was survived by his wife, Gloria, and by two stepdaughters and one stepson.

SOURCES: GABF; *Annals* 2 (1955) 162; *Newsletter* (22 April 2000); Father Edward Donoher CSB.

DONOVAN, Charles Patrick, priest, was born in Wellsville, New York (diocese of Buffalo), on 17 March 1892, one of six children of Michael Donovan and Ellen Curtin. He died in Toronto on 14 October 1981 and is buried in the Basilian plot of Holy Cross Cemetery, Thornhill, Ontario.

'Charlie' attended Immaculate Conception Parish Grade School in Wellsville and the high school section of St Michael's College, Toronto, 1907–10. He did his university studies at St Michael's College (B.A., University of Toronto, 1914) and earned a teaching certificate from the Ontario College of Education, Toronto, in 1915. That same year he entered St Basil's Novitiate, Toronto, and was professed on 17 September 1916. He did two years of theology courses, 1916–18, at St Basil's Scholasticate, Toronto, and the remaining two years, 1918–20, in Windsor, where the scholasticate had been relocated in 1918. He was ordained to the priesthood on 29 February 1920 in St Peter's Cathedral, London, Ontario, by Bishop Michael Fallon.

Father Donovan's forty-five-year teaching career began at St Michael's College School in September 1920, followed by six years at Assumption College School, 1921–7, where he taught mathematics and coached football. In August 1927 he was one of the group sent to establish the Basilian presence at Aquinas Institute, Rochester, but in 1928 he began a four-year stint at Catholic Central, Detroit (at that time, Holy Name Institute), before returning to Assumption College School, 1932–6. He was on sick leave from 1936 to 1939, spending the year 1936–7 at Strawberry Island in Lake Simcoe. He returned to Aquinas to teach mathematics and to head that department. After some twenty years there, a painful condition of varicose veins obliged him to reduce his schedule, and in 1965 he officially retired from teaching, though he remained available to lend a hand where he could and to advise and encourage beginning teachers. He celebrated his golden jubilee of priesthood in 1970 at Aquinas, but in 1974 moved to the Basilian Fathers infirmary in Toronto.

Charlie Donovan was an inspiring, versatile, even fascinating teacher – so ready was his wit and so apt his comments. He was a big man of fine appearance and genial manner. He was the first to recognize his weaknesses and to accept the consequences of his actions. He lived less concerned about the theory of religious life than about its daily, faithful practice. His success was predicted as early as 1917 when his pastor in Wellsville, Monsignor O'Brien, wrote in his letter of recommendation of Charles for the Basilian novitiate, 'Our boy Charles will prove one of your most successful workers in the vineyard of the Lord.'

SOURCES: GABF; *Annals* 4 (1971) 184–5, 5 (1981) 536, 6 (1982) 105–6; *Newsletter* (29 October 1981).

DORE, James WILFRID, priest, was born in Toronto on 5 January 1901, the eldest of eight children of James William Dore and Louise McAuliffe. A nephew, Paul Burns, was ordained as a Basilian in 1968 but later withdrew from the Congregation. Another nephew, the late Michael Burns, withdrew from the Congregation as a scholastic. Wilfrid Dore died in Toronto on 20 June 1981 and is buried in the Basilian plot of Holy Cross Cemetery, Thornhill, Ontario.

When 'Wilf' was one year old the family moved from Toronto to Hamilton, Ontario, where he attended St Patrick's Separate School and St Mary's High School, 1913–17. From there he went to St Michael's

College, Toronto, where he played football in the university intercollegiate league and, during his last two years of study, taught in the high school. Upon graduation (B.A., University of Toronto, 1922), he entered St Basil's Novitiate, Toronto, making first profession on 27 September 1923. He did theological studies at St Basil's Scholasticate, Toronto, and in 1924–5 also attended the Ontario College of Education (high school teaching certification, 1925). In 1925 he also received an M.A. in educational psychology from the University of Toronto. On 18 December 1926 he was ordained to the priesthood in St Basil's Church, Toronto, by Bishop Alexander MacDonald.

Father Dore had four one-year appointments teaching mathematics: Assumption College School, Windsor, 1927–8, Catholic Central High School, Detroit, 1928–9, 1930–1, and St Thomas High School, Houston, 1929–30. In 1931 he moved to St Michael's College, Toronto, where he taught mathematics for some years. Continuing his higher studies he obtained a B.Paed. (University of Toronto, 1937) and a Ph.D. in philosophy (University of Ottawa, 1941; thesis: 'The Intellectualistic Foundation of Freedom in the Doctrine of St Thomas Aquinas').

For the next twenty years Father Dore lectured in philosophy at St Michael's College. For ten of those years he was also dean of residence. He served as moderator of scholastics, 1952–4, and as councillor for the local Basilian community, 1954–60. He also represented the teaching staff of St Michael's College on the senate of the University of Toronto. In addition to these responsibilities Father Dore was active in adult education programs, co-operative housing, credit unions, rural life movements, and the Young Christian Worker movement. He was an expert and devoted gardener: the beautiful rockery which graces the front of Brennan Hall at St Michael's was created and maintained by him for many years.

In 1963, at the age of sixty-two, he was appointed the first Basilian rector and principal of St Joseph's College, Edmonton, Alberta, at the request of Father Henry *Carr. In 1965 he relinquished his administrative responsibilities but continued his teaching there and took great interest in developing the library that became his pride and joy. His fine taste in liturgical art found its scope in the renovations that he supervised in the chapel.

The arthritic condition which had plagued him for many years required him in 1975 to return to Toronto, where he took up residence at St Basil's College. Here he tutored a novice, Dr John *LaCroix, in theology, and cared for his plants; but declining health made it necessary in 1980 for him to move to the Basilian Fathers Residence (Infirmary).

Father Wilf Dore, a big man, impressive in his huge black cape, was a formidable, clear, and intense teacher. He held his opinions strongly and professed them in the same way. He used to say jokingly that his mother called him a 'Catholic bigot.' He was indeed a man dedicated to the Church and the Basilian community. Many were attracted to him as confessor and spiritual director. The young, the ill, and the socially abused found him a man of compassion and peace.

SOURCES: GABF; *Annals* 5 (1974) 14, 5 (1977) 196, 6 (1982) 94–6; *Newsletter* (7 July 1981); Brian F. Hogan, 'Salted by Fire: Studies in Catholic Social Thought and Action in Ontario, 1931–61,' Ph.D. diss. (University of Toronto, 1986); Kirley, *Congregation in France* 235.

DORSEY, Joseph Barrett, priest, was born in Syracuse, New York, on 10 May 1915, the eldest of three children of John Dorsey and Margaret Barrett. He died in Rochester on 28 December 1988 and is buried there in the Basilian plot of Holy Sepulchre Cemetery.

'Joe' attended elementary school and Most Holy Rosary High School in his home town. After two years, 1933–5, in the arts course at St Michael's College, Toronto, he entered St Basil's Novitiate, Toronto, made first profession on 15 August 1936, and returned to St Michael's College (B.A., University of Toronto, 1938). After one year of theology courses at St Basil's Seminary, Toronto, he went to Catholic Central High School, Detroit, for two years of teaching, of theological studies, and of graduate work in English at the University of Detroit. He returned to St Basil's Seminary in 1941 and was ordained to the priesthood in St Basil's Church, Toronto, on 15 August 1942 by Archbishop James Charles McGuigan.

Father Dorsey spent the year 1943–4 at Catholic University of America, Washington, D.C. (M.A., English, 1945). From 1944 to 1947 he taught English and coached basketball at Aquinas Institute, Rochester. In 1947 he became assistant professor of English at St Michael's College, and was on the local council of the Basilian Fathers. He also did two additional years of graduate studies at the University of Ottawa.

He returned to Rochester in 1961 to take on the duties of vice-president and dean, as well as associate professor of English, at St John Fisher College. During the next quarter-century he served in various other capacities in the college, such as dean of student life and vice-president for alumni affairs. His interests and talents found scope beyond St John Fisher: he was appointed to several college accreditation teams, was a member of numerous professional societies in higher education, served as chairman of the Monroe and Wayne counties chapter of the March of Dimes, 1976, and was elected chairman of the Rochester Diocesan Priests' Council, 1977. He became the first Roman Catholic priest to run for political office in New York State when he was nominated by the Democratic Party for the state senate in the elections of 1976. In 1977 he was elected to the general council of the Basilian Fathers as regional representative for Eastern United States, a position he held until 1985. While in this office he continued his involvement with St John Fisher College on a part-time basis, except for one year when he was fully occupied as interim president during the search for a new president, 1980. In 1985 he was appointed assistant pastor at Christ the King Church, Rochester, where cancer gradually restricted his ministry but not his enthusiasm for life, literature, friends, the Basilian community, and the world of the spirit.

Joe Dorsey was the most generous of men with his time and talents. His faith was the well-spring of the enthusiasm which he brought to all he did. He kept abreast of literature and poetry, scriptural studies, and world events. New books on education, the Church, and scientific discoveries would excite him to animated conversation, an art he enjoyed to the fullest.

BIBLIOGRAPHY: 'Catholic Thinking and Modern Problems,' *Basilian* 3 (December 1937) 133–4; 'Preliminaries,' *Benedicamus* 1 (June 1947) 2, 7; 'Retreats Should Have a New Format,' *Forum* 3 (November 1964) 18–19.
SOURCES: GABF; *Annals* 1 (1943) 27–8, 6 (1987) 494, 6 (1989) 803–4; *Newsletter* (30 December 1988).

DOUGHERTY, John Roger, priest, was born in Rochester on 30 January 1928, one of four children of Harry F. Dougherty and Veronica Lynch. He died in Windsor on 9 August 1996 and is buried in the Basilian plot of St John the Baptist Cemetery, Amherstburg Ontario.
'Jack' Dougherty came to know the Basilian Fathers during his years at Aquinas Institute, Rochester, where he graduated in 1946 and entered St Basil's Novitiate, which was located on the same grounds as Aquinas. After his first profession of vows on 15 August 1947, he was appointed to Holy Rosary Seminary, Toronto, for the first year of his undergraduate studies, which he continued in 1948 at Assumption

College, Windsor (B.A., University of Western Ontario, 1951). He taught at Assumption College for the academic year 1951-2, and began theological studies at St Basil's Seminary, Toronto. He was ordained to the priesthood in St Basil's Church, Toronto, on 29 June 1955 by Bishop Francis Allen.

After completing his theology course, Father Dougherty did a year of graduate studies in biology at Cornell University, 1956-7. He taught biology at Assumption College School, Windsor, before being appointed to the staff of Assumption University, 1958-62. After teaching one year, 1962-3 at St Thomas High School, Houston, he returned to Windsor to the staff of the newly created University of Windsor.

In 1974, with Father Robert Howell and Father Joseph Quinn, he founded Chelsea House, a centre for community life where, along with his teaching at the University of Windsor, he engaged in ministries of retreats and spiritual renewal. When he retired from teaching at the University of Windsor, he assumed responsibility for Star of the Sea Mission on Pelee Island in Lake Erie.

Jack Dougherty looked at life positively and creatively. In his later years he became a potter, delighting in fashioning from clay. He felt liberated by the passage in Jeremiah, 18:1-11, the image of the Lord as the potter and us as the clay. It revealed to him that, as the Lord can remake what is defective or broken, so could he, too, share in that image by a ministry of compassion towards the broken. He had a strong appreciation and love of the beauty and variety of all forms of life. They were to be cherished when healthy, nursed when sick, and mourned at death. To reject one part of life was to diminish the whole, to reject the gift of life itself. Such contemplative gifts explain the impact he had on the many persons who approached him.

For several years Jack Dougherty suffered from osteosarcomas which eventually metasticized to his internal organs. He was hospitalized for the last few months of his life, with alternating periods of intensive and palliative care, during all of which he showed admirable patience.

SOURCES: GABF; *Annals* 2 (1955) 198, 8 (1997) 111; *Newsletter* (20 October 1996).

DROHAN, Richard Patrick, priest, was born in Toronto on 17 March 1873, the son of David Drohan and Mary Rowan. He died in Houston on 19 December 1908 and was buried in the Basilian plot of St Michael's Cemetery, Toronto.

Richard Drohan grew up on a farm near Elora, Ontario, and there attended St Mary's Separate School. He did his high school course at De La Salle Institute in Toronto and in 1892 joined the Christian Brothers, receiving the name in religion of Brother Richard. Subsequently he took courses at the Toronto Normal School. In 1896 he withdrew from the Christian Brothers in order to study for the priesthood at St Michael's College, Toronto. Five years later he entered St Basil's Novitiate, Toronto, where he was professed on 15 August 1902. He did theological studies at St Basil's Scholasticate, Toronto, taught at St Basil's College in Waco, Texas, 1904–6, and was ordained priest on 27 December 1905.

In 1906 Father Drohan moved to St Thomas College in Houston, where he taught mathematics and physics. Strongly built and a natural athlete, he frequently joined in the games of the students. His death in 1908 resulted from injuries sustained while playing football with them.

SOURCES: GABF; Charles Collins, 'Basilians I Have Known,' transcribed in Robert J. Scollard, 'Historical Notes C.S.B.' 10 113–17 (GABF).

DROUILLARD, Clarence Joseph, priest, member of the Congregation 1939–75, relative of Father Louis *Bondy CSB, was born on 14 July 1921 in Windsor, the only son of Ovilla Drouillard and Josephine Bondy. He died suddenly on Paradise Island, Nassau, on 14 May 1979.

Clarence made the first three years of his high school course at the University of Ottawa High School and completed it at Assumption College, Windsor. At the end of his novitiate year he professed his first vows on 15 August 1939, and then obtained his Honours matriculation at St Michael's College School prior to enrolment in the Honours Moderns course at the University of Toronto (B.A., 1944). In obtaining the M.A. in French literature from Toronto in 1947, he was awarded the Quebec *Bonne Entente* prize for French and the college Gold Medal in Moderns. He completed his studies in theology at St Basil's Seminary, Toronto, and was ordained to the priesthood on 29 June 1948 in St Basil's Church, Toronto, by Cardinal James Charles McGuigan.

Father Drouillard did further graduate studies leading to a Ph.D. degree at Laval University, 1971, submitting a thesis entitled 'Le réalisme de Corneille.' After a further year at the University of Paris, he taught at St Michael's College, Toronto, and St John Fisher College, Rochester, before joining the staff of Assumption University in 1956 as professor of French language and literature. He became head of the department in 1958 and continued in these positions at the University of Windsor until 1969. In 1975 he was accepted by the diocese of London and eventually incardinated therein while continuing to teach at the university.

As head of the French department, Father Drouillard placed emphasis on the development of literary and linguistic skills, and it was because of his initiative that the department became one of the first in Ontario to introduce laboratory methods.

BIBLIOGRAPHY: 'Apostolate of the Laity,' *Benedicamus* 2 (November 1948) 4–5; 'The Teaching of Modern Languages,' *Basilian Teacher* 2 (January 1958) 15–17.
SOURCES: GABF; *Annals* 1 (1948) 220; Memo, University of Windsor Information Services.

DUGGAN, William John, priest, was born in Wellsville, New York (diocese of Buffalo) on 27 August 1910, the son of Cornelius Duggan and Teresa Freaney. He died in Houston on 1 December 1973 and is buried in the Basilian plot of Holy Sepulchre Cemetery, Rochester.

Bill Duggan did his elementary and secondary education in Wellsville before going to St Michael's College in 1927. In 1931, before completing his arts degree, he entered St Basil's Novitiate, Toronto, and took his first vows on 15 August 1932. He returned to St Michael's College for one year (B.A., Honours History, University of Toronto, 1933). After graduation he was appointed to St Basil's Scholasticate, Toronto, for theology, 1933–8, with an interval of a one-year teaching assignment, 1935–6, at Catholic Central High School, Detroit. He was ordained to the priesthood on 18 December 1937 in St Basil's Church, Toronto, by Archbishop James Charles McGuigan.

In 1938, Father Duggan was appointed to Aquinas Institute, Rochester, where he taught and served as superior and principal, 1944–9. In 1949 he was appointed to Assumption High School, Windsor, 1949–52, and in 1952 to St Thomas High School, Houston, 1952–9, superior and principal 1955–9. In 1959 he was appointed as the founding superior and principal of Andrean High School, Gary (now Merrillville), Indiana. In 1961 he returned to St Thomas High School, where he remained for the rest of his life. An inveterate golfer, he took advantage of the proximity of the links on many Saturdays and holidays.

Father Duggan held a master's degree in education from the University of Rochester as well as teacher qualification credits from the University of Michigan and the University of Texas. He gave himself unsparingly to all he undertook. His extensive knowledge of American history and vital interest in American politics made him an inspiring and effective teacher. He had a commanding presence, being a big man of fine appearance. His manner was habitually gentle and benevolent, though never lacking in firmness.

In his eleven years as a local superior in three different houses, Bill Duggan strove to make community life a positive experience for all. He had a genuine interest in his confreres and a readiness to go out to those in need. He seemed to embody the best of Basilian traditions, just as he embodied much that was solidly traditional in the Church itself. His strong devotion to the Mother of God inspired his appeal at the 1973 general chapter to reaffirm Basilian devotion to the Blessed Virgin Mary, expressing the opinion that success in recruitment was in direct proportion to the community's devotion to Mary. At that same chapter his interventions at plenary sessions were always clear and cogent, never lacking in sensitivity to opinions differing from his own.

BIBLIOGRAPHY: 'Mathematics in Basilian Schools [forum],' *Basilian Teacher* 4 (December 1959) 66–7.
SOURCES: GABF; *Annals* 5 (1974) 51–2; *Newsletter* (2 December 1973).

DuMOUCHEL, Albert Pierre, priest, was born at Grand Marais, Sandwich West (now Windsor), on 8 September 1856, the son of Jérôme DuMouchel and Jeanne Côté. He died in Windsor on 2 May 1925 and is buried there in the Basilian plot of Assumption Cemetery.

Albert DuMouchel (Dumouchelle) was one of the first students to enrol at Assumption College in Windsor when the Congregation returned there in 1870. By 1874 he was teaching elementary Latin as well as studying for the priesthood. He entered St Basil's Novitiate, then located at Assumption College, in September 1876 but withdrew in January 1877 to go to the Grand Séminaire de Montréal. There he again failed to settle his vocation, and in 1879 he sailed for France, where he re-entered the Basilian novitiate at Feyzin (Isère, now Rhône) on 30 July 1879. He returned to Canada the following year, finished theological studies at St Michael's College, Toronto, and was ordained priest on 17 June 1883.

Father DuMouchel remained at St Michael's College until 1888, when he was appointed to the College of Mary Immaculate at Beaconfield House, Plymouth, England. Two years later he was back at St

Michael's College as director of studies. In 1895 he went to Assumption College in the same capacity, but returned to St Michael's College in 1901. The year 1909–10 was spent at Ste Anne's Parish in Detroit, but again he moved back to St Michael's College, 1910, where in addition to teaching he also served as master of scholastics until 1916, when he moved to Ste Anne's Parish. In 1921 he went to St Basil's Scholasticate, Toronto, and in 1923 he was transferred to Assumption Parish in Windsor, where he died two years later.

The *Golden Jubilee Volume of Assumption College* referred to Father DuMouchel as 'a man of extraordinary talent, which he devoted unselfishly to the welfare of the College.' There and at St Michael's College he drew up the first modern catalogues describing the courses taught in these institutions. He was a traditionalist in education and did not approve of the trend away from the old classical course.

Father DuMouchel was involved in administration for many years as director of studies, councillor, and treasurer, and on several occasions he served for some months as acting superior at Assumption College and St Michael's College. The general chapter of 1910 elected him treasurer general, a post he filled with distinction until 1922. In the conflict which arose between the Province of France and that of Canada the sympathies of 'Doumie,' as he was often called, were divided and neither side could claim him as a partisan. He strongly opposed any change in the vow of poverty; and, when the greater part of the Congregation adopted the stricter vow in 1922, he was one of three priests who chose to retain the old one while remaining a Basilian.

SOURCES: GABF; *Jubilee, Assumption*; Kirley, *Congregation in France* 14, 29, 33–4, 57; *Purple and White* (10 May 1925).

DUPLAY, Jean-Marie, priest, was born 18 April 1839 at Saint-Victor (Haute-Loire, diocese of Le Puy).

Jean-Marie was one of the first group of Basilians who founded the Collège Saint-Charles at Blidah, Algeria, in 1868. He then taught at the Ecole cléricale de Périgueux (Dordogne), 1869–75. He was ordained a priest on 20 September 1873 at the Collège du Sacré-Coeur, Annonay. After the year 1875–6 at the Collège Saint-Pierre at Châteauroux (Indre), he withdrew from the Congregation but came back a few months later and accepted an appointment as prefect in the Collège de Privas (Ardèche). Unsure of his vocation in a teaching community, he changed schools four times in four years: Collège du Sacré-Coeur,

Annonay, 1878–9 and 1880–1, and the Collège Saint-Pierre in Châteauroux, 1879–80 and 1881–2. Records show that in August 1889 he was a chaplain in Saint-Etienne (Loire), archdiocese of Lyon. Eventually he was granted permission to live outside the community at his own expense, still under vows.

SOURCE: Pouzol, 'Notices.'

DURAND, Eugène, priest, younger brother of Fathers Hilaire *Durand and Noël *Durand in the family of six boys and two girls of Victor Durand and Henriette Chaudanson, was born at Montpezat-sous-Bauzon (Ardèche) on 30 November 1855. He died in Annonay on 23 January 1932 and is buried there in the cemetery on the grounds of the Collège du Sacré-Coeur.

Eugène Durand studied at the Collège de Privas and then at the Collège du Bourg-Saint-Andéol where his brother Father Hilaire *Durand was superior. He had completed secondary school when he went to the Basilian novitiate at Feyzin (Isère, now Rhône). In 1881 he went to Paris where he completed a *licence ès sciences* at the Institut catholique. He was ordained to the priesthood by Archbishop Armand de Charbonnel in the chapel of the Collège du Sacré-Coeur on 23 September 1882. He was appointed to Sainte-Barbe, the Basilian minor seminary in Annonay.

In 1884 Father Durand became the superior of the College of Mary Immaculate, Beaconfield House, Plymouth, England, where he taught until the college closed in 1903. He remained in England serving as military chaplain to the British army at Plymouth until 1914. In 1901 and 1907 he accompanied his brother Noël, who was then superior general, on his canonical visits to North America, probably acting as his interpreter. From 1903 when anticlerical laws took effect in France, Basilian houses in North America were advised to address all mail to the superior general in care of his brother 'Eugène Durand, Beaconfield House, Plymouth.'

On the eve of the 1914 war, Father Durand returned to France, where he did pastoral ministry in the southern Ardèche, especially at the Parish of Saint-Pierre-du-Colombier, canton of Bourget. He was mobilized and served as *brigadier d'artillerie* in the active army during the war. On 26 April 1922 he was elected assistant to Father Julien *Giraud, the provincial superior. After the separation of the French and North American communities that same year, Father Durand was elected *économe général* of the French Basilians at the general chapter on 12 August 1922. He was re-elected in 1928 and held this position until his death. He also continued to be the correspondent for the Basilians in France with those in America.

In 1923 the bishop of Viviers confided the Petit Séminaire de Saint-Charles, Annonay, formerly the Institution des Dames du Sacré-Coeur, to the Basilian Fathers. Father Durand spent the rest of his life there, as bursar, 1923-8, and as spiritual director, 1928-32. He was a short man with a little beard, methodical, intelligent, and deeply spiritual. He had the habit of doing morning gymnastic exercises.

SOURCES: GABF; Kirley, *Community in France* 110, 152n388, 165n421, 201; Kirley, *Congregation in France* 3, 12, 40, 42, 68-9, 79-83, 87-8, 90, 93, 97-8, 119, 122-4, 126-7, 130, 137, 140-4, 149, 155, 157-8, 160, 174, 175, 207; Pouzol, 'Notices'; *Semaine religieuse de Viviers* (12 February 1932) 96.

DURAND, Hilaire, priest, was born on 19 February 1836 at Montpezat-sous-Bauzon (Ardèche), elder brother of two other Basilians, Fathers Eugène *Durand and Noël *Durand, in a family of six boys and two girls of Victor Durand and Henriette Chaudanson. He died at Châteauroux (Indre) on 5 August 1880 and is buried in the local cemetery.

Hilaire Durand did his early studies at the Petit Séminaire d'Aubenas (Ardèche), which opened in 1852. He entered the Basilian novitiate at Privas (Ardèche) on 1 November 1856, and worked at the same time as recreation and study-hall master in the Collège de Privas. At the end of January 1857 he was moved to the Collège des Cordeliers, Annonay, where he was put in charge of the *classe de sixième* and also helped with the supervision of recreation and study hall. He made his first profession in 1858 and taught in Basilian schools while doing theological studies. He was *professeur de cinquième* at the Collège de Privas, 1858-60, and worked as supply teacher at the Collège des Cordeliers, 1860-1. He was ordained to the priesthood on 23 February 1861 in Avignon.

Father Durand received appointments to teach *seconde* at the Collège des Cordeliers, 1861-2, at the Collège de Privas, 1862-6, and at the Ecole cléricale at Périgueux (Dordogne), 1866-7. In the year 1867-8 he was *professeur de philosophie* at the Ecole cléricale, Périgueux. The following year he was made superior of the Basilian community which opened the Collège Saint-Charles in Blidah, Algeria, but the climate proved deleterious to his health. He returned to Annonay during the year 1869-70 to recuperate, then went to Vernoux as director of the minor seminary. He was *professeur de philosophie* at the Petit Séminaire d'Aubenas, 1870-1, and was then appointed superior of the college at Bourg-Saint-Andéol (Ardèche), 1871-7. When the Basilians opened the Collège Saint-Pierre at Châteauroux, diocese of Bourges, in 1877, Father Durand was appointed superior, an office he held until 1880.

Hilaire Durand was forty-four years old when he died. In spite of ill health he had twice been entrusted with opening new foundations for the community (Blidah and Châteauroux), and for ten years had served as superior in three different institutions.

SOURCES: GABF; Kirley, *Community in France* 34, 70n178; *Ordo*, diocese of Viviers, 1864; Pouzol, 'Notices.'

DURAND, Noël, priest, sixth Basilian superior general, 1898-1910, middle brother of Fathers Hilaire *Durand and Eugène *Durand, in a family of six boys and two girls of Victor Durand and Henriette Chaudanson, was born at Montpezat-sous-Bauzon (diocese of Viviers) on 25 December 1845. He died there on 16 April 1922 and was buried in the local cemetery.

Noël Durand was a student at the Collège des Cordeliers, section Sainte-Barbe, 1857-8, and then attended the Collège de Privas, where his elder brother Hilaire was a professor, in the years 1858-60 and 1862-5. He made his novitiate at Feyzin (Isère, now Rhône), probably in 1865-6, and did his theology course while teaching mathematics, 1866-9, at the Ecole cléricale de Périgueux (Dordogne). He attended the Institut catholique de Paris, 1869-70, and the following year he was at the Collège du Sacré-Coeur, Annonay. He was ordained priest on 4 March 1871 in the chapel of the college by Bishop Armand de Charbonnel.

Father Durand was director of studies and professor of mathematics at the Collège du Bourg-Saint-Andéol (Ardèche), 1871-7, and was superior from 1877 to 1879. The following twelve years he was at the Ecole cléricale de Périgueux as superior, replacing Father Adrien *Fayolle, who had been elected superior general on 11 December 1879. When Father Fayolle died on 29 July 1898, Father Durand was elected superior general on 17 September 1898. He was adventuresome, opening St Basil's College, Waco, Texas, 1899, St Thomas College, Houston, 1900, and accepting responsibility for St Mary's Seminary at LaPorte, Texas, for the diocese of Galveston (now Galveston-Houston), 1901. He made two visits to North America in 1901 and 1907 accompanied by his brother Eugène. But his term of office was also marked by the suppression of religious orders in France and by internal divisions in the Basilian community. Like other communities, the Basilians requested the status of legal association; but this was denied by the anticlerical government in France, and in 1903 the Basilians were dissolved and dispossessed of the Calvaire at Prades, the Collège du Sacré-Coeur in Annonay, the Pension Sainte-Barbe, and the Collège Saint-Charles at Blidah, Algeria. The Congregation was also obliged to abandon the direction of the minor seminaries of Vernoux and Aubenas and the Ecole cléricale de Périgueux. All of these had been confided to them by their local bishops. These institutions were allowed to continue under diocesan direction, and Basilians were allowed to teach in them if their status was changed to that of diocesan priests.

Father Durand returned to live with his family at Montpezat-sous-Bauzon, from where he supervised the Basilian community as best he could. About half the Basilians remained in the diocese of Viviers, where they served in parishes and chaplaincies, appointed by Bishop Joseph-Michel-Frédéric Bonnet. The rest, over forty of them, worked in different dioceses in France.

The political and religious difficulties in France were paralleled by internal difficulties in the Basilian community itself, where a conflict had developed between the French Basilians and the North American Basilians. From 1904 the authority of the general council had been modified, though Rome delayed implementation of the changes until the next general chapter convened in Geneva in 1910. In 1908 three French scholastics were not called to renewal of vows by the provincial council in Canada because of their lack of knowledge of English. Father Durand deposed the councillors. They appealed to Rome and were reinstated on 30 November 1909. On 5 July 1910, at the Geneva general chapter, Father Victorin *Marijon was elected superior general, and the generalate was transferred to Detroit. Two provinces, France and America, were officially constituted. Father Noël Durand became provincial of the French Basilians and held that office until his death in 1922.

In May 1913 an extraordinary general chapter was held in Rome, chiefly for the purpose of refining the Constitutions. In 1914 Rome asked Father Marijon to resign and ruled that Father M.V. *Kelly be disenfranchised for six years. Father James *Player became acting superior general, a position he held until 1922.

Father Durand died on Easter Sunday, 1922, just a few weeks after calling for a provincial council in France to request separation from the North American Basilians. Rome consented to this request, erecting two separate congregations: The Congregation of the Priests of St Basil of the diocese of Viviers and The Congregation of the Priests of St Basil of the archdiocese of Toronto.

SOURCES: GABF; Kirley, *Community in France* 165, 172, 257 and passim; Kirley, *Congregation in France* iii, 3, 6, 12, 22, 35, 40, 49–51, 54, 56, 61, 66–9, 70–4, 76, 79–80, 82, 84, 88, 91, 104, 118, 269; Pouzol, 'Notices.'

DURET, Jacques VINCENT, priest, one of the ten founding members, was born in Annonay on 6 July 1762, the son of Louis Duret, a physician, and Marianne Jacquier. His brother Louis became Mayor of Annonay. Vincent died in Annonay on 3 June 1841 and was buried in the Saint-Jacques cemetery. In 1869 his remains were reinterred in the Basilian cemetery on the grounds of the Collège du Sacré-Coeur, Annonay.

Vincent Duret received his early schooling privately from his uncle, Canon Duret. He went to study in Paris with a bursary at the Collège d'Autun, which was shortly afterwards merged with the Collège Louis-le-Grand. There he was a classmate of Maximilien Robespierre. He received his Master of Arts degree from the University of Paris and studied theology at the Sorbonne. In 1785 while still a deacon he was appointed a canon of the collegiate church of Notre-Dame in Annonay. He was ordained a priest for the diocese of Viviers in 1786.

In 1790, when revolutionary decrees dissolved all cathedral chapters and religious orders, and when all priests were obliged to take the oath to the Civil Constitution of the Clergy, Father Duret first went to live with his family but later was compelled to hide in various places, finally settling in Lyon. In 1793, when the city was besieged by a revolutionary army, he escaped to Annonay, where he remained in hiding but secretly administered the sacraments. With the arrest and execution of Robespierre the 'Reign of Terror' was over, and persecution abated even further in 1797 under the Directory. Father Duret was named assistant at Notre-Dame Parish; but in September of that year the persecution was revived and Father Duret went into hiding near Saint-Symphorien-de-Mahun. In 1798 things were once again less severe, and he returned to Notre-Dame in Annonay. On 11 November 1800 the Collège-Séminaire de Saint-Symphorien-de-Mahun was opened and, as a result of the Concordat of 1801, moved to Annonay in 1802 with the name Le Collège des Cordeliers, since it was located in a former Franciscan monastery. Father Duret established the Pension-Petit Séminaire Sainte-Barbe, a residence for students of the college who had a religious vocation and whose parents were unable to pay full tuition. He was also instrumental in the Sisters of Providence establishing a house in the area. For Father Duret, Sainte-Barbe and Notre-Dame parish were the centre of his life; but in 1816 he resigned his position at Notre-Dame to devote more time to his school projects. He joined the others at the college in forming the Association of Priests of St Basil and was elected first assistant at the general chapter in November 1822. He also helped to bring the Ursuline Sisters, the Christian Brothers, and the Trinitarian Sisters to Annonay.

Father Adrien *Chomel described Father Duret as a priest 'who was remarkably prudent and never acted on the spur of the moment. He was calm and, in the minds of some, even slow. ... His walk, appearance, voice, everything denoted the wisdom and moderation which mark the man of sound principles. He had the confidence of the clergy and faithful. He was never happier than when he discovered an opportunity of doing good for someone.' He was active right up to the time of his death, which came from a stroke suffered at Sainte-Barbe. The Sisters of Providence were granted permission to encase his embalmed heart in a metal container placed in their Chapel.

SOURCES: GABF; Chomel, *Collège d'Annonay* 137–51, 203–25, 437; Kirley, *Community in France* 59, 150n383; Pouzol, 'Notices'; Roume, *Origines* 80, 96, 100–2, 104, 159, 161, 167, 272, 354, 401, 403–4.

DWYER, John WILFRID, priest, was born on 17 January 1898, on a farm near Woodstock, Ontario (diocese of London), the son of Daniel Dwyer and Sarah McNamara. He died in Toronto on 22 December 1991, and is buried in the Basilian plot of Holy Cross Cemetery, Thornhill, Ontario.

After elementary and secondary education in or near Woodstock, Wilfrid was sent by his parents to Assumption College, Windsor, Ontario (B.A., Honours Philosophy, University of Western Ontario, 1922). He entered St Basil's Novitiate, Toronto, a member of the first class of novices of the newly constituted Congregation of Priests of St Basil of Toronto. After taking his first vows on 13 August 1923 he taught at St Thomas High School, Houston, for one year. He studied theology at St

Basil's Scholasticate, Toronto, 1924-7, concurrently earning teacher certification at the Ontario College of Education, 1925. He was ordained to the priesthood on 18 December 1926 in St Basil's Church, Toronto, by Bishop Alexander MacDonald. During his final year of theology he taught English at St Michael's College in the University of Toronto.

In 1927 Father Dwyer was appointed to Aquinas Institute, Rochester, and served as local superior, 1928-32. While there he obtained an M.A. from the University of Rochester, 1932, submitting the thesis 'The Literary Reputation of John Henry Cardinal Newman' (later published; see below). He was appointed to graduate studies at the Université de Louvain, Belgium, 1932-4 and 1935-6, with the intervening year 1934-5 spent teaching at Assumption College. He was awarded the Ph.D. in philosophy, *summa cum laude*, from Louvain, submitting a critical edition of Siger of Brabant's treatise on the eternity of the world.

Father Dwyer was appointed to the staff of the Institute of Mediaeval Studies, residing at St Michael's College until the Institute House was formed in 1942. He remained at the Institute until 1944, when he was transferred to St Michael's College. In 1945 he was appointed to St Thomas High School, Houston, where he taught and served as first councillor in the Basilian community. With the announcement by Bishop Christopher Byrne of Galveston that the Basilian Fathers would open a Catholic college in Houston, Father Dwyer was appointed to present the reasons and urgency of this project to the people of Houston. He considered this assignment one of the greatest privileges of his life. When the University of St Thomas opened in 1947 he was named its vice-president and a member of the teaching faculty.

He was then assigned to Assumption College, 1948-53, and again to St Michael's College. In 1954 he was appointed to St John Fisher College in Rochester, where he taught philosophy until 1961. In that year, at sixty-three years of age, he launched into a new apostolate as chaplain of the Newman Club at Carleton University, Ottawa, and served as assistant at St Basil's Parish in that city. In 1968, now conscious of the age gap between himself and the students, and in spite of his popularity with them, he asked to be relieved of the chaplaincy. Archbishop Joseph Aurèle Plourde then invited Father Dwyer to accept the position of secretary general of the Diocesan Synod in Ottawa, a position he held until 1973. In that year he retired to Assumption College

School, Windsor, where he remained active in the life of the community and continued reading and research.

One of his dreams was to write a biography of Father Francis *Forster, whom he greatly admired; but the troubles that Father Forster had experienced were so emotionally draining to him that he could not continue. At community gatherings 'Domini,' a nickname he acquired in his college years at Assumption, was a noted raconteur of Basilian history, which he cherished and strove to preserve. He spent many summers at Strawberry Island in Lake Simcoe, the summer retreat of the Basilian Fathers, where conversation was his favourite pastime, especially with his good friend Father Edmund *McCorkell. In 1986 he organized the 'Simcoe Club' of donors from Basilian families for the refurbishing of the island chapel. Father Dwyer is remembered as a man who overcame difficulties, persevering with interest, enthusiasm, and joy in service of God and the community.

BIBLIOGRAPHY:
Books: Ed. *L'opuscule de Siger de Brabant 'De aeternitate mundi.' Introduction critique et texte.* Louvain, 1937. *Literary Reputation of John Henry Cardinal Newman.* Rochester, N.Y., 1981.
Article: 'Catholic Action in a Catholic College,' *Basilian* 1 (March 1935) 4–5.
SOURCES: GABF; *Annals* 5 (1974) 13, 5 (1977) 196–7, 7 (1992) 137–9; *Newsletter* (27 December 1991).

E

ECKERT, Vincent Conrad, priest, was born at Dublin, Ontario (diocese of London), on 9 May 1915, the son of Peter Eckert and Theresa O'Connor. He died on 5 February 1978 in Merrillville, Indiana, and is buried in the Basilian plot of Holy Cross Cemetery, Thornhill, Ontario.

Vincent Eckert attended the local elementary school and then Dublin High School, 1930–3, St Jerome's College, Kitchener, Ontario, 1933–4, and Assumption High School, Windsor, for one year, 1934–5. He entered St Basil's Novitiate, Toronto, and took first vows on 15 August 1936. He was assigned to Assumption College, Windsor (B.A., University of Western Ontario, 1940). As a scholastic he taught for one year at Assumption High School, then went in 1941 to St Michael's College,

Toronto, earning high school teaching certification in 1942 at the Ontario College of Education. He studied theology at St Basil's Seminary, Toronto, and was ordained to the priesthood on 20 August 1944 in St Basil's Church, Toronto, by Archbishop James Charles McGuigan.

In 1945 Father Eckert was appointed to Aquinas Institute, Rochester, where he taught and, from 1946 to 1960, also served as treasurer. In 1960 he moved to Andrean High School, Merrillville. There he filled the office of treasurer until shortly before his death, in spite of his struggle with cancer during the last few years.

'Vince' Eckert was a peaceful and prayerful man – valuable traits for house meetings dealing with the liturgical changes and adaptations in religious life coming out of the Second Vatican Council. He held his own opinions firmly, though he respected those of others. He had a talent and a taste for fixing things and maintaining them in good repair, which made him much appreciated in the houses in which he served. Though not tall he was strongly built and had extraordinary stamina.

SOURCES: GABF; *Annals* 1 (1945) 99–100, 5 (1979) 404–5; *Newsletter* (14 February 1978); *Acropolis*, Andrean High School (7 February 1978) 1–2.

EMBSER, James William, priest, was born on 5 May 1905 at Hornell, New York (diocese of Buffalo), the son of James William Embser and Agnes O'Boyle. He died in Toronto on 20 December 1984 and is buried in the Basilian plot of Holy Sepulchre Cemetery, Rochester.

'Jim' Embser attended the local parochial school in Hornell and did one year of high school at Immaculate Conception School, Wellsville, New York, but in 1920 transferred to St Michael's College, Toronto, taking his high school diploma in 1923. He entered St Basil's Novitiate, Toronto, made first profession on 11 August 1924, and began his arts course at St Michael's College, living at the scholasticate. In 1925 he moved to Assumption College, Windsor (B.A., University of Western Ontario, 1928). The next year, while living at Ste Anne's Parish, Detroit, he taught with the original Basilian group at Holy Name Institute, Detroit. He studied theology at St Basil's Scholasticate, Toronto, 1929–32, and during his first year of theology he also attended the Ontario College of Education (teaching certification, 1930). He was ordained to the priesthood in St Basil's Church, Toronto, on 19 December 1931 by Bishop Alexander MacDonald.

In 1932 Father Embser returned to Holy Name Institute (later, Catholic Central High School), Detroit, where he remained until 1946, teaching Latin and serving as second councillor, 1935–6, first councillor, 1936–40, and superior and principal of the school, 1940–6. He obtained his Michigan Life Teacher's Certificate from the University of Detroit, 1934, and an M.A. in philosophy from the University of Western Ontario, 1942, submitting a thesis entitled 'Training the Adolescent.'

From 1946 to 1948 he was principal of St Thomas High School, Houston, and first councillor of the Basilian community. In 1948 he was appointed master of novices at St Basil's Novitiate, Rochester, and remained in this post until 1955. He taught Latin at St John Fisher College, Rochester, 1955–62, and then returned to Catholic Central, Detroit, 1962–6.

His final appointment, 1966, was to the University of St Thomas, Houston, where for the next eighteen years he taught Latin, gave retreats to sisters and lay groups, was chaplain to several associations, and became a much beloved figure at the university and beyond. The local community elected him to the local council for ten consecutive years, 1969–79. Failing health brought him, quite unwillingly, to the Basilian Fathers Residence (Infirmary), Toronto, in September of 1984, just four months before his death.

Father Embser taught Latin for fifty-two years. Though classes were small in his later years, his enthusiasm for his subject never abated. He kept busy doing things for others, and was extremely grateful for favours done to him. He had an intense love for the Basilian community and an equally intense prayer life. He always remembered his former students and novices in his prayers and kept their names in his breviary.

BIBLIOGRAPHY:
Book: *God's People in Wellsville: The First One Hundred and Twenty-Five Years of Immaculate Conception Parish*. Wellsville, N.Y. 1973.
Pamphlet: *Immaculate Conception, 1824–1974: One Hundred and Fifty Years of Immaculate Conception Parish, Wellsville, New York*. Wellsville, N.Y., 1975.
Articles: 'Ste Anne de Detroit,' *Basilian* 1 (October 1935) 96–7. In *Benedicamus*: 'On Teaching Religion,' 3 (November 1949) 1–5, 8; 'Father Moylan,' 4 (March 1951) 26–7, 29; 'Reflected Light,' 5 (May 1952) 4–5. In *Basilian Teacher*: Daniel L. Dillon,' 1 (April 1957) 9–11; 'Edmund T. Burns,' 2 (April 1958) 17–19; 'Michael P. Christian,' 3 (December 1958) 76–9; 'Henry S. Bellisle,' 4 (January 1960) 116–19; 'Any Virtue Is a Delicate Thing,' *Forum* 1 (December 1964) 34–5; 'The Value of a Retreat Depends upon the Preacher,' *Forum* 2 (January 1966) 2–3.

SOURCES: GABF; *Annals* 5 (1975) 65, 6 (1982) 11–12, 6 (1985) 383–5; *Newsletter* (30 December 1984).

EPITALON, Antoine, priest, was born in Saint-Etienne (Loire, archdiocese of Lyon, now diocese of Saint-Etienne), on 26 October 1873, the son of Damien Epitalon and Rosalie Gourbon. He died in Annonay on 12 January 1965 and is buried there in the Basilian cemetery on the grounds of the Collège du Sacré-Coeur.

Antoine Epitalon was educated at the Collège Saint-Michel, Saint-Etienne, and then at the Grand Séminaire Saint-Sulpice at Issy-les-Moulineaux (Seine, now Hauts-de-Seine). He entered St Basil's Novitiate at Vernoux (Ardèche) and was professed on 18 September 1896. For the following five years he taught and studied theology successively at the Petit Séminaire d'Aubenas, the Petit Séminaire de Vernoux (Ardèche), the Ecole cléricale de Périgueux (Dordogne), and the Collège du Sacré-Coeur, 1898–1901. In 1900 he went to Lyon to prepare a *licence ès sciences*. He was ordained priest at the Collège du Sacré-Coeur on 21 September 1901 by Bishop Hilarion-Joseph Montéty, titular bishop of Beirut, who was replacing Bishop Joseph-Michel-Frédéric Bonnet of Viviers. In 1903 with the expulsion of religious orders from schools in France he interrupted his studies and returned to Saint-Etienne. He was mobilized in the health services during the First World War, and afterwards served as military chaplain and *Directeur de Scoutisme* at Saint-Etienne. From 1925 to 1952 he was chaplain for Les Petites Soeurs de l'Assomption, also at Saint-Etienne.

When Father Edouard *Aureille died on 5 April 1934, Father Octave *Descellière called on Father Epitalon to replace him as économe général. He was confirmed in this post in the chapter of 1938 and reelected in 1944, holding this position until 1950. In the early 1950s he was a strong advocate of the reunion of the French and North American Basilian communities. He lived in retirement at Maison Saint-Joseph, Annonay, from 1952 until his death.

Antoine Epitalon was a distinguished, precise, and aristocratic priest with a marked aversion for the excesses of the Third Republic in France and a preference for the monarchy. He possessed a remarkable gift for expressing his thoughts and opinions with elegance and verve.

SOURCES: GABF; *Annals* 3 (1961) 74, (1965) 380–1; *Newsletter* (18 January 1965); Kirley, *Congregation in France* 156, 177, 184–5, 196–7, 208, 220, 256, 262; Pouzol, 'Notices.'

F

FAMY, Jean, priest, member of the Congregation 1860–73, was born at Saint-Champ (Ain, diocese of Bellay). Basilian records of his life cease with his withdrawal from the Congregation in 1873 and his incardination into the diocese of Saint Augustine, Florida.

Jean Famy entered St Basil's Novitiate at Privas (Ardèche), making religious profession on 5 February 1860. On 22 December of that year he was ordained deacon at Valence, and on 25 May 1861 he was ordained priest in Lyon, the bishop of Viviers being indisposed after a serious carriage accident. In 1862 he was called from the Collège de Privas to accompany Father François-Xavier *Granottier to Canada. They sailed from Liverpool on 15 August 1862 in the company of John Joseph Lynch, bishop of Toronto. Father Famy taught French and music at St Michael's College, Toronto, while studying English. In February 1864 he was appointed assistant at St Mary's of the Assumption Parish, Owen Sound, Ontario, where he remained for six years. In 1870 he returned to France and went to assist as prefect of discipline at the Collège Saint-Charles, Blidah, Algeria, for three months.

In January 1871, he temporarily replaced Father Antoine *Bord at the Calvary of Prades (Ardèche). After some months in the scholasticate he returned to Canada seeking work on the missions, July to September 1872. He went back to the Basilian novitiate at Feyzin (Isère, now Rhône), and in October 1873 asked to be relieved of his religious vows so that he could apply for incardination into a diocese in the United States. He was accepted by Bishop Augustin Vérot of Saint Augustine, Florida, an alumnus of the college in Annonay. Father Famy became pastor of St Louis Parish, Tampa, Florida and later moved to St Joseph's Parish, Mandarin, Florida.

SOURCES: GABF; *Centennial, St Mary's*; *Jubilee, St Mary's*; Kirley, *Community in France* 7n28, 12, 234n561; Pouzol, 'Notices'; Spetz, *Waterloo*.

FARRELL, John Matthew, priest, member of the Congregation 1949–71, was born in Rochester on 16 April 1930, the son of James Farrell and Nora Burke and the brother of Father William Farrell OSA. He died at Bowie, Maryland, on 3 May 1980.

John attended Blessed Sacrament parochial school and Aquinas Institute, Rochester, 1944–8. He entered St Basil's Novitiate, Rochester, in

1948 and made his first profession on 15 August 1949. He attended Assumption College, Windsor, 1949–53 (B.A., University of Western Ontario, 1953). While teaching at Catholic Central High School Detroit, 1953–5, he received teaching certification for Michigan and then studied theology at St Basil's Seminary, Toronto, 1955–9 (S.T.B., St Michael's College, 1958). He was ordained to the priesthood by Cardinal James Charles McGuigan on 29 June 1958 in St Basil's Church, Toronto.

Father Farrell taught at Andrean High School, Gary (now Merrillville), Indiana, 1959–64. He was an assistant at Ste Anne's Parish, Detroit, in 1964–5. He was a chaplain with the rank of captain in the American Air Force from 1965 to 1968. In 1971, he was dispensed from the obligations of the priesthood and religious profession. He was employed for some time in the Department of Vocational Rehabilitation in Washington, D.C.

SOURCES: GABF; *Annals* 2 (1958) 355; *Newsletter* (13 May 1980).

FAUGHT, Donald Thomas, priest, was born in North Bay, Ontario (diocese of Sault Ste Marie), on 16 June 1915, the son of Samuel John Faught and Agnes Brown. He died at Pompano Beach, Florida, on 19 February 1975 and is buried in the Basilian plot of Heavenly Rest Cemetery, Windsor.

Donald Faught attended the local grade school, North Bay Collegiate Institute, 1928–30, the high school section of St Michael's College, Toronto, 1930–1, and Assumption College School, Windsor, 1931–2. He entered St Basil's Novitiate, Toronto, making first profession on 15 August 1933. His first appointment after profession was to St Michael's College, Toronto, 1933–5, for first- and second-year arts. From 1935 to 1938 he lived at St Basil's Scholasticate ('Seminary' from 1937), Toronto, where he completed his arts course (B.A., University of Toronto, 1937) and took his first and second years of theology. In the fall of 1938 he returned to St Michael's College for two years to complete his third year of theology, concurrently earning a teacher's certificate from the Ontario College of Education. He was ordained to the priesthood on 15 August 1940 in St Basil's Church by Archbishop James Charles McGuigan.

In 1941 Father Faught was appointed to St Michael's College, where he began a long and distinguished career teaching mathematics. He earned an M.A. in mathematics from the University of Michigan in 1944. In 1954 he moved into the Basilian community at Assumption

University. He became the first head of the Department of Mathematics at the University of Windsor, a position he held until 1974. No math course of any level was beyond him. He served on the Ontario Mathematical Committee as Chair, 1960, as Executive member, 1960–2, and as member, 1961–3. He promoted the 'new math' in schools in the province of Ontario.

Father Faught served the local Basilian community in Windsor at O'Connor House as first councillor from 1963 to 1967. In 1970 he moved to the rectory of Assumption Parish while remaining on the staff of the University of Windsor. He was a man of order and logic, thorough in his work and priestly life, with a keen ability for seeing everything in proper perspective. A competent teacher of religion and of math, he was often a man of action with a pastoral sense: he once crawled under a train to attend a young man whose legs had been crushed, baptized him then and there, and later instructed him in the faith. His personal interest in each student inspired several men to pursue a religious vocation.

Don Faught had a keen interest in sports, especially hockey, and a talent for the game of bridge in which he became a Life Master. He prepared his classes to the accompaniment of classical music. His love of order did not exclude an excitability and ebullience. He enlivened every Basilian gathering by his quick wit, his expansive gestures, and, above all, his universal kindness.

In 1974, Father Faught began his first sabbatical leave in twenty years of teaching and administration. In February 1975, on a holiday with his mother in Florida, he suffered a fatal heart attack as he went into the water for an afternoon swim.

BIBLIOGRAPHY:
Book: *Calculus and Matrix Algebra: Applications to Business, Social and Life Science.* 2 vols. Toronto, 1954.
Pamphlet: *Polar Coordinates.* Ontario Mathematics Commission. Toronto, n.d.
Articles: 'Mathematics Today,' *Basilian Teacher* 1 (January 1960) 86–94; 'Religious as Mathematicians,' *Basilian Teacher* 5 (October 1960) 29–31.
SOURCES: GABF; *Annals* 5 (1976) 182–3; *Newsletter* (24 February 1975).

FAURE, Charles Joseph, priest, was born on 30 July 1818 at Entre-Deux-Guiers (Isère, now Rhône, diocese of Grenoble). He died on 16 December 1887, but the places of his death and burial are not recorded.

Charles Faure was received as a novice on 29 September 1855, at the age of thirty-seven, and taught *huitième, septième,* and *sixième* for two years in the Collège de Privas (Ardèche). He did not take vows. In July 1857, he left the Basilians to seek employment elsewhere, but returned in December of that year and taught *septième* at the Collège des Cordeliers, Annonay, 1857-8. In July 1858 he entered the Congregation of the Priests of Christian Doctrine at Cavaillon (Vaucluse), and remained with them for eight years, 1858-66. Bishop Louis Delcusy of Viviers ordained him subdeacon on 2 June 1860, but the dates of ordination to the diaconate and priesthood remain unknown. In 1866, as a priest, he sought admission once again to the Basilians. He taught *sixième* at the Petit Séminaire d'Aubenas, 1866-8, and *cinquième,* 1868-70. On 31 August 1870 he made his profession of vows as a Basilian at the age of fifty-two and left France for Canada in the company of a Mr Foy, who had spent some time at the college in Annonay and had been a novice at Feyzin.

Father Faure served as curate at Assumption Parish, Windsor, for sixteen years, 1870-86. Two years after his arrival in the parish he caught smallpox while attending the sick but made a successful recovery. His health failed, however, in 1885, and in February 1886 he returned to France. Basilian records show that he attended the annual retreat in Annonay with his confreres in the summer of 1886.

SOURCES: GABF; *Jubilee, Assumption*; Kirley, *Community in France* 218n524, 219n526, 235n562; Lajeunesse, *Assumption College*; Pouzol, 'Notices.'

FAYARD, Louis, priest, was born on 6 September 1847 at Gluiras (Ardèche), canton Saint-Pierreville. He died on 5 June 1905 in Lyon and was buried in the cemetery at Vernoux (Ardèche).

After his high school studies at the Petit Séminaire de Vernoux, Louis made his novitiate at Feyzin (Isère, now Rhône), with final profession on 20 September 1872. While studying for the priesthood he taught mathematics at the Ecole cléricale de Périgueux (Dordogne), 1870-4. He received major orders at the hands of Bishop Armand de Charbonnel in the chapel of the Collège du Sacré-Coeur, Annonay: subdiaconate, 21 September 1872; diaconate, 20 September 1873; and priesthood, 19 September 1874.

After ordination he continued to teach mathematics at the Ecole cléricale at Périgueux, 1874-7, before moving to the Collège du Sacré-Coeur, where he was professor of mathematics, senior division. In 1878 he went on graduate studies at the Faculté catholique de Lyon, where he received the *licence* in mathematics and physics, 1879. For the next seventeen years, 1879–96, he was professor of physics and chemistry at the college in Annonay. In 1896 he moved to Aubenas (Ardèche), where he taught science in the minor seminary for seven years.

With the suppression of religious orders in 1903 he was forced to leave the Petit Séminaire, going first to Félines (Ardèche) as curate in the local parish, then to Lyon, where he taught mathematics at the Ecole libre de la Trinité and was a supervisor of the day pupils. During the Easter vacation of 1904 he fell ill while visiting at Vernoux and was brought to the Hôpital Saint-Joseph in Lyon where he died a year later. A large crowd of clergy and faithful who attended the funeral on 8 June 1905 heard the pastor of Vernoux describe him as 'a very gifted priest, a scholar, an artist, a musician, known for his modesty and goodness.' People referred to him as 'the good Father Fayard.'

SOURCES: GABF; Kirley, *Community in France* 110, 184, 188n469, 209; Kirley, *Congregation in France* 68; Pouzol, 'Notices'; *Semaine religieuse de Viviers* (16 June 1905) 188–9.

FAYOLLE, Adrien, priest, fifth superior general, was born at Montréal (Ardèche) on 20 February 1837, the son of Jean-Louis Fayolle and Marie Ayme. He was an elder brother of Father Léopold *Fayolle and a nephew of Father André *Fayolle, one of the Basilian founders as well as a nephew of Father Pierre *Tourvieille, also a founder and second superior general. He died in Annonay on 29 July 1898 and is buried there in the Basilian cemetery on the grounds of the Collège du Sacré-Coeur.

Adrien Fayolle was a student at the Collège de Privas, where his uncle Father André *Fayolle was superior, before entering the novitiate in Annonay on 1 November 1856. He taught at the Collège des Cordeliers from 1856 to 1861 while studying theology. He was ordained priest in Lyon on 25 May 1861, and then taught for five years at the Collège de Privas (Ardèche). In 1866 he was named the first Basilian superior at the Ecole cléricale de Périgueux, where he remained for thirteen years. On 11 December 1879 he was elected superior general for a term of twelve years. He was re-elected in 1892 and remained in this office until his death in 1898. One of his first official acts was to consecrate the Community to the Sacred Heart of Jesus and to erect the statue of Jesus on the west side of the college in Annonay.

Father Fayolle's years as superior general proved to be difficult ones for the Basilians and for all religious orders in France. The French prime minister Léon Gambetta had resolved to act on his slogan: 'Le cléricalisme, voilà l'ennemi.' In 1880 the Jesuits were dissolved and other religious were required to have their statutes approved by the civil authorities. On 10 August 1880 Basilians who were teaching were officially secularized by the government but canonically remained religious. In November 1880 the sub-prefect of Vienne closed the novitiate at Feyzin, leaving the Community with no novitiate for three years. In July 1881 the municipal council of Bourg-Saint-Andéol expelled the Basilians from their college there, and in 1882 the community withdrew from the Collège Saint-Pierre at Châteauroux (Indre). These closures had been preceded by the withdrawal of the Basilians from the day school in Privas, 1878, and the Petit Séminaire d'Aubenas, 1879. As a result a large number of Basilian teachers were left unemployed.

In the summer of 1883 Father Fayolle travelled to North America and established a provincial council to assist the provincial there, Father Charles *Vincent. He defined the powers of the provincial and provided for an endowment fund to look after provincial expenses. In the fall of 1883 he opened a novitiate at Beaconfield House, Plymouth, England, and named Father Michael *Ferguson master of novices, followed shortly after by Father Victorin *Marijon. The next year the community opened the College of Mary Immaculate in Beaconfield House with Father Eugène *Durand as superior. In 1885 the Community assumed responsibility for a parish at Cadouin (diocese of Périgueux), and the following year accepted the parish of Ste Anne, Detroit, the first permanent Basilian foundation in the United States.

Father Fayolle was strongly committed to the Basilian involvement in education. However, even though affiliation of St Michael's College with the University of Toronto took place during his term of office, he discouraged attendance of Basilian scholastics at the university. As a result, for many years the only members with degrees from the University of Toronto were those who had obtained them prior to entering the Congregation. In 1887, however, Father Fayolle published a letter to the whole community on the importance of receiving solid theological training.

In 1889 he travelled a second time to North America with Father Victorin *Marijon in an attempt to deal with the difficulties which had developed between the North American and French branches of the community. In 1890 he and his council closed the novitiate at Plymouth, and in 1892, the year in which Father Fayolle was re-elected superior general, they built a novitiate in Toronto at Holy Rosary parish. In 1894 a scholasticate was established at St Michael's College, which was later moved to the novitiate. Also in 1894, the Constitutions which had been sent back from Rome for modifications (chiefly with regard to the vow of poverty) were revised, translated into Latin, and resubmitted for approval. To Father Fayolle's deep disappointment, the Congregation of Bishops and Regulars returned it on 22 June 1897 for further changes. He thus did not live to see the approval of the Congregation's basic document which he had so ardently desired. In 1895 the Basilians abandoned the Collège Saint-Augustin in Bône, Algeria; but that same year they returned to the Petit Séminaire d'Aubenas, which they had left in 1879.

Father Adrien Fayolle died suddenly. The funeral services on 1 August at the Collège du Sacré-Coeur were presided over by Monseigneur Battendier, vicar general of the diocese of Viviers. The Mass was celebrated by Father Joseph *Hilaire, superior of the Petit Séminaire de Vernoux, in the presence of 150 priests. The final commendation was given by Father Dubonnet, superior of the Grand Séminaire de Viviers. A similar service was held at the Ecole cléricale de Périgueux on 24 November 1898, with a large gathering of priests and former students. The bishops of Périgueux, Viviers, and Algiers had all named Father Fayolle an honorary canon of their cathedrals.

SOURCES: GABF; Chomel, *Collège d'Annonay* 517; Kirley, *Community in France* 70–150 and passim; Kirley, *Congregation in France* 50; Pouzol, 'Notices.'

FAYOLLE, André, priest, one of the ten founding members, was born at Montréal (Ardèche, diocese of Viviers [from 1801 to 1822 of Mende]), on 12 October 1791, the son of Pierre Fayolle and Marie Tourvieille. He was the nephew of Pierre *Tourvieille, the second superior general, and the uncle of Adrien *Fayolle, the fifth superior general, and of Léopold *Fayolle. He died at Privas (Ardèche) on 27 April 1867 and was buried in the local cemetery.

André Fayolle was a student at the Collège des Cordeliers from 1807 to 1811. He taught grammar there for five years while also studying theology. He was ordained to the priesthood on 30 March 1816. From 1819 to 1822 he directed the Ecole française in the classrooms of Sainte-

Claire, a school founded by his uncle Pierre *Tourvieille, while teaching humanities at the Collège des Cordeliers. Father Fayolle was one of a group of the staff made up of himself, Fathers Jean-François *Pagès, Julien *Tracol, and Henri André *Martinesche, who had formed a society for their mutual advancement in perfection under the direction of Father Augustin *Payan. Fayolle did not sign the original petition to form a community because vows were not included, but he did join the association when it formed.

Father Fayolle had been named superior of the school at Maison-Seule in 1822 and was assisted there by Father *Martinesche. They voted by mail at the first general chapter on 21 November 1822, when Father Joseph *Lapierre was elected superior general. On 28 December 1822 Bishop Claude Jean-Joseph de la Brunière designated Sainte-Barbe and Maison-Seule, where the students followed the rule of the Collège des Cordeliers, as his minor seminaries. Father Fayolle remained superior of Maison-Seule until 1828; but financial difficulties plagued that institution, and the new bishop, André Molin, closed it in 1828 and designated the schools at Bourg-Saint-Andéol and Vernoux as the minor seminaries of the Ardèche.

From 1828 to 1867 Father Fayolle was superior of the Collège de Privas. He succeeded in creating a truly fraternal community there and he had excellent relations with successive governments, whether of the Bourbon Restoration, the July Monarchy, the Second Republic, or the Second Empire. While he was pleased when Bishop Joseph-Hippolyte Guibert confided the minor seminaries of Bourg-Saint-Andéol in 1844 and Vernoux in 1846 to the Basilians, the transfer of the minor seminary of Bourg-Saint-Andéol to Aubenas in 1852 inhibited the recruitment of students at the Collège de Privas. Thus, beginning in 1853, the municipality of Privas granted an annual subsidy of four thousand francs to the college.

Father Fayolle suffered from severe rheumatism in his hands and feet. From 1862 until his death in 1867 Father Henri *Coupat helped him in running the college. Of Father Fayolle's teaching at Privas, Father Adrien *Chomel wrote, 'He was beloved by his pupils to whom he was more a father than a master, and for the greater number of whom he remained a friend.' Father Charles *Roume quotes Julien *Actorie's report of the visitation made in April 1849: 'Father Fayolle occupied for many years a rather small room at the end of the courtyard. In it were held the usual religious exercises. ... There also on

Thursday the staff gathered round their superior and presented the most intimate picture of family life that I have ever witnessed.'

SOURCES: GABF; Chomel, *Collège d'Annonay* 74, 75n2, 145, 149; Kirley, *Community in France* 33, 34, 70; Pouzol, 'Notices'; Roume, *Origines* 133, 156, 160, 161, 210–13, 232–9, 288–9, 346.

FAYOLLE, Léopold, priest, was born on 15 November 1843, the son of Jean-Louis Fayolle and Marie Ayme, at Montréal (Ardèche). He was a brother of Adrien *Fayolle and nephew of André *Fayolle. He died at Privas (Ardèche) on 23 June 1905 and is buried in the cemetery there beside his uncle.

Léopold entered the Petit Séminaire Sainte-Barbe, Annonay, in 1854 and attended class at the Collège des Cordeliers for five years. In 1859 he went to the Basilian college at Privas for the final three years of his classical studies, 1859–62. He made his novitiate at Feyzin (Isère, now Rhône), 1862–3, made first profession on Easter Sunday, 27 March 1864, and final profession on 22 September 1865. He received the subdiaconate on 23 September 1865 and the diaconate on 22 September 1866, both in the chapel of the Collège des Cordeliers, Annonay. By the following year the Basilians had moved the college to a new site above the town formerly used by the religious Sisters of the Sacred Heart. The Basilian school would henceforth be known as the Collège du Sacré-Coeur. Léopold was ordained priest in the school chapel on 21 September 1867 by Bishop Armand de Charbonnel. While taking his theology courses he taught the *classe de sixième* at the Collège des Cordeliers, 1863–6, and at the Collège de Privas, 1866–7.

After ordination Father Léopold Fayolle remained in Privas for eleven more years, teaching *cinquième*, first in the Collège de Privas, 1867–72, then in the *externat* (day-pupils school), 1872–8, which the Basilians conducted after they had to leave the college. During these years he also served as chaplain to a community of nuns. He taught one more year at the Petit Séminaire d'Aubenas, 1878–9, and then returned to the Collège du Sacré-Coeur, Annonay, where he was *professeur de quatrième*, 1879–81, and of *troisième*, 1881–93. In 1893 he was appointed master of novices at Sainte-Barbe, Annonay, a post he held for ten years, and was appointed superior there on 15 September 1901. When the Basilians were forced out of that institution in 1903, he accepted the chaplaincy of the Hôpital Sainte-Marie at Privas. The

Semaine religieuse de Viviers described him as a 'humble, lovable, charming priest.'

SOURCES: GABF; Kirley, *Community in France* 70, 124n305, 150n383, 163n416, 182n464, 184, 188n469, 205; Pouzol, 'Notices'; *Semaine religieuse de Viviers* (30 June 1905) 218–19.

FERGUSON, Michael Joseph, priest, first Canadian ordained for the Congregation, uncle of Father Thomas *Heydon, was born on a farm in Adjala Township, Ontario (archdiocese of Kingston, after 1841 diocese of Toronto) on 23 March 1839, the sixth child of Hugh Ferguson and Rose Colgan. He died in Windsor on 30 April 1913 and is buried in the Basilian plot of Mount Hope Cemetery, Toronto.

Michael Ferguson came to St Michael's College in Toronto on 23 October 1852, six weeks after it opened. He was a brilliant student, but after three years interrupted his studies to teach in a rural school and to clerk in a village store. Then he returned to St Michael's, where he was received as a novice on 1 November 1859 and made his final vows on 24 May 1861. He was ordained priest on 23 October of the same year. After ordination Father Ferguson taught at St Michael's College until 1872. During the summer months of 1863 he was acting pastor of St Mary's of the Assumption Parish in Owen Sound, Ontario, and for some years was delegate pastor of St Basil's Parish in Toronto. In 1872 Father Ferguson was transferred to Assumption College, Windsor, where he served until his death.

During the eleven years that he taught at St Michael's College, Father Ferguson was perhaps the most outstanding young priest in central and western Ontario. Tall, talented, a good-looking redhead, he was widely known and counted among his host of friends Sir John A. Macdonald, the first prime minister of Canada. At the time of the Fenian Raids, Sir John asked Father Ferguson to do something about the bitterly anti-English attitude of the Irish clergy in Toronto. Archbishop Lynch, a native Irishman, took offence at the ensuing appeal. His displeasure was the cause of Father Ferguson's transfer to Assumption College in 1872.

Compared with his early life, the life of Father Ferguson at Assumption College was that of a recluse. Two attempts were made to change its course. In 1883 he was appointed founding superior of the College of Mary Immaculate at Beaconfield House, Plymouth, England. By the end of November of the same year he was back at Assumption College, the English climate and the responsibility proving too much for his health. In 1889 he was named provincial, but declined the appointment. He was elected to the provincial council in 1883 and again in 1901. During the year 1876–7, when the novitiate was located at Assumption College, he served as master of novices.

At Assumption College Father Ferguson communicated to his classes his own unbounded admiration for the writings of Cardinal Newman and Orestes Brownson. The *Golden Jubilee Volume of Assumption College* boasted, 'As a student of pure English undefiled, he excelled, and it is a matter of sincere regret that he was so opposed to any exhibition of his gifts in the form of literary productions. He frequently contributed to Catholic publications, but always on the condition that his name should not be subscribed to them. The students of his classes, however, received the benefits of his marvellous literary gifts, and it was an education itself to listen to the flow of the choicest thoughts clothed in classic diction, while he gave life and charm to the subjects of study, as was his custom, by a profusion of illustrations drawn from every conceivable source: now from history, now from the classics of Greece or Rome, now from Catholic philosophy or theology, and most frequently of all, by personal anecdotes vividly and elegantly narrated. His memory was marvellous, and his acquired knowledge encyclopedic.' His sermons to the students of Assumption College during the month of May were greatly anticipated and long remembered. To promote public speaking among the students he founded St Basil's Literary Society in 1873.

Father Ferguson's flower garden was an institution at Assumption College until the land was required in 1907 as the location for the present chapel. He kept a diary for many years and in its volumes recorded events of the day. It was his custom to read a few pages before meals and with his memory so refreshed to lead the conversation around to the events he had recorded in his diary.

SOURCES: GABF; *Centennial, St Mary's*; *Jubilee, Assumption*; *Jubilee, St Mary's*; Hoskin, *St Basil's*; M.V. Kelly, *Rev. M.J. Ferguson CSB* (Toronto, [1914]); R.J. Scollard, *The Diaries and Other Papers of Michael Joseph Ferguson CSB: A Bibliography* (Toronto, 1970); *Yearbook SMC* 5 (1914). Samples of correspondence between Ferguson and contemporaries (among them Sir John A. Macdonald) have been published by Power, *Assumption College* 2 116–30; see also xiii–xiv, 20, 50, 58, 61, 72, 82, 88, 143, 147.

FINN, Robert William, priest, was born on 12 December 1919 at Medicine Hat, Alberta (diocese of Calgary), the son of William Finn and Mary Frances Quinlan. He died in Toronto on 24 January 1995 and is buried in the Basilian plot of Holy Cross Cemetery, Thornhill, Ontario. Robert graduated from St Mary's Boys' High School, Calgary, in 1939. That same year he entered St Basil's Novitiate, Toronto. After first profession on 15 August 1940, he was appointed to Assumption College, Windsor, where he majored in philosophy (B.A., University of Western Ontario, 1943). He taught for one year at St Thomas High School, Houston, 1943-4, before beginning theological studies at St Basil's Seminary, Toronto. Along with his theology he did graduate studies in philosophy at the Pontifical Institute of Mediaeval Studies (M.A., Philosophy, University of Toronto, 1947). On 29 June 1947 he was ordained to the priesthood in Sacred Heart Church, Calgary, by Bishop Francis P. Carroll. Father Finn was then appointed to the Pontifical Institute to complete theology and to continue his philosophical studies (M.S.L., 1949; thesis: 'William of Alnwick on the Divine Ideas').

Appointed in 1949 to St Thomas More College, Saskatoon, he began nineteen years of teaching, campus ministry, student counselling, glee club direction, and other college activities with remarkable energy and success. He served as second councillor, 1960-4, and as first councillor, 1964-6, for the Basilian house. In 1965 he was elected regional representative for Western Canada, an office to which he was re-elected in 1967. In 1968 he left Saskatoon to serve as principal of St Mark's College, Vancouver, for a few months, and subsequently as acting superior of St Joseph's College, Edmonton, also for a few months. He returned to St Mark's in 1969 and remained there as principal until 1975. He then taught for two years at Lethbridge, Alberta, before taking up pastoral ministry with the Basilian Fathers of Kelowna, British Columbia, 1978-85, and later with the Basilian Fathers of Calgary, 1985-6. He was admitted to the Basilian Fathers Residence (Infirmary) in 1986.

Father Finn's last years were darkened by a gradual weakening of his powers, both of body and mind, attributable to residual effects of an accidental inundation of his family's home with natural gas when he was a boy. It was a great sorrow for his confreres and friends to witness the decline of one so gifted with faith, intelligence, administrative ability, and wit.

BIBLIOGRAPHY: 'Teach Me Goodness. A Commentary,' *Basilian Teacher* 6 (November 1961) 55-9; 'Our Student Today: Problem and Potential [forum],'

Basilian Teacher 7 (December 1962) 112; 'Technological Innovations and Student Attitudes,' *Basilian Teacher* 7 (February 1963) 173–6.
SOURCES: GABF; *Annals* 1 (1947) 152, 8 (1996) 95–6; *Newsletter* (20 March 1995).

FINNIGAN, Joseph TERENCE, priest, was born in Toronto on 19 September 1875, the youngest child of Patrick Finnigan and Mary Gilson. He died in Toronto on 28 September 1918 and is buried there in the Basilian plot of Mount Hope Cemetery.

Terence Finnigan was crippled by an infection in his right knee when he was two years old. During the next five years his parents were faced with the possible necessity of the amputation of the leg in order to save his life. In the course of a novena made at the Monastery of the Precious Blood, Toronto, by Mother Catherine Aurélie, the foundress of this contemplative community, a steady improvement was noticed in his condition. Later the infection completely cleared up, although the right leg was considerably shorter than the left.

After this cure Terence Finnigan began his education at Loretto Convent, Toronto. In 1888 he entered St Michael's College. His leg now needed only the support of a cane, and he became agile enough to play goal in lacrosse games. He was admitted to St Basil's Novitiate, Toronto, on 3 October 1893. In 1894–5 he taught at Ste Anne's Parish School, Detroit, and at the same time studied philosophy at Assumption College. In 1895 he returned to Toronto and did theological studies at St Basil's Scholasticate. He was ordained priest on 15 August 1899.

Father Finnigan's priestly life was spent in teaching Latin, at which he excelled. In some schools he also served as treasurer. He taught at Assumption College, 1899–1900 and 1915–18, St Basil's College, Waco, Texas, 1900–6 and 1907–12, St Michael's College, 1906–7, and St Thomas College in Chatham, New Brunswick, 1913–15. He spent the year 1912–13 at St Basil's Scholasticate, and in 1918 he was appointed assistant master of novices. Usually called 'Ted' or 'Jerry' by his associates, Father Finnigan possessed the knack of winning the good will of all who had dealings with him.

SOURCES: GABF; Charles Collins, 'Basilians I Have Known,' transcribed in Robert J. Scollard, 'Historical Notes C.S.B.' 10 56–61 (GABF);

FIRTH, John Joseph FRANCIS, priest, was born on 1 July 1914, in Barrie, Ontario (archdiocese of Toronto), the son of Wilfred Firth and Mary

Geraldine Spearin, and the half-brother of Father Wilfred Firth of the archdiocese of Toronto. Father Francis Firth died in Toronto on 6 December 1999, and is buried in the Basilian plot of Holy Cross Cemetery, Thornhill, Ontario.

'Frank,' or 'Frankie,' Firth attended St Mary's Parochial School, Barrie, and Barrie Collegiate. In 1932 he began his undergraduate studies in philosophy at St Michael's College, Toronto. After one year he transferred to St Francis Xavier China Mission Seminary, Scarborough, Ontario, where he took two more years of philosophy and one of theology before returning to St Michael's College in 1936. He won the Hanrahan Prize in 1937, the Kernahan Scholarship in 1938, and the Cardinal Mercier Gold Medal in 1939. He graduated (B.A., Honours Philosophy, University of Toronto, 1939), submitting a thesis on 'The Definition of Life.' That same year he entered St Basil's Novitiate. After profession on 12 September 1940, he was appointed to St Basil's Seminary for theological studies, and concurrently took graduate courses in philosophy, obtaining an M.A. from the University of Toronto in 1942 for his thesis 'The Agent in the Operation of Abstraction in the Philosophy of St Thomas Aquinas.' He was ordained to the priesthood on 18 December 1943 in St Basil's Church, Toronto, by Bishop Roderick Macdonald of Peterborough. During his final year of theology at the seminary in 1944, he also obtained the M.S.L. from the Pontifical Institute of Mediaeval Studies, Toronto (thesis: 'The Doctrine of Sensation in Plotinus and St Augustine').

Father Firth's first appointment as a priest was to the Pontifical Institute of Mediaeval Studies, where he began his research on Robert of Flamborough, who in the period 1208 to 1215 published an influential manual for confessors. Father Firth's characteristic thoroughness and his many teaching assignments delayed the completion of his thesis until 1969, when he was awarded the Institute's prestigious M.S.D., a degree awarded only twelve times in the previous forty years. His teaching record spans nearly fifty years: St Basil's Seminary, Church history, moral and sacramental theology, 1944–60; St Augustine's Seminary and Scarborough China Mission Seminary, Church history, 1947–50; University of British Columbia, patristics and history of medieval philosophy, 1962–7; St Joseph's College, University of Alberta, Edmonton, philosophy, the history of theology and Christian thought, 1969–93; Newman Theological College, Edmonton, patristics, 1982–6. At St Joseph's College he worked so well with the Student Volunteer Campus Community of the University of Alberta, and with the Chinese community as a whole, that on the third anniversary of his death the SVCC dedicated a book to him and featured him in its website. In 1993 Father Firth became fully retired but continued contributing monthly articles on the Fathers of the Church to the *Canadian Catholic Review*.

Diminutive in body, mighty in mind, timid and self-effacing in manner, guileless and single-minded in his preoccupation with the knowledge of God and the history of the Church, Francis Firth was thorough and relentless in his quest for understanding, and ever disposed to explain and clarify. An excellent homilist, he communicated vividly and convincingly the mercy of God, his most frequent theme. As a confessor he extended that same mercy to penitents. He loved the story of Zacchaeus (Luke 19:1–10), the story of a little man 'who was up a tree!' Although his numerous and humorous personal antics will be remembered and recounted in the community with ever-renewed amusement, his presence as a man of brilliant intellect and of holiness will always be his outstanding attribute.

BIBLIOGRAPHY:
Book: Ed. Robert of Flamborough. *Liber Poenitentialis. A Critical Edition with Introduction and Notes*. Toronto, 1971.
Articles: 'The Importance of St Augustine,' *CCR* 4 (1986) 288–94. In that same journal, over the space of ten years (1988–97), he contributed exactly one hundred short articles on the lives and doctrine of the Fathers of the Church.
SOURCES: GABF; *Annals* 1 (1944) 55, 4 (1969) 118, 7 (1991) 8, 8 (1994) 11–12, 9 (2000) 90–1; *Newsletter* (15 December 1999); *Early History of Student Volunteer Campus Community and Father Francis Firth, 1980–85* (Edmonton, 2003); www.geocities.com/svcchistory

FISCHETTE, Robert Matthew, priest, brother of Sister Pierre S.Sp.S.,was born in Newark, New York (diocese of Rochester), on 10 May 1913, the son of Rocco Fischette and Mary Buttaccio. He died in Rochester on 7 December 1970 and is buried there in the Basilian plot of Holy Sepulchre Cemetery.

Robert attended his parish school and Aquinas Institute, Rochester, and entered St Basil's Novitiate, Toronto, in 1931. After professing his first vows on 15 August 1932, he was appointed to St Michael's College (B.A., University of Toronto, 1936). He did one year of theology at St Basil's Scholasticate, Toronto, and two years of teaching at Catholic Central High School, Detroit, 1937–9, earning concurrently a Michigan secondary school teacher's certificate. He returned to Toronto to complete his theology courses and was ordained to the priesthood on 15 August 1940 in St Basil's Church by Archbishop James Charles McGuigan.

In 1941 Father Fischette was assigned once again to Catholic Central, Detroit, where he taught for the next five years. During this time he obtained an M.A. from the University of Detroit, 1943, submitting a thesis entitled 'The Philosophy of Education of Father Henry S. Bellisle.' In 1946 he was transferred to Aquinas Institute, Rochester, where for ten years he was director of studies. In 1958 he obtained a doctorate in education from the University of Buffalo, submitting a thesis entitled 'A Study of the Professional Sequence of Teacher Education Programs in Catholic Institutions of Higher Learning of New York State.' In 1958 he was appointed to St John Fisher College, Rochester, first as professor of education and later as dean of studies. In 1961 he was elected to the general council of the Basilian Fathers, serving as director of studies with admirable efficiency for seven years. His hobby, stamp collecting, led him to write articles for a journal of philately.

He returned to St John Fisher College in 1968, somewhat slowed in his pace of work as the result of two heart attacks in 1962 and in 1967, though not diminished in his efficiency or devotion. He obeyed his doctors to the letter so that he might continue to work as long as possible. But on the morning of his death he over-exerted himself by straining to open a faulty garage door. He proceeded to his appointment as inspector of a student teacher in a Rochester high school, but collapsed in the course of the morning and died immediately.

Concentration and thoroughness marked every phase and task of Robert Fischette's life and work, whether as student, teacher, administrator, religious, or priest. He was strict without being rigid; exacting but never unkind. He held his opinions strongly and expressed them with conviction, yet never offensively. Small of stature and of kindly appearance, with evident devotion and zeal in his priesthood, he was a cheerful man whose company was always a pleasure.

BIBLIOGRAPHY:
Book: *Futureville – A School Study*. Buffalo, 1957.
Articles: 'The *Paradiso* of Dante's *Divine Comedy*,' *Basilian* 3 (November 1937); 'Know Your Students' TV Interests,' *University of Buffalo Educational Journal* (November 1958); 'College Pedagogy,' *Basilian Teacher* 5 (March 1961) 225–30; 'Spain Honors Velásquez – on Postage Stamps,' *Spectrum* (July–August 1969)

24–9; 'Spain Honors Goya – on Postage Stamps,' *Spectrum* (September–October 1969) 54–6.
SOURCES: GABF; *Annals* 4 (1971) 206–8; *Newsletter* (8 December 1970).

FITZPATRICK, Edward Francis, priest, member of the Congregation 1908–12, was born in Armagh, Ireland, on 7 March 1879, the youngest of ten boys of Patrick Fitzpatrick and Catherine McNaughton. He died at Bar Harbor, Maine, on 3 December 1958 and was buried there in Holy Redeemer Parish Cemetery.

Edward Fitzpatrick's parents emigrated in 1882 to Providence, Rhode Island, where he attended Tyler Public School, Sts Peter and Paul Parochial School, and La Salle Academy. After a year at Holy Cross College in Worcester, Massachusetts, 1899–1900, he went to Rochester to study for the priesthood at St Andrew's Preparatory Seminary, 1900–2, and St Bernard's Seminary, 1902–4. In 1904 he went to St Michael's College in Toronto to study theology, and was ordained priest on 2 July 1907.

The bishop of Providence gave Father Fitzpatrick a missionary appointment to the diocese of Lincoln, Nebraska, where he served half a year as assistant at St Mary's Parish, Wymore, until he entered St Basil's Novitiate, Toronto, on 19 March 1908. After profession in 1909 he taught at St Michael's College until the summer of 1910 when he was transferred to Assumption College in Windsor. Early in 1911 he obtained a leave of absence and returned to the diocese of Lincoln, where he was given charge of St Helena's parish in Grafton. At the end of the summer he returned to the Congregation and was appointed to St Thomas High School in Houston.

In June 1912 Father Fitzpatrick withdrew from the Congregation and was incardinated in the diocese of Portland, Maine, where he worked until his death in 1958: as assistant at St Patrick's parish, Lewiston; as pastor of St Benedict's parish, Benedicta, 1916–22, and St Michael's parish, South Berwick, 1922–4; as assistant at St Joseph's parish in Woodford Station, Portland, 1924–7; and as pastor of Holy Redeemer parish, Bar Harbor, where he died in 1958. Father Fitzpatrick was a lifelong friend of Father Joseph *Muckle.

SOURCE: GABF.

FLAHIFF, George Bernard, priest, superior general, archbishop, cardinal, brother of Sister Margaret Flahiff, SC, was born on 26 October 1905 at Paris, Ontario (diocese of London), the fourth son of the nine children of John Francis Flahiff and Eleanor Fleming. He died in Toronto on 22 August 1989 and is buried in the priests' plot of St Mary's Cemetery, Winnipeg, Manitoba.

George Flahiff attended Sacred Heart Parochial School, Paris, and Paris High School, 1917-22, with the exception of 1920-1 at St Jerome's College, Kitchener, Ontario. In 1922 he went to St Michael's College, Toronto, to study Honours English and History. He played intercollegiate football and O.H.A. hockey, was active in the debating club and in other activities, and won the Newman gold medal for oratory in 1925. His tutor, Lester B. Pearson, urged him to pursue a career in diplomacy; but, upon graduation (B.A, University of Toronto, 1926), he entered St Basil's Novitiate, Toronto, making first profession on 30 September 1927. While studying theology at St Basil's Scholasticate, he also taught English at St Michael's College and attended the Ontario College of Education, earning teaching certification, 1927. He was ordained to the priesthood, with special dispensation before completion of his theological studies, on 17 August 1930 in St Basil's Church, Toronto, by Archbishop Neil McNeil.

Just weeks after ordination, Father Flahiff began graduate studies at Strasbourg and then in Paris (Ecole des chartes, Diplôme d'archiviste-paléographe, 1935), presenting as his thesis 'Le bref royal de prohibition aux cours d'église en Angleterre, 1187-1286.' He returned to lecture on the history of institutions and on the history of art and architecture in medieval Europe at the Institute of Mediaeval Studies, Toronto, and was cross-appointed to the Department of History in the School of Graduate Studies of the University of Toronto in 1940. From 1943 to 1954 he was secretary (registrar) of the Institute, an office which also involved academic counselling. He served on the executive of the American Catholic Historical Association, 1940-7. Intensely interested in contemporary developments in liturgy, religious art, and architecture, he contributed frequently to *Liturgical Arts*, the journal of the Liturgical Arts Association of New York, of which he was a member.

In 1948 he was elected to the general council of the Basilian Fathers, and was appointed Basilian superior at the Institute House, 1951-4. The 1954 general chapter elected him superior general. In this office he completed the negotiations, begun by his predecessor Father E.J. *McCorkell, for the reunion of the Basilian Fathers of Viviers with the Basilian Fathers of Toronto into one single Congregation again, and began to appoint young Basilians to bolster the staff of the Collège du

Sacré-Coeur in Annonay. He later planned a Basilian residence near Paris, where scholastics and priests could live while studying theology at the Séminaire Saint-Sulpice or the Institut catholique de Paris. He extended the Basilian Latin-American missionary apostolate from Texas into Mexico itself, assuming responsibility for the suburban Mexico City parish of San Juan Crisóstomo. Reaching beyond the Basilian Congregation, he helped found the Canadian Religious Conference, of which he was president from 1958 to 1961.

Re-elected as superior general in 1960, he was but nine months into his second term when Pope John XXIII named him archbishop of Winnipeg. Consecrated bishop in St Michael's Cathedral, Toronto, on 31 May 1961, he took possession of his see on 26 June. Just before his ordination he was named to the preparatory Commission on Religious Life for the Second Vatican Council. He attended all the sessions of the council, 1962–5, but spoke only once, on ecumenism. Throughout the council he worked on the Commission on Religious Life, contributed to the council document *Perfectae caritatis*, and continued on that post-conciliar Commission. In 1967 he was also appointed to the Congregation for Religious and Secular Institutes, and served on the Congregation for Catholic Education. In travelling to and from Rome in those years he frequently interrupted his journey to visit the Maison Saint-Basile at Issy-les-Moulineaux, the Basilian house of studies near Paris that he had helped plan.

George Flahiff was an eminently pastoral archbishop, though he never thought himself up to the charge that had been laid upon him. His happiest moments were in ministering to his flock in the remote areas of his vast archdiocese. But he was much occupied with Church affairs in Canada and on the larger world scene, serving as president of the National Conference of Catholic Bishops of Canada, 1963–5. Twice, in 1967 and in 1971, he was elected as a representative of the Canadian bishops at the Synod in Rome, and travelled much in Canada and the United States explaining and promoting the teachings of the council. Pope Paul VI made him a cardinal in 1969, with Santa Maria della Salute a Primavalle as his titular church. His speech at the Roman Synod of bishops in 1971, delivered in the name of the Canadian bishops, called for the establishment of a committee to examine the role of women in church ministries, causing a world-wide stir that gave him the unjustified reputation of being an advocate for the ordination of women. His reputation as an ecumenist and as a champion for social justice were proven in many ways. Dozens of academic, religious, and civic honours were conferred upon him, among them the designation as a Companion of the Order of Canada, 1974. In 'the year of three popes,' 1978, he participated in the conclaves which elected John Paul I and then John Paul II.

After serving as archbishop of Winnipeg for twenty-one years, Cardinal Flahiff retired in 1982 to St Michael's College, Toronto, living as a confrere with his Basilian brothers. When his health declined rapidly in 1989 he went to live at the Basilian Fathers Residence (Infirmary).

He was a tall man of fine appearance and gracious manners. The influence he exercised in the Church in Canada was considerable, though more in the moral order than in the legislative or innovative. His legacy of writings has, as of 2003, yet to be made available or studied. His legacy of example – a zealous pastor, a humble religious, a faithful churchman, and an admirable human person – strongly endures.

BIBLIOGRAPHY: A list of forty of his articles and reviews published in *Mediaeval Studies*, *Liturgical Arts*, *Donum Dei*, and other journals can be found in *Mediaeval Studies* 52 (1990) vi–viii. The following items, all in the *Basilian Teacher*, do not appear there: 'Christmas Greetings,' 1 (December 1956) 3; 'Summary, Christmas Educational Conference, 1956,' 1 (January 1957) 22–4; 'Christmas Greetings,' 2 (December 1957) 3; 'Towards a Theology of Sports,' 2 (February 1958) 22–5; 'Guidance: Its Nature, Purpose, and Area of Coverage,' 3 (January 1959) 84–9; 'The Religious Priest,' 10 (1966) 327–40. As superior general he published a letter to the community each year, 1954–60, in *Basilian Annals*. As archbishop of Winnipeg, he published about one hundred pastoral letters on liturgy, ecumenism, social and moral issues, education, and the implementation of the directives of the Second Vatican Council. A number of unpublished addresses are extant in the General Archives of the Basilian Fathers, Toronto.
SOURCES: GABF; *Annals* 4 (1970) 150–1, 5 (1978) 267, 5 (1981) 537–8, 7 (1990) 120–2; *Newsletter* (24 October 1989); Kirley, *Congregation in France* 231n24, 250–4, 257–62, 264–5, 267; Jean LeBlanc, *Dictionnaire biographique des évêques catholiques du Canada* (Montreal and Ottawa, 2002) 464–5; *Mediaeval Studies* 52 (1990) iv–viii; P. Wallace Platt, *Gentle Eminence: A Life of Cardinal Flahiff*. Montreal and Kingston, 1999.

FLANAGAN, Edward Francis, priest, was born in Toronto on 20 October 1913, the son of Edward Flanagan and Winifred McPherson. He died in Toronto on 15 December 1977 and is buried in the Basilian plot of Holy Cross Cemetery, Thornhill, Ontario.

'Ted' Flanagan attended Our Lady of Perpetual Help parochial school, Toronto, and the high school section of St Michael's College, Toronto. Graduating in 1932, he entered St Basil's Novitiate, Toronto, and, after first profession on 15 August 1933, was appointed to Assumption College, Windsor (B.A., University of Western Ontario, 1936). Living at St Michael's College, Toronto, 1937, he earned teaching certification at the Ontario College of Education. He taught at Catholic Central High School, Detroit, 1937–8, while beginning the study of theology, which he completed at St Basil's Seminary, Toronto, 1938–41. Ordination to the priesthood was conferred by Archbishop James Charles McGuigan on 15 August 1940 in St Basil's Church.

Father Flanagan's teaching career was spent chiefly at St Michael's College School, 1941–2, 1943–57, 1960–77, with three short appointments at St Thomas High School, Houston, 1942–3; Assumption College School, Windsor, 1957–8; and Michael Power High School, Etobicoke, Ontario, 1958–60. His remarkable charism for inspiring his students carried over into his coaching of football and hockey. He brought out the best in young men by his close interest and understanding, his personal charm and his generosity in giving his time and efforts. His office of Athletic Director swarmed with students, some to receive help with math, some to address and stuff envelopes, and some just to hang about. He had a saying, 'Get a boy to do something for you and you have a friend for life.' He organized the Quarterback Club among the parents and friends of the students to raise money for sports equipment. In 1943 and 1944 he coached the senior high school football team at St Michael's in undefeated seasons against the best teams in the Toronto-Hamilton Region and then against St Paul's and St John's in Winnipeg. He organized team Mass on the morning of a game, and saw that there were confessors on hand. He was a fiery, inspirational coach and a demanding disciplinarian with a sense of humour. One of his players, Father Brian Higgins CSB, recalls: 'When I was in the middle of the line I could feel his eyes burning into my soul and asking, "Are you a man?"' He would not spare himself; everything he did was for the boys. During the hockey season, prior to the day's teaching, he would be at Maple Leaf Gardens from 5:30 to 8:30 a.m. for a practice which the boys found more gruelling than the games. A weekday game meant that he would return home after midnight, but he would meet his classes as usual the next day. A sign on his desk read, 'If you are dog-tired at night, you have been barking too much all day.' To a discouraged young teacher he once said, 'Don't worry too much about the subject matter. Remember that you are looking at a classroom filled with unformed souls and just try to lead them to think for themselves.' After this advice, teaching became a joy for the young teacher.

Ted Flanagan is gratefully remembered by many as the person who could perceive the talent latent in a youth and bring it forth, whether in academics or sports. The ill health of his last years with the sadness it entailed in all who knew him did not dim the bright achievements of his better years.

BIBLIOGRAPHY: 'A Religious Bulletin for Our Schools,' *Benedicamus* 3 (October 1950) 100; 'Jump, Run, Bump and Yell,' *Benedicamus* 5 (May 1952) 6–7.
SOURCES: GABF; *Annals* 5 (1978) 333–4; *Newsletter* (22 December 1977); Brian Higgins CSB.

FLANAGAN, John Berchmans, priest, was born in Wallaceburg, Ontario (diocese of London), on 24 February 1902, the son of Edward Flanagan and Mary O'Neill. He died at Dearborn, Michigan, on 3 May 1942 and is buried in the Basilian plot of Assumption Cemetery, Windsor.

After primary and secondary schooling in his home town, John completed his last year of high school at Assumption College School in Windsor. He began his arts course at Assumption College, interrupting it in 1921–2 to teach at St Thomas College in Chatham, New Brunswick. He returned to Assumption, and in 1923 completed the B.A. from the University of Western Ontario. After graduation he entered St Basil's Novitiate, Toronto, and was professed on 11 August 1924. He did theological studies at St Basil's Scholasticate, Toronto, and also received teacher certification from the Ontario College of Education in 1926. He was ordained priest on 30 June 1928 in St Basil's Church, Toronto, by Archbishop Neil McNeil.

While teaching Latin and Greek at Aquinas Institute, Rochester, 1928–32, he suffered increasingly severe attacks of asthma, first noticed in the scholasticate. He went on sick-leave in 1930 and in the course of the next four years sought help at various sanatoriums and in changes of climate. This brought temporary relief, and he was assigned to assist in various ways at Assumption College and at St Michael's College. In 1934 a chronic, racking cough and consequent loss of sleep brought on a nervous breakdown, and he became a patient at St Joseph's Retreat, Dearborn, Michigan, where he died.

Father Flanagan, always called 'J.B.' from his initials, was outstanding for his cheerfulness and leadership during his few active years. At the Ontario College of Education in Toronto the staff ranked him as one of the most promising teachers in his class.

SOURCES: GABF; *Purple and White* (15 December 1927); *Yearbook SMC* 16 (1925).

FLANNERY, William, priest, member of the Congregation, 1850–7, was born in Nenagh, County Tipperary, Ireland (diocese of Killaloe), in 1830. He died at Borrisokane, Ireland, on 21 December 1901 and was buried in the parish cemetery there.

William Flannery was educated at the Collège des Cordeliers, Annonay, in France. While still a scholastic he volunteered for appointment to the nascent St Michael's College in 1852. After ordination as a priest in Toronto in the Loretto convent on 22 May 1853, he taught at St Michael's College until 1857. During these years he wrote and directed the plays which were presented as part of the annual commencement exercises. He was also a musician and had been urged to bring his violin and books of music when he came to Canada. When religious vows were proposed in 1852, however, Father Flannery did not take them. In 1857, when differences with the bishop arose over his care of St John the Evangelist Parish in Weston, Ontario, he withdrew from the Congregation.

Father Flannery subsequently returned to Ireland and received an appointment in the parish of Toumevara; but, when Bishop Armand de Charbonnel resigned as bishop of Toronto, Father Flannery returned and joined the diocese of Toronto. He was appointed pastor of St Patrick's Parish, Dixie, Ontario, and served there from 1861 until February 1867, when he moved to St Francis de Sales Parish, Pickering, Ontario. Shortly afterwards differences with Bishop Lynch over the validity of a Canadian Mass wine caused him to withdraw once again from the diocese and return to Ireland; but he returned to Canada in 1868 and joined the diocese of London. He was put in charge of St John the Baptist Parish, Amherstburg, Ontario, from January to November 1870, and was then made pastor of Holy Angels Parish, St Thomas, Ontario, 1870–98. He died in 1901, on a visit to a married sister at Borrisokane.

As pastor at St Thomas, Father Flannery did a good deal of writing. For some years he was editor of the *Catholic Record* and of the *Catholic Weekly Review* (both published in London, Ontario). Georgetown University conferred an honorary Doctor of Divinity on him in 1897.

During his years in Canada, Father Flannery collected money for the restoration of a castle near his birthplace. This and other marks of interest led the authorities of Nenagh to name the street on which he was born William Street in his honour. Father Flannery kept up friendly relations with his former confreres and was one of the speakers at the laying of the cornerstone of St Basil's Novitiate, Toronto, in May 1892.

SOURCES: GABF; J.F. Boland, 'An Analysis of the Problems and Difficulties of the Basilian Fathers in Toronto, 1850–1860,' unpublished doctoral thesis (University of Ottawa, 1955); William Perkins Bull, *From Macdonell to McGuigan, the History of the Growth of the Roman Catholic Church in Upper Canada* (Toronto, 1939); John Gleeson, *History of the Ely O'Carroll Territory* 2 vols. (Dublin, 1915; repr. Kilkenny 1982); Edmund C. Phelan, *The Parish of St Francis de Sales, Pickering, Ontario, a Short History* (Pickering, 1966); Pouzol, 'Notices'; Laurence K. Shook, 'St Michael's College, the Formative Years, 1850–1853,' in *CCHA Report* 17 (1950) 37–52; John Read Teefy, *Jubilee Volume, 1842–1892, of the Archdiocese of Toronto* (Toronto, 1892).

FLOOD, Francis De Sales, priest, was born on 20 August 1911 in Youngstown, Ohio, the son of Joseph M. Flood and Mary A. Starrs. He died in Detroit on 19 May 1977 and is buried there in Holy Sepulchre Cemetery.

After early education in Youngstown and Cleveland, Ohio, 'Frank' enrolled at Assumption College School in 1925 and graduated in 1929. On 2 September he entered St Basil's Novitiate, Toronto, and took first vows on 12 September 1930. He was appointed to St Basil's Scholasticate, Toronto, and later to St Michael's College for his undergraduate studies (B.A., University of Toronto, 1935). For his B.A. thesis he translated Thomas Aquinas's *De articulis fidei et ecclesiae sacramentis*. After one year of teaching at Catholic Central High School, Detroit, he returned to St Basil's Scholasticate ('Seminary' from 1937) for theology. In 1938 he was appointed to Aquinas Institute, Rochester, where he continued his theological studies while serving as secretary to Father Wilfred *Murphy. He returned to the seminary in 1939 and was ordained to the priesthood on 15 August 1940 in St Basil's Church by Archbishop James Charles McGuigan. During his final year of theology, 1940–1, he earned a B.L.S. from the University of Toronto.

Father Flood's first appointment as a priest was to Catholic Central, Detroit, as librarian. Two years later he was moved to Assumption College to work in that same capacity, and he earned an M.A. in education from the University of Michigan, 1947. In 1952 he was appointed to St John Fisher College, Rochester, functioning for ten years both as librarian and professor of English. He resumed the position of librarian at Catholic Central, Detroit, in 1962, where his work was thoroughly professional, his manner ever courteous. Under his direction, the library became outstanding among school libraries in the area.

Of medium height with a tendency to heaviness, Frank was keenly intelligent, humorous, and casual in his manner. He was both the source and the object of a great deal of community humour. His lightheartedness, however, did not hide his deep concern for the community and for his confreres individually. Nor did his casual manner hide his devotion to community life and things of the spirit. He would go to great inconvenience, wherever he was, to say Mass each day. He could talk about death and the afterlife with an ease that bespoke considerable meditation on those mysteries. He was the first to volunteer when a priestly service was needed or when the superior was seeking a leader for community prayer.

SOURCES: GABF; *Annals* 5 (1978) 326–7; *Newsletter* (25 May 1977).

FLOOD, Robert Henry, priest, was born on 20 September 1919 in Syracuse, New York, the son of Charles Flood and Marion Edgeworth. He died on 3 April 1974 at Marcy, New York, and is buried in the Basilian plot of Holy Sepulchre Cemetery, Rochester.

'Bob' Flood attended St Vincent de Paul parochial school and high school in Syracuse, going to St Michael's College, Toronto, in 1937 for his university studies. One year later he entered St Basil's Novitiate, Toronto, and made first profession on 15 August 1939. From the novitiate he was appointed to St Michael's College to complete his arts course (B.A., University of Toronto, 1942). He taught English at Aquinas Institute, Rochester, for one year, and at Catholic Central, Detroit, also for one year. He took courses at the University of Detroit as well as at Wayne State University, earning Michigan teaching certification, 1944. He returned to Toronto in 1944 for theological studies at St Basil's Seminary and was ordained to the priesthood on 29 June 1947 in St Basil's Church, Toronto, by Cardinal James Charles McGuigan.

In 1948 Father Bob Flood was again appointed to Aquinas Institute to teach English. Two years later he was sent on graduate studies to Catholic University of America, Washington, D.C. (M.A., Library Science, 1951). He joined the pioneer staff of St John Fisher College, Rochester, as librarian and lecturer in English. He launched the library of the new college on a soundly academic and useful course by his organizational skills and his discerning appreciation of literature.

In 1960 he was appointed to Assumption University, Windsor, as a member of the English staff. As had been the case at St John Fisher, he enjoyed a remarkable rapport with the students, who were attracted by his unconventional manner, his wit, his love of conversation, and his stimulating approach to literature. More than one student transferred from sciences to literature as a result of Father Flood's courses, and the memory of his classes, of his opinions on literature and life, and of his witty remarks persisted long after he had left Assumption.

In 1964 Father Flood went to the University of St Michael's College as assistant librarian. It was here that his health began to fail, though there was difficulty in determining the cause. In 1968 he was appointed to St Charles College, Sudbury, Ontario, where he also worked as librarian and where he was welcomed as an occasional lecturer in English to the senior students and into the wider community of friends of St Charles College. He continued his voracious reading, mastering whole texts quickly while exhibiting an incredible level of retention, even well into his illness. He liked to read a book twice, the first time to master content, the second to analyse the author's craft. His adherence to this approach was clearly evinced in his effortless and luminous literary comments.

During his holidays in Syracuse in the late summer of 1971 he suffered a nervous collapse from which he never recovered. His condition was finally diagnosed as Huntington's chorea, a genetic affliction which leads to rapid aging. His remaining years were spent at St Vincent's Hospital, Harrison, New York, and then at Marcy Hospital, Marcy, New York, where he died.

Bob Flood's wide reading, even much beyond English literature, made his conversation, seasoned by his wit, rich and interesting. He related well to everyone, and always had time for others, time to do what anyone asked of him, always appreciative of what was done for him. His remarkable memory, especially of things concerning confreres and friends, was proof of his deep and sincere interest in them. Ironically and sadly, in his final years he was deprived of the things he loved most, reading and conversation.

BIBLIOGRAPHY:
Books (poetry): *The Bashful Chair*. Rochester, 1952. *A World Elsewhere*. Windsor, 1961. *On Strange Track*. Philadelphia, 1967.

Articles: In *Benedicamus*: 'The Sodality at Aquinas,' 2 (February 1949) 18–19, 24; 'High School Is a Vocation,' 3 (November 1949) 6–7; 'The Sodality in Action,' 3 (December 1949) 10, 13. In *Basilian Teacher*: 'The Sinner's Christmas, a Poem,' 2 (December 1957) cover; 'Man of Leisure, a Poem,' 8 (December 1963) 129; 'Seasons,' 9 (November 1964) 72; 'Timely Poetry,' 10 (January 1968) 29.
SOURCES: GABF; *Annals* 1 (1947) 152, 5 (1975) 117–18; *Newsletter* (5 April 1974); Brian F. Hogan.

FOGERON, Joseph, priest, was born on 1 March 1867 at Satillieu (Ardèche). He died on 15 April 1944 and was buried in the cemetery at Satillieu.
After entering the Petit Séminaire Sainte-Barbe in Annonay at the age of thirteen, Joseph took his classes at the Collège du Sacré-Coeur, Annonay, completing his final year in 1885. After courses in philosophy and theology at the Grand Séminaire at Viviers, he received the subdiaconate on 21 December 1889 and the diaconate on 19 December 1891 at Viviers, intending to serve in that diocese. On 23 June 1892, however, he left the seminary to transfer to the diocese of Valence but decided after that summer to help the Basilians in their school Saint-Augustin in Bône, Algeria. He remained three years there, working as disciplinarian and teaching grammar. This experience induced him to become a postulant and then a novice. He made his final profession of vows on 20 September 1895, and was ordained a priest the following day in the chapel of the Collège du Sacré-Coeur by Bishop Joseph-Michel-Frédéric Bonnet of Viviers.
After ordination Father Fogeron taught the *classe de quatrième* in the Ecole cléricale de Périgueux (Dordogne), 1895–6, and then returned to the college in Annonay where he was in charge of the commercial class, 1896–1900. He went again to Périgueux to teach *sixième* in the Ecole cléricale in 1900–1 and *quatrième* in 1901–3. When the 1903 suppression forced the Basilians to abandon the school at Périgueux, he received his certificate of 'secularization' on 29 September from the chancery of the diocese of Viviers. This allowed him to accept a teaching position, first in the Collège de l'Oratoire at Juilly (Seine-et-Marne), and later at the Institution Saint-Michel, Saint-Etienne (Loire). In this period of his life, 1903–22, he was also for a time a private tutor in the family of the Marquis d'Agrève at Chifflet, Saint-Jeure-d'Ay, canton of Satillieu (Ardèche).
In 1922 Father Fogeron joined the staff of the Collège du Sacré-Coeur, Annonay. He was placed in charge of the senior students as study-hall and recreation master, 1922–6; then he became *professeur de*

quatrième (section moderne) for the next fourteen years, 1926-40. He finished his teaching career as *professeur de quatrième* in 1940-1. After retirement he continued to live at the college, and for many years he celebrated Sunday Mass at Toissieux (Ardèche). At a general chapter of the Basilians held at the Maison Saint-Joseph, Annonay, on 27 January 1944, Father Fogeron was elected to the general council; but he died shortly afterwards at his family home.

SOURCES: GABF; Kirley, *Community in France* 185, 209; Kirley, *Congregation in France* 184, 196-8, 208; Pouzol, 'Notices.'

FORESTELL, Daniel Leo, priest, uncle of Father Terence *Forestell, was born in Springbrook, Ontario (diocese of Peterborough), on 15 July 1890, the son of James Forestell and Bridget O'Donnell. He died in Toronto on 24 April 1966, and was buried in the Basilian plot, Holy Cross Cemetery, Thornhill, Ontario.

'Dan' Forestell was raised in Campbellford, Ontario, and attended high school there, 1905-9. He enrolled at St Michael's College, Toronto (B.A., University of Toronto, 1913). The next year he attended the Ontario College of Education, Toronto. In 1914 he entered St Basil's Novitiate, Toronto, and after profession on 17 August 1915 he studied theology at St Basil's Scholasticate and was ordained priest on 21 December 1918 in St Peter's Cathedral, London, Ontario, by Bishop Michael Fallon.

Father Forestell taught French at Assumption College, Windsor, until 1922, when he was appointed assistant at Assumption Parish. Two years later he was named pastor of St John the Baptist Parish, Amherstburg, Ontario. When smallpox struck the district he would not permit his assistants to attend victims of this contagious and lethal disease, reserving that duty to himself. He was transferred to Toronto in 1925 to serve as pastor of St Basil's Parish and in 1928 he moved to Holy Rosary Parish in the same capacity. Father Forestell returned to school work in 1930 as principal of St Michael's College School in Toronto. He was superior at Catholic Central High School in Detroit, 1931-3, and from 1933 to 1942 he taught at St Michael's College and was a member of the local council. The appointments of 1942-3 took him back to parochial work as pastor of St Basil's Parish. He was pastor of St Anne's Parish, Houston, 1947-8. Appointments as assistant followed: Assumption Parish, 1948-54, St John the Baptist Parish, 1954-5, and Holy Rosary Parish, 1955-8. He went back to St John the

Baptist Parish as pastor for the year 1958-9. His last active post was assistant at St Basil's Parish, 1959-62. In 1962 he suffered the first of a series of strokes and retired to St Basil's Seminary, where he remained for the last four years of his life.

When talking with parishioners and former students, Father Forestell would amaze his listeners with his ability to recall their names and even to trace relationships. Despite his nickname, 'Frosty,' he was a warm-hearted priest who always had time for a friendly chat. He was active in urging young men to consider a vocation to the priesthood.

BIBLIOGRAPHY: 'Signs of a Priestly Vocation,' *Proceedings of the Basilian Vocation Meetings* 2 (1956) 34-6; 'Father Michael V. Kelly, *Laudemus viros gloriosos*,' *Basilian Teacher* 4 (October 1959) 22-4; 'The Basilian and Vocations to the Diocesan Clergy,' *Proceedings of the Basilian Vocation Meetings* 6 (1960) 93.
SOURCES: GABF; *Annals* 3 (1965) 371, (1966) 463-4; *Newsletter* (25 April 1966); Madden, *St Basil's*; *Yearbook SMC* 3 (1913), 22 (1931).

FORESTELL, James TERENCE, priest, was born on 22 November 1925 at Bridgeburn (now Fort Erie), Ontario (archdiocese of Toronto, now diocese of St Catharines), the eldest of three children of Tobias Frederick Forestell and Agnes Irene O'Driscoll. He was the nephew of Father Daniel Leo *Forestell. He died in Toronto on 31 July 2000 and is buried in the Basilian plot at Holy Cross Cemetery, Thornhill, Ontario.

After attending public schools in his home town, 'Terry' attended the high school section of St Michael's College, Toronto, 1942-3, on the Sir Bertram Windle Memorial Scholarship. He entered St Basil's Novitiate, Toronto, in 1943, making first profession on 15 August 1944. After doing the Honours French and Latin course at the University of Toronto (B.A., 1948), he took first-year theology at the Grand Séminaire, Quebec City, and three additional years at St Basil's Seminary, Toronto. Cardinal James Charles McGuigan ordained him to the priesthood on 21 December 1951 in St Basil's Church, Toronto.

Father Forestell began graduate studies in theology in Rome in 1952, obtaining the licence in theology in 1953 and the licence in Sacred Scripture at the Pontifical Biblical Institute ('Biblicum') in 1955. After a further year of advanced study at the Ecole biblique, Jerusalem, he was appointed in 1956 to teach at St Basil's Seminary, Toronto, where he ushered in a new era of modern approaches to the Bible that he had learned in Rome and Jerusalem. His innovative lectures were inspiring, courageous, and welcomed by most, but not without opposition from some.

In 1965 he returned to Jerusalem to begin doctoral studies. The 1967 War forced him to flee Jerusalem, and he became seriously ill while in a cholera quarantine camp in Iraq. After recuperation at the Basilian scholasticate of Maison Saint-Basile, Issy-les-Moulineaux (Hauts-de-Seine), he continued his research at Harvard Divinity School and successfully defended his thesis before the Pontifical Biblical Commission (Rome). He was awarded a doctorate in Sacred Scripture upon defence and publication of his thesis, 'The Presentation of Salvation in the Fourth Gospel: An Exegetical and Theological Study.' Though he taught courses in both the Old and New Testaments, he eventually specialized in the latter.

Father Forestell taught in the Faculty of Theology at the University of St Michael's College from 1968 to 1985. For two years, 1971–3, he served as master of novices while continuing to teach, and for one year, 1977–8, he did research at the Biblical Institute in Rome. He became internationally known as a scholar, teacher, and author. In 1981 he was awarded an honorary Doctor of Humanities by St Michael's College, Winooski, Vermont, in acknowledgment by the Edmundite Fathers of his teaching of their scholastics in Toronto.

In 1984 debilitating chronic back pain and unsuccessful surgery forced him to leave full-time teaching. He did a year of research at Stanford University, 1985–6, and then joined the staff of St Joseph's College, Edmonton, in the University of Alberta. He became fully retired in 1989 but remained with the St Joseph's community until 1994, when he moved to the Orsini House Retirement Community in Toronto. There new electric treatments gave him relief from his chronic pain so that he could give occasional lectures and retreats and do pastoral ministry. He collapsed on Saturday morning, 30 July 2000, while shopping with confreres at the St Lawrence Market, Toronto. Though resuscitated, he died some twenty-four hours later.

Father Forestell was the object of great respect and affection among his students and of unstinting gratitude for the understanding and love of the Bible he gave them. Though his method of interpretation was based on the best scholarship, his approach was always pastoral and aimed at inculcating love of Christ and the Church. His influence went well beyond the classroom into parishes, priests' gatherings, and his Basilian confreres. The chronic pain which he faced for years, as well as a bout with cancer, never overcame his pursuit of learning, his zeal to proclaim the Word, or his willing service to his friends and community.

BIBLIOGRAPHY:
Books: Ed. and comment. *Book of Proverbs*. Pamphlet Bible Series. New York, 1960. *Word of the Cross. A Study of the Theology of Salvation in St John's Gospel*. Analecta Biblica 57. Rome, 1974. *As Ministers of Christ: The Christological Dimension of Ministry in the New Testament. An Exegetical Study*. New York, 1991. (With Donald McLeod) *Pentecost 2*. Philadelphia, 1975. *Targumic Traditions and the New Testament*. Chico, Calif., 1979.
Chapters in books: (With E.C. Blackman) 'Scripture Scholars Analyze Basic Reformation Texts.' In John F. Madden CSB and Gregory Baum OESA, eds. *Churchmen in Dialogue: Reprinted from the Canadian Register*. Toronto, 1965. In *Jerome Biblical Commentary*, ed. Raymond Brown, Joseph Fitzmyer, et al. Englewood Cliffs, N.J., 1968: 'Proverbs,' 1 495–505; 'Epistles to the Thessalonians,' 2 227–35. 'Jesus and the Paraclete in the Gospel of John,' *Word and Spirit: Essays in Honor of David Michael Stanley SJ*. Toronto, 1975.
Articles: 'Why St Francis?' *Benedicamus* 3 (December 1949) 16; 'St Joseph: Basilian Patron,' *Benedicamus* 3 (February 1950) 32; 'St Thomas Aquinas,' *Benedicamus* 3 (March 1950) 40; 'Devotion to the Crib,' *Benedicamus* 4 (Christmas 1950) 24; 'Christian Perfection and Gnosis in Philippians 3:7–16,' *Catholic Biblical Quarterly* 18 (1956) 123–36; 'Christian Revelation and the Resurrection of the Wicked,' *Catholic Biblical Quarterly* 19 (April 1957) 165–89; 'Hear, O Israel, the Word of the Lord,' *Occasional Papers, St Basil's Seminary* 6 (April 1957); 'The Limitation of Inerrancy,' *Catholic Biblical Quarterly* 20 (January 1958) 9–18; 'St Paul, Teacher of the Christian Life,' *Clergy Review*, new series, 45 (August 1960) 456–65; 'Old Testament Background of the Magnificat,' *Marian Studies* 12 (1961) 205–44; 'I Am the Resurrection and the Life,' *Bible Today* (March 1963) 330–6; 'An Event in North American Biblical Scholarship. A Review Article,' *Canadian Journal of Theology* 9 (1963) 196–200; 'Hear, O Israel, the Word of the Lord,' *Bible Today* (October 1964) 838–44; 'Bible, II: Inspiration,' *New Catholic Encyclopedia* (New York, 1967) 2 381–6; (with T.J. Hanrahan CSB), 'Evangelical Poverty: Its Scriptural and Theological Basis,' *Aspects of Basilian Spirituality* (Toronto, 1972) 59–79; 'Preferential Option for the Poor,' *Occasional Paper* 5 (15 October 1985) [repr. *CCR* 4 (1986) 6–12]; 'Without Error: Fundamentalism and the Bible,' *CCR* 5 (December 1987) 405–12; 'A View of the Landscape,' *Religious Studies and Theology* 8 (January–May 1988) 9–23; 'The Church and the Bible: Interpretation of the Bible in the Church,' *CCR* (July/August 1995) 11–21; 'Myth and Biblical Revelation,' *CCR* (February 1995) 19–21; 'The Church and the Bible: The Interpretation of the Bible in the Church,' *CCR* 13 (July/August

1995) 11–21. He published scriptural commentary for homilists in *Discover the Bible* (Montreal), no. 964 (27 December 1987), no. 990 (26 June 1988), and no. 1007 (25 December 1988). In *Basilian Teacher*: 'Sacred Scripture and Our Students,' 2 (April 1958) 6–10 and 2 (May 1958) 16–19; 'What Is the Bible?' 4 (April 1960) 193–7; 'The Bible and the Church,' 4 (May 1960) 245–50; 'Inspiration and Inerrancy,' 5 (October 1960) 15–19; 'Reading the Word of God,' 5 (December 1960) 91–5; 'The Circumstances, Background, and Principles of the New Developments in Scripture Study,' 5 (February 1961) 145–52; 'What Are the Synoptic Gospels?' 5 (May 1961) 294–6; 'The Apostolic Preaching,' 6 (December 1961) 87–92; 'The Formation of the Gospels,' 6 (March 1962) 234–7; 'The Gospel according to St Mark,' 6 (March 1962) 234–7; 'The Bible as History,' 6 (October 1962) 3–8; 'The Gospel according to St Matthew,' 7 (November 1962) 58–66; 'The Gospel according to St Luke,' 7 (January 1963) 150–7; 'The Gospel according to St John' (April 1963) 253–61; trans. with commentary, 'Pontifical Biblical Commission: Instruction on the Historical Truth of the Gospels,' 8 (May 1964) 449–60; 'The Biblical Idea of Man,' 9 (December 1964) 111–23; 'New Testament View of Man,' 9 (February 1965) 229–37; 'The Priest as Minister of the Word,' 12 (1968) 295.

SOURCES: GABF; *Annals* 2 (1952) 58, 8 (1995) 11–12, 9 (2001) 97–9; *Newsletter* (20 August 2000).

FORNER, Benjamin Nicholas, priest, member of the Congregation 1918–37, was born in Monroe, Michigan (archdiocese of Detroit), on 22 May 1899, the son of Francis Joseph Forner and Anna Rosa Müller. He died at Skiatook, Oklahoma, on 27 February 1948.

Benjamin Forner attended St Michael's School, Monroe, then in 1913 went for high school to Assumption College in Windsor. Four years later he entered St Basil's Novitiate, Toronto, and was professed on 10 August 1918. His university studies at St Michael's College, Toronto, were interrupted by two years of teaching at St Thomas College, Houston, 1919–21. He graduated from the University of Toronto in 1924 with a B.A. in modern history. During his university course he also studied theology at St Basil's Scholasticate, Toronto. He was ordained priest on 24 June 1924.

Teaching assignments of Father Forner were: St Michael's College, 1924–6; Assumption College, 1926–31, where he was also secretary-treasurer of the Alumni Association; and St Michael's College, 1931–7, where he was also chaplain to the Precious Blood Convent. In 1937 he withdrew from the Congregation and joined the diocese of Oklahoma City in Tulsa, where he was formally incardinated on 24 July 1940. He was appointed pastor of St William's Parish in Skiatook. He suffered a heart attack in 1946 from which he never fully recovered.

Father Forner, affectionately called 'Big Ben,' was a well-built, tall football player whose ability as a kicker was outstanding. Those who lived with him remember his kind nature and his fund of stories.

BIBLIOGRAPHY:
Book: *Story of the Church: A Brief Account of the Life and Growth of the Catholic Church.* Detroit, 1935.
Articles: 'Struggle and Death' (short story), *Basilian* 2 (May 1936) 88–90; 'Vert Vert' (short story), *Basilian* 2 (October 1936) 106–7; 'Father Robert McBrady,' *Basilian* 2 (May 1936) 83.
SOURCES: GABF; *Annals* 1 (1948) 197–8; *Basilian* 1 (June 1935) 80, (November 1935) 118; *Basilides, Assumption College* (Windsor, 1930); *Yearbook SMC* 15 (1925), 16 (1925).

FORSTER, Robert FRANCIS, priest, ninth superior general, first superior general of the Basilian Fathers of Toronto and a 'second founder' of the Congregation, was born on a farm in Norfolk County, near Simcoe, Ontario (archdiocese of Toronto), on 16 May 1873, the eleventh of the twenty children of John Forster and Rosanna Harvey. He died in Montreal on 11 November 1929 and is buried in the Basilian plot of Mount Hope Cemetery, Toronto.

After primary education in a one-room rural school at Smokey Hollow, Ontario, Francis Forster attended Simcoe High School before going in 1890 to Assumption College, Windsor. There he won first prize in every subject from the beginning to the end of his course. W.E. Kelly (*The Canadian Magazine*) described him there as a boy 'who laughed heartily, played football vigorously, handed in his exercises with scrupulous attention to neatness and developed the provoking capacity of inevitably gaining the highest marks in examinations.' In 1897 he entered St Basil's Novitiate, Toronto, was professed on 28 August 1898, and was ordained priest on 30 June 1901.

Of his twenty-eight years as a priest, Father Forster spent only two without administrative responsibility. He taught at St Michael's College, Toronto, 1901–3, then was appointed superior at St Basil's College, Waco, Texas. In 1907 he became superior at Assumption College and remained there until 1919, when he moved to the provincial curial residence in Toronto. At Assumption his predecessors Fathers Denis *O'Connor, Daniel *Cushing, and Robert *McBrady had concentrated on preparing students to enter seminaries and be ordained priests. Father Forster sought to extend the curriculum and enhance the degree it could offer to students preparing careers as laymen. He changed the curriculum in the high school department to make it conform to that of the Ontario high school system. He initiated negotiations with the University of Western Ontario, London, Ontario, to grant the B.A. degree to Assumption students; but his plans were to be forestalled by the Great War, the influenza outbreak of 1918–19, and by opposition, on several issues, with the bishop of London, Michael Francis Fallon OMI (see below).

Even early in life Francis Forster's talent for leadership enabled him to influence not only those of his own age but also many who were his elders. A contributor to the *Golden Jubilee Volume of Assumption College* remarked: 'The essential requisite of a leader of men in any walk of life is [first] that he can read and understand the mind and temperament of those under him, and, second, that he can adapt himself to deal with them accordingly. Father Francis Forster possessed this faculty in a striking degree. In my observation of him that is the one thing which struck me most forcefully, and I have heard others remark the same thing. Even before I came to College, I heard him spoken of, and this remark still lives in my memory: "There are one hundred and eighty students in Assumption College, and Father Forster is a different man to every one of them."'

Forster became a member of the provincial council in 1911, was elected provincial in 1916, and re-elected in 1919. He was chosen ninth superior general in 1922 and was re-elected in 1928. In the management of men and of material things, he could be both forward-looking and cautious. Problems were of interest to him only in so far as they could influence the future. He was prepared to break with the past should changing conditions warrant it. At the same time he was extremely wary of any initiatives that might contravene the Code of Canon Law or incur the disapproval of Rome. For example, he opposed the changes in the philosophy curriculum that Father Henry *Carr was attempting to make at St Michael's College. As superior general, he refused Father Vincent L. *Kennedy's proposal in 1928–9 to meet a crisis in student enrolment by admitting women and non-Catholic male students to Assumption College. Nevertheless, as superior general he supported Father Carr's proposal for the establishment of the Institute of Mediaeval Studies in 1929.

A practical man, Father Forster paid off the debt for the Assumption

College chapel, which had been built just prior to his coming. He then built a heating plant, a residence, and a gymnasium. He had a disdain for the local politicians who failed to recognize the contributions of Assumption to the town. As superior general he bought a former orphanage building near St Michael's College, at 21 St Mary Street, which he remodelled to meet the needs of St Basil's Scholasticate. He paid close attention to the details of all buildings constructed under his administration.

Father Forster had entered the Congregation just when the Holy See had refused approbation of the existing Constitutions. The ensuing years had not been favourable for making the needed revisions. Thus, as provincial he began a careful study of the new code of canon law issued in 1917, with the dominant purpose of bringing the Constitutions of the Basilian Fathers into conformity with it. He gradually interested others in bringing about the needed revision and approbation. Local conditions in France had been one obstacle, but in 1921 the French province suggested the separation of the two provinces into two distinct religious congregations. Father Forster led the ensuing negotiations and in 1922 brought them to a conclusion that was satisfactory to both parties.

After his election as first superior general of the Basilian Fathers of Toronto, as the Canadian province was now called, he convinced the general chapter to defer dealing with the vow of poverty until a revision of the Constitutions had been finished. His grasp of the issues and the strength of his personality carried the majority of the capitulants with him without infringing upon the rights of others and always respecting those who differed from him. The chapter therefore accepted the new simple but stricter vow of poverty with total dependence on a common life in place of the former practice which had provided members with their support and also gave them a small salary. Still, opposition to the chapter decision was sufficiently widespread in the Congregation to require Father Forster to spend the year 1922-3 explaining it to the entire Congregation. With untiring patience and gentlemanly courtesy he advanced his arguments, and, the difficulties cleared away, 90 per cent of the members accepted the change.

A conviction of justice, joined to a streak of stubbornness, brought Father Forster victory in two legal battles with episcopal jurisdictions. Court judgments sustained his opinions in litigation over the property of St Basil's College, Waco; and he obtained from the Holy See a favourable reply in a series of differences with Bishop Michael Francis

Fallon of London, some of which dated from Forster's term as superior of Assumption College. Subsequent events cancelled out the benefits of both these decisions, however, and left the feeling that he had won the battles but lost the wars. As Michael Power has remarked, 'The fallout was an unqualified disaster for both sides.'

On 11 November 1929, Father Forster went to Montreal to meet Father James *Player, who was arriving from England. That night, as the ship was mooring, he apparently slipped on the dock and fell into the frigid water. His body was recovered only in the spring of 1930.

Father Forster's role as a 'Second Founder' of the Basilian Fathers was recognized in November 1954, when Father George *Flahiff, then superior general, issued a circular letter to commemorate the twenty-fifth anniversary of Francis Forster's tragic death.

SOURCES: GABF; H. Carr, 'Sermon Preached at the Funeral of Father Francis Forster,' *Yearbook SMC* 22 (1931); *Jubilee, Assumption*; W.E. Kelly, 'Rev. Father Forster,' *Canadian Magazine* (January 1917), repr. *St Joseph Lilies* 19 (June 1930) 35–9; Kirley, *Congregation in France* iii, 2, 12, 14, 15–16, 31, 33, 38–40, 42–8, 51–4, 56–7, 88, 95–8, 106–7, 122, 143–4, 157–8; McMahon, *Pure Zeal* 17–82, passim; *Newsletter* (21 November 1979); Michael Power, 'Fallon vs Forster: The Struggle over Assumption College, 1919–1925,' *CCHA Report* 56 (1989) 49–66; W.J. Roach, 'Father R.F. Forster CSB,' *Basilian Teacher* 1 (March 1957) 9–11. For documentation about his presidency of Assumption College and his differences with Bishop Michael Fallon, see Power, *Assumption College* 3 xvii–xxv and passim, 3 viii–ix, 25–6, 39, 41–3, 48–51, 234.

FOUILLAND, Irénée, priest, was born on 25 July 1838 at Montagny (Loire, archdiocese of Lyon). The date of death and place of his burial are unknown.

Irénée made his novitiate at Feyzin (Isère, now Rhône) and professed final vows on 22 September 1865. Bishop Armand de Charbonnel ordained him subdeacon on 23 September 1865, in the chapel of the Collège des Cordeliers, Annonay, and deacon on 21 September 1867 in the chapel of the Collège du Sacré-Coeur, Annonay. While studying theology, 1864–8, he was also *professeur de cinquième* at the Petit Séminaire de Vernoux (Ardèche). He was ordained to the priesthood by Bishop Armand de Charbonnel on 19 September 1868 in the chapel of the Collège du Sacré-Coeur and immediately left France with the founding community of the Collège Saint-Charles in Blidah, Algeria.

Community records are incomplete concerning Father Fouilland. He seems to have remained in Blidah for four years, and then returned to the minor seminary at Vernoux, where he taught *quatrième*, 1872–3, and *troisième*, 1873–7. Several teaching appointments followed: Aubenas as *professeur de quatrième*, 1877–9; Bourg-Saint-Andéol, *troisième*, 1879–81; the Collège Saint-Pierre in Châteauroux (Indre), 1881–2; the Ecole cléricale de Périgueux (Dordogne), *septième*, 1882–1900.

The Basilian records are unclear as to his whereabouts after 1900. When the anticlerical laws of 1903 forced the school in Périgueux to close, he may well have stayed to minister in that diocese.

SOURCES: GABF; Kirley, *Community in France* 185, 210; Pouzol, 'Notices.'

FOURNIER, Frédéric Bernard, priest, son of Saint-Pierre-César Fournier and Rose Sophie Vernet, was born on 22 October 1839 at Bourg-Saint-Andéol (Ardèche). He died at Bourg-Saint-Andéol on 19 December 1895.

After his high school years, spent probably at the Petit Séminaire d'Aubenas, Frédéric worked as disciplinarian, 1860–1, at the Petit Séminaire at Vernoux, and then entered the Basilian novitiate at Feyzin (Isère, now Rhône). He made his final profession of vows on 18 September 1863 at Feyzin, where the following day he was ordained subdeacon. Bishop Armand de Charbonnel ordained him to the priesthood on 23 September 1865 in the chapel of the Collège des Cordeliers, Annonay. During the years of his theological studies he served in various Basilian schools: prefect of discipline at the Petit Séminaire de Vernoux, 1862–3, and at the Petit Séminaire d'Aubenas, 1863–4, and as *professeur de septième* at the Collège des Cordeliers, Annonay, 1864–5.

After ordination Father Fournier spent his life teaching: *quatrième* at the Petit Séminaire de Vernoux, 1865–6, at the Basilian school at Privas (Ardèche), 1866–71, at the Collège du Bourg-Saint-Andéol, 1871–7, at the Collège du Sacré-Coeur, Annonay, 1877–8, and *cinquième* at the Petit Séminaire d'Aubenas, 1878–9. In 1879–95 he was *professeur de troisième* at the Petit Séminaire at Vernoux.

Father Fournier willingly lent his musical talents to both academic and liturgical celebrations in all those places where the community asked him to serve. Ill health forced him to take time off with his family at Bourg-Saint-Andéol, where he died of a rheumatic infection. A large number of confreres, including the superior general, Father Adrien *Fayolle, attended his funeral.

SOURCES: GABF; ABA; Pouzol, 'Notices.'

FRACHON, François-Régis, priest, was born on 5 September 1835 at Saint-Bonnet-le-Froid (Haute-Loire, diocese of Le Puy). He died in Toronto on 12 April 1916 and was buried there in the Basilian plot of Mount Hope Cemetery.

François-Régis Frachon attended the Collège des Cordeliers, Annonay, section Sainte-Barbe, 1849–54, and the Grand Séminaire de Viviers. He was received as a novice on 30 May 1858 and ordained to the priesthood at Valence on 22 December 1860. Prior to his ordination he had taught at the Collège des Cordeliers, 1858–60, and continued to do so until 1865. For six months, along with Father François-Regis *Hours, he studied English under Father Patrick *Molony at Feyzin (Isère, now Rhône) in preparation for ministry in Canada.

In 1866 he arrived in Toronto and taught philosophy at St Michael's College for several years. He was master of novices, 1868–73, chaplain to the Sisters of the Precious Blood, 1869–72, and chaplain to the Sisters of St Joseph, 1872–86, and was a popular confessor in St Basil's Church, Toronto. He served as assistant at Ste Anne's, Detroit, 1886–91, with Father Jean-Pierre *Grand as pastor and Father François-Xavier *Granottier as assistant. In 1891 he returned to Toronto and resumed his duties as chaplain to the Sisters of St Joseph until his death in 1916.

Three times he returned to France, each time with Father Jean Joseph Marie *Aboulin, on which occasions he always made a pilgrimage to Rome. Father Frachon was twice elected to the provincial council, in 1883 and 1898. He was a man of medium height with thinning hair and bushy whiskers. His confreres referred to him affectionately as 'Billy.' After his death, a Sister of St Joseph wrote in *St Joseph Lilies*: 'He never seems to have given offence to anyone, nor to have incurred anyone's censure. ... None who knew Father Frachon intimately could forget his kindness, his interest in personal matters, or his genuine sympathy. He was very sparing of compliments and of formal etiquette, as he knew how often they concealed totally different sentiments. He was very guarded in his language, though he never failed to act the part of a truly Christian gentleman.'

SOURCES: GABF; ABA; Chomel, *Collège d'Annonay* 516; Charles Collins, 'Basilians I Have Known,' transcribed in Robert J. Scollard, 'Historical Notes C.S.B.' 10 71–5 (GABF); Hoskin, *St Basil's*; Kirley, *Congregation in France* 45; S.M.P., 'In Memoriam, Rev. F.R. Frachon,' *St Joseph Lilies* 5 (June 1916) 17–22; Pouzol, 'Notices.'

FRACHON, Jean-Marie, priest, was born in Saint-Bonnet-le-Froid (Haute-Loire, diocese of Le Puy), on 14 November 1871, the son of Auguste Frachon and Sophie Pichon. He died in Annonay on 6 November 1945 and was buried there in the cemetery on the grounds of the Collège du Sacré-Coeur.

Jean-Marie Frachon was a student at the Collège du Sacré-Coeur, section Sainte-Barbe, in 1883. Illness forced him to interrupt his studies for the year 1889–90. He entered the novitiate in 1893 and made first profession on 21 September 1894. He was ordained priest on 18 September 1897 by Bishop Joseph-Michel-Frédéric Bonnet. He had been a prefect at the Collège du Sacré-Coeur, 1890–3, and at the Petit Séminaire de Vernoux (Ardèche), 1893–7. After his ordination he was at the Collège du Sacré-Coeur until the dispersal of the community in 1903. At that time he was welcomed into the diocese of Versailles (Yvelines), where he served as pastor of Villebon (Essonne) and of Bures-sur-Yvette (Essonne). He was mobilized into an ambulance corps during the First World War.

In 1938 he went to the Maison Saint-Joseph in Annonay in semi-retirement while overseeing the bursar's office. After the death of Father Léon *Guigon on 9 February 1941 Father Frachon looked after the novices. On 24 January 1944 he was elected councillor, but died twenty months later of stomach cancer at Maison Saint-Joseph.

SOURCES: GABF; ABA; Kirley, *Congregation in France* 151, 156, 194, 196–7, 199, 208–9; Pouzol, 'Notices.'

FRENCH, John GERALD, priest, was born on 28 May 1908 at Brechin, Ontario (archdiocese of Toronto), the son of William James French and Mary Ann Furguson. He died in Toronto on 23 October 1996 and is buried in the Basilian plot of Holy Cross Cemetery, Thornhill, Ontario.

'Gerry' French received his early education at Brechin and at St Jerome's College, Kitchener, Ontario, before going to high school at St Michael's College, Toronto, 1924–6. He entered St Basil's Novitiate, Toronto, made first profession on 30 September 1927, and was then appointed to St Basil's Scholasticate, Toronto, to study at the University of Toronto (B.A., 1931). He began theological studies and at the same time attended the Ontario College of Education, earning teaching certification in 1932. After a year of teaching at Holy Name Institute, Detroit, he returned to St Basil's Scholasticate to continue his theology course. He was ordained to the priesthood on 17 December 1933 in St Basil's Church, Toronto, by Bishop Alexander MacDonald.

Beginning in 1934, Father French filled three one-year appointments: teacher at St Thomas High School, Houston, 1934–5, assistant pastor at St John the Baptist Church, Amherstburg, Ontario, 1935–6, and teacher at Assumption College School, Windsor, 1936–7. He went to Aquinas Institute, Rochester, to teach in 1937, where he remained three years before his appointment to Catholic Central High School, Detroit, where he remained fifty-three years.

Gerry French lived the Basilian way of life. He was regular in his habits, generous in his service, and exemplary in his devotion to the Mass, prayer, and the sacrament of penance. He was sought after as a confessor for his prudence and compassion. 'He was a teacher who taught his students to be humble before truth and beauty, whether the class was on a proof for the existence of God, some difficult period in Church history, a proposition in solid geometry, or a poem by Wordsworth' (Father M. Owen Lee CSB). He lived poorly, one evidence being his clothes, which he picked up at rummage sales. He was eminently a community man, often the centre of enjoyment with his stories of Brechin and the Scottish songs which he rendered in a rich bass voice. As athletic director at the school he could be seen on his knees taping the ankles of his players before the game or washing uniforms when it was over. When his boxing team became well known and sports writers came to him asking how he as a priest knew so much about boxing, he replied, 'I read a book.' Any further discussion would, for him, offend against the strictures of the Basilian Rule to avoid publicity. He enjoyed serving as cook for the Basilians at Catholic Central or at Strawberry Island, the community summer retreat in Lake Simcoe.

After the celebration of his diamond jubilee as a priest in 1993 he moved to the Basilian Fathers Residence in Toronto, where he lived as humbly and simply as he ever had, and where his health needs were more easily attended to for the three years of life which remained to him.

SOURCES: GABF; *Annals* 5 (1978) 267, 6 (1984) 205, 8 (1997) 115–16; *Newsletter* (8 November 1996).

FULLERTON, Vincent Joseph, priest, was born in Toronto on 14 April 1910, the eldest of six children of James Vincent Fullerton and Margaret Mary Hayes. He died in Windsor on 4 September 1967 and is buried in the Basilian plot of Holy Cross Cemetery, Thornhill, Ontario.

Vincent attended St Joseph's Separate School and the high school section of St Michael's College, Toronto. In 1926 he entered St Basil's Novitiate, Toronto, making first profession on 18 September 1927. After attending the University of Toronto (B.A., 1931) and the Ontario College of Education, 1932–3, he studied theology at St Basil's Scholasticate, Toronto, and was ordained priest on 21 December 1935 in St Basil's Church, Toronto, by Archbishop James Charles McGuigan.

After a further year of theology, he was appointed to teach at St Thomas High School, Houston, 1936–8, and then at Catholic Central High School, Detroit. When his health failed at the end of summer 1938, he went on sick-leave until early 1939. He was appointed assistant at St Anne's Parish, Houston, and in 1940 to Ste Anne's Parish, Detroit.

In 1941, he went to Mexico City to learn Spanish and the cultural background of the Mexican people. At Our Lady of Guadalupe Mission Center in Rosenberg, he was assistant, 1941–6, and then pastor, 1946–8. In 1948 he was named mission procurator, but resided at St Michael's College. From 1949 until 1960 he remained as mission procurator while teaching at Aquinas Institute, Rochester. His health failed again in 1960, and he spent a year on sick-leave before going back to teaching at Assumption College School, Windsor, in 1961. He died unexpectedly seven years later from complications arising out of a chronic bronchial ailment.

Father Fullerton was an exceptionally fine preacher who was frequently called upon to give retreats for students. He had a lifelong interest in sports, particularly baseball, in which he had played catcher as a student and young priest. As mission procurator he was responsible for the printing of promotional literature.

BIBLIOGRAPHY: 'The Mystery of Grace,' *Basilian* 1 (October 1935) 93.
SOURCES: GABF; *Annals* 4 (1968) 54–5; *Newsletter* (5 September 1967).

FUMA, Gabriel, priest, was born at Saint-Pierreville (Ardèche) on 29 January 1864 (his Detroit obituary says 29 September), the son of Claude Fuma and Jeanne Goutard. He died at Marine City, Michigan, on 29 March 1932 and was buried in the priests' plot of Holy Cross cemetery there.

Gabriel was a student at the Collège du Sacré-Coeur, Annonay, section

Sainte-Barbe, 1877–82. From 1882 to 1884 he served as prefect there and began his studies in philosophy and theology. He made his novitiate at Beaconfield House, Plymouth, England, 1884–5, under Father Victorin *Marijon. He then spent a year at the Collège du Sacré-Coeur as prefect, and in 1886 he was assigned to teach at the Ecole cléricale de Périgueux (Dordogne), where he spent two years. In 1888 he returned to the Collège du Sacré-Coeur where he was ordained to the priesthood by Bishop Joseph-Michel-Frédéric Bonnet of Viviers on 21 September 1889 (his Detroit obituary says December 1888).

For the next eight years Father Fuma taught at the College of the Immaculate Conception at Plymouth. In 1897–8 he taught at the Ecole cléricale de Périgueux, and in the summer of 1898 he and Father Alphonse *Colomb were sent to study in Regensburg, Germany. He then spent another five years at the Collège du Sacré-Coeur. After the dispersal of the Congregation from that school in 1903 he spent a year doing research in the Vatican Library in the employ of the J. Pierpoint Morgan family.

In 1904, at the age of forty, Father Fuma went to North America, where he spent the last twenty-eight years of his life. After two years teaching at St Michael's College, Toronto, he received a series of parish appointments: St Mary's of the Assumption, Owen Sound, Ontario, for a year; St John the Baptist Parish, Amherstburg, Ontario, for eight years; and Ste Anne's, Detroit, for seven years. Fluent in English and German as well as his native tongue, Gabriel Fuma chose in 1922 to remain with the community in North America but worked under the aegis of the archbishop of Detroit, who appointed him on 8 September 1922 to Holy Cross Parish, Marine City, Michigan. He remained there ten years before his sudden death, which followed a heart attack suffered after he celebrated early morning Mass.

SOURCES: ABA; GABF; Pouzol, 'Notices'; Archives, archdiocese of Detroit.

G

GALLERANO, Victor, priest, member of the Congregation 1966–9, was born on 14 September 1933 in Houston, the son of Salvador Gallerano and Catherine Emmete. He died in Houston on 20 April 1988.

After graduating in 1950 from St John's High School, San Antonio,

Texas, Victor entered St Mary's Seminary, Houston, in 1951, taking the prescribed courses in philosophy and theology. He was ordained to the priesthood for the diocese of Galveston on 24 May 1958 by Bishop Wendelin J. Nold.

After six years of ministry in the diocese, Father Gallerano asked to be associated with the Congregation of Saint Basil, and was assigned to teach at Andrean High School, Gary (now Merrillville), Indiana, 1964–5. He made the novitiate year at Pontiac, Michigan, and was professed in August 1966. He taught again at Andrean in 1966–7 and then at Aquinas Institute, Rochester, 1967–9, but withdrew from the Congregation at the end of that school year and returned to his diocese, where he lived at St Mary Cathedral, Galveston until late 1969, then spent the next few years in Chile, Peru, and a parish in Spotswood, New Jersey. By 1976 his diocese had lost trace of him. An undocumented report states that he lived for a time in a 'hippie commune,' and was institutionalized for several years prior to his death.

SOURCES: GABF; *Annals* 3 (1966) 367, (1967) 449; Archives, diocese of Galveston-Houston.

GALLON, Henri, priest, was born on 14 November 1846 at Dorel'Eglise (Puy-de-Dôme, diocese of Clermont-Ferrand). He died on 25 July 1910 in his native parish and is buried there.

In 1878, at the age of thirty-two, Henri Gallon went from the major seminary of his native diocese to the Basilian novitiate at Feyzin (Isère, now Rhône), and in December of that year was appointed to replace a recreation master at the Collège du Sacré-Coeur, Annonay. He made his final profession of vows on 16 December 1880 and received the subdiaconate two days later at Viviers from Bishop Joseph-Michel-Frédéric Bonnet. He was ordained deacon on 24 September 1881 and priest on 23 September 1882 by Archbishop Armand de Charbonnel in the chapel of the Collège du Sacré-Coeur. He worked as study-hall and recreation master at Sacré-Coeur, 1880–4 and 1890–5, and at the Ecole cléricale de Périgueux (Dordogne), 1884–90.

From 1895 to 1901 Father Gallon was the treasurer at the Petit Séminaire d'Aubenas (Ardèche); but excessive zeal and ill temper led to tension between him and the superior, Father Julien *Giraud, who obtained his reappointment to Annonay as supply teacher, 1901–3. After the implementation of anticlerical laws forbidding members of religious congregations to teach, he remained in Annonay for two years. In 1909 he was chaplain at the psychiatric hospital at La Celette-par-Eygurande (Corrège), and died the next year.

SOURCES: GABF; Kirley, *Community in France* 185, 206; Pouzol, 'Notices.'

GARVEY, Edwin Charles, priest, younger brother of Wilfrid Francis *Garvey, was born on 18 April 1907 at Kingsbridge, Ontario (diocese of London), one of ten children of Thomas Garvey and Margaret Donnelly. He died on 7 September 1996 in Toronto and is buried in the Basilian plot of Holy Cross Cemetery, Thornhill, Ontario.

After early education in Kingsbridge, Ed Garvey enrolled in St Michael's College, Toronto (B.A., University of Toronto, 1928). From 1928 to 1930 he was employed by General Motors at Oshawa, Ontario. Shortly after the sudden death of his Basilian brother Wilfrid in 1930, he entered St Basil's Novitiate, Toronto, and was professed on 1 November 1931. He did theological studies at St Basil's Scholasticate, Toronto, 1931–5, and graduate studies in philosophy (M.A., University of Toronto, 1932), and was ordained to the priesthood on 16 December 1934 in Assumption Church, Windsor, by Bishop Thomas Kidd.

In 1935 Father Garvey was appointed to continue his graduate studies in philosophy at the University of Toronto, taking most of his courses at the Institute of Mediaeval Studies, Toronto (Ph.D., 1937), where he became a lifelong disciple of the French philosopher Jacques Maritain. His thesis topic was 'A Study of St Thomas' Interpretation of Aristotle on the Questions of Creation and God.' He taught philosophy for the next twenty-four years, 1937–61, at Assumption College, Windsor, serving as head of the department from 1939 to 1961. A strong believer in applying philosophical principles in society, his lively classes in social justice dealt with many contemporary problems, e.g., the injustices suffered by the Catholic school system in Ontario through the provincial government's narrow interpretation of the British North America Act of 1867. Father Garvey's trenchant criticism of these injustices impressed his students, many of whom entered the legal profession. One of these, Peter Cory, became a Justice of the Supreme Court of Canada and supported the 1987 decision, in which the other Justices concurred, which authorized Ontario to fund fully Catholic high schools, thus reversing a previous decision of the House of Lords. Father Garvey also founded at Assumption and directed, in the 1940s, the Pius XI Labour School for the formation of lay persons in social justice and social action, a work which produced labour union leaders who influenced the course of labour unionism in Ontario. He insisted that social justice and labour unionism were natural developments of the principles of democracy, and had nothing to do with leftist or socialist labour principles. Though he became a personal friend of Walter Reuther, the head of the United Auto Workers, he was convinced that the role of the priest was one of instruction and advice, not of active participation in the labour movement.

In 1952 Ed Garvey was an active participant in the successful movement to obtain a charter for Assumption College, to allow conferring of degrees in its own name. In 1961, partly because he opposed the ceding of Assumption University's degree-granting powers in all disciplines except theology to the newly created University of Windsor, Father Garvey was moved to Vancouver to be principal and superior of St Mark's College, where he established the first board of directors. He lectured particularly to groups of teachers and wrote on the philosophy of education. His teaching was hard-hitting, authoritative, and effective, though not always as clear to his students as it was to himself. He was an indefatigable promoter of the philosophy of St Thomas Aquinas and of Jacques Maritain, whom he considered the greatest philosopher of modern times. Edwin Garvey was one of a generation of Basilians in the mid-twentieth century who, inspired by their study of Aquinas through the teaching of Maritain and Etienne Gilson, exerted a notable influence on the Basilian community and in wider areas of education, sport, and politics.

In 1964 he was appointed to the University of St Michael's College, Toronto, where he taught philosophy for four years. He then went as visiting professor to the University of St Thomas, Houston, initially for one year, though he remained there for eighteen years. Already in his sixtieth year, his teaching schedule was gradually reduced, and he retired from the classroom after three years. He nevertheless remained a vocal presence on the campus; and, with the exception of one year of sabbatical leave, 1971–2, he was active at the university in writing and controversy. He stridently opposed process theology, writing in such publications as the *Wanderer*, the *Priest*, and the *Homiletic and Pastoral Review*. An ardent proponent of the teaching of Vatican II, he opposed what he saw as abusive interpretations of it. He was aggressive in his writing and speaking. There were few grey areas, and the opposition was usually described as 'totally wrong.' In September 1965 he delivered a paper, 'Catholic Education in a Pluralistic Society,' to the Canadian Catholic Trustees' Association meeting in Saint John, New

Brunswick. In April 1978 he spoke on 'Christianity and Democracy' at the International Conference on 'Cooperation of Democratic Countries' in Washington, D.C. Bishop John Ryan of Hamilton, Ontario, wrote to him after he had given a workshop in that diocese: 'The impact of your talks will be felt for many a day. It did us all more good than anything we have had in the diocese in my thirty-four years.'

'Garv,' as he was familiarly called, was a person about whom stories are told. He lived much in the world of ideas: a brilliant mind, but not always a practical one. He was habitually draped in a blanket, for he was always cold. His fingers and forelock were nicotine-stained from heavy smoking. Garv loved to talk, though conversation with him was often one-sided. In the breadth of his reading, the depth of his insight, and in his passion for truth and justice he was admirable. Ahead of his time in promoting the laity in the mission of the Church, he was outstanding among his contemporaries in the community and beyond as a champion for social justice. Though his integrist positions and ineptitude at tolerating opposing opinions often created tensions in community life, he loved the community and worked in his own way to preserve its values.

BIBLIOGRAPHY:
Book: *Process Theology and Secularization*. Houston, 1972.
Articles: 'Truth ... the Basis of Action,' *Basilian* 1 (May 1935) 47–9; 'Approach to an Integral Philosophy of Education,' *Education Past the Crossroads* (Windsor, 1957) 3–9; 'Pluralism in the University,' *Commonweal* (27 January 1961) 458–62; 'The Illusion of On-going Revelation,' *Proceedings of the Ninth Wanderer Forum* (1973) 22pp; 'Process Theology and the Crisis in Catechetics,' *Homiletic and Pastoral Review* 74 (July 1974) 6-17. In *Basilian Teacher:* 'A Philosophy of Sports,' 3 (April 1959) 184–7; 'Communications and Education [forum],' 3 (May 1959) 214–15; 'Basilian Religious Life and Intellectual Excellence,' 5 (May 1959) 285–9; 'Education and Democracy,' 7 (April 1963) 242–50; 'Teaching: A Communion of Persons,' 8 (Supplement 1964) 20–35; 'Catholic Education in a Pluralistic Society,' 10 (January 1966) 6–17;
SOURCES: GABF; *Annals* 6 (1982) 13, 6 (1985) 309, 8 (1997) 112–14; *Newsletter* (25 October 1996); Brian F. Hogan, 'Catechising Culture: Assumption College, Pius XI Labour School, and the United Automobile Workers, 1940–50,' *CCHA Historical Studies* 54 (1988) 79–95; idem, 'Salted with Fire: Studies in Catholic Social Thought and Action in Ontario, 1931–1961,' Ph.D. diss. (University of Toronto, 1986) 186–223; Power, *Assumption College* 6 2, 138, 184; Shook, *Catholic Education* 286–7, 352, 386.

GARVEY, Wilfrid Francis, priest, elder brother of Father Edwin *Garvey, was born at Ashfield, Ontario (diocese of London), on 14 October 1899, the son of Thomas Garvey and Margaret Donnelly. He died in Rochester on 5 April 1930 and is buried in the Basilian plot of Mount Hope Cemetery, Toronto.

After early education in local schools, Wilfrid went in 1913 to Assumption College, Windsor, for high school and arts (B.A., University of Western Ontario, 1921). He entered St Basil's Novitiate, Toronto, and made profession on 11 August 1922. He taught for one year at St Thomas High School, Houston, attended the Ontario College of Education, Toronto, and studied theology at St Basil's Scholasticate, Toronto. He was ordained priest on 7 June 1925.

Father Garvey did graduate studies in Rome for three years, obtaining doctorates in philosophy and theology. For the doctorate in theology he presented a thesis entitled 'De sacerdotio Christi.' In the summer of 1928 he was appointed to the staff of St Basil's Scholasticate. Shortly afterwards he experienced a recurrence of a heart ailment that had first manifested itself in Rome. In February 1930 he went on sick leave to the Basilian residence at Aquinas Institute, Rochester, where he died two months later.

SOURCES: GABF; *Yearbook SMC* 21 (1930).

GAUCHERAND, Marie-Florimond, priest, member of the Association of Priests of Saint Basil 1843–55, was born on 15 August 1822 at Saint-Barthélemy-le-Meil, canton of Le Cheylard (Ardèche).

Marie-Florimond studied at Sainte-Barbe and the Collège des Cordeliers, Annonay, and then in 1841–2 at the Grand Séminaire de Viviers. Admitted as a novice to the Association of Priests of Saint Basil on 20 October 1842, he studied theology while teaching in the Collège de Privas (Ardèche), 1842–6. Unsure of his vocation, he spent the year 1846–7 teaching *quatrième* at the Collège des Cordeliers. Ill health due to typhoid fever interrupted his work from 1847 to 1849, during which time his mother cared for him. Restored to health, he taught *seconde* at the Collège des Cordeliers, 1849–51. Bishop Joseph-Hippolyte Guibert ordained him a priest on 23 February 1851 in the chapel of the college in Annonay. Four days later Father Gaucherand made his profession by promise, but did not take vows in 1852 as most of the confreres did.

In the summer of 1851 his mother fell sick, and he went to care for her and to help provide for the family. Father Pierre *Tourvieille, superior general, had asked him to be assistant to the novice master Father Germain *Deglesne in Annonay, but he spent most of his time with his family. From 1851 to 1855 he taught *première* at the Petit Séminaire de Vernoux (Ardèche), and helped in the parish there. He withdrew from the community in the summer of 1855.

SOURCE: Pouzol, 'Notices,' Supplément 1.

GAUGHAN, John James, priest, was born in Detroit on 17 October 1928, the son of Francis Gaughan and Ann Raune. He died in Toronto on 25 October 2000 and is buried in the Basilian plot of Holy Cross Cemetery, Thornhill, Ontario.

John Gaughan was educated at Longfellow Elementary and Visitation Parochial schools and Catholic Central High School, Detroit. He entered St Basil's Novitiate, Rochester, and made first profession on 15 August 1946. After graduation from the University of Toronto (B.A., 1950), he taught for one year at Catholic Central and earned his teaching certification for Michigan, 1951. He taught at St Thomas High School, Houston, 1951–2, while also doing a year of theological studies there. He taught a third year, 1952–3, at St Michael's College School, Toronto, before completing three more years of theology at St Basil's Seminary, Toronto. He was ordained to the priesthood on 29 June 1955 in St Basil's Church, Toronto, by Bishop Francis Allen.

Father Gaughan taught mathematics and religion at Catholic Central, 1956–7, and at Assumption College School, Windsor, 1957–60. In the general chapter of 1960, much to his surprise (and in his absence), he was elected to the office of treasurer general of the Basilian Fathers, a position he was to hold for the next thirteen years. During those years he earned an M.B.A. from the University of Detroit – the first Basilian to take this degree. As treasurer general he lived at the curial house, Toronto, for ten years, at the Basilian Residence, a small house of studies on Huron Street, Toronto, for two years, and at St Basil's College, Toronto, for one year. In 1973 he was appointed director of the Newman Centre in the University of Toronto, and in 1978 was sent to assist Father Gordon Judd at St Basil's Center, Pontiac, Michigan, a retreat and renewal facility established in the former Basilian novitiate. In 1981 he was named director of the Center, but in 1983 joined the Basilian community at O'Connor House, Windsor, as treasurer of Assumption University, member of the board of trustees, one of the three university chaplains, and superior for a three-year term. In 1986 he was appointed chaplain at the University of St Michael's College. While there the early signs of the illness that would incapacitate him became evident in his difficulty with concentration and memory. He left St Michael's in 1989 to serve as assistant at Assumption Parish, Windsor. From 1991 to 1994 he lived with the Basilian community at Assumption College School, moving from there to the Basilian Fathers Residence in Toronto to receive the care he needed. During the last four and a half years of his life he was cared for at Providence Centre, Scarborough, Ontario, having lost his power of speech and his ability to recognize family, confreres, or friends.

'Johnny' was short in stature, ruddy in complexion, and gifted with a winning smile. He tended to look on the humorous side of things. The lengthy deterioration in his health was all the more poignant for those who had known his customary cheerfulness and fine spirit.

BIBLIOGRAPHY: 'A Certain Insurance to the Effectivity of Any Organization,' *Forum* 2 (May 1966) 66–7; 'We Are Asked to Face a Responsibility,' *Forum* 3 (May 1967) 73–4.
SOURCES: GABF; *Annals* 2 (1955) 198, 9 (2001) 101–2; *Newsletter* (25 November 2000).

GENCA, Allen James, priest, was born on 20 February 1932 in Detroit, the son of Wallace Genca and Genevieve Pankowski. He died in Detroit on 25 January 1994 and is buried there in the Basilian plot of Holy Sepulchre Cemetery.

Graduating from Catholic Central High School, Detroit, in 1950, 'Al' Genca placed sixth in a class of 170. After a year at St Basil's Novitiate, Rochester, he was professed on 12 September 1951, and was appointed to St Basil's Seminary, Toronto, where he began undergraduate studies, transferring the following year to Assumption College, Windsor (B.A., University of Western Ontario, 1955). As an undergraduate he taught religion and English at Assumption College School. He taught English, religion, and typing at Catholic Central, 1955–6, and obtained a temporary Michigan High School teaching certification from the University of Detroit. After a year of theological studies at St Basil's Seminary, Toronto, he taught general science at Aquinas Institute, Rochester, 1957–8, then returned to theology at the seminary in 1958 and was ordained to the priesthood on 29 June 1960 in St Basil's Church, Toronto, by Bishop Francis Allen.

Father Genca was appointed to Andrean High School, Gary (now

Merrillville), Indiana, 1961–2, to Aquinas Institute, 1962–3, and again to Andrean, 1963–9, where he taught computer science and supervised the science labs. In the summer months he studied at the University of Detroit, earning an M.A. in Education and English in 1966. The following summer he received a permanent teacher certification in Michigan.

In 1970 he was appointed to Catholic Central, where he was to work until his death at the age of sixty-one. He served as assistant principal and house treasurer, as well as guidance counsellor, which was the work he preferred and at which he excelled. He encouraged the students to choose Catholic colleges, but would go to great lengths to help them get into the college of their choice. He also helped out weekly at the nearby parish of St Mel's, both in liturgical and social events. His hobby was the College of Cardinals; he could supply immediate details on its history and all its members. He was an avid collector and purveyor of community news. After suffering many years from thyroid cancer, he was admitted early in 1994 to Providence Hospital, Southfield, Michigan, where he died two weeks later.

SOURCES: GABF; *Annals* 3 (1960) 27, 8 (1995) 95–6; *Newsletter* (20 February 1994).

GENESTON, Fernand Paul André, priest, was born on 3 April 1922 at Saint-Germain (Ardèche), the eldest of three children of Gaston Geneston and Berthe Roume. He died in Annonay on 22 April 1994 and is buried there in the Basilian cemetery on the grounds of the Collège du Sacré-Coeur.

After primary education at the village school, Fernand went as a boarding student to the Petit Séminaire Saint-Charles, Annonay, 1932–5; but he also attended classes at the Collège du Sacré-Coeur on a bursary from the Basilian Fathers. In 1935 he went to live at the Basilian Maison Saint-Joseph, Annonay, and continued his secondary studies at the college, taking the cassock in 1938. In 1939–40 he did one year of philosophy and prefect duty at the college, before becoming a Basilian novice at Maison Saint-Joseph on 5 September 1940. He took his first vows on 6 September 1941. His second year of philosophy was curtailed by service in the French Youth Camps (March–October 1942). He began theology in 1942, still at Maison Saint-Joseph, and received tonsure on 19 June 1943, but was immediately conscripted and transported to Chemnitz, Germany, where he did forced labour for nine months. After resuming his study of theology in Annonay in March

1944, he made final profession on 21 December 1945 and was ordained to the priesthood on 6 April 1946 in the cathedral of Viviers (Ardèche) by Bishop Alfred Couderc.

Father Geneston did two years of graduate studies, 1946–8, at the Faculté catholique de Lyon, majoring in Latin and Greek. In 1948 he returned to Annonay where for one year he served as prefect of the study hall, dormitory, and recreation for the juniors at Maison Saint-Joseph. In 1949 he began his distinguished teaching career of four decades at the Collège du Sacré-Coeur.

Father Geneston was tall, full-bodied, dignified but not distant, gentle-mannered, and hospitable. He worked tirelessly for his students, correcting their written work far into the night, always prepared for his classes, always disposed to help. His moments of anger were tremendously effective because they were so rare, so intense, and so sharply in contrast with his usual placid manner. Students acquired from his example a love of learning. His other interests were few and simple: walking in the countryside, gardening, reading novels, and conversation. His ire could be aroused by injustices of any kind, whether in education, business, the Church, and especially in government, both in France and in the world. Students and colleagues rejoiced when the French government awarded him the *Palmes académiques* in recognition of his services as an educator, on 28 July 1988.

'Père Geneston' suffered his first heart attack in 1974, but continued teaching until 1987, after which he worked as a replacement teacher, presided over examinations, and was textbook distributor. In 1989 he suffered a more serious heart attack, and during the year 1991 was hospitalized four times for cardiac irregularities. Celebration of the Eucharist sustained him in this time of trial. The last two years of his life at Maison Saint-Joseph were serene and happy, enlivened by visits of students grateful for what Père Geneston had taught them about what it means to know and to be free.

SOURCES: GABF; *Annals* 7 (1992) 8, 8 (1995) 99–103; *Newsletter* (16 May 1994); Kirley, *Congregation in France* 194–5, 198, 219, 220, 256, 262.

GEORGE, Gerald Fitzgerald, scholastic, was born at East Lake, Michigan (diocese of Grand Rapids), on 24 July 1905, the son of John George and Elizabeth Stapleton. He died in Windsor on 1 May 1933 and was buried there in the Basilian plot of Assumption Cemetery.

Gerald George was nine years old when his parents moved to Detroit. There he graduated from Cass Technical School. Friendship with Catholic young men led to his reception into the Catholic Church on 14 November 1925. Later he married and soon afterwards suffered the loss of his wife as she gave birth to a daughter. When his wife's parents adopted the baby, Gerald turned his thoughts towards the priesthood. He applied for admission to Sacred Heart Seminary in Detroit but was advised that he must first learn Latin. He spent the year 1930-1 living at Assumption College, Windsor, where he studied Latin at night while continuing to work at his job in the treasurer's office, City of Dearborn. In 1931 he entered St Basil's Novitiate, Toronto, was professed on 23 October 1932, and returned to Assumption College to begin his university course. Towards the end of the academic year 1932-3, he contracted pneumonia from which he died.

SOURCE: GABF.

GÉRY, Benoît, priest, member of the Congregation 1872-95, was born on 2 September 1849 in Annonay. He died in Lyon (Rhône) on 23 March 1935.

Enrolled in Sainte-Barbe Petit Séminaire, Annonay, Benoît Géry studied at the Collège des Cordeliers, 1864-7, and at the Collège du Sacré-Coeur, Annonay, 1867-70. After one year as guard in a mobile unit during the Franco-Prussian War, he entered the Basilian novitiate at Feyzin (Isère, now Rhône) in early April 1871. He made final profession on 19 September 1873.

While studying theology he worked in Basilian schools: as study-hall and recreation master at Bourg-Saint-Andéol (Ardèche), 1871-2; as professor of French at the Petit Séminaire d'Aubenas, 1872-3; and at Vienne (Isère), where he assisted Father Patrick *Molony (Moloney) at the Ecole paroissiale (later named the Institution Robin), 1873-5. Bishop Armand de Charbonnel conferred major orders on him in the chapel of the Collège du Sacré-Coeur: subdiaconate, 20 September 1873; diaconate, 19 September 1874; and priesthood, 18 September 1875.

Father Géry was appointed to the Collège Saint-Pierre in Châteauroux (Indre), where he served as bursar, 1875-80. He taught courses in commerce at Bourg-Saint-Andéol, 1880-1. During the first phase of the suppression of religious orders in France he went to the Collège du Sacré-Coeur, Annonay, where he taught commercial for the next three years. After one year as principal of the Basilian school at Beaconfield House, Plymouth, England, 1884–5, he set out for Canada with Father Jean-Pierre *Grand, and joined the staff of Assumption Parish, Windsor, in 1886. Three years later he moved to Ste Anne's Parish, Detroit. After spending the summer of 1890 at St Mary's of the Assumption Parish, Owen Sound, Ontario, he was moved to the parish of St Charles, Newport, Michigan. When the Basilians withdrew from this French-speaking parish, Father Géry sought incardination in the diocese of Detroit, and in November 1895 he was appointed pastor of St Catherine's Parish, Algonac, Michigan. There he built a new church in 1896, and in the following year he built St Mark's Mission Church in the St Clair Flats. In 1898 he established a parish cemetery. He retired as pastor on 27 April 1924 and returned to France. He was living at the Maison de Santé de Saint-Jean-de-Dieu in Lyon at the time of his death.

The life of Father Géry at Algonac was the subject of a novel, *Faith in the Root* (New York, 1942; repr. 1945), by Barbara Frances Fleury, the June 1942 selection of the Catholic Book of the Month Club. It focused on his last years at Algonac when on account of failing health and advancing years he was debating whether to stay on in his parish or resign and return to his native France.

During his years in England, Canada, and the United States Father Géry acquired a good knowledge of English, but a strong accent made it difficult for many to understand him.

SOURCES: GABF; Lajeunesse, *Assumption Parish*; Pouzol, 'Notices.'

GIBBONS, William Joseph, priest, uncle of Father Dennis Noelke CSB, was born on 28 February 1925 in Detroit, one of six children of William Gibbons and Ellen Boyle. He died on 5 June 1981 in Toronto and is buried in the Basilian plot of Holy Sepulchre Cemetery, Detroit.

After eight years at Epiphany parish school, Detroit, Bill enrolled in Catholic Central High School in September 1937, graduating in 1941. He entered St Basil's Novitiate, Toronto, and made first profession on 15 August 1942. He was appointed to Assumption College, Windsor, and one year later to St Michael's College, Toronto, to complete his undergraduate studies (B.A., University of Toronto, 1946), where he was a scholarship student and gold medallist. After a year of teaching at St Michael's College School, Toronto, he did his theological studies at St Basil's Seminary, Toronto, and was ordained to the priesthood on 29 June 1950 in St Basil's Church by Cardinal James Charles McGuigan.

In 1951 Father Gibbons began his varied career of teaching and administration at St Michael's College School, where he taught mathematics for three years. In 1954 he was appointed to St Michael's College in the University of Toronto to teach and serve as assistant registrar. During this time he also did graduate studies at Columbia University (M.A., Mathematics, 1961). In 1964 he was appointed to Catholic Central High School as principal and local superior. The following year he was elected first regional representative for eastern United States. His re-election at the general chapter of 1967, which elevated the regional representatives to membership on the general council, forced his withdrawal from responsibilities at Catholic Central.

In 1970 he was re-elected to the office of regional representative; but the general chapter of 1973 elected him vicar general (first assistant to the superior general). For the next four years he was special visitor to the Basilian apostolate in Mexico and represented the general council on the formation team. In 1977, the end of his term as vicar general, he was appointed to St Anne's Parish, Houston, as pastor and local superior. His three years there brought out pastoral qualities in him which had not to that time found their full scope. He saw to the poor and to the Hispanic immigrants with courage and compassion. In 1980 he was named master of scholastics and superior at St Basil's College, Toronto. He underwent treatment for high blood pressure during his first year, a year which he never completed. He died of a heart attack in his sleep.

Bill Gibbons responded to the many demands made of him with intelligence, efficiency, and wholehearted devotion. He related particularly well with scholastics and served as a highly effective interpreter and mediator between young Basilians and the older hierarchy of interest and opinion during a period of complex, accelerated transition for both Church and society.

SOURCES: GABF; *Annals* 1 (1950) 286, 6 (1982) 91–3; *Newsletter* (26 June 1981).

GIBRA, Louis, priest, member of the Congregation 1856–61, was born in Sury-en-Vaux (Cher, diocese of Bourges), on 15 August 1826. He died in Toronto on 27 October 1896 and was buried there in St Michael's Cemetery.

Having done his classical and philosophical studies at Bourges (Cher), Louis went to Canada at the invitation of the bishop of Toronto, Armand de Charbonnel, and studied theology at the Grand Séminaire in Montreal. He was received as a Basilian novice in 1856 at St Michael's College, Toronto, the first novice admitted in Canada. He made his final vows on 21 November 1857 and was ordained to the priesthood one week later.

Father Gibra taught French and singing at St Michael's College until 1861 when he withdrew from the Congregation and was incardinated in the diocese of Toronto. He served as pastor of Ste-Croix Parish, Lafontaine, Ontario, until 1872, when he was transferred to St Mary's Parish, Barrie, Ontario, and placed in charge of the mission parishes at Brentwood and Belle Ewart, both dedicated to Our Lady of the Assumption. He retired in September 1895 to the House of Providence, Toronto, where he died one year later.

SOURCES: GABF; Kirley, *Community in France* 7n28, 233n560, 23n568; John Read Teefy, *Jubilee Volume of the Archdiocese of Toronto, 1842–1892* (Toronto, 1892).

GIGNAC, Thomas Frédéric Ferdinand, priest, uncle of Father John Ernest *Pageau, was born in Windsor on 29 January 1868, the son of Richard Gignac and Marie Durocher. He died in Detroit on 4 April 1915 and was buried in the Basilian plot of Assumption Cemetery, Windsor.

Thomas Gignac enrolled at Assumption College, Windsor, in 1882. As a young man he was an ardent outdoorsman and an excellent marksman with rifle and shotgun. Upon the completion of his classical course he entered St Basil's Novitiate, Toronto, on 23 August 1892. He was ordained to the priesthood on 15 August 1898.

After ordination Father Gignac taught Latin and Greek at Assumption College and also served as assistant at Assumption Parish until 1903, when he moved to St Michael's College, Toronto. He was appointed superior of St Thomas High School, Houston, 1906–7, of St Mary's Seminary, LaPorte, Texas, 1907–11, and of St Basil's College, Waco, Texas, 1911–14. During a short-lived reorganization of the Congregation, 1910–11, he served as head of an American vice-province in Texas. In 1914 he was called back to Assumption College. Less than a year later he was stricken with meningitis and died within a few days.

The *Golden Jubilee Volume of Assumption College* said of Father Gignac: 'Few men were his equal as a conversationalist when he was in company that he found congenial, and his store of amusing anecdotes was a constant source of amusement to his friends.' An obituary notice in the *Dionysian* added that he 'was a man of splendid native talent and of tireless energy.'

SOURCES: GABF; Charles Collins, 'Basilians I Have Known,' transcribed in Robert J. Scollard, 'Historical Notes C.S.B.' 10 36–40 (GABF); *Dionysian, Assumption College* (Windsor, 1915); *Jubilee, Assumption*; *Yearbook SMC* 6 (1915) 84.

GIRARD, Auguste, priest, member of the Congregation 1863–77, was born on 12 January 1845 at Charbieux, canton of Serrières (Ardèche), the son of Antoine Girard and [Christian name unknown] Badel. He died at Charbieux on 23 October 1909, and was buried in the family vault in the cemetery of Bogy, near Serrières. His uncle, Father Pierre Girard (1828–89), the *curé* of Saint-Jacques d'Atticieux, was the great-uncle of Father Félix *Pouzol.

Auguste Girard studied at the Collège des Cordeliers, Annonay, while enrolled in the Petit Séminaire Sainte-Barbe. He graduated as *bachelier ès sciences* in July 1866 and went to the Institut catholique in Paris for higher studies in science. He made his novitiate at Feyzin (Isère, now Rhône) in 1862–3, and took final vows 18 September 1868. He was ordained a priest at Périgueux (Dordogne) on 4 March 1871.

Father Girard taught science and mathematics at the Collège de Privas, 1866–7 and 1871–2, and at the Ecole cléricale de Périgueux, 1869–71. Illness in 1873 obliged him to recuperate for several months in his family home at Charbieux and later at the scholasticate in Annonay. For some years he served as chaplain to the Confraternity of Saint Trachin in Annonay. He withdrew from the Congregation on 17 April 1877 to devote himself to parochial ministry in the diocese of Viviers. After serving as pastor of Saint-Georges-les-Bains (Ardèche) from 1881 to 1897, he retired to the family home, where he died twelve years later.

SOURCE: Pouzol, 'Notices,' Supplément 3.

GIRARD, Uldège Joseph, priest, was born at Cobalt, Ontario (vicariate-apostolic of Temiskaming, now diocese of Timmons) on 2 April 1910, the son of Edouard Joseph Girard and Rose Anne Paquette. He died in Toronto on 27 January 1966 and is buried in the Basilian plot of Holy Cross Cemetery, Thornhill, Ontario.

Uldège Girard attended Patterson Collegiate Institute, Windsor, 1924–7, and Assumption College School, Windsor, 1927–9. He entered St Basil's Novitiate, Toronto, in 1929 and was professed on 15 August 1930. After grade XIII at St Michael's in Toronto, 1930–1, he went to Assumption College, Windsor, for arts (B.A., University of Western Ontario, 1935). During his theological studies at St Basil's Scholasticate he also attended the Ontario College of Education, Toronto, 1935–6, which inaugurated that year a new program of practice teaching for student teachers that he described in several articles in the *Basilian* (see below). As French was his mother tongue, he organized in 1937 the new Basic French courses in the high school section of St Michael's College, and taught them with verve and great success. He was ordained to the priesthood on 17 December 1939 in St Basil's Church, Toronto, by Archbishop James Charles McGuigan.

In the summer of 1940 Father Girard returned to Assumption College School to teach French, and founded a school paper and a yearbook there. In 1953 he was transferred to Catholic Central High School in Detroit, where he continued to teach French, and developed an interest in driver education. He went back to Assumption College School in 1958, but poor health had taken away much of his former vigour. In the hope that a change of climate might benefit him, he was appointed to Our Lady of Mount Carmel Mission Center, Wharton, Texas, in 1962. He was moved, on sick leave with a serious heart condition, to Holy Rosary Parish, Toronto, in May 1964, and died there two years later.

BIBLIOGRAPHY: 'Cum Pedagogis,' *Basilian* 1 (November 1935) 117; 'The Old Order Changeth,' *Basilian* 2 (March 1936) 55–6; 'Basic French,' *Basilian* 4 (April, May, June 1938) 65–6, 96–7, 108–9.
SOURCES: GABF; *Annals* 3 (1966) 464–5; *Newsletter* (27 January 1966).

GIRAUD, Benoît, priest, half-brother of Father Julien *Giraud, and nephew of Father Jean Jacques *Giraud, was born on 21 March 1872 at Saint-Julien-en-Saint-Alban (Ardèche), the son of Louis Giraud and Clémence Servant. He died on 1 September 1946 at Saclas (Essonne) and was buried in the local cemetery.

Benoît Giraud completed secondary school, 1888–9, at the Collège du Sacré-Coeur, Annonay, as a resident of the Petit Séminaire Sainte-Barbe, Annonay. After the Basilians closed the novitiate at Beaconfield House, Plymouth, England, 1890, French candidates made their novitiate either in Annonay or in one of the schools where Basilians taught. Benoît joined the community in Algeria. He was a postulant, then a novice at the Collège Saint-Augustin, Bône, 1891–3 and 1894–5, where he worked as recreation master. (There is no record of his duties for the year 1893–4, which could have been the year of his compulsory military service.) He made first profession of vows and received tonsure on 20 and 21 September 1898 at the Collège du Sacré-Coeur. With a dispensation he professed final vows less than two years later on 17 September 1897. He received the subdiaconate at the Collège du Sacré-Coeur, Annonay, on 18 September 1897; the diaconate at the Maison-Carrée near Algiers on 1 April 1899, conferred by Bishop Léon Lévinhac, superior general of the White Fathers; and the priesthood in the college chapel in Annonay on 23 September 1899 at the hands of Hilarion-Joseph Montéty, titular archbishop of Beirut. When the community decided to withdraw from the Collège Saint-Augustin, Bône, in 1895, Benoît Giraud went to the Collège Saint-Charles, Blidah, Algeria, where he worked for eight years, 1895–1903, first as recreation and study-hall master, then as *professeur de troisième*. With the passage of anticlerical laws forbidding members of religious congregations to teach, the Collège Saint-Charles was closed on 13 July 1903.

Father Giraud then began parish ministry in the diocese of Viviers. He was appointed curate at Vesseaux in August 1903 and then at Jaujac, both parishes in the lower Ardèche. In 1905 he accepted an appointment in the diocese of Versailles. From correspondence it is known that on 20 September 1905 he was at Créteil (Val-de-Marne). Later he was curate at Livry (Nièvre). In 1909 he was given charge of two parishes, Saclas and Boissy-la-Rivière (Seine-et-Oise). During the First World War he was mobilized into the ambulance corps. On 11 September 1934 he celebrated twenty-five years as pastor of these same parishes.

SOURCES: GABF; Kirley, *Community in France* 185, 203; Pouzol, 'Notices.'

GIRAUD, Jean Jacques, priest, uncle of Father Julien *Giraud, was born on 10 October 1817 at Rompon (Ardèche). He died on 12 December 1891 at Privas (Ardèche) and was buried in the cemetery of Saint-Julien-en-Saint-Alban (Ardèche).

After spending his early years farming, Jean Jacques went to Annonay in 1843, at the age of twenty-six, to begin studies for the priesthood. He was a student at the Collège des Cordeliers, section Sainte-Barbe, until

1847. He completed his secondary studies while also working as recreation master at Sainte-Barbe, 1847–51. He entered the novitiate in Annonay in September 1851, also serving that year as recreation master at the Collège des Cordeliers, then in 1852–3 with the day-school pupils, and with the novices in 1853–4. He was ordained to the priesthood on 25 May 1854 by Bishop Joseph-Hippolyte Guibert of Viviers in the chapel of the Collège des Cordeliers.

Father Giraud spent nine years, 1854–63, at the Collège de Privas, one year as recreation master, five years as professor, and three years as bursar. During the year 1863–4 he was chaplain, along with Father Antoine *Bord, at the Calvary shrine of Prades, which Father Julien *Actorie, the superior general, had begun to restore. From 1864 to 1891 he was in Annonay, at the scholasticate on the Montée du Château, having been replaced at Prades by Father Jean-Louis *Ranc. He was the chaplain and spiritual director of the Sisters of La Providence and the Ursulines at Sainte-Marie, Annonay. Father Adrien *Chomel wrote of him in *Le Collège d'Annonay*, 'He led an edifying and devoted life, going from one convent to another bringing the example of a solid piety and patriarchal faith and the teachings of the religious life along with words of peace, encouragement and consolation. Harsh and severe toward himself he was extremely mild toward the souls confided to him.'

In the course of 1879 he wrote several times to the bishop of Viviers to give his opinion of the Constitutions of the Congregation, of the general council, the general chapter, the superior general, his authority and the length of his mandate, and on the matter of spiritual direction. He participated in the annual community retreat until his death. As the result of an illness he went to the Hospice at Privas on 4 December 1891 and died there eight days later.

SOURCES: Chomel, *Collège d'Annonay* 319–20; Kirley, *Community in France* 70n178; Pouzol, 'Notices.'

GIRAUD, Julien, priest, superior general of the Community in France for one year after the separation of the French and American communities, 1922–3, nephew of Father Jean Jacques *Giraud and half-brother of Father Benoît *Giraud, was born at Saint-Julien-en-Saint-Alban (Ardèche) on 26 March 1848, the son of Louis Giraud and Jeanne Servant. He died in Annonay on 22 January 1931 and is buried in the Basilian cemetery on the grounds of the Collège du Sacré-Coeur.

Julien Giraud lost his mother when he was four years old. His father then married a sister of his first wife, and had ten more children. The youngest boy, Benoît, also became a Basilian. Julien was a student at the Collège de Privas (Ardèche) from 1858 to 1865. He entered the novitiate at Feyzin (Isère, now Rhône) in 1865, then studied philosophy and prepared his *baccalauréat* while performing duties at the Collège des Cordeliers, at the Petit Séminaire d'Aubenas (Ardèche), and at Sainte-Barbe, the Basilian minor seminary in Annonay. From 1868 to 1871 he studied theology while teaching at Privas and at the Ecole cléricale de Périgueux (Dordogne). He was ordained to the priesthood on 23 September 1871 in the chapel of the Collège du Sacré-Coeur by Bishop Armand de Charbonnel.

Father Giraud taught for two years at the Ecole cléricale de Périgueux, then for a year at the Petit Séminaire de Vernoux, a year in Annonay and five more years at Vernoux. He completed a *licence* at the Université de Grenoble in 1880. From 1886 to 1888 he was a private tutor in a family at Arcachon (Gironde). He was superior at the Collège Saint-Augustin, Bône, Algeria, 1888–95, and at the Petit Séminaire d'Aubenas, 1895–1903. The Basilians had moved from Bône to Aubenas when Bishop Joseph-Michel-Frédéric Bonnet offered them the minor seminary there.

In 1896 Father Giraud was named an honorary canon of the cathedral of Viviers. In 1901 the Congregation requested the necessary authorization from the civil authorities to continue teaching as Basilians even though Bishop Bonnet had suggested they become priests of the diocese of Viviers. After the government prohibited members of religious congregations to teach in any school (7 July 1904), Father Giraud was named chaplain of the convent of Sainte-Marie in Annonay; but in 1905 the convent was dissolved and the sisters went to Italy. Father Giraud lived for a while at the Good Shepherd Convent and then left Annonay. From 1906 to 1909 he was a private tutor at Virazeil (Lot-et-Garonne) of a boy preparing his *baccalauréat*. In 1910 he was named titular canon of the cathedral of Viviers.

From 1910 to 1926 Father Giraud was superior of institutions for the diocese of Viviers: the *Maîtrise* (choir school) in Viviers, 1910–13, and the Petit Séminaire d'Aubenas, 1913–26. During this time he constructed the imposing clock tower on the seminary building. After the separation of the North American and French communities in 1921, he was elected provincial on 26 April 1922 and on 14 June 1922 became superior general when Rome recognized two separate congregations. When the new French congregation held its general chapter on 12

August 1922 at Aubenas he was elected superior general, but he resigned shortly afterwards.

From 1926 to 1929 Father Giraud lived in retirement at the minor seminary, Saint-Charles, Annonay. In 1929 he took up residence at Maison Saint-Joseph, which had been recently refurbished for older confreres. He died there eighteen months later. Father Charles Roume described him as a 'remarkable superior, with beard and olympian majesty.'

SOURCES: GABF; Kirley, *Community in France* 135, 175, 257–8, 260, and passim; Kirley, *Congregation in France* 12, 42, 75, 76n35, 77, 80, 82–8, 90–5, 98–9, 101–2, 103–17, 123–7, 129–30, 133, 135, 138, 140, 143, 154–7, 158, 160, 174, 182, 209, 212, 269–71; Pouzol, 'Notices'; Charles Roume, 'Ernest Martin, a Biography,' *Basilian Teacher* 4 (April 1960) 206–11; *Semaine religieuse de Viviers* (13 February 1931).

GLAVIN, Basil Francis, priest, nephew of Fathers John *Glavin and Basil *Sullivan and cousin of Father Vincent *Guinan, was born on 18 February 1921 at Mount Carmel, Ontario (diocese of London), the son of Charles Glavin and Mary Sullivan. He died in Toronto on 8 April 1985 and is buried in the Basilian plot of Holy Cross Cemetery, Thornhill, Ontario.

After elementary schooling and four years of high school, 1936–40, at Mount Carmel, Basil Glavin took grade XIII at St Michael's College School, Toronto. In 1941 he began a course in Honours Philosophy at Assumption College, Windsor. Two years later he entered St Basil's Novitiate, Toronto, where he took first vows on 15 August 1944. He returned to Assumption and completed his arts course (B.A., University of Western Ontario, 1946). He was appointed to St Thomas High School, Houston, where he taught while doing his first year of theological studies. In 1948 he went to St Basil's Seminary, Toronto, to complete his theology course, and was ordained to the priesthood on 29 June 1950 in St Basil's Church by Cardinal James Charles McGuigan.

Father Glavin worked first as a teacher and then as a pastor. He had five teaching assignments: Catholic Central, Detroit, 1951–3; St Thomas High School, Houston, 1953–4; Assumption College School, Windsor, 1954–6, during which time he also attended the Ontario College of Education, earning a Type B teaching certification; St Joseph's High School, Ottawa, 1960–1; and St Charles College, Sudbury, Ontario, 1962–7. Twice he was appointed to St Basil's Novitiate: once at Richmond Hill, Ontario, as spiritual director and, for his last year there, also treasurer, 1956–60, and once at Erindale, Ontario, as treasurer, 1961–2.

His apostolate in the parishes began at St Mary's of the Assumption, Owen Sound, Ontario, 1967–71, and extended to three other Basilian parishes: St Pius X, Calgary, 1971–3, St Basil's, Ottawa, 1974–6, and St Augustine's, Saskatoon, 1980–3. He was appointed to St Thomas More College, Saskatoon, in 1979, from where he was chaplain to religious sisters and to senior citizens' homes, and gave retreats for students. Perhaps his most effective work, well suited to his gentle, charitable nature, was the chaplaincy at St Vincent's Hospital, Vancouver, 1976–9, while living at St Mark's College.

Twice Father Glavin undertook special apostolates. He was a founding member of L'Arche Community at Barfrestone, England, 1973–4, and, in 1983–4, a member of the Galilee Community at Arnprior, Ontario. In his later years, when he was struggling with cancer, he went briefly in 1984 to Henry Carr Farm, Beeton, Ontario, but soon had to retire to the Basilian Fathers Residence (Infirmary), where he died a few months later.

Father Basil Glavin was a man of quiet conversation, and kindness to all. He lived humbly and served humbly. He often brought comfort and assurance. A gentle sense of humour never deserted him. He cherished the support of prayer communities, joining them wherever he was appointed. Friendship and the beauty of nature brought him the sense of God.

BIBLIOGRAPHY: 'Latin Baseball,' *Basilian Teacher* 1 (December 1956) 7–9; 'There Is Need of an Education Here,' *Forum* 2 (May 1966) 67–8.
SOURCES: GABF; *Annals* 1 (1950) 287, 6 (1986) 476–8; *Newsletter* (15 April 1985).

GLAVIN, John Joseph, priest, uncle of Father Basil *Glavin and cousin of Father Vincent *Guinan, was born on 2 September 1895 at Mount Carmel, Ontario (diocese of London), one of four children of Michael Joseph Glavin and Ellen Kilgalen. He died in Toronto on 31 December 1978 and is buried in the Basilian plot of Holy Cross Cemetery, Thornhill, Ontario.

After primary education at Our Lady of Mount Carmel Separate School, John attended high school at Assumption College, Windsor, 1910–14, and continued in the university course there immediately afterwards. Two years later he entered St Basil's Novitiate, Toronto, and was professed on 24 August 1917. His first appointment was to St Michael's College, Toronto, where, for one year, he continued his undergraduate studies. He returned to Assumption College to complete his university studies (B.A., University of Western Ontario, 1920) and to begin theological studies. In 1921 he was appointed once more to St Michael's College, where he completed his theology course and was ordained to the priesthood on 17 December 1921 in St Basil's Church, Toronto, by Bishop Félix Couturier of Alexandria.

Father Glavin was appointed to St Thomas College, Chatham, New Brunswick, for one year, 1922–3, and then joined the staff of Assumption College, where he remained until 1926. During this time he became involved in coaching, and attended the coaching school at Notre Dame University in the summer of 1924. In 1926 he was transferred to St Thomas College, Houston, where his talent for teaching and coaching football found its full scope. His career as a coach, however, was to be short-lived.

In 1928 Bishop Christopher E. Byrne of the diocese of Galveston (now Galveston-Houston) asked the Basilians to take charge of the young parish of St Anne in Houston. Father Glavin was appointed the first Basilian pastor. His organization, planning, and fund-raising abilities put St Anne's on an enduringly sound basis. In 1932 he was appointed pastor of St John the Baptist Parish, Amherstburg, Ontario, where the same skills became further evident. The following year he was named treasurer of St Michael's College, Toronto – a daunting task in the Depression of the early 1930s. He served on the general council from 1936 to 1948, remaining at St Michael's until 1940, when he returned to St Anne's, Houston, as pastor. From 1942 to 1948 he was pastor of Ste Anne's Parish, Detroit, then returned to St Anne's, Houston, as assistant and then as pastor in 1950.

In 1958 he was asked to go north again, this time to St Mary's of the Assumption Parish, Owen Sound, Ontario, the next year to St John the Baptist Parish, Amherstburg, and in 1960 to St Basil's, Toronto, where he remained until 1962. In each of these appointments, although not the pastor, he had charge of finances. After St Basil's he was appointed to St Anne's, Houston, for the fourth time. Having raised money there already for the new Seminary in Toronto, 1950, and a new novitiate in Pontiac, Michigan, 1959, he again undertook a successful campaign for funds to build a house of studies in Houston. When the decision to build was reversed, Father Glavin conscientiously contacted all the donors to ascertain their wishes.

In June 1970, Father Glavin took up residence at St Basil's College, Toronto, and was there for the opening of the 'Infirmary.' In 1974 arteriosclerosis and painful arthritis developed, and during subsequent years his memory faded and he became quite withdrawn, his condition causing abrupt mood changes which were painful to him and to those who cared for him. In November of 1978 he was hospitalized for a time, returning to St Basil's more serene and even cheerful. He died peacefully in the early hours of the morning of the last day of the year.

Rotund and solidly built, John Glavin was a man of principle, conviction, and devotion to duty. Although jovial by nature, he could at times be a difficult task master, yet he asked no more of others than he demanded of himself. He was at home in the pulpit. One parishioner said he used the 'Dizzy Dean style of delivery: he just reared back and smoked 'em over.' His Good Friday sermons at St Anne's, Houston, during which altar boys carried rough-hewn beams, a crown of long thorns, and long iron nails down the centre aisle, were famous. He found strength for his ministry in his devotion to the Blessed Sacrament. The decline in vocations in the community during the late 1960s and the 1970s was a great sorrow for him.

SOURCES: GABF; *Annals* 4 (1968) 45–6, 4 (1972) 221–2, 5 (1978) 265, (1979) 419–21; *Newsletter* (8 January 1979); Kirley, *Community in France* 216n518, 222n531, 232n559, 241n570.

GODARD, Jean-Marie, priest, was born at Ailleux (Loire, archdiocese of Lyon), on 19 May 1846. He died in Annonay on 15 February 1924 and was buried there in the Basilian cemetery on the grounds of the Collège du Sacré-Coeur.

Jean-Marie's father Antoine, the mayor of Ailleux, was constantly under attack by the Freemasons there. At twelve years of age Jean-Marie attended the Ecole des Salles at the Ecole cléricale (Loire). He remained there until *classe de quatrième*, when he went to the Petit Séminaire de Montbrison (Drôme). He did his philosophy and mathematics at the Séminaire d'Alix (Rhône) and then took theology at the Grand Séminaire de Lyon. Wishing to work in Christian education, he entered the Basilian novitiate at Feyzin (Isère, now Rhône), made final profession on 20 September 1872, and was ordained to the priesthood on 20 December 1873 at Viviers by Bishop Louis Delcusy.

Father Godard's entire priestly life was dedicated to education, especially of future Basilians and other priests. From 1870 to 1877 and from 1878 to 1897 he taught mathematics and was spiritual director at the Petit Séminaire de Vernoux (Ardèche). From 1897 to 1903 he was at the Collège du Sacré-Coeur (Annonay), as assistant to the master of novices, Father Léopold *Fayolle. In 1903, when governmental anticlerical legislation forbade members of congregations to teach, he 'secularized' and became assistant parish priest at Coux near Privas (Ardèche). He still continued his work as spiritual director at Vernoux, which was then under diocesan direction. When it was closed by civil authorities in December 1906, many of its seminarians went to the Collège du Sacré-Coeur, and Father Godard went with them. The college had been purchased by the Société Immobilière d'Annonay, a group of laymen, to prevent its confiscation by the state. It began receiving students in October 1905 and remained under diocesan direction until 1956, when it was returned to the Basilians. Minor seminarians, for whom Father Godard was spiritual director, were grouped under the section Saint-Charles, named for the patron of the former Petit Séminaire de Vernoux. Many seminarians owed perseverance in their vocation to him. He also directed the Sodalities of the Holy Angels and of the Blessed Virgin Mary. His catechism classes with 'magic lantern' illustrations were much appreciated.

Father Godard served as a member of the Basilian general council from 11 September 1898 to 13 April 1910, but resigned to allow a younger confrere to succeed him in view of the general chapter to be held in Geneva in July 1910.

SOURCES: GABF; Kirley, *Community in France* 124n305, 163n416, 172, 182n464, 184, 197, 198, 205, 244, 255n600; Kirley, *Congregation in France* 62, 76n34; Pouzol, 'Notices.'

GOETZ, Michael Alphonsus, priest, was born on 10 June 1920 at Kenilworth, Ontario (diocese of Hamilton), one of seven children of Alexander Joseph Goetz and Mary Costello. He died in Toronto on 12 June 1980, and is buried in the Basilian plot of Holy Cross Cemetery, Thornhill, Ontario.

'Mike' Goetz attended Derry Nane Grade School, Kenilworth. At the age of eight, while playing a family game, he sustained a hip injury. Complications set in, and amputation of the leg seemed called for. Although extensive treatment saved the leg, a limp and frequent pain would accompany him for the rest of his life. His secondary education began under the Sisters of St Joseph at the Kenilworth Continuation

School. He attended St Mary's College, Brockville, Ontario, 1937–40, before completing his senior matriculation at St Michael's College School, Toronto. He enlisted in the Canadian army but served only briefly before being discharged because of his earlier injury. He worked to pay his way through Assumption College, Windsor (B.A., University of Western Ontario, 1948), and was elected vice-president of the Students' Administrative Council in his senior year. He entered St Basil's Novitiate, Richmond Hill, Ontario, making first profession on 15 August 1949.

As a scholastic he taught mathematics at St Thomas High School, Houston, and began theological studies, 1949–50. He taught at Aquinas Institute, Rochester, 1950–1, after which he completed his theological courses at St Basil's Seminary, Toronto. He was ordained to the priesthood on 29 June 1953 in St Basil's Church, Toronto, by Cardinal James Charles McGuigan.

Father Goetz lived at St Michael's College, 1954–5, while earning teacher certificaation at the Ontario College of Education. He taught mathematics at Assumption College School until 1957, when a severe asthmatic condition forced a respite from work and a search for a Basilian house in a climate where he might survive and work. He eventually returned to rest at the newly opened Michael Power High School, Etobicoke, Ontario, where he found that with proper care and medication he could function effectively. He would live there for the rest of his life. While teaching mathematics there, 1957–73, he founded the Sodality of the Blessed Virgin Mary, the Dads' Club, the Math Club, and the Old Boys' Association, and served as school and house bursar for fifteen years. His contribution to the development of Michael Power High School in its early years of precarious financial condition was crucial.

In 1973 he embarked on a 'missionary venture' with the Dufferin-Peel Separate School Board, Mississauga, Ontario. He established the guidance department at St Paul's Junior High School and became an education consultant to the 'Parents for Catholic Education in Peel County.' In 1978 he went to St Martin's Junior High School as head of the mathematics department and advisor to the Board in extending the junior high school to a complete secondary school. His encouragement, vision, and personality, but even more his love for students, staff, and parents, contributed greatly to the success of the venture. In recognition of his service to Catholic education, the Dufferin-Peel Separate School Board in 1987 named a large new school 'The Father Michael Goetz Secondary School.'

Late in the night of 11 June 1980, after returning from a family celebration of his sixtieth birthday, Father Goetz experienced difficulty breathing. He sought help from Father Richard Sheehan. Setting out by car for Queensway Hospital, they had gone but a short distance when Father Goetz slumped over dead.

Mike Goetz was a gentle, unpretentious man. His promotion of gatherings of family and community helped establish the reputation for hospitality at Michael Power. Curtailed in some projects by health problems, he eschewed the category of invalid. He ministered to many persons with problems who came to him knowing they would find a gentle welcome and good counsel. His funeral in St Basil's Church, Toronto, was packed to overflowing with friends, relatives, and former students.

BIBLIOGRAPHY: 'Mathematics in Basilian Schools [forum],' *Basilian Teacher* 4 (December 1959) 68.
SOURCES: GABF; *Annals* 2 (1953) 108–9, 5 (1981) 608–10; *Newsletter* (24 June 1980).

GORMAN (O'GORMAN), Michael F., novice and postulant, was born in Toronto on 25 September 1846, the son of David Gorman and Margaret O'Hearn. He died in Windsor on 31 December 1878 and was buried in Assumption Cemetery prior to the opening of the Basilian plot.

After his early education in Toronto, Michael Gorman (O'Gorman) was a brilliant student at St Michael's College, excelling notably in mathematics. He entered the Grand Séminaire in Montreal, but failing health forced him to withdraw. On 15 August 1873, he entered St Basil's Novitiate, Toronto; but, when the novitiate was transferred in September to Assumption College, Windsor, he was taken out to teach First Commercial there. He died from tuberculosis at the age of thirty-two, never having finished his novitiate year.

SOURCES: GABF; Archives, Assumption Parish, Windsor.

GOURGEON, Marius, priest, was born at Lespéron (Ardèche) on 26 July 1849. He died at Puy-en-Velay (Haute-Loire) on 20 October 1936.

Marius Gourgeon was probably a relative of Father Paul *Gourgeon, who taught at the Petit Séminaire d'Aubenas (Ardèche), 1863–79, where Marius could have been a student. It seems that he made his novitiate at Feyzin (Isère, now Rhône), 1870-1. He was at the Petit Séminaire de Vernoux (Ardèche) from 1871 to 1873, and was probably at the Collège Saint-Charles, Blidah, Algeria, 1873-5. He was definitely at the Collège du Sacré-Coeur, Annonay, during the year 1875-6, and perhaps back in Blidah, 1876-9. He was ordained to the priesthood on 21 September 1878 and was certainly in Blidah, 1879-85.

He taught at the Petit Séminaire de Vernoux, 1885-90, and, after a year at the Collège du Sacré-Coeur, Annonay, returned to Vernoux for a ten-year period. From 1901 to 1903 he was back at Sacré-Coeur; but when French legislation forbade members of congregations to teach, and the Basilians were expelled from the college, he became chaplain to the Orphelinat agricole and then to the Religieuses de l'Instruction at Puy-en-Velay. From 1923 until his death thirteen years later he returned each year to Annonay for the retreat with his confreres.

SOURCES: GABF; Kirley, *Community in France* 184, 209, 240n569; Pouzol, 'Notices.'

GOURGEON, Paul, priest, the son of Victor Gourgeon and Agathe Benoît, was born in Lespéron (Ardèche) on 3 December 1834. He was probably a relative of Father Marius *Gourgeon. He died on 13 May 1899 in Annonay and was buried in the cemetery on the grounds of the Collège du Sacré-Coeur.

Paul Gourgeon was a student at the Collège de Langogne (Lozère) and at the Petit Séminaire d'Aubenas (Ardèche). He went to the Grand Séminaire de Viviers for a year and a half; but, following a desire to be involved in the education of youth, he requested entrance into the Basilian community and minor seminary of Sainte-Barbe in Annonay. He attended the Collège de Privas (Ardèche), where the novitiate was then located, first as a postulant, then as a novice, and made first profession on 16 December 1859. He was ordained to the priesthood on 18 May 1862 in the chapel of the Grand Séminaire de Viviers by Bishop Louis Delcusy.

Prior to his ordination, while studying theology, he spent a year at the Petit Séminaire de Vernoux (Ardèche) as a prefect, a year at the Collège du Sacré-Coeur as a professor of French, and a year at Privas as professor of mathematics. After ordination he taught mathematics at the Collège de Privas for one year and at the Petit Séminaire d'Aubenas for six years until the Marists took over the school. Father Gourgeon then went to Bourg-Saint-Andéol (Ardèche) for four years until it was closed in 1881 by the suppression of religious orders. He spent the following year at the Collège Saint-Pierre in Châteauroux (Indre).

A nervous ailment compelled Father Gourgeon to give up teaching, but he continued to work with students and share their recreation. His last three assignments were to institutions which the community either abandoned or was forced to abandon – an experience which shook his courage and aggravated his illness. He had an inquisitive mind and lived an austere life, drawing on his simple and strong piety to sustain him in many trials, especially physical ones, during the last months of his life.

SOURCES: GABF; Pouzol, 'Notices'; *Semaine religieuse de Viviers* (19 May 1899) 123–4.

GOUTTE, Antoine, priest, was born on 14 July 1843, the son of Jean Goutte and Jeanne Marie Chazel, at Saint-Georges-en-Couzan (Loire, archdiocese of Lyon). He died in Annonay on 7 February 1901 and was buried there in the cemetery on the grounds of the Collège du Sacré-Coeur.

Antoine Goutte did his secondary studies and the beginning of his theological studies in the archdiocese of Lyon. He made his noviatiate at Feyzin (Isère, now Rhône), probably in 1867. He worked as prefect at the Collège de Privas (Ardèche) while studying theology, 1868–70, and as prefect and teacher at the Petit Séminaire de Vernoux (Ardèche), 1870–2. He was ordained to the priesthood in the chapel of the Collège du Sacré-Coeur on 21 September 1872 by Bishop Armand de Charbonnel. After ordination he spent a year at Vernoux, a year at Bourg-Saint-Andéol (Ardèche), and four years at the Petit Séminaire d'Aubenas (Ardèche). He returned to Bourg-Saint-Andéol in 1878 and remained until 1881, when the anticlerical laws expelled the Congregation from that institution. Father Goutte went to Prades (Ardèche) to work in the pilgrimage apostolate. In 1883 he went to the Collège du Sacré-Coeur, remaining there until 1888, when he transferred to the Ecole cléricale de Périgueux (Dordogne). In 1899, illness forced his retirement to Sainte-Barbe, Annonay, where he died a short time later.

SOURCE: Pouzol, 'Notices.'

GRAND, Jean Pierre, priest, was born on 12 January 1845 in Montrond, Kingdom of Savoy, in the Piedmont region. He died in Detroit on 13 May 1922 and was buried in the Basilian plot of Assumption Cemetery, Windsor.

Pierre Grand became a French citizen at age fifteen in 1860 when the people of Savoy voted to join the French nation. He did his secondary studies from 1862 to 1869 at the Collège des Cordeliers and the Collège du Sacré-Coeur, Annonay, working as prefect, 1867–9. He made his novitiate at Feyzin (Isère, now Rhône) in 1869–70, then studied theology, 1870–2, while teaching at the Collège du Sacré-Coeur. He went to Canada on 13 August 1872 while still in temporary vows, made final profession in 1873, and was ordained to the priesthood on 30 May 1874. His priestly ministry was devoted mainly to the parish apostolate. He served at St Joseph's Parish, Chatham, Ontario, and at St John the Baptist Parish, Amherstburg, Ontario, going to reside at the Basilian novitiate at Beaconfield House, Plymouth, England, 1884–6, where he was director of the school.

Father Grand was named the first Basilian pastor of Ste Anne's Parish, Detroit, and spent a total of thirty-five years in ministry there, 1886–1908 and 1909–22. He was elected North American provincial in 1907 and spent the year 1908–9 at the novitiate in Toronto. In 1908 he published an English translation of the Basilian Constitutions. He attended the general chapter in Geneva in 1910 and was elected assistant, a post he held until his death.

Father Grand always rose early in the morning. He was a cultured and courteous priest. Although welcoming and affable he rarely dominated a conversation, being of a placid nature and possessing a calm rarely disturbed.

SOURCES: GABF; Kirley, *Community in France* 186, 235, 236n564, 246, 250, 251; Kirley, *Congregation in France* 6, 12, 14, 29, 32–4, 44–5, 53; Pouzol, 'Notices.'

GRANGEON, Marius, priest, nephew of Father Jean-Marie *Tarabout, was born at Saint-Pierre-du-Champ (Haute-Loire, diocese of Le Puy), on 17 March 1867. He died there on 22 April 1953 and was buried in the local cemetery.

After studies at the Collège du Sacré-Coeur, Annonay, section Sainte-Barbe, Marius Grangeon entered the novitiate at Beaconfield House, Plymouth, England, on 1 September 1888; but illness cut short his novitiate on 31 July 1889. While studying theology he taught for two years at the Petit Séminaire de Vernoux (Ardèche), another year at the Ecole cléricale de Périgueux (Dordogne), a third year at the Collège du

Sacré-Coeur, and then for two years at the Collège Saint-Augustin, Bône, Algeria. He made final profession on 23 September 1892, and was ordained to the priesthood on 21 September 1895 in the chapel of the Collège du Sacré-Coeur by Bishop Joseph-Michel-Frédéric Bonnet of Viviers.

After ordination he worked at the Ecole cléricale, Périgueux, 1895–7, at the Collège Saint-Charles, Blidah, Algeria, 1897–8, at the Petit Séminaire d'Aubenas, 1898–1901, and at the Collège du Sacré-Coeur, 1901–3. From 1903 on, despite the anticlerical laws forbidding members of congregations to teach, he was able to work in different colleges which continued to function in Melun, Neuilly, and Paris. He retired to his native village of Saint-Pierre-du-Champ. He continued to make his annual retreat with the community and to spend the winters at Maison Saint-Joseph, Annonay. He had the gift of recounting anecdotes and of mimicking those he had known during his life. Short in stature, he was given the nickname 'Little John' at Beaconfield House.

SOURCES: Kirley, *Community in France* 184, 208; Kirley, *Congregation in France* 156, 196, 209–10, 220; Pouzol, 'Notices.'

GRANOTTIER, Benoît, priest, member of the Congregation 1877–95, younger brother of Father François-Xavier *Granottier, was born at Valfleury (Loire, archdiocese of Lyon, now diocese of Saint-Etienne), on 31 May 1852, the son of Joseph Granottier and Marie Perrichon. He died at Plattsburgh, New York, on 1 January 1931 and was buried in St Augustine's Parish Cemetery.

Benoît Granottier was educated at the Collège du Sacré-Coeur, Annonay, and later followed his older brother François-Xavier into the Basilian novitiate. He took final vows on 22 September 1877, and was ordained to the priesthood on 18 September 1880.

Shortly thereafter Father Granottier was appointed assistant pastor at St Mary's of the Assumption Parish, Owen Sound, Ontario. One of his duties was the spiritual care of the Indians living on the Saugeen Reserve. In 1886 he spent four months, August to November, at St John the Baptist Parish, Amherstburg, Ontario. Early in 1889 he moved from Owen Sound to Assumption Parish, Windsor.

On 8 April 1895 he withdrew from the Congregation and became pastor of Sacred Heart Parish and Missions, Crown Point, New York. In 1899 he spent several months at St Joseph's Parish in Coopersville, New York. He was incardinated in the diocese of Ogdensburg, New

York, in August 1899 and was appointed pastor of St Alexander Parish, Morrisonville, where he remained until 1910, when he was transferred to St Augustine's Parish, Peru, New York. He died at the Champlain Valley Hospital, Plattsburgh. An obituary notice in the Plattsburgh newspaper stated, 'Father Granottier was an active participant in the community life of Peru and was held high in the esteem of his parishioners and friends in the community.'

SOURCES: GABF; *Centennial, St Mary's*; *Jubilee, St Mary's*; Kirley, *Community in France* 219n526, 220n528, 234n561, 235n562.

GRANOTTIER, François-Xavier, priest, elder brother of Father Benoît *Granottier, was born on 5 October 1836, at Valfleury (Loire, archdiocese of Lyon, now diocese of Saint-Etienne), the son of Joseph Granottier and Marie Perrichon. He died in Owen Sound, Ontario, on 2 March 1917 and was buried in the parish cemetery there.

François-Xavier Granottier did his secondary studies at Sainte-Foy-l'Argentière (Rhône) and theological studies at the Grand Séminaire in Algiers. He was a novice at Privas (Ardèche) in 1860 when he was summoned to replace Father Jacques Collange, who had been injured in an accident. He continued his novitiate while working as prefect at the Collège des Cordeliers. He received minor orders and was professed in 1861; he was ordained to the priesthood at Privas by Bishop Louis Delcusy of Viviers on 18 May 1862.

On 15 August 1862 Father Granottier left France for Canada with Father Jean *Famy. In 1863 he was appointed to St Mary's of the Assumption Parish, Owen Sound, Ontario, and became pastor the next year. In October 1887, after a prolonged visit in France, he went to Ste Anne's Parish, Detroit, as assistant. In July 1888 he was put in charge of Sacred Heart Parish, Warrensburg, Missouri, when the Congregation agreed to open a college at Sedalia, Missouri. Both projects were abandoned in September 1888. Father Granottier returned to Ste Anne's and in 1889 went back to Owen Sound as pastor. He built eight churches in the Owen Sound area including St Mary's, which he modelled after his own parish church of Valfleury. He was constantly on the move, visiting the various mission churches. The *Golden Jubilee Volume* of St Mary's Parish said: 'He had the real Gallic spirit of the old voyageur or *courier [sic]-de-bois*. He was a great traveller, visiting Ontario, France, Algiers, Switzerland, Italy, the Holy Land, Texas and Mexico.'

Father Granottier also served as a member of the provincial council,

1883–98, and of the general council, 1910–17. Even though the general council resided in Detroit from 1910 to 1921, Father Granottier continued to live in Owen Sound, commuting to Detroit for council meetings. He was a charming and intelligent man. It was at his suggestion that the general council legislated in 1884 the celebration of a Requiem Mass for deceased confreres during the annual retreat, a practice the Congregation has maintained ever since. His final years were marred by failing eyesight.

SOURCES: GABF; *Centennial, St Mary's*; Kirley, *Community in France* 7n28, 134n335, 135n342, 163n416, 186, 211n507, 224, 233, 234n561, 237n565, 252n589; Kirley, *Congregation in France* 14, 29, 31, 34, 36, 45, 51; Pouzol, 'Notices'; R.J. Scollard, 'François Granottier,' *Basilian Teacher* 1 (December 1956) 19–21; Spetz, *Waterloo*.

GRANT, Alexander John, priest, was born on 15 December 1910 in Winnipeg, Manitoba (archdiocese of St Boniface, since 1915 of Winnipeg), the son of Alexander Grant and Sarah McCullogh. He died in Phoenix, Arizona, probably on 1 June 1973, and is buried in the Basilian plot of Heavenly Rest Cemetery, Windsor.

Alexander Grant's father served in the First World War with the rank of major and was decorated for heroism. After the war the family moved to Toronto, where, in St John's Church, Kingston Road, 'Alex' was baptized into the Catholic Church on 9 July 1921. He attended St Michael's College School, Toronto, 1924–8, and then entered St Basil's Novitiate, Toronto, making first profession on 12 September 1929. He lived at St Basil's Scholasticate, Toronto, during his undergraduate studies, with the exception of one year at St Michael's College (B.A., University of Toronto, 1933). He studied theology at St Basil's Scholasticate, 1933–7. During the year 1934–5 he also attended the Ontario College of Education and received teaching certification for Ontario. He was ordained to the priesthood on 19 December 1936 in St Basil's Church, Toronto, by Archbishop James Charles McGuigan.

Father Grant was appointed to Aquinas Institute, Rochester, in 1937, the year in which the Basilians took over responsibility for that school. There he taught general science and mathematics while also earning an M.A. in biology from St Bonaventure's College, Olean, New York, in 1944. Biology became his chief interest and teaching subject and the academic area in which he made a notable contribution.

When, in 1945, he was appointed to Assumption College, Windsor, the biology department consisted of one person: himself. Over the years he expanded it from one course to full honours and graduate programs. He built greenhouses on the campus with his own hands, collaborated with Father Francis *Ruth in planning the Memorial Science Building, and planned the biology building, which was completed after he left Windsor. He remained head of the Department of Biology for two years after the University of Windsor came into existence (1963) and held faculty status until his death, though absent from the campus for his last eight years.

Father Grant combined keen academic ability with a deep interest in everyone with whom he associated, most of whom he called by their first name. His gentle manner disguised a relentless will and steady drive in his work, but those who worked with him found him always kind and encouraging.

Alex Grant suffered for many years from a painful and crippling combination of arthritis and psoriasis which, in 1965, finally forced him to seek a warm, dry climate. He took up pastoral work in the diocese of Phoenix, Arizona, first at Ash Fork, then at Kingman, and finally at St Margaret Mary Parish, Bullhead City. His warmth and simplicity endeared him to the people whom he left with regret when his health failed completely early in 1972. He moved into Phoenix to be closer to the medical services he needed, and died in the apartment where he had been living alone for some months.

SOURCES: GABF; *Annals* 5 (1974) 50–1; *Newsletter* (4 June 1973).

GRAY, Marie Denis Philémon, priest, was born at Saint-Julien-Labrousse (Ardèche) on 1 June 1838. He died at Châteauroux (Indre) in 1900 and was buried there.

Marie Denis Gray was a novice at Feyzin (Isère, now Rhône), and then was prefect at the Petit Séminaire d'Aubenas (Ardèche), 1869–72. He was ordained to the priesthood on 21 September 1872 in the chapel of the Collège du Sacré-Coeur, Annonay, by Bishop Armand de Charbonnel. After ordination he spent two years at Sacré-Coeur, two years at the college at Bourg-Saint-Andéol (Ardèche), and six years at the Collège Saint-Pierre, Châteauroux, until that school was given up by the Basilian community in 1882.

It appears that Father Gray remained in that locality in different apostolates. His name does not appear among the Basilians involved in education after 1882. He was a chaplain in 1889. Father Noël *Durand indicates in the Basilian necrology that Father Gray died and was buried at Châteauroux, after twenty-nine years of religious profession, at the age of sixty-two. This reckoning would indicate that he was thirty when he made his novitiate in 1868.

SOURCE: Pouzol, 'Notices.'

GRESCOVIAK, Francis Joseph, priest, was born on 29 January 1918 at Fredonia, New York (diocese of Buffalo), the son of Ludwig Grescoviak and Mary Tarkowski. He died in Toronto on 26 August 1995 and is buried in the Basilian plot of Holy Cross Cemetery, Thornhill, Ontario.

'Gus' – a name used so commonly that few of his confreres knew his Christian name – went to St Michael's College, Toronto, in 1935, where he enrolled in the Western course. In 1936 he entered St Basil's Novitiate, Toronto, making first profession on 15 August 1937, and then lived at St Basil's Seminary, Toronto, 1937–9, and at St Michael's College, 1939–40 (B.A., University of Toronto, 1940). He taught one year at Aquinas Institute, Rochester, and one year at Catholic Central, Detroit, where he also did graduate studies in education (M.Ed., Wayne State University, 1943). He studied theology in Toronto, living for two years at St Michael's College, 1942–3, 1944–5, and for two years at St Basil's Seminary, 1943–4, 1945–6. He also taught for two years at St Michael's College School during his theological studies. He was ordained to the priesthood on 15 August 1945 in St Basil's Church, Toronto, by Archbishop James Charles McGuigan.

Father Grescoviak taught high school for fifteen years, was novice master for six, and a parish priest for twenty-four. He taught at Aquinas Institute at two different periods: 1946–55 and 1961–7. Between these two periods he was novice master, first at St Basil's Novitiate, Rochester, 1955–9, and then in Pontiac, Michigan, after the novitiate was moved there, 1959–61. He lived at the Basilian House of Studies in Rochester, 1967–9, engaged in retreat work and teaching German. In 1969 he began his long service at St Basil's Parish, Toronto, which continued until his health failed in 1993.

Gus Grescoviak was a tall man with a good preaching voice and an amiable manner. Despite a serious diabetic condition with which he coped for fifty years, he gave himself unstintingly to pastoral care – confessing, preaching, directing the Legion of Mary, and hospital visitation. He served as vice-president of the Ontario Catholic Hospital

Chaplains Association, 1974–8, and gave several radio talks on spiritual matters. In his preaching he drew on an impressive collection of stories, both serious and humorous, and recommended this usage to his novices.

He was an ardent sports spectator, with considerable emotional attachment to the Toronto Maple Leafs and the Toronto Blue Jays. Each July would find him at Strawberry Island, where he passed his days fishing. He made a collection of carillon Christmas Carols, which he would broadcast from the tower of St Basil's Church when Advent came round each year. He moved reluctantly to the Basilian Fathers Residence (Infirmary) in 1993, because of his rapidly deteriorating health. In August, 1995, with members of his family and his confreres, he celebrated his golden jubilee of ordination and died two weeks later.

BIBLIOGRAPHY: 'Our Ear Should Be Attuned to God's Voice, Not Merely Man's,' *Forum* 2 (December 1965) 167–8.
SOURCES: GABF; *Annals* 1 (1946) 118, 6 (1988) 592, 8 (1996) 102–3; *Newsletter* (12 October 1995).

GUEY, Marius, priest, was born in 1872 at Réauville (Drôme, diocese of Valence), the son of Marius Guey and Marie Brun. He died on 29 March 1900 in the Sainte-Barbe minor seminary, Annonay, and was buried there in the cemetery on the grounds of the Collège du Sacré-Coeur.

Marius Guey taught grammar and worked as prefect at the Collège Saint-Charles, Blidah, Algeria, 1892–9, as a postulant, a novice, and theology student. He was away from the college for one year, 1893–4, probably for his military service. His parents were living in Algeria at that time. He was ordained to the priesthood on 23 September 1899 by Bishop Hilarion-Joseph Montéty, titular bishop of Beirut. He had no appointment for 1899–1900, probably because of serious illness, and died at the age of twenty-seven.

SOURCE: Pouzol, 'Notices.'

GUIGAL, Jean Henri, priest, was born at Vinzieux (Ardèche) on 26 June 1842, the son of Laurent Guigal and Marie-Anne Roux. He died at the Hospice d'Annonay on 26 October 1921 and was buried at Vinzieux.

Henri Guigal was a student at the Collège des Cordeliers, Annonay, section Sainte-Barbe, 1855–8. After his novitiate at Feyzin (Isère, now

Rhône), in 1862–3, he taught while studying theology at the Collège des Cordeliers, 1863–6, at the Petit Séminaire d'Aubenas (Ardèche), 1866–7, and at the Petit Séminaire de Vernoux (Ardèche), 1867–9. He was ordained to the priesthood by Bishop Armand de Charbonnel in the chapel of the Collège du Sacré-Coeur, Annonay, on 18 September 1869.

Father Guigal received appointments to the Ecole cléricale de Périgueux (Dordogne), 1869–73, the Collège du Bourg-Saint-Andéol (Ardèche), 1873–8, the Collège du Sacré-Coeur, 1878–9, the Petit Séminaire de Vernoux, 1879–80, and the Collège Saint-Pierre in Châteauroux (Indre), 1880–2. When that school was closed in 1882 because of anticlerical laws in France, Henri Guigal remained to work in the diocese of Bourges with several Basilian confreres from the college. He was pastor at Limiez-par-Vatan (Indre) after 1903. He retired to Vinzieux, but died in Annonay.

SOURCES: Kirley, *Community in France* 185, 208; Pouzol, Notices.'

GUIGON, Léon, priest, younger brother of Father Régis *Guigon, was born at Andance (Ardèche) on 29 November 1872, the son of Auguste Guigon and Marie-Thérèse Champet. He died in Annonay on 9 February 1941 and was buried there in the cemetery on the grounds of the Collège du Sacré-Coeur.

Léon Guigon was a student at the Collège du Sacré-Coeur, Annonay, section Sainte-Barbe, 1885–92. After a year of study to discern his vocation, he received tonsure on 23 September 1893 and entered the Basilian novitiate in Annonay. He made first profession of vows on 21 September 1894, and final profession a year later. While studying theology at the Petit Séminaire d'Aubenas he worked as a prefect of discipline, 1895–6, and taught *cinquième*, 1896–8. Major orders were conferred on him by Bishop Joseph-Michel-Frédéric Bonnet of Viviers at the Collège du Sacré Coeur: the diaconate on 18 September 1897 and the priesthood on 25 September 1898, along with James *Player, future acting superior general.

Father Guigon was *professeur de seconde* at the Petit Séminaire d'Aubenas, 1898–1902, during which time he completed the requirements for the *licence ès lettres*. After the exclusion of members of congregations from teaching in 1903, he served as assistant pastor at Boulieu (Ardèche), 1903–4, then taught at the Petit Séminaire d'Aubenas, 1904–6. From 1906 until 1919 (with the exception of the war years, 1914–18, when he served in an ambulance corps) he was assistant pastor at Vals-les-Bains (Ardèche), then curé at La Chapelle-sous-Aubenas

(Ardèche), 1919-25. When St Basil's Novitiate opened in Bordighera, Italy, in 1926, he was appointed master of novices and remained in that office when the novitiate moved to Maison Saint-Joseph, Annonay, from 1935 until his death in 1941.

Father Léon Guigon's valiant efforts to promote community life earn him a prominence in the restoration of the Basilians in France after 1922 comparable to that of Father Charles *Roume.

SOURCES: GABF; Kirley, *Community in France* 185, 204, 255n600; Kirley, *Congregation in France* 42, 72, 81-2, 144-5, 151n21, 154, 156, 174, 182, 184-5, 194, 206, 208-11, 213; *Semaine religieuse de Viviers* (14 February 1941).

GUIGON, Régis, priest, elder brother of Father Léon *Guigon, was born in Annonay on 29 March 1868, the son of Auguste Guigon and Marie-Thérèse Champet. He died on 6 July 1928 in Saint-Etienne (Loire).

Régis Guigon was a student at the Collège du Sacré-Coeur, Annonay, section Sainte-Barbe, 1879-84. He went to study for two years at the College of the Immaculate Conception, Beaconfield House, Plymouth, England, where he made his novitiate under Father Victorin *Marijon. He remained at Beaconfield House for another year, followed by a year at Sainte-Barbe and a year at the Petit Séminaire de Vernoux (Ardèche). From 1883 to 1896 he was at the Collège Saint-Charles, Blidah, Algeria, and the next year at the Ecole cléricale de Périgueux (Dordogne). During these years he was prefect as well as student of theology. He was ordained to the priesthood on 29 June 1897 at Périgueux.

After ordination Father Guigon worked for one year at Vernoux, one year at Périgueux, and one at Beaconfield House, with two more at Vernoux before returning for one year to Périgueux. After the governmental expulsions of teaching congregations from schools in 1903, he spent several years as chaplain to the Sisters of the Assumption at Saint-Etienne, and taught modern languages at the Collège de Saint-Chamond (Loire) and in various schools in Saint-Etienne. During the First World War he served in an ambulance corps. At Easter of 1928, while visiting his brother Léon at the novitiate in Bordighera, Italy, he fell seriously ill. He was taken back to Saint-Etienne, where he died the following summer.

SOURCES: GABF; Kirley, *Community in France* 185, 208, 240n569; Kirley, *Congregation in France* 211; Pouzol, 'Notices.'

GUINAN, Vincent Joseph, priest, brother of Sister Saint Michael Guinan OSU, was born on 15 January 1899 at Mount Carmel, Ontario (diocese of London), the son of Joseph Guinan and Margaret Sullivan. He died in Houston on 25 February 1973 and is buried there in the Basilian plot, Garden of Gethsemane, Forest Park Lawndale Cemetery.

After grade school at Mount Carmel, Vincent Guinan went in 1912 to Assumption College, Windsor, for secondary and university studies (B.A., Honours Philosophy, University of Western Ontario, 1920). When he entered St Basil's Novitiate, Toronto, in 1920, the Basilian Fathers reimbursed the bishop of London the $1150.00 subsidy he had paid for the last four years of Vincent's education. After his first profession on 23 August 1921, Vincent immediately began his theology course at St Basil's Scholasticate, located at that time in the old Elmsley House on the grounds of St Michael's College, Toronto. He also attended the Ontario College of Education, earning teaching certification in 1923. He was ordained to the priesthood in St Basil's Church, Toronto, on 23 August 1924 by Bishop Alexander MacDonald.

Father Guinan was appointed to Assumption College, where he taught in his own highly distinctive way in both the high school and the college. He also coached college teams, taking great delight in confusing referees; he ran various societies, and did Sunday ministry in Detroit parishes and graduate work on the side (M.A., Philosophy, University of Ottawa, 1929 [thesis: 'The Elizabethan Age of Literature']). From 1932 to 1940 he was the registrar of Assumption during the difficult Depression years. In 1940, when appointed to succeed Father T.A. *Macdonald as superior and president, he protested that he lacked the capacity and the training for the job. Nevertheless he succeeded in guiding Assumption through the trying years of the Second World War; and, in 1944, he began a fund drive that was strategic for Assumption not only in raising the necessary funds but also in involving the civic community. He began the construction of the Memorial Science Building, the first new building in many years. Already in 1938 his predecessor T.A. *MacDonald had called him a 'foundation stone' of Assumption. His tenure as president amply bore this out, and his services were recognized by an honorary LL.D. conferred on him by Assumption University of Windsor in 1963.

In 1946 Father Guinan was named founding president of the University of St Thomas, Houston, which held its first lectures on 24 September 1947. The university began on a tenuous financial basis, but Father Guinan's faith and enthusiasm kept the school alive and fostered its growth. He successfully resisted those in Toronto who wanted to suspend classes during the Korean War, 1950-3. His oblique approach was usually successful in eliciting both financial and other kinds of support. An early beneficiary of his scholarship program was Ricardo Ramírez, future Basilian and bishop of Las Cruces, New Mexico; and, for John McCarthy, the future bishop of Austin, Texas, he arranged a special program of studies at a time when diocesan seminarians were not obtaining degrees. He retained the scholarship and alumni portfolios when he stepped down from the presidency in 1959. A student residence built in 1970 and rebuilt in 2002-3 was named in his honour.

Vincent Guinan's contribution to the University of St Thomas was not primarily financial. Far more important was his fostering of a spirit of dedication to UST in the many communities with which he was involved. Nothing could dampen his enthusiasm, and no work for UST seemed to him unrewarding. He would cheerfully promote the university to small, sometimes indifferent groups in outlying towns, and count such evenings successful. He faithfully accompanied the Knights of Columbus, the Legion of Mary, the Siena Club (a professional women's group which he founded), the Catholic Literature Society, and the monthly Nocturnal Adoration Society. He had personal friends in all walks and ranks of life who helped the university in one way or another. They were all tied into the ambit of friendship and prayer that characterized Father Guinan's approach to life. For some twenty-five years he said the student Mass at 7:00 a.m. each day and then taught his class in first-year economics at 8:00. Even at the busiest times he did Sunday ministry in various parishes in the diocese. He suffered the loss of one eye in an automobile accident as he was being driven to celebrate Mass in a parish.

Father Guinan's usually robust health began to fail in the summer of 1972, though he continued teaching until the end of the fall term. He entered the hospital on his seventy-fourth birthday, thinking his persistent and severe back pain was due to an old injury. The diagnosis was cancer, which brought his death some five weeks later.

BIBLIOGRAPHY: 'Our Student Today: Problem and Potential [forum],' *Basilian Teacher* 7 (December 1962) 112; 'St Thomas, University of,' *New Catholic Encyclopedia* 12 (New York, 1967) 950-1.
SOURCES: GABF; *Annals* 4 (1972) 224, 5 (1974) 54-5; McMahon, *Pure Zeal* 127-255; *Newsletter* (2 March 1973). For extensive documentation relating to his presidency of Assumption College, Windsor, see Power, *Assumption College* 6 1-116.

GUINANE, James Joseph, priest, was born in Toronto on 5 February 1854, the son of William Guinane and Margaret Gleeson. He died in his native city on 3 July 1905 and was buried there in the Basilian plot of St Michael's Cemetery.

James Guinane went to St Michael's College, Toronto, at the age of eleven. He interrupted his studies there at the age of eighteen to enter St Basil's Novitiate where he was received as a novice on 29 September 1872. He did theological studies at St Michael's College, took final vows on 8 December 1878, and was ordained priest on 13 July 1879.

For ten years after ordination Father Guinane taught mathematics at St Michael's College. In July of 1888 he was appointed superior of a college to be opened at Sedalia, Missouri. When the project was abandoned in September, he returned to St Michael's College to serve as treasurer, 1892–5. During the year 1898–9 he taught at the College of Mary Immaculate, Beaconfield House, Plymouth, England, but returned to Canada to teach philosophy at Assumption College, Windsor, until his death from cancer in 1905.

Father Guinane was a fine athlete in his student days, and as a priest served as director of athletics at St Michael's College. The Assumption Jubilee volume spoke of 'his kind attention ... simple every-day advice ... his wide experience and his cheerful remonstrances.'

SOURCES: GABF; Charles Collins, 'Basilians I Have Known,' transcribed in Robert J. Scollard, 'Historical Notes C.S.B.' 10 83–91 (GABF); *Jubilee, Assumption.*

H

HAFFEY, Hugh James, priest, brother of Sister Mary Ethelburge CSJ, was born on 23 June 1905 at Welland, Ontario (archdiocese of Toronto, now diocese of St Catharines), the son of James J. Haffey and Mary T. McNeff. He died in Houston on 7 January 1975 and is buried in the Basilian plot of Holy Sepulchre Cemetery, Rochester.

After attending public schools at Welland, Hugh went in September 1924 to St Michael's College, Toronto (B.A., University of Toronto, 1927). He entered St Basil's Novitiate, Toronto, in September 1927 and took first vows on 2 October 1928. He took his theology courses at St Basil's Scholasticate, Toronto, and was ordained to the priesthood by

Bishop Alexander MacDonald on 19 December 1931, in St Basil's Church, Toronto.

Father Haffey began his long teaching career in 1932 at St Michael's College, Toronto, where he taught chemistry, both in the high school and the college. In 1937 he was appointed to Aquinas Institute, Rochester, to teach chemistry and public speaking. The next twelve years were to be momentous ones for the Basilian community in Rochester, owing in large part to Father Haffey's inspiration and dedication. He developed the school's mission crusade to an extraordinary degree and was instrumental in the building of the Aquinas Memorial Stadium.

In 1947 he was appointed executive director of the nascent St John Fisher College in Rochester and, while living at Aquinas, spent two years drumming up support for the new college and establishing it on a sound financial basis. His vision and enterprise are seen in the choice of the site for the college, which is one of the most beautiful of all Basilian institutions. His own detailed account of the long-range planning for the college can be read in the on-line *History of St John Fisher College* noted below. On 11 December 1966, he was present at the dedication of a residence on the campus named in his honour.

Father Haffey never allowed his active life to preclude study, to which he devoted many of his summers. He earned an M.A. from the Université Laval in 1939 and a Ph.D. from the University of Ottawa in 1949, his thesis topic being 'The Philosophy of a Liberal Education.' He enrolled in Columbia University, New York, in the summer of 1940. In 1971–2 he took a year's sabbatical in Cambridge and Paris to do research about the life and thought of St John Fisher and to write the history of the college named for him.

In 1949 he left Rochester to teach at Catholic Central, Detroit, remaining there for two years before being appointed to the University of St Thomas, Houston, where he was to spend the rest of his life. There he established the Department of Education to train both elementary and secondary school teachers, and became widely known in the state educational organizations. In later years he taught political science and remained active in the life of the university after retirement.

Father Haffey exuded a contagious enthusiasm in all that he undertook, and was invariably the centre of conversation. He was a dynamic teacher, carefully prepared and never dull, with a gift for language, both imaginative and precise. In preparing homilies, he taped them and asked others for criticism. He preached every Sunday for several years at Corpus Christi Church, Houston. From his earliest days in the Basilian community he was appreciated for the good humour and light-heartedness which he brought to any gathering. One of the oft-repeated Basilian stories recounted his ceremony of first vows, which at that time was done in Latin. His loud stentorian voice intoned, 'Ego Hugo ... ,' which elicited laughter from his fellow novices that put the solemnity of the occasion at serious risk. A diabetic condition and a heart attack late in 1974 made him vulnerable to pneumonia of which he died early in January 1975, some two months short of his seventieth birthday. The homily at his funeral Mass in Rochester, preached by Father Charles J. *Lavery CSB, has been published at the end of the web-site indicated below.

BIBLIOGRAPHY:
Books: *Beginnings of St John Fisher College.* Rochester, 1977 (also on line at http://www.sjfc.edu/). *The American School. Readings.* Houston, [privately printed] n.d. *Student Teaching and Guide Book for Student Teachers.* Houston, [privately printed], 1969.
Articles: 'En été,' *Basilian* 3 (October 1937) 88–9; 'En hiver,' *Basilian* 4 (January 1938) 6–7; 'Preaching and Our Students,' *Basilian Teacher* 2 (February 1958) 16–19; 'Dramatics in the High School,' *Catholic School Journal* (December 1958) 26–7; 'Communication and Education,' *Basilian Teacher* 3 (May 1959) 216–27; 'Letter to the Editor [re: Western U.S. Regional Meeting of January 1966],' *Forum* 2 (April 1966) 60.
SOURCES: GABF; *Annals* 5 (1975) 125–7; *Newsletter* (13 January 1975).

HALE, Robert Barr, priest, was born on 17 October 1937 in Kitchener, Ontario (diocese of Hamilton), the son of Emmett Cecil Hale and Rita Mary Norman. He died in Windsor on 16 February 2000, and is buried in the Basilian plot of Holy Cross Cemetery, Thornhill, Ontario.
Bob Hale attended St Mary's grade school in Kitchener. When the family moved to St Catharines, Ontario, he completed his primary education and enrolled in St Catharines Collegiate. The family then moved to Calgary, Alberta, where Bob graduated from St Mary's Boys' High School. In 1962 he took a degree in business administration at the University of Western Ontario, and then worked for two years in sales and advertising. He entered St Basil's Novitiate, Erindale, Ontario, in 1964 and was professed on 15 September 1965. He taught two years at

Aquinas Institute, Rochester, before beginning his theology courses at St Basil's Seminary, Toronto, in 1967. He was ordained to the priesthood on 12 December 1970 in St Basil's Church, Toronto, by Cardinal George Bernard *Flahiff.

After completing theological studies in 1971 Father Hale stayed on at St Basil's College (formerly St Basil's 'Seminary') as college bursar, a charge he had assumed in 1971. In 1973 he was appointed to St Basil's Parish, Toronto, as assistant pastor, then as pastor in 1975. In 1982 he was moved to Christ the King Parish, Rochester, where he spent but one year before being called back to Toronto to the office of treasurer of the Pontifical Institute of Mediaeval Studies. In 1984 he became bursar of the University of St Michael's College, in which office he served for four years. In 1988 he returned to Christ the King in Rochester as pastor, which turned out to be the longest of his appointments. In 1999 he was moved to St John the Baptist Parish, Amherstburg, Ontario, where he served only six months before his unexpected death from a coronary attack at the age of sixty-two.

Bob Hale served willingly and efficiently as administrator; but pastoral work proved to be his true calling. A gentle and humorous man, he saw that each sick person in the parish was visited at least fortnightly. He would share important moments with his people, dropping in on weddings, baptism and confirmation parties, graduations, the bowling league nights, coffee hours, and the Rosary Guild meetings, 'just to say hello.' He was ever a teacher in his homilies, and strove to keep abreast of developments in theological and pastoral renewal. He was a much-appreciated chaplain to the police force, both in Irondequoit, near Rochester, and in Toronto. Representatives of the Ontario Provincial Police, the Metropolitan Toronto Police, and the Irondequoit Police served as pallbearers at his funeral, and the flag at the Irondequoit Town Hall flew at half mast after news of his death.

SOURCES: GABF; *Annals* 4 (1971) 175, 9 (2001) 86–7; *Newsletter* (9 March 2000).

HALL, Robert Alphonse, priest, was born on 18 January 1931 in Rochester, one of twin sons of Gerard Hall and Gladys Sherman. He died at Angleton, Texas, on 16 June 1989 and is buried in the Basilian plot of Holy Sepulchre Cemetery, Rochester.

Bob Hall attended St John the Evangelist parochial school and Aquinas Institute, Rochester, where mission appeals were taken seriously. His study there of Spanish and participation in the Spanish Club sparked his interest in Hispanic ministry. In 1948 he entered St Basil's Novitiate, Rochester, making first profession on 15 August 1949. He spent one year at Holy Rosary Seminary, Toronto, and then three years at Assumption College (B.A., University of Western Ontario, 1953). During those years at Assumption he taught mathematics in the high school section. Following graduation he taught world history for one year at St Thomas High School, Houston, before beginning theological studies at St Basil's Seminary, Toronto, in 1954 (S.T.B., University of St Michael's College, 1957). He was ordained to the priesthood on 29 June 1957 in St Basil's Church, Toronto, by Cardinal James Charles McGuigan.

In 1958, Father Hall began thirty-one years entirely devoted to the Hispanic ministry. His various appointments were as follows: Mission Center, Angleton, Texas, 1958–9; Mission Center, Rosenberg, Texas, 1959–63; San Juan Crisóstomo, Mexico City, 1963–4; Ste Anne's Parish, Detroit, 1964–7; St Theresa's Church, Sugar Land, Texas, 1967–74; pastor of Holy Family Parish, Stafford, Texas and Holy Family Parish, Missouri City, Texas, 1974–80; pastor of Our Lady of Mount Carmel Parish, Wharton, Texas, 1980–8; pastor of St Basil's Parish, Angleton, 1988–9.

The most noteworthy period of his life was his thirteen years as pastor of Holy Family Parish, where he planned and built the new complex in Missouri City when the parish centre moved from Stafford. A big man with a big heart and a talent for friendship, Father Hall won the respect of the people he served and of the wider ecumenical and secular community. When he was leaving the parish in 1980 the mayor of Missouri City declared 'Father Hall Week,' and presented him with a key to the city. Stafford also observed a 'Father Hall Day.' The local press referred to him as 'the gentle bear of a man who seems to be known by almost everyone, regardless of religious affiliation.' Another editorial noted, 'His generosity is widely known as is his work in the predominantly Spanish-speaking neighborhoods.' He opened the church facilities to many community organizations. He spent many hours translating election ballots and legal notices into Spanish for local precincts. His last appointment, to St Basil's and Santo Tomás de Aquino, Angleton, was destined to be short, for quite unexpectedly he died in his sleep, two weeks short of one year in the parish.

SOURCES: GABF; *Annals* 2 (1957) 317, 7 (1990) 117–18; *Newsletter* (29 June 1989).

HANRAHAN, John Patrick, priest, was born on 15 January 1915 in Windsor, the only child of John William Hanrahan and Anna Tiernan. He died in Toronto on 23 June 1993 and is buried in the Basilian plot of Holy Cross Cemetery, Thornhill, Ontario.

John ('Jack' or 'Hanny,' as he was called at various times) attended St Alphonsus Separate School and Assumption College School, Windsor. In August 1932, he entered St Basil's Novitiate, Toronto, making first profession on 15 August 1933. He was then appointed to St Michael's College, Toronto, and in 1935 to St Basil's Scholasticate (B.A., University of Toronto, 1937). During his first year of theology at St Basil's Seminary, 1937–8, he taught Latin and English at St Michael's College School, Toronto, and in his second year, 1938–9, he attended the Ontario College of Education (interim teaching certification, 1939). He taught Latin and English in the high school during his third year, 1939–40, and was ordained to the priesthood on 15 August 1940 in St Basil's Church, Toronto, by Archbishop James Charles McGuigan.

Except for one year of parochial ministry at St John the Baptist Parish, Amherstburg, Ontario, 1949–50, and a half-year at Our Lady of Guadalupe Parish, Rosenberg, Texas (January–June 1952), Father Hanrahan's ministry was chiefly in the high school setting. He taught French and Latin at Assumption College School, 1941–3, 1944–9, 1963–71. He taught the same subjects at Catholic Central High School, Detroit, 1950–1, and French, Spanish, and religion at Michael Power High School, Etobicoke, Ontario, 1959–63.

In December 1952, at that time stationed at Assumption College School, he withdrew from the community and from priestly ministry, entering into a civil marriage in Houston, where he found employment as a shipping clerk, and then moved to Galveston, Texas. In the summer of 1957 he petitioned the Basilian community for readmission, at least to the sacraments. His partner agreed, and they proceeded with a civil divorce. He remained in Galveston, living as a Catholic layman, until the spring of 1958 when he moved into the Basilian community at Wharton, Texas, where he continued to live as a layman, though he had resumed the obligation of the Divine Office. He worked in the parish office and assisted with chores around the church. In late 1958 the Holy See authorized Father Hanrahan to be readmitted to the Basilian community and to wear clerical garb, though he was not allowed to celebrate Mass. He received these decisions gratefully, and patiently awaited full integration and authorization, which came in 1970. By that time he had been back teaching since 1959, first at Michael Power and then at Assumption College School. In 1971 he retired from teaching and was given time for special ministry and renewal, while living for various periods at St Michael's College School, Assumption College School, and St Basil's College, Toronto. In his return to the community he brought the same gentleness of spirit, regard for others, and humble service which his confreres had known in his earlier life – now enhanced by a deep sense of gratitude. He lived in retirement at Assumption College School from 1974 to 1987, helping out in the guidance department. Serious deafness brought him to the Basilian Fathers Residence (Infirmary) in 1987. His death from a stroke was sudden: he was found dead in his room early in the morning, dressed and ready for the day.

BIBLIOGRAPHY: 'Nationalism,' *Basilian* 3 (March 1937) 48–9.
SOURCES: GABF; *Annals* 6 (1984) 208, 7 (1991) 4, 8 (1994) 133–5; *Newsletter* (5 August 1993).

HARRISON, Gerald Francis CANNING, priest, was born on 18 July 1905 in Toronto, the son of John Harrison and Hannah Moning. He died in Toronto on 3 January 1991, and is buried in the Basilian plot of Holy Cross Cemetery, Thornhill, Ontario.

Canning Harrison attended St Joseph's Separate School and the high school section of St Michael's College, Toronto. He worked for two years, 1925–7, in Detroit for the Pennsylvania Railway. He entered St Basil's Novitiate, Toronto, in September 1927, and was professed on 2 October 1928. During the next seven years of arts (B.A., University of Toronto, 1932) and theological studies he lived at the scholasticate or at St Michael's College, changing from one to the other at different times, and earning interim teaching certification from the Ontario College of Education in 1933. He was ordained to the priesthood on 15 June 1935 in St Basil's Church, Toronto, by Archbishop James Charles McGuigan.

In 1935 Father Harrison was appointed to Assumption College, Windsor, where he taught for two years. He received a permanent Ontario teaching certification in 1937. He spent one year teaching at Aquinas Institute, Rochester, before returning to Assumption for a period of fourteen years. There he taught French, Latin, music, and religion, and directed the band. During these years he spent the summers with the Royal Canadian Air Force in administration and drill work. In 1943 a squadron of the Air Cadets of Canada was organized at Assumption. Father Harrison was named its first commanding officer with the rank of Air Force Lieutenant. His band joined the cadets as a unit.

In 1952 he was appointed to Catholic Central High School, Detroit, where he was to spend the next thirty-three years, with the exception of one year, 1970–1, of sabbatical leave in France. At Catholic Central, along with his other teaching, he was in charge of the band, developing the latter into one of the most accomplished in the State of Michigan. He spent several summers at a variety of institutions to improve his knowledge of music: the Pius X School of Liturgical Music, New York, the Cincinnati Conservatory of Music, the Fred Waring School of Music, and St John's University, Collegeville, Minnesota. In 1973 he was asked to take over the Alumni Association at Catholic Central, a work he carried on until his departure from the school in 1985. By his inspiring messages in the *Aluminator*, his attendance at reunions, wakes, and funerals, and his open-door policy, he created a strong and spirited organization, which benefited the school immensely. In 1990 the Alumni Association initiated an 'Outstanding Alumni Award' named for him.

In 1985, his health failing, he was moved to the Basilian Residence (Infirmary), Toronto, leaving behind a host of friends in Detroit and a legacy of long and selfless priestly service to the school and the Church.

SOURCES: GABF; *Annals* 5 (1979) 341–2, 6 (1986) 395, 7 (1992) 124–5; *Newsletter* (19 January 1991).

HART, Leon George, priest, was born on 15 April 1925 in Rochester, the third of eight children of Leon George Hart and Rosemary Bauman. He died in Windsor on 28 January 1990 and is buried there in the Basilian plot of Heavenly Rest Cemetery.

Leon Hart attended St Charles parochial school and Aquinas Institute, Rochester. He entered St Basil's Novitiate, Rochester, in 1943 and was professed on 15 August 1944. He was then appointed to St Michael's College, Toronto (B.A., University of Toronto, 1948). He taught as a scholastic for three years: at Catholic Central High School, Detroit, 1948–9, during which he acquired Michigan teaching certification from the University of Detroit; at St Thomas High School, Houston, 1949–50, where he taught English and Latin and completed a year of theological studies; and at Aquinas Institute, 1950–1. He completed his theology courses at St Basil's Seminary, Toronto, and was ordained to the priesthood on 29 June 1953 in St Basil's Church, Toronto, by Cardinal James Charles McGuigan.

In 1954 Father Hart began twenty-one years at Aquinas Institute, where he became executive vice-principal in 1956 and principal in 1964. He attended summer sessions at the Catholic University of America and at the University of Rochester (M.Ed., 1958), and participated in seminars for principals organized by the University of Rochester. In 1968 he was chosen to be a participant in the I/D/E/A Fellows Program for School Administrators. After he completed his term as principal in 1970, the diocese of Rochester appointed him Associate Superintendent of Schools and Director of Public Relations for the academic year 1970-1. In 1974 he was appointed vice-principal of Assumption College School, Windsor, and was elected to the Basilian local council. He was named local superior in 1984 and 1987. He was due to retire in June 1990, and was planning to take courses in theological renewal, but a stroke that year proved fatal.

Leon Hart was known as one who cared for the struggling student. He promoted vocations to the priesthood and the involvement of the laity in the life of the Church. He was a strong advocate of the Basilian Lay Associate program in Windsor. He organized outings for the teaching staff for skiing and golf, and often served as cook for these groups.

BIBLIOGRAPHY: 'The School Newspaper,' *Basilian Teacher* 1 (May 1956) 7-8; 'Entrance Examinations,' *Basilian Teacher* 3 (March 1959) 169-71; 'Mathematics in Basilian Schools [forum],' *Basilian Teacher* 4 (December 1959) 68-9.
SOURCES: GABF; *Annals* 2 (1953) 109, 7 (1991) 139-41; *Newsletter* (28 February 1990).

HARTMANN, Edward Joseph, priest, was born at Brantford, Ontario (diocese of Hamilton) on 12 July 1904, the son of John Hartmann and Ellen McCusker. He died in Windsor on 28 April 1957 and was buried there in the Basilian plot of Assumption Cemetery.

Edward Hartmann attended St Basil's Separate School in Brantford and Brantford Collegiate Institute before going to St Michael's College, Toronto (B.A., University of Toronto, 1928). He entered St Basil's Novitiate, Toronto, and made first profession on 12 September 1929. He attended the Ontario College of Education in Toronto, 1929-30, taught at Catholic Central High School, Detroit, 1930-1, made his theological studies at St Basil's Scholasticate, Toronto, and was ordained to the priesthood on 21 December 1932 in St Basil's Church by Bishop Alexander MacDonald.

Father Hartmann was appointed to the first Basilian staff at St Mary's Boys' High School, Calgary, Alberta. He taught there from 1933 until 1941, when he enlisted as a chaplain in the Royal Canadian Air Force. In one of his letters from England he wrote of ministering to nine boys he had taught in Calgary, one of whom he buried in an English cemetery. At the end of the war he was appointed Dean of Residence at St Michael's College. The next year he went to teach at Catholic Central High School, and while there obtained an M.A. in English at the University of Detroit. He was appointed to Assumption University, Windsor, in 1949. At the time of his death from a heart attack in 1957 he was assistant professor of English, dean of men, director of placement, and beadle for the University Convocation.

Father Hartmann had the endearing knack of turning routine and dull situations into occasions for humour. In reminiscences written for the *Alumni Times* of Assumption University, however, Father Cornelius *Crowley pointed out another side of Father Hartmann's life. An elderly couple who had known Father Hartmann in Detroit told Father Crowley, 'It may seem odd to say this, but he had such elegance.' This led Father Crowley to write, 'His specialty was the literature of the eighteenth century, the culture of an age of balance and decorum. He joked a lot about carrying the mace at Convocation, but he carried it with grace and a dignity in keeping with the ancient academic ceremony. Actually, he had a great love of tradition.'

BIBLIOGRAPHY: 'St Mary's Boys' School, Calgary,' *Basilian* 1 (November 1935) 108–9.
SOURCES: GABF; *Annals* 1 (1944) 51–2, (1945) 88, 2 (1957) 296–7; C.P. Crowley, 'Rev. Edward Hartmann CSB,' *Alumni Times, Assumption University* 2 (Summer 1957) 11–12; *Yearbook SMC* 19 (1928).

HAYES, Thomas James, priest, member of the Congregation 1886–1923, was born on a farm in Oro Township, Simcoe County, Ontario (archdiocese of Toronto), on 2 October 1862, the son of James Hayes and Mary Balf. He died at Kalamazoo, Michigan, on 12 May 1928 and was buried in Mount Hope Cemetery, Toronto.

Thomas attended the local rural school, but at the age of fourteen left home and worked at Holland Landing, Ontario, until 1881, when he went to St Michael's College, Toronto, to study for the priesthood. On 20 October 1886 he entered St Basil's Novitiate at Beaconfield House, Plymouth, England. After profession in 1887 he made his theological studies at St Michael's College, pronounced his final vows on 16 December 1890, and was ordained a priest on 16 December 1891 at St Basil's Church, Toronto, by Archbishop John Walsh.

Father Hayes taught at St Michael's College until January 1893, when he was sent for six months to Assumption College, Windsor. During the year 1893–4 he was in charge of Holy Rosary Parish, Toronto. In August 1894 he returned to Assumption College where he remained until 1898, when he was appointed assistant at St Mary's of the Assumption Parish, Owen Sound, Ontario. One year later he was named founding superior of St Basil's College, Waco, Texas. The business acumen he showed in this post, 1899–1903, was next used as treasurer first at Assumption College, 1903–7, and then at St Michael's College, 1907–14. During the year 1910–11 Father Hayes was also named acting superior of St Michael's College. From 1914 until 1922 he served as pastor of St Basil's Parish, Toronto, and in 1922 as pastor of St Mary's of the Assumption Parish in Owen Sound. In October of that year he went on sick leave. A few months later he decided against taking the new, stricter vow of poverty, withdrew from the Congregation, and was incardinated in the archdiocese of Detroit on 23 May 1924. He was appointed assistant at St Augustine's Parish in Kalamazoo, Michigan, where he died four years later.

Father Hayes was just under six feet tall and powerfully built. For years he had two nicknames, 'Guy' and 'Daddy.' He was an outstanding teacher. The centennial booklet of St Basil's Parish, Toronto, listed him as a pastor in 'The Golden Age' of the parish and went on to say, 'He is remembered as a devoted, energetic pastor. ... He guided the parish through the years of the First War and was beloved for his kindness and friendliness to all.' He was a fine preacher with a 'great voice.' From Waco he went out to preach missions as a way of making St Basil's College known and of financing it as well. At Assumption College he founded the St Dionysius Literary Society in 1896 to encourage public speaking among high school students. For some years he served as provincial treasurer. He was always popular with the diocesan clergy.

SOURCES: GABF; Archives, Archdiocese of Detroit; *Centennial, St Mary's*; *Jubilee, Assumption*; *Jubilee, St Mary's*; Kirley, *Congregation in France* 4, 12, 57; Madden, *St Basil's*; *Purple and White* (10 June 1928).

HENNESSEY, Wilfrid BRIAN, priest, was born on 21 February 1919 in Ottawa, the son of Hugh Hennessey and Eveleen McCann. He died in Toronto on 23 May 1993 and is buried in the Basilian plot of Holy Cross Cemetery, Thornhill, Ontario.

Brian Hennessey attended Corpus Christi Separate School, De La Salle High School (Bond Street), and Riverdale Collegiate, Toronto, graduating in 1937. In 1941 he enlisted in the Royal Canadian Navy, serving for four years and reaching the rank of Petty Officer. Upon discharge in 1945 he worked as a supply officer for the United Nations Relief and Rehabilitation Administration (UNRRA), which took him to different towns and cities in West Germany for the next two years. In the fall of 1947 he enrolled in Queen's University, Kingston, Ontario, where he obtained an Honours English B.A. in 1951.

During his summer months while at the university he worked in the newsroom of Kingston's *Whig Standard*. In 1951 he enrolled in graduate courses in philosophy at St Michael's College, Toronto, and one year later entered St Basil's Novitiate, Richmond Hill, Ontario, being professed on 12 September 1953. From the novitiate he was appointed to St Basil's Seminary, Toronto, for theological studies, which he did concurrently with graduate studies in philosophy (M.A., University of Toronto [thesis: 'A Treatise on Image as Sign in the Doctrine of the Concept according to St Thomas Aquinas']; S.T.B., University of St Michael's College, 1956). He was ordained to the priesthood on 8 December 1956 in the chapel of St Basil's Seminary by Bishop Francis Allen.

In 1957 Father Hennessey was appointed to St Michael's College, where he was to remain for thirty-four years. With the exception of two years as registrar of the college, he gave himself entirely to the teaching of English literature, which he loved and at which he excelled, 'communicating his spontaneous enthusiasm for the ideas and insights he saw in what he taught, providing an inspiring example of what it is to be a teacher, and coming across with an unpretentious humanity that made him always ready to be not only a teacher but a friend' (Father Frederick *Black in the funeral homily). A sharp wit and a ready sense of humour, often expressed in short verse or limericks, enlivened his classes and his company.

Brian Hennessey was a rather private person and one not readily fathomed. He struggled with belief and with the circumstances of community life, though his sincere love for the Basilian community was undoubted. His geniality in company was offset by a certain angst which was evident at times to others but which never found explanation or relief. He retired from full-time teaching in 1984, but continued on a part-time basis until the leukemia which had been sapping his strength for some six years necessitated his move to the Basilian Fathers Residence (Infirmary) in 1991. Two years later, on the feast of the Ascension of the Lord, he died peacefully in his sleep.

BIBLIOGRAPHY: 'Checkpoints for Teachers,' *Basilian Teacher* 8 (December 1963) 130–1; 'Heavens Above,' *Basilian Teacher* 8 (December 1963) 148–50; 'Art and the Pawnbroker,' *Basilian Teacher* 9 (November 1965) 546–8.
SOURCES: GABF; *Annals* 2 (1957) 314, 8 (1994) 128–30; *Newsletter* (8 June 1993).

HEYCK, Eugene Adams, priest, was born on 30 August 1921 in Houston, the son of Eugene Heyck and Leonora Adams. He died in Houston on 6 April 1989 and is buried there in the Basilian plot, Garden of Gethsemane, Forest Park Lawndale Cemetery.

'Gene' Heyck completed his elementary education at parochial schools in Houston. He was valedictorian in his graduating class of seventy-six at St Thomas High School, Houston, in 1939. He enrolled at Rice Institute, Houston, where he completed four years of a five-year course in mechanical engineering. He served in the U.S. Army Air Corps, 1942–6, part of this time at the Pentagon. In the absence of the commanding general, Gene was asked to do a facsimile of the general's signature and thus signed his own discharge papers. He returned to Rice Institute, graduated with a B.Sc. degree in 1947, and entered St Basil's Novitiate, Rochester, that same year. He made first profession on 15 August 1948. He was appointed to Assumption College, Windsor, for one year of philosophy and then to St Michael's College, Toronto, where he did two years of theology, transferring to St Basil's Seminary for his final two years. He was ordained to the priesthood on 14 June 1952 in St Anne's Church, Houston, by Bishop Wendelin J. Nold.

Father Heyck did graduate studies at the University of Toronto (B.Com., 1955). He taught accounting, algebra, engineering drawing, and calculus at the University of St Thomas, Houston, for two years. In 1957 he joined the staff of St Anne's Parish as assistant pastor, also serving as guidance counsellor and chaplain at Marian High School, Houston. He spent one year, 1962–3, as chaplain of the Newman Centre, University of Toronto, and was then asked to help plan and establish the new Basilian scholasticate on the campus of St John Fisher College, Rochester. Here he served as master of scholastics for the years 1963–6. For the year 1966–7 he taught religion at Andrean High

School, Gary (now Merrillville), Indiana, where he was also guidance counsellor for junior and senior boys.

After one more year at the University of St Thomas, his desire to serve in a parish led to his appointment again to St Anne's Parish as assistant in 1968 and then as pastor of St Basil's Parish, Angleton, Texas, in 1970. In 1977 he went as assistant to Holy Family Parish, Missouri City, Texas. During a half-sabbatical in 1981, he toured Australia and New Zealand, helping out at various parishes as he travelled. On his return in 1982, he was assistant pastor to Monsignor Leroy Braden first at St Christopher's Parish, Houston, and from 1984 at St Helen's Parish, Pearland, Texas, while associated with the Basilian community at the University of St Thomas. In 1988 ill health forced his retirement.

Gene Heyck worked tirelessly up to his last years, when a heart condition first reduced his activity and then caused his death. He was especially drawn to counselling and convert instruction. At St Helen's he was chaplain to the Knights of Columbus and Faithful Friar of the Bishop Nold Fourth Degree Assembly. His training in engineering and accounting afforded valuable aid in building the Rochester scholasticate and the rectory at St Helen's Parish. He was well versed in liturgy, even from his earliest years as a priest, proposing a revision of the *Roman Breviary* based on an extensive study and sounding of opinion, ten years prior to the Second Vatican Council.

SOURCES: GABF; *Annals* 2 (1952) 59, 7 (1990) 117–18; *Newsletter* (21 April 1989).

HEYDON, Thomas Joseph, priest, nephew of Father Michael *Ferguson, was born in Elmgrove, a pioneer settlement near Adjala, Ontario (archdiocese of Toronto), on 17 June 1857, the son of James Heydon and Katherine Ferguson. He died in Toronto on 9 March 1935 and was buried there in the Basilian plot of Mount Hope Cemetery.

Thomas Heydon attended rural schools and, in 1875, went to St Michael's College, Toronto. In October 1879 he transferred to Assumption College, Windsor, where he taught junior classes, took his turn on recreation duty, and completed two years of theology before entering St Basil's Novitiate at Beaconfield House, Plymouth, England. After first profession on 19 December 1884 he spent two years at the College of Mary Immaculate, Beaconfield House, completing his course in theology. He returned to Canada in the summer of 1886 and was ordained priest on 10 October of that year.

Father Heydon, who suffered from anaemia all his life, spent the first months after ordination on sick leave. On his return to Assumption in 1887 he taught until 1894, when he was appointed master of novices at St Basil's Novitiate, Toronto. Then he taught at St Michael's College, 1895-6, after which he went back to Assumption College. He served as assistant at St Mary's of the Assumption Parish, Owen Sound, Ontario, 1899–1901, and during the year 1902–3 was on the staff of St Basil's Scholasticate, Toronto. From 1903 until 1910 he was on loan to the diocese of Hamilton, Ontario, where he served as pastor of St Martin's Parish, Drayton. He returned to St Michael's in 1910 and in 1916 went again to Assumption, where his lifelong love of books brought him the post of librarian. From 1922 to 1925 he was assistant at St John the Baptist Parish, Amherstburg, Ontario. He retired to St Michael's in 1925.

Father Heydon was called 'Buck' from his love of horses. He was known as well for his love of playing the violin. Though never an athlete himself, he promoted the athletic programs at Assumption with gifts of equipment. When he decided against taking the new, stricter vow of poverty in 1923, he wrote to Father Francis Forster of his attachment to the Congregation: 'I have belonged to it for full fifty years. ... I purpose to remain on, obedient to its rules, trying to live in peace and good fellowship with all, and doing what I can in its best interests.'

SOURCES: GABF; *Basilian* 1 (April 1935) 36; *Centennial, St Mary's*; Charles Collins, 'Basilians I Have Known,' transcribed in Robert J. Scollard, 'Historical Notes C.S.B.' 10 107–12 (GABF); *Jubilee, Assumption*; *Jubilee, St Mary's*; Kirley, *Congregation in France* 10; Spetz, *Waterloo*; *Yearbook SMC* (1935).

HIGGINS, Albert LELAND, priest, cousin of Father John *Hussey, was born on 31 March 1908 in Buffalo, New York, the son of John Higgins and Lillian Lyons. He died in Toronto on 10 August 1991, and is buried in the Basilian plot of Heavenly Rest Cemetery, Windsor.

When 'Lee' was a child, the family moved to Detroit, though he attended Assumption College, Windsor. Upon graduation from the high school in 1926 he entered St Basil's Novitiate, Toronto, and was professed on 11 August 1927. He was then appointed to Assumption College (B.A., Honours Philosophy, University of Western Ontario, 1931). Following graduation he was appointed to St Basil's Scholasticate, Toronto, for theological studies, during the first year of which he also attended the Ontario College of Education, earning teaching certification, 1932. During the academic year 1932–3 he lived at St Michael's College, and taught in the high school section. He was ordained to the priesthood on 16 December 1934, in Assumption Church, Windsor, by Bishop John Kidd.

In 1935 Father Higgins was appointed to St Thomas High School, Houston, where he was to remain for seven years and where, in 1937 at twenty-nine years of age, he was named superior and principal of the school. He planned and oversaw the move from the Austin Street school to the new campus on the banks of Buffalo Bayou. He earned an M.A. from the University of Houston in 1942 and was awarded an honorary LL.D. from St Edward's University, Austin, Texas, the same year. In 1943 he joined the United States Army Chaplain Corps with the rank of captain, and attended the Military Chaplain School at Harvard. For his three years of service he was awarded the American Theater Campaign Medal and the Victory Medal. On returning to community life in September 1946 Father Higgins was appointed to Assumption High School for two years and then to St Anne's Parish, Houston, as pastor and rector, 1948–50. It was during this time that he made the front page of the Houston papers when from the pulpit he denounced the air-conditioning of the monkey cages at the city zoo while indigent patients of the city tuberculosis hospital languished in squalid conditions. He taught at Catholic Central High School, Detroit, 1950–2, and once more at Assumption High School, 1952–5.

In 1954 Father Higgins was elected to the general council of the Basilian Fathers, which meant regular meetings in Toronto and periodic visits to the various houses of the Congregation. In 1955 he took up residence at Ste Anne's Parish, Detroit, where he served as assistant pastor as well as first councillor for the local community. Moving to Catholic Central in 1957, he taught part-time while planning what was to become Andrean High School, Gary (now Merrillville), Indiana. In 1958 he was appointed to Gary for two years to supervise the construction of the new school. In 1960 he went to Aquinas Institute, Rochester, to teach and serve as Director of Vocations.

In 1962 Father Higgins began twenty-two years as procurator for the Basilian Fathers Missions, which at that time were extending from Texas into Mexico itself. More than any of his other successful apostolates this stands out particularly for the zeal, energy, imagination, and total dedication he brought to it. He was tireless in mission appeals up and down the continent, and his animated, humorous, and gospel-filled sermons made the Basilian Missions known and supported throughout North America. Once, when asked what was his greatest wish, he replied, 'I should like to die in the pulpit,' adding, 'Think of the collection!'

In 1983 a severe stroke deprived him of speech – except for the single phrase *per omnia saecula saeculorum* (the closing words of Latin prayers that he had employed so often), which he would utter or shout on any and every occasion. It was ironic that so fine an orator should be reduced to but one phrase, but it was a touching witness to his vocation in life.

BIBLIOGRAPHY: 'Restoring Right Order in Athletics,' *Basilian* 2 (March 1936) 49–50.
SOURCES: GABF; *Annals* 1 (1945) 90, 5 (1978) 268, 6 (1985) 307, 7 (1992) 133–5; *Newsletter* (5 September 1991).

HILAIRE, Firmin, priest, was born on 24 April 1865 at Montréal (Ardèche), the son of Firmin Hilaire and Mélanie Fayolle. He died in Annonay on 3 February 1893 and was buried there in the cemetery on the grounds of the Collège du Sacré-Coeur.

Firmin Hilaire was a student at the Ecole cléricale in Lyon and from there went to the Collège du Sacré-Coeur, section Sainte-Barbe, Annonay, for the years 1880–4. He made his novitiate at Beaconfield House, Plymouth, England, 1884–5. While studying theology he worked at Sacré-Coeur for one year, at the Petit Séminaire de Vernoux (Ardèche) for two years, at the Ecole cléricale de Périgueux (Dordogne) for one year, and at Sainte-Barbe, Annonay, for one year. He was ordained to the priesthood in the chapel of the Collège du Sacré-Coeur by Bishop Pierre Dufal CSC, former coadjutor of Galveston, Texas, on 20 September 1890.

Father Hilaire taught for one year at the Petit Séminaire de Vernoux, 1890–1, and was then named to the parish of Saint-Félix-de-Châteauneuf (Ardèche). After two months, however, he was forced to give up this post because of serious illness. He returned to Sacré-Coeur as prefect and professor and died there a year and a half later in his twenty-eighth year. The *Semaine religieuse de Viviers* said of Father Hilaire: 'He left to his students a most favourable memory of his presence among them.'

SOURCES: GABF; Pouzol, 'Notices'; *Semaine religieuse de Viviers* (10 February 1893).

HILAIRE, Joseph, priest, brother of Father Louis *Hilaire and of Father Régis Hilaire, a diocesan priest who became vicar general of the diocese of Viviers, was born at Montréal (Ardèche) on 11 June 1838, the son of Joseph Hilaire and Victoire Anne Mouraret. He died on 13 June 1915 at Montréal, and was buried in the parish cemetery there.

Joseph Hilaire did his studies at the Collège de Privas, attracted there by his compatriot André *Fayolle, one of the ten founders of the Basilians and superior of the college at that time. Joseph worked as prefect and professor, 1859–62. He was at the Collège du Sacré-Coeur, Annonay, for one year prior to his ordination to the priesthood on 19 September 1863, seemingly at Feyzin (Isère, now Rhône), by Bishop Armand de Charbonnel. This was the first ordination by the bishop after his resignation from the see of Toronto in 1860.

Father Hilaire taught at the Petit Séminaire de Vernoux (Ardèche) until 1872, though his whereabouts during the year 1864–5 are obscure, since he is not mentioned in the *Ordo* of Viviers for that year. He spent the years 1872–5 at the Collège de Privas (Ardèche) and then one year at the Petit Séminaire de Vernoux. He worked as director of studies at the Collège du Sacré-Coeur, 1876–96, and as superior of the Petit Séminaire de Vernoux, 1896–1903. In 1903, with the expulsion of religious congregations from schools, he was forced to leave Vernoux, though the institution continued under diocesan direction until 1906. After his expulsion Father Hilaire became chaplain to the Religieuses de l'Immaculée Conception at Meysse (Ardèche). In 1914, stricken with a long and painful illness, his ministry to the nuns was much curtailed, and his last days were spent with his family at Montréal.

SOURCES: GABF; Kirley, *Community in France* 70n178, 142, 147n373, 163n416, 165n421, 172, 184, 200n492, 201, 205; Pouzol, 'Notices'; *Semaine religieuse de Viviers* (2 July 1915) 164–5.

HILAIRE, Louis, priest, brother of Father Joseph *Hilaire and of Father Régis Hilaire, a diocesan priest who became vicar general of the diocese of Viviers, was born at Montréal (Ardèche) on 11 August 1844, the son of Joseph Hilaire and Victoire Anne Mouraret. He died at Montréal on 12 September 1935 and was buried in the cemetery there.

Louis Hilaire attended the Collège de Privas (Ardèche) because his brother Joseph was there, as was his compatriot Father André *Fayolle, one of the ten founders of the Basilians and superior of the college at that time. He remained at Privas until 1863, when he began his novitiate at Feyzin (Isère, now Rhône). While studying theology he taught successively at the Collège des Cordeliers, Annonay, 1864–5, the Petit Séminaire de Vernoux (Ardèche), 1865–7, and the Collège du Sacré-Coeur, Annonay, 1867–9. In December of 1868 he replaced Father Julien *Tracol in producing the *Journal du Collège*, but his health prevented him from continuing that work. In October of 1869 he went to the Petit Séminaire de Vernoux where his brother Joseph was working, and remained there until 1871, when he was ordained to the priesthood on 8 April 1871 in the cathedral at Viviers by Bishop Louis Delcusy.

Father Hilaire was stationed at the Collège du Bourg-Saint-Andéol (Ardèche) for nine years. He spent twenty-three years as bursar, first at Vernoux, 1880–8, then at Sacré-Coeur, 1888–91, and again at Vernoux, 1891–1903. When anticlerical laws in 1908 excluded the Basilians from teaching, he worked in parish ministry at Vernoux for a year, at Grospierres (Ardèche) for a few months, at Chalencon (Ardèche) for a year, and then at Les Vans (Ardèche) for six years. He was treasurer general of the Congregation from January 1907 to July 1910. He took part in the general chapter in Geneva, 5–11 July 1910. In 1911 he retired but continued helping out in the parish at Les Vans. In June of 1922 Bishop Joseph-Michel-Frédéric Bonnet of Viviers named him an honorary canon of his cathedral. In June 1931 he celebrated his sixtieth anniversary of ordination and died three months later.

Chanoine Fromenton described Father Louis Hilaire as a man of many talents: a painter, a musician, a choir leader, and a most capable treasurer.

SOURCES: GABF; Chomel, *Collège d'Annonay* 516; Chanoine Fromenton, *Petit séminaire de Vernoux* (Aubenas, 1922); Kirley, *Community in France* 150n384, 182n464, 184, 204; Kirley, *Congregation in France* 12, 42, 82; Pouzol, 'Notices'; *Semaine religieuse de Viviers* (3 July 1931) 316.

HOLMES, Arthur Joseph, priest, brother of Father Robert Holmes CSB, was born on 6 May 1930 in Toronto, one of four sons of Arthur Holmes and Mary Helen Kernahan. He died in Syracuse, New York, on 12 July 1994 and is buried in the Basilian plot of Holy Cross Cemetery, Thornhill, Ontario.

'Art' attended Blessed Sacrament Separate School and the high school section of St Michael's College, Toronto. In 1948 he registered at St Michael's College for undergraduate studies, with a major in mathematics, at the University of Toronto. In 1950 he entered St Basil's Novitiate, Richmond Hill, Ontario, where he made first profession on 15 August 1951. He was then appointed to St Basil's Seminary, Toronto, to complete his degree (B.A., University of Toronto, 1953). He taught part-time at St Michael's College School, while studying theology, and full-time during the academic year 1954-5. He was ordained to the priesthood on 29 June 1957 in St Basil's Church, Toronto, by Cardinal James Charles McGuigan.

Father Holmes taught mathematics all his priestly life in two Basilian schools: St Michael's College School, 1958-65 and 1976-94, and St Charles College, Sudbury, 1965-76. He employed a method and discipline that challenged students to discover and then immediately apply mathematical principles. Strict in method, manner, and assignment, he was at the same time the patient servant of his students. He is considered as possibly the most remarkable teacher of mathematics the Basilians have produced.

An avid athlete who had played and coached both football and hockey, his spirit, cleverness, toughness, and agility amply compensated for what he lacked in size and weight. He brought to coaching the same skill in method and precision that made his classes so remarkable. Although rather shy and taciturn in company, he was by no means withdrawn. He did not take comfortably to the changes in customs and liturgy which followed the Second Vatican Council. In his last ten years Father Holmes became very involved with Alcoholics Anonymous, finding in this community both healing for himself and a new ministry of healing and spiritual counsel for others with addictions.

SOURCES: GABF; *Annals* 2 (1957) 317, 8 (1995) 103-4; *Newsletter* (21 September 1994).

HOUDE, Adelore Louis, priest, member of the Congregation 1937-55, was born in Sault Ste Marie, Ontario, on 25 January 1915, the son of Carus and Isabelle Houde. He died in Orange County, California, in 1986.

Adelore was educated at a Catholic grade school and public high school in the Sault. Three years after graduation he entered the Basilian novitiate in Toronto, making first profession in 1937 (final profession,

1940). He did Honours Mathematics and Physics at the University of Toronto (B.A., 1941). He taught for one year at St Thomas High School, Houston, did his theological studies at St Basil's Seminary, Toronto, 1942–6, being ordained to the priesthood on 15 August 1945 in St Basil's Church, Toronto, by Archbishop James Charles McGuigan.

After teaching for two years at St Michael's College, Toronto, 1946-8, Father Houde began graduate studies, first in Toronto (M.A., 1949), and then at the University of Notre Dame, Indiana (Ph.D., 1951). He was assigned to teach at St John Fisher College, Rochester. At the end of the school year 1954–5, he left the Congregation to contract a civil marriage. He moved to Manhattan Beach, California, and had two daughters, Lori Martha and Marcelline Elinor. He taught physics one year, 1957–8, at California Polytechnic College in San Luis Obispo. In 1958 the family moved to Los Alamitos, California, and he took a job with Ford Aeronautics in Newport Beach. In 1962 he was divorced and immediately made overtures to return to the Basilians and the priesthood. A correspondence of nearly ten years attests to the negotiations on his behalf, and it was only in December of 1971 that his status was regularized and that further steps could be taken for his return to the Congregation. In the end, however, he himself decided not to go forward with the process, resolving to live as a layman in full communion with the Church.

'Ad' Houde was a man of multiple talents. A fine oil painting that he did of a view of St Michael's College campus, when the tennis courts were in the present-day Quadrangle, hangs in the faculty dining room there.

BIBLIOGRAPHY: (With E.G. Brock and E.A. Coomes). 'Periodic Deviations in the Schottky Effect for Molybdenum,' *Physical Review* 89 (15 February 1953) 851–4.
SOURCE: GABF.

HOURDIN (OURDIN), Henri, priest, was born at Vernoux (Ardèche) on 2 May 1838. He died on 26 June 1878 at the Petit Séminaire d'Aubenas (Ardèche).

Henri Hourdin did his classical studies at the Petit Séminaire de Vernoux. He made his novitiate at Privas (Ardèche) in 1858–9 under Father Auguste de *Montgolfier, then taught at the Collège de Privas from 1859 to 1863 while studying theology. He was ordained to the priesthood on 30 May 1863 at Viviers by Bishop Louis Delcusy.

Father Hourdin spent the year 1863–4 at the Collège des Cordeliers,

Annonay, before teaching three years at the Petit Séminaire d'Aubenas, 1864–7, and then six years at the Collège de Privas, the last year being at the Juvénat which had replaced the college. Of the year 1873–4 he spent the first two trimesters at the novitiate at Feyzin (Isère, now Rhône) and the third as bursar at the Petit Séminaire d'Aubenas. From 1874 to 1878 he was director and bursar at Sainte-Barbe, Annonay, assisting Father André *Charmant.

In June 1878, after treatment for a liver ailment at Vals-les-Bains (Ardèche) failed to improve his condition – which, in fact, worsened – Father Hourdin moved to the Petit Séminaire d'Aubenas, where, the day after his arrival, he died in the arms of Father Patrick *Molony (Moloney), who administered the last rites.

SOURCES: GABF; Pouzol, 'Notices.'

HOURS, Basile, priest, elder brother of Father François-Régis *Hours, was born at Malbosc (Ardèche) on 29 November 1817, the son of Jean-Pierre Hours and Agathe Robert. He died in Annonay on 30 May 1898 and was buried there in the cemetery on the grounds of the Collège du Sacré-Coeur.

Basile Hours was a student at the Collège des Cordeliers, Annonay, section Sainte-Barbe, from 1834 to 1836. He studied at the Grand Séminaire de Viviers (Ardèche) where he received minor orders. He spent the year 1841–2 at the Collège de Feyzin (Isère, now Rhône) as a teacher, and the following year he made his novitiate there under Father Henri *Coupat. He was ordained to the priesthood by Bishop Joseph-Hippolyte Guibert of Viviers in the church at Vernoux (Ardèche) on 25 May 1852. Prior to ordination, while completing theological studies, he taught at the Collège de Privas (Ardèche), 1843–7, and at the Petit Séminaire de Vernoux, 1847–52.

After ordination his teaching assignments were as follows: Vernoux, 1852–3, 1856–7, and 1860–6; Collège des Cordeliers, Annonay, 1853–6; Collège de Privas, 1857–60 and 1866–71; and the Petit Séminaire d'Aubenas (Ardèche), 1871–5. For the next two years he was assistant master of novices at Feyzin and from then on his activity was mainly in the domain of spiritual direction, although from October 1875 to February 1876 he taught in Annonay, replacing Father Victorin *Marijon, who had been injured in an accident. Father Hours was then sent again to Vernoux for one year, and from there back to the novitiate for two years until it was closed in 1880 by the anticlerical laws of the Third

Republic. In that year he returned to Annonay, but from 1882 to 1885 he was spiritual director at the Petit Séminaire de Vernoux while also teaching theology. From 1885 to 1893 he was spiritual director at the Collège du Sacré-Coeur, Annonay. For the last five years of his life he was assistant at the novitiate in Annonay.

Father Hours was a pious, courageous, and dedicated priest, timid and, in his youth, somewhat scrupulous, as his belated ordination at the age of thirty-five might indicate.

SOURCES: GABF; Chanoine Fromenton, *Petit séminaire de Vernoux* (Aubenas, 1922); Kirley, *Community in France* 70n178, 124n305; Pouzol, 'Notices'; Roume, *Origines* 346.

HOURS, Charles, aspirant, nephew of Father Basile *Hours and of Father François-Régis *Hours, was born at Alès (Haute-Garonne, diocese of Nîmes), in 1851. He died in Annonay on 21 March 1878 and was buried there in the cemetery on the grounds of the Collège du Sacré-Coeur.

Charles Hours had health problems early in life, and the reception of tonsure was deferred for that reason. From 1875 to 1878 he was working at the Collège du Sacré-Coeur as prefect and teacher. At the beginning of February 1878 he fell seriously ill and died shortly thereafter. His uncle Father Basile *Hours conducted the funeral service. His other Basilian uncle, Father François-Régis *Hours, was stationed in Canada at that time. Although admission to the novitiate had been postponed for reasons of health, he still appears to have been considered a 'confrere.'

SOURCE: Pouzol, 'Notices.'

HOURS, François Régis, priest, younger brother of Father Basile *Hours, was born in Malbosc (Ardèche) on 9 March 1832, the son of Jean Pierre Hours and Agathe Robert. He died on 23 April 1897 in Detroit, and was buried in Assumption Cemetery, Windsor.

After studies at the Collège des Cordeliers, Annonay, François Régis entered the Basilian novitiate in 1851. He studied theology while teaching at the college, 1851–5. He was ordained priest by Bishop Joseph-Hippolyte Guibert on 21 October 1855 in the chapel of the Collège des Cordeliers.

After ordination he taught at the Collège de Privas (Ardèche) for two years, then in Annonay for six years, and was bursar at Privas, 1863–5. He spent the first six months of 1866 at Feyzin (Isère, now Rhône) under Father Patrick *Molony (Moloney) preparing for ministry in Canada. He left France on 12 May 1866 and spent a year at St Michael's College, Toronto, as bursar. He was the founder and superior of St Louis College, Louisville, Ohio, 1867–73. When this foundation was closed in 1873 he was appointed master of novices at Assumption College, Windsor. In 1874 he was named pastor of St Joseph's Parish, Chatham, Ontario, and served there until the Congregation withdrew from this parish in 1878. He served at St Mary's of the Assumption Parish, Owen Sound, Ontario, 1883–6, and then as special assistant to the provincial, Father Charles *Vincent, 1886–90. He was stationed at St Charles Parish, Newport, Michigan, 1890–1, and in the latter year was appointed to Ste Anne's Parish, Detroit, where he remained for the rest of his life.

In temperament Father Hours was a mild-mannered priest, sociable in a quiet way, and able to fit in anywhere.

SOURCES: GABF; *Centennial, St Mary's*; *Jubilee, St Mary's*; *Ordo*, diocese of Viviers (1864); Kirley, *Community in France* 33, 35, 70, 124n304, 204nn515–16, 219n526, 234n561, 235, 237n565, 238, 239; Kirley, *Congregation in France* 45; Pouzol, 'Notices.'

HOWARD, Patrick Joseph, priest, was born in Worcester, Massachusetts, on 6 March 1866, the son of Thomas Howard and Mary Redican. He died in Windsor on 30 May 1929 and was buried there in the Basilian plot of Assumption Cemetery.

Patrick Howard attended local Worcester schools and graduated from the high school division of Holy Cross College. Years later Holy Cross College conferred upon him an honorary degree of Master of Arts. When he finished high school, he worked as a barber until November 1893, when he went to St Michael's College, Toronto, to study for the priesthood. On 3 September 1894 he entered St Basil's Novitiate, Toronto, and after first profession in 1895 he continued his studies at St Michael's College. He pronounced his final vows on 6 August 1898, and was ordained priest on 25 June 1900.

Father 'Pat' Howard taught at St Michael's College, where he was also in charge of dramatics and ran a program for public speaking. In 1902–3 he served as assistant at St Mary's of the Assumption Parish,

Owen Sound, Ontario. In 1907 he began his long association with Assumption College, Windsor, where he died twenty-two years later.

Father Howard rarely had an idle hour. A booming voice and a colourful New England accent made him a popular preacher. During 1928, the last full year of his life, he preached eighteen Forty Hours Devotions, eleven retreats, and gave twenty-one special addresses. Wherever he went, he was zealous in hearing confessions.

When not on the road preaching, he was in charge of the study hall at Assumption, where he regularly spent time with the students during their recreations, smoking a cigar and entertaining them with stories.

SOURCES: GABF; *Centennial, St Mary's*; *Jubilee, Assumption*; *Jubilee, St Mary's*; W.J. Roach CSB, 'Laudemus viros gloriosos,' *Basilian Teacher* 3 (January 1959) 114–18.

HOWARD, Thomas CYRIL, priest, member of the Congregation 1941–72, was born in Sussex, New Brunswick (diocese of Saint John), on 26 July 1921, the son of Francis Howard and Alexa McDonough. He died at Moncton, New Brunswick, on 14 October 1999, and was buried in St Francis Xavier Cemetery, Sussex.

'Cy' attended Sussex Public High School and then St Thomas College, Chatham, New Brunswick, for two years before entering St Basil's Novitiate, Toronto, in 1940. After making his first profession of vows on 15 August 1941, he was appointed to Assumption College, Windsor, 1941–3 (B.A., University of Western Ontario, 1943). He taught at St Thomas High School, Houston, in 1943–4. While earning teacher certification at the Ontario College of Education he resided at St Michael's College, 1944–5. He taught at Aquinas Institute, Rochester, 1945–7 and 1950–2. After theological studies at St Basil's Seminary, Toronto, 1947–50, he was ordained to the priesthood by Bishop Patrick Bray of Saint John, New Brunswick, on 16 June 1949.

Father Howard was an assistant at St Mary's of the Assumption Parish, Owen Sound, Ontario, 1952–4. He served as a chaplain with the rank of Captain in the Canadian Army, 1954–6. He was an assistant at St Anne's Parish, Houston, 1956–8, and at Ste Anne's Parish, Detroit, 1958–65. He taught at Assumption High School, Windsor, 1965–6, and was assistant in Blessed Sacrament Parish, Windsor, 1966–8. In 1968 he was appointed to Holy Spirit Parish, Saginaw, Michigan, and in 1972 he was incardinated into the diocese of Saginaw. He served as pastor at St Joseph's Church, Unionville, Michigan, and at St Denis Church, Lexington, Michigan. In 1980 he retired to Moncton.

SOURCES: GABF; *Annals* 1 (1949) 261.

HURLEY, Albert Edward Joseph, priest, member of the Congregation 1895–1924, was born at Hastings, Ontario (vicariate-apostolic of Northern Canada, since 1882 diocese of Peterborough), on 29 March 1874, the son of Timothy Hurley and Mary Teresa Ford. He died at Duarte, California, on 7 December 1966 and was buried in the priests' plot of Calvary Cemetery, Los Angeles.

Albert Hurley grew up in Peterborough, Ontario, where he attended St Peter's Separate School. In 1890 he went to St Michael's College, Toronto. Five years later, on 9 September 1895, he was received as a novice at St Basil's Novitiate, Toronto. He made his final vows on 14 August 1899, and was ordained priest on 24 August 1899.

Father Hurley taught first at Assumption College, Windsor, 1899–1900. He was a member of the founding staff of St Thomas College (High School), Houston, 1900–3. In 1903 he was appointed superior of St Mary's Seminary, LaPorte, Texas. In 1907 he went to St Michael's College, where he taught until 1914, when he went to Rome for graduate studies in theology. He obtained an S.T.L., but the First World War delayed his return to Canada until 1920. He taught at Assumption College, 1920–1, then was on staff of St Basil's Scholasticate, Toronto, 1921–3. The year 1923–4 was spent teaching at St Michael's College.

Father Hurley decided not to take the new, stricter vow of poverty in 1922 and withdrew from the Congregation in 1924 to join the archdiocese of Los Angeles. He was assistant at St John's Parish, Hyde Park, Los Angeles, 1925, assistant editor of the *Tidings* (the archdiocesan newspaper) in 1926, administrator of St Mary's Parish, El Centro, 1928–31, rector of St Mary's of the Assumption Parish, Santa Maria, 1931–2, pastor of Nativity Parish, El Monte, and then of St Ann's Parish, Seal Beach. His last active duty was chaplain to the Little Sisters of the Poor at St Ann's Home in Los Angeles. In 1955 he retired to Santa Teresita Hospital, Duarte, where he suffered a stroke in 1964 and died two years later.

Father Hurley, always full of energy, put life into the students in his classes. His was of an impetuous nature; if he found a book interesting he could not put it down until he had read it to the end. Erect in his bearing and a meticulous dresser, he personified the dignity of his calling.

BIBLIOGRAPHY: Ed. *Jubilee, St Mary's.*
SOURCES: GABF; *Annals* 4 (1968) 63; *Newsletter* (14 May 1962, 12 December 1966); Kirley, *Congregation in France* 10, 57; *Yearbook SMC* 16 (1925).

HUSSEY, John Michael, priest, cousin of Father Leland *Higgins, was born at Melbourne, Middlesex County, Ontario (diocese of London), on 2 December 1909, the son of James Hussey and Delia McManus. He died in Windsor on 6 October 1966 and was buried there in the Basilian plot of Assumption Cemetery.

John Hussey grew up in Alvinston, Ontario, and in Windsor, where he attended Assumption College School, 1923–7. He entered St Basil's Novitiate, Toronto, in 1927 and after profession on 11 August 1928 took his arts course at St Michael's College (B.A., Classics, University of Toronto, 1932). He attended the Ontario College of Education in Toronto, 1932–3, did his theological studies at St Basil's Scholasticate, Toronto, and was ordained priest on 21 December 1935 in St Basil's Church, Toronto, by Archbishop James Charles McGuigan.

Father Hussey taught at the Lee Avenue high school branch of St Michael's College, 1935–6. He earned an M.A. in education at the Catholic University of America, Washington, D.C. in 1937, submitting as his thesis 'Catholic Action in the Schools and Colleges of Quebec.' He taught Latin at Aquinas Institute, Rochester, 1937–41 and 1945–7, and at Assumption College, 1941–5 and 1947–66. During his latter tenure there Assumption College became Assumption University of Windsor from 1956 to 1963, and, after 1963, Assumption University, federated with the University of Windsor. His death in 1966 was the result of a chronic heart ailment.

As a young man 'Jocko' Hussey had excelled in baseball. As a priest he coached various teams and for some years served as chairman of the Board of Athletics at Assumption University of Windsor.

BIBLIOGRAPHY: 'The Case for Educational Psychology,' *Basilian* 4 (February 1938) 25–6; 'The "What" and "How" of Educational Psychology,' *Basilian* 4 (March 1938) 46–7; 'Organization of Abilities vs. "Faculty Theory,"' *Basilian* 4 (April 1938) 70–2; 'The Dull Student,' *Basilian* 4 (May 1938) 92–4.
SOURCES: GABF; *Annals* 3 (1966) 500; *Newsletter* (7 October 1966).

I

IVERSEN, Norman Martin, priest, was born on 9 May 1927 at Trois-Rivières, Quebec, the son of Thurston Iversen and Florence Comeau. He died in Toronto on 21 January 1993 and is buried in the Basilian plot in Holy Cross Cemetery, Thornhill, Ontario.

'Ivy' attended primary and secondary schools in Trois-Rivières, Port Mellon and Vancouver, British Columbia, Montreal, and Toronto. He enrolled in McGill University for pre-university courses; but, when the family settled in Espanola, Ontario, he went to St Michael's College, Toronto, for grade XIII. He entered St Basil's Novitiate, Richmond Hill, Ontario, in 1948, and made first profession of vows on 30 September 1949. He did his undergraduate studies at St Michael's College while living at Holy Rosary Seminary, Toronto, 1949–50, then at St Michael's College, 1950–2, and finally at St Basil's Seminary, Toronto, 1952–3 (B.A., Honours Philosophy and History, University of Toronto, 1953; S.T.B., St Michael's College, 1956). He was ordained to the priesthood on 29 June 1956 in St Basil's Church, Toronto, by Cardinal James Charles McGuigan.

In 1957 Father Iversen was appointed to Michael Power High School, Etobicoke, Ontario, where he taught part-time and began graduate studies. The next year he was appointed bursar of St Basil's Seminary, where he continued his studies. In 1960 he received an M.A. in history from the University of Toronto and was appointed to St Michael's College School to teach and to serve as bursar. Two years later he began thirty-one years at St Michael's College as treasurer of the college and of the local Basilian community, and as part-time teacher in the Western course and in the Faculty of Theology. For reasons of health he resigned the office of bursar of the college in 1984, but continued to serve as bursar of the Basilian community. He was scrupulously attentive to the working conditions and needs of the staff whom he supervised. Proud of his Scandinavian heritage, he was for many years an active member of St Ansgar's League.

In 1984 he suffered an aneurysm in the brain while on vacation in Kelowna, British Columbia, and was flown to hospital in Vancouver, where he remained in a coma for a month. He recovered consciousness, but the last decade of his life was a time of deteriorating health, though these conditions did not dampen his love of life or his readiness to oblige colleagues, confreres, and others who sought his services.

SOURCES: GABF; *Annals* 2 (1956) 251, 8 (1994) 122–3; *Newsletter* (21 January 1993).

J

JAMES, Paul McEvoy, priest, was born on 1 March 1930 in Toronto, the son of William James and Katherine McEvoy. He died in Toronto on 17 January 2001 and is buried in the Basilian plot of Holy Cross Cemetery, Thornhill, Ontario.

Paul attended Holy Rosary elementary school, St Michael's College School, and St Michael's College, Toronto (B.A., University of Toronto, 1953). He entered St Basil's Novitiate, Richmond Hill, Ontario, in September 1953 and made first profession on 12 September 1954. He took one year of theology at St Basil's Seminary, Toronto, 1954–5, then taught at Michael Power High School, Etobicoke, Ontario, 1955–6, and then at St Charles College, Sudbury, Ontario, 1956–7. He completed his theology courses at St Basil's Seminary, 1957–60, being ordained to the priesthood on 28 June 1959 in St Basil's Church, Toronto, by Bishop Francis Allen.

Paul James, or 'Doc,' as he was called, spent a total of thirty-seven years at Michael Power High School, 1960–87, 1988–98, with the intervening year in a renewal program. He taught mathematics and physics, coached intramural football, tutored students, and made himself present to them in many ways. His joyful disposition elicited a ready response from them. He served two terms as principal of the school, 1982–7 and 1989–1998, and was the local superior or rector of the Basilian community, 1988–98. Each year, before school began in the fall, he hosted a dinner for Basilians at Michael Power which featured fresh produce from the James family farm.

For many years Father James suffered intensely from arthritis, a condition which did not improve with a hip replacement. Failing health in his last years at Michael Power was exacerbated by the great sadness he felt at the termination of the Michael Power Basilian community and the sale of the school property in 1998. Father James moved to St Michael's College School in that year, and then to Anglin House (Basilian Infirmary) in the fall of the year 2000, where, in spite of a seeming recovery of the good spirits which had characterized his life, he died within three months.

SOURCES: GABF; *Annals* 2 (1959) 419, 10 (2002) 91; *Newsletter* (15 February 2001).

JANNIN, Jules, priest, member of the Congregation 1873–7, was born on 27 April 1837 at Gex (Ain, diocese of Bellay).
Jules Jannin entered the Congregation as a priest, ordained in 1861, and made final profession of vows on 19 September 1873. At the Collège du Sacré-Coeur, Annonay, he taught senior classes: *seconde*, 1872–3 and *première*, 1873–5. After two years at the Collège Saint-Charles, Blidah, Algeria, 1875–7, he received a telegram from the superior general recalling him to France. He was appointed to the novitiate at Feyzin (Isère, now Rhône) on 8 May 1877; but no further mention is made of him in Basilian records.

SOURCE: Pouzol, 'Notices,' Supplément 3.

JEFFERY, Richard Joseph, priest, was born on 18 March 1924 in Rochester, the son of Raymond Edward Jeffery and Marie Elizabeth Klem. He died in Toronto on 25 March 1978 and is buried in Holy Sepulchre Cemetery, Rochester.
Richard attended Holy Rosary School and Aquinas Institute, Rochester. In September 1942 he joined the first class in the new St Basil's Novitiate established in Rochester and was professed on 12 September 1943. At Assumption College, 1943–7, he took his B.A. (University of Western Ontario, 1947), then taught at Aquinas Institute, 1947–8, and at St Thomas High School, Houston, 1948–9, where he began to study theology. He completed the theology course at St Basil's Seminary, Toronto, and was ordained to the priesthood in St Basil's Church, Toronto, on 29 June 1951 by Cardinal James Charles McGuigan.

Father Jeffery taught at Aquinas Institute, 1952–4, before beginning the parish apostolate, in which he remained for the rest of his life: at Our Lady of Mount Carmel Church, Wharton, Texas, 1954–5; Our Lady of Guadalupe, Rosenberg, Texas, 1955–60; Ste Anne's, Detroit, 1960–2; St Theresa's, Sugar Land, Texas, 1962–3; Our Lady of Mount Carmel, Wharton, 1963–71. In June of 1971 he was named pastor of St Theresa's, Sugar Land, a post he held until 1975. In June of that year, because of failing health, he moved to St Anne's, Houston, where he remained until March of 1978.

A quiet and unassuming man, Father Jeffery was by nature friendly, putting at ease all who came into contact with him. He welcomed visitors and was particularly responsive to children, and they to him, for they often gathered about him after church services. His love of liturgical music led him to attend the St Michael's Choir School in Toronto for two summers. His last project at St Anne's was to found and train a youth choir, but he would never hear it perform. A severe heart attack in November 1977 forced his move to St Basil's Infirmary, Toronto, on 1 March 1978, where his rapidly deteriorating condition twice brought hospitalization. The second time was on Good Friday, and he died in his sleep early in the morning of Holy Saturday.

BIBLIOGRAPHY: 'A New Mission Centre for Angleton,' *Basilian Teacher* 2 (November 1957) 6–7.
SOURCES: GABF; *Annals* 2 (1951) 36, 5 (1979) 406–7; *Newsletter* (28 March 1978).

JOANNY, Régis, scholastic, was born at Prades (Ardèche) on 4 February 1869, the son of Jean-François-Régis Joanny and Rosalie Roussel. He died in Annonay on 11 June 1894 and was buried in the cemetery on the grounds of the Collège du Sacré-Coeur.

After studies at the Collège du Sacré-Coeur, section Sainte-Barbe, 1882–4, Régis Joanny continued his studies at the College of Mary Immaculate, Beaconfield House, Plymouth, England, where he made his novitiate in 1887 and then remained for a year at the scholasticate. In 1888 he went to the Collège du Sacré-Coeur to teach and do theological studies, but became ill in June 1889 and went to his family to rest. He continued for one more year in Annonay and then went to the Collège Saint-Charles, Blidah, Algeria, for three years, 1890–3, but his health deteriorated there. After returning to the Collège du Sacré-Coeur, he died in minor orders at the age of twenty-five. By his goodness and affability, his love of work, and his intelligence, he had given promise of a fruitful ministry.

SOURCES: GABF; Kirley, *Community in France* 240n569; Pouzol, 'Notices.'

JOBERT, Eugène, priest, was born at Lamastre (Ardèche) on 12 November 1865, the son of Benjamin Jobert and Marie Escoffier. He died in Annonay on 27 July 1933 and was buried at Lamastre.

Eugène Jobert studied at the Grand Séminaire de Viviers and was already a deacon when he entered the Basilian novitiate at Beaconfield House, Plymouth, England, in 1888. He was ordained to the priesthood in the chapel of the Collège du Sacré-Coeur by Bishop Joseph-Michel-Frédéric Bonnet of Viviers on 21 September 1889. Several teaching appointments, in mathematics and science, followed: the Collège du Sacré-Coeur, 1889–90, 1896–9, the Collège Saint-Augustin in Bône, Algeria, 1890–5, and the Petit Séminaire d'Aubenas (Ardèche), 1895–6. After a year of studies in Lyon, 1899–1900, he obtained a *Certificat d'études supérieures* in physics. He returned to the college in Annonay for the next three years. After the expulsion of the Basilians from their schools in 1903, he was appointed curate at Gilhoc-sur-Ormèze (Ardèche). He was then officially 'secularized,' conforming to the anticlerical laws, and taught mathematics, first at the Petit Séminaire de Vernoux (Ardèche), 1904–7, and then once again at the Collège du Sacré-Coeur, 1907–33. He served on the general council of the Basilians in France, 1922–33.

Father Jobert was a small, energetic man who communicated to his pupils his own love for mathematics and science. He was a witty, charming, and cultured conversationalist. Talented in music, for many years he directed the choir and other musical productions at the Collège du Sacré-Coeur. When he became partially paralysed on the right side, he taught himself to write with his left hand.

SOURCES: GABF; Kirley, *Community in France* 205, 240n569, 255n600; Kirley, *Congregation in France* 42, 76n34, 81–2, 87, 116, 119, 136, 139, 154–5, 175, 211; Pouzol, 'Notices'; *Semaine religieuse de Viviers* (11 August 1933) 293–4.

K

KEHOE, Wilfrid Martin, priest, was born on 3 January 1909 at Marlbank, Ontario (diocese of Peterborough), the son of Martin Kehoe and Theresa Brown. He died on 3 March 1977 in Sudbury, Ontario, and is buried in the Basilian plot of Holy Cross Cemetery, Thornhill, Ontario.

His family having moved to Port Credit, Ontario, shortly after his birth, 'Wilf' Kehoe attended elementary school there and De La Salle Collegiate in Toronto, graduating in 1926. He entered St Basil's Novitiate, Toronto, and was professed on 11 August 1927. At St Basil's Scholasticate, Toronto, he completed his upper school and began studies at the University of Toronto. In 1930 he moved to St Michael's College, Toronto (B.A., University of Toronto, 1932). He earned teaching certification at the Ontario College of Education, 1933. He also began theological studies during this time. He taught at Catholic Central High School, Detroit, 1933-4, while continuing his study of theology. In 1934 he returned to the scholasticate and was ordained to the priesthood on 16 December 1934 in Assumption Church, Windsor, by Bishop John Kidd.

In 1935 Father Kehoe was appointed to St Michael's College School, Toronto. In 1937 he went to Aquinas Institute, Rochester, one of the first group of Basilians who took over the direction of that school. He was a member of the local council, 1946-50. In 1950 he was appointed to Catholic Central once again, and was principal and superior from 1958 to 1964. In August 1964 he moved to St Charles College, Sudbury, to teach and serve as treasurer. He retired in 1975 for reasons of health.

In his younger years Wilfrid Kehoe was an excellent athlete, and his interest in sports continued through his life. At the age of sixty he learned to play the piano. He made a point of visiting friends and confreres in Rochester and Detroit each year. He was planning a visit to the Basilians in Houston when death came suddenly in the community room of St Charles College, Sudbury.

SOURCES: GABF; *Annals* 5 (1978) 318-19; *Newsletter* (10 March 1977).

KELLY, Anthony John, priest, was born in Toronto on 30 August 1921, one of three children of Michael Kelly and Anna Gough. He died in Toronto on 29 September 2001, and is buried in the Basilian plot of Holy Cross Cemetery, Thornhill, Ontario.

'Tony' Kelly attended St Clement School at Center Line, Michigan, and, on his family's return to Toronto, St Peter's School and St Michael's College. He entered St Basil's Novitiate, Toronto, and was professed on 15 August 1941. He took the honours course in classics (B.A., University of Toronto, 1945), taught at St Michael's College School, 1945-6, and obtained teaching certification from the Ontario College of Education in 1947. He studied theology at St Basil's Seminary, Toronto, and was ordained to the priesthood on 29 June 1950 in St Basil's Church, Toronto, by Cardinal James Charles McGuigan.

Father Kelly was appointed to St Michael's College School, where he taught Latin, Greek, and religious studies for thirty years, with an interval of one year of renewal in theology at St Basil's Seminary, 1971-2. A capable and convinced teacher of the classics, which he loved, Father Kelly worked with other classics teachers in the private and public high schools to keep Latin and Greek studies alive on the secondary level, and a paper he delivered on this subject was later published. Interest in his students continued beyond their years at the school.

In 1982 he was appointed to the Basilian community at Lethbridge, Alberta. There he served as chaplain at St Michael's Hospital, rector of the local Basilian community, and pastor at St Joseph's parish, Coalhurst, Alberta. In 1992, his health failing, he was assigned to the Basilian Fathers Infirmary, Toronto. He lived there until shortly before his death, when he was moved to Providence Centre, Scarborough, Ontario.

Tony's well-known enthusiasm for the Toronto Blue Jays inspired his confreres, on an occasion of his absence, to decorate one wall of his room with Blue Jay wallpaper. His kindness reached out to the aged and the lonely, and his support of the Legion of Mary and of the missions was encouraging to many students. His engaging simplicity was not incompatible with a wisdom and common sense which made him an agent of peace in heated discussions and a shrewd judge of character. In the community he was what Father Owen Lee said of him in his funeral homily, a *joculator*, one who spreads joy.

Father Kelly had a fine and true singing voice and was known particularly for his earnest rendition of the hymn 'Gift of Finest Wheat,' which he had learned at the World Eucharistic Congress at Philadelphia in 1976. He organized liturgies for Anglin House, and loved to preach at the Masses.

BIBLIOGRAPHY: 'It's All Greek to Me' (pamphlet), Ontario Educational Association, Classics Section. Toronto, 1963.
SOURCES: GABF; *Annals* 1 (1950) 285, 7 (1992) 9, 9 (2001) 17; *Newsletter* (8 October 2001).

KELLY, Charles Michael, priest, nephew of Father Michael Vincent *Kelly, was born on a farm near Athlone in the Adjala Township, Ontario (archdiocese of Toronto), on 30 March 1900, the son of John Kelly and Elizabeth Morrow. He died there on 12 August 1963 and is buried in the Basilian plot of Assumption Cemetery, Windsor.

'Charley' Kelly attended a rural school before coming to St Michael's College, Toronto, in 1915. Three years later he entered St Basil's Novitiate, Toronto, and was professed on 7 October 1919. After further studies at St Michael's College and St Basil's Scholasticate, Toronto, he was ordained to the priesthood on 19 December 1926 in St Basil's Church by Bishop Alexander MacDonald.

His first appointment after ordination was that of treasurer of St Basil's Novitiate, January–August 1927. Several parish appointments followed: assistant at Assumption Parish, Windsor, 1927–32, and Ste Anne's Parish, Detroit, 1932–3; pastor of St John the Baptist Parish, Amherstburg, Ontario, 1933–4 and 1940–8, of Ste Anne's Parish, Detroit, 1834–7 and 1948–55, and of St Mary's of the Assumption Parish, Owen Sound, Ontario, 1937–40. In 1955 he remained at St Mary's as assistant, and two years later returned to Assumption Parish in Windsor. He died suddenly in 1963 from a heart attack while visiting his brother at the family homestead.

The *Basilian Centennial* volume, Owen Sound, singled out his untiring efforts with Father James *Murphy to complete a city-wide census of Catholics and his particular attention to the Chatsworth and Southampton mission churches, where he also restored and cared for the neglected cemeteries. His outstanding achievement was the guidance of parishes through difficult years of the great Depression and the Second World War.

Father Kelly was blunt in imparting common-sense advice and possessed an exceptional memory for faces. The St Michael's *Yearbook* commented at the time of his ordination on his ability to make and keep friends. It was a trait he retained and developed. Careful study of parish records, followed up by the visiting of homes, gave him a remarkable knowledge of the families he served.

SOURCES: GABF; *Annals* 3 (1963) 219–20; *Newsletter* (13 August 1963); *Centennial, St Mary's*; Kirley, *Community in France* 216n518, 222n531, 241n570; *Yearbook SMC* 18 (1927).

KELLY, Francis Paul, priest, member of the Congregation 1933–64, was born on 9 March 1915 in Orlando, West Virginia (diocese of Wheeling-Charleston), the son of James Kelly and Agnes Carney. He died in San Diego, California, on 10 January 1993 and was buried there in the diocesan priests plot in Holy Cross Cemetery.

Frank Kelly attended St Mary's High School, Clarksburg, West Virginia, in 1928–9 and Catholic Central High School, Detroit, in 1929–32. He entered St Basil's Novitiate, Toronto, making his first profession on 12 September 1933. He attended St Michael's College, Toronto, 1934–8 (B.A., University of Toronto, 1938). He studied theology at St Basil's Seminary, 1938–41 and 1943–4. In 1942, while teaching at Catholic Central High School, Detroit, he received permanent Michigan teaching certification from Wayne State University, and in 1943 received an M.A. in classics from the University of Toronto. He was ordained to the priesthood by Archbishop James Charles McGuigan on 15 August 1943.

Father Kelly taught at Catholic Central High School in 1944–9 and again in 1953–62. He taught at Assumption High School, Windsor, in 1949–53.

In 1964 Father Kelly began the process of incardination into the diocese of San Diego. For the remainder of his life while doing pastoral work in his diocese, Frank remained close to his Basilian friends and to the Community.

SOURCES: GABF; *Annals* 1 (1944) 53; *Newsletter* (22 January 1993).

KELLY, James Joseph, priest, was born on 27 November 1939 in Rochester, the son of John J. Kelly and Julia Daly. He died in Merrillville, Indiana, on 22 June 1992 and is buried in the Basilian plot of Holy Sepulchre Cemetery, Rochester.

'Jim' Kelly attended Immaculate Conception elementary school, Corpus Christi middle school, and Aquinas Institute, Rochester, where he graduated in the upper tenth of his class in 1957. Throughout his schooling he took music lessons and developed an interest in dramatics, talents which he put to use in his later ministry. He entered St Basil's Novitiate, Rochester, in 1957 and was professed on 15 August 1958. He lived at St Basil's Seminary, Toronto, during his Western year and undergraduate studies at St Michael's College (B.A., Honours English Language and Literature, University of Toronto, 1963), and then taught English and French at St Michael's College School, Toronto, 1963–6. During summers he took courses at the University of Rochester (M.A., English, 1969). He studied theology at St Basil's Seminary, 1966–70, and was ordained to the priesthood on 13 December 1969 in Sacred Heart Cathedral, Rochester, the first priest ordained by Bishop Joseph Hogan.

In 1970 Father Kelly began doctoral studies at the University of

Rochester while residing with the Basilian community of East Rochester. During the academic year 1972–3 he taught English at St Thomas More College, Saskatoon. In 1973 he was appointed to St Basil's College, Toronto, for graduate studies in theology; but, having expressed a desire to return to the classroom, was assigned to Andrean High School, Merrillville, Indiana, where he remained for eight years, teaching and putting to good use his musical and dramatic skills. In 1982 he was appointed to Aquinas Institute, but in 1988 returned to Andrean as superior. He accepted this office with some reluctance, informing the general council of his doubts about himself as a spiritual leader. Though a sensitive, conscientious, and appreciated superior, he asked not to be renamed to the office when his three-year term ended in 1991. He continued teaching at Andrean until the day he died.

Jim Kelly was much given to reading and study. An inveterate book buyer, he is reputed to have built up several libraries which he abandoned in each place he left. He was mild-mannered but not soft where student homework and discipline were concerned. Yet he could procrastinate: the journal *Basilian Teacher* became moribund under his direction. This may have been an early sign of his diabetes, a condition to which he might have given more attention. On Monday, 22 May 1992, he excused himself from a meeting, told the cook that he would miss supper, and was later found dead on the floor of his room.

SOURCES: GABF; *Annals* 4 (1970) 139, 7 (1993) 130–3; *Newsletter* (17 July 1992).

KELLY, James Scott, priest, brother of Father Thomas Kelly CSSR and of Abbot Timothy Kelly OCSO, was born on 27 December 1924 at Sandwich (now Windsor), Ontario, the son of Irving Kelly and Monica Scott. He died on 1 March 1996 in Toronto and is buried in the Basilian plot of Holy Cross Cemetery, Thornhill, Ontario.

James Kelly graduated from St Rose High School, Amherstburg, Ontario, in 1943. After two years of arts at Assumption College, Windsor, he entered St Basil's Novitiate, Toronto, making first profession on 15 August 1946. He resumed studies at Assumption College (B.A., University of Western Ontario, 1948). He later earned an Ontario Type B teaching certification from the Ontario College of Education and a B.Ed. from the University of Toronto, with a specialist certificate in geography, and studied business administration at the University of Omaha during two summers. After teaching general science at Aquinas Institute, Rochester, 1948–9, he studied theology at St Basil's

Seminary, Toronto, 1949–53, living two of those years with the Basilian community at St Michael's College. He was ordained to the priesthood on 29 June 1952 in St Basil's Church, Toronto, by Cardinal James Charles McGuigan.

Father Kelly remained a further year at St Basil's Seminary as bursar, 1953–4, then became bursar at St Michael's College, 1954–62. During this time he gave attention and care to a fine lakeside property near Parry Sound, Ontario, which had been given to the community by Doctor Jack Egan. In 1962 he was appointed to Assumption College School, Windsor, again as bursar and also to teach math and science. In 1967 he was moved to Michael Power High School, Etobicoke, Ontario, to teach math and science and to head the science department. He remained there until 1989 when his deteriorating health obliged him to retire to the Basilian Fathers Residence (Infirmary), Toronto.

'Jim' Kelly was rotund, jovial, and infinitely obliging. He was thorough and completely professional in all his duties, often economizing by doing many jobs like landscaping and lawn care himself. He was particularly attentive to lay staff with regard to wages, benefits and general well-being. After his retirement to the Basilian Fathers Residence he continued to express his concern for the employees, often reminding the administration of the moral obligation to just wages and suitable working conditions. Sister Olga Warnke IBVM, whom he helped in establishing Loretto College on St Mary Street, Toronto, wrote of him: 'I always felt I could seek his advice and feel confident that it would point in the right direction. He always made me feel welcome with good cheer and readiness to listen. We are deeply grateful.'

SOURCES: GABF; *Annals* 2 (1952) 60, 8 (1997) 104–6; *Newsletter* (15 March 1996).

KELLY, John Michael, priest, was born in Scranton, Pennsylvania, on 27 July 1911, the second eldest of four brothers and one sister, children of John Kelly and Mary McAndrews. He died at Camp Hill, Pennsylvania, on 26 September 1986 and is buried in the Basilian plot of Holy Cross Cemetery, Thornhill, Ontario.

After elementary and secondary school at St John the Baptist Parish in Scranton, John Kelly went to St Michael's College, Toronto (B.A., Honours Philosophy, University of Toronto, 1932). He entered St Basil's Novitiate in 1932 and was professed on 12 September 1933. He studied theology at St Basil's Scholasticate, Toronto, while also taking graduate courses (M.A., Philosophy, University of Toronto, 1935), submitting as his thesis 'The Doctrine of the *Bonum* in St Thomas.' He was ordained to the priesthood on 19 December 1936 in St Basil's Church, Toronto, by Archbishop James Charles McGuigan.

Father Kelly received three short appointments to Catholic Central High School, Detroit, to Aquinas Institute, Rochester, and to Assumption College, Windsor, before being appointed in 1940 to St Michael's College, where he was to remain for the next forty-five years. There he taught philosophy and also earned a Ph.D. in philosophy from the University of Toronto in 1948, submitting as his thesis 'The Animistic Materialism of William Pepperell Montague.' That same year he became dean of men. In 1958 he was named president and vice-chancellor of the University of St Michael's College. He held these positions until 1978, while at the same time serving as principal of St Michael's College (the undergraduate arts division) until 1976. Even after 1978 he continued to exercise a degree of control over the affairs of St Michael's by remaining as director of its alumni association and president of the St Michael's College foundation until declining health forced him to relinquish these influential positions in 1985 and 1986, respectively.

John Kelly's dynamic personality, booming voice, and prominent shock of white hair made his presence a dominant one in any gathering. He became internationally known as an energetic and colourful academic administrator. He held his convictions strongly and implemented them fearlessly, even when these were idiosyncratic, e.g., his opposition to pensions for the Basilian members of the faculty and to the development of the Bay Street frontage as a source of revenue. He was generally popular with his peers in academe, with the students, and with the alumni.

Two enduring legacies of his presidency are the northward extension of Brennan Hall, completed in 1967, which made possible an enlarged student centre, and the spacious library, completed in 1969, which today bears his name and by the year 2000 housed four hundred thousand volumes. But history will regard as Father Kelly's outstanding achievement his successful advocacy, in concert with the University of Toronto's President John Evans, of the *Memorandum of Understanding, 1974,* which radically changed the University of Toronto's academic and financial relationships with its federated universities (Trinity, Victoria, and St Michael's). John Kelly single-handedly persuaded the governing board of Victoria University, initially opposed to the *Memorandum,* to support it. The *Memorandum* replaced college departments by university departments. It assigned to the University of Toronto all tuition fees and grants generated by federated college students. In return, the University of Toronto paid the salaries and benefits of full-time faculty hired up to 1974, raising them to par with its own, and helped defray the expenses of libraries, classrooms, offices, and other college facilities. At the same time, however, it determined that all future appointments would be made by the University of Toronto. The severity of this decree was softened somewhat by a provision which made possible, under strictly limited conditions, cross-appointment of faculty from the University of Toronto to the federated colleges. The immediate effect of the *Memorandum* was to save St Michael's from impending bankruptcy; but its long-term result was to reduce the federated arts colleges from independent teaching institutions to institutions where teaching is done by University of Toronto faculty in whose appointment those colleges have no voice.

Many honours came to Father Kelly. In the space of eight years, 1970–8, he was granted honorary doctorates from St Thomas University, Fredericton, New Brunswick; Victoria University, Toronto; St John Fisher College, Rochester; the University of Toronto; and Trinity College, Toronto. He was made an Officer of the Order of Canada in 1984. He received the Georgetown Medal from Georgetown University, Washington, D.C.; the Centennial Medal from the Government of Canada; the City of Toronto Civic Award; and the Sesquicentennial Medal from the Association of Part-Time University of Toronto Students. He was made an honorary member of the Paris Foreign Missions Society, a religious community of missionaries with which he had been associated since 1958. The editors of the *Mike*, the student newspaper of the University of St Michael's College, made him 'Editor Emeritus, 1982' for 'contributions, not only those to the college and university, but also those that are on a bit more of a personal level.'

On the occasion of the conferring of the honorary degree from the University of Toronto, Dr Lawrence E. Lynch, the first lay principal of St Michael's College, 1976–81, described John Kelly as 'a Basilian Father committed to pastoral care, whether it be exercised in the civic or university community, who devoted hours of his time to the personal sufferings, problems and turmoil of people outside the university involved in crime and drugs.' Dr Lynch had in mind episodes such as Father Kelly's ministry in the Death Row of Toronto's Don Jail to Leonard Jackson and Steve Suchan, preparing them for execution, and anointing them after they were hanged on 16 December 1952 – acts which earned him the respect of many inside and outside the Church.

An intense man, he remained an inveterate smoker; but through sheer willpower he abruptly terminated a problem in the use of alcohol. In his last days, after suffering a stroke while visiting his brother-in-law at Camp Hill, Pennsylvania, he became serene and peaceful, taking delight in the beauty of the Mass celebrated there by Father Joseph *Dorsey, and in the encyclical of Pope John Paul II on the Holy Spirit. He awaited death with faith and confidence.

BIBLIOGRAPHY: 'Virtues and Gifts,' *Basilian* 1 (November 1935) 110; 'Catholic Totalitarianism,' *Basilian* 3 (February 1937) 33; 'The Christian Sacrifice,' *Basilian* 3 (March 1937) 46–9; 'How to Produce "an Integrated Personality,"' *Ontario English Catholic Teachers' Association News* 8 (1953) 6–13; 'Theology in Our Colleges,' *Basilian Teacher* 5 (October 1960) 71–5; 'The Basilian Attitude towards High School,' *Basilian Teacher* 6 (December 1961) 81–6; 'Educational Purpose and the Modern Student,' *Basilian Teacher* 7 (March 1963) 204–8; 'Love All Men As We Love Ourselves,' *Gazette* (Law Society of Upper Canada) 9 no. 4 (December 1975) 291–6.
SOURCES: GABF; *Annals* 6 (1984) 209, 6 (1987) 579–81; *Newsletter* (3 October 1986); Marjorie Lamb and Barry Pearson, *The Boyd Gang* (Toronto, 1976) 241–9; Shook, *Catholic Education* 196–209; Peter J.M. Swan CSB.

KELLY, Leroy NEIL, priest, was born on 15 August 1930 in Vancouver, British Columbia, the son of Leroy Victor Kelly (a newspaper reporter and a Lutheran) and Sarah MacNeil, a Roman Catholic. He died in Vancouver on 13 August 1999 and is buried there in Garden of Gethsemane Cemetery.

Neil attended Lord Kitchener and Immaculate Conception grade schools and Vancouver College High School, graduating in 1948. That summer he played professional baseball on a Rio Grande League team in Haney, British Columbia, and he spent the summers of his university years as a catcher and outfielder. He would later list 'professional baseball player' under 'unusual employments' on his application for the Basilian novitiate. He earned a B.A. from the University of British Columbia in the spring of 1953, his certification in secondary education from the same institution in 1954, and taught for a year at Viscount Alexander Junior High at Port Coquitlam, British Columbia. He entered St Basil's Novitiate, Richmond Hill, Ontario, in October 1955, and was professed on 18 November 1956. (The delay in his profession was due to the obligation to make up time spent away from the novitiate after his father's death the previous January.) As a scholastic he taught one year at St Michael's College, Toronto, one at St Michael's College School, and one year at St Thomas High School, Houston. He did his theological studies at St Basil's Seminary, Toronto, 1959–63, and earned an M.A. from the University of St Michael's College in 1963, submitting as his thesis 'Social Doctrine Is *Sacra Doctrina*.' He was ordained to the priesthood in St Basil's Church, Toronto, on 16 December 1962, by Archbishop Philip Francis Pocock.

In 1963 Father Kelly was appointed to St Mark's College, Vancouver, where he served as treasurer, 1963–77, and as superior, 1977–80. Seven years in chaplaincy at the University of Lethbridge, 1980–7, were followed by a year as president and rector of Athol Murray College of Notre Dame, Wilcox, Saskatchewan. During the next three years he was associate pastor, first at St Augustine Parish, Saskatoon, Saskatchewan, then at St Basil's Parish, Toronto. After a one-year individual apostolate, he was appointed plant manager at St Basil's College, Toronto, and supervised with notable success the renovations to the forty-year-old building to accommodate the curial offices on the second floor and what was to become Orsini House on the third floor. The next year he returned to St Mark's, serving as rector, 1992–5, and again from 1996 until his death. He was also treasurer from 1992 to 1999.

Neil Kelly's intellectual interests covered a wide scope – mathematics, English, philosophy, theology – though in later years at St Mark's his focus narrowed to what one might call practical theology and spirituality. He loved to converse with students and to challenge them from the point of view of faith on the issues of the day. A student particularly of St Augustine, he frequently attended the annual Patristic Conference at Oxford University. The year before his death he began a series of articles in the *St Mark's Bulletin* in which he strove to clarify and integrate two elements of Church life: the seven sacraments and the liturgical movement which in part gave rise to the Second Vatican Council. The new chapel which he planned at St Mark's is a striking statement of that integration of liturgy and sacrament in his own life and in the life of the Church.

BIBLIOGRAPHY: 'The Integrity of Sports and Mastery by the Spirit,' *Basilian Teacher* 6 (May 1962) 307–12; 'Saint Augustine: Congress in Rome,' *CCR* 5 (1987) 309–13.

SOURCES: GABF; *Annals* 3 (1963) 215–16, 9 (2000) 88–9; *Newsletter* (7 September 1999); T.J. Hanrahan CSB.

KELLY, Michael Vincent, priest, uncle of Father Charles *Kelly, was born on a farm in Athlone, Ontario (diocese of Toronto), on 31 July 1863, the fourth of the nine children of John Kelly and Anne McLaughlin. He died in Toronto on 24 July 1942 and was buried there in the Basilian plot of Mount Hope Cemetery.

After early education in a rural school, Michael Kelly went in 1879 to the high school section of St Michael's College, Toronto. Four years later he enrolled in the University of Toronto and graduated with the class of 1887. He entered St Basil's Novitiate at Beaconfield House, Plymouth, England, on 9 August 1887. Returning to Toronto, he studied theology at St Michael's College, 1888–91, and was ordained priest on 21 September 1891.

During his fifty years as a priest Father 'M.V.' Kelly worked in parishes, schools, and administrative duties: St Mary's of the Assumption Parish, Owen Sound, Ontario, 1891–4, pastor 1902–4; Assumption College, Windsor, 1894–6, 1900–1; St Michael's College, 1896–1900; superior of St Basil's Scholasticate, Toronto, and at the same time pastor of Holy Rosary Parish, 1901–2; pastor of St Basil's Parish, 1904–14. In 1914 he was appointed to St Thomas College, Houston (see below), but went on sick leave – a period which he used to promote the publicity and sale of the *St Basil's Hymnal*, travelling as far as Australia, India, and the Philippines. In 1920 he returned to parish ministry: St John the Baptist Parish, Amherstburg, Ontario, as assistant, 1920–1 and 1928–9, and as pastor, 1921–2 and 1932–4; St Basil's Parish, Toronto (as pastor 1922–8, as assistant 1929–31); Ste Anne's, Detroit, as assistant, 1931–2 and 1934–41. In 1941 he retired to St Michael's College, where he died from cancer in 1942.

M.V. Kelly's administrative duties in the Congregation were not without controversy. As a member of the provincial council from 1907 until 1914 he pushed his partisan views so vigorously that he was admonished by the Congregation of Religious in 1912, and in 1914 he was relieved of his office, deprived of active and passive voice, and ordered to live in a community house outside the Province of Ontario – penalties which remained in effect until 1920. Many of the policies he had advocated were later adopted. In 1922, when the Basilians divided into two congregations, one French and one North American, he was elected to the general council and held office until 1942. From the death of Father Francis *Forster in November 1929 until the election of Father Henry *Carr in July 1930 he was acting superior general.

Father Kelly supported Father Henry Carr's policies to strengthen the educational profile of St Michael's College. His own advocacy of university degrees for Basilians and of pedagogical training in state universities met with considerable opposition at that time, and he co-authored a strong letter of protest to a University of Toronto Commission criticizing the University's failure to integrate St Michael's fully as a federated college. It was he who negotiated the Basilian foundation of St Thomas College in Chatham, New Brunswick, in 1910; but by 1922 he was a leading proponent of the Congregation's withdrawal from it. A splendid preacher, he was credited with receiving more than a thousand converts into the Church. In parochial visitation he was assiduous and, regardless of rebuffs, was persistent in seeking out Catholics who were not practising their religion. Father Daniel *Forestell wrote of him, 'Zeal is perhaps the word that summarizes most consistently Father Kelly's life.'

M.V. Kelly loved the give-and-take of community recreation. He was a fine storyteller, but group conversation was his preference. He would test his or others' theories, or stimulate others to discuss a problem, by posing questions such as: 'You are a learned man. Can you tell me ... ?' or 'You are a man of experience. Have you ever ... ?' Never dull, he loved arguments and had plenty of them.

In the midst of parochial and administrative duties, M.V. Kelly made time to exercise his gift of writing. Aside from manuals of prayer and doctrine he wrote widely on social questions such as the movement of peoples from the farm to the city – a development he greatly lamented. His prose was lucid and fluid. He founded and carried on for years the direction of the Basilian Press, where he saw about forty printings of the *St Basil's Hymnal* and the *St Basil's Hymnbook* through the press, the sale of which financed the training of Basilian seminarians for years.

BIBLIOGRAPHY:

Books: *Zeal in the Classroom: Pastoral Theology for Clergy and Religious Engaged as Teachers.* Toronto, 1922. (With Canon J.B. Geniesse) *Efficax antidotum ad matrimonium mixta praecavenda.* Rome, 1923. *Treasure of the Faithful.* Montreal, 1924. *A Catechism of Christian Doctrine Prepared and Enjoined by Order of the Third Plenary Council of Baltimore.* Montreal, 1924; repr. Chicago 1929. *Some of the Pastor's Problems.* Toronto, 1923; repr. Chicago, 1924. *Scripture Treasures: Short Passages from Holy Scripture Selected for Memorisation in High School.* New York, 1926. *Frequent Communicant's Prayer Book.* Toronto, 1930;

repr. 1931. *Basilian Vademecum*. Toronto, 1930. *Remarked in Passing*. Toronto, 1934.

Pamphlets: [A Father of the Society of St Basil]. *What Every Christian Father Can and Should Do*. Toronto, c.1910. *The Family Teacher*. Toronto, c.1916. *Rev. M.J. Ferguson CSB, A Memoir*. Toronto, [1916]. *A Great Christian Layman: A Memoir of John Eldridge, Hepworth, Ont*. Toronto, 1920. *The Moral Danger of the City to the Youth of the Farm*. [Toronto, c.1920]. *'Some Fell among Thorns': Open Letter to a Farmer*. Toronto, 1921. *Catechism Teaching*. Grand Rapids, Mich., 1921. *Bolshevism in Our Schools*. Grand Rapids, Mich., 1923. *The First Communicant's Catechism, Prepared Conformably to the Decree on First Communion*. English and Spanish. Chicago, 1923; English ed. repr. Toronto 1923, Detroit c.1930; Spanish ed. repr. Detroit, 1936; Slovak trans. n.d. *A Catechism of Christian Practice*. Toronto, 1924. *Junior Catechism [from Seven to Nine Years]*. Detroit, 1927. *The Kellys of Monasterevan and Adjala*. Toronto, 1942.

Articles: 'What Is Wrong with the Farmer,' *Centralblatt* 23 (December 1930) 299–301; 'A Lamentable Neglect,' *Emmanuel* 42 (March 1936) 66–7; 'Wolf in Sheep's Clothing,' *Orate Fratres* 14 (February 1949) 173; 'Rich Paupers and Poor Paupers,' *Catholic Worker* 3 (May 1935) 4. In *American Ecclesiastical Review*: 'On Parents' Training of Children,' 54 (1916) 158; 'On Attending Scattered Missions,' 58 (1918) 174, 428; 'Life of St Francis Xavier,' 59 (1918) 109; 'On Paris Societies,' 59 (1918) 390; 'On Catechisms,' 60 (1919) 23, 157, 281; 'On Country Pastors,' 61 (1919) 502, 686; 'Does City Life Necessarily Tend to Undermine Faith?' 84 (April 1931) 350–9; 'Rejoinder,' 85 (September 1931) 305–6; 'Pulpit on Excess Profit-taking,' 89 (September 1933) 270–6; 'Clandestine Marriages,' 94 (1936) 628–30; 'Weekday High Mass of Requiem,' 96 (1937) 619–21; 'How Shall Priests Improve the Home?' 97 (1937) 290–2. In *Basilian*: 'St Basil's Novitiate in Beaconfield,' 1 (October/November 1935) 94–5, 112–15; 'A Word with Our Scholastics,' 1 (December 1935) 133–5; 'Another Word on Preaching,' 2 (April 1936) 65, 74; 'Our Parishes,' 2 (December 1936) 147; 'Other Days,' 3 (February 1937) 29; 'The Owen Sound Mission in 1893,' 4 (March 1938) 49. In *Homiletic and Pastoral Review*: 'A Question That Is Never Answered: Unintelligibility of the Catechism,' 31 (May 1931) 874; 'A Question of Justice,' 35 (February 1935) 381–4; 'A Case of Distributive Justice,' 36 (December 1935) 285–8; 'I Know Mine and Mine Know Me,' 37 (June 1937) 952; 'The First Friday and Children's Confessions,' 37 (October 1936) 65–7; 'The Leakage, Its Chief Cause,' 39 (February 1939) 503–5; 'Again the Forgotten Man,' 41 (September 1941) 1214–15; 'Why Not a Change of Interest,' 41 (November 1940) 122–6; 'Negligence in the Home: Prevention and Cure,' 42 (July 1942) 919. In the *Journal of Religious Instruction*: 'Catechism Problem, Teaching the Public School Child,' 1 (March 1931) 186–8; 'Shall the Catechism Disappear, Teaching the Public School

Child,' 2 (September 1931) 71–7; 'Studying the Prayerbook,' 4 (March 1934) 599–601; 'Lessons in Christian Doctrine,' 5 (March 1935) 627–30; 'Memorizing Prayers,' 6 (May 1936) 829. In *St Joseph Lilies*: 'St Basil's Novitiate in Beaconfield,' 18 (March 1936) 34–7; 'Rev. Vincent J. Murphy,' 22 (June 1933) 34–6. In the *Yearbook* (St Michael's College): 'Patrick Langan,' 22 (1931) 17–18.

SOURCES: GABF; *Annals* 1 (1943) 22–5; William Perkins Bull, *From Macdonell to McGuigan, the History of the Growth of the Roman Catholic Church in Upper Canada* (Toronto, 1939); *Centennial, St Mary's*; Daniel L. Forestell, 'M.V. Kelly,' *Basilian Teacher* 4 (October 1959) 22–4; Hoskin, *St Basil's*; *Jubilee, St Mary's*; Kirley, *Community in France* 240–50 and passim; Kirley, *Congregation in France* 4, 7, 11, 13–14, 17–19, 21, 23–4, 88; Madden, *St Basil's*; *Land and Home* 6 (June 1943) 56; *New Catholic Encyclopedia* (New York, 1967) 8 146; Shook, *Catholic Education* 114–19, 151–2.

KELLY, William Howard, priest, member of the Congregation 1950–91, nephew of Father Donald Gillen OMI, was born in Calgary, Alberta, on 29 July 1928, the son of William Kelly and Elizabeth Gillen. He died at Lethbridge, Alberta, on 4 September 2000 and was buried there in Mountain View Cemetery.

After graduation from St Mary's Boys' High School, Calgary, Bill enrolled at St Michael's College (B.A., University of Toronto, 1949). He entered St Basil's Novitiate, Richmond Hill, Ontario, and made his first profession on 12 September 1950. He taught at St Michael's College School, Toronto, 1950–2, and studied theology at St Basil's Seminary, 1952–5. He was ordained to the priesthood by Cardinal James Charles McGuigan on 29 June 1954.

Father Kelly taught at St Michael's College School in 1955–7 and at St Mary's Boys' High School, Calgary, in 1957–67. He received a B.Ed. from the University of Alberta in 1959 and an M.A. in religious education from Fordham University, New York, in 1970. He was employed by the Lethbridge (Alberta) Separate School Board from 1967 to 1991 chiefly on the staff at Catholic Central High School, Lethbridge, residing with the Basilian Fathers of Lethbridge from 1967 to 1985 and subsequently at Our Lady of the Assumption Parish, Lethbridge. He served with distinction as a general councillor and regional representative for Western Canada from 1981 to 1989. He withdrew from the Congregation in 1991 and was later dispensed from the obligations of the priesthood and religious profession. He was survived by his wife, Marion Hart, three stepdaughters, and one stepson.

SOURCES: GABF; *Annals* 2 (1954) 163; *Newsletter* (1 November 2000).

KENNEDY, Edward J., priest, died in Toronto, on 23 June 1876, in his twenty-eighth year. He was buried there in the Basilian plot of St Michael's Cemetery.

Edward Kennedy was a student at St Michael's College, Toronto, who went in 1865 to study in France. He made his novitiate there before returning to Toronto in 1869. He pronounced his final vows on 2 December 1871, and was ordained priest on 1 May 1872. After ordination Father 'Ned' Kennedy taught at St Louis College, Louisville, Ohio, 1872–3, and at St Michael's College from 1873 until his death from tuberculosis. Father Kennedy was an artist, and taught drawing and painting at St Michael's.

SOURCES: GABF; Hoskin, *St Basil's*; Kirley, *Community in France* 214n515.

KENNEDY, Joseph Mullaly, priest, was born at Lindsay, Ontario (diocese of Toronto, since 1882 of Peterborough), on 22 July 1869, the son of John Kennedy and Mary Anne Wheeler. He died in Toronto on 11 October 1938 and is buried there in the Basilian plot of Mount Hope Cemetery.

Joseph Kennedy attended St Dominic's School, Lindsay, before going to St Michael's College, Toronto, in 1883. At the end of the school year he collected several prizes, then went back to Lindsay, so timid and homesick that he remained out of school until 1891 when he came back to St Michael's to complete his classical course. In 1893 he went to the Petit Séminaire Ste-Thérèse, and from there to the Grand Séminaire, Montreal. During these years he became fluent in French. He entered St Basil's Novitiate, Toronto, in 1897 and was professed on 22 August 1898. He completed his theological studies at St Michael's College and was ordained priest on 24 August 1900 in St Basil's Church, Toronto, by Archbishop Denis *O'Connor.

Father Kennedy was appointed assistant at Assumption Parish, Windsor. In 1902 he moved to St Michael's College. He taught at St Thomas High School in Houston, 1904–6 and 1909–11, at Assumption College, Windsor, 1906–9, and at St Basil's College, Waco, Texas, 1911–14. Further appointments were to Assumption Parish, 1915–16 and 1921–4, Assumption College, 1916–17 and 1920–1, St John the Baptist Parish, Amherstburg, Ontario, 1917–20, St Michael's College, 1924–34, and assistant at St Mary's of the Assumption Parish, Owen Sound, Ontario, 1934–7. He returned to St Michael's College in 1937 on sick leave and died there one year later.

Father Kennedy paid three visits to the land of his forefathers, sailing directly to Ireland and returning without going to England or the continent. The *Basilian Centennial* volume of St Mary's of the Assumption Parish stated, 'Father Kennedy was a keen student of Irish history and loved to visit cemeteries, looking for Irish names and for unusual inscriptions. He is remembered by the parishioners as being particularly kind and gentle in the confessional.'

During his later years he wrote a considerable amount of poetry, much of it in Latin.

BIBLIOGRAPHY: 'Carmen hiemale,' *Basilian* 2 (April 1936) 72; 'Fabrum semper,' *Basilian* 1 (March 1935) 12; 'Gestantes viride,' *Basilian* 2 (March 1936) 53; 'Sanctus Casimir,' *Basilian* 2 (March 1936) 57.
SOURCES: GABF; *Centennial, St Mary's*; *Centennial Volume, 1859–1959, St Mary's of the Purification Parish* (Lindsay, 1959).

KENNEDY, Thomas VERNON, priest, uncle of former Basilian scholastic Oswald Kennedy, was born at Dunrobin, Ontario (archdiocese of Ottawa), on 27 September 1907, the son of Patrick Kennedy and Rose Ann Williams. He died in Toronto on 7 April 1949 and is buried there in the Basilian plot of Mount Hope Cemetery.

Vernon Kennedy attended Lisgar Collegiate Institute, Ottawa, 1921–6, and was awarded a scholarship to St Michael's College, Toronto. He was a brilliant student in philosophy and took part in student activities. He graduated in 1930, entered St Basil's Novitiate, Toronto, and was professed on 13 September 1931. He studied theology at St Basil's Scholasticate, Toronto, 1931–4, obtained an M.A. in philosophy from the University of Toronto in 1932, and was ordained priest on 23 September 1934 in the chapel of St Peter's Seminary, London, Ontario, by Bishop John Kidd.

Father Kennedy was then sent to the International Pontifical Institute (Angelicum), Rome (S.T.L., 1936; S.T.D., 1937). His thesis was entitled 'The Axiom: *Bonum est diffusivum sui*: A Historical Study.' He spent the year 1937–8 in post-doctoral studies in theology at the Ecole pratique des hautes études, Université de Paris, and at the Institut catholique, Paris. On his return to Toronto, he taught at St Basil's Seminary, and was chaplain at St Mary's Hospital and at the Mercer Reformatory for Women. In 1943 he was appointed to the staff of the Pontifical Institute of Mediaeval Studies, Toronto. A promising career as a teacher and research scholar came to an end in 1946 when he was found to be suffering from a brain tumour. In 1947 he was appointed to St Basil's Seminary, where he was cared for by the seminarians during the two years preceding his death.

Father Kennedy was a brilliant theologian. As a teacher at St Basil's Seminary he was somewhat aloof and reserved, but in the years of his illness he grew very close to the scholastics and was much loved by them.

BIBLIOGRAPHY: 'In the Eternal City,' *Basilian* 1 (June 1935) 73.
SOURCES: GABF; *Annals* 1 (1949) 241–2; *Yearbook SMC* 21 (1930).

KENNEDY, Vincent Lorne, priest, was born on 24 January 1899 at Kinkora, Ontario (diocese of London), the son of Denis Kennedy and Agnes Malloy. He died in Houston on 25 March 1974 and is buried there in the Basilian plot, Garden of Gethsemane, Forest Park Lawndale Cemetery.

Vincent Kennedy attended school at Stratford, Ontario, before enrolling at Assumption College, Windsor. In 1917 he entered St Basil's Novitiate, Toronto, made first profession on 10 August 1918, and was appointed to St Basil's Scholasticate, Toronto, for university and theological studies. He did a brilliant course in classics at the University of Toronto (B.A., 1923), earned a specialist's teaching certificate from the Ontario College of Education in 1924, and took an M.A. in classics from the University of Toronto in 1925. He did theological studies concurrently with these other studies and was ordained to the priesthood on 20 December 1924 in the chapel of St Augustine's Seminary, Toronto, by Bishop John McNally.

In 1925 Father Kennedy was appointed to Assumption College to teach and serve as registrar. In 1927 he became the principal of the high school at St Michael's College, but the next year he returned to Assumption as superior and president, a position he held for three years. In that office he did not experience the same confidence of the superior general, Francis *Forster, that his predecessor Daniel *Dillon had enjoyed. Academic initiatives that he proposed, such as extension courses, and a pre-medical program, were rejected. Then, thirteen months after his installation, October 1929, the stock market crash occured, leading to declining revenue, a more than 50 per cent cut in enrolment, and serious indebtedness. Father Kennedy's health failed, and he was forced to resign.

In 1931 he began graduate studies in the history of liturgy and in archaeology, first in Strasbourg, 1931–3, and then in Rome, 1933–5, at the Pontifical Institute of Christian Archaeology (A.C.L, 1934, A.C.D, 1935). The publication of his thesis, 'The Saints of the Canon of the Mass,' established Father Kennedy's reputation in Europe and America as an authority on ancient liturgy, and later led to his being named to the Liturgical Commission of the Second Vatican Council by Pope Paul VI.

Father Kennedy returned to St Michael's College in 1935 to teach at the Institute of Mediaeval Studies and to fill for a time the office of secretary (registrar) of the Institute. By his industry the yearly journal of the Institute, *Mediaeval Studies*, was put on a firm basis after commercial editors had given it up. He promoted the idea of erecting the 'Institute House' into a Basilian community separate from the St Michael's house, 1942, and was named its first superior. In 1951 he moved to the Curial House in Toronto and in 1957 to Holy Rosary Parish, where he resided while continuing to teach at the Institute. In later years he would spend periods of time at St Anne's in Houston for reasons of health, and he was there at the time of his death.

Father Kennedy served as procurator general at the Holy See for the Basilian Fathers for two periods, 1937–42 and 1961–7. During the first period of this office he would visit Rome frequently. He worked closely with Father Henry *Carr, the superior general, in obtaining the approval of the Basilian Constitutions in 1938. During his second period as procurator general he resided for some years in Rome, working with the Liturgical Commission and teaching Christian Archaeology.

V.L. Kennedy was a member of the general council of the Basilian Fathers for eighteen years, 1942–60. His remarkable talent for penetrating swiftly to the heart of a problem, seeing its implications, and proposing a solution with the utmost clarity made him an invaluable member of council and of general chapters. Though quiet and reserved, he loved the company of his confreres. He knew ill-health, disappointment, and failure, but no cynicism tainted his outlook or coloured his appreciation of the talents of others. A few hours before his death, while still completely lucid and aware that the end was approaching, he proclaimed his faith in Christ the Lord, then said no more, wishing those words to be his last.

BIBLIOGRAPHY:
Book: *The Saints of the Canon of the Mass.* Rome, 1938; repr. Rome, 1963.
Chapter in book: 'For a New Edition of the *Micrologus* of Bernold of Con-

stance,' *Mélanges en l'honneur de Monseigneur Michel Andrieu*. Strasbourg, 1956, pp. 229–41.

Articles: 'The Catacombs of Rome,' *Basilian* 3 (February, 1937) 25–7, 32. In *Ephemerides liturgicae*: 'The Pre-Gregorian "Hanc igitur," 50 (1936) 349–58; 'The "De officiis divinis" of MS Bamberg lat. 134,' 52 (1938) 312–26. In *Orate Fratres*: 'The Offertory Rite,' 12 (March 1938) 193–8; 'The Decline of the Offertory Rite from the Eighth to the Twelfth Century (II),' 12 (April 1938) 244–9; 'The Offertory Rite from the Late Middle Ages to the Present (III),' 12 (May 1938) 294–8; 'Questions and Answers: Active Participation in [the] Middle Ages,' 12 (April 1938) 276–7; 'The Corpus Christi Procession,' 14 (May 1940) 297–301. In *Mediaeval Studies*: 'The "Summa de officiis ecclesiae" of Guy d'Orchelles,' 1 (1939) 23–62; 'The Franciscan *Ordo Missae* in the Thirteenth Century,' 2 (1940) 204–22; 'The Handbook of Master Peter, Chancellor of Chartres,' 5 (1943) 1–38; 'The Moment of Consecration and the Elevation of the Host,' 6 (1944) 121–50; 'Robert Courson on Penance,' 7 (1945) 291–336; 'The Date of the Parisian Decree on the Elevation of the Host,' 8 (1946) 87–96; 'The Content of Courson's *Summa*,' 9 (1947) 81–107; 'The Lateran Missal and Some Allied Documents,' 14 (1952) 61–78; 'The Calendar of the Early Thirteenth-Century Curial Missal,' 20 (1958) 113–26.

SOURCES: GABF; *Annals* 4 (1969) 116, 5 (1975) 115–16; *Newsletter* (27 March 1974); Kirley, *Congregation in France* 249; McMahon, *Pure Zeal* 61–83. For documentation relating to his presidency at Assumption see Power, *Assumption College* 5 106–38.

KILLAIRE, Frederick Joseph, priest, was born on 16 May 1944 in Windsor, the son of Theodore Joseph Killaire and Shirley May Ryckman. He died in Sault Ste Marie, Ontario, on 21 June 1976, and is buried in the Basilian plot of Heavenly Rest Cemetery, Windsor.

'Rick' Killaire attended De La Salle elementary school and Assumption College School, Windsor, graduating in 1962. In August of that year he entered St Basil's Novitiate, Pontiac, Michigan, and was first professed on 15 August 1963. As an undergraduate he lived for two years at Assumption University and two years at the Basilian House of Studies, Windsor (B.A., University of Windsor, 1967). He taught at Michael Power High School, Etobicoke, Ontario, 1967–8, and at Assumption College School, 1968–70. His theological studies were taken at St Basil's College, Toronto (M.Div., University of St Michael's College, 1973). He served as a deacon at St Basil's Parish, Toronto, 1973–4, and was ordained to the priesthood in Ste Anne's Church, Detroit, on 11 May 1974 by Bishop Walter Schoenherr.

Father Killaire's first and only appointment was to St Mary's College, Sault Ste Marie. The life of teaching to which he had looked forward was cut short by his death two years later from a weak and enlarged heart.

Rick Killaire loved literature, music, and art. His gift for conversation was enriched by extensive reading. An enthusiastic teacher, he was particularly well informed in the history of the Church. He shone in small groups, and is remembered for his joviality and good humour, which was sometimes attenuated by uneasiness about being overweight. Only in the last days of his life did he seem to find peace from an angst which he had suffered for years.

SOURCES: GABF; *Annals* 5 (1975) 68, 5 (1977) 252–3; *Newsletter* (25 June 1976).

KILLORAN, Matthew Ambrose, priest, was born on 2 February 1901 at Belledune, New Brunswick (diocese of Chatham, since 1938 of Bathurst), the son of Ambrose Killoran and Catherine McDonald. He died in Detroit on 12 October 1977 and is buried there in the Basilian plot of Holy Sepulchre Cemetery.

After primary education in his home town, 'Matt' Killoran graduated in 1923 from St Thomas College, Chatham, New Brunswick, which was under Basilian direction at that time. He entered St Basil's Novitiate, Toronto, and made first profession on 11 August 1924. He lived another year at the novitiate while completing grade XIII of the Ontario system, after which he took up residence at St Michael's College, Toronto, for three years, 1925–8, of his university studies. In 1928 he moved to St Basil's Scholasticate where he studied theology while completing arts (B.A., University of Toronto, 1929) and earning teacher certification from the Ontario College of Education in 1930. He was ordained to the priesthood on 21 December 1932 in St Basil's Church, Toronto, by Bishop Alexander MacDonald.

Father Killoran's first appointment was to Assumption College, Windsor, where he taught in the high school, 1933–5. In 1935 he was the first Basilian to be appointed to the mission apostolate among the Spanish-speaking peoples in the diocese of Galveston (now Galveston-Houston), Texas. In 1936 he was reassigned to Assumption College as treasurer, a position he filled until 1942. That year, after residing four months at St Michael's College, Toronto, he finished the year as assistant at St Mary's of the Assumption Parish, Owen Sound, Ontario (January 1943) and was then sent to teach at Catholic Central High School,

Detroit. In August 1944 he was appointed to Ste Anne's, Detroit, where he served for the rest of his life, with but one interlude as pastor at Blessed Sacrament Parish, Windsor, 1947–9.

Matt Killoran, rotund of figure and naturally pleasant, contributed much to community life by his jovial manner and his dedication to duty. He was always at home ready to answer the phone or the door. He had an admirable patience with difficult people. His humour, imbued with charity and never offensive, brought peace and a sense of well-being to any group. The humbler folk of Ste Anne's found in him understanding and welcome.

SOURCES: GABF; *Annals* 5 (1975) 64, 5 (1978) 332–3; *Newsletter* (18 October 1977).

KOEHLER, Charles RALPH, priest, was born on 19 November 1913 in Detroit, one of fourteen children of Richard William Koehler and Julia Cronin. He died in Windsor on 18 July 2000 and is buried there in the Basilian plot of Heavenly Rest Cemetery.

Ralph attended parochial school, and from 1928 to 1932 was in one of the first classes of Catholic Central High School, Detroit. He entered St Basil's Novitiate, Toronto, made first profession on 15 August 1933, and graduated in Honours Philosophy from the University of Western Ontario in 1937. He studied theology at St Basil's Seminary, Toronto, 1937–41, and was ordained to the priesthood on 15 August 1940 in St Basil's Church, Toronto, by Archbishop James Charles McGuigan. He earned a B.L.S. from the University of Toronto in 1942 and an M.A. in education from the University of Houston in 1943.

During sixty years of priestly life Father Koehler received three rather lengthy assignments and eight shorter ones. The former: teacher of religion and librarian, Catholic Central, Detroit, 1944–62, treasurer, Basilian Fathers of East Rochester, 1969–82, and Andrean High School, Merrillville, Indiana, 1982–98. The shorter appointments: St Thomas High School, Houston, 1941–4, St Charles College, Sudbury, Ontario, 1962–4, Aquinas Institute, Rochester, 1964–5, St Basil's Novitiate, Pontiac, Michigan, as confessor, 1965, Ste Anne's Parish, Detroit, as assistant, 1965–8, Windsor House of Studies ('La Pointe'), as treasurer, 1968–9, St Joseph's Center, Sugar Land, Texas, 1998–9, and Assumption College School community, 1999–2000.

Soft-spoken and gentle-mannered, Ralph Koehler brought unobtrusive service to every assignment. In summer holidays at Strawberry

Island in Lake Simcoe, he was a familiar, solitary figure, waiting a hundred yards off shore for the fish to bite. In a pre-ecology era he had once sunk an old stove in the lake to create a fishing 'spot,' apparently with success. His health was delicate, though he was eighty-one years old when he died, just one month short of his sixtieth anniversary of priesthood.

SOURCES: GABF; *Annals* 6 (1984) 206–7, 7 (1991) 7, 9 (2001) 96–7; *Newsletter* (18 August 2000).

KRAUS, John Louis, priest, member of the Congregation 1951–68, was born in Grayling, Michigan (diocese of Grand Rapids, since 1971 of Gaylord), on 13 September 1927, the son of Emil Kraus and Leone Lennon. He died in Detroit on 13 December 1986.

John graduated from Assumption High School, Windsor, in 1946. After serving in the United States Army, 1945–6, he attended the University of Detroit, 1947–8, St Joseph's Diocesan Seminary, Grand Rapids, Michigan, 1948–9, and Assumption College, Windsor, 1949–50 (B.A., University of Western Ontario, 1950). He entered St Basil's Novitiate, Rochester, in 1950 and made his first profession on 15 August 1951. After studies in theology at St Basil's Seminary, 1952–6, he was ordained to the priesthood on 29 June 1955 in St Basil's Church, Toronto, by Bishop Francis Allen.

Father Kraus taught at Aquinas Institute, Rochester, in 1956–7. He was then assigned to St Basil's Seminary in 1957–9 as treasurer and as first councillor, 1958–9. He taught philosophy at St John Fisher College, Rochester, 1959–63 and 1965–8, doing graduate studies in the interim at the University of Ottawa (Ph.D., 1966), submitting as his thesis 'Locke's Theory of Universals and Its Relation to the Question of a Science of Physical Things.'

In 1968 Father Kraus received from the Holy See a dispensation from all the obligations of the priesthood and religious profession. He taught for a time at St Mary's College, Leavenworth, Kansas, and was chairman of the philosophy department at Marian College, Indianapolis, in 1969–72. He was survived by his wife, Catherine LaCoste, and their children Leone, John Jr, Mark, and Lennon.

BIBLIOGRAPHY: *John Locke: Empiricist, Atomist, Conceptualist, and Agnostic*. New York, 1969.

SOURCE: GABF; *Annals* 2 (1955) 199.

L

LACEY, Lawrence James, priest, was born at Amherstburg, Ontario (diocese of London), on 8 March 1908, the eldest of five children born to James Lacey and Cecilia Robidoux. He died in Hamilton, Ontario, on 15 May 1968 and is buried in the Basilian plot of Holy Cross Cemetery, Thornhill, Ontario.

'Larry' Lacey attended St Anthony's Separate School and General Amherst High School, Amherstburg. He took courses at Western Business College, Windsor, 1924–5, after which he worked for the Detroit Gas Company until he entered St Basil's Novitiate, Toronto, in 1928. After profession on 15 August 1929, he attended St Michael's College, Toronto (B.A., University of Toronto, 1932). He studied theology at St Basil's Scholasticate, Toronto, and was ordained priest on 21 December 1935 in St Basil's Church, Toronto, by Archbishop James Charles McGuigan.

Father Lacey taught for ten years: at St Michael's College School, Toronto, 1936–7, at St Thomas High School, Houston, 1937–44, and at Aquinas Institute, Rochester, 1944–6. He obtained an M.A. in education from the University of Houston in 1943. The rest of his appointments were to parish work: St Anne's, Houston, as assistant, 1946–50, 1955–8, and as pastor, 1958–64; Holy Rosary, Toronto, as assistant, 1950–5 and 1968, and as pastor, 1967–February 1968; Our Lady of the Assumption, Lethbridge, Alberta, pastor, 1964–7. In February 1968 he was asked to assist at St Basil's Parish, Ottawa, for a few months. In May, he died from a heart attack while driving to visit relatives in Hamilton.

A placid and cheerful priest who was usually unhurried in his way of life, he was guided by a fine aesthetic sense in the decoration and adornment of the churches where he served. His love of Houston was well known. Until his first heart attack in the early 1960s he was a powerful and regular swimmer.

BIBLIOGRAPHY: 'Catholics of Houston,' *Basilian* 3 (November 1937) 114, 120; 'Letter to the Editor,' *Basilian* 4 (February 1938) 36; 'Ave Maris Stella,' *Benedicamus* 2 (May 1949) 37.
SOURCES: GABF; *Annals* 4 (1969) 127–8; *Newsletter* (16 May 1968).

LACOSTE, Paul, priest, was born at Fons (Ardèche) on 5 January 1868. He died on 7 February 1930 at Fons and was buried in the cemetery there.

Paul Lacoste made his novitiate at Beaconfield House, Plymouth, England, 1887-8. After a year at Sainte-Barbe, Annonay, he was appointed to the Collège du Sacré-Coeur, Annonay, 1889-91. Two years later he went to the Collège Saint-Charles, Blidah, Algeria, 1891-4, and then to the Collège Saint-Augustin, Bône, Algeria, 1894-5. He returned to Sacré-Coeur in 1895 and was ordained to the priesthood on 19 September 1896 in the chapel of the Collège du Sacré-Coeur by Bishop Joseph-Michel-Frédéric Bonnet of Viviers.

Father Lacoste spent a year each at Sacré-Coeur, the Ecole cléricale de Périgueux (Dordogne), and the Collège Saint-Charles, Blidah, before returning for a longer time to Périgueux, 1899-1903. After the anticlerical laws excluded Basilians from teaching, he remained in the Périgueux region until 1919 – from 1911, it appears, as the pastor at Saint-Gérac. He was at the Petit Séminaire d'Aubenas (Ardèche) from 1919 to 1926, when the Basilians left Aubenas. He replaced Father Octave *Descellière as superior of the *Maîtrise* (choir school) in Viviers for the year 1928-9. He fell ill and died in 1930 at Fons. His funeral service was presided over by Father Descellière, then superior of the Petit Séminaire Saint-Charles, Annonay.

Father Lacoste had taken part in the provincial chapter at Aubenas in April 1922 and, on the death of Father Noël *Durand, superior general, he was a delegate to the general chapter held at Saint-Charles, Annonay, in 1928.

SOURCES: GABF; Kirley, *Community in France* 185, 207, 240n569; Kirley, *Congregation in France* 42, 76n35, 82, 135, 151, 154, 211; Pouzol, 'Notices'; *Semaine religieuse de Viviers* (21 February 1930) 96.

LACROIX, John Robert, priest, father of Father John Robert Stephen LaCroix CSB, was born on 25 July 1912 at Tisdale, Saskatchewan (diocese of Prince Albert), the son of George J. LaCroix and Rose E. Hurtubise. He died in Toronto on 16 July 1985 and is buried in the Basilian plot of Holy Cross Cemetery, Thornhill, Ontario.

John LaCroix attended public school at Tisdale, 1918-24, and then took high school and university at Campion College, Regina, Saskatchewan. After obtaining a B.A. from the University of Manitoba in 1931, he began studies there in medicine, and received the M.D. in 1939. On

26 May 1939 he married Mary Findlay Stephens in the archbishop's residence, Winnipeg. They had four children: Stephen, Virginia, Veronica, and Margot. From 1939 to 1970 he was a member of the Royal Canadian Army Medical Corps, serving in England during the Second World War as a surgeon. The family lived at different times in Sheffield, England, Montreal, and Hamilton and Kapuskasing (Ontario), in which places Dr LaCroix practised as a surgeon and taught at various medical schools. In Hamilton he worked for a time as Chief of Staff at St Joseph's Hospital. After the death of his wife on Christmas Day 1969, he did some travelling and then asked to live with the Basilians at St Basil's College, Toronto.

On 10 July 1974 Dr LaCroix began his novitiate with the Basilian Fathers at St Basil's College, Toronto, with Father Robert Madden, rector of the college, as novice master and Father Wilfrid *Dore as instructor in spiritual theology. After first profession on 11 July 1975, he studied theology privately at St Basil's College, 1975–9, under the direction of the theology staff, taking scripture classes at the Toronto School of Theology. He was ordained to the priesthood on 2 June 1979 by Cardinal George Bernard *Flahiff in St Basil's Church, Toronto.

Father LaCroix was appointed to live at St Basil's College, from where he gave pastoral assistance at St Basil's Church, especially in the ministry of the sacrament of reconciliation. He had a gift for dealing with people, who found in him the healing art of the doctor extended to the realm of the spirit. Father Manuel Chircop, in the funeral homily, said, 'He had a way of lifting people's spirits and imparting to them that same hope which he found invaluable in his own life.'

John LaCroix was a gentleman in every sense of the word, a trait which made him accessible and easy of conversation. He loved the Basilian community, expressing himself always in superlatives when speaking of his vocation and of those who had helped him on his journey.

SOURCES: GABF; *Annals* 5 (1980) 453–4, 6 (1986) 481–2; *Newsletter* (22 July 1985).

LADET, Casimir, scholastic, was born on 2 August 1855 at Prades (Ardèche) and died on 15 September 1877 at Prades.
Casimir was a student at the Collège de Privas (Ardèche) and then, from 1872 to 1875, at the Collège du Sacré-Coeur, Annonay, section Sainte-Barbe. He made his novitiate at Feyzin (Isère, now Rhône), 1875–6. In 1876 he began theological studies while teaching at the Col-

lège Saint-Charles, Blidah, Algeria, where he fell ill. He returned to his family at Prades, and died shortly afterwards at the age of twenty-two.

SOURCES: GABF; Pouzol, 'Notices.'

LADREYT, Henri, priest, was born on 12 May 1833 at Tournon (Ardèche), the son of Jean Antoine Romain Ladreyt and Marie Olivier. He died on 6 April 1915 at Tournon (Ardèche), and was buried there.

Henri Ladreyt was brought up by his father, who impressed on him the basic traits of love and respect for God and for one's parents. A late vocation, he was twenty years old when he began studies at the Collège des Cordeliers, Annonay, section Sainte-Barbe, in 1853. He remained there for six years until he entered the Grand Séminaire de Viviers, where he experienced misgivings about his vocation to parish ministry and was advised to enter a religious community. He made his novitiate at Feyzin (Isère, now Rhône) but does not appear to have made profession until 1868. He spent the year 1866–7 at the Collège des Cordeliers, Annonay, and in 1867 he began five years at the Collège du Sacré-Coeur, Annonay. He was ordained to the priesthood in the chapel there by Bishop Armand de Charbonnel on 21 September 1872.

From 1872 to 1903 Father Ladreyt taught at the Collège Saint-Charles, Blidah, Algeria. He was one of the pillars of the institution and was named a canon of the cathedral by the archbishop of Algiers. After anticlerical legislation forced Basilians from schools in 1903, Father Ladreyt returned to Tournon, where he spent the last twelve years of his life in parish ministry.

SOURCES: GABF; Kirley, *Community in France* 124n305, 163n416, 205; Pouzol, 'Notices'; *Semaine religieuse de Viviers* (23 April 1915) 44–7.

LAJEUNESSE, Ernest Joseph, priest, was born on 2 December 1901 at LaSalle, Ontario (diocese of London), the son of Clément Lajeunesse and Claire Pajot. He died in Windsor on 23 December 1991 and is buried there in the Basilian plot of Heavenly Rest Cemetery.

'Laj,' as Ernest Joseph Lajeunesse came to be called, attended Assumption College School and Assumption College, Windsor (B.A., University of Western Ontario, 1923). He entered St Basil's Novitiate, Toronto, and, after first profession on 11 August 1924, was appointed to St Michael's College, Toronto, for first year of theology, moving to St Basil's Scholasticate in 1925. He was ordained to the priesthood on 21 December 1927 in St Basil's Church, Toronto, by Bishop Alexander MacDonald. He completed his theological studies in 1928, and in that same year received an M.A. in French from the University of Toronto.

In 1928 Father Lajeunesse was appointed to Assumption College, where he remained on the faculty until 1946, with a one-year interval, 1938–9, as assistant at Blessed Sacrament Parish, Windsor. In 1946 he was appointed superior and master of scholastics at St Basil's Seminary, Toronto. With Father Hubert *Coughlin he was largely responsible for the planning and building of the new seminary at 95 St Joseph Street (later the Cardinal Flahiff Centre), designed by the prominent architect Ernest Cormier, and for the transfer there from 21 St Mary Street (officially 65 St Nicholas Street) in 1951. In 1952 he returned to Assumption College. In addition to teaching there, he served on the local council. In 1959 he returned to St Basil's Seminary to teach there and at St Michael's College.

In 1966 Father Lajeunesse began twenty-five years of parish ministry at Assumption Parish, Windsor, with the exception of but four months at Blessed Sacrament Parish, Windsor. His activities, however, ranged farther than the rectory or the church. He served many times as canonical visitor on behalf of the general council. For many years he oversaw the operation of Strawberry Island, the summer home of the Basilian Fathers in Lake Simcoe near Orillia, Ontario, and wrote its history in 1962, with brief updates in 1974 and 1981. He also researched, wrote, and delivered talks about the history of Essex County, Ontario, the genealogy of the French families there, and Assumption Church.

A school in Windsor was named for him 'Ecole secondaire E.J. Lajeunesse,' and the Essex County Historical Society established 'The Reverend Ernest J. Lajeunesse Award' for persons making unique and significant contribution to the study of the history of Windsor and Essex County.

Laj was humble and self-effacing. In the regular interviews with scholastics called upon by his charge of them, he would not only point out areas for the seminarian to address but would invite him to comment on ways that he himself might better carry out his job. His patient and prudent manner made him a centre of peace in the community throughout his life.

BIBLIOGRAPHY:
Book: *The Windsor Border Region: Canada's Southernmost Frontier. A Collection of Documents*. Champlain Society 4. Toronto, 1960.
Pamphlets: *Strawberry Island in Lake Simcoe*. Toronto, 1962, 1974, 1981, 1983. *Outline History of Assumption Parish, 1797–1967*. Windsor, 1967.
Articles: 'H.S.R.,' *Basilian* 2 (February 1938) 30–1; 'The Coming of the First Nun to Upper Canada,' *CCHA Report* 22 (1955) 27–37; 'The First Four Years of the Settlement on the Canadian Side of the Detroit River,' *Ontario History* 47 (1955) 122–31; 'Assumption Parish, 1781,' *Basilian Teacher* 3 (April 1959) 196–8.
SOURCES: GABF; *Annals* 5 (1975) 65, 5 (1978) 259–60, 7 (1992) 140–1; *French Studies U. of T.* 125–6; *Newsletter* (27 December 1991); Kirley, *Congregation in France* 243.

LALONDE, Patrick Alfred, priest, brother of Father Gerald Lalonde CSB, was born on 15 November 1927 at Capreol, Ontario (diocese of Sault Ste Marie), the son of Alfred Lalonde and Mary Agnes Helferty. He died in Toronto on 9 October 1987 and is buried in the Basilian plot of Holy Cross Cemetery, Thornhill, Ontario.

After primary school and two years of secondary school at Capreol, 'Pat' enrolled in 1944 at Assumption College School, Windsor, and the following year transferred to St Michael's College, Toronto, where he completed high school. In 1946 he entered St Basil's Novitiate, Toronto, making first profession on 15 August 1947. He was appointed to Assumption College, Windsor, for undergraduate studies in science (B.A., University of Western Ontario, 1950). He taught science and health for one year at Aquinas Institute, Rochester. In 1951 he began theological studies at St Basil's Seminary, Toronto, moving to St Michael's College one year later, and attending the Ontario College of Education, where he earned Type B teaching certification and Type A certification in physical education, 1953. He returned to St Basil's Seminary in 1953 and was ordained to the priesthood on 29 June 1955 in St Basil's Church, Toronto, by Bishop Francis Allen.

Father Lalonde was appointed to join Father Matthew *Mulcahy at St Mary's College, Sault Ste Marie, Ontario, forming the pioneer Basilian staff at that school. He brought to St Mary's not only extraordinary gifts as teacher and coach but also a youthful enthusiasm and love of the community. He remained at the school for fifteen years, serving as local councillor for the Basilian community, 1960–6, and as superior, 1966–71. In 1971 he was appointed to St Charles College, Sudbury, Ontario, where he remained for one year. In 1972 he was named principal of Assumption College School, a position he held until 1978, serving as local councillor for the Basilian community the whole time.

In 1978 Father Lalonde returned to St Mary's in the Sault as principal for two years and was then appointed to Michael Power High School, Etobicoke, Ontario, as teacher and chaplain. In 1985 he was named superior of the local community there.

At this time it was discovered that he suffered from leukemia. Although he had periods of remission, it weakened him to the point that he requested to be relieved of the office of superior. He was appointed to St Basil's College in 1986, where he assisted in the formation of young Basilians while remaining on the guidance and chaplaincy staff of Michael Power. Sickness could not suppress his pleasant character or his universal kindness.

In co-operation with Mrs Rose Marie McIsaac and others, Pat Lalonde fostered the lay associate movement in the Basilian community. His life was marked by a spirit of adventure. He often organized outings and trips among the confreres, one of which was intended for Egan Lake on the weekend which followed his death. At St Basil's College he was an example of courage and patience. In a homily there he said, 'We can expect that the Lord will ask us for difficult things in our lives and we don't like hard things; but ... it is simply a demonstration of his confidence in us.' In an address to a Cursillo group he once said: 'Devoted parents, good friends: good books, great music, beautiful scenery, indeed anything at all may be used by God to lead us toward life. Even sickness, failure, pain, sorrow may be graces by which God directs those whom he loves towards eternal happiness.'

SOURCES: GABF; *Annals* 2 (1955) 199, 6 (1988) 706–8; *Newsletter* (26 October 1987); Gerald Lalonde CSB.

LAMB, Robert Emmett, priest, was born on 13 September 1915 in Detroit, the son of John Aloysius Lamb and Isabel Agnes Guina. He died in Toronto on 29 January 2000 and is buried in the Basilian plot of Holy Cross Cemetery, Thornhill, Ontario.

Bob Lamb attended Visitation grade school and Catholic Central High School in Detroit, where he graduated in 1933. He entered St Basil's Novitiate, Toronto, and made first profession on 15 August 1934. After undergraduate studies at Assumption College, Windsor (B.A., University of Western Ontario, 1938), he taught for one year at Catholic Central High School while studying for permanent teaching certification for Michigan, which he received in 1939. He was appointed to St Basil's Seminary, Toronto, for theology, interrupting those studies to teach another year at Catholic Central, 1941–2. He was ordained to the priesthood on 15 August 1943 in St Basil's Church by Archbishop James Charles McGuigan, and in 1944 obtained an M.A. in philosophy from the University of Toronto, submitting as a thesis 'The Teaching of Saint Thomas Aquinas on Economics.'

Father Lamb taught history at St Thomas High School, Houston, 1944–7, and again at Catholic Central, Detroit, 1947–52. During the year 1952–3 he did graduate studies in history at the University of Ottawa (Ph.D., 1954), with a thesis on the Riel Rebellion in western Canada. In 1953 he was appointed to the University of St Thomas, Houston, where he was to remain for forty-two years. In 1996 he moved to the Basilian Fathers Residence (Infirmary), Toronto.

Father Lamb maintained the highest standards for himself. His lectures were prepared with meticulous, if dry, precision. He had 'Mabillon' and 'Europa' medals struck to honour the best essays of his students. For many years he produced *History Pursuits*, a departmental bulletin and venue for student papers. He typed it personally and took it to the bus station for delivery to his printer in Galveston. So important was it to him that, on waking from a two-week coma induced by asphyxiation, his first words were a request that the newsletter be picked up at the depot. He brought prestigious historians to give the annual B.K. Smith History Lecture, and edited its annual publication. A high point in his professional life was securing the celebrated British historian Christopher Dawson for that lecture in 1960. Later that year he was invited to accompany Archbishop-elect George Bernard *Flahiff to a private audience with Pope John XXIII. Conversation turned on the preparation of Vatican Council II, a subject fed by his insatiable interest in history and the Church. That same interest prompted him, on his way to the Congress of Historical Sciences in Bucharest in 1967, to take the Orient Express from Paris to Istanbul. There he called unannounced on the Patriarch Athenagoras, and the two engaged in an animated discussion about St Basil, Church reunion, and Texas. The historian in him noted and carefully reported the books, pictures, and other aspects of the patriarch's simple office.

The asphyxiation which he had suffered years earlier affected his motor skills more severely as time passed; but he was iron-willed in continuing his routines, making his way painfully each day to the dining room, the chapel, and even, two blocks away, to his office. Obedience alone effected his move to the infirmary in Toronto, where his mind remained clear and his interest keen. His strength and power of speech ebbed continuously but not his gentleness or his attention to the things of the spirit.

BIBLIOGRAPHY:
Book: *Thunder in the North: Conflict over the Riel Risings, 1870–1885*. New York, 1957.
Pamphlets: *Middle Civilization. Presentation and Analysis*. Houston, 1978. *Crossroads Civilization. Exposition and Examination*. Houston, 1980. *Spiritual Discussions* (excerpts from Christopher Dawson). Houston, 1988.
Articles: In *Basilian*: 'Recent American Terrorism,' 2 (November 1936) 132–4; 'Assumption Lecture League,' 3 (December 1937) 139; 'Christian Contemplation vs. Marxian Action,' 4 (April 1938) 104–5; 'Attracting to Our Life,' *Benedicamus* 3 (February 1950) 26, 31; 'St Basil,' *Benedicamus* 4 (October 1950) 8; 'Troops to Red River,' *Mid-America* 39 (January 1957) 21–38; 'Thinking about Proclaiming,' *Southwestern Journal of Social Education* 15 (Spring/Summer 1985) 26–8; 'Epilogue,' in Raphael O'Loughlin, *Basilian Leaders from Texas* (Houston, 1990), 78–9; 'Thirty Summers with the Poor,' *Stirrings* 5 (August 1991) 7. In *Basilian Teacher*: 'Preface to Liberalism,' 3 (December 1958) 57–60; 'European Christendom – The Focus of History Teaching,' 4 (October 1959) 54–7; 'A Basilian *Ratio Studiorum*? Why Not?' 5 (October 1960) 13–14; 'The Future of American Education,' 6 (November 1961) 69–73; 'The Presence of France,' *Social Studies* 65 (August 1974) 168–70. Over many years he wrote numerous articles in *Cauldron*, the UST student ewspaper. For the *New Handbook of Texas in Six Volumes* (Austin, 1996) he wrote: 'Basilian Fathers,' 1 407–8, 'St Basil's College' 5 755, and 'St Thomas High School,' 5 770; (cf. *Handbook of Texas Online* http://www.tsha.utexas.edu/handbook/online/articles).
SOURCES: GABF; *Annals* 1 (1944) 54, 6 (1985) 310, 9 (2001) 83–4; *Newsletter* (18 February 2000).

LAPIERRE, Joseph Bovier (Bouvier), priest, one of the ten founding members and first superior general, was born on 25 February 1757 in the arrondissement of La Tour-du-Pin (Isère, diocese of Grenoble), the son of Louis Lapierre and Marguerite Monavon. He died on 16 August 1838 in Annonay and was buried in the now defunct Saint-Jacques Cemetery, Annonay. On 11 November 1869 his body was reinterred in the cemetery on the grounds of the Collège du Sacré-Coeur, Annonay.

Joseph Lapierre received his early education from his parish priest. He attended schools at Pont-de-Beauvoisin (Isère) and Valence (Drôme). He studied philosophy in Lyon with the Oratorians and theology with the Sulpicians at the Séminaire Saint-Irénée, Lyon, and was ordained to the priesthood in March 1782.

Father Lapierre began his ministry in what is now the diocese of Valence, probably as an assistant at Clérieux (Drôme) until late in 1786, when he went to Tain-l'Hermitage (Drôme). The revolutionary Civil Constitution of the Clergy, demanding an oath of allegiance from each cleric, was legislated by the Constituent Assembly in France on 12 July 1790. Two days later Father Lapierre took the constitutional oath in good faith; but on 22 August 1790 Archbishop Charles-François d'Aviau of Vienne informed his priests that the oath was schismatic, and on 21 October 1790 Father Lapierre informed the civil authorities that he was retracting his oath. He continued his ministry at Tain until 29 January 1791, when danger of arrest forced his escape to Tournon (Ardèche). There a certain Mme de Clavière offered him asylum and, when persecution became more severe, he hid out near her château at Vaudevant between Satillieu and Saint-Félicien, villages of the Ardèche. He secretly celebrated Mass and instructed her son. Under the new Directory government in 1795 persecution eased somewhat, and in 1796 Father Lapierre began cautiously serving the parish of Sarras (Ardèche), but was soon forced to leave because of threats from revolutionaries. It appears that in 1797 he was at Saint-Symphorien-de-Mahun (Ardèche) as pastor, and was officially given charge of the parish during the summer by Archbishop d'Aviau, who had returned from exile and spent six weeks at Saint-Symphorien.

A relative religious peace followed the coup d'état of 18 Brumaire of Year VIII (9 November 1799) when Napoleon Bonaparte overturned the Directory and established the Consulate with himself as First Consul. When Archbishop d'Aviau decided to establish a seminary-college at Saint-Symphorien, Father Lapierre suggested he call on Father Joseph Actorie to be the director. He, too, had taken the oath and later retracted. Father Léorat-Picansel, the pastor of Notre-Dame, Annonay, who was also in hiding at Saint-Symphorien, drew up a rule for the priest-teachers there. A notice of the opening of the school was circulated on 23 August 1800 without mentioning the locale. The seminary-college opened on 11 November 1800 and continued clandestinely there until 1802, when it became safe to teach openly. Father Lapierre resigned as pastor of Saint-Symphorien when the school moved to the former Franciscan convent on the Place des Cordeliers in Annonay, taking the name Collège des Cordeliers. Father Lapierre served as bursar and also undertook chaplaincy to the Ursuline Sisters, a post he held until his death. In 1805, because of his anti-revolutionary leanings, Father Actorie was forced to resign, and Father Lapierre became director.

A growing pessimism about the future of the college inspired Father Lapierre and five members of the college to write on 15 September 1822 to Bishop Charles-Joseph Brulley de la Brunière, bishop of Mende, asking permission to form a religious association of priests teaching at the college. (From 1801 to 1822 Annonay was in the diocese of Mende. In 1822 Viviers regained its status as a diocese, but the new bishop took control of the see only in 1823.) The bishop granted this request with the proviso that the new association also accept responsibility for the minor seminary at Maison-Seule (Ardèche). Eventually ten priests formed the new Association of Priests of Saint Basil. On 21 November 1822 they held their first general chapter, electing Father Lapierre superior general, with nine votes out of ten.

The ensuing years were difficult for Father Lapierre and the association, especially after the arrival of Bishop André Molin (Mollins) to the see of Viviers in the summer of 1823. His vicar general, Monsignor Joseph Laurent Régis Vernet, who was also the Sulpician superior of the Grand Séminaire de Viviers, had his own plans for seminaries in the diocese. Bishop Molin thus reacted negatively to the new association and was reluctant to support Maison-Seule as his minor seminary; but he died on 25 July 1825, just before signing the act of dissolution of the Association. Though the Basilians had to abandon Maison-Seule in 1828, Father Lapierre made new foundations at Vernoux (Ardèche), Privas (Ardèche), and Bourg-Saint-Andéol (Ardèche). Also, after consulting the community, he prepared a new draft of the Constitutions of the Association and in 1836 sent the document to Rome, where it received provisional approval.

Father Lapierre's health began to fail in 1837. He lived to see the definitive decree of praise from Rome for the Constitutions, which reached Annonay on 4 June 1838. He died two months later, having served as superior general for sixteen years.

A man more of thought than of action, Father Lapierre could take decisive steps when needed, as his retraction of the schismatic oath, his role in the foundation of the school in Saint-Symphorien, its transfer to Annonay, and the establishment of the new religious Association testify. In his negotiations with civil authorities his well-known patriotism was an asset. He looked after the material interests of the college quietly and efficiently. He seldom preached in parish churches, finding a more modest outlet for his priestly zeal as chaplain of the Ursuline sisters for thirty-five years.

SOURCES: GABF; Chomel, *Collège d'Annonay* 56-9, 97, 137-45, 438; Kirley, *Community in France* 36, 58, 239; Pouzol, 'Notices'; Roume, *Origines* 58-65, 76-83, 92, 117-19, 122-31, 159.

LAVALETTE, Jules-Jean, priest, member of the Congregation 1856-78, was born on 21 May 1830 at Montpezat (Ardèche). A brother was a secular priest in that diocese. Jules-Jean died in Viviers on 30 June 1891.

Before entering the Congregation Jules-Jean Lavalette had taught and worked as prefect at the Petit Séminaire d'Aubenas (Ardèche) in 1853-4 and at the *Maîtrise* (choir school) in Viviers, 1854-5. He was admitted as a Basilian novice on 29 September 1855. During his novitiate and theological studies he taught *seconde* at the Petit Séminaire de Vernoux (Ardèche), 1858-60. He was ordained a priest on 18 June 1859, and made final profession of vows on 29 September 1860.

Father Lavalette taught *seconde* at the Collège de Privas (Ardèche) from 1860 to 1862 and *première* at the Petit Séminaire d'Aubenas, 1862-70. After six years, 1870-6, as director of the Collège du Sacré-Coeur, Annonay, and two years, 1876-8, as superior of the scholasticate at Montée du Château, Annonay, he withdrew from the Congregation in September 1878 and took up residence at the *Maîtrise* (choir school) in Viviers, where he served as second organist in the cathedral.

SOURCE: Pouzol, 'Notices,' Supplément 3.

LAVERY, Charles Joseph, priest, was born in Toronto on 1 May 1915, the son of Charles Lavery and Ellinor Bradley. He died in Rochester on 3 December 1985 and is buried there in the Basilian plot of Holy Sepulchre Cemetery.

'Charlie' Lavery attended St Vincent de Paul parochial school, Toronto, and in 1928 enrolled in the high school section at St Michael's College, Toronto, graduating in 1933. He received his B.A. in Honours Philosophy from the University of Toronto in 1937, and entered St Basil's Novitiate. After first profession on 15 August 1938, he was appointed to St Michael's College for theological studies, moving to live at St Basil's Seminary the following year. During this time he did graduate studies in philosophy (M.A., University of Toronto, 1940; thesis: 'St Thomas and Trade'). After teaching a year at Aquinas Institute, Rochester, 1940-1, he was ordained to the priesthood on 15 August 1942 in St Basil's Church, Toronto, by Archbishop James Charles McGuigan.

In 1943 Father Lavery returned to graduate studies, this time at the University of Chicago (Ph.D., Political Science, 1950), submitting as his thesis topic 'The Classical Doctrine of Human Rights in International Law.' Whether from the many years he took to gain his degree or because of his confident manner, his confreres called him 'Chicago Charlie.' From 1949 to 1958 he taught at St Michael's College. He also served as registrar during this period and as a Basilian local councillor from 1950 to 1958. His talents for administration, educational development, and public service were to find full scope in his appointment in 1958 as president of St John Fisher College, Rochester, a position he held until 1980, after which he was named chancellor of the college, which title he retained until his retirement in 1985.

As president, Father Lavery oversaw the construction of eleven college buildings. During his time the college became co-educational, its enrolment increased dramatically, and ten academic majors were added to the curriculum. He was a prominent spokesman for higher education to the wider community, and was invited to sit on the White House Conference on Education. He was a founder of the Rochester Area Colleges, Inc., and served as its first chairman and then as a member of its executive committee.

First an educator but also a community activist, Father Lavery was a member of the Rochester Chamber of Commerce, the Rochester Area Educational Association, the Rochester Philharmonic Orchestra, the Inter-faith Committee for Israel, and the Board of Overseers of Strong Memorial Hospital. He had time, withal, for the students, and kept his door open to them, and presided at weddings, funerals, and other gatherings for alumni. In 1971 he was named Kiwanis Citizen of the Year, and in 1977 the Phi Delta Kappa Educator of the Year, and received honorary degrees from Hofstra University, Hobart College, William Smith College, Nazareth College, and the University of Rochester.

BIBLIOGRAPHY: 'Off on Another "100,"' *Basilian* 6 (December 1952) 7–10; 'Lay Professors on the Catholic Campus,' *Basilian Teacher* 5 (January 1961) 111–14. He left an unpublished typescript, 'St Thomas Aquinas' *Commentary on the Pol-*

itics of Aristotle: A Literal Translation' (1940) (Toronto, Kelly Library MS/Misc/ 4to/67).
SOURCES: GABF; *Annals* 1 (1943) 28, 6 (1986) 484–5; *Newsletter* (11 December 1985).

LAWLOR, Thomas Anthony, priest, was born on 13 June 1918 in Orillia, Ontario (archdiocese of Toronto), the son of Leo Lawlor and Catherine Chambers. He died in Toronto on 19 April 1983 and is buried in the Basilian plot of St Mary's Cemetery, Owen Sound.

Tom Lawlor attended elementary school in Orillia, Orillia Collegiate, and finished high school at St Michael's College, Toronto. He entered St Basil's Novitiate, Toronto, in 1941, making first profession on 15 August 1942. He was appointed to Assumption College, Windsor, for undergraduate studies (B.A., University of Western Ontario, 1946), during which time he also taught at Assumption College School. He taught for one year at Aquinas Institute, Rochester, studied theology at St Basil's Seminary, Toronto, 1947–51, and was ordained to the priesthood on 29 June 1950 in St Basil's Church, Toronto, by Cardinal James Charles McGuigan.

Father Lawlor worked for nineteen years in the high school apostolate: Aquinas Institute, 1951–2, teaching; St Michael's College School, 1952–4, teaching and treasurer; St Charles College, Sudbury, Ontario, 1954–7, teaching and treasurer; Aquinas Institute, 1957–8, teaching; St Charles College, 1958–64, teaching; St Mary's College, Sault Ste Marie, 1964–70, teaching. In 1970 he began twelve years as assistant pastor and councillor for the Basilian community serving St Mary's of the Assumption Parish, Owen Sound, Ontario, and its numerous missions. His ministry was cut short when leukemia was diagnosed in the early 1980s. With his usual willingness to serve he remained on the job until 1982, when his illness compelled his move to the Basilian Fathers Residence (Infirmary), Toronto, where he died less than a year later.

Father Lawlor made it a point to know personally the people to whom he ministered. He was cheerful and good-natured, enjoying a joke on himself and ready to play one on his friends.

SOURCES: GABF; *Annals* 1 (1950) 285, 6 (1984) 290–1; *Newsletter* (19 April 1983).

LEBEL, Eugene Carlisle, priest, was born on 27 July 1899 at Sarnia, Ontario (diocese of London), the son of Eugene Albert LeBel and Catherine Mahoney. He died in Toronto on 11 August 1986 and is buried in the Basilian plot of Holy Cross Cemetery, Thornhill, Ontario.

'Nig' LeBel (a nickname deriving from his baseball skills as a catcher, with reference to Justin 'Nig' Clarke, an alumnus of Assumption and popular player of the time) took his elementary schooling in Sarnia and four years of high school, 1913–17, at Assumption College School, Windsor. He entered St Basil's Novitiate, Toronto, was professed on 15 August 1918, and then completed senior matriculation at St Michael's College, Toronto, and at Assumption College School. He did the Honours English and History course at the University of Toronto, distinguishing himself by winning two gold medals (B.A., 1922). He obtained a specialist's teaching certificate in English from the Ontario College of Education. His theological studies at St Basil's Scholasticate, Toronto, brought him to priestly ordination on 19 December 1925 in St Basil's Church, Toronto, by Bishop Michael O'Brien of Peterborough, Ontario.

Father LeBel taught English at St Michael's College from 1925 to 1939, and obtained an M.A. from the University of Chicago in 1931 (thesis: 'Christian and Medieval Theology in Spenser's "Hymne of Heavenly Love" and "Hymne of Heavenly Beautie"'). He taught at St Thomas More College, Saskatoon, Saskatchewan, 1939–41. His next assignment was to Assumption College, where he served first as head of the English Department, 1941–7, then as dean, 1947–52, and finally as superior, 1952–8, and president, 1952–64, through the various changes the institution underwent in name and character. Aided by other Basilians, he wrote the 'Brief on University Charter' that was submitted to the general council on 25 January 1952. He became the principal negotiator with Premier Leslie Frost and G.E. Hall, president of the University of Western Ontario. These efforts led to the acquisition of degree-granting power for Assumption College in 1953. Three years later, following affiliation of Assumption with Holy Names College and Holy Redeemer College (Catholic), with Canterbury College (Anglican), and with the non-denominational and provincially funded Essex College, the creation of Assumption University of Windsor was accomplished, 1956. But concerns about the ability of this new Catholic university to meet the needs of the Windsor community led to the creation of the secular University of Windsor, which purchased most of the property and buildings of Assumption University. Father LeBel served as its first president, 1963–4. The Fine Arts Building at the University of Windsor is named for him.

In 1964 Father LeBel was assigned to St Mark's College, Vancouver, as superior and principal. He held these offices until 1971, when he retired to St Michael's College, Toronto. He lived there only a short time before moving to St Basil's Residence (Infirmary), Toronto. In spite of his declining health, he maintained the same gentle spirit, interest in people, and love for the Basilian community which had characterized his life.

As a young man, though slight of build, 'Nig' LeBel had been an outstanding athlete and coach. He was designated 'Captain and Star' of the St Michael's College Intermediate Intercollegiate Football championship team in 1925. As a priest, administrator, and superior he achieved an admirable blend of courtesy and humanity, love for the Church and for learning, and care for institutions. During the Second World War, though he never saw overseas service, he was chaplain to the Essex Scottish Regiment, and maintained the chaplaincy until 1955, when he received the Canadian Forces Decoration. Father Norbert *Ruth, speaking on the occasion of Father LeBel's fiftieth anniversary of priesthood, said, 'In his life, in his words and his actions, in Toronto, in Saskatoon, in Windsor, and Vancouver, on the football field, in the classroom, in his administrative duties, and in the sanctuary and the pulpit, he has carried on Christ's work.'

BIBLIOGRAPHY: 'Dryden's Conversion to Catholicism,' *Basilian* 1 (December 1935) 127–9, 2 (February 1936) 34–5; 'The History of Assumption, the First Parish in Upper Canada,' *CCHA Report* 21 (1954) 23–38; 'The Basilian Educational Ideal,' *Five Letters* (Chapter Documents) (1960) 22–4; 'The Catholic University and the Dialogue,' *Basilian Teacher* 5 (March 1961) 199–206; 'Obedience Is a Great Aid to Poverty,' *Basilian Forum* 1 (December 1964) 40–3.
SOURCES: GABF; *Annals* 4 (1969) 116, 5 (1976) 132, 5 (1979) 340, 6 (1987) 577–9; *Newsletter* (15 August 1986); Shook, *Catholic Education* 287–92; *Toronto Star* 20 November 1925, 13 August 1986; *Windsor University Magazine* 7 no. 2 (1986) 4. For his role in seeking independence of Assumption University see Power, *Assumption College* 6 198–205.

LEE, Edward Gregory, priest, brother of Monsignor Frederick Lee of the archdiocese of Toronto, was born in Ottawa on 7 July 1901, the son of William J. Lee and Mary Brady. He died on 24 April 1976 in Houston and is buried in the Basilian plot of Holy Cross Cemetery, Thornhill, Ontario.

Edward Lee attended elementary school in Ottawa and did his high school and university studies at St Michael's College, Toronto (B.A.,

University of Toronto, 1924). He entered St Basil's Novitiate, Toronto, made first profession on 11 August 1925, and was appointed to St Basil's Scholasticate, Toronto to study theology and obtain teaching certification at the Ontario College of Education. In 1926 he was moved to St Thomas High School, Houston, to teach and continue studying theology. He returned to the scholasticate in Toronto in 1927 and was ordained to the priesthood on 29 June 1929 in St Basil's Church, Toronto, by Archbishop Neil McNeil.

In August 1929 Father Lee was sent to Assumption College, Windsor. He taught there and sometimes served as librarian as well until 1944, spending summers studying at Harvard University, the University of Michigan, and the University of Chicago, leading to reception of an M.A. in English from Chicago in 1944. For the next four years he continued his graduate studies in Chicago, but did not receive the doctorate he was seeking. In 1948 he was appointed to the University of St Thomas, Houston, where he remained until his death, a total of twenty-eight years.

Father Ed Lee was a big man with a strong, agile, inquiring mind. He shared with his students the conclusions of his thoughtful study and the questions to which he himself had not yet found answers. He was witty, provocative, and never dull. Books, theatre, music, poetry, and art all enriched his life and the courses in English literature which he taught for over forty years. He had a host of admirers among his students and former students. At the University of St Thomas he founded the English Club, which one joined only by invitation. He was always available to students, whether to further their studies or to listen to their problems, in his much-frequented office in Shadwell Hall, the house where the Department of English, which he chaired for many years, was located. His culinary talents provided delicious luncheons for many students and colleagues. For more than twenty-five years he spent Sunday afternoons typing, mimeographing, and distributing a weekly bulletin, *This Week for Students*, which provided a schedule of noteworthy cultural, religious, and academic events as well as television programs and movies he deemed worthy of the students' time. One former student rated it as 'a better cultural listing than achieved by any of the three daily newspapers.' It could be enjoyed as much for its wit as for its information.

Despite his active life Father Lee rarely missed a religious exercise. He rose early, said Mass, recited his breviary, and then assisted at morning prayer with the community. Each Sunday he went to one or the other of the local parishes, according to the assignment given him by his superior, to celebrate Mass and preach. He was a man of God to whom nothing truly human was alien. An annual lectureship was established in his memory at the University of St Thomas.

BIBLIOGRAPHY: 'Composition in First-Year High School,' *Basilian* 3 (March 1937) 58–60; 'Forty-three Bishops Can't Be Wrong,' *Basilian* 3 (October 1937) 85–6; 'Prayer and Poetry,' *Basilian* 4 (March 1938); 'Methods, Manners and Modes,' *Basilian* 4 (May 1938) 90–1; 'New Trends and New Emphasis in the Teaching of English,' *Basilian Teacher* 4 (December 1961) 111; 'Contemporary Literature: A Strategy of Approach,' *Basilian Teacher* 6 (February 1962) 191–3; 'Eight and One-Half,' *Basilian Teacher* 8 (January 1964) 202–4.

SOURCES: GABF; *Annals* 5 (1976) 140, 5 (1977) 246–7; *Newsletter* (30 April 1976); 'Tribute to Father Edward Gregory Lee CSB, 1901–76: Priest, Teacher, Friend,' *This Week for Students* (Special Issue, May 1976); 'Remembering Father Edward Gregory Lee CSB (July 7 1901–April 24, 1976),' http://www.stthom.edu/alumni.

LEGOUX, Louis, priest, was born at Saint-Agrève (Ardèche) on 30 March 1855, the son of François Gaston Legoux and Marie Cécile Cros. He died on 25 April 1935, and was buried in the cemetery on the grounds of the Collège du Sacré-Coeur, Annonay.

Louis Legoux was a student at the Collège des Cordeliers, Annonay, 1866–7, and then at the Collège du Sacré-Coeur, section Sainte-Barbe, 1867–74. He entered the novitiate at Feyzin (Isère, now Rhône). He was prefect and professor, while studying theology, at the Petit Séminaire de Vernoux (Ardèche), 1875–8, at the Ecole cléricale de Périgueux (Dordogne), 1878–9, and at Vernoux once again, 1879–80. He was ordained priest on 24 September 1881 by Bishop Joseph-Michel-Frédéric Bonnet of Viviers in the chapel of the Collège du Sacré-Coeur.

Father Legoux then taught for three years in Annonay, six years at Vernoux, one year at Blidah, Algeria, five years at the Collège du Sacré-Coeur again, and seven years at the Petit Séminaire d'Aubenas. In 1903, with governmental exclusion of members of congregations from teaching, Father Legoux found himself without a ministry, according to a complaint he made to Father Julien *Giraud on 16 May 1904, while on a visit to Annonay. There are records of Father Legoux's presence at Tain (Ardèche) in the years 1909, 1910, and 1913. He was at Laurac (Ardèche) in 1922. In 1931 he was hospitalized in Marseille, but it is not known where he died.

A big man of ruddy complexion, Louis Legoux had a speech defect. Between 1929 and 1935 he visited the Basilian curial house at Maison Saint-Joseph, Annonay, several times.

SOURCES: GABF; Kirley, *Community in France* 184, 201, 206; Kirley, *Congregation in France* 72; Pouzol, 'Notices.'

LEMAN, Thomas Walthall, scholastic, was born on 7 July 1942 at Crosby, Texas (diocese of Galveston, now Galveston-Houston), into a family of five boys and one girl of Arthur Louis Leman and Eleanor Barnes. He died at Issy-les-Moulineaux (Hauts-de-Seine), France, on 24 February 1970, and is buried in the Basilian plot, Garden of Gethsemane, Forest Park Lawndale Cemetery, Houston.

Tom Leman received his elementary education at Crosby, a town about thirty miles northeast of downtown Houston. He enrolled at St Thomas High School, Houston, commuting from the family farm every day with his brothers. He was an outstanding student with a quiet and steady manner, a warm friend and a good athlete who distinguished himself in cross-country running under the training of Father John *Barry. Immediately after graduation from high school in 1960, he entered St Basil's Novitiate, Pontiac, Michigan, making first profession on 15 August 1961. He was appointed to undergraduate studies at the University of St Thomas, Houston (B.A., 1965), and then to teach at St Thomas High School, 1965-7, and at Catholic Central High School, Detroit, 1967-8. During these years he worked each summer at Basilian mission parishes in Texas. He did his first year of theological studies, 1968-9, at St Basil's Seminary, Toronto, but was appointed to continue those studies at the Séminaire Saint-Sulpice (the archdiocesan seminary for Paris), Issy-les-Moulineaux, with residence nearby at Maison Saint-Basile, the Basilian house of studies. His life was tragically cut short in February 1970 in a fall from his third-floor room.

Tom was an earnest and pleasant young man whose home life had given him impeccable manners and a gentlemanly deportment admired by all who knew him.

SOURCES: GABF; *Annals* 4 (1970) 208; *Newsletter* (24 February 1970).

LEVACK, David Alfred, priest, was born in Windsor on 26 May 1922, the only son of Victor Levack and Elizabeth Verville. He died at Sudbury, Ontario, on 5 June 1960 and is buried in the Basilian plot of Assumption Cemetery, Windsor.

'Dave' Levack was educated at St Rose Separate School, Riverside, Ontario, University of Ottawa High School, 1935–8, St Joseph's High School, Windsor, 1938–9, and Assumption College School, Windsor, 1939–40. He entered St Basil's Novitiate, Toronto, in 1940; after profession on 15 August 1941, he was appointed to Assumption College, Windsor (B.A., University of Western Ontario, 1945). He taught at St Michael's College School, Toronto, 1945–6, and in 1946–7 attended the Ontario College of Education, Toronto. After theological studies at St Basil's Seminary, Toronto, 1946–51, he was ordained a priest on 29 June 1950 in St Basil's Church, Toronto, by Cardinal James Charles McGuigan.

Father Levack's short priestly life was spent in teaching French and Spanish: at Assumption College School, 1951–4, St Michael's College School, 1954–7, St Mary's College, Sault Ste Marie, Ontario, 1957–9, and St Charles College, Sudbury, where he died from the recurrence of an earlier heart ailment at the age of thirty-eight.

Father Levack was an exceptionally fine basketball coach. He enlivened both his teaching and his community life by his love of fun and his ready wit.

SOURCES: GABF; *Annals* 1 (1943–50) 285, 3 (1960) 20.

LEWIS, Patrick Joseph, priest, was born at Oil City, Pennsylvania (diocese of Erie), on 5 February 1910, the son of Earle Lewis and Beatrice McLaughlin. He died in Toronto on 2 June 1988, and is buried in the Basilian plot of Holy Cross Cemetery, Thornhill, Ontario.

The Lewis family moved to Royal Oak, Michigan, when Pat was a young boy. During elementary school he regularly served Mass for the former Basilian Father Charles E. *Coughlin, of radio fame, at the Shrine of the Little Flower, Royal Oak. In 1925 he enrolled at Assumption College School, Windsor, and continued on at Assumption College for two years of his arts course. In 1930 he entered St Basil's Novitiate, Toronto, was professed on 15 August 1931, and then appointed to Assumption College (B.A., University of Western Ontario, 1933). While an undergraduate he taught part-time at Assumption High School. In 1933 he began theology at St Basil's Scholasticate, Toronto. During his second year of theology he took courses at the Ontario College of Education and obtained teacher certification in 1935. He also taught part-time at St Michael's College School during his years of theology. He was ordained to the priesthood in St Michael's Cathedral, Toronto, on 11 June 1938 by Archbishop James Charles McGuigan.

In his forty-seven-year apostolate in Basilian high schools, Father Lewis had four appointments: Aquinas Institute, Rochester, 1938–48, teaching general science, economic geography, and drawing; Catholic Central High School, Detroit, 1948–51; Assumption High School, 1951–63, teaching United States history and religion; and Catholic Central once again, 1963–85. In all of these places he combined his teaching with coaching, especially football. During the 1946 football season he also coached at Michigan Central College. His long years at Catholic Central made him a fixture there, popular on the playing field as well as in the classroom. He was demanding in both areas, and was appreciated for his standards.

To keep abreast of developments in his teaching areas Father Lewis attended courses at various times at the Rochester Institute of Technology and the University of Buffalo. He was chaplain to the United States Coast Guard in Detroit as well as to the Burtha Fisher Home, also in that city. While a scholastic, through his talent in art, he had prepared for publication several maps for Father Benjamin *Forner's *Story of the Church* (Toronto, 1935).

In the spring of 1972 he was assaulted on the grounds of Catholic Central and lost the sight in one eye. This experience did not, however, hamper the dedication or the enthusiasm which he brought to all he did. After retirement from the classroom in 1980, he helped maintain the grounds of the school, especially the football field. He continued his chaplaincy at the Burtha Fisher Home and his weekly ministry at St Monica's Church, Detroit, where he organized a women's group to help the missions. He is remembered as an affable man and a great storyteller.

SOURCES: GABF; *Annals* 6 (1982) 14, 6 (1989) 805–6; *Newsletter* (17 June 1986).

LIOGIER, Emile, priest, was born on 4 June 1853 at Le Cheylard (Ardèche). He died on 5 May 1909 at Saint-Christol, near Le Cheylard, where his funeral took place.

Emile Liogier was a student at the Collège du Sacré-Coeur, Annonay, section Sainte-Barbe, 1871–3. He went to the Grand Séminaire de Viviers for one year. He was a novice at Feyzin (Isère, now Rhône),

1874–5. He next spent four years at the Collège du Bourg-Saint-Andéol (Ardèche) as prefect while studying theology, and was ordained a priest on 20 September 1879 by Bishop Armand de Charbonnel.

Father Liogier worked a year at the Petit Séminaire de Vernoux (Ardèche), eleven years at the Collège du Sacré-Coeur, and another twelve years at the Petit Séminaire de Vernoux. In 1903, as a result of governmental exclusion of religious orders from teaching, he went as curate to the parish in Ecclassan, diocese of Viviers, to assist his brother Théophile, who was pastor, and then to care for him in his last illness. The brother died in 1908, one year before Emile himself died.

Father Liogier's funeral was attended by many parishioners from Le Cheylard, Saint Christol, and Ecclassan. Present too were Fathers Noël *Durand and Denis *Mouraret and Chanoine Fromenton, who had written a history of the Petit Séminaire de Vernoux where Father Liogier had worked many years.

SOURCES: GABF; Kirley, *Community in France* 184, 204; Pouzol, 'Notices.'

LOCOCO, Anthony Vincent Philip, priest, distant cousin of Father Donald Lococo CSB, was born on 18 October 1907 at Niagara Falls, Ontario (archdiocese of Toronto, since 1958 diocese of St Catharines), the son of Philip Lococo and Loretto Scarlata. He died in Toronto on 29 August 1987 and is buried in the Basilian plot of Holy Cross Cemetery, Thornhill, Ontario.

'Tony' Lococo received his primary and secondary education at Niagara Falls and then enrolled in St Michael's College, Toronto (B.A., University of Toronto, 1932). He entered St Basil's Novitiate, Toronto, was professed on 15 August 1933, and began theology at St Basil's Scholasticate, Toronto. In 1935 he moved to St Michael's College while he took courses at the Ontario College of Education, earning teacher certification in 1936. He resumed theological studies and was ordained to the priesthood on 18 December 1937 in St Basil's Church, Toronto, by Archbishop James Charles McGuigan.

In 1938 Father Lococo was appointed to Aquinas Institute, Rochester, where he remained for the next twenty years. There he taught Latin, worked as master of scholastics, and completed studies in Latin and history at St Bonaventure's College, Olean, New York (M.A., 1942). During the war years he was chaplain at the Sampson Naval Base on Seneca Lake in New York State.

In 1958 he was appointed superior of the Basilian community at St

Charles College, Sudbury, Ontario, and three years later was appointed master of novices at St Basil's Novitiate, Erindale, Ontario. When the Erindale and Pontiac novitiates were combined in 1965, he became master of novices in Pontiac, and then worked out the return of the novitiate to Erindale in 1967.

In that same year, a time of trouble and uncertainty in high school education, he was named principal of St Charles College. In 1971 he requested an appointment to Michael Power High School, Etobicoke, Ontario, where, even though officially retired, he taught Latin and worked in the guidance department and was a regular attendant at faculty meetings and in the faculty lounge. His classroom and guidance activities were gradually reduced as his health deteriorated. In 1986 he moved to the Basilian Fathers Residence, Toronto, for the one year of life which remained to him.

Tony Lococo had a fine appearance and an energetic manner. His teaching was forceful – some even said fearful. Congenial and warm in company, he particularly enjoyed family and community gatherings. In his wake service eulogy Father Edward *McLean described him as 'a happy warrior,' full of enthusiasm for the challenge of each day, even when given assignments that were a cross for him. Two days before his death he asked to be released from the hospital, for he wanted to be with his confreres. At two o'clock on the afternoon of his death he called the nurse to ask that he be prepared for death. The confreres gathered in his room, administered the sacrament of the dying, and joined in prayer. He died peacefully shortly after three.

BIBLIOGRAPHY: 'Aiding the Inexperienced Teacher,' *Basilian Teacher* 1 (May 1956) 17–20; 'The Teaching of Classics,' *Basilian Teacher* 2 (January 1958) 8–12; 'Communications and Education [forum],' *Basilian Teacher* 3 (May 1959) 217.
SOURCES: GABF; *Annals* 6 (1984) 206, 6 (1988) 704–6; *Newsletter* (10 September 1987).

LODATO, Joseph Anthony, scholastic, was born at Niagara Falls, New York (diocese of Buffalo), on 13 December 1893, the son of Anthony (another source calls him Leonard) Lodato and Maria Guesepa. He died in Windsor on 7 November 1918 and was buried there in the Basilian plot of Assumption Cemetery.

Joseph Lodato's parents moved to Toronto when he was six months old and then settled in Woodstock, Ontario (diocese of London), when he was two. There he attended Woodstock Collegiate Institute. He enrolled in Assumption College, Windsor, in 1912, and became captain of the football team. Three years later he entered St Basil's Novitiate, Toronto, was professed on 13 August 1916, and appointed to St Basil's Scholasticate, Toronto. He enrolled in the Honours Classics course at the University of Toronto. In 1917, when St Basil's Scholasticate was transferred to Assumption College, Windsor, he began the study of theology there. He contracted influenza during the epidemic of 1918, and died shortly after – one of three Basilians at Assumption to fall victim to it at that time.

Joseph Lodato was a sturdily built, athletic man who at the time of his death was captain of the Assumption College football team.

SOURCE: GABF; Power, *Assumption College* 3 xxi, 158, 279, 284.

LOOBY, Arthur Rynold, priest, was born on 14 December 1915 at Dublin, Ontario (diocese of London), the son of Louis Looby and Ann Marie Ryan. He died in Toronto on 20 October 1993 and is buried in the Basilian plot of Holy Cross Cemetery, Thornhill, Ontario.

'Art' Looby attended St Patrick's Separate School, Dublin, and Dublin Continuation School before enrolling in Assumption College School, Windsor, for grade XIII. After one year of university studies at Assumption College, Windsor, he entered St Basil's Novitiate, Toronto, in 1937, was professed on 15 November 1938, and returned to Assumption College to complete his undergraduate studies (B.A., History, University of Western Ontario, 1941). During the year 1941–2 he taught at Aquinas Institute, Rochester, and also studied pedagogy at the University of Rochester. He did theological studies at St Basil's Seminary, Toronto, 1942–7, during the first year of which he also attended the Ontario College of Education, earning teaching certification in 1943. During his second year of theology he took history courses at the Pontifical Institute of Mediaeval Studies, Toronto. He was ordained to the priesthood on 15 August 1946 in St Basil's Church by Cardinal James Charles McGuigan.

Father Looby worked for twenty-two years in the high school apostolate: he taught at Aquinas Institute, 1947–55, at St Thomas High School, Houston, where he was also treasurer, 1955–9, at St Joseph's High School, Ottawa, in the same capacities, 1959–63, at Assumption College School, teaching U.S. History to the American students as well as doing prefect duty in the student residence, 1963–7, and at St Michael's College School, Toronto, 1967–9. He received permission to join the Canadian Armed Forces as chaplain. In his nine years in that service he achieved the rank of Major, with postings at Clinton, London, Toronto, Trenton, Kingston, and Petawawa (all in Ontario), at Edmonton, Alberta, and at Holberg, British Columbia. On the occasion of Father Looby's transference from Kingston, the commanding officer wrote to the Command Chaplain of the Canadian Armed Forces: '[Father Looby's] unfailing support and tireless efforts more than met our requirements and won the admiration of all members of the Church community. The tact and discretion which he demonstrated in the pursuit of his daily activities, at times under the most trying circumstances, was noteworthy, and his record of performance was a credit to the Service.'

After discharge from the military, Father Looby returned to live at St Michael's College School, where he undertook the pastoral care of the four hundred families associated with St Eugene's Chapel, an auxiliary chapel of St Margaret of Scotland Parish, Toronto. His pastoral instincts and experience and his simple, natural goodness found their full scope in this ministry and built up a vibrant faith community at St Eugene's. On the occasion of the fiftieth anniversary of the chapel, Father Looby wrote its history. While being treated for a heart condition at St Joseph's Health Centre, Toronto, he died suddenly and alone in his room.

BIBLIOGRAPHY:
Book: *The Flowering of a Community: The History of St Eugene's, North York Township.* Toronto, 1991.
Articles: 'Extra-Curricular Activities,' *Basilian Teacher* 1 (December 1956) 12; 'Scripture and Our Students [forum],' *Basilian Teacher* 5 (December 1960) 83–4.
SOURCES: GABF; *Annals* 1 (1946) 120, 6 (1989) 721, 8 (1994) 140–2; *Newsletter* (19 November 1993).

LOUPIAS, Théophile-François, priest, member of the Congregation 1895?–1903, was born on 2 October 1875 in the diocese of Rodez (Aveyron). He died at Rodez on 11 November 1961.

Having made final profession on 21 May 1901, Théophile-François was ordained to the priesthood at Viviers (Ardèche) on 12 October 1902. He was the last Basilian ordained in France prior to the government's exclusion of members of congregations from teaching in 1903. Father Loupias then withdrew from the Congregation and was incardinated in the diocese of Périgueux (Dordogne). After nearly sixty years of priestly service he returned to his native diocese of Rodez, where he died in 1961.

SOURCES: GABF; *Newsletter* (23 January 1962); Kirley, *Community in France* 184, 211n570; Pouzol, 'Notices.'

LOWREY, Robert Emmett, priest, was born on 19 December 1897 in Ottawa, the son of John Lowrey and Mary McGrath. He died in Toronto on 23 August 1974 and is buried in the Basilian plot of Holy Cross Cemetery, Thornhill, Ontario.

Educated at St Patrick's School, Ottawa, and St Michael's College, Toronto, Robert Lowrey entered St Basil's Novitiate, Toronto, in 1917 and was professed on 10 August 1918. He completed high school matriculation and took one year of arts at the University of Toronto. In 1920 he was appointed to Assumption College, Windsor (B.A., University of Western Ontario, 1923). He studied theology at St Basil's Scholasticate, Toronto, 1923–6, and was ordained to the priesthood on 19 December 1925 in Blessed Sacrament Church, Ottawa, by the apostolic delegate to Canada, Archbishop Pietro de Maria.

In 1926 Father Lowrey was appointed to St Thomas High School, Houston, where he taught until 1934, serving as first councillor of the Basilian community there during his last two years. He taught for one year at Catholic Central High School, Detroit, after which he returned to St Thomas in Houston, teaching and coaching there for the next seven years. In 1942 he was released to enlist as chaplain in the Canadian Armed Forces. He went in with the troops in Normandy, and came under fire. In a letter of 9 May 1945 to Father E.J. *McCorkell, superior general, he wrote: 'To get as close as possible to the men during action I moved out of Headquarters. ... so I was not able to get Mass in every morning even when action was static. Before action I went from tank to tank and heard Confessions and gave Holy Communion. With the Motor Regiment I moved from slit trench to slit trench. ... no place was safe from shells.' In another letter he wrote: 'I carry the Blessed Sacrament with me when there is a chance to see my men. I go from tank to tank or carrier to carrier and ask for the Catholics. When they were in a resting place one weekend they were continually shelled, so I had to slide into a slit trench with the men a number of times. In one good slit trench I had a dozen men come to me individually for confession and communion. I kept the names, so it was a bit of consolation when I had to bury a few of them later in the week.' He was in Germany for V-E

Day, and was awarded the Military Cross for distinguished gallantry in the field. In the citation we read: 'He has been a tower of strength to his units, not only as a chaplain but as a man amongst men. ... The brigadier remarked ... "That man has done as much, if not more, for the success of this show than any other officer under my command."'

From the time of his release from the armed forces in 1946 until 1974 Father Lowrey engaged in parish work: assistant at Holy Rosary Parish, Toronto, 1946–9, pastor at Blessed Sacrament Parish, Windsor, 1949–54, pastor of St John the Baptist Parish, Amherstburg, 1954–8, and pastor of St Theresa's Parish, Sugar Land, Texas, 1958–61. In 1961 he joined the staff of St Basil's Parish, Toronto, as assistant, where he remained until his sudden death in 1974.

Athletic ability and interest ran in his family: one of his brothers coached the Ann Arbor football team for many years and another brother was sports editor of the *Ottawa Journal*. Bob was a star hockey player for De La Salle High School, and became even more famous as a football player on St Michael's College Intermediate Intercollegiate Team, which won the championship twice, 1924 and 1925, in the three years he played. He introduced hockey to Houston when he went there in 1926, playing in the city league and coaching the juniors, while carrying a full load of teaching and priestly ministry. The sports editor of the *Houston Post* compared Father Lowrey's contribution to hockey in Houston in the late 1920s and early 1930s to Gordie Howe's efforts to revitalize Houston hockey in the 1970s.

Father Lowrey's priestly zeal never abated. Daily he was in his confessional at St Basil's, where many sought his advice and absolution. Talking was a compulsion with him, and he appreciated jokes about his 'motor-mouth.' His compulsion, however, sprang from his love of people, abundantly evident in his visits to the aged at St Raphael's Home, Toronto, and in his daily contacts with confreres, parishioners, and students.

sources: GABF; *Annals* 1 (1944) 48–9, (1945) 86–7, (1946) 131–2, 4 (1969) 117, 5 (1975) 119–20; *Newsletter* (24 August 1974); Clark Nealon, *Houston Post* (19 February 1974).

LYNCH, Martin Stanley, priest, was born on 28 July 1902 in Windsor, the son of Thomas Lynch and Margaret Silver. He died in Windsor on 28 May 1969 and is buried there in the Basilian plot of Assumption Parish Cemetery.

After attending St Alphonsus Parish School and Assumption College, Windsor, 'Stan' Lynch entered St Basil's Novitiate, Toronto, in 1921, made first profession on 14 August 1922, and was appointed to Assumption College (B.A., University of Western Ontario, 1924). He taught at St Thomas High School, Houston, for one year, 1924–5, before returning to Toronto to study theology at St Basil's Scholasticate. In the fall of 1927 he took up residence at St Michael's College, joining the staff there as director of studies in the high school. He was ordained to the priesthood on 21 December 1927 in St Basil's Church, Toronto, by Bishop Alexander MacDonald. In that same year he also obtained an M.A. in classics from the University of Toronto.

In 1929 he was diagnosed as having tuberculosis, which obliged him to spend one year in a sanatorium in New York State followed by one year of convalescence at St Basil's Novitiate, Toronto. His next appointments were: St Mary's of the Assumption Parish, Owen Sound, Ontario, 1931–2, St Basil's Scholasticate, 1932–4, and St Michael's College, 1934–41, as professor of classics and inspector of Basilian schools for the general council.

In 1941 Father Lynch enlisted in the Royal Canadian Air Force. He served in England until the spring of 1945, when he was sent to Calcutta, from where his letters speak of working in the jungle. He returned to civilian life in 1946; but before leaving the service he persuaded an RCAF pilot to 'buzz' Strawberry Island in Lake Simcoe, Ontario, the summer home of the Basilian Fathers. He was appointed to Houston to prepare, with Fathers Vincent *Guinan, Wilfrid *Dwyer, and Norbert *Ruth, the opening of the University of St Thomas, where he was registrar and professor of classics until 1952. He worked in the parish apostolate at St Anne's Parish, Houston, 1952–5, Ste Anne's Parish, Detroit, 1955–61, as superior and pastor, and Blessed Sacrament Parish, Windsor, 1964–8. From 1961 to 1964 he was treasurer at St Basil's Novitiate, Pontiac, Michigan. He spent the last year of his life at the Basilian House of Studies, Windsor, where, though ill himself, he carried on an apostolate to the sick. He composed a booklet of prayers for hospital use and was working on a second publication on Christian hope when he died.

Stan Lynch was an ardent sportsman, an able coach and a gifted organizer. Under his direction St Michael's College hockey team won the Memorial Cup in 1934. For several years in the 1930s he was president of the Ontario Rugby-Football Union. He was a warm and friendly person, noted for his generosity and quiet sense of humour.

When asked a question on which his knowledge was sparse or nil, rather than say 'I don't know' he would compose an answer – historical, geographical, statistical, or philosophical – with great imagination and a straight face. This manner, when used by others, came to be known in the community as 'a Lynch answer.'

BIBLIOGRAPHY:
Pamphlet: *Hospital Prayer Book.* Toronto, 1966.
Articles: In *Basilian*: 'The Place of Athletics in Our Schools,' 1 (March 1935) 13–14; 'Father Lynch's Problem,' 2 (March 1936) 48; 'Teaching the Catechism,' 2 (December 1936) 132–4; 'Methods in Teaching the Catechism,' 3 (March 1937) 45, 56; 'Homework Assignment,' 3 (November 1937) 118, 120; 'H.S.R.: Letter to the Editor,' 4 (April 1938) 74.
SOURCES: GABF; *Annals* 1 (1944) 50–1, 1 (1945) 88, 4 (1969) 163–4, 5 (1979) 342; *Newsletter* (29 May 1969).

LYONS, Charles FRANCIS, priest, was born on 5 November 1903 in Kingston, Ontario, the son of Edward Lyons and Mary O'Brien. He died in Toronto on 15 April 1987 and is buried in the Basilian plot of Holy Cross Cemetery, Thornhill, Ontario.

Francis Lyons was educated in Windsor, where the family had moved when he was a boy. He graduated from Windsor Collegiate, entered the work force for a brief time, and then enrolled in Assumption College, Windsor. After one year of arts he entered St Basil's Novitiate, Toronto, making first profession on 11 August 1928. He returned to Assumption to complete his arts course (B.A., University of Western Ontario, 1931). He studied theology at St Basil's Scholasticate, Toronto, 1931–5, while also earning teaching certification from the Ontario College of Education. He was ordained a priest in Assumption Church, Windsor, by Bishop John Kidd on 16 December 1934.

With the exception of three years of teaching at St Thomas High School, Houston, 1940–3, Father Lyons's apostolate was in Basilian parishes: Assumption Parish, Windsor, 1935–6, Holy Rosary Parish, Toronto, 1936–40, 1943–50, St John the Baptist Parish, Amherstburg, Ontario, 1950–2, St Mary's of the Assumption Parish, Owen Sound, Ontario, as rector and pastor, 1952–8, and St Anne's Parish, Houston, 1958–72. During his short stint at St Thomas High School he earned an M.A. in education from the University of Houston.

'Beer' Lyons (as he was popularly called in the Basilian community, the origin of the name being obscure) was gentle and friendly. His manner, solicitude, and talent for remembering names, faces, and situations earned him the appellation of 'dear friend' by many parishioners. His devotion to prayer intensified in his retirement years, when he was customarily found in the chapel of St Basil's College, no longer able to work but now supporting his brothers spiritually. When someone told Father T.A. *MacDonald in his illness that Father Lyons was praying for him, he remarked, 'He does that well.' He entered St Basil's Infirmary, Toronto, in 1972 and lived the last fifteen years of his life there, still exhibiting the qualities which had endeared him to many.

SOURCES: GABF; *Annals* 5 (1975) 342, 6 (1985) 307, (1988) 700-1; *Newsletter* (18 April 1987).

M

MACDONALD, Daniel GORDON, priest, brother of Sister Catherine Marie Macdonald CSJ, was born on 4 February 1927 at Theodore, Saskatchewan (archdiocese of Regina), the son of Judge Alexander Macdonald and Veronica Boyle. He died in Saskatoon, Saskatchewan, on 28 June 1996 and is buried there in the Basilian plot of Woodlawn Catholic Cemetery.

Gordon Macdonald was a proud descendant of the Catholic Highlanders who came to Nova Scotia after their expulsion from Scotland in the eighteenth century. His parents moved to Saskatchewan shortly after their marriage, where his father was named judge in Rosetown. Gordon completed his primary and secondary school in that town and then, at the age of sixteen, travelled to Toronto to enrol in St Michael's College. After one year of arts he entered St Basil's Novitiate, Toronto, and was professed on 12 September 1945. He was appointed to St Michael's to complete his undergraduate degree in Honours Philosophy and History (B.A., University of Toronto, 1948), and then to Aquinas Institute, Rochester, where he taught for one year before returning to Toronto for theological studies at St Basil's Seminary, 1949–53. During his theological studies he also earned an M.A. in philosophy from the University of Toronto. He was ordained to the priesthood on 20 December 1952 in St Michael's Cathedral, Toronto, by Cardinal James Charles McGuigan.

In 1953 Father Macdonald undertook graduate studies in Greek and medieval philosophy at the University of Toronto and the Pontifical Institute of Mediaeval Studies. During this period he also taught part-time at St Michael's College. From 1953 to 1958 he was chaplain to the Ontario Hospital at 999 Queen Street West, Toronto. In 1958 he was appointed to Assumption University to teach philosophy and Latin; he moved from there to St Thomas More College, Saskatoon, to teach philosophy. In 1966 he was appointed to St Charles College, Sudbury, teaching on the high school level until 1975. He was then appointed to St Joseph's College, Edmonton, Alberta, and in 1986 returned to St Thomas More, where he remained until his death. Fittingly and movingly his funeral procession from the chapel was accompanied by highland bagpipe music.

'Gord' or 'Gordie' or 'Big Mac,' as he was known at one time or other by his confreres, was indeed a big man, both in body and in mind. With his wide and imaginative, even brilliant vision he played with ideas as he played with words and numbers, commenting whimsically on the human condition. His mind was ever active, always seeking, though what he saw was often hard for his listener to grasp and hard for him to put into writing. Behind a facade of gruffness he was a shy and sensitive man habitually concerned about the lot of the oppressed and the defenceless. He was ready to help anyone in spiritual difficulties, having known struggles and failures himself. He made himself regularly available for the sacrament of reconciliation, absolving in the name of Jesus and the Church but adding a philosophic comment or a quotation on the human condition.

BIBLIOGRAPHY: 'Chesterton and the Diasporas: A Reply to Owen Edwards,' *Chesterton Review* 7 (1981) 50–6.
SOURCES: GABF; *Annals* 2 (1953) 107, 8 (1997) 109–11; *Newsletter* (19 October 1996).

MacDONALD, Ralph James, priest, was born on 9 July 1915, at Watertown, New York (diocese of Ogdensburg), one of four children of Donald J. MacDonald and Rose Lucas. He died in Toronto on 19 May 1982 and is buried in the Basilian plot of Holy Cross Cemetery, Thornhill, Ontario.

Ralph attended Holy Family School, Watertown, and Regiopolis College, Kingston, Ontario, 1928–33, where the family had relocated in 1927. In the fall of 1933 he enrolled in St Michael's College, Toronto, and after one year of arts entered St Basil's Novitiate, Toronto. Following profession on 15 August 1935, he completed his undergraduate courses at St Michael's College, (B.A., Honours Philosophy, University of Toronto, 1938), working part-time in the library of the Pontifical Institute of Mediaeval Studies. He won the Hanrahan Prize in philosophy in 1936, the Kernahan Prize in 1937, and the Silver Medal in Philosophy in 1938. That year he began his theology courses at St Basil's Seminary, simultaneously doing graduate studies in philosophy (M.A., University of Toronto, 1940; thesis: 'St Thomas Aquinas and the Primacy of Intellection'). At this time he completed a translation of Etienne Gilson's *Le christianisme et la philosophie*. During the year 1940–1 he lectured in philosophy at Assumption College, Windsor, but then returned to Toronto to complete his theological studies at St Basil's Seminary. He was ordained to the priesthood in St Basil's Church, Toronto, on 15 August 1942 by Archbishop James Charles McGuigan.

In 1943 Father MacDonald began doctoral studies in philosophy at the University of Toronto while living at the Pontifical Institute of Mediaeval Studies. He was granted the Ph.D. in 1946, with the thesis topic 'Gregory of Rimini and *Notitia simplex*.' During the year 1945–6 he was once again lecturer in philosophy at Assumption College, Windsor.

In 1946 he began his career as a professor of philosophy at St Michael's College. His most popular course, 'True Humanism' (known as 'Tru Hu' among the students), was a presentation of the philosophy of Jacques Maritain, of whom Ralph MacDonald was an ardent disciple. He assisted in the revised translation of Maritain's *Les degrés du savoir*. On 6 February 1950 he spoke on the Radio League of St Michael on the topic 'Wandering between Two Worlds,' a title which could be taken as a summary of his own life. On 6 December 1965 he was a speaker on the Newman Lecture Series with the topic 'The Foundation of Christian Philosophy.' He was appointed Associate Professor of Philosophy at the University of St Michael's College in 1964.

Father MacDonald's work at the college was not limited to teaching. In 1961 he took on the duties of space controller and marshall. From 1976 to 1981 he was Awards Officer and Director of Financial Aid. Early in 1982, Father MacDonald was diagnosed with cancer. He was moved to the Basilian Fathers Residence (Infirmary), Toronto, on 2 April 1982 and began treatment at Princess Margaret Hospital; but his condition deteriorated quickly, and he died within seven weeks.

Though shy and gentle, Ralph MacDonald could become fired up by ideas and the defence of truth. He loved philosophical discussion, showing great firmness in his convictions while respecting the opinions of others. He was a purveyor of the genius of others, particularly of Maritain. Uneasy in the company of persons unknown to him, his deferential manner and shyness were possibly responsible for his not being fully appreciated as the thinker and philosopher he was.

BIBLIOGRAPHY:
Book: Trans. Etienne Gilson. *Christianity and Philosophy.* New York, 1939.
Article: 'The Meaning of Knowing,' *Basilian* 3 (April 1937) 64–6.
SOURCES: GABF; *Annals* 1 (1943) 27, 6 (1983) 192–3; *Newsletter* (25 June 1982).

MACDONALD, Thomas Aloysius (baptismal certificate: Thomas Alexander), priest, was born on 5 November 1897 at Auburnville, New Brunswick (diocese of Chatham, since 1958 of Bathurst), one of the four boys and two girls of Alexander MacDonald and Bridget Power. He died in Toronto on 30 June 1986 and is buried in the Basilian plot of Holy Cross Cemetery, Thornhill, Ontario.

'T.A.' MacDonald attended St Thomas College in Chatham, which was at that time under Basilian direction. He entered St Basil's Novitiate, Toronto, in 1916 and was professed in September of the following year. In 1917 he was appointed to live at St Basil's Scholasticate, Toronto, while doing undergraduate studies at St Michael's College (B.A., Honours Science, University of Toronto, 1921) and then theology. He was ordained to the priesthood on 22 December 1923 in the chapel of St Augustine's Seminary, Scarborough, Ontario, by Bishop Alexander MacDonald. He said his first Mass on Christmas Day in his home parish of St Michael's at Bay Side, New Brunswick.

In September 1924 Father MacDonald was appointed to the faculty of Assumption College, Windsor, to teach science. He undertook a program of summer study at Columbia University, New York City, which led to an M.A. (1930). At Assumption he served as registrar, religious superior, and, for the last eight years, as president of the college. His careful husbanding of resources is credited with the survival of Assumption College through the difficult years of the Great Depression. At the same time he had to find ways to upgrade the academic credentials of the Assumption staff and its affiliated Holy Names College, in order to satisfy the demands of both the University of Western Ontario and the Basilian superior general Henry *Carr.

In 1940 he was appointed to St Michael's College, Toronto, as treasurer, again a challenging assignment at a time when the nation was at war. He personally supervised the running of a four hundred-acre farm north of Toronto which served as a food source for the college. In 1946 he moved into the parish apostolate with an appointment to Holy Rosary Church, Toronto, as pastor. He vigorously undertook the physical improvement of the parish plant, completing the northeast entrance, constructing a baptistry on the west side, and building the new rectory. While still pastor, he was elected treasurer general of the Basilian Fathers in 1948, a responsibility he held for the next twelve years.

In 1957 he took up residence at St Michael's College, having been named the first Basilian director of the Newman Centre in the University of Toronto. He retired as director in 1965, but remained as treasurer until 1973. Assumption University recognized its debt to him by conferring on him an LL.D., *honoris causa*, 1962, and the University of St Thomas, Fredericton, New Brunswick – the successor to St Thomas College, Chatham – conferred another honorary doctorate on him in 1972. At the age of seventy-six, Father MacDonald returned to Holy Rosary as an assistant, and continued working there as his health and age permitted, until suffering a fatal stroke in his eighty-ninth year.

'T.A.' MacDonald was a man of great energy and quick decision. Some found him gruff and enormously self-willed, and with good reason. But his basic kindness and devotion were estimable, and his administrative skills proved invaluable in the institutions where he served.

SOURCES: GABF; *Annals* 4 (1967) 46, (1973) 297, 5 (1974) 7, 5 (1978) 265, 6 (1987) 575–7; *Newsletter* (12 July 1986); McMahon, *Pure Zeal* 86–126; Shook, *Catholic Education* 170–1, 198–9, 284–6. For documentation relating to his presidency of Assumption see Power, *Assumption College* 5 140–84.

MAGEE, Ernest Paul, priest, was born on 12 August 1908 in Houston, one of five children of Frederick Magee and Christine Helfrich. He died in Toronto on 11 August 1997, and is buried in the Basilian plot of Holy Cross Cemetery, Thornhill, Ontario.

Graduating from St Thomas College, Houston, in 1927, Ernest entered St Basil's Novitiate, Toronto, and was professed on 11 August 1928. He was appointed to Assumption College for undergraduate studies (B.A., University of Western Ontario, 1932), during which time he also taught in the high school section of the college. He was assigned to St Basil's Scholasticate, Toronto, for theology, and also attended the Ontario College of Education for teacher certification, which he gained in 1933. For one year, 1933–4, he taught at St Thomas High School, Houston, while continuing his theological studies. He finished the theology course at the scholasticate in Toronto and was ordained to the priesthood on 21 December 1935 in Annunciation Church, Houston, by Bishop Christopher E. Byrne.

In 1936 'E.P.' or 'Jim' (he had both nicknames) Magee returned to St Thomas High School for a nineteen-year period, where, in addition to teaching algebra, he became certified for teaching in Texas and earned an M.A. from the University of Houston in 1942. After serving as house treasurer and councillor he was appointed superior and principal of the school, 1952–5, and was then appointed to the same two offices at Aquinas Institute in Rochester. There he earned an M.Ed. from the University of Rochester in 1961. In that year he was appointed to Andrean High School, Gary (later Merrillville), Indiana, to teach and serve as first councillor. This appointment was cut short when he was elected to the general council in September 1961 to fill a position left vacant by the sudden death of Father Blake *Coll. He finished the year at Andrean, then moved to St Basil's Seminary, Toronto, and in 1964 to the Curial House, Toronto, where he was local councillor and treasurer in addition to his job as general councillor. After six years, Father Magee returned in 1967 to St Thomas High School, where he taught until his retirement in 1975. In failing health, he was appointed to the Basilian Fathers Residence (Infirmary), Toronto, in 1983.

One of Father Magee's former students, later a faculty member at St Thomas, called him 'the "discipline" in the Basilian motto "Teach me goodness, discipline and knowledge."' He was a man of few words but of powerful presence. A chain-smoker, he would listen, puffing away, to a student's reasons or excuse, and then mutter a phrase or two which decisively concluded the interview. His own life was extremely ordered and disciplined. Always available, he seemed unflappable; but at the report of some hazing at St Thomas High School, he assembled the entire student body, and in a most uncharacteristic show of anger, by gesture and words, made it clear that such activity was not acceptable. There was no more hazing. On another occasion, having surprised some boys shooting dice, he allowed them to throw dice against the wall in his office to determine how many days of punishment each would undergo.

Father Magee's last thirteen years in the Basilian Fathers Residence were years of peace and contentment, where his quiet but affable presence was a blessing to the house. He loved to play bridge and did so regularly, but he stopped abruptly just a few months before his death, when he realized his usual acuity had deserted him.

SOURCES: GABF; *Annals* 5 (1979) 342, 6 (1986) 395, 9 (1998) 77–8; *Newsletter* (25 September 1997).

MAISONNEUVE, Joseph Louis DANIEL, priest, was born on 25 August 1846 at Monts-sur-Guesnes (Vienne, diocese of Poitiers). His death probably occurred in 1913.

Daniel entered the Basilian novitiate at Feyzin (Isère, now Rhône) in 1868 or 1869 and professed final vows on 19 September 1873. Bishop Joseph-Michel-Frédéric Bonnet of Viviers ordained him to the priesthood on 12 May 1878 in the chapel of the Collège du Sacré-Coeur, Annonay.

Prior to ordination he had worked as supply teacher in various Basilian institutions. During the year 1873–4 he helped Father Robin, pastor of Saint-Maurice, Vienne (Isère), to establish the day school which later developed into the renowned Institut Robin. In May 1877 he was assigned to the Collège Saint-Charles, Blidah, Algeria, where he remained on the teaching staff until 1880. He spent the next four years at the Petit Séminaire de Vernoux (Ardèche) teaching classics in *sixième* and *cinquième*. He was appointed to the Collège du Sacré-Coeur, Annonay, in 1884 to teach French in the junior grades, remaining there until 1899, when he moved to the Ecole cléricale at Périgueux (Dordogne) to teach the *cinquième*.

With the exclusion in 1903 of members of congregations from teaching, and after the closure of the Ecole cléricale, Father Maisonneuve seems to have remained for some time in the diocese of Périgueux. Basilian records state that in 1910 and 1913 he was living at Agen (Lot-et-Garonne), but nothing more is known of him.

SOURCES: GABF; Kirley, *Community in France* 185, 207; Pouzol, 'Notices.'

MALBOS, Jean MICHEL, priest, younger brother of Father Joseph *Malbos, was born on 29 September 1839 at Saint-Paul-le-Jeune (Ardèche). He died on 20 September 1907.

After completing early studies at the Saint-Barbe section of the Collège des Cordeliers, Annonay, Michel entered the Basilian novitiate at Feyzin (Isère, now Rhône), in 1862. He made final profession of vows at Annonay on 22 September 1865. During his initial formation he taught Latin in the lower grades at the Collège des Cordeliers. He was ordained to the priesthood by Bishop Armand de Charbonnel on 21 September 1867 in the chapel of the Collège du Sacré-Coeur, Annonay. His was the first ordination in the newly acquired premises on Mont Saint-Denis.

Father Malbos taught *sixième* at the Collège du Sacré-Coeur during the years 1867–71, and during the four years following taught *cinquième* at the Ecole cléricale de Périgueux (Dordogne). With signs of failing health he spent the year 1874–5 as spiritual director at the Feyzin novitiate. His health once restored, he went to the parish at Prades (Ardèche), where he remained for almost twenty-eight years, 1875–10 February 1903, as curate under Father Antoine *Bord. He retired to Aubenas (Ardèche), where he assisted in a parish until his death.

SOURCES: GABF; Kirley, *Community in France* 184, 186, 205; Pouzol, 'Notices.'

MALBOS, Joseph, priest, elder brother of Father Jean Michel *Malbos, was born at Saint-Paul-le-Jeune (Ardèche) on 17 September 1822. He died on 6 January 1885 in Annonay and is buried there in the cemetery on the grounds of the Collège du Sacré-Coeur.

Joseph Malbos attended the Collège des Cordeliers, section Sainte-Barbe, 1837–43. After studies in theology at the Grand Séminaire de Viviers, he received the subdiaconate and then taught for a year at the Collège de Privas (Ardèche) before entering the Basilian novitiate in 1847. He taught at the Collège des Cordeliers, 1848–52, and was ordained to the priesthood on 22 September 1849 at Viviers.

On Sunday 25 July 1852 Father Malbos, accompanied by Father Jean Mathieu *Soulerin and a young seminarian Charles *Vincent, left Annonay for Le Havre where they were joined by an Irishman, William *Flannery. The four sailed to Canada, where Father Patrick *Molony had preceded them, to open the minor seminary of St Mary in Toronto. On 20 November 1852 Father Soulerin took the new Basilian vows in the presence of the bishop of Toronto, Armand de Charbonnel, a former student of the Basilians in Annonay. The following day Father Malbos made his vows before Father Soulerin. The minor seminary soon grew to include a college founded by the Christian Brothers, and took the name St Michael's College, because it was located next to the cathedral of that name. Father Malbos was its treasurer.

In 1857, at the invitation of Bishop Pierre-Adolphe Pinsonneault of the newly established diocese of London, Ontario, Father Malbos was sent to Windsor to explore the possibility of opening Assumption College (named for the parish in which it was located). He applied for incorporation and received royal assent on 16 August 1858. But, faced with opposition in this by Bishop Armand de Charbonnel of Toronto, the Congregation withdrew from the project, and Malbos returned to Annonay on 27 November 1858. During the year 1858–9 he spent a month at Aubenas (Ardèche) recovering from an illness. The rest of the year he was at the Collège des Cordeliers, and then from 1859 to 1862 taught at Aubenas. For the following five years he was the director of the Collège des Cordeliers. He continued in that work until 1870, effecting the move of the school in 1867 and renaming it the Collège du Sacré-Coeur.

In 1866 Father Malbos negotiated with the bishop of Périgueux (Dordogne) for the Basilians to assume direction of the Ecole cléricale at Périgueux. From 1870 to 1880 he was director of the Petit Séminaire de Vernoux (Ardèche). In 1880 he took up residence at Sainte-Barbe, Annonay, where he died on 6 January 1885 after a short illness.

Father Malbos was an energetic man of brilliant mind, facile speech, and independent spirit. Both in Canada and in France he gave numerous retreats and missions. He used his talents in fund-raising. Father Adrien *Chomel wrote of him: 'He had the gift of eloquence; his language was so beautiful that he might easily have become an orator had he accustomed himself to writing, instead of improvising after only a short preparation. He had all the qualities of a good prefect of studies, especially a knowledge of boys as well as the firmness necessary for managing them.'

SOURCES: GABF; J.F. Boland, 'An Analysis of the Problems and Difficulties of the Basilian Fathers in Toronto, 1850–1860,' unpublished Ph.D. thesis (University of Ottawa, 1955); Chomel, *Collège d'Annonay* 481–2; Chanoine Fromenton, *Petit Séminaire de Vernoux* (Aubenas, 1922); Kirley, *Community in France* 1, 7, 28, 29, 31, 36, 70n178, 150n384, 184, 217; Kirley, *Congregation in France* 1, 45, 235; McMahon, *Pure Zeal* 3–4; Pouzol, 'Notices'; Roume, *Origines* 302, 327, 347; L.K. Shook, 'St Michael's College, the Formative Years, 1850–1853,' *CCHA Report* 17 (1950) 37–52; L.K. Shook, 'The Coming of the Basilians to Assumption College – Early Expansion of St Michael's College,' *CCHA Report* 18 (1951) 59–73; L.K.

Shook, *Catholic Education* 131–2, 136, 276–7, 289. For documentation relating to his years at Assumption College, see Power, *Assumption College* 1 43–70 passim.

MALLEY, Eugene Robert, priest, brother of Father John Malley of the diocese of Rochester, was born on 31 July 1924 in Rochester, one of the four children of James Malley and Anna Dunheir. He died on 10 April 1980 in Windsor, Ontario, and is buried in the Basilian plot of Holy Sepulchre Cemetery, Rochester.

After attending St Augustine's Parochial School and graduating from Aquinas Institute, Rochester, in 1942, 'Gene' Malley entered the newly opened St Basil's Novitiate in Rochester and was professed on 10 October 1943. His novitiate year had to be extended by a month because a snow-ball injury necessitated removal of his left eye. He was appointed to St Michael's College, Toronto, for undergraduate studies (B.A., University of Toronto, 1948), studied theology at St Basil's Seminary, Toronto, 1948–52, and was ordained to the priesthood on 29 June 1951 in St Basil's Church, Toronto, by Cardinal James Charles McGuigan. During his theology course he also pursued graduate studies in Spanish (M.A., University of Toronto, 1952).

Father Malley was sent to Rome for graduate studies in theology at the International Pontifical Institute (Angelicum), Rome (S.T.L., 1953; S.T.D., 1954, after defending his thesis entitled 'Piety'). He joined the faculty of St Basil's Seminary in 1954, where he became first councillor, 1955–8, and was named superior and master of scholastics, 1958–64. His next appointment was to Assumption University, Windsor, where he became assistant professor of religious studies as well as head of the religious studies department. He was promoted to full professor in 1968.

From 1967 to 1972 Father Malley served as superior of the Basilian community at Assumption University and from 1967 to 1973 also served as president of Assumption University. From 1969 to 1974 he was vice-dean of Humanities of the University of Windsor, and in 1974 he became dean of the Faculty of Arts. Upon resigning this office in 1978 he was elected head of the religious studies department. He was also elected to the Senate of the University of Windsor as well as to the office of co-ordinator of European Studies in the Faculty of Arts. He exercised these positions of administration and authority with wisdom and humanity.

On 27 March 1980, during a meeting of the United Way Executive

Committee at Hiram Walker's, Windsor, he felt ill, excused himself, and went outside, where he was seen walking in the area. The next morning he was found comatose in a garden a few blocks away. He was taken to Windsor Western Hospital, but died two weeks later without gaining consciousness.

A dynamic priest and teacher, Gene Malley was a loyal friend and an understanding man with a winning smile which tended to cover an inner turmoil caused in no small measure by the changes in religious life and community living.

SOURCES: GABF; *Annals* 2 (1951) 36, 5 (1981) 606–7; *Newsletter* (17 April 1980); Shook, *Catholic Education* 205, 290.

MALLON, Hugh Vincent, priest, brother of Fathers Paul *Mallon, Gregory *Mallon, and Francis Mallon CSB, was born on 5 July 1910 in Toronto, the second youngest of the seven children of John Francis Mallon and Catherine Teresa Mulvey. He died in Toronto on 28 October 1978, and is buried in the Basilian plot of Holy Cross Cemetery, Thornhill, Ontario.

Hugh Mallon attended Holy Rosary School and the high school section of St Michael's College, Toronto, graduating in 1926. That same year he entered St Basil's Novitiate, Toronto, and was professed on 18 September 1927. He was assigned to live at St Basil's Scholasticate during university studies (B.A., Honours English and History, University of Toronto, 1931). While remaining at the scholasticate, he earned a specialist's certificate in English and history from the Ontario College of Education, 1932. He studied theology, 1931–5, and was ordained to the priesthood on 16 December 1934 in Assumption Church, Windsor, by Bishop John Kidd.

In 1935 Father Mallon was appointed to Assumption College, Windsor. After a year of serious health problems he was assigned in 1936 to teach English and to fill the office of director of athletics. In 1940 he went to St Michael's College in the same two capacities. Under his coaching the St Michael's Majors hockey team won the Memorial Cup in 1945 and 1947. During the summer months of successive years he attended the University of Michigan, earning an M.A. in English in 1944.

In 1952 Father Mallon was named co-director of the St Michael's College Centennial Campaign. He was appointed vice-president and registrar of the University of St Michael's College in 1958, but in 1961 he was named vice-president of Assumption University, where he also taught in the department of English. He returned to Toronto in 1963 to his former offices of vice-president and registrar. During these years at St Michael's and at Assumption he was frequently a member of the local council of the Basilian community.

In 1973 Father Mallon twice underwent major surgery from which he never fully recovered. He was nevertheless appointed superior of the Basilian community at the University of St Michael's College in 1976. In addition to that onerous position, he kept in touch with former students by editing and publishing the *St Michael's Alumni Newsletter*, for which service he was recognized by an award from the University of Toronto Alumni Association in 1975. He also received the university's Sesquicentennial Award in 1977.

In August 1978 Father Mallon was admitted to hospital with diagnosis of leukemia. He underwent chemotherapy which greatly taxed his strength. In September he resigned his position as superior. His last month was spent in the Basilian Fathers Residence (Infirmary), where his strength ebbed rapidly. On 27 October, he was fully conscious and alert when his brothers Greg and Frank administered the sacrament of the sick, in the company of a large number of his confreres. He died peacefully the following afternoon.

Hugh Mallon was a gentle man, patient and understanding of the needs of others, even-tempered and trusting. Although frequently in the spotlight, he neither sought it nor gloried in it.

BIBLIOGRAPHY: 'Joyce Kilmer,' *Basilian* 4 (April 1938) 67–8.
SOURCES: GABF; *Annals* 5 (1978) 268, 5 (1979) 416–18; *Newsletter* (3 November 1978); J. Francis Mallon, *The Mallons of Spadina Road* (Toronto, 1982); Shook, *Catholic Education* 176, 187, 190, 201.

MALLON, John PAUL, priest, brother of Fathers Gregory *Mallon, Hugh *Mallon, and Francis Mallon CSB, was born on 28 April 1900 in Toronto, the eldest of the seven children of John Francis Mallon and Catherine Teresa Mulvey. He died on 10 February 1974 and is buried in the Basilian plot of Holy Cross Cemetery, Thornhill, Ontario.

Paul Mallon attended Holy Rosary School, Toronto, and St Michael's College, Toronto, for both high school and university (B.A., Modern Languages, University of Toronto, 1921). He entered St Basil's Novitiate, Toronto, on 3 October 1921. In 1922 the Basilians reorganized into two congregations, one in France and one in North America, with the latter adopting a new, stricter vow of poverty. Among Father Mallon's papers was found a handwritten testimonial stating that he accepted the Constitutions of the 1922 general chapter of the new Basilian Congregation in North America.

After his profession on 13 October 1922, he taught for one year at St Michael's College. He then began theology studies at St Basil's Scholasticate, living for the last three years of these studies at St Michael's and qualifying during the last year for a Teacher's Certificate from the Ontario College of Education. He obtained an M.A. in French and Italian studies from the University of Toronto in 1925. He was ordained to the priesthood in St Basil's Church, Toronto, on 18 December 1926 by Bishop Alexander MacDonald.

In 1927 Father Mallon went with the first group of Basilians to Aquinas Institute, Rochester, where he taught until 1932. He spent the year 1932–3 at St Michael's and then, in August 1933, he once again formed part of a founding group of Basilians, this time for St Mary's Boys' High School, Calgary, Alberta. He returned to Aquinas in 1937 for two years and then was freed for graduate studies at Laval University, Quebec City. The year 1940 saw him back to full-time teaching at Aquinas. He continued his studies in the summers and was awarded a Ph.D. from Laval in 1942.

That same year Father Mallon went to St Thomas More College, Saskatoon, Saskatchewan. There he was to remain for twenty-eight years, and there his talents and his tireless activity found their broadest scope. He served as councillor in the local community and registrar for the college. It was said that no one knew the Catholic population of Saskatchewan as he did, and his interest in students and friends went far beyond official demands. He was a great believer in the power of the written word and steadily promoted Catholic literature, both by making it easily available at the college and by seeming to know what a person might be interested in. He was himself a devoted and discerning reader. He was deeply attached to the teaching of the Church and would brook no deviation from it. His faith was strong, serene, and simple, while at the same time reasoned and informed.

Paul Mallon's dedication to learning remained unabated through his life. When he left St Thomas More College at seventy years of age, it was not to retire. He asked to be appointed to the Basilian community in Annonay, where he could nourish his interest in French, work with Père Félix *Pouzol on the archives, and be close to Italy, for he was fluent in Italian and always enjoyed Italian people and conversation. He served as community librarian during his three-year stay in Annonay, 1970–3.

He was appointed to St Basil's College in the summer of 1973, where quietly and unobtrusively he set about getting to know the students and renewing his own theology. He attended lectures, discussed books and courses, and took on ministerial duties such as hearing Italian confessions in one of the Toronto parishes. He was generous with his time but was discreet to a fault in imposing on that of another. He died quietly, alone in his room, apparently while reading his breviary.

BIBLIOGRAPHY: 'The Teaching of Elementary French,' *National Catholic Education Association. Proceedings* (1929; repr. *Basilian* 1 [May 1935] 51–2); 'St Thomas More College,' *Basilian Teacher* 1 (March 1957) 18–21.
SOURCES: GABF; *Annals* 4 (1973) 272, 5 (1975) 111–13; *Newsletter* (12 February 1974); Kirley, *Congregation in France* 235; J. Francis Mallon, *The Mallons of Spadina Road* (Toronto, 1982); Shook, *Catholic Education* 348, 351.

MALLON, Thomas GREGORY, priest, brother of Fathers Paul *Mallon, Hugh *Mallon, and Francis Mallon, was born on Toronto's Centre Island on 27 June 1908, the third youngest of the seven children of John Francis Mallon and Catherine Teresa Mulvey. He died in Toronto on 11 December 1991 and is buried in the Basilian plot of Holy Cross Cemetery, Thornhill, Ontario.

'Greg' Mallon attended Holy Rosary Separate School and the high school section of St Michael's College, Toronto. He continued at St Michael's College for his university studies (B.A., University of Toronto, 1931). After graduation he entered St Basil's Novitiate, Toronto, making first profession on 12 September 1932. He immediately began theological studies at St Basil's Scholasticate, Toronto, during the first year of which he also attended the Ontario College of Education, earning teaching certification in 1933. He was ordained to the priesthood on 21 December 1935 in St Basil's Church, Toronto, by Archbishop James Charles McGuigan. Greg was the last of the four Mallon brothers to be ordained.

In 1936 Father Mallon began thirty-nine years of teaching and administration at various Basilian schools. From 1936 to 1943 he taught English at St Thomas High School, Houston, and obtained Texas teaching certification in 1942 and an M.A. in education (University of Houston, 1943). He taught at St Mary's Boys' High School, Calgary, Alberta,

1943–54, and earned the Alberta teaching certificate from the University of Calgary. He also took on the chaplaincy of the Royal Canadian Navy Reserve and was treasurer of the local house. In 1954 he returned to Toronto as bursar of St Michael's College School, and in 1960 accepted the same charge at St Thomas More College in the University of Saskatchewan, Saskatoon, retiring in 1978. He returned to Toronto once more, to be assistant treasurer at St Basil's College.

Greg Mallon's administrative experience and financial skills proved invaluable in the reorganization of the Basilian Fathers infirmary, which involved major construction on the fourth floor of St Basil's College. Greg personally oversaw and monitored the work, which resulted in an excellent facility. He was smaller of stature than his three Basilian bothers but very much like them in his generous community spirit.

BIBLIOGRAPHY: 'Catechetical Action,' *Basilian* 3 (January 1937) 7, 10.
SOURCES: GABF; *Annals* 6 (1983) 116, (1986) 396, 7 (1992) 135–7; *Newsletter* (18 December 1991); J. Francis Mallon, *The Mallons of Spadina Road* (Toronto, 1982).

MALONE, Felix CLARE, priest, was born on 12 August 1929, at Guelph, Ontario (diocese of Hamilton), the only child of Felix Malone and Anna Saul. He died in Toronto on 14 September 1977 and is buried in the Basilian plot of Holy Cross Cemetery, Thornhill, Ontario.

When Clare was still very young the family moved from Guelph to Holy Rosary Parish, Toronto, where he attended the parish school and was well known to the parish staff and the neighbouring novices. Upon graduation from St Michael's College School in 1950, he entered St Basil's Novitiate, Richmond Hill, Ontario, and was professed on 15 August 1951. He was appointed to St Basil's Seminary, Toronto, 1951–2, and then to St Michael's College, 1952–4, for his undergraduate studies (B.A., University of Toronto, 1954). He taught for two years at St Charles College, Sudbury, Ontario, before taking his theological studies at St Basil's Seminary, 1956–60. During these years he also studied at the Ontario College of Education, producing a thesis, 'Secondary Education Conducted by the Basilian Fathers in the Province of Ontario.' He was ordained to the priesthood in St Basil's Church, Toronto, on 28 June 1959, by Bishop Francis Allen. In that same year he obtained an S.T.B. from the University of St Michael's College.

In 1960 Father Malone was appointed to the novitiate at Richmond Hill as treasurer while doing graduate studies at the University of Toronto (M.Ed., 1961). In August 1961 he was assigned to Michael Power High School, Etobicoke, Ontario, where he remained until 1968, holding positions of teacher, director of athletics, and, from 1964 to 1968, principal. In August 1968 the Metropolitan Toronto Separate School Board appointed him to supervise its programs in grades IX and X. During the time he held this position, 1968–70, he lived at St Basil's Seminary. In 1970 he returned to work in Basilian schools: to Assumption College School, Windsor, 1970–2, and St Mary's College, Sault Ste Marie, Ontario, 1972–3, as teacher, and Michael Power, as principal, from 1973 until ill health required his resignation in January 1976. He continued to teach until his death some twenty months later.

Clare Malone was a man of immense talent and energy. Even his deteriorating heart condition seemed to spur him on as though he were racing against time. He had a habitual cheerfulness with a ready and infectious laugh. He could work long hours at difficult and complicated tasks, for his incisive, analytical mind went immediately to the heart of a problem. With students he was patient in explaining problems and solutions. His certainty of an early death never cast a shadow over his habitual good humour and enjoyment of work and community life.

BIBLIOGRAPHY: 'There Must Be Conveyed a Distinctly Basilian Spirituality,' *Forum* 1 (May 1965) 118–20.
SOURCES: GABF; *Annals* 2 (1959) 420, 5 (1978) 330–1; *Newsletter* (20 September 1977).

MALONEY, Donald ANDREW**,** priest, member of the Congregation 1948–72, was born in St Andrews' West, Ontario (diocese of Alexandria, since 1976 of Alexandria-Cornwall), on 12 September 1925, the son of Vincent Maloney and Marcella Campbell. He died on 26 August 1978, and is buried in the cemetery of his native town.

'Andy' Maloney came to St Michael's College from St Andrew's High School in 1943, and then joined the Canadian Army for service in the Second World War. He completed his degree (B.A., University of Toronto, 1947) and then entered St Basil's Novitiate, Richmond Hill, Ontario, making first profession on 15 August 1948. He studied theology at St Basil's Seminary, 1948–52, and was ordained to the priesthood by Bishop Rosario Brodeur in St Finian's Cathedral, Alexandria, Ontario, on 22 December 1951.

Father Maloney received an M.A. in philosophy from the University of Toronto in 1953. He pursued further graduate studies at the University of Toronto while residing at the Institute House, 1953–4, and at St Michael's College, 1954–5 and 1957–8. Throughout his undergraduate and graduate studies he was supported financially by the Department of Veterans' Affairs. He taught at Assumption University of Windsor in 1955–7. In 1958–60 he attended the Angelicum in Rome (S.T.D., 1960). He was second councillor at St Basil's Seminary, 1961–3, and then was an assistant at St John the Baptist Parish, Amherstburg, Ontario, 1963–4. A number of different teaching appointments followed, first at the University of Windsor, 1964–5, and then at St Mark's College, Vancouver, 1965–6. He spent a year, 1966–7, at the Jesuit-operated al-Hikma University, Baghdad, Iraq, but had to leave there at the outbreak of the 1967 Israeli-Arab War. After another year at St Mark's, he returned to Baghdad in the fall of 1968, hoping to remain there; but the coup that eventually brought Saddam Hussein to power broke out at that time, and the al-Hikma University was confiscated and its members expelled. Father Maloney taught theology at St Peter's Seminary, Cape Coast, Ghana, 1969–70, and was then appointed to the University of St Thomas, Houston, 1970–2. He withdrew from the Congregation in 1972, and subsequently worked at the University of South Carolina, Columbia, as a government grants administrator. He is survived by his wife, Linda Mitchell Maloney, and a son, Vincent.

BIBLIOGRAPHY: 'Jesus as the Horizon of Human Hope,' 97–112 of *Does Jesus Make a Difference?* ed. Thomas M. McFadden. Proceedings of the College Theological Society. New York, 1974. In *Basilian Teacher:* 'Undergraduate Theology,' 2 (November 1957) 8–13; 'For the Sake of Argument,' 6 (March 1962) 221–3; 'For the Sake of Another Argument,' 6 (April 1962) 280–4; 'The Theologian and the Cinema,' 7 (May 1963) 271–4; 'Studiousness,' 7 (November 1962) 45–51; 'Sacrament and Salvation History,' 8 (February 1964) 244–9; 'Safeguarding Personal Values in Religious Life,' 8 (May 1964) 435–51; 'Birth Regulation and Population Problems,' 8 (November 1963) 69–74; 'In Hoc Signo Vinces,' 9 (October 1964) 25–8; 'A Tribute: Albert Schweitzer,' 9 (February 1965) 242–3; 'Ecce Lignum Crucis,' 10 (February 1966) 76–84; 'Theology in the University,' 10 (October 1966) 278–88; 'Sacraments and Sacramental Rites,' 11 (October 1967) 310–20.
SOURCES: GABF; *Annals* 2 (1952) 58; Linda M. Maloney.

MARCEAU, William Charles, priest, was born in Rochester on 22

February 1927, the first of two children of Charles William Marceau and Melinda Frances Fritz. He died in Toronto on 6 August 2000 and is buried in the Basilian plot of Holy Sepulchre Cemetery, Rochester. Bill Marceau attended Sacred Heart parochial school and Aquinas Institute, Rochester, where he graduated in June 1945. He enlisted in the U.S. Naval Reserve for two years. He entered St Basil's Novitiate, Rochester, was professed on 15 August 1948, and was appointed to Assumption College, Windsor (B.A., University of Western Ontario, 1952). After two years of teaching and coaching football, basketball, and track at Aquinas Institute, he studied theology and French at the Grand Séminaire in Quebec, 1954–5, and at St Basil's Seminary, Toronto, 1955–8, and was ordained to the priesthood on 29 June 1957 in St Basil's Church, Toronto, by Cardinal James Charles McGuigan.

In 1958 he was assigned to Aquinas Institute for one year and then to the Institution Secondaire du Sacré-Coeur, Annonay, for two years. He returned to Aquinas in 1961 and taught there for four years, during that time also earning an M.A. in French literature from the Université Laval, Quebec. In 1965 he began doctoral studies at Laval (Ph.D., 1968), submitting a thesis on 'L'optimisme dans les oeuvres de Saint-François de Sales.'

In 1967 Father Marceau was assigned to the Basilian Fathers of East Rochester, where he remained attached for the rest of his life, with the exception of two years, 1968–9, at the Basilian House of Studies, Rochester, and 1973–4 at Laval. He taught French at St John Fisher College. His insatiable quest for learning coupled with his outgoing manner fostered a remarkable career of study, lecturing, publishing, retreat preaching, and spiritual direction. He obtained a post-doctoral diploma (I.P.F.E.) in French literature from the Université de Paris in 1969, and returned frequently during research leaves to Laval (M.A., Philosophy, 1975), to the Université de Paris-Sorbonne, the Institut catholique and the Ecole pratique des hautes études in Paris, and to Oxford University to study French philosophy. He loved French culture and sought to instil that love in his students, even with ski trips to Quebec. The Ministry of Education of France recognized his work by naming him *Titulaire des Palmes académiques* in 1978. He earned the M.Th. conferred conjointly by the University of St Michael's College and the University of Toronto, 1990, with a thesis entitled 'The Notion of the Eucharist in Théodore de Bèze and François de Sales,' and in 1996 received the S.T.L. from the University of St Thomas (Angelicum),

Rome, where he subsequently enrolled in 1997 in the doctoral program.

Father Marceau was a visiting professor at St Peter's Seminary, Bangalore, India, at St Thomas More College, Saskatoon, in the Christianity and Culture program at St Michael's College, Toronto, and at the University of St Thomas, Houston. His focus on French literature, philosophy, and spiritual theology produced several books and numerous articles on St Francis de Sales, on whose life and teaching he was an internationally acknowledged authority. He was a member of the editorial team for publication of the critical edition of the letters of Ste Jeanne de Chantal. Much in demand as a spiritual director and retreat preacher, he worked with the Sisters of the Visitation in both France and India.

Father Marceau's zest for life, for seeking new plateaus and new friends, was abruptly curtailed late in 1999 by a heart attack, a serious fall, and subsequent illnesses that necessitated moving him to Anglin House, the Basilian Fathers infirmary in Toronto. In July 2000 his rapidly deteriorating condition demanded a move to Providence Centre, Toronto, where he died shortly after.

BIBLIOGRAPHY:

Books: *L'optimisme dans l'oeuvre de saint François de Sales*. Paris, 1973; repr. Paris, 1993; trans. *Optimism in the Works of St Francis de Sales*. Visakhapatnam, India, 1983; repr. Toronto Studies in Theology. Lewiston/Queenston, 1989. *Stoicism and St Francis de Sales*. Hyattsville, Md., 1973; repr. S.F.S. Publications, Visakhapatnam, 1979; repr. Toronto Studies in Theology 44, Lewiston/Queenston, 1990; trans. *Stoïcisme et Saint François de Sales*. Saint-Etienne, 1983. *Henri Bergson et Joseph Malègue: la convergence de deux pensées*, Stanford French and Italian Studies 50. Saratoga, Calif. 1987. *The Eucharist in Théodore de Bèze and François de Sales*. Toronto Studies in Theology 67. Lewiston/Queenston, 1991. *St Francis de Sales' Theology of Eucharist*. Bangalore, India, 1992.

Articles: 'Claudel – Dramatist of Humanity,' *Basilian Teacher* 9 (October 1965) 483–9; 'St Francis de Sales – Spiritual Director,' *Salesian Studies* 6 (Summer 1969) 87–92; 'Russia As Seen by Rev. Dr. William Marceau,' *Tower Chronicle* 2 (November 1969) 11–19; 'La théorie de la bonté naturelle dans l'*Emile* de Jean-Jacques Rousseau,' *Modern Language Studies* 1 (Summer 1971) 30–3; 'Overseas Studies as a Motivating Force for College Students,' *Midwest Education Review* 6 (Fall 1973) 1–4; 'Un américain au stade de Vanves,' *Tribune régionale* 14 (May 1975) 12; 'Le renouveau par l'indifférence,' *Annales salésiennes* 1 (1977) 14–15; 'La religion de Voltaire d'après le *Dictionnaire philosophique*,' *Bulletin de la Société des professeurs français en Amérique* (1978) 17–24; 'Salesian Confidence in

God and Man,' *Review for Religious* 40 (January 1981) 54–69; 'L'héritage augustinien chez saint François de Sales,' *Papers on French Seventeenth-Century Literature* (Tübingen) 9 (1981) 137–50; 'Salesian Voluntarism,' *Review for Religious* 41 (November–December 1982) 898–922; 'Role of Prayers in the Apostolate, according to St Francis de Sales,' *Studies in Salesian Spirituality* 2 (1983) 43–52; 'Authority and Obedience,' *Jyothidhara* 4 (October 1984) 43–52; 'St Francis de Sales and the Fathers,' *Studies in Salesian Spirituality* 4 (1985) 48–60; 'Salesian Peace and Joy,' *Jyothidhara* 6 (December 1985) 3–9; 'Prayer in Salesian Spirituality,' *Studies in Salesian Spirituality* 5 (August 1986) 9–28; 'La philosophie spirituelle de Henri Bergson,' *Laval théologique et philosophique* 42 (February 1986) 35–55; 'The Influence of Italian and Spanish Mystics on St Francis de Sales,' *Spirituality Today* 39 (Summer 1987) 148–62; 'L'oeuvre spirituelle de Joseph Malègue,' *Bulletin de la Société des professeurs français en Amérique* (1987–8) 99–138; 'Jacques Etienne Montgolfier and Joseph-Michel Montgolfier,' *Great Lives from History. Renaissance to 1900*, ed. F.N. Magill (Pasadena, Calif., c.1989) 3 1656–60; 'The Blessing of Old Age (I),' *Salesian Journal of Spirituality* 1 (March 1988) 12–24; 'The Blessing of Old Age (II),' *Salesian Journal of Spirituality* 1 (June 1988) 152, 162; 'Salesian Prayer,' *Salesian Journal of Spirituality* 2 December 1989) 373–82; 'The Christianity of Mme de LaFayette,' *Papers on Seventeenth-Century Literature* 17 no. 32 (1990) 171–84; 'Fénelon – Epigone of St Francis de Sales,' *Indian Journal of Spirituality* 3 (1990) 376–85; 'Théodore de Bèze et François de Sales: Deux spiritualités de l'Eucharistie,' *XVIIe Siècle* 170 (January–March 1991) 5–11; 'Spiritual Theology Today,' *Indian Journal of Spirituality* 5 (December 1992) 349–57; 'La volonté salésienne et son rôle,' *Francographies* 1 (1993) 61–7; 'St Irenaeus of Lyon and the Theory of Recapitulation,' *Indian Journal of Spirituality* 6 (December 1993) 467–76; 'The Incarnation and Francis de Sales,' *Indian Journal of Spirituality* 6 (1994); 'Early English Translations of Salesian Writings,' *Indian Journal of Spirituality* 8 (August 1995) 155–64; 'St Francis de Sales – Liberation Theologian,' *Indian Journal of Spirituality* 8 (September 1995) 301–15; 'St Francis de Sales – Missionary,' *Indian Journal of Spirituality* 8 (December 1995) 459–69; 'Réponse au Père Scott,' *Biblio* 17, Actes du Lexington (1995) 374; 'St Francis de Sales and his Doctrine of Love,' *Indian Journal of Spirituality* 9 (June 1996) 143–57; 'Recusant Translations of Saint Francis de Sales,' *Downside Review* 114 no. 396 (July 1996) 221–33. He published fifty-six book reviews in *Emmanuel, French Review, Laval théologique et philosophique, Journal of Ecumenical Studies, Theological Studies, Romanic Review, Papers on French Seventeenth-Century Literature, Canadian Catholic Review, Nineteenth-Century French Studies,* and *Christianity and Literature.*
SOURCES: GABF; *Annals* 2 (1957) 318, 9 (1999) 6–7, (2001) 99–100; Basilian Archives, East Rochester, N.Y.; *Newsletter* (25 August 2000).

MARCOUX (MARCOU), Auguste, priest, was born on 19 October 1905, at Saint-Julien-Vocance (Ardèche), the son of Joseph Marcoux and Marcelline Chareyron. He died in Annonay on 20 August 1974, and is buried there in the Basilian cemetery on the grounds of the Collège du Sacré-Coeur.

Auguste Marcoux entered the Basilian Novitiate at Bordighera, Italy, on 31 January 1929 and made first profession on 12 February 1930. After his final profession on 5 July 1933 he completed his theological studies and was ordained to the priesthood by Bishop Pierre-Marie Durieux in the cathedral at Viviers on 6 July 1934.

Father Marcoux worked as prefect at the Collège du Sacré-Coeur, 1934–44, but the remainder of his active ministry was in parish work. He was curate at Dessaignes (Ardèche) and then pastor at Monestier (Ardèche), 1944–8. Failing health forced a long period of hospitalization and rest. In 1955, however, he was able to return to parish work in a limited way at Cuers (Var), 1955–7, and later at Saint-Sauveur-en-Rue (Haute-Loire), 1959–60.

From 1960 on Father Marcoux lived at the hospital at La Teppe, Tain-l'Hermitage (Drôme), where he served in a group of chaplains until a fall in May 1974 initiated a decline in health which brought him to the hospital in Annonay in July. There he was attended by his confreres until his death a month later. His funeral took place in the chapel of the Collège du Sacré-Coeur.

Despite a life of poor health, notably epilepsy, Father Marcoux persevered eagerly in the exercise of his priestly ministry.

SOURCES: GABF; *Annals* 5 (1975) 118–19; *Newsletter* (3 September 1974); Kirley, *Congregation in France* 159, 176, 185, 196, 220, 256, 262; Pouzol, 'Notices.'

MARIJON, Victorin, priest, seventh superior general of the Congregation, 1910–14, and second superior general of the French Congregation, 1923–31, was born in Vernoux (Ardèche) on 5 July 1851. He died on 21 October 1931 in Annonay and is buried there in the cemetery on the grounds of the Collège du Sacré-Coeur.

Victorin Marijon studied at the Petit Séminaire de Vernoux. He made his novitiate at Feyzin (Isère, now Rhône) and took final vows in 1872. He was ordained to the priesthood by Bishop Armand de Charbonnel in the chapel of the Collège du Sacré-Coeur on 19 September 1874. He taught in Annonay until the end of 1883, when he was named master of novices at Beaconfield House, Plymouth, England. Forty-seven novices, French and North American, made their novitiate under his direction. In the summer of 1889 he accompanied the superior general, Father Adrien *Fayolle, on his canonical visitation of the houses in North America. At the end of November 1890, at the age of thirty-nine, Father Marijon was named provincial in North America, residing at St Michael's College, Toronto, and held the office until 1907, when he was appointed novice master at St Basil's Novitiate, Toronto.

In 1910 the general chapter in Geneva elected Father Marijon superior general, with eleven out of fifteen votes, and directed him to take up residence at Ste Anne's Church, Detroit. Deep divisions in the Congregation, stemming from differing interpretations of leadership roles and religious life itself, led to a special chapter in 1913 in Rome to modify the Constitutions. In 1914, under pressure from Rome, Father Marijon resigned and Father James *Player, the first assistant, was elected acting superior general, a position he held until the separation into two communities in 1922. On the death of Father François-Xavier *Granottier in 1917, Father Marijon was again elected to the general council. At this time, and until he returned to France in 1921, he was doing parish work at Ste Anne's.

On 14 June 1922 the decree from Rome creating two congregations, one for France and one for North America, came into effect. Father Julien *Giraud was elected superior general of the French community; but when he resigned a year later the French community elected Father Marijon in his place, and he held the position until his death in 1931. He was also superior of the Petit Séminaire Saint-Charles in Annonay until 1928. In 1926 he opened the novitiate in Bordighera, Italy, and spent part of a year there while expansion and reparations were made at Maison Saint-Joseph, Annonay, as a retirement house and scholasticate. In 1929 he presented in Rome a draft of the new Constitutions for the French community.

Father Marijon was a major figure in Basilian history. As master of novices he was motivated by zeal for the traditions of the Congregation. Father Michael Vincent *Kelly, who made his novitiate under Father Marijon, described him as 'a man of deep faith and fervent piety, strictly observant of every requirement of religious life, exemplary and edifying in every detail, at once zealous and discreet, retiring, gentle, urbane, kind and considerate of everyone.' Ironically, Father Kelly would be the chief opponent of Father Marijon some years later.

As provincial, Father Marijon wrote several circular letters recalling Basilian customs and their observance. Following the practice in the college in Annonay he reserved to himself many of the duties which had been exercised by the superior of St Michael's and the pastor of St Basil's parish. It was during his tenure as provincial that the first Basilian houses in Texas were opened at Waco, Houston, and LaPorte.

As superior general living in America he was less effective. He wished to assure French control of the growing province in North America. Two apostolic visitors in 1910 and 1912 failed to resolve the differences between himself and the Canadian Basilians who were led by M.V. *Kelly. In the same directive from Rome that forced Father Marijon's resignation, Kelly was disenfranchised, relieved of membership on the provincial council, and ordered to live outside of the province of Ontario. When elected to the general council in 1917, Father Marijon proved a difficult and even recalcitrant member, openly opposed to the acting superior general, Father James *Player.

Father Marijon was looked upon as a second founder of the Basilians in France. He did a great deal to keep together the members who had been expelled from teaching in 1903, and remained in communication with Father Player, who had been made acting superior general in his place in 1914. Commenting on his tenure as superior general from 1923 to 1931, the *Semaine religieuse de Viviers* described him as 'a worthy successor of the venerable founders of the Community of St Basil: Actorie, Duret, Tourvieille and many others, men of rule and duty, wisdom and goodness, whose virtue and merits had their source in simplicity and modesty, and whose memory is cherished by those who had them for teachers and examples.'

SOURCES: GABF; M.V. Kelly, 'Beaconfield,' *Basilian* 1 (October and November 1935) 94–5, 112–15; Kirley, *Community in France* 134–5, 244–60 and passim; Kirley, *Congregation in France* 3–6, 13, 14–18, 20–9, 32–6, 45, 48, 50, 52, 54, 55–6, 72, 74, 76, 79–80, 82–3, 86–90, 94–6, 102, 114, 116; 119, 125–37, 139–44, 147–51, 155–6, 159–61, 174, 209, 211–12, 221, 262, 269–70; Pouzol, 'Notices'; *Semaine religieuse de Viviers* (6 November 1931).

MARIN, Charles Augustin, priest, member of the Association of Priests of Saint Basil 1834–44, was born on 5 November 1811 at Beaumes-de-Venise (Vaucluse, diocese of Avignon).

Augustin Marin attended the Christian Brothers' school in Lyon, where his parents had moved in 1814. After a retreat in 1823 preached by Father Pierre *Tourvieille, the Brothers recommended twelve-year-old Augustin to him. Father Tourvieille enrolled the boy at Sainte-Barbe and then at the Collège des Cordeliers in Annonay. Augustin excelled in his studies, including philosophy and theology. He paid all his tuition by teaching a class in writing five hours a week. On 30 November 1834 he was admitted as a novice to the Association, and was ordained a priest on 23 September 1837 at Le Puy (Haute-Loire). In October of that year he made his profession by promise, not by vows, following the custom at the time.

Father Marin taught the senior grades at the Collège de Privas, the Collège des Cordeliers, and the Collège de Feyzin (Isère, now Rhône). Much to the regret of his confreres, especially Father Tourvieille, he withdrew from the Association in September 1844 and was incardinated in the diocese of Avignon, where he taught *seconde* in the Petit Séminaire.

SOURCE: Pouzol, 'Notices,' Supplément 1.

MARTARESCHE, Frédéric, priest, was born on 20 February 1834 at Saint-Pierre-la-Roche (Ardèche), the son of Alexis Martaresche and Jeanne Vignal. He died on 22 November 1905 at Rochemaure (Ardèche) and was buried in the village of his birth.

Frédéric Martaresche entered the novitiate of the Marist Brothers in 1852 and was professed in that community. In 1866 he went to the Collège des Cordeliers, Annonay, to teach commercial, and decided to become a priest. After studying Latin, philosophy and theology, he made final profession in the Basilian Congregation on 20 September 1872 and was ordained to the priesthood on 20 September 1873 by Bishop Armand de Charbonnel in the chapel of the Collège du Sacré-Coeur, Annonay.

He remained at the college in Annonay teaching the commercial classes from 1874 to 1899. When the Basilians were expelled from the school in 1903, he assisted the pastor of Rochemaure until his sudden death two years later. The *Semaine religieuse de Viviers* said of him, 'The piety, religious spirit and dedication he showed in all his priestly functions justified the esteem in which he was held by his confreres.'

SOURCES: GABF; Chomel, *Collège d'Annonay* 145; Kirley, *Community in France* 185, 188n469, 204; Pouzol, 'Notices'; Roume, *Origines* 156, 160, 161, 210, 402; *Semaine religieuse de Viviers* (1 December 1905) 568.

MARTIN, Arsène, priest, nephew of Fathers Ernest *Martin and Joseph *Martin, was born in Prades (Ardèche) on 18 March 1862. He died at Amherstburg, Ontario, on 15 October 1909, and is buried in the Basilian plot of Assumption Cemetery, Windsor.

Arsène Martin studied up to the *classe de troisième* at the Sainte-Barbe section of the Collège du Sacré-Coeur, Annonay. In 1884 he went to Mary Immaculate College, Beaconfield House, Plymouth, England, where he remained for four years and made his novitiate in 1886-7. In 1888 he set sail for Canada and continued his studies in philosophy and theology at St Michael's College, Toronto, and then at Assumption College, Windsor. He took final vows on 8 January 1891 and was ordained to the priesthood on 14 December 1892.

After ordination Father Martin returned to St Michael's College to teach the natural sciences and serve as librarian and as treasurer, 1901-5. In 1907 he was transferred to St John the Baptist Parish, Amherstburg, where he was assistant until his death in 1909.

'Père Martin,' as he was usually called, seemed never to have lost his youth. At St Michael's College he took part in the recreations of the students, which made him popular with them.

SOURCES: GABF; Kirley, *Community in France* 186, 211n507, 214n516, 216n518, 219n526, 220n528, 236n564, 240n569; Pouzol, 'Notices.'

MARTIN, Ernest, priest, brother of Father Joseph *Martin and uncle of Father Arsène *Martin, was born at Prades (Ardèche) on 8 January 1856, the son of Jean Martin and Anne Veyrand. He died on 9 October 1935 in Annonay and is buried there in the cemetery on the grounds of the Collège du Sacré-Coeur.

After attending the Collège des Cordeliers, section Sainte-Barbe, 1866-74, Ernest Martin made his novitiate at Feyzin (Isère, now Rhône), 1874-5. He taught during his theological studies and was ordained priest on 24 September 1881 in the chapel of the Collège du Sacré-Coeur by Archbishop Armand de Charbonnel. From 1875 to 1882 he was prefect or teacher at the Basilian schools at Privas, Bourg Saint-Andéol, and Vernoux, all in the Ardèche, and in Blidah, Algeria. He spent the year 1882 obtaining the *licence ès sciences*. For the next twenty years he was professor of mathematics and science at the college in Blidah where his brother Joseph was superior. With the 1903 laws forbidding members of congregations to teach, the Basilians were expelled and the building was sold to become a school for girls.

Father Martin then spent five years teaching at St Michael's College, Toronto, two years at Assumption College, Windsor, and then another year at St Michael's. In 1906 his brother Joseph died in Blidah, and in 1909 his nephew Arsène died at Amherstburg, Ontario. In 1910 Ernest Martin returned to France, teaching for a time in Grenoble (Isère) at the Pensionnat Saint-Michel and at the Externat Notre-Dame. He then went to live with a niece in the canton d'Aubenas (Ardèche). In 1915 he undertook to teach mathematics at the Petit Séminaire d'Aubenas, and in 1923 retired to the Petit Séminaire Saint-Charles, Annonay, where he looked after the gardens. From 1929 to 1935 he lived at Maison Saint-Joseph, Annonay, again making use of his gardening skills. He was elected to the general council in 1932, serving until his death three years later.

Father Charles *Roume described Father Martin as 'a small man, thin and brittle as a match-stick. His countenance of swarthy complexion was lit by eyes in whose glint occasionally shone a hint of mischief that rarely, if ever, became outwardly manifest. A thin beard tapered his chin. His body was a bundle of nerves, which he heroically, though not always successfully, strove to keep in check. The students had nicknamed him "Calvin," and it must be admitted that he bore a striking resemblance to the Geneva reformer.'

The lifetime of Father Ernest Martin extended over several crises in France: the anticlerical laws of 1883 and 1903–4, the war of 1914–18, and the division of the Congregation in 1922. But whenever he heard anyone express anxiety over the future, he would quote the proverb, 'God tempers the wind to the shorn lamb.'

SOURCES: GABF; Kirley, *Community in France* 70n179, 172, 185, 186, 188, 202, 214n516, 216n518, 221n531; Kirley, *Congregation in France* iii, 42, 45, 81–2, 127, 137–8, 154, 174–5; Pouzol, 'Notices'; Charles Roume, 'Ernest Martin, A Biography' (trans. Kevin J. Kirley), *Basilian Teacher* 4 (April 1960) 206–11.

MARTIN, James Edward, priest, was born on 13 March 1906 at Chatham, New Brunswick (diocese of Chatham, since 1938 of Bathurst), the son of James Martin and Sarah Fernando. He died in Toronto on 3 February 1992, and is buried in the Basilian plot of Holy Cross Cemetery, Thornhill, Ontario.

'Jimmy' Martin attended St Joseph's Preparatory School and St Thomas College, Chatham, which was at that time under the direction of the Basilian Fathers, and began his undergraduate studies there. After his second year he entered St Basil's Novitiate, Toronto, was professed on 10 August 1924, and was appointed to Assumption College, Windsor, to complete his undergraduate studies (B.A., University of Western Ontario, 1927). He was a born athlete. The June 1927 edition of Assumption College's *Purple and White* reported: 'His efficiency on the gridiron has merited him the coveted "A." For two years Jim has captained and starred on the College hockey team. His baseball qualifications have numbered him amongst the College Nine.' He studied theology at St Basil's Scholasticate, Toronto, 1927–31, during the first year of which he also attended the Ontario College of Education, earning teacher certification in 1928. He was ordained to the priesthood on 12 June 1931 in St Michael's Cathedral, Toronto, by Archbishop Gerald Murray CSSR.

In September 1931 Father Martin was appointed to Catholic Central High School, Detroit, where he was to remain for the next eighteen years as teacher, coach, and sports celebrity. He was second councillor of the local community in 1936–40 and 1941–6, taught Latin and algebra on a full-time basis, was director of athletics, and coached football, basketball, and baseball. He attended the University of Detroit during three summers, 1935–7, earning a Michigan Teachers Life Certificate. He perfected his coaching skills by attending summer courses at Butler University, Indiana, and Lawrence Tech, Michigan.

Jimmy Martin put Catholic Central, a relatively unknown school when he went there, on the map. Under his leadership, and in partnership with the legendary Father Flanagan, the annual Boys' Town Football Game was begun, which on one occasion attracted some forty-four thousand spectators to Briggs Stadium. Father Martin's forte, however, was baseball: his teams won the Catholic league championship seventeen out of eighteen years. He also coached American Legion teams in the summer. Thirty-five of his players turned professional, and five of these played in the major leagues. On the occasion of his leaving Catholic Central in 1949 he was the subject of several newspaper and magazine feature articles in the Detroit-Windsor area. Each noted that Jimmy Martin's success with young men was more than athletic: he was recognized for his ability to integrate sports skills with Christian education and personal growth. Father Martin was inducted into the Michigan Sports Hall of Fame in 1978.

In 1949 he was appointed assistant pastor at Holy Rosary Parish, Toronto, and in 1952 he was appointed, for a two-year period, to teach at Aquinas Institute, Rochester. He returned to Holy Rosary in 1954 and ministered there for five years, serving for two of those years on the local council. In 1959 he was named pastor of St John the Baptist Parish, Amherstburg, Ontario, a position he held until 1971, serving also as rector of the local community in 1959–61 and again in 1964–7. In 1971, while still residing with the community at St John the Baptist Parish, he began to function as assistant pastor at St Anthony's Parish, Harrow, Ontario. To his work in parishes Father Martin brought the same enthusiasm, joy, and full devotion that he had shown in his academic and coaching years. The Amherstburg area Chamber of Commerce instituted 'The Father James E. Martin AAM Citizen of the Year Award,' presented annually and bearing his picture.

Jimmy Martin, for all his success and fame, was the most unassuming and congenial of persons. He loved to laugh, saw the bright and humorous side of life, was extremely docile to those to whom he owed obedience, and had a gift for friendship and interpersonal relations. Of those in his charge when he was pastor or superior he was ever thoughtful. In proclaiming the Gospel he was zealous and carefully prepared.

By 1985, for reasons of health, he retired to the Basilian Fathers Residence (Infirmary), Toronto, where he spent the remaining seven years of his life.

SOURCES: GABF; *Annals* 5 (1975) 66, 6 (1982) 12, 7 (1993) 119–21; *Newsletter* (14 February 1992).

MARTIN, John Joseph, priest, member of the Congregation 1940–9, was born in Syracuse, New York, on 8 March 1914, the son of Michael Martin and Catherine Fitzgerald. He died in Syracuse on 23 May 1967, and is buried in St Mary's Cemetery, DeWitt, New York.

John Martin attended St John's Cathedral Academy and Powelson Business College in Syracuse before he came to St Michael's College, Toronto, in 1938. The following year he entered St Basil's Novitiate, Toronto, and was professed on 15 August 1940. He returned to St Michael's College (B.A., University of Toronto, 1943), studied theology at St Basil's Seminary, Toronto, 1943–7, and was ordained priest on 15 August 1946 in St Basil's Church, Toronto, by Cardinal James Charles McGuigan.

Father Martin was appointed to Aquinas Institute, Rochester, in 1947. In February 1948 he was transferred to St Anne's Parish in Houston, and in the summer of 1948 he moved to Assumption College School, Windsor.

He withdrew from the Congregation in 1949 to work in the diocese of Syracuse, where he was incardinated on 21 June 1955. He served as assistant at St Catherine's Parish, Binghamton, St John the Baptist Parish, Rome, New York, St Mary's Parish, Jamesville, New York, and St Paul's Parish, Whiteboro, New York. In 1965 he suffered a heart attack and went on sick leave at St Pius X Home in Syracuse.

SOURCES: GABF; *Annals* 1 (1946) 120, 4 (1968) 63–4; *Newsletter* (2 June 1967).

MARTIN, Joseph, priest, brother of Father Ernest *Martin and uncle of Father Arsène *Martin, was born on 19 March 1840 at Prades (Ardèche), the son of Jean Martin and Anne Veyrand. He died in Blidah, Algeria, on 7 January 1906, and was buried in the priests' cemetery there.

Joseph Martin studied at the Petit Séminaire d'Aubenas (Ardèche) and then at the Collège des Cordeliers, Annonay. He made his novitiate at Feyzin (Isère, now Rhône), 1862–3, and was ordained a priest on 21 September 1867 in the chapel of the Collège des Cordeliers by Bishop Armand de Charbonnel. While preparing for the priesthood he taught at Privas (Ardèche) and at the college in Annonay. During the year 1867–8 he attended the Institut catholique, Paris, where he obtained the *licence ès sciences*.

In 1868 he was appointed to Blidah, Algeria. Archbishop (later Cardinal) Charles Lavigerie of Algiers wanted him there to teach at the Collège Saint-Charles, along with Father Hilaire *Durand and four other Basilians who would join him later that month. Father Martin spent the rest of his life at Saint-Charles, becoming superior in 1869 when ill health forced Father Durand to return to France. He remained superior for thirty years.

From 1899 to 1903 Father Martin lived at Blidah as honorary superior. As one of the legal owners of the college, he fought its closure in 1903 when members of congregations were forbidden to teach, but was expelled on 25 September 1903. Despite two years of litigation, the Republic took over the property. Father Martin remained in the rectory of a parish in Blidah where he had been welcomed.

A former student eulogized him: 'Beneath a gruff exterior there lay a delicate firmness, a tender devotion and an intense goodness.'

SOURCES: GABF; Kirley, *Community in France* 70n178, 124n305, 165n421, 172, 182n464, 185, 186, 188, 209; *Ordo*, Diocèse de Viviers, 1864; Pouzol, 'Notices';

Charles Roume, 'Ernest Martin, a Biography' (trans. Kevin J. Kirley), *Basilian Teacher* 4 (April 1960) 206–211.

MARTINESCHE, Henri, priest, one of the ten founding members of the Congregation, was born on 15 July 1797, the son of Jean Martinesche and Rose-Marie Térisse, at Vinezac (Ardèche, diocese of Viviers [from 1801 to 1822 of Mende]). He died on 24 February 1879 at Vaudevant (Ardèche) and is buried in the cemetery there.

Henri Martinesche enrolled in the Collège des Cordeliers, Annonay, as an aspirant to the priesthood and was ordained a priest on 1 June 1822. Already as a teacher in the college in 1820 he had begun to live a form of religious life with three other young members of the staff, but he did not sign the petition to the bishop of Mende on 15 September 1822 asking permission to found an Association of teaching priests, because it made no mention of vows. However, on 21 November 1822, he became one of the ten founders who bound themselves to the common life and the teaching apostolate. He taught at Maison-Seule (Ardèche) from 1822 to 1828 with Father André *Fayolle as superior. When the vicar general of the diocese of Viviers, Father Vernet, opened a school at Vernoux (Ardèche) for young seminarians, Maison-Seule was forced to close, and Father Martinesche returned to Annonay, where he taught until his eyesight began to fail. In 1833 he became chaplain to the Dienne family at Vaudevant and remained there until his death. Up until 1864 he came regularly to the annual Basilian retreat in Annonay, despite nearly total blindness.

The register of burials kept at the parish of Vaudevant, where he spent almost half a century, said that Father Martinesche was 'a man who loved the poor and deprived himself of necessities in order to help them. ... In the parish he was loved as a father and venerated as a saint.' The people of the parish and surrounding countryside flocked through heavy snow to his funeral.

SOURCES: GABF; Pouzol, 'Notices'; Roume, *Origines* 404.

MAZENOD, Jean-Claude-Marie, priest, was born on 11 November 1849 at Saint-Christo-en-Jarey, near Saint-Etienne (Loire, archdiocese of Lyon). He died at Lyon (Rhône) on 26 November 1922 and is buried there in the Cimetière Loyasse.

After secondary and theological studies in his home diocese, Jean-Claude was received as a novice on 21 November 1876 at the Collège du Sacré-Coeur, Annonay, where he had been teaching. He made his final profession on 18 May 1877 and was ordained a priest on 18 September 1880 by Bishop Joseph-Michel-Frédéric Bonnet of Viviers in the chapel of the Collège du Sacré-Coeur. He taught grammar classes at the college and in the scholasticate in Annonay, 1876–83, and then went to Canada, where he served as assistant at Assumption Parish, Windsor, for three years. He spent the year 1886–7 as curate at Ste Anne's Parish, Detroit, before joining the teaching staff at Mary Immaculate College, Beaconfield House, Plymouth, England, for the year 1887–8. His next assignments were to the Collège Saint-Augustin, Bône, Algeria, 1888–92, and to the Ecole cléricale, Périgueux (Dordogne), teaching the senior grades. In 1897 he returned to Beaconfield House for one year and then went to the school in Périgueux as teacher of English, 1899–1902. He was appointed to the Petit Séminaire de Vernoux (Ardèche) to teach English in 1902 but remained there one year only. His teaching career came to an end with the expulsion of Basilians from their schools in 1903. His whereabouts are uncertain after this date. He lived for some time in his home town of Saint-Christo-en-Jarey, and in 1915 he was received into the Maison de Vernaison (Rhône), near Lyon, a house of retirement run by the Camillian Fathers.

SOURCES: GABF; Kirley, *Community in France* 70n179, 184, 210, 219n526, 235n562, 237n565; Pouzol, 'Notices.'

MAZET, Louis, priest, was born on 23 August 1873, at Quintenas, canton of Satillieu (Ardèche), the son of Pierre Mazet and Virginie Rouby. He died in Annonay on 9 December 1967 and is buried there in the Basilian cemetery on the grounds of the Collège du Sacré-Coeur.

Louis Mazet enrolled in the Petit Séminaire de Vernoux (Ardèche) in 1887 and went to the Grand Séminaire de Viviers (Ardèche) in 1892. After his compulsory year of military service, 1894–5, he entered the Basilian novitiate in late June 1896, took final vows on 28 October 1898, and was ordained to the priesthood on 23 September 1899 in the chapel of the Collège du Sacré-Coeur, Annonay, by Bishop Hilarion-Joseph Montéty.

Father Mazet's teaching years ran from 1896 to 1903: at the Petit Séminaire de Vernoux, 1896–8, the Collège du Sacré-Coeur, 1899–1900, where he taught theology, at the Collège Saint-Charles, Blidah, Algeria, 1900–1, and again at Sacré-Coeur, Annonay, 1901–3, as teacher of languages. In 1898–9 he obtained a *licence en théologie* from the Faculté catholique de Lyon.

With the legislation in 1903 excluding Basilians from teaching, Father Mazet undertook parish ministry in the Ardèche which was to last for thirty-four years until his retirement in 1937. He served as curate at Dessaignes, 1903–7, at Roiffieux, 1907–9, and at Saint-Barthélemy-le-Plain, 1909–11. He was pastor at Saint-Michel-de-Chabrillanoux, 1911–13, and spent the war years 1914–18 as assistant at Satillieux. In 1918 he was appointed pastor of Saint-Romain-d'Ay, a post he held for nineteen years in spite of delicate health. A master of plain chant and with a good ear for music, he formed a first-class parish choir at Saint-Romain which under his direction executed Gregorian chant to perfection. Father Mazet also made a special study of French politics and never tired of teaching his parishioners how to live as good Catholics and good citizens in the uncertain years between the First and Second World Wars. In the general chapter of the French Basilians in 1938 he was elected general councillor and was re-elected in the chapter of 1944, but he took no part in the chapter of 1950 at which Father Charles *Roume was chosen superior general.

In 1937 he retired to Maison Saint-Joseph, Annonay, where he remained largely confined to his small room, which he kept heated the year round with a coal stove, as he suffered from drafts and cold air. In spite of multiple maladies and infirmities, some of which baffled local doctors, his mind remained alert to the last, permitting him to receive the visits of confreres and former parishioners and to converse intelligently with them.

SOURCES: GABF; *Annals* 2 (1959) 414, 4 (1968) 55–6; *Newsletter* (11 December 1967); Kirley, *Community in France* 183, 204; Kirley, *Congregation in France* 156, 184–5, 196–7, 212, 220, 256, 262; *Mon Collège* (Annonay) 58 (February 1968) 7; Pouzol, 'Notices.'

McALPINE, Joseph GERALD, priest, was born in Marysville, Ontario (archdiocese of Kingston), on 17 June 1907, the son of Thomas James McAlpine and Mary Elizabeth Anderson. He died in Toronto on 30 September 1957 and is buried in the Basilian plot of Holy Cross Cemetery, Thornhill, Ontario.

Gerry McAlpine received his early education at Marysville, then took his high school courses at St Michael's College in Toronto, 1920–3 and

1924–5. He spent one year in arts, 1925–6, before entering St Basil's Novitiate, Toronto. After profession on 11 August 1927, he returned to St Michael's College, where he completed his arts course (B.A., University of Toronto, 1931) and was also an assistant to Father Vincent L. *Kennedy. The following year he attended the Ontario College of Education in Toronto. He did his theological studies at St Basil's Scholasticate, Toronto, and was ordained priest on 17 December 1933 in St Basil's Church, Toronto, by Bishop Alexander MacDonald.

Father McAlpine had eight appointments in twenty-one years: teaching at St Thomas High School, Houston, 1934–5, assistant at St Anne's Parish, Houston, 1935–7, assistant at Ste Anne's Parish, Detroit (August–November 1937), teaching at Assumption College School, Windsor (November 1937–spring 1938), assistant at Ste Anne's, Detroit, 1938–40, and at St Anne's, Houston, 1940–5, teaching at St Michael's College School, 1945–50, assistant principal 1950–5, and assistant at St John the Baptist Parish, Amherstburg, Ontario, 1955. Shortly after this appointment he went on sick leave, and died at St Basil's Seminary, Toronto.

Father McAlpine was a quiet, soft-spoken, self-effacing priest. An obituary in the *Basilian Teacher* stated, 'Teachers can hope to find no better example of the patience and perseverance required in a truly Christ-like pedagogue.'

SOURCES: GABF; *Annals* 2 (1957) 294; *Basilian Teacher* 2 (December 1957) 5; *Yearbook SMC* 22 (1932).

McBRADY, Robert, priest, was born at Audley, a tiny hamlet north of Whitby, Ontario (archdiocese of Toronto), on 24 January 1848, the son of Daniel McBrady and Ellen Broderick, pioneer Irish settlers. He died in Toronto on 4 May 1936 and was buried there in the Basilian plot of Mount Hope Cemetery.

Robert McBrady obtained his first schooling in Whitby Grammar School, then presided over by Dr Eastwood, a celebrated teacher in early Ontario. He enrolled in St Michael's College, Toronto, in September 1864 and remained until November 1865 when he withdrew to continue his education in France. In 1867 he entered St Basil's Novitiate at Feyzin (Isère, now Rhône), France. He was preparing for the *licence* at the University of Paris when the outbreak of the Franco-Prussian War in 1870 forced his return to Canada. He was appointed to Assumption College, Windsor. There he taught Latin and studied theology. He was ordained priest on 30 May 1874 in the chapel of Assumption College, Windsor, and that same afternoon was back teaching in the classroom.

Father McBrady's sixty-two years of priesthood were in three Basilian houses: Assumption College, 1874–9, 1883–9 and 1901–7, St Basil's Scholasticate, Toronto, 1894–7 and 1907–9, and St Michael's College, 1879–83, 1889–94, 1897–1901, and 1909 until his death in 1936. He was superior of St Basil's Scholasticate, 1894–7, and principal and superior of Assumption College, 1901–7, and St Michael's College, 1912–15. At Assumption he planned and began construction of the chapel that, nearly a hundred years later, is still considered the 'architectural jewel' of the Windsor campus. During his last term at St Michael's College women from Loretto College and St Joseph's College were enrolled for the first time at St Michael's, in order to qualify for degrees from the University of Toronto, although it was not an innovation he had proposed. He was twice a member of the provincial council, 1898–1901 and 1904–16. He was said to have all the qualities of a good administrator, save one: he was too much of a gentleman to question others closely about the practical side of their proposals.

'Bobby' McBrady was at home especially in the classroom, where he taught with enthusiasm. For over fifty years he carried a full schedule and taught, at one time or another, every subject except music. He could understand stupidity but would not put up with indolence. Writing of Father McBrady in the *Golden Jubilee Volume of Assumption College* 'Tabellarius '01' recorded that 'the asperity of the rebuke would be lost in the beautifully rounded sentence hurled at the head of the thoughtless one, from lips scarcely restraining a smile and amused eyes looking over berimmed spectacles.' A famous comment was, 'Eh, eh, young man, you know about as much about the construction of that sentence as I do about the architecture of the dome of heaven.' In some reminiscences gathered by Father Henry *Bellisle and published in *Basilian*, Father McBrady counselled new teachers: 'In dealing with students, be polite with them. They are your guests in the classroom. Prepare your work carefully. Assign tasks judiciously and correct exercises with care.'

Love of learning caused Father McBrady to spend most of his leisure time in reading. He once avowed, 'When I became a priest, I continued to study. I studied Latin and Greek. ... Newman appealed to us all.' He knew theology well and taught it for some years, but speculative thought never attracted him. His heart was given to literature, to the ring of the polished sentence.

Father McBrady was in demand as a preacher in both English and French. As a pulpit orator the beautiful expression of a thought fascinated him, and he seldom preached extemporaneously lest in so doing he fall short of his classical ideal. He wrote his sermons, memorized them, then burned them to avoid using them a second time. An extract from his sermon at the funeral of Father Laurence *Brennan (1904) was published in *Benedicamus* 3 (January 1950) 24.

In an obituary notice for the *Basilian*, Father Benjamin *Forner wrote of Father McBrady: 'Gifted with a high mind and a true sensibility of what was great and beautiful, he will live in the memory of those who knew him as a man of warmth and energy. Grammarian, linguist, orator, he was pre-eminently the priest. In him, scholarly attainment was adorned by simplicity and humility. Here was a priest who never taught a class without preparing it, never preached a sermon without writing it. His greatest achievement, according to his own estimation, was that he said his prayers and did his work.'

BIBLIOGRAPHY: 'Reminiscences,' ed. H.S. Bellisle, *Basilian* 1 (April 1935) 23–4, 34.
SOURCES: GABF; Charles Collins, 'Basilians I Have Known,' transcribed in Robert J. Scollard, 'Historical Notes C.S.B.' 10 99–106 (GABF); B.N. Forner, 'Father McBrady, Obituary,' *Basilian* 2 (May 1936) 83; *French Studies U. of T.* 55–6; *Jubilee, Assumption*; 'Golden Jubilee, 1874–1924, or, Our Reverend Chaplain, Father McBrady,' *Saint Joseph Lilies* 13 (June 1924) 87–89; Kirley, *Community in France* 9, 37, 214nn515, 516, 216n518, 218n524, 220n528, 225, 242, 246; Kirley, *Congregation in France* 4, 7, 12–14; McMahon, *Pure Zeal* 15–17; Edmund C. Phelan, *The Parish of St Francis de Sales, Pickering, Ontario, a Short History* (Pickering, 1966); W.J. Roach, 'R.W. McBrady, a Biography,' *Basilian Teacher* 1 (November 1956) 9–11; E.L. Rush, 'Golden Jubilee of Father McBrady,' *Yearbook SMC* 15 (1921); L.K. Shook. 'The Coming of the Basilians to Assumption College – Early Expansion of St Michael's College,' *CCHA Report* 18 (1951) 59–73; Shook, *Catholic Education* 155. For documentation regarding his years at Assumption College see Power, *Assumption College* 3 XIII–XVII, 7–11, 45, 81.

McCABE, Patrick Francis, priest, was born on 28 December 1928 at Arthur, Ontario (diocese of London), the son of Patrick McCabe and Lena Herriot. He died in Toronto on 12 May 1992 and is buried in the Basilian plot of Holy Cross Cemetery, Thornhill, Ontario.

Frank McCabe attended Sacred Heart parochial school at Kenilworth, Ontario, and Arthur High School. Following the suggestion of his high school principal, Mr Pat Brown, whom he had consulted about the priesthood, he entered St Basil's Novitiate, Toronto, in 1948 and made first profession on 15 August 1949. He was appointed to live at Holy Rosary Seminary, Toronto, during his university studies in Toronto, but in 1950 he was transferred to Assumption College, Windsor (B.A., University of Western Ontario, 1953). After spending the year 1953-4 at the Grand Séminaire de Québec studying theology, he taught French one year at St Michael's College School and then at Assumption College School. He finished his theology studies at St Basil's Seminary, Toronto, 1956-9, and was ordained to the priesthood on 29 June 1958 in St Basil's Church, Toronto, by Cardinal James Charles McGuigan.

In 1959 Father McCabe was appointed once more to St Michael's College, again for only one year. In 1960 he was named to St Mary's College, Sault Ste Marie, where he spent fourteen years and where, besides teaching, he was local councillor, 1961-4, 1967-9, treasurer, 1961-4, superior, 1971-4, head of the French department and director of athletics. He spent a sabbatical year, 1974-5, with the Basilian community in Annonay. In 1975 he returned to the classroom at Assumption College School, Windsor, where he taught French, coached, and was local councillor and principal, 1978-82. In 1981 he was elected regional representative for Eastern Canada, an office to which he was twice re-elected and in which he was notable for attention to the confreres, good judgment in council meetings, and strong devotion to the Basilian mission of education. While on the council he was principal of St Michael's College School for two years, 1986-8, and was the canonical visitor to the Basilians in France.

Father McCabe saw teaching, coaching, and administration as equally important in education, and exercised all three wholeheartedly. He earned certification as a principal and in counselling and guidance.

After being diagnosed with inoperable prostate cancer in 1991, he survived for slightly less than a year, working as long as he could and meeting death with the equanimity and faith which had characterized his life.

BIBLIOGRAPHY: 'Poverty Has to Be a Personal Thing,' *Basilian Forum* 1 (December 1964) 43-4.
SOURCES: GABF; *Annals* 2 (1958) 359, 7 (1993) 128-30; *Newsletter* (21 May 1992).

McCANN, Leonard Albert, priest, was born at Maidstone, Ontario (diocese of London), on 2 May 1908, the son of John McCann and

Theresa Lawson. He died in Toronto on 21 August 1966 and is buried in the Basilian plot of Assumption Cemetery, Windsor.

Leonard McCann grew up in Windsor, Ontario, attended Assumption College School, 1922–6, and completed one year of university before entering St Basil's Novitiate, Toronto. After profession on 11 August 1928 he returned to Assumption College (B.A., University of Western Ontario, 1931). He attended the Ontario College of Education, Toronto, during his first year of theology at St Basil's Seminary, Toronto. He was ordained to the priesthood by Bishop John Kidd on 23 September 1934 in the chapel of St Peter's Seminary, London, Ontario.

Father McCann was appointed to graduate studies in theology in Rome (S.T.L., Angelicum, 1936). In September 1936 he began teaching at St Basil's Scholasticate ('Seminary' from 1937), Toronto. During the year 1942–3 he resumed graduate studies in Quebec City (S.T.D., Université Laval, 1943). He was assistant superior at St Basil's Seminary in 1938–42 and 1943–52. In 1952 he was appointed to Assumption University, Windsor, where he taught until 1964, when he was named master of novices at Annonay. When the opening of this novitiate was delayed, he spent the year 1964–5 following courses in spiritual theology at the Institut catholique de Paris. In 1965 he was appointed rector of Maison Saint-Basile, Issy-les-Moulineaux; but shortly afterwards, diagnosed with advanced cancer, he returned to St Basil's Seminary, where he died within a year.

Father McCann loved music and had a fine singing voice. He demanded much of himself and of his students. His good-humoured vehemence of expression brought him the nickname 'Toughie.'

BIBLIOGRAPHY:

Book: *Doctrine of the Void as Propounded by St John of the Cross and as Viewed in the Light of Thomistic Principles.* Toronto, 1955.

Articles: In *Basilian*: 'The Albertinum,' 2 (February 1936) 30–2; 'A Spiritual Problem,' 3 (October 1937) 89; 'The Fruits of Meditation,' 4 (May 1938) 83–4; 'A Mere Suggestion,' 4 (June 1938) 112. In *Benedicamus*: 'Some Reflections on Apostolate of Religious,' 2 (June 1949) 42–3; 'True Devotion to Mary,' 3 (May 1950) 42–3, 45; 'Birth of a Seminary,' 5 (February 1952) 2–4; 'The Role of Prefects and Retreats in Fostering Vocations,' *Proceedings of the Basilian Vocation Meetings* 6 (1960) 78–80; 'Scripture and Our Students [forum],' *Basilian Teacher* 5 (December 1960) 84.

SOURCES: GABF; *Annals* 3 (1966) 465–66; *Newsletter* (2 September 1966).

McCARROLL, Edward GERARD, scholastic, was born at Alliston, Ontario (archdiocese of Toronto), on 18 July 1914, the son of Edward McCarroll and Mary O'Hara. He died in Toronto on 26 August 1939 and was buried in the family plot in St Paul's Cemetery, Alliston.

Gerard was educated at Alliston Public School and Alliston Secondary School. In the spring of 1930, while in grade X, he suffered an attack of rheumatic fever which took him out of school. During the next five years he was able to attend school only on a part-time basis and wrote two or three papers each year. By 1935 he had regained sufficient strength to complete a course offered in Alliston by the Orangeville Business College, obtained employment in Toronto with Stafford Industries in 1936, and completed high school in evening courses. He lived in St Basil's Parish, where he took an active part in its societies and joined the Third Order of St Francis. At length he felt that his health was strong enough to study for the priesthood. On 2 September 1938 he entered St Basil's Novitiate, Toronto; but in March of 1939 illness made necessary his removal to St Joseph's Hospital, where he died five months later after pronouncing his first vows.

SOURCE: GABF.

McCARTHY, Arthur John, priest, was born on 31 January 1945 in Rochester, the son of Thomas McCarthy and Grace Marguerite Wade. He died in San Francisco, California, on 28 January 1991, and is buried in the Basilian plot of Holy Sepulchre Cemetery, Southfield, Michigan.

Art McCarthy attended St Monica's grade school and Aquinas Institute, Rochester, and entered St Basil's Novitiate, Pontiac, Michigan, in 1963. After profession on 15 August 1964, he was appointed to the Basilian House of Studies on the campus of St John Fisher College, Rochester, where he majored in history, philosophy, and English (B.A., 1968). During the summer months he taught catechism at the Basilian missions in Texas. In 1968 he spent some time living and working at the Centro Cultural in Mexico City. That same year he was appointed to Catholic Central High School, Detroit, where he taught English for three years and earned an M.Ed in 1969 and teacher qualification for Michigan in 1972 at Marygrove College. He began theological studies at St Basil's College, Toronto, in 1971 (M.Div., University of St Michael's College, 1974), and worked with the pastoral team of St Basil's Parish while also assisting in the bursar's office of the college.

He spent the summer of 1974 studying Spanish in Mexico City, and for his diaconate year was appointed to Our Lady of Guadalupe Parish, Rosenberg, Texas. He was ordained to the priesthood by Bishop Joseph Hogan on 24 May 1975 in the chapel of Becket Hall at St John Fisher College.

In 1975 Father McCarthy was appointed to Catholic Central once again, to teach English literature at the senior level, to serve as head of the English Department, and to assist as a guidance counsellor. In the summers he preached for the Basilian missions. In 1980 he was named superior of the Basilian community at Catholic Central, assuming as well the duties of treasurer. He undertook the renovation of the Basilian residence. At the expiration of his term as superior, he requested graduate studies, and spent one year in make-up course work at San Francisco State University. He was appointed again to Catholic Central, 1987–9, but resumed his studies in September 1989, defraying their cost by teaching English as a second language to Latin American immigrants. In January 1991 he was stricken with a mysterious infection which doctors could neither identify nor isolate, and which proved fatal in a few days. A quiet and private person, an excellent teacher, Art McCarthy was a compassionate and devoted religious superior.

SOURCES: GABF; *Annals* 5 (1976) 137, 7 (1992) 126–8; *Newsletter* (1 March 1991).

McCARTHY, Thomas, deacon, was born in Ireland in 1841. He died in Toronto on 5 April 1865. His was the first burial in the Basilian plot of St Michael's Cemetery, Toronto.

Thomas McCarthy attended St Michael's College, Toronto, 1856–60. He became a novice in the Congregation on 26 March 1860, and made his final vows on 23 May 1861. He taught elementary English at St Michael's College, 1862–3, where he contracted tuberculosis which proved to be fatal.

SOURCE: GABF.

McCARTY, Francis John, priest, brother of Sister Anne McCarty IBVM, was born on 6 September 1914, at Stratford, Ontario (diocese of London), the son of Matthew McCarty and Jessie Smith. He died in Toronto on 24 May 1998, and is buried in the Basilian plot of Holy Cross Cemetery, Thornhill, Ontario.

Educated in Stratford and at Assumption College School, Windsor,

Frank McCarty entered St Basil's Novitiate, Toronto, in 1934 and made first profession on 15 August 1935. He did undergraduate studies at St Michael's College (B.A., University of Toronto, 1938) and began his theological studies at St Basil's Seminary, Toronto, in 1938. He taught at St Thomas High School, Houston, 1939–40, while continuing his theology courses. During his third year of theology he attended the Ontario College of Education (high school assistant certification, 1941). Archbishop James Charles McGuigan ordained him to the priesthood on 15 August 1942 in St Basil's Church, Toronto.

Father McCarty spent the first twenty years of his priesthood in four Basilian high schools teaching Latin, mathematics, and history and, in some places, filling administrative positions: St Michael's College School, 1943–5, teaching; St Thomas High School, 1945–50, teaching; Assumption College School, 1950–5, teaching, councillor, principal, 1953–5; St Charles College, Sudbury, Ontario, 1955–8, superior and principal; Michael Power High School, Etobicoke, Ontario, 1958–63, teaching, councillor, vice-principal. He obtained an M.A. in education from Columbia University in 1952.

Father McCarty spent four years in parish work: Blessed Sacrament, Windsor, first as assistant, then as rector, 1963–5; and Assumption Parish, Windsor, as pastor, 1965–7. He returned to teaching in high schools: first at Michael Power High School, 1967–71, and then at St Michael's College School, 1971–3.

Appointed by the general council to find a location for a Basilian retirement house, he scouted various sites in the southwestern United States, finally choosing Phoenix, Arizona, where a house had been left by the late Father Alexander *Grant. There he worked as chaplain to various retirement facilities and was named the first rector of the Basilian Fathers of Phoenix in 1976. In 1983 he was appointed administrative assistant at St Thomas High School, Houston, and then served a year as assistant novice master at St Basil's Novitiate, Sugar Land, Texas. From 1985 he lived in retirement in six different Basilian houses: Basilian Fathers of Phoenix, 1985–7, Basilian Fathers Residence, Toronto, 1987–9, Assumption Parish, 1989–92, Assumption College School, 1992–4, Orsini House, Toronto, 1994–7, and Basilian Fathers Residence (Infirmary), 1997–8. He provided a gentle, affable presence, an example of a prayerful and peaceful religious and priest.

BIBLIOGRAPHY: 'Spoonfielder's Law,' *Basilian Teacher* 1 (May 1956) 3–6; 'Mathematics in Basilian Schools [forum],' *Basilian Teacher* 4 (December 1959) 70; 'The

Christian Educator Today,' *Basilian Teacher* 7 (March 1963) 201–3; 'The Ways of God,' *Aspects of Basilian Spirituality* (1972) 81–5. Unpublished: 'In Her Hands' (autobiography).
SOURCES: GABF; *Annals* 1 (1943) 27, 6 (1986) 398, 7 (1993) 4–5, 9 (1999) 91–2; *Newsletter* (11 June 1998).

McCORKELL, Edmund Joseph, priest, superior general, 1942–54, was born on 4 January 1891, on the family farm in the Township of Mara, near Brechin, Ontario (archdiocese of Toronto), one of ten children of Joseph McCorkell and Mary O'Donnell. He died in Toronto on 9 March 1980, and is buried in the Basilian plot of Holy Cross Cemetery, Thornhill, Ontario.

After attending the local public school, Edmund became the first person from the Brechin area to enter high school when he enrolled in Orillia Collegiate Institute in the fall of 1904. In 1907 he entered the Faculty of Education, Toronto, where he obtained a teacher's certificate. With the encouragement of Father Nicholas *Roche he taught in the high school section of St Michael's College, Toronto, while attending university (B.A., 1911) – a member of the first class of St Michael's after its federation with the University of Toronto. He entered St Basil's Novitiate, Toronto, and was professed on 15 August 1912. He studied theology at St Basil's Scholasticate, first in Toronto and later in Windsor. Archbishop Neil McNeil ordained him to the priesthood in St Basil's Church, Toronto, on 29 June 1916.

After a year of graduate studies in philosophy and theology at the Catholic University of America, Washington, D.C. (M.A., 1917), he returned to lecture in English at St Michael's College, especially nineteenth-century literature, and even as an administrator he always found time to teach. In 1922 he was named professor of English and registrar, and in 1925 superior and president, at St Michael's College. In 1931 he became master of novices at St Basil's Novitiate, Toronto, and then returned to the offices of superior and president of St Michael's, which he held until 1940. During the year 1940–1 he taught at Assumption College, Windsor.

After receiving an honorary LL.D. from the University of Ottawa, spring 1941, he was appointed superior and principal of St Thomas More College, Saskatoon, Saskatchewan, but in July 1942 was elected superior general of the Basilian Fathers. Convinced of the importance of education in the Church's mission and perceiving the growing numbers of vocations, he was constantly planning for the future. He took time to imbue the scholastics with academic goals and with the conviction of their importance in the Basilian apostolate. He accepted the invitations of two bishops to found universities – St Thomas in Houston and St John Fisher in Rochester – and was responsible for the building of the new St Basil's Seminary in 1951. After re-election in 1948, he initiated and fostered the reunion of the North American Basilians and the Basilians in France, though it was his successor, George B. *Flahiff, who officially executed the act of reunion in September 1955 that healed a separation of thirty-three years.

A number of academic appointments followed his second term as superior general: professor of English at St John Fisher College, 1954–5, president of the Pontifical Institute of Mediaeval Studies, Toronto, 1955–61, superior of the Basilian community at Assumption University, 1961–4, lecturer and special assistant to the president, St John Fisher College, 1964–9. He retired to St Michael's College in 1969 to study and to write. He was named 'Officer of the Order of Canada' in 1972, and in 1977 received an honorary D.S.L. from the University of St Michael's College. On Saturday, 8 March 1980, he experienced a weak spell after the evening meal, was taken to St Michael's Hospital, Toronto, and died shortly after midnight.

'Gus,' as he was popularly called (though rarely to his face), fulfilled the highest positions in the community with both dignity and humility. He remembered his humble origins with pride and gratitude, and sought to ensure that the Basilians were mindful of the poor and disadvantaged. He had friends in all walks of life, and was nationally esteemed as an educational leader and priest. As the principal speaker at the centennial ceremonies at Martyrs Shrine, Midland, Ontario, 1948, Father McCorkell was introduced as 'the most beloved priest in Ontario.' Eschewing praise, he would humorously relate stories of his own embarrassments or failures in a long career that had clarified the educational ideal and widened the horizons of the Basilian Fathers.

BIBLIOGRAPHY:

Books: *Captain The Reverend William Leo Murray, B.A., M.C., 1890–1937; A Memoir.* Toronto, 1939. *Henry Carr, Revolutionary.* Toronto, 1969. *The McCorkell Family and Its Affiliates; Memoirs of Rev. E.J. McCorkell CSB.* Toronto, 1975; 2nd ed. 1976.
Pamphlets: *Father Carr's Approach to Ethics.* Vancouver, 1973; *The Mysticism of Wordsworth,* Pamphlet series 4. Toronto, 1933. *Cardinal Newman and the Christian Philosophic Tradition,* Pamphlet series 27. Toronto, 1933. *Catholic Approach to*

English Literature, Pamphlet series 28. Toronto, 1933. Cistercian Influence in 'The Quest of the Holy Grail,' Pamphlet series 29. Toronto, 1933.

Articles: 'The Significance of Newman for Our Time,' *CCHA Report* 12 (1944–5) 103–8; 'Bertram Coghill Alan Windle,' *CCHA Report* 25 (1957–8) 53–8; 'Humanism and the Middle Ages,' *Speculum* 24 (1949) 516–19; 'Letter [response to Father Maurice Farge], "Rule as Function,"' *Forum* 2 (April 1966) 57–8; 'The Really Vital Confrontation Was That of Each Delegate with Himself,' *Forum* 2 (October 1966) 88; 'Chesterton in Canada,' *Chesterton Review* 2 (1975–6) 39–54; 'Chesterton and Thomism,' *Chesterton Review* (1979) 311–16. In *Basilian:* 'The New St Michael's,' 1 (May 1935) 47, 57; 'St Thomas and Human Liberty,' 2 (February 1936) 23–5; 'The Most Reverend Francis P. Carroll,' 2 (March 1936) 37–8; 'Truth in Higher Education [Graduation Address, Assumption College, June 1937],' 3 (November 1937) 105–6. In *Benedicamus:* 'Two Monsignors,' 3 (March 1950) 38–9; 'Patience and Progress,' 5 (April 1952) 7–8; 'A New Look ... And Looking Back,' 6 (December 1952) 2–6. In *Basilian Teacher:* 'Laudemus viros gloriosos: James L. Ruth,' 3 (March 1959) 152–3; 'The Spirit of the Pontifical Institute,' 5 (November 1960) 37–40; 'Our Student Today: Problem and Potential [forum],' 7 (December 1962) 113; 'Federation: The Legacy of Father Carr,' 8 (March 1964) 301–7; 'A Meditation on Renewal,' 10 (April 1966) 203–8. In *St Joseph Lilies:* 'Reverend Frederick Daniel Meader, CSB,' 13 (December 1924) 44–7; 'Spain and the Modern World,' 23 (December 1934) 272–5.

SOURCES: GABF; *Annals* 1 (1943) 36, 3 (1962) 139, 3 (1966) 520, 5 (1981) 603–5; *Newsletter* (14 March 1980); *Heartwood* 64, 73, 77, 85; Kirley, *Congregation in France* 45n40, 200–1, 232–4, 236–8, 240–1, 244–5, 248–50, 252, 256, 261; Shook, *Catholic Education* 165–79, 222–4 and passim.

McEVOY, James J.O., priest, was born in Drumcondra, County Meath, Ireland (diocese of Meath), on 18 September 1842. He died in Jersey City, New Jersey, on 31 October 1911, and was buried there from St Patrick's Church.

His family having settled in Jersey City, James McEvoy first attended schools there, then St Peter's College, New York, and St Charles College, Ellicott City, Maryland. In 1861 he went to St Michael's College, Toronto, where he studied philosophy and did one year of theology. He was a student at the Grand Séminaire in Montreal, 1864–5. From there he went to France, where he entered St Basil's Novitiate at Feyzin (Isère, now Rhône). As a scholastic he taught at St Charles College, Blidah, Algeria, and at the Collège du Sacré-Coeur, Annonay. He made his final vows on 27 October 1869, and was ordained priest two days later.

Father McEvoy spent the winter of 1869–70 in New Orleans, Louisiana, on sick leave. He taught at St Michael's College, 1870–1, then went again on sick leave, 1871–3. He returned to St Michael's College and taught there until 1876. During the next six years poor health precluded any regular appointment, but in 1882 he was named assistant at St Basil's Parish, Toronto. In 1890 he went with Father Laurence *Brennan to Aiken, near Charleston, South Carolina, where a new foundation was being considered. While there he fell and sustained an injury that left him partially paralysed. He received permission to live with his brother in Jersey City, where he died.

SOURCE: GABF.

McGAHEY, Joseph Edward, priest, was born in Toronto on 21 September 1902, the son of Robert McGahey, D.D.S., and Catherine Davis. He died in Toronto on 2 December 1945 and is buried in the Basilian plot of Mount Hope Cemetery.

Educated at Riverdale Collegiate Institute, Toronto, 1915–20, and St Michael's College, Toronto, 1920–4 (B.A., University of Toronto, 1924), prominent in sports and in university debating, 'Joe' McGahey entered St Basil's Novitiate, Toronto, in 1924 and was professed on 12 September 1925. He studied theology at St Basil's Scholasticate, Toronto, attended the Ontario College of Education in Toronto, 1926–7, obtained an M.A. in philosophy from the University of Toronto in 1929, and was ordained priest on 29 June 1929 in St Basil's Church, Toronto, by Archbishop Neil McNeil.

Father McGahey was appointed to St Michael's College where he served as principal of the high school in 1929–30. He was named to the Newman Foundation at the University of Illinois in Urbana in 1931, but returned to St Michael's early in 1932 when the Congregation withdrew from Urbana. In 1932–4 he was assistant at St Mary's of the Assumption Parish, Owen Sound, Ontario. Again at St Michael's College in 1934 he taught and was active in the work of St Michael's Social Guild. During the years 1937–9 he drew large crowds to a series of talks in Teefy Hall on social justice. He had a lasting influence on many students and others in his promotion of justice, especially for labour. He gave a series of radio talks on justice and peace which he published as pamphlets. In 1940 he enlisted as a chaplain in the Canadian Army, but a severe heart attack forced his resignation in 1941. After a period of rest, he went to St Thomas More College in Saskatoon, Saskatchewan. In 1944 his health failed again and he spent some months on sick leave at St Thomas High School, Houston. Returning to St Michael's College in September 1945, he suffered a fatal heart attack three months later.

Joe McGahey was a man of remarkable energy. As a player and later as a coach he fired athletes with a determination to win. Writing in the *Chelsea Annual*, Dean Francis Leddy said that he 'should be likened to a blazing meteor, shooting across our line of vision, dazzling us by his bright light, and alas, all too soon burned out in his swift passage. Physically and mentally Father McGahey lived for years at a tempo which no ordinary man could have sustained for even a few months and died having accomplished in a short life more than most people do in twice the time.'

BIBLIOGRAPHY: *A Broadcast on Peace Given over Station CBL, November 6, 1938*. Toronto, 1939. *Three Broadcasts on Liberty Given over Station CBL, November 13, 20, 27, 1938*. Toronto, 1939.
SOURCES: GABF; *Annals* 1 (1946) 128–30; Eugene A. Cullinane, 'Father McGahey,' *Benedicamus* 6 (April 1953) 2–4; J.F. Leddy, 'Two Great Priests, a Tribute,' *Chelsea Annual* (Saskatoon, 1956); Shook, *Catholic Education* 154, 162, 347–8.

McGEE, William Patrick, priest, was born on 27 November 1888, at Lucan, Ontario (diocese of London), the son of Patrick McGee and Mary Ann Kehoe. He died in Toronto on 16 November 1975 and is buried in the Basilian plot of Holy Cross Cemetery, Thornhill, Ontario.

'Billy' McGee attended elementary and high school in Lucan, graduating in 1908. He enrolled in the Stratford Normal School and for a number of years taught at S.S. No. 12 in Carrick, Ontario. In January 1917 he entered St Basil's Novitiate, Toronto, and was professed on 23 January 1918. He was assigned to St Thomas College, Chatham, New Brunswick, freeing Father Michael *Pickett for chaplaincy service in the army. In July 1918 he was appointed to Assumption College, Windsor, for undergraduate courses in arts and theology. In August 1922 he went to the Basilian scholasticate, Toronto, to take his fourth year of theology and to complete his undergraduate work. He was ordained to the priesthood by Bishop Michael O'Brien of Peterborough, Ontario, in St Michael's Cathedral, Toronto, on 24 February 1923, and in June of that same year was awarded a B.A. from the University of Toronto.

In 1923 Father McGee began sixteen years of teaching at Assumption College. He earned an M.A. in education from Columbia University, New York City, 1929. In the Windsor area he was best known, however, as a sports coach, and was an early promoter of basketball in Ontario. His team won the Michigan-Ontario Championship and the Ontario Championship, 1933-4, and the Ontario and Eastern Canadian Championships, 1934-5. Alumni from these teams formed the nucleus of the Canadian Olympic team of 1936 which won the Silver Medal in Berlin. Ever since those years the trophy presented to the winning university team in the Canadian Basketball Championship is named the W.P. McGee Trophy.

In 1939 Father McGee was assigned to Aquinas Institute, Rochester, and in 1946 was moved to Catholic Central High School, Detroit, where he supervised the building of the new school plant on Outer Drive. A variety of appointments followed: St John the Baptist Parish, Amherstburg, Ontario, 1952-3; assistant treasurer at St John Fisher College, Rochester, 1953-5; first Basilian pastor of St Theresa's Church, Sugar Land, Texas, 1955-8; councillor and confessor, St Basil's Novitiate, Rochester and then Pontiac, Michigan, 1958-66. He retired first to 'La Pointe,' the Basilian House of Studies in Windsor, 1966-9, then to Assumption University, Windsor, 1969-74, but in 1974 moved to St Basil's Infirmary, Toronto, where he remained until his death a year later.

During his fifty-six years as a Basilian, Billy McGee brought to his work enthusiasm, interest in the young, and cheerfulness. Witty, even-tempered, open to all, he was interested in everything Basilian.

BIBLIOGRAPHY: 'Do Athletics Help to Educate Our Boys,' *Basilian* 1 (November 1935) 103-5; 'Community Relations: An Apostolate,' *Benedicamus* 1 (March 1948) 2-3; '*Laudemus viros gloriosos*: John M. Ryan,' *Basilian Teacher* 4 (December 1959) 79-82.
SOURCES: GABF; *Annals* 4 (1968) 6, 5 (1974) 6, 5 (1976) 189-90; *Newsletter* (21 November 1975); McMahon, *Pure Zeal* 125.

McGILLIS, Thomas Rodric, priest, was born on 12 December 1912 at St Andrew's West, Ontario (diocese of Alexandria, since 1976 of Alexandria-Cornwall), the son of Hugh McGillis and Hanna McDonald. He died in Toronto on 25 November 1987 and is buried in the Basilian plot of Holy Cross Cemetery, Thornhill, Ontario.

After completing grade VIII at St Andrew's School, 'Tom' McGillis went to work on his mother's farm. Four years later, one of his sisters, who was a schoolteacher, persuaded him to return to school. He enrolled in St Andrew's Catholic High School, where, while working part-time as janitor, errand boy, and chauffeur for the nuns who ran the school, he completed grade XII. Through the influence of two Basilians, Fathers Terence and John *McLaughlin, he took grade XIII at St Michael's College, Toronto. He entered St Basil's Novitiate, Toronto, in 1937, was professed on 15 August 1938, and was appointed to Assumption College, Windsor, where he majored in English and mathematics (B.A., University of Western Ontario, 1942). After teaching mathematics and religion at St Thomas High School, Houston, 1942–3, he studied theology at St Basil's Seminary, Toronto, 1943–7, and was ordained to the priesthood on 15 August 1946 in St Basil's Church, Toronto, by Cardinal James Charles McGuigan.

Father McGillis taught at Aquinas Institute, Rochester, 1947–51, at Assumption College School, 1951–2, and at St Thomas High School, Houston, 1952–4. He served at St Anne's Parish, Houston, 1954–8, and taught again at St Thomas High School, 1958–61.

It was during his first year in Houston as a priest that Father McGillis underwent a spinal operation for a painful condition of calcium deposit. The operation failed. For the rest of his life he had to walk haltingly with arm crutches and suffered continuous pain. That suffering is important to understanding his character and manner, for at times he seemed severe and forbidding, though he enjoyed jokes and the pleasantries of community life, and had a ready and warm smile.

In 1961 he joined the staff of Andrean High School, Gary (now Merrillville), Indiana, and five years later returned to Assumption College for one year, 1966–7. From 1967 to 1970 he taught at Iona Academy at St Raphael's West, near his home town, but then was appointed to St Michael's College School, 1970–6. He became chaplain to the sisters of the Monastery of the Holy Redeemer at Fort Erie, Ontario, 1976–9, but his health forced his return to St Michael's College School for a year and then a move to the Basilian Fathers Residence (Infirmary), where he would spend the last seven years of his life.

Tom McGillis was a private man but a demanding teacher. While he excoriated sloth in students, and communicated this clearly to them, he also gave them an example of striving for excellence. When the 'new math' was introduced, he quickly became certified for it. In his last years when his sufferings became more complex he nevertheless wanted to be kept informed of events and developments in the Basilian community.

SOURCES: GABF; *Annals* 1 (1946) 120, 6 (1988) 708–10; *Newsletter* (11 December 1987).

McGINN, James GERRARD, priest, member of the Congregation 1951–71, was born on 23 February 1931 in Toronto, the son of Arthur McGinn and Dorothy Young. He died at Blind River, Ontario, on 25 October 2002, and is buried there.

'Jerry' McGinn attended St Bridget's, St Anselm's, and Blessed Sacrament Separate Schools, and then enrolled first in the high school section of St Michael's College, 1945–9, and then at Lawrence Park Collegiate Institute, Toronto, 1949–50. He entered St Basil's Novitiate, Richmond Hill, Ontario, and made his first profession of vows on 15 August 1951. He did Honours Philosophy and English at St Michael's College (B.A., University of Toronto, 1955). During his first year of theology at St Basil's Seminary, Toronto, he also obtained Type B certification from the Ontario College of Education, 1956. He taught at St Michael's College School in 1955–6 and at Aquinas Institute, Rochester, in 1957–8. He finished his theological studies at St Basil's Seminary, 1958–61, and was ordained to the priesthood on 29 June 1960 by Bishop Francis Allen in St Basil's Church, Toronto.

Father McGinn taught at Assumption High School, Windsor, 1961–7. He was granted leave of absence in 1967. In 1971 the Holy See granted him dispensation from the obligations of the priesthood and religious profession. At his death he was survived by his wife, Judy, and three children. Father Thomas Mohan CSB preached the homily at his funeral Mass at St James the Greater Parish, Blind River.

SOURCE: GABF; *Annals* 3 (1960) 29–30; Thomas Mohan CSB.

McGOUEY, James THOMAS, priest, was born on 24 August 1904 in Saint John, New Brunswick, the son of James Thomas McGouey and Mary Ann Bradley. He died on 26 March 1969 in Windsor, and is buried there in the Basilian plot of Assumption Parish Cemetery.

Having been educated by the Basilians at St Thomas College, Chatham, New Brunswick, 'Tom' McGouey entered St Basil's Novitiate, Toronto, in 1923 and made first profession on 14 August 1924. He studied at Assumption College, Windsor (B.A., University of Western

Ontario, 1928) and took theology at St Basil's Scholasticate, Toronto. Bishop Alexander MacDonald ordained him to the priesthood on 19 December 1931 in St Basil's Church, Toronto. During his final year of theology he lived at St Michael's College and obtained teacher certification from the Ontario College of Education.

Father McGouey taught for one year at Assumption College, 1932–3, before being appointed to St Mary's Boys' High School, Calgary, where he taught mathematics and physics for the next fourteen years. During the Second World War he served as part-time chaplain to the Royal Canadian Air Force in Calgary. He was first councillor for the Basilian community from 1937 to 1947, and then returned to Assumption College in 1947 to teach mathematics and psychology.

Although a serious fall in 1962 left him lame, Father McGouey continued to teach until his retirement in 1968, when he undertook ministry to the aged at Huron Lodge, Windsor. He paid particular attention to visitors and new members of the house. After visiting a confrere in Hôtel Dieu Hospital, he contracted a chill which developed into congestive heart failure. He died a week later.

SOURCES: GABF; *Annals* 4 (1970) 161–2; *Newsletter* (27 March 1969).

McGRADY, Leo Victor, priest, was born in Toronto on 10 December 1920, the son of Leo John McGrady and Frances Agnes Maiden. He died in Toronto on 13 July 1965 and is buried in the Basilian plot of Holy Cross Cemetery, Thornhill, Ontario.

Leo McGrady attended St Monica's and Our Lady of Perpetual Help Separate Schools, Toronto, before completing high school at St Michael's College, Toronto. He spent the year 1940–1 at the Redemptorist Juniorate, Brockville, Ontario, before entering St Basil's Novitiate, Toronto. After profession on 15 August 1942 he was appointed to Assumption College, Windsor (B.A., University of Western Ontario, 1945). He taught at Catholic Central High School, Detroit, 1945–7, and obtained teacher certification for the State of Michigan through Wayne State University, Detroit. He studied theology at St Basil's Seminary, Toronto, continuing his studies in education during the summer months (M.A., University of Detroit, 1949). Cardinal James Charles McGuigan ordained him to the priesthood on 29 June 1950 in St Basil's Church, Toronto.

Father McGrady was a splendid teacher of English who promoted public speaking and gave lessons in voice training. He taught at Catholic Central High School, Detroit, 1951–5. During these years he began graduate studies in speech at the University of Michigan at Ann Arbor (M.A., 1960). Subsequent appointments took him to Aquinas Institute, Rochester, 1955–6, St Basil's Seminary, 1956–7, St Charles College, Sudbury, Ontario, 1957–8, Assumption College School, Windsor, 1958–62, and St Michael's College School, 1962.

Early in 1963 he was found to be suffering from cancer of the tongue. Treatment brought relief and in September of 1964 he went to St John Fisher College, Rochester; but, after a few months of teaching, the cancer reappeared, and he moved to St Basil's Seminary. He died less than a year later in Toronto General Hospital.

BIBLIOGRAPHY: 'Report on Vocation Activities at Aquinas Institute, Rochester,' *Proceedings of the Basilian Vocation Meetings* 1 (1955) 5; 'Techniques in Teaching Religion,' *Educational Bulletin* (June 1955) 5–7; 'The Art of Teaching Religion,' *Basilian Teacher* 1 (February 1956) 2–6; '"... but Yearbooks Go on Forever,"' *Basilian Teacher* 1 (May 1957) 9–11.
SOURCES: GABF; *Annals* 1 (1950) 285, 3 (1965) 381–2; *Newsletter* (19 July 1965).

McGUIGAN, Gerald Frederick, priest, was born on 24 June 1925 at Powell River, British Columbia (archdiocese of Vancouver), the son of William McGuigan and Gertrude Frederickson. He died in Toronto on 24 July 1988 and is buried in the Basilian plot of Holy Cross Cemetery, Thornhill, Ontario.

'Gerry' McGuigan received his elementary and secondary education in Vancouver, where the family had located when he was still young. After finishing high school he joined the Royal Canadian Navy, serving in the North Atlantic in 1944–5 on a corvette assigned to convoy duty. In 1945 he began undergraduate studies in general arts at the University of British Columbia. Two years later he entered St Basil's Novitiate, Toronto, and was professed on 12 September 1948. After profession he was appointed to St Michael's College to complete his undergraduate studies (B.A., University of Toronto, 1950). He taught at St Thomas High School, Houston, 1950–1, while also doing his first year of theology. In 1951 he moved to St Basil's Seminary, Toronto, to continue his theological studies, and was ordained to the priesthood on 29 June 1953 in St Basil's Church, Toronto, by Cardinal James Charles McGuigan (who was a distant relation).

In 1954 Father McGuigan began graduate studies at the University of Toronto (M.A., Political Science, 1955), and subsequently did three years of doctoral studies in economics at Laval. In 1958 he was appointed to the Basilian community at St Mark's College, Vancouver, to teach economics at the University of British Columbia, while continuing his studies. He was awarded a *Doctorat ès sciences sociales* by the Université Laval in 1962, after defending his thesis, 'Land Policy and Land Disposal under Tenure of Free and Common Socage. Quebec and Lower Canada, 1763–1809: A Collection of Pertinent Documents with Commentaries and Interpretive Conclusions' (4 volumes).

While at St Mark's Father McGuigan taught an innovative interdisciplinary program called 'Arts I–II' at the University of British Columbia. During one summer in the mid-1960s he travelled extensively in Eastern Europe, at that time behind the 'Iron Curtain,' on a motorbike. Moving to Toronto in 1969 he inaugurated another program at Erindale College, University of Toronto, to provide students with an opportunity to study themes of broad fundamental human concern. For the first year of this experiment he lived at the Basilian novitiate at Glenerin Hall, Erindale, Ontario, and for the remaining two years he was in residence at the University of St Michael's College.

From his travels in the Far East in 1972–3, Father McGuigan left an unpublished manuscript, 'Overland to India, or Eastward Ho! or Wagons East!' He then conceived the idea of ISAID (Institute for the Study and Application of Integrated Development), which he founded in 1974. It sought to teach native peoples to be self-sustaining by using technologies that completely respected their particular culture. The ISAID volunteers joined a French program, 'Projet Tapis Vert,' in a small village in the southwest corner of the Republic of Niger, aimed at restoring land threatened by desertification to food production. It expanded to include sixteen villages in the region. Father McGuigan lived and worked with the people. His expertise and innovations were recognized world-wide, and his work was funded by both Canadian and United States government agencies. In 1985 he was invited to deliver a paper at the UNESCO conference in Medellín, Colombia, on 'Drought and Desertification: The Natural and Human Causes.' The Faculty of Architecture at the National University in Medellín asked him to repeat the paper there.

After he returned to live in Basilian houses in the Toronto area in August 1980, he taught part-time and continued to work with ISAID, making frequent trips to Africa to oversee expanding projects. In 1986 he resigned as director of ISAID and requested a year of sabbatical leave, which he spent at Mount Saviour Monastery in upstate New

York, and after which he was appointed to the Basilian community in Sudbury, Ontario. He set about making plans for a new development project in Latin America. In July 1988 he took up residence at St Basil's College, Toronto, to complete his plans and to launch the project. He was there only two weeks when he suddenly collapsed and was rushed to hospital but died soon after arrival.

An imaginative teacher, a lover of humanity, a thinker and a doer, Gerry McGuigan went to the ends of the earth to help others learn to help themselves. This involved hands-on experience in their society, to evaluate 'appropriate technology' for them. He urged his Basilian confreres in schools and parishes to foster awareness of the issues of social justice both by teaching and by providing experience in needy countries.

Gerry McGuigan's zeal was balanced by a warmth and gentleness of character, a ready sense of humour, a love of the community, and a humility which did not allow him to take himself too seriously.

BIBLIOGRAPHY:
Book: (With George Payerle and Patricia Horrobin) *Student Protest*. Toronto and London, 1968.
Pamphlet: *Report on Arts Two Seminar: 1968–1969*. Vancouver, 1970.
Articles: 'Problems of Structure,' *Forum* 1 (October 1965) 133–44; 'Letter to the Editor [response to Father Francis Orsini, 'Poverty'],' *Forum* 1 (January 1965) 55–8.
SOURCES: GABF; *Annals* 2 (1953) 109, 6 (1989) 807–9; *Newsletter* (28 July 1988); Gail Burns, 'Innovative Basilian Left Legacy of Effective Aid,' *Catholic New Times* (4 December 1988) 3.

McGUIRE, Thomas JOHN, priest, was born in Marquette, Michigan, on 16 May 1891, the son of William McGuire and Jennie Maties. He died in Toronto on 30 January 1964 and is buried in the Basilian plot of Holy Cross Cemetery, Thornhill, Ontario.

When John McGuire was one year old, his parents moved to a farm in Sydenham township, Ontario, near Hoath Head, about ten miles east of Owen Sound. He attended a local public school and Owen Sound Collegiate Institute, after which he taught for two years, 1909–11, at Vibank, Saskatchewan, before enrolling in St Michael's College, Toronto (B.A., University of Toronto, 1915). He entered St Basil's Novitiate, Toronto, in 1915 and was professed on 26 August 1916. He took courses at the Ontario College of Education, Toronto, and studied theology at St Basil's Scholasticate. He was ordained priest on 29 February 1920 in St Peter's Cathedral, London, Ontario, by Bishop Michael Fallon.

Mature beyond his years, Father McGuire was soon given responsibilities. After one year of teaching at St Thomas High School, Houston, 1920–1, in successive years he was appointed treasurer then local superior and principal. Under his guidance the school observed in 1925 its silver jubilee. In 1927 he became superior of the Basilian community at Aquinas Institute, Rochester. In the following year he was named pastor of St Basil's Parish, Toronto, and in 1934 was transferred to St Mary's of the Assumption Parish, Owen Sound. He went back to St Thomas High school in 1937. In 1939 he was sent to St John the Baptist Parish in Amherstburg, Ontario, as assistant.

The last twenty-two years of Father McGuire's life were spent with the young members of the Congregation: confessor at the Rochester novitiate, 1942–4 and 1955–8, master of novices at the Toronto and Richmond Hill novitiates, 1944–55, confessor at St Basil's Seminary, 1958–9, and at St Basil's Novitiate, Richmond Hill and Erindale, from 1959 until his death, which followed a long series of cardiac ailments.

Father McGuire's dominant characteristic was gentleness. The *Basilian Centennial* volume of St Mary's of the Assumption Parish noted, 'Father John will always be remembered for his quiet dignity, his kindliness and his Irish wit.' In him mildness was coupled with firmness. The responsibilities and problems of administration did not frighten him. Unassuming yet observant, he smiled his way quietly through life.

BIBLIOGRAPHY: 'Losses in the Novitiate,' *Proceedings of the Basilian Vocation Meetings* 2 (1956) 36–8; 'Father Neil J. McNulty,' *Basilian Teacher* 3 (November 1958) 42–7.
SOURCES: GABF; *Annals* 1 (1944) 55, 3 (1964) 299–300; *Newsletter* (31 January 1964); *Centennial, St Mary's*.

McGWAN, Thomas James, scholastic, nephew of Father John *Ryan, was born in Cobourg, Ontario (diocese of Peterborough), on 11 March 1890, the son of Andrew McGwan and Margaret Ryan. He died in Windsor on 25 October 1918 and is buried there in the Basilian plot of Assumption Cemetery.

After early education at local schools Thomas McGwan went to St Michael's College, Toronto, in 1907. He taught at St Basil's College in

Waco, Texas, during the greater part of the school year 1911-12. After graduating from the University of Toronto in 1913 he attended the Ontario College of Education in Toronto, 1913-14. Two years of teaching followed at De La Salle High School in Toronto. On 3 October 1916, he was received as a novice at St Basil's Novitiate in Toronto. After his profession he was sent to Assumption College, Windsor, to study theology. There he was fatally stricken during the influenza epidemic of 1918 – one of three Basilians at Assumption to be its victims.

SOURCES: GABF; *Yearbook SMC* 9 (1918), 14 (1923).

McINTYRE, John Clement, priest, younger brother of Father Viator *McIntyre and uncle of Father John Murray CSB, was born in Dorchester, Ontario (diocese of London), on 23 November 1905, the son of James McIntyre and Margaret Clifford. He died in Windsor on 28 April 1945 and is buried there in the Basilian plot of Assumption Cemetery.

Educated at St Peter's Separate School, London (where the family had moved), Assumption College School, Windsor, 1920-3, and Assumption College, 1923-7 (B.A., University of Western Ontario, 1927), 'Johnny' McIntyre entered St Basil's Novitiate, Toronto, and was professed on 11 August 1928, along with his brother Viator. He attended the Ontario College of Education, Toronto, 1928-9, did theological studies at St Basil's Scholasticate, Toronto, 1928-32, being ordained priest on 19 December 1931 in St Basil's Church, Toronto, by Bishop Alexander MacDonald.

Father McIntyre was appointed to teach mathematics at Catholic Central High School, Detroit, 1932-8. As treasurer there from 1933 to 1938 he oversaw three moves of the Basilian residence. In 1936 he obtained teaching certification for the State of Michigan, and earned an M.A. in English at the University of Detroit in 1939. He taught at St Michael's College School, Toronto, 1938-41, and at St Thomas High School in Houston, 1941-2. When hypertension compelled him to give up teaching, he was named assistant at St John the Baptist Parish, Amherstburg, Ontario; but from 1943 he lived at Assumption College on sick leave until his death.

'Johnny Mac' was a cheerful community man who could also be frank and outspoken. Despite his short stature, he had been a formidable football player, and he taught his teams to play the same fearless game that he had played.

SOURCES: GABF; *Annals* 1 (1945) 84–5; *Purple and White* (6 June 1927); *Silver Anniversary, Catholic Central High School, 1928–53* (Detroit, 1953); *Yearbook SMC* 22 (1931).

McINTYRE, Viator Ignatius, priest, older brother of Father John *McIntyre and uncle of Father John Murray CSB, was born on 11 July 1904 at Dorchester, Ontario (diocese of London), the son of James McIntyre and Margaret Clifford. He died in Toronto on 30 January 1974 and is buried in the Basilian plot of Holy Cross Cemetery, Thornhill, Ontario.

'Vi,' as he was known all through life, did his early schooling in London, Ontario, moving on to Assumption College, Windsor, at the age of fourteen, where he completed high school and university (B.A., Honours Philosophy, University of Western Ontario, 1926). After one year of theology he entered St Basil's Novitiate, Toronto, and was professed on 11 August 1928, along with his brother John. He completed his theology studies at St Basil's Scholasticate, Toronto, 1928–31, and was ordained a priest on 28 February 1931 in St Basil's Church, Toronto, by Bishop Alexander MacDonald. During his theological studies he also obtained teacher certification from the Ontario College of Education.

In August 1931 Father McIntyre was appointed to Assumption College. For two years he carried a heavy teaching schedule: six periods a day in a variety of subjects including history of philosophy, political economy, algebra, geometry, French, and religious knowledge. He also filled the office of director of athletics. In 1935 he was chosen all-star coach by the Ontario Rugby Football Union. He obtained an M.A. in philosophy from the University of Toronto in 1932. In 1933, at twenty-nine years of age, he became principal of Assumption College School, a post he held for two years.

In 1935 he was appointed to St Michael's College, Toronto, and one year later he became principal of its high school section, 1936–46. He remained on staff for one year after relinquishing that post, then moved into the parish apostolate, first at St John the Baptist Parish, Amherstburg, Ontario, as assistant, 1947–9, and then at Blessed Sacrament Parish, Windsor (assistant 1949–54, rector 1954–64, and pastor 1954–65). In failing health, he lived for four years at the Amherstburg Parish, two years at Assumption College School, and in 1970 became one of the first members of St Basil's Infirmary, Toronto.

An educator in the fullest sense, Vi McIntyre worked efficiently and without fanfare. He was a clear and demanding teacher, a successful administrator, and an outstanding coach. His students admired, feared, and loved him, and his friendship with numbers of them persevered through many years. An accident in his youth deprived him of sight in one eye, which later had to be removed; yet this did not curtail his studies or his later work. From 1966 on he was beset with internal troubles aggravated by high blood pressure, and during his last years he was in almost continuous discomfort. None of this extinguished his notable smile or his gentle sense of humour.

BIBLIOGRAPHY: 'The Truth about Study,' *Basilian* 2 (May 1936) 86–8.
SOURCES: GABF; *Annals* 5 (1975) 110–11; *Newsletter* (31 January 1974); Shook, *Catholic Education* 162, 176, 180.

McKINNON, Robert Oliver, priest, was born on 11 March 1925 in Sudbury, Ontario (diocese of Sault Ste Marie), the son of Alexander McKinnon and Bernadette Acquin. He died in Toronto on 18 February 1999, and is buried in the Basilian plot of Holy Cross Cemetery, Thornhill, Ontario.

After senior matriculation at Sudbury High School, 1943, 'Bob' McKinnon served in the Royal Canadian Naval Reserve for two years and then taught all grades in the Monetville, Ontario, country school before turning to the formal study of fine art at the Ontario College of Art, 1948–51. He taught art in the elementary schools for the Sudbury District Separate School Board. He received interim first class certification in 1954 after two summer sessions at the Toronto Normal School on Pape Avenue. That same year he entered St Basil's Novitiate, Richmond Hill, Ontario, and made first profession on 15 August 1955. He was appointed to live at St Basil's Seminary while completing his undergraduate and theological studies. He was ordained to the priesthood on 29 June 1960 in St Basil's Church, Toronto, by Bishop Francis Allen. After completing his theology studies in 1961 he taught a year at St Joseph's High School, Ottawa, and in 1962 went to Andrean High School, Gary (now Merrillville), Indiana, where for the next eleven years he taught religion and fostered the fine arts.

Bob McKinnon was a painter of considerable talent, but dramatic production became his true avocation. His skill here was already evident in his seminary days with such productions as *The Music Man* and *Little Mary Sunshine* and during his one year in Ottawa with *Our Town*. But it was at Andrean that this talent found its great richness and astonishing variety. He produced and directed the following: *The*

Music Man and *Our Town*, 1962–3; *Little Mary Sunshine*, 1963–4; *The Diary of Anne Frank* and *My Fair Lady*, 1964–5; *The Unsinkable Molly Brown* and *A Man for All Seasons*, 1965–6; *The Sound of Music* and *Detective Story*, 1966–7; *Arsenic and Old Lace* and *West Side Story*, 1967–8; *Oliver* and *Marat/Sade*, 1968–9; *Mame* and *Up the Down Staircase*, 1969–70; *Funny Girl* and *Hello Dolly*, 1970–1. Several of the students he directed at Andrean became professional actors on Broadway.

In 1972 Father McKinnon began his long association with St Michael's College School, Toronto, where he staged over fifty dramas and musicals during his twenty-two years there, 1971–84 and 1985–94, with the intervening year at the Basilian Fathers of Calgary. He repeated many of the successes named above and added to his repertoire *The King and I, Camelot, JB, Guys and Dolls, The Boy Friend, Fiddler on the Roof, Brigadoon, Antigone, Amadeus, Riel,* and *Johannes Reuchlin and the Talmud*. Michael Higgins, president of St Jerome's College, University of Waterloo, wrote in his eulogy that Father McKinnon's production of *Reuchlin* exemplified his deep conviction that theatre was a 'pastoral mandate' and was 'his principal mode of education, of enlightenment, of liberation' (*Toronto Star*, 6 March 1999). Bob's confreres and friends recognized that his dedication to the fine arts and particularly to theatre was integral to his vocation as a Basilian priest-teacher for both academic and pastoral reasons, though it was by no means the only outlet for his zeal. He spent many summers as a military chaplain, first at the Trenton Air Force Base and then at the Ipperwash Army Cadet Camp.

Father McKinnon left St Michael's in 1994 to live at the new retirement community (later, Orsini House) at the Cardinal Flahiff Centre, because deteriorating health was taking its toll. Even there, at great effort he commuted to St Michael's College School to continue his dramatic productions. The last few months of his life were spent in the Basilian Fathers Residence (Infirmary). The presence at his funeral of many former drama students and members of the Toronto arts community witnessed to the impact he had on many lives.

BIBLIOGRAPHY: 'The Question of Media and Art,' *Basilian Teacher* 4 (March 1960) 175–7.
SOURCES: GABF; *Annals* 3 (1960) 28, 9 (2000) 85–6; *Newsletter* (16 March 1999).

McLAUGHLIN, John Redmond, priest, younger brother of Father Terence *McLaughlin and brother of Sister Mary Joanna CSJ, was born at Northfield, Ontario (diocese of Alexandria, since 1976 of Alexandria-Cornwall), on 13 November 1916, the son of John H. McLaughlin and Anna Maria Wheeler. He died in Detroit on 20 December 1954 and is buried in the Basilian plot of Assumption Cemetery, Windsor.

Upon graduation from St Andrew's High School, St Andrew's West, Ontario, John McLaughlin entered St Basil's Novitiate, Toronto, and was professed on 12 September 1936. After studies at St Michael's College, Toronto (B.A., University of Toronto, 1940), his theological studies, begun in 1940 at St Basil's Seminary in Toronto, were interrupted by two years of teaching, first at Catholic Central High School, Detroit, 1942–3, and then at Aquinas Institute, Rochester, 1943–4. During the summers of 1944 and 1945 he earned high school teaching certification at the Ontario College of Education, Toronto. He was ordained to the priesthood on 15 August 1945 in St Basil's Church, Toronto, by Archbishop James Charles McGuigan.

In 1946 Father 'Shorty' McLaughlin was appointed to Aquinas Institute to teach Latin and to counsel students. He was in charge of the Aquinas Annex during the year 1951–2. In 1953 he was transferred to Catholic Central High School, where he taught until his sudden death in 1954 from coronary thrombosis. His smallness of stature was no obstacle to the respect and esteem he won from the students he taught and the athletes he coached.

SOURCES: GABF; *Annals* 1 (1946) 117, 2 (1955) 226–7.

McLAUGHLIN, Terence Patrick, priest, older brother of Father John Redmond *McLaughlin and brother of Sister Mary Joanna CSJ, was born on 30 April 1903 at St Andrew's West, Ontario (diocese of Alexandria, since 1976 of Alexandria-Cornwall), the second son of John H. McLaughlin and Anna Maria Wheeler. He died in Toronto on 15 September 1970 and is buried in the Basilian plot of Holy Cross Cemetery, Thornhill, Ontario.

'Terry' attended School Section 22, Cornwall Township, and Cornwall Collegiate Institute, winning the Carleton scholarship and the Edward Blake scholarship to St Michael's College, Toronto, in 1922. He took employment in the summer of 1923 and during the year 1924–5 in an automobile plant in Detroit, finally taking his B.A. from the University of Toronto in Honours Philosophy in 1926 and winning the Mercier Gold Medal. He entered St Basil's Novitiate, Toronto, and was professed on 30 September 1927. While studying theology at St Basil's Scholasticate, Toronto, he taught physics to grade XIII at St Michael's, and earned interim certification in physical culture and interim high school assistant's certification, 1928, at the Ontario College of Education. He was ordained to the priesthood on 17 August 1930 in St Basil's Church, Toronto, by Archbishop Neil McNeil.

A month after his ordination Father McLaughlin sailed with Father George B. *Flahiff to Europe, where he began five years of studies in canon law and history at the Université de Strasbourg and the Faculté de Droit and the Ecole pratique des hautes études in Paris, with summer work at Salzburg in exegesis, ethics, and metaphysics. During these years he kept a longhand journal totalling 784 pages. Working under the direction of Gabriel Le Bras, he obtained the doctorate in the history of canon law from the Université de Strasbourg in 1935 with a thesis, 'Le très ancien droit monastique de l'occident: étude sur le développement général du monachisme et ses rapports avec l'église séculière et le monde laïque, de saint Benoît de Nursie à saint Benoît d'Aniane.'

In August 1935 he was appointed to St Michael's College, Toronto, and began a thirty-year-long career teaching the history of canon law at the Institute (from 1939 Pontifical Institute) of Mediaeval Studies, Toronto. He saw canon law not as something imposed arbitrarily but as developing to serve the needs of the Church. The context of history, he wrote, showed that 'A Law is not to be substituted for the human conscience but must leave room for it to form and develop itself' (*Basilian* 1 [1935] 84). His abiding respect for authority in the Church did not keep him from observing the human qualities of those who make the laws as well as of those who keep or fail to keep them. He once remarked that Romans had a need to get the law down in writing; its application and observance were quite other matters.

In 1940, at the age of thirty-seven, he became superior and president of St Michael's College. He held these positions for six years, guiding the college through the difficult days of the Second World War, when enrolment of American students fell from 160 to 1 and when the Government of Ontario pondered closing all faculties of arts. Father McLaughlin arranged tutoring for fifty students who volunteered to harvest wheat in Saskatchewan. He brought Benedictine scholastics from New Hampshire into residence at St Michael's so that their monastery could be used in the war effort. By nature diffident, except on matters on which he could speak as an authority, he was a careful, impartial, and authoritative superior. It was during this time that the Basilians appointed to the Pontifical Institute of Mediaeval Studies formed a *domus formata* separate from that of St Michael's, 1942. He also led the way in purchasing land and making long-range plans for the physical separation of the high school section of St Michael's from the undergraduate college.

His term as superior completed in 1946, he joined the Institute house, resuming his research work. Although elected procurator general in 1942, the Second World War made it impossible that he represent the Basilian Fathers at the Holy See; but from 1946 on he regularly taught at the Institute in the first semester, then spent from February to July or August in Rome, a city he loved and of which he gave exhausting but illuminating tours to visiting confreres and friends. He participated in negotiations in 1956 to regain the Collège du Sacré-Coeur in Annonay for the Basilians. From 1955 until 1970 he served on the Advisory Board of the Institute of Medieval Canon Law. For sixteen years he was one of the three judges for the marriage tribunal in the archdiocese of Toronto.

Terry McLaughlin was indefatigable in his study and research. Both in Rome and in Toronto he followed a regular schedule, rising early and spending long hours at his desk. In an article 'Why Should We Work?' he called attention to St Basil's view of work as a powerful means of sanctification. He did not disdain, even as superior and president, to wash floors when help was hard to get during the war. As editor of the Institute journal *Mediaeval Studies* for eight years he personally did the painstaking work of proof-reading to his own exacting standards, and he compiled two index volumes covering thirty-five years. Seldom in good health, all his life he suffered from ulcers, more than once undergoing surgery, until little of his stomach remained. One of his lungs was prone to collapse; he had emphysema in both lungs and a chronic heart condition. His death prevented publication of the several thousand pages of his transcription and collation of the manuscripts of the *Summa decretorum* of Huguccio of Pisa and of the *Summa super decretum Gratiani* of Simon of Bisignano. In 2005 the University of Toronto's Centre for Medieval Studies inaugurated and named in his honour a new lecture series on the history of law in the Middle Ages.

Among his confreres he was a warm and witty companion and loved a good story. He and Father Simon *Perdue, one playing the role of professor and the other that of parish priest, brightened many a gathering of confreres as they pitted wits on summer evenings at the entrance to the Clover Hill building. His piety was deep and unobtrusive. The night before he died, characteristically unwilling to be fussed over, he told Father Donald Finlay CSB, his superior who was attending him, to go home, as there was nothing more he could do at the hospital. Asked if he would like his rosary, he replied, 'No thanks, I'm concentrating on the crucifix.'

BIBLIOGRAPHY:

Books: *Le très ancien droit monastique de l'occident: de Saint Benoît de Nursie à Saint Benoît d'Aniane.* Archives de la France monastique, 38. Paris, 1935. Ed. *Summa Parisiensis on the Decretum Gratiani.* Toronto, 1952. Ed. *Church and the Reconstruction of the Modern World: The Social Encyclicals of Pope Pius XI.* Garden City, N.Y., 1957. *Mediaeval Studies, General Index,* vols. 1–25 (1939–63), vols. 26–30 (1964–8). Toronto, 1964, 1968.

Articles: In *Basilian:* 'A Letter about Law,' 1 (October 1935) 83–5; 'Oblates in Mediaeval Monasteries,' 3 (April, October 1937) 70–2, 74, 92–5; 'Why Should We Work?' 3 (June 1938) 102–3; 'The War in the Queen's Park–Bay Street Sector,' *St Michael's College Year Book* (Toronto, 1946) 14. In *Mediaeval Studies*: 'The Teachings of the Canonists on Usury (XII, XIII, and XIV Centuries),' 1 (1939) 81–147, 2 (1940) 1–22; 'The Prohibition of Marriage against Canons in the Early Twelfth Century,' 3 (1941) 94–100; trans. Angelo Mercati, 'The New List of the Popes,' 9 (1947) 71–80; 'The Formation of the Marriage Bond according to the *Summa Parisiensis,*' 15 (1953) 208–12; 'Abelard's Rule for Religious Women,' 18 (1956) 241–92; 'The *Extravagantes* in the *Summa* of Simon of Bisignano,' 20 (1958) 167–76. In *New Catholic Encyclopedia* (New York, 1967): 'Bazianus,' 2 183; 'Joannes Faventius,' 7 996; 'Paucapalea,' 11 1; 'Simon of Bisignano,' 13 220; 'Summa Parisiensis,' 13 791.

SOURCES: GABF; *Annals* 4 (1971) 209–10; *Newsletter* (18 September 1970); Kirley, *Congregation in France* 231n24, 242, 249, 252, 255, 258–61, 264, 266–7; Larry McDonald, 'T.P. McLaughlin of St Michael's College: A Bio-Bibliographical Consideration' (unpublished); *Mediaeval Studies* 33 (1971) 1–5; Shook, *Catholic Education* 174–9, 204, 216–17, 225.

McLEAN, Louis Charles EDWARD, priest, was born on 24 December 1925 in Oakville, Ontario (diocese of Hamilton), the second youngest of eight children of Martin McLean and Greta Woodward. He died in Toronto on 27 November 1990, and is buried in the Basilian plot of Holy Cross Cemetery, Thornhill, Ontario.

'Ted' McLean attended Blessed Sacrament Separate School and the high school section of St Michael's College, Toronto. As captain and defenceman, he led the St Michael's Junior OHA hockey team to the Memorial Cup in his final year of high school, 1944–5. After one year of arts at St Michael's College, he entered St Basil's Novitiate, Richmond Hill, Ontario, in 1946 and made first profession on 12 September 1947. He was appointed to St Michael's College to complete his undergraduate studies, majoring in Latin and philosophy (B.A., University of Toronto, 1950). His first appointment was to teach Latin at St Michael's College School, relocated in 1950 on Bathurst Street at St Clair Avenue. During his second year there he also attended the Ontario College of Education, earning a Type B teacher certification, 1952. From 1952 to 1956 he studied theology at St Basil's Seminary, Toronto, being ordained to the priesthood on 29 June 1955 in St Basil's Church, Toronto, by Bishop Francis Allen.

In 1956 Father McLean returned to St Michael's College School. In 1957 he was one of the founding fathers of Michael Power High School, Etobicoke. There he taught Latin and history and headed the departments of classics and physical education. During the summers he took graduate courses in Latin at the University of Ottawa. In 1962 he assumed the office of treasurer at St Basil's Novitiate, Erindale, Ontario, and three years later was appointed to St Mary's College, Sault Ste Marie, Ontario. In 1967 he was named superior of the Basilian community at St Charles College, Sudbury, Ontario, a position he held until elected regional representative for Eastern Canada in 1970. He maintained his residence at St Charles and also took on part-time work with the Sudbury Separate School Board as a counsellor. In 1977 he moved to Michael Power High School and worked as part-time chaplain at St Thomas Aquinas School, Bramalea, Ontario. At the end of his term as regional representative in 1981 Father McLean was named principal of Father Henry Carr Secondary School and rector of the Basilian Fathers of Rexdale. In 1987 he returned to live with the Basilian community at Michael Power, continuing as chaplain at Father Henry Carr Secondary School.

Father McLean's chief concern as regional representative was the spiritual well-being of his confreres. He once reported to his superiors: 'What local houses need more than representation ... is someone to visit them regularly to instruct them in spiritual renewal. They need a representative who is informed in matters biblical, theological and spiritual to help them build communities that are more vigorous and better able to cope with the stress in religious life today.' He himself regularly took courses in theological renewal.

Ted McLean's fame as an athlete never affected his openness to others, or his enthusiasm and warm humanity. He died in his sixty-fifth year after being struck by a car as he was taking his daily exercise of jogging.

BIBLIOGRAPHY: 'Spiritual Reading: Recommendations,' *Benedicamus* 1 (May 1948) 6; 'Requirements of a Good Defenseman,' *Basilian Teacher* 4 (December 1959) 83; 'The Discussion Period Should Be Optional [response to Father Robert Madden, 'Student Retreats'],' *Basilian Forum* 2 (December 1965) 168–9; 'Prayer,' *Aspects of Basilian Spirituality* (1972) 33–8.
SOURCES: GABF; *Annals* 2 (1955) 199, 7 (1991) 151–3; *Newsletter* 22 (30 December 1990).

McMAHON, Edward Joseph, priest, was born on 31 December 1906 at Fitzroy Harbour, Ontario (archdiocese of Ottawa), the son of Thomas McMahon and Eleanor Warnock. He died in Ottawa on 8 April 1970 and is buried there in the priests' plot of Notre-Dame Cemetery.

After attending public school in his home town, and later Arnprior High School, Edward McMahon enrolled in the University of Ottawa in September 1924 (B.A., Licence in Philosophy, 1929). After a year at St Joseph's Seminary, Edmonton, Alberta, he decided on religious life in a teaching community and entered St Basil's Novitiate, Toronto, making first profession on 12 September 1931. During his theological studies he lived first at St Michael's College, 1931–2, and then at St Basil's Scholasticate, 1932–5. He obtained a teaching certificate from the Ontario College of Education in 1933. He was ordained to the priesthood on 16 December 1934 in Assumption Church, Windsor, by Bishop John Kidd.

In 1935 Father McMahon was appointed to Catholic Central High School, Detroit, where he taught physics and mathematics for the next fifteen years in the senior grades. He found time in 1941 and 1942 to pursue graduate courses in science and mathematics at Notre Dame, Marquette, and the University of Michigan. In 1950 he was appointed to St Mary's Boys' High School, Calgary, to teach mathematics and science in the senior grades, and was elected to the local council. In 1957 he was named principal of the newly founded St Francis High School, Lethbridge, Alberta, and rector of the Basilian house. One year later he joined Fathers A. John *Ruth and Basil *Regan in the founding of St Joseph's High School, Ottawa. Once again he taught in the senior grades and served on the local council until just a few days before his death in 1970.

As a teacher Father McMahon was exacting of his students and of himself. He kept in contact with former students and always welcomed their visits. He had a cheerfulness that warmed the lives of his confreres and the lives of the sick whom he habitually visited in hospitals in Calgary and Lethbridge. He was an ardent sportsman, particularly for tennis and golf, and a great enthusiast for the Montreal Canadiens hockey team. The example he gave of regular work, prayer, and congeniality found expression in the designation 'Steady Eddy' by which he was familiarly known.

On Saturday, 4 April 1970, Father McMahon suffered an attack of what he deemed to be indigestion. He did not do his usual Sunday parish ministry, but taught his classes on Monday morning. That evening, in hospital, his condition was diagnosed as a severe heart attack. He died peacefully on Wednesday afternoon, attended by the superior general, Father Joseph *Wey, and his confreres.

BIBLIOGRAPHY: 'Mathematics in Basilian Schools [forum],' *Basilian Teacher* 4 (December 1959) 71; 'Testing,' *Basilian Teacher* 4 (February 1960) 133–4; 'Scripture and Our Students [forum],' *Basilian Teacher* 5 (December 1960) 85–6.
SOURCES: GABF; *Annals* 4 (1971) 211; *Newsletter* (9 April 1970).

McMANUS, John Edward, priest, was born on 8 March 1927 in Rochester, one of two sons of Paul T. McManus and Anna Standfest. He died in Houston on 27 March 2000, and is buried there in the Basilian plot, Garden of Gethsemane, Forest Park Lawndale Cemetery.

John, or 'Guts,' as he was called for his hardihood in sports, attended Our Lady of Good Counsel School and Aquinas Institute, Rochester. He entered St Basil's Novitiate, Rochester, was professed on 15 August 1946, and was appointed to St Michael's College, Toronto (B.A., University of Toronto, 1950). He taught for two years, first at Aquinas Institute, 1950–1, and then at Assumption High School, Windsor, 1951–2. He studied theology at St Basil's Seminary, Toronto, 1952–6, and was ordained to the priesthood on 29 June 1955 in St Basil's Church, Toronto, by Bishop Francis Allen.

In 1956–8 Father McManus earned an M.A. in German at the University of Toronto. He taught a year at Aquinas Institute before being appointed to the University of St Thomas, Houston, where he remained for the rest of his life, a total of forty-two years. He taught German and Spanish until 1968, and after that only German. He headed the German program from 1958 and served as chair of the Modern Languages Department from 1966 to 1978. In addition to full-time teaching and departmental duties he worked in other capacities, including campus ministry, dormitory prefect, and bookstore manager. He supervised the installation of three successive language labs. In 1961 he was appointed the first master of scholastics at the University of St Thomas and supervised the opening of the scholasticate on campus.

Father McManus attended many seminars in the United States, Germany, and Austria. He received Fulbright, Goethe Institute, and National Endowment for the Humanities scholarships. He maintained close contacts with his relatives on his mother's side in Germany. He gave papers annually at professional conferences, especially the South Central Conference on Christianity and Literature. From 1987 to 1997 he hosted the regional meetings of the Institute on Religious Life at the University of St Thomas.

John McManus's stolid, single-minded, and determined ways showed the characteristics of his maternal background. He tended to be taciturn, a trait which lent credence to the few words he did speak. All his life he maintained his upper New York State accent.

BIBLIOGRAPHY: 'Letter to the Editor [response to Father Joseph Trovato, 'Community Prayer'],' *Forum* 1 (May 1965) 129–31; 'St John Neumann,' *CCR* 4 (1986) 175–9.
SOURCES: GABF; *Annals* 2 (1955) 199, 8 (1997) 11–12, 9 (2001) 91–2; *Newsletter* (20 April 2000).

McNEIL, Donald Joseph, priest, was born in Toronto on 28 September 1916, the only child of William McNeil and Jeanette McDonald. He died in Toronto on 24 November 2001 and is buried in the Basilian plot of Holy Cross Cemetery, Thornhill, Ontario.

After graduating from the high school section of St Michael's College, 1935, 'Don' McNeil entered St Basil's Novitiate, Toronto, and was professed on 15 August 1936. He lived at St Basil's Seminary, 1936–45, with the exception of a year of teaching high school at St Michael's College, 1942–3. He did undergraduate studies, 1936–40 (B.A., Honours Classics, University of Toronto, 1940), and theology, 1941–5, and was ordained to the priesthood on 15 August 1944 in St Basil's Church, Toronto, by Archbishop James Charles McGuigan.

Father McNeil took two years of graduate studies, 1945-7, one at the University of Toronto and one at Harvard University. He joined the staff of St Michael's College, where he remained for fifty-two years, teaching Greek and Latin until retirement, serving as superior of the Basilian community at St Michael's, 1962-7, and devoting himself to the liturgical life of the community during the post–Vatican II period of change and adaptation. He was particularly concerned about the correctness and the beauty of the place of worship, giving untold hours of labour, both mental and manual, to ensure these. For many years he celebrated the early weekday Mass at St Basil's Church.

To all he did Don MacNeil brought a thoroughness and persistence. Though quiet and retiring by nature, he was lively and congenial in community. His chief recreation took the form of long walks, usually by himself, to the amazement of those who spotted him at unbelievable distances from the college, moving at a jaunty pace and seemingly tireless. He enjoyed good health; there is no record of his ever having visited a dentist. His physical condition was reflected in a habitual cheerfulness and a ready smile, though his last two years – spent at Anglin House (Infirmary) – were darkened by times of depression, as painful to all as they were uncharacteristic.

BIBLIOGRAPHY: 'Oratio classica prima – Pro Homero,' *Basilian* 3 (December 1937) 136-8; 'Experimentation to Be Attempted,' *Forum* 1 (November 1964) 24-6.

SOURCES: GABF; *Annals* 1 (1945) 100, 6 (1987) 494, 8 (1997) 7-8, 10 (2002) 93; *Newsletter* (7 December 2001).

McNULTY, Neil Jerome, priest, was born in the village of Asphodel, near Norwood, Ontario (diocese of Toronto, since 1882 of Peterborough), on 14 October 1862, one of eleven children born to Neil McNulty and Mary O'Leary. He died in Toronto on 7 December 1934 and is buried there in the Basilian plot of Mount Hope Cemetery.

After early education in local schools, Neil attended the Model School at Newmarket, Ontario, where he obtained teaching certification for elementary schools. He taught for three years in Douro, Ontario, then went into the grocery business in Peterborough, Ontario. In 1892 he enrolled in St Michael's College, Toronto, to study for the priesthood. One year later he went to the Basilian College of Mary Immaculate at Beaconfield House, Plymouth, England, where he taught while continuing his studies. He entered St Basil's Novitiate, Toronto, on 9 September 1895, and there his fellow novices began calling him 'the major' for his military bearing. After profession he studied at Assumption College, Windsor, 1896–1900, then completed his theological courses at St Basil's Scholasticate, Toronto. He was ordained priest on 6 January 1902.

His first appointment as a priest took Father McNulty to St Thomas College (High School), Houston, 1902–4, where he taught English and took a lively interest in school athletics. He served as assistant at St John the Baptist Parish, Amherstburg, Ontario, 1904–7, returned to teaching at St Thomas High School, 1907–8, and then taught at Assumption College, 1908–9. In 1909 he was sent to Holy Rosary Parish, Toronto, as assistant, and the following year was appointed to St Mary's of the Assumption Parish, Owen Sound, Ontario, where he remained until 1934, when he moved to St Michael's College, on sick leave, a few months before his death.

During his twenty-four years as assistant at St Mary's in Owen Sound, Father McNulty attended at one time or another all the missions attached to this parish. After a few years he went regularly to St Michael's Church, Irish Block; St Vincent's Church, Meaford; and St Francis Church, Thornbury. At each place he would hear confessions on Saturday and Sunday morning, say or sing Mass with sermon, teach catechism in the afternoon, and close the day with rosary, sermon, and Benediction of the Blessed Sacrament. On Monday morning, he said Mass, took Holy Communion to the sick, and visited homes before returning to Owen Sound. He was noted for his special concern for ministry to the sick and dying.

An obituary notice in the *Owen Sound Sun-Times* stated: 'Father McNulty was one of the most beloved priests who ever came to Owen Sound. ... he quickly found a place in the hearts of the parish.' He was unhurried and methodical in his undertakings, and made a holy hour before the Blessed Sacrament every day. Father Charles *Collins explained Father McNulty's love of prayer in these words: 'He often remarked to me in our little walks on the verandah after meals, "I long ago decided that a man had to sanctify himself, and prayer was the great means within the reach of all to attain perfection."'

BIBLIOGRAPHY: *'Laudemus viros gloriosos*: T.J. McGuire,' *Basilian Teacher* 3 (November 1958) 42–7.
SOURCES: GABF; *Centennial, St Mary's*; Charles Collins, 'Father McNulty,' *Basil-*

ian 2 (April 1936) 68–70; *Jubilee, St Mary's*; T.J. McGuire, 'Neil J. McNulty,' *Basilian Teacher* 3 (November 1958) 42–7; Spetz, *Waterloo*; *Yearbook SMC* 26 (1935).

McREAVY, John Joseph, priest, elder brother of Father Thomas Joseph McReavy CSB, was born on 31 May 1922 at Owen Sound, Ontario (diocese of Hamilton), one of a family of nine children born to John Joseph McReavy and Mary Butler. He died in Saskatoon, Saskatchewan, on 26 September 1978 and is buried in the Basilian plot of St Mary's Cemetery, Owen Sound.

'Jack' McReavy completed his elementary schooling at St Mary's School, Owen Sound. In 1937 the family moved to Blind River, Ontario, returning to Owen Sound in 1942. During this time Jack attended Scollard Hall, North Bay, Ontario, and the high school section of St Michael's College, Toronto. In 1943 he entered St Basil's Novitiate, Toronto, was professed on 15 August 1944, and was appointed to St Michael's College (B.A., University of Toronto, 1947). He remained at St Michael's for the first year of his theological studies, and then moved to St Basil's Seminary in 1948, the same year in which he received an M.A. in philosophy from the University of Toronto. He was ordained a priest on 29 June 1950 in St Basil's Church, Toronto, by Cardinal James Charles McGuigan.

Father McReavy taught philosophy at several Basilian schools: St John Fisher College, Rochester, 1951–5, 1956–9, with the intervening year on graduate studies in philosophy at the University of Ottawa; University of St Thomas, Houston, 1959–66; and St Thomas More College, Saskatoon, where he remained for the rest of his life. There he gave special attention to foreign students and to student drama. In later years, failing health curtailed his activities drastically. A few months before his death he was elected as the Basilian representative on the priests' senate of the diocese of Saskatoon.

Jack McReavy was a well-read and reflective philosopher who set little store by the common university dictum 'publish or perish.' He had a keen, questioning mind, and students found him to be a colourful, provocative, and stimulating professor. He could not ignore the elements and incidents of life, needing to wrestle meaning out of them. This gnawing inquisitiveness tended to rob him of his peace of mind. About the year 1975 he entered a period of inner turmoil, not unlike that expressed by St Paul in the words 'we ourselves, who have the first fruits of the Spirit, groan inwardly as we wait for adoption as sons, the redemption of our bodies' (Rom. 8:23). His countervailing confidence in his confreres and a ready sense of humour allowed him to share, in his own way, this confusion with them so that both he and they could grow and slowly resolve the difficulties. Ultimately he seemed to have found peace.

He was deeply gratified at being elected to the Basilian local council, and an abiding concern for the community motivated him to spend considerable time on a critical analysis of the *Basilian Way of Life*. He died suddenly, alone in his room at St Thomas More College, after having taken his Irish setter 'Shanna' for an afternoon walk.

BIBLIOGRAPHY: 'Christmas Lessons,' *Benedicamus* 4 (Christmas 1950) 20; 'Obedience Seemed to Elude Me [response to Father Elliot Allen, 'Obedience'],' *Forum* 2 (April 1966) 54–5.
SOURCES: GABF; *Annals* 1 (1950) 288, 5 (1979) 414–15; *Newsletter* (4 October 1978).

MEADER, Frederick DANIEL, priest, was born in South Bend, Indiana (diocese of Fort Wayne, since 1960 of Fort Wayne–South Bend), on 2 August 1880, the eldest of nine children born to Theodore Meader and Mary Murphy. He died in Toronto on 6 October 1924 and was buried there in the Basilian plot of Mount Hope Cemetery.

Daniel was raised in Orillia, Ontario. He completed the high school course at the Orillia Collegiate Institute and, after Normal School in Collingwood, Ontario, taught for two years at Byng Inlet, Ontario, and at the Separate School in Orillia. In 1901 he entered the University of Toronto and graduated first of firsts in mathematics and physics, 1905. At the urging of his mentor Professor John McLennan, he accepted a teaching fellowship in mathematics for 1905–6, but he resigned this position to enter St Basil's Novitiate, Toronto. He was professed on 15 August 1907, studied theology at St Basil's Scholasticate, Toronto, and was ordained priest on 30 July 1911.

Father 'Dan' Meader taught philosophy and religious knowledge at St Michael's College, Toronto. In 1914 he was appointed to graduate studies at the University of Louvain, but the outbreak of the First World War forced his return to St Michael's, where he was appointed registrar, and in 1916 he added to his duties the office of treasurer. Four years later, 1920, he was named principal and superior at St Thomas College, Chatham, New Brunswick, and was the first to propose that it develop into a university. His draft for a university charter was rejected by the superior general, Father Francis *Forster. When the Congregation withdrew from Chatham in 1923 he returned to Toronto and joined the staff of St Basil's Scholasticate. Shortly afterwards he suffered a fatal heart attack.

Father Meader was a man of remarkable industry. As a university student he had worked almost full-time to pay his tuition and fees, was active in student associations, and in his graduating year was president of the Catholic Students' Union. During these years he first manifested his social conscience by helping members of a working-boys' club to continue their education. He was never heard to say an unkind word.

At St Michael's College Father Meader frequently handled two jobs and took only four hours' sleep. His social activism found priestly expression as a confessor at the Good Shepherd Convent, a school for delinquent girls. He still made time for a tremendous amount of reading. He warned against the materialistic philosophy and ideology which he saw infiltrating the University of Toronto. At the time of his death he left an unfinished manuscript textbook on metaphysics.

BIBLIOGRAPHY: 'Philosophy at St Michael's College,' *Yearbook SMC* (1914) 50.
SOURCES: GABF; E.J. McCorkell, 'Reverend Frederick Daniel Meader, CSB,' *St Joseph Lilies* 13 (December 1924) 44–7; Shook, *Catholic Education* 118–19, 159–61; *Yearbook SMC* 12 (1921), 16 (1925).

MEGAN, James ARNOLD, priest, was born on 27 August 1915 in Montreal, one of three children of Francis Megan and Regina Quinn. He died in Toronto on 13 September 1990 and is buried in the Basilian plot of Holy Cross Cemetery, Thornhill, Ontario.

'Arnie,' or 'Meeg,' attended St Dominic's parochial school and D'Arcy McGee High School, Montreal, and then took a two-year course in analytical and quantitative chemistry at Sir George Williams College, Montreal. He developed an early interest in farming, since his parents were raised on farms and he spent summers on the farm of an uncle. In 1937 he went to the Marylake Farm School, operated by St Michael's College, Toronto, under the direction of Father Michael *Oliver, where he remained for one year. In 1938 he entered St Basil's Novitiate, Toronto, and was professed on 15 August 1939. He was then appointed to Assumption College, Windsor, where he completed his university studies, majoring in mathematics and science (B.A., University of Western Ontario, 1943). He taught for one year at Aquinas Institute,

Rochester, and for one year at St Michael's College School, Toronto. In the summers he attended the Ontario College of Education, earning a permanent Type B teaching certification, 1945. He studied theology at St Basil's Seminary, Toronto, 1945–9, and was ordained to the priesthood on 29 June 1948 in St Basil's Church, Toronto, by Cardinal James Charles McGuigan.

In 1949 Father Megan began four decades of teaching in Basilian high schools: St Michael's College School, 1949–54 and 1955–71, Aquinas Institute, Rochester, 1954–5, and St Joseph's High School, Ottawa, as both teacher and community treasurer, 1971–3. In 1973 he was transferred to St Mary's College, Sault Ste Marie, Ontario, where he remained until failing health obliged his move in 1990 to the Basilian Fathers Residence (Infirmary) in Toronto.

Meeg was a man of inexhaustible energy and thoroughness. He instilled inquisitiveness in his students, for he himself was unceasingly questioning, seeking, experimenting, and venturing. He claimed to have worked out the formula for better colour photography before Kodak came to the same conclusion, though this would be hard to substantiate. He paddled a canoe from Lake Superior to Strawberry Island in Lake Simcoe, though he did not know how to swim. He explored woods and rivers, abandoned mine shafts, animal physiology, human conception rhythms, and map-drawing for scientific experiments as they related to biology. On retirement in 1986 he was presented with a computer, and in short order was writing programs and teaching others. At the request of the general council he made a valuable study of Basilian superannuation and pensions in Ontario, and helped draw up a detailed and just account of Basilian ownership and services for the sale of St Mary's College.

When diagnosed with cancer in 1987, he continued to inquire and explore in the measure his failing health permitted; but in 1990 he 'surrendered' to the cancer and retired to Toronto, where he told his confreres that, intrigued to know what was on the other side, he was ready to die. On his seventy-fifth birthday, just seventeen days before his death, he wrapped his computer in a large bow and presented it to the confreres at the residence.

SOURCES: GABF; *Annals* 1 (1948) 219, 7 (1991) 144–6; *Newsletter* (2 October 1990).

MELOCHE, Paul Joseph, priest, was born on 28 April 1927 at LaSalle, Ontario (diocese of London), the son of Claude Meloche and Marie

Nadeau. He died in Toronto on 21 May 1975 and is buried in the Basilian plot of Holy Cross Cemetery, Thornhill, Ontario.

Having attended St Theresa's School at River Canard, Ontario, and Assumption High School, Windsor, Paul Meloche enrolled in pre-dentistry at the University of Detroit in 1944, but withdrew in 1947 to enrol in the O'Neill Business College, Windsor. One year later he entered St Basil's Novitiate, Richmond Hill, Ontario, taking first vows on 22 September 1949. He was assigned to Assumption College, Windsor (B.A., University of Western Ontario, 1951). After teaching one year at Catholic Central High School, Detroit, he studied theology at St Basil's Seminary, Toronto, 1952-6, receiving an S.T.B. from the University of St Michael's College in 1955. He was ordained to the priesthood on 29 June 1955 in St Basil's Church, Toronto, by Bishop Francis Allen.

Father Meloche taught French in five Basilian schools: Assumption High School, Windsor, 1956-7, St Mary's Boys' High School, Calgary, Alberta, 1957-64, also as treasurer 1960-4, St Michael's College School, also as treasurer, 1964-7, St Charles College, Sudbury, Ontario, 1967-71, and St Francis High School, Lethbridge, Alberta, 1971-3. In that last year, having been appointed superior, he was an *ex officio* delegate to the general chapter that summer. Before assuming the office, however, mental disorientation set in rapidly, to the extent that continuing in the chapter was impossible. His loss of memory, particularly in recalling his confreres' names, was an acute suffering to him. His condition was diagnosed as premature senility, and he entered the Basilian Fathers Infirmary in Toronto.

Paul Meloche was particularly known for fidelity to the traditions of the Basilian community and its spiritual exercises. His delicate sensitivity alerted him to sadness or depression in others, and he had a talent for bringing them help. He spent his time at home, ready to show hospitality to guests and kindness to those with whom he lived.

SOURCES: GABF; *Annals* 2 (1955) 200, 5 (1976) 185-6; *Newsletter* (23 May 1975).

MENUT, Pierre, priest, was born on 30 June 1839 at Vernosc-les-Annonay. He died in Périgueux (Dordogne) on 18 December 1895 and is buried there.

Pierre Menut studied at the Collège des Cordeliers, Annonay, in the Sainte-Barbe section, and made his novitiate at Feyzin (Isère, now Rhône). He took final vows on 25 September 1864 and was ordained to the priesthood by Bishop Armand de Charbonnel on 24 September

1866 in the chapel of the Collège des Cordeliers. While doing his theology he taught and supervised students at the Petit Séminaire de Vernoux (Ardèche) and at the Collège de Privas (Ardèche) as well as at the college in Annonay. Right after ordination he went to the Ecole cléricale de Périgueux (Dordogne), where he taught for twenty-nine years, 1866–95, mostly in the higher grades. Each summer he would return to Vernosc for vacation.

Pierre Menut was known as a humble and simple priest, easy to talk to. He died suddenly at the age of fifty-six.

SOURCES: GABF; Kirley, *Community in France* 31; Pouzol, 'Notices.'

MERLE, Hilarion, priest, was born on 25 June 1832 at Malons (Gard, diocese of Nîmes), the son of Alexis Merle and Marie Bernard. He died on 21 February 1913 in Annonay and is buried in the priests' plot of the Annonay cemetery.

Having entered the novitiate on 29 September 1857 in Annonay, Hilarion Merle made his profession of vows on 31 August 1859. Bishop Louis Delcusy of Viviers ordained him to the priesthood on 30 May 1863. During his years of initial formation and after ordination until 1903 he had worked as prefect of discipline, first at Sainte-Barbe minor seminary, 1857–73, and later at the Externat (day school) of the Collège du Sacré-Coeur, near Sainte-Barbe, 1873–1903. He insisted on good order and worked tirelessly to help young people form their consciences. He was also a successful fund-raiser for Sainte-Barbe, where poor students who could pay no tuition were educated. In appreciation of his many years of supervision and spiritual guidance his former students organized a gala dinner on 20 July 1899 and presented him with a vestment of Gobelins cloth woven with gold thread, which remained among the treasures of the Basilian community in Annonay for over a century.

When the Basilians were expelled in 1903 from teaching in the Collège du Sacré-Coeur and Sainte-Barbe, Father Merle found a lodging in the rue de Sauzéat, Annonay, near Sainte-Barbe, and served as chaplain to the orphanage run by the Trinitarian Sisters in the rue des Jardins, Annonay.

SOURCES: GABF; Kirley, *Community in France* 184, 201 206; Pouzol, 'Notices.'

MEYER, John Wilbert, priest, was born on 25 October 1906, at Francesville, Pulaski County, Indiana (diocese of Lafayette, Indiana), the son of Henry F. Meyer and Wilhelmina Karstens, both of Lutheran faith. He died on 10 December 1969 in Houston and is buried there in the Basilian plot, Garden of Gethsemane, Forest Park Lawndale Cemetery.

John Meyer attended Winamac High School, Winamac, Illinois, and Ball State Teachers College, Muncie, Indiana, 1924–6 (Indiana State Teacher's Licence, 1925). For two years, 1926–8, he taught high school at Aurora, Illinois. He was received into the Catholic Church on 27 June 1928, and in 1929 he went to Assumption College, Windsor, where he enrolled in Honours Philosophy. Two years later he entered St Basil's Novitiate, Toronto, making first profession on 15 August 1932. He returned to Assumption College, where he completed his arts course (B.A., University of Western Ontario, 1934). He taught in 1934–5 at Catholic Central High School, Detroit, and then began his theological studies at St Basil's Scholasticate, Toronto. In 1937 he was appointed to Aquinas Institute, Rochester, and completed his theology while teaching. He was ordained to the priesthood on 17 December 1939 in St Basil's Church, Toronto, by Archbishop James Charles McGuigan.

In 1940 Father Meyer returned to Aquinas to teach and work as librarian. In 1950 he was appointed to the University of St Thomas, Houston, as librarian, a position he held for nineteen years until his sudden death from a heart attack.

John Meyer devoted many summers to graduate work in library science at the University of Michigan (B.L.S., 1944, M.L.S., 1948). In every Basilian house in which he lived he took on the task of sacristan with his quiet faith and piety. Although diminutive in stature and of very mild temperament, he attracted students of every type. He had a keen and lifelong interest in rodeo riding, and was for years the chaplain and an honorary member of the National Rodeo Association. Students grew accustomed to seeing bronco and steer riders coming to his library office during the Houston Fat Stock Show and Rodeo every year. Shortly before his death a new operation restored his hearing, which a childhood disease had destroyed. He had been forced to wear a metal hearing device clamped across the top of his head – a cross that he had borne most of his life with habitual cheerfulness.

BIBLIOGRAPHY: 'Safeguarding Our Health,' *Basilian* 2 (October, November 1936) 114, 118, 135–6.
SOURCES: GABF; *Annals* 4 (1970) 167–8; *Newsletter* (11 December 1969).

MEYZONNIER, Camille, priest, was born in Annonay on 18 December 1843, the son of Etienne Meyzonnier and Joséphine Pradier. He died in Annonay on 8 December 1891 and was buried there in the Basilian cemetery on the grounds of the Collège du Sacré-Coeur.

Camille Meyzonnier attended the Externat (day school) of the Collège des Cordeliers, Annonay, 1853–60, and the Sainte-Barbe section, the minor seminary, for rhetoric, 1860–1. He was a brilliant and studious young man, as well as mischievous and sociable. He made his novitiate at Feyzin (Isère, now Rhône) during the year 1861–2, and took final vows on 20 September 1867. Bishop Armand de Charbonnel ordained him to the priesthood on 18 September 1869 in the chapel of the Collège du Sacré-Coeur, Annonay.

While studying for the priesthood he taught at the Collège de Privas (Ardèche), 1862–6, at the Collège des Cordeliers, 1866–7, and at the Collège du Sacré-Coeur as professor of *seconde*, 1867–9. After ordination he remained at Sacré-Coeur in the same capacity for two years before taking charge of the highest class, philosophy, which he taught with verve for the next twenty years, 1871–91. At the age of forty-seven, he died suddenly of a heart attack at the college. A large crowd of clergy, notables of the city, and students attended his funeral.

Father Meyzonnier had the qualities of mind and heart of a dedicated French scholar. A charming conversationalist and talented teacher, his jolly and lovable disposition won the affection of many faithful friends.

SOURCES: GABF; Chomel, *Collège d'Annonay* 517; Pouzol, 'Notices'; *Semaine religieuse de Viviers* (18 December 1891) 606–7.

MICHEL, Louis, priest, member of the Congregation 1862–c.1872, was born at Issoudun (Indre, diocese of Tours), but the date is not known.

Louis entered the novitiate at Feyzin (Isère, now Rhône) on 8 April 1861. In September of that year he was summoned to teach the Commercial class at the Collège des Cordeliers, Annonay, and in 1862–3 taught at the Collège de Privas (Ardèche). He made his profession of vows on 18 September 1863, and was ordained to the priesthood on 23 September 1865. After remaining a year at the scholasticate in Annonay, he taught *septième* at the Ecole cléricale in Périgueux (Dordogne), 1866–9, and served as treasurer there 1869–72. He left the Congregation between 1872 and 1876, and nothing else is known of him.

SOURCE: Pouzol, 'Notices,' Supplément 2.

MICHELON, Elie, priest, member of the Congregation c.1890–c.1896, was born on 24 June 1868 at Saint-Basile, canton of Lamastre (Ardèche).
Elie probably studied at the Petit Séminaire de Vernoux (Ardèche), and entered the novitiate at Beaconfield House, Plymouth, England, on 26 September 1889; but ill health forced his return to France in August 1890. He did his theological studies in Annonay while helping out as prefect of discipline in the *Externat* (day school), 1890–1. He taught *huitième* at the Collège du Sacré-Coeur, Annonay, 1891–2, and made final profession of vows on 23 September 1892. He taught the French course from 1892 to 1895, and was ordained to the priesthood on 21 September 1895 by Bishop Joseph-Michel-Frédéric Bonnet of Viviers. After an additional year at the college, he seems to have been absent during the annual retreat in 1896, and no further mention of him occurs in Basilian records.

SOURCE: Pouzol, 'Notices,' Supplément 2.

MILLER, John Joseph, priest, was born on 29 January 1915 at Smethport, Pennsylvania (diocese of Erie), the son of John Miller and Bessie Hussey. He died in Miami, Florida, on 12 May 1978, and is buried in the Basilian plot, Garden of Gethsemane, Forest Park Lawndale Cemetery, Houston.
The Miller family having moved to Toronto soon after his birth, John was educated at Holy Family Parish School and then in the high school section of St Michael's College, graduating in 1933. He entered St Basil's Novitiate, Toronto, taking first vows on 15 August 1934. He studied at Assumption College, Windsor (B.A., University of Western Ontario, 1937); and, after one year of teaching mathematics at Aquinas Institute, Rochester, 1937–8, he did his theological studies at St Basil's Seminary, Toronto, 1937–42. Archbishop James Charles McGuigan ordained him to the priesthood on 17 August 1941 in St Basil's Church, Toronto.
In 1942 Father Miller was appointed to teach at Aquinas Institute, Rochester. After one semester, a lung condition forced his removal to a dryer climate. He taught with the Franciscan Fathers at St Mary's High School, Phoenix, Arizona, but in 1943 became a chaplain in the United States Air Force and was on active duty until 1946, when he was assigned to St Thomas High School, Houston. After one year of teaching he began graduate studies at the University of Arizona, but in 1949

returned to active duty in the Air Force, where he served at three domestic Air Force bases (Bergstrom, Austin, Texas; Homestead, Florida; and Chanute, Illinois) and in foreign posts (Korea and French Morocco).

Upon discharge in 1967 he studied Spanish and undertook promotional work for the Basilian Missions. He served as pastor of Our Lady of Mount Carmel Parish, Wharton, Texas, 1968–70, where he had hopes of founding a training school for missionaries. When that failed to materialize, he moved to Florida to do pastoral ministry, first in the diocese of Orlando and then in the archdiocese of Miami, where he died.

Jack Miller was a man of fine appearance and radiant personality with extraordinary energy and enthusiasm. Father Gerald Martin, who had served with him in Korea, described him, in the homily at his funeral in Key Biscayne, Florida, as 'a model of genuine priestliness who knew how to adjust to new conditions in the modern world without losing one bit of genuine priestly character.' A number of priests came from long distances to be present at the funerals in Florida and in Houston. The lay catechists of St Agnes Parish, Key Biscayne, had unstinting praise for the quality and comprehensiveness of the program that Father Miller had designed and directed.

Though his work kept him apart from the Basilian community for so many years, he made it a point to attend Basilian celebrations and funerals whenever he could. The ill health that plagued him through his life never dampened his enthusiasm for his work and the people he encountered.

SOURCES: GABF; *Annals* 5 (1979) 408–9; *Newsletter* (19 May 1978).

MILLER, Robert Grace, priest, brother of the late Father Richard Miller SJ and of Father Thomas Miller CSB, was born on 5 February 1912 in Rochester, one of five sons of William Francis Miller and Margaret Grace Nelligan. He died in Toronto on 21 December 1997 and is buried in the Basilian plot of Holy Cross Cemetery, Thornhill, Ontario.

Bob Miller was educated at Nazareth Hall, and at Aquinas Institute, Rochester. In 1930 he enrolled in St Michael's College, Toronto (B.A., Honours Philosophy, University of Toronto, 1934). His Honours thesis was a translation of Thomas Aquinas's commentary on the *Peri hermeneias* of Aristotle. He participated actively in dramatics and athletics, held a Carnegie Research Scholarship from 1934 to 1938, and won both the McBrady and the Mercier medals. He did graduate studies at the Institute of Mediaeval Studies, Toronto (M.A., University of Toronto, 1935). His Ph.D. thesis (University of Toronto, 1938) was entitled 'The Notion of the Agent Intellect in Saint Albert the Great.' He entered St Basil's Novitiate, Toronto, in August 1938 and was professed on 15 August 1939. Theological studies followed at St Basil's Seminary and at the Institute (since 1939 'Pontifical Institute'), interrupted by one year of teaching, 1941–2, at Assumption College, Windsor. He was ordained to the priesthood on 15 August 1943 in St Basil's Church, Toronto, by Archbishop James Charles McGuigan.

Father Miller's forty-six years in university work began with an appointment in 1943 to St Thomas More College, Saskatoon, where he rose to the rank of professor of philosophy at the University of Saskatchewan. During this time he was also appointed diocesan director of Catholic Action, founding and editing the *Catholic Action Priests' Magazine*. In 1948 he was appointed to the University of St Thomas, Houston, as head of the department of philosophy. In addition to his academic duties, he served as director of development and in that capacity founded the 'U.S.T. Mardi Gras,' an annual fund-raising event which featured famous cinema and entertainment personalities. In 1951 he was assigned to St Michael's College for post-doctoral work. During this time he began his career of public lecturing and of publishing. His book (see below) was widely used as a textbook in both state and private universities. In 1953 he was appointed to Assumption University, Windsor, where he taught and continued to give public lectures. He remained in Windsor until 1959, when he was appointed to St John Fisher College, Rochester, as chairman of the department of philosophy. After mandatory retirement in 1977, Father Miller undertook a reduced schedule of teaching at Nazareth College, Rochester, until 1989. Though failing eyesight curtailed his activities, his interest in philosophy never abated. As late as 1994 he was preparing for publication a work on the notion of causality in the work of St Thomas Aquinas. During his retirement years he was faithfully assisted by his brother, Father Thomas Miller CSB, until in the spring of 1997 when he was moved to the Basilian Fathers Residence, Toronto, nine months before his death.

Though philosophy was his occupation – even his obsession – Bob Miller was an active participant in the society around him. He was an impressive speaker, clear and confident in his manner, disposed to see the humour in the various situations and ironies of life. He was firm in his principles and convictions – some would have said rigid – though always a seeker of the truth.

BIBLIOGRAPHY:
Book: *Philosophy and Language: The Linguistic Turn.* Albany, N.Y., 1968.
Articles: 'The Roots of Economics,' *Quarterly Review* (February 1942); 'Methodology of Normative Sciences,' *Quarterly Review* (June 1942); 'Some Legal Threats to Peaceful Democracy,' *Culture* 4 (June 1945) 284–93; 'Problems of the Spiritual and Temporal Orders,' *Catholic Action Priests' Magazine* (January, March, May, September, December 1947; January, February, March, May, June 1948); 'Areas of Action,' *Forum* (September 1948); 'The Philosophy of Personality,' *Messenger* (March 1948); 'An Aspect of Averroes' Influence on St Albert,' *Mediaeval Studies* 16 (1954) 57–71; 'The Ontological Argument in St Anselm and Descartes,' *Modern Schoolman* 32 (May 1955) 341–9, 33 (November 1955) 31–8; 'The Empiricist's Dilemma: Either Metaphysics or Nonsense,' *Proceedings of the American Catholic Philosophical Association* 29 (1955) 151–76; 'Empiricisms and Varieties of Metaphysics,' *Papers of the Michigan Academy of Science, Arts & Letters* 42 (1957) 309–28; 'The Philosophy of History,' *Proceedings of the Canadian Philosophical Association* (1958); 'Linguistic Analysis and Metaphysics,' *Proceedings of the American Catholic Philosophical Association* 34 (1960) 80–109; 'St Anselm on the Existence of God,' *Readings in Ancient and Medieval Philosophy*, College Readings Series 6 (Westminster, Md., 1960) 185–80; 'Realistic and Unrealistic Empiricisms,' *New Scholasticism* 35 (1961) 311–37; 'Conceptualism,' *New Catholic Encyclopedia* 4 (New York, 1967) 108–9; 'Universals, Position of Modern Thinkers,' *New Catholic Encyclopedia* 14 (New York, 1967) 454–7, 2d ed. 14 (New York, 2002) 325–8; 'Gilson, Etienne Henry,' *Encyclopedia of Philosophy* 3 (January 1967) 332–4; 'Philosophy of Science: Explanation in History,' *Proceedings of the American Catholic Philosophical Association* 43 (1969) 195–203.
SOURCES: GABF; *Annals* 1 (1944) 54–5, 7 (1990) 14, 8 (1994) 13–14, 9 (1998) 82–3; *Newsletter* (29 December 1997).

MIRABEL, Léon, scholastic, was born at Chapias, commune of Labeaume (Ardèche), c.1875–8. He died on 28 February 1899 and was probably buried in the cemetery on the grounds of the Collège du Sacré-Coeur, Annonay.

Léon studied at the Sainte-Barbe section of the Collège du Sacré-Coeur, Annonay from 1889 to 1895, and made his first profession of vows on 17 September 1897. He supervised the students at Sainte-Barbe for a while, but became afflicted with a painful illness which led to his death. The community records contain no additional information on this young Basilian.

SOURCES: GABF; Pouzol, 'Notices.'

MOFFIT, John Richard, scholastic, was born in Louisville, Ohio (diocese of Youngstown), on 3 March 1853, the son of James and Julia Moffit. He died in Toronto on 2 April 1876 and is buried there in the Basilian plot of St Michael's Cemetery.
After attending local schools and St Louis College, which the Basilians founded in 1867 and directed until 1873 in his native city, John Moffit entered St Basil's Novitiate, Toronto, on 29 September 1872. He resumed his studies at St Michael's College, Toronto, after profession in 1873. Stricken with tuberculosis, he was permitted to take final vows on his deathbed.

SOURCE: GABF.

MOLIN, Dominique Florentin, priest, was born on 18 November 1840 at Issarlès (Ardèche), the son of Hippolyte Molin and Marie Liabeuf.
He died at Labastide-de-Juvénas (Ardèche) on 25 February 1921.
Dominique made his novitiate at Feyzin (Isère, now Rhône) and professed final vows on 6 April 1871 at the Collège de Privas (Ardèche). He taught while studying theology, first at the Petit Séminaire d'Aubenas (Ardèche), 1867–9, then at the Collège de Privas (Ardèche), 1869–71, and finally at the Collège du Sacré-Coeur, Annonay, 1871–3. Bishop Louis Delcusy ordained him to the priesthood on 7 June 1873 in the cathedral of Viviers (Ardèche).

After ordination he remained at the college in Annonay, 1873–7. The community records show him next at the Collège Saint-Pierre in Châteauroux (Indre) in January 1880, where he may have gone in 1877. He was appointed to the Ecole cléricale at Périgueux (Dordogne) in 1880. There he taught *sixième* for four years. In 1884 he returned to the Collège du Sacré-Coeur to *sixième* for another four years. From 1888 to 1891 he served as bursar in the Petit Séminaire de Vernoux (Ardèche). From 1893 he was director at Sainte-Barbe minor seminary, Annonay, serving also as chaplain to the Trinitarian Sisters at the orphanage, rue des Jardins, Annonay. With the exclusion of religious congregations from teaching in 1903, he took refuge in the rectory at Labastide-de-Juvénas (lower Ardèche), where his brother was pastor.

He was appointed assistant to his brother by the bishop on 20 September 1904.

SOURCES: GABF; Pouzol, 'Notices.'

MOLLARET, Elie, scholastic, was born on 5 February 1855 at Montrond, near Saint-Jean-de-Maurienne (Savoy), which at that time was part of the kingdom of Piedmont-Sardinia. He died in Windsor on 5 July 1881 and is buried there in the Basilian plot of Assumption Cemetery.

When he was five years old, Elie Mollaret became a French citizen following the plebiscite held on 22 April 1860, in which the Savoyards voted, 130,533 to 235, in favour of joining France. In the course of the year 1871-2 Elie went to the Collège du Sacré-Coeur, Annonay, Saint-Barbe section, where his brother Marc was already enrolled. Both young men helped with the supervision of the study-hall and recreation periods.

Elie's brother Marc entered the Basilian novitiate at Feyzin (Isère, now Rhône) in 1875 and was professed in 1876, but did not persevere in the community. Elie Mollaret went to Canada in 1876 and made his novitiate at Assumption College, Windsor, where Father Michael *Ferguson was his novice master. While continuing his studies for the priesthood, 1877-81, he taught at Assumption College until he fell victim to a painful illness which brought about his death on 5 July 1881. It was said of Elie Mollaret that, although outwardly reserved, inwardly he was not lacking in warmth and generosity.

SOURCES: GABF; Kirley, *Community in France* 219n526, 239n568; Pouzol, 'Notices.'

MOLLIER, Victorin, priest, was born on 30 April 1838, at Aubenas (Ardèche), the son of Alexandre Laurent Mollier and Jeanne-Marie ('Jenny') Jouve. The registry office in Privas (Ardèche) recorded his name as Régis-Victor Mollier. He died on 13 September 1888 and was buried in the Basilian cemetery on the grounds of the Collège du Sacré-Coeur, Annonay.

After studies at the Petit Séminaire d'Aubenas and at the Collège des Cordeliers, Annonay, Victorin was received as a novice on 19 March 1861. Bishop Louis Delcusy ordained him to the priesthood on 10 June 1865 in the cathedral at Viviers (Ardèche). While studying theology he supervised students in the study hall and on recreation, first at the Collège des Cordeliers, 1861–7, and then in the new location of the Collège du Sacré-Coeur on Mont Saint-Denis, Annonay, 1867–9. For the next nineteen years, 1869–88, he served as bursar at the Collège du Sacré-Coeur.

SOURCES: GABF; Chomel, *Collège d'Annonay* 517; Kirley, *Community in France* 241n570, 246n576, 247n580; Pouzol, 'Notices.'

MOLONY (MOLONEY), Patrick, priest, the first Basilian to go to North America, was born in the diocese of Killaloe, Ireland, on 18 April 1813. He died in France in Annonay on 8 April 1880 and is buried there in the cemetery on the grounds of the Collège du Sacré-Coeur.

Patrick Molony was sent at an early age to the Irish Seminary in Paris. There an acquaintance invited him to teach English at the Collège des Cordeliers, Annonay, where he went in December 1835. He was ordained a priest on 24 December 1841, then joined the Basilians on 25 August 1842. Shortly afterwards he returned to Ireland where he spent two years fulfilling obligations to his native diocese. Upon his return to France in 1846 he was appointed to the Basilian college at Feyzin (Isère, now Rhône) and in 1847 he went to the Petit Séminaire de Vernoux (Ardèche) to be assistant to the master of novices and pastor of the parish of Saint-Apollinaire.

When a former student, François Armand de Charbonnel, was named bishop of Toronto in 1850, he asked Father Molony to accompany him to Toronto and to work with his Irish immigrant flock there. With permission of the superior general he accepted. In a letter to a confrere in Vernoux he describes the two-week crossing from Southhampton, England, to New York City, where his sisters and brother already lived. The party then travelled up the Hudson River and Lake Champlain, crossing overland to Montreal, and finally up the St Lawrence and Lake Ontario to Toronto, where, on the morning of 21 September 1850, a crowd of 'fine people, poor children of Erin, made much ado' at their arrival. Toronto had thirty-five thousand inhabitants, of which seven thousand were Catholics. Father Molony was named assistant at St Michael's Cathedral, where he became well known for his preaching. He also served as chaplain to the Catholic troops in the Toronto Garrison, and taught in an ecclesiastical school that Bishop Charbonnel had opened in the episcopal residence. He writes, 'I am at the same time superior, recreation master, professor of *huitième, sixième*, and *troisième*, in short a true Basilian in every sense of the word. ... I devote five hours a day to providing them with class.'

When the school, known since 1852 as St Michael's College, outgrew the confines of the cathedral rectory, Father Molony and four other Basilians moved with it to Clover Hill, north of the city, in 1856. But, when differences with the bishop about his approach to pastoral duties developed, he was appointed to return to France. He was named first to the Collège de Privas (Ardèche), where volunteers for work in English-speaking Canada were taught English. Later he was stationed at the novitiate at Feyzin. In 1878 he was called back to the Collège du Sacré-Coeur, where he died.

SOURCES: GABF; J.F. Boland, 'An Analysis of the Problems and Difficulties of the Basilian Fathers in Toronto, 1850–1860,' unpublished Ph.D. thesis (University of Ottawa, 1955); Chomel, *Collège d'Annonay* 318–19; Hoskin, *St Basil's*; Kirley, *Congregation in France* 1, 234; Madden, *St Basil's*; Pouzol, 'Notices'; Roume, *Origines* 300, 316–26, 347; L.K. Shook, 'St Michael's College, the Formative Years 1850–1853,' *CCHA Report* 17 (1950) 37–52.

MONAGHAN, Francis Emmett, priest, was born on 9 November 1920 in Houston, the son of Joseph Monaghan and Margaret Folse. He died in Houston on 7 April 1995 and is buried there in the Basilian plot, Garden of Gethsemane, Forest Park Lawndale Cemetery.

'Frank' Monaghan met the Basilians in his teens when the family moved to St Anne's Parish, Houston, where he was to become pastor many years later. He attended St Thomas High School, Houston, after which he spent one year at the University of Houston. He entered St Basil's Novitiate, Toronto, in 1939, making first profession on 12 September 1940. He was then appointed to St Basil's Seminary, Toronto, for university studies (B.A., University of Toronto, 1944) and for theology, 1944–8. During his theology course he also studied music at the Royal Conservatory of Music in Toronto (A.R.T.C.M., 1947). He was ordained to the priesthood on 22 June 1947 in St Anne's Church, Houston, by Bishop Christopher E. Byrne.

Father Monaghan remained at St Basil's Seminary as professor of music and treasurer from 1949 to 1953. He was then appointed to the University of St Thomas, Houston, where he exercised the same two functions. In 1958 he went to St Anne's Parish as assistant. He continued to teach at the university until 1964, when he was named pastor and rector of St Anne's, offices he held until 1973. His remarkable pastoral talents helped make St Anne's a model parish in the diocese for the spirit of community and the generosity of the parishioners.

In 1973 Father Monaghan returned to St Thomas and became an integral part of the life of the university, serving at various times as lecturer in music, director of alumni services, university treasurer, vice-president of community services, scholarship director and a member of the board of directors. He was very much a public figure in Houston, where he was involved in the Texas Conference of Churches, Division of Research and Planning, and served on the Diocesan Commission on the Arts. He was named Knight Commander of the Equestrian Order of the Holy Sepulchre of Jerusalem and a Knight of the Military and Hospitaller Order of Saint Lazarus of Jerusalem. In 1968 the Seminary of Our Lady of Penafrancia in the Philippines conferred on him the degree of Doctor of Humanities, *honoris causa*. New pipe organs at both St Anne's Church and the Chapel of St Basil at the University of St Thomas were subscribed and named in his honour, and a scholarship at St Anne's School was established in his memory.

An accomplished pianist and gifted with a fine singing voice, Frank Monaghan had his own radio program in Houston before entering the Basilians. In the community on many happy occasions he led his Basilian confreres, gathered around the piano, in lively sing-songs of popular music or entertained them with flawless renditions of Chopin. Always ready to help others, he once said: 'I have received too much from the Lord, I could never give enough to repay it all. So I try to use every opportunity, be it serious or frivolous, to serve and help others.' Father William Young amplified this in his homily at Father Monaghan's funeral: 'He never refused to make his priesthood available to anyone who asked. He never said no even though the past few years had made everything, even walking, difficult for him. ... Like all of us he was not perfect, but he was a generous and caring priest.'

BIBLIOGRAPHY: 'Spirit of Plain Chant,' *Benedicamus* 4 (October 1950).
SOURCES: GABF; *Annals* 1 (1947) 151, 7 (1991) 10, 8 (1996) 98–100; *Newsletter* (1 June 1995).

MONIN, Jean, priest, was born on 2 November 1829 at Moras, near Anneyron (Drôme, diocese of Valence), the son of Jean Monin and Marie Pupat. He died in Annonay on 6 April 1899 and is buried there in the cemetery on the grounds of the Collège du Sacré-Coeur.

After attending the Collège du Bourg-de-Péage (Drôme), Jean Monin enrolled in the Sainte-Barbe section of the Collège des Cordeliers, Annonay, in 1846, where he took rhetoric and philosophy and successfully passed the baccalaureate examination. He was received as a novice on 1 November 1849 and was ordained to the priesthood on 25 May 1854 in the chapel of the Collège des Cordeliers by Bishop Joseph-Hippolyte Guibert of Viviers, later archbishop of Tours and then cardinal archbishop of Paris.

From 1849 to 1857 Jean Monin taught French in the lower grades at the Collège de Privas (Ardèche), the Collège des Cordeliers, and at the Petit Séminaire de Vernoux (Ardèche). From 1857 to 1879 he was professor of humanities, rhetoric, and philosophy successively in the Basilian colleges in Annonay and Privas (Ardèche) and at the Petit Séminaire de Vernoux. He was the director of the college at Bourg-Saint-Andéol, 1879–81. With the closure of this school he became chaplain to the Ursuline Sisters at the Couvent Sainte-Marie, Annonay, and remained in that position for eighteen years, 1881–99. He died at Sainte-Barbe after a brief illness.

When vows were proposed in 1852 to replace promises, Jean Monin delayed his profession until 14 February 1869. He was elected to the general council in 1883 and was a member of it until his death. As a teacher he had a reputation for clarity and methodical presentation and for kindness to his students, and was a popular and effective spiritual director.

SOURCES: GABF; Kirley, *Community in France* 70n178, 71n181, 79, 124n305, 137n347, 147n373, 244; Pouzol, 'Notices'; Roume, *Origines* 347; *Semaine religieuse de Viviers* (14 April 1899).

MONOT, Louis Michel, priest, was born on 30 August 1814 in Annonay, the son of André Monot and Anne Roux. He died at Privas (Ardèche) on 4 October 1877 and is buried in the Basilian plot of the cemetery at Privas.

Louis Michel Monot studied at the Collège des Cordeliers, Annonay, from 1827 to 1835, in the *externat* (day school) and later in the Sainte-Barbe section, the Basilian minor seminary. While studying theology he taught grammar and literature at the Collège de Privas (Ardèche) and at the Collège des Cordeliers, Annonay. He did his novitiate year,

1838–9, as a deacon under the direction of Father Germain *Deglesne in Annonay, and was ordained a priest on Holy Saturday, 16 March 1839, in Grenoble (Isère).

Father Monot taught humanities at the Collège des Cordeliers, 1839–41, and rhetoric and philosophy at the Collège de Feyzin (Isère, now Rhône), 1841–6. He was to spend the next twenty-eight years teaching in minor seminaries, first at Bourg-Saint-Andéol (Ardèche), 1846–52, and then at Aubenas (Ardèche), 1852–74. He served as superior of the Petit Séminaire d'Aubenas from 1859 to 1874, but relinquished the office out of obedience when the diocesan administration judged him to be too lenient with the students. Humbly he accepted a move to the *externat* (day school) of the Collège de Privas in 1874, where he died three years later.

Father Monot was a superb Latin scholar who held a licence in classics from the Université de Montpellier, where his examining jury congratulated him for his original composition of Latin verse. He translated into Latin the Basilian Constitutions in 1863, and into Latin verse the *Fables de Florian* as well as passages from the great tragedies of Corneille and Racine. He was a member of the Basilian general council from 1868 to 1877. His approach to teaching and preaching retreats could be summed up in the words *dulcis et humilis cordis*.

SOURCES: GABF; Chomel, *Collège d'Annonay* 72, 300–2; Kirley, *Community in France* 32, 59, 150n384; Pouzol, 'Notices'; Roume, *Origines* 346.

MONTAGUE, Robert Michael, priest, was born in West Saint John, New Brunswick, on 21 December 1918, the fourth of seven children of Hugh Montague and Catherine Barry. He died in Edmonton, Alberta, on 27 October 1968 and was buried in the Basilian plot of Holy Cross Cemetery, Thornhill, Ontario.

After attending St Patrick's Grade School and Saint Vincent's High School, Saint John, Bob Montague worked for a time, but in January 1941 enlisted in the Royal Canadian Navy. He quickly rose to the command of HMCS *Port Hope*, a mine-sweeper on convoy duty in the North Atlantic, and by the end of the war held the rank of lieutenant commander. Following his discharge he enrolled in St Michael's College, Toronto, and in September of 1946 entered St Basil's Novitiate at Richmond Hill, Ontario. After first profession on 3 October 1947, he resumed his studies (B.A., University of Toronto, 1950). During his senior year he began the study of theology at St Basil's Seminary, Toronto. He was ordained priest on 29 June 1952 in St Basil's Church, Toronto, by Cardinal James Charles McGuigan.

Western Canada was the scene of Father Montague's priestly work. He taught at St Thomas More College in Saskatoon, Saskatchewan, from 1953 to 1956. During the year 1956–7 he attended the graduate school at Assumption University of Windsor (M.A., Psychology, 1957). Returning to St Thomas More College he resumed teaching and also served as chaplain to the Newman Association at the University of Saskatchewan. In 1965 he obtained a sabbatical leave for studies in sociology, but before he began these he was appointed rector and superior at St Joseph's College, Edmonton, Alberta. One year later his health failed and he underwent surgery for stomach ulcers. In the spring of 1968 he was found to be suffering from cancer of the esophagus, and died in October of the same year.

During his student years Bob Montague was active in dramatics, and was long remembered for striking performances as Thomas à Becket in *Murder in the Cathedral*. He possessed a fine tenor voice and was fond of singing Irish songs. Always a humble, unobtrusive, and ever-capable gentleman, the qualities of leadership that he displayed as a young naval officer brought him community responsibilities: local councillor, St Thomas More College, 1955–6 and 1957–65, and the headship of St Joseph's College from 1965. He was elected to the priests' senate of the archdiocese of Edmonton. An obituary notice said of him that students loved him 'for his qualities as a person – his warmth, his wit, his gentleness.'

BIBLIOGRAPHY: 'Seminarians Meet at St Michael's College,' *Benedicamus* 3 (January 1950) 21.
SOURCES: GABF; *Annals* 1 (1947) 116, 2 (1952) 59, 4 (1969) 130–1; *Newsletter* (29 October 1968).

MONTGOLFIER, Auguste de, priest, was born on 9 January 1800 at Vidalon-les-Annonay (diocese of Viviers [from 1801 to 1822 of Mende]), the son of Jean-Baptiste and Méranie de Montgolfier. He died at Privas on 26 October 1859 and was buried in the family plot at Saint-Marcel-les-Annonay.

Auguste, the grand-nephew of the inventors of the hot-air balloon, called '*montgolfière*' in their honour, was a student at the Collège des Cordeliers in the early years before the Association of Priests of St Basil was established. In the academic year 1816–17 he was awarded the prize in physics and chemistry. He interrupted his studies to serve an apprenticeship in the family paper mill at Saint-Marcel-les-Annonay, and spent a year in Germany and England to become more proficient in this industry. On his return to France he was director of a paper manufactory at Saint-Maur, near Paris, where he introduced several modifications in making paper.

In 1829 he resumed his studies at Sainte-Barbe, the Basilian minor seminary, where he would remain for fifteen years. He studied philosophy, 1829-30, under Father Germain *Deglesne, and theology, 1830-6, while assisting at Sainte-Barbe in various capacities. At thirty-six years of age he was ordained priest at Viviers by Bishop Abdon Bonnel on 17 December 1836. The preceding summer he had obtained certification at Privas to become director of the Ecole moderne de Français, which had been transferred in 1827 from Sainte-Claire to the Collège des Cordeliers. He continued to live at Sainte-Barbe until 1844, as bursar until 1841 and as superior, 1841-4, replacing Father Vincent *Duret, who had died in 1841. When Bishop Joseph-Hippolyte Guibert confided the direction of his minor seminaries to the Basilians, Montgolfier became superior of the Petit Séminaire de Saint Charles at Vernoux (Ardèche), 1844-6. There the students were impressed by the deep piety of their superior. For his part Father de Montgolfier was concerned about the finances of the school and the lack of receptivity of the students to mathematics. From 1846 to 1848 he was superior of the Petit Séminaire in Bourg-Saint-Andéol and then returned to Vernoux, 1848-56. During the year 1848-9 he was director of the novitiate, which had been moved to Vernoux. In 1856 when Father Germain *Deglesne died, he once again became master of novices, first at Sainte-Barbe, 1856-7, and then at the new location at Privas (Ardèche), 1857-9.

Father Charles *Roume referred to Auguste de Montgolfier as 'a most obedient religious, the humblest of superiors.' Father Adrien *Chomel stressed how effective he was at instilling the love of God and neighbour in his novices. Father André *Fayolle, superior at Privas, said, 'During the two years I lived with Father de Montgolfier I saw him do everything one reads about in the lives of the saints.'

SOURCES: ABA; Chomel, *Collège d'Annonay* 216, 222, 226-48; Chanoine Fromenton, *Petit Séminaire de Vernoux* (Aubenas, 1922); Pouzol, 'Notices'; Roume, *Origines* 216, 222, 226-48, 288, 302, 346-7, 354-62, 366-71.

MONTREUIL, Antoine, priest, member of the Congregation 1889-

1902, was born in Windsor on 17 January 1870, the son of Jean Montreuil and Charlotte Lajeunesse.

Antoine Montreuil made a brilliant course at Assumption College, Windsor, before making his novitiate year at Beaconfield House, Plymouth, England, 17 August 1889–1 September 1890. He did his theological studies at the Petit Séminaire de Vernoux (Ardèche), 1890–2, while working as prefect of discipline. He returned to Canada at the end of the school year, made his profession of final vows on 23 August 1892, and was ordained priest on 15 July 1894.

Father Montreuil taught at Assumption College, 1894–5, then served as assistant at Assumption Parish in Windsor until 1899, when he was transferred to St Michael's College, Toronto. Instead he took up residence at the Canadian College, Rome, in 1900, and on 25 March 1902 the general council approved his request for secularization.

SOURCES: GABF; Kirley, *Community in France* 214n516, 220n528, 235n562, 240n569; Pouzol, 'Notices,' Supplément 2.

MOONEY, Donald Richard, priest, brother of Fathers John, Paul, and Thomas Mooney of the diocese of London, Ontario, was born on 3 October 1925 in Windsor, the son of Frederick Mooney and Frances Helen Moran. He died in Houston, Texas, on 15 September 1992 and is buried in the Basilian plot of Heavenly Rest Cemetery, Windsor.

Don (later 'Moon' to his confreres) received his elementary and secondary education at public schools in Woodslee, Ontario, where the family had relocated from Windsor. He took grade XIII at St Joseph's High School, East Windsor, 1942–3, and then enrolled in Assumption College as a Basilian 'junior.' He entered St Basil's Novitiate, Toronto, in 1944, was professed on 15 August 1945, and returned to Assumption College (B.A., University of Western Ontario, 1947). He was appointed to St Thomas High School, Houston, for one year of teaching and first year of theology. He completed his theology courses at St Basil's Seminary, Toronto, 1948–51, and was ordained a priest on 15 August 1951 in St Basil's Church, Toronto, by Cardinal James Charles McGuigan.

Father Mooney began his forty-year apostolate in Basilian parishes and missions with an appointment to Ste Anne's Parish, Detroit, serving as assistant for two years, 1951–3, during which time he also studied Spanish. He was to return to Ste Anne's some years later as pastor and rector, 1968–71. His other appointments were: Our Lady of Mount Carmel Parish, Wharton, Texas, as assistant, 1953–7, as pastor and rector, 1965–8, and again as pastor, 1971–80; St Basil's Parish, Angleton, Texas, as assistant, 1957–60, and councillor, 1958–60, then again as assistant and councillor, 1962–5; St Theresa's Parish, Sugar Land, Texas, as assistant and councillor, 1960–2; Holy Family Parish, Missouri City, Texas, 1980–3.

In 1983 Don Mooney joined the Basilian mission apostolate in Mexico, with an appointment to the parish of Santa María de la Asunción, Caltepec, where he worked for the next nine years, coping with a heart condition which finally proved fatal. He gave himself entirely to his people, striving to live as they lived in the poorest of conditions, being constantly at their service – a good shepherd. Never highly organized, he adopted rather easily, it might be said, the attitudes to time and pace of life of his flock. Though he might well have survived longer had he taken more care of his health, he would not be constricted in his devotion, tramping up and down rugged hills and desert areas to minister and to bring the word of God. His memory lived on among his people: a full eight years after his death, the mere mention of his name by Bishop Ricardo Ramírez CSB at an ordination ceremony raised a loud and lengthy cheer.

SOURCES: GABF; *Annals* 2 (1951) 37, 7 (1993) 138–40; *Newsletter* (8 October 1992).

MORLEY, Arthur Joseph, priest, was born in England on 15 November 1876, the son of Henry Morley and Elizabeth Dorsey. He died at Windsor on 6 November 1914 and was buried there in the Basilian plot of Assumption Cemetery.

Arthur Morley emigrated as a boy to the United States and spent four years working in the cotton mills at Lowell, Massachusetts. He was received into the Catholic Church at Immaculate Conception Parish there on 20 June 1895. Two years at Huntsville, Ontario, preceded his enrolling in 1899 in the high school section of St Michael's College, Toronto, to begin study for the priesthood. In 1901 he entered St Basil's Novitiate, Toronto, and was professed on 21 July 1902. Undergraduate studies at Assumption College, Windsor, and theological courses at St Basil's Scholasticate, Toronto, preceded ordination to the priesthood on 18 August 1907.

Father Morley served as assistant at Ste Anne's Parish, Detroit, 1907–9. He was then appointed to Assumption College, where he taught history until his death in 1914 from cancer.

Short and slight of build, Father Morley's favourite recreation was walking. The *Golden Jubilee Volume of Assumption College* stated, 'From early youth, he waged ceaseless warfare against ill health, but no one ever heard him make a complaint, nor did he ever fail to be at his post when it was physically possible for him to be there.' The Assumption *Dionysian* (the 1915 yearbook), added: 'He spent his recreations among the students and his conversations were not only charming but instructive, uplifting and edifying. His heart was big and his charity unbounded.'

SOURCES: GABF; Charles Collins, 'Basilians I Have Known,' transcribed in Robert J. Scollard, 'Historical Notes C.S.B.' 10 62–5 (GABF); *Dionysian* (Windsor, 1915); *Jubilee, Assumption.*

MORRISSEY, John BERTHOLD, priest, was born on 8 September 1898 in Hamilton, Ontario, one of two children of James Morrissey and Laura McDonald. He died in Toronto on 7 October 1981 and is buried in the Basilian plot of Holy Cross Cemetery, Thornhill, Ontario. 'Bert' attended St Patrick's Separate School and St Mary's High School, Hamilton, where he held a scholarship and graduated with honours in 1914. He attended St Michael's College, Toronto, maintaining a standing with distinction in classics. In 1918 he entered St Basil's Novitiate, Toronto, and made first profession on 27 May 1919. He was appointed to Assumption College, Windsor, where he studied theology and concurrently took undergraduate courses. In 1922 he was moved to the Basilian Scholasticate, Toronto, to continue the two streams of study. He was ordained to the priesthood by Bishop Michael O'Brien of Peterborough, Ontario, on 24 February 1923 in St Michael's Cathedral, Toronto, and received a B.A. from the University of Toronto in May of the same year. A few months later he was granted interim high school assistant's certification from the Ontario College of Education.

In August 1923 Father Morrissey returned to Assumption College to teach part-time and to assist at Assumption Parish. After only one year, however, suffering from psychological anxieties, he suddenly left Windsor. Despite wide publicity, his whereabouts were unknown for thirteen years, but in 1937 he asked to be readmitted to community life. After a period of treatment in Montreal he was appointed to Holy Rosary Seminary, Toronto, and then to St Basil's Novitiate, Richmond Hill, to teach Latin to the novices. In 1956 he was appointed assistant pastor at Ste Anne's Parish, Detroit, and was local councillor there in

1964–5. He was appointed in July 1965 as house and school librarian at St Michael's College School, Toronto, and was sacristan of the chapel and a popular confessor to the students. He retired from the library in 1975, but continued to give assistance there and to be a faithful fan at the Junior B hockey games on Sunday nights.

Despite his earlier anxieties, Father Morrissey grew old gracefully. His classroom reached beyond the school to the neighbourhood and even farther afield. His attention to the needs and well-being of others, given with humour and kindness, strengthened the community. He was much devoted to the Blessed Virgin Mary and to praying the rosary. Having developed a serious heart condition, he died peacefully in hospital on the feast of the Most Holy Rosary.

SOURCES: GABF; *Annals* 4 (1970) 135, 5 (1974) 6, (1980) 458, 6 (1982) 103–4; *Newsletter* (29 October 1981); McMahon, *Pure Zeal* 45–9.

MORRO, James Peter, priest, was born on 19 May 1930 in Philadelphia, Pennsylvania, one of twin sons of James V. Morro and Margaret DeStefano. He died in Toronto on 10 October 1992 and is buried in the Basilian plot of Holy Cross Cemetery, Thornhill, Ontario.

After attending St Monica's Parish School and La Salle College High School in Philadelphia, 'Jim' enrolled in La Salle College, majoring in French and education (B.A., 1951). After a year as a substitute teacher in art, drawing, English, and history in Philadelphia schools, he won a scholarship from the French government, 1952. He studied at the Sorbonne and also taught English at the Lycée Jacques-Amyot, Auxerre (Yonne). He returned to the United States in 1954 and found employment in the Lower Moreland Township School District, Huntingdon Valley, Pennsylvania, where he taught French and dramatics. He obtained permanent Pennsylvania teaching certification from Pennsylvania State University in 1956. While with the school district he was active in French Teachers' Associations on the local and regional level. During the summers he attended the Université Laval, Quebec City, and Villanova University in Philadelphia. While at Laval he learned about the Basilian Fathers from Father William *O'Brien, and entered St Basil's Novitiate, Rochester, in 1958. He moved with it to the new site in Pontiac, Michigan, where he made his first profession of vows on 12 September 1959. His appointment to St Basil's Seminary, Toronto, to study theology was interrupted by a year of teaching French and English at Michael Power High School, Etobicoke, 1960–1; and, after resuming his theology course, he was ordained a priest on 15 December 1963 in St Basil's Church, Toronto, by Cardinal James Charles McGuigan.

Father Morro completed studies for a *maîtrise ès arts* at Laval in 1963, submitting a thesis on 'Les traductions anglaises des pièces de Jean Anouilh.' He served as director of publications for the Pontifical Institute of Mediaeval Studies, Toronto, 1964–74, and was treasurer of the Institute for the first six of those years. In 1974 he was allowed to accept an invitation from Bishop Leonard Crowley, auxiliary of Montreal, to work as chaplain in the English Catholic School System, first at Marymount High School, 1974–85, and then at both D'Arcy McGee High School and St Pius X Comprehensive School, 1985–9. He also served as chaplain to the Sisters of the Precious Blood, preached retreats to seminarians and sisters, and served on various committees for the school board, the archdiocese, and the Canada Council. He was active as well in the Montreal Ministry to Priests Program. For most of his years in Montreal he lived at St Patrick's Parish and regularly helped with liturgies.

After a preparatory six-month study program in 1989 he took charge of the Basilian Fathers Residence (Infirmary), Toronto, but his own failing health forced him to resign in 1991. He lived for a time at Scarborough Court, a retirement facility, where he explored the possibility of establishing a community of retired or infirm Basilians. In August 1992, he was hospitalized for serious circulatory problems which two months later proved fatal.

Father Morro was a man of huge bodily dimensions with equally huge dimensions of affability, humour, and generosity. He taught, preached, conversed, and ate with gusto. He struggled with his weight, but joked about it at his own expense. Asked by a doctor if he had trouble swallowing, his reply was, 'Would to God I did!' A gourmet cook himself, his pastry recipes had to include 'Lots of sugar, lots of butter, lots of cream.' He accepted with good nature the fun and confusion caused by occasional visits from his identical twin brother, Ferdinand. A truly magnanimous soul, Jim Morro gave encouragement to everyone, especially the young.

BIBLIOGRAPHY: 'Language Labs. Two Views,' *Basilian Teacher* 4 (May 1960) 242–4.
SOURCES: GABF; *Annals* 3 (1964) 292, 7 (1993) 145–7; *Newsletter* (26 October 1992).

MORROW, John M., priest, was born on a farm in Tecumseh Township, Simcoe County, Ontario (diocese of Toronto), on 20 July 1845, the son of George Morrow and Elizabeth Caperly. He died in Toronto on 1 August 1878 and was buried there in the Basilian plot of St Michael's Cemetery.

After education in local schools, John Morrow went to St Michael's College, Toronto, in 1861. He entered St Basil's Novitiate, Toronto, on 25 July 1868, took final vows on 2 December 1871, and was ordained to the priesthood on 1 May 1872. At the time of his ordination Father Morrow was in poor health. He was sent on sick leave to France, where he lived for a time at the Collège du Sacré-Coeur, Annonay, but the climate did little for him. He returned to St Michael's College as prefect of discipline. He died in 1878 from tuberculosis.

Father John Morrow's retiring disposition, coupled with his poor health, hindered his reputation from spreading beyond the confines of St Michael's College.

SOURCE: GABF.

MOULIN, Jean Paul Emile, was born on 14 September 1830 at Mende (Lozère, diocese of Mende). He died on 6 June 1873 and is buried on the grounds of the Collège du Sacré-Coeur, Annonay. Two of his sisters became religious, one in the community of the Coeur-Agonisant-de-Jésus in Lyon, the other with the Trinitarians in Valence.

Ordained to the priesthood for his own diocese in 1855, then later attracted to the education of youth, Father Moulin decided to become a Basilian in Annonay. He made his novitiate at Feyzin (Isère, now Rhône) in 1863–4 and professed final vows on 21 September 1866. He taught at various institutions staffed by the Basilians: the Collège des Cordeliers, Annonay, 1864–5, the Collège de Privas, (Ardèche), 1865–7, the Petit Séminaire de Vernoux (Ardèche), 1867–8, and the Ecole cléricale de Périgueux (Dordogne), 1868–72.

In June 1872 he fell sick and returned to the scholasticate at Sainte-Barbe, Annonay, where he was cared for by the Sisters of Providence. His health improved to the extent that by September 1872 he was able to serve for a few months as chaplain to the church of Trachin, Annonay. He experienced renewed heart trouble with palpitations and shortness of breath, however, so that by Christmas of 1872 he could no longer lie down but had to remain in an armchair. After six more months of resignation in suffering, he died at the age of forty-two.

SOURCES: GABF; Pouzol, 'Notices.'

MOURARET, Casimir, priest, member of the Congregation from about 1868 to 1882, the son of Etienne Mouraret, a farmer, and Victoire Sophie Roure, was born in the Mas Gau, commune of Montréal, canton of Largentière (Ardèche), on 4 March 1848.
Casimir studied philosophy at the Collège des Cordeliers, 1865–6, and entered the novitiate at Feyzin (Isère, now Rhône), making final profession of vows on 3 March 1871. Bishop Louis Delcusy of Viviers ordained him a priest on 23 December 1871. He taught in various schools staffed by Basilians: the Petit Séminaire d'Aubenas (Ardèche), 1867–8, the Petit Séminaire de Vernoux (Ardèche), 1868–72, the Ecole cléricale de Périgueux (Dordogne), 1872–3, the *externat* (day school) at Privas (Ardèche), 1873–5, and the Collège Saint-Pierre in Châteauroux (Indre), 1875–82. In the latter school he taught rhetoric from 1875 to 1879, and was superior of the local house from 1880 to 1882. When the Basilians withdrew from the school in 1882, Father Mouraret withdrew from the community and, apparently, from the priesthood, after which nothing more is known of his life.

SOURCES: Kirley, *Community in France* 31; Pouzol, 'Notices,' Supplément 3.

MOURARET, Denis, priest, uncle of Father Jean Roure CSB, was born on 27 July 1866 at Montréal (Ardèche), canton of Largentière. He died in Annonay on 25 March 1938 and is buried there in the cemetery on the grounds of the Collège du Sacré-Coeur.
Denis Mouraret did his secondary studies at the Collège du Sacré-Coeur, Annonay, in the Sainte-Barbe section. He entered the novitiate at Beaconfield House, Plymouth, England, on 24 September 1887. Bishop Pierre Dufal CSC, former coadjutor bishop of Galveston, Texas, ordained him to the priesthood on 20 September 1890 in the chapel of the Collège du Sacré-Coeur. He earned a *licence ès lettres* from the Institut catholique de Paris in 1888 and taught humanities, rhetoric, and philosophy in various Basilian schools: the Collège Saint-Charles, Blidah, Algeria, 1888–9, the Collège du Sacré-Coeur, Annonay, 1889–91, the Collège Saint-Augustin, Bône, Algeria, 1891–5, and the Petit Séminaire d'Aubenas (Ardèche), 1895–1903.

When the Basilians were expelled from teaching in 1903, he served as curate in the parish at Jaujac (Ardèche) for one year, and then returned to the Petit Séminaire d'Aubenas, a secular priest in the eyes of the state, to teach rhetoric, 1904–26. He became its director, 1907–13, and bursar, 1919–26.

When the Basilians opened their novitiate at Bordighera, Italy, in 1926, Father Denis Mouraret was the assistant novice master until 1935, and also acted as chaplain to communities of French sisters who had moved to Italy when their convents were confiscated. He retired to Maison Saint-Joseph in Annonay in 1935. He had a priest-nephew, a teacher in the Grand Séminaire de Viviers, who was killed during the First World War.

Father Mouraret was a member of the general council in France, 1922–8 and 1935–8. A tall man, slightly stooped, he always wore tinted glasses to protect his eyesight and as a result looked older than he really was. Quiet, gentle, humble, with a keen intelligence, he kept his good humour and lively sense of community to the end.

SOURCES: GABF; Kirley, *Community in France* 172, 184, 197, 204, 240n569, 239n568; Kirley, *Congregation in France* 42, 76n35, 81–2, 87, 116, 119, 125, 135, 139, 144, 146–7, 154, 156, 174, 184–5, 212–13; Pouzol, 'Notices.'

MOURGUE, Marcel, priest, younger brother of Father Xavier *Mourgue, was born on 17 December 1859 at Saint-Bonnet-le-Froid (Haute-Loire, diocese of Le Puy), the son of Cyprien Mourgue and Marie Desmartin. He died in Annonay on 2 December 1935 and was buried there in the cemetery on the grounds of the Collège du Sacré-Coeur. Marcel Mourgue studied at the Sainte-Barbe section of the Collège du Sacré-Coeur, Annonay; and, when the anticlerical government closed the Basilian novitiate at Feyzin in 1880, he made his novitiate while helping out as recreation master at the *externat* (day school) of the college, 1882–4. He took final vows on 19 September 1884 and went to Beaconfield House, Plymouth, England, for two years to prepare for ordination to the priesthood. While there, he helped supervise students at Mary Immaculate College. He was ordained to the priesthood on 18 September 1886 by Bishop Joseph-Michel-Frédéric Bonnet in the chapel of the Collège du Sacré-Coeur.

For seventeen years after ordination he taught in various Basilian schools: the Collège du Sacré-Coeur, 1886–8, the Petit Séminaire de Vernoux (Ardèche), 1888–9, the Collège Saint-Augustin, Bône, Algeria,

1889–95, the Petit Séminaire d'Aubenas (Ardèche), 1895–6, the Collège Saint-Charles, Blidah, Algeria, 1896–7, and the Ecole cléricale, Périgueux (Dordogne), 1897–1903.

With the governmental exclusion in 1903 of Basilians from teaching, he worked in parish ministry in the diocese of Périgueux until 1922, when he resumed teaching in the Petit Séminaire d'Aubenas (Ardèche), 1922–4. He assisted the pastor in the parish of Vanosc (Ardèche), 1924–31, before retiring to Maison Saint-Joseph, Annonay.

A victim of diabetes, Father Mourgue consumed a lot of fruit in his room, throwing the pits out the window. From them peach, apricot, and cherry trees sprang up in the yard, which still served as an orchard in the early twenty-first century. He also loved to play the bugle with the school band.

SOURCES: GABF; Kirley, *Community in France* 185, 207, 240n569; Kirley, *Congregation in France* 156, 174, 213; Pouzol, 'Notices.'

MOURGUE, Xavier, priest, older brother of Father Marcel *Mourgue, was born on 7 June 1852 at Saint-Bonnet-le-Froid (Haute-Loire, diocese of Le Puy), the son of Cyprien Mourgue and Marie Desmartin. He died at Saint-Arnaud-de-Belvès, diocese of Périgueux (Dordogne) on 13 February 1912.

Xavier Mourgue studied at the Collège des Cordeliers, Annonay, 1864–7, and at the Sainte-Barbe section of the Collège du Sacré-Coeur, Annonay, 1867–71. He made his novitiate at Feyzin (Isère, now Rhône) and took final vows on 8 December 1875. Bishop Armand de Charbonnel ordained him to the priesthood on 21 September 1878 in the chapel of the Collège du Sacré-Coeur. While studying philosophy and theology Xavier Mourgue taught classes at the Petit Séminaire de Vernoux (Ardèche). After ordination he went to teach for the year 1878–9 at the Ecole cléricale de Périgueux (Dordogne), and was then appointed to the Collège Saint-Pierre in Châteauroux (Indre), where he taught commercial courses, 1879–81. For the next nineteen years he taught in three Basilian schools: the Collège du Sacré-Coeur, Annonay, 1881–4 and 1889–96, the Ecole cléricale de Périgueux, 1884–8 and 1896–1900, and the Collège Saint-Charles, Blidah, Algeria, 1888–9. In the Périgueux diocese he served as assistant at Théviers (Dordogne), 1900–3, and also at Corgnac (Dordogne), 1903–10. He was appointed pastor at Saint-Arnaud-de-Belvès, where he died two years later. Neither he nor his brother Marcel was ever registered as a secular priest in their native diocese of Le Puy; hence their application for a clergy salary after 1903 in accordance with the terms of the concordat was turned down. It mattered little, in fact, as the complete separation of Church and State in 1905 annulled all such clerical salaries.

SOURCES: GABF; Kirley, *Community in France* 185, 207; Pouzol, 'Notices.'

MOYLAN, Thomas Vincent, priest, was born in Toronto on 27 October 1879, the son of William Moylan and Penelope Mulcahy. He died in Toronto on 5 April 1942 and is buried there in the Basilian plot of Mount Hope Cemetery.

Thomas Moylan had a distinguished record at St Basil's Separate School, Toronto, and continued to win prizes in the high school section of St Michael's College, Toronto, 1894-7, and at St Michael's College, 1897-1901. He entered St Basil's Novitiate, Toronto, was professed on 15 August 1902, studied theology at St Basil's Scholasticate, Toronto, and was ordained to the priesthood on 5 August 1906.

Father Moylan was appointed to Assumption College in both teaching and administration, but in 1914 was sent to St Basil's College, Waco, Texas. When the Basilians left there in 1915 he returned to Assumption College as vice-president and director of studies. After a term as master of novices, 1922-5, he again returned to Assumption College. Sleeping sickness, contracted in Texas, gradually diminished his abilities, and in 1930 he retired to St Basil's Scholasticate ('Seminary' from 1937), where he died twelve years later.

Father James *Embser wrote of Father Moylan's 'refinement of manner which made him the perfect religious gentleman.' The *Basilides* said that, during his many years as prefect of studies, the students 'knew it was folly to try to put anything over on him. They remember the eyes that seemed always upon them. ... the unruffled manner, even temper and impartial justice, always strict but never too severe ... ever ready for a friendly chat or to give what help he could.' He understood boys and men and was skilled in assessing their capabilities. At Assumption College he guided many towards the priesthood. In his last years in the scholasticate, though much afflicted by his illness, he was ever an exemplary model of patience and devotion to community life.

BIBLIOGRAPHY: 'Father Plourde As I Knew Him,' *Basilian* 1 (June 1935) 67-9, 79.
SOURCES: GABF; *Basilides, Assumption College* (Windsor, 1930); Charles Collins,

'Basilians I Have Known,' transcribed in Robert J. Scollard, 'Historical Notes C.S.B.' 10 66–70 (GABF); J.W. Embser, 'Father Moylan, a Biography,' *Benedicamus* 4 (March 1951) 26–7, 29; Hoskin, *St Basil's*; Kirley, *Congregation in France* 8; *Jubilee, Assumption*; Power, *Assumption College* 5 22–4, 28, 32, 69, 90.

MUCKLE, Joseph Thomas, priest, brother of Fathers Charles and Francis Muckle of the diocese of Rochester, of Father William Muckle of the archdiocese of Toronto, and of Sister Mary Charles (baptized Elizabeth) of the Sisters of Mercy, Rochester, was born at Middlesex, New York (diocese of Rochester), on 22 January 1887, one of nine children born to Thomas Muckle and Margaret Delaney. He died at Fort Lauderdale, Florida, on 9 May 1967 and is buried in the Basilian plot of Holy Cross Cemetery, Thornhill, Ontario.

Joseph Muckle received his early education at Penn Yan, New York. He attended East High School in Rochester, 1903–4, and St Michael's College, Toronto, 1904–7, before entering St Basil's Novitiate, Toronto. After profession on 15 August 1908, he enrolled in Honours Classics at the University of Toronto, winning the Campbell prize. At the end of three years he withdrew from this course to begin the study of theology at St Basil's Scholasticate, Toronto, and was ordained to the priesthood on 29 June 1915.

Father Muckle was appointed to graduate studies in the School of Letters at the Catholic University of America, Washington (M.A., 1916). His first teaching appointment was to St Michael's College, where he remained until 1919, when he was named superior and principal of Assumption College, Windsor. In October of the same year he finalized the agreement, first proposed by his predecessor Francis *Forster, by which students at Assumption College would be granted degrees from the University of Western Ontario. His other plans for expansion were, however, curtailed by jurisdictional disputes between Bishop Michael Fallon of London and the Basilian superior general, Francis *Forster. For reasons of health he resigned in the fall of 1922 and went to St Thomas High School, Houston. In 1926 he returned to St Michael's College.

In anticipation of the founding of the Institute of Mediaeval Studies, Toronto, Father Muckle spent the year 1927–8 studying Latin palaeography at Harvard University and in Europe. He spent some time at the University of Chicago, but the exact time in question is not clear. He taught at the Institute from 1929 until 1957, when he became Professor Emeritus. An obituary notice in *Mediaeval Studies* notes: 'he introduced a serious study of the classical sources of patristic and mediaeval culture. For many years he lectured on this phase of the classical heritage in such a way that students became interested in the Classics. At heart, he was a philologist and concerned primarily with language and literature rather than with history and philosophy. He was a careful scholar and demanding of students who, at first, often considered him something of an ogre, but later appreciated the fact that *admonere voluit, non mordere.*'

Joseph Muckle was elected a Fellow of the Royal Society of Canada in 1946. The University of Western Ontario conferred on him an LL.D. *honoris causa*, in 1947, and in that same year he was a member of the presidential committee which issued the Innis Report on the reorganization of the School of Graduate Studies in the University of Toronto. At the time of his retirement in 1957 Assumption University of Windsor bestowed on him an honorary LL.D.

Within the Congregation Father Muckle served on the general council, 1932–6, and on local councils. Plagued all through his life by ill health, he spent a good part of his last years on sick leave. He died in 1967 from pulmonary edema. His colleague J.R. *O'Donnell wrote of him that he was 'a man of deep convictions and quite capable of expressing them without counting the odds.'

BIBLIOGRAPHY:

Books: Ed. *Algazel's Metaphysics, a Mediaeval Latin Translation.* Toronto, 1933. Ed. and trans. *Story of Abelard's Adversities.* Toronto 1954; several reprints.
Articles: 'Sterilization: Why Is It Wrong?,' Pamphlet series 26 (Toronto, 1933); 'Purpose of the Institute of Mediaeval Studies,' *Basilian* 2 (December 1936) 143–4; 'The Early Church and the Classics,' *Basilian* 3 (February, March 1937) 30–2, 50–2, 55. For a list of seventeen articles that he published in *Archives d'histoire doctrinale et littéraire du moyen-âge, Mediaevalia et Humanistica, Mediaeval Studies,* and *Transactions of the Royal Society of Canada,* see *Mediaeval Studies* 29 (1967) vi–vii, and R.J. Scollard, *Dictionary of Basilian Biography* (Toronto, 1969) 108–9.
SOURCES: GABF; *Annals* 2 (1955) 395, 3 (1966) 366, 4 (1968) 56–7; *Newsletter* (9 May 1967); *Basilides,* Assumption College (Windsor, 1930); Kirley, *Congregation in France* 237; *Mediaeval Studies* 29 (1967) v–vii; J.R. O'Donnell, 'Joseph Thomas Muckle, 1887–1967,' *Proceedings and Transactions of the Royal Society of Canada* 4th series, 5 (1967) 107–9; Shook, *Catholic Education* 215–16, 219, 225, 282–3, 294, 378. For documentation dealing with Father Muckle's presidency of Assumption College, see Power, *Assumption College* 3 327–31, 336–8, 341–6, 348 and Appendix V, 4 1–32, 221–5.

MULCAHY, Matthew Thomas, priest, grandnephew of Father Michael Joseph *Mulcahy and of Father John Read *Teefy, was born on 7 January 1911 in Orillia, Ontario (archdiocese of Toronto), the son of Matthew Teefy Mulcahy and Gertrude Rolland. He died in Toronto on 18 February 2000 and is buried in the Basilian plot of Holy Cross Cemetery, Thornhill, Ontario.

After graduation from Orillia Collegiate Institute in 1929 'Matt' Mulcahy attended St Michael's College, Toronto (B.A., University of Toronto, 1932), enrolled in the Ontario College of Education, and began teaching high school in Ontario, first at Penetanguishene (three years) and then at South Porcupine (four years). He obtained a specialist's certification in physical education in 1937 and an Ontario High School principal's certification in 1942. By special permission, he delayed his entrance to St Basil's Novitiate, Toronto, until 29 December 1941 (the usual date was 5 August) in order first to earn enough money to pay his income tax. Professed on 8 January 1943, he spent the next six months teaching at St Michael's College School. He studied theology at St Basil's Seminary, Toronto, 1943–7, and was ordained to the priesthood on 15 August 1946 in St Basil's Church by Cardinal James Charles McGuigan.

In 1947 Father Mulcahy was appointed once again to St Michael's College School, where he taught and was Basilian second councillor. In 1951 he was sent to Sudbury, Ontario, to found St Charles College, and where he served as principal and religious superior. During his last year there, 1955–6, he supervised the founding and building of St Mary's College in Sault Ste Marie. As its first principal and superior, he set out to win for St Mary's a reputation for academic excellence and school spirit. In 1961 he returned to St Charles to teach, but in 1962 was appointed to St Paul's High School, Saskatoon, where he taught for one year while living at St Thomas More College. After spending the years 1963–6 as an exchange professor at St Lawrence College, Quebec City, he returned to St Michael's College School, where he remained actively involved for the next thirty-three years.

With all his gifts for administration and human relations, Matt Mulcahy was essentially a teacher, whether of English literature or mathematics, archery or skiing. His greatest joy was to see his students surpass him and achieve excellence. He loved the out-of-doors and participative sports of all kinds. He supervised Strawberry Island several summers, making it more attractive as a gathering place for all

Basilians. His sisters in Orillia helped acquire property on the mainland canal, subsequently named 'Mulcahy Landing,' from where the Basilian boats serviced the Island.

'Matt' was ready to learn from others, and office, prestige, or compliments were matters of indifference to him. During the early years of St Mary's College, as he was scrubbing floors, a visitor approached and asked to see the principal. 'I'm the principal,' he said. 'Oh,' said the visitor, 'I thought you were the janitor.' 'That, too,' said Matt. Such was this priest, teacher, and admirable human being who enriched Basilian education for half a century. He was deeply touched by the honorary degree of Doctor of Divinity conferred on him by the University of St Michael's College in 1994. He understood and accepted the honour as a recognition not only of his service but also of the Basilian contribution to Catholic secondary education.

In 1999, at the age of eighty-eight, Father Mulcahy fell with a collapsing scaffold while putting up a net in the school gymnasium. Treatment for a broken hip at a Toronto hospital and a period of recuperation at his sisters' home at Orilla, Ontario, allowed him to return to St Michael's before the end of the year. Increasing frailty, however, required his moving to Anglin House, the Basilian infirmary, early in 2000. His good spirits never failed, nor did his interest in the community and sense of humour. He died suddenly one morning after returning to his room from breakfast.

SOURCES: GABF; *Annals* 1 (1946) 121, 8 (1994) 23–6, 8 (1997) 5–6, 9 (2001) 87–9; *Newsletter* (20 March 2000); Michael Higgins, 'Lives Lived,' *Globe and Mail* (5 September 2000); E.J. Lajeunesse, *Strawberry Island in Lake Simcoe* (Toronto, 1962, 1974, 1983, 1984) 76–7.

MULCAHY, Michael Joseph, priest, great-uncle of Father Matthew *Mulcahy, was born at Carrig-Na-Var, parish of Glammire, County Cork, Ireland, on 23 December 1841, the son of Dennis Mulcahy and Catherine Murphy. He died in Toronto on 30 April 1905 and was buried there in the Basilian plot of St Michael's Cemetery.

After the death of his father, Michael Mulcahy's mother emigrated to Oshawa, Ontario, where young Michael attended the local Grammar School taught by Alexander Begg. In 1853 he enrolled in St Michael's College, Toronto, where he soon proved himself to be a fine athlete and the best handball player in the college. On 8 December 1859, he entered the Basilian novitiate, Toronto, and took final vows on 8 March 1862. He spent the year 1863–4 in France, and was ordained to the priesthood in Lyon on 21 May 1864.

Except for two short teaching appointments, one at St Louis College, Louisville, Ohio, and one at the College of Mary Immaculate in Beaconfield House, Plymouth, England, 1887–8, Father Mulcahy's priestly life was spent at St Michael's College. There he was known as the strict master of the study hall, and as a patriotic Irishman who would not tolerate the least slight on his native land. During the early years of his priesthood he frequently served as assistant in St Basil's Parish, Toronto. He died of a stroke in 1905.

SOURCE: GABF.

MULLINS, John Brian, priest, was born on 6 March 1922 in Bathurst, New Brunswick (diocese of Chatham, since 1938 of Bathurst), the son of Joseph Brian Mullins and Josephine Power. He died in Houston, Texas, on 1 August 1993, and is buried there in the Basilian plot, Garden of Gethsemane, Forest Park Lawndale Cemetery.

'Mully,' as he came to be called, attended Dalhousie Convent School and Bathurst High School, graduating in 1939. He worked for a year at the Royal Bank before entering St Basil's Novitiate, where he made first profession on 12 September 1941. After undergraduate studies at Assumption College, Windsor, majoring in English, French, and history (B.A., University of Western Ontario, 1945), he taught at St Michael's College School, Toronto, 1945–6. He studied theology at St Basil's Seminary, Toronto, 1946–50, and was ordained to the priesthood on 29 June 1949 in St Basil's Church, Toronto, by Cardinal James Charles McGuigan.

After seven more years, 1950–7, as French teacher at St Michael's College School, Father Mullins was named founder, principal, and superior of Michael Power High School, Etobicoke, Ontario. In his seven years there he set the school on a sound academic basis with a province-wide reputation for excellence. In 1964 he took the position of chaplain of D'Arcy McGee High School, Montreal, assisting as well as guidance counsellor and religion teacher. In 1964–5 he was assistant chaplain at the Newman Club of McGill University, and was also administrator of Our Lady of Good Counsel Parish, Montreal, 1965–9, where he hosted numerous Basilian visitors to Expo '67. After suffering his first heart attack, he accepted a pastoral position at Transfiguration Parish, Montreal, 1969–71, but was appointed to St Basil's Parish, Toronto, 1971–3, and then to St Anne's Parish, Houston, where he ministered for the next twenty years in spite of continuing heart problems that included open-heart surgery. He collapsed one evening after helping to clear away the supper dishes, remaining comatose for the ten days preceding his death.

John Mullins was a joyful and energetic person who recognized the humorous side of things with an infectious laugh. He preached well and convincingly, and never sought special consideration because of his poor health.

BIBLIOGRAPHY: 'The Mission Society in Our High Schools,' *Benedicamus* 3 (May 1950) 46–7.
SOURCES: GABF; *Annals* 1 (1949) 262, 7 (1992) 10–11, 8 (1994) 137–9; *Newsletter* (12 September 1993).

MULVIHILL, Daniel Joseph, priest, brother of Monsignor Claude Mulvihill of the archdiocese of Toronto and of Sister Mary Avila CSJ, was born on 7 November 1915 in Peterborough, Ontario, the son of Patrick Mulvihill and Laura McSweeney. He died in Toronto on 21 January 1987, and is buried in the Basilian plot of Holy Cross Cemetery, Thornhill, Ontario.

'Dan' attended elementary school in Peterborough and completed his secondary education at St Michael's College, Toronto, in 1933. In that year he entered St Basil's Novitiate, Toronto, making first profession on 15 August 1934. He was then assigned to Assumption College, Windsor (B.A., University of Western Ontario, 1937). For the next two years he taught history in the high school section of Assumption, and during the year 1938–9 he took first-year theology. In 1939 he was moved to St Michael's College to continue his theological studies and also took courses at the Ontario College of Education, earning teacher's certification in 1940. He moved to St Basil's Seminary in 1940 and was ordained to the priesthood on 17 August 1941 in St Basil's Church, Toronto, by Archbishop James Charles McGuigan.

In 1942 Father Mulvihill was appointed to Assumption College once again, where he was to serve for many years in both teaching and administration. For the first year he taught history. In 1943 he was appointed treasurer of the college while continuing his teaching. In 1945 he was released for graduate studies at the University of Michigan (M.A., 1946; Ph.D., 1953), having defended his thesis entitled 'Juan de Zumárraga, First Bishop of Mexico.' Meanwhile, in 1950, he returned to Assumption to head the department of history. He served on the board of governors of Assumption University from 1952 and became vice-president for development in 1958. He was elected president of the Canadian Catholic Historical Association in 1961–2, and was honorary president in 1962–3. He was named superior of the Basilian community and president of Assumption University, 1964–7. With the exception of a sabbatical year in 1973–4, he continued to teach history at the University of Windsor until 1978, when he was appointed principal of St Mark's College, Vancouver, 1978–81. He then spent a year with the Basilian Fathers of Rexdale, Ontario. From 1983 to 1986 he served in the chaplaincy office at Brescia Hall, University of Western Ontario. In June of 1986 he took up residence at Holy Rosary Parish, Toronto, to recuperate from surgery; but his health continued to decline. Released from hospital after a short respite in late December 1986, he had to be readmitted on 14 January 1987, and died a week later.

Dan Mulvihill was a man of impressive build and energy. His manner of speech was rather stentorian, though not pompous. Extensively read in his field of history, he could be counted on for accuracy of the record and for provocative reflections. As superior of the religious community, he unified and encouraged. As an administrator and president he was at times distressed, even depressed, by the problems of office.

BIBLIOGRAPHY: 'The First Bishop of North America,' *CCHA Report* 24 (1957) 13–22.
SOURCES: GABF; *Annals* 6 (1985) 310, 6 (1988) 694–5; *Newsletter* (27 January 1987); Shook, *Catholic Education* 287, 290–1.

MUNGOVAN, Michael Joseph, priest, was born at Stratford, Ontario (diocese of Toronto, since 1856 of London), on 16 July 1846, the son of Thomas Mungovan and Mary Quinlivin. He died in Toronto, on 2 March 1901 and was buried there in the Basilian plot of St Michael's Cemetery.

Michael Mungovan enrolled in St Michael's College, Toronto, in 1869. Two years later he left to study at Montreal College. In 1872 he became a Basilian postulant and was assigned to teach at St Louis College, Louisville, Ohio. He entered St Basil's Novitiate, Toronto, on 15 August 1873. The novitiate was transferred a few months later to

Assumption College, Windsor, where he was professed, studied theology, and was ordained to the priesthood on 15 February 1878.

Father Mungovan taught at Assumption College until 1887, when he was appointed assistant at St Mary's of the Assumption Parish, Owen Sound, Ontario. The summer of 1890 brought him back to Assumption College in the dual role of director of studies and treasurer. In 1899 he moved to Toronto to fill the same offices at St Michael's College. A liver condition caused his death two years later.

Father Mungovan knew how to meet people, and they liked him for his sense of humour. Many a student considered him a good friend. Among themselves they called him 'Mun' and at times 'Pardee,' though they took no liberties with him. A biographical sketch in the *Golden Jubilee Volume of Assumption College* states: 'He was naturally genial, but sparing in his confidences, and his confreres enjoyed his company. ... his interests were within the College walls – a fact which enabled him to use his exceptional ability wholly to the advantage of the school.' He spoke Gaelic fluently and French passably. From 2 February 1883 he kept a diary to which he was faithful for many years. Extracts written in 1890, when he was at St Mary's of the Assumption Parish in Owen Sound, were published in *Basilian* 4 (February 1938) 28.

SOURCES: GABF; *Centennial, St Mary's*; Charles Collins, 'Father Mungovan,' *Basilian* 4 (April 1938) 73, 80; *Jubilee, Assumption*; *Jubilee, St Mary's*; Kirley, *Congregation in France* 52. Selections from his diary, 1890–95, have been published in Power, *Assumption College* 2 100–14.

MUNNELLY, Leo Joseph, priest, was born on 1 January 1916 in Toronto, the eldest of the family of one son and three daughters of John Munnelly and Catherine McKeon. He died in Houston on 7 May 1981 and is buried in the Basilian plot of Holy Cross Cemetery, Thornhill, Ontario.

Leo attended parochial schools in Toronto and took high school at St Michael's College, graduating in 1933. That same year he entered St Basil's Novitiate, Toronto, and was professed on 15 August 1934. He lived at St Michael's College for one year of his university studies and then at St Basil's Scholasticate ('Seminary' from 1937), Toronto, for three years (B.A., University of Toronto, 1938), winning the Sir Bertram Windle Gold Medal in Philosophy. While doing his theological studies he also pursued graduate studies in philosophy (M.A., University of Toronto, 1940), with the thesis 'Exemplarism in the Doctrine of Saint

Bonaventure,' and then taught as a scholastic in 1940–1 at Catholic Central High School, Detroit. He was ordained to the priesthood on 15 August 1942 in St Basil's Church, Toronto, by Archbishop James Charles McGuigan.

In 1943 Father Munnelly was appointed to graduate studies at the Pontifical Institute of Mediaeval Studies, Toronto (M.S.L., 1944). After teaching history during the spring term of 1945 at St Thomas More College, Saskatoon, he was appointed to Assumption College, 1945–6, before returning to St Thomas More College for 1946–9. He once again took up graduate studies, this time at Fordham University, 1949–52, after which he was appointed to St John Fisher College, Rochester. He taught at St Michael's College School from 1961 to 1966, when he was moved to the University of St Thomas, Houston.

Father Munnelly collapsed on the academic mall from a heart attack as he was walking to administer the last examination of his teaching career. Though in great pain he remained lucid as he received absolution and the sacrament of the dying from his colleague Father Janusz Ihnatowicz, whom he asked to help him to pray. He died just as the paramedics arrived.

Leo was blessed with a fine physical appearance, a phenomenal memory, and a mastery of the long view of history, which had become his teaching specialty. Pastimes he excelled in were tennis and golf.

SOURCES: GABF *Annals* 1 (1943) 26–7, 6 (1982) 86–7; *Newsletter* (16 May 1981).

MURPHY, Francis Leo, priest, was born on 16 October 1903 in Ottawa, the son of Patrick Murphy and Jane Daly. He died in Houston on 3 September 1974, and is buried there in the Basilian plot, Garden of Gethsemane, Forest Park Lawndale Cemetery.

Francis attended St Patrick's Elementary School and Lisgar Collegiate Institute, Ottawa, graduating in 1923. He began the study of law at Osgoode Hall, Toronto, in 1925, was called to the bar in 1930, and practised law in Toronto until 1937, when he entered St Basil's Novitiate on Kendal (now Tweedsmuir) Avenue. After making first profession on 15 August 1938, he spent one year at St Michael's College studying philosophy, and then began theological studies at St Basil's Seminary, while also taking courses at Shaw's School of Business, Toronto. He was ordained to the priesthood on 23 August 1942 in Blessed Sacrament Church, Ottawa, by Archbishop Alexandre Vachon.

His first appointment in 1943 resulted in the nickname by which he would always be known. In obedience to his appointment, Father Murphy moved to St Michael's College, only to find that there was no room for him. He returned to St Basil's Seminary, where he found that his former room there was already occupied. Back to St Michael's he went, then back to the seminary, then back to St Michael's again, before he was finally sent to Assumption College, Windsor, where he taught for one year. These changes in appointment earned him, from that time on, the name 'Shifty' Murphy. In 1944–5 he worked as assistant at Blessed Sacrament Church, Windsor, and in 1945 he was appointed to St Thomas High School, Houston, where he remained until his death thirty years later. At an undetermined time he suffered a slight stroke which caused him to drag one leg as he walked.

Father Murphy became extremely attached to St Thomas High School and to his adopted city of Houston. In order to prepare for an upcoming evaluation of the school, he was asked to become a certified librarian. By attending summer school at St Mary's University, San Antonio, he earned the B.L.S. in 1950. He often cited this experience as an example of the fruits of religious obedience.

Father Murphy never forgot kindnesses done to him, and was careful to return them. Visitors to the school found him an attentive and pleasant host. An inveterate traveller, he visited most of North America, Europe, and the Caribbean Islands. He was planning a trip to Australia in 1974 when, late in August, he fell and broke his thigh. Recuperating from the subsequent operation, he died suddenly at St Anthony's Convalescent Home of cardiac arrest.

SOURCES: GABF; *Annals* 1 (1943) 28, 5 (1975) 121–2; *Newsletter* (5 September 1974).

MURPHY, James Joseph, priest, was born in Detroit on 30 November 1888, the son of Arthur Murphy and Elizabeth McEnery. He died at Owen Sound, Ontario, on 23 November 1967 and was buried there in St Mary's Cemetery.

Raised on a farm near Oxford, Michigan, James Joseph Murphy worked as a farmer until the age of thirty-five. He then went to Assumption College, Windsor, to begin studies for the priesthood. From 1923 to 1932 he completed high school and undergraduate studies, then entered St Basil's Novitiate, Toronto, and was professed on 15 August 1933. He did his theological studies at St Basil's Scholasticate,

Toronto and was ordained to the priesthood on 19 December 1936 in St Basil's Church, Toronto, by Archbishop James Charles McGuigan.

The priestly life of Father 'Jim' Murphy was spent in parish work as an assistant: at St John the Baptist Parish, Amherstburg, Ontario, 1937–8; at Ste Anne's Parish, Detroit, 1938–40; at Assumption Parish, Windsor, 1940–4; and at St Mary's of the Assumption Parish, Owen Sound, from 1944 until his death in 1967, after a year and a half of suffering from cancer.

During his twenty-three years in Owen Sound, Father Murphy regularly ministered at two mission churches each Sunday. In 1944 he completed construction of St Michael's Church in the Irish Block and served this mission until 1948, when he was put in charge of St Thomas Church, Wiarton and St Mary's Church, Hepworth. In the early 1960s he served St Patrick Church in Southampton and St Stanislaus Church in Chatsworth. The *Basilian Centennial* volume of St Mary's of the Assumption Parish said, 'Father Murphy is best known for his untiring efforts as chaplain of the Owen Sound General and Marine Hospital. During the past sixteen years, he has been visiting the hospital as often as five or six times each day ... a familiar and welcome sight to all patients, both Catholic and non-Catholic.' The amputation of one leg in the summer of 1966 put an end to his active ministry.

SOURCES: GABF; *Annals* 4 (1968) 57–8; *Centennial, St Mary's*; *Newsletter* (24 November 1967).

MURPHY, John Francis, priest, younger brother of Father Joseph Stanley *Murphy and first cousin of Fathers Norman Joseph *Murphy and Wilfred *Murphy, was born on 27 March 1909 at Woodslee, Ontario (diocese of London), the son of Patrick Joseph Murphy and Ellen Dunn. He died on 26 February 1975 in Windsor, and is buried there in the Basilian plot of Heavenly Rest Cemetery.

John Francis Murphy graduated from Woodslee Continuation School in 1927 and enrolled in Assumption College, Windsor (B.A., University of Western Ontario, 1931). He entered St Basil's Novitiate, Toronto, and was professed on 15 August 1932. He spent the following year at St Basil's Scholasticate, Toronto, studying theology. In 1933–4 he taught at Holy Name Institute, Detroit, while continuing his theological studies. In 1934 he returned to Toronto and was ordained to the priesthood on 21 December 1935 in St Basil's Church, Toronto, by Archbishop James Charles McGuigan.

Father Murphy taught English and history at St Michael's College School, Toronto, 1936-8, and English literature at Aquinas Institute, Rochester, 1938-44. Every summer he did graduate studies in English at the University of Ottawa (M.A., 1942, with the thesis: 'The Failure of Wordsworth's Mysticism'; Ph.D., 1944, with the thesis: 'Francis Thompson: A Catholic Poet of Nature'). He was appointed to Assumption College in 1944 to teach and to serve as registrar. In 1950 he was named as the first president and superior of the newly established St John Fisher College, Rochester, working in these capacities until 1958. In 1964 St John Fisher College conferred on him an honorary LL.D in recognition of his services.

In 1958, Father Murphy was appointed to the ten-year-old University of St Thomas, Houston, Texas, and was named its president in 1959. He retired from the position in 1966, and was named chancellor. He served as local councillor for the Basilian community from 1958 to 1967, and as superior for the year 1967-8 in replacement of Father Edward *Sullivan, who had died unexpectedly. In August of 1968 he was appointed chaplain at Assumption University, Windsor, where he remained until his death.

John Murphy exuded optimism for his work and for the institutions he served. A gift for language enabled him to sum up a complex situation in an apt and colourful turn of phrase. He took pains to know students personally. A trait of 'confiding' identical news to a number of them amused him and them as well. As an administrator he maintained a fine harmony between his Basilian and professional life. The success of two Basilian universities owes much to his administration during difficult formative years. Both named buildings in his memory.

Father John Murphy's habitual enthusiasm remained constant in his final years as chaplain in Windsor. One month short of his sixty-sixth birthday, after several days of distress that he attributed to pleurisy, he suffered a heart attack. Father Stanley *Murphy, his brother, and Father Arthur *Weiler administered the last rites and accompanied him to hospital, where he died a few minutes after admission.

BIBLIOGRAPHY: 'The Radiator Club,' *Basilian* 1 (April 1935) 35; 'Domus sacerdotum,' *Basilian* 1 (November 1935) 111-12; 'Bearding the Barber,' *Basilian* 2 (January 1936) 16; 'Annesi ... according to the Scholastic Method ... ,' *Basilian* 2 (May 1936) 101-3; 'Safeguarding Our Health,' *Basilian* 2 (October, November 1936) 114, 118, 135-6; 'Letter to the Editor,' *Basilian* 3 (March 1937) 59; 'The Letter-Box: (Why the *Basilian* Should Not Be Allowed to Die),' *Basilian* 4 (February

1938) 39; 'It's a Long Way from Home,' *Benedicamus* 5 (April 1952) 4–6; 'Mathematics in Basilian Schools [forum],' *Basilian Teacher* 4 (December 1959) 71–2; 'Science and the Liberal Arts in Catholic Colleges,' *Basilian Teacher* 5 (May 1961) 281–4.

SOURCES: GABF; *Annals* 5 (1976) 184–5; *Newsletter* (1 March 1975).

MURPHY, Joseph STANLEY, priest, elder brother of Father John Francis *Murphy and first cousin of Fathers Norman Joseph *Murphy and Wilfred Joseph *Murphy, was born on 4 June 1904 at Woodslee, Ontario (diocese of London), the son of Patrick Joseph Murphy and Ellen Dunn. He died in Windsor, Ontario, on 22 May 1983 and is buried there in the Basilian plot of Heavenly Rest Cemetery.

'Stan' was educated in his home town of Woodslee and at Assumption College School, Windsor, graduating in 1924. He entered St Basil's Novitiate, Toronto, was professed on 11 August 1925, and returned to Assumption College (B.A., University of Western Ontario, 1928). He taught for one year, 1928–9, at Catholic Central High School, Detroit, while also doing his first year of theological studies. In 1929 he was appointed to St Basil's Scholasticate, Toronto, to continue his theological studies and to earn certification at the Ontario College of Education, 1930. He was ordained to the priesthood on 19 December 1931 in St Basil's Church, Toronto, by Bishop Alexander MacDonald.

Father 'Stan,' as he was popularly and universally known, had but one appointment in his life as a Basilian priest: Assumption College, where he began teaching philosophy in 1932. In 1934 he was awarded an M.A. in philosophy from the University of Toronto, submitting as his thesis 'Mediaeval Doctrines and Robert Herrick.' He was principal of the high school for two years and registrar of Assumption College from 1940 to 1946. In this position he brought Wyndham Lewis and then Marshall McLuhan to Assumption, and indeed gave McLuhan his first teaching position in Canada.

The great work of his life was the Christian Culture Series, which he founded in 1934. Born of his desire to bring Christian culture to an economically depressed society, this lecture series brought great scholars, artists, politicians, and social activists to Windsor not only from North America but also from Europe. Its popularity has endured unbroken since its foundation. For his contributions to university and cultural life in Canada, Father Murphy was awarded a *doctorat ès lettres* from the Université Laval (1965) and an LL.D. from the University of Windsor (1979). That latter year he was made a member of the Order of Canada. He was the first Canadian member of the Detroit Symphony Orchestra Board, a vice-president of the Windsor branch of the National Ballet of Canada, and an honorary president of the Windsor branch of the Canadian Opera Guild. He was vice-president of the Detroit Frédéric Chopin Society and chaplain to the Windsor First Saturday Club of Catholic Business and Professional Women. He served for a time on the Senate of the University of Western Ontario, London, and was a member of the Windsor Centennial Committee, as well as of other cultural and civic groups in Windsor and Detroit.

Father Stan's unfailingly pleasant disposition and ready smile won him countless friends. He had time for everyone, especially the bewildered new student. His simplicity and candour put him at ease with intellectuals, artists, social activists, and politicians on both sides of the Atlantic.

BIBLIOGRAPHY:
Book: Ed. *Christianity and Culture*. Baltimore and Montreal, 1961.
Articles: In *Basilian*: 'Assumption Lecture League,' 1 (April 1935) 27–8; 'The Divine Prodigal,' 1 (June 1935) 79; 'Lord of the Twentieth Century,' 1 (November 1935) 116; 'Light and Shade in Catholic Character (Reflections on Father Feeney's Lecture),' 3 (December 1937) 132; 'Glad Tidings,' 4 (January 1938) 16; 'Nigra sum sed formosa,' 4 (May 1938) 87; 'I Found a Queen,' 4 (June 1938) 106; 'The Significance of Jacques Maritain,' preface to Jacques Maritain, *The Natural Law and Human Rights*. Windsor, 1942, 3–8; 'Communications and Education [forum],' *Basilian Teacher* 3 (May 1959) 219–20; 'The Born, the Unborn, the Stillborn,' *Basilian Teacher* 7 (January 1963) 281–4; 'Wyndham Lewis at Windsor,' *Canadian Literature* (Winter 1968): 9–19; Introduction, *The Diaries and Other Papers of Michael Joseph Ferguson CSB: A Bibliography Complied by Robert J. Scollard* (Toronto, 1970).
Other: He supervised publication of E.J. Pratt, *Brébeuf and His Brethren* (Toronto, 1942), and of Raïssa Maritain and Margaret Sumner, *The Divine Ways: A Little Work on St Thomas Aquinas* (Toronto, 1942), both published by the Basilian Press, Toronto.
SOURCES: GABF; *Annals* 5 (1976) 141, 6 (1982) 13, 6 (1984) 294–6; *Newsletter* (9 June 1983).

MURPHY, Norman Joseph, priest, younger brother of Father Wilfred Joseph *Murphy, and first cousin of Fathers John Francis *Murphy and Joseph Stanley *Murphy, was born on 1 October 1905 in Windsor, the son of William J. Murphy and Emma Mailloux. He died at

Crown Point, Indiana, on 17 March 1985, and is buried in the Basilian plot of Heavenly Rest Cemetery, Windsor.

Educated at St Francis Grade School, Norman graduated from the high school of Assumption College, Windsor, in 1922. He did a year of university studies at Assumption before entering St Basil's Novitiate, Toronto, where he was professed on 11 August 1924. He was appointed to St Basil's Scholasticate, Toronto, while taking courses at the University of Toronto. In 1925 he returned to Assumption College to complete his university studies (B.A., University of Western Ontario, 1927). He studied theology at St Basil's Scholasticate, Toronto. During the year 1928–9 he also attended the Ontario College of Education, earning teaching certification in 1929. He was moved to St Michael's College for his final year of theology, 1930–1, and was ordained to the priesthood on 20 December 1930 in St Basil's Church, Toronto, by Bishop Alexander MacDonald.

In his fifty-four years of Basilian priesthood Father 'Norm' Murphy had eleven appointments involving eight institutions: teaching, Assumption College School, 1931–4, 1935–7, 1946–9; teaching and treasurer, St Mary's Boys' High School, Calgary, Alberta, 1934–5; teaching and second councillor, 1938–42, and earning Alberta teaching certification in 1935; teaching at Aquinas Institute, Rochester, 1942–6; teaching and moderator of scholastics, Assumption College, 1949–55; teaching, St John Fisher College, Rochester, 1955–62; assistant pastor, St Theresa's Parish, Sugar Land, Texas, 1962–5; teaching, St Thomas High School, Houston, 1965–7; chaplain, Andrean High School, Merrillville, Indiana, 1967–85.

Norman Murphy had a particular devotion to the Blessed Sacrament. He was much interested in the formation of the young in religious life, and was often asked to give retreats to scholastics. He was an ardent gardener: as moderator he detailed several scholastics to plant flowers abundantly around the campus of Assumption College. He loved to talk about community experiences in times past, whether or not anyone was listening closely, and could pick up the thread of a story a day later as though there had been no interruption.

SOURCES: GABF; *Annals* 5 (1975) 66, 5 (1981) 538–9, 6 (1986) 475–6; *Newsletter* (29 March 1985).

MURPHY, Vincent Joseph, priest, was born in Toronto on 10 July 1877, the son of Joseph Murphy and Frances McNaughton. He died in Montreal on 28 March 1933 and was buried in the Basilian plot of Mount Hope Cemetery, Toronto.

Vincent Murphy grew up in St Basil's Parish, Toronto, and attended St Basil's Separate School and St Michael's College, 1888-9. He entered St Basil's Novitiate, Toronto, late in 1897 and was professed on 6 January 1899. His theological studies were made at St Basil's Scholasticate, Toronto, and he was ordained to the priesthood on 21 December 1903.

An outstanding Latin teacher at St Michael's College, 1903-7, and then at Assumption College, Windsor, Ontario, Father Murphy rose through a succession of positions to be vice-president of Assumption. He got results by putting extra effort into the simplest duty, but the strain of such efforts led to a nervous breakdown in 1915. When treatment and rest at St Basil's Scholasticate restored him to health, he was appointed treasurer at St Michael's College in 1920, and in 1922 he was elected treasurer general and later in the same year was named pastor of Holy Rosary Parish, Toronto. When his health failed again, two years later, he was withdrawn from parish work. Rest brought another improvement, and in 1928 he was re-elected treasurer general and was also appointed treasurer of St Basil's Scholasticate. Late in 1929 the tragic death of Father Francis *Forster, a lifelong associate, had an upsetting effect on Father Murphy. Doctors recommended institutional care. He was taken to La Retraite Saint-Benoît, Montreal, where he died in 1933.

The story of Father 'Vinnie' Murphy's priestly life divides into two parts, the first replete with accomplishments and promise for the future, the second and slightly longer part filled with patient suffering. Of his early years in the priesthood Father M.V. *Kelly wrote, 'Succeeding years showed the teacher whose pupils achieved the best results, the organizer whose baseball or football team always seemed to win, later the financier entrusted with the temporal interests of his college and evincing a rare efficiency which apparently took little time to acquire, finally the preacher possessed of all the gifts required to make a great pulpit orator.'

SOURCES: GABF; *Jubilee, Assumption*; M.V. Kelly, 'Reverend Vincent J. Murphy CSB,' *St Joseph Lilies* 22 (June 1933) 34-6; Kirley, *Congregation in France* 88; E.J. McCorkell, 'Sermon Preached at the Funeral of Father V.J. Murphy,' *Yearbook SMC* 24 (1933).

MURPHY, Wilfred Joseph, priest, elder brother of Norman Joseph *Murphy and first cousin of Fathers John Francis *Murphy and

Joseph Stanley *Murphy, was born on 10 August 1903 in Windsor, the son of William J. Murphy and Emma Mailloux. He died in Houston on 26 October 1970, and is buried there in the Basilian plot, Garden of Gethsemane, Forest Park Lawndale Cemetery.

Wilfred Murphy attended Assumption Parish School, Windsor, Assumption College School, and Assumption College. After his second year of arts he entered St Basil's Novitiate, Toronto, and was professed on 11 August 1922. He returned to Assumption College (B.A., Honours Philosophy, University of Western Ontario, 1924). He taught for one year at St Thomas High School, Houston, before doing his theological studies in Toronto at St Basil's Scholasticate, 1925–7, and St Michael's College, 1927–8. He held teaching certification from the Ontario College of Education, 1926, and an M.A. in philosophy from the University of Toronto, 1929. He was ordained to the priesthood on 21 December 1927 in St Basil's Church by Bishop Alexander MacDonald.

In 1928 Father Murphy was appointed to work with the Basilians in Rochester who were teaching at Rochester Academy, which would later come under Basilian direction as Aquinas Institute. Four years later he was appointed to St Thomas High School, Houston, 1932–7, but would return twice to Aquinas, 1937–40 and 1951–4. Other teaching assignments included Catholic Central High School, Detroit, 1940–4, and St Thomas High School, Houston, 1954–70.

In the midst of these teaching appointments Father Murphy spent six years on the Basilian Missions in Texas at Our Lady of Guadalupe Parish, Rosenberg, 1944–50, and became fluent in Spanish. He continued his Hispanic ministry at Ste Anne's Parish, Detroit, 1950–1.

Wilfred Murphy was careful to make visitors welcome and give them of his time. He often served as community sacristan, but no task was too menial for him. He suffered for many years from asthma and from violent fits of coughing. In September 1958 a severe heart attack forced him to abandon all duties for five months, but he returned to the classroom and then to the school office for another ten years. He died quietly in his room of a massive heart attack.

BIBLIOGRAPHY: 'Spiritual Reading,' *Basilian* 2 (April 1936) 70–2.
SOURCES: GABF; *Annals* 4 (1970) 212–13; *Newsletter* (28 October 1970); Power, *Assumption College* 5 167.

MURRAY, Edmund Francis, priest, was born in Toronto on 30 May 1844, the son of Charles Murray and Mary Pollard. He died in Toronto on 4 May 1925 and was buried there in the Basilian plot of St Michael's Cemetery.

Edmund Murray enrolled as a day pupil at St Michael's College, Toronto, in 1855 when the school was still located in the rectory of St Michael's Cathedral. On 8 September 1865 he entered St Basil's Novitiate, Toronto, and made his final vows on 29 September 1870. He was ordained to the priesthood on 1 May 1872.

Father 'Fish' Murray, as he was often called, grew up without growing old. With his boyish enthusiasm went exceptionally good health. He was a priest everyone seemed to love; he was courteous and affable and a popular confessor. In every gathering he radiated cheerfulness and good fellowship. St Michael's College was for him heaven on earth. All his priestly life was spent there, except for the years 1910–14, when he was stationed at Assumption College, Windsor, and for some months during the First World War, when he helped out in various parishes of the diocese of Hamilton, Ontario. An obituary notice in the *Yearbook, St Michael's College* states: 'No priest was ever loved more for his own sake. He was the kindest, the saintliest, and the funniest of men.' Father Murray showed great concern for the poor. For a number of years he was chaplain at Sacred Heart Orphanage in Toronto. He taught music and also directed the choir and played the organ in St Basil's Church.

SOURCES: GABF; W.R. Harris, 'Tribute to Father Edmund Murray,' *Yearbook SMC* 13 (1922); Hoskin, *St Basil's*; E. Kelly, *The Story of St Paul's Parish, Toronto, 1822–1922* (Toronto, 1923); *Purple and White* (10 May 1925); *Yearbook SMC* 16 (1925).

MURRAY, William Hudson, priest, uncle of Fathers John Clifford Murray CSB and William Coughlin CSB and of former Basilian Daniel Coughlin, was born on 4 January 1888 on a farm near Wilton Grove, Ontario (diocese of London), the son of George Murray and Ella Flood. He died in Toronto on 23 June 1976 and is buried in the Basilian plot of Holy Cross Cemetery, Thornhill, Ontario.

William Murray attended a school near the family farm and then entered London (Ontario) Collegiate Institute in 1902, where he remained only for the first semester before transferring to the high school section of Assumption College, Windsor, graduating in 1905. He held a job until 1909, when he entered St Basil's Novitiate, Toronto, making first profession on 24 October 1910, after which he was appointed to St Michael's College, Toronto, for undergraduate studies (B.A., University of Toronto, 1915) simultaneously with his studies in theology. After ordination to the priesthood on 18 September 1914 in St Basil's Church, Toronto, by Archbishop Neil McNeil, he taught at St Michael's College, 1914–22.

In 1922, the year in which the Basilians in North America separated from the Basilians in France, Father Murray was sent to the Institut catholique, Paris (*Licence en philosophie*, 1925). In the arrangements made between the two communities, he worked in the archives in Annonay to find documents important to the North American congregation. While in Paris he studied under Jacques Maritain, whom he recommended to Father Henry *Carr, then superior of St Michael's, as a possible visiting professor. In 1925 he returned to St Michael's, teaching for three years and serving as dean of residence, 1927–8. In 1928 he was appointed master of novices.

In 1931 Father Murray returned to teach at St Michael's and was named second councillor. In 1936–7 he was in charge of four Basilians who spent the winter at Strawberry Island in Lake Simcoe. In 1937 he was named superior of the curial house, though he continued to do some teaching at St Basil's Seminary and at St Michael's. In 1940 he was named pastor of St Mary's of the Assumption Parish, Owen Sound, Ontario, where he spoke every Tuesday evening on the local radio station. In 1946 he returned to teaching at Assumption College. The next year he was named confessor at Holy Rosary Seminary, Toronto, 1947–8, and, the following year, confessor and treasurer at St Basil's Novitiate, Richmond Hill, Ontario, where he remained until 1959.

Father Murray took up residence at Assumption University, Windsor, in 1959. No longer teaching, he served as extraordinary confessor to the novices at St Basil's Novitiate, Pontiac, Michigan. In 1967 he retired completely, was appointed to St Basil's Seminary, Toronto, where, his memory having seriously deteriorated, he became the first member of the newly established St Basil's Infirmary.

Basilians always called him 'Pike Murray,' even when the title 'Father' was prefixed. He liked order and decorum, an interest which perhaps stemmed from his service as community master of ceremonies in the years just after his ordination and from his insistence on good pronunciation of both English and French. His fluency in the latter language reflected his concern that lack of communication might lead to divisions among Canadians. He read widely in spirituality and was one of the first Basilians to promote the works of Blessed Abbot Columba Marmion OSB. In the final years of his life his memory was so severely impaired that he lived literally from moment to moment – a condition that supplied amusing incidents and stories, though it was regrettable that one who had experienced so much of Basilian history was not able to pass it on. A broken hip, suffered in mid-June 1976, proved too much for his fragile system, and brought his death a week later. He was at that time the oldest Basilian both by age and by religious profession.

SOURCES: GABF; *Annals* 1 (1944) 65, 3 (1960) 23, 3 (1964) 106–7, 5 (1977) 254–5; *Newsletter* (30 June 1976); Kirley, *Congregation in France* 95, 231n24.

N

NICHOLSON, Joseph SYLVESTER, priest, was born in Kinkora, Ontario (diocese of London) on 19 March 1892, the son of John Nicholson and Mary Prendible. He died at Fostoria, Ohio, on 9 May 1933 and was buried in the Basilian plot of Assumption Cemetery, Windsor.

Sylvester Nicholson grew up in Logan, Ontario, and attended school there. In 1909 he went to St Michael's College, Toronto, where he studied until 1914, when he went to St Thomas College in Chatham, New Brunswick, to teach and, with Father Jack *Spratt, began a successful hockey tradition there. One year later he entered St Basil's Novitiate, Toronto, and was professed on 13 August 1916. He studied theology at Assumption College, Windsor, and at the Catholic University of America, Washington, D.C. (M.A., Theology, 1921). He was ordained to the priesthood on 19 February 1921 in St Peter's Cathedral, London, Ontario, by Bishop Michael Fallon.

Father Nicholson returned to St Thomas College as treasurer. When the Basilians withdrew from there in 1923, he was appointed to that office at Assumption College, which was then in the midst of an expansion program. In 1929 he moved to Catholic Central High School, Detroit, again as treasurer. There, although a man of tremendous physical strength, he overtaxed and permanently damaged his heart while moving a piano. In 1932 he was relieved of the office of treasurer. He died in 1933 while on a visit to his sister in Ohio.

Father 'Nick' had been raised among people who made do with very little, and he carried a good deal of this habit of life into his administration of temporalities. He was excellent in handling boys, both in the classroom and in his administrative duties. The *Silver Anniversary Booklet of Catholic Central High School* stated, 'Former students of Father "Nick" will best remember the big heart which he tried to hide beneath a rough exterior.'

SOURCES: GABF; Shook, *Catholic Education* 116–19; *Silver Anniversary, Catholic Central High School 1928–1953* (Detroit, 1953); *Yearbook STC* (1922).

NICOLAS, Etienne Elie, priest, member of the Congregation 1860–70, was born on 19 March 1835 in Annonay.

Etienne began secondary schooling at age nineteen in the Petit Séminaire Sainte-Barbe, Annonay, studied for a time in the Grand Séminaire of Viviers, and then entered the Basilian novitiate at Privas (Ardèche) on 5 February 1860. After final profession of vows on 29 November 1861, he was ordained a priest on 20 September 1862 at Romans (Drôme) by Bishop Jean-Paul-François-Marie Lyonnet of Valence.

Father Nicolas served in Basilian institutions for ten years: the Petit Séminaire de Vernoux (Ardèche), 1860–1; the Collège des Cordeliers, Annonay, where he taught Commercial, 1861–3; the Collège de Privas, as teacher, 1863–6, and bursar, 1866–7; Sainte-Barbe, Annonay, bursar, 1867–8; the Ecole cléricale de Périgueux (Dordogne), bursar, 1868–9; and the Collège du Sacré-Coeur, Annonay, teaching *septième*. He withdrew from the Congregation in October 1870. Records in the diocesan archives in Viviers show that he became chaplain to the Ursuline sisters at Boulieu-les-Annonay and was later chaplain in the prison and in the Hôpital Sainte-Marie, Privas. In December 1883 he was in Nice (Alpes-Maritimes).

SOURCE: Pouzol, 'Notices,' Supplément 2.

NICOLAS, Hippolyte Gustave Pierre Mathieu, priest, member of the Congregation 1873–89, was born on 6 January 1836 at Bourg-Saint-Andéol (Ardèche).

Hippolyte Nicolas first entered the community of the Brothers of Christian Doctrine. After teaching the commercial course at the Collège du Sacré-Coeur, Annonay, he decided to join the Basilians. He taught one year at the Basilian college at Privas (Ardèche) and then at the Collège du Sacré-Coeur before entering the novitiate in 1872 and taking final vows on 17 September 1875. Bishop Armand de Charbonnel ordained him to the priesthood on 22 September 1877 in the chapel of the Collège du Sacré-Coeur. For eleven years he taught at Sainte-Barbe, the minor seminary of the Basilian Fathers in Annonay; but in 1888 Father Nicolas went on sick leave to Monaco and withdrew from the Basilian community in June 1889.

SOURCES: GABF; Pouzol, 'Notices,' Supplément 3.

NIGH, William Francis, priest, brother of Brother Baptist Nigh of the Presentation Brothers, Montebello, Quebec, was born on 13 February 1902 at Seaforth, Ontario (diocese of London), the son of William Nigh and Mary Barry. He died on 18 November 1974 in Sudbury, Ontario, and is buried in the Basilian plot of Holy Cross Cemetery, Thornhill, Ontario.

'Bill' Nigh attended elementary and secondary schools in his home town, graduating from Seaforth Collegiate Institute in 1919. In the fall of 1920 he enrolled in Assumption College, Windsor, Ontario (B.A., University of Western Ontario, 1923). He entered St Basil's Novitiate, Toronto, in 1923, was professed on 11 August 1924, and was appointed to St Michael's College for theological studies. He moved to St Basil's Scholasticate in 1925, but went back to St Michael's in 1927. He was ordained to the priesthood on 21 December 1927 in St Basil's Church, Toronto, by Bishop Alexander MacDonald.

In 1928 Father Nigh was appointed to St Thomas High School, Houston, where he remained until 1946, teaching a number of subjects, serving as first councillor, 1941–4, and earning an M.A. in education from the University of Houston in 1943. In 1946 he was moved to Assumption College, Windsor, to teach mathematics, and served as department head, 1950–5. In 1969 he was appointed to St Charles College, Sudbury, where he continued teaching until the day he died.

Young people were attracted by 'Bill' Nigh's wisdom of years and youthful enthusiasm. He liked to share with them his own faith and his love for the Mother of God. Students had confidence in him not only to get them through the exams but also because he saw them as persons with aspirations, problems, and human potential. Many have called him the exemplar of the Basilian priest-teacher. He was also much interested in the physical plant of the houses where he was appointed. Late in life he took on the summertime chore of cutting the extensive park areas of Strawberry Island, the summer home of the Basilian Fathers in Lake Simcoe; and every day he celebrated Mass for the Sisters of St Joseph at Invermara nearby on the mainland. He never slowed down, not even for death, which came suddenly just after he had finished an evening meal with his confreres.

BIBLIOGRAPHY: 'Silence,' *Basilian* 1 (December 1935) 124–5.
SOURCES: GABF; *Annals* 5 (1975) 124–5; *Newsletter* (22 November 1974); E.J. Lajeunesse, *Strawberry Island in Lake Simcoe* (Toronto, 1962, 1974, 1981) 75.

NOLAN, Hugh Philip, priest, was born on 27 April 1908 at Luogan, Northern Ireland (diocese of Clogher), one of twelve children of John Joseph Nolan and Margaret McGrillen. He died in Toronto on 23 June 1969 from injuries suffered in a car accident, and is buried in the Basilian plot of Heavenly Rest Cemetery, Windsor.

Having attended schools in Belfast and in Quebec City, Hugh Nolan enrolled in Assumption College, Windsor, where his family had settled in 1922. He entered St Basil's Novitiate, Toronto, in 1927 and was professed on 13 August 1928. He was appointed to St Michael's College, Toronto, for undergraduate studies (B.A., University of Toronto, 1932), then began theological studies, with residence one year at St Michael's College and another at St Basil's Scholasticate. Along with his theology he took courses at the Ontario College of Education, earning teaching certification for Ontario in 1933. Bishop John Kidd ordained him to the priesthood on 16 December 1934 in Assumption Church, Windsor.

In 1935 Father Nolan was appointed to Catholic Central High School, Detroit, where he was to spend the next thirteen years. He obtained a Michigan teaching certification in 1936; and, working in summers, earned an M.A. in chemistry from St Bonaventure University, Olean, New York, 1943. He served as treasurer of the school for two years, 1944–6. In 1948 he was assigned to Aquinas Institute, Rochester, returning to Catholic Central in 1950 for a period of four years. Two parish assignments followed: St John the Baptist Parish, Amherstburg, Ontario, 1954–7, and St Mary's of the Assumption Parish, Owen Sound, Ontario, 1957–8. He returned to the classroom at St Thomas High School, Houston, for three years, 1958–61. He joined the staff of Assumption Parish, Windsor, in 1961. Five years later, his health failing, he took up residence at St Michael's College School, Toronto, where he worked to the extent his physical condition allowed.

A splendid athlete in his youth, Hugh Nolan nourished a keen interest in sports all his life. He would jokingly boast: 'I was the best left half on the Assumption High School football team'; but the boast was well justified, for few were so fast or so dependable. During his years at Catholic Central he proved himself an able and successful coach.

Hugh Nolan had many dark moments, long periods of depression and personal suffering; but nothing dimmed his faith or the joy of being a priest. On the morning of his death, with his strength failing rapidly, he told a nurse who found him on his knees, 'I am saying my last Mass.'

SOURCES: GABF; *Annals* 4 (1969) 164–5; *Newsletter* (23 June 1969).

NORMANDEAU, Joseph LEO, novice, was born at Cobalt, Ontario (diocese of Haileybury, since 1938 of Timmins), on 22 April 1917, the son of Louis Normandeau and Alma Poirier. He died in Toronto on 21 April 1936 and is buried there in the Basilian plot of Mount Hope Cemetery.

Leo Normandeau moved to Windsor at an early age and there attended high school at Assumption College, 1930–5, where he was remembered for his big, boyish smile. At that time he was an orphan, living with an older brother. Upon completion of his high school course he entered St Basil's Novitiate, Toronto, where he received the religious habit on 14 August 1935. He died eight months later after a mastoid operation. One of Mr Normandeau's teachers wrote in 'A Letter to Father Tighe,' published in the *Basilian*, 'Your words to Father Carr suffice to tell us all that we need know about him: "He died as we would expect a novice to die."'

SOURCES: GABF; Tom (pseud.), 'Letter to Father Tighe,' *Basilian* 2 (May 1936) 91.

O

O'BRIEN, Austin David, priest, brother of Sister Emerentius CSJ, uncle of Father William *O'Brien and cousin of Father Fergus *Sheehy, was born at Peterborough, Ontario, on 26 June 1898, the youngest of eight children of Michael O'Brien and Johanna Sheehy.

He died in Toronto on 22 February 1949 and was buried there in the Basilian plot of Mount Hope Cemetery.

Educated at St Peter's Separate School and Peterborough Collegiate Institute, 1912–16, Austin O'Brien went to St Michael's College, Toronto, in 1917 and, except for some months in the Canadian Army, continued there until he entered St Basil's Novitiate, Toronto, in 1919. After profession on 2 October 1920, he returned to St Michael's College, graduated from the University of Toronto in Honours Philosophy in 1924, and then attended the Ontario College of Education in Toronto, 1924–5, to earn teacher certification. He studied theology at St Basil's Scholasticate, Toronto, and was ordained a priest on 19 December 1925 in St Basil's Church by Bishop Michael O'Brien of Peterborough.

Father O'Brien's appointments were many and varied: St Thomas High School, Houston, 1926–8; St Michael's College, 1928–9, 1930–2, 1937–42; Ste Anne's Parish, Detroit, 1929–30, 1933–4, 1935–6, 1946–7; Catholic Central High School, Detroit, 1932–3; Assumption Parish, Windsor, 1934–5; St Mary's of the Assumption Parish, Owen Sound, Ontario, 1942–3; Aquinas Institute, Rochester, 1943–6; and St Basil's Parish, Toronto, from 1947 until his sudden death in 1949 from a heart attack.

Father 'Sham' O'Brien, as he was called, was a colourful and outgoing man who enlivened every group he entered. A gifted athlete in his student days, he remained keenly interested in sports all his life. The Basilian Centennial volume for St Mary's of the Assumption Parish described him as 'a kindly, lively, good natured person, with a love for children.' In parishes he seemed to attract the most troubled and would spend hour after hour with them.

SOURCES: GABF; *Annals* 1 (1943–50) 242–3; *Centennial, St Mary's*; *Purple and White* (15 December 1925); *Yearbook SMC* 15 (1924).

O'BRIEN, William Hilary, priest, nephew of Father Austin David *O'Brien and of Sister Emerentius CSJ, was born on 13 August 1922 in Toronto, the son of William Joseph O'Brien and Mary Josephine Corrigan. He died in Toronto on 8 December 1998, and is buried in the Basilian plot of Holy Cross Cemetery, Thornhill, Ontario.

Bill O'Brien attended St Clare's Separate School, 1928–35, and the high school section of St Michael's College, Toronto. Graduating in 1940, he went on to earn a B.A. from the University of Toronto, and in February

1943 he enlisted in Royal Canadian Artillery, which later brought him the nickname 'Gunner.' He served in the Second World War in England from December 1943 to May 1945. He had been posted for action in Europe in January 1945, but fell ill with influenza. He attended the Ontario College of Education, 1945–6, and taught as a layman at St Michael's College School, 1946–8. He entered St Basil's Novitiate and was professed on 15 August 1949. His first appointment was to St Michael's College, where he resided while studying theology. In 1951 he moved to St Basil's Seminary to continue his theological studies, and was ordained to the priesthood on 20 December 1952 in St Michael's Cathedral, Toronto, by Cardinal James Charles McGuigan.

In 1953 Father O'Brien received the first of three appointments to St Michael's College School, 1953–6, 1957–62, 1982–98, a total of twenty-four years. He also taught fifteen years at St Thomas More College, Saskatoon, 1967–82, with an interval in 1969 at the Université Laval. He had three shorter appointments: St Charles College, Sudbury, Ontario, 1956–7, the Université Laval and St Lawrence College, Québec, 1962–5, and Basilian Fathers of East Rochester, 1965–7, where he taught French at St John Fisher College.

Bill O'Brien was a man of encyclopedic knowledge, incisive wit, analytic mind, and generous heart. He was a dynamic, not to say an electrifying, teacher. Fluent in French, he subsequently added Latin, Russian, Italian, and Hebrew to his linguistic repertory. He tutored applicants and M.S.L. students in Latin at the Pontifical Institute of Mediaeval Studies. He loved to talk; and, though witty and rather intense, his conversation was never trifling. His military experience marked him for life – rhythmic gait, clipped speech, punctuality, and the neatness of room, office, and dress all bearing witness. When directing the Loretto Abbey two-hundred-strong choir and the St Michael's Band at Massey Hall, all preparatory movements were timed so that the bandmaster mounted the podium precisely at 8:00 p.m. He served as part-time military chaplain all his Basilian life, both in western Canada and at Downsview Air Base, Toronto. He was the moving spirit behind the planning and execution of the memorial to fallen alumni which is incised in the stone of the slype at St Michael's College. His association with the Canadian Parachute Battalion involved him in 'jumping with the best of them' until a broken leg ended his aerial exploits.

Father O'Brien's love and reverence for Basilian history, tradition, and heritage made him a diligent archivist of St Michael's College

School in the 1980s and 1990s. He rescued from a coal bunker the bits and pieces of the stained glass window that had surmounted the main entrance to the old college building on Bay Street. He had it repaired and remounted over the entrance to the college on Bathurst Street, where it serves not only as a link with the past but also as a monument to one of St Michael's most dedicated Basilians.

BIBLIOGRAPHY: 'Languages in High Schools,' *Basilian Teacher* 2 (December 1957) 8, 19, 12, 24–5; 'Breaking the Sound Barrier,' *Basilian Teacher* 5 (January 1961) 121–4.
SOURCES: GABF; *Annals* 2 (1953) 107, 9 (1999) 83–4; *Newsletter* (15 January 1999).

O'CONNOR, Denis, priest, bishop of London, archbishop of Toronto, was born on a farm in Lot 1, Concession 3, Pickering Township, Ontario (diocese of Kingston, since 14 December 1841 of Toronto), on 26 February 1841, the eldest of three children born to Denis O'Connor and Mary O'Leary, pioneer Irish immigrants. He died in Toronto on 30 June 1911, and is buried there in the Basilian plot of Mount Hope Cemetery.

After education in a rural school, Denis O'Connor was the eleventh pupil and second boarder to enrol at St Michael's College when it opened in Toronto in 1852. He followed the classical and philosophical curriculum until 1859, when he entered the novitiate in Toronto. After profession on 24 June 1860, he continued his studies at St Michael's College until 1861 when, at the instigation of Father Jean Mathieu *Soulerin, he and Francis Mary *Walsh spent one year at the Basilian house at Feyzin (Isère, now Rhône) and another at the scholasticate in Annonay. His piety and judgment attracted attention, and there was great disappointment when he contracted tuberculosis. The disease was well advanced by the time he returned to Toronto in September 1863. Fearing the worst, he was granted an indult to be ordained priest at the age of twenty-two, on 8 December 1863, after which he went on sick leave.

Father O'Connor's mother had died young, and his father had married Bridget Callaghan, who bore him ten children. His stepmother nursed the young priest back to health. By September 1864 he was strong enough to do light office work and substitute for absent teachers at St Michael's College. Three years later, when his health failed a second time, he spent the greater part of 1867 on sick leave. In 1868 he became acting superior of St Michael's College for several months, but on 28 July 1870 was appointed superior of Assumption College, Sandwich (now Windsor). 'The challenge seemed to restore his entire being, both body and soul, for with only three hundred dollars in his pocket, and no hope of obtaining a government grant, he arrived at Sandwich on July 20, 1870, fully confident in God's power and his own abilities' (Michael Power, *Assumption College. 2: The O'Connor Years 1870–1890* [Windsor, 1986] viii). He was so successful in enhancing the college physically and in reputation that he was looked on as its second founder. Pope Leo XIII conferred an honorary Doctor of Divinity upon him on 20 September 1888, the year of his silver jubilee as a priest. He was ordained bishop of London, Ontario, on 18 October 1890. Nine years later, on 27 January 1899, he was transferred to the archdiocese of Toronto and took possession of his new see on 3 May 1899. He resigned as archbishop of Toronto on 22 May 1908, and retired to St Basil's Novitiate, Toronto, where he died in 1911.

'A Pioneer Alumnus' wrote in the *Golden Jubilee Volume of Assumption College* that the second founder 'was made of sterling stuff. Physically handsome, mentally vigorous, kind of heart, severely strict in discipline both toward himself and others, he was a born leader and a prudent administrator. Students instinctively recognized his natural authority and did his bidding.' Father Charles *Collins, who was one of his students, wrote: 'He was the embodiment of all the powers and prerogatives that go with the position of superior. His spirit dominated the whole college. ... His word was law and that law was obeyed, or one knew the reason why. He impressed me as being a section of the Rock of Gibraltar. ... His voice was hard and his manner of speech very laconic and all was business.' While at Assumption College Denis O'Connor was on good terms with the bishop of Detroit, and it was a disappointment to him when the Congregation did not accept the offer of a high school there in 1877. He was instrumental in the Congregation's taking charge of St John the Baptist Parish, Amherstburg, Ontario, in 1878, and of Ste Anne's Parish, Detroit, in 1886. Within the Congregation, Father O'Connor was elected to the provincial council in 1883 and re-elected in 1886 and 1889.

Upon becoming a bishop, he tendered his resignation as councillor, but it was not accepted. Although he no longer took an active part in its deliberations he was always ranked as an *ex officio* member of the provincial chapter. Following his episcopal ordination Bishop O'Connor changed his residence but not his way of life. He continued to live frugally and to work industriously. All his correspondence was attended to personally. He observed no office hours, being at home to every caller from early morning until evening. The only time he reserved for himself was half an hour outdoors in the early afternoon, and that only out of consideration for his weakened lungs. He guided his life by three rules: prayer, work, and the instruction of the young. Rev. J.V. Tobin (diocese of London), who gave the eulogy at his funeral, described his preaching in the *Golden Jubilee Volume of Assumption College*, 'In season and out of season he fed his spiritual children on the bread of God's word, broken to them in sermons and instructions of great depth of thought, carefully prepared, forcibly if not eloquently delivered, as redolent of piety as the homilies of the early Fathers of the Church, and made intelligible to the simplest minds and to the minds of children by the absence of all obscure terms and by a wealth of apt illustration.' As an administrator he was convinced that nine-tenths of a bishop's energy must be devoted to keeping up existing works, and he was slow to initiate new institutions, requiring a feasible plan for the financing of all new undertakings. In his dealings with both priests and laity he retained something of the schoolmaster, delegating very little authority to them. Whether as priest, bishop, or archbishop, Denis O'Connor shrank from press publicity, regarding it as incompatible with humility. The only photograph for which he posed was taken in 1883 to form part of a collection being presented to his classmate and lifelong friend, Father Michael *Ferguson. His human side was known to his friends, among whom he threw off his natural reserve. After his retirement he lived in almost complete isolation from the world and gave himself to prayer in preparation for death.

SOURCES: GABF; Charles Collins, 'Archbishop O'Connor, 1841–1911,' *Basilian* 4 (June 1939) 107, 120; *Golden Jubilee, Assumption College*; Hoskin, *St Basil's*; E. Kelly, *The Story of St Paul's Parish, Toronto, 1822–1922* (Toronto, 1923); Jean LeBlanc, *Dictionnaire biographique des évêques catholiques du Canada* (Montreal and Ottawa, 2002) 704–5; McMahon, *Pure Zeal* 6–16; F.A. O'Brien, *Life Work of a Saintly Prelate, Most Reverend Denis O'Connor* (Kalamazoo, 1914); Edmund C. Phelan, *The Parish of St Francis de Sales, Pickering, Ontario, a Short History* (Pickering, 1966); Michael Power and Mark McGowan, in *Dictionary of Canadian Biography* 14 (1998) 789–92; R.J. Scollard, 'Most Reverend Denis O'Connor, CSB, DD,' *Basilian* 4 (May 1938) 88–9; Shook, *Catholic Education* 279–81. For documentation relating to Denis O'Connor's administration of Assumption College see Power, *Assumption College* 2 37–74.

O'DONNELL, Bernard Joseph, priest, was born on 7 February 1899, in Bathurst, New Brunswick (diocese of Chatham, since 1938 of Bathurst), the son of Stephen O'Donnell and Margaret Cullen. He died in Windsor, Ontario, on 27 March 1977, and was the first Basilian to be buried in St John the Baptist Cemetery, Amherstburg, Ontario,

Bernard O'Donnell attended primary and secondary schools in Bathurst and then enrolled at St Thomas College, Chatham, New Brunswick, which at that time was under the direction of the Basilian Fathers. After completing two years of arts and doing some teaching he entered St Basil's Novitiate, Toronto, was professed on 11 August 1922, and was assigned to live at the Basilian Scholasticate, Toronto, while completing his arts course (B.A., University of Toronto, 1926). In 1927 he obtained teaching certification for Ontario. He had begun his theology course in parallel with his other studies in 1924, and continued through 1927, being ordained to the priesthood on 18 December 1926 in St Basil's Church, Toronto, by Bishop Alexander MacDonald.

Father O'Donnell taught at Assumption High School, 1927-8, St Thomas College, Houston, 1928-33, and St Michael's High School, Toronto, 1933-6. In 1936 he began a long and distinguished career in Basilian parishes: Assumption Parish, Windsor, 1936-7, St Basil's Parish, Toronto, 1937-46, St John the Baptist Parish, Amherstburg, 1946-54, 1957-8, and 1965-77, St Mary's of the Assumption Parish, Owen Sound, Ontario, 1954-7, Blessed Sacrament Parish, Windsor, 1958-65, and Ste Anne's Parish, Detroit, summer 1965.

'Bernie' O'Donnell had been a member of the St Michael's Varsity Intermediate Championship Football Team of 1925, yet his was a gentle presence. He had a keen sensitivity to the poor, the elderly, and the lonely, and much of his time was spent visiting shut-ins. As he did not drive he always walked, no matter what the distance, to make such visits. In Amherstburg, where he spent over twenty years of his ministry, everyone of every faith knew and admired him. His low-key but sharp wit and his many kindnesses in the community were greatly admired. Weakened by a lengthy struggle with cancer, which involved a major operation in 1976, he entered Hotel-Dieu Hospital in mid-March 1977, needing treatment but not thought to be critical. Two weeks later he died as he had lived, peacefully and unobtrusively, in his sleep.

SOURCES: GABF; *Annals* 4 (1973) 272, 5 (1977) 197, (1978) 322-3; *Newsletter* (31 March 1977).

O'DONNELL, James REGINALD, priest, was born on 19 August 1907 at Jarvis, Ontario (archdiocese of Toronto, since 1958 of St Catharines), the son of John O'Donnell and Mary Hunks. He died in Toronto on 5 February 1988 and is buried in the Basilian plot of Holy Cross Cemetery, Thornhill, Ontario.

'Reg' O'Donnell completed junior matriculation at Cayuga High School, Cayuga, Ontario. Arrangements were made for him to enrol at St Michael's College, Toronto, but on the advice of his parish priest he spent two years doing senior matriculation and first year of arts at St Jerome's College, Kitchener, Ontario. He transferred to St Michael's College, and in 1927 entered St Basil's Novitiate, Toronto, making first profession of vows on 11 August 1928. He completed his undergraduate studies (B.A., University of Toronto, 1931) while living first at St Michael's and then, in 1929, at St Basil's Scholasticate, where he concurrently began theological studies. He was ordained to the priesthood on 21 December 1932 in St Basil's Church, Toronto, by Bishop Alexander MacDonald. In May 1933, he was awarded an M.A. degree in philosophy and classics from the University of Toronto.

Father O'Donnell left for graduate studies in Europe in 1933 in preparation for teaching at the Institute of Mediaeval Studies, Toronto. He spent one year at the University of Cracow, Poland, and one year at the Ecole pratique des hautes études, Paris. He returned to St Michael's in 1935 and began teaching at the Institute while continuing graduate studies (Ph.D., Philosophy, University of Toronto, 1946), submitting his thesis on 'The *De bono et malo* of William of Auvergne: Text, Introduction, and Brief Analytical Studies.'

Father O'Donnell was a precise and painstaking scholar and a demanding teacher, but his students 'soon came to realize that he was only requiring of them what he always required of himself: constant care and precision in the reading of the manuscripts, respect for the scribes, and first an interest in the work itself, the thought of the author in its whole context' (citation at his reception of an honorary doctorate from the Pontifical Institute in 1979). Other honours that came to him were his election as a Fellow of the Royal Society of Canada in 1960, a Canada Council Senior Fellowship at Florence and Rome, 1960–1, and a Fellowship of the Institute for Advanced Study, Princeton, 1968–9.

Besides his work at the Pontifical Institute of Mediaeval Studies, Father O'Donnell taught in the Department of Classics and in the School of Graduate Studies in the University of Toronto. For many years he was editor of *Mediaeval Studies*, the annual journal of the Pontifical Institute, maintaining rigorously its high standard of scholarship.

Reg O'Donnell was one of the original members of the Basilian Institute House when it was formally established in 1942, and served as local councillor, 1952–68. He kept in contact with alumni and professors, and did much to foster scholarship and higher studies in the community. Even after moving to the Basilian Fathers Residence (Infirmary) in 1982 and suffering the amputation of one leg, he still made every effort to participate in community events and celebrations, cheerfully moving about in his motorized wheelchair.

BIBLIOGRAPHY:
Books: Ed. Nicolas of Autrecourt, *Exigit ordo*. Toronto 1939. Ed. *Nine Mediaeval Thinkers: A Collection of Hitherto Unedited Texts*. Toronto, 1955. Ed. *Essays in Honour of Anton Charles Pegis*. Toronto, 1974. He left unpublished a transcription of the *Sapientiale* of Thomas of York.
Articles: A list of his twenty-three articles and three translations in scholarly journals and books can be consulted in *Mediaeval Studies* 50 (1988) ix–x. That list does not include the following: 'An Attack on M. Maritain,' *Basilian* 4 (March 1938) 43, 53.
SOURCES: GABF; *Annals* 5 (1979) 343, 6 (1983) 115, 6 (1989) 809–11; *Newsletter* (15 February 1988); Shook, *Catholic Education* 217, 221n, 223, 225, 429n.

O'DONNELL, Joseph Leo, priest, was born on 2 March 1900 in London, Ontario, the son of Hugh O'Donnell and Elizabeth Trainor. He died in Toronto on 18 December 1984 and is buried in the Basilian plot of Holy Cross Cemetery, Thornhill, Ontario.

After attending London Collegiate Institute, 1915–20, Joseph O'Donnell enrolled in Assumption College, Windsor (B.A., University of Western Ontario, 1923). He entered St Basil's Novitiate, Toronto, making first profession on 11 August 1924. He began theological studies, living first at St Michael's College, Toronto, 1924–5, then at St Basil's Scholasticate, and also attended classes at the Ontario College of Education, earning teacher certification in 1926. He returned to St Michael's for his final year of theology, 1927–8, and was ordained to the priesthood on 21 December 1927 by Bishop Alexander MacDonald in St Basil's Church, Toronto.

Father O'Donnell was appointed to Aquinas Institute in 1928, a member of the first group of Basilians there. In 1932 he returned to St Michael's to teach English, particularly Shakespeare. He served on the local council of the Basilian community while continuing studies (M.A., University of Western Ontario, with a thesis on 'Ethical Principles of the Middle Ages in Shakespeare'). In 1945 he was appointed to St Thomas More College, Saskatoon. While teaching a full schedule, he served on the local Basilian council, was treasurer of the college, 1948–52, and superior and principal, 1955–61. As treasurer he collaborated with Father Basil *Sullivan in planning the splendid main building of the campus. For years he produced and directed student performances of plays, both old and new, that were famous for their professional character.

From 1967, when he retired, he lived in London, Ontario, with his sister Margaret, and did pastoral work at St Michael's Parish, London, and chaplaincy service at the motherhouse of the Sisters of St Joseph. A stroke suffered in March 1984 necessitated a move to the Basilian Fathers Residence (Infirmary), Toronto, where he suffered several more strokes before his death in December.

Both at St Michael's and St Thomas More, Joe O'Donnell directed plays of Shakespeare and of modern dramatists. He was so enthralled by the beauty and richness of the Bard's work that his whole manner became dramatic. His teaching was not so much a course as an experience. He affected a great black cape, which he wore about the campus and loved to unfurl as he swung it over his shoulders or turned to look majestically behind him. An excellent preacher, he taught predication to the Basilian scholastics. As one who loved to sing he organized glee clubs, and was never so pleased as when playing the piano and singing with a group of students or with members of the community. Wherever he served the memory of him lingered long after.

BIBLIOGRAPHY: 'A Catholic Approach to English,' *Basilian* 1 (April 1935) 29–30.
SOURCES: GABF; *Annals* 5 (1975) 64, 5 (1978) 260, 6 (1985) 382–3; *Newsletter* (19 December 1984); Kirley, *Congregation in France* 235; Shook, *Catholic Education* 350–2; *Heartwood* 78–9, 95, 98–100, 104–6, 111, 133.

O'DONOGHUE, John Curtis, priest, was born on 22 September 1919 in St Catharines, Ontario (archdiocese of Toronto, since 1958 diocese of St Catharines), the son of Joseph Patrick O'Donoghue and Katharine Grobb. He died in Windsor, Ontario, on 15 September 1978, and is buried in the family plot in Victoria Lawn Cemetery, St Catharines.

John completed his elementary and secondary education in his home city and then enrolled in St Michael's College, Toronto, where for one year he studied commerce at the University of Toronto. In 1939 he entered St Basil's Novitiate, Toronto. After profession on 15 August 1940, he was appointed to St Basil's Seminary, Toronto, for undergraduate studies (Honours B.A., Modern Languages, University of Toronto, 1944). As a scholastic he taught at St Thomas High School, Houston, 1944–5, and at Catholic Central High School, Detroit, 1945–6. He returned to St Basil's Seminary in 1946 for theological studies and was ordained to the priesthood on 29 June 1949 in St Basil's Church, Toronto, by Cardinal James Charles McGuigan.

In 1950–1, Father O'Donoghue earned an M.A. in Romance languages from the University of Toronto. He taught at the University of St Thomas, Houston, from 1951 to 1958. He did a further year of graduate studies at the University of Toronto, 1958–9, before moving to Assumption University, Windsor, where he taught until 1968. After earning a second Master's degree (A.M., Harvard University, 1969), he returned to teach in Windsor at Assumption University and subsequently at the University of Windsor.

'Ajax' O'Donoghue read widely and enjoyed conversation about history and ideas. He found beauty everywhere: in the cosmos, music, art, poetry, and people. This sensitivity and his faculty for expressing it made him a fascinating teacher, but persons less sensitive to beauty and life than he was sometimes found themselves the target of an articulate volley of Irish wrath. His interest in languages extended beyond his specialty, Spanish, to include research in Celtic language and literature.

Father O'Donoghue looked to the welfare of confreres and visitors, though his shyness made this an effort. His only complaint in the long months of his final illness was that he could not say Mass each day. His sisters came to Windsor to attend him during that time, and the family requested that he be buried in the family plot.

SOURCES: GABF; *Annals* 1 (1949) 261, 5 (1979) 412–13; *Newsletter* (20 September 1978).

O'DONOHUE, Peter, priest, was born in County Cavan, Ireland (diocese of Kilmore), on 4 May 1846. He died in Toronto on 5 March 1915 and was buried there in the Basilian plot of Mount Hope Cemetery.

Peter O'Donohue emigrated to Canada at the age of eighteen. He enrolled in St Michael's College, Toronto, in 1866, then entered St Basil's Novitiate, Toronto, on 25 July 1868. After profession he studied again at St Michael's College until 1871, when he was sent to Assumption College, Windsor, for theology. He was ordained a priest on 13 June 1875.

Father O'Donohue received frequent changes of appointment: assistant at St Mary's of the Assumption Parish, Owen Sound, Ontario, 1875-83; Assumption College, 1883-6; pastor of St Mary's of the Assumption, 1886-9; pastor of St Basil's Parish, Toronto, 1891-2; treasurer of St Michael's College, 1891-2; assistant at Ste Anne's Parish, Detroit, 1892-3; pastor of St Charles Parish, Newport, Michigan, 1893-5; administrator of Holy Rosary Parish, Toronto, 1895-1900. He was on loan to the diocese of London as pastor of St Patrick's Parish, Raleigh, 1900-1, and of Sacred Heart Parish, Lambton, 1901-9. In 1909 he was appointed assistant master of novices and assistant at Holy Rosary Parish, posts he held until his death in 1915.

Father O'Donohue was a good-natured Irishman with a head of thick, wavy, pure white hair. He had a peculiar semi-English accent and was known for his quaint sayings. An obituary notice in the St Michael's College *Yearbook* declared that 'All who ever knew Father O'Donohue now remember him as a man of gentle, genial and affable character, especially devoted to children.'

SOURCES: GABF; *Centennial, St Mary's*; *Jubilee, St Mary's*; Hoskin, *St Basil's*; Spetz, *Waterloo*; *Yearbook SMC* 6 (1915).

O'GORMAN, George DONAL, priest, was born on 16 November 1923 in Toronto, the son of George O'Gorman and Ethel Lanthier. He died on 2 February 1996 at Henry Carr Farm, Beeton, Ontario, and is buried in the Basilian plot of Holy Cross Cemetery, Thornhill, Ontario.

Donal attended Blessed Sacrament Separate School and secondary school at St Michael's College, Toronto, doing his grade XIII at Lawrence Park Collegiate, Toronto. He worked for two years before serving for nearly three years, 1943-5, in the Royal Canadian Air Force as pilot and navigator. After two years at St Michael's College, Toronto, majoring in modern languages, he entered St Basil's Novitiate, Richmond Hill, Ontario, and was professed on 15 August 1948. He was appointed to St Michael's College (B.A., Honours Modern Languages, University of Toronto, 1950). After a year of teaching at St Michael's College School while concurrently studying theology, he was appointed to St Basil's Seminary, where he completed his theology course while doing graduate studies in French (M.A., University of Toronto, 1952). He was ordained to the priesthood on 29 June 1953 in St Basil's Church, Toronto, by Cardinal James Charles McGuigan.

In 1954, Father O'Gorman began a long teaching career at the University of St Michael's College, interrupted by three years of graduate studies at Columbia University, one year of which, 1958–9, was spent in Paris, where he lodged with the Eudist Fathers. He obtained the Ph.D. from Columbia University in 1960, with the thesis topic 'Diderot's Satire.' He continued teaching at St Michael's from 1959 to 1985, with one sabbatical year in Paris, 1972–3, and was the superior of the Basilian community, 1978–81.

In 1985, after experiencing a certain disappointment with the reception of his published work, Father O'Gorman accepted an appointment as rector of Henry Carr Farm and then as pastor of Our Lady of the Assumption Parish, Lethbridge, Alberta, 1987–94. There he helped found the Martha Native Ministry, a program for the integration of the rituals of native peoples into the Eucharist. During the last six months of his pastorate he went to Bolivia to study Spanish, probably with a view to ministry in Latin America; but he was reappointed in 1994 as rector of Henry Carr Farm, where he spent the last eighteen months of his life, dying suddenly after the evening meal.

Donal O'Gorman was a man of fine appearance and manners who graced any gathering. He spoke French fluently and elegantly. Widely read and thoughtful, his conversation never lacked interest or wit. He had a spirit of adventure that found outlets in his co-operation with Father Gerald *McGuigan's work in Africa, in his interest in the native peoples of Canada, and in his sojourn in Bolivia. At the university he did a good deal of spiritual counselling, for students found him understanding and wise. His own quest in matters spiritual was marked by a certain reverent questioning of rules and structures, though it was unusual for him to be sad or pessimistic.

BIBLIOGRAPHY:
Book: *Diderot the Satirist: Le neveu de Rameau and Related Works: An Analysis.* Toronto, 1971.
Articles: (With Otis Fellows) 'Another Addition to the *Salon de 1767*?,' *Diderot Studies* 3 (1966) 215–17; (With Otis Fellows) 'A Note concerning Diderot's Mathematics,' *Diderot Studies* 10 (1968) 47–50; 'Myth and Metaphor in *Rameau's Nephew*,' *Diderot Studies* 17 (1973) 117–30; Ed. (with Jean Mayer) 'Sur deux mémoires de d'Alembert: l'un concernant le calcul des probabilités, l'autre

l'inoculation (1761),' *Philosophie et mathématique. Idées I* in *Didérot. Oeuvres complètes* 2 (Paris, 1975) 339–61; 'Diderot and the Formica-leo Incident: A Demystification,' *Diderot Studies* 20 (1981) 219–24; 'Hypotheses for a New Reading of *Jacques le Fataliste*,' *Diderot Studies* 19 (1978) 129–43; 'Henry James's reading of *The Turn of the Screw*,' *Henry James Review* 1 (1980): 125–38, 228–56.

SOURCES: GABF; *Annals* 2 (1953) 110, 8 (1997) 101–2; *French Studies U. of T.* 172; *Newsletter* (12 February 1996).

O'LEARY, Arthur Jennings, priest, was born on 30 September 1910 in Toronto, the son of Frederick O'Leary and Mary Jennings. He died in Toronto on 16 June 1976, and is buried in the Basilian plot of Holy Cross Cemetery, Thornhill, Ontario.

'Art' O'Leary attended Holy Name Separate School and the high school section of St Michael's College, Toronto, graduating in 1928. He attended St Michael's College for one year before entering St Augustine's Seminary, Scarborough, Ontario, where he spent two years. He returned to St Michael's and completed his studies (B.A., University of Toronto, 1933), and attended the Ontario College of Education for one year. In October 1934 he entered St Basil's Novitiate, Toronto, making first profession on 26 October 1935, after which he studied theology at St Basil's Scholasticate ('Seminary' from 1937) and was ordained to the priesthood on 17 December 1938 in St Basil's Church, Toronto, by Archbishop James Charles McGuigan.

In 1939 Father O'Leary was appointed to St Michael's College School and then, in 1940, to Aquinas Instutute, Rochester. He took summer courses at St Bonaventure University, Olean, New York, to earn an M.A. in English, 1942. He was the priest later described by his teacher Thomas Merton as belonging to 'some teaching Order in Canada' who 'just sat there and gave me black looks' (*Seven Storey Mountain* [New York, 1948] 339). In 1953 he was transferred to Assumption College School, Windsor, and two years later was appointed once more to St Michael's College School, 1955–61. In August 1961, he entered the parish apostolate with an appointment to St Basil's Parish, Toronto, 1961–2, and then to St Mary's of the Assumption Parish, Owen Sound, 1962–5. He began serving in the Basilian Hispanic missions in Texas in August 1965, first at St Basil's Parish, Angleton, 1965–9, and then at Our Lady of Guadalupe Parish, Rosenberg, 1969–74. Wishing to become more fluent in Spanish, he went to Mexico City in 1974, and during the last two years of his life he commuted between the Mexican capital and the parishes in Texas. He had just received an appointment to St Theresa's Parish, Sugar Land, when, visiting his brother in Etobicoke, Ontario, he suffered two heart attacks in three days, the second of which proved fatal.

Art O'Leary was a quiet, reserved man who gave the impression of sternness – whence his nickname 'Cheery' and Thomas Merton's impression of 'black looks.' In the classroom he was a strict disciplinarian and a demanding teacher; but the initial fear which his manner inspired soon turned to respect and admiration as the students came to realize his interest in them and in the subject he was teaching. He had a dry sense of humour and was able to pinpoint the foibles of others immediately. It was impossible to put on a false front in his presence. His years as a parish priest were perhaps his richest and happiest, if happiness could ever properly be associated with Father O'Leary. His love for the poor Latin Americans to whom he ministered was shown by his willingness at sixty years of age to go to language school so that he could better minister to them.

SOURCES: GABF; *Annals* 5 (1977) 250–1; *Newsletter* (22 June 1976).

OLIVER, Michael Joseph, priest, was born on 29 October 1888 at Barrie, Ontario (archdiocese of Toronto), the son of John Oliver and Maria Maloney. He died in Toronto on 11 February 1977 and is buried in the Basilian plot of Holy Cross Cemetery, Thornhill, Ontario.
After early education in Barrie, Mike Oliver enrolled in St Michael's College, Toronto (B.A., University of Toronto, 1910). In August 1910 he entered St Basil's Novitiate, Toronto, and made his first profession on 17 September 1911. After three years of theological study at St Basil's Scholasticate, Toronto, he was ordained to the priesthood on 18 September 1914 in St Basil's Church, Toronto, by Archbishop Neil McNeil.

Father Oliver went immediately for studies at the Catholic University of America, Washington, D.C. (Ph.M., 1915). His first school appointment was to St Michael's College, 1915–23, where he was both teacher and administrator in the high school section. In 1923 he was named to Assumption College, Windsor, for one year of teaching, and was then appointed to Holy Rosary Parish, Toronto, as pastor, 1924–8. He undertook the building of the present church, modelled on the English church of St Neat's in Huntingdonshire that he had seen and admired. Opened in 1927, it remains one of the most beautiful of Toronto churches. In 1928 he returned to St Michael's, where he directed the Diamond Jubilee Expansion Campaign. He was appointed once more to Holy Rosary as pastor, 1930–4, and then as pastor of St Basil's Parish, Toronto, 1934–7. In 1937 he was appointed to St Michael's College once again, this time to undertake a program of social work, particularly the direction of the Marylake Farm School and land settlement projects. He was named to Holy Rosary for a third time, 1942–6, and was then made pastor of St Mary's of the Assumption Parish, Owen Sound, Ontario, 1946–52. During this time, a parish couple, undecided about which one of several Latvian refugee children to adopt into their family, asked Father Oliver's advice. His choice, whom they raised as Paul McGill, was later ordained as a Basilian priest and became pastor of Holy Rosary Parish in 1993.

A new chapter opened with his appointment in 1952 to the new foundation of St Mark's College, Vancouver. He was treasurer and local councillor, and oversaw construction of the college buildings. He was chaplain of the Newman Club at the University of British Columbia, 1952–61. In 1968–70 he was administrator and then assistant of St Pius X Parish, Calgary, Alberta, then returned to Vancouver, where he undertook chaplaincy work, parish ministry, and publication of the annual *Catholic Directory for British Columbia and the Yukon*. After a series of minor strokes, he was moved to St Basil's Infirmary, Toronto, on 7 December 1976; but on Christmas day he had to be taken to hospital, where he died seven weeks later.

When he died Father Oliver was the oldest Basilian, both by age and by profession. He had known the crises and changes in the community in the early part of the century and especially the separation from France in 1922. His readiness to undertake a diversity of apostolic works contributed to the character and customs of the present community. He enjoyed working but never hesitated to draw others into his projects, and became known as 'Father Woudya.' Many Basilians owe their vocation to his example. A man of distinguished appearance and manners, he was at ease with everyone.

BIBLIOGRAPHY:
Book: Ed. Henry Carr. *The Heart of the Matter* (twenty papers of a projected thirty, mimeographed, privately circulated).
Pamphlets: *Marylake Farm School, King, Ontario: An Outline of Its Work and Objects*. Toronto, 1939. Ed. *Catholic Directory for British Columbia and the Yukon*. 8th ed. Vancouver, 1968 (also contains three poems by Father Oliver). *The Question and the Answer: 'A Matter of Consequence' for Adults Only (Parents and Priests)*. Vancouver, 1969.

Articles: 'Children's Concepts,' *Separate Public School Review* 1 no. 3 (January 1922); 'Baccalaureate Sermon to Graduates of 1922,' *Loretto Rainbow* 29 no. 3 (July 1922) 110–11; 'Flee to the Country!' *Basilian* 1 (March 1935) 7–8, 14; 'The Vancouver Story,' *Basilian Teacher* 8 (March 1964) 315–22; 'A Mountain Stream (poem),' *Basilian Teacher* 10 (January 1966) 29; 'Father Henry Carr CSB and the University of British Columbia,' in *Were the Dean's Windows Dusty?*, ed. Gerard Mulligan (Montreal, 1966) 2 209–39; 'Letter [on various forms of the apostolate],' *Forum* 3 (March 1967) 46–8.
SOURCES: GABF; *Annals* 3 (1962) 75, (1964) 306–7, 5 (1978) 314–15; *Newsletter* (16 February 1977); Brian F. Hogan, 'Salted with Fire: Studies in Catholic Social Thought and Action in Ontario, 1931–1961,' Ph.D. diss. (University of Toronto, 1986), 75–87.

O'LOANE, John Henry, priest, was born in Toronto on 17 April 1897, the son of John Thomas O'Loane and Ellen Teresa McCarthy. He died in Toronto on 22 May 1966 and is buried in the Basilian plot of Holy Cross Cemetery, Thornhill, Ontario.

John O'Loane grew up in Our Lady of Lourdes Parish, Toronto. He enrolled in the high school section of St Michael's College in 1910 and in 1914 registered in the college department (B.A., University of Toronto, 1918). He served for six months in the Royal Flying Corps, then entered St Basil's Novitiate, Toronto, and was professed on 18 January 1920. He was appointed to teach at Assumption College in Windsor, 1920–1, and at St Thomas High School, Houston, 1921–2, and then to study theology at St Basil's Scholasticate, Toronto. He also attended the Ontario College of Education, 1922–3. He was ordained priest on 30 June 1923 in St Basil's Church, Toronto, by Bishop Alexander MacDonald.

Father O'Loane taught at Assumption College and served as director of athletics, 1923–8. His appointment in 1928 as principal of the high school there was followed by other heavy responsibilities: superior and principal of St Thomas High School, 1931–7, superior and first Basilian principal of Aquinas Institute, Rochester, 1937–43 and 1952–5, superior and master of scholastics, St Basil's Seminary, 1943–6, and superior and president of Assumption College, 1946–52. In this latter capacity, and aided by Father E.C. *LeBel, he initiated the move to obtain a university charter for Assumption, thus separating it from its affiliation with the University of Western Ontario that had been in effect since 1921.

Father O'Loane was a member of the general council, 1948–54, and master of novices at St Basil's Novitiate, Richmond Hill, Ontario, 1955–61. He retired to St Michael's College School and died in 1966, several months after suffering a stroke.

Father O'Loane liked to be 'on top' of his work. When made director of athletics at Assumption College he attended coaching schools at the University of Michigan and at Notre Dame. When appointed high school principal he obtained an M.A. in education from Columbia University, 1931. He made a point of knowing personally every student. As a religious superior he was known for his regularity, his invariable fairness, and his constant devotion to the Rule.

BIBLIOGRAPHY: 'St Thomas College, Houston,' *Basilian* 1 (March 1935) 11–12; 'New Attitudes for New Situations,' *Basilian* 4 (May 1938) 82–3; 'To Rome and Back,' *Benedicamus* 4 (November 1950) 10–11; 'Leonard J. Dolan, a Biography,' *Basilian Teacher* 1 (May 1957) 6–8. 'Communications and Education [forum],' *Basilian Teacher* 3 (May 1959) 220–1.

SOURCES: GABF; *Annals* 3 (1966) 466–7; *Newsletter* (24 May 1966); *Basilides, Assumption College* (Windsor, 1930); Edmund C. Phelan, *Parish of St Francis de Sales, Pickering, Ontario. A Short History* (Pickering, 1966); *Yearbook SMC* 9 (1918). For documentation relating to his presidency at Assumption see Power, *Assumption College* 6 116–97.

O'LOUGHLIN, Simon RAPHAEL, priest, was born on 7 May 1916 in Ashfield Township, Ontario (diocese of London), the son of Joseph O'Loughlin and Mary Griffin. He died in Toronto on 19 March 1998 and is buried in the Basilian plot of Holy Cross Cemetery, Thornhill, Ontario.

Raphael, at times called 'Ralph' (though in later life he insisted on 'Raphael'), began his education locally. When he was eleven his parents moved to Detroit, where he attended St Agnes Grade School. After a first year of high school at Sacred Heart Seminary, Detroit, he graduated three years later at Catholic Central High School, Detroit, 1933. He entered St Basil's Novitiate, Toronto, and was professed on 15 August 1934. He was appointed to Assumption College, Windsor (B.A., Honours Philosophy, University of Western Ontario, 1938). He taught for one year at Catholic Central High School, Detroit, while also attending Wayne State University, Detroit, for teacher certification for the State of Michigan. He studied theology at St Basil's Seminary, Toronto, and philosophy at the Pontifical Institute of Mediaeval Studies, Toronto, 1939–43. He was ordained to the priesthood on 15 August

1942 in St Basil's Church, Toronto, by Archbishop James Charles McGuigan. During his final year of theology, 1942–3, he also taught at St Michael's College School, Toronto.

Father O'Loughlin's priestly ministry over forty-three years in four countries presents a varied pattern. Formal classroom teaching in a Basilian school was limited to one year at St Thomas High School, Houston, 1943–4. He served as assistant in two Basilian parishes, Ste Anne's, Detroit, 1948–50, and Assumption Parish, Lethbridge, Alberta, 1970–3. His real life's work, however, was in the Hispanic ministry in Texas and Mexico, in the following appointments: assistant in Basilian Hispanic parishes in the Houston area, 1944–8; assistant at the Rosenberg, Texas, Mission Center, 1950–7; pastor at St Basil's Mission Center, Angleton, Texas, 1957–62; assistant at San Juan Crisóstomo Parish, Mexico City, 1973–7; chaplain of the Capilla Santa Irene and assistant at the Iglesia Jesús Obrero, Mexico City, 1977–82; assistant at Holy Family Parish, Missouri City, Texas, 1982–5.

In the course of these ministries Father O'Loughlin was always seeking new ways of making pastoral ministry more effective. Urged by this quest, he spent three years of graduate study in ministry, 1962–5, while in residence at Ste Anne's Parish, Detroit. He took summer courses in pastoral theology at the Catholic University of America, Washington, D.C.; but he spent the summer of 1963 at the University of Munich, and then visited catechetical centres in Lyon, Paris, and Brussels. In 1964–5 he attended courses at the Pius XII Catechetical Center at Monroe, Michigan. It was after this that he went to teach at St Meinrad Seminary, Indiana, for four years, 1965–9, and then accepted a one-year position as a catechetics resource person for the diocese of Evansville, Indiana, 1969–70, while also serving as pastor of St Patrick's Church, Corning, Indiana.

In 1985–6 he spent a year at St Joseph's Mission Center, Sugar Land, Texas, doing research in the mission archives. He retired to St Thomas High School, Houston, in 1986, where he continued his research and preaching for the Basilian missions and was called upon occasionally to assist in Spanish-speaking parishes, including the Basilian parish in Cali, Colombia. He moved into Dillon House, Houston, in 1993, where he remained until his transfer to the Basilian Fathers Residence (Infirmary), Toronto, in January 1998.

Raphael O'Loughlin stood six-foot-eight in stature but was gentle in manner and speech. He thought broadly and benevolently. Though he regretted not having been chosen for doctoral studies, bitterness was not part of his way. He was popular with children, first by his size and then by his playful manner. All his life he was afflicted with back pain caused by herniated discs, for which he underwent two major operations, 1969 and 1972, and suffered limited mobility in his later years. His affability and optimism, however, remained undiminished.

BIBLIOGRAPHY:
Book: *Basilian Leaders from Texas.* Houston, 1991.
Articles: 'Our Lady of Guadalupe,' *Benedicamus* 3 (May 1950) 48; 'Mobility Can Be a Sign of the Christian as Pilgrim,' *Forum* 3 (March 1967) 37; 'Diomedio Cardinal Falconio (1842–1917),' *Occasional Paper* 18 (December 1993), 1–4. He left in mimeographed format 'An Overview of the Basilian Fathers' Apostolate among the Spanish-Speaking: Texas–Detroit–Mexico, 1936–1986.'
SOURCES: GABF; *Annals* 1 (1943) 27, 6 (1985) 311, 7 (1993) 5–7, 9 (1999) 84–6; *Newsletter* (13 April 1998).

O'MEARA, John Patrick, priest, was born on 16 May 1914 in Rochester, the son of Patrick J. O'Meara and Bridget O'Neill. He died in Windsor, Ontario, on 11 February 2000, and is buried there in the Basilian plot of Heavenly Rest Cemetery.

Educated at Corpus Christi School and Aquinas Institute, Rochester (graduation, 1932), John O'Meara entered St Basil's Novitiate, Toronto, and was professed on 15 August 1933. He was appointed to St Michael's College, Toronto, where he completed senior matriculation in 1934. He was then appointed to St Basil's Scholasticate ('Seminary' from 1937) for undergraduate studies (B.A., University of Toronto, 1938). Three years of teaching and further studies followed: St Michael's College School, 1938–9, where he taught United States history and modern history and did his first year of theology; Assumption College School, Windsor, 1939–40, where he taught English and history while doing his second year of theology; and Catholic Central High School, Detroit, 1940–1, where he taught while also earning teaching certification for Michigan and an M.Ed. from Wayne State University, 1941. He returned to the scholasticate in Toronto in 1941 to complete his theology course and to teach history at St Michael's College School. He was ordained to the priesthood on 15 August 1942 in St Basil's Church, Toronto, by Archbishop James Charles McGuigan.

Father O'Meara taught history at Aquinas Institute, 1943–7. In 1947 he undertook graduate studies (Ph.D., University of Ottawa, 1948), and presented a thesis, 'The Right of Sanctuary, Its Origins in Western

Europe and Its Development in England.' He taught for one year at Aquinas before going to the recently founded University of St Thomas, Houston, where he functioned as registrar for the year 1949–50. In 1950 he was transferred to Rochester, to teach at St John Fisher College while living at Aquinas Institute. He moved into the new college in 1951 as vice-president and dean and first councillor of the Basilian community. He was an advocate of setting high standards at St John Fisher College.

In 1959 Father O'Meara was moved to Assumption University of Windsor, just as it was initiating changes which would lead to the establishment of the University of Windsor in 1963. His experience and advice contributed in no small way to these developments. He held various posts, including professor of history both at Assumption University and at the University of Windsor. He was a member of the American Historical Association and of the American Catholic Historical Association. He served as an assessor of research projects for the Canada Council.

During the late 1960s and early 1970s, when conflict arose in the Basilian community at Assumption University about independent ways of living the canonical vow of poverty, Father O'Meara's differences with both the local and general Basilian authorities resulted in his living apart from the community for seven years, 1974–81. Having retired from the University of Windsor in 1979 he returned to living with the Basilian community at O'Connor House in 1981. He was a man accustomed to independence, but yet was conscious that conflict could have hurtful consequences. His later years were marked by a preoccupation with compassion and forgiveness, with the hope that he had been reconciled with all those with whom he had clashed in the past. He served as chief financial officer for Assumption University, 1985–7, and as a member of its board of governors, 1984–91. After 1991 ill health, including two hip surgeries, a stroke, several infections, and a bout with pneumonia, seriously curtailed his activities.

BIBLIOGRAPHY:
Book: *Student Guide for American History*. Windsor, 1976.
Articles: 'Aquinas Institute,' *Basilian* 3 (March 1937) 43, 56; 'A Re-evaluation of Christian Liberal Education,' *Basilian Teacher* 6 (November 1961) 60–3; 'Our Student Today. Problem and Potential [forum],' *Basilian Teacher* 7 (December 1962) 114; 'The Key to Renewal Is Listening,' *Forum* 2 (May 1966) 71–2.
SOURCES: GABF; *Annals* 1 (1943) 26, 6 (1984) 207, 7 (1993) 8–9, 9 (2001) 84–5; *Newsletter* (8 March 2000).

O'NEILL, Edward John, priest, was born on a farm at Hickory Grove, Ontario, near the crossroads village of Nanticoke (diocese of Hamilton, since 1958 of St Catharines), on 20 March 1856, the son of Patrick and Catherine O'Neill. He died in Toronto on 23 August 1935 and is buried there in the Basilian plot of Mount Hope Cemetery.

Having attended Nanticoke Public School, Edward O'Neill went to St Michael's College, Toronto, in 1874. After graduation in 1882, he studied medicine for a few months in Buffalo before deciding to enter St Basil's Novitiate, and was received as a novice on 14 October 1883 at Beaconfield House, Plymouth, England. Following his profession in 1884 he studied theology in France and was ordained to the priesthood on 24 September 1887. Father O'Neill taught at St Michael's College, 1887–91, and at the College of Mary Immaculate, Beaconfield House, Plymouth, England, where he also served as chaplain to the Catholic troops stationed nearby. He taught at St Basil's Scholasticate, Toronto, 1898–1901, before going to teach first at St Mary's Seminary, LaPorte, Texas, and, in 1911, at St Basil's College, Waco, Texas. He returned to St Michael's College in 1915, and in 1923 was appointed to the staff of St Basil's Parish, Toronto. He died from cancer of the stomach.

Father 'Pep' O'Neill, so nicknamed for his unhurried and deliberate manner, had been a brilliant student at St Michael's College with a preference for English. During his years in England he was a correspondent for the *Catholic Register* in Toronto. The academic promise of his youth was never fully realized because of indifferent health. During the last twenty years of his life he was looked upon as a model of regularity, one who had a set schedule for almost every minute of the day and who adhered to it faithfully.

BIBLIOGRAPHY: 'Scholastic Sport,' *Basilian* 2 (January 1936) 13; 'I Hunted Snipe – As Told to Fra Juniper,' *Basilian* 2 (October 1936) 117, 120.
SOURCE: GABF.

O'NEILL, James Francis, priest, was born on 24 October 1915 in Windsor, Ontario, the son of George O'Neill and Alma Bondy. He died in Windsor on 27 August 1997 and is buried there in the Basilian plot of Heavenly Rest Cemetery.

Having attended parochial schools in Windsor, James Francis O'Neill enrolled in Assumption College School, Windsor, in 1930. He early acquired the nickname 'Steve,' when one of his Basilian teachers noticed a resemblance to the legendary Detroit Tiger catcher of that name. From then on he was called 'Steve' by everyone except his mother, who called him 'Francis.' Upon graduation from high school he entered St Basil's Novitiate, Toronto, was professed on 15 August 1937, and was appointed first to St Basil's Seminary, Toronto, and then, in 1939, to St Michael's College for undergraduate studies (B.A., Philosophy, History, and Languages, University of Toronto, 1940). There he won the McBrady Prize in Latin. He taught mathematics and religion at St Thomas High School, Houston, for one year before returning to St Michael's in 1941. He began theological studies and attended courses at the Ontario College of Education, earning teacher certification in 1942. Moving to St Basil's Seminary in 1943 to complete theology, he was ordained to the priesthood on 20 August 1944 in St Basil's Church, Toronto, by Archbishop James Charles McGuigan.

Father O'Neill's priestly life was spent in the high school apostolate at Assumption College School and Michael Power High School, Etobicoke, Ontario, with the exception of one year at Assumption University as dean of residence and university chaplain, 1965–6. During his first period at Assumption, 1945–65, he taught, served as first councillor in the Basilian community, and was principal of the school from 1960 to 1965. His second period there, 1980–97, included several years as teacher, as superior, 1992–5, and retirement. Between those periods he taught at Michael Power High School, where he co-founded the guidance department and served as superior, 1977–80.

All his life Father O'Neill maintained the ready and winning smile which had won him the name 'Steve' in 1930. He had a gift for working with people and for engaging parents and others in support of the school. He was a successful fund-raiser. The present Assumption High School, separated from the university campus, is a monument to his efforts and resourcefulness. The move from Assumption to Michael Power might have been a severe cross had it not been for the prospect of nearby golf courses to be conquered on his days off. He did actually, on one occasion, make a hole-in-one.

SOURCES: GABF; *Annals* 1 (1945) 100, 6 (1988) 593, 8 (1995) 9, 9 (1998) 78–9; *Newsletter* (1 October 1997).

ONORATO, John Francis, priest, was born in Geneva, New York (diocese of Rochester), on 23 June 1906, the son of Alexander Onorato and Adelaide DiNictio. He died in Houston on 9 September 1963, and is buried there in the Basilian plot of Garden of Gethsemane, Forest Park Lawndale Cemetery.

John Onorato was educated in both the elementary and high schools of St Francis de Sales parish. In 1925 he went to St Michael's College, Toronto, and one year later entered St Basil's Novitiate, Toronto. Professed on 18 September 1927, he was appointed to Assumption College in Windsor (B.A., University of Western Ontario, 1930). He studied theology at St Basil's Scholasticate, Toronto, concurrently attending the Ontario College of Education, 1931–2. He was ordained to the priesthood on 17 December 1933 in St Basil's Church, Toronto, by Bishop Alexander MacDonald.

Father Onorato's priestly life took him into high school classrooms and college lecture halls, to military chaplaincy, and to the mission fields of southwest Texas. He taught at St Thomas High School in Houston, 1934–7, and at Aquinas Institute in Rochester, 1937–43. During this period he also obtained an M.A. in Italian from Columbia University, New York City. During the Second World War he was a chaplain with the United States Navy from 1943 to 1946, serving with contingents at Plymouth and Dartmouth in England. He returned to teach at Aquinas Institute, 1946–50. After a year of advanced studies at the University of Florence in Italy, he taught at St John Fisher College in Rochester, 1951–5, but then moved into Basilian mission apostolate first at St Theresa Mission Center, Sugar Land, Texas, 1955–62, and then at St Basil's Mission Center, Angleton, Texas, the year prior to his death.

Father 'Johnnie' Onorato was a gentlemanly priest, attentive to his dress and grooming. His confreres referred to him jokingly as 'the noblest Roman of them all.' He possessed a fine tenor voice. Before going to St Michael's College he had been apprenticed to a barber and as a student paid part of his expenses by cutting hair of other students.

SOURCES: GABF; *Annals* 1 (1945) 89, 3 (1963) 220–1; *Newsletter* (12 September 1963); *Basilides, Assumption College* (Windsor, 1930).

O'REILLY, Edward Augustine, priest, elder brother of Father Eugene O'Reilly CSB, was born on 21 January 1924 on Wolfe Island, Ontario (archdiocese of Kingston), the son of James O'Reilly and Helen Finn. He died in Toronto on 4 May 1997 and is buried in the Basilian plot of Holy Cross Cemetery, Thornhill, Ontario.

Having come to know the Basilian Fathers at Marylake Farm, Ontario,

Ed enrolled in the high school section of St Michael's College, Toronto, in 1941. He entered St Basil's Novitiate, Toronto, in 1944 and made first profession of vows on 15 August 1945. He was then appointed to Assumption College, Windsor (B.A., University of Western Ontario, 1948). He taught at Catholic Central High School, Detroit, 1948–9, at St Thomas High School, Houston, 1949–50, where he also began his theological studies, and then at St Michael's College School, 1950–1, before completing his theology at St Basil's Seminary, Toronto. He was ordained to the priesthood on 29 June 1953 in St Basil's Church, Toronto, by Cardinal James Charles McGuigan.

Father O'Reilly taught for thirty-three years in six Basilian high schools: Aquinas Institute, Rochester, 1954–7, concurrently earning an M.Ed. from the University of Rochester, 1957; St Charles College, Sudbury, Ontario, 1957–8, where he also served as treasurer; Aquinas Institute once again, 1958–62, with summer graduate courses in history, his teaching specialization, at Canisius College, Buffalo, New York; Michael Power High School, Etobicoke, Ontario, 1962–5; Andrean High School, Gary (now Merrillville), Indiana, 1965–7; and St Mary's College, Sault Ste Marie, Ontario, 1967–87. He was granted a sabbatical year in 1987, which he spent at St Albert the Great Parish, Las Cruces, New Mexico. This was followed by an appointment to St Mary's of the Assumption Parish, Owen Sound, Ontario, where he resided for two years. In 1990, because of failing health, he was appointed to the Basilian Fathers Residence (Infirmary) in Toronto, where he lived until January 1997, when it became necessary to move him to Providence Centre, Scarborough, Ontario, to receive the care his condition now demanded and where he died peacefully in his sleep some four months later.

Ed O'Reilly was a gentle, affable, and very sociable man. In later years he grew a long and full beard. During his long tenure in Sault Ste Marie he was active in the charismatic movement, much to the satisfaction of Bishop Alexander Carter. The degeneration of his health over a period of years was as painful to observe as it was painful to endure. Robert Barbeau, a colleague in the Sault, wrote, 'Colourful Father O'Reilly brings many fond and humorous memories to mind, when we think back to his classroom in portables, with the raccoons under the floorboards and the students adjusting grades in his marks book.'

Preaching at his brother's funeral, Father Eugene O'Reilly said in part: 'He strove to ensure that the Christ who linked His life with his in baptism ... did not remain a shadowy figure on the margins of his life, but became a friend in whom he confided more and more.'

BIBLIOGRAPHY: 'Human-Christian-Religious Development,' *Forum* 2 (May 1966) 76–7.
SOURCES: GABF; *Annals* 2 (1953) 110, 9 (1998) 76–7; *Newsletter* (25 June 1997).

O'REILLY, Joseph Alfred, priest, was born on 26 March 1917 in Ottawa, Ontario, the son of George O'Reilly and Edith Lee, and the brother of Fathers John and Frank O'Reilly of the diocese of Hamilton, Ontario. He died in Toronto on 21 March 1993 and is buried in the Basilian plot of Holy Cross Cemetery, Thornhill, Ontario.

His parents having moved to Toronto when he was two, Joe attended St Helen's Separate School and the high school section of St Michael's College. He entered St Basil's Novitiate, Toronto, making first profession on 12 September 1937, and was assigned to Assumption College where, along with a double major in history and Latin (B.A., University of Western Ontario, 1941), he taught part-time in the high school section. After teaching full-time there in 1941–2 and at St Thomas High School, Houston, 1942–3, he studied theology at St Basil's Seminary, Toronto, 1943–7, while also teaching part-time at St Michael's College School. He was ordained to the priesthood on 15 August 1946 in St Basil's Church, Toronto, by Cardinal James Charles McGuigan.

In 1947 Father O'Reilly was appointed to Aquinas Institute, Rochester, to teach religion, business, and Latin. When appointed as director of the business department, he took courses in business at Niagara University. In 1960 he obtained an M.A. in education from the University of Rochester. He studied speech at both Northwestern and Marquette Universities, and his work with the students as director of speech and debating was recognized by an award from the National Forensic League. He served as vice-principal at Aquinas and as spiritual director of the scholastics in the local Basilian house. His promotion of the Catholic School Bowling League in the Rochester area was recognized by an award.

After twenty years at Aquinas Father O'Reilly was moved to Lethbridge, Alberta, where he taught for ten years at Catholic Central High School. In 1977 he left the classroom to devote himself full-time to parish ministry in the diocese of Calgary, Alberta, first in the town of Raymond, where his outgoing manner and warm humanity won the respect and affection of the predominately Mormon population. In

1987 the Mormon community joined heartily with the Catholics to celebrate his fiftieth anniversary of religious profession. He actively ministered to three congregations until, weakened by cancer, he retired to the Basilian Fathers Residence (Infirmary) in January 1993, where he died a few weeks later.

BIBLIOGRAPHY: 'Factors in a Speech Program,' *Basilian Teacher* 1 (February 1957) 3–5; 'Getting Started,' *Basilian Teacher* 1 (March 1957) 22–4; 'Challenge to Be Met,' *Basilian Teacher* 1 (April 1957) 20–2.
SOURCES: GABF; *Annals* 1 (1946) 120, 6 (1988) 593, 8 (1994) 126–8; *Newsletter* (26 March 1993).

O'ROURKE, Thomas Patrick, priest, first native Texan ordained in the Basilian Congregation, was born in Lorena, Texas (diocese of Galveston [in 1890 of Dallas, since 1948 of Austin]), on 22 May 1889, the son of William Joseph O'Rourke and Brigid White. A nephew, Father John O'Rourke, was a priest in the diocese of Dallas. He died in Houston on 21 March 1955 and was buried there in the Basilian plot of Garden of Gethsemane, Forest Park Lawndale Cemetery.

Thomas O'Rourke received his early education in various small-town schools in central Texas, as the family moved about with his father, who worked as a railroad crew foreman. In 1904 he went as a boarder to St Basil's College, Waco, Texas, for high school and one year of college. He took a second year at Assumption College, Windsor, 1908–9, then returned to St Basil's College for two years of philosophy before entering St Basil's Novitiate in Toronto. After profession on 19 September 1912 he studied theology at St Basil's Scholasticate, Toronto, and was ordained to the priesthood on 29 June 1916 in St Basil's Church by Archbishop Neil McNeil.

Father 'T.P.' O'Rourke spent only five years away from his native state. He taught at St Thomas College, Houston, 1916–24, where he was also football and baseball coach, prefect of discipline and, in 1922–4, treasurer. Although he never obtained a B.A. or finished his theology course, he went to the Catholic University of America, Washington, D.C., spending summers in New York with Francis Patrick Duffy, an alumnus of St Michael's College and famous chaplain of the 'Fighting 69th' in the First World War. He received an M.A. in 1925 with a thesis, 'The Memorials of Fray Alonzo Benavides,' and the Ph.D., 1927, after further work in the Library of Congress, Washington, D.C., and archives in Austin, Texas. His director, Rev. Peter Guilday, wrote that several publishers wanted 'first shot' at publishing his thesis on the Franciscan Missions in Texas, 1690–1794. Father Guilday, who was head of the American Catholic Historical Society, wanted to engage O'Rourke as his assistant; but the Congregation appointed him superior and principal of St Thomas College (High School), 1927–31. There his expression 'Don't let them fence your goodness in' became familiar to the students. During these years he decided against further expansion of the school on its Austin Street downtown site and purchased an extensive tract of land for a new campus on the northeast junction of Shepherd Drive and Buffalo Bayou.

In 1931 Father O'Rourke was appointed to Assumption College, but a year later was back in Houston as pastor of St Anne's Parish, where in 1940 he opened the magnificent new Spanish-mission-style church in the planning and decoration of which he had a strong role. Already in his eighth year as pastor, he was then appointed to Ste Anne's Parish, Detroit. There he gave a series of radio talks on CKLW, Windsor, on the theme of the dignity of work and the worker, and applied the social teachings of Popes Leo XIII and Pius XI to the local labour unrest. He returned to St Anne's, Houston, in 1941 as assistant; but two years later he went to live at St Thomas High School, now located on the extensive new site he had purchased. There much of his time was given to serving on a Wartime Labor Relations Board. Although his health was declining he was involved in plans for opening the University of St Thomas, and he procured its Montrose Boulevard site. The former science building there was later named for him. In 1947 he was appointed to Our Lady of Guadalupe Mission Center, Rosenberg, Texas, a Basilian apostolate that he had strongly supported in the 1930s. His health did not improve, and in the following year he retired to St Thomas High School, where he died in 1955 from a long-standing diabetic and heart condition. On 22 May 1989, the centennial of O'Rourke's birth, John McCarthy, bishop of Austin and a former student of Father O'Rourke, presided and preached at a memorial Mass for him at St Anne's.

Father O'Rourke was big of body and heart. An obituary article in the *Houston Chronicle* recalled him as 'a man of absolute candor. No matter what problems confronted him, he could be relied upon to speak his mind with frankness, always with diplomacy and frequently with humor.' The *Houston Press* referred to him as 'an excellent speaker, threading his Irish good humor throughout his remarks or giving them impetus with his forcefulness.' St Edward's University,

Austin, Texas, recognized his contributions to the history of the Catholic Church in Texas by conferring an honorary LL.D. on him in 1934.

BIBLIOGRAPHY:
Book: *The Franciscan Missions in Texas (1690–1793)*, Studies in American Church History 5. Washington, D.C., 1927; repr. New York, 1974.
Article: 'A Study of the "Memorial" of Fray Alonso De Benavides,' *Records of the American Catholic Historical Society of Philadelphia* 39 no. 3 (September 1928) 237–59.
SOURCES: GABF; *Annals* 2 (1955) 227–8; *Aquin* (Yearbook St Thomas High School) 11 (1955); *The Father O'Rourke Scholarship Association, University of St Thomas* (Houston, 1955); S.R. O'Loughlin, *Basilian Leaders from Texas* (Houston, 1991) 30–45.

ORSINI, Francis Alphonsus, priest, elder brother of former Basilian priest Gerald Orsini and of the late Sister Eleanor Orsini CSJ, was born on 27 September 1918 in Toronto, the second eldest son of the five children of Emilio Orsini and Sarah Feeheley. He died in Toronto on 13 April 1987 and is buried in the Basilian plot of Holy Cross Cemetery, Thornhill, Ontario.

Frank attended Holy Rosary Separate School and the high school section of St Michael's College, Toronto. He was recommended for St Basil's Novitiate as a 'cheerful but not boisterous' young man known to the Basilian community for his piety, academic standing, and athletic ability, especially in hockey. After first profession on 15 August 1936, he was appointed to St Basil's Scholasticate ('Seminary' from 1937), Toronto, for studies at the University of Toronto (Honours B.A., Latin and French, 1940). He taught Latin and modern history for one year at St Thomas High School, Houston. In 1941 he began his theological studies while living at St Michael's College, Toronto. Concurrently he taught French and Latin at St Michael's College School, and during summers earned interim high school specialist's certification, awarded 1944, at the Ontario College of Education as well as graduate courses in French. He moved to St Basil's Seminary in 1943 and was ordained to the priesthood on 20 August 1944 in St Basil's Church, Toronto, by Archbishop James Charles McGuigan.

Father Orsini's varied talents and ready obedience brought him some fifteen appointments in his forty-three years of priestly ministry: St Anne's Parish, Houston, assistant pastor, 1945–6; St Basil's Seminary, professor, 1946–7; Lateran University, Rome, graduate studies, canon law (J.C.B, 1948, J.C.L., 1949, J.C.D., 1950; thesis: 'The Common Life in Religious Institutes, in Societies of the Common Life and in Secular Institutes'); St Basil's Seminary, professor, 1950–8, rector, 1952–8; University of St Michael's College, professor and dean of men, 1958–61; general councillor, with three years as rector of the curial house and one year as assistant at Holy Rosary Parish, 1960–7; first regional representative for Eastern Canada, with residence at St Michael's College, 1967–9; St John the Baptist Parish, Amherstburg, Ontario, assistant in charge of the Italian-speaking community, 1969–71, pastor, 1971–4; St Basil's College, working in the marriage tribunal of the archdiocese of Toronto, 1974–9; St Mary's of the Assumption Parish, Owen Sound, Ontario, assistant pastor, 1979–80; St John the Baptist Parish, Amherstburg, assistant pastor, 1980–3; St Basil's Novitiate, Detroit, assistant novice master, 1983–5; St Basil's College, assistant rector, 1985–6; St Basil's Novitiate, Sugar Land, Texas, assistant novice master, 1986.

While rector of the seminary Frank Orsini was in charge of the summer leisure and work of up to a hundred scholastics at Strawberry Island in Lake Simcoe. A special project of his was the creation of a clearing on the south side of the Island, now known as Orsini Park. Some scholastics found him strict and too conservative, but they respected his integrity. At the 1967 general chapter a group of 'liberal' delegates, whose theology he did not embrace, made a concerted effort to elect him to the general council, but ultimately failed after each series of votes. A few months later he was elected the first regional representative for Eastern Canada.

Just months into his last appointment Father Orsini was diagnosed with inoperable cancer. After undergoing treatment for a time, he asked that it be stopped and that he be moved to the Basilian Fathers Residence (Infirmary) in Toronto. There, though in constant pain, he maintained the cheerfulness which had characterized his life. To those who asked about his condition, his response 'Just fine!' was no false optimism but a witness to faith and hope.

BIBLIOGRAPHY:
Pamphlet: Ed. *Pictorial Directory, St John the Baptist Parish, Amherstburg* (Amherstburg, 1972).
Articles: 'The Personnel Required for Forming Religious,' Canadian Religious Conference, Ottawa (1956) 1–10; 'Poverty,' *Forum* 1 (December 1964) 29–33; 'A Beginning Has Been Made,' *Forum* 2 (November 1966) 114–15.
SOURCES: GABF; *Annals* 1 (1945) 100, 2 (1951) 105, 6 (1987) 495, (1988) 698–9;

Newsletter (15 April 1987); E.J. Lajeunesse, *Strawberry Island in Lake Simcoe* (Toronto, 1962, 1974, 1981, 1983) 73.

O'TOOLE, William Bernard, priest, was born at Painesville, Ohio (diocese of Cleveland), on 18 April 1897, the son of John J. Toole and Gertrude Bush. He died in Houston on 25 July 1968 and was buried in the Basilian plot of Holy Sepulchre Cemetery, Rochester.

'Marty' O'Toole (born Toole) grew up in Geneva, New York. He won a scholarship at the end of grammar school and a New York State Regents Scholarship when he graduated from Geneva High School, 1916. That same year he went to St Michael's College, Toronto, to study classics. Two years later he entered St Basil's Novitiate, Toronto. After profession on 7 October 1919, he was appointed to St Thomas High School, Houston, where he taught Latin and at the same time studied philosophy. In 1921 he resumed his studies at the University of Toronto (B.A., 1924), and began theology at St Basil's Scholasticate. He was ordained priest on 20 December 1924 at St Augustine's Seminary, Scarborough, Ontario, by Bishop John McNally.

From 1918 through 1923 he signed his name either 'Toole' or 'O'Toole,' but by 1924 he signed only 'O'Toole.' Documentation about an official change is not extant.

After a year at the Ontario College of Education in Toronto, 1924–5, Father O'Toole resumed his career as a teacher of Latin and Greek. He taught at Assumption College, Windsor, 1925–6 and 1933–4, St Michael's College, 1926–9, and Catholic Central High School, Detroit, 1929–33. He attended summer courses at the University of Chicago in 1926 and 1931. In 1934 he began twenty-five years of teaching at St Michael's College, where for many years he was dean of American Freshmen. His strong personality made him both the friend and counsellor to many students. Although short of stature, he played second base during his student days and as a young priest coached basketball teams. In later years golf was his favourite sport. In 1938 he obtained an M.A. in classics from the University of Toronto.

As chaplain in the United States Army, January 1943–August 1946, Father O'Toole served overseas with distinction, rising to the rank of Major. Excerpts from his letters describing his life as a chaplain in England with troops preparing for the Normandy invasion and later in hospitals near the front were published in the *Basilian Annals* (see below). This experience marked him for life: he would post notices for students in military form, and always told time by a twenty-four-hour clock.

In 1959 Father O'Toole retired from teaching and was appointed to St Anne's Parish, Houston, where he died in 1968 after a series of heart attacks. To the end his rapport with young people, as during his teaching days, continued to be a feature of his ministry.

SOURCES: GABF; *Annals* 1 (1944) 49–50, 1 (1945) 87–8, 4 (1969) 128–9; *Newsletter* (27 July 1968); *Yearbook SMC* 15 (1924).

OUDIN, Joannès Etienne, priest, was born on 9 October 1851, at Monistrol (Haute-Loire, diocese of Le Puy). He died at Privas (Ardèche) on 27 October 1913 and is buried in the cemetery there.
Having gone to Annonay in 1876 to teach at the Collège du Sacré-Coeur, Joannès Oudin was received as a novice on 2 February 1877. He took final vows on 6 January 1878 and was ordained a priest on 18 September 1880 by Bishop Joseph-Michel-Frédéric Bonnet of Viviers in the chapel of the Collège du Sacré-Coeur. He taught at various Basilian schools: Ecole cléricale, Périgueux (Dordogne), 1878–82; Collège Saint-Charles, Blidah, Algeria, 1882–4 and 1889–90; Collège du Sacré-Coeur, 1884–9. Ill health obliged him to take some time off in his native parish of Monistrol. He resumed his teaching duties in 1895 at the Petit Séminaire d'Aubenas (Ardèche), where he remained until government laws in 1903 forbade members of congregations to teach in schools. He returned to the Haute-Loire and took up residence in Bas-en-Basset, near Monistrol, where he assisted the local pastor. By February 1910 his health had failed to the point where he needed psychiatric care. His sister, an Ursuline nun, brought him to Saint-Etienne (Loire) for treatment in March 1910. Two years later he was admitted to the Hôpital Sainte-Marie, a psychiatric institution in Privas, where he remained for one year before his death. Abbé Louis de Lavareille, who knew him after 1903, attributed the gravity of his illness to the anticlerical laws and sanctions of the day.

SOURCES: GABF; Kirley, *Community in France* 210; Pouzol, 'Notices.'

OZIL, Ferdinand, priest, was born on 24 January 1851 at Villeneuve-de-Berg (Ardèche). He died in Annonay on 27 November 1901 and is buried in the Basilian cemetery there on the grounds of the Collège du Sacré-Coeur.
After secondary school at Aubenas, Ferdinand Ozil entered the novitiate at Feyzin (Isère, now Rhône), and took final vows on 19 February

1875. Bishop Armand de Charbonnel ordained him to the priesthood on 23 September 1876 in the chapel of the Collège du Sacré-Coeur, Annonay. He taught at the Ecole cléricale, Périgueux (Dordogne), 1871–2 and 1874–85, and at the Petit Séminaire de Vernoux, 1872–4. In 1886 he went to Mary Immaculate College, Beaconfield House, Plymouth, England, where he was assistant to the novice master, 1886–9, and bursar of the college, 1889–95. Upon returning to Annonay he was appointed superior of Sainte-Barbe minor seminary, 1895–1901. At the general chapter of 1898 he was elected treasurer general.

SOURCES: GABF; Chomel, *Collège d'Annonay* 517; Kirley, *Community in France* 150n383; Pouzol, 'Notices'; *Semaine religieuse de Viviers* (24 November 1901) 571.

P

PACHER, Florian Edmund, priest, was born on 14 May 1914 at Cheboygan, Michigan (diocese of Grand Rapids, since 1971 of Gaylord), the son of Joseph Paciorkowski and Anna Romczak. He died in Toronto on 8 April 1977, and is buried in the Basilian plot of Holy Cross Cemetery, Thornhill, Ontario.

Florian attended elementary school in Cheboygan. When the family moved to Detroit, he attended Catholic Central High School, graduating in 1932. He entered St Basil's Novitiate, Toronto, was professed on 15 August 1933, and was appointed to St Michael's College, Toronto, for undergraduate studies (B.A., University of Toronto, 1937). During the year 1937–8 he studied theology while also teaching at St Michael's College School. He taught for one year at St Thomas High School, Houston, 1938–9, and for one year at Catholic Central High School, 1939–40, concurrently earning teaching certification for Michigan in 1940. After resuming his theology courses at St Basil's Seminary, Toronto, he was ordained to the priesthood on 15 August 1942 in St Basil's Church, Toronto, by Archbishop James Charles McGuigan.

Father Pacher – his Polish name had been abbreviated before he entered the Basilian community – received ten appointments in his thirty-five years of Basilian priesthood: Aquinas Institute, Rochester, 1943–4; Catholic Central High School, 1944–52; St Thomas High School, Houston, 1952–3; Assumption College School, Windsor, 1953–

5; Catholic Central High School, 1955–6; Ste Anne's Parish, Detroit, 1956–64; St Charles College, Sudbury, 1964–5; St Basil's Parish, Toronto, 1965–70; the Curial House, Toronto, 1970–3, where he served as second councillor; and St Michael's College School, 1973–7.

Though his manner was eccentric and sometimes trying, 'Patch' (as he was called) was pleasant in conversation and interested in the achievements of his confreres. In 1976 he suffered a heart attack which left him seriously weakened. A second attack one year later proved fatal. The tragedy of his dying alone and undiscovered for some time was attenuated by the special nature of the day on which he was called home, Good Friday.

SOURCES: GABF; *Annals* 1 (1943) 265, 5 (1978) 324–5; *Newsletter* (15 April 1977).

PAGEAU, Jean ERNEST, priest, member of the Congregation 1895–1923, nephew of Father Thomas *Gignac and uncle of Fathers Rolland Janisse CSB, John Janisse CSB, and Lawrence Janisse CSB, was born in Windsor on 3 February 1874, the son of Jean Pageau and Marie Ann Gignac. His sister was the mother of Archbishop Leonard Wall (archdiocese of Winnipeg). He died in Montreal on 4 September 1941 and is buried in St Alphonsus Cemetery, Windsor.

After early education in Windsor, 'Ernie' Pageau went to St Michael's College, Toronto, in 1890. On 9 September 1895, he entered St Basil's Novitiate, Toronto. Following profession he studied at St Michael's College and St Basil's Scholasticate. He was ordained to the priesthood on 25 July 1901.

Father Pageau taught from 1901 to 1908 at St Thomas High School, Houston, and was principal and superior there, 1910–14. He taught at St Michael's College, 1908–10 and 1914–18. Transferred to St Thomas College, Chatham, New Brunswick, Father Pageau taught there until the school was temporarily closed following the disastrous fire in March 1919. He returned to St Michael's College where he taught English and French until 1923.

In 1923, when the Congregation adopted the new, stricter vow of poverty, he withdrew from the Basilians and was incardinated in the diocese of London, Ontario, on 11 February 1924. After serving at St Alphonsus Parish, Windsor, he was placed in charge of a mission that grew into the parish of Christ the King, Windsor. Later he was pastor of Annunciation Parish at Stoney Point. In this charge he suffered a nervous breakdown and required hospitalization until his death in 1941.

Father Pageau was a short, jovial priest, inclined to stoutness. He walked with a severe limp, the result of a broken hip suffered when, after helping students to exit the burning school building in Chatham, he had to jump from the top storey. He was a fine singer with a powerful voice. Despite his withdrawal from the Congregation he was happy to be invited to community functions, especially those at Assumption Church, Windsor.

SOURCES: GABF; Kirley, *Community in France* 214n516, 216n518, 227, 233n559, 240n570; A.F. Pagès, *A History of the Basilian Order in Canada* (Toronto, 1924); Shook, *Catholic Education* 117. *Yearbook STC*; Rolland Janisse, CSB.

PAGES, Alphonse Auguste, priest, was born at Saint-Sauveur-de-Cruzières (Ardèche) on 24 February 1841. He died on 16 August 1892 at Grenoble (Isère) and is buried in the cemetery on the grounds of the Collège du Sacré-Coeur, Annonay.
Alphonse Pagès was a student at the Collège des Cordeliers, section Sainte-Barbe, 1856–61. He entered the novitiate at Feyzin, and after profession studied theology and taught at the Collège de Privas (Ardèche). He was ordained priest on 21 September 1867 in the chapel of the Collège du Sacré-Coeur, Annonay, by Bishop Armand de Charbonnel.
Father Pagès taught at the Ecole cléricale de Périgueux, 1867–74. A second seven-year period was spent at the Collège du Bourg-Saint-Andéol (Ardèche). It ended with the Basilian expulsion from the college as a consequence of the anticlerical laws. He was appointed to the Collège du Sacré-Coeur from 1881 to 1891, but spent the final year of his life at St Charles College, Blidah, Algeria. He died at Grenoble during the summer vacation of 1892.

SOURCES: GABF; Chomel, *Collège d'Annonay* 312–14; Pouzol, 'Notices.'

PAGES, Jean-François, priest, one of the ten founding fathers, was born in Malbosc (Ardèche, diocese of Viviers [from 1801 to 1822 of Mende]), on 8 March 1793, the son of Louis-François Pagès and Marie Christine Dumazart. He died in Annonay on 27 August 1861 and was buried in the cemetery of Saint-Jacques but in November 1869 was reinterred in the cemetery on the grounds of the Collège du Sacré-Coeur.
After early studies at a local school, Jean-François was encouraged by his parish priest, a brother of Father Pierre *Tourvieille, to enrol in the Collège des Cordeliers, Annonay, where he lived in a private boarding-house. In 1812 he became prefect at Sainte-Claire, the school for

day-scholars, while continuing his studies in philosophy and theology. He was ordained to the priesthood in 1818 and appointed to the parish at Vanosc (Ardèche). The following year Father Julien *Actorie asked the bishop to reappoint him to the staff of the college in Annonay. After teaching there from 1819 to 1822, he joined the other members of the new Association of Priests of Saint Basil on 21 November 1822, even though he had not signed the petition requesting its founding two months earlier.

From 1822 to 1832 he served as director of Sainte-Claire and chaplain at the local hospital, as well as professor at the Collège des Cordeliers. In 1832 Sainte-Claire was closed and the students were transferred to Sainte-Barbe, the minor seminary. Placed in charge of a section of the bursar's office, 1831-4, Father Pagès continued teaching at the college until 1849. That year he succeeded Father Germain *Deglesne as chaplain of the Dames du Sacré-Coeur. In 1852 he did not take the proposed vows but continued to live under the promises made in 1822. He served as chaplain to the Christian Brothers, 1852-61.

Father Pagès was described as a giant with the air of a monk. Orderly and methodical in his work as a professor, he had an attraction for the rigours of penance and fasted strictly during Lent. He was generous to those in need among his family members and to other religious, especially to the 'Trappistines,' an order of nuns at Maubec, where he often went for days of recollection.

SOURCES: GABF; Chomel, *Collège d'Annonay* 145, 267-71, 438; Kirley, *Community in France* 29; Pouzol, 'Notices'; Roume, *Origines* 160, 347, 402.

PAGES, Lucien, priest, was born either at Valaurie, canton of Grignan, or at Granges-Gontardes, canton of Pierrelatte (Ardèche) on 17 August 1858. He died on 11 February 1928 at Cadouin (Dordogne), diocese of Périgueux, and was buried in the local cemetery.

Lucien Pagès was a student at the Collège du Sacré-Coeur, section Sainte-Barbe, 1870-7. He was ordained to the priesthood in the chapel of the Collège du Sacré-Coeur by Archbishop Armand de Charbonnel on 22 September 1882. He taught at the Collège du Sacré-Coeur, 1879-1901. From 1901 to 1928 he did pastoral ministry at a shrine and place of pilgrimage at Cadouin where a shroud, declared unauthentic by church authorities in 1934, was venerated.

SOURCES: GABF; Kirley, *Community in France* 185, 208; Pouzol, 'Notices.'

PAGES, Pierre, priest, member of the Congregation 1873–c.1876, was born on 12 April 1846 in the mountain village of Loubaresse, canton of Valgorge (Ardèche).
Pierre Pagès studied at the Collège du Sacré-Coeur, Annonay, from 1872 to 1874, and made his profession of vows on 19 September 1873. He was ordained a priest on 18 September 1875, and withdrew from the Congregation probably in 1876.

SOURCE: Pouzol, 'Notices,' Supplément 2.

PAPPERT, Edward Cecil, priest, was born on 13 February 1914 in Rochester, the son of Frederick J. Pappert and Isabella Stoll. He died in Windsor on 18 November 1990, and is buried there in the Basilian plot of Heavenly Rest Cemetery.
Edward attended St Boniface parochial school and Aquinas Institute, Rochester. At his graduation from Aquinas in 1932, he received the best attendance award. He entered St Basil's Novitiate, Toronto, in 1932 and was professed on 15 August 1933. He did the 'Western year' at St Michael's College, Toronto, followed by two years of undergraduate studies, after which he was appointed to St Basil's Scholasticate ('Seminary' from 1937), Toronto, both as undergraduate and student of theology (B.A., University of Toronto, 1938). Appointed to Catholic Central High School, Detroit, he taught grade X English, continued theological studies, and took courses at the University of Detroit, earning high school provisional certification, Michigan, 1941. He returned to Toronto to complete his theology courses, and was ordained to the priesthood on 15 August 1942 in St Basil's Church by Archbishop James Charles McGuigan.

In 1943 Father Pappert, or 'Pappy' as he came to be called, was appointed to teach at Aquinas Institute. While there he also earned an M.A. from the University of Detroit, 1944, submitting a thesis, 'The Literary Career of Cyril Tourneur.' In 1948 he began doctoral studies in English at the University of Ottawa, but a year later was appointed to teach at St Michael's College School. In 1950 he went to Assumption College, Windsor, where he would remain for the rest of his life, but managed to finish his Ph.D. at the University of Ottawa in 1953 (thesis: 'The Evolution of Cicero's Orator into Sir Philip Sidney's Poet'). He made a rich contribution to Assumption, to the University of Windsor, and to the city of Windsor.

Father Pappert's most outstanding work was in the area of education extension, which was a tradition at Assumption going back to 1933. Heavy immigration from Europe following the Second World War created in the late 1940s a vastly increased demand for extension work, to the point where a full-time director was required. Father Pappert occupied that positon with distinction from 1950 to 1979. His expertise in this field reached beyond Assumption University. Through the years 1960 to 1965 he served terms as secretary, treasurer, and president of the Canadian Association of Directors of Extension and Summer School. He also served on the executive of the U.S.-based Association of University Evening Colleges, 1963–5. In 1965 he represented the Canadian universities at the first International Congress on University Adult Education in Copenhagen.

Father Pappert was a member of the Board of Governors of Assumption University. He also worked for the Marriage Tribunal of the diocese of London. At the invitation of Bishop Gerald Emmett Carter, he collaborated in establishing the John XXIII Centre for Adult Education, offering both Catholic and inter-faith programs. He was a member of the City of Windsor's Adult Education Co-ordinating Committee. From the Industrial Management Clubs of Canada he received the Award of Merit, 1966, for his contribution to supervisory management training, and in 1975 received from the Board of Commissioners of Police an award for his work on the Police Study Program. In that same year the Ontario Council for University Continuing Education recognized his outstanding service.

Father Pappert served one term, 1975–8, as superior of O'Connor House, bringing to the office the same diligence, wisdom, and affability that had characterized his life even during the vicissitudes of rapid changes in living religious life in the post–Vatican II years. During the last ten years of his life a series of heart attacks curtailed his activities.

BIBLIOGRAPHY: 'Whither Spain?,' *Basilian* 2 (October 1936) 112; 'Tension in the Pacific,' *Basilian* 3 (January 1937) 8–10.
SOURCES: GABF; *Annals* 1 (1943) 266, 6 (1984) 207, 7 (1991) 146–8; *Newsletter* (21 December 1990).

PARÉ, Vincent Alton, priest, was born on 24 January 1927 in Windsor, the son of Armand Paré and Laura Antaya. He died in Toronto on 28 March 1998 and is buried in the Basilian plot of Heavenly Rest Cemetery, Windsor.

'Veeg' Paré attended St Francis Separate School and Assumption College School, Windsor, completing grade XIII in 1945. He continued at

Assumption College for one year of arts, after which he entered St Basil's Novitiate, Rochester, making first profession on 15 August 1947. He returned to Assumption College to complete his undergraduate studies (B.A., University of Western Ontario, 1950), concurrently teaching French in the high school. He was appointed to Aquinas Institute, Rochester, for one year of teaching and coaching, especially basketball. In 1951 he began theological studies at St Basil's Seminary, Toronto, and also taught French at St Michael's College School. He was ordained to the priesthood on 29 June 1955 in St Basil's Church, Toronto, by Bishop Francis Allen. He received an S.T.B. from the University of St Michael's College in 1956.

Father Paré had but two appointments in his life as a Basilian priest-teacher. The first was to St Charles College, Sudbury, Ontario, 1956–60, teaching and coaching. He brought his basketball team to the All-Ontario Finals. In 1960 he was appointed to Assumption College School, where he was to serve as teacher, vice-principal, and disciplinarian for eighteen years. He was organized, strict, and demanding but always fair, patient, and humorous. He also spent six years as prefect of the boarders' residence. Two massive heart attacks in 1966 put an end to his coaching and reduced his teaching, though for some years he continued as vice-principal, and was first councillor of the Basilian community, 1969–72. He remained very much a part of the life of the school by his interest in the students, his counselling, his sacramental ministry, and his attendance at school events. He never complained about his weakened health.

Veeg Paré created and fostered bonds of friendship with former students, and many of them asked him to officiate at their weddings or came to him for counsel. He considered the fraternity and common prayer of community life a source of strength, and served on the local council at both St Charles and Assumption. During the short time that he spent in the Basilian Fathers Residence (Infirmary), December 1997 until his death, the staff referred to him as the perfect patient.

SOURCES: GABF; *Annals* 2 (1955) 200, 9 (1998) 9–10, (1999) 86–8; *Newsletter* (14 April 1998).

PAYAN, Augustin, priest, one of the ten founding fathers, was born on 1 October 1771 at Chassiers, near Largentière (Ardèche, diocese of Viviers [from 1801 to 1822 of Mende]), the son of Joseph Payan and Suzanne Soulerin. He died in Annonay on 8 April 1847 and was buried in the Saint-Jacques Cemetery. He was later reinterred in the

Basilian cemetery on the grounds of the Collège du Sacré-Coeur, Annonay.

An excellent student at the Collège d'Aubenas, and inspired by the example and martyrdom during the Revolution of Father François-Augustin Rouville SJ, one of his teachers, Augustin Payan first sought to fulfil his vocation with the Jesuits. This not being possible, and hearing of the clandestine seminary-college of Saint-Symphorien-de-Mahun (Ardèche), he went there with a letter of recommendation, dated June 1801, from his parish priest. He was then thirty years of age. He taught at the seminary-college while studying theology under Father Marie-Joseph Actorie. When the seminary-college moved to Annonay in 1802 he continued to teach and to study theology, and was ordained to the priesthood by Jean de Belmont, bishop of Saint-Flour, on 22 September 1804.

While teaching he also did chaplaincy work at the hospital in Annonay, 1811–20. He did Sunday ministry and often preached in the church of Notre-Dame in Annonay.

Father Payan had become the spiritual leader of a small group of priest-teachers at the Collège des Cordeliers. This group prepared the way for the new association which came into being on 21 November 1822. Father Payan was elected to the council of the new community and remained a councillor until his death. During the years 1822 to 1834 he could be considered the first novice master, as he oversaw the period of probation of new members, even though he did not support the idea of a more formal novitiate in 1835.

In 1825 he was named bursar of the college, and later also served as prefect of studies, 1829–32. From 1832 until his death he was the chaplain for the Dames du Sacré-Coeur, whom he had helped get established in Annonay. For more than thirty years Father Payan was also the confessor and spiritual director for most of the students and some teachers at the college.

Father Payan offered his last Mass on Easter Sunday, 4 April 1847, just four days before his death. Father Adrien *Chomel wrote in his history of the college: 'Gifted with a sweet, affable and easy temperament, Father Payan was, in the eyes of his former students, goodness personified.'

SOURCES: GABF; Chomel, *Collège d'Annonay* 61–5, 117, 121–2, 144; Kirley, *Community in France* 59; Pouzol, 'Notices'; Roume, *Origines* 80, 92, 156, 166–7, 159, 401.

PENDERGAST, Russell Anthony, priest, brother of Father Paul Pendergast SFM, was born on 24 September 1921 in Toronto, the eldest of three sons and two daughters of Francis Anthony Pendergast and Catherine Russell. He died in Toronto on 9 February 1997 and is buried in the Basilian plot of Holy Cross Cemetery, Thornhill, Ontario.

'Russ' Pendergast attended St John's Separate School and graduated from the high school section of St Michael's College, Toronto, in 1940. He articled for the accounting firm of Clarkson and Gordon (Toronto) but was subsequently seconded for intelligence work with the Canadian armed forces. In 1942 he entered St Basil's Novitiate, Toronto, and was professed on 15 August 1943. He was appointed to residence at St Basil's Seminary and later at St Michael's College during his university studies (B.A., Honours Political Science and Economics, University of Toronto, 1947). He studied theology at St Basil's Seminary, Toronto, 1947–51, and was ordained to the priesthood on 29 June 1950 in St Basil's Church, Toronto, by Cardinal James Charles McGuigan.

In 1951 Father Pendergast was appointed to the newly founded St John Fisher College, Rochester, where he taught economics, assisted in chaplaincy, and was treasurer of the college from 1959 to 1963. He also pursued graduate studies at the University of Ottawa (Ph.D., University of Ottawa, 1955), submitting as his thesis 'The XY Company: A Study of the Economics of the Montreal Based Fur Trade in Western Canada at the Beginning of the Nineteenth Century.' His research was done largely in the archives of the Grand Séminaire de Québec.

In 1963 Father Pendergast accompanied Father Wilfrid *Dore to Edmonton, Alberta, to assume Basilian responsibility for St Joseph's College in the University of Alberta. In his typical canny way he claimed the special rate for shipping his belongings west that railroads had granted, and never officially rescinded, to western settlers in the late nineteenth century. Father Pendergast reorganized the college and placed it on a sound financial basis. He joined the faculty of the university in the department of economics and became an esteemed colleague and outstanding professor. He always wore his clerical collar when teaching. His disarming ways and interest in the students made him a widely appreciated figure on the campus, and he won the university's Rutherford Award in 1985 for best teacher of the year. He served as treasurer of St Joseph's College, 1964–77, regional representative of the Basilian Fathers for western Canada, 1973–7, and local superior, 1985–91. Though he never taught at St Joseph's, he was the centre of that institution, with the door of his main-floor office always open to any and all.

Father Pendergast was active as an economist in university and governmental affairs. His conclusions were clear, hard-hitting, and colourfully expressed. He was a constant reader in his field, but his faith was the source of his vision and wisdom. What sorrows he faced and failures he suffered never overcame his good humour.

BIBLIOGRAPHY:

Book: *The XY Company, 1798 to 1804*. Rochester, 1957.
Article: 'Retreats for Students,' *Basilian Teacher* 1 (May 1957) 3–5; 'Report on an Experiment,' *Basilian Teacher* 3 (May 1959) 205–7.
SOURCES: GABF; *Annals* 1 (1950) 287, 2 (1952) 114, 8 (1994) 23–4, 9 (1998) 74–6; *Newsletter* (15 March 1997).

PENNY, Joseph Gerard, priest, was born on 8 June 1926 in Halifax, Nova Scotia, the only son in a family of three of Joseph Penny and Vera Courtney. He died in Toronto on Pentecost Sunday, 11 June 2000, and is buried in the Basilian plot of Holy Cross Cemetery, Thornhill, Ontario.

Joe Penny attended St Thomas Aquinas grade school and St Mary's High School in Halifax. At the suggestion of his spiritual counsellor, Father Lawrence O'Neill, he entered St Basil's Novitiate, Toronto, in 1944, taking first vows on 12 September 1945. He was appointed to St Michael's College, Toronto, for undergraduate studies (B.A., University of Toronto, 1948). He taught for a year at Aquinas Institute, Rochester, and spent a year at the Ontario College of Education while living at Holy Rosary Seminary, Toronto. During the year 1950–1, he lived and taught at St Michael's College School, Toronto. From 1951 to 1954 he studied theology at St Basil's Seminary, Toronto, and was ordained to the priesthood on 29 June 1953 in St Basil's Church, Toronto, by Cardinal James Charles McGuigan.

As a priest Father Penny had several appointments: St Michael's College School, teaching English, moderator of scholastics, 1954–66; St Charles College, Sudbury, Ontario, teaching, 1966–8; graduate studies (M.A., University of Windsor, 1969); St Michael's College School, teaching, 1970–6, 1977–9, superior, 1970–6; University of St Michael's College, chaplain, 1976–7. In 1979 he was appointed to the Basilian Fathers of Wilcox, Saskatchewan, to teach at the Athol Murray College of Notre Dame. From 1981 to 1993 he taught at St Thomas More College, Saskatoon, Saskatchewan, with the year 1990-1 off for pastoral and professional development. He worked as hospital chaplain in Saskatoon, 1993-5, and then in St Augustine's Parish, Saskatoon, 1995-7.

Joe Penny loved the English language and enthusiastically taught its literature to his students. His manner was constantly friendly, an engaging smile and humorous quip ever at the ready. He could turn tension into rollicking laughter.

Shortly after attending the Basilian general chapter of 1997, Father Penny was found to have lymphoma. During a period of remission in 1998, he moved to Henry Carr Farm, Beeton, Ontario, but intense suffering required frequent visits to the Basilian Fathers Residence (Infirmary), Toronto. On the Sunday before his death, while concelebrating Mass, several cries of pain escaped him. After Mass, his native courtesy undiminished, he quietly apologized for the disturbance.

BIBLIOGRAPHY: 'Obedience Is Orientation towards Others,' *Forum* 2 (April 1966) 55; 'We Witness to ... No Schizophrenic Split between Sanctity and Secularism,' *Forum* 3 (May 1967).
SOURCES: GABF; *Annals* 2 (1953) 110, 9 (2001) 92-3; *Newsletter* (10 July 2000).

PERBET, Séraphin, priest, was born on 26 July 1868 at Saint-Martin-de-Valamas (Ardèche), the son of Louis Perbet and Rosalie Chambrier. He died in Annonay on 13 January 1951 and is buried there in the Basilian cemetery on the grounds of the Collège du Sacré-Coeur.

Séraphin made his novitiate at Beaconfield House, Plymouth, England, 1888-9, took final vows on 18 September 1891, and was ordained to the priesthood by Bishop Joseph-Michel-Frédéric Bonnet of Viviers on 22 September 1893 in the chapel of the Collège du Sacré-Coeur, Annonay. He taught in Basilian institutions for fourteen years: at Sainte-Barbe minor seminary, Annonay, 1889-90, at the Ecole cléricale, Périgueux (Dordogne), 1890-1 and 1896-7, and at the Collège du Sacré-Coeur, 1891-6 and 1897-1903.

With the dispersal of Basilians in 1903 following governmental exclusion of members of congregations from teaching in schools, Father Perbet took up parish work as assistant at Chanéac, near Saint-Martin-de-Valamas, 1903-4. He taught for two years at the Petit Séminaire de Vernoux (Ardèche), 1904-6. For the next forty-two years he served successively as curate of Saint-Martial, pastor of Saint-Cierge-sous-le-Cheylard, and pastor at Saint-Jean-Roure, Rochessauve, and

Accon (all places in the Ardèche). In 1948 he retired to Maison Saint-Joseph in Annonay.

In retirement he devoted himself to prayer and recollection. Despite his four decades in remote parishes, he felt very attached to the Basilian community and contributed what money he could to help educate young students. He died of a cerebral haemorrhage in the hospital in Annonay.

SOURCES: GABF; Kirley, *Community in France* 184, 204, 240n569; Kirley, *Congregation in France* 156, 192, 213, 220; Pouzol, 'Notices.'

PERBOST, Antoine VICTOR, priest, was born on 5 June 1824 at Chapias, commune of La Beaume, canton of Joyeuse (Ardèche), the son of Pierre Perbost. His mother's name was Thérèse (family name not known). He died at Prunet, canton of Largentière (Ardèche), on 31 July 1903 and was buried in the local cemetery.

Victor taught for a year at the Collège des Cordeliers, Annonay, 1855–6, before entering the novitiate at Vernoux (Ardèche) at the age of thirty-two. He made final profession of vows in 1858 and was ordained to the priesthood on 17 December 1859 by Bishop Louis Delcusy of Viviers. He spent his entire priestly life teaching in minor seminaries: at Vernoux, 1860–2 and 1874–91, at Aubenas (Ardèche), 1862–74, and, for a few months, at the Collège du Bourg Saint-Andéol. He lived in retirement at the Basilian minor seminary, Sainte-Barbe, Annonay, 1891–1903. The exclusion in 1903 of members of congregations from teaching in schools forced him to take refuge in the parish of Prunet, where a Father Perbost, probably a relative, was pastor.

SOURCE: Pouzol, 'Notices.'

PERDUE, Simon Andrew, priest, was born in Downeyville, Ontario (diocese of Peterborough), on 27 March 1893, the youngest of nine children of Simon Perdue and Margaret Brick. He died in Toronto on 7 March 1966 and is buried in the Basilian plot of Holy Cross Cemetery, Thornhill, Ontario.

Simon Perdue attended School No. 6, Emily, in Downeyville Parish, and obtained a normal entrance certificate at Ennismore High School in 1912. He enrolled in Normal School (as Ontario teachers' colleges were then called) and qualified as an elementary school teacher. He taught in a number of small rural schools, among them Douro and

Springhill. In 1918 he resumed his education, first at the University of Ottawa, then at St Michael's College, Toronto, 1919–21. He entered St Basil's Novitiate, Toronto, in 1921 and was professed on 12 August 1922. His theological studies at St Basil's Scholasticate, Toronto, were interrupted by a year of teaching at St Thomas College (High School) in Houston, 1923–4. He was ordained priest on 18 December 1926 in St Basil's Church, Toronto, by Bishop Alexander MacDonald.

Father 'Si' Perdue taught for two years at St Thomas High School, Houston; but, after the first of a long series of illnesses, he went on sick leave to St John the Baptist Parish, Amherstburg, Ontario. A series of parish appointments followed: Ste Anne's, Detroit, 1933–4, St Basil's, Toronto, 1934–5, Holy Rosary, Toronto, 1935–43, and Assumption Parish, Windsor, 1943–9. He returned to St Basil's Parish, Toronto, in 1949 and remained there until his death in 1966 from a brain tumour.

Father Perdue took time to talk with parishioners and to entertain visitors to St Michael's College. Those who confided in him found in him a prudent guide. His verbal jousting with Father Terry McLaughlin, in which he playfully vaunted parish work over the academic, enlivened many a community recreation.

SOURCES: GABF; *Annals* 3 (1966) 468–9; *Newsletter* (7 March 1966); *Yearbook SMC* 18 (1927).

PERRY, Harold Charles, priest, was born on 18 August 1923 in Rochester, the son of Harold A. Perry and Mary McKelvey. He died in Houston on 25 January 1978 and is buried there in the Basilian plot of Garden of Gethsemane, Forest Park Lawndale Cemetery.

Harold attended Holy Rosary grade school and Aquinas Institute, Rochester, graduating in 1942. After wartime service in the United States Army he enrolled in the State University of New York (B.S., Education, 1949). He went on to Lehigh University, Bethlehem, Pennsylvania, where he earned an M.A. in history in 1950. In September of that year he returned to Aquinas as a teacher. One year later he entered St Basil's Novitiate, Rochester, making first profession on 15 August 1952. He was then assigned to Assumption College School, Windsor, where he taught while studying philosophy. He took his theology courses at St Basil's Seminary, Toronto, 1953–7, earned the S.T.B., St Michael's College, 1956, and was ordained to the priesthood on 29 June 1956 in St Basil's Church, Toronto, by Cardinal James Charles McGuigan.

Father Perry taught at Aquinas Institute, 1957–61, and then began graduate studies in political science at Syracuse University. His studies were interrupted in 1963 by his appointment to St John Fisher College, Rochester, where he remained until 1969, when he returned to Syracuse University for two more years. In the fall of 1971 he was assigned to the University of St Thomas, Houston, where he remained until his death. He was superior of the Basilian community from 1974 to 1977.

Harold Perry was a warm, welcoming priest who was especially attentive and encouraging to younger Basilians. His generosity and gregarious personality made him a popular man on the campus as well as a unifying influence. He was a person of fine tastes who appreciated things well done, whether in art, cuisine, teaching, community life, or liturgy. He loved to travel, and was an indefatigable sightseer. His death from a stroke at the age of fifty-four shocked and saddened the university community.

SOURCES: GABF; *Annals* 2 (1956) 252, 5 (1979) 402–3; *Newsletter* (30 January 1978).

PETREY, Paul Francis, priest, member of the Congregation 1933–50, was born in Wellsville, New York (diocese of Buffalo), on 4 May 1913, the son of Peter Petrey and Elizabeth Markey. He died in Dallas, Texas, on 6 August 1965, and is buried there in Calvary Hill Cemetery.

Paul Petrey was educated in Immaculate Conception School, the high school section of St Michael's College, Toronto, 1929–30, and St Michael's College (B.A., University of Toronto, 1933). After a year at St Basil's Novitiate, Toronto, he made first profession on 27 September 1934. He did his theological studies at St Basil's Scholasticate, Toronto, and was ordained priest on 17 December 1938 by Archbishop James Charles McGuigan in St Basil's Church, Toronto.

A forceful and engaging personality made Father Petrey an effective teacher of mathematics at Catholic Central High School, Detroit, 1934–5 and 1938–43, and at St Thomas High School, Houston, 1947–50. During his early years as a teacher he attended courses in education at the University of Detroit and qualified as a secondary school teacher in the State of Michigan.

In 1950 Father Petrey withdrew from the Congregation, changed his name to William Mitchell, married Margaret Murphy, the sister of the wife of another former Basilian, Thomas *Slattery, and moved to Dallas, Texas. He raised a son (John) and a stepdaughter (Anne). He was killed in an automobile accident and was buried from his parish church of St Pius X, Dallas.

SOURCES: GABF; John O'Leary.

PEYREPLANE, Hippolyte, priest, was born on 4 May 1874 at Labégude, canton of Aubenas (Ardèche), the son of Hippolyte and Marie Peyreplane. He died at Aubenas (Ardèche) on 2 May 1908 and is buried in the family plot at Prades (Ardèche).

Hippolyte went to Annonay in 1887 to enrol as a minor seminarian in the Sainte-Barbe section of the Collège du Sacré-Coeur. He did all his secondary schooling there and passed the baccalaureate exams in 1895. He made his novitiate at Sainte-Barbe in 1893–4 under the direction of Father Léopold *Fayolle, and took final vows on 17 September 1897. Bishop Hilarion Montéty ordained him to the priesthood on 23 September 1899 in the chapel of the Collège du Sacré-Coeur, Annonay. During his years of theology he had taught commercial, 1895–6, and humanities, 1896–9, at Sacré-Coeur, and remained on staff until the Basilians were excluded from teaching there by the anticlerical laws in 1903.

Father Peyreplane served as curate at Saint-Paul-le-Jeune (Ardèche) for a few months before going to the Petit Séminaire d'Aubenas (Ardèche), where he taught humanities, 1903–6. When religious priests were forced out of the minor seminary in 1906 he went to help minister in his native parish of Labégude. When the minor seminary at Aubenas reopened in 1907 in the college that had belonged to the Marist Brothers, Father Peyreplane took up teaching the humanities. His untimely death after a brief illness nine months later deprived the Basilians and the diocese of a devout young priest and an outstanding teacher, much beloved by his students.

SOURCES: GABF; Kirley, *Community in France* 184, 197, 205, 255n600; Pouzol, 'Notices.'

PHELAN, George Raymond, priest, was born in Chatham, New Brunswick, on 12 July 1914, the son of Thomas Phelan and Mary Murdock. He died in Windsor on 7 February 1965 and is buried there in the Basilian plot of Assumption Cemetery.

George Phelan attended elementary school and then St Thomas College, 1926-32, in his native city. He spent the year 1933-4 at Assumption College, Windsor, before entering St Basil's Novitiate, Toronto. After profession on 15 August 1935, he returned to Assumption College (B.A., University of Western Ontario, 1939). He taught at Catholic Central High School, Detroit, in 1939-40, then attended the Ontario College of Education, Toronto, 1940-1, for teacher certification. He studied theology at St Basil's Seminary, Toronto, 1941-5, and was ordained to the priesthood on 20 August 1944 in St Basil's Church, Toronto, by Archbishop James Charles McGuigan.

Father Phelan taught French in three Basilian schools: St Michael's College School, Toronto, 1945-52, Catholic Central High School, Detroit, 1952-3, and Assumption College School, 1953-60. In the latter year a severe heart attack led to five years of restricted activity and frequent hospitalization before his death. Through it all he remained cheerful and optimistic.

Intensely interested in dramatics, he was a skilful director and indefatigable producer of student plays, and had a gift for attracting to dramatics students who were not participating in other student activities. His classroom quips were long remembered by his students.

SOURCES: GABF; *Annals* 1 (1945) 99, 3 (1965) 382-3; *Newsletter* (9 February 1965).

PHILIPPON, Marius, priest, was born on 9 September 1865 at Baix (Ardèche), the son of Frédéric Philippon and Rosalie Salles. He died on 1 October 1937 at Baix and is buried in the cemetery there.

Marius entered the novitiate at Beaconfield House, Plymouth, England, on 1 September 1885 and took final vows on 21 September 1888. Upon returning from the novitiate in England he taught in 1886-7 at the Collège du Sacré-Coeur, Annonay, and successfully passed the exams for the first part of the *baccalauréat.* He went to the Collège Stanislas in Paris to complete his degree, but fell ill and returned to Annonay in December 1887. He completed the school year as recreation master in the junior division of the college in Annonay and successfully passed the second part of the *baccalauréat* in the spring of 1888. Bishop Joseph-Michel-Frédéric Bonnet of Viviers ordained him to the priesthood on 19 September 1891 in the chapel of the Collège du Sacré-Coeur, Annonay.

Father Philippon then taught at the Collège du Sacré-Coeur, 1888-9, at the Collège Saint-Charles, Blidah, Algeria, 1889-92, and again at

Sacré-Coeur, 1892–1903, where he taught the philosophy class. When the anticlerical laws in 1903 excluded Basilians from teaching, he went to live with his family at Baix, where he assisted in ministry at the parish and where he died thirty-four years later.

Through this period his connection with the Basilians remained. He had been elected to the general council in 1900 when Father Jean-Claude *Savoye resigned. He attended the general chapter in Geneva in 1910 and served as councillor to the provincial, Father Noël *Durand, until 1922. In 1934 he was again elected general councillor in France when Father Eugène *Jobert died. In his latter years he occasionally visited the confreres at Maison Saint-Joseph, where the community was gathered in Annonay.

SOURCES: GABF; Kirley, *Community in France* 147n373, 172, 182n464, 183, 201 205, 240n569; Kirley, *Congregation in France* 12, 42, 80–3, 87, 154, 156, 171, 213–14; Pouzol, 'Notices.'

PICKETT, Michael Joseph, priest, was born at Berkeley, Ontario (diocese of Hamilton), on 11 February 1876, the son of John Pickett and Mary McLelland. He died in Toronto on 30 July 1949 and is buried there in the Basilian plot of Mount Hope Cemetery.

After attending Berkeley Public School, Michael went in 1893 to St Michael's College, Toronto, for his secondary education. In 1900 he entered St Basil's Novitiate, Toronto, and was professed on 8 September 1901. As a scholastic he taught at St Mary's Seminary, LaPorte, Texas, 1901–2, and then completed his theological studies at St Basil's Scholasticate, Toronto. He was ordained to the priesthood on 3 September 1905 in St Basil's Church, Toronto, by Archbishop Denis *O'Connor.

Father Pickett taught once again at St Mary's Seminary, LaPorte, 1905–10, at St Michael's College, 1910–11, and at St Thomas College, Chatham, New Brunswick, 1911–15. With the outbreak of the First World War he applied to be a chaplain in the Canadian Army, and lived at St Michael's College in 1915–16 while awaiting induction. He spent over two years as a chaplain with the Canadian Overseas Expeditionary Force in France, and suffered in his later years from the effects of mustard gas. His post-war appointments were to St Mary's of the Assumption Parish, Owen Sound, Ontario, as assistant, 1919–20, St Thomas College, Chatham, 1920–3, and Assumption College, Windsor, where he taught commercial subjects, 1923–6. He retired to St Basil's

Seminary, Toronto, where he died twenty-three years later of heart disease.

From his father, an early railroad contractor, Father Pickett inherited a booming voice that made his sermons memorable events – perhaps on occasion more than memorable: his sermon at Redford, Michigan, on Good Friday, 1926, was reported to have lasted three hours and fifteen minutes. A somewhat rough exterior – probably reinforced by wartime experiences – marked him as a man's priest, inspiring confidence and drawing to him for counsel and encouragement students, soldiers, and parishioners. The *Basilian Centennial* volume of St Mary's of the Assumption Parish recorded, 'He was affectionately called "the gruff padre with the heart of gold."'

SOURCES: GABF; *Annals* 1 (1949) 239–40; William Perkins Bull, *From Macdonell to McGuigan, the History of the Growth of the Roman Catholic Church in Upper Canada* (Toronto, 1939); *Centennial, St Mary's*; *Jubilee, St Mary's*; McMahon, *Pure Zeal* 32–3.

PLAYER, James Frederic, considered as the eighth superior general, was born in Weymouth, England (diocese of Plymouth), on 9 July 1871, the son of Alfred Player and Ann Champ. He died in Toronto on 1 March 1931 and is buried there in the Basilian plot of Mount Hope Cemetery.

James Player received his early education in local schools and at the Basilian College of Mary Immaculate, Beaconfield House, Plymouth, England. In 1892 he and another Englishman, John *Plomer, entered St Basil's Novitiate in Toronto with the first class of novices received in the new novitiate on Kendal (now Tweedsmuir) Avenue. After his profession on 18 September 1893, he returned to the College of Mary Immaculate and later completed his theological studies in France. He was ordained priest in Annonay on 24 September 1898.

Father Player's first appointment in Canada was as assistant at Holy Rosary Parish, Toronto, January–August 1901. His next appointment, as superior of St Mary's Seminary, LaPorte, Texas, 1901–3, was cut short when ill health brought him back to Holy Rosary Parish where, in 1911, he was well enough to be named pastor. He was transferred to St Basil's Parish, Toronto, in 1922. Three years later he was named spiritual director at St Basil's Novitiate, an office he held at the time of his death from a heart ailment in 1931.

Writing in the *Parishioner*, Mr George Dawson described Father

Player as 'tall and handsome; friendly, yes! but with that certain reserve so often a part of the English gentleman.' The bright promise of his early years in the priesthood was diminished by his health: a stomach ulcer tended to make him fussy about little things, and later a heart condition restricted his activities. It was nevertheless he who was instrumental in having Holy Rosary Separate School built on the parish grounds. He opened two missions that grew into parishes: St Monica's in 1906 and St Clare's in 1912. He also looked after St John the Evangelist Parish, Weston, Ontario, 1908–11. He introduced a large number of statues into the novitiate chapel, which served at that time as the church for Holy Rosary parish.

Aside from those several appointments, James Player assumed responsibilities that affected the whole Congregation. With good friends on both sides of the Atlantic he was looked upon as being above the disputes that disturbed the Congregation during the first two decades of the twentieth century. He was elected provincial treasurer in 1905, and in 1911 was chosen to fill the position of first councillor left vacant by the death of Father John Read *Teefy. When his lifelong friend, Father Victorin *Marijon, resigned as superior general in 1914, Father Player became acting superior general of the whole Congregation. Because this interregnum lasted until the separation from the French community in 1922, he is considered the eighth superior general. In 1920, on a visit to Rome, he was instructed to convene a general chapter in Toronto on 14 June 1921. It was never held because the province of France proposed, and the province of Canada welcomed, the transformation of the two provinces into separate religious communities. Father Player was elected to the general council of the Basilian Fathers of Toronto in 1922 and served until 1928.

SOURCES: GABF; G.H. Dawson, 'The Story of Holy Rosary Parish,' *Parishioner* (September 1964–January 1965); Kirley, *Community in France* ii, 216n518, 229n550, 237n566, 240n570, 251n587, 252, 253n592, 254; Kirley, *Congregation in France* 2, 21, 29–30, 32–3, 36–40, 42–4, 47–9, 55, 57, 88; *Yearbook SMC* 22 (1931).

PLOMER, John Clifton, priest, member of the Congregation 1892–1922, was born in Falmouth, England (diocese of Plymouth), on 8 February 1875, the son of John Plomer and Elizabeth Pearce. He died in Detroit on 16 July 1926 and was buried there in Mount Olivet Cemetery.

Educated at Falmouth Grammar School and at the Basilian College of

Mary Immaculate, Beaconfield House, Plymouth, England, John Plomer and his compatriot James *Player entered St Basil's Novitiate, Toronto, on 23 August 1892, in the first class in the new novitiate on Kendal (now Tweedsmuir) Avenue. After profession the following year he remained in Toronto, studying at St Michael's College and St Basil's Scholasticate until 1897, when he was sent to Annonay in France to complete his theological studies. He was ordained to the priesthood on 23 September 1899 in the chapel of the Collège du Sacré-Coeur by Bishop Hilarion Montéty.

Father Plomer taught at St Michael's College, 1900–1 and 1904–7, and at St Mary's Seminary, LaPorte, Texas, 1901–4 and 1907–11. In 1911 he was appointed to St Basil's Scholasticate. In 1916 he returned to Texas as principal and superior of St Thomas High School, Houston. In 1919 he moved to Assumption College, Windsor, where he taught history.

Father Plomer and Father Charles *Coughlin, both members of the Assumption staff, withdrew from the Congregation in 1922, and used the occasion to launch an acrimonious attack on the Community that was countered by an equally acrimonious reply from a lay member of the Assumption faculty. Incardinated in the archdiocese of Detroit on 26 February 1923, Father Plomer taught at Sacred Heart Seminary, Detroit, until his death following an operation for gallstones. Father Vincent *Donnelly, a lifelong friend, described Father Plomer as 'a man of many and excellent talents. ... His specialties were mathematics, the languages and sciences. ... He had a great love for outdoor sports and was always to be found among the leaders.' He left a library of over two thousand volumes to Sacred Heart Seminary.

BIBLIOGRAPHY: 'Basilian Fathers,' *Catholic Encyclopedia* (New York, 1907–13) 2: 324–5; two unpublished manuscripts: Eng. trans. Adrien *Chomel, *Le Collège d'Annonay*; Eng. trans. Adrien Chomel, unpublished biography of Father Julien *Tracol.
SOURCES: GABF; Lambert M. Lavoy, 'In Memoriam,' *Gothic*, Sacred Heart Seminary (November 1926) 6; *Makers of the Catholic Encyclopedia* (New York, 1917) 138 (with portrait); *Purple and White* (15 October 1926); Shook, *Catholic Education* 283–4.

PLOURDE, Emil J., priest, was born in Detroit on 2 November 1879, the son of Arthur Plourde and Liliosa Dumontier. He died in Windsor on 20 December 1934 and is buried there in the Basilian plot of Assumption Cemetery.

Emil Plourde grew up in River Rouge, Michigan, and from there attended Ste Anne's School, Detroit. In 1895 he went to Assumption College, Windsor, where as a baseball pitcher he acquired the nickname 'Jig' that stayed with him for the rest of his life. In 1899 he entered St Basil's Novitiate, Toronto, was professed on 29 September 1900, and resumed his studies at St Michael's College in Toronto, 1900-2. After two years of theological courses at Assumption College and two at St Basil's Scholasticate, Toronto, he was ordained to the priesthood on 5 August 1906.

Father Plourde taught commercial subjects and supervised athletics at a number of Basilian schools: St Basil's College, Waco, Texas, 1906-10; St Thomas High School, Houston, 1910-13 and 1922-7; Assumption College, 1913-16 and 1920-2; St Thomas College, Chatham, New Brunswick, 1916-19. He also served in several parishes: Assumption Parish, Windsor, 1919-20 and 1928-9; Ste Anne's Parish, Detroit, 1927-8 and 1929-31. In 1931 he was appointed spiritual director at St Basil's Novitiate, Toronto. After an operation for stomach ulcers in 1934, he went to recuperate at Ste Anne's Parish, Detroit; but, during a visit to Assumption College, he suffered a fatal heart attack.

Although somewhat under medium height, Father Plourde was an exceptional athlete who participated in every sport during his student days and for years afterwards. Writing of him in *The Basilian*, Father Thomas *Moylan said, 'Youth was something permanent with him. He never grew old. ... In the things that win the admiration of boys and men, and women too, he was blessed with skill and accomplishments that would have given many every reason for pride and a sense of superiority. There was never anything of this in Father Plourde.' An obituary notice in the *Yearbook*, St Michael's College, 1935, remarked that within the Congregation 'he was loved by all from the youngest scholastic to the oldest priest.'

SOURCES: GABF; Charles Collins, 'Basilians I Have Known,' transcribed in Robert J. Scollard, 'Historical Notes C.S.B.' 10 50-5 (GABF); T.V. Moylan, 'Father Plourde As I Knew Him,' *Basilian* 1 (June 1935) 67-9, 79; Power, *Assumption College* 3 364; *Yearbook SMC* (1935); *Yearbook STC*.

POKRIEFKA, Edward Leo, priest, was born in Detroit on 1 April 1896, the son of August Pokriefka and Frances Bohl. He died in Detroit on 28 October 1954 and is buried in the Basilian plot of Assumption Cemetery, Windsor.

Edward Pokriefka left school at an early age and worked as a labourer until he was twenty-six, when he went back to school as a boarder in first-year high school at Assumption College, Windsor. Eight years later he entered St Basil's Novitiate, Toronto, and was professed on 15 August 1931. After theological studies in Toronto at St Basil's Scholasticate he was ordained to the priesthood on 16 December 1934 in Assumption Church, Windsor, by Bishop John Kidd.

After a year as assistant to the treasurer of St Michael's College, Toronto, 1935–6, Father Pokriefka served at St Mary's of the Assumption Parish, Owen Sound, Ontario, 1936–7 and 1940–3, looking after the mission churches: St Michael's, Irish Block, and St Mary's, Hepworth. From 1945 to 1950 he worked in the development of Assumption College, especially the drive for a Memorial Science Building. Half his priestly life was spent at Ste Anne's Parish, Detroit, 1937–40, 1943–6, and 1950 until his death from a cerebral haemorrhage.

Father Pokriefka, whose name was usually shortened to 'Poke,' was big, strong, and remarkably light on his feet. He had the gift of getting others to work with him. The *Basilian Centennial* volume of St Mary's of the Assumption Parish noted, 'His memory is still very much alive here as a good speaker, but above all as a good worker.' His language was blunt, on occasion forceful, and at all times picturesque. He was by nature a man of business rather than a thinker. Much of Father Pokriefka's work in Detroit was done in outreach from Ste Anne's Parish. For some years he was chaplain to the Good Shepherd Sisters. Later he frequently replaced pastors of small parishes who were on sick leave.

BIBLIOGRAPHY: *A History of St Michael's Church and the Irish Block, 1852–1937* (Meaford, Ont., 1937).
SOURCES: GABF; *Annals* 2 (1954) 183–4; *Centennial, St Mary's*; *Basilides, Assumption College* (Windsor, 1930).

POLLY, Jean-Baptiste, priest, one of the ten founding fathers, uncle of Father Jean François *Polly, was born at Saint-Symphorien-de-Mahun (Ardèche, diocese of Viviers [from 1801 to 1822 of Mende]) on 19 April 1772, the son of Jean Polly and Marguerite Deglesne. He died in Annonay on 28 March 1846, was buried in the cemetery of Saint-Jacques, and reinterred in 1869 in the cemetery on the grounds of the Collège du Sacré-Coeur, Annonay.

Jean-Baptiste Polly began his education by studying Latin with Father

Besset, curate at Quintenas (Ardèche). Later he went to the Grand Séminaire at Le Puy (Haute-Loire). In April or May of 1793 the seminary was forced to close, and Jean-Baptiste returned to his family. After the death of his father on 18 July 1793 he became mayor of 'Mahun-Libre,' as the revolutionaries, suppressing saints' names, had called the village. He did not hesitate to deceive the anticlerical inspectors by hiding priests who refused to swear the schismatic revolutionary oath. Still wanting to become a priest, he studied theology secretly with a Sulpician in Lyon for five months, then returned to Saint-Symphorien, probably in 1797. After further studies in theology at the clandestine seminary at Monestier near Vanosc (Ardèche), he was ordained secretly to the priesthood in the church at Vanosc in 1801.

Father Polly served as assistant at La Louvesc (Ardèche) for a year and a half, at Préaux, 1803–4, and at Satillieu, 1804–6. In 1806 he joined the staff at the Collège des Cordeliers, Annonay, where he was for a time bursar and where he taught sciences, theology, and philosophy until his death.

In 1822 he joined with nine other secular priests engaged in teaching at the Collège des Cordeliers, Annonay, in seeking permission to found the Association of Priests of St Basil. He was elected second assistant at the first general chapter in 1822.

Father Polly was known as a conscientious and methodical teacher with a rough exterior, an iron constitution, and a warm heart. From 1815 he did Sunday ministry at the parish at Toissieux (Ardèche), going there on foot. He often walked to Tournon (Ardèche) and back, a total of thirty kilometres, in order to consult a book in the library.

SOURCES: GABF; Chomel, *Collège d'Annonay* 65–73, 111, 117, 131, 144, 438; Kirley, *Community in France* 59; Pouzol, 'Notices'; Roume, *Origines* 54–7, 133, 159, 401.

POLLY, Jean FRANÇOIS, priest, nephew of Father Jean-Baptiste *Polly, was born on 13 December 1803 at Saint-Symphorien-de-Mahun (Ardèche, diocese of Mende, since 1822 of Viviers), the son of Jean François Charles Polly and Jeanne Marie Buisson. He died on 28 July 1854 in Annonay and was buried there in the cemetery of Saint-Jacques. In 1869 his remains were reinterred in the Basilian cemetery on the grounds of the Collège du Sacré-Coeur.

François Polly attended the Collège des Cordeliers as a boarding student, doing the rhetoric course in 1822-3 just after the Basilian Community was founded. He taught at the Collège des Cordeliers, 1823-9, and at the Collège de Privas (Ardèche) in 1829-34, making his novitiate informally while teaching. He was professed on 3 September 1830 and ordained to the priesthood in 1833.

Father Polly held the position of professor of philosophy at the Collège des Cordeliers from 1834 to 1854. During the first six months of 1836 he studied in Paris at the Collège Stanislas and the Sorbonne; he was also absent from the college during the year 1840-1. He served as bursar at the Collège des Cordeliers, 1838-54, and from 1838 until his death he was also chaplain for the Ursuline Sisters.

On the death of Father Germain *Deglesne he became treasurer general of the Congregation. In 1836 he accompanied Father Pierre *Tourvieille to Rome, 10-23 October, to present the Constitutions of the community to the Holy See. In March of 1846 he was elected to the Basilian general council, replacing his uncle Jean-Baptiste *Polly, who had died. He remained on the council until 1854.

Father Adrien *Chomel wrote of Father François Polly: 'He was gifted with remarkable ease in speaking, and his clear, methodical teaching made his class very interesting, while his lively, brilliant and unhesitating utterance impressed the most abstract truths indelibly on the minds of his hearers.'

SOURCES: GABF; Chomel, *Collège d'Annonay* 199, 270-2; Pouzol, 'Notices.'

POPE, Joseph William, priest, was born on 26 July 1909 in Lindsay, Ontario (diocese of Peterborough), the eldest of eight children of Patrick George Pope and Albina Picard. He died in Houston on 22 September 1979 and is buried in the Basilian plot of Heavenly Rest Cemetery, Windsor, Ontario.

Joseph Pope attended St Dominic's Parochial School, Lindsay, and then Assumption College School, Windsor, graduating in 1927. While working for Sylvester's Farm Machinery that summer, he was one of the first mechanics sent to service combines in western Canada. He entered in St Basil's Novitiate, Toronto, was professed on 11 August 1928, and was appointed to St Basil's Scholasticate and then to St Michael's College, but never finished his university course. During his theological studies, 1931-5, he lived at the Scholasticate, except for the year 1933-4 at St Michael's College, and in summers was one of the principal builders of the stone shrine at Strawberry Island in Lake Simcoe. He was ordained to the priesthood on 16 December 1934 in Assumption Church, Windsor, by Bishop John Kidd.

Father Pope's forty years of active priesthood were spent exclusively in Basilian parishes, with the exception of two years of study, 1971–3, at the Toronto School of Theology, when he lived at St Basil's College. His appointments were as follows: St Mary's of the Assumption Parish, Owen Sound, Ontario, 1935–6, 1941–8, 1959–71, a total of twenty years; Assumption Parish, Windsor, 1936–40; Ste Anne's Parish, Detroit, 1940–1, 1948–53; St Anne's Parish, Houston, 1953–9; and Our Lady of Mount Carmel Parish, Wharton, Texas, 1973–5. He served as second councillor in the local community while at St Anne's, Houston, 1956–9, and as first councillor at St Mary's, Owen Sound, 1960–8. He never took on the function of pastor.

Joe Pope was a quiet, retiring person, though not lacking in a sense of humour, which would flash out in company in which he felt himself at ease. He promoted devotion to the Blessed Virgin Mary and was an early proponent of the Catholic Family Movement. Never idle outside of prayer, preaching, or ministry, he cultivated hobbies such as philately, shell collecting, and photography. He gave his collection of Vatican stamps, which he said was a complete set, to the University of St Thomas.

In 1975 Father Pope went to live at St Thomas High School, Houston, from where he ministered to senior citizens at St Dominic's Center, visiting the lonely and teaching hobbies, such as making rosaries to send to the missions. In 1977 he underwent successful surgery for cancer. A stroke suffered in 1978 while on holiday in Owen Sound, Ontario, slowed him down; but he recovered once again and returned to Houston. A year later, consonant with his quiet and self-effacing manner, he died in his sleep.

SOURCES: GABF; *Annals* 5 (1979) 343, (1980) 520–1; *Newsletter* (1 October 1978).

POUZOL, Auguste, priest, great-uncle of Father Félix *Pouzol, was born on 14 April 1845 in Annonay, the son of Jean-Pierre Pouzol and Elisabeth Vernet (Vernay). He died in Annonay on 28 March 1915 and was buried in the priests' plot of the cemetery in Annonay.

Auguste Pouzol completed his studies at the Collège des Cordeliers, Annonay, in 1865 and made his novitiate at Feyzin (Isère, now Rhône), in 1867–8. He was ordained to the priesthood on 20 September 1873 by

Bishop Armand de Charbonnel in the chapel of the Collège du Sacré-Coeur.

Auguste Pouzol worked in five geographic departments of France, including Algeria, as well as in Canada and England. He studied and taught theology at the Petit Séminaire d'Aubenas (Ardèche), 1868–74, he taught at the Ecole cléricale de Périgueux (Dordogne), 1874–80, the Petit Séminaire Saint-Charles, Vernoux (Ardèche), 1880–1, the Collège Saint-Pierre in Châteauroux (Indre), 1881–2, and in Canada for two years, 1882–4, one at St Michael's College, Toronto, and one at Assumption College, Windsor. He spent the summer of 1884 at St Mary's of the Assumption Parish, Owen Sound. He was at the College of Mary Immaculate at Beaconfield House, Plymouth, England, in 1885. He taught at the Collège du Sacré-Coeur as professor of English until 1896 and then at the Collège Saint-Charles in Blidah, Algeria, where he remained until the expulsion of teaching religious in 1903. From 1903 to 1909, under the legal status of a secular priest, he taught at the Institution Sainte-Marie at Riom (Puy-de-Dôme) before returning to Annonay. Father Pouzol was a linguist who composed a dictionary of Esperanto.

The war of 1914, the mobilization of a nephew, and the death of a grandnephew affected him a great deal. He died in his apartment on 28 March 1915 of uraemic poisoning. The newspaper *La Croix de l'Ardèche* said of him, 'He was a pleasant and very original person.'

SOURCES: GABF; Kirley, *Community in France* 185, 201, 209, 214n515; Kirley, *Congregation in France* 67; Pouzol, 'Notices.'

POUZOL, Félix Jules, priest, grandnephew of Father Auguste *Pouzol, was born on 18 October 1911 in Annonay, the son of Auguste Pouzol and Marie Servonet. He died in Annonay on 6 December 2000 and is buried there in the cemetery on the grounds of the Collège du Sacré-Coeur.

Félix was baptized in the old church of Notre-Dame parish, Annonay. All his life he maintained an intense loyalty to that parish, and it was from that parish, although not from the original church, that he was buried. He was educated in its parish school and at the Petit Séminaire de Saint-Charles, Annonay. He entered the Basilian novitiate at Bordighera, Italy, on 20 February 1928, receiving the habit from Father Victorin *Marijon, and made first profession on 25 February 1929. From the novitiate he went to Maison Saint-Joseph, Annonay, where he did two years of philosophy and four of theology, 1929–35. He made final profession on 25 May 1934, and was ordained to the priesthood on 6 July 1935 by Bishop Pierre-Marie Durieux in the cathedral of Viviers.

Father Pouzol taught in Annonay for many years at three institutions: Maison Saint-Joseph, the Collège du Sacré-Coeur, and the Petit Séminaire de Saint-Charles. He formed a whole generation of both Basilians and secular clergy in philosophy, theology, and spirituality. His mannerisms were amusing, but his teaching was clear, complete, and gratefully received. He was an 'Annonéen' to the marrow of his bones, loving the town, knowing its history and people, and daily treading its tortuous medieval streets. His weak eyesight exempted him from military service and from forced labour during the war. It did not, however, prevent him from doing thorough research over many years on the lives of the deceased French Basilians. Not satisfied with the brief treatment accorded them in the 1969 *Dictionary of Basilian Biography*, he composed in longhand 'Notices biographiques' which have served as the basis for most of the biographies of French Basilians in the present volume. Nor did his myopia inhibit his passionate love of hunting for mushrooms or his singular success therein.

At his funeral in the church of Notre-Dame, Annonay, Father Bernard Buisson CSB spoke to a full congregation of Father Pouzol's former students and friends about the five salient features of his life: his fidelity to the Church, his total consecration to the mission of education, his zeal in encouraging priestly vocations, his passion for Basilian history, and his ardent devotion to the Mother of God.

BIBLIOGRAPHY: 'History and Memories of a Minor Seminary (*Histoire et souvenirs d'un petit-séminaire*),' *Basilian Teacher* 3 (March 1959) 149–60; 'Un anniversaire à signaler,' *Mon Collège* (December 1972) 3–4; 'Our Lady of Lourdes: "I Am the Immaculate Conception,"' *CCR* 6 (1988) 53–4.
SOURCES: GABF; *Annals* 5 (1980) 458–9, 6 (1986) 397, 9 (2000) 3, (2001) 102–4; *Newsletter* (22 January 2001); Kirley, *Community in France* 211n507; Kirley, *Congregation in France* v, 67n14, 129, 137n53, 156, 159, 166n14, 167n16, 176, 184–5, 195–6, 203–7, 209–15, 219–20, 231, 256, 262, 271.

POWELL, Francis Gerald, priest, member of the Congregation, 1898–1922, was born in London, Ontario, on 10 March 1878, the son of Michael Powell and Catherine Dunn. He died in Montreal, Quebec, on 24 February 1951 and is buried in St Peter's Cemetery, London.

Educated in London, Ontario, Francis Powell went to Assumption College, Windsor, in 1891. With a record of seven years as a good student, and despite offers to play professional baseball, he entered St Basil's Novitiate, Toronto, and was professed on 6 August 1899. He did his theological courses at St Basil's Scholasticate, Toronto, and at Assumption College, and was ordained to the priesthood on 20 September 1902.

Father Powell taught at Assumption College until 1907, when he was appointed principal and superior of St Thomas College, Houston. In 1910 he was named principal and superior of St Michael's College, Toronto, but poor health prevented his active exercise of this office, and in 1911 he went to Assumption College. Two years later he returned to St Michael's College to teach philosophy, 1913-21. He was a member of the provincial council from 1916 until 1921, when he resigned for reasons of health. After one year on sick leave he served at Ste Anne's Parish, Detroit, 1922-3. Exercising his canonical option when the new, stricter vow of poverty was adopted in 1922, he withdrew from the Congregation and was incardinated in the diocese of London, Ontario, on 17 July 1924. For some years prior to his death in 1951 he lived in retirement at St Joachim's Rectory, Pointe-Claire, Montreal.

SOURCES: GABF; *Annals* 2 (1951) 42; *Jubilee, Assumption*; Kirley, *Congregation in France* 34, 40.

PRAT, Jean Henri, priest, member of the Congregation 1823-c.1858, was born on 13 July 1794 at Rocles (Ardèche).
Jean Henri Prat was received as a novice on 5 June 1823 in the newly formed Association of Priests of Saint Basil in Annonay (Ardèche). After ordination to the priesthood he taught at the minor seminary of Maison-Seule (Ardèche), which the Basilians operated for the diocese of Viviers from 1822 to 1844, the date on which the bishop moved that seminary to Vernoux (Ardèche). Father Prat later served as bursar in the minor seminary at Bourg-Saint-Andéol (Ardèche). Roume describes him as 'a schemer and mischief-maker ... up to complicated and underhanded intrigues ... a troublesome, muddle-headed bursar.' He seems to have left the Congregation at the beginning of the school year 1857-8, after which all trace of him was lost.

SOURCES: Pouzol, 'Notices,' notes supplémentaires; Roume, *Origines* 186 and passim.

PRECHEUR, Henri Louis, priest, member of the Congregation 1941–55, was born on 28 February 1921 in Annonay. He died on 6 January 1987 at the Collège du Sacré-Coeur, Annonay, and is buried there in the cemetery on the college grounds.

Henri Prêcheur entered the Basilian novitiate in Annonay in 1940 and made his first profession of vows on 6 September 1941. He was ordained a priest on 17 March 1945. For the next ten years he taught natural science and religious knowledge at the Collège du Sacré-Coeur as a member of the Congregation of Priests of Saint Basil of Viviers; but, at the time of the reunion of the French Basilians with the Congregation in North America in 1955, he opted for incardination in the diocese of Viviers. Bishop Alfred Couderc, ordinary of that diocese, granted him permission to continue living with the Basilians at the college, where he taught science and religion until his death from a heart attack thirty-two years later.

SOURCES: GABF; *Newsletter* (21 January 1987); Kirley, *Congregation in France* 194, 198, 219–20, 256, 257n68, 262.

PREVOST, Denis, priest, nephew of Father Etienne *Prévost, was born on 19 July 1852 at Montréal, canton of Largentière (Ardèche), the son of Victor Prévost and Victorine Velay. He died at Montréal (Ardèche) on 4 September 1930 and was buried in the local cemetery.

After secondary school, probably at the Petit Séminaire d'Aubenas (Ardèche), Denis Prévost entered the Basilian novitiate at Feyzin (Isère, now Rhône), in 1868 at the age of sixteen and took final vows on 19 September 1873. Bishop Joseph-Michel-Frédéric Bonnet ordained him to the priesthood on 26 May 1877 in the cathedral at Viviers. During his years of study, Denis Prévost had taught at various Basilian schools: the Collège du Sacré-Coeur, Annonay, 1869–70, the Petit Séminaire d'Aubenas (Ardèche), 1870–4, and the Collège du Bourg-Saint-Andéol (Ardèche), 1874–7. After ordination he remained at the school in Bourg-Saint-Andéol until the Basilians were forced out by the municipality in 1881, the result of the anti-religious legislation of 1880.

He joined the staff of the Collège du Sacré-Coeur in 1881 and taught there until 1886, when he was appointed to teach rhetoric at the Petit Séminaire Saint-Charles at Vernoux (Ardèche). His students much appreciated the family atmosphere that reigned in his classroom. With the exclusion of religious in 1903 from teaching in schools, he retired to live with his family in Montréal. His health was never robust, and in his later years he lived almost entirely in seclusion, reading, praying, serenely accepting his infirmities.

SOURCES: GABF; Kirley, *Community in France* 206; Kirley, *Congregation in France* 159; Pouzol, 'Notices.'

PREVOST, Etienne, priest, uncle of Father Denis *Prévost, was born on 3 August 1805 at Montréal, canton of Largentière (Ardèche, diocese of Mende, since 1822 of Viviers), the son of Victor Prévost and Rose Hilaire. He died in Annonay on 9 May 1886 and is buried there in the Basilian cemetery on the grounds of the Collège du Sacré-Coeur.

Etienne Prévost learned Latin from the local parish priest. He went on to study at the Collège des Cordeliers, Annonay, while living at Sainte-Claire, the residence for day students. He helped supervise the study hall and recreation periods while doing his own studies, and taught French in the moderns section in 1828–9. He was ordained to the priesthood on 17 December 1831, and two years later bound himself by promise to the young Association de Saint-Basile, which had been formed in 1822. When the substitution of vows for promises was proposed in 1852 he readily accepted.

Father Etienne Prévost spent twenty-one years at the Collège de Privas (Ardèche), first teaching *troisième*, 1836–41, then as house bursar, 1841–57. He also served as bursar at the Petit Séminaire d'Aubenas (Ardèche), 1857–61. In 1861 he was appointed novice master at Feyzin (Isère, now Rhône), a post he fulfilled until 1880. In November of that year, as part of a long-range government policy to exclude members of congregations from teaching in schools, the sub-prefect of Vienne and a squadron of police expelled the priests and novices. Father Prévost and his two assistants took refuge in Annonay. There his health began to fail. Confined to bed with agonizing pains in his limbs, he continued to pray and read until his death.

SOURCES: GABF; Kirley, *Community in France* 70; Pouzol, 'Notices.'

PRINCE, Raymond Louis, priest, was born on 28 January 1906 at Ford City (later Windsor), Ontario, the son of Alphonse Prince and Seraphine Christe. He died in Windsor on 18 December 1992 and is buried there in the Basilian plot of Heavenly Rest Cemetery.

'Pooch' Prince attended St Joseph's Separate School and Assumption College School, Windsor. Upon graduation in 1927 he entered St Basil's Novitiate, Toronto, and was professed on 12 September 1928. He was appointed to Assumption College for undergraduate studies (B.A., University of Western Ontario, 1932), and studied theology at St Basil's Scholasticate, Toronto, 1932–6. During his first year of theology he also attended the Ontario College of Education, earning teaching certification in 1933. He lived at St Michael's College during his second year of theology, 1933–4, and at the scholasticate for the final two years. He was ordained to the priesthood on 21 December 1935 in St Basil's Church, Toronto, by Archbishop James Charles McGuigan.

In 1936 Father Prince was appointed assistant at Ste Anne's Parish, Detroit. In 1939 he began thirty-six years of teaching and student counselling at Aquinas Institute, Rochester. In 1963 he was asked by the community to serve as rector of the French scholasticate, Maison Saint-Basile, at Issy-les-Moulineaux near Paris. Although popular with the scholastics, he asked to be relieved after two years. He returned to Aquinas, where he taught for five more years, 1965–70, before his retirement. In 1973 he was appointed to the Basilian community at Assumption College School, where he remained until his death nearly twenty years later.

Father Prince was humble, affable, and extremely conscientious in his work. In retirement he undertook regular tasks of a lighter kind. He particularly enjoyed the work of sacristan, as he was devoted to the Blessed Sacrament and the Mass. He referred to himself as 'just a foot-soldier'; but in his unassuming way he touched the lives of many.

SOURCES: GABF; *Annals* 5 (1979) 344, 6 (1986) 396, 7 (1993) 147–9; *Newsletter* (30 December 1992).

PRINCIPE, Walter Henry, priest, elder brother of Father Charles Principe CSB, was born on 15 October 1922 in Rochester, the son of Arthur Principe and Louise Masnaghetti. He died in Houston on 8 May 1996, and is buried in the Basilian plot of Holy Sepulchre Cemetery, Rochester.

Walter attended St John the Evangelist parochial school and Aquinas Institute, Rochester, graduating third in the 1940 class of 248. He entered St Basil's Novitiate, Toronto, was professed on 15 August 1941, and was appointed to live at St Basil's Seminary, Toronto, for undergraduate studies (B.A., Honours Political Science and Economics, University of Toronto, 1946, first class honours). He studied theology at St Basil's Seminary, 1946–50, while concurrently doing graduate studies in philosophy (M.A., University of Toronto, 1951). He was ordained to the priesthood on 29 June 1949 in St Basil's Church, Toronto, by Cardinal James Charles McGuigan.

In 1950 Father Principe took courses at the Pontifical Institute of Mediaeval Studies leading to the M.S.L, 1952, with the thesis 'Gerson's Attitude towards the Occult Sciences.' In 1951–3 he pursued studies at the Ecole pratique des hautes études, Université de Paris, earning the Diplôme des sciences religieuses, 1954, with the thesis 'La question, "Utrum Pater et Filius diligant se Spiritu Sancto," de Pierre Lombard à S. Thomas d'Aquin.' His years in Paris acquainted him with the work of Marie-Dominique Chenu, Henri de Lubac, and Yves Congar, all of whom remained models for him of the priest-theologian. Returning to Toronto in 1954, he taught for two years at St Basil's Seminary. From 1956 to 1961 he continued research at the Institute and in European libraries in the field of thirteenth-century systematic theology. His thesis, 'The Theology of the Hypostatic Union in the Early Thirteenth Century,' earned him the Institute's rarely granted M.S.D., *summa cum laude*, 1963, and was later published in four volumes (see below).

As the first dean of theology of St Michael's, 1955–65, he saw the creation of a full-fledged Faculty of Theology as well as the graduate Institute of Christian Thought, which later gave way to the ecumenical, multi-institutional Toronto School of Theology. From 1961 to 1967 he was based at St Basil's Seminary; but in the latter year he returned to the Pontifical Institute, where, as a senior fellow since 1964, he taught patristic and medieval theology and spirituality, especially as expounded by Thomas Aquinas and Bonaventure. He directed the doctoral work of thirteen students and the M.A. work of numerous others at the University of Toronto's Centre for Medieval Studies and its Centre for Religious Studies.

Walter Principe became an internationally known figure in the theological world. He combined scholarly work and success with service to other organizations and communities, accepting responsibilities which others in his position might have avoided in the interest of scholarship. Among many other duties, he was a consultant to the Canadian Conference of Catholic Bishops, a member of the Vatican's International Theological Commission, the first president of the Canadian Corporation for Studies in Religion, chairman of the Canadian Federation for the Humanities, president of the Canadian Theological Society, member of the U.S. Catholic-Lutheran dialogue, a member of the United Church of Canada–Catholic dialogue, and, in 1990–1, president of the Catholic Theological Society of America. In these later years, as he increasingly became a voice for liberal theologians, he resigned from the Vatican's International Theological Commission, which he judged to be narrowly conceived and confined in its deliberations.

Among the awards and distinctions he received were a Guggenheim Fellowship, 1967, Fellowship in the Royal Society of Canada, 1984, the John Courtney Murray Award from the Catholic Theological Society of America, 1987, and a Doctorate in Humane Letters, *honoris causa*, from St John Fisher College, Rochester, 1988. In addition to papers at learned conferences, he lectured at twenty universities in North America and abroad, including Jerusalem, Tokyo, and Beijing. His publications include six books and about a hundred book chapters and articles in historical and contemporary theology, especially on the Trinity, Christology, the Church, and spirituality (see below).

Far from being isolated by his scholarship and achievements, Walter Principe was a friendly and affable person who loved the Basilian community, ever acknowledging that all he had achieved he owed to his membership in it. In his high school days he had developed an interest in music, especially in playing the clarinet and oboe. He used this talent in a ministry to the aged.

In 1993, he was appointed to residence at Dillon House, Houston. There he was engaged in research to write a history of Christologies of the twelfth and thirteenth centuries; but a quadruple bypass operation, which followed a similar procedure ten years earlier, led to complications that caused his death a month later.

BIBLIOGRAPHY:

Books: *William of Auxerre's Theology of the Hypostatic Union*. Toronto, 1963. *Alexander of Hales' Theology of the Hypostatic Union*. Toronto, 1967. *Hugh of Saint-Cher's Theology of the Hypostatic Union*. Toronto, 1970. *Philip the Chancellor's Theology of the Hypostatic Union*. Toronto, 1975. *Introduction to Patristic and Medieval Theology*. Toronto, 1980; 2nd ed. 1982; repr. 1987. Ed. (with Jonathan Black) *Quodlibetal Questions of Guerric of Saint-Quentin*. Toronto, 2002.

Pamphlets, chapters in books, articles: For a list of his 130 journal articles, book chapters, booklets, book reviews, miscellaneous pieces, and fifteen tape recordings see *Mediaeval Studies* 58 (1996): xvii–xx.

SOURCES: GABF; *Annals* 1 (1949) 262, 8 (1997) 106–8; *Newsletter* (1 August 1996);

J.K. Farge, 'Walter Henry Principe CSB (1922-1996),' *Mediaeval Studies* 58 (1996): v-xx; Kirley, *Congregation in France* 212, 231n24, 234; Armand Maurer, *Proceedings of the Royal Society of Canada*, series 6, vol. 7 (1996) 181-2.

PRIOU, Jean-Baptiste, priest, member of the Congregation 1880-c.1886, was born in 1856 or 1857 at Curac, arrondissement of Barbezieux (Charente, diocese of Angoulême).

Jean-Baptiste made his novitiate at Feyzin (Isère, now Rhône), 1879-80, and studied at the scholasticate in Annonay, 1880-1 under the direction of Father Julien *Giraud. He worked as prefect of discipline at the Collège du Sacré-Coeur, Annonay, while studying theology. He made his final profession of vows on 5 January 1883 during an appointment to the Collège Saint-Charles, Blidah, Algeria, 1882-3. Archbishop Armand de Charbonnel ordained him to the priesthood on 19 September 1885 in the chapel of the Collège du Sacré-Coeur, where he taught *quatrième*, 1883-4, prior to an appointment to the Ecole cléricale de Périgueux (Dordogne), 1884-6. He probably withdrew from the Community at the end of the 1886 school year, as the Basilian records make no further mention of him.

SOURCE: Pouzol, 'Notices,' Supplément 2.

PURCELL, John Joseph, priest, was born in Kerry, County Kerry, Ireland, on 7 January 1878, the son of Patrick Purcell and Christina Walsh. He died in Windsor, Ontario, on 14 November 1918 and is buried there in the Basilian plot of Assumption Cemetery.

John Purcell's parents emigrated to Canada when he was nine years old. He grew up in St Basil's Parish, Toronto, and in 1891 enrolled at St Michael's College, Toronto. He wanted to be a Basilian; but his parents needed his support, and he went to the Séminaire de philosophie, Montreal, 1897-9, and then to the Grand Séminaire for theology. When his mother died in 1902, he entered St Basil's Novitiate, Toronto. After first profession on 9 October 1903, he returned to the Montreal Grand Séminaire with the intention of taking a degree in theology. Poor health, however, intervened; he left Montreal in June 1904 – his course in theology completed, but without a degree. He taught at St Mary's Seminary, LaPorte, Texas in 1904-5 and at St Thomas College, Houston, in 1905-7. After making his final vows on 17 December 1906, he was ordained to the priesthood in St Mary's Cathedral, Galveston, Texas, on 22 December 1906.

Father Purcell continued to teach at St Thomas College (High School) until the summer of 1907, when he moved to St Basil's College, Waco, Texas. In 1910 he was transferred to St Michael's College, Toronto, where he taught philosophy until 1913. His final appointment was to teach at Assumption College, Windsor, where he also became master of scholastics in 1916. He died during the influenza pandemic of 1918, one of its three Basilian victims at Assumption.

The *Golden Jubilee Volume of Assumption College* described Father Purcell as 'a man of many attainments,' adding that 'his familiarity with the [Latin] Vulgate was astounding. ... he had the whole of the New Testament by heart, and this familiarity extended not only to the matter but to the meaning of the text.' A splendid teacher of philosophy, he imparted his personal enthusiasm for it to his students. He spoke Latin and French fluently. In an obituary notice published in the *Year Book of St Michael's College*, 1919, Father Henry Carr wrote of Father Purcell's 'helplessness in practical matters,' his 'weakness for cigars and contempt of the pipe,' of his 'big-hearted generosity which kept him continually in trouble,' and of his unique wit which diffused good nature and good humour.

SOURCES: GABF; Charles Collins, 'Basilians I Have Known,' transcribed in Robert J. Scollard, 'Historical Notes C.S.B.' 10 45–9 (GABF); *Jubilee, Assumption*; Hoskin, *St Basil's*; *Year Book SMC* 10 (1919); Power, *Assumption College* 3 284–5, 317–18.

PURCELL, Louis Francis, priest, brother of Sister Leona Purcell CSJ, was born on 22 September 1912 at Seaforth, Ontario (diocese of London), the son of Thomas Purcell and Catherine McFadden. He died in Windsor, Ontario, on 26 August 1983 and is buried in the Basilian plot of Holy Cross Cemetery, Thornhill, Ontario.

'Lou' Purcell received his early education at Seaforth and graduated from Seaforth Collegiate in 1932. He attended Assumption College, Windsor, for one year, entered St Basil's Novitiate, Toronto, and made his first profession of vows on 15 August 1934. Appointed to Assumption College, he completed his undergraduate studies (B.A., University of Western Ontario, 1936). One year of graduate studies followed at the University of Alberta, where he received teaching certification for Alberta in 1937. He studied theology at St Basil's Seminary, Toronto, 1937–41, and was ordained to the priesthood on 15 August 1940 in St Basil's Church, Toronto, by Archbishop James Charles McGuigan.

In 1941 Father Purcell began thirty-six years of teaching, study, and administration in seven different Basilian high schools: Catholic Central High School, Detroit, teaching, 1941–2; graduate work at the University of Detroit and Wayne State University, Detroit, 1942–3; Aquinas Institute, Rochester, teaching, 1943–4; Catholic Central once again, teaching English and history, 1944–8; St Thomas High School, Houston, 1948–52, where he received a teaching certification for Texas in 1950 and directed school dramatics; St Mary's High School, Calgary, Alberta, teaching and treasurer, 1952–60; Assumption College School, Windsor, teaching and treasurer, 1960–2; St Michael's College School, Toronto, teaching and treasurer, 1962–4; St Mary's College, Sault Ste Marie, Ontario, teaching and treasurer, 1964–77. In 1977 Father Purcell was appointed assistant pastor at St Basil's Parish, Toronto, where he remained until his death six years later.

Lou Purcell was a man for others, ever open and available to students, colleagues, or parishioners. His manner was gracious and friendly and his Irish wit and sense of humour, though sharp, were never offensive. He gave himself wholeheartedly to the instruction of converts and the ministry of sacramental confession.

SOURCES: GABF; *Annals* 6 (1984) 298–9; *Newsletter* (8 September 1983).

Q

QUEALEY, Brian Thomas Joseph, priest, member of the Congregation 1955–69, younger brother of Francis MICHAEL Quealey, also a former Basilian, was born in New Toronto, Ontario, on 12 June 1936, the son of Francis Quealey and Lillian Gain. He died at Penetanguishene, Ontario, on 17 November 2000; his remains were cremated.

Brian attended St Michael's College School, Toronto, 1949–54. He entered St Basil's Novitiate, Richmond Hill, Ontario, in 1954 and made his first profession on 15 August 1955. While attending St Michael's College, 1955–8, he resided one year, 1955–6, at St Basil's Seminary, Toronto, and obtained his B.A. from the University of Toronto in 1958. He taught at St Charles College, Sudbury, 1958–60, and at Michael Power High School, Etobicoke, Ontario, 1960–1. After his theological studies at St Basil's Seminary, Toronto, 1961–5 (S.T.B., University of St

Michael's College, 1964), he was ordained to the priesthood by Archbishop George Bernard *Flahiff CSB on 13 December 1964.

Father Quealey was an assistant in St Anne's Parish, Houston, 1965-6, and at San Juan Crisóstomo, Mexico City, 1966-8. He was given leave of absence in 1968, and in 1969 was dispensed from the obligations of the priesthood and religious life. He is survived by his wife, Luchi Moreno, and their children Natalie and Patrick.

BIBLIOGRAPHY: 'We Only Ask to Create Anew,' *Forum* 1 (May 1965) 122.
SOURCES: GABF.

QUINLAN, Leonard Clarence, priest, was born on 6 January 1903 in Gibraltar, the son of James Thomas Quinlan and Helen Frances Dwyer. He died in Houston on 21 February 1983, and is buried there in the Basilian plot of Garden of Gethsemane, Forest Park Lawndale Cemetery.

Leonard entered the Army School in Gibraltar at the age of four. His father, a lieutenant and quartermaster in the Royal Engineers, was transferred in 1908 to the Curragh Camp, Ireland, and in 1911 to Dublin. There Leonard entered 'The High School.' On 31 December 1913 the family sailed for Jamaica, British West Indies, where Leonard enrolled in Jamaica College, a secondary school. In September 1915 he was sent to St George's College, Kingston, Jamaica, where, upon completion of the course in 1918, he received three certificates for the exams set by Cambridge University. He worked for fifteen years in Jamaica in the insurance business and in Canada in an accounting firm. While in Canada he took a course in journalism and began selling freelance articles to the *Toronto Star Weekly*. He won first prize in an essay contest with an entry entitled 'The History of Fire Insurance in Canada.'

In 1934 he applied for an executive position with a chemical firm, but was also pondering a vocation to the priesthood. When the position did not materialize he took it as a sign. He entered St Basil's Novitiate, Toronto, and made first profession on 25 August 1935. Appointed to residence at St Basil's Scholasticate, Toronto, he began studies in political science and economics while doing his theological studies concurrently (B.A., 1940; M.A., 1942, University of Toronto, submitting a thesis on 'William Stanley Jevons, 1835–1882'). He was ordained to the priesthood in St Basil's Church, Toronto, on 17 August 1941 by Archbishop James Charles McGuigan.

Father Quinlan taught first at Assumption College, Windsor, 1942–4, and then at St Thomas More College, Saskatoon, Saskatchewan, 1944–5. He did graduate studies in economics at the University of Chicago, 1945–8, without completing the doctorate, and returned to Assumption College in 1948 for a period of four years. In 1952 he was appointed to the University of St Thomas, Houston, where he was a full-time member of the department of economics until 1970 and then taught part-time for an additional year. He served as Basilian treasurer, 1969–76, librarian, 1976–7, and sacristan, 1977–83. From 1966 to 1969 he lived in the Basilian House of Studies, Houston, as assistant rector and confessor.

Leonard Quinlan was a man of many parts. Both in the seminary and at Assumption he directed performances of Gilbert and Sullivan musicals. At Strawberry Island he built the front porch of the original 'bunkhouse' to serve as a stage for plays. At the fledgling University of St Thomas he often did repairs or renovations to the houses which at that time constituted the major part of its physical plant. For many years he was the photographer for the *Summa*, the UST yearbook. He was also an accomplished portraitist and muralist. For a holiday, he liked to take bus trips into Mexico, where he would photograph landscape or village and, on his return, transmit a favourite scene to canvas. He was a knowledgeable collector of coins and medals, and he made his collections available to colleagues for classroom use.

'Quinny' conversed in a straightforward manner but with a mixed British-Jamaican accent that was not always comprehensible. He spoke gruffly, irony being often his manner of expression. 'He always came down hard on the side of truth. Chips then had to fall where they might,' said Father Robert *Lamb in his funeral eulogy. Yet he had a fine sense of humour, ever amused by the follies of humanity.

BIBLIOGRAPHY: 'Infirmary Interlude,' *Basilian* 2 (February 1936) 36–7; 'The New Spain,' *Basilian* 4 (January 1938) 11, 20; 'Communications and Education [forum],' *Basilian Teacher* 6 (May 1962) 320–5. He edited *Basilian*, 1936–8.
SOURCES: GABF; *Annals* 6 (1984) 288–90; *Newsletter* (8 March 1983).

QUINN, John Francis, priest, was born on 7 May 1925 in Dublin, Ireland, the son of Joseph Edward Quinn and Mary Kelly. He died in Toronto on 20 May 1996 and is buried in the Basilian plot of Holy Cross Cemetery, Thornhill, Ontario.

Although John's parents had moved to England, he was educated in

Ireland by the Sisters of Mercy and the Irish Christian Brothers. He entered the Irish Civil Service in 1939 and served in the Irish Defence Forces, 1943–5. He enlisted in the Royal Air Force in Great Britain and served as a mechanic in the motor pool of the British Commonwealth Occupational Forces in Japan. He used his release pay in 1948 to emigrate to Toronto, where he completed his secondary education at night school while working full-time by day. In 1950 he enrolled at St Michael's College, and after one year of university studies entered St Basil's Novitiate, Toronto, making first profession on 15 August 1952, and then completed his undergraduate course at St Michael's College (B.A., Honours Philosophy, University of Toronto, 1955). During the following year he held the position of reader in philosophy at St Michael's College. For the year 1956–7 he taught Latin and religious knowledge at St Michael's College School. He studied theology at St Basil's Seminary, Toronto, 1957–61 (S.T.B., University of St Michael's College, 1960), and earned an M.A. in philosophy from the University of Toronto in 1961. He was ordained to the priesthood on 29 June 1960 in St Basil's Church, Toronto, by Bishop Francis Allen.

In 1964 Father Quinn was awarded an M.S.L. from the Pontifical Institute of Mediaeval Studies, Toronto, with the thesis, 'The Analogical Similitudes of God in the Created Universe. A Study in the Christian Metaphysics of Saint Bonaventure.' Two years later he received a Ph.D. from the University of Toronto, submitting as his thesis 'St Bonaventure and the Notion of Christian Philosophy in Modern Scholarship, An Introduction to St Bonaventure and the Divine Immutability.' He taught courses in medieval philosophy from 1966 and also served as secretary (registrar) of the Institute.

John Quinn became an authority on the thought of St Bonaventure, and was chosen to compose the article on Bonaventure in the *New Encyclopedia Britannica*, Macropaedia (Chicago, 1973). Bonaventure's emphasis on knowing God with the heart provides a key to Father Quinn's later life, spirituality, and ministry. He suffered ill health all his life; and, as he was less able to teach and write, he turned to charismatic prayer and ministry. He clung as long as he could to his Sunday ministry at Precious Blood Parish, Scarborough, Ontario, and to his apostolate at Madonna House in Toronto. His counsel and intercessory prayer were sought by many childless couples, many of whom attributed their subsequent success in bearing children to his prayers.

'Sean' returned annually for holidays to Ireland, where he visited a large coterie of friends who were devoted to him. At his death, he had no living relatives. He was mourned, however, by scores of people who had been sustained and helped by his deep faith, his simple kindly manner, and his desire to bring peace and joy to others.

BIBLIOGRAPHY:
Book: *The Historical Consciousness of St Bonaventure's Philosophy.* Toronto, 1973.
Articles: For a list of his nineteen articles on the philosophy and theology of St Bonaventure see *Mediaeval Studies* 58 (1996) xxiii–xxiv.
SOURCES: GABF; *Annals* 3 (1960) 28, 8 (1997) 108–9; *Newsletter* (12 August 1996); J.A. Raftis, 'John Francis Quinn, CSB (1925–1996),' *Mediaeval Studies* 58 (1996) xxii–xxiv.

R

RAFFERTY, Francis Andrew, priest, was born in Princetown, Devon, England (diocese of Plymouth), on 18 May 1879, the son of Joseph Rafferty and Ann McDermott. He died in Montreal on 30 January 1960 and is buried in the Basilian plot of Holy Cross Cemetery, Thornhill, Ontario.

Francis Rafferty was educated in local schools and at the College of Mary Immaculate in Beaconfield House, Plymouth, England. He entered St Basil's Novitiate, Toronto, was professed on 8 September 1897, and was appointed to studies at Assumption College, Windsor, 1897–8. He did his theological course at St Basil's Scholasticate, Toronto, and was ordained to the priesthood on 29 June 1902.

After a visit to his parents in England, Father Rafferty was appointed to teach at St Basil's College, Waco, Texas. There a mental illness, attributed to a head injury sustained while at St Basil's Scholasticate, became noticeable, along with incidents of violent behaviour, and he was recalled to Toronto. After short stays on sick leave at St Michael's College, St Mary's of the Assumption Parish in Owen Sound, Ontario, and St Basil's Novitiate, institutional care became necessary. He entered La Retraite Saint-Benoît, Montreal, on 7 October 1906, where he remained until his death in 1960. For nearly fifty-four years Father Rafferty lived in a confused, sometimes catatonic state. He was visited regularly by Basilian superiors general; but it was only shortly before his death that he became lucid for about a week, during which time he conversed with Father George B. *Flahiff, the superior general, and was able to receive Holy Communion. His last night was spent largely walking about while praying his rosary.

SOURCES: GABF; *Annals* 3 (1960) 19–20.

RANC, Jean Louis, priest, younger brother of Jean Pierre *Ranc, was born on 20 March 1821 at Montselgues, canton of Valgorge (Ardèche, diocese of Mende, since 1822 of Viviers), the son of Pierre Ranc and Marie Ayglon. He died in Annonay on 28 June 1902 and was buried there in the cemetery on the grounds of the Collège du Sacré-Coeur.

Louis Ranc did his classical studies at the Collège de Privas (Ardèche), where his brother Father Jean Pierre Ranc was a teacher. He made his novitiate in Annonay and at Privas, 1847–8, and did his theological studies while teaching and serving as prefect at the Collège des Cordeliers, Annonay, and at the Petit Séminaire de Vernoux (Ardèche), 1850–2. He was ordained to the priesthood by Bishop Joseph-Hippolyte Guibert of Viviers in the parish church of Vernoux on 23 May 1852, and made his final profession on 1 October of the same year.

Father Ranc remained at Vernoux for three years as prefect of discipline. He taught at the Collège des Cordeliers, 1855–64, and was elected to the general council in 1862. Named pastor of the parish at Prades (Ardèche) in 1864, he directed the Calvary pilgrims' shrine there, and in the year 1867–8 enlarged the parish church.

Father Ranc was entrusted with the opening of the Collège Saint-Pierre de Châteauroux (Indre), 1875–7. In 1878 he was appointed bursar at the Petit Séminaire d'Aubenas (Ardèche). This appointment was brief, as he was soon sent to replace Father Michel *Monot, who had died in October 1877, as superior of the day school at Privas. When this school was closed the next year, Father Ranc went to Aubenas; but the Basilians withdrew from the Petit Séminaire there in 1879. (They would return in 1895.) From 1879 to his death in 1902 Father Ranc resided at Sainte-Barbe, the Basilian minor seminary in Annonay. He was chaplain to religious and to the personnel of the Rochebrune factory in Annonay.

SOURCES: GABF; Chanoine Fromenton, *Petit Séminaire de Vernoux* (Aubenas, 1922); Kirley, *Community in France* 29, 41, 70n178, 124n305, 150n384, 163n416; Pouzol, 'Notices'; Roume, *Origines* 346.

RANC, Jean Pierre, priest, elder brother of Father Jean-Louis *Ranc, was born on 1 January 1816 at Montselgues in the canton of Valgorge (Ardèche), the son of Pierre Ranc and Marie Ayglon. He died on 25 January 1894 in Annonay and was buried there in the cemetery on the grounds of the Collège du Sacré-Coeur.

Pierre Ranc was a student at the Collège des Cordeliers, Annonay, section Sainte-Barbe, 1829–36, and then spent a year teaching as a postulant at the college. In 1837 he entered the novitiate, which appears to have been located at Privas (Ardèche) at that time. He remained at Privas until his ordination to the priesthood on 5 June 1841 and continued there as professor of philosophy until 1852, when the philosophy course was suppressed owing to falling enrolment following the transfer of the minor seminary from Bourg-Saint-Andéol (Ardèche) to Aubenas (Ardèche). He worked at the minor seminary at Vernoux (Ardèche) from 1852 to 1857, and then returned to Privas, where he served until 1862 as spiritual director of the Sisters of the Congregation of the Trinity. He was then superior successively at Vernoux, 1862–70, the Collège de Privas, 1870–2, and the day-school there, 1872–4.

In 1868 he had been elected to the general council, and in 1878 he became vicar general under Father Jean Mathieu *Soulerin. He had in the meantime served as superior of the minor seminary at Aubenas from 1874 to 1879. Though he retired in the latter year he continued to be part of the administration of the community while living at Sainte-Barbe. He presided over the general chapter convened on 11 December 1879 after the death of Father Soulerin, as well as the one convened on 4 August 1892.

SOURCES: GABF; Chanoine Fromenton, *Petit Séminaire de Vernoux*; Kirley, *Community in France* 55, 61n160, 64n164, 134n339, 150n384; Pouzol, 'Notices'; Roume, *Origines* 346.

RAPHANEL, Jules, priest, was born on 17 January 1857 at Rocles, near Largentière (Ardèche), the son of André Raphanel and Anne Vaschalde. He died in Annonay on 24 June 1887 and was buried there in the cemetery on the grounds of the Collège du Sacré-Coeur. Having done early studies, probably at the Petit Séminaire d'Aubenas, Jules made his novitiate at Feyzin (Isère, now Rhône) (the year is not known). He was assigned to the Collège du Sacré-Coeur, Annonay, for the year 1877–8, but in the third trimester went to the Petit Séminaire de Vernoux (Ardèche) as a replacement. He taught mathematics at the

Ecole cléricale de Périgueux (Dordogne), 1879–80, and made final profession of vows on 17 September 1880. He continued to teach mathematics at the Ecole cléricale as he studied theology, and was ordained to the priesthood on 3 June 1882 in Périgueux. After ordination, in failing health, he returned to Annonay and helped supervise students both at the Collège du Sacré-Coeur and in the day-school on the Montée du Château, until his death at the age of thirty.

SOURCES: GABF; Kirley, *Congregation in France* 78n197; Pouzol, 'Notices.'

REATH, Vincent Bernard, priest, was born at St Thomas, Ontario (diocese of London), on 10 July 1869, the youngest of five boys and one girl born to Moses Reath and Eleanor Bolger. He died in Toronto on 20 January 1929 and was buried in the Basilian plot of Mount Hope Cemetery, Toronto.

After attending school in his home town, Vincent Reath worked as a telegrapher until 1887, when he went to Assumption College, Windsor, to study for the priesthood. He entered St Basil's Novitiate, Toronto, on 15 August 1892. After profession he continued his studies at St Michael's College and St Basil's Scholasticate, Toronto, and was ordained to the priesthood on 15 August 1898.

In his first appointment to Assumption College, Father Reath taught Latin and supervised student recreation. In 1907 he was transferred to St Basil's Novitiate and in 1908 to St Michael's College. He also taught at St Thomas College, Chatham, New Brunswick, 1914–19, then came back to St Michael's College. He died in 1929 from pneumonia, after injuries sustained in a fall on an icy pavement.

Within the Congregation Father Reath was affectionately called 'Pop.' As a student he had been an outstanding baseball player; all his life he was noted for his piety, and was a popular confessor.

SOURCES: GABF; Charles Collins, 'Basilians I Have Known,' transcribed in Robert J. Scollard, 'Historical Notes C.S.B.' 10 92–4 (GABF); *Jubilee, Assumption; Yearbook SMC* 20 (1929); *Yearbook STC.*

RECORD, Maurice ADRIAN, priest, brother of Sister Eleanor IBVM, was born on 18 January 1913 at Owen Sound, Ontario (diocese of Hamilton), the son of Francis Record and Agnes Walsh. He died in Toronto on 31 January 1997 and is buried in the Basilian plot of Holy Cross Cemetery, Thornhill, Ontario.

'Zak,' as he was known in the Basilian community, attended elementary school in Owen Sound and Assumption College School, Windsor, 1926–30. The superior of Assumption at the time, Father Vincent *Kennedy, described him as 'distinctly above average.' He entered St Basil's Novitiate, Toronto, in 1930 and was professed on 30 August 1931. After the arts course at Assumption College (B.A., University of Western Ontario, 1936), he was appointed to St Michael's College, Toronto, for his first year of theology and for studies at the Ontario College of Education, earning high school certification in 1937. The following year he taught at Catholic Central High School, Detroit. In 1938 he was appointed to St Basil's Seminary, Toronto, to continue his theology course, and was ordained to the priesthood on 15 August 1940 in St Basil's Church, Toronto, by Archbishop James Charles McGuigan.

Father Record taught in the high school at St Michael's College, Toronto, 1941–2, and then at St Thomas High School, Houston, 1942–7, where he became the first Basilian to qualify for a civilian pilot's licence and taught a course in aeronautical science. He obtained an M.A. in psychology from the University of Toronto in 1949 with a thesis 'Study of Mathematical Achievement of Controlled Groups of Fourth-Year Students in New York and Ontario,' and then did additional studies at the University of Montreal until 1952. While studying in Toronto he did research for the Royal Canadian Air Force at the Institution of Aviation and Medicine, and while in Montreal he worked at Ste-Anne-de-Bellevue Mental Hospital and in the psychiatric ward of Queen Mary Veterans' Hospital. He was a licensed clinical psychologist.

In 1952 he joined the faculty of Assumption College. The following year he was called upon to found the college's department of psychology, and he also established the Guidance Clinic. As the status of that college evolved he was co-opted successively into the faculty of Essex College of Assumption University and then, in 1963, into that of the University of Windsor. Apart from his teaching and clinical work, Father Record was actively involved in many professional societies, including the psychology associations of Ontario and Michigan. He was a founding member and president of both the Ontario Group Psychology Association and the Mental Health Council of Windsor and Essex County. He also held office in the Canadian University Counselling Association, the American Group Psychotherapy Association, and the Ontario Association for Retarded Children. He was a board member of the Victorian Order of Nurses, the Red Cross, and the Family Life Bureau of the diocese of London.

In 1974 he retired from Assumption University and the University of Windsor to begin a private practice of clinical psychology at Belle River, Ontario. He took the year 1977–8 to work as a staff member of the Department of Education and Training of the South Beach Psychiatric Center on Staten Island, New York, serving as liaison resource person between the mental health professionals and the clergy of Staten Island, and was also the first chaplain-in-residence at this institution. He resumed practice in his Belle River clinic and continued until his retirement to Assumption High School in 1992. Four years later he moved to the Basilian Fathers Residence (Infirmary) in Toronto and shortly thereafter to Providence Centre in Scarborough, Ontario, where the special care he required was available, and where he died.

Adrian Record was energetic and determined – some would say reckless – in the pursuit of his goals. He held his opinions firmly and confidently, a quality which made for success in his profession but not in ordinary human relations. He was fiercely independent, even as his health failed; yet he managed successfully his two professions as priest and psychologist.

BIBLIOGRAPHY: 'Basilian Missions,' *Basilian* 2 (January 1936) 9; 'Impractical Pragmatism,' *Basilian* 4 (June 1938) 116.
SOURCES: GABF; *Annals* 6 (1982) 15, 9 (1998) 73–4; *Newsletter* (15 February 1997).

REDMOND, John Michael, priest, was born on 10 April 1934 at Weston, Ontario (archdiocese of Toronto), the only child of Alphonsus Redmond and Rita LePage. He died in Toronto on 21 September 1981 and is buried in the Basilian plot of Holy Cross Cemetery, Thornhill, Ontario.

After attending St John the Evangelist Separate School, Weston, and St Michael's College School, Toronto, where he graduated in 1953, 'Johnny' Redmond entered St Basil's Novitiate, Richmond Hill, Ontario, and made first profession on 12 September 1954. He studied at Assumption College, Windsor (B.A., University of Western Ontario, 1957) and did three years teaching, first at St Michael's College School, 1957–8, and then at Michael Power High School, Etobicoke, 1958–60. In those summers he supervised the transport of three hundred tons of crushed gravel as a base for tennis courts at Strawberry Island in Lake Simcoe. He did his theological studies at St Basil's Seminary, Toronto, 1960–4, receiving an S.T.B. from the University of St Michael's College in 1963. His ordination to the priesthood on 15 December 1963 was at the hands of Archbishop George Bernard *Flahiff in St Basil's Church, Toronto.

Father Redmond's only appointment in his life was to Michael Power High School, where he taught religion and became director of athletics. For the year 1967–8 he was first councillor of the local Basilian community. His remarkable talent for forming young men in discipline, determination, and spirit brought fame to his track and field program at Michael Power. His teams were victorious in both Canadian and American meets. Under his direction Michael Power won fifteen consecutive Toronto and District Colleges Athletic Association track championships and nine out of ten championships in the Ontario Federation of Secondary Schools Association. A spin-off from the high school track teams was the 'Power Track Club,' whose membership included both graduates and freshmen.

In 1976 Father Redmond was appointed principal of Michael Power High School. He strengthened all departments and initiated programs for special needs. He strove to develop the spirituality of the school community by his strong support of the COR (Christ in Others Retreat) Program and by instituting a school chaplaincy service.

After experiencing pain in his arm and in the area of his heart during the summer of 1981, he was admitted to St Michael's Hospital, Toronto, on 11 September, where surgery was scheduled for 23 September. Two days before that date he suffered a massive heart attack. Emergency surgery was at first thought successful, but he died some six hours later.

John Redmond was humble in his manner, frugal in his life style, and sensitive to the needs of others. In spite of his many duties, he took time for anyone in difficulty. He inspired affection and loyalty in the students and staff, who attended his funeral Mass at Michael Power. The next day a second funeral, which filled St Basil's Church to overflowing, was attended by three bishops and civic dignitaries. It bore striking witness to the esteem in which Father Redmond was held, and to the sorrow felt at his untimely death. His father died just one month later.

The 'Father John Redmond Catholic Secondary School,' established by the Catholic Separate School Board in Etobicoke in September 1985, preserves his memory.

SOURCES: GABF; *Annals* 3 (1964) 293, 6 (1982) 100–2; *Newsletter* (20 October 1981); E.J. Lajeunesse, *Strawberry Island in Lake Simcoe* (Toronto, 1962, 1974, 1981, 1983) 74.

REGAN, Bernard Michael, priest, brother of Fathers Oscar *Regan and Basil *Regan, was born in Toronto on 23 May 1909, the eldest of four sons of Charles Herbert Regan and Marie A. Neales. He died in Toronto on 26 November 1979 and is buried in the Basilian plot of Holy Cross Cemetery, Thornhill, Ontario.

'Barney' Regan was educated at St Joseph's Separate School and in the high school section of St Michael's College, Toronto. He entered St Basil's Novitiate, Toronto, immediately after high school, was professed on 18 September 1927, and was appointed to live at St Basil's Scholasticate, Toronto, for undergraduate studies (B.A., University of Toronto, 1931). He began his theology studies at St Basil's Scholasticate, during the first year of which he also attended the Ontario College of Education, earning teaching certification in 1932. He taught at Catholic Central High School, Detroit, 1932–3, while continuing to study theology. He was ordained to the priesthood on 17 December 1933 in St Basil's Church, Toronto, by Bishop Alexander MacDonald.

Father Regan's appointments were mostly in the high school apostolate: St Michael's College School, teaching, 1934–5; Assumption College School, Windsor, teaching, 1935–6; Catholic Central High School, Detroit, teaching, second councillor in the Basilian community, 1950–2, superior and principal, 1952–8; St Mary's College, Sault Ste Marie, Ontario, teaching and second councillor, 1958–9; Andrean High School, Gary, Indiana, teaching, 1961–5; and Michael Power High School, Etobicoke, Ontario, teaching, 1965–76.

Father Regan was treasurer of St Basil's Novitiate, Pontiac, Michigan, 1959–61. In 1970 he was granted sabbatical leave for one year, after which he returned to the classroom. In 1973 he accepted the position of moderator of the Dads' Club at Michael Power, a responsibility he continued to carry until his death. In 1976 he underwent throat surgery for the removal of a cancerous growth. This affliction necessitated his retirement from the classroom, though he retained residence at Michael Power.

Bernard Regan's motto was 'Go big!' An intense competitor, he always tried for excellence and enjoyed good rapport with his students. Although a sensitive man with a gift for relating well, he could become quite acerbic in an argument. He loved the world of sports, both as spectator and as participant. As a scholastic at Strawberry Island in Lake Simcoe he was known as 'the power hitter to left field.' He was a staunch advocate of Catholic education and of the charism and calling of the Basilian Fathers in that apostolate.

SOURCES: GABF; *Annals* 5 (1978) 269, 5 (1980) 522–3; *Newsletter* (4 December 1979).

REGAN, Herbert BASIL, priest, brother of Fathers Bernard *Regan and Oscar *Regan, was born in Toronto on 2 February 1912, the third of four sons born to Charles Herbert Regan and Marie A. Neales. He died in Ottawa on 3 December 1958 and is buried in the Basilian plot of Holy Cross Cemetery, Thornhill, Ontario.

Basil Regan attended St Joseph's Separate School and the high school section of St Michael's College, Toronto, 1925–9. He entered St Basil's Novitiate, Toronto, and after profession on 29 September 1930 studied at St Michael's College (B.A., University of Toronto, 1934). He taught at St Thomas High School, Houston, 1935–6, did his theological studies at St Basil's Scholasticate ('Seminary' from 1937), Toronto, and was ordained priest on 18 December 1937 in St Basil's Church, Toronto, by Archbishop James Charles McGuigan.

Father 'Bas' Regan taught in the high school section of St Michael's College for twenty years, 1938–58, serving as principal, 1945–58, and as superior, 1950–6. In 1958 he was appointed founding principal of St Joseph's High School, Ottawa; but in December of that year he collapsed in his classroom from a heart attack just prior to the first morning class, and died shortly afterwards.

Father Regan was a cheerful community man who bore his own burdens without complaint and who helped others to carry theirs. In his student days he was a top calibre hockey player and softball pitcher. He was an excellent Latin teacher, and as a principal kept abreast of developments in education. At the time of his death he was a member of the Atkinson Foundation Committee studying high school education.

SOURCES: GABF; *Annals* 2 (1959) 425–6.

REGAN, William OSCAR, priest, brother of Fathers Bernard *Regan and Basil *Regan, was born on 20 November 1910 in Toronto, the second of four sons of Charles Herbert Regan and Marie Neales. He died in Thunder Bay, Ontario, on 31 August 1994 and is buried in the Basilian plot of Holy Cross Cemetery, Thornhill, Ontario.

Oscar Regan attended St Joseph's Separate School and the high school section of St Michael's College, Toronto, graduating in 1927. He entered St Basil's Novitiate, Toronto. After first profession on 10 August 1928, he was appointed to live at St Basil's Scholasticate, Toronto, for undergraduate and theological studies (B.A., University of Toronto, 1932). He earned Type B teaching certification at the Ontario College of Education in 1933. He was ordained to the priesthood on 16 December 1934 in Assumption Church, Windsor, by Bishop John Thomas Kidd.

Father Regan taught English and mathematics at Catholic Central High School, Detroit, 1935–7, and at Aquinas Institute, Rochester, 1937–57. He obtained an M.Ed. from the University of Rochester in 1944, and was on the local Basilian council from 1950 to 1957. He taught at Assumption College School, Windsor, from 1957 to January 1959, when he was appointed principal of St Joseph's High School, Ottawa, to replace his brother Basil *Regan, who had died suddenly two weeks before. He remained in that job until 1962 and was Basilian first councillor, 1959–60, and superior, 1960–2. In 1962 he was appointed to St Thomas More College, Saskatoon, where he was to spend the next thirty-two years, as teacher, local councillor, 1966–7, superior, 1967–73, and, long into retirement, director of alumni. He was chaplain to the Knights of Columbus, member of the Saskatchewan Diocesan Priests' Council, and judge for annulment cases in the diocesan marriage tribunal.

Oscar Regan had a buoyant personality. Hospitality to both visitors and his confreres came natural to him. He made an annual summer trip by car to the family cottage north of Toronto. He enjoyed such good health at the age of eighty-four years that his death, which occurred suddenly as he was returning to Saskatoon with his travelling companion Father Joseph *Penny, came as a shock. In their conversation at supper the previous evening, Oscar had expressed his gratitude for his vocation as a Basilian priest.

BIBLIOGRAPHY: 'The Epiphany,' *Basilian* 2 (January 1936) 20; 'A Confrere Sleeps,' *Basilian* 2 (February 1936) 32; 'The Priest at Bethlehem,' *Basilian* 4 (January 1938) 2; 'Letter to the Editor [on the Western Canada Regional Meeting],' *Forum* 2 (March 1966) 38–9; 'Studying Students through Test Results,' *Basilian Teacher* 1 (November 1956) 3–7; 'Guidance – How Its Administrators See It,' *Basilian Teacher* 3 (January 1959) 91–5.

SOURCES: GABF; *Annals* 5 (1979) 334, 6 (1985) 308, 8 (1995) 305–6; *Newsletter* (7 October 1994).

RENAUD, Luke, priest, uncle of Father Luke *Beuglet, was born at River Canard, Ontario (diocese of Toronto, since 1856 of London), on 14 September 1850, the son of Joseph Renaud and Florence Bondy. He died in Detroit on 9 February 1925 and was buried in the Basilian plot of Assumption Cemetery, Windsor.

Luke Renaud (Renault) entered the first English class at Assumption College, Windsor, on 10 January 1871. As a student he regularly received the top ranking in the weekly 'testimonials.' He made his novitiate at Assumption College, 1878–9, pronounced his final vows on 26 March 1884, and was ordained priest on 19 June 1884. As a scholastic Luke had been employed as recreation master. After ordination he was in charge of the study hall at Assumption College, and introduced handball there in 1887. In 1889 he began a series of parish assignments: St John the Baptist, Amherstburg, as assistant, 1888–99, and then as pastor, 1901–7; Ste Anne, Detroit, 1899–1901, as assistant, and 1907–20, as pastor. He lived five years at Ste Anne's in retirement and with failing eyesight until his death.

Father Renaud served as a member of the provincial council in 1909. In 1910 he was elected to the general council and continued in this office until 1922. Failing health kept him from attending the 1922 general chapter. The *Golden Jubilee Volume of Assumption College* stated that 'he excelled as a student of mathematics' and that 'many an alumnus will recall with satisfaction the thorough instruction he received in Father Renaud's classes.' Later in his life his love for Assumption College caused him to establish the Renaud Bursary. At Ste Anne's Parish Father Renaud inaugurated the annual novena in honour of St Anne. In the rectory he maintained the tradition of hospitality established under Father Pierre *Grand. Father Renaud was a placid, unhurried soul, one of the most patient and sympathetic of his generation of Basilians. He took things as they came, went about his work and his prayers methodically, and in his unassuming way accomplished much.

BIBLIOGRAPHY: 'A Diary of Rev. Luke Renaud, CSB on the Beginning of St Anthony of Padua Roman Catholic Church, Harrow, Ontario, May 9, 1905–August 5, 1907' (unpublished).
SOURCES: GABF; Charles Collins, 'Basilians I Have Known,' transcribed in Rob-

ert J. Scollard, 'Historical Notes C.S.B.' 10 41–4 (GABF); *Jubilee, Assumption*; Kirley, *Congregation in France* 14, 29, 32–4; *Purple and White* (15 February 1925).

REUSS, Norbert Clarence, priest, was born on 6 February 1912 in Cleveland, Ohio, the son of Joseph Reuss and Elizabeth Shoen. He died in Houston on 2 June 1999 and is buried there in the Basilian plot of Garden of Gethsemane, Forest Park Lawndale Cemetery.

'Dutch' Reuss attended St Philip Neri School in Cleveland, 1919–26, and Assumption College School, Windsor, 1926–30. After graduation he entered St Basil's Novitiate, Toronto, made first profession on 15 August 1931, and was appointed to Assumption College for university studies (B.A., Honours Philosophy, University of Western Ontario, 1935). He studied theology at St Basil's Scholasticate ('Seminary' from 1937), Toronto, 1935–9, and was ordained to the priesthood on 17 December 1938 in St Basil's Church, Toronto, by Archbishop James Charles McGuigan.

After completing his theology course in 1939, Father Reuss was appointed to teach at Assumption College School for one year, and then to parish work at Our Lady of Guadalupe Church, Rosenberg, Texas, where he remained for four years. In 1944 he was assigned to St Thomas High School, Houston, to teach chemistry and mechanical drawing. He continued to study and improve his skills: in 1948 he took a course in drafting at the University of Houston; in the year 1951–2 he took six courses in education to earn permanent teaching certification for Texas; and in 1955 he obtained his Professional Life Certificate for Elementary and High School. Having received a National Science Foundation grant in 1959, he studied chemistry at Notre Dame University and then took a course in oil chemistry at the University of Houston in 1960.

In 1962, after twenty-three years in Texas, Father Reuss was appointed to Aquinas Institute, Rochester, a move which surprised him but which he considered a good thing for a Basilian to undergo. There he taught chemistry, general science, and religion for ten years. He was reassigned to St Thomas in 1972, and remained there for the rest of his life.

'Dutch' Reuss's kindness and thoughtfulness of the community, notable all his life, increased in later years despite the decline in his health. He was hospitable to visitors, and showed special care for Basilians newly assigned to St Thomas. He accepted failing eyesight and arthritis without complaint. In retirement he looked after many needs in the house. He regularly made himself available to students for the sacrament of reconciliation, and provided the same ministry for an infirmary of nuns.

SOURCES: GABF; *Annals* 6 (1982) 15, 6 (1989) 719, 9 (2000) 86–8; *Newsletter* (24 June 1999).

REVERSADE, Justin, priest. One record says he was born on 15 February 1857 at Ladouze, canton of Saint-Pierre-de-Chignac (Dordogne); another says he was born on 5 February 1857 at Breuilh (Dordogne, diocese of Périgueux), and died on 24 April 1926 at Terrasson (Dordogne).
Justin probably did his secondary studies at the Ecole cléricale, Périgueux, which the Basilians had taken over in 1866. He made his novitiate at Feyzin (Isère, now Rhône) in 1875 and took final vows on 11 September 1880. Archbishop Armand de Charbonnel ordained him to the priesthood on 25 September 1882 in the chapel of the Collège du Sacré-Coeur, Annonay. From ordination until 1903 he taught rhetoric, first at the Collège du Sacré-Coeur, 1882–4, then at the Ecole cléricale de Périgueux, 1884–1903. In 1902 he was awarded the title of honorary canon of the cathedral of Périgueux.

With the implementation in 1903 of laws forbidding religious to teach in schools, he remained in his home diocese, but it is not known where. One address, with no date, was Institution Saint-Front, Fraysse-par-Vergt (Dordogne). In 1907 he is listed as chaplain to the Couvent du Saint-Sauveur, Terrasson (Dordogne).

Even though geographically detached, Father Reversade remained a member of the Basilian Community. He attended the general chapter of 1910 in Geneva as a delegate and sided with the North American confreres who wanted a more equitable representation at general chapters.

SOURCES: GABF; Kirley, *Community in France* 70n179, 185, 208, 248n581; Kirley, *Congregation in France* 12, 14; Pouzol, 'Notices.'

REYNAUD, Claude, priest, member of the Congregation 1856–72, was born on 6 May 1830 in the commune of Présailles, canton of Le Monastier (Haute-Loire, diocese of Le Puy).
Claude received a classical education 'under the guidance of Father [Julien] *Actorie' before going to the Grand Séminaire in Viviers. He

was a postulant at Sainte-Barbe, Maison du Peloux, Annonay on 10 April 1856, and was received as a novice on 29 June that year. From October 1856 to the end of January 1857 he combined the duties of a novice with those of prefect of discipline at the Collège des Cordeliers. While studying theology he worked at the Petit Séminaire de Vernoux (Ardèche) as prefect, 1857–9 and 1862–4, and at the Collège de Privas (Ardèche), teaching, 1859–62. After ordination to the priesthood on 30 May 1863, he taught *septième* at the Petit Séminaire d'Aubenas (Ardèche), 1864–6, and *quatrième* at the Collège de Privas, 1866–7. At the Collège du Sacré-Coeur, Annonay, he taught *sixième*, 1867–71, and Commercial, 1871–2. In April 1872 he petitioned Rome to be released from the obligations of his religious vows in order to minister as a secular priest, and withdrew from the Congregation at the end of that school year.

SOURCE: Pouzol, 'Notices,' Supplément 2.

REYNOUARD, Georges Louis, priest, was born on 1 January 1921, at Rosières (Ardèche), the eldest of three sons of Paul Reynouard and Marie-Louise Maigron. He died in Annonay on 14 January 1995 and is buried there in the Basilian cemetery on the grounds of the Collège du Sacré-Coeur.

Georges went to Annonay in 1934, first as a student at the Petit Séminaire Saint-Charles, and then, in 1935, as a junior with the Basilians at Maison Saint-Joseph, taking classes at the Collège du Sacré-Coeur. In 1940 he became a Basilian novice, making first profession on 6 September 1941. After completing his *baccalauréat*, he began the study of philosophy, which was twice interrupted, first by obligatory participation in the Youth Camps of France at Die (Drôme), March–October 1942, and then by forced labour at Chemnitz, Germany, July 1943–March 1944. On his return to Annonay in 1944 he continued his theological studies and was ordained to the priesthood on 19 January 1947 in the cathedral at Viviers (Ardèche) by Bishop Alfred Couderc.

Father Reynouard spent the whole of his active ministry as a Basilian priest at the Collège du Sacré-Coeur. He began with two years, 1947–9, as prefect of boarders. In 1949 he was given charge of the *classe de cinquième* where he taught the full gamut of basic subjects. He was a lively, conscientious, and interesting professor, especially in his teaching of natural science, for he not only knew nature in all its aspects but he also loved, respected, and constantly wondered at its life and beauty. An example of his science presentations each year was his collection of silkworms, which he kept in boxes to spin their cocoons. He taught about the mulberry leaves the worms required to feed on, the silk they weave in the cocoon, and how one kept the long skein from breaking. He was an avid soccer fan and player, not above an infraction of a rule here and there in his zeal to win. He served the students in many ways beyond the classroom: cinema clubs, youth camps, nature excursions, retreats, and sports events. They caught from him an enthusiasm and joy in life which flowed from his faith and his desire to minister. His sense of humour, which enlivened any gathering, never failed. His adventurous spirit carried over into his love for driving motorcycles and automobiles at speeds which at times proved terrifying for his passengers.

Georges Reynouard was much attached to his native southern Ardèche, with its distinctive terrain, Occitan language, and customs. When he retired from teaching in 1986, he obtained permission to reside in the Basilian vacation home, 'Villa Saint-Patrice,' at Saint-Alban-sous-Sampzon. There he happily received and cooked for confreres and friends and did pastoral ministry, especially in a senior citizens' home. For reasons of health he returned in 1992 to Maison Saint-Joseph, where his condition steadily degenerated during the next two and a half years, with Alzheimer's disease denying him the joy in life which he had shared so long with others.

SOURCES: GABF; *Annals* 7 (1992) 11–12, 8 (1996) 89–94; *Newsletter* (1 March 1995); Kirley, *Congregation in France* 194–5, 198, 205–12, 215–20, 256, 262.

RIEUBON, Joachim, priest, was born on 14 April 1871 at Saint-Cirgues-de-Prades, canton of Thueyts (Ardèche). He died on 31 March 1952 at Berroughia, Algeria, and was buried in the local cemetery.
Joachim Rieubon made his novitiate in 1894–5 at the Institution Saint-Augustin, Bône, Algeria, while helping with the supervision of the students. He took final vows on 17 September 1897 and was ordained to the priesthood on 23 September 1898 in the chapel of the Collège du Sacré-Coeur, Annonay, by Bishop Hilarion Montéty.

From 1895 to 1903 Father Rieubon taught Arabic in the Collège Saint-Charles, Blidah, Algeria. When the school was closed in 1903 and the Basilians forbidden to teach in schools, Father Rieubon remained in Algeria in pastoral ministry, first at Damiette, then at Berroughia, West Algeria. He was a zealous priest, and was made an honorary canon of the cathedral of Algiers. He paid occasional visits to his Basilian confreres at Maison Saint-Joseph, Annonay, but continued his ministry in Algeria until his death.

SOURCES: GABF; Kirley, *Community in France* 185, 209; Kirley, *Congregation in France* 220; Pouzol, 'Notices.'

RILEY, Wilfred Samuel, priest, was born on 23 March 1903 in Chatham, Ontario (diocese of London), the son of Anthony Riley and Annie Withers. He died in Toronto on 15 May 1984 and is buried in the Basilian plot of Holy Cross Cemetery, Thornhill, Ontario. In 1923, when 'Bill' Riley was twenty years of age, his family moved to Detroit, where he worked as a plasterer and paperhanger. He was received into the Catholic Church on 18 March 1928 at St Rose Church, Detroit, and became a citizen of the United States the following year. In February 1930, at the age of twenty-seven, he began the high school course at Assumption College, Windsor, and completed it in one and a half years. He entered St Basil's Novitiate, Toronto, was professed on 15 August 1933, and was appointed to Assumption College (B.A., University of Western Ontario, 1936). He studied theology at St Basil's Seminary, Toronto, living for one year, 1938–9, at St Michael's College, Toronto, and teaching in St Michael's high school. He was ordained to the priesthood on 17 December 1939 in St Basil's Church, Toronto, by Archbishop James Charles McGuigan.

Father Riley worked in both the teaching and parish apostolates: Catholic Central High School, Detroit, 1940–1, as teacher and treasurer; St Anne's Parish, Houston, 1941–2, as assistant; St Mary's of the Assumption Parish, Owen Sound, 1942–4, as assistant; Assumption College School, 1944–50, as teacher; Aquinas Institute, Rochester, 1950–7, as teacher and prefect of discipline; St Thomas High School, Houston, 1957–83, as teacher.

Bill Riley was a warm-hearted and friendly man who enjoyed company. His hearty handshake surprised the recipient by its firmness and strength. He was a tough disciplinarian, teaching mathematics and mechanical drawing using a four-inch-wide yardstick that he applied to students from time to time. But no one considered him unfair, and students who returned to the school usually asked first after Father Riley.

Father Riley's early skills as a tradesman were put to use as a Basilian. When stationed at St Mary's of the Assumption he laid brick at the

Irish Block Mission church (later demolished). At Aquinas he spent his summers filling in cracks in the concrete of the Memorial Stadium; and in Houston he painted the steel grandstands of the old Eagle Stadium more than once, going out early in the morning with a lunch pail and returning late in the afternoon. He humbly accepted the consequences of his personal weaknesses and strove constantly to be faithful to the religious life and the priesthood. In 1983 deteriorating health forced his move to St Basil's Residence (Infirmary), Toronto, where he lived for some ten months before his weakened heart gave out.

SOURCES: GABF; *Annals* 6 (1984) 206, 6 (1985) 378–9; *Newsletter* (28 May 1984).

RIVARD, Joseph Leo, priest, was born on 6 May 1906 in Windsor, one of a family of five born to Napoléon Rivard and Cécile Menard. He died in Toronto on 4 July 1981 and is buried in the Basilian plot of Holy Cross Cemetery, Thornhill, Ontario.

After attending Immaculate Conception Separate School and high school at Assumption College, Windsor, 1924–7, Joe Rivard entered St Basil's Novitiate, Toronto, and made first profession on 11 August 1928. He was appointed to Assumption College (B.A., University of Western Ontario, 1931), studied theology at St Basil's Scholasticate, Toronto, 1931–5, and was ordained to the priesthood on 16 December 1934 in Assumption Church, Windsor, by Bishop John Thomas Kidd.

In 1935, Father Rivard began thirty years in the parish apostolate, with but one brief interval, 1946–8, at Aquinas Institute, Rochester, where he taught French and supervised the main office. His parish assignments and occupations were to Assumption Parish, Windsor, 1935–42, 1944–6, assistant, directing the youth group and ministering to the French community; Ste Anne's Parish, Detroit, 1942–4; 1948–50; 1953–5, assistant; St Anne's Parish, Houston, 1950–3, assistant and second councillor, director of the Catholic Youth Organization group, and coach of grade-school basketball; Blessed Sacrament Parish, Windsor, 1955–7, assistant; St John the Baptist Parish, Amherstburg, Ontario, 1957–63, assistant and second councillor.

In 1963 Father Rivard returned to St Anne's in Houston. After some years his health deteriorated and diabetes was diagnosed – the prelude to fifteen years of suffering and incapacitation. In 1975 he was admitted to St Thomas Nursing Home, Houston, where he remained for four months before being moved to the Basilian Fathers Residence (Infirmary) in Toronto, where, with occasional hospitalization, he remained until his death.

Joe Rivard was a shy and unassuming man. Although ill during much of his priestly life, he was uncomplaining and frequently expressed gratitude to those who cared for him. In his better days he was a devoted parish priest, especially in his ministry to the sick and dying. When a call came he responded immediately, no matter the time of day or night.

SOURCES: GABF; *Annals* 5 (1979) 345, 6 (1982) 97–9; *Newsletter* (21 July 1981).

ROACH, Michael THOMAS, priest, elder brother of Father William *Roach, was born in Mara Township, Ontario (archdiocese of Toronto), on 31 July 1872, the son of Thomas Roach and Cecilia McGrath. He died in Toronto on 27 September 1936 and is buried there in the Basilian plot of Mount Hope Cemetery.

Tom Roach began his education at a local school, but his parents moved to Toronto. He entered St Michael's College in 1889 and, on 9 September 1895, was received as a novice at St Basil's Novitiate. After first profession he continued his studies at St Michael's College, 1896–8, Assumption College in Windsor, 1898–1900, and St Basil's Scholasticate, Toronto, 1900–1. With his brother Father William *Roach he was ordained to the priesthood on 28 July 1901.

Father Roach taught mathematics at St Michael's College until 1907, when he was sent to Kalamazoo, Michigan, to open Gibbons Hall; but the Congregation withdrew from that high school after two years, and Father Roach was appointed to St Thomas College (High School), Houston. When the Basilians took over the direction of St Thomas College, Chatham, New Brunswick in 1910, he was sent there as treasurer. Four years later he went to St Basil's College in Waco, Texas. When the Basilians withdrew from there in 1915 he was appointed to Assumption College for a year. Three parish appointments followed, with an interim, 1927–9, as treasurer of St Basil's Novitiate, Toronto: St Mary's of the Assumption Parish, Owen Sound, Ontario, pastor, 1916–25; Assumption Parish, Windsor, as assistant, 1925–7; Ste Anne's Parish, Detroit, 1929–33. In 1933 he was found to be suffering from diabetes, and at the time of his death in 1936 was being treated in Toronto for cancer.

With his talent for finances, Father Tom Roach served as treasurer in every house to which he was appointed. The partiality he had for concrete floors, walks, and verandas was expressive of his physique and personality – rugged, strong, enduring. In his younger days he was a fine athlete. The *Basilian Centennial* volume of St Mary's of the Assumption Parish noted: 'Father Roach still maintained an enthusiasm for outdoor life, especially hunting. Year after year he took his holidays during the deer season, and usually brought back a supply of venison.' He was notably popular with country people, and his preaching contained practical advice suited to the needs of his hearers.

BIBLIOGRAPHY: *Golden Jubilee, 1871–1921, St Mary's of the Assumption Parish.* Owen Sound, 1921.
SOURCES: GABF; *Basilian* 2 (November 1936) 139; *Jubilee, St Mary's*; *Centennial, St Mary's*; Kirley, *Congregation in France* 57; Spetz, *Waterloo*; *Thurible* (1937).

ROACH, William Joseph, priest, younger brother of Father Michael Thomas *Roach, was born in the rural parish of Brechin, Ontario (diocese of Toronto), on 1 January 1875, the son of Thomas Roach and Cecilia McGrath. He died in Toronto on 12 February 1961 and is buried in the Basilian plot of Holy Cross Cemetery, Thornhill, Ontario.

'Willie' Roach began his education in a local school. When his family moved to Toronto he attended St Michael's College, 1888–96 (B.A., University of Toronto, 1896). He entered St Basil's Novitiate, Toronto, and was professed on 29 September 1897. He studied theology at St Basil's Scholasticate, Toronto, and Assumption College, Windsor. He was ordained to the priesthood at the same time as his brother, Father Michael Thomas *Roach, on 28 July 1901.

He taught for a year at Assumption College, but in 1902 was sent to the Catholic University of America, Washington, D.C., for graduate studies. He returned to teach at Assumption College, 1904–11; in 1911 he began eight years as principal and rector of St Thomas College, Chatham, New Brunswick. His promotion of hockey there and his building of a rink for the school and the town drew disapproval from the provincial, Father Francis *Forster, but it raised Chatham to national notice. After the fire in the school, 1919, he became master of scholastics at St Basil's Scholasticate, Windsor, 1919–25. Subsequent appointments were to St Michael's College, 1925–6 and 1928–32, the Curial House, 1926–8, St Mary's of the Assumption Parish, Owen Sound, Ontario, pastor, 1932–4, Holy Rosary Parish, Toronto, 1934–6, and Assumption College, 1936–42. In 1942 he was appointed spiritual director at St Basil's Seminary, Toronto, where he remained for his eighteen remaining years. During sixteen of those years he continued to teach philosophy and theology.

Assumption University bestowed on him an honorary LL.D. in 1954, and St Thomas College, Chatham (now University of St Thomas, Fredericton), New Brunswick, where he had taught when it was a Basilian high school, honoured him with the same degree in 1955.

Father Roach possessed a splendid physique and health that enabled him to play tennis and to swim almost to the end of his life. As a student he had participated in school sports, and as a teacher he promoted them. In 1908 he introduced basketball at Assumption College. The *Basilian Centennial* volume of St Mary's of the Assumption Parish noted that, 'Though he was kept occupied with teaching, pastoral and administrative duties, Father Roach never lost his interest in athletics: he was elected honorary chaplain of St Michael's Hockey Club in 1954, and even at the age of seventy-five would join the occasional hockey practice with the team.' As master of scholastics he brought about the purchase of Strawberry Island in Lake Simcoe as a summer home for the community. He retained a lifelong interest in this place and made it a point to spend as much time as possible there each summer. Well into his seventies, it was not unusual for him to swim around the island – about one mile.

Father Roach was a member of the Basilian provincial council from 1919 to 1922. He was elected general councillor and secretary general of the Basilian Fathers of Toronto in 1922, and continued in these offices until 1928. He attended the 1954 general chapter which reunited the French and North American Congregations, and chapter ordered his intervention on this matter to be circulated to the entire Congregation.

A *Basilian Teacher* editorial written after his death noted: 'Father Roach never grew "old." In both thought and activity he long kept abreast of the groups of scholastics whom he served and loved so deeply. The intensity of his devotion to the community kept pace with its physical expansion.'

BIBLIOGRAPHY:
Book: *Golden Jubilee, Assumption College* [1870–1920]. Sandwich, Ont., 1920.
Articles: 'The Seminary and the Priest,' *Benedicamus* 3 (June 1950) 54; 'Strawberry Island,' *Benedicamus* 4 (October, December 1950) 2–3, 18–19; 'Father R.F. Forster,' *Basilian Teacher* 1 (March 1957) 9–11; 'R.W. McBrady,' *Basilian Teacher*

1 (November 1956) 9–11; 'Patrick J. Howard,' *Basilian Teacher* 3 (January 1959) 116–18; 'Strawberry Island,' *Basilian Teacher* 4 (May 1960) 253–5. 'Basilians in Chatham, N.B.,' *Basilian Teacher* 5 (January 1961) 136–7.
SOURCES: GABF; *Annals* 1 (1946) 116, 2 (1951) 32, 3 (1961) 90–1; *Basilian Teacher* 5 (March 1961) 195–8; *Basilides, Assumption College* (Windsor, 1930); *Centennial, St Mary's*; *Jubilee, Assumption*; Kirley, *Congregation in France* 9–10, 57, 88; Shook, *Catholic Education* 115–16; *Yearbook, STC*.

ROCHE, Marie-LUDOVIC, priest, bishop, member of the Association of Priests of Saint Basil 1849–53, was born 5 February 1828 at Serrières (Ardèche). He died on 6 October 1880 in Orléans, and was buried in the cemetery of his native parish at Serrières.

Marie-Ludovic Roche studied at the Collège des Cordeliers, Annonay, 1839–46, and then at the Grand Séminaire de Viviers, 1846–9. When he was already a subdeacon he was admitted to the Basilian novitiate on 14 October 1849, and was ordained a priest on 20 December 1851 in the cathedral at Viviers. He made his profession by promise, but did not take vows in 1852 when most of his confreres did. He taught in the Collège des Cordeliers (*cinquième*, 1849–51 and *quatrième*, 1851–3). Although deeply attached to his confreres, he found teaching class an ordeal and withdrew from the Association on 5 August 1853.

Father Roche then pursued higher studies, attaining a *licence ès lettres* and a *doctorat en théologie*, submitting a thesis on the controversy between St Stephen and St Cyprian on the baptism of heretics. For some years he lectured in ecclesiastical history at the Sorbonne, and served as a chaplain at Sainte-Geneviève, Paris. He was consecrated bishop of the diocese of Gap (Hautes-Alpes) in 1879. He maintained close ties with the Basilians until his death, which occurred in 1880 while preaching the priests' retreat at Orléans. A nephew, Jules Roche, represented the Ardèche for many years at the Assemblée Nationale in Paris.

BIBLIOGRAPHY:
Book: *De la controverse entre saint Etienne et saint Cyprien au sujet du baptême des hérétiques.* ... Paris, 1858.
Sermons and pastoral letters: 'Oraison funèbre du R.P. Jandel, prononcée à Paris, dans la chapelle des PP. Franciscains de Terre-Sainte, le 22 janvier 1873.' Paris, 1873. 'Oraison funèbre du très honoré Fr. Philippe, secrétaire général des Frères des écoles chrétiennes, prononcée dans la chapelle de la Maison Mère, par M. l'abbé Roche, ... le 5 février 1874.' Versailles, 1874. 'Acte. 1879 11-30

(Mandement de Mgr l'Evêque de Gap à l'occasion de son arrivée dans le diocèse.' Gap, 1879. 'Lettre pastorale et mandement de Mgr l'Evêque de Gap prescrivant des prières publiques à l'occasion de la rentrée du Sénat et de la Chambre des Députés.' Gap, January 1880. 'N° 3. Lettre pastorale et mandement ... pour le saint temps de Carême.' Gap, [1880]. 'Circulaire à l'occasion d'une lettre apostolique accordant la bénédiction au clergé de Gap pendant la retraite ecclésiastique.' Gap, 6 September 1880. 'Lettre circulaire de Monseigneur l'Evêque de Gap, invitant les prêtres de son diocèse à la retraite ecclésiastique.' Gap, 16 July 1889 [sic!].
SOURCE: Pouzol, 'Notices,' Supplément 1'; Catalogue collectif de France http://www.ccfr.bnf.fr/accdis/accdis.htm.

ROCHE, Nicholas Ernest, priest, was born in the diocese of Wexford, County Cork, Ireland, on 7 February 1866. He died at Owen Sound, Ontario, on 16 May 1932 and is buried in the Basilian plot of Mount Hope Cemetery, Toronto.

His family having emigrated to Canada when he was a boy, Nicholas grew up on a farm on Vaughan Road, just south of Eglinton Avenue, now in Toronto. He went to work at the age of thirteen and was twenty-one when in 1887 he enrolled in the high school section of St Michael's College, Toronto, to study for the priesthood. Six years later he entered St Basil's Novitiate, Toronto and was professed on 24 August 1894. He studied theology at Assumption College, Windsor, 1894–5, St Basil's Scholasticate, Toronto, 1895–7, and St Michael's College, 1897–8. He was ordained to the priesthood on 17 December 1897.

Father 'Nick' Roche taught at St Michael's College until 1 May 1900, when he was sent to Houston as founding superior and principal of St Thomas High School. He operated the school in two different downtown locations before building a new school and Basilian residence on Austin Street. In 1907 Father Roche returned to Toronto as superior of St Michael's College, but in 1910 he was appointed as the founding principal and rector of St Thomas College, Chatham, New Brunswick. After one year he was called back to Toronto to serve as provincial. He lived at St Michael's College but spent much time replacing ailing members of the novitiate staff and in supply ministry at St Mary's of the Assumption Parish, Owen Sound. In 1916 he was named Master of Novices and held this position until 1922, when he was appointed again to St Michael's College. In 1925 he was named pastor of St Mary's of the Assumption Parish. He died there seven years later from a cerebral aneurysm.

In the general administration of the Congregation Father Roche served as provincial, 1911–16, as a member of the provincial council, 1916–22, and as a member of the general council, 1930–2. His diary reveals what went into the making of this man of faith and prayer: 'Sense of duty. Kinder to all, especially my own' (1 January 1916). 'I must learn to offer all my crosses up to God' (2 January 1916). Father Roche had a strong power of winning and holding love: in a few minutes he could change a total stranger into an acquaintance, and in two or three meetings could form a bond of friendship. He used this power to help young people discern a religious or priestly vocation.

As a student at St Michael's College, Father Roche won prizes for public speaking. As a priest he quickly gained a reputation for his preaching. Father Charles *Collins wrote of him: 'He had the gift of holding his audience in rapt attention. ... He was so intensely earnest, and yet so simple in expression. His language just flowed along.' Father T.P. *O'Rourke wrote: 'He exerted lasting influence on his hearers. In him, nature and grace did combine to make a manly priest and a priestly man.' After his return to St Michael's in 1922 he was left free to accept preaching engagements in the measure that his health permitted. His sermon on the occasion of the golden jubilee of St Mary's Church is found in the commemorative volume published on that occasion (Owen Sound, 1921) 67–75.

BIBLIOGRAPHY: 'Guides to Sanctity,' *Basilian* 1 (1935) 105, 125, 2 (1936) 10, 25, 56, 75, 90, 107, 125, 150; 'The Priest and the Divine Office,' ed. V.L. Kennedy, *Basilian* 4 (April 1938) 69, 80.
SOURCES: GABF; *Centennial, St Mary's*; Charles Collins, 'The Shepherd of Owen Sound, Nicholas E. Roche,' in *Basilian* 1 (April 1935) 31–2; Kirley, *Congregation in France* 16–17, 19–20, 57; Shook, *Catholic Education* 114; *Thurible*; *Yearbook, STC* 1 (1922).

ROE, Charles Francis, scholastic, was born in Detroit on 19 November 1916, the son of George Roe and Bertha Wolfstyn. He died in Toronto on 26 March 1939 and is buried there in the Basilian plot of Mount Hope Cemetery.

Charles Roe attended St Leo's Parochial School and Catholic Central High School, Detroit, before entering St Basil's Novitiate, Toronto, in 1934. After profession, 12 September 1935, he studied at St Michael's College, Toronto, 1935–8, and then began theological studies at St Basil's Scholasticate ('Seminary' from 1937), Toronto. He died nine months later after an operation for appendicitis.

As a novice Charlie Roe found some of the rules very hard. As a scholastic he experienced academic difficulties which kept him from completing his university course. He nevertheless left the memory of a cheerful and obliging confrere.

SOURCE: GABF.

ROGERS, William George, priest, member of the Congregation 1906–22, was born at Barrie, Ontario (archdiocese of Toronto) on 29 December 1886, the son of George Rogers and Mary Dunn. He died while on vacation at Bar Harbor, Maine, on 17 August 1950 and was buried in St Mary's Cemetery, Lindsay, Ontario.

William Rogers grew up in Lindsay, where he attended Lindsay Collegiate Institute before coming to St Michael's College, Toronto, in 1903. He entered St Basil's Novitiate, Toronto, on 15 August 1906. After profession in 1907 he was appointed to Assumption College, Windsor. He was ordained to the priesthood on 30 July 1911 in Ste Anne's Church, Detroit, by auxiliary bishop Edward D. Kelly.

Father Rogers taught science at Assumption College until 1913, when he went to Ste Anne's Parish, Detroit, as assistant. In 1914 he was transferred to St Thomas College, Chatham, New Brunswick, where he taught until 1919. He returned to Assumption College and, while teaching, took advantage of the recent affiliation of the College with the University of Western Ontario to complete the requirements for a B.A. in Honours Philosophy. Towards the end of 1922, with the adoption by the Congregation of the new, stricter vow of poverty, Father Rogers opted to withdraw, and was incardinated in the archdiocese of Detroit on 26 February 1923. He was appointed to the staff of Sacred Heart Seminary and taught there until his death, which followed a heart attack as he was preparing to say Mass in Holy Redeemer Church, while on vacation in Bar Harbor.

During his years as a priest of the archdiocese of Detroit, Father Rogers kept up his association with Assumption College, serving as president of the alumni association, 1940–7. The University of Western Ontario conferred an LL.D. degree on him in 1945.

SOURCES: GABF; Archives, Archdiocese of Detroit; *Annals* 1 (1950) 283; *Centennial Volume, St Mary's of the Purification Parish* (Lindsay, 1959); *Jubilee, Assumption*; *Yearbook STC*.

ROMANS, Louis, priest, was born on 28 September 1850 at Saint-

Félicien (Ardèche), son of Augustin Romans and Thérèse Fombonne. He died at Champagne, canton of Serrières (Ardèche) on 28 December 1922, and was buried in the local cemetery.

Louis did his early studies at the Collège des Cordeliers, Annonay, 1863–7, and at the Collège du Sacré-Coeur, Annonay, 1867–70, in the Sainte-Barbe section. He made his novitiate at Feyzin (Isère, now Rhône), 1870–1, and professed final vows on 19 September 1873. Bishop Armand de Charbonnel ordained him to the priesthood on 18 September 1875 in the chapel of the Collège du Sacré-Coeur. While studying theology he helped supervise and teach students at the Petit Séminaire de Vernoux, 1871–5. After ordination he continued to teach there until 1879, when he was appointed to the Collège Saint-Pierre in Châteauroux (Indre). When the Basilians withdrew from that school in 1882, he remained in the diocese of Bourges helping in various parishes. The community records show that he was pastor at Chezal-Benoît (Cher) in 1889, and that he had been authorized to live outside the community, although still under vows. He taught at the Petit Séminaire de Saint-Gaultier (Indre) in 1894–5, and then became pastor at Montlevicq (Indre) in October 1895. He was still there in 1903. In 1913 he was residing at Champagne, where he died nine years later.

SOURCES: GABF; Kirley, *Community in France* 185, 203n506, 208; Pouzol, 'Notices.'

RONAN, Edward Xavier, priest, cousin of Monsignor John Edward Ronan of the archdiocese of Toronto, was born in Adjala Township, Ontario (archdiocese of Toronto), on 27 April 1924, the son of William Ronan and Mary Florence Malone. He died in Toronto on 4 July 2000 and is buried in the Basilian plot of Holy Cross Cemetery, Thornhill, Ontario.

Having attended the parish school of St James in Colgan, Ontario, and Tottenham Continuation School in the nearby village, 1936–40, 'Eddie' Ronan completed upper school at St Michael's College, Toronto, and in 1941 entered St Basil's Novitiate, Toronto. He left the novitiate in June of 1942 but re-entered in August of 1943, making first profession on 15 August 1944. He was appointed to St Michael's College for undergraduate studies (B.A., University of Toronto, 1947). He was then appointed to teach at Aquinas Institute, Rochester, while also attending night school in industrial arts at Edison Technical School. At Holy Rosary Seminary, Toronto, 1948–50, he did a year of theology courses and then attended the Ontario College of Education. In 1950 he introduced the industrial arts option at the newly opened Bathurst Street location of St Michael's College School, while also doing a second year of theology. In 1951 he was in the first group to move into the new St Basil's Seminary at 95 St Joseph Street, Toronto. With the help of Richard Kinsky, Frederick Sohn, and other volunteers he constructed the 110 bookcases and desk lamps required for the new building. He was ordained to the priesthood on 29 June 1952 in St Basil's Church, Toronto, by Cardinal James Charles McGuigan.

Father Ronan taught industrial arts and history at St Michael's College School from 1953 to 1978, except for one year, 1964–5, at St Charles College, Sudbury and a year of study leave, 1967–8, during which he pursued studies in industrial arts at the Gloucester College of Arts in the United Kingdom and observed similar programs in other countries. He also taught for a time at the Elliott Lake School of Arts. For thirteen summers he took courses, obtaining an M.A. in history (1957), a Type A certification in art (1963), and specialist's certification in history (1972), all from the University of Detroit.

In 1972 Father Ronan began programs on Judge Jean-Claude Couture's farm at Bond Head (Beeton), Ontario, to give his students firsthand experience of farming and the manual arts. The next year the Basilians purchased the site and named it Henry *Carr Farm. Father Ronan and other Basilians appointed to the farm worked to improve it and to make it a place of discovery and learning for students. 'Here [he wrote] the students are learning that they have power over matter. Most important of all, they are learning to respect themselves and the work they do.' He passed on his inherited love of the land and his inherent love of building to hundreds of young people and gave them hands-on experience in driving horses, ploughing, haying, and producing maple syrup and honey. He forged links between Henry Carr Farm and Basilian projects at Meriden, Connecticut, and St Lucia, West Indies, travelling to both sites despite crippling arthritis in later years.

In 1978 Father Ronan was appointed to Henry Carr High School at Rexdale, Ontario, teaching there until 1984, when he introduced the industrial arts at St Thomas High School, Tottenham, Ontario. After 1985 he assisted the pastor of St James, Colgan, Ontario. The last two years of his life were spent at Anglin House, the infirmary of the Basilian Fathers in Toronto, where even cancer could not prevent his setting up a workshop to practise his arts.

Ed Ronan inherited a love for poetry from his mother, who was a published poet. His artistic instinct made him seek the beautiful in all he did, and he communicated the patience and the wonder of nature. The eucharistic ciboria used for the papal visit to Toronto in 1984 were of his design.

BIBLIOGRAPHY: 'From the Workshop,' *Basilian Teacher* 2 (December 1957) 20–1; 'The Student – A Maker?' *Basilian Teacher* 3 (April 1959) 190–1; 'The Manual Arts,' *Basilian Teacher* 6 (January 1962) 138–40; 'Henry Carr Farm,' *Chesterton Review* 7 (1981) 88–9.
SOURCES: GABF; *Annals* 2 (1952) 61–2, 8 (1995) 13–14, 9 (2001) 94–5; *Newsletter* (20 July 2000).

ROUDIL, Elie, priest, was born on 19 January 1870 at Aubenas (Ardèche), the son of Henri-Louis Roudil, a member of the French military mounted police, and Emilie Anne Gilles. He died at Largentière (Ardèche) on 5 January 1939 and is buried in the family vault at Saint-Sernin (Ardèche).
Elie studied at the Collège du Sacré-Coeur, Annonay, in the minor seminary section of Sainte-Barbe, 1881–8. He made his novitiate at Beaconfield House, Plymouth, England, 1888–9, under the direction of Father Victorin *Marijon, and professed final vows on 19 December 1895. Bishop Joseph-Michel-Frédéric Bonnet of Viviers ordained him to the priesthood on 4 June 1898. During his studies he had taught in the Collège Saint-Charles, Blidah, Algeria, 1889–92 and 1893–7. He passed the baccalaureate exams in July 1896 and taught humanities in the *classe de seconde* at the Collège du Sacré-Coeur, 1897–8. After ordination he taught senior students rhetoric and history at that college until 1903, at which date the anticlerical laws excluded Basilians from teaching.

After 1903 he exercised various ministries as chaplain and teacher. With a fictive certificate of diocesan status, he taught history and geography at the Collège de l'Assomption, Nîmes (Gard), and served as chaplain to the Sisters of Sainte-Eugénie, Nîmes. Conscripted at the outbreak of war in 1914, he was assigned to an ambulance corps and sent to Salonica (formerly Thessalonica), Greece, where he remained four years. After the war he taught at Saint-Paul-Trois-Châteaux (Drôme) and at the Petit Séminaire de Valence (Drôme). In the early 1930s he made occasional brief visits to the confreres at Maison Saint-Joseph, Annonay, where the confreres remembered him as very cultured, well read, and well travelled. In his latter years he was chaplain at the hospital at Largentière (Ardèche).

SOURCES: GABF; Kirley, *Community in France* 184, 210, 240n569; Kirley, *Congregation in France* 42, 72, 82, 156; Pouzol, 'Notices.'

ROUME, Charles Léon Luc, priest, superior general of the Basilian Fathers of Viviers, 1950–5, was born on 11 October 1901 at Ruoms (Ardèche), the son of Ernest Roume and Berthe Etienne. He died in Annonay on 25 May 1966, and is buried there in the cemetery on the grounds of the Collège du Sacré-Coeur.

Charles Roume studied under the Assumptionists at Miribel-les-Echelles (Isère) and then at the Petit Séminaire d'Aubenas (Ardèche), at that time located in the Maison des Frères Maristes, 1916–19. He was briefly on military service at Mainz in occupied Germany after the First World War, then entered the Grand Séminaire de Viviers, receiving tonsure in 1924. For a time he taught with the Marists in their college at Montluçon (Allier), but on 7 November 1926 he entered the Basilian novitiate at Bordighera in Italy. He studied theology in Rome at the French seminary and the Gregorian University, 1927–31, and was ordained to the priesthood on 21 September 1929 in the seminary chapel at Ventimiglia, Italy, by Bishop Ambrogio Daffra. He taught moral theology, sacred scripture, canon law, and church history at the Basilian scholasticate, Maison Saint-Joseph, Annonay, 1931–9, and he taught Italian to the students at the Petit Séminaire Saint-Charles, Annonay.

In 1939 Father Roume was elected to the general council of the Basilian Fathers in France. Briefly mobilized at the beginning of the Second World War, 1939–40, he resumed teaching at Maison Saint-Joseph, 1940–56. In 1941 he was appointed director of the juvenate, and held the office until 1944. His term on the council expired on 27 January 1944, though he resumed his place on the council the following April on the death of Father Joseph *Fogeron.

On 5 January 1950 Father Roume was elected superior general of the French Basilians. As an advocate of reunion of the French Basilians with the North American Congregation, he attended the celebrations marking the centenary of St Michael's College, Toronto, in 1952. Two years later, the Basilian general chapter in Toronto unanimously approved the reunion, which was granted by Rome on 14 June 1955.

On 29 September 1955 the new superior general, Father George Bernard *Flahiff, presided at the ceremony of reunion in the chapel of Maison-Saint-Joseph. From 1955 to 1958 Father Roume served as local superior in Annonay, and from 1956 to 1958 as superior of the Collège du Sacré-Coeur, the college having been returned to the direction of the Basilian Fathers by Bishop Alfred Couderc of Viviers in 1956. Father Roume served as bursar of the college, 1958–62, before retiring to Maison Saint-Joseph. He was present for the opening of the Paris house of studies, Maison Saint-Basile, in 1961. He died as the result of an automobile accident on his way to visit the former superior of the college. His funeral took place in the chapel of the Collège du Sacré-Coeur in the presence of the new bishop of Viviers, Jean Hermil.

The history of the Congregation was a personal interest of Father Roume. When the 1960 general chapter appointed him historian of the Congregation, he wrote two historical articles. At the request of the superior general, Father Joseph *Wey, he wrote the authoritative history of the Congregation to 1864 (see below).

Father Roume's precise language and style reflected the French literature of the seventeenth century, which he knew very well. He communicated a richness of perception to his students. He loved his native southern Ardèche, and was never quite at home in the northern part of it where Annonay is located. He was sensitive to a fault, given to moods of depression, though in normal conditions he was a man of warmth, wit, and charm. He left his mark on the Congregation he loved by his teaching, administration, and the reunion of its two branches into one.

BIBLIOGRAPHY:
Book: *Origines et formation de la Communauté des Prêtres de Saint-Basile*. Privas, 1965 (Eng. trans. K.J. Kirley and W.J. Young. *A History of the Congregation of St Basil to 1864*. Toronto, 1975).
Articles: 'News from Annonay,' *Benedicamus* 5 (June 1952) 11–12; 'Histoire des origines. Saint-Symphorien-de-Mahun, Annonay, 1800–1822,' *Basilian Teacher* 2 (May 1958) 8–13; 'Ernest Martin, a Biography' (trans. K.J. Kirley), *Basilian Teacher* 4 (April 1960) 206–11.
SOURCES: GABF; *Annals* 3 (1966) 469–470; *Newsletter* (26 May 1966); Kirley, *Community in France* ii; Kirley, *Congregation in France* ii, 1, 146–8, 156, 159, 162, 168, 176, 180, 184–5, 194, 196–8, 200–1, 208–11, 213, 215, 219–22, 224–7, 229, 231–2, 234–45, 248, 250–1, 253–4, 256–65, 267–8, 271; *Mon Collège*, Collège du Sacré-Coeur, 55 (July 1966) 19; Pouzol, 'Notices.'

ROURE, Auguste, scholastic, was born on 7 July 1836 at Joyeuse (Ardèche). He died at Joyeuse on 23 April 1860 and was buried there.

Auguste Roure studied at the Petit Séminaire d'Aubenas (Ardèche) and made his novitiate in 1858-9 at Privas (Ardèche). He taught French at the Collège des Cordeliers, Annonay, from September 1859 to 19 March 1860, when tuberculosis obliged him to take sick leave with his family at Joyeuse, where he died one month later. He died as a scholastic, having received tonsure, but the date of his first profession of vows is not recorded.

SOURCES: GABF; Pouzol, 'Notices.'

ROUX-SAGET (ROUSSAGET), François, priest, was born on 26 August 1817 at Grenoble (Isère, now Rhône). His mother's family name was Michon. He died in Annonay on 25 February 1890, and is buried there in the Basilian cemetery on the grounds of the Collège du Sacré-Coeur.

François taught the primary grade in the Collège de Feyzin (Isère, now Rhône), 1841-2, and received tonsure on 4 June 1842 at the hands of Bishop Joseph-Hippolyte Guibert, future cardinal archbishop of Paris, in the chapel of the Ursuline convent, Annonay, along with four other young men who did not persevere in the Basilian community. He was formally received as a novice on 23 October 1842 at Feyzin and taught school while studying theology, first at the Collège de Feyzin, 1842-5, and then at the Collège des Cordeliers, Annonay, 1845-6. Bishop Guibert ordained him to the priesthood on 27 December 1846 in the chapel of the Collège des Cordeliers. Two days later he made his profession of perpetual promises as a Basilian.

Father Roux-Saget received many appointments, mostly in administration: bursar at the Petit Séminaire de Vernoux (Ardèche), 1846-54; bursar at the Collège des Cordeliers, Annonay, 1854-6; superior and bursar at the Petit Séminaire de Vernoux, 1856-9, concurrently serving as curate at the parish of Saint-Félix-de-Châteauneuf, near Vernoux; assistant director at Sainte-Barbe minor seminary, Annonay, 1859-61; bursar at the Petit Séminaire d'Aubenas (Ardèche), 1861-5; chaplain to the Calvary pilgrimage at Prades (Ardèche), 1865-7; superior of the Collège de Privas (Ardèche), 1867-70; director of the novitiate at Feyzin, 1870-2 and 1874-80; and bursar at the Ecole cléricale de Périgueux (Dordogne), 1872-4. When the first wave of anticlerical laws of the Third Republic closed the novitiate in 1880, and priests and novices were put out by force, Father Roux-Saget retired to the scholasticate in Annonay for the next ten years. Basilians remembered him as tall, affable, distinguished in his manner, and something of a character.

SOURCES: GABF; Kirley, *Community in France* 70n178, 150n384; Pouzol, 'Notices'; Roume, *Origines* 346.

ROY, Norman Francis, priest, was born on 31 December 1911 in Toronto, the son of Agesilaus Roy and Josephine Begy. He died in Rochester on 1 June 1985 and is buried there in the Basilian plot of Holy Sepulchre Cemetery.

Having attended St Peter's parochial school and De La Salle High School, Toronto, Norman began the Honours Philosophy course at St Michael's College, Toronto, in 1929. He interrupted his studies to enter the Paulist Fathers' novitiate, but left the Paulists after fifteen months in order to help his family. He was employed for a number of years by the T. Eaton Company as a clothing salesman. While working he took courses through the extension program at the University of Toronto (B.A., 1939). In 1940 he entered St Basil's Novitiate, Toronto, and was professed on 15 August 1941. He studied theology at St Basil's Seminary, Toronto, and was ordained to the priesthood on 26 May 1945 in St Basil's Church, Toronto, by Archbishop Ildebrando Antoniutti, the apostolic delegate to Canada.

After completing his theology courses in 1946 Father Roy was appointed to teach at Catholic Central High School, Detroit, where he also served as treasurer for the local Basilian community. In 1949–50 he taught at St Michael's College, and in 1950–3 at St Michael's College School. He taught again, 1953–62, at Catholic Central, concurrently earning Michigan teaching certification in 1954 and an M.A. in English from the University of Detroit in 1962. Appointed to Aquinas Institute, Rochester, in 1962, he taught commercial and English until retirement in 1976. At both Catholic Central and Aquinas he organized bookstores which were a considerable asset to the schools.

Norman Roy was a modest, gentle, and constantly cheerful man of culture and talents, being both a linguist and an expert in electronics. Intrigued and amused by his refreshing manner, his students benefited from the clarity and devotion of his teaching. His manner was eccentric but never offensive, and was the source of community stories which he enjoyed as well. When his health in later years restricted his activities, his inability to be in active service of the community was a source of suffering, but he retained his sense of joy. He died as the result of a heart attack suffered in May 1985.

SOURCES: GABF; *Annals* 1 (1945) 102, 6 (1986) 479–80; *Newsletter* (6 June 1985).

RUS, Svatopluk STEPHEN, priest, was born on 4 February 1925 in Zlonice, Czechoslovakia (now Czech Republic), one of two sons of Wenceslaus Rus and Mary Sadlackova. He died in Toronto on 10 May 1992 and is buried in the Basilian plot of Holy Cross Cemetery, Thornhill, Ontario.

After his secondary education at the Realgymnasium in Středočeský Kraj (Slany, district of Kladno), 1944, 'Steve' Rus entered the Technical University in Prague to study engineering, but this was interrupted when the Soviet occupation of his country stirred him to find his way into West Germany. During two years' residence in a displaced persons camp at Schwäbisch Gmünd, he received instruction in the Catholic faith and baptism from Father Simon Zuzka OFM in September 1948. Shortly afterwards he lived in various cities in England before emigrating to Canada in 1951. He lived first at Kapuskasing, Ontario, then moved to Toronto, where he took up once more the study of engineering (B.Sc., University of Toronto, 1954) and then worked for a year with Westinghouse in Hamilton, Ontario. He entered St Basil's Novitiate, Richmond Hill, Ontario, in 1956 and made first profession on 12 September 1957. He studied philosophy for a year at St Basil's Seminary, Toronto, while teaching part-time at St Michael's College School. The next year he taught mathematics at Assumption High School, Windsor, before beginning theology at St Basil's Seminary in 1959.

During his third year of theology Steve requested leave of absence to live in the Trappist Monastery of Our Lady of Gethsemani in Kentucky; but when his novice master there, Brother Louis (Thomas Merton), advised him to pursue a more active apostolate, he returned to the Basilians in January 1963 to continue his theology course at St Basil's Seminary and to teach part-time at Michael Power High School, Etobicoke, Ontario. He was ordained to the priesthood on 14 June 1964 in the chapel of the Jesuit Seminary, Toronto, by Archbishop Philip Pocock.

Stephen Rus's twenty-eight years of ministry as a priest included the following appointments: Blessed Sacrament Parish, Windsor, 1964–6; Assumption Parish, Windsor, 1966–71, 1973–5, as pastor 1986–9; graduate studies in theology, Regensburg, West Germany, 1971–2; Director of the Newman Centre, Toronto, 1972–3; Our Lady of the Assumption Parish, Lethbridge, Alberta, 1975–8; pastoral ministry in the diocese of London, Ontario, at Chatham, 1978–80; St Charles Garnier Parish, Kelowna, British Columbia, as pastor, 1980–6; renewal, 1989–90; St Michael's College School, with pastoral ministry at St Wenceslaus Parish, archdiocese of Toronto, 1990–2. Father Rus also ministered to the Czech communities in each place in Canada where he worked in Basilian institutions. He died shortly after being diagnosed with prostate cancer.

Steve Rus was a large, heavy-set man of gentle manners and deliberate speech. He never lost the accent of his native tongue. All his life he strove to understand the harmony of the divine with human life and the cosmos. Writing to the superior general in 1986 he commented: '[This transcendent design] forms a coherent pattern of truth, a pattern which is living and capable of receiving and ordering within myself any experience of past, present or future.'

BIBLIOGRAPHY: 'East, West, and the Spirit,' *Basilian Teacher* 4 (March 1960) 188–91; 'St Basil and Eastern Monasticism,' *Basilian Teacher* 5 (December 1960) 103–8; 'The Eastern Schism,' *Basilian Teacher* 5 (April 1961) 267–72; '"Velvet" Revolution. A Miracle for Czechoslovakia,' *Catholic Register* (18 August 1990), 12.
SOURCES: GABF; *Annals* 3 (1946) 294, 7 (1993) 126–8; *Newsletter* (19 May 1992).

RUSH, Edward LEONARD, priest, was born on 26 November 1894 in Toronto, the son of Edward F. Rush and Elizabeth Ahearn. He died in Toronto on 24 December 1979 and is buried in the Basilian plot of Holy Cross Cemetery, Thornhill, Ontario.

The eldest son in a prominent Toronto family, Leonard graduated from Harbord Collegiate Institute and then enrolled in the University of Toronto, where he was active in the recently founded Newman Club on St Joseph Street. He spent one year at St Mary's College, a Redemptorist school at North East, Pennsylvania. Against his father's wishes but with the support of his mother he entered St Basil's Novitiate, Toronto, in January 1917, making first profession one year later. He was then appointed to Assumption College, Sandwich, Ontario, where the scholasticate had been moved from Toronto, to complete his undergraduate studies and begin the study of theology. In 1921 he returned to Toronto for another full year of theology, and then was sent with Father William *Murray in 1922 to Paris for studies at the Institut catholique. He took lessons in elocution from a member of the Comédie Française, a fact of which he was proud. On 31 March 1923 he was ordained to the priesthood in the Eglise des Carmes by Bishop Alfred Baudrillart, rector of the Institut catholique. This, too, was an event which Father Rush was fond of recalling all through his life.

On his return to Canada he was appointed to St Michael's College, Toronto, where he taught French for five years. During this time he spent his summers at Columbia University (M.A., French, 1927). In 1928 he was named one of the first group of Basilians sent to take charge of Holy Name Institute, Detroit, which would become Catholic Central High School. He continued his summer courses at Columbia. In 1931 he was appointed to Ste Anne's Parish, Detroit, for one year, returning to Holy Name Institute as superior and principal in 1932, and continued in these offices when the school changed its name in 1933 to 'Catholic Central.' He returned to St Michael's College for a teaching stint of two years, 1934-6.

In 1936 Father Rush and Father Gerald *Anglin were sent to found St Thomas More College in Saskatoon. He did not consider himself the man for the job, and more than once asked to be relieved; but the superior general, Father Henry *Carr, would not hear of it, and Father Rush remained there for five years.

In 1941 he returned to St Michael's once more and taught there until 1946. His students recall the theatrical energy he expended to help them learn. He served on the Basilian local council and also undertook graduate studies at the Université Laval, where he received the doctorate in 1944, submitting as this thesis 'Francis Jammes, poète chrétien.' In 1946, while continuing to teach at St Michael's, Father Rush was named rector of the newly established Holy Rosary Seminary (a residence for scholastics), located in the former novitiate building on Kendal (now Tweedsmuir) Avenue, Toronto. In 1948 he was named once more to a new foundation, the University of St Thomas in Houston, where for ten years he taught French and Spanish and was vice-president and a member of the local council. His talents as preacher and musician also found scope at St Anne's Parish, Houston, where he returned in later life for prolonged visits.

Father Rush's late years of active teaching were spent at St John Fisher College, Rochester, 1958-61. He was then given reduced responsibilities at St Michael's, accepting retirement only reluctantly. In 1972 he was struck by an automobile on Bay Street. A lengthy convalescence in St Basil's Infirmary, Toronto, did not prevent his celebrating his fiftieth anniversary of priesthood in 1973. He took up permanent residence in the infirmary in 1975 and remained there until his death four years later.

Leonard Rush was noted in the community and abroad for his wit and charm. He was a brilliant linguist and musician who loved to entertain. He would readily sit down at the piano to animate a singsong, always beginning with 'The Last Time I Saw Paris.' He was much in demand as a preacher for retreats, first Masses, and other special occasions. As a teacher he kept his students working hard and always alert, for they never knew what to expect.

His last years, when his health was failing and his urbane manners were slipping away, were not happy ones for him or easy ones for the community around him. He died alone in his room in the early hours of Christmas Eve. Archbishop Philip Pocock was the main celebrant at his funeral Mass.

BIBLIOGRAPHY: 'Francis Jammes,' *Catholic World* 123 (May 1926) 162–70; 'Quid petis, frater? – A Meditation,' *Basilian* 1 (October 1937) 91–2; 'St Thomas More College,' *Basilian* 3 (February 1937) 23.
SOURCES: GABF; *Annals* 4 (1968) 47, 5 (1974) 7, 5 (1979) 340–1, (1980) 526–8; *French Studies U. of T* 122–3; *Heartwood* 68–73, 170; *Newsletter* (29 December 1979); Shook, *Catholic Education* 345–7.

RUTH, Anthony JOHN, priest, was born on 17 August 1914 at Watford, Ontario (diocese of London), one of a family of five girls and four boys of Edward Ruth and Margaret Maloney. He died in Toronto on 18 November 1998 and is buried in the Basilian plot of Holy Cross Cemetery, Thornhill, Ontario.

John Ruth's family was solidly Catholic and active in their parish. Four of his older sisters became religious. After attending local schools, he went in 1932 to St Michael's College, Toronto, for grade XIII, and the following year entered St Basil's Novitiate, Toronto. After profession on 15 August 1934, he was appointed to St Michael's College, Toronto, for undergraduate studies (B.A., University of Toronto, 1938), and then taught for one year at Catholic Central High School, Detroit. While studying his first year of theology, 1939–40, he lived at St Michael's College and also attended the Ontario College of Education, earning teacher qualification for Ontario. He moved to St Basil's Seminary, Toronto, in 1940 and was ordained to the priesthood on 15 August 1942 in St Basil's Church, Toronto, by Archbishop James Charles McGuigan.

In 1943 Father Ruth was appointed to St Michael's College School to teach. In 1949 he became assistant pastor at St Basil's Parish, Toronto, but this work was interrupted by a four-year stint as chaplain to the combat troops of the Canadian Armed Forces in Korea. On his return to civilian life in 1954 he was appointed to Blessed Sacrament Parish, Windsor, as assistant pastor for one year and then to St Basil's Parish, Toronto, as pastor, 1955–8. There he organized the centennial celebrations of the parish in 1956. He was to return to St Basil's once more in 1979 for one year.

In 1958 Father Ruth was appointed founding pastor of St Basil's Parish, Ottawa, and served there at three different periods, 1958–64, 1970–9, and 1980–7, for a total of twenty-two years. Here his pastoral instincts, his genius for friendship, and his skill for organizing found their full scope. Anticipating the spirit and the liturgical developments of the Second Vatican Council, he built a round church that was revolutionary at the time in order to involve the worshipping community more fully in the liturgical action. He emphasized the significance of baptism both in his preaching and in the physical arrangements of the church. He confidently organized the parish council, for he believed strongly in the call and role of the laity in the Church. Appointed pastor of Holy Rosary Parish, Toronto, 1964–70, he again promoted an active parish council and encouraged the Christian Family Movement. He became a leader in the liturgical movement in Canada and a respected voice in pastoral practice. He served as chairman of the Basilian Pastoral Institute, 1961–4.

In 1987, at the age of seventy-three, Father Ruth responded to the request of Archbishop Calvin Félix of Castries, Saint Lucia, and undertook pastoral work in the cathedral there. In 1992 the Archbishop confided to the Basilians St Benedict's Parish, located on higher, more salubrious ground. Father Ruth served as pastor there until his failing health necessitated retirement to the Basilian Fathers Residence (Infirmary) in 1997.

John Ruth was a talented organizer who knew how to listen to others and to delegate authority. One collaborator remarked, 'By inviting people to simple acts of generosity he led them to levels of self-sacrifice and service beyond anything they had thought themselves capable of.' His wide understanding of the Church was matched by his ardent zeal to serve the people of God. Three months before his death he organized at the Cardinal Flahiff Centre in Toronto an anointing ceremony which was also a farewell to his many friends. More than 150 persons came to celebrate Mass with him and witness the anointing of the sick at the hands of his good friend Archbishop Félix of Castries.

SOURCES: GABF; *Annals* 1 (1943) 266, 6 (1985) 310, 7 (1993) 9, 9 (1999) 94–6; *Newsletter* (8 December 1998).

RUTH, Francis Sylvester, priest, elder brother of Father Norbert *Ruth and Jerome Ruth CR, was born at Hepworth, Ontario (diocese of Hamilton), on 28 March 1902, one of a family of six boys and three girls born to Anthony Ruth and Josephine Beninger. He died in Windsor on 11 July 1964 and was buried there in the Basilian plot of Assumption Cemetery.

Francis Ruth attended Hepworth Public School, Teeswater High School, 1916–19, and St Michael's College, Toronto, 1919–20. He entered St Basil's Novitiate, Toronto, and was professed on 23 August 1921. He took the general course at the University of Toronto, majoring in physics and chemistry (B.A., 1926). Having already studied theology at St Basil's Scholasticate, Toronto, concurrently with his undergraduate course, he was ordained to the priesthood on 18 December 1926 in St Basil's Church by Bishop Alexander MacDonald. He attended the Ontario College of Education, Toronto, 1926–7.

Father Ruth was a member of the first Basilian staff at two high schools, Aquinas Institute, Rochester, 1927–8, and Catholic Central High School, Detroit, 1928–36. He was then transferred to Assumption College, Windsor, to teach chemistry and physics and to supervise the natural sciences academic program.

Francis Ruth was entrusted with the planning of several buildings at Basilian institutions: the Memorial Science Building, Assumption College, 1946; a smaller science building (later named for Father Thomas P. *O'Rourke) for the University of St Thomas, Houston, 1947; an administration building at St John Fisher College, 1950, where he became treasurer in 1951. A severe heart attack in 1953 was followed by sick leave at Assumption College, 1954–5 and at Ste Anne's Parish, Detroit, 1955–6. In 1956 he was appointed assistant treasurer at Assumption University. During the next three years he supervised the construction of a library building there and of St Basil's Novitiate, Pontiac, Michigan. He was stationed at St John the Baptist Parish, Amherstburg, Ontario, 1959–60, then at Holy Rosary Parish, Toronto, 1960–2, while planning the new parish hall there and a new Basilian residence at Assumption College School, Windsor. He returned to St John the

Baptist Parish in 1962, and before his death from cancer in 1964 had drawn preliminary plans for an addition to the rectory.

Father Ruth was thorough in each phase of planning and construction, and never submitted preliminary plans or sketches to an architect without first consulting the ideas and wishes of the Basilians who would live or work there. He maintained a lifelong interest in photography. At the time of his ordination the *Yearbook of St Michael's College* predicted that 'His sane judgment, dry humour and stoical way of looking at life's bumpy paths will always stand him in good stead.'

SOURCES: GABF; *Annals* 3 (1964) 298–9; *Newsletter* (21 July 1964); *Silver Anniversary, Catholic Central High School, 1928–1953* (Detroit, 1953); *Yearbook SMC* 18 (1927).

RUTH, James Leo, scholastic, younger brother of Father John Peter *Ruth, was born on a farm near Hepworth, Ontario (diocese of Hamilton), on 12 March 1911, the son of Leo Ruth and Mary Maloney. He died in Toronto on 15 December 1934 and was buried there in the Basilian plot of Mount Hope Cemetery.

James Leo Ruth attended local schools to the end of grade X. He went to work on his father's farm until 1928, when Father John McCall, his pastor, persuaded him to return to school. In 1930, having completed fourth year locally, he went to St Michael's College, Toronto, for grade XIII. At the end of the school year he entered St Basil's Novitiate, Toronto, making first profession on 16 August 1932. Appointed to St Michael's College, he enrolled in the Honours Philosophy course at the University of Toronto, but died in the third year of this course, following an operation for a ruptured appendix.

In a letter to his brother Father John Peter *Ruth, dated 19 August 1934, he wrote of his last annual retreat, 'I tried to make it the best retreat of my life and I hope my life will always reflect my thoughts and prayers during those days.' The *Yearbook of St Michael's College* placed over his obituary the heading, 'He lived with God.'

SOURCES: GABF; E.J. McCorkell, 'James L. Ruth,' *Basilian Teacher* 3 (March 1959) 172–3; *Yearbook SMC* (1935).

RUTH, John Peter, priest, elder brother of James Leo *Ruth, was born on 12 January 1907 at Hepworth, Ontario (diocese of Hamilton), the son of Leo Ruth and Mary Maloney. He died at Hepworth on 9 July

1971 and is buried in the parish cemetery of St Mary's of the Assumption Parish, Owen Sound, Ontario.

John Peter received his primary and two years of secondary education at Hepworth and attended Owen Sound Collegiate for one year. He took one year at Stratford Normal School, 1924-5. In August 1925 he wrote to the superior general of the Basilian Fathers, Father Francis *Forster, asking permission to live with the Basilians for a year as an associate. Replying to the request, Father Forster invited him to begin his novitiate the next month in Toronto, which he did, making first profession on 11 September 1926. He was then appointed to St Basil's Scholasticate, Toronto, to complete his senior matriculation at St Michael's College School. For the next two years, 1927-9, he lived at St Michael's College, engaged in university studies, after which he returned to the scholasticate to begin his theological studies. He received his B.A. from the University of Toronto, 1930, and teaching certification from the Ontario College of Education, 1931. He was ordained to the priesthood on 21 December 1932 in St Basil's Church, Toronto, by Bishop Alexander MacDonald.

Father Ruth was appointed to Assumption College, Windsor, to teach mathematics and serve as prefect of the boarders, 1933-50, and regularly did weekend ministry at St Theresa's Parish, Detroit. In 1950 he was appointed to Aquinas Institute, Rochester, and in 1952 joined the faculty of St John Fisher College, Rochester, where he taught mathematics until his death.

'Solid and reliable' characterize everything about John Peter Ruth: his physical appearance, his teaching, his piety, and his personality. At meetings he was more inclined to listen than to speak, though he would not hold back a gentle humorous comment. He liked to work, even to fill in for another, and became affectionately known as 'Horse Ruth.' He maintained his native love of the soil, tending to lawns and gardens wherever he was, notably at Strawberry Island, the summer home of the Basilian Fathers in Lake Simcoe. On vacation with family at Hepworth he was planning to lend a hand with the farm chores on the very morning that he experienced chest pains. Having had at least two heart attacks in the early 1960s, he obtained medication but did not think the attack required hospitalization. He died later that day in the house in which he had been born sixty-four years before.

SOURCES: GABF; *Annals* 4 (1972) 254-5; *Newsletter* (14 July 1971).

RUTH, Norbert Joseph, priest, brother of Francis Sylvester *Ruth and Jerome Ruth CR, was born on 19 June 1909 at Hepworth, Ontario (diocese of Hamilton), one of a family of six boys and three girls of Anthony Ruth and Josephine Beninger. He died in Toronto on 29 April 1998 and is buried in the Basilian plot of Holy Cross Cemetery, Thornhill, Ontario.

'Norb,' or 'Babe,' as he came to be called (possibly for his small stature but more likely with reference to the famous 'Babe' Ruth himself), attended elementary school and began high school at Hepworth, but was sent by his parents to the high school at Assumption College, Windsor, in 1924, with the understanding that they could not pay more than $100.00 for tuition, room, and board. At the end of grade XII he entered St Basil's Novitiate, Toronto, and was professed on 11 August 1927. He was appointed to St Basil's Scholasticate, Toronto, to complete grade XIII and take Honours Mathematics and Physics at the University of Toronto (B.A., 1932). Following graduation he began theological studies, but interrupted them for a year at the Ontario College of Education, earning teacher certification in 1934. He resumed his theological studies, concurrently teaching classes in both the high school and the undergraduate sections of St Michael's College. He was ordained to the priesthood on 19 December 1936 in St Basil's Church, Toronto, by Archbishop James Charles McGuigan.

Father Ruth's first appointment as a priest, 1937, was to St Michael's College, where he again taught both on the high school and university levels and served as dean of residence for five years, 1941–6. In 1946 he was appointed to Holy Rosary Seminary, Toronto, as assistant rector and spiritual director, while also doing graduate studies in physics at the University of Toronto (M.A., 1947). The following year he was named a member of the founding group of the University of St Thomas in Houston. He lived first at St Thomas High School, where he taught and served as treasurer, and then moved into the Basilian house near the university, where once again he taught and served as treasurer. In 1951 he was appointed to Assumption College, which, during the next twenty-eight years, would be the scene of his most important achievements. He began as professor of physics. In 1952 he was named dean of arts and sciences, a position he continued to hold when the college became Assumption University of Windsor in 1957.

Father Ruth's organizational and administrative skills proved invaluable in the developments which took place in the 1950s and 1960s at Assumption. He was one of the moving forces in the ecumenical federation of Canterbury, Iona, and Holy Redeemer Colleges with Assumption University of Windsor. The latter received indirect financial assistance from the Province of Ontario through its federated secular Essex College, which taught pure and applied science, business, and nursing. Ruth, doubting the long-range financial viability of the Catholic university, strongly supported the creation of a secular university to supplant Essex College and Assumption University of Windsor, with the latter becoming federated with the new University of Windsor. He persuaded the Basilian general council to move confreres who opposed this plan (Frank *Burns, Edwin *Garvey, and Peter Swan) and to replace them with others favourable to it (Hugh *Mallon and E.J. *McCorkell). As a result, in 1963 the Province of Ontario created the secular University of Windsor, with which Assumption University (no longer 'of Windsor') was federated. Ruth saw this not as 'the death of Assumption but its flowering.' He became the University of Windsor's first dean of arts and sciences, and also contributed to the establishment of new faculties and schools. When his term expired in 1970 he continued as professor of physics for five years.

After a sabbatical leave, Father Ruth became president of Assumption University, 1975. It had not yet exercised its right to teach arts and theology, but offered students of the University of Windsor a chaplaincy and scholarships and continued the successful Christian Culture Series of lectures and concerts for the public. In 1979 he undertook pastoral service in the diocese of London, the last two years of which were devoted to Holy Name of Jesus Parish, Essex, Ontario. He was a member of several professional associations and served as chairman for some of them. In 1978 the University of Windsor conferred on him the degree of LL.D. *honoris causa*. His work in the University of Windsor has been chronicled in his memoirs, *The Dean's Story* (see below). He retired to the Assumption College School Basilian community in 1984, ever maintaining his interest in the Church and in the institutions in which he had served. In 1997 he moved to the Basilian Fathers Residence (Infirmary) in Toronto where he died some ten months later.

BIBLIOGRAPHY:
Book: *From Assumption College to the University of Windsor: The Dean's Story*, ed. George A. McMahon. Windsor, 1997.
Articles: 'Science: Atheistic or Catholic?,' *Basilian* 2 (February 1936) 27–9; 'Education and the Natural Sciences,' in *Education Past the Crossroads* (Windsor, 1957) 30–8; 'The University of Windsor,' in *Were the Dean's Windows Dusty?*, ed.

Gerard Mulligan (Montreal 1966) 1 93–104; 'The University of Windsor, an Example of Ecumenical Co-operation,' *Journal of Higher Education* 38 (February 1967) 90–5. In *Basilian Teacher:* 'On Philosophy and Science,' 1 (March 1957) 3–6; 'Academic Standards in Our High Schools,' 3 (October 1958) 3–12; 'Why Some College Freshmen Fail,' 4 (October 1959) 3–8; 'Assumption University,' 8 (January 1964) 154–68.

SOURCES: GABF; *Annals* 5 (1978) 269, 5 (1981) 579–80, 6 (1987) 492, 8 (1997) 3, 9 (1999) 88–90; *Newsletter* (3 June 1998); McMahon, *Pure Zeal* 33.

RYAN, Michael JOHN, priest, uncle of Thomas *McGwan, scholastic, was born in Precious Corners, a hamlet north of Cobourg, Ontario (diocese of Toronto, since 1882 of Peterborough), on 8 November 1869, the youngest child of Michael Ryan and Bridget Salmon. He died at Richmond Hill, Ontario, on 21 November 1947 and is buried in the Basilian plot of Mount Hope Cemetery, Toronto.

Educated in a rural school and at Cobourg Collegiate Institute, John Ryan obtained a teacher's certificate and taught in rural schools until January 1891 when he resigned from his job at Rathburn, Ontario, and went to St Michael's College, Toronto, to study for the priesthood. In 1896 he entered St Basil's Novitiate, Toronto, and was professed on 20 August 1897. He made his theological studies at St Michael's College and was ordained priest on 24 August 1900.

Father Ryan taught at St Michael's College for one year. In 1901 he was sent to St Basil's College in Waco, Texas, where he taught, served as treasurer and then as superior until 1911, when his financial acumen led to his appointment as treasurer at Assumption College, Windsor. Two years later he moved to St Michael's College in the same capacity. He was the pastor of St John the Baptist Parish, Amherstburg, Ontario, 1917–21, and then of Ste Anne's Parish, Detroit, 1921–31. Ten years later he was called back to Assumption College to serve as treasurer in a time of financial crisis. In 1936 he was elected treasurer general of the Basilian Fathers and moved to St Basil's Scholasticate, Toronto. He was re-elected in 1942 and in the same year was appointed spiritual director and local treasurer of St Basil's Novitiate. He moved with the novitiate to a farm north of Richmond Hill, Ontario, in 1946 and died there one year later on the anniversary of the founding of the Basilian Fathers, 21 November.

Father Ryan had a simple formula for judging the suitability of a young man for the priesthood: a willingness to work. It described his own priesthood, whether as teacher, treasurer, or pastor.

SOURCES: GABF; *Annals* 1 (1946) 116, (1948) 194–6; Kirley, *Congregation in France* 57; W.P. McGee, 'M. John Ryan,' *Basilian Teacher* 4 (December 1959) 79–82.

RYAN, Patrick Joseph, priest, was born in Johnstown, Kilkenny County (diocese of Ossory), Ireland, on 12 March 1840, the son of Kyran Ryan and Mary Laurenson. He died in Toronto on 31 August 1917 and was buried there in the Basilian plot of St Michael's Cemetery.

Patrick Ryan and his cousin Laurence *Brennan were brought to Canada in 1864 by their uncle, Father Jeremiah Ryan of the diocese of Hamilton, Ontario, who sent them to St Michael's College, Toronto. Together they entered St Basil's Novitiate, Toronto, on 25 July 1868, made final vows on 2 December 1871, and were ordained to the priesthood on 1 May 1872.

After two years teaching at St Michael's College, 1872–4, Father Ryan received several parish appointments: assistant at St Joseph's, Chatham, Ontario, 1874–8; pastor, St John the Baptist, Amherstburg, Ontario (exchanged for St Joseph's), 1878–1901; pastor, St Mary's of the Assumption, Owen Sound, Ontario, 1901–2; and pastor, Holy Rosary, Toronto, 1902–8. In the latter year he was loaned to the diocese of Hamilton as administrator of Sacred Heart Parish, Paris, Ontario. In 1909 he retired to St Michael's College for his eight remaining years.

Father Ryan was a quiet, reserved person of average height but very heavily built. In his later years confreres affectionately called him 'Daddy.' The Golden Jubilee Volume of St Mary's of the Assumption Church recorded that in Owen Sound 'his saintly life and deeds of mercy were long remembered by Catholics and non-Catholics alike.'

SOURCES: GABF; *Centennial, St Mary's*; *Jubilee, St Mary's*.

S

SAVOYE, Jean-Claude, priest, was born on 3 August 1848 at Davézieux (Ardèche), the son of Jean-Claude Savoye and Marguerite Reboulon. He died on 17 January 1929 in Annonay and was buried there in the cemetery on the grounds of the Collège du Sacré-Coeur.

Jean-Claude Savoye attended both the Collège des Cordeliers and the Collège du Sacré-Coeur, Annonay, 1861–8, in the minor seminary section of Sainte-Barbe. He made his novitiate at Feyzin (Isère, now Rhône) in 1868–9. Having begun his theology in 1869 at the scholasticate, Montée du Château, he taught at the Petit Séminaire d'Aubenas, 1870–1, and at the Collège du Sacré-Coeur, 1871–4, where he showed himself a gifted Latin teacher. He was ordained to the priesthood on 19 September 1874 in the chapel of the Collège du Sacré-Coeur by Bishop Armand de Charbonnel.

From 1880 to 1896 Father Savoye was superior of the Petit Séminaire Saint-Charles at Vernoux (Ardèche), and of the Collège du Sacré-Coeur, Annonay, from 1896 to 1903. In 1885 he had been named an honorary canon of the diocese of Viviers. He was a progressive educator who did a great deal to raise the standard of education at Sacré-Coeur. With the passage of anticlerical legislation in 1903 excluding religious from teaching, Father Savoye managed to remain in Annonay giving Latin lessons to future priests, and for six years was chaplain at La Providence.

In addition to his teaching jobs he was elected to the general council in 1892 and became first councillor in 1895. He presided over the general chapter on 11 September 1898 that elected Father Noël *Durand superior general. Father Savoye was re-elected first councillor, but he resigned the post on 30 October 1900. He served as treasurer of the community, 1902–7; but, having resigned this office, he was postulated as general councillor. He took part in the general chapter in Geneva in 1910 which decided that the general council should live at Ste Anne's parish, Detroit. He participated in the general chapter of July 1928.

After 1922 Father Savoye lived in a house between the Cour des Marroniers of the college and the brow of the Montée du Savel. He had become almost blind and needed assistance. He was named spiritual director of the Petit Séminaire Saint-Charles when it opened in 1923 under Basilian direction. In failing health he moved to Maison Saint-Joseph in 1929, along with the other elderly confreres, and died there shortly after his arrival. His last words, upon hearing the school bell, were: 'Study has finished. I must get up and go to teach my class.'

SOURCES: GABF; Kirley, *Community in France* 124n305, 137n347, 142, 147n373, 150n384, 163n416, 165n421, 182n464, 183, 206, 244; Kirley, *Congregation in France* 12, 81, 83, 87, 93, 112, 124, 126–7, 137, 154, 214; Pouzol, 'Notices.'

SCHREINER, William Allen, priest, was born on 10 January 1935 in Rochester, the son of Wilfred A. Schreiner and Alice Mary Wilbur. He died in Toronto on 9 October 1992 and is buried in the Basilian plot of Holy Cross Cemetery, Thornhill, Ontario.

'Herbie' Schreiner attended St Michael's and Sacred Heart elementary schools and Aquinas Institute, Rochester, 1948–51. He was a brilliant student, completing high school in three years, except for one English and one health credit, which he made up during his novitiate. He entered St Basil's Novitiate, Rochester, in 1951 and was professed on 15 August 1952. He was appointed to St Basil's Seminary, Toronto, for one year and then to St Michael's College, Toronto (B.A., University of Toronto, 1956). He taught at Aquinas Institute, 1956–8, concurrently earning an M.Ed. from the University of Rochester, 1958, and at St Thomas High School, Houston, 1958–9. He studied theology at St Basil's Seminary, 1959–63 (S.T.B., University of St Michael's College, June 1962), and was ordained to the priesthood on 16 December 1962 in St Basil's Church, Toronto, by Archbishop Philip Pocock.

In 1963 Father Schreiner began twelve years of high school teaching, mostly religion courses to senior students: at Aquinas Institute, 1963–7, at Andrean High School, Gary (now Merrillville), Indiana, 1967–70, at Catholic Central High School, Detroit, 1970–1, with time off from June to December 1970, taking courses at Vanderbilt University, and at St Thomas High School, Houston, 1971–5. In the teaching of scripture he had great success, giving students a firm foundation in understanding the Word of God.

In 1975 he was granted a year's sabbatical at the Monastery of Christ in the Desert, New Mexico. During the following year, 1976–7, he studied Spanish at the Centro Cultural, a Basilian foundation in Mexico City, and was appointed to St Theresa's Parish, Sugar Land, Texas, as assistant and local councillor, 1978–80. During the year 1980–1 he taught again at St Thomas High School. He was then freed to give full time to the Monastery of Citeaux, which he founded and partially built on the Colorado River near Wharton, Texas, as a centre for prayer and reflection. Serious deterioration in health obliged him to enter the Basilian Fathers Residence (Infirmary) in Toronto in 1992, where he died a few months later.

'Herbie' Schreiner spent his life seeking God, though he never seemed to attain serenity. He had a gift for attracting people and support for the causes he espoused. The spirituality centre to which he gave the last ten years of his life was a source of some satisfaction, but it did not long survive his passing.

SOURCES: GABF; *Annals* 3 (1963) 216, 7 (1993) 143–5; *Newsletter* (19 October 1992).

SCOLLARD, Robert Joseph, priest, was born on 15 August 1908 in Toronto, the third of eight children of Robert Scollard and Lillian McFadden. His sister Lillian became Sister Mary Robert in the Congregation of the Good Shepherd. He died in Toronto on 25 June 1993 and is buried in the Basilian plot of Holy Cross Cemetery, Thornhill, Ontario.

Bob Scollard was educated at St Joseph's Separate School and in both high school and university at St Michael's College, Toronto (B.A., University of Toronto, 1928). He entered St Basil's Novitiate, Toronto, in 1928 and made first profession on 11 September 1929. He studied theology at St Basil's Scholasticate, Toronto, 1929–33, during the first year of which he also attended the Ontario College of Education, receiving high school assistant certification and elementary physical culture certification in 1930. He was ordained to the priesthood on 21 December 1932 in St Basil's Church, Toronto, by Bishop Alexander MacDonald.

Father Scollard served for many years as librarian of the Pontifical Institute of Mediaeval Studies, 1932–51, of St Michael's College, 1933–55, 1969–75, and of St Basil's Seminary, 1951–9. He attended summer courses, 1939–42, at the University of Michigan Library School, obtaining an A.M. in library science in 1942. He earned Ontario Class A Librarian Certificate No. 258 in 1946. His work in establishing these various libraries remains unique in Basilian annals. He was the first librarian in the University of Toronto to adopt the Library of Congress classification. In 1975 he was appointed to the University of St Michael's College as Archivist and Librarian Emeritus.

The general chapter of the Basilian Fathers elected Bob Scollard to the office of secretary general in 1954 and again in 1960 and 1961. When the office was no longer elective, the general council appointed him to it for the year 1967–8. He also served as community archivist during these years, collecting, collating, and preserving documentation on Basilians and on the history of the Congregation. His typescript 'Historical Notes C.S.B.' fills sixty-one bound volumes and six volumes of indexes, some parts of which were mined for his published pamphlet series of 'Historical Bulletins' and for the *Dictionary of Basilian*

Biography (Toronto, 1969). A two-volume typescript, 'Lives of the Brethren,' was a forerunner of the *DBB*.

Robert Scollard helped found the Canadian Catholic Historical Association. He served as a member of the Ontario Library Association, the Canadian Library Association, the Association of Canadian Archivists, and the Toronto Area Archivists Group. He received the George Edward Clerk Medal of the Canadian Catholic Historical Association, 1975, the Alumni and Faculty Medal from St Michael's College, 1978, an honorary D.Litt.S. from the University of St Michael's College, 1983, the *Pro Ecclesia et Pontifice* Cross from Pope John Paul II, 1987, and the Arbor Award from the University of Toronto, 1989. During the last ten years of his life he gave one day a week to the project of indexing the complete run of *Varsity*, the student newspaper of the University of Toronto.

To his duties as priest and religious Father Scollard brought the same search for perfection that characterized his professional work. He was always available to his confreres and others for the sacrament of reconciliation. In his last will he requested that the usual two Masses to be offered for the repose of his soul by each confrere be offered instead for the pope and all bishops in union with him and for the local ordinary and the local Church. He was a man of clear and strong opinions, firmly expressed but never forced on others. His most constant form of recreation was gardening. A semi-cloistered area on the grounds of St Michael's College, between St Basil's Church and Brennan Hall, has been designated 'Scollard Park' to commemorate his work and devotion to the community.

BIBLIOGRAPHY:

Book: *Dictionary of Basilian Biography. Lives of Members of the Congregation of Priests of Saint Basil from Its Beginnings in 1822 to 1968*. Toronto, 1969.

Pamphlets: *Basilian Historical Bulletin* series: 1: *Basilian Serial Publications, 1935–1969* (Toronto, 1970); 2: (With James A. Donlon, CSB) *Sources for the History of St Basil's Parish, Toronto* (Toronto, 1970); 3: (With Harold B. Gardner, CSB) *A Catalogue of the Manuscripts in the Library of St Basil's Seminary, Toronto* (Toronto, 1970); 4: (With Frederick A. Black, CSB) *A Register of the Letters of Bishop Charbonnel in the General Archives of the Basilian Fathers, Toronto* (Toronto, 1970); 5: (With Introduction by J. Stanley Murphy, CSB) *The Diaries and Other Papers of Michael Joseph Ferguson, CSB* (Toronto, 1970); 6: *The Diaries and Other Papers of Michael Joseph Mungovan, CSB* (Toronto, 1971); 7: *Basilian Novitiates in France, England and Italy. An Annotated Bibliography* (Toronto, 1971); 8: *Basilian Novi-*

tiates in Canada and the United States. An Annotated Bibliography (Toronto, 1972); 9: (With Introduction by J. Francis Mallon, CSB) *A Bibliography of the Writings of Charles Collins, CSB* (Toronto, 1974). Regarding Basilian history he also published: (With J.R. O'Donnell CSB). *Two Hundred Years of Basilian Ordinations to the Priesthood, 1782–1982*. Toronto, 1982; *An Interesting Community: Lives of Fifty-Year Basilian Priests*. Toronto, 1983; *Authentic Basilians ... Superiors General of the Basilian Fathers, 1822–1955*. Toronto, 1985. In the *University of St Michael's College Archives* series: *A Holdings List of the Administrative, Student, and Other Serial Publications of the University of St Michael's College, Toronto*. Toronto, 1976. *Footprints in the Sand of Clover Hill: Anniversaries and Notable Events in the History of St Michael's College, 1852–1977*. Toronto, 1977. (With Sister Geraldine M. Thompson CSJ) *Something Accomplished: The Story of the Class of 1928, Saint Michael's College in the University of Toronto, Written in Its Golden Year*. Toronto, 1978. *A Register of Convocations and the Graduates in Theology of the University of St Michael's College, 1955–1979*. Toronto, 1979. *A Register of Graduates in Arts, 1910–1940, St Michael's College in the University of Toronto*. Toronto, 1981. *A Register of Graduates in Arts 1941–1951, St Michael's College in the University of Toronto*. Toronto, 1982. *Handbook to the Archives of the University of Saint Michael's College*. Toronto, 1983. *Members of the Corporation, the Collegium and the Administrations of the University of St Michael's College, 1852/1853–1984/1985*. Toronto, 1985. Other pamphlets include: *The Basilian Fathers: A Short Account of the History, Life and Works of the Congregation of Priests of St Basil*. Toronto and Detroit, 1940. *Prayers for Students*. Toronto, 1943. *Union List of Serials in the Basilian Libraries of the City of Toronto*. Preliminary edition. Toronto, 1957. *Diaries Kept for the Years 1915, 1916, 1920 and 1922 by Nicholas E. Roche*. Toronto, 1965. *A Calendar of the Deceased Bishops and Priests of the Archdiocese of Toronto, December 1841–May 1974*. Toronto, 1974. *Roman Catholic History and Archives in the Province of Ontario*. Toronto, 1974. *A Calendar of the Deceased Bishops and Priests of the Archdiocese of Toronto, December 1841–October 1975*. 2nd ed. Toronto, 1975. *Dean William Harris, 1846-1923*. Newmarket, Ont., c.1976. *A Variety of Achievements: A History of the Class of 1939, Faculty of Library Science, University of Toronto*. Toronto, 1979. *A Young and Holy Priest: The Life of Rev. Michel Moncoq, 1827-1856*. Toronto, 1979. *A Calendar of the Deceased Bishops, Priests and Deacons of the Archdiocese of Toronto* 3rd ed. Toronto, 1981. *A Register of Graduates in Arts 1952–1959, St Michael's College in the University of Toronto*. Toronto, 1986. *Papal Medal Investitures, Archdiocese of Toronto, 1937–1987*. Toronto, 1987. *A Register of Graduates in Arts 1960-1965, St Michael's College in the University of Toronto*. Toronto, 1987. *They Honoured the Vestments of Holiness: A Calendar of the Deceased Bishops, Priests, and Deacons of the Archdiocese of Toronto, 1792–1990*. 4th ed. Toronto, 1990. As secretary general he also edited the *Basilian Annals* from 1954 to 1968.

As archivist of St Michael's he prepared several four-page finding lists and site guides: see *Annals* 6 (1984) 278.

Articles: In *Basilian:* 'Blessings,' 1 (April 1935) 53–4; 'The Institute Library,' 3 (December 1937) 128–9; 'Most Reverend Denis O'Connor CSB, DD,' 4 (May 1938) 88–9; 'A List of Photographic Reproductions of Mediaeval Manuscripts in the Library of the Pontifical Institute of Mediaeval Studies,' *Mediaeval Studies* 4 (1942) 126–38, 5 (1943) 51–74; 'The Mediaeval Library: A Laboratory for Ideas,' *Catholic Library World* 18 no. 4 (April 1947) 213–5; 'The Basilian Fathers Not from Brazil,' *Catholic Digest* (April 1948) 84–6; 'A Veritable Laboratory: The Library of the Pontifical Institute of Mediaeval Studies,' *Canadian Library Association Bulletin* (May 1951) 3 pp.; 'In 19 Hundred & 52,' *Benedicamus* 6 (December 1952) 11–12; 'F.X. Granottier, *Laudemus viros gloriosos*,' *Basilian Teacher* 1 (December 1956) 19–21; 'Assumption College, 1883,' *Basilian Teacher* 3 (May 1959) 223–7; 'Soulerin, Jean Mathieu,' *Dictionary of Canadian Biography* (Toronto, 1965–) 10 662–3. For the *New Catholic Encyclopedia* (New York, 1967): 'Basilian,' 2 149–51; 'Charbonnel, Armand François Marie de,' 3 459; 'Carr, Henry,' 3 146; 'Denomy, Alexander Joseph,' 4 774; 'Kelly, Michael Vincent' 8 146; 'Soulerin, Jean Mathieu,' 13 474; 'Vaschalde, Adolphe Arthur,' 14 541.

SOURCES: GABF; *Annals* 5 (1980) 459–60, 6 (1983) 115, 6 (1984) 276, 7 (1993) 64–5; 8 (1994) 135–7; *Newsletter* (11 September 1993); Kirley, *Congregation in France* 200.

SCOTT, Walter Winthrop, priest, was born on 21 March 1925 in San Francisco, California, the son of Walter Scott and Mary Vandegaer. He died in Houston on 13 September 1988 and is buried there in the Basilian plot of the Garden of Gethsemane, Forest Park Lawndale Cemetery.

His family having moved to Houston shortly after Walter's birth, he attended St Thomas High School. Graduating in 1942 he entered the newly opened St Basil's Novitiate, Rochester, and was professed on 2 September 1943. After university studies at St Michael's College, Toronto (B.A., University of Toronto, 1947), he taught Latin and religion at St Thomas High School for one year, concurrently beginning his theological studies, then taught a second year at Catholic Central High School, Detroit. He completed his theology course at St Basil's Seminary, Toronto, 1949–52, being ordained to the priesthood on 29 June 1951 in St Basil's Church, Toronto, by Cardinal James Charles McGuigan.

Father Scott returned to St Thomas High School to teach English and religion and to produce and direct student theatre (he called the drama club SCITAMARD – 'dramatics' spelled backwards). He earned an M.Ed. from the University of Houston in 1954, and in 1963 was appointed assistant principal at St Thomas and then, the following year, principal, a position he held until 1968. That year the community appointed him principal of Pius X High School, Albuquerque, New Mexico, of which the Basilians had just assumed direction.

In 1972 he obtained permission to return to graduate studies at the University of Houston, and requested relief from administration in future. But the following year the Basilians of the Western United States Region elected him regional representative, and re-elected him in 1977. He founded a house for Basilian Associates at the University of St Thomas, and lived there himself.

In 1979, when he was appointed rector of St Basil's College, Toronto, and master of scholastics, he resigned as regional representative. Not long after he suffered a serious heart attack during a retreat at Invermara, the Lake Simcoe home of the Sisters of St Joseph. Father George Freemesser CSB was able to revive him; but a second, later attack obliged him to resign his post, and in 1980 he moved to the Basilian house in Phoenix, Arizona. His health having improved by 1982, he was appointed assistant novice master at St Basil's Novitiate, Sugar Land, Texas. The following year a stroke obliged him to convalesce at the Basilian Fathers Residence (Infirmary) in Toronto. In 1986 he was well enough to join the Basilian community at St Thomas High School. There he brought the cheerfulness and affability, the confidence and optimism, which had characterized his life. He died suddenly from a massive heart attack two years and two months later.

BIBLIOGRAPHY: 'Experimentation Will Enable Us to Determine the Best Retreat Forms,' *Forum* 2 (December 1965) 169–70.
SOURCES: GABF; *Annals* 2 (1951) 37, 6 (1989) 811–13; *Newsletter* (29 September 1988).

SEMANDE, François-Xavier Denis Alfred, priest, was born in Loiselville, now River Canard, Ontario (diocese of Toronto, since 1856 of London), on 24 January 1855, the son of Antoine Semande and Mathilde Lafferté. He died in Sandwich (now Windsor) on 21 June 1922 and was buried there in the Basilian plot of Assumption Cemetery.

François Semande attended local schools, and in 1870 (the first year of Basilians at Assumption) went to Assumption College, Windsor, as a student in Second Latin. Six years later he entered the Basilian novitiate at Assumption College for the year 1876-7. He studied theology at Assumption College, pronounced his final vows on 17 April 1881, and was ordained a priest on 16 June 1881.

Assumption College remained the scene of Father Semande's labours until 1893, with the exception of 1886-7 as assistant at St Mary's of the Assumption Parish, Owen Sound, Ontario. From 1893 to 1907 he was pastor (and from 1916 to 1922 assistant) of Assumption Parish, Windsor. In the intervening years he was treasurer of Assumption College, 1907-9, and pastor of St John the Baptist Parish, Amherstburg, Ontario, 1909-16. He returned as assistant to Assumption Parish in 1916, and died there six years later from a heart attack, just after celebrating Mass.

Father E.J. *Lajeunesse wrote of Father Semande, 'He seemed to know what changes [at Assumption Parish] should be made, and he wasted no time in undertaking them.' He built the rectory in 1896 and made a number of improvements in the church. In 1901, when Bishop McEvay pressed for the establishment of separate schools wherever there was a sufficient number of Catholic families, Father Semande overcame stubborn opposition, born from the prospect of higher taxes, to build three schools at Petite Côte, Grand Marais, and Sandwich. He was one of the best-known and admired priests in the Windsor area. His step was deliberate, his whole manner suggested business, and even his humour admitted nothing frivolous.

SOURCES: GABF; Charles Collins, 'Basilians I Have Known,' transcribed in Robert J. Scollard, 'Historical Notes C.S.B.' 10 31-5 (GABF); *Jubilee, Assumption*; *Jubilee, St Mary's*; Lajeunesse, *Assumption Parish*.

SENIAWSKI, John Walter, priest, was born on 29 April 1947 in Rochester, the son of Walter Seniawski and Evelyn Radel. He died in Rochester on 20 June 1991, and is buried there in the Basilian plot of Holy Sepulchre Cemetery.

'Jack' attended St Theodore's elementary school and Aquinas Institute, Rochester, graduating in 1965. He entered St Basil's Novitiate, Rochester, that same year; but in June 1966 an interruption for reasons of health postponed his profession until 17 February 1967. He lived these intervening months at the Basilian House of Studies on the campus of St John Fisher College, where he continued to live during his undergraduate years (B.A., June 1970). Appointed to Aquinas Institute to teach and to manage the sports equipment, he developed an easy rapport with the students, a talent he maintained through life. In 1973 he began theological studies at St Basil's College, Toronto. During this time he spent one summer as assistant administrator of the Columbus Boys' Camp at Orillia, Ontario. He was assigned to Michael Power High School, Etobicoke, for his diaconate year, to teach while completing his theology course, and was ordained to the priesthood on 21 May 1977 in his home parish of St Theodore's, Rochester, by Bishop Dennis Hickey, his former pastor, then auxiliary bishop of Rochester, who would also celebrate his funeral Mass.

In 1977 Father Seniawski was appointed once more to Aquinas Institute to teach history and theology. He involved himself fully in the life of the school. It was said of him that 'his was the gift of being able to reach those whom others were unable to motivate or influence.' An avid outdoorsman, he organized wilderness fishing trips for the students and enjoyed hunting. As a member of the National Rifle Association, he dedicated himself to teaching the safe use of arms. In his high school days he had been an apprentice instructor at a rifle club. From 1977 he served as chaplain to the Gates, New York, Auxiliary Police Force. His full-time teaching ended abruptly in May 1986 when he suffered a debilitating stroke. He was able to continue as house bursar, to supervise the textbook loan program and ground maintenance, and to assist in the chaplaincy to the sisters at Nazareth Academy, until he was hospitalized in May 1991, a month before his death.

Jack Seniawski was a shy person, but this did not hinder his effectiveness. He saw himself as a team player who knew his strengths and his limitations.

SOURCES: GABF; *Annals* 5 (1978) 263, 7 (1992) 130–2; *Newsletter* (18 July 1991).

SEREY, Benjamin, priest, was born on 27 December 1868, at Montréal (Ardèche), the son of Vincent Serey and Sylvie Blachère. He died on 5 October 1939 at Privas (Ardèche) and was buried in the local cemetery.

Benjamin studied in the Sainte-Barbe minor seminary section of the Collège du Sacré-Coeur, Annonay, 1882–8. After completing rhetoric there in 1888 he went to the novitiate at Beaconfield House, Plymouth, England, where he made his first profession of vows. During his years of preparation for the priesthood he taught and supervised students at various Basilian schools: the Ecole cléricale at Périgueux (Dordogne), 1889–90, 1892–3, Sainte-Barbe minor seminary, 1890–2, and the Collège du Sacré-Coeur, 1893-5. He made final profession of vows on 22 September 1892. Bishop Joseph-Michel-Frédéric Bonnet of Viviers ordained him to the priesthood on 21 September 1895 in the chapel of the Collège du Sacré-Coeur.

After ordination, Benjamin Serey spent almost his entire priestly life teaching the senior grades: at the Petit Séminaire d'Aubenas (Ardèche), 1895-8; at the Collège du Sacré-Coeur, Annonay, 1898-9; at the Collège Saint-Charles, Blidah, Algeria, 1899-1902; and at the Petit Séminaire d'Aubenas, 1902-3.

Like other Basilians he had to abandon teaching in 1903 after the implementation of anticlerical laws. He served as curate at Berrias (Ardèche), 1903-6. In 1906, because he had been legally declared a 'secular' priest, he began to teach humanities at the Petit Séminaire de Vernoux (Ardèche); but on 23 December of that year the teachers and seminarians were expelled by the French mounted police from Valence (Drôme), and the building was converted into a *gendarmerie*, despite lively opposition from the Catholic people of Vernoux. In early 1907 the teachers and seminarians were received into the Collège du Sacré-Coeur, Annonay, which had reopened its doors under diocesan direction in 1905. Father Serey went to Aubenas in 1907, where he taught in the Institution Saint-Michel for two years before going to the Collège du Sacré-Coeur in Annonay in 1909. Here he taught for the next twenty-two years, 1909-31, with the exception of four years at the Institution Saint-Michel at Aubenas (Ardèche), 1915-19.

In 1931 Father Serey went to the Basilian novitiate at Bordighera, Italy, where for four years he helped the master of novices and served as chaplain to the Sisters of the Presentation; but attacks of epilepsy gradually became more frequent. He retired to Maison Saint-Joseph, Annonay, in March 1935, hoping to be able to help out with supervision and spiritual direction in the new combined novitiate and juniorate which opened there that year. His condition worsened, and he had to be admitted to the Hôpital Sainte-Marie at Privas (Ardèche), where he died four years later.

Through his experience of being twice expelled by the state because of his status as a religious, Father Serey remained devoted to the formation of young seminarians and to the Basilian community.

SOURCES: GABF; Kirley, *Community in France* 184, 197, 204, 240n569, 255n600; Kirley, *Congregation in France* 42, 76n34, 82, 148, 149, 154, 156, 214-15; Pouzol, 'Notices.'

SEVEYRAC, Félix, priest, was born on 12 April 1872 at Aubenas (Ardèche). He died on 5 March 1932 at Viviers (Ardèche) and was buried in the local cemetery.

Félix Séveyrac did his high school studies probably at Aubenas. Because of his mastery of music he is most likely the Séveyrac whom the *Ordo* of the diocese of Viviers lists at the *maîtrise* (choir school) at Viviers in 1892 or the one at Vernoux in 1893. Félix Séveyrac took part in the annual Basilian retreat of September 1897 and entered the novitiate on the seventeenth of that month. He taught at the Collège du Sacré-Coeur, Annonay, 1897–1903, and was ordained to the priesthood at Viviers on 6 June 1903, the last Basilian ordained before the expulsion of Basilians from schools as a result of anticlerical laws.

Father Séveyrac went to live at the Petit Séminaire de Vernoux and ministered at the small parish of Saint-Félix-de-Châteauneuf, where he remained as pastor when the Vernoux school was closed in December 1906. In 1913 he became the organist at the cathedral of Viviers. He was mobilized in the First World War. One report has him in the ambulance corps, another in the artillery at Nîmes (Gard). After the war he returned to Viviers to a variety of duties: director of the *Semaine religieuse de Viviers*, chronicler for the review *Jeanne d'Arc*, secretary for the diocesan administration, professor of design at the *maîtrise* de Viviers, and professor of organ at the Grand Séminaire. He published a collection of pen sketches notably of Viviers and the surrounding region. He was a modest person with the soul of an artist. He had a youthful heart which affected all he said and did. He died suddenly at his desk in his sixtieth year.

BIBLIOGRAPHY: *Manuel de chants à l'usage du diocèse de Viviers. Motets et Cantiques avec accompagnement d'orgue ou d'harmonium*. Viviers, 1931; *Histoire de la Congrégation des soeurs gardes-malades de Saint-Roch à Viviers*. Viviers, 1934.
SOURCES: GABF; Catalogue collectif de France http://www.ccfr.bnf.fr/accdis/accdis.htm; Kirley, *Community in France* 184, 206; Pouzol, 'Notices'; Kirley, *Congregation in France* 78, 215; *Semaine religieuse de Viviers* (11 March 1932).

SHARPE, Gerald Vincent, priest, younger brother of Fathers Joseph *Sharpe and Wilfrid *Sharpe, was born on 1 August 1896 at Point Edward (now part of Sarnia), Ontario (diocese of London), the son of Michael Sharpe and Anna Kane. He died at Owen Sound, Ontario, on 4 September 1977 and is buried there in the Basilian plot of St Mary's Cemetery.

Gerald attended local schools in Sarnia and then spent two years, 1916–18, at Assumption College, Windsor. In 1918 he joined the Canadian Army, spending one year in the service, mostly in England. He returned to Assumption College in 1919 and the following year entered St Basil's Novitiate, Toronto, making first profession on 23 August 1921. He was appointed to St Basil's Scholasticate, Toronto (B.A., University of Toronto, 1924) and earned teaching certification from the Ontario College of Education in 1925. He was also studying theology during these years and was ordained to the priesthood on 18 December 1926 in St Basil's Church, Toronto, by Bishop Alexander MacDonald.

In 1927 Father Sharpe was appointed to teach at St Michael's College; he was moved in March 1932 to finish the year at Catholic Central High School, Detroit. He remained in Detroit for two years at Ste Anne's Parish, returned to the classroom at St Michael's for the year 1934–5, and then, for the next seven years, was confessor at St Basil's Novitiate, Toronto, while teaching part-time at St Michael's. In 1942 he began thirty-five years of parochial ministry: Assumption Parish, Windsor, 1942–3, 1946–62, St Mary's of the Assumption Parish, Owen Sound, Ontario, 1943–6, 1968–77, and Our Lady of the Assumption Paris, Lethbridge, Alberta, 1962–8.

'Gerry' Sharpe shared his two Basilian brothers' love and talent for music. Rather small of stature compared to them, he was a man of unflagging energy and enthusiasm. He accepted each obedience with equanimity. He prepared his sermons and homilies carefully, usually writing them out. On the day of his death, having prepared a homily on the importance of being ready for death whenever it might come, he set out to celebrate Mass at a local hospital. The homily was delivered by graphic example, for he was killed in an automobile accident on the way. He was eighty-one years of age, yet still eager and ready to minister.

SOURCES: GABF; *Annals* 4 (1972) 224, 5 (1977) 198, 5 (1978) 328–9; *Newsletter* (8 September 1977).

SHARPE, Joseph Patrick, priest, eldest brother of Fathers Gerald *Sharpe and Wilfrid *Sharpe, was born in Point Edward (now part of Sarnia), Ontario, on 13 March 1875, the son of Michael Sharpe and Anna Kane. He died at Owen Sound, Ontario, on 29 November 1918 and was buried in the Basilian plot of Assumption Cemetery, Windsor.

Joseph Sharpe was educated in local schools and at Assumption College, Windsor, 1892–7. In 1897 he entered St Basil's Novitiate, Toronto, and was professed on 22 August 1898. Following theological studies at Assumption College and at St Basil's Scholasticate, Toronto, he was ordained to the priesthood on 23 August 1903.

Father Sharpe taught at Assumption College until 1904 when he was appointed to St Thomas High School, Houston. He was transferred to St Basil's College, Waco, Texas, 1906–13, returned to Assumption College, 1913–14, then went back to St Basil's College. When the Basilians left Waco in 1915, he returned again to Assumption College and from there went in 1916 to St Mary's of the Assumption Parish, Owen Sound, where he had charge of St Michael's Church in the Irish Block. He died at Owen Sound during the influenza epidemic of 1918.

Joseph Sharpe was an outstanding athlete, excelling in track and field, and had a magnificent physique. He taught many subjects, but principally modern languages. He spent the summers of 1908–10 in Mexico learning Spanish. Love of music, a trait characteristic of his family, found expression in his work with the Assumption College Orchestra and Glee Club.

SOURCES: GABF; *Centennial, St Mary's*; *Jubilee, St Mary's*; *Purple and White* (15 January 1927).

SHARPE, Wilfrid Clarence, priest, middle brother of Fathers Joseph *Sharpe and Gerald *Sharpe, was born on 22 September 1891 at Point Edward (now part of Sarnia), Ontario (diocese of London), the son of Michael Sharpe and Anna Kane. He died in Houston on 1 January 1976 and is buried there in the Basilian plot of Garden of Gethsemane, Forest Park Lawndale Cemetery.

Wilfrid, or 'Willy,' as he was called in the family and in the community, attended the local elementary school and, in the year 1902–3, Sarnia Collegiate Institute. He transferred to the high school section of Assumption College, Windsor, graduating in 1906. After two more years at Assumption College he took a teaching position for two years with the Basilian Fathers at St Basil's College, Waco, Texas. In September 1910 he entered St Basil's Novitiate, Toronto, making first profession on 17 September 1911. He immediately began theological studies while at the same time completing his undergraduate courses (B.A., Honours Classics, University of Toronto, 1914). He was ordained to the priesthood on 18 September 1914 in St Basil's Church, Toronto, by Archbishop Neil McNeil.

Immediately after ordination Father Sharpe went to the Catholic University of America, Washington, D.C., to study Latin and theology (M.A. and S.T.B., 1915). He was assigned to Assumption College, where he taught for the next ten years. In 1925 he began three years as master of novices in Toronto. When the Basilian general chapter of 1928 elected him to the general council, he took up residence at Catholic Central High School, Detroit, where, in addition to his council duties, he taught classics. In 1929 he moved to the curial house in Toronto. He was re-elected councillor in the chapter of 1930, and from 1930 to 1936 he was also secretary general. At the end of his term in 1936 he was appointed pastor of Holy Rosary Parish, Toronto, and in 1942 he was again named master of novices, this time at the newly founded St Basil's Novitiate in Rochester. In 1948 he became superior of the Basilian community at St Thomas High School, Houston, but in 1952 moved to the University of St Thomas, Houston, where he taught for the next eleven years. In 1963 he was appointed to the Rochester House of Studies as councillor for the community and confessor for the scholastics, while also teaching at St John Fisher College. In 1966 he returned to the University of St Thomas and remained active up until his death at the age of eighty-four, on New Year's Day 1976.

Wilfrid Sharpe was soft-spoken and fine-mannered. He was an accomplished classicist and a lover of music with a remarkable knowledge of classical opera, comic opera, musicals, and popular songs, all of which he could play on the piano and sing. His memory for the names and accomplishments of theatre and sports personalities was phenomenal, yet he was the most unassuming of men, a trait which increased his influence on parishioners, students, and his confreres.

BIBLIOGRAPHY: 'Wanted: A Spiritual Man,' *Basilian* 1(December 1935) 123–4.
SOURCES: GABF; *Annals* 3 (1961) 75, (1964) 306–7, 5 (1976) 190–2; *Newsletter* (7 January 1976).

SHAUGHNESSY, Patrick James, priest, member of the Congregation 1887–1923, was born in Oakville, Ontario (diocese of Hamilton), on 21 March 1861, the son of Patrick Shaughnessy and Ellen O'Boyle. He died at Oakville on 22 November 1935 and was buried there in St Mary's Cemetery.

Patrick Shaughnessy was educated in Oakville and at St Michael's College, Toronto, 1881–7. He entered St Basil's Novitiate at Beaconfield House, Plymouth, England, on 9 August 1887. Following first profession in 1888 he returned to Canada, studied theology at Assumption College, Windsor, and was ordained to the priesthood on 19 December 1891.

Father Shaughnessy's appointments were to both teaching and parish work: St Michael's College, 1892–4; assistant at St Mary's of the Assumption Parish, Owen Sound, Ontario, 1894–8, in charge of St Michael's Church in the Irish Block; Assumption College, 1898–1904; and St John the Baptist Parish, Amherstburg, Ontario, 1915–16. He had returned to St Mary's of the Assumption Parish, 1904–15, and was given the privilege of laying the cornerstone for the mission at Hepworth. After a year on loan to the diocese of Hamilton, Father Shaughnessy became assistant at Ste Anne's Parish, Detroit, 1917–23. When the Congregation adopted the new, stricter vow of poverty, he opted for incardination in the archdiocese of Detroit (20 June 1924) under the title of patrimony. Father Shaughnessy served as assistant at St Patrick's Parish, Wyandotte, Michigan, until 1930, when he retired to live with his brother Peter and sister Anne in Oakville.

Patrick Shaughnessy was a tall Irishman whose striking appearance and storytelling commanded attention. Ahead of his time, he was a strong advocate of administering Extreme Unction as the sacrament of the sick. The *Golden Jubilee Volume of Assumption College* noted that 'no one had more loyal admirers than Father Shaughnessy among the students of his class, to whom he devoted not only the class hours, but much of his recreation time.'

SOURCES: GABF; Archives, Archdiocese of Detroit; *Centennial, St Mary's; Jubilee, Assumption; Jubilee, St Mary's.*

SHEAHAN, Francis Michael, priest, uncle of Father Joseph Redican CSB, was born on 26 July 1912 in Toronto, the son of Joseph Sheahan and Loretta Hayes. He died in Toronto on 2 December 1997 and is buried in the Basilian plot of Holy Cross Cemetery, Thornhill, Ontario.

Frank Sheahan attended St Joseph's Separate School and the high school section of St Michael's College, Toronto, graduating in 1929. He entered St Basil's Novitiate, Toronto, and was professed on 15 August 1930. He was appointed to St Basil's Scholasticate, and a year later to St Michael's College for undergraduate studies (B.A., Honours Philosophy, 1934). He returned to St Basil's Scholasticate in 1934 for theology and pedagogical studies, earning teacher certification at the Ontario College of Education in 1935, and was ordained to the priesthood on 17 December 1938 in St Basil's Church by Archbishop James Charles McGuigan.

Father Sheahan had a long and varied career of teaching (chiefly history, Latin, and religion) and of administration: St Thomas High School, Houston, 1939–42, 1943–6; Aquinas Institute, Rochester, 1942–3; director of Camp Loma Linda, Kerrville, Texas, 1945 and 1946; St Michael's College School, Toronto, 1946–8; Holy Rosary Seminary, Toronto, 1948–50, rector; St Michael's College, 1950–2, treasurer; Aquinas Institute, 1952–7; Assumption College School, 1957–81 (first councillor 1959–60, superior 1960–7, treasurer 1967–73); St John the Baptist Parish, Amherstburg, Ontario, 1981–4, assistant; Basilian Fathers Residence (Infirmary), Toronto, 1984–90, superior.

After three years' retirement at Michael Power High School, 1990–3, Father Sheahan returned to the Basilian Fathers Residence because of deteriorating health. He was cheerful and co-operative, a man for others. He loved conversation, and could be seen at the west entrance chatting with passers-by or reciting his rosary. His sense of humour never deserted him, nor did his serenity and peaceful manner. He had many friends and acquaintances, especially among boarding students at Assumption High School and their parents, many of whom came to his funeral. At his death he was in his eighty-sixth year, sixty-seven years of them as a Basilian and fifty-nine as a priest.

BIBLIOGRAPHY: 'H.S.R.,' *Basilian* 4 (April 1938) 75–6; 'We Must Have a Real Concern for Others and for the Community,' *Forum* 2 (May 1966) 72–4.
SOURCES: GABF; *Annals* 5 (1981) 540–1, 6 (1989) 719, 9 (1998) 81–2; *Newsletter* (23 December 1997).

SHEEDY, Matthew Patrick, priest, was born on 16 March 1913 in Toronto, the son of Matthew Sheedy and Florence Hynes. He died in Windsor on 9 February 1989 and is buried there in the Basilian plot at Heavenly Rest Cemetery.

'Matt' Sheedy attended Holy Rosary School and the high school section of St Michael's College, Toronto, graduating in 1932. One year later he entered St Basil's Novitiate, Toronto, and was professed on 12 September 1934. He was appointed to Assumption College for university studies (B.A., University of Western Ontario, 1936), concurrently teaching health, algebra, and geometry in the high school of Assumption College. He obtained teaching certification from the Ontario College of Education during his first year of theology, 1936–7, and taught one year at Catholic Central High School, Detroit, before moving to St Basil's Seminary, Toronto, for theological studies, 1938–41. During this time he also taught English at St Michael's College School, and managed to play hockey, at which he excelled. He was ordained to the priesthood on 15 August 1940 in St Basil's Church, Toronto, by Archbishop James Charles McGuigan.

Father Sheedy devoted forty-eight years to teaching, coaching, and administration in four Basilian high schools: Catholic Central, 1941–7, teaching English, while concurrently taking courses at the University of Detroit (M.A. in English); St Thomas, Houston, 1947–55, teaching English and coaching baseball; Assumption College School, 1955–8; St Michael's College School, 1958–65, as superior and principal; and again at Assumption College School, as principal, 1965–71. At the expiration of his term he stayed on at Assumption to teach English and religion. He wrote poetry and encouraged his students to do so by distributing mimeographed booklets of their work. He worked in the guidance office and was moderator of the Mothers Club. In forming the Windsor Catholic High School Board, consisting of representatives of Windsor's three senior Catholic secondary schools and the Windsor Roman Catholic Separate School Board, which funded and operated grades IX and X, he helped pave the way for the funding of grades XI, XII, and XIII by the provincial government. Assumption University recognized his leadership in education by conferring on him an honorary LL.D., and a gymnasium at Assumption High School was named for him.

Matt Sheedy seemed to have unlimited resources of energy, and he spent them generously. He was a leader who bred confidence in those who worked with him, just as he was a teacher who inspired love of learning and courage in his students. He worked literally to the end of his days. Diagnosed with cancer of the liver during the Christmas holidays in 1988, he died six weeks later.

BIBLIOGRAPHY: 'Jocism,' *Basilian* 3 (April 1937) 67, 80; 'H.S.R.,' *Basilian* 4 (April 1938) 74–5; 'Coaching Basketball,' *Basilian Teacher* 2 (December 1957) 26–8; 'Basketball Training,' *Basilian Teacher* 3 (March 1959) 166–8; 'New Trends and New Emphasis in the Teaching of English,' *Basilian Teacher* 6 (December 1961) 113–14; 'Give Young People Responsibility as Soon as Possible,' *Forum* 3 (March 1967) 42.

SOURCES: GABF; *Annals* 6 (1984) 209, 7 (1990) 113–14; *Newsletter* (6 March 1989).

SHEEHAN, Cornelius J., priest, elder brother of Father William Alexander *Sheehan, was born in Cleveland, Ohio, on 17 April 1902, the son of John Sheehan and Catherine Ahern. He died at Winsted, Connecticut, on 7 February 1939 and was buried in the Basilian plot of Mount Hope Cemetery, Toronto.

'Con' Sheehan was an exceptional child, strong in body, gifted in mind, and endowed with remarkable piety. From Immaculate Conception Parochial School he went to St Joseph's Preparatory Seminary, Cleveland, then in 1916 to Assumption College, Windsor. During the following years he built up an 'all-time' reputation in athletics and at the same time lived up to his promise as a student (B.A., University of Western Ontario, 1924). He entered St Basil's Novitiate, Toronto, in 1924 and was professed on 11 October 1925. He studied theology at St Basil's Scholasticate, Toronto, attending also the Ontario College of Education during the year 1926–7, and was ordained to the priesthood on 29 June 1929 in St Basil's Church, Toronto, by Archbishop Neil McNeil.

Father Sheehan taught at Catholic Central High School, Detroit, 1929–31, St Michael's College School, Toronto, 1931–4, and St Thomas High School, Houston, 1934–5. He was active in promoting athletic programs. Plagued by a problem with alcohol, he was on leave in his home diocese of Cleveland in 1935–6, then spent the year 1936–7 at Strawberry Island in Lake Simcoe, and was on leave again from 1937 until his death in 1939 from injuries sustained in an automobile accident while driving with a priest friend to visit his sister in Newton, Massachusetts.

SOURCES: GABF; *Yearbook SMC* 20 (1929).

SHEEHAN, Michael McMahon, priest, was born on 29 January 1925 at Renfrew, Ontario (diocese of Pembroke), the first child and only son of Gerald Sheehan and Cecilia Lena McMahon. He died in Toronto on 23 August 1992 and is buried in the Basilian plot of Holy Cross Cemetery, Thornhill, Ontario.

Michael (or 'Mac,' as he was called by his family and some confreres), attended Renfrew Separate School, 1931–7, and Renfrew Collegiate Institute. In 1942 he enrolled at St Michael's College in the University of Toronto in Philosophy (English or History). After passing his first year with first-class honours, he entered St Basil's Novitiate, Toronto, making first profession on 15 August 1944. Upon completing his university course (Honours B.A., 1947, first of firsts), he did his theological studies at St Basil's Seminary, Toronto, 1947–51, while also doing graduate work (M.A., Philosophy, University of Toronto, 1951). He was ordained to the priesthood on 29 June 1950 in St Basil's Church, Toronto, by Cardinal James Charles McGuigan.

Father Sheehan was sent to study medieval history at the Ecole pratique des hautes études, Paris, 1951–3. He returned to Toronto to teach history of the Church and history of art at St Basil's Seminary while continuing graduate studies (M.S.L, Pontifical Institute, 1954, with a thesis, 'The Variations and Significations of English Terms Implying Feudalism'). In 1955 he was transferred to the Institute House, and would remain a member of it the rest of his life, serving as second councillor, 1969–71, 1985–7, first councillor, 1987–92, and treasurer, 1991–2. He taught at the Institute, at the Centre for Medieval Studies of the University of Toronto, and at St Basil's Seminary. In 1962 he was awarded the Institute's rarely granted doctorate in Mediaeval Studies (M.S.D.) for his thesis 'The Last Will in England, from the Conversion to the End of the Thirteenth Century.' He was visiting professor at the University of British Columbia, Vancouver, January–June 1976, and again at the University of St Thomas, Houston, January–May 1991. The year of his death he was designated second vice-president of the Medieval Academy of America, and would have acceded to its presidency in two years.

Michael Sheehan's extensive research into medieval civil and Church court archives made of him a pioneer in the field of women's history and the history of the family, but he never lost his interest in art and archaeology. He put together an extensive collection of colour slides for the Institute library, and he twice went to Turkey to participate in digs. He wrote five books, eighty-three articles and reviews, and served as speaker or panellist at many scholarly conferences. For all his learning and fame, Mike Sheehan dwelt in no ivory tower. He was generous with his time counselling, encouraging, and directing the theses of students. He loved outings, rock collecting, and other activities such as carpentry and gardening.

For the last few years of his life Michael Sheehan was receiving experimental treatment for malignant melanoma, and occasionally experienced brief 'black-outs.' It was perhaps one of the latter which brought about a fall from his bicycle, causing severe head injuries which proved fatal a few hours later.

Two books, containing articles composed by former students and colleagues, appeared in homage after his death: *Wife and Widow in Medieval England*, ed. Sue Sheridan Walker (Ann Arbor, 1993); and *Women, Marriage, and Family in Medieval Christendom: Essays in Memory of Michael M. Sheehan, CSB*, ed. Constance M. Rousseau and Joel T. Rosenthal (Kalamazoo, 1998).

BIBLIOGRAPHY:
Books: *The Will in Medieval England: From the Conversion of the Anglo-Saxons to the End of the Thirteenth Century.* Toronto, 1963. Ed. (with R.W. Keyserlingk) *The Condition of Man.* Montreal, 1965. (With Kathy D. Scardellato) *Family and Marriage in Medieval Europe: A Working Bibliography.* Vancouver, 1976; repr. 1978. Ed. *Aging and the Aged in Medieval Europe.* Toronto, 1990. (With Jacqueline Murray) *Domestic Society in Medieval Europe: A Select Bibliography.* Toronto, 1990. *Marriage, Family, and Law in Medieval Europe. Collected Studies*, ed. James K. Farge CSB. Toronto and Cardiff, 1996; repr. 1997.
Articles: For the Bibliography of his fifty-three articles and thirty book reviews, see *Mediaeval Studies* 55 (1993) xi–xvi.
Other: During six years, 1964–9, he gathered and published a complete bibliography on the Church in Canada for the *CCHA Report* (1964–5) and *CCHA Study Sessions* (1966–9).
SOURCES: GABF; *Annals* 1 (1950) 288, 7 (1993) 136–8; *Newsletter* (11 September 1992); Kirley, *Congregation in France* 212, 231n24, 234, 261; W.H. Principe CSB, 'Michael McMahon Sheehan, CSB, MSD,' *Mediaeval Studies* 55 (1993) vii–xi; idem, 'Introduction,' *Women, Marriage, and Family in Medieval Christendom: Essays in Memory of Michael M. Sheehan CSB*, ed. Constance M. Rousseau and Joel T. Rosenthal (Kalamazoo, 1998) 1–10; J.A. Raftis CSB, 'The Interdisciplinary Context of a Career,' in ibid., 11–16.

SHEEHAN, Paul Thomas, priest, younger brother of Father Peter *Sheehan, was born on 7 March 1931 in St Catharines, Ontario (archdiocese of Toronto, since 1958 of St Catharines), one of the family of six sons and four daughters of Simon Edward Sheehan and Mary Olef Woodcroft. Three sisters, Mary, Antoinette and Theresa, joined the Congregation of Saint Joseph. Paul died at Parry Sound, Ontario, on 4 November 1996 and is buried in the Basilian plot of Holy Cross Cemetery, Thornhill, Ontario.
Paul attended St Mary's Separate School and St Catharines Collegiate Institute in his home town. He enrolled at St Michael's College, Toronto, in grade XIII, 1947, and in first year of arts, 1948. The following

year he entered St Basil's Novitiate, Toronto, making first profession on 15 August 1950. He was appointed to St Michael's College to continue his arts course, 1950–2. In 1952–3, while residing at St Basil's Seminary, he completed his university course (B.A., University of Toronto, 1953), did his first year of theology, and taught part-time at St Michael's College School. He moved back to the seminary while earning teacher certification at the Ontario College of Education, 1953–4, and then moved to St Michael's College School to teach for a year, 1954–5. He completed his theological studies at St Basil's Seminary, 1955–8, continuing to teach part-time at St Michael's. Cardinal James Charles McGuigan ordained him to the priesthood on 29 June 1957 in St Basil's Church, Toronto.

In 1958, and each year for the rest of his life, Father Paul Sheehan was appointed to St Michael's College School. There he developed a unique credit course in construction techniques for students in industrial arts. His method was to train them through the hands-on remodelling of a residence for working women in the heart of the city. He was also head of the physics department at the school, and served as a member of the Science Committee set up by the Ontario Ministry of Education which chose teachers from the primary to the university level to develop a new integrated science curriculum. With the aid of his students Father Sheehan designed, produced, and distributed across the province science equipment at a minimal cost to elementary school science classes. He communicated to many a love for carpentry and construction not simply as skills but as art. He remodelled the student chapel at St Michael's College School, adding a gallery built by himself. Among his other projects is a two-storey, fifty-bed residence at Strawberry Island in Lake Simcoe, Ontario, which he built for the Basilian Fathers during one summer – again aided by a group of his students. This was the building where Pope John Paul II spent his vacation prior to World Youth Day, July 2002.

Though not renowned for music as was his brother Peter, Paul played the piano well and took great pleasure in recalling the popular songs of the 1930s and 1940s. Proud of his origins in a working-class family, he sympathized with the labour movement and with the aspirations of workers. He personally carried meals to the home of a former employee of the college who found herself without sufficient means, and made provisions for the person were he to be absent. His competence in manual arts carried over into his preparation of his homilies, which were always written out for careful delivery.

Paul Sheehan held his opinions strongly, even passionately, especially those concerning the policies, maintenance, and future of St Michael's College School. This caused him a good deal of suffering in his later years when he witnessed decisions and developments which to him seemed inappropriate.

His death at the age of sixty-five was strikingly consistent with his life and character. He had gone to Parry Sound to help with repairs at the summer home of Our Lady's Missionaries. While working on their dock, alone, he suffered a fatal heart attack and died instantly.

BIBLIOGRAPHY: 'Testing,' *Basilian Teacher* 1 (February 1956) 17–18.
SOURCES: GABF; *Annals* 2 (1957) 319, 8 (1997) 116–17; *Newsletter* (22 November 1996).

SHEEHAN, Peter Edward, priest, elder brother of Father Paul *Sheehan, was born on 11 September 1927 in St Catharines, Ontario (archdiocese of Toronto, since 1958 of St Catharines), one of the family of six sons and four daughters of Simon Edward Sheehan and Mary Olef Woodcroft. Three of his sisters, Mary, Antoinette, and Theresa, joined the Congregation of St Joseph. Peter died in Toronto on 26 July 1972 and is buried in the Basilian plot of Holy Cross Cemetery, Thornhill, Ontario.

Peter attended St Mary's Separate School and St Catharines Collegiate Institute in his home town, then in 1943 went to St Michael's College, Toronto, for his final year of high school. The following year he entered St Basil's Novitiate, Toronto, making first profession on 12 September 1945. He studied at the University of Toronto, living for one year at St Michael's College, then for two years at Holy Rosary Seminary, Toronto, returning to St Michael's for his final year (B.A., Honours Music and History, 1949). Still residing at St Michael's he began his theological studies while at the same time studying at the Royal Conservatory of Music, Toronto (A.R.T.C and A.T.C.M. in organ and speech, 1950). He taught a year at St Michael's College School before resuming his theological studies at St Basil's Seminary. He was ordained to the priesthood on 29 June 1953 in St Basil's Church, Toronto, by Cardinal James Charles McGuigan.

In 1954 Father Sheehan was sent to Rome for graduate studies in theology (S.T.D., Angelicum, 1956), submitting a thesis on 'The Realization of the Divine Presence through the Indwelling of the Trinity according to John Henry Cardinal Newman.' In August 1956 he was appointed to St John Fisher College, Rochester. He remained there for eleven years as head of the theology department, and for some years as dean of men. He helped considerably in the design and furnishing of some of the new college buildings. He was active in musical circles in Rochester and served on the executive of the National Association of Theology Teachers.

In 1967 he was asked to take over the direction of the Newman Centre, University of Toronto. He moved easily and successfully into this work, which gave scope for his exceptional talents for friendship and guidance of young people. He was imaginative and zealous in his preaching and in the liturgy, promoting the use of art in the liturgy and striving to make the Centre a focus of an authentic Christian spirit on the campus. He was one of the founding members of the Campus Ministries Foundation, attempting to inaugurate ecumenical co-operation among the various campus ministers.

Peter Sheehan was an accomplished pianist, organist, and composer. At the request of his Basilian superiors, he undertook a new edition of the *Saint Basil Hymnal*, which won accolades for its selections and presentation but which appeared unfortunately just prior to drastic innovations in church music. Gifted with a clever wit and ready sense of humour, his lighthearted approach to life was an asset in his work with the young – an attitude all the more admirable in retrospect, for he was clearly aware that his own life would be short. In 1968, at the age of forty-one, he suffered his first serious heart attack, and death came four years later. He was the only Basilian to die in the year 1972. A commemorative edition of psalms was hand printed in his memory: *XII Psalms in memory of Peter Sheehan*, printed by Nelson Adams (Toronto, 1976).

BIBLIOGRAPHY:
Book: Ed. *The New Saint Basil Hymnal*. Organ and singing editions. Toronto, 1958.
Articles: 'The Clouds Hang Thick o'er St Basil's Camp,' *Basilian Teacher* 2 (October 1957) 3–6; 'Scripture and Our Students [forum],' *Basilian Teacher* 5 (December 1960) 86; 'College's Art Collection,' *Tower Chronicle* (St John Fisher College) 2 no. 3 (May 1966), 1,6; 'St John Fisher College,' *New Catholic Encyclopedia* 12 (New York, 1967) 890–1; 'Can Theology Change?' *Faith Now* (supplement to *Our Sunday Visitor*, September 1968), 3 pp.; 'A Commentary on the Letters of the Basilians from University of St Thomas, April 1971 [and the] Basilian Fathers, Rochester, May 1971 [open letter format]' (Toronto, 26 May

1971); 'Priesthood and Liturgy: On Those Who Would Be Leaders of Common Prayer,' *Living Worship* 9 no. 2 (1973) 1–4.
SOURCES: GABF; *Annals* 2 (1953) 111, 4 (1973) 306–7; *Newsletter* (4 August 1972); Sister Antoinette Sheehan CSJ.

SHEEHAN, William Alexander, priest, younger brother of Father Cornelius *Sheehan, was born in Cleveland, Ohio, on 24 February 1904, the son of John Sheehan and Catherine Ahern. He died in Houston on 10 November 1967 and is buried there in Garden of Gethsemane, Forest Park Lawndale Cemetery.

Bill (sometimes, to his confreres, 'Wild Bill') Sheehan attended Immaculate Conception Parochial School, Cleveland, and then worked for some years before resuming his education in the high school section of Assumption College, Windsor, 1922–6. He entered St Basil's Novitiate, Toronto, in 1926 and was professed on 11 August 1927. He returned to Assumption for undergraduate studies (B.A., Honours Philosophy, University of Western Ontario, 1931). He studied theology at St Basil's Scholasticate, Toronto, 1931–5, also attending the Ontario College of Education, Toronto, 1931–2, and was ordained to the priesthood on 16 December 1934 in Assumption Church, Windsor, by Bishop John Thomas Kidd.

Father Sheehan taught mathematics at Catholic Central High School, Detroit, 1935–7 and 1952–3, and at Aquinas Institute, Rochester, 1937–46, where he also served as treasurer, 1943–6. In 1946 he was moved to St Thomas High School, Houston, and taught mathematics there until a severe heart attack in 1959 forced his retirement. He expressed his views strongly but in a manner that did not offend, and unfailing good humour made him a fine community man.

BIBLIOGRAPHY: 'Is This Group C?,' *Basilian* 1 (June 1935) 77, 79.
SOURCES: GABF; *Annals* 4 (1968) 58–9; *Newsletter* (13 November 1967); *Purple and White* (15 October 1926).

SHEEHY, Fergus Joseph, priest, was born on 26 April 1906 in Peterborough, Ontario, the son of Richard Sheehy and Mary Anne Kelly. He died in Toronto on 20 January 1985 and is buried in the Basilian plot of Holy Cross Cemetery, Thornhill, Ontario.

'Ferg' Sheehy attended the elementary and high school of St Peter's Cathedral in Peterborough. While working for a local construction company rebuilding a church which had burned, the church's pastor,

Father John McAuley, encouraged him to return to school and to think about the priesthood. Following this advice, Ferg completed high school at St Michael's College, Toronto, in 1926, entered St Basil's Novitiate, Toronto, and made first profession on 11 August 1927. He was appointed to St Michael's College, where he lived for two years doing undergraduate studies. In 1929 he moved to St Basil's Scholasticate, Toronto, completed his undergraduate work (B.A., University of Toronto, 1932), and began his theological studies. In 1933 he obtained teacher certification from the Ontario College of Education and was ordained to the priesthood on 21 December 1935 in St Basil's Church, Toronto, by Archbishop James Charles McGuigan.

Father Sheehy began a thirty-eight-year career in the high school apostolate at Assumption College School in 1936. Two years later he was moved to Aquinas Institute, Rochester, where he served for thirteen years, the last four as principal of the Aquinas Annex. In 1950 he returned to Toronto for one year of teaching at St Michael's College School, after which he went to teach at St Thomas High School, Houston, where he also earned Texas teaching certification, and served as moderator of scholastics during the last five years. In 1961 he was appointed superior of the community at Aquinas Institute and was principal of the school, 1961–4. In 1967 he returned to Assumption to teach until retirement in 1974.

In the fall of 1982, faulty circulation necessitated amputation of a leg, and he moved to the Basilian Fathers Residence (Infirmary), Toronto, where he remained until his death two years later.

Ferg Sheehy was a patient and compassionate man who loved the give and take of community life. He had a passion for sports, having been an outstanding football player in his younger days. Later, when retired and infirm, he took pleasure from sports events on the radio and television.

SOURCES: GABF; *Annals* 5 (1978) 270, 6 (1986) 472–3; *Newsletter* (25 January 1985).

SHEEHY, John Dennis, priest, was born in St Louis, Missouri, on 14 April 1908, the son of John M. Sheehy and Margaret Fitzgibbons. He died in Houston on 25 January 1967 and is buried there in the Basilian plot of Garden of Gethsemane, Forest Park Lawndale Cemetery. Growing up in Detroit, John Sheehy attended Blessed Sacrament Parochial School, then high school at Assumption College, 1922–6. A letter from his mother to Father Daniel *Dillon provides a picture of the family's financial straits, and another letter reveals a poor showing in an examination. After one year of arts at Assumption John entered St Basil's Novitiate, Toronto, and was professed on 15 August 1929. He returned to Assumption to complete his university studies (B.A., University of Western Ontario, 1932). He attended the Ontario College of Education, Toronto, 1932–3, then taught for one year at Holy Names Institute, Detroit, a school later absorbed into Catholic Central High School. He studied theology at St Basil's Scholasticate in Toronto and was ordained priest on 19 December 1936 in St Basil's Church, Toronto, by Archbishop James Charles McGuigan.

Father Sheehy taught at St Thomas High School, Houston (January–June 1937), then moved to Aquinas Institute, Rochester, 1937–8. He began a long appointment at Catholic Central High School, 1938–52, where he was superior and principal from 1946 to 1952. At the same time he studied history and pedagogy at the University of Michigan, taking an M.A. in education in 1952. In the office of principal, Father Sheehy was an organizer who knew how to pick the right persons to carry out his ideas. He built the main wing of the new Catholic Central High School plant in 1950–1. For several years he wrote a daily religious bulletin for the students.

In 1952 Father Sheehy was appointed to the University of St Thomas, Houston, where he taught both educational theory and United States history. He was an imaginative teacher who made the subject come alive by relating it to current events. In history he insisted that students write papers using primary sources. The Piper Foundation selected him in 1964 as one of the ten outstanding professors in the State of Texas.

Among confreres and students Father John Sheehy stood out for his height – he was six foot six – and for his gifts as a jovial conversationalist. His death from a brain tumour was the first of three Basilian deaths at the University of St Thomas that year (Fathers Leslie *Vasek and Edward *Sullivan followed him) – losses which constituted a serious blow to the university.

BIBLIOGRAPHY: 'The Breviary,' *Basilian* 1 (December 1935) 130; 'Virgo sacerdos,' *Basilian* 2 (April 1936) 73–4; 'Our Lady of Good Counsel,' *Basilian* 3 (January 1937) 15; 'Educational Guidance,' *Benedicamus* 1 (April 1948) 2–3; Power, *Assumption College* 5 196–202.
SOURCES: GABF; *Annals* 4 (1968) 59–60; *Newsletter* (26 January 1967).

SHERIDAN, John Joseph, priest, member of the Congregation 1910–23, was born at Brechin, Ontario (archdiocese of Toronto), on 4 August 1886 (or 1888; the documents vary), the son of James Sheridan and Bridget Gaughan. He died in Montreal, Quebec, on 3 March 1943, and was buried in the Basilian plot, Mount Hope Cemetery, Toronto.

After attending local schools, John went to St Michael's College, Toronto, to take a commercial course, 1903–4. In 1905 he returned to St Michael's to enrol in the high school course, and proved to be a brilliant student. He enrolled in 1908 in the university class of 1912, but in January 1910 withdrew from the University of Toronto to teach at Assumption College, Windsor. That summer he entered St Basil's Novitiate, Toronto, and was professed on 15 August 1911. He resumed his university studies while taking theology at St Basil's Scholasticate, Toronto, and graduated in 1915. He was ordained to the priesthood on 26 September 1915 by Archbishop Neil McNeil at St Basil's Church, Toronto.

Father 'Jack' Sheridan taught first at St Thomas College, Chatham, New Brunswick, 1915–16. In 1916 he went to the Catholic University of America, Washington, D.C. (M.A., 1917). He taught at St Michael's College, 1917–19, and Assumption College, 1919–21, returning there briefly after the year 1921–2 as assistant at St John the Baptist Parish, Amherstburg, Ontario. He was one of four Basilians at Assumption who exercised the canonical option of withdrawing from the Congregation when the new, stricter vow of poverty was adopted in 1922, and he was incardinated in the archdiocese of Detroit on 26 February 1923. After serving in a number of parishes there, among them St Catherine's, and serving as chaplain of St Joseph's Mercy Hospital, Ann Arbor, Michigan, 1930, he received permission on 24 January 1939 from his bishop to reside with the Basilians at Catholic Central High School, Detroit. At the invitation of Father Edmund *McCorkell, he returned to St Michael's College to teach – a move he termed 'my long cherished and prayerful desire.' Some months later he went on sick leave to St Mary's of the Assumption Parish, Owen Sound, Ontario. In January 1941, while residing at St Gregory's Parish, Oshawa, Ontario, where he was living while attending his dying mother, he requested a letter from the Detroit chancery in order to return to the United States. His own health did not improve, and he entered La Retraite Saint-Benoît in Montreal, where he experienced a fatal heart attack.

sources: GABF; *Annals* 1 (1943) 32; Archives, Archdiocese of Detroit.

SHOOK, Laurence Kennedy, priest, was born on 6 November 1909 in Toronto, the son of Richard Conrad Shook and Mary Kennedy. He died in Toronto on 23 October 1993 and is buried in the Basilian plot of Holy Cross Cemetery, Thornhill, Ontario.

'Larry' Shook attended three parochial schools in Toronto – St Clare's, St James's, and St Cecilia's and then undertook the high school courses at St Michael's College, Toronto, 1922–6. He entered St Basil's Novitiate, Toronto, making first profession of vows on 30 September 1927. For the next nine years he lived at St Basil's Scholasticate, Toronto, during which time he completed grade XIII, did Honours English and History (B.A., University of Toronto, 1932), and studied theology while also completing an M.A. in philosophy at the University of Toronto, 1933. He was ordained to the priesthood on 21 December 1935 in St Basil's Church, Toronto, by Archbishop James Charles McGuigan.

In 1936 Father Shook was sent on graduate studies to Harvard University (A.M., 1937, Ph.D., English Philology, 1940). He was appointed to St Michael's College, Toronto, in 1940 to begin thirty-five years teaching in the department of English, serving as head of the department, 1942–61. During the early 1940s he did part-time chaplaincy for the Royal Canadian Air Force. Though much devoted to reading and study, he enjoyed but one year of formal studies after 1940, with a sabbatical in Paris, 1948–9. During that year he was asked by the superior general of the time, Father Edmund *McCorkell, to attend the golden jubilee of Father Octave *Descellière, the superior of the French Basilians in Annonay, the cradle of the Basilian Congregation (see 'Letter from Annonay,' *Annals* 1 [1949] 244–8). This was the beginning of the process of reunion of the French Basilians with the Basilian Congregation in North America, which took place formally in September 1955.

Father Shook served as second councillor for the Basilian community at St Michael's, 1949–50, as first councillor, 1950–2, and as superior and president of the college, 1952–8. His last academic appointment was to the Pontifical Institute of Mediaeval Studies, where he taught and served as first councillor, 1958–61, 1968–71, and *praeses* (president), 1961–71.

Laurence Shook was a scholar, a dynamic teacher, an educator in the fullest sense, and an able administrator. In a radio lecture in 1952 he stated, 'No man is completely alive until he is in possession of knowledge, and has learned to think. In this sense, it is education which gives life; and it is higher education which makes possible a full and complete life.' That same year, the centennial year of St Michael's College, he carried through the integration of St Michael's, St Joseph's, and Loretto Colleges into one cohesive institution under a centralized administration. In 1954 he initiated provincial legislation amending the century-old College Act to enable the conferring of civil degrees in theology. He was the moving force behind another act in 1958 which conferred university status on St Michael's College. As *praeses* of the Pontifical Institute he was instrumental in setting up the Mediaeval Studies Foundation to put the Institute on a viable financial basis, and he worked with the University of Toronto to establish its own Centre for Mediaeval Studies, working out a collaboration between it and the Pontifical Institute.

In 1965 the bishops of Canada invited Father Shook to serve as a *peritus* at the final session of the Second Vatican Council. In this role he organized the 'International Congress on the Theology of Renewal in the Church' which the bishops sponsored as their contribution to the celebration of the Canadian centennial in 1967. Leading theologians from all parts of the world gathered with 2200 participants. Father Shook then edited (in English and in French) the two-volume proceedings of the congress.

In the course of his career as administrator and scholar he held membership in the Senate of the University of Toronto, the National Conference of Canadian Universities, the Association of British Universities, and the Association of Catholic Universities and Colleges. In 1977 the University of Toronto conferred a D.Litt. and the University of Michigan conferred a Ph.D. *honoris causa*. He was named a Fellow of the Mediaeval Academy of America, and served twice as its president. He became an Officer of the Order of Canada, 1975, and received a Doctorate of Sacred Letters, *honoris causa*, from St Michael's College, 1980. To recognize his contributions, the Pontifical Institute named its Common Room in memory of him in 2001.

Father Shook remained intellectually active and occupied into his eighties. During his later years he preferred living and working in the country property of St Michael's, 'Hockley Hall,' Orangeville, Ontario, where he welcomed the visits of confreres and friends.

BIBLIOGRAPHY:
Books: Trans. Etienne Gilson. *The Christian Philosophy of St Thomas Aquinas.*

New York, 1956. Trans. Etienne Gilson. *Heloise and Abelard.* Chicago, 1951; repr. Ann Arbor, Mich. and Toronto, 1960. Ed. *Theology of Renewal. Proceedings of the Congress on the Theology of the Renewal of the Church.* 2 vols. Montreal and New York, 1968. French ed. (with Guy-M. Bertrand). *La théologie du renouveau.* 2 vols. Montreal, 1968. *Catholic Post-Secondary Education in English-Speaking Canada: A History.* Toronto, 1971. *Etienne Gilson.* Toronto, 1984; Italian trans. Maria Stefania Rossi. Milan, 1991.

Articles: For forty-two of his articles and chapters in books see *Mediaeval Studies* 56 (1994) x–xii. The following do not appear there: 'Reverence and Fear,' *Basilian* 1 (March 1935) 18; 'Thoughts on Faith,' *Basilian* 1 (April 1935) 33; 'She's Probably Right,' *Basilian* 4 (May 1938) 35–7; 'Personal Prayer,' *Basilian* 12 (1968) 244; 'In His Image: Etienne Gilson,' *CCR* 2 (1984) 455–6; 'The Pontifical Institute of Mediaeval Studies,' in *Were the Dean's Windows Dusty?*, ed. Gerard Mulligan (Montreal 1966) 1 T1–T31.

SOURCES: GABF; *Annals* 5 (1978) 270, 6 (1986) 397, 8 (1994) 142–4; *Newsletter* (30 November 1993); James K. Farge, Laurence Kennedy Shook, CSB,' *Mediaeval Studies* 56 (1994) vii–xii; Kirley, *Congregation in France* 201–2, 230, 231n24, 235, 261.

SILVESTER, George Ernest Joseph, priest, was born in Toronto on 7 August 1920, the son of George Ernest Silvester and Elesha Eleanor O'Connor. He died in Toronto on 15 October 2001 and is buried in the Basilian plot of Holy Cross Cemetery, Thornhill, Ontario.

George attended De La Salle, Oaklands, in Toronto. He enrolled in St Michael's College in 1937 for university studies (B.A., University of Toronto, 1940) and entered St Basil's Novitiate, Toronto, making first profession on 15 August 1941. He was assigned to St Basil's Seminary, Toronto, for his theology courses, 1941–2, 1943–7, and for classes at the Ontario College of Education, 1942–3. He was ordained to the priesthood on 15 August 1946 in St Basil's Church, Toronto, by Cardinal James Charles McGuigan.

Father Silvester spent the first twelve years of his priestly life teaching in three Basilian schools: St Thomas High School, Houston, 1947–50, Aquinas Institute, Rochester, 1950–2, and St Charles College, Sudbury, Ontario, 1952–9. From then on he worked in six Basilian parishes: St Basil's, Ottawa, 1959–63, 1964–70, Holy Rosary, Toronto, 1963–4, 1971–3, 1980–6, St Pius X, Calgary, 1973–80, St Augustine's, Saskatoon, 1986–92, St John Fisher, Richmond, Texas, 1992–3, and St Theresa's, Sugar Land, Texas, 1993–2001. A sabbatical leave in 1970–1 was spent taking classes in pastoral spirituality in Louvain. He was imaginative in his methods and worked with enthusiasm and a ready sense of humour. He is remembered especially for his vivid homilies. He could deal with all classes and kinds, from the underprivileged children at Columbus Boys Camp, Orillia, Ontario, to well-educated parish congregations, to Latino immigrants in Texas. In later years various illnesses cramped his activity but not his spirit, and made it necessary for him to take up residence at Anglin House (the Basilian infirmary), Toronto, in 2001. At the end he spent three months in Mount Sinai Hospital, Toronto, and a few weeks at Providence Centre, Toronto, where he died.

BIBLIOGRAPHY: 'Come Follow Us,' *Benedicamus* 2 (May 1949) 36–7; 'Communications and Education [forum],' *Basilian Teacher* 3 (May 1959) 222; 'Catechetics ... Is Surely Our Area,' *Forum* 3 (1967) 39.
SOURCES: GABF; *Annals* 1 (1946) 120, 7 (1992) 12, 8 (1997) 6–7, 10 (2002) 94; *Newsletter* (24 October 2001).

SLATTERY, Thomas, priest, member of the Congregation 1932–50, was born on 11 August 1911 in Syracuse, New York, the son of John Slattery and Florence McCarthy. He died in Dallas, Texas, on 18 October 1978, and is buried there in Calvary Hill Cemetery.

Tom Slattery attended Most Holy Rosary High School, Syracuse, 1925–9. After two years, 1929–31, at St Michael's College, Toronto, he entered the Basilian novitiate and made first profession of vows on 15 August 1932. After finishing his arts course at St Michael's (B.A., University of Toronto, 1935), he taught in the high school section of St Michael's College, 1935–6, and at Catholic Central High School, Detroit, 1936–7. During this latter year he also took courses in education at the University of Detroit, and completed the work for a Michigan teaching certification in two summers, 1937 at Wayne State University, Detroit, and 1940 at the University of Detroit. His theological training took place in Toronto, 1937–9, during which time he also taught part-time at St Michael's College School. He was ordained to the priesthood in St Basil's Church, Toronto, by Archbishop James Charles McGuigan on 17 December 1938.

Father Slattery was appointed to teach at Catholic Central High School, 1939–42, and then at Aquinas Institute, Rochester, 1942–50. He withdrew from the Congregation and changed his name legally in Texas to Frank J. O'Leary. He married Dorothy Ann Murphy and had four children (Dorothy Ann, Margaret, and twin sons Thomas and

John). He lived in Dallas, Texas, near another former Basilian, Paul *Petrey, who had married the sister of his wife. They were visited frequently by Fathers Art *O'Leary and Charles *Lyons. In 1966 the Holy See dispensed him from the canonical obligations of the priesthood and religious life, and his marriage was validated in the Church. He was buried from his parish church of St Pius X, Dallas.

SOURCES: GABF; *Annals* 1943–50; John O'Leary.

SMITH, Charles Casper, priest, was born on 29 January 1933 at Centerline, Michigan, the son of Herbert Smith and Elizabeth de Smet. He died in Farmington Hills, Michigan on 21 September 2002 and is buried in Holy Sepulcher Cemetery, Southfield, Michigan.

'Charlie' Smith attended Holy Name School, Detroit, 1938–46, then Catholic Central High School, Detroit, 1946–50. He entered St Basil's Novitiate, Rochester, making first profession on 15 August 1951. His undergraduate studies were taken in Toronto, 1951–5, where he lived for one year at St Basil's Seminary and for three years at St Michael's College (B.A., University of Toronto, 1955). There followed two years of teaching, one at St Thomas High School, Houston, and the second at Catholic Central. He returned to St Basil's Seminary for theology, 1957–61, being ordained to the priesthood by Cardinal James Charles McGuigan on 29 June 1960 in St Basil's Church, Toronto.

Father Smith was appointed to Andrean High School, Gary (now Merrillville), Indiana, where he remained for fourteen years, teaching English and Latin. In 1966 he obtained an M.A. in English from the University of Detroit. In 1975 he was appointed to return to St Thomas High School, where he taught until 1987. In that year he requested a change of apostolate, and was accordingly appointed to Holy Rosary Parish, Toronto, as assistant pastor. During his final year there he served as acting pastor. In 1993 he returned to Catholic Central, where he worked chiefly in the treasurer's office.

Charlie Smith was retiring, though not unsocial. As a teacher he was methodical, demanding of his students and unsparing of himself. In his priestly ministry in schools and parishes his homilies were notable for their careful preparation and clear delivery. A lover of things small and beautiful, he was an inveterate collector – mostly from church bazaars and yard sales. His annual Christmas tree was a magnificent display of ornaments, the provenance and value of which he delighted to explain. He had a strong devotion to the Mother of God, making at one time a European trip consisting exclusively of pilgrimages to various Marian shrines. He visited Lourdes more than once. It is not accidental that his memorial card bears a copy of the 'Virgin of the Nativity' by Fra Filippo Lippi.

In 1981 Charles had quadruple bypass surgery, and in 1994 he underwent radiation therapy for prostate cancer. He faced with equanimity the possibility of an imminent death. Entering the hospital on a Friday afternoon for prescribed tests, he suffered a heart attack the next morning and died on Sunday.

SOURCES: GABF; *Newsletter* (30 September 2002).

SOLEILHAC, Jean-Baptiste, priest, elder brother of Father Jean-Louis *Soleilhac, was born on 21 January 1848 at Alleyrac (Drôme, diocese of Valence). He died on 30 March 1920 and was buried in the canton of Monastier (Haute-Loire).

Jean-Baptiste did his secondary and theological studies in his native diocese. He made his novitiate at Feyzin (Isère, now Rhône), 1872–3. He taught at the Ecole cléricale de Périgueux (Dordogne), 1873–4, and at the Collège du Sacré-Coeur, Annonay, 1874–6. Bishop Joseph-Michel-Frédéric Bonnet of Viviers ordained him a priest on 23 September 1876 in the chapel of the Collège du Sacré-Coeur.

Father Soleilhac taught at the Petit Séminaire d'Aubenas (Ardèche) for three years and for one year at the Ecole cléricale de Périgueux. In 1880 he returned for a year to the college in Annonay.

In 1881 he spent a year of study in Paris at the Institut catholique. Subsequent appointments were to the Ecole cléricale de Périgueux, 1882–4; a brief stay in Paris; Beaconfield House, Plymouth, England, 1885–90, as assistant novice master; the Collège Saint-Augustin, Bône, Algeria, 1890–1; and the Collège du Sacré-Coeur, 1891–1903. In Annonay he also taught at the scholasticate and the novitiate and served as chaplain to the Ursuline sisters. With the 1903 implementation of government laws excluding members of congregations from teaching, he returned to Alleyrac, where he exercised his priestly ministry until his death at the age of seventy-two.

SOURCES: GABF; Kirley, *Community in France* 184, 210; Pouzol, 'Notices.'

SOLEILHAC, Jean Louis, priest, younger brother of Father Jean-Baptiste *Soleilhac, was born on 11 March 1861 at Alleyrac (Drôme,

diocese of Valence). He died on 31 January 1948 at Saint-Etienne.
Louis Soleilhac was a student at the Collège du Sacré-Coeur, Annonay, Sainte-Barbe section, 1879–82. From 1883 to 1885 he served as prefect at the Collège Saint-Charles, Blidah, Algeria. After a novitiate year at Beaconfield House, Plymouth, England, 1885–6, he did some teaching and theological studies at the Collège Saint-Augustin, Bône, Algeria, 1886–9. He was ordained to the priesthood on 21 September 1889 in the chapel of the Collège du Sacré-Coeur by Bishop Joseph-Michel-Frédéric Bonnet of Viviers.

Father Soleilhac then served for three years in Bône and for six years in Blidah. After a year at the Ecole cléricale de Périgueux he spent four years at the Collège du Sacré-Coeur. With application of the laws excluding religious from teaching, he returned to the Loire *département*, where he did various ministries, among them teaching at the Institution Sainte-Marie, Saint-Chamond, and chaplaincy at Saint-Etienne. He made the annual retreat in Annonay and frequently visited the confreres at Maison Saint-Joseph there. He was a delegate to the general chapter of 1938.

SOURCES: GABF; Kirley, *Community in France* 184, 210, 240n569; Kirley, *Congregation in France* 156, 184, 215; Pouzol, 'Notices.'

SOSULSKI, Michael Carl, priest, member of the Congregation 1955–c.1967, was born in Weyburn, Saskatchewan (archdiocese of Regina) on 10 February 1928, the son of John Sosulski and Marie Jenny. He died at Winfield, Illinois, on 20 September 1994. He was cremated at River Hills Crematory, Batavia, Illinois.

Michael attended Weyburn Collegiate in his home town in 1941–5, and then attended Teachers' College in Moose Jaw, Saskatchewan. Later he enrolled at the University of Saskatchewan, Saskatoon, where he obtained a B.Ed. in 1952, an M.Ed. in 1954. His thesis was 'A Comparison of the Performance of Matched Pairs of Old-Dull and Young-Bright Children on Some Items of the Wechsler Intelligence Scale for Children.' During those studies he acquired teaching experience in Saskatchewan and Alberta. He entered St Basil's Novitiate, Richmond Hill, Ontario, made his first profession on 12 September 1955, and studied philosophy and theology at St Basil's Seminary, 1955–60. He obtained an S.T.B. from the University of St Michael's College in 1958 and was ordained to the priesthood by Bishop Francis Allen on 28 June 1959.

In 1960–1 Father Sosulski did graduate studies at Assumption University of Windsor (M.A., 1961). He taught educational psychology at

St John Fisher College, Rochester, 1961–6. From June to August 1966 he was treasurer at St Joseph's College, Edmonton, Alberta, but then withdrew from the Congregation. In 1970 he settled in DuPage County, Illinois, where he was professor of psychology in the College of DuPage and, at the time of his death, acting dean of social and behavioral sciences. He was survived by his wife, Mary Regina, and four children, Michael, John, Carla, and Marya.

BIBLIOGRAPHY: 'A Basilian Way,' *Basilian Teacher* 1 (November 1956) 20–2; 'Do Your Tests Test?' *Basilian Teacher* 4 (April 1960) 217–23.
SOURCE: GABF; *Annals* 2 (1959) 421.

SOULERIN, Jean Mathieu (Matthieu), priest, founding superior of St Michael's College, Toronto (1852), fourth superior general, 1865–79, was born at Ailhon (Ardèche, diocese of Mende, since 1822 of Viviers), on 5 or 6 June 1807, the son of Matthieu Soulerin and Marie Pigeyre. He died in Annonay on 17 October 1879 and was buried there in the cemetery on the grounds of the Collège du Sacré-Coeur.

At the age of five, Jean Mathieu Soulerin was enrolled in the Sainte-Claire section of the Collège des Cordeliers, Annonay, by his maternal relative Father Pierre *Tourvieille. He made a brilliant course, obtaining a *baccalauréat ès lettres* and a *baccalauréat ès sciences*. He taught philosophy at the Collège des Cordeliers, 1827–8, and then at the Grand Séminaire de Grenoble, 1828–30. He probably entered the Basilian community in 1830, and taught Greek that year at the Collège des Cordeliers. He worked five years at the Collège de Feyzin under the direction of Father Julien *Actorie, and was ordained to the priesthood on 20 December 1834.

In 1836 he went to Paris for advanced studies but did not complete the *licence*. From 1837 to 1841 he was once again at Feyzin, and the following year went to teach history at the Grande-Sauve (Gironde), archdiocese of Bordeaux, on loan to Archbishop François Donnet, who was a former student in Annonay. From 1842 to 1852 Father Soulerin was at the Collège des Cordeliers as director of studies.

Father Soulerin had been elected to the general council in 1844 and re-elected in 1847 and 1850. Father Tourvieille looked upon him as his successor in the office of superior general. But in 1850, at the request of Armand de Charbonnel, a former student at the Collège des Cordeliers who had been named bishop of Toronto, Canada, the Basilians sent Father Patrick Molony, an Irishman, to help him look after the three thousand Irish Catholics among Toronto's population of thirty thousand. Two years later the Congregation complied with Charbonnel's request to staff a school in Toronto, and on 25 July 1852 Father Soulerin was named its superior. Also appointed to the new foundation were Father Joseph *Malbos and a young scholastic, Charles *Vincent. As neither was English-speaking, they joined William *Flannery, an Irish Basilian scholastic, at Le Havre and embarked for Canada on 4 August 1852. On 15 September 1852 they opened the minor seminary of St Mary in the episcopal residence in Toronto with twenty-one students. Among them were Michael *Ferguson, who would be the first Basilian priest ordained in Canada, and Denis *O'Connor, who later became bishop of London, Ontario, and archbishop of Toronto. Father Soulerin took the new Basilian vows on 20 November 1852, with Bishop Charbonnel presiding, and the following day Father Malbos took his vows, with Father Soulerin presiding.

The Christian Brothers had already begun a Catholic school in Toronto named St Michael's. In 1853, because of small enrolments, St Michael's school and St Mary's minor seminary merged to form one institution under the direction of the Basilians, with the name of the former (because of its proximity to St Michael's Cathedral). As the temporary quarters were not suitable, Captain John Elmsley donated in 1854 a generous property on Clover Hill, north of the city and to the east of the University of Toronto, and the Basilians purchased some adjacent lots. Construction began on a new college and a new St Basil's Church, and both were opened in September 1856. Father Soulerin was named pastor of the church and superior of the college.

To meet other needs of the local church, Soulerin accepted the care of St John's Parish, Weston, Ontario, in 1853; and in 1863 he sent priests to take charge of St Mary's of the Assumption Parish, Owen Sound, Ontario, and its mission chapels. When, in 1856, Bishop Charbonnel went on a two-year *ad limina* visit to Rome, he named Father Soulerin as administrator of the diocese. He also served as master of novices in Canada in 1856, 1858, 1859, and 1860.

Father Soulerin persuaded Bishop Charbonnel and the superior general, Father Tourvieille, to broaden the scope of St Michael's to include not only candidates for the priesthood but also young men preparing for the professions and commerce. He would later make innovations in policy and curriculum in Annonay, and in both places he made provision for good athletic programs.

On 10 January 1865, Father Soulerin was elected superior general, and returned to France the following June. During his fourteen years in office he fostered a notable expansion of the Congregation. In Annonay, on 6 September 1867, he moved the Collège des Cordeliers from the centre of the town to a building on the Colline Saint-Denis formerly used by the Religieuses du Sacré-Coeur. The college took as its new name Collège du Sacré-Coeur. On 11 November 1869 the remains of the confreres buried in the Cimetière Saint-Jacques, Annonay, were reinterred in a new cemetery created on the grounds of the college.

Under Soulerin's rule there was an increase in the exchange of members between France and Canada, and he took on a number of new commitments: the Ecole cléricale de Périgueux (Dordogne), 1866; St Louis College, Louisville, Ohio, 1866; the Collège Saint-Charles, Blidah, Algeria, 1868; Assumption College, Sandwich (now Windsor), Ontario, 1870; the college at Bourg-Saint-Andéol, 1871; St Joseph's Parish, Chatham, Ontario, 1873, which five years later would be exchanged for St John the Baptist Parish, Amherstburg, Ontario; and the college Saint-Pierre at Châteauroux (Indre), diocese of Bourges, 1875.

Jean Mathieu Soulerin died at the age of seventy-two. As a founder in Canada and as an administrator in France, he had displayed a remarkable equanimity. Neither success nor failure seemed to make any difference to him. He was a calm and reserved person, warm-hearted but not expansive. Father Robert *McBrady described Father Soulerin as 'a good man and a good scholar and in some respects quite brilliant. He formed quite a friendship with Dr McCaul, the President of the University of Toronto' – although the latter was known to regret that Soulerin 'had not a more progressive religion.' He was not a man who sought friendships, but he made them nonetheless: Bishop John Farrell of Hamilton and Bishop Joseph Guigues OMI of Ottawa were not only friends but also sought his advice. Bishops John Lynch of Toronto and Adolphe Pinsonneault of London appointed him vicar general, as did later the bishop of Viviers.

As superior general Father Soulerin took up the work of revising the Constitutions begun by Father Julien *Actorie. In 1878 he published a French text to which he added Father Actorie's circular letter of 26 January 1863, a letter of his own dated 11 May 1873, and a Litany of St Basil in Latin. An English translation of Father Soulerin's letter was published in the *Basilian Vademecum* edited by Father M.V. *Kelly (Toronto, 1931, pp. 106–14). The *Golden Jubilee Volume of the Archdiocese of*

Toronto noted of Father Soulerin: 'His extensive learning, his deep humility and simple piety won for him the esteem and confidence of his equals, the love and respect of all his confreres and students.' In the year 2000 the retirement house at St Michael's College School, Toronto, was named 'Soulerin House' in memory of him.

BIBLIOGRAPHY:
Book: *Constitutions de la Congrégation de Saint-Basile.* Lyon, 1878.
Article: 'Missions du Canada,' *Annales de la propagation de la foi* (Lyon) 28 (April 1856) 308–19.
SOURCES: GABF; J.F. Boland: 'Father Soulerin, Founder and Administrator,' *CCHA Report* 23 (1956) 13–27; L.D. Burns, *Father Jean Soulerin*, unpublished manuscript (1964); Chomel, *Collège d'Annonay* 199, 483–517; Kirley, *Community in France* 259 and passim; Kirley, *Congregation in France* 1, 45, 84, 234, 243–4; *New Catholic Encyclopedia* (New York, 1967) 13, 474; Robert McBrady, 'Reminiscences,' *Basilian* 1 (April 1935) 23–4; Pouzol, 'Notices'; Roume, *Origines* 327–40, 347; R.J. Scollard, *Dictionary of Canadian Biography* 10 662–3; L.K. Shook: 'The Coming of the Basilians to Assumption College, Early Expansion of St Michael's College,' *CCHA Report* 18 (1951) 59–73; Shook, *Catholic Education* 129–38. John Read Teefy, *Jubilee Volume 1842–1892 of the Archdiocese of Toronto* (Toronto, 1892). For documentation relating to his connections with the opening of Assumption College, Windsor, see Power, *Assumption College* 1 42–70 and passim.

SPECK, Paul Stanley, priest, member of the Congregation 1953–66, was born on 22 July 1931 at St Catharines, Ontario (diocese of Hamilton, since 1958 of St Catharines), one of twelve children of Ernest Speck and Irene Smith and a cousin of former Basilian Neil Smith. He died in Toronto 22 June 1993. His remains were cremated.
Paul attended Notre Dame High School, Welland, Ontario, 1947–51, and did grade XIII at St Michael's College School, Toronto, 1951–2. He entered St Basil's Novitiate, Richmond Hill, Ontario, and made first profession on 15 August 1953. After his arts course at Assumption College, Windsor (B.A., University of Western Ontario, 1956), he taught at Assumption High School, Windsor, 1956–8, and then studied theology at St Basil's Seminary, Toronto, 1958–62, obtaining an S.T.B. from the University of St Michael's College in 1961. He was ordained to the priesthood, one year later than his classmates, by Archbishop Philip Pocock on 17 June 1962 at the Jesuit seminary, Toronto.
Father Speck taught English literature at Michael Power High

School, Etobicoke, Ontario, 1962 to 1965. In this latter year he began graduate studies in English at Fordham University. In 1966 he withdrew from the Congregation and from the Church.

For many years Paul was owner and headmaster of the Annex Village Campus, a small 'alternative' high school in Toronto. He also acquired the Henry of Pelham Family Estate Winery and other properties in the Niagara Peninsula. During this time he distressed his many friends by publishing newspaper articles which were highly critical of the Church, the priesthood, and the Basilian Fathers. In 1992, however, he sought and obtained canonical laicization from the Holy See and was reconciled to the Church. At his death, the result of cancer, he was survived by his wife, Barbara Schroetter, and by his sons Paul, Matthew, and Daniel.

BIBLIOGRAPHY: In *Basilian Teacher:* 'New Trends and New Emphasis in English,' 6 (December 1961) 114; 'The Gladly Dead,' 8 (December 1963) 106–13; 'The Night of the Iguana,' 9 (December 1964) 147–50; 'Curiosity in Hamlet,' 9 (January 1965) 181–6; 'Fortune in King Lear,' 9 (February 1965) 244–9.
SOURCES: GABF; *Annals* 3 (1962) 141; 'Confessions of an Ex-Priest,' *Globe and Mail, Weekend Magazine* (3 March 1979) 10; 'The Ex-Believer,' *Toronto Star* (4 February 1990) D1.

SPRATT, John Cantius, priest, was born on 20 October 1890 in Lindsay, Ontario (diocese of Peterborough), the son of Richard Patrick Spratt and Mary Podser. He died in Toronto on 2 June 1981 and is buried in the Basilian plot of Holy Cross Cemetery, Thornhill, Ontario.

'Jack' Spratt attended St Dominic Separate School, Lindsay, and Lindsay Collegiate Institute, before transferring to St Michael's College, Toronto. Though small in stature he was a superb athlete. In 1911 he played hockey with St Michael's Senior O.H.A. team. When the team played in New York, the *New York Globe* described him as 'the particular bright star on the Canadian team.' When in Boston, on that same trip, the team won again. He received the most valuable player award, and the St Michael's team was declared 'Amateur Champs of America and the World.' After these exciting days at St Michael's, he continued his education at Assumption College, Windsor (B.A., 1914). Prior to joining the Basilians he taught with them in 1914–15 at St Basil's College, Waco, Texas. In the annual baseball game against the local Baptist Baylor University, his pitching and a few fluke hits allowed St Basil's its first and only victory over Baylor. In 1915 he entered St Basil's Novitiate, Toronto, and was professed on 17 September 1916. After theological studies at St Basil's Scholasticate, which was moved to Windsor in 1918, he was ordained to the priesthood on 29 February 1920 in St Peter's Cathedral, London, Ontario, by Bishop Michael Fallon.

Father Spratt's first appointment was to teach at St Thomas College, Chatham, New Brunswick, where he spent only one year. With Father William *Roach's support, he laid a strong foundation for the Chatham hockey team. In 1921 he was appointed to Assumption College, Windsor, where he continued his involvement in sports. As coach and captain of the college hockey team, he scored both goals in the victory over the University of Michigan in Ann Arbor, January 1925. Later that year he was appointed to St Thomas High School, Houston, and in the latter part of 1926 to St Mary's of the Assumption Parish, Owen Sound, Ontario. The local hockey team there was badly in need of a coach. In one year he fashioned a team which won the Memorial Cup and the Canadian Championship, and Father Spratt became the town hero. For the next ten years, 1927–37, he alternated between Assumption and St Michael's, spending a total of six years in the former and four in the latter. In 1937 he returned to St Mary's in Owen Sound for a period of three years and was then appointed to St John the Baptist Parish, Amherstburg, Ontario, where he served for eight years, the last seven as local councillor. In 1948 he was appointed to Aquinas Institute, Rochester, where he remained for twenty-six years as teacher, coach, and director of the physical education program. At the age of seventy-five, on the point of retiring, he introduced hockey to Aquinas and was also instrumental in doing the same for St John Fisher College, Rochester. Though he retired officially in 1965 he stayed at Aquinas until 1974, when he moved to the Basilian Fathers Residence (Infirmary) in Toronto, taking on the role of chief raconteur. Visitors were entertained by Peter, his small parakeet, which had learned phrases voiced in the inimitable intonation of Jack Spratt himself.

Father Spratt had a genius for friendship, and the ill-treated and misunderstood found in him compassion and encouragement. From his youth he loved nature, the outdoors, the rustic, and the peaceful.

SOURCES: GABF; *Annals* 3 (1966) 456, 4 (1971) 184–5, 5 (1981) 526–7, 6 (1982) 88–90; *Newsletter* (18 June 1981); McMahon, *Pure Zeal* 27–8; Ruth Mugglebee, *Father Coughlin of the Shrine of the Little Flower* (Boston, 1933; New York, 1937) 79; Shook, *Catholic Education* 116.

STALEY, Arthur James, priest, member of the Congregation 1895–1908, was born on Wolfe Island, Ontario (archdiocese of Kingston), on 9 September 1873, the son of Daniel Staley and Sarah Spoor. He died in Toronto on 27 April 1922 and was buried in St Mary's Cemetery, Kingston, Ontario.

Arthur Staley attended local schools until he was sixteen years old, then went to St Michael's College, Toronto. Six years later he entered St Basil's Novitiate, Toronto, and was professed on 14 August 1896. He continued his studies for the priesthood at Assumption College in Windsor, 1896–8 and 1900–1, and at St Michael's College, 1898–1900. He was ordained to the priesthood on 28 July 1901.

Father Staley taught at Assumption College, 1901–2, and at St Michael's College, 1902–8. In 1908 he withdrew from the Congregation to work in the archdiocese of Toronto and was incardinated on 26 November 1910. He served as assistant in various parishes until 1916 when he was appointed pastor of St John the Evangelist Parish, Weston – a parish that Father Jean Mathieu *Soulerin had originally taken as a Basilian work. Father Staley died from injuries sustained in an automobile accident.

SOURCES: GABF; William Perkins Bull, *From Macdonell to McGuigan, the History of the Growth of the Roman Catholic Church in Upper Canada* (Toronto, 1939); Kirley, *Community in France* 214n516, 216n518, 220n528, 240n570.

STAPLETON, John Francis, priest, member of the Congregation 1941–77, was born in Fitzroy Harbour, Ontario (archdiocese of Ottawa), on 24 November 1921, the son of L.J. Stapleton and Mary McDermott. He died in Collingwood, Ontario, 19 June 1997 and is buried there.

John attended Collingwood Collegiate Institute and then enrolled in the Honours Philosophy course at St Michael's College, Toronto. In 1940 he entered St Basil's Novitiate, Toronto. After first profession of vows on 15 August 1941, he finished his course at St Michael's, 1941–4 (B.A., University of Toronto, 1944). He taught at Aquinas Institute in 1944–5 and then began theological studies at St Basil's Seminary, 1945–9. He was ordained to the priesthood on 29 June 1948 in St Basil's Church, Toronto, by Cardinal James Charles McGuigan.

Father Stapleton was appointed to the Institute House in 1949, and remained there until 1962. He obtained his degree in library science from the University of Toronto in 1950, was appointed assistant librarian at the Pontifical Institute of Mediaeval Studies for the year 1950–1, and then served as librarian from 1951 to 1962. In 1962 he was appointed librarian of St Basil's Seminary, 1962–7, and then master of novices, 1968–71 – a time of turmoil in the Church and in religious congregations. He was an assistant pastor at St Mary's of the Assumption Parish, Owen Sound, 1972–6. In 1976 he joined the diocese of Hamilton, citing his desire to minister in a 'one-man parish.' He was incardinated in 1977 and did parochial ministry first in Linwood, Ontario (from where he wrote to Bishop Paul Redding that he found joy and acceptance by both Catholics and Protestants), then in Mildmay, Ontario, early 1980s–1990, and finally at St Peter's Parish, Durham, 1990–June 1994. A condition of hypertension forced his retirement that year.

BIBLIOGRAPHY: 'True Dialogue May Never Be Reached,' *Forum* 1 (October 1964) 11–12.
SOURCES: GABF; *Annals* 1 (1948) 221–2; Archives, diocese of Hamilton.

STOREY, William Joseph, priest, cousin of Father Vincent *Kennedy, was born at Stratford, Ontario (diocese of London), on 2 September 1895, the son of John Storey and Mary Malloy. He died in Windsor on 28 June 1944 and was buried there in the Basilian plot of Assumption Cemetery.

Bill Storey attended local schools before enrolling in Assumption College, Windsor, in 1912 to complete his high school course. He also completed two years of college before entering St Basil's Novitiate in Toronto, with Father Nicholas *Roche as master. After profession on 24 August 1917 he finished his arts course at St Michael's College (B.A., University of Toronto, 1920), then attended the Ontario College of Education in Toronto, 1921–2. From 1917 he had also been studying theology at St Basil's Scholasticate. He was ordained to the priesthood in St Basil's Church, Toronto, on 17 December 1921 by Bishop Félix Couturier of Alexandria.

Father Storey taught chemistry and physics in the high school section of St Michael's College and was in charge of the athletic program. In 1929 he was appointed treasurer of Assumption College. Two years later he was transferred to Catholic Central High School, Detroit, but returned to St Michael's College in 1932. He worked for one year at Ste Anne's Parish, Detroit, then went back to teaching in 1935 at St Thomas High School, Houston. During the building of the new school plant on Buffalo Bayou he served as treasurer of the building committee and was responsible for examining all plans and checking all building materials and equipment. In 1942 he moved back to Assumption College, where he cared for the grounds and from where he did much preaching. He died suddenly from a heart attack.

sources: GABF; *Annals* 1 (1944) 64–5, *The Basilides, Assumption College* (Windsor, 1930); *Yearbook SMC* 21 (1930).

SUCHET, Emile, priest, was born on 5 March 1854 at Tauriers, canton of Largentière (Ardèche). He died at Prades (Ardèche) on 18 December 1929 and was buried in the local cemetery.

Emile attended school at Sainte-Barbe, the minor seminary section of the Collège du Sacré-Coeur, Annonay, and passed his baccalaureate exams brilliantly in 1875. He made his noviciate at Feyzin (Isère, now Rhône), 1873–4, and professed final vows on 21 September 1877. Bishop Armand de Charbonnel ordained him to the priesthood on 20 September 1879 in the chapel of the Collège du Sacré-Coeur. During his preparation for the priesthood he taught classes in the Ecole cléricale de Périgueux (Dordogne), 1875–8, and at the Petit Séminaire de Vernoux (Ardèche), 1878–9.

For one year after ordination Father Suchet studied at the Catholic Faculty in Lyon, and then was appointed to teach rhetoric at the Collège Saint-Pierre in Châteauroux (Indre), 1880–1. His subsequent teaching appointments included the following: the Collège du Sacré-Coeur, 1881–5; the Ecole cléricale de Périgueux, 1885–8; the Petit Séminaire de Vernoux, 1888–9; the Collège Saint-Augustin, Bône, Algeria, 1889–95; and the Petit Séminaire de Vernoux, 1895–1903. With the exclusion in 1903 of members of congregations from teaching in schools, Father Suchet entered the parochial ministry and served as a curate at Les Vans (Ardèche). In 1910 he was co-pastor at Prades (Ardèche), where he assisted at the Calvary Chapel and where he died.

sources: GABF; Kirley, *Community in France* 70n179, 184, 204; Kirley, *Congregation in France* 42, 81–2; Pouzol, 'Notices.'

SULLIVAN, Basil Francis, priest, cousin of Father John *Glavin and of Father Vincent *Guinan and uncle of Father Basil *Glavin, was born on 12 May 1894 at Mount Carmel, Ontario (diocese of London), the son of Patrick Sullivan and Mary Guinan. He died in Toronto on 24

June 1983 and is buried in the Basilian plot of Holy Cross Cemetery, Thornhill, Ontario.

Basil did high school studies at Crediton, Ontario, and then at Assumption College. He began university studies at Assumption in 1912, but after two years entered St Basil's Novitiate, Toronto, and was professed on 17 August 1915. He was appointed to St Michael's College to complete his university course (B.A., University of Toronto, 1917). He returned to Assumption to study theology until 1920, when he was sent to the Catholic University of America, Washington (M.A., Theology, 1921). He was ordained to the priesthood on 19 February 1921 in St Peter's Cathedral, London, Ontario, by Bishop Michael Fallon.

Father Sullivan spent the next twenty-eight years, 1921–49, teaching at St Michael's College, and was registrar there from 1925 to 1949. He was appointed principal and superior at St Thomas More College, Saskatoon, in 1949, returned to St Michael's to teach, 1955–7, and then went back to St Thomas More for nine more years in various capacities: chaplain to the University Hospital, moderator of the Confraternity of Christian Doctrine at Saskatchewan Teachers' College, and professor of sociology for the nurses at St Paul's Hospital. In 1966 he retired to St Joseph's College, Edmonton, returning to St Michael's in 1971. In 1980 he moved into the Basilian Fathers Residence (Infirmary) where he spent the last three years of his life.

As registrar of St Michael's during the Great Depression years, Father Sullivan came up with the solution to a potentially crippling economic crisis. The Ontario Department of Education decided to move first-year university students into a grade XIII of high school. This would have eliminated the large contingent of American students whose tuition was vital to St Michael's. Father Sullivan proposed to the superior, Father *Bellisle, the idea of introducing the 'Western course' at St Michael's. With the co-operation of Assumption College, Windsor, it allowed American students at St Michael's to be enrolled extramurally at Assumption and thus to get college credit for the first year through Assumption's agreement with the University of Western Ontario.

Father Sullivan dealt on a personal level with everybody he encountered in his work. His memory for their names, faces, situations, and problems was legendary, and he found innovative ways to deal with their problems. New undertakings, whether personal or institutional, never frightened him. He was an insatiable reader, always eager to share his knowledge with others. His desk was a clutter of books and papers sprinkled with cigarette ash, from which he could readily find what he needed. Answering a break-in at Teefy Hall in the late 1940s, the investigating officer, looking with horror at Father Sullivan's desk, heard him say, 'Why, he didn't touch a thing.' Because he was one of the most experienced registrars in all the colleges and schools of the University of Toronto, his counterparts found his suggestions and his co-operation invaluable.

BIBLIOGRAPHY: 'St Thomas and Property,' *Basilian* 1 (May 1935) 43-4, 56.
SOURCES: GABF; *Annals* 3 (1965) 371, 4 (1972) 222-3, 6 (1982) 11, (1984) 296-8; *Newsletter* (30 June 1983); *Heartwood*, 85, 88-92, 98-102, 106-7; Kirley, *Congregation in France* 58.

SULLIVAN, Edward John, priest, was born in Syracuse, New York, on 9 November 1918, the son of John Sullivan and Anna Whalen. He died in Houston on 20 November 1967 and is buried in the Basilian plot of Holy Sepulchre Cemetery, Rochester.

'Eddie' Sullivan graduated from Holy Rosary High School, Syracuse, in 1936. He came to St Michael's College, Toronto, for the 'Western' course and one year of Honours Philosophy before entering St Basil's Novitiate, Toronto. After profession on 15 August 1939, he resumed his studies at the University of Toronto (B.A., 1942, M.A., 1947). He taught at Catholic Central High School, Detroit, 1942-3, and at St Thomas High School, Houston, 1943-4, before his appointment to study theology at St Basil's Seminary, Toronto. He was ordained to the priesthood on 29 June 1947 in St Basil's Church, Toronto, by Cardinal James Charles McGuigan.

Graduate studies in philosophy followed ordination and brought him an M.S.L. from the Pontifical Institute of Mediaeval Studies, Toronto, in 1949, and a Ph.D. in philosophy from the University of Toronto in 1951. His doctoral thesis was entitled 'The Doctrine of Divine Ideas According to William of Ockham. Study and Text.' He was appointed to the University of St Thomas, Houston, where, except for a sabbatical leave in 1961-2, which he spent at Maison Saint-Basile, Issy-les-Moulineaux, France, he taught philosophy until his sudden death from a massive heart attack at the age of forty-nine.

Edward Sullivan was an extraordinary teacher who made philosophy a living force in the core curriculum and the academic community of the university. He went to extreme measures of animation and concocted images to make philosophical concepts come alive for his students, frequently invoking Father Leonard *Quinlan's cat Deega.

Father Sullivan was a delegate to the 1966 Basilian convention and again to the month-long 1967 general chapter. In both assemblies he took an active part, pleading for the right of new ideas to a sympathetic hearing. In other interventions he urged the union in Basilian life of the best standards in education and the highest spiritual ideals. Shortly before his death he was appointed superior of the Basilian community at St Thomas. His death, coming in the same year as those of Fathers John *Sheehy and Leslie *Vasek, was a serious blow to the University of St Thomas. An editorial in the *Houston Post* described him as 'a scholar who played tennis and golf and painted for his own pleasure. ... He was approachable, shock-proof, compassionate. ... As a city, Houston benefitted from the achievements – tangible and intangible – of this stimulating teacher. His loss will be felt by those who knew and loved him, but his work will endure in the university he helped create.' The building which houses the departments of philosophy and theology at UST was named 'Sullivan Hall' in his memory.

sources: GABF; *Annals* 1 (1947) 152, 4 (1968) 60–1; *Newsletter* (20 November 1967); *Houston Post* (23 November 1967) section 2 5; Kirley, *Congregation in France* 235.

SULLIVAN, John Aloysius, priest, was born at Fall River, Massachusetts, on 7 June 1873, the son of Daniel and Hannah Sullivan. He died in Toronto on 3 February 1913 and was buried at Fall River.

John Sullivan attended local schools and in 1888 went to St Michael's College, Toronto. Four years later he entered St Basil's Novitiate, Toronto, and was professed on 23 August 1893. Studies in theology followed at St Michael's College and St Basil's Scholasticate, Toronto. He was ordained to the priesthood on 15 August 1898.

Father Sullivan taught at St Michael's College until 1903, when he moved to St Basil's College, Waco, Texas. In March of 1907 he was transferred to St Mary's of the Assumption Parish, Owen Sound, Ontario. In 1910 he returned to St Michael's College, where he died from pneumonia three years later at the age of thirty-nine.

Students loved Father Sullivan for his interest in athletics. In parochial work and as a chaplain his kindness to the sick and dying seemed inexhaustible. Among Basilians he was known for his interest in everything going on in the community.

sources: GABF; *Centennial, St Mary's*; *Jubilee, St Mary's*; *Yearbook SMC* 4 (1913).

SULLIVAN, John Joseph, priest, was born at Dundas, Ontario (diocese of Hamilton), on 3 May 1892, the son of Michael and Margaret Sullivan. He died in Toronto on 6 December 1967 and is buried in the Basilian plot of Holy Cross Cemetery, Thornhill, Ontario.

John Joseph Sullivan attended school in Dundas and in 1907 went to St Michael's College, Toronto, for high school. He continued in the college department (B.A., University of Toronto, 1915). He entered St Basil's Novitiate, Toronto, and after first profession on 26 August 1916, made his theological studies at St Basil's Scholasticate, Toronto. He was ordained to the priesthood on 29 February 1920.

Father Sullivan's first years as a priest were spent in teaching: St Thomas College, Chatham, New Brunswick, 1920–2, St Thomas College, Houston, 1922–8, and Assumption College, Windsor, 1928–32. He received several parish appointments as assistant pastor: Ste Anne's, Detroit, 1932–3, Holy Rosary, Toronto, 1940–6, and St Mary's of the Assumption Parish, Owen Sound, Ontario, 1933–4, 1935–40, and 1946–61. He served often as local councillor. In 1961 he retired to Michael Power High School, Etobicoke, Ontario, where for a few years he served as relief chaplain at St Joseph's Hospital in Toronto. As an inveterate reader, the partial blindness of his later years was a heavy affliction.

Parishioners remember his disarming forgetfulness and his cheering visits to the sick. The *Basilian Centennial* volume of St Mary's of the Assumption Parish noted his scholarship, his friendliness, his love of the city, and his effervescent good humour as qualities displayed in conjunction with a gruff kindliness.

SOURCES: GABF; *Annals* 3 (1966) 455, 4 (1968) 61–2; *Newsletter* (7 December 1967); *Centennial, St Mary's; Yearbook SMC* 6 (1915).

SULLIVAN, Walter Vincent, priest, was born on 7 August 1911 in Rochester, the son of John Michael Sullivan and Margaret Lucille Sullivan. He died in Toronto on 1 June 1978 and is buried in the Basilian plot of Holy Cross Cemetery, Thornhill, Ontario.

Walter Sullivan attended Immaculate Conception grade school and took two years of high school at Aquinas Institute, Rochester. He transferred to St Andrew's Preparatory Seminary, Rochester, for the rest of his high school, entering St Bernard's Seminary, Rochester, upon graduation in 1930. After two years of philosophy and three years of theology there, he was told by the diocesan authorities that his lameness, the result of an ankle injury, was an obstacle to his ordination to the priesthood. He withdrew from the seminary in 1935. Two years later, after a series of operations had mitigated the condition, he was admitted to St Basil's Novitiate, Toronto, where he made first profession of vows on 15 August 1938. After teaching for one year at St Thomas High School, Houston, and for one year at Aquinas Institute, he returned to Toronto for his fourth year of theology, 1940–1. He taught one more year in Houston before his ordination, which took place in Rochester on 6 June 1942 at Sacred Heart Pro-Cathedral at the hands of Bishop James Kearney.

Father Sullivan continued to teach at St Thomas High School for nine years, with two brief interruptions. Increasing lameness and a tendency to stutter, however, made this work more and more difficult. In 1951 he began a period of twenty-one years of parish ministry, with nineteen years at St Anne's, Houston, and one year each at Angleton and Sugar Land. In this work his zeal truly flourished. Despite severe pain, decreasing mobility, and his speech impediment, he managed to show seemingly limitless concern for others, and painstakingly applied his talent for helping them.

By 1972 he was so severely crippled that even a limited parish apostolate was beyond his strength. His mission then became one of suffering and solitary prayer. He resided with relatives in Rochester from the summer of 1972 until the spring of 1977, when he moved to St Basil's Infirmary, Toronto, for the remaining year of his life.

SOURCES: GABF; *Annals* 5 (1979) 410–11; *Newsletter* (5 June 1978).

T

TALLON, John David, priest, was born on 9 June 1938 in Detroit, the son of Edmund Tallon and Margaret Stewart. He died in Detroit on 16 January 1982 and is buried in the Basilian plot of Heavenly Rest Cemetery, Windsor.

John attended St Luke's and St Alphonsus's grade schools and graduated from Catholic Central High School in 1956. He entered St Basil's Novitiate, Rochester, and was professed on 15 August 1957. He was appointed to St Michael's College, Toronto, for university studies, but transferred in 1961 to Assumption University, Windsor (B.A., University of Windsor, 1963). He taught at Assumption College School, 1961–3, and at Michael Power High School, Etobicoke, 1963–4, and then studied theology at St Basil's College, Toronto (S.T.B., University of St Michael's College, 1967). He was ordained to the priesthood on 9 December 1967 in Blessed Sacrament Cathedral, Detroit, by Bishop Joseph Breitenbeck.

Father Tallon taught for one year, 1968–9, at Aquinas Institute, Rochester. In the fall of 1969 he undertook graduate studies (M.A., Social Work, University of Windsor, 1970), and began his work at Hôtel-Dieu Hospital, Windsor, that led to his establishing there in 1971 the Department of Social Work, of which he was the director until his death. He was on the Board of Governors of Villa Maria Home for the Aged and of Assumption University, but resigned the latter position in 1975 when he was appointed educational co-ordinator of seminars and institutes by the Ontario Hospital Association Social Work Section as well as editor of its newsletter journal. He was a sessional instructor at the University of Windsor School of Social Work and School of Nursing as well as an associate field supervisor of clinical students of the university. Amid these administrative duties he also attended to persons from broken homes or crumbling marriages, to battered women and children, to those with suicidal tendencies, and to the dying and the bereaved. Three days before his sudden death in a head-on collision during a heavy snowfall, he had delivered a paper, 'Coping with Bereavement.'

John Tallon was a cheerful man with a talent for listening and for bringing out the best in people. He enjoyed life and loved the company of his family, where his ebullient nature found its full scope. In all his dealings he was conscious of his priesthood, and had the habit of adding a short phrase of his own to the prayer at Mass just prior to the communion, 'Keep me faithful to your teaching *and to my priesthood*, and never let me be parted from you.' The Hôtel-Dieu Hospital established the John Tallon Memorial Fund for furnishing the chapel in its chronic care wing, where a plaque preserves his memory.

SOURCES: GABF; *Annals* 4 (1968) 52, 6 (1983) 189–91; *Newsletter* (8 February 1982).

TALLON, Joseph EDWARD, subdeacon, was born in Cornwall, Ontario (diocese of Alexandria, since 1978 of Alexandria-Cornwall), on 12 February 1897, the son of James Tallon and Agnes Bradley. He died in Toronto on 16 October 1925 and is buried there in the Basilian plot of Mount Hope Cemetery.

'Eddie' Tallon attended schools in his native city and enrolled in St Michael's College, Toronto, in 1915. During the First World War he spent several months with the Canadian Army at Seaforth in England. After the war he returned to St Michael's College, graduated with the class of 1919, and in the following year attended the Ontario College of Education, Toronto. He taught at Assumption College School, Windsor, 1920–1, then entered St Basil's Novitiate, Toronto, and was professed on 11 August 1922. He taught for one year, 1922–3, at St Thomas College (High School), Houston, before beginning his theological studies at St Basil's Scholasticate, Toronto. He was ordained subdeacon on 19 September 1925, and was living in anticipation of ordination to the priesthood on 19 December when he died from pneumonia following an operation for appendicitis.

SOURCES: GABF; *Purple and White* (1 November 1925); *Yearbook SMC* 17 (1926).

TARABOUT, Jean-Marie, priest, uncle of Father Marius *Grangeon, was born on 15 January 1840 (one community record reads 1841) at Saint-Pierre-du-Champ (Haute-Loire, diocese of Le Puy). He died in his home town on 14 November 1930 and is buried in the local cemetery.

After secondary studies at the Petit Séminaire de Monistrol near his home town, Jean-Marie Tarabout entered the Basilian novitiate at Feyzin (Isère, now Rhône) and professed final vows on 20 September 1867. Bishop Armand de Charbonnel ordained him to the priesthood on 18 September 1869 in the chapel of the Collège du Sacré-Coeur, Annonay.

Father Tarabout taught in various Basilian schools: the Ecole cléricale de Périgueux (Dordogne), 1867–71; the Petit Séminaire de Vernoux, 1871–3; the Collège du Bourg-Saint-Andéol, 1873–5; and the Petit Séminaire d'Aubenas, 1875–9. When the Basilians withdrew from there in 1879 he went to the scholasticate in Annonay. Further appointments brought him as a teacher to the Collège Saint-Pierre in Châteauroux (Indre), 1880–2, and to the Collège du Sacré-Coeur, Annonay, 1883–1903. For two of these years, 1889–91, he lived at Sainte-Barbe, and from 1891 to 1903 he served as bursar at the Collège du Sacré-Coeur. When anticlerical legislation excluded Basilians from the school in 1903, he went to his home parish of Saint-Pierre-du-Champ, where he died. Father Tarabout had been chosen to be a member of the general council, 7 May 1899, after the death of Father Jean *Monin, and he remained on the council until his resignation on 21 April 1910.

SOURCES: GABF; Kirley, *Community in France* 163n416, 172, 182n464, 183, 211; Kirley, *Congregation in France* 155; Pouzol, 'Notices.'

TASTEVIN, Antoine Alphonse, priest, was born on 9 September 1843 in the Mas-des-Salles at Balazuc, canton of Vallon (Ardèche), the son of Antoine Laurent Tastevin and Rose Ursule Guigon. He died at his place of birth on 1 September 1911 and is buried in the local cemetery.

After studies at the Petit Séminaire d'Aubenas (Ardèche), Antoine Tastevin went to the Collège du Sacré-Coeur, Annonay, where the records say he served as infirmarian, 1867–71, while also taking classes. He entered the novitiate at Feyzin (Isère, now Rhône) in 1871, and made final profession of vows on 18 September 1874. Bishop Joseph-Michel-Frédéric Bonnet of Viviers ordained him to the priesthood on 23 September 1876 in the chapel of the Collège du Sacré-Coeur, Annonay.

Father Tastevin taught at various Basilian schools: the Petit Séminaire d'Aubenas, 1874–6; the Ecole cléricale de Périgueux (Dordogne), 1876–9; the Collège du Bourg-Saint-Andéol (Ardèche), 1879–80; the Collège du Sacré-Coeur, 1880–4. For some years after this last date only occasional mention is made of Father Tastevin in the community records. He came each year from 1884 to 1888 to the retreat in Annonay, perhaps from Avignon (Vaucluse). There is some evidence that he taught in the Collège Saint-Charles, Monaco, in 1889, and he probably stayed there until 1892. He was definitely on the teaching staff of the Collège Saint-Augustin, Bône, Algeria, 1892–4, then at the Petit Séminaire d'Aubenas, 1895–8, and at the Petit Séminaire de Vernoux (Ardèche), 1898–1902. He may have gone for one year, 1902–3, to the Collège Saint-Charles, Blidah, Algeria. With the anticlerical legislation in 1903 excluding members of congregations from teaching, he found employment as chaplain at a sanatorium at Hauteville (Ain), but he contracted tuberculosis and went to live with his family at Balazuc. The *Semaine Religieuse de Viviers* said of him that he was remarkable for 'his piety and zeal, a man of simple tastes and love of solitude.'

SOURCES: GABF; Kirley, *Community in France* 201, 208; Pouzol, 'Notices.'

TEEFY, John Read, priest, grand-uncle of Father Matthew *Mulcahy, was born at Richmond Hill, Ontario (diocese of Toronto), on 21 August 1848, the second of nine children born to Matthew Teefy and Elizabeth Clarkson. He died in Toronto on 10 June 1911 and is buried there in the Basilian plot of Mount Hope Cemetery.

John Teefy received his early education in the one-room Richmond Hill Grammar School under Mr A.M. Lafferty, who was a silver medallist in both classics and mathematics. In 1867 John matriculated at the University of Toronto and four years later graduated with the silver medal in mathematics. Afterwards he taught at Port Rowan, Beamsville, and Hamilton Collegiate Institute, all in Ontario. A sermon preached by Bishop John Farrell on the scarcity of priestly vocations motivated him to enter the Grand Séminaire Saint-Sulpice, Montreal, on 11 September 1874. Realizing his attachment to school life, however, he left that seminary on 5 April 1877 and entered St Basil's Novitiate, which was then located at Assumption College in Windsor. He made his profession on 12 June 1878, and was ordained to the priesthood on 20 June, eight days later.

During the summer of 1878 Father Teefy was appointed to St Michael's College, Toronto, where he taught until 1886, when he was transferred to the College of Mary Immaculate at Beaconfield House, Plymouth, England. He returned to St Michael's College in 1888 and was named superior for the period 1889–1903. His principal achievement at St Michael's College was to bring it into affiliation with the University of Toronto, thus enabling Catholic students to proceed towards university degrees under Catholic auspices. The University Senate gave its approval on 14 March 1881. Writing in the *University of Toronto Monthly* (July 1911), Professor Alfred Baker, a lifelong friend of Father Teefy, said, 'The effect of Dr. Teefy's character on his Protestant friends, and they were many, was to make them think and speak with profound respect of the Church to which he belonged.' In the last years of his office, however, Father Teefy paid less attention to the affiliation with the University of Toronto.

During his term as superior of St Michael's, Father Teefy, with a group of editors of existing Catholic diocesan publications, founded in 1893 the *Catholic Register* (Toronto), which was to be 'the voice of English-speaking Catholics in Canada.' He was its editor for the first two years.

His term at St Michael's culminated in the celebration of its golden jubilee, 1852–1902, celebrated 28–30 April 1903, at which time the East

Wing on Bay Street was opened. He also found time during his term to earn an M.A. from the University of Toronto, 1894, presenting a thesis, 'Life of the Rt. Rev. Dr. de Charbonnel,' on the second bishop of Toronto, who had brought the Basilians to North America. Two years later the University of Toronto conferred an honorary LL.D. on him. He was appointed to its Board of Governors in 1906.

Father Teefy twice served on the Basilian provincial council, 1898–1901 and 1907–10. In 1904 he was appointed superior of St Basil's Scholasticate, which at that time was housed in the novitiate building on Kendal (now Tweedsmuir) Avenue. Father Teefy became a prominent public personality, preacher, and speaker much in demand. In 1908 he became the first canonical pastor of Holy Rosary Parish, Toronto, which met for worship in the Basilian novitiate chapel. He attended the first Plenary Council of Canada in Quebec City, 1909, and was elected first assistant to the superior general in 1910.

Father Teefy's health began to fail after 1908, and he died in 1911 from diabetes. An obituary notice in the 1912 *Yearbook* of St Michael's said of him that 'no one ever formed even a slight acquaintance with him who did not feel his own character strengthened and enlivened.' Writing in the *Catholic Record*, Hugh McIntosh recalled his friend's filial piety: 'To his father, who in the halo of a patriarchal age survives him, his devotion was in full keeping with the Christian ideal.'

BIBLIOGRAPHY:
Books: (With William Richard Harris) *Jubilee Volume, 1842–1892: The Archdiocese of Toronto and Archbishop Walsh*. Toronto, 1892. *Worship of God: A Course of Lenten Sermons*. New York, 1902.
Articles: Sermon, in *Golden Jubilee of the Diocese of Hamilton*, ed. M.J. O'Reilly (Hamilton, 1906) 32–50.
Other: In addition to his editing of the *Catholic Register* (Toronto) in 1894–6, he was chief editorial writer for the *Catholic Record* (London, Ontario).
SOURCES: GABF; A. Baker, 'Rev. John Read Teefy, M.A., LL.D,' *University of Toronto Monthly* (July 1911), repr. *Catholic Record* (London, Ontario) 12 August 1911; Henry Carr, 'The Very Reverend J.R. Teefy, C.S.B., LL.D.,' *CCHA Report* 7 (1939) 85–95; Kirley, *Congregation in France* 2, 12–14; H.F. McIntosh: 'Father Teefy,' *Catholic Record* July 1911; Shook, *Catholic Education* 146–7; *Yearbook SMC* 3 (1912).

THOMPSON, George James, priest, brother of Fathers Vincent Thompson CSB and Joseph Thompson (member of the Congregation

1937–55), was born on 31 August 1904 at Teeswater, Ontario (diocese of Hamilton), the eldest of the eleven children of Charles James Thompson and Lillian Shields. He died in Toronto on 26 July 1969 and is buried in the Basilian plot of Holy Cross Cemetery, Thornhill, Ontario.

George Thompson was educated at Culross Public School near his home town, and at Teeswater Collegiate. He spent the year 1921–2 at St Jerome's College, Kitchener, Ontario, after which he farmed for a year before going to St Michael's College, Toronto (B.A., University of Toronto, 1927). While at the university he won the All-Canadian Intercollegiate Wrestling Championship and a Varsity Letter. After graduation he entered St Basil's Novitiate, Toronto, making first profession on 2 October 1928. Theological studies followed immediately at St Basil's Scholasticate, Toronto. Concurrently he obtained teaching certification from the Ontario College of Education, 1928, and taught for one year at Catholic Central High School, Detroit, 1930–1. He was ordained to the priesthood on 19 December 1931 in St Basil's Church, Toronto, by Bishop Alexander MacDonald.

Father Thompson spent his priestly life in teaching and academic administration, mostly at Assumption College, Windsor, 1932–3, 1934–49, and 1955–60. He was principal of the high school section from 1937 to 1946, and was the first superior and principal of the newly independent Assumption High School, 1957–60. He taught for one year at Catholic Central, Detroit, as a priest, 1933–4, and for six years, 1949–55, was superior and principal of St Mary's Boys' High School, Calgary, Alberta. A serious heart attack in 1960 reduced his activity. This curtailment of his teaching and formation of the young was a great sacrifice for him. He spent a year of convalescence at St Basil's Seminary, 1960–1, and then joined the staff of St Michael's College School, Toronto, where he taught, as his health allowed, until his death eight years later.

While strict and demanding, he was always fair and friendly. During the Second World War he regularly wrote and sent a newsletter to his former students serving in the military, wherever they were in the world.

BIBLIOGRAPHY: 'New Teachers and the Classroom Situation,' *Basilian Teacher* 5 (January 1961) 118–20.

SOURCES: GABF; *Annals* 4 (1970) 165–6; *Newsletter* (28 July 1969); Vincent Thompson CSB.

THOMSON, Vincent Alexander, priest, was born in Toronto on 19 July 1902, the fourth of seven children born to Alexander Thomson and Ellen Boland. He died in Toronto on 7 October 1968 and is buried in the Basilian plot of Holy Cross Cemetery, Thornhill, Ontario.

Vincent Thomson attended Our Lady of Lourdes Separate School, De La Salle High School, 1916–21, and St Michael's College (B.A., University of Toronto, 1925). He entered St Basil's Novitiate, Toronto, was professed on 11 September 1926, and did theological studies at St Basil's Scholasticate, Toronto, while concurrently attending the Ontario College of Education, 1928–9. He was ordained to the priesthood on 21 December 1929 in St Basil's Church, Toronto, by Archbishop Neil McNeil.

Father Thomson's first assignment was to the high school section of St Michael's College, Toronto, where for three years he served as teacher, prefect of discipline, and assistant principal. In 1933 he was a member of the first Basilian staff appointed to St Mary's Boys' High School, Calgary, Alberta, and in 1934 qualified for permanent Alberta teaching certification. Graduate studies in sociology brought him an M.A. degree in 1940 from Gonzaga University, Spokane, Washington. At St Mary's Father Thomson taught a full schedule, was treasurer, 1935–7, of the Basilian residence, and was superior and principal of the school from 1937 to 1943. He was a chaplain in the Royal Canadian Air Force, 1943–5, successively at Rivers, Manitoba (Navigation School), at Saskatoon, and at Calgary (Service Flying Training School). At the end of the War, he was named treasurer of St Michael's College. From there he moved to St John the Baptist Parish, Amherstburg, Ontario, as pastor, 1948–54, then became the founding pastor of Our Lady of the Assumption Parish, Lethbridge, Alberta. He was pastor of Holy Rosary Parish, Toronto, 1961–4, and then treasurer at St Basil's Seminary, 1964–early 1966. Three appointments as assistant pastor followed: Assumption Parish, Windsor, 1966, St Pius X Parish, Calgary, 1966–7, and St Basil's Parish, Toronto, where he served but one year before his sudden death from arterial sclerotic heart disease.

During his college days Vincent Thomson distinguished himself in football and hockey. He played tennis for many years after his ordination. He took a special interest in the material plant of the houses where he lived and worked. At Calgary he supervised the building of the Basilian residence, and his ability as a gardener made the grounds noted for their beauty. At St Michael's College he made extensive alterations to Brennan Hall in 1948; and during the following two years, as pastor of St John the Baptist Parish, he renovated and redecorated the church. In Lethbridge he built Our Lady of the Assumption church in 1957. He was an open-hearted priest who made and kept friends.

BIBLIOGRAPHY: 'The Faith in Peril Here!,' *Basilian* 2 (April 1936) 67–8; 'Lethbridge,' *Basilian Teacher* 1 (December 1956) 16–18.
SOURCES: GABF; *Annals* 4 (1969) 129–30, *Newsletter* (7 October 1968); *Yearbook SMC* 16 (1925).

TIGHE, Edward Joseph, priest, was born on a farm outside of Clinton, Hallett Township, Ontario (diocese of London), on 28 December 1890, the son of Thomas Tighe and Margaret Quigley. He died in Toronto on 10 July 1944 and was buried there in the Basilian plot of Mount Hope Cemetery.

Edward Tighe attended local schools and Stratford Normal School, and taught until 1913 before resuming his education at Assumption College in Windsor. Four years later he entered St Basil's Novitiate, Toronto, and was professed on 10 August 1918. He studied theology at St Basil's Scholasticate when it was temporarily located at Assumption College, Windsor. In 1921 he completed the requirements for a B.A. degree from the University of Western Ontario. He was ordained priest on 28 August 1921 in St Peter's Cathedral, London, Ontario, by Bishop Michael Fallon.

Father Tighe taught Latin in the high school of Assumption College and philosophy at the arts level. In 1929 he obtained an M.A. in philosophy from the University of Ottawa. Five years later he was appointed master of novices and served in this post at St Basil's Novitiate, Toronto, from 1934 until his death in 1944 from a cerebral haemorrhage.

Father Tighe was rich in mannerisms, some native and some acquired, which gave him a legendary character. At an early date he was given the nickname 'The Colonel.' Behind his eccentricities was a capacity for hard work and the ability to make students work. Outside the classroom he coached baseball and football, shared the recreations of the boarding students, and taught them how to get along with others and to cope with the problems of everyday life. As master of novices, Father Tighe lived in almost total seclusion from the world, seldom leaving the novitiate grounds. He taught his novices that the 'fear of the Lord was the beginning of wisdom.' He brought them to love the Blessed Virgin under the title of 'Our Lady Help of Christians' and urged devotion to St John Bosco, who was the modern propagator of this title of Our Lady. It was at his suggestion that the general chapter of 1942 adopted St John Bosco as a patron of the Congregation. His conferences to the novices mingled profound spiritual insights with brilliant sorties of wit. He preached the annual retreat for scholastics in August 1934. James *Ruth described it in a letter written to his brother, Father John P. *Ruth, on 19 August 1934: 'The conferences were given by Father Tighe, who was not only instructive, but very inspiring and admonishing. He is a great man for using illustrations and telling little stories in his talks, which were so interesting that they made everyone laugh but himself. Above all, his conferences were practical and you didn't have to think long before you could apply them to your own case.' Fifty years later, Father Tighe's retreats to Basilians were still considered by many the best they ever made.

BIBLIOGRAPHY: 'A Letter to Jim,' *Basilian* 1 (April 1935) 25, 34; 'An Answer to Jim,' *Basilian* 1 (November 1935) 107-8.
SOURCES: GABF; *Annals* 1 (1945) 82-4.

TIMMONS, Joseph Jeremiah, priest, was born in Milltown, New Brunswick (diocese of St John), on 8 August 1912, the son of Joseph Francis Timmons and Hellena Maud Coughlin. He died in Toronto on 7 December 1956 and is buried in the Basilian plot of Holy Cross Cemetery, Thornhill, Ontario.

Joseph Timmons grew up in St Catharines, Ontario, where he attended the Separate School and the Collegiate Institute. In 1928 he enrolled in St Michael's College, Toronto, as a high school student and continued in arts with the class of 1935. He entered St Basil's Novitiate, Toronto, and was professed on 26 September 1936. He received teacher training at the Ontario College of Education in Toronto, 1938-9, studied theology at St Basil's Seminary, Toronto, and was ordained priest on 15 August 1940 in St Basil's Church, Toronto, by Archbishop James Charles McGuigan.

Father 'Joe' Timmons was an exceptional Latin teacher first at Catholic Central High School, Detroit, 1941-4, and then at St Michael's College School, 1944-56. His untimely death was the result of a coronary thrombosis. An obituary notice in the *Basilian Teacher* described his 'happy ability, born of a sincere spirituality, of drawing, at once, both respect and love from his pupils. He could instill a just reverential fear and yet make it a joy to obey.' At clerical and community gatherings he was usually the centre of a group. Beneath his sparkling wit was a solid sense of responsibility, but only close associates were aware of the depths of seriousness in his character.

sources: GABF; *Annals* 2 (1957) 297–8; *Basilian Teacher* 1 (January 1957) 7.

TODD, Gerard William, priest, was born on 8 June 1896 in Toronto, one of twins born to Charles Albert Todd and Annie Cotter, who also had three daughters. He died in Detroit on 24 June 1980 and is buried in the Basilian plot of Holy Sepulchre Cemetery, Southfield, Michigan.

'Gerry' Todd attended St Basil's Elementary School and enrolled in the high school section of St Michael's College, Toronto, in 1912. He finished his secondary education at Assumption College, Windsor, in June 1916 and then entered the rhetoric class there. In the spring of 1918 he joined the Canadian Army Field Artillery, but the armistice was signed before he was called to active service. He returned to his course at Assumption in February 1919, and in August entered St Basil's Novitiate, Toronto, making first profession on 30 August 1920. For the next five years he studied philosophy and theology at the Basilian Scholasticate, Toronto, and coached the St Michael's College Nine to recognition as one of the best in Toronto. He was ordained to the priesthood on 6 June 1925 in St Basil's Church, Toronto, by Archbishop Neil McNeil.

Father Todd was appointed assistant pastor at Ste Anne's Parish, Detroit, 1925–9 and 1933–4, Assumption Parish, Sandwich, Ontario, 1929–33, and Holy Rosary Parish, Toronto, 1934–5. In 1935 he was appointed pastor of St John the Baptist Parish, Amherstburg, where the parish records reveal that he 'took on a variety of chores. Besides his great passion for fire trucks and uniforms ... he was self-appointed Sunday morning traffic director in front of the Church.'

In the summer of 1940 he was transferred to St Michael's College School, Toronto, where he taught religion and served in his own benevolent fashion as prefect of discipline. In August 1941 he moved to Assumption College School as religion teacher and recreation supervisor. He would regularly be on the 'little walk' on Sunday afternoons to greet the parents of boarders who came to visit their sons. He was secretary, confidant, and friend to Bishop Charles Leo Nelligan, retired ordinary of the Canadian military forces, who was resident there. Father Todd himself had become a part-time chaplain in the Royal Canadian Air Force in 1942.

In August 1955 he was appointed to Catholic Central High School, Detroit, as confessor and counsellor. There, as in other places, he eagerly accepted the post of chaplain for the Detroit Fire Department. During this time the initial signs of Menière's disease became apparent: as his spinal column deteriorated so did his hearing and his eyesight. Compelled to retire, he moved to the Burtha Fisher Home, Detroit. With difficulty he accepted the incapacity and confinement to a wheelchair, and saw his apostolate as one of prayer. His death came quickly after an acute myocardial infarction suffered at the age of eighty-four.

Gerry Todd concerned himself with the humble and the needy. A personal sensitivity never stifled his jovial and rather boisterous manner, which won the hearts of young and old alike.

SOURCES: GABF; *Annals* 4 (1971) 171, 5 (1976) 132, 5 (1981) 611–13; *Newsletter* (11 July 1980).

TOURVIEILLE, Alphonse, scholastic, grandnephew of Father Pierre *Tourvieille, was born at Joannas (Ardèche) on 8 October 1864, the son of Henri Tourvieille and Emilie Suchet. He died on 12 February 1888 in Annonay and was buried there in the cemetery on the grounds of the Collège du Sacré-Coeur.

Alphonse Tourvieille was educated at the Collège du Sacré-Coeur, section Sainte-Barbe, 1877–85. He made his novitiate at Beaconfield House, Plymouth, England, 1885–6. For the next two years he served as prefect at Sainte-Barbe. In September of 1886 he received tonsure and, the next year, minor orders. On Sunday 12 February 1888 in a 'moment of delirium he threw himself from the balcony overlooking the courtyard of the scholasticate, and died fifteen minutes later.'

SOURCES: GABF P1 25A; Kirley, *Community in France* 240n569; Pouzol, 'Notices.'

TOURVIEILLE, Pierre, priest, one of the ten founding members of the Congregation, second superior general, uncle of Father André *Fayolle and of Alphonse *Tourvieille, was born at Joannas, near Largentière (Ardèche, diocese of Viviers, from 1801 to 1822 diocese of Mende), on 5 June 1780, the son of Charles Tourvieille and Marie Reynaud. He died in Annonay on 6 August 1859 and was buried in the Cimetière Saint-Jacques, Annonay. In 1869 his body was reinterred in the cemetery on the grounds of the Collège du Sacré-Coeur.

Pierre Tourvieille received his early education during the French Revolution from his brother Charles, who was a priest some twenty years his elder. After 1796 he studied philosophy and mathematics at Grenoble, then in March 1802 went to the clandestine college-seminary in the hills of the Ardèche at Saint-Symphorien-de-Mahun. With the signing of the Concordat between Napoleon Bonaparte and the Holy See, that school moved to Annonay later in 1802, and assumed the new name of Collège des Cordeliers. Pierre continued his studies in philosophy and theology and was ordained to the priesthood on 14 March 1807 by Etienne de Mons, bishop of Mende.

Father Tourvieille taught mathematics at the Collège des Cordeliers. In 1811 he opened Sainte-Claire as an overflow boarding-house for clerical students who could not be accommodated at Sainte-Barbe, the minor seminary. Later he enlarged the scope of Sainte-Claire to make it a school for students preparing for the professions and the business world, and merged it with the Collège des Cordeliers in 1827. The French Government awarded him a silver medal in 1821 in recognition of his work at Sainte-Claire. In 1825 he was named *Officier de l'Instruction publique*, and in 1854 was promoted to *Chevalier de la Légion d'Honneur*.

In 1822 he directed the reorganization of the college and was one of the ten founding members of the Association of Priests of Saint Basil. On 2 December 1822 he was elected to the general council at the second session of the first general chapter. He began to draw up a set of Constitutions in 1822, and carried the first draft to Rome for approval in 1836. A decree of praise came from Rome later after he had become superior general, on 27 October 1838, but during his time in office he did not push for a definitive edition of the Constitutions.

As superior general Father Tourvieille was a paradox of daring enterprise and rigid adherence to earlier practices. He foresaw the anticlerical trend in French civil legislation and prepared for it by sending priests to Canada at a time when human prudence counselled strengthening the staffs of existing schools. Earlier, as director of studies at the college, he arranged for Basilians to study in Lyon or Paris; but as superior general he was less inclined to send priests away for advanced studies.

In his relations with the general public, Father Tourvieille was urbane and affable. He met people graciously and quickly put them at their ease. Parents noted with satisfaction his interest in the progress of their children and appreciated both his letters and the reception they received when they visited the college. In his dealings with the Ministry of Public Instruction he was uniformly successful. Within the college he was always careful to consult not only the director of studies but also senior teachers before implementing new policies.

Within the Basilian community, however, Father Tourvieille was more autocratic. He often found his own experience setting him against the views of younger members. Perhaps imbued with Jansenist tendencies, he had a horror of comfort. He rebuffed appeals to human weakness with the reply that, as he had lived through persecution and trials, so would austerity be good for seminarians and their teachers. He resisted separating the novitiate and scholasticate from the general community and separating the office of superior general from that of local superior at the Collège des Cordeliers. Only reluctantly did he consent to the taking of a mitigated simple vow of poverty in 1852. Father Adrien *Chomel wrote, 'Father Tourvieille was undoubtedly much attached to the past, especially the old religious practices in which he had been brought up.' Father *Roume wrote that 'rigid and austere in his youth, he remained so to the end.'

Father Tourvieille was much in demand as a preacher for retreats and special occasions. He followed the classical tradition: solid matter, text carefully prepared, points outlined and subdivided, the whole memorized to the last word and the least gesture. During the school year he accepted few invitations to preach, preferring to give full time to his college duties; but from 1820 until 1845 his summers were filled with a succession of retreats.

Pierre Tourvieille opens his written reminiscences (1855) in this way: 'In the month of March 1802, I entered the first ecclesiastical house opened in the diocese and have never left it. For fifty-three years, I have followed all the changes in this house. ... There is no position I have not occupied, under different circumstances in the training of youth, and I can assert that my entire life has been spent in their midst.' At the time of his death he had held the office of superior general for twenty-one years. His influence on the community, enriching in the areas of administration and educational practice but restrictive in the area of religious life, was enormous.

BIBLIOGRAPHY: 'Instructions upon the General and Particular Duties of Teachers in the Education of Youth' (unpublished, Eng. trans. of the French), 306 pp.

SOURCES: GABF; Chomel, *Collège d'Annonay* 128–31, 137–51, 152–202, 388–421; Kirley, *Community in France* 1, 6, 9, 10, 12, 22, 23, 39, 40, 58, 59, 150n383, 166, 182, 217, 242; Pouzol, 'Notices'; Roume, *Origines* 111, 159, 161, 164–7, 263–4, 268, 346, 348–53, 384–6. For documentation on him and the Basilian undertaking of Assumption College, Windsor, see Power, *Assumption College* 1 44–64 passim.

TRACOL, Julien, priest, one of the ten founding fathers, was born on 6 June 1796 in Annonay, the son of Julien Tracol, wholesale merchant, and Anne Lagrange, a Protestant. He died on 3 June 1885 in Annonay and was buried in the cemetery on the grounds of the Collège du Sacré-Coeur.

Julien Tracol's first teacher was a Father Charvet, a former Franciscan. He studied at the Collège des Cordeliers, 1808–11, where he was always at the top of his class. In 1811 he expressed the desire to become a priest, but his father thought that at fifteen he was too young, and put him to work in the family business. In 1813 Julien returned to the college to study philosophy and theology. He was ordained to the priesthood for the diocese of Viviers on 28 March 1819. In September of that year, he was appointed assistant at Notre-Dame parish, but his delicate conscience found parish work too difficult. In 1820 he returned to the college. Two years later he was one of the ten members of the college staff who began the Association of Priests of Saint Basil in 1822. At the end of the 1824 academic year he went to the Jesuit novitiate in Avignon but stayed less than a month, and was back at the college after the summer. Besides teaching he served as chaplain to the sisters and orphans at La Providence. From 1837 to 1842 he filled the office of director of studies, but after that his health curtailed full-time work. He filled in at the school as needed, looked after the library and the sacristy, and trained altar boys. He did a good deal of writing, edited the *Journal du Collège*, preached numerous retreats, wrote the biographies of some of the confreres, and was secretary general for thirty-seven years, until 1859. On the advice of his spiritual director he did not take vows in 1852, but kept the promises of 1822. In 1867 he retired to Sainte-Barbe. The last fifteen years of his life were very painful. He was eventually unable to say Mass or to recite his breviary. A sister of Providence assisted him and read to him if he asked. He died at Sainte-Barbe at the age of eighty-nine.

Father Robert McBrady wrote: 'I knew Tracol. He was the last of the old guard. All looked upon him as a saint, and justly so.' A self-effacing person, he was troubled often by scruples which made his priestly ministry difficult. He contributed a great deal to the history of the Congregation by the records he kept as secretary general and as editor of the *Journal du Collège*. Father Adrien Chomel, both in his *Collège d'Annonay* and in his unpublished biography of Father Tracol, praises his literary style as 'simple, free, pure and lucid ... we find hardly a correction in the fourteen or fifteen volumes of his private diary and the Journal of the College, though he wrote but one copy of them.' The personal diary, kept from 1824 to 1865, survived him only on the insistence of his spiritual director. He also wrote spiritual tracts and a commentary on the Rule drawn up for the priests at the college by Father Léorat-Picansel, pastor of Notre-Dame parish in Annonay.

SOURCES: Chomel, *Collège d'Annonay* 145, 249–56, 437, 438; Adrien Chomel, 'Father Julien Tracol 1796–1885' (unpublished), trans. J.C. Plomer (Toronto, 1904); Kirley, *Community in France* 29, 30, 70; R. McBrady, 'Reminiscences,' *Basilian* 1 (April 1935) 23–4, 34; Pouzol, 'Notices'; Roume, *Origines* 104, 155, 159, 168–71, 347, 403.

TROUILLET, Henri, priest, was born on 10 October 1864 at Félines (Ardèche). He died at Serrières (Ardèche) on 7 May 1941 and is buried at Félines.

Henri studied at Sainte-Barbe minor seminary in Annonay, 1876–84, and spent one year as prefect at the Collège Saint-Charles, Blidah, Algeria, 1885–6, before entering the Basilian novitiate at Beaconfield House, Plymouth, England. He professed final vows on 21 September 1888 and was ordained to the priesthood by Bishop Joseph-Michel-Frédéric Bonnet of Viviers on 19 September 1891 in the chapel of the Collège du Sacré-Coeur.

While doing his theological studies, he taught at the Collège Saint-Charles, Blidah, 1887–8, 1889–90, and at the Collège du Sacré-Coeur, Annonay, 1888–89, 1890–1. After ordination he taught at the Ecole cléricale de Périgueux (Dordogne), 1891–6, and at the Collège du Sacré-Coeur, Annonay, 1896–1902. He seems not to have had a teaching assignment in 1902–3. With the dispersal of the Basilians in 1903, following governmental exclusion of religious from teaching, he served as chaplain at the hospital at Serrières, a post he held until his death thirty-eight years later.

Father Trouillet also assumed responsibility for the parish of Serrières during the war, 1914–18. He made a point of teaching Latin to boys who gave signs of a vocation to the priesthood, one of these being the young Pierre Tiollier, who became a diocesan priest and taught for several decades at the Collège du Sacré-Coeur.

Short in stature, shy and self-effacing, Father Trouillet came regularly after 1923 to make the retreat with the Basilians at the Petit Séminaire Saint-Charles, Annonay.

SOURCES: GABF; Kirley, *Community in France* 206, 240n569; Kirley, *Congregation in France* 81–2, 174, 184; Pouzol, 'Notices.'

U

UDALL, Cyril Ronald, priest, member of the Congregation 1946–67, was born on 7 July 1927 at Dauphin, Manitoba (archdiocese of Winnipeg), the son of Francis Udall and Anne Halowski. He died at Santa Cruz, California, on 21 October 1995. He was buried there from his parish of Holy Cross.

After attending Assumption High School and Assumption College, Windsor, 'Cy' entered the Basilian Novitiate and made his first profession on 15 August 1946. He returned to Assumption College (B.A., University of Western Ontario, 1949), taught at Aquinas Institute, Rochester, and St Thomas High School, Houston, and then did his theological studies at St Basil's Seminary, Toronto. He was ordained to the priesthood in St Basil's Church by Cardinal James Charles McGuigan on 29 June 1953.

Father Udall studied music at the Ursuline School of Music, Windsor, at Wayne State University, Detroit, at the Eastman School of Music, Rochester, and at the Royal Conservatory of Music, Toronto, where he obtained the A.R.T.C. He returned to Aquinas Institute and directed its band from 1954 to 1966.

Father Udall was dispensed from the obligations of the priesthood and religious profession in 1967. He became a computer programmer for a large corporation, and was very active in his parish. He was survived by his wife, Theresa, and by their children Cecilia, Frank, and Cyril.

BIBLIOGRAPHY: 'Music in High School,' *Basilian Teacher* 3 (April 1959) 180–3; 'O

Jesus Living in Mary (Father Olier),' *Basilian Teacher* 4 (December 1959) 84; 'Bop Can Lead to Bach,' *Basilian Teacher* 5 (October 1960) 23–6.

SOURCES: GABF; *Annals* 2 (1953) 111; *Newsletter* (19 December 1995); *Aquinas Landmark* (January 1996).

V

VACHER, Régis, priest, member of the Association of Priests of Saint Basil 1823–c.1836, was born on 14 December 1798 or 1799 at Prades, near Aubenas (Ardèche, diocese of Viviers [from 1801 to 1822 of Mende]).

Régis Vacher became a novice on 18 May 1823 and made his profession by promise, not by vows, as was the custom at the time, on 30 August 1826. He was ordained a priest on 22 September 1827 in Viviers. Father Vacher worked in the Basilian college at Feyzin (Isère, now Rhône), and was bursar there from 1832 to 1836. He probably withdrew from the Association that year, as there is no further mention of him.

SOURCE: Pouzol, 'Notices,' Supplément 1.

VADNAIS, Ernest Lucien Pierre, priest, was born on 16 November 1933 in Windsor, Ontario, the son of Philemon Vadnais and Beatrice Duval. He died in Toronto on 21 September 1975, and is buried in the Basilian plot of Holy Cross Cemetery, Thornhill, Ontario.

'Ernie' Vadnais attended Our Lady of the Rosary School and Assumption College School, Windsor. In 1952 he entered St Basil's Novitiate, Toronto, and was professed on 15 August 1953. He was appointed to Assumption University of Windsor (B.A., 1957). He taught for two years at Assumption College School and for one year at Michael Power High School, Etobicoke, Ontario. In August 1960, along with James Carruthers CSB and Ulysse Paré CSB, he went to the Grand Séminaire de Québec to begin theological studies. The next year all three were sent to France as part of the founding group of Maison Saint-Basile, Issy-les-Moulineaux (Seine, now Hauts-de-Seine), along with Jacques Deglesne CSB and Fathers Wallace Platt CSB, superior, and Edward *Sullivan CSB. The four scholastics took their theology at the Séminaire Saint-Sulpice, Issy-les-Moulineaux. After two years in Paris, Ernie returned to Canada for his fourth year of theology at St Basil's Seminary, Toronto (S.T.B., University of St Michael's College, 1964). He was ordained to the priesthood on 15 December 1963 in St Basil's Church, Toronto, by Archbishop George Bernard *Flahiff CSB.

In July 1964 Father Vadnais was appointed to Michael Power High School, Etobicoke, Ontario, where he taught for six years. During summers he attended Middlebury College, Vermont (M.A., French, 1970). He enrolled in Rosary College, Chicago (M.A., Library Science, 1971). Towards the end of his studies he began to experience neck pains and some paralysis in the left arm. He continued to work, however, and was appointed to the library staff at the University of St Thomas, Houston. On the point of leaving for his new appointment he learned that he was afflicted with amyotrophic lateral sclerosis. His appointment was changed to St Michael's College, Toronto, where he worked in the library as long as he could. In 1973 he entered the Basilian Fathers Infirmary, where he lived in gradual debilitation for two years, an example of patience in suffering to all, especially to the scholastics, with whom he had great rapport.

Ernie Vadnais was a cheerful, amiable man who took a good deal of teasing for his ingenuousness. He had great devotion to Saint Thérèse of Lisieux, whose spirituality he reflected. He brought a deep sense of order to all he said and did. Neatness and grooming were for him a mark of respect for others. All through his sickness and suffering he maintained this care of his person and his appearance. Though he did not complete a dozen years of priesthood he left a cherished memory.

SOURCES: GABF; *Annals* 3 (1964) 293, 5 (1976) 187–8; *Newsletter* (24 September 1975).

VAHEY, Thomas James, priest, was born in Youngstown, Ohio, on 23 February 1898, the eldest son of William Vahey and Mary Burns. He died in Toronto on 4 December 1955. He was the first Basilian to be buried in the Basilian plot of Holy Cross Cemetery, Thornhill, Ontario.

Tom Vahey attended local schools, but in 1913 left Royen High School, Youngstown, after one year, to go to work. He returned to school, however, at Assumption College, Windsor, in 1914, completed high school, and entered St Basil's Novitiate, Toronto. After profession on 10 August 1918 he was appointed to St Michael's College, Toronto, and took honours classics at the University of Toronto (B.A., 1924) and theology at St Basil's Scholasticate, while concurrently attending the Ontario College of Education, 1924–5, and continuing his studies in classics (M.A., 1925). He was ordained to the priesthood on 19 December 1925 in St Basil's Church, Toronto, by Bishop Michael O'Brien of Peterborough, Ontario.

Father Vahey taught at Assumption College, 1926–33, and at St Michael's College, 1933–4, and was assistant at St John the Baptist Parish, Amherstburg, Ontario, 1934–6. He spent the year 1936–7 on sick leave at Strawberry Island, Lake Simcoe, Ontario. He returned to teaching at Aquinas Institute, Rochester, 1937–9, then moved to St Michael's College for the years 1939–41 and to St Thomas High School, Houston, 1941–3. Three years of parish work at Ste Anne's Parish, Detroit, were followed by two years of teaching at Assumption College, 1946–8. He spent the year 1948–9 at the Pontifical Institute of Mediaeval Studies, Toronto, translating works of St John Chrysostom. From 1949 to 1952 he lived at the Curial House, Toronto, and taught at St Basil's Seminary and St Michael's College, being appointed to St Michael's in 1952. He was a dynamic, at times an overpowering, teacher who communicated his enthusiasm for the classics to his students. His death came from a heart attack.

BIBLIOGRAPHY: 'St Michael's College,' *St Joseph Lilies* 22 (June 1933) 7–14.
SOURCES: GABF; *Annals* 2 (1955) 246–7; *Purple and White* (15 December 1925); *Yearbook SMC* 15 (1924).

VALLANSON, Jean Fleury, priest, was born on 12 September 1841 at Vinzieux (Ardèche). He died in Lyon on 28 March 1926 and was buried there in the cemetery of Loyasse.

Jean Fleury Vallanson studied at the Collège du Sacré-Coeur, section Sainte-Barbe, Annonay from 1856 to 1863, and made his noviitiate at Feyzin (Isère, now Rhône) in 1863–4. He professed final vows on 21 September 1866 and was ordained to the priesthood by Bishop Louis Delcusy on 17 December 1870 in the cathedral of Viviers. While studying theology he had worked in various Basilian schools: the Petit Séminaire de Vernoux (Ardèche), as study-hall and recreation master, 1864–5; the Collège des Cordeliers, Annonay, 1865–6; and the Petit Séminaire d'Aubenas (Ardèche), as professor in the minor grades, 1866–70. After ordination he remained at the Petit Séminaire d'Aubenas, 1870–7, and then was appointed to the Collège Saint-Charles, Blidah, Algeria, where he taught French grammar classes, 1877–1903.

When the government excluded Basilians from teaching in 1903, he returned to France, probably to Annonay, though no precise records exist for this period. He is listed in 1909 in the Archives départementales (Privas) as chaplain at La Providence and living alone in a room on Rue Saint-Georges, Annonay. One of the convent sisters brought him his meals. By 1922 he was in residence at the Maison de Retraite des Camilliens, Route de Francheville, Lyon (Rhône), where he died at the age of eighty-four.

SOURCES: GABF; Kirley, *Community in France* 185, 206; Pouzol, 'Notices.'

VALLON, Jean Antoine, priest, one of the ten founding fathers, was born at Lafarre (Ardèche, diocese of Vienne, since 1822 of Viviers), on 20 December 1775, the son of Pierre Vallon and Jeanne Granjon. He died on 13 August 1840 at Lafarre and was buried in the local cemetery.

It is not known where Jean Antoine did his studies. He appears to have been ordained for the diocese about 1800. He was listed among the teachers at Saint-Symphorien-de-Mahun in August 1802, and moved later that year with the school to the Collège des Cordeliers, Annonay. He did not sign the original petition to form the Association of Priests of Saint Basil, but he did join the others on 21 November 1822. He was prefect of discipline until he left the college in 1827 after serving for nearly twenty-five years. In the *Journal du Collège* Father *Tracol speaks of Pierre Vallon's 'douleureuse maladie.' After exercising different ministries he retired to his native region at Lafarre, and died at the foot of the altar where he was about to offer Mass.

Father Adrien Chomel described Father Vallon as 'a living example of the Rule, setting an example of hard, mortified life; and to his onerous duties he added mortifications which certainly enfeebled his constitution.' Bishop Armand de Charbonnel said of him, 'He was a holy priest – but to be classed among those saints who inspired fear in their subjects.' He always had a strong affection for the college and in his will left a small legacy to Sainte-Barbe, the minor seminary.

SOURCES: GABF; Chomel, *Collège d'Annonay* 59–61, 117, 144; Pouzol, 'Notices'; Roume, *Origines* 80, 92, 160, 401, 404.

VASCHALDE, Adolphe Arthur, priest, was born at Saint-Pons (Ardèche) on 10 March 1871, the son of Bélime Vaschalde and Honorine Mercoyrol. He died in Toronto on 31 January 1942 and was buried there in the Basilian plot of Mount Hope Cemetery.

Adolphe was a student in the Sainte-Barbe (minor seminary) section of the Collège du Sacré-Coeur, Annonay, in 1885–6. The following year he made his novitiate at Beaconfield House, Plymouth, England, and remained there for a year as a scholastic. On 23 August 1888 he went to North America, where he would spend most of his life. He studied for two years at Assumption College, Windsor, three years at St Michael's College in Toronto, and two years at Catholic University of America, Washington, D.C., where he obtained S.T.B. and S.T.L. degrees. He was ordained to the priesthood on 14 July 1895.

Adolphe Vaschalde taught philosophy for five years at St Michael's College (Scollard, *DBB* 162, says these years were at Assumption). He returned to the Catholic University of America to study oriental languages. In 1902 he obtained a doctorate and spent the next year on a post-doctoral fellowship in Washington. From 1903 to 1910 he taught philosophy at St Michael's. In 1910 he joined the staff in Semitic languages at Catholic University and remained there until he retired to St Michael's in 1939, receiving that year the *Bene Merenti* Medal from Pope Pius XII.

Father Vaschalde remained a member of the province of France. The internal difficulties of the Congregation in the early twentieth century were distasteful to him. It was to escape them that he received permission from his provincial to teach at the Catholic University of America. As long as international conditions permitted, however, he went to France each summer to visit his relatives and his Basilian confreres, to consult colleagues in his field, and to do research in libraries. During these years he spent the Christmas vacation with his confreres in America, going in alternate years to Assumption College and to St Michael's College.

Adolphe Vaschalde acquired an international reputation for his editing of Coptic and Syriac patristic texts. The *Corpus Scriptorum Christianorum Orientalium* series counted him as a contributor from its formation in 1903, and in 1930 named him editor in charge of its Coptic texts. Browsing in bookshops in search of books in his specialized field was a lifelong recreation of Father Vaschalde; his library later went partially into the Department of Oriental Languages at the Catholic University of America and partly to the library of the Pontifical Institute of Mediaeval Studies, Toronto. When he died, W.R. Taylor, chairman of the Department of Oriental Languages at the University of

Toronto, wrote: 'Each time I was privileged to meet him, I was impressed by the richness of his character. Though possessed of full and accurate knowledge in his field, he bore it all with rare humility and sweet charity.' An obituary in the *Catholic Historical Review* said that 'he endeared himself to those who came to know him well by an unfailing habit of kindliness. ... He had the directness and candour which accompany a devotion to truth, and which flow from the highest Christian ideals. Evidence of shoddy scholarship, false principles, or deliberate wrong-doing always provoked in him deep indignation.'

BIBLIOGRAPHY:
Books: Ed. *Three Letters of Philoxenus, Bishop of Mabbôgh, 483–519*. Rome, 1902. Ed. (with J.-B. Chabot) *Philoxeni Mabbugensis Tractatus tres De Trinitate et incarnatione*, 2 vols. CSCO, Scriptores Syri, series 2, vol. 27. Paris, 1907. Ed. *Babai Magni Liber de unione*, 2 vols. CSCO 79–80. Rome and Louvain, 1915. *Iacobi Edesseni Hexaemeron: seu, In opus creationis libri septem*, 2 vols. CSCO, Scriptores Syri, series 2, vol. 56. Louvain, 1932. Ed. with I. Sedlacek and J.-B. Chabot. *Dionysii bar Salibi Commentarii in Evangelia Marc*, 2 vols. CSCO Scriptores Syri, series 2, vol. 98. Louvain, 1933.
Articles: 'Ce qui a été publié des versions coptes de la Bible,' *Revue Biblique* 28 (1919) 220–43, 513–31, 29 (1920) 241–58, 30 (1921) 237–46, 31 (1922) 234–58; repr. *Muséon. Revue d'études orientales* 43 (1930)–46 (1933). For the *Catholic Encyclopedia* (New York, 1907) he wrote the following articles: 'Mesrob,' 'Nerses I–IV,' 'Nerses of Lambron,' 'Philoxenus of Mabbogh,' 'Serapion of Thmuis, Saint,' and 'Tell-el-Amarna Tablets.'
Unpublished: 'Biblical Introduction' (250 pp.); 'Hebrew Archaeology' (154 pp.); 'Notes on Assyria, Israel, Juda' (119 pp.).
SOURCES: GABF; *Catholic Historical Review* 28 (April 1942) 126–8; 'Adolphe A. Vaschalde, Priest and Scholar,' *Catholic University of America Bulletin* 9 (May 1942); Kirley, *Community in France* 186, 214n516, 216n518, 219n526, 220n528, 240n569, 242; Kirley, *Congregation in France* 45, 199; *Makers of the Catholic Encyclopedia* (New York, 1917) 177; *New Catholic Encyclopedia* (New York, 1967) 14: 541; Pouzol, 'Notices.'

VASCHALDE, Auguste, scholastic, was born at Rocles (Ardèche) on 19 January 1873, the son of Martin and Julie Vaschalde. He died at his place of birth on 28 January 1898 and was buried in the local cemetery.

Auguste Vaschalde received his early education from two priests in his native village. After studies at the Collège du Sacré-Coeur, Annonay, in the Sainte-Barbe (minor seminary) section, 1887–93, he entered the novitiate and made first profession on 21 September 1894. He did one year of military service with the Troisième Zouaves. After two years, 1895–7, teaching at the Collège Saint-Charles in Blidah, Algeria, he went to live with his family because of illness. He died there at the age of twenty-five.

SOURCES: GABF; Pouzol, 'Notices.'

VASCHALDE, François Jean, priest, was born at Saint-Pons (Ardèche) on 1 March 1828, the son of François Vaschalde, a tailor, and Marguerite Barnier. He died in Annonay on 16 November 1892 and was buried there in the cemetery on the grounds of the Collège du Sacré-Coeur.

François Vaschalde studied first at the Collège des Cordeliers, Annonay, in the Sainte-Barbe (minor seminary) section, 1845–9, and then at the Grand Séminaire de Viviers. On 7 April 1854 he returned to Annonay and entered the Basilian community. He was ordained to the priesthood on 19 December 1857 in the chapel of the Grand Séminaire by Bishop Louis Delcusy of Viviers. For three years prior to his ordination he had been prefect and professor at the Collège des Cordeliers. As a priest he taught at the Petit Séminaire de Vernoux (Ardèche), 1857–63 and 1864–7, and at the Collège des Cordeliers, 1863–4. In 1867 he returned to the Collège du Sacré-Coeur, the new name for the Collège des Cordeliers after it moved to a new location in Annonay, where he taught theology and remained for the rest of his life.

On 25 March 1878 Father Vaschalde was appointed to the general council by Father Jean Mathieu *Soulerin to replace Father André *Charmant, who had died. In the chapters of 1880, 1883, 1886, and 1889 he was re-elected to the council. He suffered from chronic asthma and died after a short illness. The *Semaine religieuse de Viviers*, which called him François-Xavier Vaschalde, described him as 'a peaceful, modest and faithful priest.'

SOURCES: GABF; Chomel, *Collège d'Annonay* 517; Kirley, *Community in France* 55, 70n178, 124n305; Pouzol, 'Notices'; *Semaine religieuse de Viviers* (2 December 1892) 568.

VASEK, Leslie Joseph, priest, was born in Houston on 4 January 1923, the son of John Vasek and Martha Gully. He died in Houston on 16

October 1967 and was buried there in the Basilian plot of Garden of Gethsemane, Forest Park Lawndale Cemetery.

'Les' Vasek attended St Joseph's Parochial School and St Thomas High School, Houston, and then entered St Basil's Novitiate in Toronto. After his profession on 15 August 1942, he was appointed to St Michael's College, Toronto, where he fulfilled the brilliant promise of his high school record, graduating with honours (B.A., University of Toronto, 1946). The following year was spent teaching at St Thomas High School. He studied theology at St Basil's Seminary, Toronto, 1947–51, while concurrently taking further studies in physics at the University of Toronto (M.A., 1951). He was ordained to the priesthood on 29 June 1950 in St Anne's Church, Houston, by Bishop Louis Reicher of Austin, Texas.

In 1951 Father Vasek was appointed to the University of St Thomas, Houston, where he taught physics and also served as treasurer, 1951–3. In 1955 he returned to the University of Toronto for graduate studies, earning a Ph.D. in physics (1958) for his thesis, 'The External Photo-electric Effect in Insulators.' After returning to the University of St Thomas, he once again taught physics and served as treasurer. His health began to fail in 1965, and he was relieved of the office of treasurer. He died in 1967 from a heart attack at the age of forty-four – the second of three Basilian priests teaching at the University of St Thomas to die that year.

Father Vasek had an innate shyness which he hid with an outgoing manner. His friendly way won the confidence of all who had dealings with him.

SOURCES: GABF; *Annals* 1 (1950) 289, 4 (1968) 62–3; *Newsletter* (17 October 1967).

VERGER, Jules, priest, was born on 13 June 1864 at Bourg-les-Valence (Drôme, diocese of Valence), the son of Joseph Verger and Rose Cappuccini. He died at Privas (Ardèche) on 11 January 1934 and was buried in the Basilian plot of the cemetery at Privas.

His family having moved to Tournon (Ardèche), Jules attended the Lycée de Tournon and then went to the Petit Séminaire d'Aubenas (Ardèche). He made his novitiate at Beaconfield House, Plymouth, England, 1884–5, and professed final vows as a Basilian on 17 September 1886. Bishop Joseph-Michel-Frédéric Bonnet of Viviers ordained him to the priesthood on 21 September 1889 in the chapel of the Collège du Sacré-Coeur, Annonay. While doing his theological studies he had taught and supervised students, first at Sainte-Barbe, the minor seminary in Annonay, 1885–6, and then at the Collège Saint-Charles, Blidah, Algeria, 1886–9. He obtained a *licence ès lettres* in July 1889, and did a doctoral thesis on St Augustine.

For ten years Father Verger taught philosophy at the Collège Saint-Charles, Blidah. He returned to Annonay, and taught rhetoric at the Collège du Sacré-Coeur, 1899–1903. After the 1903 legislation excluding religious from teaching, he served as chaplain at the Collège municipal, Privas, from 1904 to 1933, and for some time was chaplain as well to the Sisters of the Sacred Heart, Privas. He died suddenly as he was preparing to say Mass. Well known for his teaching and spiritual direction, he was honoured by the presence of a large crowd of clergy, former students, and lay people at his funeral.

SOURCES: GABF; Kirley, *Community in France* 205, 240n569; Kirley, *Congregation in France* 72, 81–2; Pouzol, 'Notices.'

VERMILLION, René Marcel, priest, was born on 15 October 1928 at Villefagnon (Charente, diocese of Angoulême), the son of René Valarche and Yvonne Marenelli. He died in Galveston, Texas, on 4 July 1992 and is buried in the Basilian plot of Garden of Gethsemane, Forest Park Lawndale Cemetery, Houston.

René's parents having divorced when he was quite young, his mother married Burke Vermillion, a Lieutenant-Commander in the United States forces stationed in France, who adopted René. The places of his early education varied according to his stepfather's assignments: France, Norfolk, Virginia, Houston, and the Canal Zone, Panama. This multilingual exposure was the basis of René's pursuit of language studies both before and after he entered the Basilians. He graduated from Balboa High School, Canal Zone, although most of his secondary education was taken at Stephen F. Austin High School, Houston. He attended Canal Zone Junior College and in 1949 the University of Houston. He taught for one year in Guam, after which he returned to Houston, where he enrolled in the University of St Thomas (B.A., 1953). Upon graduation he entered St Basil's Novitiate, Rochester, and made first profession on 24 September 1954. He taught religion, history, and Latin for two years at St Thomas High School, Houston, and then did his theological studies at St Basil's Seminary, Toronto, 1956–60. Bishop Francis Allen ordained him to the priesthood on 28 June 1959 in St Basil's Church, Toronto.

In 1960 Father Vermillion returned to St Thomas High School, where for the next sixteen years he was engaged in teaching (French, Spanish, and religion), counselling, and administration. In 1962 he obtained an M.Ed. from the University of Houston and became certified in the State of Texas as counsellor. He took summer and night courses in psychology and special education to improve his skills. For a number of years he served as assistant principal, registrar, and disciplinarian, and was coach of the swimming team. He was named president of the Diocesan Guidance Counsellors Association, Houston, and held office in the Houston branch of the American Guidance and Personnel Association. He provided chaplaincy service to the NASA astronauts at Ellington Air Force Base, and was invited to lead a service of prayer at one of the early space launchings at Cape Kennedy (Canaveral). In the local Basilian community he served as treasurer and actively promoted vocations to the Basilians. Proud of his French heritage and a promoter of French culture, he served as president of the Alliance Française in Houston. He was invested as *Titulaire des Palmes Académiques* by the consul-general of France on Bastille Day 1979.

In 1976 Father Vermillion joined the staff of O'Connell School, Galveston, as counsellor and teacher. The following year he became dean of students and executive assistant to the principal. In 1978 he was appointed director of development. While in Galveston he did chaplaincy service for various convents of sisters. In 1980 he transferred to Bishop McGuiness High School, Oklahoma City, becoming in 1981 vice-principal and director of guidance. He continued in that ministry until, in December 1991, a condition of terminal brain cancer caused his hospitalization in Galveston and his death six months later.

René Vermillion was an eminently social man, an organizer of parties and a man whose company was enjoyable. Archbishop Charles Salotka presided over a memorial Mass in the cathedral of Oklahoma City on 14 July 1992, and Father Robert Boyer spoke in gratitude for Father Vermillion's years of service there.

SOURCES: GABF; *Annals* 2 (1959) 422, 7 (1993) 133–5; *Newsletter* (23 July 1992).

VERNEDE, Auguste, priest, was born on 17 November 1846 at Saint-Germain (Ardèche), the son of Jean Vernède and Lucie Débannet.

He died in Annonay on 21 January 1881, and is buried there in the Basilian cemetery on the grounds of the Collège du Sacré-Coeur.

After secondary studies at the Petit Séminaire d'Aubenas (Ardèche), Auguste entered the Basilian novitiate at Feyzin (Isère, now Rhône) in 1865 and made his final profession of vows on 17 September 1869. He was ordained a deacon by Bishop Louis Delcusy of Viviers on 17 December 1870. The date of his ordination to the priesthood is not known. He taught in Basilian schools while doing his theology courses: the Collège des Cordeliers, Annonay, October–December 1866; the Petit Séminaire de Vernoux (Ardèche), December 1866–July 1868; the Collège du Sacré-Coeur, Annonay, 1868–9; and the Collège de Privas (Ardèche), 1869–70.

Father Vernède accompanied Daniel Cushing to Canada in August 1871 and was appointed to Assumption College, Sandwich (now Windsor), Ontario, to teach; but his limited facility in English obliged him to move to pastoral ministry in 1872 at Assumption Parish, Sandwich, which was largely French at the time. Father Vernède was plagued by ill health, so that early in September 1879 he returned to Annonay, suffering from tuberculosis of lungs and bone. He spent his last days at Sainte-Barbe, where the confreres and sisters of a nearby convent cared for him. The college journal describes him upon his return from Canada as being 'in a sad state,' shaken by 'a heart-rending cough' and suffering from 'decay in the bone of the left knee.' After his death an entry in the same journal reads, 'This young priest had won the esteem and the affection of his confreres and of all who knew him.'

SOURCES: GABF; Kirley, *Congregation in France* 45; Pouzol, 'Notices.'

VERON, Louis, priest, member of the Congregation 1886–c.1901, the son of Louis Véron and Marie Cotillon, was born on 13 May 1864 in Le Puy (Haute-Loire).

Louis studied at the Collège du Sacré-Coeur, Annonay, and then made his novitiate at Beaconfield House, Plymouth, England, 1884–5. After a few months of illness and recuperation in his family he professed the vows on 17 September 1886. Bishop Joseph-Michel-Frédéric Bonnet ordained him a priest on 21 September 1889 in the chapel of the Collège du Sacré-Coeur.

Father Véron's main work in Basilian institutions was that of prefect of discipline: at the Collège du Sacré-Coeur, Annonay, junior division,

1886–7; at the Petit Séminaire Sainte-Barbe, Annonay, 1887–8; at the Petit Séminaire de Vernoux (Ardèche), 1888–9; at the Collège du Sacré-Coeur, senior division, 1889–90; and at the Ecole cléricale de Périgueux, 1890–1.

He probably withdrew from the Community in 1901. Letters from the superior general, Father Noël *Durand, that were sent in February, March, and April 1900, summoning him to return to Annonay, went unanswered.

SOURCE: Pouzol, 'Notices,' Supplément 2.

VIELFAURE, Auguste, priest, was born on 28 August 1855 at Joannas (Ardèche). He died on 27 July 1908 at Largentière and is buried in the cemetery at Joannas.

Auguste studied at the Collège du Bourg-Saint-Andéol (Ardèche), and entered the Basilian novitiate at Feyzin (Isère, now Rhône) in 1876 or 1877, taking final vows on 17 September 1880. Archbishop Armand de Charbonnel ordained him to the priesthood on 23 September 1882 in the chapel of the Collège du Sacré-Coeur, Annonay. While studying theology he taught and served as prefect of discipline, first at the Ecole cléricale de Périgueux (Dordogne), 1879–80, and then at the Collège du Sacré-Coeur, Annonay.

After ordination Father Vielfaure continued to teach at the Collège du Sacré-Coeur, Annonay, 1882–5. He returned to Périgueux in 1885 to serve as curate, 1885–93, at the Shrine of the Holy Shroud in the parish of Cadouin (Dordogne). From 1893 to 1895 he taught in the Ecole cléricale de Périgueux. His next appointment brought him to Mary Immaculate College, Beaconfield House, Plymouth, England, as bursar of the college – a post he held for five years, 1895–1900. For the next three years he divided his time between working as prefect of discipline and as bursar at the Petit Séminaire d'Aubenas. With the exclusion in 1903 of Basilians from their schools, he retired to his place of birth at Joannas to live with his aged mother, and died in the hospital at Largentière nearby at the age of fifty-two.

SOURCES: GABF; Kirley, *Community in France* 184; Pouzol, 'Notices.'

VINCENT, Charles, priest, provincial in North America, 1874–90, was born on 30 June 1828 at Vallon (Ardèche). He died on 1 November 1890 in Toronto and was buried there in the Basilian plot in St

Michael's cemetery, the first of the early French Basilians to be buried in Canada.

Charles Vincent studied at the Petit Séminaire at Bourg-Saint-Andéol (Ardèche) and then did one year of philosophy at the Collège des Cordeliers in the Sainte-Barbe (minor seminary) section. He made his novitiate at Vernoux (Ardèche) under Father Auguste de *Montgolfier in 1848–9, and then taught at the Petit Séminaire de Vernoux, 1849–50, and at the Collège des Cordeliers, 1850–2. He professed final vows in 1851 and received minor orders in April 1852.

While still a scholastic Charles Vincent was chosen, along with Fathers Jean Mathieu *Soulerin and Joseph *Malbos and another scholastic, William *Flannery, to help staff a minor seminary in Toronto at the request of Bishop Armand de Charbonnel, a former student of the college. They reached Toronto in August 1852. Together with Father Patrick *Molony, a Basilian who had preceded them in 1850, and a Christian Brother, they began what was to become St Michael's College. Charles Vincent did not take the vows with the community in 1852, but held to the formula of promises of 1822. He continued his theology course and was responsible for discipline at the new school, although in the beginning he understood not a word of English – a situation which his Irish students in study hall exploited at his expense. He was ordained to the priesthood along with William Flannery by Bishop Charbonnel on 22 May 1853.

In the summer of 1857 Father Vincent returned to France to visit his family, whom he had not informed of his departure in 1852, fearing the emotional strain. He took the new Basilian vows on 29 September 1857 at the end of the annual retreat.

After his return to Toronto, St Michael's College and its collegiate church St Basil's Parish were to occupy the rest of Father Vincent's life. In 1857 he was named treasurer, and from 1865 to 1886 he served as superior of the college. Along with teaching and administration, he took on the duties of pastor of St Basil's, 1865–80, and in 1869 he became confessor and benefactor to the cloistered Sisters of the Precious Blood in Toronto. In 1868 he had once again returned to France for the annual retreat.

From 1874 to 1890 he was provincial in America, even though provinces had not been canonically erected. In a sense he was head of the Basilians in America from 1865 to 1890. This was not an easy time. After 1870 there were serious difficulties with Archbishop John Lynch of Toronto. Father Vincent was dissuaded by his confreres from resigning. The archbishop fell ill, and peace was gradually restored. In 1878 Father Vincent was named a vicar general of the archdiocese of Toronto and in 1875 he had attended the first provincial council in Canada as theologian for Bishop Jean-François Jamot of Peterborough, who was a native of Aneyron (Ardèche), a place near Father Vincent's home town of Vallon.

As pastor of St Basil's Church Father Vincent undertook major renovations in 1876, adding on the present-day sanctuary. In 1878, to mark the silver jubilee of his ordination, a stained glass window of his patron St Charles was placed above the main altar. He supported the efforts of Father John Read *Teefy to affiliate with the University of Toronto, and in 1881 he was the first Basilian to be a member of the University of Toronto Senate. He died of diabetes at the age of sixty-two.

The *Golden Jubilee Volume of the Archdiocese of Toronto* said of him: 'He was a man of great simplicity, of quick, practical judgment and deep insight into character. He was kind and gentle, easy to approach, more loved than feared.' He had a beautiful singing voice and was in charge of the choir at St Basil's. Without being eloquent he preached well. A high school established by the Basilians in Sudbury in 1951 was named 'St Charles College' in his memory.

SOURCES: GABF; *French Studies U. of T.* 30; Hoskin, *St Basil's Parish*; Madden, *St Basil's*; *Jubilee Volume 1842–1892 of the Archdiocese of Toronto* (Toronto, 1892); 'Very Reverend C. Vincent,' *Irish Canadian* (5 September 1889), repr. *Basilian Teacher* 4 (February 1960) 145–7; T.J. Hanrahan, *Dictionary of Canadian Biography* (Toronto 1965, etc.) 11 903–4; Kirley, *Community in France* 33 and passim; Kirley, *Congregation in France* 1, 45, 51, 96, 234; Pouzol, 'Notices'; Roume, *Origines* 326–37, 347. For documentation on Vincent relating to the Basilians assuming charge of Assumption see Power, *Assumption College* 2 27–37.

VINCENT, Claude Louis, priest, member of the Congregation 1949–79, cousin of Father Donald C. Furlong CSB, was born in Ottawa on 10 November 1925, the son of Walter Vincent and Anne Furlong. He died on 10 December 1996 in Windsor and was buried in Sacred Heart Cemetery, Lasalle, Ontario

After obtaining his B.A. from the University of Toronto in 1948, Claude entered the Basilian Novitiate and made his first profession on 15 August 1949. He taught at St Michael's College School, Toronto, and at St Thomas High School, Houston. He did his theological studies at St

Basil's Seminary, Toronto, and was ordained to the priesthood on 29 June 1953.

Father Vincent taught at Aquinas Institute, Rochester, St Charles College School, Sudbury, Ontario, and Michael Power High School, Etobicoke, Ontario. He obtained an M.A. in sociology from Loyola University, Chicago, in 1965. From 1964 until his retirement in 1991 he taught in the department of sociology at the University of Windsor. He had withdrawn from the Congregation in 1979. He was survived by his wife, Marilyn Venney, and several stepchildren.

SOURCES: GABF; *Annals* 2 (1953) 111; *Newsletter* (23 December 1996).

W

WALIGORE, Arthur Francis, priest, was born on 6 February 1924 in Detroit, the son of Joseph Waligore and Frances Partyka. He died at Springhill, Florida, on 17 February 1977, and is buried in the Basilian plot of Holy Cross Cemetery, Thornhill, Ontario.

'Art' or 'Tammy,' as he came to be called, attended St Thomas the Apostle parochial school and Catholic Central High School, Detroit, graduating in 1942. He entered St Basil's Novitiate, Rochester, a member of the first group of novices there, was professed on 12 September 1943, and was appointed to St Michael's College, Toronto, for undergraduate studies (B.A., Honours Classics, University of Toronto, 1948). As a scholastic he taught for two years, first at Catholic Central, 1948–9, and then at St Thomas High School, Houston, 1949–50, where he also did his first year of theology. He spent the next year at St Michael's doing his second year of theology and then moved to the new St Basil's Seminary to continue his theological studies. He was ordained to the priesthood on 29 June 1952 in St Basil's Church, Toronto, by Cardinal James Charles McGuigan.

Father Waligore was appointed to Aquinas Institute, Rochester, where he taught for three years. During the summers he studied at the University of Michigan (M.A., Classics, 1956). He was then appointed to St Michael's College, where he spent the next fourteen years as teacher, moderator of scholastics, 1958–60, assistant registrar, assistant dean of residence, 1960–6, and second councillor for the Basilian community, 1966–9. In 1970 he moved to Michael Power High School, Etobicoke, as teacher, assistant principal, and second councillor, 1972–3. In August, 1973, he was named treasurer general of the Basilian Fathers, a position he held until his death four years later.

Tammy Waligore was a quiet, unassuming man of quick intelligence. He loved to be home, where he entered into community activities wholeheartedly. After supper he would often recruit two or three confreres to go skating at a nearby city rink, and in spring or summer he organized Basilian baseball games. He was an ardent bridge player who brought excitement to the table by his skill and his speed of play. He had a deep concern about the observance of the vow of poverty, and urged this on the general community. He found it difficult to discuss theological matters, especially controversial ones, but he read widely and was constantly seeking greater understanding. He died in his sleep while on vacation with his mother, visiting his sister in Florida. An autopsy revealed an astonishing condition of arterial sclerosis.

SOURCES: GABF; *Annals* 2 (1952) 62, 5 (1978) 316–17; *Newsletter* (24 February 1977).

WALSH, Francis Anthony, priest, younger brother of Father Joseph Basil *Walsh, was born at Parkhill, Ontario (diocese of London), on 16 July 1901, the youngest of eight children born to Thomas Walsh and Theresa McKenna. He died in Houston on 9 June 1952 and was buried in the Basilian plot of Assumption Cemetery, Windsor.

Francis Walsh attended local schools and then the high school section of Assumption College, Windsor, 1917–21. A heart ailment forced interruption of his studies, but in 1925 he returned to Assumption College (B.A., University of Western Ontario, 1929). He entered St Basil's Novitiate, Toronto, was professed on 12 September 1930, and made his theological studies at St Basil's Scholasticate, Toronto. Bishop Alexander MacDonald ordained him to the priesthood on 21 December 1933 in Assumption Church, Windsor.

Father Frank Walsh taught at Assumption College School, 1934–6. He was on sick leave during the year 1936–7, then served as assistant at Ste Anne's Parish, Detroit. In 1946 he returned to Assumption College School. Deterioration of his health in ensuing years left him almost a complete invalid. He was assigned to St Thomas High School, Houston, where he died two years later.

During the 1940s as director of the Basilian Press, Father Walsh made plans to expand its operations, but ill health and wartime paper shortages prevented their implementation. He had a lifelong interest in baseball, although he never played the game himself and did but little coaching. He was, however, an active organizer of intramural baseball leagues in the schools to which he was attached. He was a friend of Ty Cobb of the Detroit Tigers, and Connie Mack never failed to visit when he brought his Philadelphia Athletics to town. No matter the state of his health or his active schedule, he always found time to talk to anyone who sought him out.

SOURCES: GABF; *Annals* 2 (1952) 66–7.

WALSH, Francis Mary I., priest, was born at Miramichi, New Brunswick (diocese of Saint John), on 3 October 1842. He died in Toronto on 28 May 1914 and is buried there in the Basilian plot of Mount Hope Cemetery.

The family having moved to Highland Creek, Ontario (east of Toronto) when he was a child, Francis was sent to St Michael's College, Toronto, in 1855. In due course he entered St Basil's Novitiate, which was then located at St Michael's College, and was professed on 23 May 1861. In August 1861 he went with Denis *O'Connor to France, where both studied at the novitiate at Feyzin (Isère, now Rhône) until October 1862, when they moved to the scholasticate on the Montée du Château, Annonay. In August 1863 he returned to Canada with Father Louis *Ranc. He completed his course in theology at St Michael's College, and in 1867 was appointed to St Louis College, Louisville, Ohio, where he was ordained to the priesthood on 20 October 1867.

After ordination, 'Père Walsh,' as he wanted to be called, taught again at St Louis College, 1867–72, with an interval of several months at Assumption College, Windsor. He taught French at St Michael's College from 1872 to 1876, and assisted at St Mary's of the Assumption Parish, Owen Sound, Ontario, until the end of 1879 or the beginning of 1880, when he replaced Father Patrick *Molony, who was ill, as teacher of English at the Collège du Sacré-Coeur, Annonay. He remained in France until 1885. From 1885 to 1891 he was absent from the Congregation, serving as a missionary in the mining camps of the Dakotas. He returned to St Michael's College in 1891 and remained there until his sudden death in 1914.

Father Walsh was completely bilingual and frequently preached at the francophone parish of Sacré-Coeur, Toronto. He judged that his most rewarding work was done in his last years in Toronto when he attended the Central Prison, the Mercer Reformatory, and the Ontario Hospital. He was also chaplain at St John's Industrial School. When he died the superintendent of the Central Prison wrote to Father Nicholas *Roche, 'Father Walsh by his long, faithful, and loving service here endeared himself to every member of the Central Prison staff, and was respected and looked up to by the inmates.' The Golden Jubilee Volume of St Mary's Church described Father Walsh as 'a thorough French scholar, a striking orator, a man of faith, humble and kind.' An obituary in the *Yearbook* of St Michael's College described him as 'a humble man of inspiring faith, affable and kind in demeanour, and his deportment was marked by a genuine *politesse*.'

SOURCES: GABF; *Centennial, St Mary's; Jubilee, St Mary's; Yearbook SMC* 6 (1915).

WALSH, Joseph Basil, priest, member of the Congregation 1911–48, elder brother of Father Francis Anthony *Walsh, was born at Seaforth, Ontario (diocese of London), on 14 June 1888, the second of eight children born to Thomas Walsh and Theresa McKenna. He died at Waco, Texas, on 20 July 1965 and was buried in the Basilian plot of Assumption Cemetery, Windsor.

Joseph Walsh attended local schools at Seaforth and Parkhill High School. He taught school for one year. In 1907 he enrolled in Assumption College, Windsor, and one year later transferred to St Michael's College, Toronto. He entered St Basil's Novitiate Toronto in 1911 and, after profession on 15 August 1912, completed his university course while studying theology. He graduated in June 1915 and was ordained to the priesthood on 26 September 1915.

Father Walsh was sent to study at the Catholic University of America, Washington, D.C. (M.A., 1916). He was appointed to Assumption College, 1916–19, and then to St Michael's College as treasurer, 1919–34, which led to his election as treasurer general of the Congregation, 1933–6. He spent the year 1934–5 at Assumption College and the year 1935–6 in Toronto supervising the construction of the Queen's Park buildings (More, Fisher, Teefy, and the Institute wing) at St Michael's College. He spent the year 1936–7 as assistant at St John the Baptist Parish, Amherstburg, Ontario, and then was named pastor of St Basil's Parish, Toronto, 1937–42. After serving five years as pastor of St Anne's Parish, Houston, 1942–7, he was transferred to Catholic Central High School, Detroit. Early in 1948 he withdrew from the Congregation and was incardinated in the diocese of Austin (Texas), where he was the founding pastor of St Joseph's Parish, Waco, Texas. He died there in 1965, stricken with a cerebral haemorrhage while locking up the church he had built. At the request of his five surviving sisters, he was buried next to his Basilian brother Francis.

While still quite young Father Walsh lost all the hair on the top of his head and was generally called 'Baldy.' He possessed an endless supply of energy, with a habit of working from early morning until late at night.

SOURCES: GABF; *Annals* 3 (1965) 383; *Newsletter* (4 August 1965); Kirley, *Congregation in France* 159; Madden, *St Basil's*.

WARE, John Francis, priest, was born on 12 July 1925 at Mineola, Long Island (diocese of Brooklyn, since 1957 of Rockville Center), one of four sons of Francis Ware and Helen Ignatia Loyola Doyle. He died in Toronto on 28 March 1995 and is buried in the Basilian plot of St John the Baptist Cemetery, Amherstburg, Ontario.

After graduating from Chaminade High School, Mineola, John served in the United States Army Air Corps until 1946. Thinking of the priesthood, he spent one year specializing in Latin at St Charles College, Catonsville, Maryland, before enrolling in Assumption College, Windsor, where he continued his undergraduate studies. He entered St Basil's Novitiate, Rochester, in 1948, making first profession on 15 August 1949. He returned to Assumption College to complete his arts course (B.A., University of Western Ontario, 1951) while concurrently teaching at Assumption College School. He taught in 1951 at Catholic Central High School, Detroit, and in 1952–3 at Aquinas Institute, Rochester. He studied theology at St Basil's Seminary, Toronto, 1953–7 (S.T.B, University of St Michael's College, 1956), while also teaching part-time at St Michael's College School. He was ordained to the priesthood on 29 June 1956 in St Basil's Church, Toronto, by Cardinal James Charles McGuigan.

In 1957 Father Ware was appointed to Aquinas Institute once more and taught there for eight years. In 1965 he was appointed to Andrean High School, Gary (now Merrillville), Indiana, 1965–8. Outside the classroom John coached sports, counselled students, and moderated clubs. He gave conferences and retreats especially on the theme of vocations.

In 1968 he undertook studies in psychology at the University of Notre Dame (M.A., 1969). He began doctoral studies, but from January to June 1970 he filled a counselling position at Quincy College, Illinois. In July of 1970 he was appointed to St John the Baptist Parish, Amherstburg, Ontario, where for seventeen years his remarkable talents for working with young people found their full scope. In 1987 he took a year for professional development and renewal, and in 1988 he was appointed to St John Fisher Parish, Richmond, Texas. He spent two years at Dillon House, Houston, 1992–4, before severe emphysema demanded his move in 1994 to the Basilian Fathers Residence (Infirmary), Toronto, where he spent the few remaining months of his life.

John Ware's founding of Shalom House in Amherstburg as a place of meeting, recreation, and counsel for teenagers brought him recognition from the Amherstburg community at large, who named him 'Man of the Year' in 1987 and who granted funding for his work by the United Way of Windsor-Essex County.

SOURCES: GABF; *Annals* 2 (1956) 253, 6 (1987) 529–30, 8 (1996) 96–8; *Newsletter* (31 May 1995).

WARREN, John Arthur, priest, was born on 30 January 1909 at Niagara Falls, Ontario (archdiocese of Toronto, since 1958 of St Catharines), the son of Arthur Warren and Irene A. Flynn. He died at Wainfleet, Ontario, on 4 May 1985 and is buried in the Basilian plot of Holy Cross Cemetery, Thornhill, Ontario.

'Jack' Warren began high school at Niagara Falls Collegiate Institute, but in 1926 he enrolled at St Michael's College, Toronto, where he completed high school and remained for university studies. In 1931 he entered St Basil's Novitiate, Toronto, making profession on 15 August 1932, and was appointed to St Michael's College (B.A., University of Toronto, 1933). Jack played football on the varsity intercollegiate team. He studied theology at St Basil's Scholasticate, Toronto, while concurrently taking courses at the Ontario College of Education and earning teaching certification, 1935. He taught French and history at St Michael's College School, 1935–6, returning to the scholasticate in 1936 to complete his theology. Archbishop James Charles McGuigan ordained him to the priesthood on 18 December 1937 in St Basil's Church, Toronto.

In 1938 Father Warren moved back to St Michael's College School to teach French in all grades for the next eight years. During the summers he studied at the Université Laval (M.A., French, 1945). It was during these years that his long association with the Royal Canadian Air Force began as part-time chaplain, 1943-6. In 1946 he was appointed to Assumption College School, Windsor, to teach French. He taught for one year at Aquinas Institute, 1951-2, and for one year at St Charles College, Sudbury, Ontario, 1952-3. In September 1953 he became a full-time chaplain with the R.C.A.F. He was posted in 1955 to Station Clinton, Summerside, Prince Edward Island, in 1957 to Marville, France, and in 1960-5 to Camp Borden, Ontario. He was named pastor of Blessed Sacrament Parish, Windsor, 1965-6, and then assistant at St Basil's Parish, Toronto, 1966-7. He returned to chaplaincy duty with the R.C.A.F. for the years 1967-71. After his second retirement he undertook pastoral work in the diocese of St Catharines, serving at both St Mary's Parish and St Andrew the Apostle Parish, Welland, Ontario. In 1984 he retired from full-time parish duties.

Jack Warren was a tall, finely built man, gentle and courteous of manner. Though he lived away from the community for many years, his Basilian identity and loyalty remained constant. He died in an automobile accident at the age of seventy-six.

SOURCES: GABF; *Annals* 6 (1983) 116, 6 (1986) 478-9; *Newsletter* (15 May 1985).

WEILER, Arthur Jerome, priest, was born on 2 December 1904 at Mildmay, Ontario (diocese of Hamilton), one of sixteen children (eight daughters and eight sons) of George Weiler and Theresa Fedy. He died in Toronto on 18 August 1995 and is buried in the Basilian plot of Holy Cross Cemetery, Thornhill, Ontario.

'Art' (or, as he became known for his teaching of geology, 'Rocky') Weiler attended Sacred Heart elementary school in Mildmay and Walkerton High School, graduating in 1921. He obtained elementary teaching certification from Stratford Normal School in 1924, and taught for the next two years before entering St Michael's College, Toronto, in September 1926. During his arts course he taught part-time at St Michael's College School (B.A., Honours Philosophy, University of Toronto, 1930) and attended the Ontario College of Education, earning secondary school teaching certification, 1930. He began teaching full-time at St Michael's College School, then entered St Basil's Novitiate, Toronto, in 1932, and made first profession on 12 September 1933. He studied theology at St Basil's Scholasticate, Toronto, 1933-7, and was ordained to the priesthood on 19 December 1936 in St Basil's Church, Toronto, by Archbishop James Charles McGuigan.

In September 1937 Father Weiler was appointed to Assumption College, and would remain in the Windsor area for the next fifty-eight years, working at both the high school and the college for thirty years and then in ministry to the sick and aged for twenty-eight years. At Assumption College he taught German, geology, mathematics, and science.

His devotion to the Mother of God dated from his youth and characterized his whole life. In her honour he founded the Marian Centre at the Assumption College and, as a countersign to the annual May Day parade sponsored by the Communist Party in Moscow, organized the annual May Day parade through the streets of Windsor.

After retiring from teaching in 1967 and taking up residence at O'Connor House, Windsor, he became chaplain in three hospitals, two nursing homes, and a chronic care facility. In 1986 failing health caused his move to the Villa Maria Nursing Home, Windsor, where he was both patient and minister. In July 1995 he was moved to the Basilian Fathers Residence (Infirmary), Toronto, where he died one month later at the age of ninety, the oldest Basilian at that time.

BIBLIOGRAPHY:
Pamphlets: *Lord, the Man You Love Is Ill.* Windsor, 1969. *Walk in Love.* Windsor, 1973.
Articles: 'Prayer,' *Basilian* 2 (January 1936) 10; 'Prayer, Mass and the Apostolate,' *Benedicamus* 2 (November 1948) 2–3; 'Apostolate and the Cross,' *Benedicamus* 3 (November 1949) 2–3; 'The Priest Teacher and His Relations to Extra-Curricular Activities,' *Basilian Christmas Educational Conference* (1956) 16–19; 'The Priest Teacher and His Relations to Extra-Curricular Activities,' *Basilian Teacher* 1 (January 1957) 16–18.
SOURCES: GABF; *Annals* 6 (1984) 208, 6 (1987) 492, 8 (1996) 103–4; *Newsletter* (15 October 1995).

WELTY, Emil Jerome, priest, was born in Cleveland, Ohio, on 18 April 1888, the son of Frederick Welty and Josepha Zeller. He died in Toronto on 22 March 1962 and in buried in the Basilian plot of Holy Cross Cemetery, Thornhill, Ontario.

Emil Welty lived from 1893 to 1901 with relatives in Germany, where he began his education. After rejoining his parents, who had immigrated to Salem, Ohio, he continued his education but then went to work in a steel mill. In 1909 he enrolled in Assumption College, Windsor, to study for the priesthood. Six years later he entered St Basil's Novitiate, Toronto, and was professed on 13 August 1916. He studied theology at St Basil's Scholasticate, which was then located temporarily at Assumption College, and at the same time completed the requirements for a B.A. from the University of Western Ontario. He was ordained priest on 29 February 1920 in St Peter's Cathedral, London, Ontario, by Bishop Michael Fallon.

Father Welty taught at Assumption College in 1920–1, then served as its treasurer, 1921–3. Appointed in 1923 to St Michael's College, Toronto, he received an M.A. in philosophy from the University of Toronto in 1924. During the year 1925–6 he was a student at the Universität München, Germany, and during the year 1926–7 at the Université de Fribourg, Switzerland, where he obtained a Ph.D. His thesis was entitled *'De simplicitate Dei*, Based on the Thomistic Principles of Theism.' He returned to teach at St Michael's College, 1927–9, and then at Assumption College, 1929–32. He was assistant at St Mary's of the Assumption Parish, Owen Sound, Ontario, 1932–4, and at Ste Anne's Parish, Detroit, 1934–6, then returned to St Michael's College to teach philosophy, religious knowledge, and German until the early 1950s, when asthma and a heart condition forced his retirement from teaching. He spent the last ten years of his life in the college infirmary.

In his younger years at Assumption College, Father Welty had excelled in sports. Later he cultivated many pastimes and skills. He played the violin with a fine style, and photography was a lifelong enthusiasm – his work gracing many school yearbooks. He created garden spots at St Michael's College and in Owen Sound. The *Basilian Centennial* volume of St Mary's of the Assumption Church called Father Welty a true worker: 'He built the stone wall that runs up 15th Street hill. He [did] all the landscaping himself. One of his greatest joys was a flower garden along the path leading from the back of the church to the bottom of the hill, and also along the stone wall.'

BIBLIOGRAPHY:
Book: *De simplicitate Dei*. Fribourg, 1927.
Article: 'Photographs Taken at Strawberry Island. Memories,' *Basilian* 3 (1937) 82.
SOURCES: GABF; *Annals* 3 (1962) 159–60; *Newsletter* (23 March 1962); *Centennial, St Mary's*.

WESLEY, John MICHAEL, priest, was born on 11 June 1940, in Rochester, one of two sons of John Casimir Wesley and Mary Martha

Tucker. He died in Toronto on 1 November 1980 and is buried in the Basilian plot of Holy Sepulchre Cemetery, Rochester.

Upon completion of his elementary education at Blessed Sacrament Parish School, Rochester, Michael was awarded a four-year scholarship to Villanova High School, which he declined in order to enter Aquinas Institute, Rochester, in September 1953. As a freshman he won a trip to Texas for being high salesman in the school's magazine drive. He graduated in June 1957, fourth in his class of 267 with an average of 93 per cent. He attended Villanova University, Villanova, Pennsylvania, and was valedictorian of the graduating class of 1961. He entered St Basil's Novitiate, Pontiac, Michigan, and was professed on 15 August 1962. He taught for one year with the first group of scholastics to be appointed to Andrean High School, Gary (now Merrillville), Indiana, and then taught two additional years at Aquinas, 1963–4. In 1965 he was appointed to Maison Saint-Basile, Issy-les-Moulineaux (Hauts-de-Seine), and began his theological studies at the Séminaire de Saint-Sulpice. He completed his theology course at St Basil's Seminary, Toronto, 1966–9 (S.T.B., University of St Michael's College, 1969). He was ordained to the priesthood on 14 December 1968 in Sacred Heart Cathedral, Rochester, by Bishop Dennis Hickey.

Father Wesley returned to his alma mater, Aquinas Institute, in 1969 to teach theology, Latin, French, mathematics, and typing. He became meet director for the Aquinas Relays, which he developed during the ensuing years into an international event. He joined the Genesee Valley Track and Field Certified Officials Association in 1971 and became its president in 1977.

As early as 1974 Father Wesley had begun to experience blackouts of varying duration. A series of tests revealed a brain tumour, for which in 1978 he underwent surgery followed by radiation. In 1979 he returned to the classroom on a part-time basis, having accepted his condition with a dissembling insouciance. He continued teaching during the year 1979–80 on a reduced schedule and was chairman for the Relays. He underwent steroid treatment in June and July of 1980 and then moved to the Basilian Fathers Residence (Infirmary), Toronto, in August. He was deeply disappointed at not being able to attend the opening Aquinas football game, having missed but one (his year in France) since the age of seven.

Mike Wesley was a formidable defender of traditional doctrines and practices of the faith. He approached his priesthood, the Basilian community, his teaching and coaching, and his recreational hours with a vibrant intensity; but he was at the same time patient in tutoring the slow learner and in coaching the less gifted. He came to view his suffering not as a matter for complaint or defeat but as a fulfilment of his priesthood, achieving spiritual serenity in his last days. He died peacefully in his room while his confreres were celebrating the liturgy for the feast of All Saints.

SOURCES: GABF; *Annals* 4 (1969) 103–4, 5 (1981) 617–19; *Newsletter* (19 November 1980).

WEY, Joseph Charles, priest, thirteenth superior general, was born on 18 March 1910 at Hammond, Indiana (diocese of Gary), the son of Linus Gregory Wey and Mary Clara Wruck. He died in Toronto on 10 December 2000, and is buried in the Basilian plot of Holy Cross Cemetery, Thornhill, Ontario.

When 'Joe' was three years old the family moved to a farm near Riviera, situated in the Rio Grande Valley in South Texas. In 1917 they moved again to the Heights district of Houston, where Joe attended All Saints Parochial School, Heights Junior High School, 1923–4, and St Thomas College, graduating in 1927. There and in summer leagues in the parks of Houston he was a formidable baseball pitcher. He entered St Basil's Novitiate, Toronto, and was professed on 11 August 1928. Appointed to St Basil's Scholasticate, Toronto, he did classics at St Michael's College in the University of Toronto (Honours B.A., 1933), studied theology, 1933–7, and earned an M.A. in classics. He was ordained to the priesthood on 19 December 1936 in St Basil's Church, Toronto, by Archbishop James Charles McGuigan.

Father Wey taught Latin and Greek at St Michael's College, Toronto, 1937–40. He began graduate studies at the University of Chicago, but was then asked to teach at Assumption College, Windsor, 1940–1, and again at St Michael's, 1941–7, with particular interest in Greek and Roman drama, especially Latin comedy. After termination of the Second World War, he studied at Cambridge University, England, 1947–9, where he developed a keen talent for reading medieval Latin manuscripts. He put these skills at the service of countless students and colleagues over a total of thirty-six years, in two periods, 1949–60 and 1973–98, at the Pontifical Institute of Mediaeval Studies, Toronto, serving as registrar for a time, but at the same time teaching and doing research. He worked for years on a critical edition of the *Collectio canonum Hibernensis*, an early source of Irish secular and ecclesiastical law, but relinquished all his work on it to a European colleague to complete when, in 1960, he was elected vicar general of the Basilians and, in the following year, superior general, a post he held for the next twelve years.

In a prophetic letter to the community, printed in the *Basilian Annals*, 1961, he warned of the divisiveness that threatened Basilian life because of changes of deep significance taking place in almost every sphere of human endeavour, and urged a spirit of unity and a commitment to truth. His years as superior general were extremely difficult, encompassing the turbulence of change in Church and society, leading to the questioning of the basic values of religious life by many and to massive withdrawals of members. Though he suffered greatly during this period, he maintained an exemplary calm and patience, ever seeking, as had been his wont, the good of the individual person.

His two terms at an end, he returned as emeritus Fellow at the Institute, and published critical editions of William of Ockham and of Ockham's strongest critic, Walter Chatton. For this he was the first recipient of the 'Scholarship in Franciscan Studies' Medal awarded by the Franciscan Institute at St Bonaventure's University, Olean, New York, in 1987. When he foresaw that he would not have the years to finish his work on Chatton, he sent the four volumes he had transcribed and begun to edit to a colleague to complete. Still wanting to work, however, he proceeded to assist another colleague by reviewing his transcriptions of manuscripts of the eighth-century Irish theologian Johannes Scotus Eriugena.

Joe Wey's habits were admirably frugal, his recreation limited to reading, fishing, and watching nature programs and baseball on television. In the latter his patience often gave way to strongly expressed opinions about the game and especially about the umpire who was calling balls and strikes.

BIBLIOGRAPHY:
Books: Ed. William of Ockham. *Quodlibeta septem*, in *Guillelmi de Ockham Opera philosophica et theologica ad fidem codicum manuscriptorum edita*. Opera theologia 9. St Bonaventure, N.Y., 1980. Ed. William of Ockham. *Principium bibliae sive Quaestio de connexione virtutum*, in *Quaestiones variae*, Opera theologica 8. St Bonaventure, N.Y., 1984. Ed. Walter Chatton. *Reportatio et Lectura super Sententias: Collatio ad Librum primum et Prologus*. Toronto, 1989. Ed. (with Girard Etzkorn) Walter Chatton. *Reportatio super Sententias*, 4 vols. Toronto, 2002–5. Ed.

(with Girard Etzkorn) *Lectura. A Second Commentary on Lombard's Sentences (1328–1330)*. Toronto, 2006.
Article: 'The *Sermo Finalis* of Robert Holcot,' *Mediaeval Studies* 11 (1949) 219–24. He also wrote annual letters to the Community, published in *Basilian Annals*, 1961–72.
SOURCES: GABF; *Annals* 5 (1979) 345, 6 (1987) 493, 8 (1997) 3–4, 9 (1999) 2, (2001) 104–6; *Newsletter* (24 January 2001); J.K. Farge, 'Joseph Charles Wey C.S.B. 1910–2000,' *Mediaeval Studies* 63 (2001) vii–ix.

WHELAN, James Hugh, priest, was born at Westport, Ontario (archdiocese of Kingston), on 27 April 1902, the son of John Whelan and Maryanne Lynett. He died in Detroit on 5 June 1940 and was buried in the Basilian plot of Assumption Cemetery, Windsor.

James Whelan attended St Michael's College, Toronto, for both high school and university education (B.A., University of Toronto, 1925). He planned a career in law, but shortly after classes had begun he withdrew from Osgoode Hall and entered St Basil's Novitiate, Toronto. After profession on 13 October 1926 he attended the Ontario College of Education, Toronto, 1926–7. He did his theological studies at St Basil's Scholasticate, Toronto, and was ordained to the priesthood on 21 December 1929 in St Basil's Church, Toronto, by Archbishop Neil McNeil.

Father 'Jim' Whelan taught at Aquinas Institute, Rochester, 1930–2, while concurrently studying to obtain an M.A. in philosophy from the University of Toronto. In 1932 he moved to Holy Name Institute in Detroit, and in 1933 was appointed superior and principal. When Holy Name Institute was amalgamated with Catholic Central High School in 1934 he became superior and principal of the combined schools. He acquired a secondary school teaching certification for the State of Michigan in 1936, having taken courses at the University of Detroit. He strengthened the educational policies of Catholic Central, and under his administration it became the largest Catholic high school in the state. For several summers he spent some weeks in New York State recruiting students for St Michael's College. He died from a heart attack at the age of thirty-eight.

Into his short life, Father Whelan crowded a great deal of zealous work and spread a cheerful brightness among his colleagues and students. The bulletin of Blessed Sacrament Parish, Detroit, commented: 'People liked him instinctively because they recognized in him a friend. ... They were attracted by his sense of humor ... the genial humor that bespeaks an intelligent good nature.' As both religious superior and principal he had a way of making people sense that they were working with him rather than under him. His interests extended beyond the walls of the schools in which he worked.

SOURCES: GABF; *Hour* (Bulletin of Blessed Sacrament Parish, Detroit [13 June 1940]); *Silver Anniversary, Catholic Central High School, 1928–53* (Detroit 1953); *Yearbook SMC* 16 (1925).

WHELAN, Maurice Francis, priest, was born on 1 April 1909 in Ottawa, the son of Lawrence Whelan and Harriet Meloche. He died in Toronto on 22 March 1990 and is buried in the Basilian plot of Holy Cross Cemetery, Thornhill, Ontario.

'Mo' Whelan, as he was known in the community, attended Holy Name School in Toronto, where the family had moved from Ottawa. In 1925 he enrolled in high school at De La Salle College, Toronto, but transferred in 1927 to St Michael's College as a boarder. He excelled in academics and athletics, and was the goalie for the league-winning St Michael's Junior A Hockey Team in the 1927–8 season. He entered St Basil's Novitiate in 1928 and was professed on 15 August 1929. Appointed to live at St Basil's Scholasticate, he completed his high school studies at St Michael's College School in 1930. He took one year of undergraduate studies at St Michael's College before transferring to Assumption College, Windsor, (B.A., Philosophy and English, University of Western Ontario, 1934), where he played quarterback for the intercollegiate football team. He studied theology at St Basil's Scholasticate, concurrently attending the Ontario College of Education (teaching certification, 1935). His studies were interrupted by a teaching assignment at Aquinas Institute in 1937–8. He was ordained to the priesthood on 17 December 1939 in St Basil's Church, Toronto, by Archbishop James Charles McGuigan.

Father Whelan began forty-five years of work in secondary education with four short appointments: Aquinas Institute, 1940–2, St Michael's College School, 1942–3, St Thomas High School, Houston, 1943–5, and Assumption College School, 1945–50. In 1950 he returned to St Michael's College School, where he was to remain for the next thirty-six years, teaching, coaching, counselling, supervising the publication of the yearbook, and instilling the traditional spirit of St Michael's which he cherished. He taught chiefly mathematics, and studied three summers at St Bonaventure University, Olean, New York, to improve his math skills. He was demanding as a teacher and equally demanding as a coach, for that approach seemed the only one worthy of the sublime vocation to form young men to live as Christians. Though he retired from teaching in 1978 he maintained his involvement in the life of the school until 1986, when he was moved to the Basilian Fathers Residence (Infirmary) for the last four years of life.

BIBLIOGRAPHY: 'Catholic Ideals in Teaching History,' *Basilian* 1 (March 1935) 9–10, 12; 'Thoughts on Church History,' *Basilian* 2 (January 1936) 5; 'Mathematics in Basilian Schools [forum],' *Basilian Teacher* 4 (December 1959) 73.
SOURCES: GABF; *Annals* 5 (1980) 460, 7 (1991) 141–3; *Newsletter* (30 April 1990).

WHELIHAN, James Austin, priest, was born on 6 April 1902 at Lucan, Biddulph Township, Ontario (diocese of London), the son of Patrick Whelihan and Bridget Collison. He died in Toronto on 15 November 1986 and is buried in the Basilian plot of St Mary's Cemetery, Calgary, Alberta.

Jim Whelihan attended elementary school in his home town and did two years at Lucan High School before going to Assumption College, Windsor, where he first met the Basilians. He continued on to university studies at Assumption (B.A., University of Western Ontario, 1926), and then entered St Basil's Novitiate, Toronto. After profession on 11 August 1927, he was appointed to St Basil's Scholasticate, Toronto, for theology and for graduate work in philosophy. He also attended the Ontario College of Education, earning teacher certification and participating in the athletic program of the University of Toronto Schools. For his final year of theology, 1930–1, he was appointed to live at St Michael's College, Toronto. He was ordained to the priesthood on 21 December 1930 in St Basil's Church, Toronto, by Bishop Alexander MacDonald.

In 1931 Father Whelihan was appointed to St Thomas High School, Houston, to teach mathematics and Spanish. In 1933, with his appointment to St Mary's Boys' High School in Calgary, he began his fifty-two-year apostolate in Western Canada, of which thirty-nine years were spent in Calgary. He was one of the founders of the Basilian house in that city. In 1935 he became a certified teacher for Alberta. The only break in his long tenure in the West came in 1941–2 when he was sent to Assumption College to study philosophy but ended up teaching full time. Returning to Calgary and immersing himself in the life of the school, he quickly became a major influence on the youth there by his inspired teaching, his genuine love for students, his insistence on hard work and hard play, and his habitual joyful spirit. He coached the whole gamut of sports: football, track and field, basketball, hockey, and boxing. Any young man willing to do his best was given a role: player, waterboy, manager, or time-keeper. Scores of students, some of whom rose to positions of importance in the Church, in politics, and in business, would later recall with gratitude the good teaching, example, and devotion of Father Whelihan.

The work and influence of Jim Whelihan extended beyond his own school to the wider community. In sports he guided the Calgary Tornadoes to the Western Canada Junior Football Championship in 1946 and to the finals in Vancouver the following year. He served on the Athletic Board for the City of Calgary and on the city's Planning Commission. In 1954 he was named 'Sportsman of the Year' by the Booster Club of Calgary. After retirement in 1969 he continued to coach city teams of boys twelve and thirteen in flag football. In 1985 he was inducted into the Order of Canada and into the Alberta Sports Hall of Fame and Museum. The citation for the the Order of Canada read in part: 'His influence extended beyond those directly involved in his classes, his teams and his religion. Believing and teaching that every individual has a responsibility to develop himself to his fullest potential and to make a contribution to mankind, he has instilled a love of good citizenship in generations of students.'

From 1971 to 1984 Father Whelihan was appointed to St Mark's College, Vancouver, and served as chaplain and counsellor to the students at Vancouver College. From 1984 to June 1986 he lived in retirement in the Basilian community until failing eyesight made necessary his transfer to the Basilian Fathers Residence (Infirmary), Toronto, where he brought the same joyful spirit that had characterized his life. He died five months later as the result of a stroke.

BIBLIOGRAPHY: 'Coaching Track,' *Basilian Teacher* 5 (March 1961) 215–18.
SOURCES: GABF; *Annals* 5 (1978) 271, 5 (1981) 539, 6 (1987) 583–5; *Newsletter* (28 November 1986).

WIECZOREK, Conrad Thomas, priest, member of the Congregation 1951–69, was born in Toronto on 10 May 1932, the son of Conrad Wieczorek and Josephine O'Neill. He died in Toronto on 30 November 1995. After a funeral Mass in St Basil's Church, Toronto, he was buried in the Basilian plot of Holy Cross Cemetery, Thornhill, Ontario.

Conrad attended high school at St Michael's College, Toronto, 1945–50. He entered St Basil's Novitiate, Richmond Hill, Ontario, in 1950 and made his first profession in August 1951. He lived at St Basil's Seminary while attending St Michael's College, 1951–2 and 1954–5, and resided at St Michael's College, 1952–4 (B.A., University of Toronto, 1955). He taught at St Charles College, Sudbury, 1955–7. After theological studies at St Basil's Seminary, Toronto, 1957–61, he was ordained to the priesthood by Bishop Francis Allen on 29 June 1960.

Father Wieczorek obtained an S.T.B. from the University of St Michael's College in 1960 and an M.A. in philosophy from the University of Toronto in 1961, submitting as his thesis 'The Motivation of the Will in the Philosophy of Duns Scotus.' He taught at St John Fisher College, Rochester, 1961–3. He was then assigned to graduate studies in theology at the Institut catholique, Paris, 1963–4, where he resided at the Basilian house of studies, Maison Saint-Basile, Issy-les-Moulineaux. From 1964 to 1968 he studied at Marquette University, Milwaukee, Wisconsin.

Father Wieczorek was dispensed from the obligations of priesthood and religious profession in 1969. He worked at a variety of jobs including at least one in the publications industry. For some ten years prior to his death he suffered from dementia caused by a series of strokes.

SOURCES: GABF; *Annals* 3 (1960) 29–30; *Newsletter* (19 December 1995).

WILBUR, Gerard HARVEY, priest, uncle of Father Joseph *Willett, was born in Bathurst, New Brunswick (diocese of Chatham, since 1938 of Bathurst), on 17 December 1898, the son of Percy Wilbur and Mary Richardson. He died in Bathurst on 15 July 1947 and was buried in the Basilian plot of Assumption Cemetery, Windsor.

Harvey Wilbur attended Sacred Heart School in Bathurst and St Thomas College in Chatham, New Brunswick, 1917–21. There he completed two years of college and served as an apprentice teacher, 1920–1. 'Harry,' as he was then called, entered St Basil's Novitiate, Toronto, in 1921 and was professed on 15 August 1922. He resumed his education in Toronto, taking philosophy at St Michael's College and theology at St Basil's Scholasticate. He was ordained to the priesthood on 19 December 1926 in Sacred Heart Church, Bathurst, by Bishop Patrick Chaisson.

Father 'Pete' Wilbur, as he had come to be called in Toronto, was appointed to St John the Baptist Parish, Amherstburg, Ontario, 1927–9. He taught at St Thomas High School, Houston, 1929–30. During the year 1930–1, while a staff member of Ste Anne's Parish, Detroit, he took courses at Assumption College, Windsor, to complete the requirements for a B.A. from the University of Western Ontario. In the year 1931–2 he attended the Ontario College of Education, Toronto, then taught at St Michael's College School, Toronto, 1932–3, and at Catholic Central High School, Detroit, 1933–4. In 1934 Father Wilbur moved to Assumption Parish, Windsor, and was placed in charge of Blessed Sacrament Church, where he organized the first credit union in the Windsor area (1938), which was named for him. From it developed six credit unions of the Ford Motor Company of Canada and five of the Chrysler Corporation of Canada.

Father Wilbur possessed a simplicity of manner which enabled him to work well with the cosmopolitan population of his parish. In 1947, while visiting relatives in New Brunswick, he was stricken with a heart attack and died four days later. An obituary notice in the *Gloucester Northern Light* said that 'Father Wilbur was supremely content in his sacred calling. He radiated happiness and cheerfulness. He "went about doing good" and giving himself in the service of others.'

BIBLIOGRAPHY:
Pamphlet: *Our Parish.* Windsor, 1947. (A memorial to the parishioners who served in the Second World War.)
Article: 'The New Church at Windsor,' *Basilian* 3 (November 1937) 102–3.
Unpublished: A History of Blessed Sacrament Parish, Windsor.
SOURCES: GABF; *Annals* 1 (1947) 160–1; *Gloucester Northern Light*, Bathurst, New Brunswick (17 July 1947); *Yearbook SMC* 18 (1929).

WILLETT, Joseph Lineham, priest, nephew of Father Harvey *Wilbur, was born in Ruby Lake, Manitoba (archdiocese of St Boniface, since 1915 of Winnipeg), on 19 November 1911, the son of Harry Willett and Rita Wilbur. He died in Houston on 1 January 1958 and was buried there in the Basilian plot of Garden of Gethsemane, Forest Park Lawndale Cemetery.

Joseph's family moved from Manitoba to Bathurst, New Brunswick, where he attended local schools. He did part of his high school and two years of university studies at St Thomas College, Chatham, New

Brunswick. In 1929 he entered St Basil's Novitiate, Toronto, was professed on 15 August 1930, and took the Honours Philosophy course at St Michael's College (B.A., University of Toronto, 1934). His qualifying Honours thesis was an English translation of Thomas Aquinas's commentary on the *Liber de causis*. He attended the Ontario College of Education in 1934–5 and studied theology at St Basil's Scholasticate ('Seminary' from 1937), Toronto, 1935–9. He was ordained to the priesthood on 17 December 1938 in St Basil's Church, Toronto, by Archbishop James Charles McGuigan.

Father Willett taught first at Aquinas Institute in Rochester, 1939–54. During the wartime years he learned to fly, obtained a private pilot's licence, and taught courses in aviation. In 1954 he was transferred to St Thomas High School, Houston, where he taught mathematics. Two years later he moved to Assumption College School, Windsor, but a severe heart attack incapacitated him for most of the year 1956–7. He returned to St Thomas High School in 1957 and died suddenly on New Year's Day 1958, at forty-six years of age.

Joe Willett was blessed with the physique of an athlete, and in his younger days took keen enjoyment in competitive sports. After ordination, however, his six-foot-three body began to break down, and various ailments required hospital care. Through all of these he retained his competitive spirit. Somewhat shy, Father Willett kept his own counsel. An obituary in the *Basilian Teacher* said of him: 'He went about his work with the proficiency of an expert. Father Willett possessed a penetrating insight regarding the problems of modern youth, and exercised great patience and charity in all his dealings with them, especially towards those not so quick to learn.'

SOURCES: GABF; *Annals* 2 (1959) 350–1; *Basilian Teacher* 2 (January 1958) 19.

WILSON, James Francis, priest, was born on 1 August 1912 at Massey, Ontario (diocese of Sault Ste Marie), one of a family of three girls and seven boys of William J. Wilson and Theresa Killoran. His brother Clarence became a Paulist Father and his sister Pauline a member of the Loretto Sisters. He died in Toronto on 19 January 1997 and is buried in the Basilian plot of Holy Cross Cemetery, Thornhill, Ontario.

Jim Wilson attended St Peter's Separate School and high school at St Michael's College, Toronto. He entered St Basil's Novitiate in 1928 and was professed on 15 August 1929. He began undergraduate studies immediately, living at St Basil's Scholasticate for three years of these studies and at St Michael's College, 1931–2 (B.A., Honours French, University of Toronto, 1934). He taught as a scholastic for the year 1934–5 at St Thomas High School, Houston, and then began his theological studies in Toronto, living for the first year at St Michael's College and then, from 1936 to 1938, at St Basil's Scholasticate ('Seminary' from 1937). At the same time he attended the Ontario College of Education. In 1938 he was appointed once again to St Thomas High School, where he completed his theology while teaching. He was ordained to the priesthood on 29 June 1939 in St Michael's Cathedral, Toronto, by Archbishop James Charles McGuigan.

Father Wilson lived and worked at St Thomas High School from 1938 to 1991, with the exception of one year, 1971–2, of residence at Our Lady of Mount Carmel Parish, Wharton, Texas. He taught languages, having set about learning Spanish when he was assigned to St Thomas, and built up an outstanding Spanish department at the school. He also taught English and in so doing developed an extraordinary talent for quoting Shakespeare. His reputation as a baseball coach spread through the city of Houston and beyond, though he learned the sport only when he went to the South. His method both in teaching and in coaching was always calm, clear, and, above all, encouraging. He taught as much by his manner and courtly bearing as by his words. From his earliest years he suffered from weak eyesight, which was also painful. His one letter of doubt about his ability to continue his work, written to the superior general in 1938, went unanswered. He persevered against the odds and became an effective teacher, even famous and esteemed.

Father Wilson was a prominent, much-loved figure in Houston. He was active in the Rotary Club and served on the Education Committee of the Chamber of Commerce and on the President's Council of the Houston Grand Opera Association. In the Basilian Congregation he was elected the first regional representative for Western United States and was twice re-elected to the office. He was one of the first members of the Priests Senate of the diocese of Galveston-Houston. A surprise tribute to Father Wilson in 1981 drew more than a thousand admirers to a banquet at the Shamrock Hotel chaired by the mayor of the city, who was one of his former students and baseball players.

With reluctance he moved in 1992 to Dillon House, the Basilian Fathers retirement home in Houston, and with even greater reluctance to the Basilian Fathers Residence (Infirmary), Toronto, in 1993. At the wake service for him on Toronto on 21 January 1997, Father William Irwin CSB aptly applied to his former teacher and coach a text from the letter of St James about the wisdom from above which is 'first pure, then peaceable, gentle, open to reason, full of mercy and good fruits without a trace of partiality or hypocrisy.'

BIBLIOGRAPHY: 'The Social Justice Club,' *Basilian* 2 (November 1936) 140; 'Scripture and Our Students [forum],' *Basilian Teacher* 5 (December 1960) 87.
SOURCES: GABF; *Annals* 5 (1980) 460–1, 7 (1990) 11–12, 8 (1998) 72; *Newsletter* (27 January 1997).

WOOD, Richard Shakeshaft, priest, was born in Houston on 26 June 1916, the son of L.B. Wood and Helen Davey. He died in Windsor on 21 November 1956 and was buried there in the Basilian plot of Assumption Cemetery.

'Dick' Wood attended St Thomas High School, Houston. Upon graduation in 1934 he entered St Basil's Novitiate, Toronto, was professed on 12 September 1935, and was appointed to Assumption College, Windsor, for undergraduate studies (B.A., University of Western Ontario, 1940). He taught mathematics there in 1939–40, and then studied theology at St Basil's Seminary, Toronto. Archbishop James Charles McGuigan ordained him to the priesthood on 15 August 1943 in St Basil's Church, Toronto.

In 1944 Father Wood returned to Assumption College, where he taught for one year before his appointment as treasurer, 1945. For eleven years he guided the finances of Assumption through a period of expansion that took the institution from a small classical college, dependent on the University of Western Ontario to confer degrees on its graduates, to independence, 1953, and then to incorporation as Assumption University of Windsor, 1956.

Richard Wood died at forty years of age after a two-year struggle with cancer. Orderliness and thoroughness were the dominant characteristics of his personal life and of his work as treasurer. In his sermon preached at Father Wood's funeral, Father Ernest *Lajeunesse said of him, 'To those who knew him best, his dignified bearing and affable manner in his dealings with all classes of people were the outward manifestation of a well disciplined character.'

SOURCES: GABF; *Annals* 1 (1943) 54, 2 (1956) 299–300; Power, *Assumption College* 6 201.

Y

YOUNG, Edmund Michael, priest, was born on 20 November 1907 at Chatham, New Brunswick (diocese of Chatham, since 1938 of Bathurst), the son of Michael Young and Sarah MacDonald. He died in Toronto on 3 November 1997 and is buried in the Basilian plot of Holy Cross Cemetery, Thornhill, Ontario.

'Ed' Young attended local elementary schools and enrolled in St Thomas College, Chatham, in 1920, shortly before the Basilians withdrew from that school. He entered St Basil's Novitiate, Toronto, in 1923 and was professed on 12 August 1924. He was then appointed to St Basil's Scholasticate, Toronto, where he completed grade XIII, took his B.A. degree in Honours English and History (University of Toronto, 1930), and completed two years of theology. He was an outstanding kicker on St Michael's intermediate intercollegiate football team, 1926-8. He obtained teaching certification from the Ontario College of Education in 1930, and spent the year 1932-3 in residence at St Michael's College while continuing his theology, but returned to the scholasticate for his final year. He was ordained to the priesthood on 17 December 1933 in St Basil's Church, Toronto, by Bishop Alexander MacDonald.

In 1934 Father Young began a thirteen-year stint teaching at Assumption College. He used the summers from 1938 to 1942 to do graduate studies in history at Columbia University in New York City (M.A., 1943). Eleven other assignments followed: St Thomas High School, Houston, 1947-9, teaching; Catholic Central High School, Detroit, 1949-57, teaching, second councillor, 1952-7; Michael Power High School, Etobicoke, Ontario, 1957-9, teaching, second councillor; St Basil's Seminary, 1959-60, teaching, first councillor; Assumption College School, 1960-5, teaching; St Basil's Novitiate, Pontiac, Michigan, 1965-6, confessor; St Basil's Seminary, 1966-71, treasurer; St John the Baptist Parish, Amherstburg, 1971-2, assistant; St Basil's College, Toronto, 1972-80, assistant director of St Basil's Infirmary; Basilian Fathers Residence, 1980-3, assistant director; Basilian Fathers Residence, 1983-97, retired.

Ed Young is remembered for accepting cheerfully these many changes in appointment, for his desire to do things well, and for his consideration of others. Though diffident about his ability, he was always willing to fill a need. He once introduced the wonders of geography to a four-year-old, captivating the child to the extent that the boy later chose geography as his university subject. In the infirmary he gave much attention and support to the staff, who called him a 'bringer of peace.' At his death he held the record for the longest span of life as a professed Basilian: seventy-three years.

BIBLIOGRAPHY: 'So Dark the Night,' *Basilian* (December 1935) 132; 'An Open Letter,' *Basilian* 3 (January 1937) 5; 'That Radical Program,' *Basilian* 3 (March 1937) 60; '20,000,000 Suckers and Some More,' *Basilian* 3 (November 1937) 106–7; 'A Just Wage,' *Basilian* 3 (December 1937) 126–7; 'The First Two Rs,' *Basilian* 3 (March 1938) 54–5.
SOURCES: GABF; *Annals* 5 (1975) 67, 6 (1984) 203, 9 (1998) 79–80; *Newsletter* (5 December 1997).

Basilians by Chronological Order of Death

The sign † indicates that the year of death, but not the date, is known.
The sign — indicates a member who withdrew from the Congregation.

1838	16 August	Lapierre, Joseph Bovier (Bouvier)
1840	13 August	Vallon, Jean Antoine
1841	3 June	Duret, Jacques VINCENT
1846	28 March	Polly, Jean-Baptiste
1847	8 April	Payan, Augustin
1849	25 October	Chalaye, Isidore
1854	28 July	Polly, Jean FRANÇOIS
1856	19 June	Deglesne, Antoine Louis GERMAIN
1859	6 August	Tourvieille, Pierre
	26 October	Montgolfier, Auguste de
1860	23 April	Roure, Auguste
1861	27 August	Pagès, Jean-François
1864	28 October	Actorie, Joseph Marie JULIEN
1865	5 April	McCarthy, Thomas
1867	27 April	Fayolle, André
1868	5 August	Coupat, Henri
	27 September	Cushing (Cushin), John B.
1870	8 December	Bonnet, Pierre
1873	6 June	Moulin, Jean Paul Emile
	5 August	Chabert, Félix
1875	23 February	Bodineau, Auguste Clément
	22 September	Cotter, George Barry
1876	2 April	Moffit, John Richard
	23 June	Kennedy, Edward J.
1877	15 September	Ladet, Casimir
	4 October	Monot, Louis Michel
1878	21 March	Hours, Charles

	24 March	Charmant, André
	23 May	Chanteloube, Alexis
	26 June	Hourdin (Ourdin), Henri
	1 August	Morrow, John M.
	31 December	Gorman (O'Gorman), Michael F.
1879	24 February	Martinesche, Henri
	17 October	Soulerin, Jean-Matthieu
1880	8 April	Molony (Moloney), Patrick
	5 August	Durand, Hilaire
	6 October	— Roche, Marie-Lᴜᴅᴏᴠɪᴄ
1881	21 January	Vernède, Auguste
	5 July	Mollaret, Elie
	23 September	Clappe, François-Xavier
1885	6 January	Malbos, Joseph
	3 June	Tracol, Julien
	22 August	— Chabert, Benjamin
1886	9 May	Prévost, Etienne
1887	24 June	Raphanel, Jules
	16 December	Faure, Charles-Joseph
1888	12 February	Tourvieille, Alphonse
	13 September	Mollier, Victorin
1890	25 February	Roux-Saget (Roussaget), François
	1 November	Vincent, Charles
1891	30 June	— Lavalette, Jules Jean
	21 August	Arnoux, Jean François Régis
	8 December	Meyzonnier, Camille
	12 December	Giraud, Jean-Jacques
1892	16 August	Pagès, Alphonse Auguste
	16 November	Vaschalde, François Jean
1893	3 February	Hilaire, Firmin
1894	25 January	Ranc, Jean Pɪᴇʀʀᴇ
	11 June	Joanny, Régis
1895	18 December	Menut, Pierre
	19 December	Fournier, Frédéric Bernard
1896	20 January	Demeure, Louis-Marie Joseph
	27 October	— Gibra, Louis
1897	23 April	Hours, François-Régis
1898	28 January	Vaschalde, Auguste
	30 May	Hours, Basile
	29 July	Fayolle, Adrien

1899	28 February	Mirabel, Léon
	6 April	Monin, Jean
	13 May	Gourgeon, Paul
1900		†Gray, Marie Denis Philémon
	29 March	Guey, Marius Denis
	11 April	— Allignol, Ferdinand
	26 November	Chambon, Jean-Louis
1901	7 February	Goutte, Antoine
	2 March	Mungovan, Michael Joseph
	13 April	Bosc, Henri
	27 November	Ozil, Ferdinand
	21 December	— Flannery, William
1902	8 February	Chavanon, Jean-Claude
	28 June	Ranc, Jean Louis
	22 October	Bord, Antoine
1903	31 July	Perbost, Antoine Victor
1904	30 June	Brennan, Laurence
	10 October	Bonnaud, Louis
1905	30 April	Mulcahy, Michael Joseph
	5 June	Fayard, Jacques Louis
	23 June	Fayolle, Léopold
	3 July	Guinane, James Joseph
	22 November	Martaresche, Frédéric
1906	7 January	Martin, Joseph
	12 February	Costello, John Joseph
	24 December	Chomel, Adrien
1907	20 September	Malbos, Jean Michel
1908	5 March	Bret, Jean-Marie
	2 May	Peyreplane, Hippolyte
	27 July	Vielfaure, Auguste
	19 December	Drohan, Richard Patrick
1909	5 May	Liogier, Emile
	15 October	Martin, Arsène
	23 October	— Girard, Auguste
1910	25 July	Gallon, Henri
	14 November	Balandreau, Jean
1911	10 June	Teefy, John Read
	30 June	O'Connor, Denis
	1 September	Tastevin, Antoine Alphonse
	15 September	Clauzel, Edouard

	31 October	McEvoy, James J.O.
1912	13 February	Mourgue, Xavier
1913	3 February	Sullivan, John Aloysius
	21 February	Merle, Hilarion
	28 March	Buckley, Patrick L.
	30 April	Ferguson, Michael Joseph
	31 July	Brunel, Louis
	27 October	Oudin, Joannès Etienne
	19 November	Bufferne, Vincent Augustin
1914	28 May	Walsh, Francis Mary I.
	6 November	Morley, Arthur Joseph
1915	5 March	O'Donohue, Peter
	28 March	Pouzol, Auguste
	4 April	Gignac, Thomas Frédéric Ferdinand
	6 April	Ladreyt, Henri
	13 June	Hilaire, Joseph
	29 October	Chalandard, Pierre Joseph
1916	12 April	Frachon, François-Régis
	16 August	Delhomme, Auguste
1917	2 March	Granottier, François Xavier
	31 August	Ryan, Patrick Joseph
1918	13 March	Bonfils, Joseph Frédéric
	28 September	Finnigan, Joseph TERENCE
	25 October	McGwan, Thomas James
	7 November	Lodato, Joseph Anthony
	14 November	Purcell, John Joseph
	29 November	Sharpe, Joseph Patrick
1919	1 March	Chambon, Léopold
	9 May	Crespin, Jean
	19 July	Bouchet, Xavier
1920	24 February	Collins, John Bernard
	30 March	Soleilhac, Jean-Baptiste
1921	25 February	Molin, Dominique Florentin
	23 April	Cru, Gustave
	26 October	Guigal, Jean-HENRI
1922	16 April	Durand, Noël
	27 April	— Staley, Arthur James
	13 May	Grand, Jean PIERRE
	21 June	Semande, François-Xavier Denis Alfred
	22 November	Descellière, Louis

	26 November	Mazenod, Jean-Claude-Marie
	28 December	Romans, Louis
1923	22 May	Chanteperdrix, Jean-Antoine
1924	15 February	Godard, Jean-Marie
	6 October	Meader, Frederick DANIEL
	23 December	Cherrier, Léon Edouard
1925	2 January	Cauvin, Ernest
	9 February	Renaud, Luke
	2 May	DuMouchel, Albert Pierre
	4 May	Murray, Edmund Francis
	16 October	Tallon, Joseph EDWARD
1926		†Alboussière, Louis
	28 March	Vallanson, Jean Fleury
	24 April	Reversade, Justin
	16 July	— Plomer, John Clifton
1928	11 February	Pagès, Lucien
	12 May	Burns, Edmund Toussaint
	12 May	— Hayes, Thomas James
	6 July	Guigon, Jean Régis
	18 December	Cushing (Cushin), Daniel
1929	17 January	Savoye, Jean-Claude
	20 January	Reath, Vincent Bernard
	2 May	Cohas, Joseph Pierre Bonnet
	30 May	Howard, Patrick Joseph
	11 November	Forster, Robert FRANCIS
	18 December	Suchet, Emile
1930	7 February	Lacoste, Paul
	5 April	Garvey, Wilfrid Francis
	4 September	Prévost, Denis
	14 November	Tarabout, Jean-Marie
	5 December	Coulet, Gustave
1931	1 January	— Granottier, Benoît
	21 January	— Corvisy, Lucien
	22 January	Giraud, Julien
	1 March	Player, James Frederic
	22 March	Charron, Victorin-Adrien
	30 August	Aboulin, Jean JOSEPH Marie
	21 October	Marijon, Victorin
1932	23 January	Durand, Eugène
	5 March	Séveyrac, Félix

	29 March	Fuma, Gabriel
	16 May	Roche, Nicholas Ernest
1933	28 March	Murphy, Vincent Joseph
	9 April	Côté, Jacques-Alfred
	1 May	George, Gerald Fitzgerald
	9 May	Nicholson, Joseph SYLVESTER
	27 July	Jobert, Eugène
	26 November	Deschanel, Jules
1934	11 January	Verger, Jules
	5 April	Aureille, Edouard
	4 December	Christian, Michael Patrick
	7 December	McNulty, Neil Jerome
	15 December	Ruth, James Leo
	20 December	Plourde, Emil J.
1935	9 March	Heydon, Thomas Joseph
	23 March	— Géry, Benoît
	25 April	Legoux, Louis
	23 August	O'Neill, Edward John
	12 September	Hilaire, Louis
	9 October	Martin, Ernest
	22 November	— Shaughnessy, Patrick James
	2 December	Mourgue, Marcel
1936	21 April	Normandeau, Joseph LEO
	4 May	McBrady, Robert
	27 September	Roach, Michael THOMAS
	20 October	Gourgeon, Marius
1937	1 October	Philippon, Marius
	2 November	Aureille, Emile
1938	25 March	Mouraret, Denis
	11 October	Kennedy, Joseph Mullaly
	28 December	Bellisle, Henry Stanislaus
1939	5 January	Roudil, Elie
	7 February	Sheehan, Cornelius J.
	26 March	Roe, Charles Francis
	26 August	McCarroll, Edward GERARD
	5 October	Serey, Benjamin
1940	5 June	Whelan, James Hugh
	1 October	Donnelly, Vincent Ignatius
1941	9 February	Guigon, Léon
	31 March	Chanteperdrix, Léopold

	7 May	Trouillet, Henri
	4 September	— Pageau, Jean ERNEST
	22 November	Burke, Richard Thomas
1942	8 January	— Costello, Paul
	31 January	Vaschalde, Adolphe Arthur
	5 April	Moylan, Thomas Vincent
	3 May	Flanagan, John Berchmans
	14 May	Cummer, William ERNEST
	24 July	Kelly, Michael Vincent
	6 December	Boucher, Maurice
1943	3 March	— Sheridan, John Joseph
	7 December	Colomb, Alphonse Marcelin
1944	15 April	Fogeron, Joseph
	28 June	Storey, William Joseph
	10 July	Tighe, Edward Joseph
1945	28 April	McIntyre, John Clement
	6 November	Frachon, Jean-Marie
	2 December	McGahey, Joseph Edward
1946	1 September	Giraud, Benoît Camille
1947	2 June	Collins, Charles
	15 July	Wilbur, Gerard HARVEY
	21 November	Ryan, Michael JOHN
1948	28 January	Dolan, Leonard Joseph
	31 January	Soleilhac, Jean LOUIS
	27 February	— Forner, Benjamin Nicolas
	7 December	Dillon, Daniel Leo
1949	22 February	O'Brien, Austin David
	7 April	Kennedy, Thomas VERNON
	8 April	Burke, James VINCENT
	30 July	Pickett, Michael Joseph
1950	9 August	Descellière, Marie Joseph OCTAVE
	17 August	— Rogers, William George
	16 November	— Bart, Peter John
1951	13 January	Perbet, Séraphin
	24 February	— Powell, Francis Gerald
1952	31 March	Rieubon, Joachim
	9 June	Walsh, Francis Anthony
1953	22 April	Grangeon, Marius
	27 October	Dillon, Joseph Patrick
1954	28 October	Pokriefka, Edward Leo

	20 December	McLaughlin, John Redmond
1955	21 March	O'Rourke, Thomas Patrick
	30 May	Deluche, Gabriel
	25 July	Beuglet, Luke Léon
	4 December	Vahey, Thomas James
1956	23 September	Crowley, Joseph FLOYD
	21 November	Wood, Richard Shakeshaft
	7 December	Timmons, Joseph Jeremiah
1957	28 April	Hartmann, Edward Joseph
	19 July	Denomy, Alexander Joseph
	30 September	McAlpine, Joseph GERALD
1958	1 January	Willett, Joseph Lineham
	3 December	Regan, Herbert BASIL
	3 December	— Fitzpatrick, Edward Francis
1959	27 August	Bobichon, Emile
1960	30 January	Rafferty, Francis Andrew
	5 June	Levack, David Alfred
1961	12 February	Roach, William Joseph
	23 July	Burns, Edmund Eugene
	28 August	Coll, Edward BLAKE
	7 September	Conway, William Joseph
	11 November	— Loupias, Théophile François
1962	22 March	Welty, Emil Jerome
	14 July	Burbott, Eugene Michael John
	5 October	Corrigan, John Vincent
1963	23 June	Bergeron, Cyril Orville
	12 August	Kelly, Charles Michael
	9 September	Onorato, John Francis
	28 November	Carr, Henry
1964	30 January	McGuire, Thomas JOHN
	11 July	Ruth, Francis Sylvester
1965	12 January	Epitalon, Antoine
	7 February	Phelan, George Raymond
	13 July	McGrady, Leo Victor
	20 July	— Walsh, Joseph Basil
	6 August	— Petrey, Paul Francis
1966	27 January	Girard, Uldège Joseph
	7 March	Perdue, Simon Andrew
	24 April	Forestell, Daniel Leo
	22 May	O'Loane, John Henry

	25 May	Roume, Charles Léon Luc
	21 August	McCann, Leonard Albert
	6 October	Hussey, John Michael
	7 December	— Hurley, Albert Edward Joseph
1967	25 January	Sheehy, John Dennis
	9 May	Muckle, Joseph Thomas
	23 May	— Martin, John Joseph
	4 September	Fullerton, Vincent Joseph
	16 October	Vasek, Leslie Joseph
	10 November	Sheehan, William Alexander
	20 November	Sullivan, Edward John
	23 November	Murphy, James Joseph
	6 December	Sullivan, John Joseph
	9 December	Mazet, Louis
1968	15 May	Lacey, Lawrence James
	25 July	O'Toole, William Bernard
	7 October	Thomson, Vincent Alexander
	27 October	Montague, Robert Michael
1969	12 January	Allnoch, Carl Mitchell
	26 March	McGouey, James THOMAS
	6 April	Boland, John FRANCIS
	28 May	Lynch, Martin STANLEY
	23 June	Nolan, Hugh Philip
	26 July	Thompson, George James
	19 October	Collins, John Francis
	10 December	Meyer, John Wilbert
1970	24 February	Leman, Thomas Walthall
	8 April	McMahon, Edward Joseph
	15 September	McLaughlin, Terence Patrick
	26 October	Murphy, Wilfred Joseph
	7 December	Fischette, Robert Matthew
1971	18 March	Carter, Cyril Francis
	9 July	Ruth, John Peter
	28 August	Beninger, Donald Bernard
1972	26 July	Sheehan, Peter Edward
1973	21 February	Cherry, John Thaddeus
	25 February	Guinan, Vincent Joseph
	1 June	Grant, Alexander John
	1 December	Duggan, William John
1974	30 January	McIntyre, Viator Ignatius

	10 February	Mallon, John PAUL
	12 February	Allor, Edward William
	25 March	Kennedy, Vincent Lorne
	3 April	Flood, Robert Henry
	20 August	Marcoux (Marcou), Auguste
	23 August	Lowrey, Robert Emmett
	3 September	Murphy, Francis Leo
	30 September	Barnes, Joseph George
	18 November	Nigh, William Francis
1975	7 January	Haffey, Hugh James
	19 February	Faught, Donald Thomas
	26 February	Murphy, John Francis
	21 May	Meloche, Paul Joseph
	21 September	Vadnais, Ernest Lucien Pierre
	16 November	McGee, William Patrick
1976	1 January	Sharpe, Wilfrid Clarence
	27 February	Cross, James Francis
	24 April	Lee, Edward Gregory
	10 June	Coyle, William Ambrose
	16 June	O'Leary, Arthur Jennings
	21 June	Killaire, Frederick Joseph
	23 June	Murray, William Hudson
1977	11 February	Oliver, Michael Joseph
	17 February	Waligore, Arthur Francis
	3 March	Kehoe, Wilfrid Martin
	26 March	Brown, Francis AUSTIN
	27 March	O'Donnell, Bernard Joseph
	8 April	Pacher, Florian Edmund
	19 May	Flood, Francis De Sales
	4 September	Sharpe, Gerald Vincent
	14 September	Malone, Felix CLARE
	12 October	Killoran, Matthew Ambrose
	15 December	Flanagan, Edward Francis
1978	25 January	Perry, Harold Charles
	5 February	Eckert, Vincent Conrad
	25 March	Jeffery, Richard Joseph
	12 May	Miller, John Joseph
	1 June	Sullivan, Walter Vincent
	26 August	— Maloney, Donald ANDREW
	15 September	O'Donoghue, John Curtis

	26 September	McReavy, John Joseph
	18 October	— Slattery, Thomas
	28 October	Mallon, Hugh Vincent
	31 December	Glavin, John Joseph
1979	14 May	— Drouillard, Clarence Joseph
	3 September	Burns, Francis Leo
	22 September	Pope, Joseph William
	26 October	— Coughlin, Charles Edward
	26 November	Regan, Bernard Michael
	2 December	Amlin, Thomas Delbert
	24 December	Rush, Edward LEONARD
1980	26 February	Caird, Alfred Page
	9 March	McCorkell, Edmund Joseph
	10 April	Malley, Eugene Robert
	3 May	— Farrell, John Matthew
	12 June	Goetz, Michael Alphonsus
	24 June	Todd, Gerard William
	26 August	Biondi, Michael Bernard
	1 November	Wesley, John MICHAEL
1981	21 January	Allen, Elliott Bernard
	7 May	Munnelly, Leo Joseph
	2 June	Spratt, John Cantius
	5 June	Gibbons, William Joseph
	20 June	Dore, James WILFRID
	4 July	Rivard, Joseph Leo
	21 September	Redmond, John Michael
	7 October	Morrissey, John BERTHOLD
	14 October	Donovan, Charles Patrick
1982	16 January	Tallon, John David
	19 May	MacDonald, Ralph James
1983	4 January	Cahill, Frederick Wallace
	21 February	Quinlan, Leonard Clarence
	19 April	Lawlor, Thomas Anthony
	6 May	Coughlin, Hubert Patrick
	22 May	Murphy, Joseph STANLEY
	24 June	Sullivan, Basil Francis
	26 August	Purcell, Louis Francis
	18 November	Benwitz, Donald Earl
	2 December	— Acosta, Rudolph
1984	15 May	Riley, Wilfred Samuel

	12 October	Brown, William MacBeath
	18 December	O'Donnell, Joseph Leo
	20 December	Embser, James William
1985	20 January	Sheehy, Fergus Joseph
	6 March	Damato, John Joseph
	17 March	Murphy, Norman Joseph
	8 April	Glavin, Basil Francis
	4 May	Warren, John Arthur
	1 June	Roy, Norman Francis
	16 July	LaCroix, John Robert
	27 August	Bondy, Louis Joseph
	3 December	Lavery, Charles Joseph
1986		† — Houde, Adelore Louis
	10 April	Batty, Thomas Dake
	2 June	Barry, John Patrick
	30 June	MacDonald, Thomas Aloysius
	11 August	LeBel, Eugene Carlisle
	26 September	Kelly, John Michael
	7 November	Delaney, Charles William Patrick
	15 November	Whelihan, James Austin
	13 December	— Kraus, John Louis
1987	6 January	— Prêcheur, Henri Louis
	21 January	Mulvihill, Daniel Joseph
	9 February	Adam, Leo Joseph
	13 April	Orsini, Francis Alphonsus
	15 April	Lyons, Charles Francis
	21 August	Bowie, James Joseph
	29 August	Lococo, Anthony Vincent Philip
	15 September	— Crowley, John Joseph
	9 October	Lalonde, Patrick Alfred
	25 November	McGillis, Thomas Rodric
	19 December	Donlon, James Alexander
1988	5 February	O'Donnell, James Reginald
	20 April	— Gallerano, Victor
	2 June	Lewis, Patrick Joseph
	24 July	McGuigan, Gerald Frederick
	13 September	Scott, Walter Winthrop
	9 November	Bauer, David William
	28 December	Dorsey, Joseph Barrett
1989	9 February	Sheedy, Matthew Patrick

	6 April	Heyck, Eugene Adams
	16 June	Hall, Robert Alphonse
	13 July	— Bourret, Marcel
	6 August	Chauvin, Robert Thomas
	22 August	Flahiff, George Bernard
	9 November	— Conway, John Thomas
1990	28 January	Hart, Leon George
	22 March	Whelan, Maurice Francis
	13 September	Megan, James ARNOLD
	18 November	Pappert, Edward Cecil
	24 November	Culliton, Joseph Thomas
	27 November	McLean, Louis Charles EDWARD
1991	3 January	Harrison, Gerald Francis CANNING
	28 January	McCarthy, Arthur John
	19 March	Brown, William James
	20 June	Seniawski, John Walter
	10 August	Higgins, Albert LELAND
	11 December	Mallon, Thomas GREGORY
	22 December	Dwyer, John WILFRID
	23 December	Lajeunesse, Ernest Joseph
1992	17 January	Crowley, Clifford Joseph
	3 February	Martin, James Edward
	6 April	Diemer, Rudolph Stephen
	10 April	Armstrong, David Linus
	10 May	Rus, Svatopluk STEPHEN
	12 May	McCabe, Patrick FRANCIS
	22 June	Kelly, James Joseph
	4 July	Vermillion, René Marcel
	23 August	Sheehan, Michael McMahon
	15 September	Mooney, Donald Richard
	1 October	Collins, James Joseph
	9 October	Schreiner, William Allen
	10 October	Morro, James Peter
	18 December	Prince, Raymond Louis
1993	10 January	— Kelly, Francis Paul
	21 January	Iversen, Norman Martin
	12 March	Burns, Daniel Vincent
	21 March	O'Reilly, Joseph Alfred
	9 May	— Bannon, J. MURRAY
	23 May	Hennessey, Wilfrid BRIAN

	14 June	Daley, Joseph JAMES Edward
	22 June	— Speck, Paul Stanley
	23 June	Hanrahan, John Patrick
	25 June	Scollard, Robert Joseph
	1 August	Mullins, John Brian
	20 October	Looby, Arthur Rynold
	23 October	Shook, Laurence Kennedy
1994	25 January	Genca, Allen James
	31 March	Allard, Richard Joseph
	22 April	Geneston, Fernand Paul André
	12 July	Holmes, Arthur Joseph
	31 August	Regan, William OSCAR
	1 September	Abend, Joseph John
	20 September	— Sosulski, Michael Carl
1995	14 January	Reynouard, Georges Louis
	24 January	Finn, Robert William
	28 March	Ware, John Francis
	6 April	— Crowley, Cornelius Patrick Joseph
	7 April	Monaghan, Francis Emmett
	4 August	Burke, John Aloysius
	18 August	Weiler, Arthur Jerome
	26 August	Grescoviak, Francis Joseph
	23 September	Cooper, Donald Theodore
	30 September	Boehm, Francis Christian
	30 September	DeBilly, Roger Foley
	14 October	Black, James BERNARD
	21 October	— Udall, Cyril Ronald
	30 November	— Wieczorek, Conrad Thomas
1996	28 January	Castillo, José ISIDRO
	2 February	O'Gorman, George DONAL
	15 February	Brot, Lucien Jules
	1 March	Kelly, James Scott
	8 May	Principe, Walter Henry
	20 May	Quinn, John Francis
	28 June	Macdonald, Daniel GORDON
	9 August	Dougherty, John Roger
	7 September	Garvey, Edwin Charles
	17 October	Anglin, Gerald Falconbridge
	23 October	French, John GERALD
	4 November	Sheehan, Paul Thomas

	10 December	— Vincent, Claude Louis
1997	19 January	Wilson, James Francis
	31 January	Record, Maurice ADRIAN
	9 February	Pendergast, Russell Anthony
	31 March	— Cullinane, Eugene Augustine
	4 May	O'Reilly, Edward Augustine
	19 June	— Stapleton, John Francis
	11 August	Magee, Ernest Paul
	27 August	O'Neill, James Francis
	3 November	Young, Edmund Michael
	2 December	Sheahan, Francis Michael
	21 December	Miller, Robert Grace
1998	19 March	O'Loughlin, Simon RAPHAEL
	28 March	Paré, Vincent Alton
	29 April	Ruth, Norbert Joseph
	24 May	McCarty, Francis John
	18 September	Agius, Grace Joseph
	6 October	— Celette, Marcel Claudius
	18 November	Ruth, Anthony JOHN
	8 December	O'Brien, William Hilary
1999	18 February	McKinnon, Robert Oliver
	2 June	Reuss, Norbert Clarence
	13 August	Kelly, Leroy NEIL
	14 October	— Howard, Thomas CYRIL
	6 December	Firth, John Joseph FRANCIS
2000	29 January	Lamb, Robert Emmett
	11 February	O'Meara, John Patrick
	16 February	Hale, Robert Barr
	18 February	Mulcahy, Matthew Thomas
	9 March	Black, Frederick Arthur
	27 March	McManus, John Edward
	5 April	— Donoher, Paul Bernard
	11 June	Penny, Joseph Gerard
	22 June	— Cashubec, James Francis Joseph
	4 July	Ronan, Edward Xavier
	18 July	Koehler, Charles RALPH
	31 July	Forestell, James TERENCE
	6 August	Marceau, William Charles
	4 September	— Kelly, William Howard
	25 October	Gaughan, John James

	17 November	— Quealey, Brian Thomas Joseph
	6 December	Pouzol, Félix Jules
	10 December	Wey, Joseph Charles
2001	17 January	James, Paul McEvoy
	29 May	Armstrong, Charles Joseph
	2 September	Butler, Albert Francis
	29 September	Kelly, Anthony John
	15 October	Silvester, George Ernest
	24 November	McNeil, Donald Joseph
2002	5 August	Beaton, Peter James
	27 August	Clemens, Henry NORBERT
	21 September	Smith, Charles Casper
	25 October	McGinn, James GERRARD

For the following neither the day nor year of death is known. The year given is the latest recorded in GABF or ABA.

1832	— Desbos, Jean-Pierre
1833	— Chaussinand, Joseph
1836	— Cartal, Julien
	— Vacher, Régis
1847	— Desbos, Jean-Baptiste
1855	— Gaucherand, Marie-Florimond
	— Marin, Charles AUGUSTIN
1857	— Prat, Jean Henri
1862	— Bard, Jean Louis
1871	— Chareyre, Régis
1872	— Reynaud, Claude
1873	— Famy, Jean
1876	— Baqué (Baquet), (Christian name unknown)
	— Michel, Louis
	— Pagès, Pierre
1877	— Jannin, Jules
1882	— Mouraret, Casimir
1883	— Nicolas, Etienne Elie
1886	— Priou, Jean-Baptiste
1889	— Décor, Joseph Louis Hippolyte
	Duplay, Jean-Marie
	— Nicolas, Hippolyte
1896	— Michelon, Elie
1900	— Brosse, Jean André

1901 — Véron, Louis
1902 — Montreuil, Antoine
1906 Fouilland, Irénée
1913 Maisonneuve, Joseph Louis DANIEL
1915 Audibert, Auguste